CRIMINAL JUSTICE ETHICS

Edited by

Paul Leighton

Eastern Michigan University

and

Jeffrey Reiman

American University

UPPER SADDLE RIVER, NEW JERSEY 07458

Library of Congress Cataloging-in-Publication Data

Criminal justice ethics / edited by Paul Leighton and Jeffrey Reiman.
    p. cm.
  Includes bibliographical references.
  ISBN 0-13-085129-9
  1. Criminal justice, Administration of—Moral and ethical aspects—United States. 2. Social justice—United States. 3. Legal ethics—United States. 4. Police ethics—United States. I. Leighton, Paul, (date) II. Reiman, Jeffrey H.

HV9950.C74316 2001
174′.9364—dc21

00–044111

for **Satoko**
and for **Sue**

Acquisitions Editor: Ross Miller
Assistant Editor: Katie Janssen
Marketing Manager: Don Allmon
Production Editor: B. Christenberry
Manufacturing Buyer: Sherry Lewis
Cover Designer: Bruce Kenselaar

This book was set in 10 point Janson by Pub-Set, Inc., and was printed and bound by RR Donnelley/Harrisonburg. The cover was printed by Phoenix Color Corp.

Prentice Hall

© 2001 by Prentice-Hall, Inc.
A Division of Pearson Education
Upper Saddle River, New Jersey 07458

10 9 8 7 6 5 4 3 2

ISBN 0-13-085129-9

PRENTICE-HALL INTERNATIONAL (UK) LIMITED, *London*
PRENTICE-HALL OF AUSTRALIA PTY. LIMITED, *Sydney*
PRENTICE-HALL CANADA INC., *Toronto*
PRENTICE-HALL HISPANOAMERICANA, S.A., *Mexico*
PRENTICE-HALL OF INDIA PRIVATE LIMITED, *New Delhi*
PRENTICE-HALL OF JAPAN, INC., *Tokyo*
PEARSON EDUCATION ASIA PTE. LTD., *Singapore*
EDITORA PRENTICE-HALL DO BRASIL, LTDA., *Rio de Janeiro*

CONTENTS

III. MORAL PROBLEMS IN POLICING   232

III.1. POLICE ETHICS

III.2. DECEPTION & INFLUENCE

III.3. SELECTIVE ENFORCEMENT

VI.2. MEDIA

APPENDIX: PROFESSIONAL CODES OF ETHICS

PREFACE

People seem to have endless interest in criminal justice. We relate immediately to the struggle between the forces of good and evil; we sympathize with the victims of crime and suffer with them the injustice they have experienced; we get satisfaction when the guilty receive their just deserts; and we identify with the wrongly accused and their struggle against the nearly overwhelming forces and resources of the government. This interest is not only a matter of our fears and hopes, but also a sign of our deep-seated concern with morality.

We are for capital punishment or against it, for laws prohibiting abortion or drug use or against them. We think that crime is caused by poverty and thus that poor criminals deserve a special break, or we think that crime is caused by plain old orneriness and that no allowance should be made for socially disadvantaged crooks. We wonder whether lawyers can be morally good people and what makes them behave as they do. We ask, how far can the police go in using deception or sexual enticements to catch crooks? Is it entrapment if the police tell a suspect that manufacturing PCP is "as easy as baking a cake"? Would we revive chain gangs or corporal punishment? Should prostitution be legal?

There seem to be no neutrals on these and similar issues. Everyone has strong opinions on the morality of criminal justice, from its policies and ideals to its practices and abuses. But these opinions are too frequently formed haphazardly, based on the experiences we have had, on our likes and dislikes, on the attitudes of those we admire, and perhaps on a good deal of misinformation. We might hear an argument that strikes us as sensible without considering another side of the issue. If our moral beliefs are not well formed, if we would not hold them after thoughtful examination of the other side (or sides) of the issue, then we may support harmful policies. We all can benefit from deeper reflection on our moral beliefs about criminal justice—and that is what criminal justice ethics is about.

Ethics connotes not only morality as such, but the philosophical study of moral principles—the attempt to subject our moral beliefs to careful scrutiny. That is what this book is about. It aims not to convince readers that one set of moral beliefs is superior to others, but to assist them in reflecting on their own moral beliefs. Toward this end, we have put together a collection of articles that articulate drastically different moral beliefs about important criminal justice issues. Readers, seeing how moral beliefs are examined and defended, can examine and defend their own—or, perhaps, discover shortcomings in their own beliefs and open their minds to new ones.

Toward this end, we have tried to identify particularly challenging articles, ones that argue for unpopular or unusual positions, ones that make for lively reading and discussion and that provide for thinking and rethinking. In many cases, the articles present different sides of an issue, often in the form of direct debates between experts. The reader is exposed to a variety of voices engaged in the vehement defense of principles important to them. Who better to write about prostitution law than feminist scholar Catharine MacKinnon, and who better to respond than the International Committee for Prostitutes' Rights in their "World Whores' Congress Statements"? The debate between O.J. Simpson Attorney Johnnie Cochran and Yale Law Professor Akhil Reed Amar is more engaging than a "balanced" article by a single author on whether criminal defendants have too many rights.

At other times, we have selected provocative articles and allowed them to stand alone, hoping that readers themselves will enter into the debate, putting forth their own responses to positions that strike them as wrong-headed, allowing themselves to revise their opinions in the face of new ones, and to hunt for evidence important to the issues. The case studies reflect the messiness of real-life situations requiring ethical decisions or judicial opinions. The legal cases in particular allow readers to see how legal reasoning may or may not overlap with moral reflection. We have been less interested in mechanically balancing every pro with a con than with stimulating thought and inciting debate. Numerous addresses to quality Internet sites direct readers to further data, arguments and perspectives to ensure that this book opens the door to exploration rather than being a final word.

Moreover, the selected articles reflect a broad conception of the field of criminal justice ethics. In addition to the standard issues—death penalty or abortion or recreational drug use or prostitution—we have viewed criminal justice as inextricably bound up with social justice. Since the criminal justice system protects the existing social and economic system, criminal justice can be no more just than the social and economic systems. Consequently, issues of social justice are issues of criminal justice. Likewise, the agents of criminal justice—police, lawyers, and even doctors administering lethal injections—are people following careers, trying to do their best in a difficult job. Consequently, issues of professional ethics are issues in criminal justice ethics.

And, finally, we view criminal justice as developing over time in the face of a changing society. Thus, we have tried to identify ethical issues that are just coming over the horizon—the interest in televising execution, and, of course, the problems posed by the growing presence of computers and information technology. How does the Constitution apply to cyberspace? In these areas, our concern has been to challenge the reader to do his or her own thinking about criminal justice as it is and as it will be.

To the extent we have achieved our goals in this volume, it is only with the help of many individuals. In particular, we would like to thank Paul Haskell, Jennifer Hatten, Andrew Pfeiffer, and Karen Schaumann. Thanks also to the staff of the Department of Sociology, Anthropology & Criminology at Eastern Michigan University for undertaking some of the tedious work with graciousness and thoroughness. Thanks to Karita France for getting this project under way and to Jennifer Ackerman for advice on how to navigate a range of problems; and to our editor Ross Miller and associate editor Katie Janssen.

INTRODUCTION

In "Criminal Justice Ethics," Jeffrey Reiman reviews the main approaches to ethics and suggests reasons why people should be moral. He contends that, in addition to the normal moral quandaries about police discretion and capital punishment, questions about social justice are ethical questions for criminal justice. Since the criminal justice system enforces the rules of the existing social and economic order, the criminal justice system cannot be anymore just than the social order.

In "Teaching Ethics Ethically," Robert Nash argues that the classroom itself can be a model of ethical behavior. He draws on twenty-seven years teaching professional ethics to make suggestions both students and teachers are likely to find useful about the process of discussing sensitive issues of social policy and personal morality. Additional resources on these topics are available at <http://www.paulsjusticepage.com>.

Criminal Justice Ethics

Jeffrey Reiman

1. WHY SHOULD WE WORRY ABOUT WHETHER THE CRIMINAL JUSTICE SYSTEM IS MORAL?

For some people, this question won't even arise. Obviously, the criminal justice system must be moral, they may think, because everything should be moral. That's what moral means: *the way things should be!* This answer is so general, however, that it is little more than an empty platitude, that gives us no guidance. More pointedly, this answer ignores the possibility that there are special reasons that criminal justice must be moral. These special reasons may indicate the kinds of standards by which the morality of criminal justice must be judged—as the shape of keyhole gives us a clue about the shape of the key that will open it.

By *criminal justice*, or *the criminal justice system*, more is meant here than just the police and the courts and the prisons. I mean all of that, of course, but I also mean the laws that this system enforces and the laws that determine what the criminal justice system may do to enforce those laws. The first sort of laws are most commonly criminal laws, laws prohibiting certain behavior on the part of citizens: theft, fraud, assault, use of narcotics, commerce in sex, etc. The second sort of laws are most commonly constitutional laws or principles, rules limiting what the government may do in prosecuting crime or requiring that government follow certain procedures in that prosecution: limits on search and seizure, requirements of due process, legal counsel, trial by jury for the accused, etc.

By *morality*, is meant here the standards of rightness and goodness by which we judge human behavior: fairness, non-malevolence, tolerance, truthfulness, and so on. I shall have a lot more to say about moral standards in what follows, but one thing is worth mentioning at the start. Some people distinguish between *morality* and *ethics* in the following way. While morality comprises the standards of rightness and goodness that we apply to human behavior, ethics has two special meanings: First, *ethics* means the philosophical study of morality, the search for principles that justify the moral standards that we seek to apply. Second, *ethics* means those moral standards that are appropriate to particular occupations (so we speak of legal ethics or medical ethics, rather than of legal or medical morality). In both of these senses, the study of whether and how criminal justice is moral is rightly called *criminal justice ethics:* It is a philosophical undertaking, and it seeks to understand and justify those moral standards that are appropriate to the occupations that comprise the criminal justice system. With this observation, we are brought back to the question raised above: Are there special reasons that criminal justice must be moral?

That the answer to this question is *yes* can be seen in two ways. First, consider how similar criminal justice is to crime. Both use force to get people to do things they may not want to do. Further, every punishment applied by the criminal justice system would be a crime if applied by one private citizen to another. If a citizen locks you in a prison cell that she has constructed in her basement—even if you deserve it!—this is the crime of kidnapping. If a citizen fines you, he has committed the crime of theft. If he executes you, he has committed the crime of murder. How can it be right for the criminal justice system to do what criminals do? It might seem that the answer to this is that what the criminal justice system does conforms to the law, while what the criminal does violates the law. However, this answer is less satisfactory than it first appears. Rather than answer our question, it simply

forces us to restate it: Why are acts done in conformity to law right when the same acts done in violation of the law are wrong? *What magical power does law have to make bad acts good?*

This is no idle question. We have seen in this century and in the previous one numerous examples of crimes carried out under color of law. Was persecution of Jews in Nazi Germany right because it was spelled out in the infamous Nuremberg Laws? Was subjugation of blacks under the system of *apartheid* right because it was sanctioned by South African law? Was slavery in pre-Civil War America right because it was legal in many states and even allowed by the U.S. Constitution? These examples show that law itself is not enough to make wrong acts or practices right. Indeed, the example of pre-Civil War America shows that even the law of a constitutional democracy cannot make wrong acts or practices right. *Criminal justice can only be distinguished from crime if criminal justice is moral while crime is immoral.* This is what led the great thinker and teacher, Saint Augustine, to ask rhetorically: *Without justice, what are kingdoms but great robberies?* In short, only morality can distinguish the state's force as right from the criminal's force as wrong. Only by being moral can criminal justice be distinguished from the very crime that it condemns!

There is a second (and related) way to see the special need of criminal justice for morality. Suppose a gun-toting robber approaches you and commands you to give him your wallet. You are, we might say, *obliged* to hand it over. But no one would say that you are *obligated* to do so. You don't *owe* the gunman your wallet. If you could get away from him, or overpower him, you would be within your rights to do so. Now, suppose a gun-toting police officer approaches you and commands you to hand over your car to him so that he can chase an escaping felon. The police officer is doing more than just forcing you to obey him. Assuming that he is acting within the legal limits of his authority, you should obey him, even if you could get away from the officer or overpower him. You are obligated, not merely obliged, to comply with his command. In short, the commands of criminal justice are thought to be based on more than mere force. What is this "more"? The examples above (of persecution, subjugation, and slavery) show that lawfulness is not enough. Jews in Nazi Germany, blacks under South African apartheid, and slaves in America were not obligated to accept their condition. They were victims of mere force even if legally sanctioned. Again, only morality can make the difference. Morality accounts for the obligation we have to comply with the authority of criminal justice. Morality is what makes it right, not mere might.

It may be asked: Is even morality enough to make this difference? After all, someone might object by saying that Nazi morality justified the persecution of Jews, South African morality justified the subjugation of blacks, and pre-Civil War American morality justified slavery. This is a very useful objection. It shows that if morality means only the standards that some people do accept at some time, then morality cannot make the difference we need. Thus the morality we are after is more than merely a collection of people's actual moral beliefs. It is more than the standards that people do actually accept or have actually accepted. What is this "more"? This question moves us from morality to ethics: from standards merely accepted to the reflection on and justification of standards. The morality that will make the difference between criminal justice and crime, between right and mere might, must be in some sense a morality that is rationally justifiable. That is, it must be a morality whose credentials lie not simply in being accepted, but rather a morality that can be shown *worthy* of acceptance on the basis of rational arguments.

The determination of what is rationally justifiable in morality is a philosophical inquiry into the nature and basis of moral standards themselves—in a word, *ethics*. Happily, this is not an inquiry that we must begin from zero. Philosophers from ancient times have reflected on the nature and basis of morality, and contemporary moral philosophers have continued this reflection and sifted from it what is acceptable according to modern standards. Thus, we will profit from a brief consideration of what moral philosophers have to say about ethics.

2. WHAT CAN WE LEARN FROM MORAL PHILOSOPHY ABOUT ETHICS?

By way of approaching moral philosophy, it will be helpful to start by looking at the meaning of the concept of morality and then to consider the problem of relativism. After considering the contributions of moral philosophy, we will take up the question of why one should be moral and then try to draw some conclusions about how to evaluate moral standards.

2.1. *The Meaning of the Concept of Morality*

In our attempt to understand morality as rationally justifiable standards of behavior, we can receive some guidance from what people usually mean by morality. When someone gives a moral justification for how she is acting, she means to show that her actions are not simply selfish or self-interested. This suggests that morality is a kind of neutral standard. Moreover, when someone offers a moral justification, she means, further, to show that her actions are good in some way. Thus morality refers to a neutral standard of goodness. And finally, if someone offers a moral justification, she assumes that others can understand the content of the moral principle to which she appeals. Morality is not private, not secret, not esoteric. In order to expect people to accept moral justifications, indeed, in order to expect people to be moral, we must believe that morality is something accessible to all people—at least all people sane and mature enough to be held responsible for their actions. This in turn suggests that people can understand how morality is good, how it is good for them and for others. Thus we can say—without yet having said what standards comprise the content of morality—that morality means standards of behavior that are good in ways that are neutral among people and in ways that all reasonable people can understand. For this reason, the moral philosopher Kurt Baier has wisely characterized morality as indicating "the good of all people alike."

It is easy to see that the least controversial aspects of morality, rules against killing or cheating or stealing, are good in just this way. That is, while cheating or robbing another may be good for the cheater or thief, it cannot be good for everyone. For everyone, it would be better if there were no theft, no cheating, and so on. And the ways in which this would be good are not hard to grasp. It would be good because it would protect people from loss and disappointment. With this in mind, it would not seem all that difficult to determine what sorts of moral standards can be rationally justified. All we need to do is figure out what practices it would be good for everyone to allow or to disallow, and standards providing for these permissions and prohibitions would be rationally defensible. There is an important truth here. Nonetheless, we live in an era when people seem to disagree a great deal about morality, and very few people think that there are moral standards that are rationally defensible in a universal sense. It is common enough to hear people say that morality is just a matter of personal choice, that there is no morality that is generally true or valid or justifiable for all people, that everyone must decide for him- or herself what to believe about morality. To confront and correctly assess this fact, let us consider the problem of relativism.

2.2. *The Problem of Relativism*

It is above all important to be clear about what relativism is and what it is not. Relativism is the idea that there are no generally valid or binding moral standards. Be careful, this is not the same as the empirical fact that people disagree about moral standards. People can disagree about moral standards even if there are some generally valid moral standards, much as people once disagreed about whether the earth moved around the sun or vice versa, even though there is (and always was) a valid—indeed, true—resolution of this disagreement.

Moreover, the disagreement about moral standards is easy to exaggerate. While there are important disagreements, there are also many moral principles that are found in virtually all cultures among virtually all people: For example, all moral traditions have some version of the Golden Rule. All cultures and just

about all individuals think it is wrong to impose violence on innocent people (or at very least that this needs a powerful justification, such as might exist in time of war); all cultures and just about all individuals distinguish between what belongs to one person and what belongs to others—even thieves don't want to be robbed and generally know that what they are doing is wrong (or needs a powerful justification, such as might be provided by urgent need or prior victimization).

Of course, there are real differences: Some people think that taking life is never justified; some think it is only justified in self-defense; others think that it is justified as punishment. Some people think that lying is never justified and others that it is easily justified. Some people think that prostitution and drug use are purely matters of personal taste not subject to moral judgment, while others think that these are serious evils. Of course there are perennial disagreements about abortion and infanticide and euthanasia, and so on.

What is important, however, is to note that such disagreements as do exist do not imply that there are no generally valid moral standards. They tell us only that people don't always agree on what the standards are or should be. Relativism is a stronger claim. It is the denial that there are generally valid moral standards. In this sense, it is not an empirical claim at all. It is not about what people *do* believe, but about what they *should* believe. That is to say, relativism cannot be proven or disproven by empirical tests, such as surveys that would show that people do or do not believe in universal moral standards. It is a philosophical claim about the existence of universal moral standards, whether or not people believe in them. Thus relativism must be proven or disproven by philosophical arguments.

A dangerous mistake is to confuse relativism with tolerance. Some people resist the belief in generally valid moral standards because they think it will lead to imposing one person's moral beliefs (held by him to be the valid ones) on others (who have different moral beliefs). But imposing one person's moral beliefs on others is only wrong if something is really wrong! Tolerance is itself a moral principle. To believe in it is to believe that tolerance is really right. This is precisely what a relativist cannot believe. He cannot believe that tolerance is right and intolerance is wrong because he cannot believe that anything is really right or wrong.

Additionally, people who believe that it is wrong to impose one person's beliefs on another usually believe that it is wrong to impose one person's will upon another, for instance, by violence or deception. It is clear that people who believe that imposing one person's beliefs on another is wrong believe that there are numerous things that are really *wrong*. Is there anyone who thinks that we should be tolerant of those who murder, cheat, and steal?

Belief in tolerance is itself a belief that there is at least one generally valid moral principle, namely, that people should not have others' views imposed on them. That moral principle is not relativism and cannot be supported by relativism. Indeed, a relativist must believe that there is nothing really *wrong* with imposing one person's views on another, because he or she feels that there are no generally valid standards to show that anything is really wrong at all.

Most people think that there are things that are really morally wrong. Most think that the Nazis committed great wrongs, that racism, sexism, violence against innocents, manipulation, deception, betrayal, and so forth are serious moral wrongs. To test your own beliefs, consider this story:

> A student in an ethics class announced that she was a relativist. The professor responded, "That's fine; however, I'm going to give you an F in this course as a result." The student protested: "But, that's not fair!" "Oh, really?" replied the professor. "I thought you were a relativist. Do you mean to tell me you think that there really is a standard of fairness? Tell me about it."

Don't you think there is a standard of fairness? Don't you think that the professor in this story is *really* being unfair?. If so, then, you, like most people, believe that there are some standards that distinguish right from wrong. Perhaps you think that this is because you share the standards of fairness in your culture. Do you think that, in another culture, it could be fair to flunk someone in a course just for his or her beliefs, rather than on the basis of performance? Suppose you answer this last question by saying that it could be fair in another culture if students knew in advance that they would be treated that way. But, then, you are still insisting on a standard of fairness, namely, that it is only fair to treat people according to principles they know and understand in advance.

There are fewer real relativists than people who say they are relativists, but this doesn't mean that relativism is not a serious problem. What it suggests rather is that the only answer to relativism lies in showing that some moral standards are generally valid on the basis of rational arguments. If this can be shown, then we may either convince the relativists or show the non-relativists that they are justified in holding the relativists to at least some moral standards. To see if any moral standards can be shown to be generally valid on the basis of rational arguments, let us look at what moral philosophers have to say.

2.3. The Main Philosophical Approaches to Morality

Philosophers trying to show that some moral standard is rationally defensible have generally done this in one of three ways: They have tried to find something that is widely accepted as good, either as a goal of action or as a motive of action; they have tried to find something that can be defended as appropriate to human nature; and they have tried to find something that can obligate people to make the sacrifices that morality demands. Since some of these strategies can be pursued in different ways, we can divide approaches to morality into five general categories: consequentialism, virtue ethics, communitarianism, deontological ethics, and contractarianism.

2.3.1. Consequentialism

Consequentialism is the view that what makes moral standards valid is the fact that acting on them tends to produce good effects.

The most familiar form of consequentialism is *utilitarianism*, formulated with different emphases by the nineteenth-century philosophers, Jeremy Bentham and John Stuart Mill, but subjected to numerous technical adjustments in the twentieth century. The basic idea is that what is good is happiness, with happiness understood as either the feeling of satisfaction or as the fact of having one's desires satisfied. Since utilitarian morality aims not simply at each individual's pursuit of his private happiness, utilitarianism holds that the moral good is found in the maximization of happiness for all people or for all creatures capable of experiencing pleasure or pain. The latter version would include sentient animals within the reach of morality.

Either way, the utilitarian supposes that we can, at least roughly, estimate how much net happiness (satisfaction minus dissatisfaction) any of our actions will produce in each person affected and then that we can add this up to arrive at an aggregate sum of net happiness that will be produced for all people affected by any of our actions. The utilitarian would have us calculate these possible outcomes for all of the actions available to us (including the action of doing nothing). Our utilitarian duty is to do that action that, among all the actions possible for us, produces the highest aggregate sum of net happiness.

Utilitarian ethics are sometimes summed up in the slogan "the greatest good for the greatest number." However, this slogan is misleading in that it does not take into account the intensity of satisfactions or dissatisfactions. A utilitarian's duty is to produce the greatest amount of net happiness. Something that produces very intense satisfaction for a few and to which most people are indifferent may produce more overall happiness than something that produces satisfaction of a milder sort for more people. Likewise, an action that makes a large number of people only mildly happy but makes a small number of people intensely miserable may produce less overall happiness than an action that makes fewer people happy but no one intensely miserable. Thus, utilitarianism will not always aim to make the largest number of people happy. However, it must be admitted that, since it is very difficult (some think impossible) to compare different people's levels of satisfaction utilitarianism may in fact aim to achieve the happiness of the greatest number in spite of itself.

There is much to be said for utilitarianism. First of all, acting on moral principles—even when doing so tends to sacrifice the agent's own satisfaction—does generally work to make most people happier than they would be if people acted simply in pursuit of their own selfish desires. Moreover, utilitarianism has a sensible and easily understandable standard of goodness. Everybody can recognize that being satisfied is better than being dissatisfied, that pleasure is better than pain. This is a broadly neutral standard in that it doesn't favor one means of producing pleasure over another. What pleases me may bore you to tears, and vice versa, but no matter. All that counts is how much pleasure I get from what pleases me and how much you get from what pleases you, and likewise for pain. And since everyone is vulnerable to pleasure and pain, this is also a universal standard. As noted before it applies even beyond the human race. Many philosophically minded vegetarians and critics of cruelty to animals act on utilitarian grounds.

Utilitarianism played an important role in modernizing criminal justice practices, largely because it insisted that the main legitimate justification of punishment lay in its tendency to deter criminals (including the one being punished) from committing crimes in the future. Since utilitarianism aims to maximize satisfaction, punishment of the guilty is—for utilitarianism—an imposition of dissatisfaction that can only be justified if it leads to an overall increase in satisfaction. Prior to utilitarianism, punishments were meted out on the basis of people's varying intuitions about the evilness of acts committed, with the result that punishments varied wildly and were often very cruel compared to the act committed. Against this, utilitarianism insisted that punishments be determined on the basis of the appeal to empirical facts, such as the effect of punishment on crime rates and the degree of dissatisfaction produced by the crime being punished. This development introduced a measure of rationality and even scientific method into criminal justice and contributed considerably to civilizing our system of punishments. When you hear people debating whether the use of marijuana should be decriminalized based on medical data about its effects on the health of users, or whether the death penalty should be abolished based on data about its tendency to deter future murders, you are hearing the effect that utilitarianism has had on rationalizing criminal justice policy.

On the other hand, utilitarianism has lately been subjected to significant criticism on two main grounds. First, it appears that some things are good not because they lead to pleasure or to the satisfaction of desires. So, for example, fairness, self-respect, truthfulness to self and others, or a sense of the meaningfulness of one's pursuits seem to be good no matter what satisfactions they lead to. This fact has led some consequentialists to broaden the notion of good from happiness to include some other things as intrinsically good. This change makes their theories more true to the diversity of people's aims but more controversial, since people have different opinions concerning what is intrinsically good. Second, utilitarianism has been criticized because its way of arriving at the moral good is by aggregating the net satisfaction of individuals. This evaluative method has the effect that actions that produce enough satisfaction for enough people will be found moral even if they impose great dissatisfaction on a small enough number of others. As a result, many contemporary philosophers think that utilitarianism cannot provide adequate protection for individual rights, since the fate of each individual is wholly dependent on how treatment of her affects the satisfaction of others. If, as many people believe, morality requires that individuals be treated in certain ways no matter how many others may profit from their mistreatment, then utilitarianism seems to miss something crucial about morality.

2.3.2. Virtue Ethics

Many philosophers have observed that, in everyday life, morality seems less a matter of producing some good consequences or of even complying with certain rules, and more a matter of being a certain sort of person—a person with a character marked by distinctively moral dispositions, such as kindness, sensitivity to the needs of others, respectfulness, fairness, courage, seriousness of purpose, and so on. These philosophers have accordingly thought that it is not the goodness of our goals or the rightness of our rules that makes us moral, but the goodness of our dispositions, traditionally called *virtues*. This approach—which stems from Aristotle and other ancient moral thinkers, such as the Stoics and Epicureans—is called *virtue ethics*. Here too, there is an important truth. The people we think of as moral do not seem to tote up consequences or to subject their actions to abstract moral rules. Rather they react morally, that is, with sensitivity to others' needs, with a desire to be fair and generous, with a courage that is less the result of reflection than the consequence of a character that would not think of shrinking from doing what is right.

But virtue ethics encounters difficulty when it tries to account for the goodness of the virtues. Why is the disposition to fairness or to kindness good while a disposition to self-aggrandizement or to callousness is not good? Without an account of the goodness of the moral dispositions, virtue ethics is less an answer to the question "What is moral?" than it is to the question "To what does morality properly apply?" Its answer is that it properly applies to people's characters rather than to their actions or to rules, but it leaves us still in need of valid standards of morality by which to distinguish good from bad character traits. Thus virtue ethics is dependent on the sort of moral reflection that we just saw in utilitarianism and will see in deontological ethics.

2.3.3. Communitarianism

Philosophers have normally identified two features of human nature that seem to make special treatment of human beings appropriate:

their rationality and their sociality. By the latter is meant the fact that human beings do not merely live in groups, as do many other animals, but that they understand themselves in light of the identities they share as members of groups and in light of the attachments they have to friends, relatives, neighbors, and coworkers. This conception of sociality has led to a position in moral philosophy called *communitarianism*, which holds that morality is constituted by the ideals that define and hold together real human groups.

However, while our social nature is not to be ignored or underestimated, it should be clear that communitarianism does not so much identify proper moral standards as accept the standards of existing groups as definitive. Its problem, then, is that morality becomes equivalent finally to the standards that people actually endorse, some of which seem patently immoral. Thus, many philosophers originally sympathetic to communitarianism have come to notice that many communities are defined by moral standards that now seem oppressive. For example, traditional religious communities have often held sexist views to the extent that they have taught that women are meant to serve and obey men, and many small-town communities have held racist views or have been intolerant of homosexuals or others who, though harmless, are different. The daily newspapers are filled with the persecutions carried out in the name of one ethnic group's historical detestation of another. Thus, in a way that is parallel to virtue ethics, communitarianism points rather to where morality should be found than to what it is, and leaves us still in need of valid moral standards to distinguish moral communities from oppressive ones.

The important truth in communitarianism is that we are not separate atoms but are necessarily linked to our fellows. Thus, the marks of morality—altruism, self-sacrifice, and commitment beyond ourselves—are part of us because we ourselves are social in nature. Even when we think of our self-interest, it is defined by the communities of which we are members. Moreover, without going so far as to accept the moral principles that are endorsed in our group simply because they are endorsed, we can recognize that the moral ideals actually accepted by a community have a special standing. Inasmuch as they shape people's identities, a community's morals are worthy of special respect and ought to be neither dismissed lightly nor accepted uncritically.

2.3.4. Deontological Ethics

The strain of moral reflection that argues that moral treatment is appropriate to humans because of their rationality has a long history. Its most popular recent incarnation is associated with the moral thinking of the philosopher Immanuel Kant. His view is of a type called *deontological* because it aims to show how there can be moral requirements that do not depend on whether the actions required produce good consequences.

Kant took it to be our special competence as rational beings to formulate general or universal laws, and this, he thought, was what gave us moral knowledge. For any act that we might contemplate doing, we can always ask whether we would be willing to endorse a universal law that permitted or required that type of action. Interestingly, such questioning is strikingly like applying the Golden Rule to a prospective action. If I contemplate cheating my neighbor, Kant would have me ask myself whether I would be willing to live in a world in which people were all permitted to cheat one another—which, of course, would mean that I too would be subject to permissible cheating. With perhaps an excess of optimism, Kant concluded that not only would no one want to live in such a world, but also no one *could* honestly will to live in one. If, then, I proceed to cheat my neighbor, I live out a kind of contradiction: I perform an action that I would not allow generally, an action that I cannot endorse as a general rule. Thus, I know at least in my heart of hearts that I am making a special exception for myself that I would not grant others and that I cannot really justify for myself.

Note that the philosophy of Kant is *not* saying that I shouldn't cheat my neighbor because doing so might lead to my getting cheated myself; it is proposing a test that one performs wholly in one's mind. I ask myself if I could will my intended action as a universal law. If I cannot, then that action is wrong even if I could do it and suffer no bad consequences at all.

Accordingly, Kant believed that our rationality alone provided a test of the morality of actions. This is not to say, as is often mistakenly said of Kant, that he thought that the full content of morality could be derived from our pure reason without reference to the facts of the world. Far from it. Reason supplies a test of morality, but it is our desires that supply the subjects of the test. My reason cannot itself tell me not to cheat my neighbor. Rather, observing in myself the desire to cheat him, I can apply reason to this desire and ask if I would be willing to live in a world where everyone was permitted to act on such desires. It is the test that is universal and derived from reason, but the test must be applied to the observed facts of human life.

Kant thought that this competence of ours was more than merely a means to figure out what is moral. Since he took it to derive from our reason alone and not from our desires, he thought it represented our unique freedom from natural forces. Human beings could guide their actions and could decide which of their desires to act on by reference to a standard found in their reason and not thus itself the product of desire. Thus, in our reason, Kant found freedom, freedom from the forces of nature, freedom from the pushes and pulls of desires and aversions. Thus his moral theory exalts human beings' free rational wills and teaches us to treat all free rational beings as "ends-in-themselves," that is, as beings that cannot rightly be subjected to forces that their own reason does not endorse. This in turn adds a new dimension to the test described above. When I ask of a prospective action whether I would be willing to live subject to a universal law permitting or requiring such things, I am asking whether I truly believe that all rational beings could freely endorse the action I have in mind.

When I contemplate cheating my neighbor, what I must ask is, "Could my action be freely and rationally endorsed by my neighbor?" It

is obvious that it could not, since the very possibility of cheating my neighbor requires bypassing her rational judgment about what I am doing. I must depend on her ignorance of what I am doing in order to succeed in cheating her. Likewise, robbing my neighbor requires bypassing or overriding her freedom. I can only rob her by acting against her will—if it were her will that I end up with the thing I take from her, then she would give it to me and it would not be robbery. Consequently, morality of this Kantian variety is sometimes identified with *respect*, respect for the freedom and rationality of one's fellows. Evil actions are actions which bypass or override or ignore the freedom and rationality of others, and thus are disrespectful of those others' most distinctive capacities. Such a moral view is deontological in that it arrives at its judgments without considering all the consequences of the acts under consideration. So, even if cheating or robbing my neighbor might in some way help my nation or even all of humanity, such acts are forbidden because they fail to respect my neighbor.

In sum, for Kant and those inspired by him, true morality is a matter of treating human beings in ways that are appropriate to their nature as free and rational beings. This means in ways that treat them as free and rational, in ways that they can freely and rationally accept. When people complain, for example, of being treated like objects or like tools, they are essentially saying that they have been treated in ways that fail to respect their freedom and rationality. They have been manipulated or pushed around, rather than appealed to for free and rational acceptance. Since freedom and rationality are taken to be the marks of *personhood*, a Kantian-type morality is sometimes called a morality of respect for persons.

Contrary to consequentialism, this kind of deontological moral approach clearly rules out using people as means to the happiness of others. For this reason, many of those who have felt that utilitarianism is not a strong enough defender of individual human rights have turned to Kantian or Kantian-inspired moral views. Nonetheless, though there is undoubtedly something about Kantian-style morality that resonates with many people's strong feelings about the treatment proper to human beings, this kind of approach has its problems as well. Unlike utilitarianism, with its emphasis on happiness or the satisfaction of desires, Kantian moral theory doesn't provide an easily grasped notion of good. The idea that certain treatment is appropriate to free rational beings is a more abstract kind of good than pleasure or satisfaction, nor is it easy to prove that it is more important to respect human beings than to bring about their happiness. And some philosophers have doubted whether we really have a capacity to make rational evaluations independent of our desires.

2.3.5. Contractarianism

Contractarianism was originally used by philosophers like John Locke and Thomas Hobbes to account for the legitimacy of political authority. The idea was that if people could be thought of as agreeing in a kind of *social contract* to the establishment of some form of government, then that form of government could not be thought of as tyrannical or oppressive. This does not imply that governments are established by real contracts, or real agreements among citizens, for the simple reason that in order to have real contracts, it is necessary to have real peace and stability, and political institutions must already exist to provide just that. The social contract is a theoretical idea, not a historical one. To say that a government satisfies the requirements of the social contract doctrine is to say that people, who were not under a government, would find it rational to give up the primitive freedom that they would have outside of states and agree freely to be subject to this kind of government. For this reason, social contract doctrines usually start from some imaginary "state of nature," which lacks governmental institutions, and try to show the sort of political constraints people in that imaginary situation would reasonably contract into.

It is this theoretical, imaginary feature of the social contract doctrine that makes it suitable as a basis for morality as well as for political institutions. Just as one can ask what form of government it would be rational for people to agree to, one can ask what moral constraints it would be rational for them to agree to. Indeed, it is a short step from Kantian moral theory to contractarian moral theory. Kant himself defended a kind of moral contractarianism at certain points, and John Rawls, the most important of twentieth-century contractarian moral philosophers, considers his own view a Kantian one. What Rawls has added to contractarianism is, first of all, replacement of the "state of nature" (an imaginary situation without governmental institutions) by the "original position" (an imaginary situation in which people must decide on basic moral principles). Rawls has also insisted that the decision in the original position be thought of as taken behind an imaginary "veil of ignorance," which keeps the people in the original position ignorant of all facts about their own situations, though they retain general knowledge of history, economics, politics, and so forth.

The effect of changing to the original position is to adapt the contract to the goal of determining moral principles rather than governmental institutions. It eliminates the state of nature as an anarchic condition that people want to escape, and thus a condition to which governments are compared when evaluating them. The original position is simply a condition in which decisions are to be taken. The effect of the veil of ignorance is that people deciding in the imaginary original position cannot tailor moral principles to their own situations—rather they must imagine that they could be in anyone's shoes and decide on principles in light of what would be best for anyone. For example, not knowing whether they are rich or poor, they cannot decide on taxation or welfare policies on the basis of whether they would personally benefit from such policies. They have to decide what would be better from the standpoint of anyone, or everyone, in the society. This feature guarantees the moral, rather than self-interested, nature of the decision that is to be made in the original position.

The basic idea of contractarian moral theory is that, inasmuch as morality requires people to forego the pursuit of their self-interest (to avoid acts that would benefit themselves at a cost to others, such as lying, cheating, or stealing), a rationally defensible morality must provide benefits to people that make it rational for them to conform to the constraints of morality. This idea dovetails with Kantian morality because it gives pride of place to the notion that treating people morally is treating them in ways that they could rationally and freely endorse. What contractarianism adds is a focus on the sacrifices that morality requires and the benefits it must provide to make moral obligation reasonable for free people.

Contractarianism can be viewed as combining the best of Kantianism and of utilitarianism. Where a Kantian moral philosophy emphasizes treating people in ways they can accept, contractarianism tries to spell out the benefits that make morality reasonable for one to accept. The benefits must be of a very general nature—such as liberty, personal security, and provision of general means to pursue one's goals—that just about anyone can be expected to regard as benefits. In this way, contractarian moral theory shares with utilitarianism the focus on important and widely desired benefits. On the other hand, contractarians insist that people would not agree to be sacrificed for the well-being of others or for the aggregate good of society. Thus, contractarianism shares with Kantianism a stronger basis for protecting people's individual rights than utilitarianism can provide.

The standard test of morality for a contractarian is whether a proposed moral standard is such that, even with the constraints it places on people's pursuit of their self-interests it would be rational for all people, deciding together as so many individuals, not knowing how they in particular will be affected, to agree to be subject to that standard. To see the plausibility of this approach consider the light it sheds on practices such as racism or sexism. Ask yourself if you would agree to either of these behind a veil of ignorance—that is, not knowing which race or sex you are. Without such knowledge, forced to judge as if one could be anyone, people will not agree to racism or sexism, since they might well be seriously

disadvantaged by either. This shows the unfairness of racism and sexism very clearly since it shows that these are policies that could only be chosen by members of the favored race or sex—thus such policies only exist because they have been forced on the disfavored ones.

The problems with contractarianism come from the difficulty of determining what people would all agree to as good behind a veil of ignorance, given the actual disagreements that people have over what is good and what is worth sacrificing for. For example, at least some people, say deeply religious fundamentalists, might not find liberty a benefit that would make it worth their while to refrain from claiming the right to stop others from acting in ways that they regard as sinful. On the other hand, the fact that contractarian morality can combine utilitarianism's emphasis on concrete benefits with Kantianism's refusal to allow the sacrifice of a few for the benefit of the rest has made contractarianism an extremely popular and powerful moral theory among contemporary moral philosophers.

2.4. *Why Be Moral?*

The contributions of moral philosophers are very impressive. Perhaps they have made enough of an impression on some skeptical readers to make them think that some moral standards can be rationally justified after all. But there is another question that might arise at this point, namely, "Even if there are valid moral standards, why should I go along with them when I could benefit from violating them?" There is no sense denying that sometimes a person might benefit from immoral behavior. If that weren't true, we wouldn't need criminal justice to persuade people to stay on the good side of the law. Nor is it enough to think that the immoral person will be tormented by his conscience. Some people have stronger consciences than others; some may be able to silence their consciences, shout them down, or neutralize them by rationalizing their immoral behavior. We need a more concrete answer as to why people should be moral.

Many times, perhaps most of the time, it is in one's self-interest to be moral. After all, if people find out that you are a liar or a thief, you may be punished, ostracized, or treated with suspicion, all of which may seriously detract from your own well-being. But this is not enough, since the real challenge comes when it seems to be in one's self-interest to be immoral. What then can be said to show that it would still be a mistake to be immoral?

The answers to this question parallel the approaches that moral philosophers have taken, but the answers may apply to more than one approach. Parallel to utilitarianism's emphasis on making everyone as happy as possible is the idea that we human beings have a natural sympathy for one another; we want our fellows to be happy, and we are naturally sad when they are unhappy. There's plenty of evidence for this. Pictures of victims of famine or subjugation naturally produce unhappiness in us, whether they are on the evening news or in the movies. We will be made happier if others are happy, and since being moral is a way of making others happy, we will be made happier by being moral even if in the short run it appears that we can make ourselves happy by being immoral.

Parallel to the emphasis in virtue ethics on good character traits is the idea that by being immoral we exercise and encourage in ourselves traits—selfishness, insensibility, pride, greed, and so on—that are not admirable. They are not traits we want in our friends or children, in fact, they are not traits we want in ourselves. So, by being immoral we lose respect for ourselves and make ourselves unlovable in our own eyes. The immoral person cannot truly believe that he or she is living well or living a life worth living. Conversely, by being moral, we exercise and encourage in ourselves traits—altruism, sensitivity, humility, generosity, and so on—that are admirable. Thus, by being moral, we make ourselves into the sorts of persons we truly want to be. We make ourselves worthy of our own respect, lovable in our own eyes.

Parallel to communitarianism's insistence on our social nature is the idea that, in being immoral, we cut ourselves off from our fellows. To lie, we must keep inside what we really think and watch the other act on a false notion of what we think. To rob or injure another, we must make ourselves insensitive to the other's loss or pain. These attitudes are forms of alienation—they open distances between us and our fellows, cut us off from genuine human contact, and make us strangers to one another. If communitarians are right about the centrality of sociality to our natures, these attitudes are ways in which we impoverish ourselves and empty ourselves of substance and identity. Even if we benefit from an immoral act, we suffer as well a diminution of our humanity, a kind of loneliness from which there is no escape.

Parallel to the deontologist's notion that morality is an expression of our nature as free and rational beings is the idea that, in being immoral, we fail to be true to our nature. As we saw earlier, for Kant, to act immorally is to make an unjustified exception for ourselves that we would not grant others—while to act morally is to govern our actions by our rational capacity to arrive at general rules and thus to manifest our special human nature as rational beings. Also, for Kant, to act immorally is to give in to self-interest when morality requires otherwise and to make oneself the mere slave of one's desires. To act morally is to rise above one's desires and manifest one's special human nature as free. When we act immorally, then, we treat ourselves as lesser beings than we are, more like non-rational and unfree animals than like humans, and we naturally disrespect ourselves for it—even if, for the moment, the benefits of our immorality crowd out the awareness of the contempt in which we hold ourselves for being less than what our nature allows us to be.

Parallel to the contractarian's notion that morality is like an agreement for each to make those sacrifices that, if made by all, would benefit all is the idea that the immoral person is a kind of parasite, a cheat who takes the benefits provided by the sacrifices of others and refuses to make his sacrifice when his turn comes. Such a person is alienated from his fellows much in the way the communitarian supposes immoral people to be. Moreover, such a person makes himself a kind of outlaw; he declares war on society by saying, in effect, I will take what I can get from my fellows but I will not cooperate in producing or providing the benefits we all need.

In sum, we should be moral because it is often in our self-interest to be so; and even where it is not, we will be made happy in the long run by being moral and thus making others happy; we will admire, respect and love ourselves more for being moral; we will feel connected and in harmony with our fellow human beings; we will regard ourselves as being true to our distinctive natures as free and rational beings; we will feel ourselves free in the sense of being more than merely the slaves of our desires and rational in the sense of being able to subject our acts to general rules; and we will feel that we are full, cooperating members of the human community rather than parasites or cheats, doing our share when our turn comes, able to live in peace with our fellows without deception or fear of discovery.

2.5. Conclusion: How Shall We Evaluate Moral Standards?

Rather than try to adjudicate between the various ethical approaches that we have just reviewed, we leave that to each reader to do for him or herself. What we draw from this overview is, rather, a set of questions that each individual may pose when trying to determine the morality of a practice or policy or rule:

Compared to the possible alternatives, does it tend to make all people overall happier in the long run?

Does it contribute generally to people's being better able to satisfy their desires?

Does it exercise and encourage people's most admirable character traits?

Does it link us more closely to our fellows?

Does it reverberate with the best values that define our shared communities?

Does it correspond to a rule that we would be willing to have made into a law for everyone, ourselves as well as others?

Does it show respect for the unique capacity of our fellow human beings to make free and rational decisions about their actions?

Does it provide benefits to all people that make reasonable the sacrifices it asks of all?

Surely a practice, policy, or rule that does well on such an examination is one that we can confidently believe is moral.

3. THE SPECIAL MORAL DEMANDS OF CRIMINAL JUSTICE

We have already seen that its use of force makes criminal justice uncomfortably like crime and imposes on us the need to show that criminal justice is different in a way that implies that its use of force is moral while that of criminals is immoral. Moreover, criminal justice claims a legitimacy such that citizens are obligated to obey it, not just forced to do so. Each of these facts points us to important features of the problem of determining the morality of criminal justice.

That criminal justice uses force reminds us that it is a creation of the state and thus its force is exercised in the name of the public as a whole. The force available to the agents of criminal justice is not simply their private power. It is the public's power entrusted to those agents by the citizenry when it, through its representatives, makes laws for the criminal justice system to enforce and follow. The use of force by criminal justice agents must thus be subject to the rule of law.

That criminal justice claims a legitimacy such that citizens are obligated to obey it suggests that criminal justice must be justified in terms that the citizens can and do accept. This justification must take into account the diversity of values in the citizenry. Perhaps there once were countries where everyone agrees on what is right and wrong, but this is surely not the case in the United States or in other modern nations. Even though, as I suggested earlier, it is easy to exaggerate the extent of moral disagreement, such disagreement does exist, and this places on criminal justice yet another burden. If criminal justice is to be obligatory to all citizens, it cannot simply impose the values of some citizens on others. It must, as far as possible, accommodate to the plurality of moral views that exist. Let us then consider in turn the requirements of the rule of law and the need to accommodate moral pluralism.

3.1. The Rule of Law

Even if a law is made in a democratic manner by a legitimate government, it may still be an immoral law. The mere fact that something is lawful does not make it right. Nonetheless, the law is not without its moral weight both for citizens and for public officers. For citizens, that something is the law, certainly that it is a democratically made law of a legitimate government, gives it at least a prima facie moral claim on our obedience. Our obligation to obey the law cannot be based on our agreeing with the law. To insist on that is to insist that laws only bind those who agree with them, and that in turn implies that there is really no law at all. People then would be required to do only what they thought was right to do, and thus there would be no set of rules that bound the whole society—and thus no law. Socrates recognized this fact when, after being unjustly condemned to death by the Athenian citizenry, he refused to disobey the law and try to escape his punishment. To do that, he thought, would harm the law, since there is no law if people believe they don't have to obey laws they dispute. To harm the law, for Socrates, was to do an injustice to the Athenian state whose legitimacy and basic goodness he acknowledged. Likewise, John Locke, writing in the seventeenth century, proclaimed that to consent to be part of a state is to consent to be governed by the majority will. This is so because to insist on more, to insist on unanimity, is to insist on one's right to follow one's own decisions at all times and thus to refuse to join a state at all.

Since one's obligation to obey the laws cannot depend on one's agreeing with them, it follows that, if a state is a generally good and just one, if its means of establishing laws are generally democratic and fair, one has an obligation to obey the law even if one disagrees with the law. Of course, it is not the only thing that counts. If the law demands action that is seriously immoral, then that fact may outweigh the law's own moral force. This may then justify civil disobedience or, in extreme cases, more extreme action against the law.

The law does not, however, only place moral requirements on citizens, it also places important and special moral requirements on public officials. They are, of course, also citizens and thus also bound to obey the laws. However, more important for our purposes is the fact that public officials, the agents of the criminal justice system in particular, have special powers that are created by the laws. This has numerous implications: First, it means that they have *only* the power given them by the laws. Lawmakers may make only those laws that the higher law of the constitution permits, and they may only make them in the way for which the higher law provides. Judges do not have discretion to do whatever they think is right. They can only sentence criminals according to the penalties in the law, after those criminals have been found guilty according to the procedures and standards stipulated by the law. Even if the judge is sure in her heart that the person before her is guilty, she may not punish that person if the jury finds him innocent; neither may she punish him more than the legal penalty for the crime of which he has been found guilty. Likewise, the police do not have unlimited authority to do whatever is necessary to stop crime. They may do only what the law says they may do.

Moreover, the law speaks in general terms. It is a system of rules that apply to a large range of individual cases. This means that the agents of criminal justice must treat people alike—not that they must treat criminals and innocents alike, but rather that they must treat similarly all who break the law in similar ways. In this sense, the rule of law demands equality of treatment.

The facts just mentioned often lead to dissatisfaction with the criminal justice system. We may be unhappy when someone whom the public is convinced is guilty escapes punishment because of failure to prove his guilt according to the legally indicated procedures and standards. We may wish that the police could go further in tailoring their treatment to the different situations of different individuals, but consider what is at stake. To allow people to be convicted because the public is convinced that they are guilty is to deprive people of the sure protection of due process. To allow the police to tailor their treatment to the different conditions of different citizens is to give up law and hand our fates over to the intuitions and perceptions of the police. For these reasons, Plato thought of the rule of law as "second best." Best, he thought, would be rule by an all-wise and perfectly moral ruler who could do whatever he thought best to bring about justice in every particular situation. But, Plato recognized, that would only work if we could be sure that our ruler was all-wise and perfectly moral, for if he wasn't he could do immense harm. Since we cannot be sure of this, Plato recommended that we be satisfied with the second best, strict rules applied in the same way to all people. Even if some injustice is done, it will be less injustice and less dangerous than handing unlimited power over to our rulers.

3.2. *Moral Pluralism*

A criminal justice system claims moral legitimacy. That is, it asserts its rules as not merely expressions of power with which the people are forced to comply, but rather as expressions of a legitimate authority that people are morally obligated to obey. Yet why should the citizens obey the rules of the criminal justice system?

One way to see the force of this question is to compare the sort of answer that can be given when the rule at issue is a widely accepted one, such as the rule against murder, to a case in which the rule is more controversial, such as a rule against homosexual sodomy. Consider the latter case first. When the practitioner of homosexual sodomy is arrested, he may understandably suspect that the criminal justice system is simply using its power to impose on him the moral opinions of the majority. Why should he feel obligated to go along with the moral opinions of the majority? Is he not being subjected to mere might disguised as right? Would he have an equal right to impose rules against heterosexual practices if homosexuals were in the majority? These sorts of questions bring us back to the uncomfortable similarity between criminal justice and crime and to the need to show that the citizens have reason to believe that they owe obedience and are not just being pushed around.

Consider how much easier it is to answer analogous questions when enforcing the rule against murder. Can the murderer complain that he is simply being forced to comply with the moral opinions of the anti-murder majority? No, for the simple reason that he also does not want to be murdered. The law against murder protects him as well as his victims. In short, one reason that a law against murder is not controversial while a law against sodomy is, is that the law against murder protects something of value to *every* citizen—his or her life—while a law against sodomy protects something of value to only *some* people. It is this fact that makes the first sort of law appear legitimate—every citizen is obligated to obey it because it protects interests that every citizen has. It makes the second sort of law suspect as mere might masquerading as right—it enforces some people's moral opinions, and does not clearly protect something of value to everyone. This is the reason that the so-called "victimless crimes" are controversial. Real victimization is something against which everyone wants to be protected and thus laws that prohibit crimes that cause clear injury and loss are laws that everyone is clearly obligated to obey.

The more general lesson here is that the law does best when it protects values that are universally shared, and it becomes more dubious—more like might and less like right—when it protects values that only some people endorse. The best laws then will be those that protect against violence and loss, laws that ensure security and liberty, because these are things that virtually all people want. This has obvious implications under the conditions of moral pluralism, where we expect people to differ on at least some moral issues. The more the law sticks to what all people value, the more legitimate it will appear to the citizens, and the more likely they are to feel obligated to obey the law and to support the law enforcers.

4. WHAT ABOUT CRIMINAL JUSTICE IS SUBJECT TO MORAL EVALUATION?

In the chapters that follow, experts from many fields will address in detail the ethical problems that are presented by criminal justice. In the remainder of this introductory essay, I mean only to sketch the overall framework within which those problems are located. Speaking generally, we can say that criminal justice presents moral problems at three levels: of laws, of practices, and of social and psychological foundations. Let us consider these in order.

4.1. The Level of Laws

The mere fact that something is a law is not sufficient to make it morally acceptable. In recent times, acts that were legally criminal have become in fact legally acceptable, either by changes in the law or by changes in enforcement practices. So, while many states have laws against fellatio engaged in even by married couples, such laws are virtually never enforced and many people do not realize that they are doing something that is technically illegal. Private gambling, playing gin rummy or poker for money with your friends, is legally criminal in many states, but almost never prosecuted. In some states, prostitution was against the law and then decriminalized, leaving the only relevant crime that of public solicitation. Of course, we have gone from a long period, the century between the Civil War and the 1970s, when abortion was illegal, to the current situation in which it is a constitutional right. Needless to say, those who think that abortion is murder feel that it is immoral even though legally permitted, and those who think that abortion is part of a woman's right to control over her body feel that it is moral and was moral even when it was legally criminal.

That legality is not the same as morality means that we must ask what acts should—morally should—be treated as crimes. Should recreational use of marijuana or cocaine be against the law? Should prostitution be against the law? Should abortion be against the law?

Should pornography be against the law? Should business actions that lead to injury or loss of life be treated as crimes? There is also a related group of questions about how serious specific crimes are. If assault is a crime, should it be treated as a more serious crime, with a more serious penalty, if it is motivated by race hatred or homophobia? Should actions of employers that increase the dangerousness of workplaces and result in loss of life be treated as forms of homicide? Should rape be treated as a form of assault or as a special crime? What standards should be used in determining whether wrongful actions, such as sexual harassment, have occurred?

Finally, the laws also provide for the punishment of criminals. At this level, we must also ask what punishments are morally acceptable. Should we administer corporal punishment to violent offenders, as some have recently recommended? Should we revive chain gangs, as some states have recently done? Should prisons provide programs of rehabilitation or just the pains of confinement as the criminal's just reward? Should prisons be turned over to private corporations if they provide more cost-effective administration? Should repeat offenders get harsher sentences than first offenders for the same crimes? Is it fair to identify former sex offenders publicly after they have served their prison sentences and presumably paid their debt to society? And, of course, there remains the age-old question of whether a state should impose the death penalty on convicted murderers.

4.2. The Level of Practices

By practices are meant the acts of individual agents in the criminal justice system and the agency policies that allow or disallow such acts. Here, then, we find questions about how police treat suspects, whether it is legitimate for the police to use deception in apprehending criminals, and what degree of force the police may use. Further, are the police discriminating—consciously or unconsciously—among citizens on the basis of race, sex, or class? Is it fair to arrest prostitutes but not their clients? Is it fair to bring middle-class juvenile delinquents home to their parents while lower-class ones are brought to the station house to be booked? Should the police exercise discretion over whom they arrest, or should they be required to arrest whomever they have reason to believe has broken the law? What limits should there be on the means—undercover agents, paid informers, and the whole range of existing and emerging technology, such as thermal imagers that "see" through walls—that the police use to get evidence against criminals?

The police are not the only agents of the system. So, we must ask as well whether the decisions made by prosecutors on whom or what acts to prosecute are made fairly and in the public interest. Should prosecutors engage in "plea bargaining," trading reductions in charges for guilty pleas? Is it fair to impose harsher penalties on someone found guilty after a trial than on someone who pleads guilty without a trial in return for a reduction in charge and thus in sentence? How far should lawyers go in defending accused criminals or in promoting the interests of individuals whose actions they find reprehensible? Should we support "the exclusionary rule," requiring that evidence obtained improperly by the state be excluded at trial even if the result is that a guilty person goes free? Should juries have the right to find people innocent if they believe that the law the individual has violated is immoral, a practice called "jury nullification"? How strong should the presumption of innocence be? Should juries convict only when criminals have been found guilty beyond a reasonable doubt, or would it suffice if most of the evidence tends to indicate guilt? On what basis should judges determine sentences? What role should members of other professions—physicians and psychiatrists, as well as representatives of the media—play in the criminal justice system?

4.3. The Level of Social and Psychological Foundations

This level is foundational because it is not directly about the criminal justice system itself, but rather about the conditions upon which, the criminal justice system functions so to speak. What is meant by social foundations relates to the social justice issues that determine the justice of criminal justice, and what is meant by psychological foundations relates to the conceptions of human freedom and responsibility that guide the operation of the system.

4.3.1. Social Justice

The simple fact is that a criminal justice system cannot be more just than the society it protects. The law against theft may seem neutral on its face: It protects everyone against theft of what they own. However, if the distribution of wealth or property in a society is unjust, then such a law protects, and thus promotes—*aids, and abets*—injustice. Suppose (an idea for which there is unhappily a considerable amount of evidence) that the removal of Native American tribes from their traditional lands was a form of violent theft. Then it follows that current possession of that land by American citizens is a continuation of that theft (a kind of ongoing possession of stolen goods). Consequently, if a latter-day Native American steals, he may be correcting an injustice rather than committing one. Morally speaking, he would not be the thief, but the rectifier of theft. Likewise, morally speaking, if the criminal justice system apprehends the Native American and returns what he has taken to its current owner, the criminal justice system is arguably an accomplice in the original theft.

Since there has been and remains considerable economic injustice in America, this notion is of wide relevance. In addition to the violent theft of Native American lands, much of American wealth was taken out of the hides of African slaves, brought here and forced to work under inhuman conditions. Moreover, there has been and continues to be wage discrimination against black and Latino workers, as well as against females. This is an injustice that enriches those who can get away with paying the members of such disadvantaged groups less than equally qualified white males are paid. Thus, even though there has been considerable progress in rectifying this discrimination, it remains the case that at least in some significant measure the distribution of wealth and income in the United States is unjust. To that same extent, the criminal justice system is arguably an accomplice in that injustice.

In addition, these injustices are reproduced in the heart of the criminal justice system itself. As wealth and income are unjustly distributed, so too is the ability to hire one's own high-quality lawyer. Consequently, defense of one's rights, of one's legal presumption of innocence, is unjustly distributed as well. As just about everyone now knows after witnessing the murder trial of O. J. Simpson, the rich are much better able to defend themselves against criminal prosecutions than the poor. Statistics bear out that, not only are the poor far more prevalent in the prison population than in the population at large, they are—for the same offense—far more likely to be arrested than the well-off; if arrested, more likely to be charged; if charged, more likely to be convicted; and if convicted, more likely to be given harsh sentences. If, as we suggested at the outset, the criminal justice system is uncomfortably like crime in its actions, here is where the problem most clearly shows. If the criminal justice system does not work for the benefit of all members of society, if it imposes its penalties more frequently on the disadvantaged in society than on the better-off, then, to that extent it loses its moral differentiation from crime. Instead of being moral because it is serving the interests of all alike, it starts to be like crime in imposing its force for the benefit of some and to the disadvantage of others.

What's more, if the poor and disadvantaged are victimized by the criminal justice system, then the status of their moral obligation to its rules also comes into question. The criminal justice system claims the obligation of all citizens on the basis of providing benefits for all. However, if the system does not provide benefits for all, but victimizes some, and if it protects the property of those who have benefited

from the unjust exploitation of the poor and disadvantaged, then, to that same extent, it is doubtful that the poor and disadvantaged are morally obligated to comply with the criminal justice system. For them, perhaps, as has been said by some, the police are no different from an occupying army, obeyed because they have greater weaponry, not because they morally deserve it. Then the same would apply to the courts and the rest of the criminal justice system.

Social injustice may transform the apparent wrongdoing of criminals into the moral equivalent of rectifying injustice, and it may undermine the guilt of the victims of injustice by weakening the degree to which they are morally obligated to obey the law.

4.3.2. Psychological Foundations

For people to be held morally and legally responsible for their acts, those acts must in some sense be in their control. This implies that, in addition to conditions of social justice underlying the operations of criminal justice, there are psychological conditions that must be in play as well. This much is recognized in laws that release the insane from criminal guilt or punishment. It is (on some accounts) also recognized in rules against entrapment that release from criminal guilt individuals who have been tempted into crime by agents of the state. But to recognize the insane and the excessively tempted, we need a theory of normal "sane" freedom, a theory that can account for how people can freely do what they know to be wrong. We need to know how responsibility and guilt function in order to know what people may be rightly held responsible for, and guilty of. This means that criminal justice ethics requires a reflection into the core of the self, the place where intentions are formed and from which actions stem.

Teaching Ethics Ethically

Robert Nash

"Ethics and aesthetics are one and the same."
　　　　Ludwig Wittgenstein, *Philosophical Investigations*

It never fails. During preregistration week, the phone calls begin: "Professor Nash, I am planning to take your ethics course this semester. I have heard so much about it that I am a little anxious. Don't get me wrong. My friends [or colleagues] really liked the course when they took it, but I still don't know what to expect. I want to be sure I can do the work given my other responsibilities this term. Will there be a lot of reading? Do you, by any chance, have a syllabus I might look at so that I know what lies ahead for me?"

Such phone calls make me happy because not only am I feeling insecure that I will have sufficient enrollment to offer a course in ethics each term, but, believe it or not, I actually enjoy writing syllabuses! In fact, I look forward to writing a completely new syllabus each semester in order to clarify for myself, in a fresh way, just why I continue to teach ethics courses and what exactly I hope to achieve in any given semester. I have never been able to understand why some colleagues fail to put together a substantial syllabus. As a student confided bitterly to me: "Too often, course syllabuses tend to be one-page jokes for one-page courses."

As a parent, I have sometimes learned the hard way that the best way to teach morality to my children is to live my life morally: Similarly, over the years, I have learned that the best way to teach ethics is to teach ethically. Thus, in the true spirit of an ethics course, I

Reprinted by permission of the publisher from Nash, R., *'Real World' Ethics*, (New York: Teachers College Press, © 1996 by Teachers College, Columbia University. All rights reserved.) pp. 15–27.

believe my syllabus should be ethically exemplary. The above caller will soon learn that I consider the course syllabus to be a binding fiduciary contract I have with each student. It actually operates on two levels: It attempts to outline and summarize the major content to be covered in a course; and it strives to fulfill students' right to know exactly what is expected of them so that they can give their fully informed consent, not merely to formal course requirements, but also to my peculiar way of doing things as a teacher. Over the years, my syllabuses have grown thicker and thicker. Students jest that if they can get through my hefty syllabus in class on opening day, then they can easily complete any subsequent reading requirements during the semester. Because of its length, I believe my syllabus sets the appropriate tone of the course from the opening moments and spells out in considerable detail, with minimal jargon, just how seriously I take the work that faces us in the weeks to come. It also begins to build the trust that I believe is necessary for effective ethics teaching.

The one drawback of a substantial syllabus, unfortunately, is that a few students incorrectly experience it as a "weeder," calculated to eliminate the faint-of-heart, as well as the philosophical novice, from my class on the first day. This disturbs me. Because I have never seen myself as one who uses his syllabus to remove undesirable elements from a course, I make it a point to acknowledge at the outset that I consider a fairly comprehensive syllabus, written in an informative and entertaining manner, my way of showing how much I look forward to working with, and getting to know, my students. This disclaimer aside, though, the groans of some students, as they plunge into a reading of my beefy syllabus, are still painfully audible on opening day.

At this point, I will present a typical syllabus for one of my more generic applied ethics courses, as an example of what I mean when I speak of teaching ethics ethically. I will omit only specific logistical information (course requirements, reading lists, etc.) that the reader might not find relevant at this juncture. What comes next, then, is essentially what students receive on the first day of class. You will be reading what they read.

SYLLABUS: ETHICS OF PROFESSIONAL RELATIONSHIPS

Greetings. As often as I have taught this course, I frequently hear the same questions from students about its purposes, content, expectations, and, yes, relevance. I will attempt to respond to many of these concerns in what follows, and I promise to be as clear and concise as I can. I will also introduce you to a basic moral framework and problem-solving approach to professional ethical dilemmas that I have been developing over a 27-year period. During the semester, I will do my best, with your assistance, to adapt my philosophical framework to your special professional issues, concerns, and dilemmas. I believe that our several readings, for example, will touch on many of your unique ethical dilemmas, whatever your profession.

Please know that, although I am a veteran teacher of sorts, I always begin a semester of ethics teaching with considerable trepidation. In my experience, students all too often harbor several unfortunate stereotypes and fears about ethics content and instruction. Permit me to try to dispel a few of these clichés and perhaps allay some personal anxieties for you. In so doing, I will also be declaring my purposes in teaching this course and clarifying my expectations of you this semester as you strive to fulfill the course requirements.

"Ethics courses are too didactic."

Rest easily. I will not be teaching you what's categorically right and wrong about particular professional practices. This is the prerogative of someone far more insightful (and dogmatic) than I. I simply cannot give you surefire answers to complex moral dilemmas. I have no neat moral formulas. Although I do believe that objective ethical analysis is possible, even desirable, what I, an applied philosopher, intend to do this semester is to introduce you to a number of ethical languages as frameworks to think about ethical issues and resolve ethical dilemmas. During class time, I will frequently be a provocateur, a clarifier, an interpreter of texts, a dispenser of information, and a user of moral languages. If all works well, at the very least, you will be able to identify and understand the central ethical issues in your life and use the appropriate languages to frame the questions, analyze the issues, resolve the dilemmas, and defend the eventual decisions and judgments you will make.

"This stuff sounds pretty philosophical. What in the world can we do with philosophy?"

You are right. The course will be *philosophical*, but in a helpful way, I hope. The way I teach philosophy is active, applied, and conversational. I believe the most practical tool any professional can have is a good ethical theory. If you know what you stand for morally, and why, you can defend your ethical practices anywhere, anytime, to anybody. While I cannot guarantee that you can ever "do" anything with philosophy per se the way you might be able to "do" something with "hands-on" professional techniques, I can offer you an important opportunity to talk together in a systematic and thoughtful way about ethical ideas, ideals, policies, and practices.

Moreover, I will try to get you actively involved in what I hope are stimulating conversations about the "big" ethical issues, not only in your work but in society as well. I am talking about the importance of taking time in our busy lives to pause and to be reflective about what is morally significant in the work we do. One of my favorite political philosophers, Michael Oakeshott, describes vividly what a university classroom experience should be. A university should "offer a moment in which to taste the mystery without the necessity of at once seeking a solution. The characteristic gift of a university is the gift of an interval" (p. 428).

It is only in this "interval," I believe, that we can step back from the daily fray and try to answer the most basic moral questions we will ever ask. While it is true that we will be learning how to resolve concrete ethical dilemmas during the semester, we will also be using the "interval" to respond to such "ultimate" moral questions as the following: Is all the effort I am making to help others (and myself) truly worth it? What is it that I believe deep down about the work I do, and why in the world, especially on my darkest, most despairing days, should I continue doing it? What exactly should I be doing to help people to be productive, self- and other-respecting, happy and responsible citizens? Do I have a vision of the good society and the good life that is both realistic and inspiring? And how can I persuasively defend that which is worth holding onto in my moral beliefs and practices, and how can I begin to dismantle that which must give way to the new?

It is important to note that a philosopher (*philo-sophia*, G.) is someone who loves the pursuit of wisdom so much that the process of discovering meaning and purpose in life is considered to be almost as important as the product. The reason why we do philosophy is simple: because we love the search for wisdom as much as the possession of it. Contrary to what you might think, a philosopher is not some calm and composed figure who attempts to cast everything in air-tight conceptual systems, or who spends inordinate amounts of time contemplating ethereal and unanswerable questions for their own sake. No, a philosopher's primary purpose is to inch ever closer to some fundamental moral truths about the human condition. This process is far from calm because fundamental truths, whether you know it or not, are the stuff we build our lives and careers on. Sadly, too many of us either take these fundamental moral truths for granted, or, worse, we dismiss them as impractical or inaccessible. We relegate them to the "metaphysical basement" and hope they never come up the stairs to the main living area to embarrass us. But these "background moral beliefs" always have a way of making an appearance and interfering with our professional practices and policies. It will be one of the pieces of business of this course to expose these "background moral beliefs" to the light of day in order to test, refine, and apply them. What, I ask you, could be more practical and valuable for professionals than this?

"Nobody's perfect. Who are you to think you can teach ethics?"

I'll be talking about who I am as a person and as a professional later when we introduce ourselves. At this point, though, let me say that *I* don't pretend to be a perfect model of professional ethical deportment or philosophical articulation, although I certainly strive to become as morally sensitive and ethically articulate as I can. Neither do I expect *you* to be a paragon of moral behavior and philosophical sophistication. One of the more embarrassing and painful advantages of teaching this course is that I become keenly aware of my own ethical confusions, inconsistencies, and compromises. The daunting task of appearing before you as an ethics "expert" attempting to clarify and resolve moral issues keeps me honest and, yes, humble. Listen respectfully to what I espouse, please, but be forgiving when I fail to live up to my own highest moral ideals. I will do the same for you. One non-negotiable expectation I will have of you, however, is to take the course seriously enough to work hard to master the ethical languages I will teach you. At the very least, I hope you have the same expectation of me.

"Don't you think that some ethical decisions are more morally correct than others? Come on, admit it. You've got your moral biases."

I do have my moral biases, and I will identify them when I think the timing is right, or when asked. But it does not follow that I will be foisting them on you, or that I will expect you to adopt my ethical views. Not only will I steadfastly refrain from issuing ethical imperatives (please call me on it when I do), but I will never insist that certain moral decisions are more politically, or philosophically, or religiously, or educationally "correct" than others. I hope you will find very little intractable orthodoxy in the various points of view I will enunciate throughout the course. If you do, confront me. While it is true that I have strong moral beliefs, some of which I hold tenaciously, I will try always to espouse my own ideals in a tentative, qualified way. I call this—teaching ethics with "tenuous tenacity."

But I do feel strongly, even uncompromisingly, about some things. I have a conversational rule I apply in my courses: Find the truth in what you oppose. Find the error in what you espouse. I will ask you to apply this rule as well. The virtue of this rule is that, in practice, every ethical pronouncement should be heard (and read) as containing some element of truth. It is our responsibility to search relentlessly for this truth (no matter how tiny) before we proceed to refute it. Moreover, everything moral is up for grabs in this seminar. All ethical propositions are arguable, including this one. In principle, no single ethical language is irrefutably the best or the most complete. My major intention this semester is to help you cultivate the richest, fullest moral language possible so that you can achieve some depth, balance, consistency, clarity, and precision in your ethical assertions and problem-solving.

Does this mean, therefore, that I will be promoting a kind of ethical neutrality, or relativism, or situationalism? Although, when discussing cases, you will hear me frequently say "It all depends . . .", you will have to wait until the term ends, I'm afraid, to get what you might consider satisfactory answers to that extremely complicated philosophical question. (We will be discussing the question often, I hope.) I will say here, though, that I believe ethical decision-making for professionals cannot simply be a matter of subjective whim or arbitrary personal preference, if it is to be defensible. This course is about normative ethical behavior and, hence, defensible ethical actions, judgments, and decision-making. At this early juncture in the course, I note, minimally, that ethical understanding and defensibility are two of my highest pedagogical and moral ideals.

"Ethics instruction sounds too technical, too complicated. Why bother with ethical reasoning? Why can't we just consult a list of simple do's and don'ts that everybody agrees on? Why don't we just appeal to a code of ethics? Why give us all this terminological grief?"

Although I will frequently be using technical terminology and referring to certain philosophical writers and their ideas throughout the course, I will do this not to show off but to provide as serious and full a context for ethical understanding and decision-making as I can. Once you make the effort to see the everyday professional world through an ethical lens, and once you begin to understand and analyze problems from a series of systematic ethical frameworks, you will find yourself using the technical language more comfortably and referring to the particular authors more frequently and accurately. And you will learn all too quickly that no ethical dilemma is merely a matter of referring to a list of professional do's and don'ts. Ethical dilemmas are far more complicated than that. *Every resolution to an ethical dilemma, I maintain, must consider the act, the intention, the circumstance, the principles, the beliefs, the outcomes, the virtues, the narrative, the community, and the political structures.* In fact, we will be using codes of ethics mainly as broad (and suggestive) normative guidelines for behavior, not as definitive specifications for ethical decision-making.

"Why then should we bother taking a course in ethics? You're obviously not going to tell us what's right and wrong—either in our personal lives or in our jobs. This seems like an unnecessarily painful way to learn about ethics."

If I am not going to be giving you any specific solutions to ethical dilemmas, then you might be thinking, when all is said and done, that the best ethical decision-making is really subjective, intuitive, and impressionistic. After all, you might be wondering, don't we learn ethics by the "seat of our pants," or by trial-and-error, or by early socialization and indoctrination, or by imitation? Isn't it up to the family, the church, temple, or mosque, and the local community to create ethical people? Isn't the test of a good ethical decision if it works, or if it feels right, or if it convinces others, or if it keeps me out of court? Who knows with any degree of certainty what someone should do in particular ethical situations? Why should we read all these books, do all this writing, come to all these classes, engage in all this philosophical discussion, if everything is up for grabs? Why not settle for a little values clarification when we find ourselves stuck with an ethical dilemma, talk to a few respected professional peers, consult Kohlberg or Gilligan for the appropriate moral stage and developmental response, strive for at least a modicum of moral self-esteem, and, if necessary, flip a coin to make a decision? Down with all of this "ethics-babble"!

Although I cannot guarantee that you will be able to satisfactorily answer all of these questions for yourselves by the end of the course, I can tell you that the challenge of thinking broadly, deeply, and systematically about ethics for an intensive semester entails many professional and personal rewards. Among the "little" rewards are reading some good texts, engaging in some stimulating conversations, clarifying some core moral beliefs, thinking deeply about the moral life in general, learning to write with precision and clarity, and exchanging moral views with some very interesting people. Among the "big" rewards are rehearsing for major ethical decision-making in the actual professional world, learning to defend controversial and complicated ethical actions and judgments, understanding what makes you "tick" morally, finding the moral courage to stand up for what you believe even while respecting the views of those who think differently, and being able to translate your background moral beliefs and principles into defensible ethical problem-solving. The "little" rewards will make your life more intellectually stimulating. The "big" rewards could someday keep you from getting sued.

"You are beginning to convince me of the importance of an applied ethics course, all right, but you haven't said anything yet about the course content. What are these 'ethical languages' and 'systematic ethical frameworks' you keep talking about? What books are we going to read? It sounds to me like you are making a molehill out of a mountain. Won't there be any real content to the course?"

This is going to take a little time, so please be patient. I will try to be brief. After all, it will be the work of the entire course to respond adequately to these content questions. First of all, applied ethics is the implementation of general ethical theories, principles, rules, virtues, structures, moral ideals, and background beliefs to problems of professional practice, including professional–client relationships, delivery of services, and policy construction and enactment. During the term, it will be essential for us to examine a wide range of actual cases involving assumptions, practices, delivery, research, and policy. These cases will not only clarify and illustrate principles, virtues, background beliefs, and their conflicts; they will test and modify these elements as well. Without the applied dimension of ethical analysis, the entire exercise could prove to be arid and nugatory. Thus it will be necessary for you to know the meaning and implications of such ethical theories as deontology, utilitarianism, and virtue ethics, as well as such principles as autonomy, beneficence, nonmaleficence, and justice.

Moreover, I will make the case that each of us lives our life in three overlapping moral worlds: a metaphysical life-space, a concrete moral world of small communities, and a secular pluralist world of large organizations. Each of these worlds features its own specialized language. The *metaphysical life-space* is the interiorized world of individual, philosophical consciousness. It is in this world that we attempt to formulate a comprehensive, coherent, and consistent account of morality grounded in a powerful set of "ultimate" background beliefs; these may be expressed in philosophical, theological, political, scientific, or other types of language. It is in this world that each of us understands and chooses to live out certain moral ideals, makes sense of the other two worlds we inhabit, and translates the messages of the other two worlds into conscious ethical practices. We often speak a very private moral *language of background beliefs* in this world.

The *concrete moral world of small communities* is the external, tangible world of moral origin and influence for most of us. Much of what we believe metaphysically and morally, and who we are as moral beings, has its roots in, and is mediated through, our various smaller, specific moral communities. We may claim membership in only a few, or in several, of these concrete moral communities. Some are permanent; others are transient. All are particular, however, and they send powerful moral messages. These intimate groupings may be ideological, religious, ethnic, racial, political, recreational, instrumental, or familial. In these concrete moral communities, we often speak a *language of character* grounded in communally sanctioned ideals, narratives, traditions, and virtues.

And the *secular pluralist world of large organizations* is the world of the workplace, the professions, the public arena. It is the setting where private individuals of diverse ideologies, values, and moral persuasions come together to make decisions of an ethical nature. The secular pluralist world requires an ethical *language of principle* rooted in mutual respect and a tolerance of moral differences. Secular pluralist language is, of necessity, an abstract language of general principles that diverse individuals and groups employ to reach mutual understanding, tolerance, and, possibly, agreement, regarding the resolution of ethical conflicts. It is the language of logic, reason, rules, and principles.

I will make the case that ethical investigation must always operate in at least these three languages. The language of background beliefs is a "foundationally rich" discourse in the sense that it grounds the other two languages. It is the vocabulary of ultimate beliefs, truth, and metaphysics. It is well suited to helping us discover deeper meaning and purpose in our moral deliberations. The language of character is a "content-rich" discourse (a form of moral examination rooted in the concrete moral viewpoints of particular persons and communities), and it helps us gain a fuller personal understanding of our moral origins, intentions, and aspirations. It is well suited to explicating the influence of our concrete moral communities on our ethical activities. The language of moral principles is a "procedurally rich" discourse (a minimum form of moral discourse that is logically deductive without establishing the absolute "correctness" of any particular point of view).

It is well suited to rational, defensible ethical decision-making in the secular pluralist society.

All three moral languages overlap and are mutually interdependent. You will learn that your understanding and application of rules, principles, and theories are deeply influenced by your particular stories, traditions, and conception of the virtues. These in turn shape and are shaped by a number of structural realities that affect all ethical decision-making. Moreover, you will see that it is crucial to become aware of those background beliefs that underlie and drive the entire ethical decision-making process. My hope is that, even though these background beliefs are sometimes most difficult for students to retrieve, you will realize they exert perhaps the most powerful influence on all of your moral thinking.

"Whew! You are going to have to go over all of the above much more slowly and carefully during the semester, if I am to understand and apply it intelligently. I will give you the benefit of the doubt, though, and assume you know what you are doing. It does sound intriguing. I must admit that I am very anxious. Do you really think you are going to get us to talk freely—using a technical language about difficult ethical issues— with virtual strangers? I'm no philosopher, you know. Moreover, why should I take the risk and disclose moral concerns I might have at my workplace or even in my personal life? Is this going to be a sensitivity group? If it is, count me out. I don't want anyone in this class to judge me, including you."

The last few years I have been developing an approach to ethics discussions I call the "moral conversation." The Latin root of the word "conversation," *conversari*, means to live with, to keep company with, to turn around, to oppose. Thus, for me, a conversation is literally a manner of living whereby people keep company with each other, and talk together, in good faith, in order to exchange sometimes agreeable, sometimes opposing, ideas. A conversation is not an argument, although it can get heated. A conversation is at its best when the participants are not impatient to conclude their business, but wish instead to spend their time together in order to deepen and enrich their understanding of an idea, or, in our case, the ideas in a text, or of a possible solution to a difficult ethical case.

A conversation that is moral, from the Latin *moralis* (custom), is one whose conventions emphasize the fundamental worth and dignity of each participant in the exchange, and this includes the authors of our texts as well. I believe the best way to get a person to talk publicly about ethical concerns is to treat that person with the utmost respect. I will always try to treat you with the highest regard in the sense that I believe all of you have a share of moral truth. No single one of us, though, has a corner on the market of ethical insight. No single one of us inhabits the moral high ground a priori. We are all moral *viators* (travelers with a purpose) on a journey to find meaning in the work we do, and because our journey is our own, it possesses intrinsic worth and is to be respected.

The primary purpose of engaging in a moral conversation this term is to test, expand, enrich, and deepen our moral languages through the disciplined examination of significant texts—and through the vehicle of pertinent ethical cases that you yourselves will construct, analyze, and resolve—so that each of us can arrive at a fuller ethical language than we now speak. With the ideal of the moral conversation in mind, I hope we can be genuinely respectful of each other's efforts to work through difficult readings, to find a common classroom language to express our individual interpretations of these readings, and to take conversational risks in constructing a more cogent moral discourse.

In brief, then, *good moral conversation starts with*

1. An honest effort to read and understand the assigned texts

2. An acute awareness that you have moral biases and blind spots

3. An open-mindedness about the possibility of learning something from both the author and your peers in the conversation

4. A willingness to improve your current moral language

5. A conscious effort to refrain from advancing your own current moral language as if it were the best one

6. An inclination to listen intently in order to grasp the meaning of other people's languages for expressing their moral truths

7. An agreement that clarifying, questioning, challenging, exemplifying, and applying ideas are activities to be done in a self- and other-respecting way

8. A realization that we will frequently get off course in our conversations because a spirit of charity, intellectual curiosity, and even playfulness will characterize many of our discussions, and because, as David Bromwich says: "The good of conversation is not truth, or right, or anything else that may come out at the end of it, but the activity itself in its constant relation to life"

9. An appreciation of the reality that it will take time for us to get to know each other, and a realization that eventually we will find ways to engage in robust, candid, and challenging conversation about ethics without being so "nice" we bore each other to death, or without being so hostile that we cripple each other emotionally and intellectually

Finally, I have devised several overlapping "ethical aphorisms" that have helped to foster moral conversation in past seminars. These aphorisms will constitute a code of ethics for our class discussions:

Do not force premature closure on the moral conversation. Genuine philosophical discourse rarely speaks in clear and unambiguous messages. Rather it speaks in subtleties, sometimes in riddles, occasionally in circles and haltingly at that, and always in ambiguities, paradoxes, and unfinished business. Beware of the tyranny of quick-fix moral directives and impatient "final" calls to action.

Find the truth in what you oppose. Find the error in what you espouse. Then and only then declare the truth in what you espouse, and the error in what you oppose.

Read as you would be read. Listen as you would be listened to. Question as you would be questioned. Pontificate only if you would be pontificated to.

Speak with, not at or separate from, each other. T. S. Eliot once said that Hell is where nothing connects. Conversational Heaven must be where every comment is a link in an unbroken chain.

If you don't stand for something, you'll fall for anything. But know how to stand up for what you believe without standing over, or on, others.

Accept no text or opinion uncritically; it might be false. Reject no text or opinion uncritically; it might be true.

Find and express your own voice, but also find the right time to lower your own voice so that others might find theirs. The paradox is that we discover what we know as much by listening as by speaking.

But speak we must! Language is the primary tool we have to make meaning together. Without language, there is no meaning. It is a resource to be recycled frequently. There can be no conversation—moral or otherwise—unless people are willing to express their ideas, no matter how erroneous, outrageous, eccentric, enfeebled, or politically and morally unorthodox. Remember John Stuart Mill's enduring insight: In a democratic society, all opinions must be heard because some of them may be true; and those that aren't true must be vigorously contested. In either case, free people only stand to gain.

Once you acknowledge your moral duty to speak up, even if your ideas are only half-formed or even half-baked, do not be afraid of appearing less than brilliant in your discourse. It will be our collective responsibility to discover if there is "brilliance" in those observations you consider merely ordinary.

Finally, remember what Ludwig Wittgenstein once observed about ethics: Ethics and aesthetics are one and the same. Thus, at times we must stop to appreciate the beauty, as well as the truth, in our ethical utterances and conversations. Any moral belief that brings intense satisfaction to the mind or senses can be a beautiful thing, something to be admired by all.

"One last question, please. What is your teaching style going to be?"

The content of this course is, by its nature, very controversial. I fully intend to follow the rules of the moral conversation outlined above, but, being human, I am a flawed practitioner. Not by intention, I assure you, I am bound to step on everyone's moral toes at least once by course's end simply because I may have beliefs different from yours and because you may not like my pedagogical style. I will be both provocateur and explicator. At times, I will be a lecturer, a discussion leader, and an active seeker of truth in our moral dialogues. You will be amazed at how few irrefutable ethical answers I have to your most disturbing ethical dilemmas. But in spite of my paucity of final answers, I believe I do have considerable clarity on many pertinent ethical questions, themes, issues, and languages. I also have a problem-solving process many professionals have found helpful. I will not be laid back. Alas, I will be pushing you to reach beyond your pet ethical shibboleths, as I hope you will push me to reach beyond my own. I will be speculating and playing with moral ideas right along with you. If I unwittingly hurt your moral feelings, please let me know—in class if possible, outside of class if not. I can assure you I mean no comment personally, and I will take none of your comments personally either.

I like to think of our weekly forays into the various readings and professional dilemmas as helpful ethical conversations we will have. Because one of my own very strong background beliefs is that the best way to teach morality is to teach morally, I make a promise to each one of you that I will respect you as fully autonomous and responsible moral agents, and I will listen attentively to your own moral languages, even though, at times, they may be different from mine. I ask, in return, that you not be morally thin-skinned and that you give my ethical system a fair hearing.

I
MORAL FOUNDATIONS
OF CRIMINAL GUILT

This section looks at the conditions under which society can hold an individual responsible for acts it considers crimes. In "The Morality of the Criminal Law," David Bazelon (former judge of the Court of Appeals for Washington, D.C.) examines the relationship between law and moral values and argues that the law should do more than merely enforce order. He takes up the question of what should be a crime and addresses the mental and social conditions of criminal responsibility. Recounting his own struggles to define a usable standard for the insanity defense, he goes on to speculate about whether unjust or oppressive social conditions ought to reduce criminal responsibility in the way that mental illness does.

Bill Lawson follows up on Bazelon's concerns about the relevance of social inequalities to criminal guilt. "Crime, Minorities, and the Social Contract" looks specifically at the obligations minorities have to obey the laws when the state fails in its obligation to protect citizens from urban crime. In general, a contractarian view of legal obligation treats it as a debt that citizens owe one another in return for the benefits (such as peace, predictability, and security) that come when most citizens obey the law and the state protects citizens against those who would break the law. Lawson contends that important features of this two-way bargain are not kept for poor inner-city residents. His reading of social contract literature leads him to "the unsettling conclusion that the fear of being a victim of crime for many urban residents releases them from an obligation to obey governmental dictates and consequently from any moral or legal obligation to obey the law."

The nature of the guilty mind is more puzzling than it might immediately seem to be. Consider that a criminal disobeys the law in order to satisfy some desire (say, for wealth). Now, if he doesn't know that he should obey the law, then he is ignorant that he is doing wrong (if not insane) and blameless. If he does know he should obey the law, then how does his desire convince him to go against what he knows he should do? If the desire is too strong to resist, then the criminal "can't help it" when he breaks the law and is, again, blameless. If his desire isn't too strong to resist, then he must be acting on it because he has decided he should do what he desires. But, if he knows that he should obey the law, how does this happen? Is he irrational enough to believe something contrary to what he knows, or does he become ignorant that he should obey the law? Either of these seems to render him blameless again. In her challenging article, "Mens Rea," Jean Hampton tries to spell out clearly what is guilty about a guilty mind and why the guilty are appropriately blamed and punished.

The section concludes with a case study, Leo Katz's "The Crime That Never Was," about impossible attempts. This article asks us to think about what it is that the law aims to punish. Normally, the law punishes attempted crimes even though they fail and thus produce no harm. Certainly the one who attempts a crime but fails is just as evil as one who attempts and succeeds, but what is an attempted crime? Suppose Bob shoots Frank, wanting to kill him, but Frank was already dead, having died minutes before of a heart attack. Has Bob committed attempted murder? Suppose Jane tries to poison Jill, giving her a substance she believes is poison but is really harmless. Has Jane committed attempted murder? Is Joe guilty of attempted murder if he is doing voodoo rituals that he thinks will bring about Kim's demise? Katz's case is about a man who tries to smuggle a painting across international borders, except that, unbeknownst to him, the painting is a forgery and taking it out of the country is not illegal. Is he guilty of a criminal attempt? Katz writes three opinions to the case that represent a balancing between the necessity of punishing inner evil (the one who tries voodoo believing it will kill his enemy is just as inwardly evil as the one who shoots a living person and misses) and protection against acts likely to be dangerous.

Readers who are interested in exploring these topics further can visit Findlaw <www.findlaw.com> and The Jurist: The Law Professors' Network <http://jurist.law.pitt.edu/>. Within the "topics" section of Findlaw and The Jurist will be resources about criminal law. The Jurist also contains links to web pages that law professors have developed for teaching criminal law. The heading "legal theory" at both pages accesses many resources that discuss the relationship of law to race and gender. A listing of these and other Internet resources is available through <http://www.paulsjusticepage.com>.

The Morality of the Criminal Law

David L. Bazelon

It is an honor for me to be giving the first of the J. Edgar Hoover Foundation lectures. Until 1946, I knew Mr. Hoover only by his imposing reputation. That year, I came from Chicago to Washington, D.C., as an Assistant Attorney General by appointment of President Truman. Soon after taking up my duties, I met Mr. Hoover for the first time. He was a great source of encouragement, assistance, and support. Just as important to a young attorney new

David L. Bazelon, *The Morality of the Criminal Law* 49 *Southern California Law Review* (1976): 385–405. Reprinted with the permission of the *Southern California Law Review*.

This address was delivered on Nov. 18, 1975, at the University of Southern California as the first of the J. Edgar Hoover Foundation Lectures. David L. Bazelon is Chief Judge of the United States Court of Appeals for the District of Columbia Circuit.

to the Capital, his help gave me confidence and a sense of sharing in work that was important to the Nation.

In 1949 I was nominated to fill a vacancy on the U.S. Court of Appeals. I was still not very well known in Washington, and more than a few persons thought that at 39 I was pretty young to be a judge of the Court of Appeals. Without being asked, Mr. Hoover went to Capitol Hill to tell some important senators that he knew me well and that he would vouch for me. I don't have to tell you how much that must have smoothed the way for my confirmation.

After I took my seat on the Court of Appeals, Mr. Hoover and I didn't see much of each other. Although he never told me so, I am certain that he was deeply disappointed, if not hurt, by some of the paths I have taken as a judge. I suppose it should go without saying that we both believed in criminal justice and we both believed in social justice. But J. Edgar Hoover, like some of my best friends, always believed that you could and must separate the two. I did not share that belief and I still do not. I believe that there can be no truly just criminal law in the absence of social justice—in other words, you can't have one without the other. In a way, the following examination of my present topic, the morality of the criminal law, is my side of a discussion that Mr. Hoover and I should have had when he was alive, but never did.

I.

I have chosen this topic because, in my judgment, the debates currently raging over a wide range of criminal law issues can best be understood by reference to a divergence of opinion on a central question: what role should moral concepts play in the administration of criminal justice? Two polar positions can be identified.[1] Each starts from the premise that

creating some kind of order is a moral imperative. Each asserts that there can be no moral development in a society in which the mighty prey on the weak. What separates the two positions are the means they would employ to achieve order and, ultimately, the types of order they seek.

The first view, which some rightly or wrongly associate with Mr. Hoover, holds that achieving order is so important that there is little room for concerns of social justice in devising means; the view explicitly suggests an amoral process, justified by a high moral end. It is thus able to endorse what seems to be the easiest means to achieving order—imposition of strong external constraints. It demands that the criminal law punish disorder and make the cost of violating the law so great that few will dare to do so. This view and the cluster of beliefs associated with it I shall call the "law-as-external-constraint" thesis.[2]

Standing against this thesis is the view that the law's aims must be achieved by a moral process cognizant of the realities of social injustice. This philosophy sees externally imposed order—repressive order—as suffering from the same basic defect as "disorder": both lack moral authority. The philosophy asserts that the moral foundation of order is tenuous at best when people obey the law solely because they fear the consequences of disobedience. As the poet Wallace Stevens wrote, "A violent order is a disorder."[3] The only truly moral order, according to this second philosophy, is order based on the internalization of control, that is, on the members of the society obeying the law because they personally believe that its commands are justified. Thus, this

[1]An excellent discussion of two similarly polarized "models" for the criminal justice system may be found in Packer, *Two Models of the Criminal Process*, 113 U. PA. L. REV. 1 (1964).

[2]Of course, to many friends and critics alike, Mr. Hoover represents more than this view of the law. He epitomizes professionalism in the field of law enforcement; and he stands as the defender of a way of life, one which could be threatened by—and could view as criminal—dissent, attitudes, and even hair lengths. But my focus is only on Mr. Hoover's association with the law-as-external-constraint thesis, and not on any other of his associations with any other values or beliefs.

[3]W. STEVENS, *Connoisseur of Chaos*, in *The Collected Poems of Wallace Stevens* 215 (1954).

view demands that the law facilitate the internalization process by becoming a moral force in the community.

Lest there be any doubt, I should state at the outset that I associate myself with the latter view. Furthermore, when I speak of moral force or morality in the law, I am not speaking of a righteous certitude or a mystical sense of authority. Rather, I am speaking about elements of human decency such as are embodied in the words, "Do unto others as you would have them do unto you." Whether phrased in religious or philosophical terms, this essential concept of reciprocal decency is what I mean by morality. My primary effort here will be to explore the implications of the internalization-of-control view, as well as the implications of the law-as-external-constraint thesis.

II.

One arena in which the conflict between the two views can be seen is the debate over the question of what acts should be made criminal. Proponents of the law-as-external-constraint philosophy translate this question into cost-benefit terms. They ask whether the resources that would be required to enforce the law are justified by the social benefits that would be reaped. Thus, proposals to decriminalize so-called "victimless" offenses such as gambling, prostitution, homosexuality, fornication, and public drunkenness stand or fall on the proposition that decriminalizing such conduct would free police, prosecutorial, and judicial resources to concentrate on more serious offenses.

Rather than posing the issue in these terms, I would ask: is the conduct in question viewed by the society as both a moral wrong and a breach of some minimum condition of social existence? In other words, although not every act regarded as immoral by the dominant community should be made criminal, no act should be made criminal if it is not viewed as immoral. I believe that the criminal code should define only the minimum conditions of each individual's responsibility to the other members of society in order to maximize personal liberty. Thus, along with minimum-condition

questions, the moral question provides an appropriate starting point for deciding when to criminalize or to decriminalize. There will be times, no doubt, when some will vehemently disagree with, and perhaps even be morally offended by, the community's decision as to what it should condemn. But unless we are willing to allow the community the freedom to reach even "wrong" decisions, there is no hope of making the criminal law a statement of moral principles to which all can aspire.

III.

Moral considerations are equally implicated in determining what should be done with people who engage in proscribed conduct. One's views on sentencing policy should reflect one's view of the role of the criminal law. Those who look to the law for external control seek sentences which will maximize order; their primary concern is to determine how harsh sentences can be without becoming so harsh that juries will stop convicting, or police and prosecutors stop charging. Those who look to the law to facilitate internal controls, however, see sentencing as a weighing of safety considerations against the dictates of what I call the "sixth sense"—the moral sense. The "internalists" may disagree whether the sixth sense would be better served by individualization and mercy on the one hand, or by uniformity and equality of punishment on the other. But at least their disagreement is over what *social justice* would require. This disagreement, they believe, must be resolved before embarking on the necessary consideration of what community safety demands. None of those who subscribe to the internal control model believe that sentencing policy should be used to achieve repressive order.

Moral considerations intrude even earlier in the process of deciding what to do with people who engage in proscribed conduct. Those who see the law as a moral force insist that the law should not convict unless it can condemn. According to this view, a decision for conviction requires the following three determinations: (1) a condemnable act was committed by the actor-defendant; (2) the actor can be condemned—that is, he could reasonably have been expected to have conformed his behavior to the demands of the law; and (3) society's own conduct in relation to the actor[4] entitles it to sit in condemnation of him with respect to the condemnable act.

To some extent the law already inquires into at least the first two of these factors. Starting in the late thirteenth century, the law went beyond its prior exclusive focus on physical acts which violated the penal code, to consider why the acts occurred.[5] Through the element of intent or *mens rea*, and the defenses of mistake, duress, and most important, insanity or lack of criminal responsibility, the modern law has sought to punish only what Roscoe Pound termed "the vicious will."[6]

But the law, like the rest of us, "promise[s] according to [its] hopes" but "perform[s] according to [its] fears."[7] Although it has been asserted repeatedly that only a free choice to do wrong will be punished, in practice the law presumes, almost irrebuttably, that proscribed behavior is the product of "a free agent confronted with a choice between doing right and doing wrong and choosing freely to do wrong."[8] In *The Common Law*, Justice Holmes recognized the conflict between certain moral pretenses and practices when he observed that if punishment

> stood on the moral grounds which are proposed for it, the first thing to be considered would be those limitations in the capacity for choosing rightly which arise from abnormal instincts, want of education, lack of intelligence, and all other

defects which are most marked in the criminal classes.[9]

In other words, if moral condemnation were the basis for criminal sanctions, we would have to consider—to take some contemporary examples from cases that have come before me— whether a free choice to do wrong can be found in the acts of a poverty-stricken and otherwise deprived black youth from the central city who kills a marine who taunted him with a racial epithet,[10] in the act of a "modern Jean Valjean" who steals to feed his family,[11] in the act of a narcotics addict who buys drugs for his own use,[12] or in the act of a superpatriot steeped in cold war ideology who burglarizes in the name of "national security."[13]

We are uneasy in contemplation of these situations and the issues Holmes raises. But we dare not shy away from them simply because they are difficult or the answers unsettling. The questions must be faced if the criminal law is to be an instrument for the reinforcement of moral obligations.

My endeavors in the area of the insanity defense have been an ongoing effort to import this kind of inquiry into the criminal law. I began in 1954, in the *Durham*[14] case, with an attempt to break the logjam that had been created by the old *M'Naghten*[15] test. The two *M'Naghten* questions—(1) whether the defendant understood the nature and quality of his act, and (2) whether the defendant knew the difference between right and wrong with respect to his act—had become obsolete in light of contemporary behavioral knowledge. For

---

[4]If, for example, society itself were responsible for any deprivations or degradations that the actor had suffered, society might not be entitled to condemn that actor.

[5]See *United States v. Barker*, 514 F.2d 208, 228 & nn. 5–7 (D.C. Cir.) (Bazelon, J., concurring), *cert. denied*, 421 U.S. 1013 (1975).

[6]Pound, *Introduction* to F. SAYRE, *Cases on Criminal Law* at xxxvi (1927).

[7]"*Nous promettons selon nos espérances, et nous tenons selon nos craintes.*" LA ROCHEFOUCAULD, MAXIMES 61 (F.C. Green ed. 1945).

[8]Pound, *Introduction* to F. SAYRE, CASES ON CRIMINAL LAW at xxxvii (1927).

[9]O.W. HOLMES, *THE COMMON LAW* 45 (1881).

[10]See *United States v. Alexander*, 471 F.2d 923 (D.C. Cir.), *cert. denied*, 409 U.S. 1044 (1973); *cf. United States v. Robertson*, 507 F.2d 1148 (D.C. Cir. 1974).

[11]*Cf.* Everett v. United States, 336 F.2d 979 (D.C. Cir. 1964).

[12]See United States v. Moore, 486 F.2d 1139 (D.C. Cir.), *cert denied*, 414 U.S. 980 (1973). See also *Easter v. District of Columbia*, 361 F.2d 50 (D.C. Cir. 1966) (en banc).

[13]See *United States v. Barker*, 514 F.2d 208 (D.C. Cir.), *cert. denied*, 421 U.S. 1013 (1975).

[14]*Durham v. United States*, 214 F.2d 862 (D.C. Cir. 1954).

[15]*M'Naghten's Case*, 8 Eng. Rep. 718 (H.L. 1843).

almost a century thoughtful psychiatrists had been vigorously complaining that they did not truly understand *M'Naghten* and, in any event, that it raised moral and legal, rather than medical questions.[16] In addition, the psychiatrists believed that they, if freed from *M'Naghten's* strait jacket, could provide extensive insights into aspects of behavior that were highly relevant to the issue of responsibility. Since the traditional tests, as narrowly construed, precluded consideration of such insights, many psychiatrists sought to include them under the cover of "yea" or "nay" answers to the twin questions posed by *M'Naghten*.

Durham sought to uncover the information and analysis that lay beneath these conclusions by using language relevant to the behavioral disciplines. We framed our test in these words: "[A]n accused is not criminally responsible if his unlawful act was the product of mental disease or mental defect."[17] Our model, the method of assessing fault in negligence cases, was one long familiar to the law. We did not see our definition of responsibility as a precise test, just as we did not see the law's definition of negligence—the failure to exercise that degree of care which would be exercised by a "reasonable man of ordinary prudence"—as a precise test. Rather, we saw our terms "mental disease or defect" as akin to "due care," "product" as akin to "proximate cause," and "responsibility" or "guilt" as akin to "fault" or "liability." We recognized that it would almost always be possible to establish some sort of causal relationship between a mental condition and a criminal act, just as carelessness could almost always be tied to some injury. In the same way that the jury decided the "fault" issue in negligence cases, we wanted the jury to decide whether the mental abnormality was too serious and the causal connection too direct to impose guilt in criminal cases. Thus, the jury not only would make factual determinations, but also would fix the legal norm against which the mental condition and its relationship to the behavior must be measured.

[16]See *Durham v. United States,* 214 F.2d at 870–73.
[17]Id. at 874–75.

The role we envisioned for the expert was for him to tell the jury anything he considered within the scope of his expertise concerning the relationship between the defendant's behavior and the defendant's state of mind. We expected, perhaps naively, that because the phrases "mental disease or defect" and "product" would be familiar to behaviorists, these terms would allow for significant development by means of expert assistance. Through this process we hoped to open the law to more sophisticated information and more sophisticated concepts of free will. If nothing else, we believed that the community would be provided with an opportunity to learn—and thereby more clearly understand—not only the complexity of the criminal responsibility issue, but also the community's responsibility both for the criminal act and for the rehabilitation of the actor. In this manner we sought to approximate the law's promise, given according to its hopes.

While *Durham* did elicit more information than *M'Naghten*, it did not do nearly enough. Usually missing from an expert's testimony was a description of his investigation and examination, and of the origin, manifestations, and development of the accused's condition. This lack of information was due, at least in part, to: (1) society's failure to provide psychiatrists in public hospitals with the time and resources needed to examine defendants carefully; and (2) the primitive state of scientific understanding of human behavior. But the experts never told us of these problems, never candidly testified to what they knew and did not know about an individual or what they could not know considering the state of knowledge in the behavioral sciences. Instead, they papered over the problems by giving testimony tantamount to "yea" or "nay" answers to the *Durham* questions. Such testimony was little different from that which we had heard in response to *M'Naghten's* inquiries. *Durham* had called upon behavioral scientists to aid in the decision of whether a person was morally blameworthy, not to usurp the decision through sterile, conclusory testimony.

We first sought to rescue the term "mental disease or defect" from the grasp of the experts. Whether behavioral scientists considered a particular mental impairment a "disease" often turned on the treatment needs of the impaired individual or on behavioral concepts of what is a "disease." Yet the behaviorists' definition of "disease" is not a scientific definition and hence is subject to widely differing views. As Nobel laureate Dr. S.E. Luria has explained:

> An open-ended, undisprovable theory is not scientific theory at all. . . . No matter how much illumination psychoanalytic theory may throw on certain aspects of human behavior, it cannot be considered a scientific theory . . . [because] it is not clear that [psychoanalytic theory] potentially could be disproved by any critical set of tests.[18]

Thus, conditions became "diseases" or "nondiseases" overnight based on majority votes of hospital staff psychiatrists or, as in the case of homosexuality, of the entire membership of the American Psychiatric Association. To the extent blameworthiness was being considered, the experts' personal views of whom should be punished controlled the decision.

In 1962, to alleviate this continued expert dominance over the term "mental disease or defect," we held in the *McDonald*[19] case that "a mental disease or defect includes any abnormal condition of the mind which substantially affects mental or emotional processes and substantially impairs behavior controls."[20] This functional definition was an heroic attempt to focus attention on the *extent* of the impairment and the impairment's *relation* to moral blameworthiness. It did not succeed. First, behavioral scientists continued to speak in conclusory terms, using psychiatric labels developed for other purposes as the equivalent of the functional *McDonald* test. But more importantly, *McDonald* pointed up a second unresolved problem: the experts were offering conclusory testimony on whether the act was a "product" of the disease.

Three years after *Durham*, in *Carter v. United States*,[21] we had explained that the "productivity" requirement was satisfied if "the accused would not have committed the act if he had not had the disease."[22] But this definition did not settle the moral issues contained in the productivity requirement, because the resolution of whether a certain mental impairment caused a particular criminal act is itself a determination with respect to moral blameworthiness. As we realized when formulating the *Durham* test, any of one's emotional conditions will have some effect on one's ability to conform to the law's demands. The issue is whether the effect of the mental impairment was so serious that the community can no longer conclude, with the requisite certainty, that the act was a product of a free choice to do wrong. This conclusion involves two moral questions: (1) how serious must one's mental defect be before it is no longer reasonable, and therefore not "just," to expect one to control one's behavior; and (2) at what point are the doubts over whether a defendant could have exercised self-control sufficiently great to preclude a finding of criminal responsibility? In the most blatant cases, as where the murderer thought the gun was a toothbrush or had such a strong impulse that he would have killed even if an entire police force had been at his elbow, the answers are not difficult. It certainly would be unjust to hold an actor criminally responsible in such situations. But in the run of cases, the answers depend on a subtle balance between the community's reluctance to impose moral condemnation on an unfree actor and its need to protect itself from his acts.

Conclusory expert testimony on the "productivity" requirement buried these moral questions and precluded their consideration by the jury. Just as psychiatric definitions of "disease" reflected the personal views of the psychiatric experts, so too behavioral descriptions of the causal relation between a mental impairment and a criminal act reflected the

---

[18]Luria, What Makes a Scientist Cheat, *Prism*, May 1975, at 15–16.

[19]*McDonald v. United States*, 312 F.2d 847 (D.C. Cir. 1962).

[20]Id at 851.

[21]252 F.2d 608 (D.C. Cir. 1957).

[22]Id. at 617.

personal judgments of behavioral experts on the moral questions I have just described. In 1967, in the *Washington*[23] case, we attempted conclusively to resolve the problem by forbidding any expert testimony in terms of the ultimate issue: namely, whether an act was the product of a mental disorder. The decision contained a model instruction, to be followed in all cases, detailing the expert's role in the legal determination of criminal responsibility.[24] The *Washington* instruction was the culmination of our struggle to fulfill *Durham's* promise. The instruction remains valid today, no matter what legal definition of "insanity" or responsibility is employed. But as detailed and explicit as the instruction was, it did not solve the problem of expert dominance, because in the vast majority of cases, the behavioral experts ignored it.

The primary victims of this unsolved problem were, and still are, defendants from disadvantaged backgrounds. These defendants received only cursory mental examinations, for the doctors in public hospitals were too overworked for anything more thorough. Some psychiatrists would then testify that these defendants did not suffer from mental diseases, reasoning that mental impairments associated with social, economic, and cultural deprivation and with racial discrimination—so-called "personality disorders"—were not "diseases." Other psychiatrists would find a mental disease, but proceed to testify that the crime was not the product of that mental condition because, "This is normal behavior for a great many people in that subculture."[25] And sometimes the judges would beat the experts to the draw by denying motions for mental examinations on the same basis. For example, in 1959 a very able and distinguished juvenile court judge denied such a motion, concluding that while a juvenile girl's "precocious sexual experiences"—including a pregnancy at age 10 and a rape at age 16—"are certainly pathetic," such experiences

---

[23]*Washington v. United States*, 390 F.2d 444 (D.C. Cir. 1967).

[24]The instruction reads, in part, as follows:

As an expert witness, you may, if you wish and if you feel you can, give your opinion about whether the defendant suffered from a mental disease or defect. You may then explain how defendant's disease or defect relates to his alleged offense, that is, how the development, adaptation and functioning of defendant's behavioral processes may have influenced his conduct. This explanation should be so complete that the jury will have a basis for an informed judgment on whether the alleged crime was a "product" of his mental disease or defect. But it will not be necessary for you to express an opinion on whether the alleged crime was a "product" of a mental disease or defect and you will not be asked to do so.

When you are asked questions which fall within the scope of your special training and experience, you may answer them if you feel competent to do so; otherwise you should not answer them. If the answer depends upon knowledge and experience generally possessed by ordinary citizens, for example questions of morality as distinguished from medical knowledge, you should not answer.

You should try to separate expert medical judgments from what we may call "lay judgments." If you cannot make a separation and if you do answer the question nonetheless, you should state clearly that your answer is not based solely upon your special knowledge. It would be misleading for the jury to think that your testimony is based on your special knowledge concerning the nature and diagnosis of mental conditions if in fact it is not.

Some final words of caution. Because we have an adversary system, counsel may deem it is his duty to

attack your testimony. You should not construe this as an attack upon your integrity. More specifically, counsel may try to undermine your opinions as lacking certainty or adequate basis. We recognize that an opinion may be merely a balance of probabilities and that we cannot demand absolute certainty. Thus you may testify to opinions that are within the zone of reasonable medical certainty. The crucial point is that the jury should know how your opinion may be affected by limitations of time or facilities in the examination of this defendant or by limitations in present psychiatric knowledge. The underlying facts you have obtained may be so scanty or the state of professional knowledge so unsure that you cannot fairly venture any opinion. If so, you should not hesitate to say so. And, again, if you do give an opinion, you should explain what you did to obtain the underlying facts, what these facts are, how they led to the opinion, and what, if any, are the uncertainties in the opinion.

Id. at 457–58.

[25]See *United States v. Brawner*, 471 F.2d 969, 1020–21 (D.C. Cir. 1972) (Bazelon, C.J., concurring in part and dissenting in part); *cf.* United States v. Carter, 436 F.2d 200, 209 n.14 (D.C. Cir. 1970) (Bazelon, C.J., concurring).

are far from being uncommon among children in her socioeconomic situation with the result that the traumatic effect may be expected to be far less than it would be in the case of a child raised by parents and relatives with different habits.[26]

At first, I was appalled at what struck me as gross insensitivity by a good and normally sensitive judge. I later realized that he may be right, *and that is the most frightening thought of all.* But if he is right, if a "socioeconomic situation" can render one impervious to trauma, would it not also render one impervious to the sanctions of law?

In less than two decades, the *Durham* experiment generated valuable experience and insights. It did not succeed, however, in its ultimate goal of eliciting relevant information for the community's determination of moral culpability. The operation was a success, but the patient died. In the 1972 decision of *United States v. Brawner*,[27] I joined with all the other members of my court in abandoning the *Durham* rule. But I could not agree with the alternative my colleagues chose. The majority in effect adopted the American Law Institute's Model Penal Code test, which requires the jury to determine whether "as a result of mental disease or defect [the defendant] lacks substantial capacity either to appreciate the criminality . . . of his conduct or to conform his conduct to the requirements of law."[28] I felt that this test, with its use of the phrases, "as the result of" and "mental disease or defect," was little more than a warmed-over amalgam of *M'Naghten* and *Durham*. However, its greatest weakness was its total failure to eliminate, or even to alleviate, the primary problem that *Durham* had sought to resolve: the problem of expert dominance.

In a separate opinion, I suggested an alternative approach, more akin to the minority proposals[29] of the ALI draftsmen or to one of the recommendations of the British Royal Commission.[30] Under my view, the jury would be instructed

> that a defendant is not responsible *if at the time of his unlawful conduct his mental or emotional processes or behavior controls were impaired to such an extent that he cannot justly be held responsible for his act.*[31]

This proposed instruction reflects what I derived from the *Durham* experience: (1) neither psychiatric experts nor appellate judges have a magic formula to determine how the balance between morality and safety should be struck in individual cases; (2) the community at large, which is both the beneficiary and the victim of these balancing decisions should, through its traditional surrogate, the jury, assess criminal responsibility in light of community standards; and (3) the legal rules were restricting the jury's inquiry into the causes of a criminal act and deflecting the jury's attention away from the central moral question. The instruction would freely allow expert and lay testimony on the nature and extent of behavioral impairments and of physiological, psychological, environmental, cultural, educational, economic, and heredity factors. Its ultimate aim, much like *Durham*'s, would be to give all of us a deeper understanding of the causes of human behavior in general and criminal behavior in particular.

Learned Hand once told me that my *Durham* opinion created more problems than it solved. Perhaps some might be inclined to level a similar criticism at my views in *Brawner*. On the one hand, my *Brawner* formulation might

---

[26]In re *Betty Jean Williams*, No. 27-220-3 (D.C. Juv. Ct., Oct. 20, 1959), quoted in United States v. Brawner, 471 F.2d at 1020 n.30 (Bazelon, C.J., concurring in part and dissenting in part).

[27]471 F.2d 969 (D.C. Cir. 1972).

[28]MODEL PENAL CODE § 4.01(1) (Proposed Official Draft, 1962), quoted in *United States v. Brawner*, 471 F.2d at 973.

[29]MODEL PENAL CODE § 4.01(1), Alternative (a) (Tent. Draft No. 4, 1955), quoted in *United States v. Brawner*, 471 F.2d at 986–87 n.24.

[30]ROYAL COMMISSION ON CAPITAL PUNISHMENT, REPORT, CMD. No. 8932, ¶ 333 (iii), at 116 (1953) (three Commissioners dissenting from this recommendation), quoted in United States v. Brawner, 471 F.2d at 986 n. 23.

[31]*United States v. Brawner*, 471 F.2d at 1032 (Bazelon, CJ., concurring in part and dissenting in part) (emphasis in original).

simply enable juries to find every defendant responsible and feel more complacent about doing so because, given the way the question would be put to them, they might view any answer they give as a moral one. But on the other hand, if my *Brawner* formulation were to elicit detailed information concerning the plight of those who live in the "other America," jurors might be so troubled as to force society to confront a difficult set of questions. What do we do with persons deemed dangerous but not responsible, and how do we accurately determine dangerousness? How do we preserve the dignity of those found to lack adequate behavioral controls? Is there any real difference between the penitentiaries and the public mental hospitals? I would say of *Brawner*, as I said of *Durham*, that Judge Hand's assessment was exactly right except for the very important word "*creates.*" My *Durham* views did not, and my *Brawner* views would not, create problems. Those opinions have simply uncovered bullets that society has always refused to bite.

In the 3 years since *Brawner* was decided, I have increasingly come to believe that no matter how an "insanity" test is formulated, the inquiry into culpability will be narrowly circumscribed by psychiatric concepts of disease. Therefore, I am increasingly attracted to the view that the insanity defense should be abolished and that the question of responsibility should be explored when the Government seeks to discharge its burden of establishing, beyond a reasonable doubt, the existence of *mens rea* or intent—an essential element of almost all crimes. Thus, unlike some abolitionists who see abolition as a way of avoiding any inquiry into responsibility, I see abolition as a way of broadening the inquiry beyond the medical model. Admittedly, our concept of *mens rea* is as primitive now as our insanity concepts were over 20 years ago. But once freed from the "insanity" label as framed by the medical model, *mens rea* offers the opportunity and hope of proving more hospitable to a broad inquiry into all forms of disabilities and motivations.

Of course, culpability and intent are not synonymous; even an individual who intentionally engages in unlawful conduct may be nonculpable when the law itself is deemed unjust by the community or when the reasons for the defendant's conduct serve as a justification or excuse. For this reason I do not feel that the jury's traditional power to "nullify" the law is a feature of the system to be reluctantly tolerated simply because of our unwillingness to set aside a jury verdict of not guilty. Rather, I view nullification as an important means of "bring[ing] to bear on the criminal process a sense of fairness and particularized justice."[32] I believe that from the John Peter Zenger trial of the 1700's to the trials of leftists in the 1970's, history generally supports that view. Therefore, I further believe, as I wrote in a dissenting opinion[33] in a case involving nine radicals who had spilled blood on records of the Dow Chemical Company, that we should not depend on sophisticated juries to intuit this power, but should be willing to instruct *all* juries as to its existence. Of course there have been, and will be, abuses such as the actions of bigoted Southern juries in acquitting whites of crimes against blacks. I doubt, however, that informing jurors of their power to nullify will increase the frequency of such actions; to the contrary, I believe a carefully framed instruction could instill in jurors a higher sense of responsibility. But more important, even the "abuses" have a positive aspect: they reveal the state of community values. For example, by exposing virulent white racism, jury nullification helped fuel a civil rights revolution and led the courts to create a right to be tried before a jury selected without bias.

Against all that I have said and believed on the importance of focusing on moral culpability is the law-as-external-constraint thesis. Applied to either the insanity or nullification context, this view asserts that the law cannot afford its moral pretenses, cannot afford to excuse all who are not culpable. The law needs to

---

[32] *United States v. Dougherty*, 473 F.2d 1113, 1142 (D.C. Cir. 1972) (Bazelon, C.J., concurring in part and dissenting in part). See generally Scheflin, *Jury Nullification: The Right to Say No*, 45 S. CAL. L. REV. 168 (1972).

[33] *United States v. Dougherty*, 473 F.2d at 1138–44 (Bazelon, C.J., concurring in part and dissenting in part).

maintain a stern visage of uncompromising force, it is said, in order to encourage those without impairment to obey all law and in order to encourage those with impairment to exercise that amount of free will which they do possess.

I strongly suspect that those who fear that my emphasis on moral culpability would jeopardize our safety are not realistic. To believe that putting the question of culpability to juries will increase sharply the number of acquittals of dangerous defendants strikes me as unrealistic. But if I am wrong in my projection—if community morality cannot condemn certain acts of dangerous actors—then those facts, and the values they reflect, should be confronted. The real question, it seems to me, is how we can afford *not* to live up to our moral pretenses and *not* to excuse unfree choices or nonblameworthy acts.

IV.

Just as moral considerations are implicated in the treatment of persons who have actually engaged in proscribed conduct, so too are they implicated in the treatment of persons *accused* of such conduct. The issue may be starkly posed: can the law afford to treat the accused with dignity and compassion, or must dignity and compassion give way to the need for efficiency?

The answer of the courts over the past two decades has been that the law can—indeed must—treat defendants humanely. The *Gideons*,[34] the *Mirandas*,[35] and the *Argersingers*[36] are not the result of the Justices of the United States Supreme Court, after 200 years, having gained new insights into the language of the Constitution or having uncovered new evidence concerning the framers' intent. Furthermore, in spite of contrary assertions by historians and political scientists, such decisions are not simply the product of the ebb and flow of personalities, pressures, and interests.

These decisions, like all great constitutional decisions, are statements of moral principle. In the words of Judge Elbert Tuttle, "[T]he only way the law has progressed from the days of the rack, the screw and the wheel is the development of moral concepts. . . ."[37]

A number of valuable precepts can be distilled from the great decisions of our times. Perhaps the most important of these is the insistence that each person should receive equal justice. Of course this ideal is not a modern discovery; it is at least as old as the Republic itself. But as our moral concepts evolve, more and more meaning is being poured into the vague words "equal justice." There was a time when the law, in its majestic equality, permitted the rich as well as the poor an "equal opportunity" to retain private counsel, to hire investigators and expert witnesses, to purchase trial transcripts, and to pay fines. We put a set of rights at our own eye level but ignored the fact that the growth of others had been stunted by many circumstances, including the accident of birth. Gradually, however, we have come to realize that "[t]here can be no equal justice where the kind of trial a man gets depends on the amount of money he has."[38] With this reminder from Justice Black, we have sought to give the stunted the assistance of a box on which to reach our own eye level.

Of course much still remains to be done before the noble ideal of equal justice will be a reality. Although we generals of the judiciary have designed magnificent insignia for the standards of criminal justice, the battles are being lost in the trenches of the station houses, courtrooms, and jails of the nation. For example, the powerful, but not the weak, have effective assistance of counsel from the earliest stages of the criminal process, enjoy freedom from confinement pending their trials and appeals, receive respectful treatment from judges, prosecutors, policemen, and probation officers, and undergo incarceration in

[34]*Gideon v. Wainwright*, 372 U.S. 355 (1963).
[35]*Miranda v. Arizona*, 384 U.S. 436 (1966).
[36]*Argersinger v. Hamlin*, 407 U.S. 25 (1972).

[37]*Novak v. Beto*, 453 F.2d 661, 672 (5th Cir. 1971) (Tuttle, J., concurring in part and dissenting in part), cert. denied, 409 U.S. 968 (1972).
[38]*Griffin v. Illinois*, 351 U.S. 12, 19 (1956).

prisons that are the least restrictive institutions possible.

Those who look to the law to impose external constraints are not especially troubled by such inequalities. They argue that the criminal law cannot be concerned with assuring that each accused fully understands his rights and has an equal opportunity to assert them. The law's mission is to acquit the innocent and to convict the guilty, and procedures are important primarily as means to that end. Convictions must not be reversed for "procedural irregularities" if the defendant-appellant was "guilty anyhow." Collateral attacks on unfair procedures should not be entertained unless the petitioner makes a colorable claim of innocence. These views are expressed with some force in a recent book, *The Price of Perfect Justice*,[39] which argues that the criminal system has spent too much effort perfecting justice and too little effort perfecting swift and certain punishment of wrongdoers.

I have always found this argument rather puzzling. I cannot understand how it can be that allowing rich defendants certain rights does not reasonably interfere with the efficient operation of the system, but that ensuring poor defendants the same rights would place an intolerable burden on it.[40] Further, I am convinced that those who fear that too much effort has been expended perfecting the quality of justice are living in a world of make-believe. Since most cases are either dismissed by police or prosecutor or else disposed of by guilty pleas, for most defendants the criminal process is nothing more than a series of discretionary, and often arbitrary decisions. But my disagreements with the attitudes on criminal procedure of those who subscribe to the law-as-external-constraint thesis extend to an even more fundamental level. First, I believe the proponents of that thesis downgrade and even ignore the important role that respect for the law—as distinguished from fear of the law—can play in achieving order. As Charles Evans Hughes warned over 50 years ago:

> A petty tyrant in a police court, refusals of a fair hearing in minor civil courts, [or] the impatient disregard of an immigrant's ignorance of our ways and language, will daily breed Bolshevists who are beyond the reach of your appeals.[41]

Second, unlike the worshippers of the great God Efficiency, I believe that the manner in which we treat those accused of crime is important as an end in itself, and not simply as a means to convicting the guilty, if only because "the guilty are almost always the first to suffer those hardships which are afterwards used as precedents against the innocent."[42]

V.

The final and most important arena in which the tension between the two polar positions on the criminal law can be felt has nothing—and everything—to do with the criminal justice system per se. The issue to which I refer is that of alternative responses to the crime problem. Those concerned with internalized controls urge actions designed to alleviate the social and economic causes of crime. Those satisfied with external constraints call for mandatory incarceration of convicted criminals in order to remove from the streets persons who would otherwise commit crimes and to deter other would-be criminals from violating the law.[43]

---

[39]M. FLEMING, *THE PRICE OF PERFECT JUSTICE* (1974).

[40]See generally Kamisar, *Has the Court Left the Attorney General Behind?—The Bazelon-Katzenbach Letters on Poverty, Equality and the Administration of Criminal Justice*, 54 KY. L.J. 464 (1966).

[41]Address by Charles Evans Hughes to the 42d Annual Meeting of the New York State Bar Association, Jan. 17, 1919, in 42 REP. N.Y. ST. B. ASS'N 224, 240 (1919).

[42]1 T. MACAULAY, *History of England*, 383 (Harper & Bros. 1849–61), quoted in *United States v. Barrett*, 505 F.2d 1091, 1115 (7th Cir. 1975) (Stevens, J., dissenting).

[43]For example, the Attorney General of California recently proposed that certain repeat offenders be sentenced to life imprisonment without possibility of parole. "[W]e," he said, "will in effect write off certain people . . . ." The Attorney General made his cost-benefit balance explicit by stating that he would "rather run the risk of keeping the wrong man a little longer than let the wrong man out too soon." L.A. Times. Nov. 15, 1975, § 2, at 12, col 3. See also J. WILSON, *THINKING ABOUT CRIME* 179–80 (1975).

I do not wish to enter the debate over whether mandatory incarceration could have a significant impact on the crime rate; in my judgment the evidence on the question is far from clear. If mandatory incarceration proves ineffective, however, I am certain that other repressive measures could be devised that would be horribly effective. A tap on every phone, a bug in every house, and a cop on every corner might well do the trick. If not, we could always incarcerate every potential criminal or perhaps mercifully put to sleep every proven criminal, thereby writing off all such persons as beyond rehabilitation.

In the short run, it may well be that mandatory incarceration or some other form of repression will have to be adopted to respond to the public demand for security. Indeed, within a single recent week such sensitive leaders as Senator Edward Kennedy of Massachusetts[44] and Governor Hugh Carey of New York[45] were each compelled to endorse mandatory sentencing. But if we adopt such measures, it should be with the painful awareness that any resulting order will be immoral, or at best amoral. In my opinion, it is simply unjust to place people in dehumanizing social conditions, to do nothing about those conditions, and then to command those who suffer, "Behave—or else!" The overwhelming majority of violent street crime, which worries us so deeply, is committed by people at the bottom of the socioeconomic-cultural ladder—the ignorant, the ill-educated, and the unemployed and often unemployable. I cannot believe that this is coincidental. Rather, I must conclude that those people turn to crime for reasons such as economic survival, a sense of excitement or accomplishment, and an outlet for frustration, desperation, and rage. We cannot produce a class of desperate and angry citizens by closing off, for many years, all means of economic advancement and personal fulfillment for a sizeable part of the population, and thereafter expect a crime-free society.

What concerns me about the wave of proposals for getting tough with criminals is that they often seem to be offered without any awareness of those underlying causes of crime that I have mentioned. I am troubled less by what is said than by what is left unsaid. President Ford's recent message on crime to Congress provides an example.[46] The President spared us from the traditional, ritualistic acknowledgment of the social causes of street crime. Consequently, he spared himself from the need to offer concrete proposals to deal with those causes. Indeed the only time the President even mentioned the poor was in his repeated calls for compassion for the victims of crime. Had the President also noted that the perpetrators of crime come from disadvantaged groups, his compassion might have led him to focus on the conditions that afflict all members of those groups, victim and offender alike.

Three intellectual justifications can be offered for the "externalists'" attempt to divorce criminal justice from social justice and to rely on "get tough" solutions to the crime epidemic.[47] First, it is argued that this society cannot afford social justice. At a time when the largest city reaches the brink of bankruptcy, notwithstanding its extremely high rate of taxation, this argument is enticing. Some localities cannot even afford adequate police protection, let alone measures to provide the educational and economic opportunities which are lacking for an alarming number of their citizens. Moreover, the experience of the 1960's teaches that the costs will be high, for we have learned the hard way that halfway measures will not work. Nevertheless, these costs must be borne, for there is no alternative consistent with the survival of a truly free democracy. I must believe that a nation whose gross national product hovers at the one trillion dollar mark can find the resources.

---

[44]N.Y. Times, Dec. 6, 1975, at 29, col. 2 (city ed.).

[45]*N.Y. Times*, Dec. 10, 1975, at 1, col. 6 (city ed.).

[46]The President's Special Message to Congress on Crime, June 19, 1975, in 11 *Weekly Compilation of Presidential Documents 652* (1975), 17 Crim. L. Rep. 3089 (1975).

[47]In 1974, this epidemic resulted in an 18% increase, the largest since such statistics were first compiled, in the rate of crime. L.A. Times, Nov. 18, 1975, § 1, at 4, col. 4.

Second, it is suggested that "we do not know, with any confidence, the causes of crime."[48] In a very narrow sense this is true. We do not understand why some poor people commit crime and others do not, why crime increases in periods of economic growth as well as in periods of economic decline, or why some cities with high unemployment experience more crime than do other cities with lower unemployment. We do not understand the effect of population growth and density on crime, and there is respected opinion suggesting that increases in population affect not only the degree but also the very nature of the problem. We do not understand the effect of age, sex, geography, race, or genetics on crime—and each of these factors may be of some relevance. In short, we do not understand *all* the causes of crime.

But rather than focusing on what we do *not* know, I suggest focusing on what we do know. We know, as I have already stated, that almost all violent crime is committed by the disadvantaged and deprived. We know, or so my expert colleagues on the National Academy of Sciences Committee for Child Development tell me, that the family is the most effective child-developing and child-socializing agent available. We know, or think we know, that the crucial period for personality formation is during infancy.[49] And we certainly know that the grinding poverty in our ghettos wreaks destruction on the family unit and makes it impossible for parents to convey a sense of order, purpose, and self-esteem to their children. In short, we know that poverty appears to be a *necessary*, though not a sufficient, condition for the occurence of most violent crime.

The real problem is that because of our limited knowledge the only apparent solution to the poverty-causes-crime problem is to alleviate the suffering of all deprived people, including noncriminals. If physical order is the only goal, this solution is undeniably wasteful since it directs resources to persons who pose

no danger of physical disorder to society. But if moral order is the aim, this solution is a necessity. The fact that some persons are resigned to their plight and that their miseries cause us no trouble is hardly a justification for allowing them to continue to suffer.

The first step down the long road to moral order is to provide a form of guaranteed income to every family as a matter of right, *not* grace or benevolence. Parents who are unable to put food on the table, or who can do so only by surrendering their self-respect, cannot be expected to raise children who are law-abiding, productive, and fulfilled members of society. But even if providing the poor with a guaranteed income or with educational and economic opportunities would have no effect on the crime rate, the call for such action would be no less urgent. We dare not demand a cost-benefit justification for these measures; they are right for their own sake and they are necessary for a humane society. One indication of how far we have strayed from our moral principles is the frequency with which proposals to eradicate injustices are defended solely in terms of their potential for reducing crime.

The third justification that is offered for divorcing crime control from social reform is a cost-effectiveness justification. It is argued that precisely because poverty is the *root* cause of crime, it is also the most difficult to deal with. Therefore, the argument goes, it would be wiser to concentrate on less deep-seated causes. The position is deficient in two respects.

In the first place, the application of cost-benefit analysis to crime control is dangerous. The more repressive the criminal law becomes, the more likely it will be to hide its "costs." Every time the criminal law erroneously confines someone on the basis of a mistaken assumption that he will recidivate unless confined, there is obviously a significant cost; but it is a hidden cost, since society rarely, if ever, learns about the error. Every time we introduce a new invasion of privacy such as wiretapping or mail opening, the invasion produces significant costs; but they, too, tend to be hidden costs, since the victims who are innocent seldom complain. The alleged costs of nonrepression,

---

[48]McKay, Criminal Justice in New York City, *City Almanac*, Aug. 1975, at 4.

[49]Of course, this insight may prove nothing more than today's wisdom, to be forgotten tomorrow.

on the other hand, are often revealed in gory detail. When the system erroneously releases someone who commits a new crime, we usually learn about it. When the search that turns up a criminal is determined to be illegal and as a result the criminal's conviction is reversed, we learn about that as well. Thus, aside from questions concerning the propriety of cost-benefit analysis for the kinds of issues dealt with by the criminal law, cost-benefit analysis, if not appropriately formulated, will provide an inadequate basis on which to make decisions regarding crime control measures.[50]

But second, even if one were to make the heroic assumption that cost-benefit analysis could work and the even more heroic assumption that the most cost-effective method of crime control is repression, the argument would hardly be ended. What ultimately is at issue in the debate over alternative responses to the crime problem is a question of the goal to be pursued: repressive order or moral order. On that question, cost-benefit analysis has nothing to say. To choose moral order is to choose a long, painful, and costly process. The only option I can imagine that is less appealing is not to choose it. Creating order through repression will not be easy, and maintaining it, as the frustrations of the deprived grow, will be more and more difficult. As the poet Langston Hughes warned:

> What happens to a dream deferred?
>> Does it dry up
>> like a raisin in the sun?
>> Or fester like a sore—
>> And then run?
>> Does it stink like rotten meat?
>> Or crust and sugar over—
>> like a syrupy sweet?
>> Maybe it just sags
>> like a heavy load.
>> *Or does it explode?*[51]

In 1930, a young official in the Justice Department, in testifying on the need for better crime statistics, told an Appropriations Subcommittee of the House of Representatives that one subject "that would be interesting in connection with crime statistics is the relation to crime of unemployment, of disease, and of the various items which make up the economic life of a country."[52] The official, as you might or might not have guessed, was the man whose memory is honored here, J. Edgar Hoover. Today, 45 years later, it is time—long past time—to confront the relationship between crime and the accident of birth.

---

[50]*Cf.* Dershowitz, *The Origins of Preventive Confinement in Anglo-American Law* (pts. 1–2), 43 U. Cin. L. Rev. 1, 781 (1974); Dershowitz, *Indeterminate Confinement: Letting the Therapy Fit the Harm*, 123 U. Pa. L. Rev. 297 (1974); Dershowitz, *Preventive Confinement: A Suggested Framework for Constitutional Analysis*, 51 Texas L. Rev. 1277 (1973); Dershowitz, *Imprisonment by Judicial Hunch*, 57 A.B.A.J. 560 (1971).

[51]L. Hughes, Dream Deferred in *The Panther and the Lash*, 14 (1967).

[52]Quoted in S. Ungar, *FBI 361* (1976).

Crime, Minorities, and the Social Contract

Bill Lawson

What is the relationship between governmental protection and our obligation to obey the law? What are the legitimate limits of the exercise of power the state can use to preserve the peace? What is meant by political obligation, if individuals are always free to decide if the state is doing its job?[1] Urban crime represents an interesting focal point for answering these important questions.

One of the most important benefits the state provides is that of protection. This protection can be either from outside invaders or from unsavory characters within the state, that is, those individuals who want to infringe on property rights by stealing, defrauding, or destroying property. Protection of property rights is one of the basic functions of the government. Indeed, governmental protection encompasses many areas of an individual's life. But physical protection, that is, protection of life and property, is a basic benefit of state membership.

In many urban areas, the residents think that the efforts of the police are ineffective in protecting them from crime. These citizens complain that the police come late or not at all to calls for assistance. Many urban residents think that they are victims twice. First, they have to contend with crime in their communities, and then they have to contend with lack of protection from the state.

Urban crime presents an interesting problem for social contract theorists, particularly for those theorists who draw on John Locke's

Bill Lawson, "Crime, Minorities, and the Social Contract" (as appeared in *Criminal Justice Ethics*, Volume 9, Number 2, [Summer/Fall 1990]; 16–24). Reprinted by permission of The Institute of Criminal Justice Ethics, 555 W. 57th St., New York, N.Y. 10019-1029.

version of the Social Contract. Locke argued that the right of self-preservation is not completely given up when one joins the state. That some citizens perceive the state as being unable to protect them from crime raises the following question: If a segment of the population thinks that the state continually fails to protect them from crime, at what point are these individuals morally justified in taking on the responsibility of protecting themselves from crime?

I will argue that certain passages in Locke's *The Second Treatise of Government* lead to the unsettling conclusion that the fear of being a victim of crime for many urban residents releases them from an obligation to obey governmental dictates and consequently from any moral or legal obligation to obey the law. If my reading of Locke is correct, the actions taken by urban residents to protect themselves can be viewed as neither civil disobedience nor vigilantism. I conclude that urban crime forces us to reassess our understanding of the relationship between a group's conception of the protection they are getting from the state and what the state claims it is doing to protect them. While my focus is urban residents, I think that my argument applies to the conception of governmental protection as seen by other members of the state as well.

Since Locke does not specifically mention urban crime, it will be necessary to tease out the implications of his version of social contract theory for this situation.

LOCKE ON POLITICAL OBLIGATIONS

Locke's *Second Treatise* is an explanation of how individuals come to have political obligations and of the extent of both the state's obligations to its citizens and their obligations to the state. According to this theory, prior to the formation of civil society, men live in a "state of nature." While descriptions of the state of nature vary, for Locke it was a place of relative peace, which lacks a civil authority. There were, however, some inconveniences in this state—disputes over property. There was no civil authority in the state of nature, so each man was his own judge, jury, and executioner.

It was clear, according to Locke, that not all men were equally suited to press their property claims against others. Some civil mechanism was needed to adjudicate property claims. Thus, free, equal, and autonomous individuals come together to form a compact in which they agreed to give up to the state certain rights they naturally possess. These rights include the right to be their own judge, jury, and executioner. By freely consenting to join with others in civil society, each is thought to be politically obligated to obey the dictates of the state.

The state is to ensure protection of their property, which includes their lives, by providing known laws, judges, and punishment for property violations. Individuals should then be able to live peaceful and secure lives with the knowledge that their property rights are respected and protected. In this manner their chances of a life free of the inconveniences of the state of nature are ensured.

Locke, like Hobbes, realized that events can conspire to cause the government or the society to dissolve. He makes the distinction between dissolution of government and dissolution of society. Of course, conquest comes immediately to mind as an event that would lead to the dissolution of society. Locke, however, thinks that it is possible that once the social contract is instituted the government can dissolve and the society still exist. For Locke, dissolution of government does not mean a return to the state of nature.

Locke discusses at length the circumstances that tend towards the dissolution of government. He also notes that usurpation and tyranny can dissolve the government but do not have to. Usurpation and tyranny, according

to Locke, justify disobeying governmental dictates. Disobeying the government in these cases is, of course, justified disobedience, and Locke thinks that the state will respond positively and restore the broken trust. Legal avenues for redress against tyrannical abuses give effect to the right of resistance without destabilizing the government.[2]

For our disscussion of urban crime, we can cite a passage in the Second Treatise that is often glossed over:

> There is one way more whereby such a government may be dissolved, and that is when he who has the supreme executive power neglects and abandons that charge, so that laws already made can no longer be put in execution. This is demonstratively to reduce all to anarchy, and so effectively to dissolve the government; for laws not being made for themselves, but to be by their own execution the bonds of the society, to keep every part of the body politic in its due place and function, when that totally ceases, the government visibly ceases, and the people become a confused multitude, without order or connection. When there is no longer the administration of justice for the security of men's rights, nor any remaining power within the community to direct the force to provide for the necessities of the public, there certainly is no government left. When the laws cannot be executed, it is all one as if there were no laws; and a government without laws is, I suppose, a mystery in politics, inconceivable to human capacity and inconsistent with human society.[3]

This is a case in which those persons entrusted to provide protection fail to uphold their obligation to protect citizens. Locke thinks that in these and like cases the government is dissolved and the people have the right to provide for their own protection.

Who decides if the trust has been broken and the government dissolved? Locke is very clear that it is the people themselves. "The people shall be judge; for who shall be judge whether his trustee or deputy act well and according to the trust reposed in him but he who deputes him and must, by having deputed him, have still a power to discard him when he fails in his trust."[4]

If the people decide the trust has been broken, they then have the moral right to protect themselves. Locke thinks that individuals are always free to protect themselves when the state is thought to no longer be able to protect them. They also have the right to choose by which means to do so, even if the means would have been illegal before the government was dissolved. Since there are no laws, their actions are not illegal. Thus, protecting oneself is neither civil disobedience nor vigilantism.

LOCKE'S THEORIES AS APPLIED TO URBAN CRIME

Locke's objective is, of course, to present a theory of political obligation. Why should we believe that an understanding of the situation of urban residents can be drawn from his work? Consider the following discussion that could take place at a neighborhood watch meeting in an urban area.

Tom: It is clear that our community isn't receiving adequate police protection. If we call the police, they come hours later or not at all. We need bars on our doors and windows. Drug dealers control the streets. There are daily shoot-outs between dealers.[5] Our children are not safe. It is unsafe to walk the streets. Life in this community can be nasty, brutish, and short. We need to arm ourselves and take back our community.

Jean: We should press for more protection from the state.

Tom: We have asked for more protection and have not received any. I think that we should protect ourselves.

Jean: But that would be wrong!

Tom: Why?

Jean: It's the state's job to provide protection for its citizens. What if everyone took the law into his or her own hands?

Tom: I'm not saying that people should take the law into their own hands. If we lived in a predominantly white neighborhood, we would receive adequate police protection. They have no need to take the law into their own hands. They receive protection from the state. The state does not provide urban Blacks and Hispanics the same protection of their property. If the state is supposed to protect our property and does not, I don't see why we can't protect it ourselves.

Jean: Wouldn't taking the law into our own hands be breaking the law? We would be committing an act of civil disobedience.

Tom: Protecting yourself is not an act of civil disobedience.

John: I remember, from my college days, talk of a social contract between the state and its citizens.

Tom: What is a social contract?

John: It is a pact by which individuals agree to give up to the state certain rights they naturally possess.

Tom: What rights?

John: The right to be their own judge, jury, and executioner.

Tom: What does the state provide?

John: The state is to provide protection of their property, which includes their lives. The citizens should then be able to live peaceful and secure lives with the knowledge that their property rights are respected and protected.

Tom: What happens if the state fails to protect them?

John: The contract is broken!

Tom: Does that mean they should protect themselves?

John: Yes!

Tom: Why doesn't that same line of reasoning apply to us. We are not protected. Why shouldn't we protect ourselves?

Tom's question goes to the heart of our discussion. If these individuals truly believe that they can do a better job protecting themselves than the government can, and they believe that the trust has been broken, then, according to Locke, they are free to protect themselves.

Thus, urban dwellers would have to be, at least in the American political context, minimal Lockeans in that they believe that the state should protect their property. Locke is clear that individuals cannot wait around for the government to do its job until they find themselves in a much worse position than they would have been in had they taken control of their communities earlier.

These individuals may be well advised to heed the words of the noted economist Walter Williams:

> Blacks can not depend on politicians. They must protect their own neighborhoods, even if that means using violence to clean up drug corners and crackhouses. They must show up on school premises to mete out instant justice to miscreants. "Williams," you say, "that sounds like vigilantism." Well," I say, "what do you do when established legal authorities refuse to do their job—just sit and take it? And for how long?"[6]

Williams's position raises a number of important questions. To what lengths, for example, should the state go to stop urban crime? Should the state abridge civil liberties to decrease crime? What in the end should be a community's response to its perception of lack of governmental protection?

STATE VS. INDIVIDUAL PREROGATIVES

If we look to Locke for answers to these questions, we find that he believes that in cases of extreme emergency the sovereign should use a political power called prerogative. For prerogative is nothing but the power of doing public good without a rule.[7] He thinks that this power—to do what is in the public good at the discretion of the sovereign—would be used in those cases where it would take too long to get laws passed.

In general, executive prerogatives can be justified by their tendency to promote a benefit or prevent harm that would not have been promoted or prevented had the power of the government been limited to the strict letter of the law.[8] The wise Prince will use this power in accordance with the public trust.

According to Locke, governments have the power to do those things which will tend toward the public good, even if it means using extra-legal means.[9] The problem for Locke is whether the use of prerogative is actually an abuse of power. Has the Prince overstepped his authority?

Would Locke permit the state to infringe on constitutionally guaranteed rights to prevent crime? Would this action be an abuse of prerogative? It appears that Locke would allow the infringement, by the state, of civil liberties to put an end to crime. Take the example of search and seizures without a warrant.

> The right of the executive to act in these instances is not different in principle from the right of any citizen who, "having the power in his hands, has by the common Law of Nature, a right to make use of it for the good of the Society" (2T. 159). For example, anyone may break into a person's home to save a child from a fire and may even have a duty to do so. The executive, having greater power at his disposal, is more likely to be in a situation where he is capable of fulfilling his duty under natural law in comparable manner.[10]

This reading of Locke puts urban residents in a precarious position. They cannot be sure that the infringement of their civil liberties would be directed only toward the criminal element. The government may want to confiscate the weapons of the victimized individuals. This action would violate the constitutional right to bear arms (assuming here that these individuals still see themselves as members of the state). This would mean that these citizens would be placed in the position of fighting the police to keep their weapon while at the same time battling the criminal element. There are cases in which patrols established by the community to keep the peace have subsequently clashed with the police.

In Los Angeles, for example, the Nation of Islam has been active in the battle against drugs in black communities. These individuals patrol communities unarmed and have had run-ins with the police. One such account of an altercation between thirteen young Muslims and twenty-four Los Angeles police officers is indicative of the problem:

Although accounts differ, Nation of Islam spokespersons say the Muslims objected to being ordered to assume a prone position on the ground. "Why do you want us to bow down to you—bow in the streets, face down, as though you were God?" a Farrakhan aide, Khallid Muhammad, said later. "You don't make the white folks of Beverly Hills bow down. . . . we bow down to God and God alone." All 13 of the Muslims were charged in the episode, and the controversy fueled mounting tensions in predominantly black south-central Los Angeles over what many residents see as harassment and the overuse of force by city police and sheriff's deputies."[11]

Here it is important to note that the actions of the state are crucial in residents' decisions as to whether their own acts of protection are supplemental, or are essential because the government has abrogated the social contract. The residents of this community thought that they were justified in having patrols. The state believed that the patrols were unjustified. When the state fails to allows citizens to perform those actions that they feel are within the legal parameters of the law, it erodes any confidence in the ability of the state to take the welfare of these citizens seriously.

Can these besieged individuals depend on other members of the state coming to their aid? Locke notes that if a segment of the population finds itself at war with the government, its particular battle may not be important to other members of the state. Locke is concerned with society-wide abuses of governmental power. But what he writes is telling.

> It being as impossible for one or a few oppressed men to disturb the government, where the body of the people do not think themselves concerned in it, as for a raving madman or heady malcontent to overturn a well-settled state, the people being as little apt to follow the one as the other.[12]

Urban residents cannot depend on other citizens coming to their aid, particularly if these other citizens think that (1) the state must infringe on the civil liberties of certain individuals to ensure the peace, and (2) the state will not one day turn on them.

In the end, urban residents are the final judges of current level of governmental protection and the likelihood of future protection. According to Locke, these individuals must either (a) continue to press for protection or (b) establish their own government, which they believe will protect them from crime. If they adopt (a), they cannot wait until their lives and property are near ruin before they move to option (b). What option (b) means in practical terms remains to be sketched out. What is clear is that they must replace the status quo. This could mean requesting either a total withdrawal of the existing government from minority neighborhoods (including nonpolice services), that is, secession, or a replacement of existing law enforcement services by local enforcement services. Locke, it seems, never thought things would get to this point.

URBAN CRIME VICTIMS AND THE SOCIAL CONTRACT

One of the fundamental reasons for continued allegiance to a government is the knowledge that the government can and will protect the individual more effectively than can (a) the state of nature or (b) some alternative political structure. Since for Locke, the dissolution of Government does not mean the end of the social contract, the state must be thought to protect one better than some other political arrangement. It is the question of when the state has failed to uphold its obligation to protect that comes to the fore in the case of urban crime.

In a number of urban areas, the efforts of the police are thought by those residents to be ineffective in protecting citizens from the criminal element. Many Americans living in urban areas feel unprotected from the criminal element in their neighborhoods.[13] Some urban areas are like battlegrounds.[14] In Washington, D.C., the violent crime (murder) rate is so high that there are calls for deploying the National Guard to protect citizens.[15] There are several cities with violent crime rates similar to those of Washington.[16]

In its 1987 summary of crime victimization, the U.S. Department of Justice reported that blacks were victims of violent crime at a higher rate than whites or members of other minority groups.[17] For both violent and personal theft crimes, the rate of victimization was greatest for central city residents. For personal crimes of violence, the rate of victimization was highest among residents in urban areas. Overall, the robbery victimization rates were higher in central cities. The assault victimization rates were higher in central cities. Households headed by blacks had higher victimization rates for all three major household crimes. Based on number of vehicles owned, white heads of household were victims of motor vehicle theft at a lower rate than blacks or members of other minority groups. The rate of victimization for burglary was generally higher for black households than for white ones regardless of annual family income. Low-income (less than $15,000) black households had higher larceny rates than low-income white households. In motor vehicle theft, black households with incomes over $30,000 had higher rates than white households in those high income categories. There were no significant differences in household larceny or motor vehicle theft victimization rates between black renters and black home owners. And for personal crimes central city households had the higher rates of crime. The Department of Justice data show very clearly that urban residents are more often victims of crime—violent or otherwise.

In America, we consider our sanctions in criminal law as being deterrents and look upon our law enforcement agencies as being protective agencies. We believe that the legal system is to ensure that an individual may go peacefully about her business without coercive interference. Many Americans living in urban areas cannot go peacefully about their business.[18] Individuals in urban areas live in fear based on personal victimization or the victimization of friends, neighbors or relatives. It is the same fear that has caused the residents of these areas to turn their houses into prisons in which they attempt to lock themselves from crime.[19]

The majority of the citizens of these communities are neither criminals nor involved in crime. Yet these individuals, many of whom are members of racial or ethnic minorities, find themselves often at the mercy of the criminal element. Members of these communities feel that the state is not protecting them.[20]

One might object that there is too much police pressure in black neighborhoods. In fact, it is argued, the extraordinarily high lifetime arrest probabilities of young, male urban blacks (35 percent of whom are arrested at least once before age 18; 47 percent before age 30) suggest that law enforcement agents have a very high profile in black urban neighborhoods. One might also cite the record high numbers of people in prison today, a substantial proportion of whom are urban black males.

While these figures may be correct, we must remember that Locke puts the decision as to whether the state is protecting the individual in the hands of the people being affected. Many urban residents think that the police are there to contain rather than to protect. There is talk of black genocide, and the above figures, rather than reassuring urban residents that they are well protected, reinforce the position that blacks are not protected.

However, the fact that individuals feel that the state is not protecting them does not mean that they are immediately free to protect themselves. We would hope that reason would dictate the behavior of these residents. Yet, as noted above, how the state responds to their attempts to supplement the social contract will have important ramifications on their view of governmental protection.

These individuals are not entirely unprotected, or else they would not be citizens in the legal sense. They are still free to join with other citizens to push for the redress of their grievances, and as long as the system tries to protect them and allows them to politically organize and "fight" for protection, they are obligated to obey the laws of the state.[21] In this regard, they should use nonviolent civil disobedience and push for better police protection.

Michael Walzer, in talking about oppressed minorities, argues that, in their push for better protection, they are not required to obey every single law, or pay every tax, even to defend the state: "These are the obligations of free and equal citizens and also, perhaps, of men who freely choose not to be free and equal citizens, who do not ask but receive all other benefits of the political community."[22]

Thus Walzer would conclude that as long as the state does not take measures to make members of this group truly equal, their obligations to the state are weakened. One cannot be expected to consent to a state in which one does not receive all of the benefits (and notably protection), especially if this political arrangement is not designed to benefit all concerned. Walzer believes that the system ultimately will change and will one day protect urban residents like other citizens. But until they are protected, these individuals have fewer obligations than those citizens who are protected. While they are waiting for the state to respond they can, of course, supplement the social contract by providing for themselves such services as neighborhood watches and voluntary police organizations or groups like the Guardian Angels to patrol their communities.

This response is troublesome for a number of reasons. First, citizenship is not limited to one important right, protection. Citizenship includes a cluster of rights, of which protection is one. If a group is unprotected to the point that it fears for its existence, its political obligations are seriously undermined. However, this view does not resolve the problem of deciding what these individuals are now not obligated to do as part of their weakened political obligations as citizens. What are the obligations of a group that receives all of the benefits of citizenship except one? What effect does not receiving a benefit have on their not paying their taxes? Which taxes? There is no one-to-one relationship between benefits and obligation.

Second, unprotected citizens have to believe that the state places importance on their lives as members of the state. When members of crime-ridden communities review their social history, can they be sure that the state will protect them? Locke and later contract theorists tacitly assumed that the state would provide equal physical protection for all members of the state. Any lack of physical protection would be closely connected with usurpation of political power and the abuses that follow.

Racial group membership, which has been a reason for political usurpation and the denial of basic political rights, adds a strange twist to our understanding of equal protection and state membership. In America, racial minorities have long claimed that the government has been remiss in protecting them from physical and political wrongs. Blacks and other racial minorities realize that the state has been slow to protect their constitutionally guaranteed rights. How can they be expected to believe that the government will look out for their interest when it comes to protecting them from crime?

Remember, Locke claims that it is the individual who decides if the state is doing or can do its job. The social and political history of blacks in America gives urban crime its racial edge. If these individuals don't think that the state will ever protect them, no argument about supplementing the social contract will convince them otherwise.

CONCLUSION

Does it matter that these crimes are committed by blacks against blacks? The answer to this question would go beyond the scope of this paper. It would involve developing a crime victimization theory. However, if it is the job of the state to protect citizens, then it is the state's job to ensure that laws are obeyed, that criminals are punished, and that citizens are protected no matter what their race.

Finally, the work of William Julius Wilson on the urban underclass has greatly influenced thinking on the problems of the urban poor.[23] Wilson thinks that there are two black communities, one of middle-class blacks who have "made it" and another of underclass blacks living in urban slums, who have not. Serious crime victimization lies mainly with this latter group, and particularly with young black males. M. Hindelang notes that an "individual's chances of personal victimization are dependent upon the extent to which the individual shares de-mographic characteristics with offenders."[24] If Wilson is correct, middle-class blacks are less likely to be victims of crime because they do not live in the area with offenders.

A *Social Science Quarterly* study on residen-tial segregation of Blacks, Hispanics, and Asians by socioeconomic status and generation concluded that "blacks are highly segregated from Anglos, and that this segregation persists regardless of black education, income, or oc-cupation status."[25] "If the black middle class is abandoning the black poor," as Wilson (1987) argued, "they are not moving to integrated Anglo-black neighborhoods."[26] According to the *Social Science Quarterly* data, middle class blacks continue to be residentially segregated and "are forced to live in neighborhoods of much poorer quality than whites with similar class backgrounds."[27]

No matter what their education or occupation achievement, and whatever their incomes, blacks are exposed to higher crime rates, less effective educational systems, higher mortality risks, more dilapidated surroundings, and a poorer socio-economic environment than whites, simply be-cause of the persistence of strong barriers to residential integration.[28]

If it is true that blacks no matter what their education or economic status are more likely to be a victim of crime, it may call into question the relationship of all blacks to the political order. This consequence of residential segre-gation needs to be explored further.

We can at least say that if equal protection is one of the basic benefits of being a member of the social contract, then urban residents are left to question the value of contract member-ship. Crime forces these individuals to reassess their obligations to the state and our under-standing of social contract theory.

However, to accept the social contract is also to accept many of its basic assumption about how individuals come to be members of the state and what type of physical protection they receive.[29] If urban residents think that they are left to fend for themselves, given this

reading of Locke, actions taken to protect their lives and property cannot be viewed as morally wrong or illegal.

While I have focused on urban residents, I think that my conclusions can be applied to any members of the state. Should the Bernard Goetzes of today's world be released from their obligations to obey the law because they feel they are inadequately protected? Should we li-cense white store owners in minority neigh-borhoods to shoot all those of whom they are suspicious? Of course not. It is meaningful to think of these individuals being protected by the state. Yet the state has also to convince them that they are adequately protected. My discussion of Locke's positions and urban crime points out that if we accept a Lockean version of the social contract, we must admit that the state has always to argue that no matter what your perceptions of governmental protection, you are really protected and thus obligated to obey the laws.

NOTES

The author gratefully acknowledges the helpful comments and suggestions of Laurence Thomas, William Oliver, the reviewers and the editorial staff of *Criminal Justice Ethics*.

[1] See, e.g., C. Pateman, *The Problem of Political Obligation* (New York, 1985).

[2] R. W. Grant, *John Locke's Liberalism 163* (1987).

[3] J. Locke, *The Second Treatise of Government* § 219 (T. P. Peardon ed. 1952).

[4] Id at § 240.

[5] Bowman, Families are Caught in Crossfire, *USA Today*, Feb. 19, 1989, at 1A.

[6] Williams, Liberals Have Sold Blacks Down the River, Special Issue: *New Dimensions*, 1989, at 77.

[7] J. Locke, supra note 3, at § 166.

[8] R. W. Grant, supra note 2, at 84.

[9] Is the Fight on Drugs Eroding Civil Right. N. Y. Times, May 6, 1990, at 5E.

[10] R. W. Grant, supra note 2, at 84.

[11] Farrakhan's Mission, *Newsweek*, March 19, 1990, at 25.

[12] J. Locke, § 208.

[13] For example, a survey in Minneapolis-St.Paul revealed that crime- and drugs-related violence were the number one concern of residents of the Twin cities. This is not surprising given the rise in drug related crimes in most American cities. Star Tribune, February 21, 1989, at 5 Be.

[14] "Whole sections of urban America are being written off as anarchic badlands, places where cops fear to go and

acknowledge: "This is Beirut, U.S.A.," *U.S. News & World Report*, April 10, 1989, at 20.

[15]President Bush has refused to call out the National Guard in Washington, D.C., despite the fact that as of this writing 114 people have been killed in the first three months of 1989.

[16]*N.Y. Times*, Aug. 13, 1989, A22.

[17]U.S. Department of Justice, Criminal Victimization in the United States, 1987 (June 1989). This and the data that immediately follow in the text are found on pp. 3–5 of this report.

[18]In a Gallup Report, when asked if "In general do you think the police in your community do a good, fair or poor job against crime," 60 percent of whites versus 39 percent of blacks answered "good." *The Gallup Poll. The Gallup Report 8* (March/April 1989).

[19]Victims of Crime, *U.S. News & World Report*, July 31, 1989, at 16.

[20]How We Can Win the War on Poverty, *Fortune*, April 10, 1989, at 125.

[21]M. Walzer, *Obligations: Essays on Disobedience, War, and Citizenship* 68 (Cambridge, Mass., 1970).

[22]Id.

[23]W.J. Wilson, *The Truly Disadvantaged* (1987).

[24]L. Hindelang, M. Gottfredson & J. Garofalo, Victims of Personal Crime: An Empirical Foundation for a Theory of Personal Victimization 257 (1974).

[25]Denton & Massey, *Residential Segregation of Blacks, Hispanics, and Asians by Socioeconomic Status and Generation*, 69 Soc. Sct. Q. 805 (1988).

[26]Id. at 814.

[27]Id.

[28]Id.

[29]See Lawson, Locke and the Legal Obligations of Black Americans, 3 *Pub. Aff.* Q. 49 (1989).

Mens Rea

Jean Hampton

The greatest incitement to guilt is the hope of sinning with impunity.

Cicero

INTRODUCTION

Accusing, condemning, and avenging are part of our daily life. However, a review of many years of literature attempting to analyze our blaming practices suggests that we do not understand very well what we are doing when we judge people culpable for a wrong they have committed. Of course, everyone agrees that, for example, someone deserves censure and punishment when she is guilty of a wrong, and the law has traditionally looked for a *mens rea*, or "guilty mind," in order to convict someone

of a criminal wrongdoing. But philosophers and legal theorists have found it interestingly difficult to say what *mens rea* is. For example, noting the way in which we intuitively think people aren't culpable for a crime if they disobey the law by mistake, or under duress, or while insane, theorists such as H. L. A. Hart[1] have tried to define *mens rea* negatively, as that which an agent has if he is not in what we consider to be an excusing state. But such an approach only circumscribes and does not unravel the central mystery; it also fails to explain why the law recognizes any excusing

Jean Hampton, "Mens Rea," *Social Philosophy and Policy* 7, Number 2 (Spring 1990): 1–28. Reprinted with permission of *Social Philosophy and Policy*.

[1]See Hart's *Punishment and Responsibility*, ch. 2, "Legal Responsibility and Excuses," pp. 28–53 (Oxford: Clarendon Press, 1968).

states as mitigating or absolving one of guilt, much less why all and only the excusing states that are recognized by the law are the right ones. Moreover, the Model Penal Code, which gives a very detailed account of the kinds of mental states which justify criminal conviction,[2] does not tell us (nor was it designed to tell us) why these states of mind (e.g., knowledge, purposiveness, intention, assumption of risk of harm, negligence) are relevant to an assessment of legal guilt.

In this article I want to try to develop a positive account of *mens rea*, or legal culpability, which explains why the mental states detailed in the Model Penal Code are relevant to recognizing it. Because negligence introduces difficulties into the discussion that I cannot properly pursue here, my focus will be on nonnegligent culpable acts, although I will have something to say about criminal negligence in the final section of the paper.

The procedure I will follow for analyzing the legally guilty mind is to clarify, first, what non-negligent culpability is more generally. People can be judged to be "at fault" in three different circumstances: when they act illegally, when they act immorally, and when they act irrationally.[3] I want to argue, however, that there is one distinctive kind of "mental act" that underlies all three kinds of culpability, and which is definitive of the (non-negligent) guilty mind. Hence, I will start by giving an analysis of rational and moral culpability, and then use these analyses as models for the explication of legal culpability.

Let me also make clear that I will merely be analyzing the concept of culpability and not justifying it. Proponents of deterrence theory and consequentialist approaches to legal blame should see this paper as robbing them of only one of their arguments against their opponents, namely that the concept of *mens rea* is not intelligible. Even if I succeed in making the notion intelligible in the context of nonnegligent culpable acts, there is still plenty of room for attacks against it as the wrong notion for our legal system to rely upon in its conceptualization of the point of criminal sanctions. Nonetheless, I am interested in formulating an intelligible conception of culpability because I am committed to it, and so wish to see a deeper understanding of an idea that is (and should be) central to our legal system and our moral practices generally.

It was common in ancient times to think that there was something about the way human beings are by nature that explains why they are invariably culpable for violations of the norms of morality, reason, and law. This article, one might say, tries to cash out that ancient view by arguing that it is because human beings are prone to a particular mental act definitive of being "at fault" in any of these three ways that they have a "fallen" nature. Nonetheless, I will contend that this natural basis for human culpability does not afford us an excuse for our wrongdoings. The following explication of *mens rea* aims to establish why we are appropriately blamed, punished, and (one hopes) finally forgiven for our culpable acts.

I. DEFIANCE OF REASON

An analysis of culpability should start not with a discussion of legal culpability, and not even with a discussion of moral culpability, but with an analysis of what I will call "rational culpability," which is a way of being rationally "at fault."

To be rationally culpable is to be irrational, but not every kind of irrationality counts as culpable irrationality, and not every mistake people make when they reason constitutes being irrational. Consider that a person who

[2]The Model Penal Code has been drafted, with commentary, by the American Law Institute and has had considerable influence upon legal reform in the United States during the past 30 years. For a presentation and discussion of the Code's minimum requirements for culpability, see *Criminal Law and its Processes*, ed. Sanford Kadish and Monrad Paulsen (Boston: Little, Brown and Co., 1975; 3rd edition), p. 95.

[3]This article builds on my initial attempts to understand moral culpability in "The Nature of Immorality," *The Foundations of Moral and Political Philosophy*, ed. Ellen Frankel Paul, *et al.* (Oxford: Basil Blackwell, 1990); also published in *Social Philosophy and Policy*, volume 7, issue 1 (Autumn 1989).

makes a mistake about how to achieve his goals fails to act rationally, but he is not for that reason alone criticized as 'irrational'. When Henry Hudson headed up the large river that emptied into the Atlantic by the island of Manhattan thinking that it was the Northwest Passage, he wasn't irrational: he was mistaken. Unlike Henry, those we consider culpably irrational are not in some sense "innocent" in their performance of the mistaken action. We think either that they knew that their action was imprudent but did it anyway or that they ought to have known that it was imprudent. Of the former, we might say they demonstrated "willful irrationality"; of the latter, we might say they demonstrated "negligent irrationality." Leaving aside negligence here, I will attempt an analysis of willful irrationality in this section. I will argue that the notion of "fault" implicit in the judgment of someone as irrational in this sense involves the attribution of a mental state to this person which is importantly similar to the mental state attributed to those who are judged morally or legally "at fault."

Being willfully irrational is also not the same as another species of irrationality, which I will distinguish with the term 'non-rational'. There are certain mistakes in reasoning that human beings commonly make and which psychologists study—mistakes in the way they process information, in the way they reason logically, and in the way they think about the world.[4] When we make such errors, we are not thinking or behaving rationally, but there is nothing intentional about our mistakes. We are "afflicted" with the disposition to make them (for reasons worthy of psychological study), and they cannot be considered "our fault" unless others consider us negligent in failing to remedy our tendency to make them. In this article I also will not discuss these non-culpable failures of reason, and henceforth when I use the word 'irrational' I will be doing so to refer to those non-negligent failures of rationality

which we believe the individual engaged in willfully in order to advance some objective, and not innocent "cognitive slips."

It is not hard to recognize this species of irrationality. "Johnny knows he won't get through college if he doesn't study," says his father, "but, for him, every night is party night. How can he be so irrational?" Johnny's persistence in behavior that we believe he knows will preclude the achievement of a preeminent goal he has is central to our perception of him as "at fault"; it is this knowledge which makes him deserving of our criticism for his behavior. It may be tempting for Johnny's father, who realizes that Johnny is aware that his behavior doesn't make sense given his goals, to explain Johnny's behavior in a way proposed by the American comedian Bill Cosby. Cosby, in order to account for his children's penchant for knowing the better but doing the worse, explains it in two words: brain damage.

The joke highlights the fact that it is difficult to make this kind of behavior intelligible. In order to try to make sense of this difficulty, let me develop and analyze an actual (and I think interesting) example of genuine irrationality. I once knew an 18-year-old who decided he wanted to live the "natural life," raising his own food, living in a house built with his own hands, in a rural area along the coast of Maine. After getting permission to use a piece of his grandmother's land, he attempted to build his house—a kind of log cabin affair—despite the fact that he knew little about building houses. His father, on the other hand, knew a great deal about house-building techniques. Nonetheless, this young man refused to take any advice from his father about how to build the house, and refused all offers of help from him because he wanted to live independently of his parents. The result, predictably enough, was disastrous: what was built was poor and did not stand up to the winter storms. In the end, the teenager had to seek refuge with his grandmother, and eventually had to go to his father and accept the help he had insisted on refusing before.

We would not, of course, consider this person immoral for what he had done, but we

[4]For examples of discussions of such failures of reasoning, see A. Tversky and D. Kanneman, "The Framing of Decisions and the Rationality of Choice," *Science* (1981), pp. 543–58; and David Pears, *Motivated Irrationality* (Oxford: Clarendon Press, 1984), esp. pp. 45ff.

would not be kind in our assessment of him: 'pig-headed', 'stupid', 'imprudent' are the sorts of descriptions we would use—words which indicate a kind of culpability in our minds, but a non-moral one.

We would make this assessment of him because we would believe of him that he "knew better." But what did he really know? If we believe that the boy wasn't insensible and thus paid attention both to the facts of the world around him and all the things that parents, teachers, and friends were telling him, then we have to believe that he knew that he didn't really have enough technical ability to build a log house himself. In particular, we think he knew, first, that he didn't have the technical ability to build a house by himself; second, that the chances of him learning to do this by winter's arrival were very bad; and third, that his father did indeed know how to build one. In virtue of these three beliefs, we can attribute to him at least the following item of knowledge:

a) attempting to build the house alone is not the most effective way, and probably not even a possible way, to achieve his goal, so that his actions are irrational.

His abysmal ignorance must have been obvious even, we think, to himself. We would say of any remarks he might make to the contrary that "he's fooling himself."

So why did he try to build the house if he knew the action was imprudent? Was he simply ignoring the counsels of prudence? To say that he was simply ignoring them would be to say that he was pursuing something else besides the prudent course of action, and that this prudent course of action therefore "lost" fair and square in his calculations about what to do. For example, we might see the son as having to choose between two incommensurable goods, being prudent, and something else, say, being independent, and finally deciding to choose the latter because he concluded somehow that he had a better reason to be independent than to be prudent.

But this isn't an accurate picture of what was going on. In this situation there was not some

neat clash of incommensurable goods, with the teenager feeling he had better reason to choose the imprudent option. Granted, the goal that the teenager had was independence; nonetheless, that goal could only be achieved if he accepted his father's help to build the house. So to live an independent life, the boy had to depend upon his father in the short term. And given that the boy was not in any way intellectually deficient, we impute to him the knowledge, supplied by reason, that to achieve independence he had to accept his father's help. Reason's directive to this effect, we think, must have had real force for him. He must have appreciated that going to his father and asking for help was what he *ought* to do, given what was necessary to achieve his ultimate goal. To put it in a different way: given his goal, this person knew that he ought to be rational and do that which would allow him to successfully achieve his goal. So reason had authority for the teenager in this situation. We conclude, then, that the teenager had the following knowledge:

b) The fact that the action he contemplates is irrational gives him not just a reason but the best reason in the circumstances not to do the action; reason's directives are "authoritative" in the situation.

But if he knew not just that his action was irrational but that he had the best possible reason in the circumstances to act rationally, why did he persist in irrational behavior? This is the standard sort of question that trips up those who try to recognize and explain akratic action. If we believe, with Aristotle, that every act we take aims at what we believe to be good, then knowing the better but doing the worse seems to be impossible.

So how do we make the teenager's action intelligible? We take seriously the natural characterization we make of him as rebellious and we make sense of his action as a rebellion. Consider that the boy knew both that building the house without his father's help was irrational, and that he hated the idea of having his father help him. Indeed, the prospects of accepting the help were sufficiently repulsive to him that he could not bear to let it happen. Hence he was faced with a choice: he could conform his actions and desires to the dictates of reason, which would mean temporarily giving up his goal of being independent of his father and accepting his help, *or* he could defy reason's authority and substitute in its place the authority of his desire to build the house by himself. He chose defiance. And, as I shall now argue, anyone whom we consider to be willfully irrational is someone whom we believe to be defiant of reason.

Those who defy reason do not merely rebel against its directives, but attempt to install another authority in its place which will endorse the action they wish to perform. To put it in an Aristotelian way, they are able to do what is worse, despite always taking action to achieve the good, by challenging the authority of that which judges the action worse, and choosing instead to respect as authoritative that which makes the action good. Of course every act we take aims at the good, but when we want to see the worse action as the better one, we can depose our reason which judges it worse and install a new authority that makes it an act that aims at the good.

What is the new authority? Normally, it will be whatever desire motivates the interest in performing the action. However, one might also want to install in the place of reason what one thought was a less authoritative norm—e.g., a moral or legal norm—to which one had allegiance and which directed one to perform an action one's reason told one not to perform. However, many theorists, particularly Kantians, argue that moral norms have more (rather than less) authority than practical reason; in any conflict between them, the right choice would be the choice to obey morality. In view of this, Kantians would believe any rebellion against the directives of reason in the name of morality would be commendable rather than wrong, and thus improperly classified as defiance (you don't defy a legitimate ruler when you support her and not a rival faction after her throne). Indeed, Kantians would expect to see defiance of morality by those who preferred

the directives of reason, rather than the reverse. It also seems strange to think that one would have more allegiance to legal norms than to the directives of practical reason, hence making it unlikely that a person would defy the latter in order to install the former. What is not strange at all, however, is the defiance of the authority of law in order to install the authority of reason, when it directs one to behave in ways that are illegal. (We will discuss this form of defiance in our discussion of legal culpability.) So the normal and natural explanation for why we would behave irrationally and defy the directives of practical reason is that those directives conflict with the satisfaction of a desire which ought not to have sway in this situation, but which we insist should be authoritative. To use an English locution, when we are defiant of reason we "would have it that" we are right to do what our desires dictate, and not what reason dictates.

There are two ways in which such defiance of practical reason call work. One can either defy the normative power of practical reason directly, or one can defy it indirectly by defying the information provided by theoretical reason on which the disliked directives of practical reason are based.

The form of reasoning constitutive of the direct defiance of practical reason is: "I want to do x but I know that doing x will not allow me to achieve y and achieving y is my preeminent goal; nonetheless, I will do x." Here the reasoner is defying the norm that tells him that he ought to do what will allow him to achieve his preeminent goal. He refuses to bow to the authority of this norm, and, as the American expression goes, "he tries to have his cake and eat it too." Children are wonderfully good at this kind of reasoning. A weary babysitter once told me that his little charge had wanted a hamburger but refused to go with him to the only place where she could get the hamburger, telling him that she wanted to "have the hamburger without getting it." She threw a kind of tantrum in the face of an unacceptable directive of practical reason.

Such childish defiance may persist into adulthood, but it is more common for an adult to try another kind of defiance of reason. Adults normally do not defy the directives issued by practical reason because, I suspect, they have learned that it doesn't work—one simply cannot have one's cake and eat it too. But a different and more sophisticated style of defiance can seem more promising: in this case, one defies any pronouncements about the world made by theoretical reason which indicate that one's desired course of action is an ineffective way to achieve one's goal. Thus one reasons, "I will perform the most effective action that I can to achieve my goal *y*, but I want to perform action *x*, and so I 'would have it that' *x* will allow me to achieve that goal." But (one might say) this kind of reasoning is crazy! The mountain won't come to Mohammed, and reality can't be altered to suit your convenience. How could anyone believe that it could?

But we all do. We all find ourselves not only wanting but demanding that the world go our way, and even expecting that it will because we have demanded it to do so. So if our teenage house-builder chose this method of defiance, he defied the pronouncement of his theoretical reason that attempting to build the house was too unlikely to succeed to be worth the risk. "I don't like to believe that this is true," he said to himself, "therefore it isn't going to be that way. I 'would have it that' I have enough expertise to build the house." This method of defiance involves an indirect way of getting around the authority of practical reason. He is accepting that he ought to do what will allow him to best achieve his preeminent goal. But he is defying the information supplied to him by his theoretical reason about what the best thing to do actually is.

There are various ways we can challenge the pronouncements of our theoretical reason about the world so as to allow us to believe that what we want to do is also what will best achieve our goals. And these various ways are reflected in the different kinds of *rationalizations* we offer to justify our irrational acts. For example, a person can postulate a kind of magical control over the world, so that doing what he wishes will also seem consistent with the commands of practical reason. This strategy amounts to saying: "My reason tells me that the world is *x*, but I don't like its being *x*, because that means I can't perform the action I want and achieve my goal. Therefore, because I want it to change, it *will* change." This characterizes the reasoning of a graduate student who once told me that even when he knows his credit card limit has been reached, he still pulls out the credit card at his favorite record store. "Because," he says, "I want the albums."

Or people can decide to believe that they are permitted to try a forbidden activity because they are exempted from the sorts of problems that normally plague those who engage in it. For example, drug-users often insist that other people get addicted to heroin, but not them. And the teenage house-builder might have insisted that although other people require instruction in the art of house-building, he was talented enough not to need it.

People can even decide to revise the rules of logic to achieve their goals. Consider the logic student who must prove a theorem on a problem set, but finds it difficult to do so if she is limited to the standard rules of inference: it is not unusual for a student in this situation to "change" these rules and "prove" the theorem using her new ones, only to wince when the problem set comes back with a bad grade. And when asked by her logic professor why she came up with this proof when she *knew* the correct rules of inference, such a student generally has nothing to say—except, perhaps, "I was hoping it would work." And, in general, we hate to answer such questions because the answer is so embarrassing: we *did* hope that we could fix the pronouncements of reason to suit our interests, and when we're caught, our hubris is brought painfully to our own attention.

So what we call the rationalizations which frequently attend our irrational actions are, in fact, expressions of our defiance of the dictates of theoretical rationality that seem to make it impossible for us to do what we want and still follow the dictates of practical reason. Those rationalizations can either be articulations of the way we defiantly see the world in conformity with our desires, or they can be ways of *bolstering* that defiance in situations where we have some doubt that we can pull it off. "Not everyone is as good with his hands as I am," our teenage house-builder might say (following a moment of doubt), "so I'm special enough to be able to do something other people can't do."

No matter which of these reason-defying strategies our teenager chose, and no matter how he rationalized what he was doing, the fact of his choosing one of them means we must attribute to him one further (false) belief:

c)   the authoritative directives of reason that tell him to do what he prefers not to do can be successfully defied, and the desire dictating the irrational action can be installed as the authority in this situation, so that this desire, and not reason, will rightly direct him as to how he should act.

His irrationality is therefore the result of his choice to respect an authority other than reason.

It is intriguing to me that in all of the discussions of akrasia and self-deception purporting to make sense of knowing the better and doing the worse, this way of rendering the phenomenon intelligible has never been proposed. (Perhaps it has been missed because those who have worked in this area have not spent a great deal of time with small children, and have therefore missed the opportunity to see the faults of humanity undisguised by the veneer of civilization. Or so it seemed to me one day as I marveled at my three-year-old son determinedly setting out to ride his tricycle to San Francisco.) Yet it is clearly a possible explanatory hypothesis: if somebody knows the better and does the worse, doesn't this suggest that *she does so because she believes she can insist that the worse is better?* Thus the smoker aware of the surgeon general's report can quit smoking, or she can insist that this report has nothing to do with her because she simply isn't going to get cancer. (Once, in presenting this account to a philosopher who smoked, I gave him this example, and he told me in dead earnest that he really wasn't going to get cancer.) And the Malibu home owner whose home is threatened every year by the winter tides—and who explains why he doesn't move from

his home on the beach by saying "Every year it gets worse, but I just bury my head in the surf"[5]—believes he has a choice between accepting the pronouncements of theoretical reason and performing the prudent action given those pronouncements, or ignoring those pronouncements so as to enjoy himself. Quite clearly he prefers the second option. "But," we say, "this is nuts! People can't make the world behave the way they want it to behave." That's true; that's why these people are irrational. But they, and we, try anyway.

But why aren't these people (i.e., us) genuinely crazy? The reason is that, on this analysis, they are genuinely ignorant of something; they are ignorant of what they can realistically accomplish in the world. But the nature of their ignorance is not the sort of thing that we normally take to be a sign of mental illness. The person who defies reason has a certain conception of who he is and what he needs which makes him treat a stupid strategy as a plausible one. His parents and friends, when they see him act irrationally, might complain "Who does he think he is?" The answer is that he thinks that he is someone special enough to have his desires prevail. The smoker who knows the statistics about cancer and smoking says "the disease won't get *me*." And the Malibu coast-dweller who knows the danger of flooding insists that the world dishes out disaster to other people, not to him. So, to use an old-fashioned word, although none of these people behaves immorally, all of them are guilty of the "sin of pride." This pridefulness is not craziness because their defiance of the pronouncements of reason occurs in situations where there is some probability that their wishes can come true. Akratic people don't jump off cliffs wishing they could fly; they do, however, smoke in situations where they know there is a chance that they won't get cancer, and they go to graduate school in philosophy when they know there is a chance (albeit small) that they will be able to get a job, and they attempt to build houses even when they don't

[5]CBS News, March 1983.

know how to do so because there is a chance that they'll be able to build something good enough before winter comes.

So when the teenager in my example realized that his makeshift house was inadequate for the winter, he learned something. He not only learned what he could plausibly accomplish and what he could not, but he also learned something about himself: his place in the world turned out not to be as high as he thought, and he realized he was a lot more like other people in power and importance than he thought.

And now we see why the defiance account can render deliberate irrationality intelligible: it explains the irrational action as that which is precipitated by a defiant act in which one installed as authoritative something other than reason which endorsed the irrational action, and it also explains that defiance as a function of the agent's ignorance about something fundamental. The agent who defies the authority of practical reason, insisting that the worse is better in a situation where he wants to perform the action his reason calls worse, does so because he does not understand that he simply cannot supplant reason's authority with something more congenial. The logic student, the drug addict, the Malibu homeowner, and the teenage house-builder all mistakenly attribute to themselves a control over reality that they simply do not and cannot have. Such ignorance is striking in the very young, and it is part of the reason we call young people 'immature'. But such immaturity persists into adulthood, albeit in a less obviously false form. Perhaps human self-love is such that we are invariably inclined to see ourselves as more powerful, more special, and more significant than we in fact are. (Perhaps we are, to borrow a phrase from Hobbes, naturally and irredeemably vainglorious.) As we grow we learn, sometimes painfully, just how much and how little we can accomplish, and thus how significant our wishes will be in determining the future course of the world.

A reader might accept that this style of explanation fits some non-negligent forms of irrationality, but not all of them. Such a critic might argue that to say that the irrational person is "defiant" appears to attribute to him a fist-shaking rebelliousness that not every irrational individual has. For example, even if the defiance account explains the proud but self-deceived smoker, does it really explain the smoker who hates the fact that he smokes, does so regretfully, and longs to quit? It does: the word 'defiance' doesn't describe the emotional attitudes of the irrational agent, but rather the kind of mental act that explains how he can know the better and do the worse. The reluctant smoker, no matter how much he claims to hate smoking and to prefer to refrain from it for the rest of his life, picks up the cigarette on this occasion because, right now, smoking this cigarette is what he badly desires and he "would have it that" doing what he desires at this moment is not the worse but the better course of action. "This cigarette won't matter that much to my health, so I might as well enjoy myself," he might say in order to bolster his defiance of the dictates of reason. Or he might say to himself, "I can't live without these things, so I might as well have one now." This way of representing things makes the better course of action impossible at this moment, so that the worse course of action is now permitted, in defiance of the information given him by his theoretical and practical reason. Even the term 'weakness of will' is itself a defiant misrepresentation of the phenomenon of incontinent action: a person who describes his actions in this way is suggesting that he was "too weak" to avoid the action that he claims to acknowledge as worse, thereby representing his action as somehow inevitable when it was not. On the view I am presenting, what he is actually doing is choosing the action he calls worse, even while understanding that it is worse from the standpoint of reason—a standpoint he knows is supposed to be authoritative—because he believes he can defy that authority and substitute in its place the authority of his desires, which direct him to perform the desired action.

There is one other very important way in which defiance can operate to make someone culpably irrational (a way that some might contend constitutes negligence, or at least what has been called "advertent negligence").[6] Suppose I perform action *x* in ignorance of the fact that it will prevent me from achieving my goal. *Prima facie*, such ignorance excuses me; but if that ignorance was something I knew that, at some earlier time, I ought to remedy, then the ignorance does not excuse me because it is itself effected by a culpable act. So if I know that I ought to have my cholesterol level checked, but fail to do so and continue to eat large quantities of beef, cheese, and ice cream, then when I have my first heart attack I cannot say that my ignorance of my high cholesterol level excuses me from charges of irrationality. I knew that I should not remain ignorant, because an extremely important desire of mine, self-preservation, could only be effectively pursued if I obtained certain information. In this example, what could explain the fact that I did not get that information? It is not hard to give a perfectly good explanation; I knew, if I got it, that I might have to give up eating the foods I loved, so therefore I did not do so. In this situation I declared that I "would have it that" these foods posed no risk to my future survival, making it unnecessary for me to procure information that might suggest otherwise. There are many ways in which I could rationalize my defiance, as we discussed previously. The point is, however, that my ignorance in this situation would be culpable precisely because it could be traced to a defiant action: I defied reason (in its theoretical or practical guise) in order to choose to remain ignorant, and for this reason my failure to procure my goals by virtue of that ignorance makes it appropriate to call me 'irrational' rather than merely 'mistaken'.

II. MORAL CULPABILITY

Whether one thinks that moral culpability even exists depends upon what one's moral theory says about the authority of moral imperatives. In particular, if one believes that moral imperatives are hypothetical rather than categorical, then one must consider irrational those people who know that these imperatives offer them the best way to satisfy their desires but who fail to follow them anyway. The term "immoral" could, at most, designate those irrational agents who violate a species of rationally-dictated imperative—e.g., the imperatives that direct people as to how to achieve peace, or cooperation, or impartial behavior. Philosophers such as David Gauthier and Philippa Foot, who have proposed that moral imperatives may be just a species of rational hypothetical imperatives, are committed to assimilating immorality to irrationality in this way.[7] And the preceding section on the defiance of reason would be, for such philosophers, all that would be necessary to capture the sense in which those who fail to follow these imperatives are culpable.

If the reader agrees with this view, the analysis to follow postulating defiance of a distinctively moral kind of authority will be at best psychologically interesting—an account of what people who postulate this nonexistent authority think they are doing when they behave immorally.

However, philosophers who are committed to the idea that morality has a distinctive authority and who describe moral imperatives as categorical want an explanation of immorality that makes it something other than irrationality. If these theorists are right that moral imperatives bind with an authority that often (and maybe always[8] supersedes even the authority of

[6]The distinction is from Glanville Williams, *Criminal Law: The General Part* (London: Stevens and Sons Ltd., 1953), pp. 49–59. For a nice overview of the controversies surrounding the topic of negligence, see the readings on negligence, recklessness, and strict liability in *Freedom and Responsibility*, ed. H. Morris (Stanford: Stanford University Press, 1961).

[7]See David Gauthier's *Morals by Agreement* (Oxford: Oxford University Press, 1986), and Philippa Foot's "Morality as a System of Hypothetical Imperatives," in *Virtues and Vices* (Berkeley: University of California Press, 1988).

[8]Kant appears to insist on the total supremacy of morality in his writings, but this idea has been challenged recently. For example, see Susan Wolf, "Moral Saints," *Journal of Philosophy*, vol. 79, no. 8 (August 1982), pp. 419–39.

reason,[9] then someone who understands that authority should also understand that she should always act from these moral imperatives—even in situations where moral behavior prevents her from satisfying her desires, and is to that extent irrational. So why would she fail to do so?

Despite enormous interest in the authority of morality, moral theorists as a whole have been not only unsuccessful at but also markedly uninterested in explaining immoral action.[10] The founder of our discipline, Socrates, was one of the few who took on the issue explicitly, but his explanation is one of the most unsuccessful. Immoral people, says Socrates, are ignorant of the good, and hence deserving of pity rather than anger, education rather than pain.[11] Yet unlike genuinely ignorant people, the immoral among us do not seem to welcome instruction! Are they really just ignorant? Moreover, it is striking that despite advocating this account of immorality, Socrates was prepared to support punishment of immoral people; clearly, punishment is an unusual educational technique! The fact that punishment rather than college courses seems to be the appropriate kind of response to those who act immorally suggests that their immoral action is a functional of a certain kind of resistance inside them, which the Socratic punishment is somehow supposed to break. Understanding immoral agents simply as ignorant fails to capture or explain this resistance.

Perhaps the most serious problem with Socrates's account, however, is that it does not seem hard to find morally culpable people who not only know but even take delight in the fact that what they are doing is wrong. In fact, isn't this knowledge just what makes us want to blame them? After all, outside of legal contexts, ignorance normally excuses.[12] Consider the foreigner who does not know that his behavior in this culture is rude, or the child who does not realize that her words to a friend are wounding, or the doctor who administers a fatal dose of medication negligently prepared by another doctor who had always been trustworthy before: such people bring about injury through their ignorance, but in view of that ignorance—an ignorance we find reasonable under the circumstances—we do not judge them culpable. If immoral people are assimilated with these kinds of folk, it is no wonder that Socrates thought pity rather than anger was the appropriate emotional response toward them. Socrate's explanation seems to destroy the moral culpability it was meant to explain.

If ignorance excuses them knowledge must convict. But once we attribute knowledge to the culpable agent, it is difficult to know how to explain his immoral action in a way that makes it both intelligible and a genuine instance of *culpable* action. Suppose we say, for example, that the person who acts immorally is genuinely indifferent to the authority of moral imperatives. If she is not making any mistake by ignoring them, then that must mean the imperatives, however wonderful we think them, do not in fact apply to this person. She is outside their scope, and hence does nothing wrong when she does not follow them. Such a person is properly called 'moral' rather than 'immoral', since we cannot say about her that "she should have done otherwise." We might hate her from a moral point of view, and wish her to be removed from our world, but this way of viewing her makes her into a kind of monster that, although worthy of our hatred and opposition, is

---

[9]Note here that the word 'reason' is used in a very narrow sense to refer to a norm of action directed at the individual intent on satisfying his desires. This is the economist's notion of reason, roughly equivalent to prudential calculation. Philosophers such as Kant use the word 'reason' more broadly to cover both prudential and moral calculation. Despite my sympathies with Kant's use of the word, I will retain the narrow use of 'reason' in this paper to mark the distinction between two quite different forms of normative reasoning.

[10]The following historical remarks are taken from a much longer and more detailed account of various theories of culpability in my "The Nature of Immorality." See note 3.

[11]See *Meno*, 77b–78b (in the translation of W. R. M. Lamb, Harvard University Press, 1924, p. 289), and *Protagoras*, 357d-e (in the translation by W. R. M. Lamb, Harvard University Press, 1924, p. 243).

[12]As the saying goes, "*Ignoratia legis non excusat.*" We will be discussing later why ignorance is not a good excuse in legal contexts.

no more a justifiable subject of moral *blame* than any other dangerous creature outside the reach of moral imperatives. So, once again, we see that what was supposed to be an explanation of culpable action actually destroys the phenomenon it was supposed to explain.

There is one more popular style of explanation, which I call the Manichean account of immorality. On this view, immoral behavior is a function of a certain "part" of us (Plato would call it the appetite or the spirited part, Freud would call it the id, St. Paul would call it "sin that has its lodging in us")[13] which fights against (and wins against) the part within us (reason, or the superego, or knowledge of God's commands) that is directing the moral action.[14] But how can this view explain a person's culpability for a bad deed when that deed was precipitated by a force about which he could do nothing? On this view, immoral action is not something chosen but something effected by an event—the event of the good part being overpowered by that of the bad part. This loss is presumably something that the good part could do nothing to prevent. But if the good part of you is too weak to win some or all battles with the bad part, then the bad action precipitated by the victory of the bad part is not chosen by the good part. And since the good part is supposed to be who you really are, this means the bad action is not chosen by you, and thus it is not something for which you are responsible. If "the devil made you do it"— where the "devil" is understood variously as your id, or your appetites, or your hormones, and "you" are associated with that within you which wanted to do good but couldn't—then "you" are not to blame. You are its victim, and hence not the appropriate recipient of our condemnation. However intelligible this style of explanation for immoral behavior is, it once again destroys the phenomenon to be explained.

After considering the way that these accounts failed to capture our conception of (non-negligent) culpability, I found myself looking for one particular kind of inner event that would be the secret of it. Clearly, there are many kinds of people who do immoral deeds, with all sorts of characters from good to bad to awful. If one undertook the project of "explaining" immorality, one would have to come to grips with the variety of motivations, character traits, and desires that are all part of the reason human beings prefer to act badly rather than morally. But despite this diversity, all people who act immorally, no matter whether they are normally saintly or devilish, have something in common which grounds the judgment that they are "at fault," and thus culpable for a wrongdoing. If it isn't ignorance, or indifference, or weakness in the face of a force for evil, then what could be present in all of them even in the actions of people whom we think have, by and large, a good character—that makes them the appropriate subjects of blame for the particular immoral action they perform?

To understand what it is, consider the following description of what is supposed to be the first morally culpable act committed by a human being:

The serpent was more crafty than any wild creature that the Lord God had made. He said to the woman, "Is it true that God has forbidden you to eat from any tree in the garden?" The woman answered the serpent, "We may eat the fruit of any tree in the garden, except for the tree in the middle of the garden: God has forbidden us either to eat or to touch the fruit of that: if we do, we shall die." The serpent said, "Of course you will not die. God knows that as soon as you eat it, your eyes will be opened and you will be like gods knowing both good and evil." When the woman saw that the fruit of the tree was good to eat, and that it was pleasing to the eye and tempting to contemplate, she took some and ate it. She also gave her husband some and he ate it. Then the eyes of both of them were opened and they discovered they

---

[13]Romans 7:14–20.

[14]This style of explanation is also popular with those who want to understand akratic behavior. See the articles discussing this style of approach in *The Multiple Self*, ed. Jon Elster (Cambridge: Cambridge University Press, 1986).

were naked; so they stitched fig-leaves together and made themselves loin-cloths.[15]

As we all know, when God found out what the two of them had done, he was furious; he punished not only the two human beings but also the serpent for their disobedience.

And that is the point of the tale: human immorality is a function of human disobedience of an authoritative command. Human beings are culpable for the commission of wrongs not because they are ignorant that what they are doing is wrong, but because they *know* they are doing wrong. Indeed, if they were ignorant of the wrongfulness of their act, this would excuse them from culpability. Eve and Adam knew that they were not supposed to eat of the fruit of the tree of knowledge; if they had been ignorant of the command, God would have been filled with sorrow rather than fury at their deed (assuming that the ignorance itself wasn't something for which they were culpable). So their knowledge is central to their culpability.

However, not only knowledge of the command, but also knowledge of the command's *authority* is central to our finding them at fault. Adam and Eve are not culpable out of indifference to an imperative which they happen not to find in their interest to follow. They know they are *supposed* to follow the command, i.e., that it is authoritative over them, that it is supposed to rule them. While the tale represents them as having no knowledge of good and evil, and thus no knowledge of moral commands generally until they eat the fruit, it does establish that they had knowledge of God's authority, and hence of the authoritativeness of his commands. (Is knowledge of God's authority moral knowledge? Part of the point of the tale may be that knowledge of this authority is not moral knowledge, so that God's authority is prior to and higher than the authority of morality.) If they had been ignorant of his authority, their ignorance would once again undercut their culpability for the act they took. If I don't know that an imperative issued by

someone gives me a better reason to act than my wishes give me, then (even though I act incorrectly) I am the appropriate subject of further education rather than blame (assuming, again, that my ignorance is something for which I am not culpable).

Finally, Adam and Eve's culpability is a function of the fact that the wrongdoing was *chosen* rather than caused. Eve was not pushed, compelled, or under duress when she ate the fruit. The snake, of course, encouraged her to do so, but, in the words of Dante, Eve herself "let Desire pull Reason from her throne."[16] In other words, she chose the action, aware that it was forbidden by an authoritative command applicable to her.

The Genesis story therefore presents the following four elements as necessary conditions of the culpable mind:

1. Making the decision to choose the action.
2. Choosing it in the knowledge that the action is forbidden by a command.
3. Choosing it in the knowledge that the action is forbidden by a command that is applicable to oneself and authoritative in this situation (i.e., it gives one the best possible reason to act in the situation).

These three elements presuppose the fourth:

4. Having both the capacity to make choices and the capacity to have knowledge of authoritative commands.

These last two capacities are necessary conditions for judging someone a moral agent.[17] A person who is either unable to choose how to act despite knowing the authoritativeness of the commands (e.g., a kleptomaniac) or unable to understand the way in which these commands are authoritative (e.g., a sociopath) cannot be considered a moral agent, and hence

[15]Genesis 3:1–7.

[16]*Inferno*, Canto V, quoted by Donald Davidson in "How is Weakness of the Will Possible?", in *Essays in Actions and Events* (Oxford: Clarendon Press, 1980), p. 35.

[17]I am indebted to Peter Arenella for pressing me to make this idea explicit in my analysis.

cannot be appropriately blamed for behavior that is not in accord with those commands. We may very well want to do something about such people—lock them up, execute them, put them into therapy—but they are not people whom we should blame or punish.[18]

But, readers might protest, if this analysis makes immorality a function of such an informed choice, doesn't it portray wrongdoing as a case of knowing the better but choosing the worse, and haven't innumerable discussions of incontinence shown that such a characterization of human action is highly problematic at best, and perhaps incoherent?

This account does indeed portray culpable wrongdoing as a case of knowing the better and doing the worse, but the preceding section on the defiance of reason aimed to establish that such a portrayal need not be understood as an incoherent account of human action. The view that I will henceforth call the "defiance" account of moral culpability incorporates these four features in a coherent and (I will argue) plausible way. In a nutshell, the view is that a culpable agent is one who chooses to defy what she knows to be an authoritative moral command in the name of the satisfaction of one or more of her wishes, whose satisfaction the command forbids. She is disobedient in the face of knowledge that obedience is expected, and a rebel in the sense that she is attempting to establish something more to her liking as authoritative over her decision-making, rather than these moral commands. Just like irrational people, immoral people know the better but do the worse because they believe they can install a new reason-giving authority over their actions that transforms the worse into the better.

I want to argue that such defiance is a distinctively human phenomenon, which normally occurs whenever following a command—which one knows is authoritative in the circumstances—interferes with the perception of what is required to achieve or do something else that one wants, in this situation, a human being has the capacity to "overthrow" the authority in her own mind, and to install a new authority which sanctions the action she wishes to take. Indeed, the previous discussion of irrationality was meant to suggest that defiance of norms generally—including rational as well as moral norms—is a distinctively human capacity, which marks out human beings from other animals and which traditional religious thinkers would consider to be the central element in their fallen natures.

How is it distinctive of human beings? Don't dogs, horses, and monkeys display the ability to break rules, sometimes even exhibiting something approximating shame when they do so? However, the defiant mental act that I claim is distinctive in human beings is not just the act of disobeying a command; it is the choice which leads to the disobedience. Specifically, *it is the choice to supplant what one knows to be an authoritative rule with a different authority that sanctions the act one wishes to to take.* Or, to put it another way, it is a rebellion against that which is taken to have final evaluative authority in the salutation, in order to install a new evaluative authority which evaluates the action one wishes to take as better and not worse.

Contrast this with the disobedience of a horse. When a horse disobeys his rider's command to canter, the horse is simply doing what he prefers until the rider can use punishments

---

[18]In "The Legal and Moral Responsibility of Organizations" (in *Criminal Justice: Nomos XXVII*, eds. J. Roland Pennock and John W. Chapman, [New York: New York University Press, 1985] pp. 267 86), Susan Wolf suggests that sociopaths, although incapable of understanding or being responsive to moral authority, are capable of the kind of responsibility (call it 'practical') which is the foundation of tort law. "We use," she says, "the practical sense when our claim that an agent is responsible for an action is intended to announce that the agent assumes the risks associated with the action. In other words, the agent is considered the appropriate bearer of damages, should they result from the action, as well as the appropriate reaper of the action's possible benefits" (p. 276). One can, according to Wolf, be capable of being practically responsible but not morally responsible; sociopaths may be one example of such an agent, organizations may be another. If she is right, there is a difference between being a moral agent and being (to coin a name) a "practical agent." One might also say, as we shall discuss in the next section, that the criminal law takes seriously the question whether or not the lawbreaker is a moral agent, whereas the tort law requires practical agency.

and rewards to induce him to prefer the behavior preferred by the rider. So what the horse does is always determined by his desires. Unless we human beings are badly wrong in our understanding of equine mental life, there is no perception of an 'ought to obey' in the horse's head which can act as a reason-giving authority that competes with his desires. But it is the ability to understand and act from the idea that "I ought to obey"—an ability which involves the appreciation of a moral command as authoritative—that distinguishes a human being from an animal. And it is our ability to challenge that authority and install a reason-giving authority that is more amenable to our interests which makes human beings' disobedience of commands distinctive.

My point is that to be morally culpable, one must be able to recognize the authority of morality even while trying to overthrow it. So wrongdoers are rebels, but rebels always understand the authority of that which they seek to depose. This is why they are, and see themselves as, rebels—people who must depose, bring down, vanquish an authority that they oppose and wish to replace.

In the name of what do they rebel? Normally, one opposes morality for the sake of self-interest, which may or may not be rationally tutored. This is why the question "Why are we immoral?" is so naturally answered by saying "Because we're selfish." A legal norm might also come to oppose the moral authority, and the agent might be tempted to serve that norm, rather than the more important moral norm. Whatever the source of temptation, the agent gives in to it when she installs that source over morality as her reason—giving authority.

As in the case of the discussion of irrationality, the combative language used to state this view may already have some readers worried that it only fits the very worst immoral people. How can the mental state of the reluctant moral offender, or the offender guilty of only a minor moral offense, be understood as some kind of defiant act?

But such a worry misunderstands the account. The defiance view is not a portrait of human character but an analysis of the "culpable act" inside the head of the agent which occurs whenever a person is guilty of a blameworthy but non-negligent action. The view does not attribute to those who are guilty of a wrongdoing the wholesale rejection of the authority of morality on every occasion. Nor does it attribute to them certain emotional attitudes characteristic of political rebels, such as anger, hatred, hostility, or resentment towards the authority they defy, although it is consistent with the view that the culpable agent have any of these emotional attitudes. All that the view says about the morally culpable agent is that inside her there was an act of "insubordination" resulting in the performance of the prohibited action, and it is that insubordination which constitutes her culpability. Specifically, what makes her the appropriate subject of blame is the choice to install as authoritative something that condones what she wishes to do, rather than to allow the relevant authoritative moral command to prevail. That act of insubordination can be done regretfully, sorrowfully, or even happily—the point is that it is *this* act which constitutes being at fault. It can be a rare occurrence in a person's life or a common one; it can occur when the directives of the moral authority are not terribly serious, or when they are very serious indeed; and it can be accompanied by a variety of emotional states. But it is this defiant act that is the basis of all morally culpable action.

So the person who is a decent member of our community but who nonetheless decides, while in a great hurry to get her shopping done at the mall, to sneak into a parking space someone else has been patiently waiting for—that person is, at that moment, defying the claims of morality and obeying the commands of her own wishes. And Peter, who betrayed his friend Jesus three times before the cock crowed and who wept with guilt after his betrayals, nonetheless believed (regretfully, sorrowfully, tearfully) when he denied he knew Jesus that it was more important for him to satisfy his desire to stay alive than it was to be loyal to his friend and the religious views to which he had previously committed himself.

So, like those who defy reason, people who are culpable for moral wrongs obey what they take to be the authority of their own wishes in defiance of the authority of the moral imperatives proscribing the actions that the satisfaction of their wishes require. Take our parking-space thief. She believes that:

a′)   taking the space herself rather than letting the other person have it (where this other person was there first) was immoral (albeit mildly so; it was at least rude).

b′)   that, given the authority which the dictates of morality have, she is supposed to have better reason to refrain from this immoral behavior than to engage in it so as to satisfy her desires.

c′)   that the authority of morality can be defied in this case, because her own wishes are too important to "lose" to it.

Unless one is insensible, everyone knows (a′). Knowing (b′) might, however, not be possible for some people, who are thereby precluded from being moral agents. Someone who cannot understand the authority of morality cannot be expected to conform her actions in accord with it when the moral dictates oppose her desires. This seems to be exactly the right thing to say about sociopaths. "Although sociopaths can achieve an intellectual understanding that cheating, stealing, murdering, etc., are *considered* to be immoral, they cannot understand why they ought not to act in these ways."[19] We might say that attributing to someone the knowledge of morality's authority is the same as attributing to him a conscience; sociopaths, therefore, lack consciences.[20] Although we lack, as moral philosophers, a good theory of what moral authority is (to the point where some doubt that it exists at all), still, if such a theory were at hand, it would tell us how one who qualifies as a moral agent has access, cognitively or emotionally, to the authority of moral commands.

In popular parlance, (c′) constitutes the parking-space thief's belief that she can and

should "get away with it" if she decides on the immoral action. It is interesting to note that, in *Paradise Lost*, Milton portrays Eve as someone who believes (c′), and who is thereby emboldened to eat the forbidden fruit. In Milton's poem, before she picks the fruit she reasons:

Here grows the cure of all, this fruit divine,
Fair to the eye, inviting to the taste,
Of virtue to make wise: what hinders then
To reach, and feed at once both Body and Mind?[21]

Eve believes there is nothing hindering her from successfully challenging God's authority, and so she eats the fruit. And all her human progeny, who are prone to immoral deeds, are represented as being inclined to reach the same conclusion about their chances of successfully defying the authority that is giving them the commands they dislike. What distinguishes moral skeptics from moral objectivists is that skeptics seriously entertain the idea that the authority or morality can be successfully challenged, whereas objectivists (perhaps out of faith alone) insist that it cannot.

The defiance account describes one kind of choice which all immoral agents share that marks them out as morally culpable. But can it help us to grade the extent to which any agent is immoral?

In answering this question, it is important to note that the defiance view denies that any offender is "devilish" in the way Kant described—and the way he refused to believe any of us were.[22] That is, immoral people are not portrayed as people who defy the authority of morality out of some kind of unmotivated hatred of that authority. Instead, they are portrayed as rebels against the authority of morality who aim to substitute as authoritative something they prefer to it. As they fight against the moral authority, they may come to despise it insofar as it persists in interfering with their

---

[19]Wolf, "The Moral and Legal Responsibility of Organizations," p. 278.

[20]Wolf says the same, ibid.

[21]*Paradise Lost*, Book IX (New York: Doubleday, 1969, p. 212.

[22]See Kant's *Religion Within The Limits of Reason Alone*, trans. Theodore M. Greene and Hoyt H. Hudson, ed. John Silber (New York: Harper and Brothers, 1960), pp. 52–53.

ability to follow the imperatives of their preferred authority, but they have no fundamental unmotivated antipathy to cooperative, other-regarding behavior. In fact, even the devil himself turns out not to be devilishly defiant on Kant's way of construing the term! The devil, remember, rebels against God not because he finds God intrinsically hateful, but because he prefers himself as ruler of the world (although, as he continues to fight and lose the battle for supremacy with God, he is generally represented as coming to despise his rival).[23]

Hence, the defiance view is not as negative as it might be in its portrayal of human immorality. Still, I believe it leaves room for distinguishing grades of immorality, which are, in essence, represented as degrees of rebellion. The point of the defiance account is that all immoral people (i.e., all people who are morally culpable) are rebels; but there is a difference between rebels who are sorry about having to rebel and rebels who have no qualms about their rebellion, and there is a difference between

petty rebellion and major insubordination. We look both to the severity of the offense and to the emotional and intellectual attitudes attending its performance to form a judgment of just how immoral a person has shown herself to be by performing the immoral action. In forming that judgment, I suspect that determining the severity of the offense usually takes precedence, and judgments about emotional attitudes are used to mark out distinctions among those who have challenged the same authoritative command. For example, we would say that two people who, in similar circumstances, betray their friends in order to advance their careers have both engaged in an offense of the same seriousness, but the person who feels no sorrow as he betrays his friend is worse, in our eyes, than the betrayer who is plagued by a bad conscience.

Why isn't the former betrayer better characterized as indifferent, rather than defiant? Some readers may worry that my account of culpability seems to leave out a perfectly good category of wrongdoer: i.e., the kind who violate moral commands without in any way flinching, who appear to have no loyalty to those commands and even express contempt for them. These people seem indifferent to the demands of morality, not defiant of them. But what does it mean to call them 'indifferent'? Does it mean that they are outside the scope of moral imperatives? That is, do those imperatives issue directives that give them *no reason to act* in the way directed? If this is so, such people made no mistake in their action, although they acted in ways we dislike. If we called them 'immoral', the description could only be a reflection of our dislike; it could not convey, as it does in the defiance account, our judgment that the wrongdoer's action has been a mistake not only from our point of view but also from his. Accordingly, if they made no mistake acting as they did, they are best described as 'amoral', where this label designates those who do not act morally and who are not the sort of creature to whom the moral imperatives apply. We may want to do something about these people—they can be greatly disruptive of societal harmony. But our response

---

[23]Because Kant wished to avoid characterizing people as devilish in this sense, he shied away from using the word 'rebel' to describe evil people. For example, he says in the *Religion Within The Limits of Reason Alone* that "Man (even the most wicked) does not, under any maxim whatsoever, repudiate the Moral Law in the manner of a rebel (renouncing obedience to it)" (p. 31). Instead, he maintains that "Man (even the best) is evil only in that he reverses the moral order of the incentives when he adopts them into his maxims," (p. 31) but this kind of "insubordination" (which is different from l1flat-out renunciation) is characterized as rebellion later on in the *Religion*, when Kant notes that were we to remove the incentive of inclination from human nature, then "though it is true that this rebellion is often stilled, the rebel himself is still not conquered, and exterminated" (p. 51n). The critical debate about whether or not Kant is right to reject the idea that we are devilish in his sense fails to take account of the way in which he does acknowledge a genuinely devilish rebellion in the hearts of all (sinful) human beings. See Silber, pp. cxxivff and cxxixff; Allen Wood, *Kant's Moral Religion* (Ithaca: Cornell University Press, 1970), p. 212n; and Philip Quinn, p. 9 and n. 3.

Those who are familiar with Kant's analysis of immoral behavior in the *Religion* will see strong similarities between his treatment of it as an act of insubordination in one's ranking of motives for action and my account of it as the defiant of something other than morality as the authority governing one's choice of action in the situation.

to them could not be condemnatory, retributive, or desert-based.

Suppose, however, that someone said of such people: "Well, of course they believe they are outside the scope of morality, and so act in ways that we see as indifferent to the authority that commands them, but we don't believe that this is true. We do see these commands as applying to them: they are assuming that they are independent of morality's rule when in fact they are not. Hence, we can correctly say of them that they should have done otherwise, and hence that they are immoral, without finding in them an explicitly defiant act."

But this way of conceiving of these agents does render them defiant in a sense: they are acting as if they are independent of morality's rule when they are not. Now do they understand that they are at least supposed to be ruled by morality, or do they not? If they *do* know about the claim these directives make to rule them (e.g., if they are aware of and can understand the force of the kinds of admonishments of immoral behavior made by parents, Sunday School teachers, judges, and so forth), then there is, in their heads, a defiant act after all. Although they take no interest in the commands, they are aware of their authority, and they are defying it. On the other hand, if they do not know about their authority then either they are themselves responsible for putting themselves in this state or else some other, external cause is responsible for their being in this state. If they put themselves in it—if they were authors of their own moral insensitivity— we have some grounds for holding them culpable for the actions committed because of that insensitivity. But if something else was the author of it (e.g., a severely impoverished childhood, a mental illness), then they are *ignorant;* why should we blame them for actions which reflect an ignorance that was not their doing? As we have discussed, ignorance excuses an agent from culpability. So, oddly enough, an account of an "immoral" agent as purely indifferent actually destroys what is necessary for that agent to be immoral.

Interestingly, one can find this very account of our blaming practices (in the context of legal norms) given by the Supreme Court of West Germany:

> As a free and moral agent and as a participant in the legal community, the individual is bound at all times to conform his behavior to law and to avoid doing the wrong thing, He does not fulfill his duty merely by avoiding that which seems to him clearly to be the wrong thing; rather he must attempt to determine whether that which he plans to do is compatible with the legal imperatives of the system. He must resolve his doubts by reflection or investigation. This requires that he apply his moral sensibility. . . . If despite the moral sensitivity that can fairly be demanded of him, the individual does not perceive the wrongfulness of the contemplated action, then his mistake is to be viewed as incluctable; the act would be, for him, unavoidable. In a case of this sort, the individual cannot be blamed for his conduct.[24]

Of course, some kind of response to the harmful acts of those "morally insensitive" people who believe themselves to be part of a different moral realm is highly appropriate, but not a blaming response coupled with retribution. We can either work to remedy their ignorance about moral authority, or, if a remedy seems impossible, we can work to neutralize the threat they pose to others (e.g., through incarceration or execution). But it is not fair to respond to them as individuals who could have acted morally, because in an important sense, they were not able to do so.

However, as the discussion above indicated, there is one kind of morally insensitive agent whose insensitivity is a function of his ignorance; on the defiance view, it does make sense to blame this agent. This is that agent who, although now incapable of conforming his actions to the demands of morality, chose to perform actions and to develop in ways that made such insensitivity likely, and was *fully aware of the risk he was taking.* Such a person

---

[24]2BGH 194 (March 18, 1952). Translation by George Fletcher, *Comparative Criminal Theory,* 72 (2nd ed. 1971, mimeo, UCLA); in Kadish and Paulsen, p. 124–5.

now acts immorally out of ignorance, but he is himself responsible for that ignorance in the sense that he chose it knowing he should not. We would call him culpably ignorant.[25] Aristotle insists, for example, that people who appear unaware that what they are doing is wrong are actually people who are

> responsible for becoming men of that kind, and . . . make themselves responsible for being unjust or self-indulgent, in the one case by cheating and in the other by spending their time in drunken bouts and the like, for it is activities exercised on particular objects that make the corresponding character . . . . Now *not to know* that it is from the exercise of activities on particular objects that states of character are produced is the mark of a thoroughly senseless person.[26]

So of course they do know what they are doing, in which case they have chosen to make themselves into people who are morally insensitive; in virtue of that choice, they are culpable far being morally insensitive later.

Indeed, perhaps we are sometimes inclined to judge morally monstrous people i.e., people who are incapable of understanding moral norms—as culpable despite their inability to act from these norms, because we believe that earlier in their lives they chose to engage in activities that they knew would likely turn them into moral monsters, and that they did so anyway, in defiance of that knowledge, in order to satisfy their desires. If they become incapable of being ruled by moral considerations thereafter, they are ignorant, but nonetheless culpably so—by virtue of this prior defiant act. Note that it is because we can trace their immoral actions to a defiant act that it becomes possible for us to call them culpable. Indeed,

insofar as it seems appropriate to call such people indifferent to morality, the defiance account will allow that there is some truth to that description. But this kind of indifference is a function of a prior defiant act, and is not itself the source of their culpability.

Other wrongdoers appear indifferent to morality in a different way, but still in a way that the defiance account illuminates. Consider that there is a difference between understanding morality's authority but consistently opposing it, and accepting that authority most of the time but fighting it off on occasion—say, when its commands oppose certain important wishes. Occasional disobedience of an authority one normally believes deserves obedience is different from full-scale disobedience of directives whose claim to be authoritative one *knows about* but never accepts. The second sort of rebel, one might say, is attempting to declare himself amoral in a society that (he knows) insists on seeing him as persistently disobedient of his proper ruler. He is attempting to make himself indifferent to the claims of morality. Because such a person continually fights to gain his independence from the authority that in his view makes a false claim to rule him, he is unlike and, from a moral point of view, worse than rebels who only occasionally fight against a realm that, on other occasions, they have admitted is entitled to govern them. We judge the former to be worse, from a moral point of view, than the latter, because the latter has significantly more allegiance to the moral authority than the former.

The cagey reader may now be aware that she can make an interesting attack on the defiance account of immorality in light of these last remarks. Why do immoral people defy the moral authority? Presumably they do so because they think they can "get away with it"—their rebellion, they think, will be successful in the sense that any costs they pay because of their defiant action will be outweighed by the benefits from it. Let me be vague about what "costs" and "benefits" refer to here, because different moral philosophers committed to the objective authority of morality will have different ways of cashing out what they are (for

---

[25]See Holly Smith, "Culpable Ignorance," *Philosophical Review*, vol. 92, no. 4 (October, 1983), pp. 543 571. Aquinas considers the culpably ignorant to include every non-negligent performer of immoral actions. See *Summa Theologica*, First Part of the Second Part, Question 6, Article 8, "Does Ignorance Render an Act Involuntary?"

[26]*Nicomachean Ethics*, 1114a 3–11; my emphasis; translation is that of W. D. Ross in *The Basic Works of Aristotle* ed. Richard McKeon (Chicago: Random House, 1941).

example, Aristotle would talk of human flourishing, Kant would talk of the persistent indictment of reason one would feel following the defiance). For present purposes, choose your favorite way of cashing out these terms. Now are moral rebels right to think they can get away with their rebellion and escape without paying any significant costs? Presumably any moral theorist committed to the authority of morality would argue that they cannot do so in any situation over which the moral authority is sovereign.

Now it may well be correct to conclude that the authority of morality has limits—that there are jurisdictions in life over which it does not rule.[27] One might also think that, either because of one's disposition or early training, one may be inclined to exaggerate the scope of morality's authority. In a situation where morality was not the ultimate authority, one's refusal to act morally would be a good thing, because it would show that one was trying to get out from under a ruler whose rule in this situation was inappropriate. Properly speaking, one is not being defiant of morality in such a case because one cannot rebel against something that has no final right of command (although it might *feel* rebellious to the agent who is struggling to overcome what she suspects is her own false sense of morality's authority).

But in situations in which morality is sovereign, moral theorists (e.g., Kantians) committed to the objective authority of morality would insist that the agent's belief that she could successfully defy its rule is false. And it is the falsity of this belief that the agent doesn't know: in this case, the defiance analysis of immorality represents such a person as ignorant of the fact that a rebellion against the authority of morality cannot succeed. Why doesn't this ignorance excuse this person from culpability?

To answer this question, consider that, on the defiance view, *the defiance itself is what makes the person culpable*, whereas the defier's ignorance of the impossibility of succeeding is the

explanation other defiance, and thus, of her culpability (and that which renders it intelligible). That is, it explains why the defiance occurred, but it does not explain away the defiance—and ignorance only excuses when it explains away the defiance. Or, to put it in another way, when ignorance excuses, it is because the fact of the ignorance shows the agent was not defiant after all. When we say "Mary was reasonably ignorant that the man she shot was a human being and nor a deer, so we can't find her guilty of murder," or "Joan had no idea that her words to the visitor brought back painful memories, so we can't blame her," we're attributing to the agent an ignorance of something relevant to her assessment of what the authoritative commands told her to perform; because she was so ignorant, she is not acting out of defiance of those commands. In contrast, the ignorance attributed to the culpable agent on the defiance view is an explanation of her defiance—it explains why she thought it made sense to engage in it; this explanation, however, in no way forces us to redescribe her choice to act contrary to the moral rules as not defiant after all. Indeed, it assumes and must assume that defiance in order to explain it. And it is the defiance which makes her culpable.

But why is our assessment of immorality entirely a function of the culpable agent's decision to defy the moral rules? This is, I find, a deep and difficult question. What are we trying to do or say when we label someone immoral? On the defiance view, it seems that we are making a negative evaluation of culpable people because of their decision to give allegiance to something other than the authority that deserves it. And this evaluation shows our own allegiance to the moral authority they flouted. But if it is their allegiance which we are attacking, then our attack is not fended off by any claim that the immoral agent thought she could succeed in evading the rule of morality. That ignorance explains why she thought she could succeed in switching her allegiance, and so explains why she acted immorally. But it does not touch or explain away the (in our eyes) awful fact that she no longer wanted to be committed to the right ruler.

---

[27]For an argument to this effect, see Susan Wolf, "Moral Saints."

And it is that failure of commitment that we are denouncing.

If this way of understanding our moral assessments of people is correct, then there are still mysteries that need to be unraveled. Suppose a person persists in acting morally, not because she respects the moral authority, but only because she is in some way afraid of it. If she could persuade herself that she could get away with defying it, she would defy it, Is such a "closet defier" already in an important sense immoral, since she lacks the allegiance to moral authority which marks out the good from the bad?

And what about the claim made by a long line of defenders of morality's authority the defiance of it is bound to fail: is such a claim really true? The defiance account of immorality assumes what moral philosophers have struggled unsuccessfully to justify for many years: the inescapable authority of moral commands. Perhaps one reason why this has been a favorite and persistent topic in moral philosophy for hundreds of years is that it is the central element upon which our blaming practices rest, and so it must be justified if those blaming practices are to be judged legitimate.

III. DEFIANCE OF LAW

It is relatively straightforward to apply this account to legal culpability. Take the tax cheat: he knows

a″   that the legal system commands him not to commit the action, i.e., that it is illegal.

b″   given the authority which legal commands have, he is supposed to have better reason to refrain from illegal behavior than to engage in it in order to do something else he wishes.

Nonetheless, he also believes

c″   the authority of the law can be defied, and something else that condones what he wishes can be enthroned in its place, thereby allowing him to act so as to satisfy them.

Given his belief in (c″), our law-breaker believes he can "get away with it." It is (c″) which is the defiance that constitutes legal *mens rea*, and which the legal system is looking for when it tries in court those who have committed illegal acts.

Thus, I am proposing that an important component of the criminal law is the defiance conception of culpability. The Model Penal Code gives us criteria for culpability that are, in essence, signs of a defiant mind: e.g., knowledge, purposiveness, and recklessness (where the last assumes a defiant choice of the action knowing the risks). And the excuses and justifications recognized by the law make sense as mental states in which no defiance has occurred.

In particular, those who are excused from legal culpability will be found not to have believed (c″). For example, the man who, misled by incompetent IRS consultants and government pamphlets, fails to pay enough tax doesn't believe (c″). His action is explained by his ignorance of the tax law—an ignorance that cannot be traced to any defiance of the law's authority on his part. And the driver who takes proper and sufficient care in her operation of a motor vehicle and who hits and kills a drunken pedestrian who has inexplicably hurled himself in front of her car in no way kills the person because of her defiance of the law's authority in order to satisfy her wishes.

Normally, however, ignorance of the law is not an excuse, because a legal system expects people to do their best to understand the legal rules of that system, and communicates that expectation to the citizenry. Hence, if someone complains that he did not know the rule, the legal system is unimpressed because it believes this person knew he should have learned of the rule but nonetheless failed to do so. In the words of one judge, "everyone is conclusively presumed to know the law."[28] He is culpably ignorant, and his culpable failure to remedy his ignorance makes him defiant of the authority of the legal system, and hence legally

[28]Judge Buttles, *State v. Woods*, Supreme Court of Vermont, 1935, 107 Vt. 354, 179 A 1, in Kadish and Paulsen, p. 110.

culpable. (So the taxpayer who did his best to comply with the law but who failed to do so because the tax code was either ambiguous or inadequately promulgated by the state such that he could not find out what the relevant tax rules were would be unfairly penalized for his failure to comply with those rules.)

As I have already mentioned, not only illegal acts of commission but also acts of recklessness are analyzed neatly by this approach. A reckless offender is another example of one who is culpable in the manner of those who are culpably ignorant. Even if he doesn't mean, for example, to drive the power boat into the dock full of people, and even if he points out, correctly in our view, that his boat was going too fast for him to control, nonetheless we believe that he had to know, as he chose to go at that high speed, that he was taking the risk that he would be unable to control the boat and possibly endanger others' lives. The fact that he did so anyway is a sign of his defiance of legal (and, in this case, also moral) pronouncements against taking that kind of risk. He is therefore culpable for running the boat into the dock not because he wanted to perform it in defiance of legal and moral imperatives (he wanted no such thing) but because he wanted to do that which entailed *risking* the kind of harm ruled out by legal and moral imperatives, so that he undertook the risk in defiance of these imperatives.

But what, the reader may wish to know, is legal authority? This famous question is one that some theorists have had trouble answering.[29] To the extent that one denies there is any authority attaching to law *qua* law, one would say either that the lawbreaker is defiant of the authority of morality upon which one supposes legal commands rely, insofar as they have any force upon us—which is the view of any classic natural law theorist—or that she is defiant

of reason, in the sense that she performs the illegal action knowing she may suffer a penalty that she finds unacceptable. On this latter view, the authority of the law (and particularly the criminal law) derives from reason, because laws are imperatives backed by negative sanctioms designed to secure a certain deterrent goal. The lawbreaker, on this view, is not defying any special authority that legal rules have, but he is being irrational (assuming that an expected utility calculation, properly performed and of which he is capable, would tell him not to violate the legal rule).

Those who insist, however, that the law does and should have a special authority will want to see the legal offender as defiant not only of reason but also of that special "positivist" authority. Why would someone want to defy the law? She might do so because she was motivated by self-interested considerations that the law opposed, or because she was motivated by what she took to be her moral duty, which conflicted with the legal requirements. Those who insist that the law has its own special authority must defend the strength and scope of that authority, in order to explain when refusal to obey the law for moral or self-interested reasons is legitimate, and when it is condemnable defiance of the proper authority. The question of which authority ought to take precedence when the legal and moral authorities are in conflict is a particularly thorny one. The conscientious objector insists that citizens must serve morality first and the law second; Hobbes is one philosopher who thought that this way of rating the two authorities was a recipe for civil strife, and who therefore insisted that legal authority come first. ("How many throats has this false position cut, that a prince for some causes may be deposed!"[30]) We have located an important point at which philosophizing about the nature and extent of the state's authority is necessary.

Nonetheless, as the quote from the West German Supreme Court shows, a legal system

---

[29]See Elizabeth Anscombe, *On the Source of the Authority of the State* in her *Collected Works, Volume III: Ethics, Religion and Politics* (Minneapolis: University of Minnesota Press, 1981), pp. 130–55; Joseph Raz. *The Authority of Law: Essays in Law and Morality* (Oxford: Clarendon Press, 1979); and Leslie Green, *The Authority of the State* (Oxford: Clarendon Press, 1988).

[30]Hobbes, *De Cive, The English Works of Thomas Hobbes*, vol. ii, ed. W. Molesworth, preface, pp. xi–xii.

normally does not want to diverge too far from morality; its architects even expect that people understand and assume the authority of morality in the system's own pronouncements and expectations of their appropriate behavior. It may even be that legal systems require that people understand and respect the authority of morality if its punitive response to them explicitly aims at making a moral point, e.g., if the punishment is intended as moral retribution, moral education, or both.

However, the state may actually want to avoid constructing its legal code in strict conformity to morality for certain important reasons. For example, even quite vicious behavior, such as libel or slander, can be merely a tort and not a criminal offense in situations where the state is concerned to pursue other values, such as the protection of free speech.[31]

Although the defiance view of legal culpability fits the facts well, it does not fit them perfectly. There are decisions (e.g., *Regina v. Prince*[32]) concerning mistake in law that suggest that the law is much more inclined toward "strict liability" than the defiance account would allow. In *Regina v. Prince*, a man married a woman who was under age without knowing it, and with the reasonable belief that she was not. It seems improper to claim that such a person is defiant of the law. Finding him guilty anyway might be justified on grounds of pursuing a deterrent goal, and, in general, the state's interest in deterring harm may lead it to convict even non-culpable (in the sense of non-defiant) offenders in the interest of making them an example for those who are contemplating the same action.

Are those people convicted of criminal negligence convicted on deterrent grounds alone? They are not if they are judged "advertently negligent," because such people really do fit the *mens rea* test of guilt. This form of negligence is essentially the same as recklessness; one who is guilty of it knew that she was risking an unacceptable level of harm when she undertook her action, but flouted that knowledge and did so anyway. She therefore displayed a defiant act prior to her crime. But an "inadvertently negligent" agent is someone who did not know that she should have done otherwise, and yet (we think) could and should have known better. There appears to be no defiant act inside the agent, but only an ignorance that we find culpable. Is that finding based entirely on the thought that conviction would have desirable deterrent consequences for this individual (or for others in the community)?

Perhaps not entirely. If we take an Aristotelian attitude towards this inadvertently negligent person, we believe that, although she did not know that what she was doing was wrong, that ignorance was a function of her faulty character—a character for which she bears primary responsibility and which she knew better than to develop in this way. So we locate the defiance not at the time of the act, but earlier, during the process of character-formation. Thus a man who is convicted of gross criminal negligence after killing a pedestrian at a crosswalk while driving 30 miles over the speed limit in a rainstorm may be legitimately culpable: not because we *now* find in him any defiance of a legal rule whose authority he understood in this situation, but because earlier in his life he had developed the character of an irresponsible driver in defiance of what he knew to be the authoritative legal and moral norms mandating safe and responsible motoring.

The inclination to try to see cases of inadvertent negligence as cases of advertent negligence or recklessness derives, I believe, from the desire to find the subjective element of defiance of the relevant norm in any person convicted of a legal offense. To convict someone

---

[31]It may also be that the stringent conditions needed to convict people of certain crimes (e.g., treason) in some legal systems—conditions that require finding not only the defiance which I call *mens rea* but also a certain kind of reason for that defiance—reflect the society's concern to control the power of the state in situations where it might be indicated to overreact and use its power excessively or arbitrarily. I am indebted to discussions with David Dolinko on this point.

[32]*Regina v. Prince*, L. R. 2 Crim. Cas. REs. 54 (1876). The defendant was convicted of marrying a girl under the age of sixteen, in violation of Victorian English Law, despite the fact that he was judged to have the "reasonable belief" that she was 18.

who is genuinely and reasonably unaware of the criminal nature of his actions in order to secure greater deterrence of social harm violates the conditions of fairness in judgment and response implicit in the defiance account. Indeed, it seems to be a (mild) instance of resorting to terror to gain social control. Now perhaps the state is sometimes justified in pursuing convictions on these grounds (although that is controversial) because it must not only exact retribution but also secure a high degree of protection for its citizens through the deterrence of certain forms of behavior. Nonetheless, these convictions offend our sense of justice—which is created, I would argue, by our acceptance of the idea that genuine culpability requires a defiant mind.

CONCLUSION

Although defiance is critical to behavior that we standardly criticize, condemn, and take action to stop, I wonder whether or not it is also critical to our success as individuals and as groups. A readiness to "take on the world" may well be what is necessary to invent new machines, concoct ambitious dreams such as going to the moon, or fight off self-doubt occasioned by racist, or sexist, or class-based perspectives on one's abilities. It may even be (as I have suggested elsewhere) that defiance is a necessary part of certain emotions such as resentment and hatred.[33] To appreciate how our capacity to defy authoritative norms may have helped us survive—as individuals, as a people, as a species—might enable us to become reconciled to something that exponents of various sorts of norms would argue that we ought bitterly to regret. And perhaps it is because we do see this capacity as important to our survival that it becomes hard to shake the thought that the first two human beings were impressive in the way they took on God.

[33]See *Forgiveness and Mercy* (written with Jeffrie Murphy), ch. 2 (Cambridge: Cambridge University Press, 1986).

CASE STUDY
The Crime That Never Was

Leo Katz

A FAKE OPINION IN A FAKE CASE INVOLVING FAKES

Commonwealth v. Omeira
Supreme Court of Wessex

Before Newson, C. J., Henchard, Hardy, Farfrae, Middlebury, J.

Newson, C. J.: The defendant, Jan Omeira, is charged with attempting to export illegally "valuable artifacts of the native culture" in violation of Section 901.34(1) of the Wessex Code.

To protect our national patrimony, the Wessex legislature twenty years ago passed a law making it illegal to export native art works produced before 1920 and worth more than 100,000 pounds. This sweeping prohibition is subject to only one ill-defined exception. The Arts Council, an agency of the Interior Department, has broad discretion to grant exemptions, that is, special licenses, when it finds that "unusual circumstances so warrant." Licenses are typically granted when a work of art cannot be sold in Wessex except at a very small fraction of its world market price or when the applicant promises to secure another "native" work of comparable worth currently in foreign hands.

The defendant is a retired businessman of considerable wealth. He owns a farm in Casterbridge, Wessex, where he spends half of the year, and a rancho in Cuernavaca, Mexico, where he spends the other half. He is a zealous

aficionado of the arts; indeed, since his retirement the acquisition of expensive paintings has become his chief preoccupation. He has opened art galleries both in his house in Casterbridge and in his villa in Cuernavaca, the one in Casterbridge for the public at large, the one in Cuernavaca almost exclusively for his own use and that of his guests.

The Constabulary has been aware for some time that not all native paintings Mr. Omeira is known to have acquired at public auctions in Wessex have made their appearance in his Casterbridge gallery and suspected him therefore of having illegally transported many of them to his gallery in Cuernavaca. Since few people have gained access to that gallery, no direct confirmation has been possible. For several years Mr. Omeira was systematically strip-searched on every one of his departures for Mexico. The searches turned up nothing and were discontinued.

In January of this year, the Constabulary received an anonymous tip that some time in March, Omeira would personally be smuggling a picture by the famous eighteenth-century landscape painter Ignacius Decameron out of the country. The picture, *Seminole Falls*, had for several years been hanging in Omeira's Casterbridge gallery and had recently been taken down for "cleaning." When Omeira left for Mexico in March, Customs scoured his luggage. They found a false bottom in one of his trunks and inside it, tightly rolled up, *Seminole Falls*.

Omeira's case was about to go to trial, when something very unusual happened. A well-known Belgian landscape painter named Flammarion remarked in an interview with the French monthly Paris Match that he thought it "rather amusing" that a Wessex art collector was being prosecuted for smuggling a Decameron landscape when in fact the painting was a forgery. How did he know it was a forgery, the astonished journalist asked. Because, replied Flammarion, he had painted it himself.

The government to whom Omeira had forfeited the smuggled picture immediately invited a panel of experts to test Flammarion's claim. They found that the painting's age crackle had a different structure from that of genuine eighteenth-century paintings. Moreover, the crackle seemed to have been artificially produced. They found that the dirt in the painting's crevices wasn't dirt at all. It had crept into the crevices very unevenly and had a different homogeneity from dirt. They suspected it was ink. With the help of radiographic studies they discovered a residue of a prior painting underneath the landscape, suggesting that this was an eighteenth-century canvas that had been recycled for forgery. They also noticed some of the paints used contained pigments not known in Decameron's day. Finally, one of the experts was struck by the reddish tinge of the painting's sky. He had been to Seminole Falls and he knew that tinge. But he was almost certain it was due to factory smoke and could not have been present in the eighteenth century. The group concluded that Flammarion was right: the picture was a fake.

Why had Flammarion forged a Decameron? When Flammarion was still a young, struggling painter living in Wessex, he entered into a feud with the influential art critic Arcadius Breitel. Breitel had published some scathing reviews of Flammarion's work, which had sent the painter into a fit of impotent rage. He wrote a letter to the magazine *Kaleidoscope*, which Breitel edited. Breitel was a snob, he wrote, who had never yet dared to praise a painting by an unknown. His sole basis for judging a painting was its age and signature. "What a delightful prank it would be," the letter concluded, "to confront this nincompoop with a picture by an unknown in the style and name of an 'Old Master,' hear him pronounce it a masterpiece, and see him squirm when the true author is revealed." The prank, tossed in at the end of the letter more as a figure of speech than a real suggestion, captured his fancy. He resolved to give it a try.

Flammarion bought a real eighteenth-century painting depicting the Last Supper by a mediocre and forgotten artist. He carefully ground the original painting off the canvas and now had a genuine eighteenth-century canvas to work on. He had taken care not to remove the painting's base which was cracked in many places, since he planned to use it when he began to age his own superimposed painting. He then retired to an inn near Seminole Falls, where he produced a rendition of the famous spot in the distinctive style of Ignacius Decameron. When he was done, he rolled it around in a cylinder to induce the age crackle. He covered the entire surface with India ink, letting it seep into the painting's cracks to simulate the fine dust that collects on an old canvas over time. Once it had dried, he removed the ink and added another layer of light brown varnish. He was ready to sell the picture.

He approached an art dealer–friend with an involved story about a former mistress of his, descended from an impoverished aristocratic Wessex family that now made its home in Uruguay. The family had only recently discovered the painting in its vaults, thought it might be a real Decameron, and wished to sell it without divulging their identity, since the sale of expensive works of art abroad was frowned upon by the government of Uruguay. The art dealer accepted the story unquestioningly and took the painting, as Flammarion expected, to none other than Arcadius Breitel for authentication. Breitel was known to be an expert on Decameron. In fact, Flammarion had painted the picture so as to fall in nicely with some of Breitel's pet theories about the painter.

Breitel not only authenticated the painting but pronounced it a major, if not the major work of Decameron. He praised it as the "ultimate synthesis of the romanticist yearnings of Decameron's early years and the naturalistic sobriety of his more mature years, the sort of synthesis I argued he was on the verge of attaining when his life was so tragically cut short by that riding accident. I was wrong. *Seminole Falls* proves that he did attain it before he died." He gushed about the way "the hard facts of topography are diffused behind pearly films of colour," found the colors "purer, more prismatic" than any other of Decameron's work, and concluded that for its brilliancy and iridescence this was perhaps the finest Decameron yet.

This was the point at which Flammarion had originally intended to step forth and expose Breitel. He didn't. A man named VanDamm had offered one million pounds for the painting. Faced with this offer and with the opportunity to see his painting forever after celebrated as a sublime example of Wessex art, he could no longer bring himself to admit the hoax. For nearly ten years the painting remained a part of the VanDamm collection. Then VannDamm, who found himself in financial straits, decided to sell it. He applied to the Arts Council for an export license so that he would be able to offer it up through Sotheby's. An expert from the Arts Council inspected the painting and concluded that it was probably a fake, worth at best 50,000 pounds. Although under the circumstances no license would have been necessary, the council issued one anyway, simply because the painting's status was still unclear.

VanDamm, however, had lost all appetite for having it sold at Sotheby's. If the painting really was a forgery, a public auction would bring that to light all too quickly. Instead, he discreetly searched for buyers among his colleagues in the business. He finally sold it to Jan Omeira for 1,200,000 pounds. Needless to say, he mentioned nothing about the painting's suspect provenance or even about the export license.

The discovery that *Seminole Falls* was a forgery put the trial judge in this case in a delicate quandary. Omeira was charged with attempting illegally to export a valuable native painting. But it is perfectly legal to export a forged Decameron. How then was the defendant guilty of any wrongdoing? The trial judge chose to slight the issue. In a disturbingly desultory opinion, he simply noted that the "defendant believed he was smuggling a real Decameron. Therefore he is guilty of attempting to export a 'valuable artifact of native culture'" and sentenced the defendant to three years in prison. The defendant appealed. I believe his appeal has merit.

A failed crime can still be a crime. That's why we have the law of attempts. The assassin who is prevented from firing a bullet by an alert bodyguard, the safecracker who is stopped short of opening the vault by an unsuspected alarm system, the rapist who is frustrated in his aim by an obstreperous victim, all have failed in completing their intended crime; yet they are guilty of a crime nonetheless, the crime of criminal attempt.

But not all failed crimes are crimes. "Suppose a man takes away an umbrella from a stand with intent to steal it, believing it not to be his own, but it turns out to be his own, could he be convicted of attempting to steal?" Baron Bramwell, who posed this hypothetical more than a century ago in a case called *Regina v. Collins*, rightly considered the question purely rhetorical.

When is a failed crime not an attempt? It behooves us to make a brief foray through some of the more typical cases and to see what general principle is to be extracted from them.

In *Commonwealth v. Dunaway* a man was charged with attempting to rape and engage in incestuous relations with his daughter. He had apparently advanced quite far in this undertaking when his wife called the police to arrest him. In the course of the trial it turned out that the girl was the man's stepdaughter. Wessex law makes consanguinity a prerequisite of incest. The defendant did not, of course, know that; he thought he was committing incest. He was convicted. On appeal the attempted rape conviction was upheld, the attempted incest conviction overturned. The court observed that even if the man had succeeded in his undertaking, even if he had actually completed an act of intercourse with his step-daughter, he would only be guilty of rape, not incest. Stephen's Digest of the Criminal Law defines an attempt to commit a crime as "an act done with intent to commit that crime, and forming part of a series of acts which would constitute its actual commission if it were not interrupted." The defendant's act, even if not interrupted, would not have constituted incest. Hence, the court reasoned, he could not be guilty of the attempt to commit incest.

The defendant in *Stephens v. Abrahams* wanted to import a certain item into Victoria (Australia) without paying the duty on it. To this end he presented the customs officer with a fake invoice for the item. Unbeknownst to him, the item was not dutiable anyway. A bill was pending in Parliament that proposed to tax such items, but it had not yet been passed. The Customs Office discovered the defendant's deception and charged him with attempt to "defraud the revenue contrary to the Commonwealth Customs Act." The Supreme Court acquitted him. Even "if the accused had succeeded in his object, he would not have succeeded in defrauding the revenue," it argued. Even if the defendant had managed to deceive the Customs office with his fake invoice, he would not have cheated them out of any money they were entitled to. So there could be no attempt to defraud them either.

Wilson received a check for $2.50. The upper right-hand corner of the check read: "2⁵⁄₁₀₀." The body of the check read: "two and ⁵⁄₁₀₀ dollars." The top of the check read: "Ten Dollars or Less." Undaunted, Wilson inserted a "1" in front of the "2⁵⁄₁₀₀" hoping to cash the check in for $12.50. Needless to say, the pathetic ploy foundered and Wilson was charged with attempting to commit check forgery. Check forgery, however, requires an alteration of a material part of the check. The number on a check itself is immaterial. Whenever there is a discrepancy between number and words, the words control. Since Wilson had done all he meant to do and it did not amount to check forgery, how, the court asked, could he be guilty of attempted check forgery? Wilson was acquitted.

In *People v. Dlugash* the defendant was charged with attempted murder because he had shot a corpse.

Defendant stated that, on the night of December 21, 1973, he, Bush and Geller had been out drinking. Bush had been staying at Geller's apartment and, during the course of the evening, Geller several times demanded that Bush pay $100 towards the rent on the apartment. According to defendant, Bush rejected these demands, telling Geller

that "you better shut up or you're going to get a bullet." All three returned to Geller's apartment at approximately midnight, took seats in the bedroom, and continued to drink until sometime between 3:00 and 3:30 in the morning. When Geller again pressed his demand for rent money, Bush drew his .38 caliber pistol, aimed it at Geller and fired three times. Geller fell to the floor.

Then, to confuse the police and to buy the defendant's silence, Bush ordered him to fire some extra bullets into Geller's body. The somewhat frightened defendant did just that, believing that Geller was still alive. The autopsy, however, revealed that Geller was almost certainly already dead. In an arcanely reasoned opinion, the New York Court of Appeals somehow reached the conclusion that the defendant could indeed be found guilty of attempted murder. Few courts, I venture to say, would accept that conclusion. Lord Reid in *Haughton v. Smith* some years ago contemplated just such a case and gave what I think is the definitive answer: "A man lies dead. His enemy comes along and thinks he is asleep, so he stabs the corpse. The theory [advanced by some] inevitably requires us to hold that the enemy has attempted to murder the dead man. The law may sometimes be an ass but it cannot be so asinine as that."

The defendant in *People v. Jaffe* had bought what he thought were stolen goods from some undercover policemen. He could not be charged with buying stolen goods since the goods weren't stolen. Instead, he was charged with attempting to buy stolen goods. The courts acquitted him: "If all which an accused person intends to do would if done constitute no crime it cannot be a crime to attempt to do with the same purpose a part of the thing intended."

In *State v. Clarissa* the defendant, a black slave, was charged with attempting to murder two white men by feeding them a substance called Jamestown weed, which she believed to be poisonous. The prosecution failed to allege or prove that it was. The Supreme Court of Alabama reversed the conviction, explaining:

[The] administration of a substance not poisonous, or calculated to cause death, though believed to be so by the person administering it, will not be an attempt to poison, within the meaning of the [murder] statute. From this analysis of the statute, it follows, that the indictment should allege, that the substance administered was a deadly poison, or calculated to destroy human life, as it is necessary that every indictment should warrant the judgment that is rendered upon it. Yet every allegation in this indictment may have been proved, and the life of the persons against whom the supposed attempt to poison was made, never had been in jeopardy; as it cannot be known as a matter of law, that the seed of the Jamestown weed is a deadly poison. The moral guilt, it is true, is as great in the one case as in the other, but that is not the offense which the law intended to punish; but the actual attempt to poison, by means calculated to accomplish it.

A notable curiosity occurred in our own jurisdiction only very recently in *Commonwealth v. Jejune*. The defendant and his wife were Haitian immigrants. The defendant's wife had grown very sick shortly after coming to this country. At the behest of a neighbor a doctor visited her. She told him that she could not be helped because her husband had cast a spell over her. Two days earlier she had found in his shaving cabinet a doll bearing her likeness with pins in it. The doctor ordered her taken to the hospital, where she quickly recovered. No organic cause for her illness was ever discovered. The woman's husband did not deny having tried to kill her by magic. He was charged with attempted murder. The trial court rightly dismissed the charge and acquitted the man. It observed, "To try to kill someone by sticking pins in a doll is to try the impossible. Even if the man had continued sticking pins in the doll for the rest of his life he could not have killed his wife. How then can we brand such an inherently innocent activity attempted murder?"

These cases establish a simple yet powerful principle. An act which, unless interrupted, constitutes a crime is a criminal attempt. But an act which, even if completed, wouldn't be a crime, is not.

The defendant in all of these cases is morally heinous. But why is he morally heinous? Because of what he did? No, because of what he thought he did. In that case to convict him "would be to convict him not for what he did but simply because he had a guilty intention." It is a fundamental tenet of our criminal law that a man cannot be convicted for his thoughts, only for his acts.

My disposition of Omeira's case should now be clear. Even if Jan Omeira had succeeded in smuggling his painting across the border, he would not have violated the export ban, since *Seminole Falls* is a forgery. If the completed act was no crime, the attempt could not possibly be one either. The trial court's verdict should be reversed.

Henchard, J.: I disagree sharply with the reasoning of Justice Newson. He would have us endorse what I think is a rather strange principle: that an "act which, although intended to be a crime, would not have amounted to one, even if it had not been interrupted, is not a criminal attempt." Taken seriously, this principle would have absurd implications. Justice Newson concedes that the assassin who is overpowered by a bodyguard, the safecracker who is caught by an unsuspecting alarm system, the rapist who is stymied by a resistant victim all are guilty of a criminal attempt. But suppose that given the way the assassin aimed his gun, he would have missed his target anyway. Justice Newson's principle would have the man acquitted. Suppose the gold bars in the vault were too heavy for the safecracker to move, even if he had gotten to them. Justice Newson's principle would have the man acquitted. Suppose the rapist was impotent and could not have achieved an erection. Justice Newson's principle would have the man acquitted. I do not see how Justice Newson can propose a principle with such consequences.

Nor can I approve of many of the decisions that seem to have endorsed this principle. If the defendant in Jaffe thought he was buying stolen goods, he was attempting to buy stolen goods. If the defendant in *Jejune* thought what he did would tend to kill his wife, he was attempting murder. By contrast, the decision of the *Dlugash* court was exactly right: If the defendant in *Dlugash* thought he was shooting a human being, he was attempting murder. In each of these cases, what the defendants were attempting was impossible only because of some unforeseen contingency. That makes them no different from the assassin, the safecracker, the rapist. They, too, failed because some unforeseen contingency stopped them in their tracks.

Justice Newson contends that to punish the defendants in cases like *Dlugash*, *Jaffe*, and *Jejune* is to punish evil thoughts, not evil acts. But that's not so. We punish the defendants there not because they wanted to commit an evil act but because they took what they thought were substantial steps toward putting those thoughts into practice. I think I can pinpoint the source of Justice Newson's confusion. He thinks that when but for the defendant's evil thought he would not be punished we are punishing him for the evil thought. That's a mistaken idea. We would not convict a murderer but for the fact that he intended to kill a human being. Yet it can hardly be said that we are punishing him only for his evil thoughts.

I do not think, therefore, that Jan Omeira is innocent of a criminal attempt to violate the export ban on art merely because what he took to be a real Decameron turned out to be a forgery. But I think there are other reasons for acquitting him.

Suppose two men furtively engage in homosexual intercourse thinking that it is illegal. In fact, state law has nothing against mutually consented-to homosexual intercourse. Are they guilty of a criminal attempt? Evidently not. You cannot invent the law against yourself. Just because you think something is illegal and then attempt to do it, you haven't yet done anything illegal. The crime you attempt is, we might say, "legally impossible" because there isn't such a crime. This is very different from the case where what you are attempting to do isn't really criminal because the facts, not the law, are different from what you took them to be: because

the man you attempt to shoot is already dead, because the goods you attempt to buy are not really stolen, because the method you adopt for killing someone won't really work. We might call these cases of "factual impossibility." In sum, attempting the legally impossible is not a crime, attempting the factually impossible is. In a way, this is a corollary to the principle that ignorance of law is no excuse. Just as thinking something is legal when it isn't won't get a defendant out of a bind, thinking it is illegal when it isn't won't get him into one.

This principle, rather than the one endorsed by Justice Newson, serves to make sense of the three cases cited in his opinion with which I agree. I agree that the defendant in *Dunaway* who thought he was committing incest should have been acquitted of the charge of attempting incest. What he attempted was legally impossible. The law does not make intercourse with one's stepdaughter part of incest. Thinking that the law does cannot make the defendant guilty of attempted incest.

I also agree that the defendant in *Stephens v. Abrahams* who thought he was smuggling a dutiable item past customs should have been acquitted of the charge of attempting to "defraud the revenue." He, too, attempted the legally impossible, since Victoria did not make the item he smuggled dutiable. Thinking that it did could not have made the defendant guilty of attempted smuggling.

Finally, I agree that the defendant in *State v. Wilson* who thought he was forging a check when he altered its numerals should have been acquitted of the charge of attempting check forgery. He thought that what he did was forgery. The law happens to define forgery differently. Thus, he, too, attempted the legally impossible. Thinking that the law prohibited what he did as forgery did not make him guilty of attempted forgery.

When the Decameron was still in Mr. VanDamm's possession, he applied for an export license to the Arts Council. The Arts Council granted him the license. In effect, they amended the export law so as to exempt this particular painting from its sway. Thus what Mr. Omeira attempted to do was to smuggle out of the country a painting under the mistaken belief that the law prohibited him from exporting it. In fact, the law specifically exempted that painting. What he was attempting to do was not merely factually impossible (because he was dealing with a forgery) but legally impossible (because the painting had been exempted from the export ban). The case is thus on all fours with *Dunaway*, *Stephens*, and *Wilson*. It is for that reason that I too would acquit Mr. Omeira, notwithstanding my wholehearted disagreement with the reasoning of Justice Newson's opinion.

Farfrae, J., with whom Hardy, J., concurs: I agree in spirit with Justice Newson's approach. I agree with him that many of the so-called impossible attempt cases should be resolved in the defendant's favor. I disagree with the particulars of his argument, for many of the reasons given in Justice Henchard's opinion. And I disagree with his resolution of this case.

I disagree both in spirit and substance with Justice Henchard's approach, and, of course, with his resolution of this case in particular. The approach hinges on a distinction that strikes me as both obscure and unimportant, that between law and fact, legal impossibility and factual impossibility.

The distinction between "law" and "fact" has proved obscure wherever it is employed. For instance, the common law used to require that a plaintiff's complaint in a civil action only state the "facts" of his case, not any "legal conclusions." Unfortunately, no one had ever been able to tell whether the allegation that "on November 9, the defendant negligently ran over the plaintiff with his car at the intersection of State Street and Chestnut Street" is a statement of fact or a legal conclusion. In fact, the distinction between law and fact is just the legal version of the philosophical distinction between "empirical" and "analytical" statements, a distinction on whose existence philosophers have been unable to agree to this day.

The distinction is as unimportant as it is obscure. It distinguishes between cases that are really alike. . . . The present case shows neatly just how unimportant it is. The defendant Omeira made two mistakes. First, he

mistakenly thought the picture was authentic. Second, he mistakenly thought it hadn't been licensed for export. Under Justice Henchard's rule, the first mistake fails to exonerate him, but the second mistake does. The first is a mistake of fact, the second a mistake of law. Yet I fail to see any profound difference between the two kinds of mistake. If Omeira's ignorance of the painting's authenticity doesn't exonerate him, then neither should his ignorance of the export license.

The proper way to approach cases like the present is to ask two questions. Let me ask them in turn, to explain why they are important, show how one goes about answering them, and answers them for the present case. The first question is this: Did the defendant really attempt something criminal?

An attempt is often mistakenly thought of as the fragment of a completed offense. Of course, that isn't so. The driver who hurtles down a slippery road at breakneck speed may be inviting a deadly accident that would qualify as involuntary manslaughter if it occurred. Nevertheless, he is not attempting to commit the crime of involuntary manslaughter. To attempt something one must not merely be on one's way to committing it, one must intend to commit it. The reckless driver clearly is not.

This obvious point has subtle implications. It means that a defendant may be thinking he is committing a crime, without actually attempting to commit it. He knows the bomb he plans to hurl into the queen's carriage will kill not only the queen, but her bodyguard, but he is only attempting to kill the queen, not the bodyguard. Killing the bodyguard is an unintended by-product of killing the queen. Of course, determining whether somebody is actually attempting something or merely engaging in conduct which he thinks will bring it about, often is hard. It depends on whether the commission of the crime is his desired end or a means toward such an end (in which case we have an attempt) or whether it is rather a by-product of bringing about some desired end. To find out which it is, one has to ask whether the defendant would change his course of conduct if he thought the commission of the crime was not tied to the achievement of his desired end.

If we apply this analysis, we will see that many defendants charged with impossible attempts are not in fact attempting the crime they are charged with attempting. They merely think they are committing a crime. The rapist in *Commonwealth v. Dunaway* is not guilty of attempted incest, because he was not intending to commit incest. He only thought he was committing incest. Had he been told that incest requires consanguinity, he would have been relieved. He would certainly not have desisted from his actions. The "smuggler" in *Stephens v. Abrahams* is not guilty of attempted smuggling because he was not intending to smuggle. He merely thought he was smuggling. Had he been told that the items he was importing weren't dutiable, he would have been relieved. He would certainly not have abstained from importing them. The "killer" in *People v. Dlugash* is not guilty of attempting murder, because he was not intending to kill the already-dead man. He merely thought he was killing him. Had he been told that he was shooting a corpse, he would have been relieved. He would certainly not have avoided shooting it. The "fence" in *People v. Jaffe* is not guilty of attempting to buy stolen goods because he was not intending to buy stolen goods. He merely thought he was buying stolen goods. Had he been told that the goods were not stolen, he would have been relieved. He would certainly not have eschewed buying them.

What now of this case? Was the defendant intending to export an authentic Decameron? Or was he merely thinking he was exporting an authentic Decameron? That depends: Had he been told that the Decameron was fake, would he have cared? Would he have changed his course of conduct? Would he not have exported it? The defendant will, of course, argue that although he thought the painting was a genuine Decameron, that was not the reason he wanted to export it. He will argue that he liked the painting for its artistic merits, not its provenance, and that he would still have wanted to take it to Cuernavaca, even if it

was a forgery. That's a tough argument to reckon with.

The record indicates that the defendant liked to keep his most exclusive and prized possessions in his Cuernavaca gallery. It also indicates that the defendant did not collect art as an investment. Very few paintings he acquired he ever resold. He collected them purely and simply for the aesthetic pleasure they afforded. Asking whether the defendant would have tried to export a forged Decameron to Cuernavaca amounts to asking whether his aesthetic enjoyment of the painting would have been diminished by his discovery that it was fake. Should it have been? Is it rational to enjoy a painting as long as you think it is a Decameron and on learning it is a mere Flammarion-imitating-Decameron cease to do so?

Some decades ago it was discovered that a widely hailed Vermeer depicting *Christ and the Disciples at Emmaus*, exhibited for may years at Rotterdam's Boymans Museum, was a forgery by a twentieth-century painter named van Meegeren. Hundreds of thousands of visitors, many of them connoissuers and critics, had enjoyed the painting. When the fraud was discovered, the picture was immediately removed from view. Was that rational? The philosopher Alfred Lessing argues that it wasn't:

What is the difference between a genuine Vermeer and a van Meegeren forgery? It is of little use to maintain that one need but look to see the difference. The fact that *The Disciples* is a forgery (if indeed it is) cannot, so to speak, be read off from its surface, but can finally be proved or disproved only by means of extensive scientific investigations and analyses. Nor are the results of such scientific investigations of any help in answering our question, since they deal exclusively with nonaesthetic elements of the picture, such as its chemical composition, its hardness, its crackle, and so on. . . .

The plain fact is that aesthetically it makes no difference whether a work of art is authentic or a forgery, and, instead of being embarassed at having praised a forgery, critics should have the courage of their convictions and take pride in having praised a work of beauty. . . .

The fact that a work of art is a forgery is an item of information about it on a level with such information as the age of the artist when he created it, the political situation in the time and place of its creation, the price it originally fetched, the kind of materials used in it, the stylistic influences discernible in it, the psychological state of the artist, his purpose in painting it, and so on. All such information belongs to areas of interest peripheral at best to the work of art as aesthetic object, areas such as biography, history or art, sociology, and psychology. I do not deny that such areas of interest may be important and that their study may even help us become better art appreciators. But I do deny that the information which they provide is of the essence of the work of art or of the aesthetic experience which it engenders.

It would be merely foolish to assert that it is of no interest whatever to know that *The Disciples* is a forgery. But to the man who has never heard of either Vermeer or van Meegeren and who stands in front of the Disciples admiring it, it can make no difference whether he is told that it is a seventeenth-century Vermeer or a twentieth-century van Meegeren in the style of Vermeer. And when some deny this and argue vehemently that, indeed, it does make a great deal of difference, they are only admitting that they do know something about Vermeer and van Meegeren and the history of art and the value and reputation of certain masters. They are only admitting that they do not judge a work of art on purely aesthetic grounds but also take into account when it was created, by whom, and how great a reputation it or its creator has.

Is Lessing right to suggest that we are being snobbish and irrational if we permit our pleasure in a painting to be decisively influenced by its identity? I will offer two examples to show that he is not. (To be sure, a bit of irrational self-suggestion is involved. The act critic takes to a famous signature like many a patient to a placebo. He will find virtues in the painting that really aren't there. This doesn't prove

that all virtues in all paintings are the invention of the art critics, just as reaction of the patient doesn't prove that the real medicine is superfluous. For unlike the forgery and the placebo, the real painting and the real medicine do their job without suggestion—which is why the medicine works for many not susceptible to the placebo's suggestive power.)

My first example is the plot of a film made some time ago by the American director Martin Ritt, written by Walter Bernstein and starring Woody Allen. It was called *The Front*. The story takes place sometime in the 1950s. Howard Prince, a man in his late twenties or early thirties, works as a cashier in a diner. He is a bright college dropout and sometime bum. One day Al Miller, a childhood pal who has become a well-known TV scriptwriter, drops in. The man is depressed. He had been ordered to appear before the House Committee on Un-American Activities, had taken the Fifth Amendment, and had been blacklisted as a result. On seeing Howard he hits upon a ruse for salvaging something of his dwindling livelihood. He proposes that Howard (Woody Allen) submit his manuscripts for him, representing himself to their author. In return, he promises Howard 10 percent of the proceeds. Howard is delighted. He is pleased to help. Besides he likes the adventure, the money, and the glamor of holding himself up as a television scriptwriter. The first, second, and third scripts are accepted without much questioning and with much acclaim. But the charade doesn't always go smoothly. Howard is not very well read and therefore hard-pressed to make conversation on literary subjects. Nor is he much good at explaining and "selling" his own scripts. Finally, disaster threatens when the director asks him to rewrite a scene on the spot. Howard finesses all of these obstacles, and so successful is the scheme that several more blacklisted authors are brought in to take advantage of Howard's ability as a front. Howard Prince soon becomes known as one of the most prolific TV scriptwriter around.

On the set Howard meets a young directorial assistant named Florence Barret, a tall, pretty, young woman with long, brunette hair and soulful eyes. Florence is involved with a stockbroker but cannot resist the charms of this outwardly rather clumsy but yet so clever and creative writer. She is a friendly, warmhearted, open-minded person, but it is clear that Howard Prince would not have had a chance with her but for his new persona—but for his reputation as an immensely talented, prolific new writer.

Months later Howard confesses his real identity to Florence. She is shocked and angry, she feels duped, and she wonders whether she really knows him. But she doesn't break with Howard. As things stand when the movie ends the two are likely to be married soon.

Why does Florence love Howard? He doesn't have the attributes she was looking for in a man. He only seemed, at some point, to have those attributes. Why does she not discard him when she discovers he doesn't? Because she has grown to love him. But why has she grown to love him? Because of attributes he doesn't have. In other words, she continues to love him for no other reason than that he is identical with the person she loved in the past. Even if a man came along who genuinely epitomized the attributes she had been looking for in a man, she would not abandon Howard for him. Do we consider her snobbish or irrational for placing such emphasis not on Howard's real attributes but the fact that he happens to be identical with someone she loved in the past? Not in the least. We might consider her snobbish if she did otherwise. Identity then is a crucial concern not only to the snob.

Evidently it doesn't much matter that the person we love possess certain attributes making him suitable for loving, but only that he be identical with a person we once considered suitable for such loving.

My second example: ABC corporation, a car-manufacturing company, is being prosecuted for negligent homicide. One of its buses has caused the death of thirty school children. The bus model, the state's attorney argues, was thrown on the market quite recklessly with only a modicum of testing. As a result, its tendency to explode readily after a head-on collision with another vehicle was never discovered and corrected. Before the indictment is officially announced, the company is reorganized top to bottom. Almost all of the management and personnel involved in the production of the fatal model are fired. Two-thirds of the board of directors, the real culprits, are tossed out. The fired and dismissed managers, employees, and board members coalesce into a new corporation of their own, called the XYZ company and also begin to produce cars. Which of the two companies will be liable for the misdeeds of the ABC corporation? Why, clearly the ABC corporation. Evidently, we don't punish the entity because we think it particularly deserving of punishment, but because it happens to be identical with an entity which sometime in the past was particularly deserving of punishment.

Why then should we only admire a Decameron painting for the aesthetic qualities it now possesses rather than because it is identical with the work of a man whose work we have come to admire? I don't think there is anything snobbish about such an attitude. A man is not irrational or unreasonable for behaving in this fashion. And I don't feel we are imputing any irrational, unreasonable or implausible trait to Mr. Omeira when we assume that he cared very much that his picture be a real Decameron rather than merely "another pretty picture."

We have established that the defendant really attempted to export an authentic Decameron. But that is not enough to show that he is guilty of a criminal attempt. Before finding him liable for that, we need to answer a second question: Did the defendant really create an unreasonable risk of a crime being committed? Why do I think this question needs to be asked?

Before we convict someone for recklessly or negligently causing harm, we require that his conduct be "unreasonable," that it be the sort a reasonable man would take exception to. In a sense, that introduces an element of luck into the law. The defendant may think that what he is doing creates an unreasonable risk, but if in fact it does not, he will not be convicted. The law does not want to trouble itself with conduct that wouldn't bother a reasonable man.

We should impose the same requirement of unreasonableness before we convict someone for intentionally or knowingly causing harm. Indeed, I think we already do. It's just that, typically, when a defendant intentionally brings about harm, there is no doubt that his conduct was such as would have bothered a reasonable man. If it wouldn't have bothered a reasonable man, the prosecutor usually decides not to press charges. That has the unfortunate effect of making us overlook this potentially important point.

Let me elucidate with an example. Suppose a father wants to kill his five-year-old son. He decides to do so by sending him to summer camp, not, as he did in past years, by train, but by plane instead. He is under the mistaken impression that plane crashes are a lot more frequent than train crashes. He hopes such a crash will occur. And indeed it does. Clearly, the father has intentionally caused his son's death. (He intended his son to die in just the manner he did, and the son wouldn't have died, if he hadn't been on that plane.) But should we convict him of murder? I don't think so. Why? Because the father did nothing a reasonable man would object to: It was not unreasonably risky to send the boy to summer camp by airplane.

Suppose the plane never crashed. But the police learn of the father's evil intentions and charge him with attempted murder. Should we convict him? I don't think so. Why? Because the father did nothing a reasonable man would object to: To repeat, it is not unreasonably risky to send the boy to summer camp by airplane.

The same analysis applies to many cases of impossible attempts. The man who tried to kill his wife by witchcraft was engaging in conduct a reasonable man would not object to. It is not unreasonably risky to stick pins into someone's likeness. Hence the defendant should be acquitted. Whether the slave who tried to kill someone with the harmless Jamestown weed created an unreasonable risk depends on the facts of that case. From what I know of the case, I cannot say. In any event, the decision is one for the jury. Whether Wilson, who tried to forge a check with ludicrous ineptitude, created an unreasonable risk is a close call.

In the present case, did the defendant Omeira create an unreasonable risk that valuable artifacts of the native culture would be exported? Would a reasonable man have objected to his conduct? I believe so. The forgery was near-perfect. A reasonable man would certainly have been worried that what Omeira was trying to export was a real Decameron. Of course, if the forgery were terribly crude, so crude that any reasonable man could detect it, the answer would be different.

I conclude that the defendant's conviction should be affirmed.

[The court being evenly divided, Justice Middlebury will cast the deciding vote. I leave it to the reader to make Justice Middlebury's decision for him.]

II
WHAT SHOULD BE A CRIME?

In his classic defense of individual freedom, *On Liberty*, the British philosopher John Stuart Mill formulated the so-called "harm principle": The only legitimate reason for using the law to limit adults' freedom of action is to prevent harm to others. On this principle, *legal paternalism* is illegitimate because paternalistic laws make actions criminal because they would harm the actor him- or herself, such as laws requiring motorcyclists to wear helmets or prohibiting adults from drinking alcohol or taking drugs. Likewise, *legal moralism* is ruled out because moralistic laws enforce prevailing moral beliefs where no clear harm to others can be shown, such as laws against prostitution or public drunkenness.

Nonetheless, many would hold that legal paternalism is justified because it protects people from unwise choices that may harm them down the road, and others hold that legal moralism is justified as expressing the democratic right of the majority to rule. Some who are sympathetic to the harm principle would hold that legal coercion is justified to protect people against behavior that is harmless but offensive (such as laws against public nudity), or to ensure collective support of valuable public goods (such as laws that require people to pay taxes for education even if they do not have children to send to school). These various and conflicting principles are set out with the arguments for and against them by David A.J. Richards in "The Moral Foundations of Decriminalization," and Joel Feinberg in "Grounds for Coercion" and "Hard Cases for the Harm Principle." The full text of Mill's work is available through <http://www.bartleby.com/>. All the Internet addresses mentioned in this text, along with additional resources, are available through <http://www.paulsjusticepage.com>.

The section then goes on to consider a number of currently debated areas of lawmaking: drug legalization, prostitution, corporate crime, hate crimes, and abortion.

Drugs: Arnold Trebach, former head of the Drug Policy Foundation, believes that many of the harms associated with drugs are related more to the laws against them than to the effects of the drugs themselves. He believes that people should have the right to choose what to put in their bodies and advocates "returning the power of individual choice to the citizens of a supposedly free country over a very intimate matter." He offers several plans for legalizing drugs.

Inciardi details many of the public health problems associated with legal drugs to highlight his concern that legalizing drugs would increase the number of people using these drugs and be detrimental to public health. He argues that there are dangers and health consequences of marijuana, cocaine, and heroin—and claims that the belief that legalization would "eliminate crime, overdose, infections, and life dislocations for its users is for the most part delusional." Inciardi details the problems of crack cocaine, especially, and emphasizes that his ideas on policy are based on visits to crack houses on the "mean and despairing streets." From his perspective, legalizing crack is unlikely to reverse the human suffering the drug has caused.

Further information on this topic is available from the National Organization for the Reform of Marijuana Laws <http://www.norml.org/home.shtml> and the Office of National Drug Control Policy <http://www.whitehousedrugpolicy.gov/>.

Prostitution: The case for prostitution laws is set forth in the American Legal Institute's 1959 Model Penal Code Comment:

> Prostitution is an important source of venereal disease . . . it is a source of profit and power for criminal groups who commonly combine it with illicit trade in drugs and liquor, illegal gambling and even robbery and extortion. Prostitution is also a corrupt influence on government and law enforcement machinery. Its promoters are willing and able to pay for police protection; and unscrupulous officials find them an easy mark for extortion. Finally some view prostitution as a significant factor in social disorganization, encouraging sex, delinquency and undermining marriage, the home, and individual character (quoted in *Cherry v. Koch* 491 NYS2d 934, 944).

In re P is a judicial decision that argues against all of these concerns and strikes down New York State's prostitution statute as unconstitutional. (It also releases a 14-year-old girl from charges that she agreed to exchange sexual acts for a fee of $10.) The judge further argues that the statute is applied in an unequal manner that disadvantages women and thus undermines any argument that such laws can be justified on the paternalistic ground that they protect women.

In her article "Prostitution and Civil Rights," feminist legal scholar Catharine MacKinnon expresses a similar concern about sex discrimination in the application of the law. She argues that, in sexist societies such as our own, *all* prostitution is forced prostitution and sexual slavery; the prostitution laws further victimize women who are already victimized by being prostitutes. MacKinnon does not favor repealing prostitution laws, but rather wants to find new legal tools to deal with women's subordination.

The International Committee for Prostitutes' Rights agrees with MacKinnon that prostitutes are denied a wide range of civil and human rights, but as their "World Charter and World Whores' Congress Statements" makes clear, they want to decriminalize "all aspects of adult prostitution resulting from individual decision." The statement claims that prostitution should be recognized as a legitimate career choice; they argue for a variety of reforms that reduce economic and social coercion on women and children to engage in prostitution and protect adults who have freely chosen to engage in prostitution from fraud, rape, violence, and extortion.

Though many additional materials on prostitution are easily accessible, the voice of the prostitutes and sex workers are frequently left out of debates. Readers interested in this perspective are referred to the Prostitutes' Education Network <http://www.bayswan.org/penet.html> and Frederique Delacoste and Precilla Alexander, eds., *Sex Work: Writings by Women in the industry*, 2nd ed. (San Francisco: Cleis

Press, 1998). The editors note that the first edition "was probably the first (and only?) book from a feminist press to be reviewed favorably in the same month in both *The Women's Review of Books* and *Hustler* magazine."

Corporate Harm & Violence: In contrast to the previous sections arguing about decriminalizing acts currently prohibited by law, the reading on corporate violence and harm raises the concern that *more* of these acts should be treated as crimes if the criminal justice system is really interested in protecting us against all harmful behavior—and not just against the harmful behavior of poor people. In "A Crime by Any Other Name," Jeffrey Reiman argues that many acts of corporations are not treated as crimes even though they cause more physical harm and death than the crimes of homicide and aggravated assault. The American Medical Association along with Stanton Glantz and his colleagues present a case study about what the tobacco industry really knew about the harmfulness and addictive nature of its product, in "Looking Through a Keyhole at the Tobacco Industry."

More information is available from Northeastern University Law School's Tobacco Control Resource Center & Tobacco Products Liability Project, <http://tobacco.neu.edu/>. Some of the legal theory used to hold tobacco manufacturers liable in the civil cases is now being used against gun manufacturers, reports *The Jurist: The Law Professor's Network* <http://jurist.law.pitt.edu/guns/index.htm>.

Hate Crimes: As the United States strives to be a more tolerant and inclusive society, hate crimes and hate speech are matters of great concern. Some believe that hate crimes are best dealt with through existing assault laws and that racist, sexist, and homophobic hate speech are simply offensive utterances protected by the First Amendment's guarantee of free expression. Others see expressions of hatred as involving an extra harm related to intimidation or terrorism. In *RAV v. St Paul* (1992), the U.S. Supreme Court invalidated a law making it a crime to display an object like a burning cross that "arouses anger, alarm or resentment in others on the basis of race, color, creed, religion or gender." But this case did not resolve questions about sentencing enhancements for bias-motivated assaults. *Wisconsin v. Mitchell* deals directly with this question, and a sharply divided Wisconsin Supreme Court strikes down the statute. We reprint this state court decision because it includes three separate opinions and a thoughtful debate, although the result was overruled by the Supreme Court in a unanimous 1993 decision. The Supreme Court decision is available through Findlaw <http.//www.findlaw.com>, as are the related cases: *RAV v. St Paul*, *Johnson v. Texas* (flag burning), and *Hustler Magazine v. Jerry Falwell* (libel).

Abortion: In a series of articles, philosophers Don Marquis and Jeffrey Reiman debate the question of the morality of abortion and its possible harms. In "Why Abortion Is Immoral," Marquis argues that abortion is wrong because it deprives a fetus of a future life much in the way that killing an adult—even in her sleep—deprives her of a future life. One feature of Marquis's defense of this position is that it accounts for most people's belief that infanticide is as wrong as the killing of adults. In "Abortion, Infanticide, and the Asymmetric Value of Human Life," Reiman holds that our beliefs about the wrongness of the killing of humans only make sense if we assume that they are meant to protect the lives of people who are already aware of being alive and caring about continuing. He thus concludes that abortion, since it happens to a fetus who is not yet aware of being alive, is morally permissible. He contends that the killing of infants—who are also not yet aware of being alive—must be condemned on other grounds. In rejoinders, Marquis and Reiman defend their own views and offer critiques of each other's argument.

Grounds for Coercion

Joel Feinberg

1. THE PRESUMPTIVE CASE FOR LIBERTY

Whatever else we believe about freedom, most of us believe it is something to be praised, or so luminously a Thing of Value that it is beyond praise. What is it that makes freedom a good thing? Some say that freedom is good in itself quite apart from its consequences. On the other hand, James Fitzjames Stephen wrote that " . . . the question whether liberty is a good or a bad thing appears as irrational as the question whether fire is a good or a bad thing."[1] Freedom, according to Stephen, is good (when it is good) only because of what it does, not because of what it is.

It would be impossible to demonstrate that freedom is good for its own sake, and indeed, this proposition is far from self-evident. Still, Stephen's analogy to fire seems an injustice to freedom. Fire has no constant and virtually invariant effects that tend to make it, on balance,

"Grounds for Coercion" and "Hard Cases for the Harm Principle" from *Social Philosophy* by Feinberg, Joel, © 1973. Reprinted by permission of Prentice-Hall, Inc., Upper Saddle River, NJ. Pp. 20–22, 25–54.

[1]James Fitzjames Stephen, *Liberty, Equality, Fraternity* (London: 1873), p. 48.

a good thing whenever and wherever it occurs, and bad only when its subsequent remoter effects are so evil as to counterbalance its direct and immediate ones. Thus, a fire in one's bed while one is sleeping is dreadful because its effects are evil, but a fire under the pot on the stove is splendid because it makes possible a hot cup of coffee when one wants it. The direct effect of fire in these and all other cases is to oxidize material objects and raise the temperature in its immediate environment; but *these* effects, from the point of view of human interests, and considered just in themselves, are neither good nor bad.

Freedom has seemed to most writers quite different in this respect. When a free man violates his neighbor's interests, then his freedom, having been put to bad use, was, on balance, a bad thing, but unlike the fire in the bed, it was not an unalloyed evil. Whatever the harmful consequences of freedom in a given case, there is always a direct effect on the person of its possessor which must be counted a positive good. Coercion may prevent great evils, and be wholly justified on that account, but it always has its price. Coercion may be on balance a great gain, but its direct effects always, or nearly always, constitute a definite loss. If this is true, there is always a *presumption* in favor of freedom, even though it can in some cases be overridden by more powerful reasons on the other side.

The presumption in favor of freedom is usually said to rest on freedom's essential role in the development of traits of intellect and character which constitute the good of individuals and are centrally important means to the progress of societies. One consensus argument, attributable with minor variations to Von Humboldt, Mill, Hobhouse, and many others, goes roughly as follows. The highest good for man is neither enjoyment nor passive contentment, but rather a dynamic process of growth and self-realization. This can be called "happiness" if we mean by that term what the Greeks did, namely, "The exercise of vital powers along lines of excellence in a life affording them scope."[2] The highest social good is then the greatest possible amount of individual self-realization and (assuming that different persons are inclined by their natures in different ways) the resultant diversity and fullness of life. Self-realization consists in the actualization of certain uniquely human potentialities, the bringing to full development of certain powers and abilities. This in turn requires constant practice in making difficult choices among alternative hypotheses, policies, and actions—and the more difficult the better. John Stuart Mill explained why:

> The human faculties of perception, judgment, discriminative feeling, mental activity, and even moral preference are exercised only in making a choice. He who does anything because it is the custom makes no choice. He gains no practice either in discerning or in desiring what is best. The mental and moral, like the muscular, powers are improved only by being used.[3]

In short, one does not realize what is best in oneself when social pressures to conform to custom lead one mindlessly along. Even more

clearly, one's growth will be stunted when one is given no choice in the first place, either because of being kept in ignorance or because one is terrorized by the wielders of bayonets.

Freedom to decide on one's own while fully informed of the facts thus tends to promote the good of the person who exercises it, even if it permits him to make foolish or dangerous mistakes. Mill added to this argument the citation of numerous social benefits that redound indirectly but uniformly to those who grant freedom as well as those who exercise it. We all profit from the fruits of genius, he maintained, and genius, since it often involves doggedness and eccentricity, is likely to flourish only where coercive pressures toward conformity are absent. Moreover, social progress is more likely to occur where there is free criticism of prevailing ways and adventurous experiments in living. Finally, true understanding of human nature requires freedom, since without liberty there will be little diversity, and without diversity *all* aspects of the human condition will be ascribed to fixed nature rather than to the workings of a particular culture.

Such are the grounds for holding that there is always a presumption in favor of freedom, that whenever we are faced with an option between forcing a person to do something and letting him decide on his own whether or not to do it, other things being equal, we should always opt for the latter. If a strong general presumption for freedom has been established, the burden of proof rests on the shoulders of the advocate of coercion, and the philosopher's task will be to state the conditions under which the presumption can be overriden.

*   *   *

4. THE CONCEPT OF HARM

If social and political coercion is a harm-causing evil, then one way to justly it is to show that it is necessary for the prevention of even greater evils. That is the generating insight of the "harm to others principle" (henceforth called simply "the harm principle") which permits society to restrict the liberty of some persons in order

---

[2]See Edith Hamilton, *The Greek Way* (New York: W. W. Norton & Company, Inc., 1942), pp. 35 ff.

[3]John Stuart Mill, *On Liberty* (New York: Liberal Arts Press, 1956), p. 71.

to prevent harm to others. Two versions of this principle can be distinguished. The first would justify restriction of one person's liberty to prevent injury to other specific individuals, and can therefore be called "the private harm principle." The second can be invoked to justify coercion on the distinct ground that it is necessary to prevent impairment of institutional practices and regulatory systems that are in the public interest; thus it can be called "the public harm principle." That the private harm principle (whose chief advocate was J. S. Mill) states at least one of the acceptable grounds for coercion is virtually beyond controversy. Hardly anyone would deny the state the right to make criminal such directly injurious conduct as willful homicide, assault and battery, and robbery. Mill often wrote as if prevention of private harm is the *sole* valid ground for state coercion, but this must not have been his considered intention. He would not have wiped from the books such crimes as tax evasion, smuggling, and contempt of court, which need not any specific individuals, except insofar as they weaken public institutions in whose "health" we all have a stake. I shall assume that Mill held both the public and private versions of the harm principle.

In its simplest formulations, the harm principle is still a long way from being a precise guide to the ideal legislator, especially in those difficult cases where harms of different orders, magnitudes, and probabilities must be balanced against one another. Even when made fully explicit and qualified in appropriate ways, however, the unsupplemented harm principle cannot be fairly assessed until it is known precisely what is meant by "harm."

i Harm as the Invasion of an Interest

It has become common, especially in legal writings, to take the object of harm always to be an *interest*. The *Restatement of the Law of Torts* gives one sense of the term "interest" when it defines it as "anything which is the object of human desire,"[7] but this seems much too broad to be useful for our present purposes.

[7]*Restatement of the Law of Torts* (St. Paul: American Law Institute, 1939), p. 1.

A person is often said to "have an interest" in something he does not presently desire. A dose of medicine may be "in a man's interest" even when he is struggling and kicking to avoid it. In this sense, an object of an interest is "what is truly good for a person whether he desires it or not." Even interest defined in this second way may be indirectly but necessarily related to desires. The only way to argue that X is in Doe's interest even though Doe does not want X may be to show that X would effectively integrate Doe's total set of desires leading to a greater net balance of desire-fulfillment in the long run. If most of Doe's acknowledged important desires cannot be satisfied so long as he is ill, and he cannot become well unless he takes the medicine, then taking the medicine is in Doe's interest in this desire-related sense.

Legal writers classify interests in various ways. One of the more common lists "Interests of Personality," "Interests of Property," "Interest in Reputation," "Interest in Domestic Relations," and "Interest in Privacy," among others. A humanly inflicted harm is conceived as the violation of one of a person's interests, an injury to something in which he has a genuine stake. In the lawyer's usage, an interest is something a person always possesses in some condition, something that can grow and flourish or diminish and decay, but which can rarely be totally lost. Other persons can be said to promote or hinder an individual's interest in bodily health, or in the avoidance of damaging or offensive physical contacts, or in the safety and security of his person, his family, his friends, and his property. One advantage of this mode of speaking is that it permits us to appraise harms by distinguishing between more and less important interests, and between those interests which are, and those which are not, worthy of legal recognition and/or protection.

ii Harm vs. Hurt: The Role of Knowledge

Is it true that "what a person doesn't know can't *harm* him"? For most cases, this maxim certainly does *not* apply, and it is one of the merits of the "interest" analysis of harm that it explains why. Typically, having one's interests violated is one thing, and knowing that one's interests have been violated is another. The rich man is harmed at the time his home is burgled, even though he may not discover the harm for months; similarly, a soldier is harmed the moment he is wounded, though in the heat of the battle he may not discover even his serious wounds for some time. The law does not permit a burglar to plead "He will never miss it" even when that plea is true, for the crime of burglary consists in inflicting a forbidden harm, whether or not it will be discovered or will hurt. It is true that not all harms *hurt*, partly because not all harms ever come to be noticed. There may well be a relatively narrow and precise sense of "harm" in ordinary usage such that "being harmed" can be contrasted with being hurt (as well as with "being shocked" and "being offended"). However, if harm is understood as the violation of an interest, and all men have an interest in not being hurt, it follows that hurt is one species of harm. Hence, even though not all harms hurt, all hurts do harm (or more accurately, are themselves harm), and the harm principle could conceivably be used to justify coercion when it is necessary to prevent hurts, even when the hurts do not lead to any *further* harm.

There are some special cases where the maxim "What a person doesn't know can't *hurt* him" seems quite sound. In these cases, knowledge of some fact, such as the adulterous infidelities of one's spouse, is itself hurtful; indeed, the whole hurt consists in the knowledge and is inseparable from it. Here knowledge is both a necessary and sufficient condition of a hurt: What the cuckolded husband doesn't know "can't hurt him." That is not to say that he cannot be *harmed* unless he is hurt. An undetected adultery damages one of the victim's "interests in domestic relations," just as an unknown libelous publication can damage his interest in a good reputation, or an undetected trespass on his land can damage his interest in "the exclusive enjoyment and control" of that land. In all these cases, violation of the interest in question is itself a harm even though no *further* harm may result to any other interests.

The distinction between hurt and (generic) harm raises one additional question. We must include in the category of "hurts" not only physical pains but also forms of mental distress. Our question is whether, in applying the harm principle, we should permit coercion designed to prevent mental distress when the distress is not likely to be followed by hurt or harm of any other kind. Some forms of mental distress (e.g., "hurt feelings") can be ruled out simply on the ground that they are too minor or trivial to warrant interference. Others are so severe that they can lead to mental breakdowns. In such cases, however, it is the consequential harm to mental health and not the mere fact of distress that clearly warrants interference on the ground of harmfulness. Thus, a convenient criterion for determining whether a hurt is sufficiently harmful to justify preventive coercion on that ground suggests itself: the hurt is serious enough if and only if it is either a symptom of a prior or concurrent harm of another order (as a pain in an arm may be the result and sign of a broken bone), or is in itself the cause of a consequential harm (e.g., mental breakdown) of another order.

iii Harm vs. Offense

The relation of offensiveness to harmfulness can be treated in much the same way as that of hurtfulness to harmfulness. The following points can be made of both:

1. Some harms do not offend (as some do not hurt).

2. All offenses (like all hurts) are harms, inasmuch as all men have an interest in not being offended or hurt.

3. Some offenses (like some hurts) are symptoms or consequences of prior or concurrent harms.

4. Some offenses (like some hurts) are causes of subsequent harms: in the case of extreme hurt, harm to health; in the case of extreme offense, harm from provoked ill will or violence. These subsequent harms are harms of a different order, i.e., violations of interests other than the interest in not being hurt or offended.

5. Some offenses, like some hurts, are "harmless," i.e., do not lead to any *further* harm (violations of any interests other than the interest in not being hurt or offended).

6. Although offense and hurt are in themselves harms, they are harms of a relatively trivial kind (unless they are of sufficient magnitude to violate interests in health and peace).

Partly because of points 5 and 6, many writers use the word "harm" in a sense that is much narrower than "the invasion of any interest." In this narrower sense, harm is distinguished from and even contrasted with "mere offense." Some distinguish "harm to one's interests" from "offense to one's feelings" (as if there were no interest in unoffended feelings). This is a permissible, even useful, way of talking, if we agree that offensiveness as such is strictly speaking a kind of harm, but harm of such a trivial kind that it cannot by itself ever counterbalance the direct and immediate harm caused by coercion. One should appreciate how radical the harm principle is when interpreted in the strict and narrow way that excludes mere offensiveness as a relevant sort of harm. Both the British Wolfenden Report and the American Model Penal Code, for example, recognize "harmless" offensiveness as a ground for preventive coercion in some circumstances. For clarity and convenience only, I shall stipulate then that "offensiveness as such" is a proposed ground for coercion distinct from harm of the sort required by the harm principle (narrowly interpreted), so that "the offense principle" can be treated as an independent principle in its own right.

Offensive behavior is such in virtue of its capacity to induce in others any of a large miscellany of mental states that have little in common except that they are unpleasant, uncomfortable, or disliked. These states do not necessarily "hurt," as do sorrow and distress. Rather the relation between them and hurt is analogous to that between physical unpleasantness and pain, for there is also a great miscellany of unpleasant but not painful bodily states—itches, shocks, and discomforts—that have little in common except that they don't hurt but are nevertheless universally disliked. Among the main sorts of "harmless but disliked" *mental* states are irritating sensations (e.g., bad smells, cacophony, clashing colors),

disgust, shocked moral sensibilities, and shameful embarrassment.

iv Harm vs. Nonbenefit

When the harm principle is unsupplemented by any other accepted ground for coercion, it decrees that state power may not be used against one person to *benefit* another, but only to prevent harm to another. One way of coercing citizens is to force them to pay taxes in support of various state activities. A partisan of the harm principle might be expected to cast a suspicious eye on all such schemes of involuntary support. Indeed, he might argue that taxing some to educate others is to coerce some merely to benefit others, or that taxing some to provide libraries, museums, theatres, or concert halls for others is to coerce some merely to amuse, inspire, or edify others, and is therefore unjustified.[8] On the other hand, an advocate of the harm principle could with consistency *deny* the foregoing propositions if he had a different way of construing the harm-nonbenefit distinction.

One muddled way of basing the distinction between harms and mere nonbenefits is to make it correspond to that between *acting* and *omitting* to act to another's detriment.[9] That will not do for the obvious reason that it is possible to harm or to benefit another either by action or omission. In other words, both actions and omissions can be the *cause* of changes in another's condition for better or worse. If we judge that Doe's failure to save the drowning swimmer Roe was the cause of Roe's death, then we can label Doe's omission the mere "withholding of a benefit" only if we judge the loss of life itself, in the circumstances, to be the loss of a benefit rather than the incurring of a harm. If, on the other hand, loss of one's life, like loss of one's health, fortune, or loved ones, is itself a harm, then anything that causes such a loss, whether it be act, omission, or fortuitous event, causes a harm.

[8]Cf. Stephen, *Liberty, Equality, Fraternity*, p. 16.
[9]See, for example, James Barr Ames, "Law and Morals," *Harvard Law Review*, XXII (1908), pp. 97–113, and Lord Macaulay, "Notes on the Indian Penal Code," *Works* (London: Longmans, Green & Co. Ltd., 1866), Vol. VII, p. 497.

Another unsatisfactory way of basing the harm-nonbenefit distinction is to hold that being without something good is a mere non-benefit, whereas being in possession of something evil is a harm. It would follow from such a view that not learning truths is not having a good and hence not being benefited, whereas being told lies is to be in possession of something bad, and is therefore to be harmed. Thus it would follow that education is a mere benefit and its lack no harm. But surely this will not do. To be effectively deprived of all food is clearly to be harmed as much as to be given poisoned food; the upshot in each case is death. Similarly, to have hardly any knowledge of the world is to be handicapped so severely as to be harmed, though perhaps not as severely as to have imposed on one a systematic set of falsehoods. In either case the result is damage to one's vital interests. Harm, therefore, is no more linked to "positive" possessions than it is to "positive" actions. It can consist in a lack as well as a presence, just as it can be caused by an omission as well as an action.

More promising correlations, at first sight, are those between harms and unmet *needs* and between benefits and unneeded goods. We harm a man when we deny or deprive him of something he needs; we fail to benefit him (merely) when we deny or deprive him of some good he does not need. An unneeded good is something a person wants which is not necessary for his welfare, something he can do without. To receive something one wants but does not need is to benefit or profit, but not to the point where loss of the gain would be a harm. Thus, if I have an annual salary of one hundred thousand dollars, and my employer gives me a fifty thousand dollar raise, I benefit substantially from his largesse. If he fails to give me a raise, I am not so benefited, but surely not harmed either (given my needs). If he reduces me to five thousand or fires me, however, he not merely fails to benefit me, he causes me harm by withholding money I *need*. These examples suggest that a statesman or legislator who is committed to an unsupplemented harm principle must have means for distinguishing authentic human needs from mere wants, and

that his problem is little different in principle from that of the ordinary householder who must often distinguish between "luxuries" and "necessities" when he plans his household budget.

The problem is more complex, however, than these homey examples suggest. The "unmet need" analysis of harm would imply, for example, that a rich man is not harmed by a minor larceny, a conclusion we have already rejected. Still another distinction can be helpful at this point: that between *being in a harmful condition* (whatever its cause or origin) and undergoing *a change in one's condition in a harmful direction*. To deprive even a rich man of money is to damage his interests, that is, to change his condition for the worse, even though not yet to the state of actual injury. Thus, it is to "harm" him in one sense, but not in another. At best, the "unmet need" criterion is a test for determining when a damaged interest has reached the threshold of "actual injury," rather than a weathervane-indicator of harmful directions. Let us stipulate at this point, for the sake of clarity and convenience, that the harm principle be interpreted in such a way that changes in the condition of a protectable interest in harmful directions, even short of the stage of "actual injury" (unmet need), count as a kind of harm, the prevention of which, in some circumstances, may justify coercion. However, when harms have to be ranked and balanced in a given application of the harm principle, an actually injurious condition should outweigh a mere change in a harmful direction.

5. LINES OF ATTACK ON MILL

Arguments against Mill's unsupplemented harm principle (his claim that the private and public harm principles state the *only* grounds for justified interference with liberty) have been mainly of two different kinds.[10] Many have argued that the harm principle justifies too much social and political interference in

[10]Cf. H. L. A. Hart, *Law, Liberty, and Morality* (Stanford: Stanford University Press, 1963), p. 5.

the affairs of individuals. Others allow that the prevention of individual and social harm is always a ground for interference, but insist that it is by no means the only ground.

i "No Man Is an Island"

Mill maintained in *On Liberty* that social interference is never justified in those of a man's affairs that concern himself only. But no man's affairs have effects on himself alone. There are a thousand subtle and indirect ways in which every individual act, no matter how private and solitary, affects others. It would therefore seem that society has a right, on Mill's own principles, to interfere in every department of human life. Mill anticipated this objection and took certain steps to disarm it. Let it be allowed that no human conduct is entirely, exclusively, and to the last degree self-regarding. Still, Mill insisted, we can distinguish between actions that are plainly other-regarding and those that are "directly," "chiefly," or "primarily" self-regarding. There will be a twilight area of cases difficult to classify, but that is true of many other workable distinctions, including that between night and day.

It is essential to Mill's theory that we make a distinction between two different kinds of consequences of human actions: the consequences *directly* affecting the interests of others, and those of primarily self-regarding behavior which only *indirectly* or *remotely* affect the interests of others. "No person ought to be punished simply for being drunk," Mill wrote, "but a soldier or policeman should be punished for being drunk on duty."[11] A drunk policeman directly harms the interests of others. His conduct gives opportunities to criminals and thus creates grave risk of harm to other citizens. It brings the police into disrepute, and makes the work of his colleagues more dangerous. Finally, it may lead to loss of the policeman's job, with serious consequences for his wife and children.

Consider, on the other hand, a hard working bachelor who habitually spends his evening hours drinking himself into a stupor, which he then sleeps off, rising fresh in the morning to put in another hard day's work. His drinking does not *directly* affect others in any of the ways of the drunk policeman's conduct. He has no family; he drinks alone and sets no direct example; he is not prevented from discharging any of his public duties; he creates no substantial risk of harm to the interests of other individuals. Although even his private conduct will have some effects on the interests of others, these are precisely the sorts of effects Mill would call "indirect" and "remote." First, in spending his evenings the way he does, our solitary tippler is *not* doing any number of other things that might be of greater utility to others. In not earning and spending more money, he is failing to stimulate the economy (except for the liquor industry) as much as he might. Second, he fails to spend his evening time improving his talents and making himself a better person. Perhaps he has a considerable native talent for painting or poetry, and his wastefulness is depriving the world of some valuable art. Third, he may make those of his colleagues who like him sad on his behalf. Finally, to those who know of his habits, he is a "bad example."[12] All of these "indirect harms" together, Mill maintained, do not outweigh the direct and serious harm that would result from social or legal coercion.

Mill's critics have never been entirely satisfied by this. Many have pointed out that Mill is concerned not only with political coercion and legal punishment but also with purely social coercion—moral pressure, social avoidance, ostracism. No responsible critic would wish the state to punish the solitary tippler, but social coercion is another matter. We can't prevent people from disapproving of an individual for his self-regarding faults or from expressing that disapproval to others, without undue restriction on *their* freedom. Such expressions, in Mill's views, are inevitably coercive, constituting a "milder form of punishment." Hence

[11]Mill, *On Liberty*, pp. 99–100.

[12]Mill has a ready rejoinder to this last point: If the conduct in question is supposed to be greatly harmful to the actor himself, "the example, on the whole must be more salutory" than harmful socially, since it is a warning lesson, rather than an alluring model, to others. See Mill, *On Liberty*, p. 101.

"social punishment" of individuals for conduct that directly concerns only themselves—the argument concludes—is both inevitable and, according to Mill's own principles, proper.

Mill anticipated this objection, too, and tried to cope with it by making a distinction between types of social responses. We cannot help but lower in our estimation a person with serious self-regarding faults. We will think ill of him, judge him to be at fault, and make him the inevitable and proper object of our disapproval, distaste, even contempt. We may warn others about him, avoid his company, and withhold gratuitous benefits from him—"not to the oppression of his individuality but in the exercise of ours."[13] Mill concedes that all of these social responses can function as "penalties"—but they are suffered "only in so far as they are the natural and, as it were, the spontaneous consequences of the faults themselves, not because they are purposely inflicted on him for the sake of punishment."[14] Other responses, on the other hand, add something to the "natural penalties"—pointed snubbing, economic reprisals, gossip campaigns, and so on. The added penalties, according to Mill, are precisely the ones that are never justified as responses to merely self-regarding flaws—"if he displeases us, we may express our distaste; and we may stand aloof from a person as well as from a thing that displeases us, but we shall not therefore feel called on to make his life uncomfortable."[15]

ii Other Proposed Grounds for Coercion

The distinction between self-regarding and other-regarding behavior, as Mill intended it to be understood, does seem at least roughly serviceable, and unlikely to invite massive social interference in private affairs. I think most critics of Mill would grant that, but reject the harm principle on the opposite ground that it doesn't permit enough interference. These writers would allow at least one, and as many as five or more, additional valid grounds for coercion. Each of these proposed grounds is

stated in a principle listed below. One might hold that restriction of one person's liberty can be justified:

1. To prevent harm to others, either
   a. injury to individual persons (*The Private Harm Principle*), or
   b. impairment of institutional practices that are in the public interest (*The Public Harm Principle*);
2. To prevent offense to others (*The Offense Principle*);
3. To prevent harm to self (*Legal Paternalism*);
4. To prevent or punish sin, i.e., to "enforce morality as such" (*Legal Moralism*);
5. To benefit the self (*Extreme Paternalism*);
6. To benefit others (*The Welfare Principle*).

The liberty-limiting principles on this list are best understood as stating neither necessary nor sufficient conditions for justified coercion, but rather specifications of the *kinds* of reasons that are always relevant or acceptable in support of proposed coercion, even though in a given case they may not be conclusive.[16] Each principle states that interference might be permissible *if* (but not *only if*) a certain condition is satisfied. Hence the principles are not mutually exclusive; it is possible to hold two or more of them at once, even all of them together, and it is possible to deny all of them. Moreover, the principles cannot be construed as stating sufficient conditions for legitimate interference with liberty, for even though the principle is satisfied in a given case, the general presumption against coercion might not be outweighed. The harm principle, for example, does not justify state interference to prevent a tiny bit of inconsequential harm. Prevention of minor harm always counts in favor of proposals (as in a legislature) to restrict liberty, but in a given instance it might not count *enough* to outweigh the general presumption against interference, or it might be

---

[13]Mill, *On Liberty*, p. 94.
[14]Mill, *On Liberty*, p. 95.
[15]Mill, *On Liberty*, p. 96.

[16]I owe this point to Professor Michael Bayles. See his contribution to *Issues in Law and Morality*, ed. Norman Care and Thomas Trelogan (Cleveland: The Press of Case Western Reserve University, 1973).

outweighed by the prospect of practical difficulties in enforcing the law, excessive costs, and forfeitures of privacy. A liberty-limiting principle states considerations that are always good reasons for coercion, though neither exclusively nor, in every case, decisively good reasons.

It will not be possible to examine each principle in detail here, and offer "proofs" and "refutations." The best way to defend one's selection of principles is to show to which positions they commit one on such issues as censorship of literature, "morals offenses," and compulsory social security programs. General principles arise in the course of deliberations over particular problems, especially in the efforts to defend one's judgments by showing that they are consistent with what has gone before. If a principle commits one to an antecedently unacceptable judgment, then one has to modify or supplement the principle in a way that does the least damage to the harmony of one's particular and general opinions taken as a group. On the other hand, when a solid, well-entrenched principle entails a change in a particular judgment, the overriding claims of consistency may require that the judgment be adjusted. This sort of dialectic is similar to the reasonings that are prevalent in law courts. When similar cases are decided in opposite ways, it is incumbent on the court to distinguish them in some respect that will reconcile the separate decisions with each other and with the common rule applied to each. Every effort is made to render current decisions consistent with past ones unless the precedents seem so disruptive of the overall internal harmony of the law that they must, reluctantly, be revised or abandoned. In social and political philosophy every person is on his own, and the counterparts to "past decisions" are the most confident judgments one makes in ordinary normative discourse. The philosophical task is to extract from these "given" judgments the principles that render them consistent, adjusting and modifying where necessary in order to convert the whole body of opinions into an intelligible, coherent system. There is no a priori way of refuting another's political opinions, but if our opponents are rational men committed to the ideal of consistency, we can always hope to show them that a given judgment is inconsistent with one of their own acknowledged principles. Then something will have to give.

Hard Cases for the Harm Principle

Joel Feinberg

1. MORALS OFFENSES AND LEGAL MORALISM

Immoral conduct is no trivial thing, and we should hardly expect societies to tolerate it; yet if men are *forced* to refrain from immorality, their own choices will play very little role in what they do, so that they can hardly develop critical judgment and moral traits of a genuinely praiseworthy kind. Thus legal enforcement of morality seems to pose a dilemma. The problem does not arise if we assume that all immoral conduct is socially harmful, for immoral conduct will then be prohibited by law not just to punish sin or to "force men to be moral," but rather to prevent harm to others. If, however, there are forms of immorality that do not necessarily cause harm, "the problem of the enforcement of morality" becomes especially acute.

The central problem cases are those criminal actions generally called "morals offenses." Offenses against morality and decency have long constituted a category of crimes (as distinct from offenses against the person, offenses against property, and so on). These have included mainly sex offenses, such as adultery, fornication, sodomy, incest, and prostitution, but also a miscellany of nonsexual offenses, including cruelty to animals, desecration of the flag or other venerated symbols, and mistreatment of corpses. In a useful article,[1] Louis B. Schwartz maintains that what sets these crimes off as a class is not their special relation to morality (murder is also an offense against morality, but it is not a "morals offense") but the lack of an essential connection between them and social harm. In particular, their suppression is not required by the public security. Some morals offenses may harm the perpetrators themselves, but the risk of harm of this sort has usually been consented to in advance by the actors. Offense to other parties, when it occurs, is usually a consequence of perpetration of the offenses in *public*, and can be prevented by statutes against "open lewdness," or "solicitation" in public places. That still leaves "morals offenses" committed by consenting adults in private. Should they really be crimes?

In addition to the general presumption against coercion, other arguments against legislation prohibiting private and harmless sexual practices are drawn from the harm principle itself; laws governing private affairs are extremely awkward and expensive to enforce, and have side effects that are invariably harmful. Laws against homosexuality, for example, can only be occasionally and randomly enforced, and this leads to the inequities of selective enforcement and opportunities for blackmail and private vengeance. Moreover, "the pursuit of homosexuals involves policemen in degrading entrapment practices, and diverts attention and effort"[2] from more serious (harmful) crimes of aggression, fraud, and corruption.

These considerations have led some to argue against statutes that prohibit private immorality, but, not surprisingly, it has encouraged others to abandon their exclusive reliance on the harm and/or offense principles, at least in the case of morals offenses. The alternative principle of "legal moralism" has several forms. In its more moderate version it is commonly associated with the views of Patrick Devlin,[3] whose theory, as I understand it, is really an application of the public harm principle. The proper aim of criminal law, he agrees, is the prevention of harm, not merely to individuals, but also (and primarily) to society itself. A shared moral code, Devlin argues, is a necessary condition for the very existence of a community. Shared moral convictions function as "invisible bonds" tying individuals together into an orderly society. Moreover, the fundamental unifying morality (to switch the metaphor) is a kind of "seamless web";[4] to damage it at one point is to weaken it throughout. Hence, society has as much right to protect its moral code by legal coercion as it does to protect its equally indispensable political institutions. The law cannot tolerate politically revolutionary activity, nor can it accept activity that rips assunder its moral fabric. "The suppression of vice is as much the law's business as the suppression of subversive activities; it is no more possible to define a sphere of private morality than it is to define one of private subversive activity."[5]

H.L.A. Hart finds it plausible that some shared morality is necessary to the existence of a community, but criticizes Devlin's further contention "that a society is identical with its morality as that is at any given moment of its history, so that a change in its morality is tantamount to

[1]Louis B. Schwartz, "Morals Offenses and the Model Penal Code," *Columbia Law Review*, LXIII (1963), 669 ff.

[2]Schwartz, "Morals Offenses and the Model Penal Code," 671.

[3]Patrick Devlin, *The Enforcement of Morality* (London: Oxford University Press, 1965).

[4]The phrase is not Devlin's but that of his critic, H.L.A. Hart, in *Law, Liberty, and Morality* (Stanford: Stanford University Press, 1963), p. 51. In his rejoinder to Hart, Devlin writes: "Seamlessness presses the simile rather hard but apart from that, I should say that for most people morality is a web of beliefs rather than a number of unconnected ones." Devlin, *The Enforcement of Morality*, p. 115.

[5]Devlin, *The Enforcement of Morality*, pp. 13–14.

the destruction of a society."[6] Indeed, a moral critic might admit that we can't exist as a society without some morality, while insisting that we can perfectly well exist without *this* morality (if we put a better one in its place). Devlin seems to reply that the shared morality *can* be changed even though protected by law, and, when it does change, the emergent reformed morality in turn deserves *its* legal protection.[7] The law then functions to make moral reform difficult, but there is no preventing change where reforming zeal is fierce enough. How does one bring about a change in prevailing moral beliefs when they are enshrined in law? Presumably by advocating conduct which is in fact illegal, by putting into public practice what one preaches, and by demonstrating one's sincerity by marching proudly off to jail for one's convictions:

> there is . . . a natural respect for opinions that are sincerely held. When such opinions accumulate enough weight, the law must either yield or it is broken. In a democratic society . . . there will be a strong tendency for it to yield—not to abandon all defenses so as to let in the horde, but to give ground to those who are prepared to fight for something that they prize. To fight may be to suffer. A willingness to suffer is the most convincing proof of sincerity. Without the law there would be no proof. The law is the anvil on which the hammer strikes.[8]

In this remarkable passage, Devlin has discovered another argument for enforcing "morality as such," and incidentally for principled civil disobedience as the main technique for initiating and regulating moral change. A similar argument, deriving from Samuel Johnson and applying mainly to changes in religious doctrine, was well known to Mill. According to this theory, religious innovators deserve to be persecuted, for persecution allows them to prove their mettle and demonstrate their disinterested good faith, while their teachings, insofar as they are true, cannot be hurt, since truth will always triumph in the end. Mill held this method of testing truth, whether in science, religion, or morality, to be both uneconomical and ungenerous.[9] But if self-sacrificing civil disobedience is *not* the most efficient and humane remedy for the moral reformer, what instruments of moral change are available to him? This question is not only difficult to answer in its own right, it is also the rock that sinks Devlin's favorite analogy between "harmless" immorality and political subversion.

Consider the nature of subversion. Most modern law-governed countries have a constitution, a set of duly constituted authorities, and a body of statutes created and enforced by these authorities. The ways of changing these things will be well known, orderly, and permitted by the constitution. For example, constitutions are amended, legislators are elected, and new legislation is introduced. On the other hand, it is easy to conceive of various sorts of unpermitted and disorderly change—through assassination and violent revolution, or bribery and subornation, or the use of legitimately won power to extort and intimidate. Only these illegitimate methods of change can be called "subversion." But here the analogy between positive law and positive morality begins to break down. There is no "moral constitution," no well-known and orderly way of introducing moral legislation to duly constituted moral legislators, no clear convention of majority rule. Moral subversion, if there is such a thing, must consist in the employment of disallowed techniques of change instead of the officially permitted "constitutional" ones. It consists not simply of change as such, but of illegitimate change. Insofar as the notion of legitimately induced moral change remains obscure, illegitimate moral change is no better. Still, there is enough content to both notions to preserve some analogy to the political case. A citizen works *legitimately* to change public moral beliefs when he openly and forthrightly expresses his own dissent, when he attempts to argue,

---

[6]Hart, *Law, Liberty, and Morality*, p. 51.
[7]Devlin, *The Enforcement of Morality*, pp. 115 ff.
[8]Devlin, *The Enforcement of Morality*, p. 116.

[9]John Stuart Mill, *On Liberty* (New York: Liberal Arts Press, 1956) pp. 33–34.

persuade, and offer reasons, and when he lives according to his own convictions with persuasive quiet and dignity, neither harming others nor offering counterpersuasive offense to tender sensibilities. A citizen attempts to change mores by *illegitimate* means when he abandons argument and example for force and fraud. If this is the basis of the distinction between legitimate and illegitimate techniques of moral change, then the use of state power to affect moral belief *one way or the other,* when harmfulness is not involved, is a clear example of illegitimacy. Government enforcement of the conventional code is not to be called "moral subversion," of course, because it is used on behalf of the status quo; but whether conservative or innovative, it is equally in defiance of our "moral constitution" (if anything is).

The second version of legal moralism is the pure version, not some other principle in disguise. Enforcement of morality as such and the attendant punishment of sin are not justified as means to some further social aim (such as preservation of social cohesiveness) but are ends in themselves. Perhaps J. F. Stephen was expressing this pure moralism when he wrote that "there are acts of wickedness so gross and outrageous that . . . [protection of others apart], they must be prevented at any cost to the offender and punished if they occur with exemplary severity."[10] From his examples it is clear that Stephen had in mind the very acts that are called "morals offenses" in the law.

It is sometimes said in support of pure legal moralism that the world as a whole would be a better place without morally ugly, even "harmlessly immoral," conduct, and that our actual universe is intrinsically worse for having such conduct in it. The threat of punishment, the argument continues, deters such conduct. Actual instances of punishment not only back up the threat, and thus help keep future moral weeds out of the universe's garden, they also erase past evils from the universe's temporal record by "nullifying" them, or making it as if they never were. Thus punishment, it is said,

contributes to the intrinsic value of the universe in two ways: by canceling out past sins and preventing future ones.[11]

There is some plausibility in this view when it is applied to ordinary harmful crimes, especially those involving duplicity or cruelty, which really do seem to "set the universe out of joint." It is natural enough to think of repentance, apology, or forgiveness as "setting things straight," and of punishment as a kind of "payment" or a wiping clean of the moral slate. But in cases where it is natural to resort to such analogies, there is not only a rule infraction, there is also a *victim*—some person or society of persons who have been harmed. Where there is no victim—and especially where there is no profit at the expense of another—"setting things straight" has no clear intuitive content.

Punishment may yet play its role in discouraging harmless private immoralities for the sake of "the universe's moral record." But if fear of punishment is to keep people from illicit intercourse (or from desecrating flags, or mistreating corpses) in the privacy of their own rooms, then morality shall have to be enforced with a fearsome efficiency that shows no respect for individual privacy. If private immoralities are to be deterred by threat of punishment, the detecting authorities must be able to look into the hidden chambers and locked rooms of anyone's private domicile. When we put this massive forfeiture of privacy into the balance along with the usual costs of coercion—loss of spontaneity, stunting of rational powers, anxiety, hypocrisy, and the rest—the price of securing mere outward conformity to the community's moral standards (for that is all that can be achieved by the penal law) is exorbitant.

Perhaps the most interesting of the nonsexual morals offenses, and the most challenging case for application of liberty-limiting principles, is cruelty to animals. Suppose that

[10]James Fitzjames Stephen, *Liberty, Equality, Fraternity* (London: 1873), p. 163.

[11]Cf. C. D. Broad, "Certain Features in Moore's Ethical Doctrines," in P. A. Schilpp. *The Philosophy of G. E. Moore* (Evanston, Ill.: Northwestern University Press, 1942), pp. 48 ff.

John Doe is an intelligent, sensitive person with one very severe neurotic trait—he loves to see living things suffer pain. Fortunately, he never has occasion to torture human beings (he would genuinely regret that), for he can always find an animal for the purpose. For a period he locks himself in his room every night, draws the blind, and then beats and tortures a dog to death. The sounds of shrieks and moans, which are music to his ears, are nuisances to his neighbors, and when his landlady discovers what he has been doing she is so shocked she has to be hospitalized. Distressed that he has caused harm to human beings, Doe leaves the rooming house, buys a five hundred acre ranch, and moves into a house in the remote, unpopulated center of his own property. There, in the perfect privacy of his own home, he spends every evening maiming, torturing, and beating to death his own animals.

What are we to say of Doe's bizarre behavior? We have three alternatives. First we can say that it is perfectly permissible since it consists simply in a man's destruction of his own property. How a man disposes in private of his own property is no concern of anyone else providing he causes no nuisance such as loud noises and evil smells. Second, we can say that this behavior is patently immoral even though it causes no harm to the interests of anyone other than the actor; further, since it obviously should *not* be permitted by the law, this is a case where the harm principle is inadequate and must be supplemented by legal moralism. Third, we can extend the harm principle to animals, and argue that the law can interfere with the private enjoyment of property not to enforce "morality as such," but rather to prevent harm to the animals. The third alternative is the most inviting, but not without its difficulties. We *must* control animal movements, exploit animal labor, and, in many cases, deliberately slaughter animals. All these forms of treatment would be "harm" if inflicted on human beings, but cannot be allowed to count as harm to animals if the harm principle is to be extended to them in a realistic way. The best compromise is to recognize one supreme interest of animals, namely the interest in freedom from cruelly or wantonly inflicted pain, and to count as "harm" all and only invasions of *that* interest.

2. OBSCENITY AND THE OFFENSE PRINCIPLE

Up to this point we have considered the harm and offense principles together in order to determine whether between them they are sufficient to regulate conventional immoralities, or whether they need help from a further independent principle, legal moralism. Morals offenses were treated as essentially private so that the offense principle could not be stretched to apply to them. Obscene literature and pornographic displays would appear to be quite different in this respect. Both are materials deliberately published for the eyes of others, and their existence can bring partisans of the unsupplemented harm principle into direct conflict with those who endorse *both* the harm and offense principles.

In its untechnical, prelegal sense, the word "obscenity" refers to material dealing with nudity, sex, or excretion in an offensive manner. Such material becomes obscene in the legal sense when, because of its offensiveness or for some other reason [this question had best be left open in the definition], it is or ought to be without legal protection. The legal definition then incorporates the everyday sense, and essential to both is the requirement that the material be *offensive*. An item may offend one person and not another. "Obscenity," if it is to avoid this subjective relativity, must involve an interpersonal objective sense of "offensive." Material must be offensive by prevailing community standards that are public and well known, or be such that it is apt to offend virtually everyone.

Not all material that is generally offensive need also be harmful in any sense recognized by the harm principle. It is partly an empirical question whether reading or witnessing obscene material causes social harm; reliable evidence, even of a statistical kind, of causal connections between obscenity and antisocial behavior is extremely hard to find.[12] In the absence of clear and decisive evidence of harmfulness, the American Civil Liberties Union insists that the offensiveness of obscene material cannot be a sufficient ground for its repression:

> . . . the question in a case involving obscenity, just as in every case involving an attempted restriction upon free speech, is whether the words or pictures are used in such circumstances and are of such a nature as to create a clear and present danger that they will bring about a substantial evil that the state has a right to prevent. . . . We believe that under the current state of knowledge, there is grossly insufficient evidence to show that obscenity brings about *any* substantive evil.[13]

The A.C.L.U. argument employs *only* the harm principle among liberty-limiting principles, and treats literature, drama, and painting as forms of expression subject to the same rules as expressions of opinion. In respect to both types of expression, "every act of deciding what should be barred carries with it a danger to the community."[14] The suppression itself is an evil to the author who is squelched. The power to censor and punish involves risks that socially valuable material will be repressed along with the "filth." The overall effect of suppression, the A.C.L.U. concludes, is almost certainly to discourage nonconformist and eccentric expression generally. In order to override these serious risks, there must be in a given case an even more clear and present danger that the obscene material, if not squelched, will cause even greater harm; such countervailing evidence is never forthcoming. (If such evidence were to accumulate, the A.C.L.U. would be perfectly willing to change its position on obscenity.)

The A.C.L.U. stand on obscenity seems clearly to be the position dictated by the unsupplemented harm principle and its corollary, the clear and present danger test. Is there any reason at this point to introduce the offense principle into the discussion? Unhappily, we may be forced to if we are to do justice to all of our particular intuitions in the most harmonious way. Consider an example suggested by Professor Schwartz. By the provisions of the new Model Penal Code, he writes, "a rich homosexual may not use a billboard on Times Square to promulgate to the general populace the techniques and pleasures of sodomy."[15] If the notion of "harm" is restricted to its narrow sense, that is, contrasted with "offense," it will be hard to reconstruct a rationale for this prohibition based on the harm principle. There is unlikely to be evidence that a lurid and obscene public poster in Times Square would create a clear and present danger of injury to those who fail to avert their eyes in time as they come blinking out of the subway stations. Yet it will be surpassingly difficult for even the most dedicated liberal to advocate freedom of expression in a case of this kind. Hence, if we are to justify coercion in this case, we will likely be driven, however reluctantly, to the offense principle.

There is good reason to be "reluctant" to embrace the offense principle until driven to it by an example like the above. People take perfectly genuine offense at many socially useful or harmless activities, from commercial advertisements to inane chatter. Moreover, widespread irrational prejudices can lead people to be disgusted, shocked, even morally repelled by perfectly innocent activities, and we should be loath to permit their groundless repugnance to override the innocence. The offense principle, therefore, must be formulated very precisely and applied in accordance with carefully formulated standards so as not to open the door to wholesale and intuitively unwarranted repression. At the very least we should require that the prohibited conduct or material be of the sort apt to offend almost everybody, and not just some shifting majority or special interest group.

---

[12]There have been some studies made, but the results have been inconclusive. See the *Report of the Federal Commission on Obscenity and Pornography* (New York: Bantam Books, 1970), pp. 169–308.

[13]*Obscenity and Censorship* (Pamphlet published by the American Civil Liberties Union, New York, March, 1963), p. 7.

[14]*Obscenity and Censorship*, p. 4.

[15]Schwartz, "Morals Offenses and the Penal Code," 680.

It is instructive to note that a strictly drawn offense principle would not only justify prohibition of conduct and pictured conduct that is in its inherent character repellent, but also conduct and pictured conduct that is inoffensive in itself but offensive in inappropriate circumstances. I have in mind so-called indecencies such as public nudity. One can imagine an advocate of the unsupplemented harm principle arguing against the public nudity prohibition on the grounds that the sight of a naked body does no one any harm, and the state has no right to impose standards of dress or undress on private citizens. How one chooses to dress, after all, is a form of self-expression. If we do not permit the state to bar clashing colors or bizarre hair styles, by what right does it prohibit total undress? Perhaps the sight of naked people could at first lead to riots or other forms of antisocial behavior, but that is precisely the sort of contingency for which we have police. If we don't take away a person's right of free speech for the reason that its exercise may lead others to misbehave, we cannot in consistency deny his right to dress or undress as he chooses for the same reason.

There may be no answering this challenge on its own ground, but the offense principle provides a ready rationale for the nudity prohibition. The sight of nude bodies in public places is for almost everyone acutely *embarrassing*. Part of the explanation no doubt rests on the fact that nudity has an irresistible power to draw the eye and focus the thoughts on matters that are normally repressed. The conflict between these attracting and repressing forces is exciting, upsetting, and anxiety-producing. In some persons it will create at best a kind of painful turmoil, and at worst that experience of exposure to oneself of "peculiarly sensitive, intimate, vulnerable aspects of the self"[16] which is called *shame*. "One's feeling is involuntarily exposed openly in one's face; one is uncovered . . . taken by surprise . . . made a fool of."[17]

[16]Helen Merrill Lynd, *On Shame and the Search for Identity* (New York: Science Editions, Inc., 1961), p. 33.
[17]Lynd, *On Shame and the Search for Identity*, p. 32.

The result is not mere "offense," but a kind of psychic jolt that in many normal people can be a painful wound. Even those of us who are better able to control our feelings might well resent the *nuisance* of having to do so.

If we are to accept the offense principle as a supplement to the harm principle, we must accept two corollaries which stand in relation to it similarly to the way in which the clear and present danger test stands to the harm principle. The first, the *standard of universality*, has already been touched upon. For the offensiveness (disgust, embarrassment, outraged sensibilities, or shame) to be sufficient to warrant coercion, it should be the reaction that could be expected from almost any person chosen at random from the nation as a whole, regardless of sect, faction, race, age, or sex. The second is the *standard of reasonable avoidability*. No one has a right to protection from the state against offensive experiences if he can effectively avoid those experiences with no unreasonable effort or inconvenience. If a nude person enters a public bus and takes a seat near the front, there may be no effective way for other patrons to avoid intensely shameful embarrassment (or other insupportable feelings) short of leaving the bus, which would be an unreasonable inconvenience. Similarly, obscene remarks over a loudspeaker, homosexual billboards in Times Square, and pornographic handbills thrust into the hands of passing pedestrians all fail to be reasonably avoidable.

On the other hand, the offense principle, properly qualified, can give no warrant to the suppression of *books* on the grounds of obscenity. When printed words hide decorously behind covers of books sitting passively on bookstore shelves, their offensiveness is easily avoided. The contrary view is no doubt encouraged by the common comparison of obscenity with "smut," "filth," or "dirt." This in turn suggests an analogy to nuisance law, which governs cases where certain activities create loud noises or terrible odors offensive to neighbors, and "the courts must weigh the gravity of the nuisance [substitute "offense"] to the neighbors against the social utility [substitute "redeeming social value"] of the defendant's conduct."[18] There is, however, one vitiating disanalogy in this comparison. In the case of "dirty books" the offense is easily avoidable. There is nothing like the evil smell of rancid garbage oozing right out through the covers of a book. When an "obscene" book sits on a shelf, who is there to be offended? Those who want to read it for the sake of erotic stimulation presumably will not be offended (or else they wouldn't read it), and those who choose not to read it will have no experience by which to be offended. If its covers are too decorous, some innocents may browse through it by mistake and be offended by what they find, but they need only close the book to escape the offense. Even this offense, minimal as it is, could be completely avoided by prior consultation of trusted book reviewers. I conclude that there are no sufficient grounds derived either from the harm or offense principles for suppressing obscene literature, unless that ground be the protection of children; but I can think of no reason why restrictions on sales to children cannot work as well for printed materials as they do for cigarettes and whiskey.

3. LEGAL PATERNALISM*

The liberty-limiting principle called legal paternalism justifies state coercion to protect individuals from self-inflicted harm, or, in its extreme version, to guide them, whether they like it or not, toward their own good. Parents can be expected to justify interference in the lives of their children (e.g., telling them what they must eat and when they must sleep) on the ground that "daddy knows best." Legal paternalism seems to imply that, since the state often perceives the interests of individual citizens better than do the citizens themselves, it stands as a permanent guardian of those interests *in loco parentis*. Put this bluntly, paternalism

seems a preposterous doctrine. If adults are treated as children they will come in time to be like children. Deprived of the right to choose for themselves, they will soon lose the power of rational judgment and decision. Even children, after a certain point, had better not be "treated as children," or they will never acquire the outlook and capability of responsible adults.

Yet if we reject paternalism entirely, and deny that a person's own good is ever a valid ground for coercing him, we seem to fly in the face both of common sense and long-established customs and laws. In the criminal law, for example, a prospective victim's freely granted consent is no defense to the charge of mayhem or homicide. The state simply refuses to permit anyone to agree to his own disablement or killing. The law of contracts similarly refuses to recognize as valid contracts to sell oneself into slavery, or to become a mistress, or a second wife. Any ordinary citizen is legally justified in using reasonable force to prevent another from mutilating himself or committing suicide. No one is allowed to purchase certain drugs even for therapeutic purposes without a physician's prescription (doctor knows best). The use of other drugs, such as heroin, for mere pleasure is not permitted under any circumstances. It is hard to find any convincing rationale for all such restrictions apart from the argument that beatings, mutilations, death, concubinage, slavery, and bigamy are always bad for a person whether he or she knows it or not, and that antibiotics are too dangerous for any nonexpert, and narcotics for anyone at all, to take on his own initiative.

The trick is stopping short once one undertakes this path, unless we wish to ban whiskey, cigarettes, and fried foods, which tend to be bad for people, too. We must somehow reconcile our general repugnance for paternalism with the apparent necessity, or at least reasonableness, of some paternalistic regulations. The way to do this is to find mediating maxims or standards of application for the paternalistic principle which restrict its use in a way analogous to that in which the universality and reasonable avoidance tests delimit the offense principle. Let us begin by rejecting

---

[18]William L. Prosser, *Handbook of the Law of Torts* (St. Paul: West Publishing Co., 1955), p. 411.

*This section reprinted from my "Legal Paternalism" in Volume I, no. 1 of the *Canadian Journal of Philosophy* (1971), by permission of the Canadian Association for Publishing in Philosophy.

the views that the protection of a person from himself is *always* a valid ground for interference and that it is *never* a valid ground. It follows that it is a valid ground only under certain conditions, which we must now try to state.

It will be useful to make some preliminary distinctions. The first is between those cases in which a person directly produces harm to himself (where the harm is the certain and desired end of his conduct), and those cases in which a person simply creates a *risk* of harm to himself in the course of activities directed toward other ends. The man who knowingly swallows a lethal dose of arsenic will certainly die, and death must be imputed as his goal. Another man is offended by the sight of his left hand, so he grasps an ax in his right hand and chops his left hand off. He does not thereby "endanger" his interest in the physical integrity of his limbs, or "risk" the loss of his hand; he brings about the loss directly and deliberately. On the other hand, to smoke cigarettes or to drive at excessive speeds is not to harm oneself directly, but rather to increase beyond a normal level the probability that harm to oneself will result.

The second distinction is that between reasonable and unreasonable risks. There is no form of activity (or inactivity, for that matter) that does not involve some risks. On some occasions we have a choice between more and less risky actions, and prudence dictates that we take the less risky course. However, what is called "prudence" is not always reasonable. Sometimes it is more reasonable to assume a great risk for a great gain than to play it safe and forfeit a unique opportunity. Thus, it is not necessarily more reasonable for a coronary patient to increase his life expectancy by living a life of quiet inactivity than to continue working hard at his career in the hope of achieving something important, even at the risk of a sudden fatal heart attack. Although there is no simple mathematical formula to guide one in making such decisions or for judging them "reasonable" or "unreasonable," there are some decisions that are manifestly unreasonable. It is unreasonable to drive at sixty miles an hour through a twenty mile an hour zone in order to

arrive at a party on time, but it may be reasonable to drive fifty miles an hour to get a pregnant wife to the maternity ward. It is foolish to resist an armed robber in an effort to protect one's wallet, but it may be worth a desperate lunge to protect one's very life.

All of these cases involve a number of distinct considerations. If there is time to deliberate one should consider: (1) the degree of probability that harm to oneself will result from a given course of action, (2) the seriousness of the harm being risked, i.e., "the value or importance of that which is exposed to the risk," (3) the degree of probability that the goal inclining one to shoulder the risk will in fact result from the course of action, (4) the value or importance of achieving that goal, that is, just how worthwhile it is to one (this is the intimately personal factor, requiring a decision about one's own preferences, that makes it so difficult for the outsider to judge the reasonableness of a risk), and (5) the necessity of the risk, that is, the availability or absence of alternative, less risky, means to the desired goal.[19]

Certain judgments about the reasonableness of risk assumptions are quite uncontroversial. We can say, for example, that the greater are considerations 1 and 2, the less reasonable the risk, and the greater are considerations 3, 4, and 5, the more reasonable the risk. But in a given difficult case, even where questions of "probability" are meaningful and beyond dispute, and where all the relevant facts are known, the risk decision may defy objective assessment because of its component personal value judgments. In any case, if the state is to be given the right to prevent a person from risking harm to himself (and only himself), it must not be on the ground that the prohibited action is risky, or even extremely risky, but rather that the risk is extreme and, in respect to its objectively assessable components, manifestly unreasonable. There are sometimes very good reasons for regarding even a person's judgment of personal worthwhileness

[19]The distinctions in this paragraph have been borrowed from Henry T. Terry, "Negligence." *Harvard Law Review*, XXIX (1915), pp. 40–50.

(consideration 4) to be "manifestly unreasonable," but it remains to be seen whether (or when) that kind of unreasonableness can be sufficient grounds for interference.

The third and final distinction is between fully voluntary and not fully voluntary assumptions of a risk. One assumes a risk in a fully voluntary way when one shoulders it while informed of all relevant facts and contingencies, and in the absence of all coercive pressure or compulsion. To whatever extent there is neurotic compulsion, misinformation, excitement or impetuousness, clouded judgment (as, e.g., from alcohol), or immature or defective faculties of reasoning, the choice falls short of perfect voluntariness.[20] Voluntariness, then, is a matter of degree. One's "choice" is *completely involuntary* when it is no choice at all, properly speaking—when one lacks all muscular control of one's movements, or is knocked down or sent reeling by a blow or an explosion—or when, through ignorance, one chooses something other than what one means to choose, as when one thinks the arsenic powder is table salt and sprinkles it on one's scrambled eggs. Most harmful choices, as most choices generally, fall somewhere between the extremes of perfect voluntariness and complete involuntariness.

The central thesis of Mill and other individualists about paternalism is that the fully voluntary choice or consent (to another's doing) of a mature and rational human being concerning matters that directly affect only his own interests is so precious that no one else (especially the state) has a right to interfere with it simply for the person's "own good." No doubt this thesis was also meant to apply to almost-but-not-quite fully voluntary choices as well, and probably even to some substantially nonvoluntary ones (e.g., a neurotic person's choice of a wife who will satisfy his neurotic needs. but only at the price of great unhappiness, eventual divorce, and exacerbated

guilt). However, it is not probable that the individualist thesis was meant to apply to choices near the bottom of the voluntariness scale, and Mill himself left no doubt that he did not intend it to apply to completely involuntary "choices." Neither should we expect antipaternalistic individualism to deny protection to a person from his own nonvoluntary choices, for insofar as the choices are not voluntary they are just as alien to him as the choices of someone else.

Thus Mill would permit the state to protect a man from his own ignorance, at least in circumstances that create a strong presumption that his uninformed or misinformed choice would not correspond to his eventual enlightened one.

> If either a public officer or anyone else saw a person attempting to cross a bridge which had been ascertained to be unsafe, and there were no time to warn him of his danger, they might seize him and turn him back, without any real infringement of his liberty; for liberty consists in doing what one desires, and he does not desire to fall into the river.[21]

Of course, for all the public officer may know, the man on the bridge does desire to fall into the river, or to take the risk of falling for other purposes. Then, Mill argues, if the person is fully warned of the danger and wishes to proceed anyway, that is his business alone, despite the advance presumption that most people do not wish to run such risks. Hence the officer was justified, Mill would argue, in his original interference.

On other occasions a person may need to be protected from some other condition that may render his informed choice substantially less than voluntary. He may be "a child, or delirious, or in some state of excitement or absorption incompatible with the full use of the reflecting faculty."[22] Mill would not permit any such person to cross an objectively unsafe

---

[20]My usage of the term "voluntary" differs from that of Aristotle in his famous analysis in Book III of the *Nicomachean Ethics*, but corresponds closely to what Aristotle called "deliberate choice."

[21]Mill, *On Liberty*, p. 117.

[22]Mill, *On Liberty*, p. 117.

bridge. On the other hand, there is no reason why a child, or an excited person, or a drunkard, or a mentally ill person should not be allowed to proceed on his way home across a perfectly safe thoroughfare. Even substantially nonvoluntary choices deserve protection unless there is good reason to judge them dangerous.

For all we can know, the behavior of a drunk or an emotionally upset person would be exactly the same even if he were sober and calm. But when the behavior seems patently self-damaging and is of a sort in which most calm and normal persons would not engage, then there are strong grounds, if only of a statistical sort, for inferring the opposite; these grounds, on Mill's principle, would justify interference. It may be that there is no kind of action of which it can be said, "No mentally competent adult in a calm, attentive mood, fully informed, and so on, would ever choose (or consent to) that." Nevertheless, there are some actions that create a powerful presumption that an actor in his right mind would not choose them. The point of calling this hypothesis a "presumption" is to require that it be completely overridden before legal permission be given to a person who has already been interfered with to go on as before. For example, if a policeman (or anyone else) sees John Doe about to chop off his hand with an ax, he is perfectly justified in using force to prevent him, because of the presumption that no one could voluntarily choose to do such a thing. The presumption, however, should always be taken as rebuttable in principle; it will be up to Doe to prove before an official tribunal that he is calm, competent, and free, and still wishes to chop off his hand. Perhaps this is too great a burden to expect Doe himself to "prove," but the tribunal should require that the presumption against voluntariness be overturned by evidence from some source or other. The existence of the presumption should require that an objective determination be made, whether by the usual adversary procedures of law courts, or simply by a collective investigation by the tribunal into the available facts. The greater the presumption to be overridden, the more elaborate and fastidious should be the legal paraphernalia

required, and the stricter the standards of evidence. The point of the procedure would not be to evaluate the wisdom or worthiness of a person's choice, but rather to determine whether the choice really is his.

This seems to lead us to a form of paternalism so weak and innocuous that it could be accepted even by Mill, namely, that the state has the right to prevent self-regarding harmful conduct only when it is substantially nonvoluntary, or when temporary intervention is necessary to establish whether it is voluntary or not. A strong presumption that no normal person would voluntarily choose or consent to the kind of conduct in question should be a proper ground for detaining the person until the voluntary character of his choice can be established. We can use the phrase "the standard of voluntariness" as a label for considerations that mediate application of the principle that a person can be protected from his own folly.

Consider a typical hard case for the application of the voluntariness standard, the problem of harmful drugs. Suppose that Richard Roe requests a prescription of drug X from Dr. Doe, and the following discussion ensues:

Dr. Doe: I cannot prescribe drug X to you because it will do you physical harm.

Mr. Roe: But you are mistaken. It will not cause me physical harm.

In a case like this, the state, of course, backs the doctor, since it deems medical questions to be technical matters subject to expert opinions. If a layman disagrees with a physician on a question of medical fact, the layman is presumed wrong, and if he nevertheless chooses to act on his factually mistaken belief, his action will be substantially less than fully voluntary. That is, the action of *ingesting a substance which will in fact harm him* is not the action he voluntarily chooses to do (because he does not believe that it is harmful). Hence the state intervenes to protect him not from his own free and voluntary choices, but from his own ignorance.

Suppose however that the exchange goes as follows:

Dr. Doe: I cannot prescribe drug X to you because it will do you physical harm.

Mr. Roe: Exactly. That's just what I want. I want to harm myself.

In this case Roe is properly apprised of the facts; he suffers from no delusions or misconceptions. Yet his choice is so odd that there exists a reasonable presumption that he has been deprived of the "full use of his reflecting faculty." It is because we know that the overwhelming majority of choices to inflict injury for its own sake on oneself are not fully voluntary that we are entitled to presume that the present choice is not fully voluntary. If no further evidence of derangement, illness, severe depression, or unsettling excitation can be discovered, however, and the patient can convince an objective panel that his choice is voluntary (unlikely event!), then our "voluntariness standard" would permit no further state constraint.

Now consider the third possibility:

Dr. Doe: I cannot prescribe drug X to you because it is very likely to do you physical harm.

Mr. Roe: I don't care if it causes me physical harm. I'll get a lot of pleasure first, so much pleasure, in fact, that it is well worth running the risk of physical harm. If I must pay a price for my pleasure I am willing to do so.

This is perhaps the most troublesome case. Roe's choice is not patently irrational on its face. A well thought-out philosophical hedonism may be one of his profoundest convictions, involving a fundamental decision of principle to commit himself to the intensely pleasurable, even if brief, life. If no third party interests are directly involved, the state can hardly be permitted to declare his philosophical convictions unsound or "sick" and prevent him from practicing them, without assuming powers that it will inevitably misuse.

On the other hand, this case may be quite similar to the preceding one, depending on what the exact facts are. If the drug is known to give only an hour's mild euphoria and then cause an immediate, violently painful death, then the risks appear so unreasonable as to create a powerful presumption of nonvoluntariness. The desire to commit suicide must always be presumed to be both nonvoluntary and harmful to others until shown otherwise. (Of course, in some cases it can be shown otherwise.) Alternatively, drug X may be harmful in the way nicotine is now known to be harmful; twenty or thirty years of heavy use may create a grave risk of lung cancer or heart disease. Using the drug for pleasure when the risks are of this kind may be to run unreasonable risks, but that is no strong evidence of nonvoluntariness. Many perfectly normal, rational persons voluntarily choose to run precisely these risks for whatever pleasures they find in smoking. To assure itself that such practices are truly voluntary, the state should continually confront smokers with the ugly medical facts so that there is no escaping the knowledge of the exact medical risks to health. Constant reminders of the hazards should be at every hand, with no softening of the gory details. The state might even be justified in using its taxing, regulatory, and persuasive powers to make smoking (and similar drug usage) more difficult or less attractive; but to prohibit it outright would be to tell the voluntary risk-taker that his informed judgments of what is worthwhile are less reasonable than those of the state, and therefore he may not act on them. This is paternalism of the strong kind, unmediated by the voluntariness standard. As a principle of public policy it has an acrid moral flavor, and creates serious risks of governmental tyranny.

4. COLLECTIVE GOODS AND COLLECTIVE ACTION

Despite the presumptive case for liberty, there seem to be numerous examples in which the modern state has no choice but to force (usually by compulsory taxation) both willing and unwilling citizens to support public projects that are clearly in the public interest. In many of these cases those who do not benefit directly from a public service are made to pay as much in its support as those who do, or even more. Thus nondrivers are taxed to support highways and nonparents to support schools.

This has the appearance of injustice, and the justification of unhappy necessity. Often the alternative to mandatory taxation—a system of purely voluntary support requiring only users to pay fees—is subject to a fatal defect that forces us to choose between universal compulsory support for the public facility or no facility at all.

Consider, for example, public municipal parks. Suppose the town of Metropolis decides to create a large public park with gardens, woods, trails, and playgrounds. John Doe appreciates living in an attractive community but has no direct personal need for such a park, since he already has a ten acre yard with gardens, picnic tables, tennis courts, and the like. Why, he asks, should he be forced to support something he doesn't need and doesn't want strongly enough to pay for? Suppose, however, that the city charges only those who wish to use the park, and that this group constitutes 90 percent of the population. The richest 10 percent opt out, thus raising the average costs to the remainder. That rise, in turn, forces some of the 90 percent to withdraw, thus raising the cost to the others, forcing still more to drop out, and so on. This process will continue until either a very expensive equilibrium is reached, or, what is more likely, the whole project collapses (as in the case of some voluntary public medical and insurance plans).

It is avoidance of this characteristic escalation effect, rather than paternalism, that provides the rationale for compulsory social security and medicare programs. Here it is important to apply the various principles of liberty distribution not to individual cases, such as the compulsory taxation of John Doe, but to rules and general financing schemes. Compulsory rather than voluntary schemes are justified when the social good in question cannot be secured in any other way. Whether compulsion on this ground accords with the harm principle depends on whether loss of the good would be classified as a social harm or the mere withholding of a benefit. Where the good is security, medical care, or education, there is little doubt that its loss would properly be called a "harm" to those who incur it.

In cases of the sort we have been considering, some people who don't want a given public service are forced to pay for it because there is no other practical way of supporting it, and its loss would be a harm to those who do want it. In a more interesting and troublesome kind of case, *all* of the members of a community or group want some good which is in fact in the interests of each individual equally, and yet it is in no individual's interest to contribute toward the goal unless all are *made* to do so. This paradoxical state of affairs has attracted considerable attention from economists who have noticed its similarity to the condition of a company in an industry that enjoys "perfect competition." So long as the price of a manufactured product on the free market exceeds the marginal cost of production, it will be in the interest of each company to increase its output and thus maximize its profit. But the consequence of increased output will be lower prices, so in the end all companies will be worse off for "maximizing profits" than they might otherwise have been. If any single firm, anticipating this unhappy result, were to restrict its own output unilaterally, it would be in still more trouble, for its restriction of output in a large industry would not prevent the fall of prices, and it would suffer lower sales in addition to lower prices. It is in the interest of each firm that *all the others* restrict output, but, in a purely competitive situation, none of the others dare do that. Where there is no coercion, we have the paradoxical result that it is "rational" for each firm to pursue policies that will destroy its interests in the end. It is more rational still to prefer general coercion.

Problems like that raised by "perfect competition" tend to occur wherever large organizations have come into existence to advance the interests of their members. A great many such organizations, from consumer societies and labor unions to (as many have claimed) the political state itself, exist primarily to advance some common interest in virtue of which the members can be supposed to have banded together in the first place. Now, some of the collective aims to which large organizations are devoted have a very special character. They are directed at goods which, if they are made available to any one member of the group, cannot feasibly be withheld from any other member. Examples of such generalized and indivisible goods are supported prices for companies in the same industry in a not-so-competitive market, the power of collective bargaining for members of a union, and certain goods provided for its citizens by the state, such as police protection, courts of law, armies, navies, and public health agencies. Perhaps it would be technically possible to "sell" these goods only to those willing to pay for them, but it would hardly be "feasible." It is not clear, for example, how an organization, private or public, could eliminate air pollution only for those willing to pay. Nonpayers would breathe the expensively purified air, and there would be no way of preventing this "freeloading" short of banishment or capital punishment. In such cases, it is in each member's interest to let the others pay the bill and then share in consumption of the indivisible benefit; since each member knows that every member knows this as well as he, each has reason to think that he may be taken advantage of if he voluntarily pays his share. Yet if each member, following his own self-interest, refuses to pay, the collective good for which they are united cannot be achieved.

Voluntarily submitting to a coercion understood by each to apply to all seems the only way out.

It is in virtue of such considerations that compulsory taxation, at least in support of collective goods and indivisible services of an essential kind, can be justified by the harm principle. That principle would not justify compulsory taxation in support of benefits to private groups, or even of public benefits of the sort whose loss would not constitute a serious harm, but that does not mean that the friends of public libraries, museums, and parks need be driven to embrace the welfare principle. When persons and groups are deprived of what they *need*, they are harmed; it may not be implausible to insist that the country as a whole, in this and future generations (including people who have no present desire for culture, history, nature, or beauty), *needs* large national parks, wilderness areas, enormous libraries, museums, atomic accelerators for physical research, huge telescopes, and so on. To argue that we need these things is to claim that we cannot in the end get along very well without them. That is the kind of case that must be made if we are to justify compulsion, on liberal principles, to the reluctant taxpayer.

The Moral Foundations
of Decriminalization

David A. J. Richards

Joel Feinberg's *Harm to Others* deepens and clarifies philosophical understanding of the interpretation and weight of arguments of harm to others in criminal justice in ways that make it the most important work of its kind since Mill's *On Liberty* and a major achievement of the political and legal philosophy of our generation. My inquiry here is intended as a tribute to Joel Feinberg and his remarkable achievement in the following vein: If arguments of harm to others, properly understood, should in this area take roughly the form that Feinberg imputes to them, what is the moral basis of the program of decriminalization that these arguments advance, and how might such an analysis advance understanding of the nature of controversies over the scope of the criminal law?

Feinberg's study aims at a middle level of generalization, somewhere between abstract metaethical and normative philosophy and a detailed casuistry. My inquiry begins at the more abstract level and tries to show how such an approach can clarify some detailed issues of moral casuistry, including the complex forms of historical and factual inquiry that inform serious discussion of these issues. My discussion thus situates the Feinberg argument in the larger perspective of the historical tradition he elaborates (namely, liberalism) and the critical discussion of what that tradition is and how it should be understood. In particular, I question the long dominance of the interpretation of this tradition in terms of utilitarian equality: the interpretation of

David A. J. Richards, "The Moral Foundations of Decriminalization," (as appeared in *Criminal Justice Ethics* Volume 5, Number 1, [Winter/Spring 1986]: 11–16). Reprinted by permission of The Institute for Criminal Justice Ethics, 555 W. 57ᵗʰ St., New York, N.Y. 10019–1029.

treating persons as equals in terms of utilitarian neutrality among ends and among people.

MORAL FOUNDATIONS: MILL'S ARGUMENT

John Stuart Mill's classic argument, invoking the harm principle as a limit on just criminal and social sanctions, rests on an extended and complex form of moral criticism of the degree to which a certain form of conventional morality has unreflectingly been permitted to require both forms of state punishment through the criminal law and larger patterns of social condemnation to be enforced through informal mechanisms of social control. The form of conventional morality at issue reflects this structure of argument: any form of conduct may be subject to state or social condemnation if an ordinary person, reflecting some statistical normalcy of sentiment and opinion of the society at large, were to experience deep revulsion and offense at the thought of the action in question *simpliciter*. Mill argues that the Anglo-American conception of public morality, reflected in the work of the purity reformers and others, rests, on examination, on this form of argument of conventional morality. If the argument from conventional morality is seriously defective, as Mill argues that it is, the effective conception of public morality must fall also.

Mill's argument for the inadequacy of conventional morality as the measure of legal and social enforcement rests on the stark failure of the relevant standard (the offense taken by an ordinary person at the thought of _____) to advert to any impact of the conduct in question on any interests of persons. Forms of conduct are to be legally and socially condemned solely because an ordinary person would take offense at the thought of certain conduct, *without more*—in particular, without any—required form of inquiry into the reasons why such conduct is condemned, the degree to which the conduct frustrates or advances human interests, the justifiability of requiring all persons similarly situated so to act, and so on. But, so understood, conventional morality will mandate legal and social prohibitions that narrow the range of permissible actions to those simply of the most unquestioned popular prejudices reflecting crude stereotypes, elementary failures of moral and human imagination, crass group stupidity, and bigotry. If the achievement of democratic government leads, Mill suggests (following De Tocqueville), to the unquestioned dominance of conventional morality so understood, the deepest values of the political theory of democracy will be betrayed: a tool intended to liberate human capacities for the enlightened pursuit of interests on terms fair to all will become an instrument for the crudest oppression of the varieties of the pursuit of happiness by Procrustean and stupid convention—rigid, unintelligent, willful.

In order to obviate this betrayal of basic democratic values, Mill argues that conventional morality as such must be rejected as the basis for legal and social condemnation; in its place, he offers the harm principle. In contrast to the standard of conventional morality, which allows anything in principle to be the object of legal and social condemnation (depending on the feelings of offense of the ordinary person), the harm principle, subject to a background theory of just distribution and of moral duties of fair contribution, imposes determinate constraints on the degree to which legal and social condemnation may be applied to acts. The harm principle, Mill argues, advances a form of reasoning which democratic majorities must observe in order justly to impose criminal sanctions in the same way that justice in punishment requires that the definition and imposition of criminal sanctions observe certain principles of legality, proportionality, concurrence of *actus reus* and *mens rea*, and the like.

Mill's argument for the harm principle correctly seeks to dispel the superficial appeal of conventional morality as the most democratic way for a society to establish enforceable moral values, for how, it may be asked, could a society more democratically decide these issues than by a kind of populist appeal to the felt values which unite democratic majorities as a people? Mill's arresting and provocative response is a deep political theory of the values fundamental to republican democracy. From this perspective, the populist moral romanticism, on which the appeal of conventional morality depends, rests not on the sound values that make democracy a defensible form of government but on an older, indeed ancient, conception of public tribal morality antecedent to the elaboration and embodiment of the values of equality and liberty in working constitutional democracies. On examination, this tribal conception is in tension, if not blatantly inconsistent, with many of these values (for example, the primacy of religious toleration and freedom of conscience, as I shall shortly argue). The values distinctive of democracy are, Mill argues, precisely values of the liberation of human capacities for the enlightened pursuit of interests on terms fair to all, which the enforcement of the tribal conception of conventional morality frustrates in deep and damaging ways. Accordingly, an alternative conception of an enforceable public morality (the harm principle) is required by democratic political theory.

Mill's arguments in *On Liberty* are the great advance in political theory which they are precisely because they connect, in a philosophically profound way, arguments for the priority of free speech and the harm principle to a deep and plausible general theory of constitutional democracy. Nonetheless, the form of Mill's defense of liberalism suffers from the intractable internal tension between Mill's sympathy for rights-based arguments of principle and his doctrinal utilitarianism. Thus, although Mill's harm principle places a constraint on the criminal law comparable to the one embodied in the French Declaration of Rights, Mill did not justify the constraint on the basis of the human rights paradigm, as did the French Declaration.

Rather, Mill appealed to a general utilitarian argument, derived from Jeremy Bentham, that failure to follow the harm principle reduces the aggregate surplus of pleasure over pain. Mill was less doctrinaire in his opposition to the language and thought of rights than Bentham, and some find in *On Liberty* rights-based arguments of personal autonomy. But, although Mill did give great weight to preserving the capacity of persons to frame their life plans independently, he appears—in accordance with his argument in *Utilitarianism*—to have incorporated this factor into the utilitarian framework of preferring "higher" to "lower" pleasures. Thus, the argument of *On Liberty* is utilitarian: the greatest aggregate sum by which pleasure exceeds pain, taking into account the greater weight accorded by utilitarianism to higher pleasures, is secured by granting free speech and observing the harm principle as the measure of criminalization.

But, to the extent that the harm principle appears to be at least a good first approximation to a significant constraint of justice on permissible criminalization, there are grave objections to grounding this perception of justice in utilitarian argument. The harm principle is not a necessary corollary of utilitarian tenets; quite the contrary. The basic desideratum of utilitarianism is to maximize the surplus of pleasure over pain. If certain plausible assumptions about human nature are made, however, utilitarianism would require the criminalization of certain conduct in violation of the harm principle. Assume, for example, that the overwhelming majority of people in a community take personal satisfaction in their way of life and that their pleasure is appreciably heightened by the knowledge that conflicting ways of life are forbidden by the criminal law. Suppose, indeed, that hatred of the nonconforming minority, legitimated by the application of criminal penalties, reinforces the pleasurable feelings of social solidarity, peace of mind, self-worth, and achievement in a way that tolerance, with its invitation to self-doubt, ambivalence, and insecurity, could not. In such

circumstances, the greater pleasure thus secured to the majority may not only outweigh the pain to the minority but, as compared with the toleration required by the harm principle, may result in a greater aggregate of pleasure. Accordingly, utilitarianism would call for criminalization in violation of the harm principle. From this perspective, James Fitzjames Stephen may be a more consistent utilitarian than Mill insofar as his argument suggests that a utilitarian political morality does not cohere with the stringent requirements of the harm principle.[1]

To the extent that recent Mill scholars have attempted to reconstruct Mill's argument on utilitarian grounds, they propose an interpretive structure which is not properly utilitarian, but rather reflective of central neo-Kantian values of the independence and integrity of the person.[2] For, to the extent that scholars tinker with utilitarian assumptions in order to yield anything as demanding as the harm principle, they confirm one's suspicions that, for them, the harm principle is a more secure moral judgment than any utilitarian rationale or assumptions designed to justify it. If so, as C. L. Ten suggests,[3] we should develop an alternative moral theory that will ground the harm principle more directly and securely and that, in any event, Mill appears to assume, albeit through a glass darkly.

MORAL FOUNDATIONS: KANT'S ETHICAL CONSTRUCTIVISM

The key to such an alternative analysis is, I believe, to be found in Kant's ethical constructivism, in which ethical principles are understood as those principles that persons impose on themselves and one another as the best expression of their natures as free, rational, and equal persons with the twin moral powers of rationality and reasonableness.[4] On this conception, ethical principles, including the principles of politics, give a central place to the inalienable right to conscience, the right of persons to form, exercise, and revise their twin moral powers of rationality and reasonableness in the construction of a life well and humanely lived. In American constitutional law, this moral right is, I believe, the background constitutional right that explains the coordinated purposes of the free exercise and anti-establishment clauses of the first amendment: the free exercise clause forbids state coercion of the expression of conscience inconsistent with respect for persons, and the anti-establishment clause insists on equal respect for the way in which persons form and revise their consciences.[5]

This kind of moral and legal right fundamentally shapes the interpretation of the morality justly enforceable by the criminal law. Respect for the independent exercise of our moral powers, reflected in the constitutional guarantees, gravitates to a certain test for required neutrality of state action, namely, that state restrictions (free exercise) or endorsements (anti-establishment) of conscience can be justified at the relevant points and in the proper way only by certain general goods that rational and reasonable persons would want, as conditions of whatever else they want (thus yielding an alternative, nonutilitarian interpretation of liberal neutrality both among ends and among persons). We can, consistent with this constructivist conception, surrender to the state only that power over our lives (including the scope of the criminal law) which is consistent with the diverse ways we may, as free and rational persons, reasonably define and pursue our ultimate personal and ethical ends. Consistent with this conception, Locke thus defines the just limits of state power in terms of "civil interests,"[6] defining such interests as general goods:

> Civil interest I call life, liberty, health, and indolency of body; and the possession of outward things, such as money, lands, houses, furniture, and the like.[7]

And, he naturally appeals to such "civil interests" in defining when the state may and may not restrict or regulate conscience: the state may, for example, require that babies be washed if washing is understood to secure health interests, but it may not do so if the aim is not such an interest, as in the instance of compulsory baptism;[8] or, the state may not stop a person from killing a calf in a religious ritual if no civil interest would be secured by such a prohibition but it may, of course, forbid taking the life of a child in such a ritual.[9] The natural contractarian idea motivating this argument and the related tests in American religion clause jurisprudence is that the pursuit of general goods by the state is unobjectionable because such pursuit is neutral among the diverse ways people may, consistent with their right to conscience, interpretively weight the pursuit of those goods in their vision of a good and decent life. But, the state pursuit of other aims not limited to these general goods would precisely abridge the freedom of conscience, for these aims (compulsory baptism, or prohibitions on killing animals in religious rituals) are reasonably authoritative only for those of one conscientious system of beliefs as opposed to another. Justice in government requires that state power remain neutral among such beliefs.

This contractarian constraint on state power was strikingly put by Locke in terms of a harm criterion: the state may not, for example, forbid killing a calf in one's religious rituals "for no injury is done to any one, no prejudice to another man's goods."[10] Jefferson put the same point crisply:

> The legitimate powers of government extend to such acts only as are injurious to others. But it does no injury for my neighbor to say there are twenty gods, or no god. It neither picks my pocket nor breaks my leg.[11]

The concept of injury or harm implicit in these contractarian views assumed the reigning moral consensus on issues of what counted, in the area of public morality, as a harm or injury which the state might forbid. Often, such public morality was assumed to be a kind of general religious or, more specifically, Protestant religious morality, so that Locke,[12] like Roger Williams,[13] could insist that such arguments for toleration, expressive of equal respect for the inalienable right to conscience, were quite consistent with the state's traditional powers in the enforcement of conventional morality.

However, the conception of "harm" (given the background conception of general goods which it assumes) takes a form itself critical of conventional morality, as it does in Mill and Feinberg, when the religious and moral conventions, which Locke and Jefferson assume, become themselves subject to criticism as resting on sectarian assumptions, not on general goods. On this view, the harm principle, in its modern form, expresses deeper and wider currents of moral pluralism associated with wide-ranging interpretive disagreements which internally divide many religious traditions (for example, over issues of Bible criticism, the relevance of modern science, and so on) and which more sharply demarcate religious and ethical argument than was formerly thought either natural or possible. Issues of unquestioned conventional morality, for Locke or Jefferson, become, from this perspective, profoundly controversial because these issues no longer correspond to any reasonable conception of general goods which the state may justly enforce on people at large. Accordingly, arguments over the limits of the criminal law, sponsored by the harm principle, themselves express deeper critical reassessments of the degree to which conventional morality corresponds to such general goods.

ARGUMENTS FOR DECRIMINALIZATION

This abstract account of the moral basis for the harm principle may usefully clarify the ways in which concrete arguments for decriminalization are properly developed, and so enhance our understanding, consistent with Feinberg's account, of how the harm principle should be understood and applied. Thus, Feinberg's account of how "harm" should be understood is strikingly consistent with the nonutilitarian constructivism of general goods here proposed as the background normative theory underlying the harm principle. That account clarifies as well two distinctive features of the ways in which this principle operates in arguments for decriminalization: first, such arguments feature a characteristic internal criticism of the

historical assumptions and conceptions underlying the criminalization of certain kinds of conduct; and second, concurrent with this, such historically self-conscious criticism freshly inquires into relevant matters of fact. Both features are clarified by the constructivist analysis here proposed.

First, successful arguments for decriminalization, based on the harm principle, often criticize the assumptions and conceptions underlying the conventional condemnation of certain acts. Arguments against the criminalization of contraceptive use, for example, criticize the exclusively procreational model of sexuality classically stated by St. Augustine, a model of ideal sexuality as serving anhedonically the iron procreational will.[14] These critical arguments bring out not only the structure of sectarian mythopoesis surrounding such views but also the background social and economic factors (high rates of infant and adult mortality, the desperate need for children as workers in the agrarian economy of the household) which made such conceptions sensible and even functional.

And second, such historical criticism is usually accompanied by current empirical research, for example, into the nature of sexuality as a form of imaginative self-expression and intimate bonding. Such research clarifies the degree to which the traditional conception of sexuality does not fairly reflect the nature of sexuality as such but reflects a highly contingent historical selection, motivated perhaps by background social exigencies, from among the possible views of legitimate sexuality.

Critical inquiries of these interconnected historical and empirical kinds center on providing good reasons for concluding that the traditional criminalization of contraception, for example, does not today rest on a general good which rational and reasonable persons would want whatever else they want. Rather, the continuing force of the condemnation must rest, today, on precisely the kind of sectarian choice among the range of possible views which violates the basic requirement of state neutrality central to the constructivist conception of the legitimate exercise of state power. In short, the inquiries which characteristically frame arguments for decriminalization precisely demarcate nonneutral sectarian aims from general goods in the way that the general constructivist conception calls for. This suggests that the kind of abstract background normative conception which I have offered as the proper moral foundation for Feinberg's interpretation of the harm principle clarifies as well the concrete structure of the decriminalization argument typically sponsored by the harm principle. If this is correct, it deepens our understanding, I believe, of what generates the harm principle, giving that principle a natural historical place in the development of liberalism, in the self-criticism of cultural traditions, and in empirical research bearing on moral and legal reform.

The larger intellectual point is that controversies over the interpretation and weight of the harm principle depend upon a kind of holistic criticism of traditional moral assumptions, questioning, in tandem, interconnected metaphysical, social, moral, and empirical assumptions. Thus, decriminalization debates familiarly move among a number of disparate critical points. We cannot, of course, critically suspend all our assumptions at once. But, we can critically examine one assumption while holding the others constant, and then examine one of the others in the same way. This pattern of critical analysis is, I believe, well exemplified in all the central decriminalization debates of the age over such issues as contraception use, abortion, consensual homosexuality, prostitution, forms of drug use, certain decisions to die, and so on.[15] Controversies over abortion, for example, turn on disagreements over what counts here as "harm," in which controversies over the metaphysics of the person and larger gender assumptions are inexplicably intertwined. A consensus on the role of women—once unquestioned—often breaks down now along sectarian lines on both sides: the metaphysics of foetal life and the natural role of women as mothers now confront a

feminist criticism of the natural order assumed by these arguments.[16] My point in this paper is that we deepen understanding of the way in which the harm principle governs such debates, consistent with Feinberg's project, when we connect intermediate level discussions of the principle both to more abstract and more concrete inquiries.

NOTES

[1] See J. Stephen, *Liberty, Equality, Fraternity*, 135–78; 227–29 (1967).

[2] See, e.g., J. Gray, *Mill on Liberty: A Defence* (1983) and F. Berger, *Happiness, Justice and Freedom* (1984).

[3] C. Ten, *Mill on Liberty* (1980).

[4] See J. Rawls, Kantian Constructivism in Moral Theory 77 *J. of Phil.* 515 (1980).

[5] See D. Richards, *Toleration and the Constitution* (forthcoming).

[6] J. Locke, A Letter Concerning Toleration, 6 *The Works of John Locke* 9 (London, 1823).

[7] Id. at 10.

[8] Id. at 30–31.

[9] Id. at 33–34.

[10] Id. at 34.

[11] T. Jefferson, *Notes on the State of Virginia* 159 (W. Peden ed. 1955).

[12] Thus, Locke insists that religious congregations would be punishable if they committed such public wrongs as to "pollute themselves in promiscuous uncleanness, or practise any other such heinous enormities," supra note 6, at 33; cf. id. at 292, 535. Locke does note, however, that not all immoralities are justly enforceable by law. Some, like "[c]ovetousness, uncharitableness, idleness," are sinful wrongs but not punishable (id. at 36); others, like "lying and perjury," are only punishable by law in certain cases where we consider not the religious or ethical wrong to God, but injury to "men's neighbours, and to the commonwealth" (id. at 37).

[13] See, e.g., The Bloudy Tenent of Persecution, 3 *The Complete Writing of Roger Williams* 108–10, 152, 155 (S. Caldwell ed. 1963).

[14] Cf. D. Richards, *Sex, Drugs, Death, and the Law* 37–38 (1982).

[15] See id.

[16] See, in general, K. Luker, *Abortion and the Politics of Motherhood* (1984). See also D. Richards, supra note 5, chs. 8, 9.

Legalize It?
Debating American Drug Policy

Arnold Trebach and James Inciardi

THE REPEAL OF DRUG PROHIBITION
Arnold Trebach

It follows that any sensible plan for legalization will work so long as it adheres to certain basic principles of realism about the manner in which people actually relate to drugs. Legalization is as much an approach to drug policy as it is a specific plan, as this section will make clear. In that spirit, I offer the following summary list of drug realisms, of new ways of thinking about drugs, that any legalization plan must take into account.

- We must stop thinking about drugs and drug users in terms of war and hate.

In the wake of the riots of 1992 and revolutionary discontent of the American public over the inability of the government to cope with harshly divisive social problems, the need for drugpeace is more vital than ever. We cannot have peace in our cities in the midst of the constant attacks and counterattacks of a drug war.

- Multitudes of people, most of them perfectly decent and respectable human beings, like drugs. Any program that demands, upon threat of criminal punishment, that these people always repress those desires so as to create a drug-free

Arnold Trebach and James Inciardi, *Legalize It? Debating American Drug Policy*. (Washington, DC: American University Press, 1993). Reprinted by permission of American University Press (Selected pages). In this edited version of the debate original footnote numbers have been retained.

society is unrealistic and harmful. It is the equivalent of attempting to repress the natural and diverse sexual appetites of our people. As the recent revelations about pedophile Catholic priests have demonstrated, the rule of sexual abstinence, even when backed by the threat of burning in hell, cannot create a sex-free clergy. Moreover, in too many cases it has perverted normal sex drives into destructive paths of sexual expression.

- The criminal law must not be allowed to occupy the center of the new drug-control system. Police and prison keepers should not be the primary agents for controlling the admittedly bad effects of many drugs. We should attempt to put parents, educators, clergy, and cultural leaders in their place. The criminal law should operate only at the edges of the system—when there is the imminent possibility of harm to an innocent third party arising from drug use. It should not be a crime to use heroin at home in your bedroom, for example, while it should remain a crime to be under the influence of any mind-altering drug, say prescribed Valium, while driving.

- "Harm reduction" should be the overarching theme of all new drug laws and drug-control policies. Harm reduction accepts the reality of both the desire for drugs by millions of people and the related fact that millions of people may be harmed by drugs every year. Accordingly, the philosophy suggests, we must bend our energy and ingenuity to convincing people that they must make careful choices and that in a free society they may choose no drugs at all (as most will), comparatively harmless ways of using drugs, or very destructive methods. Whatever their choices, they must be assured that they will not be treated as enemies of the state and that help will be available if they encounter trouble.

- The pursuit of highs and altered states of consciousness, far from being destructive as is widely assumed, is natural and good for individuals and society. The best highs are very probably those brought about without the help of chemicals—through, for example, religion, meditation, cheering on a favorite sports team, exercise, and making love. This is because natural highs avoid the risks of drugs and demonstrate to people the powerful truth that each individual has the inherent ability to achieve internal happiness. Yet, the great majority of people who use drugs, legal or illegal, to achieve highs do so without causing observable harm to themselves or others. Only a small minority of opium, heroin, cocaine, crack, and marijuana users get into trouble with the drugs (and with other elements of their lives) and come to public attention. Sadly, the universe of drug users is defined in the public mind by that tiny percentage who draw so much attention to themselves and their troubles.

- As we design new drug-control systems, we should remember our revolutionary democratic roots. For centuries, the great mass of people were considered inferior clods, certainly incapable of choosing rulers, who were instead anointed by God and the accident of royal blood. In a shocking reversal of these established, hallowed truths, the Declaration of Independence declared that the people had a natural right—based upon natural law which was superior to written law—both to throw out their divinely appointed rulers by force of arms if necessary and also to choose all future rulers. If we can put faith in the people to make the awesome choice of who will rule their nation, it seems an easy step now to ask those rulers to relinquish control once again over what substances people may choose to put in their own bodies. In the end, that is all that is involved here: returning the power of individual choice to the citizens of a supposedly free country over a very intimate matter.

MY PREFERRED PLAN OF LEGALIZATION: THE REAL TREBACH MODEL

A treasure trove of ideas on the specifics of drug-law reform has developed during the past two decades (see, for example, Trebach and Zeese 1989, 1990b, 1991, 1992). There is a great deal of disagreement among the reformers about the specifics of reform; indeed, they raise many of the same questions that prohibitionists do.

Richard M. Evans, a Massachusetts attorney and experienced reform activist, provides an excellent summary of the range of worthwhile proposals, which he places in three broad categories: decriminalization, limitation, and regulation and taxation (Evans 1990). Under decriminalization, drugs would remain illegal but the offense of possession would be treated like a traffic violation, with relatively little loss of liberty for the transgressor. Limitation models would make drugs legally available but with clearly defined limits as to which institutions and professions could distribute the drugs. Included here, for example, would be the distribution of drugs to addicts through doctors, an approach I labeled "medicalization" many years ago. Regulation and taxation models would involve a wide array of looser controls, similar to those currently applied to alcohol.

Choosing a path for future policy from among these proposals is complex. Different aspects of various models might very likely be applied to different drugs.

My preferred plan of legalization seeks essentially to turn the clock back to the last century, before we made the terrible mistake of starting the war on opium smoking. With some modern adaptations—such as sensible rules regarding purity, labeling, places and hours of sale, and age limits for purchasers—we should return to the people the freedom of choice regarding drugs which was unwisely taken from them at the turn of the century. This plan springs from a judgment that we should trust our adult citizens more than government officials to make choices as to what goes in their bodies.

In concrete terms, then, my major proposal is what we deal with virtually all illegal drugs as we now deal with alcohol. This idea, which has been suggested by many commentators, including me, during recent years, has often been derided by prohibitionists as being naive on the grounds that alcohol is allegedly less harmful and easier to control than the currently illegal drugs. There is simply no proof of this assumption; in fact, dose for dose, alcohol is one of the most toxic and violence-producing drugs human beings regularly consume. For those very good reasons, the nation prohibited alcohol from 1920 to 1933. However, we soon came to see that as bad as alcohol was, Prohibition was worse for the country and its people. National alcohol prohibition was therefore repealed.

That is where the process of reform should start now: repeal national drug prohibition. Just do it—in the same way Prohibition was repealed in 1933, in the same way its people dismantled the former Soviet Union—with speed, courage, and the confidence that the future cannot be worse than the present.

THE QUESTION OF POLITICAL REALITY

We live in cataclysmic, revolutionary times where the unthinkable today may well become the norm the day after tomorrow. Traditional ways of thinking and sacred icons are regularly and rapidly smashed. The repeal of alcohol prohibition happens to be one splendid example of this phenomenon.

Even though it was widely disliked and disregarded, there was a general belief that Prohibition was here to stay. An Associated Press story of 24 September 1930 quoted the main author of the Eighteenth Amendment, Senator Morris Sheppard of Texas, as gloating, "There is as much chance of repealing the Eighteenth Amendment as there is for a hummingbird to fly to the planet Mars with the Washington Monument tied to its tail" (as quoted in Kyvig 1985, 14). A few years later, in 1933, the Twenty-first Amendment was proposed and, quite remarkably, actually ratified the same year.

In a similar vein, it was utterly unthinkable and laughable to contemplate the dismantling of the Union of Soviet Socialist Republics and the rejection of communism by its leaders. Certainly, it would have seemed absurd to imagine that it could have been accomplished comparatively peacefully and without the use of armed force by the West. To my knowledge, not a single intelligence officer among the thousands on either side of the old Iron Curtain ever made such a prediction.

It would be a rational assessment to conclude that if one were calculating probabilities a few years before each event, the mathematical odds against either (1) the repeal of Prohibition or (2) the peaceful dismantling of the Soviet Union should have been calculated as much higher than (3) the possibility that Congress would pass a national drug-prohibition repeal law by the year 2000.

As an activist professor at The American University and as the founder and president of the independent Drug Policy Foundation, I have been more or less in the front lines of reform for two decades. I have received my fair share of both brickbats and bouquets for my heretical positions. Now the latter almost exclusively predominate. The drug-law reform movement has more and more supporters throughout the United States and the world. The movement is getting positively respectable (although not so much so as to be boring). I have never seen such high-level support for change. The Drug Policy Foundation now regularly receives letters and calls from federal and state judges and other officials prodding it to greater action and asking that it more aggressively mobilize its resources and fight more openly to repeal prohibition once and for all. At times I feel I must run to keep up with the seemingly conservative judges and others of that respectable ilk who want complete legalization now, today.

REPEAL GOALS AND OPTIONS

The major goals of the new drug laws at the national level would be, first, to eliminate the key federal laws imposing criminal penalties on the manufacture, sale, and possession of drugs;

second, to dismantle the Drug Enforcement Administration and assign some of its staff and functions to the Federal Bureau of Investigation or other federal agencies; and third, to carve out a new supportive role for the federal government that recognizes the primacy of the states in drug control. Thus the federal government would not be totally eliminated from the drug field, but rather there would be an attempt to recognize the unique contributions that national agencies could perform under the new system. The federal government should continue to play a major role in the drug field, particularly in the areas of drug education, treatment, and research—ongoing needs regardless of the legal status of drugs. Thus, we will be invoking a venerable conservative concept, states' rights, as the cornerstone idea for reform (yet another idea from the past that will help design our future).

As it did with repeal of alcohol prohibition, the federal government would return to the states the primary power to determine which drugs could be legally sold and under what conditions, a power the federal government took away early in this century. The major federal statute affecting currently illegal drugs is the Comprehensive Drug Abuse Prevention and Control Act of 1970, which has been amended numerous times in the past two decades. This prohibition statute (although not named that, of course) is listed in the United States Code starting in section 801 of volume 21. The first task is to excise that law.

Recently, Daniel K. Benjamin and Roger Leroy Miller of Clemson University faced up to that task (1991) and suggested two main legal options. Alternative 1 would change the U.S. Code to read:

THE ENHANCED STATES' CONTROL OVER DRUG ABUSE ACT

Section 1. Sections 801–904, 21 USCA are hereby repealed.

Section 2. The transportation or importation into any state, territory, or possession of the United States for delivery or use therein of any controlled substance, in violation of the laws thereof, is hereby prohibited (Benjamin and Miller 1991, 267).

This proposed law uses the language of the alcohol repeal amendment and would accomplish almost complete repeal of drug prohibition at the federal level. It would virtually put the Drug Enforcement Administration (DEA) out of business because that agency has the distinction of being perhaps the only police organization in the country with the sole responsibility to enforce only one statute, the one being repealed. Of course, under section 2 of the repeal statute, the federal government would have the duty to assist the states in the enforcement of their own prohibition laws, and this could require the work of federal drug enforcement agents.

Also, the national government would retain responsibility for international law enforcement duties in the drug field, the precise shape of which are now impossible to determine. They would certainly, however, be quite limited compared with today. In my opinion, such limited duties could well be handled by the Federal Bureau of Investigation, the major national law enforcement agency in the United States. There would seem no need, except political appearances, to pay for a separate agency in the future, whatever form of legalization statute is crafted.

Benjamin and Miller suggest a less comprehensive reform law, Alternative 2, as follows:

Amendment to 21 USCA Section 903

THE RETURN TO THE STATES CONTROL OVER DRUG ABUSE AMENDMENT Section 903, 21 USCA, shall be revised to read as follows: No provision of this subchapter shall be construed as indicating an intent on the part of the Congress to occupy the field in which that provision operates to the exclusion of any state law on the same subject matter which would otherwise be within the authority of the state. Any conflict between that provision of this subchapter and that state law so that the two cannot stand together shall be resolved by construing the law so as to give full effect to the relevant state law (1991, 268).

This alternative new statute would leave the major federal prohibition law in place but would recognize the primacy of state law wherever there was a conflict. The authors claim it would accomplish the same result as the first alternative. I much prefer the more comprehensive approach because it would definitively remove the federal government almost totally from its dominant role in prohibition enforcement. However, Alternative 2 should also be considered as a bargaining option, as should other approaches to repeal. This effort should concentrate on removing the great majority of armed federal drug police officers from American life, forever.

A logical sequence of events would be that Congress first passes a repeal bill, roughly along the lines of the Benjamin and Miller (1991) Alternative 1. This would mean that the criminal law jurisdiction of the federal government over domestic illicit drugs would largely cease. While the rapid removal of the federal government from most domestic drug control would cause uncertainties, it would not mean that drug control would cease. All states now have overlapping laws and agencies that perform many of the same functions as the federal government. Under the new system, the state systems would simply become dominant.

Congress would then pass a law, under this scenario, setting up the new national commission that would study all of the major issues about the future of drug control, but especially the various approaches being taken in the states to implement new systems. If the current approach to dealing with alcohol is any guide, it is to be expected that there would be wide variations from one state to another in drug control. (As in the first years after alcohol repeal, many states might exercise their legal option to retain drug prohibition within their borders.) It is likely that the national commission would continue working for some years, monitoring and reporting on the results of the different state models and about new American policies on the international scene.

There would be other important roles in the future for the federal government, some being simple extensions of current functions

now being carried out by research agencies such as the National Institute on Drug Abuse, which should be retained and expanded. Current federal and state drug-control systems usually take entirely separate approaches to dealing with legal and illegal drugs. This makes no sense and ought to be remedied in the future. All of the drugs present many common problems and should be considered together. For example, there is a good deal of prescription drug abuse, especially among the elderly. Existing federal grant-in-aid programs would be extended to include grants to help states to develop good models of control for all drugs, including the currently illegal ones as well as those with a long history of legal use, especially alcohol, tobacco, caffeine, and mind-altering prescription drugs, such as tranquilizers.

Another federal function that ought to be retained is the regulation of the legal drug industry. This is carried on primarily by the Food and Drug Administration, which has the responsibility to see that drugs sold in interstate commerce are "safe and effective." Thus the FDA approves new drugs for use in the country. Because the legal drug business is national, even international, it makes sense for a national agency to continue to have some control on assuring the safety, efficacy, purity, and proper labeling of these sometimes potent substances.

STATE MODELS

It is possible that once federal drug prohibition is repealed, many states would continue prohibition within their boundaries. However, I make the assumption that the same political forces that would have effected reform at the federal level would be pushing for change within many states. This certainly was the case with the repeal of alcohol prohibition. My preferred model for the states, which would be largely free from federal control, would be one that provided great freedom to adult residents to obtain the drugs they desired. At the same time there would be less stringent control on the selling and marketing of drugs. The preferred new state model could involve two options: the medical option, and the nonmedical option.

The first option would be quite similar to the current prescription system. Under this medical option, a person desiring drugs would go to a doctor or—and this is an important addition—other licensed drug expert and obtain advice and, if the expert agreed, a prescription. The prescription would then be filled by a pharmacist under many of the current rules. It is to be expected that this option would be used by the great majority of people, certainly by almost all of those who see themselves as patients in a medical setting with traditional organic illnesses, such as asthma, cancer, and heart disease. They would have the comfort and protection of familiar methods of obtaining and using drugs, which they would properly think of as medicines.

The one major change I would make in the current system is to break the monopoly that medical doctors now enjoy regarding the power to write prescriptions for drugs deemed to have the greatest potential for abuse. There is no good reason, either scientific or ethical, to retain that monopoly, and this would seem a good time to break it. While many doctors have great knowledge of drugs and medicines, many others are ignorant of all but those few they use in their practices daily. States should be encouraged to experiment with new procedures that would allow drug experts without medical degrees—including pharmacologists, pharmacists, and nurses—to be tested and licensed to write prescriptions. However, it would seem wise to prevent those who wrote prescriptions from also selling the drugs to fill them. Thus, there might be, for example, consulting pharmacists and dispensing pharmacists.

Second, the nonmedical option would avoid the prescription system altogether. It would allow an adult citizen who had passed certain modest requirements or even tests, similar to those for a driver's license, to obtain the drugs he or she wished directly from a licensed seller without the need of professional advice or prescription. Thus, the state would be treating adults like adults, responsible thinking people who are given choices and are deemed capable of making them.

Those who chose to use drugs under the second option would, in effect, be the adventurers and risk-takers because of the dangers presented by drug use. The great majority of them would be marijuana smokers, at least in the first years of legalization, since marijuana is the most popular currently illicit drug. If the truth be faced, however, few marijuana smokers will be taking great risks, unless they use the drug heavily while attempting to work, drive a car, or use other machinery. Of course, all drugs, including marijuana, present dangers which the state and private sellers would have a duty to fully disclose.

Some people might prefer to operate under neither or under both of these options. Many heroin addicts I have known see themselves simply as people who love heroin and who probably would initially choose the nonmedical option to obtain drugs. I have also known many such addicts as they got older and more troubled, at which point they might turn to the medical option in a fervent effort to stop using. Under this new system, even the lowest street addicts would be treated as basically rational people who have to make choices about their options. There are great risks in this approach, but I submit there are even greater risks in continuing the current method which assumes that all addicts have lost their ability to make rational decisions.

SENATOR GALIBER'S MODEL

There are many detailed proposals laying out how radical legalization systems might work, as outlined, for example, by Benjamin and Miller (1991). While none shares precisely the same features, all move in the direction of full legalization of drugs. One of the most far-reaching and comprehensive has been that proposed by New York State Senator Joseph L. Galiber of the Bronx. First introduced in 1988, the bill has been reintroduced and redrafted regularly and remains an active proposal before the

Senate of New York (as do similar bills before other state legislative bodies).[17]

The Galiber bill would set up a comprehensive, rational legal control system for drugs which in most vital respects would mirror New York State's system for controlling alcohol. As a State Liquor Authority now controls alcohol in New York, in the future a State Controlled Substances Authority (SCSA) would control drugs.

The law would first repeal those sections of state law that impose criminal sanctions for the possession and sale of all illegal drugs. The SCSA would move into this gap and act to determine the manner and means of dispensing controlled substances in order to promote the welfare and safety of the public. The authority would be headed by a five-person commission appointed by the governor with the advice and consent of the senate. All members and staff would be disqualified from holding an interest in any establishment being regulated.

The manufacture and sale of drugs would take place within regulations set up by the SCSA, which would bear many similarities to those now established for alcohol. While it is easy for an adult to purchase alcohol almost anywhere in the state, few people are aware of the extensive network of laws and regulations, most at the state and local level, that control the industry. Some of these controls are established by the legislature, with most being imposed by the executive rule-making power of the liquor authority. This would also be the

case with the new drug agency. The new law would establish the minimum requirements, for example, for a person to be eligible to obtain a license to manufacture or sell drugs: over 21 years of age; U.S. citizen or lawfully resident alien; no convictions of a felony other than drug offenses before the enactment of the law; and no past revocation of a liquor or drug license for cause. In addition, the law would require that drugs be sold only within the channels of the new system, that there be no house-to-house sales or sales in public parks, that manufacturers and sellers keep complete records open for inspection by the authority, that advertising be modest and subject to review by the authority, and that individual purchasers be at least 21 years of age.

The new law would also impose specific packaging and labeling requirements. For example, controlled substances would be sold only in separate, clearly labeled packages containing "no more than ten usual doses." The authority then would be delegated the responsibility to determine in each case the definition of "a usual dose" (section 43-1). It would be unlawful for any person to sell a controlled substance that did not meet any of the new labeling and packaging requirements. Each package would contain a full disclosure of the contents and the potential dangers. Samples of warning labels that would be required by the law are as follows:

WARNING: This drug is addictive. You may not be able to quit using it.

WARNING: This drug may cause seizures, convulsions, and death.

WARNING: If you are pregnant, this drug may cause serious birth defects in your child, including missing limbs and brain damage.

The law would also require that such warnings be rotated on a quarterly basis by those who package the drugs (section 43).

While the law would not require that sellers have any special professional qualifications,

[17]An earlier version of the Galiber bill appears in Trebach and Zeese (1989, 400). Also in that volume, with an introductory analysis (p. 371), is a proposed law titled, "A Bill to Reduce the Violence Associated with the Trade in Illicit Drugs," by Nancy Lord, M.D., J.D., who was the Libertarian Party candidate for Vice-President of the United States in 1992, as well as a detailed proposal (p. 429)— The Cannabis Revenue Act—that was composed originally by the National Task Force on Cannabis Regulation in 1982. Taking a lead role in that latter project is Richard Evans, Esq., of Northampton, Massachusetts. The latest version of the Galiber bill is no. 4094-A, New York State Senate, entitled in part "An Act to Establish a Controlled Substance Law," dated March 21, 1991.

there is a provision for "addiction care centers" operated by licensed physicians. Under this section, physicians could operate a treatment center and obtain a license to dispense drugs for addicts in treatment within the new system. While this may sound like the current system or the medical option I recommended above (which is my own proposal and does not appear in the Galiber bill or any of the other bills in state legislatures), it is somewhat different. Under the Galiber bill, the doctor would be licensed to dispense drugs within medical treatment but no prescription would be necessary.

The SCSA would have jurisdiction over a new "controlled substances treatment fund." Monies would be placed in this fund from general tax revenues and also from taxes imposed on controlled substances, which could be quite substantial. The new authority also would be given responsibility for coordinating, directing, and funding all public treatment programs in the state. These would cover a wide range of treatments, including those that were drug free and aimed toward complete abstinence (section 52). Not later than one year after the effective date of the law, the new authority would have to report to the legislature on changes in the crime rate, changes in the number of people in prison, the quantities and types of drugs legally sold under this law, "estimates of number of people using controlled substances in each category, with a breakdown by frequency of use," and estimates of the number of "controlled substance related motor vehicle and industrial accidents, and hospital admissions" (section 50).

There are many other provisions in this proposed law which now covers 19 single-spaced, printed pages. If the law were to be passed, the SCSA would, in accordance with directions in the law, develop additional rules for the orderly marketing and control of the newly legalized drugs. When I testified in general support of the Galiber bill on 16 June 1989, I made several specific suggestions for amendments (Trebach 1989). Among them:

- Put the law into effect and thus formally legalize all of the drugs but then allow the SCSA to

set up a timetable for gradual implementation. This could mean that a mild drug like marijuana would be placed on sale first in a few selected localities around the state. Once the SCSA had worked out the practical and administrative details with that drug in those places, the authority could then move on to other drugs and other localities.

- Experiment in the first years of legalization with a provision that drug purchasers be required to pass a test on the drugs, their dangers, and the applicable law. The test would bear some similarities to the written section of the test for a driver's license. Thus at the start of this experiment only those who had passed the test and obtained a drug user's license could purchase drugs under the new system. (I should report that Senator Galiber told me during the hearing that he thought this was a bad idea and would simply keep too many people in the black market.)

- Institute a "harmfulness tax," an idea that has been championed in recent years by Lester Grinspoon of Harvard Medical School, among others. In this context it might mean that at first taxes would be roughly equal on all drugs. The SCSA would be given power to conduct research on the relative harm caused by each drug to the health of individuals and to the general society. On the basis of that research, the SCSA would establish tax rates, none of which would be prohibitive. It is likely that, for example, crack would be in the highest tax category and marijuana in one of the lowest. Heroin, powdered cocaine, alcohol, and tobacco might well be grouped just below crack. A vote of the SCSA governing body, hopefully based upon realistic research, would decide. The new revenue would be devoted primarily to new treatment and education resources. It is possible that billions in taxes, now lost to the underworld, would be realized, even in New York State alone. Finally, there might be enough money for drug treatment on demand.

- Include exemptions for personal use. Most illegal drugs are relatively easy to produce. Given the availability of the basic ingredients, it is harder to produce, say, a good Scotch than to grow marijuana or to synthesize heroin. Another reason for such a personal-use exemption is found in basic principles. A free society should recognize that individual privacy is at the core of the democratic experience. In 1975, the Alaskan Supreme Court did recognize these factors when it interpreted the right to privacy clause in the state constitution as granting adult Alaskans the right to grow and possess marijuana in the privacy of the home for personal use and not for sale. Thus, marijuana is legal, not simply decriminalized, in the privacy of Alaskan homes. (A state recriminalization law was recently passed by referendum, which had the strong backing of former drug czar William Bennett, but the constitutionality of that law has not yet been litigated.)

In addition to the suggestions I made in my testimony, nonmedical drug stores should be subject to the same type of local community controls as are liquor stores; they should not be located in residential areas nor near schools or religious establishments. Regulations should allow the stores to be open for as long as local liquor stores are. The exteriors of the new stores should contain no advertising and the signs on them should be for purposes of identification only. Here again the concepts of moderation and of harm reduction would apply.

Moreover, publicity campaigns should be mounted that, as contradictory as it may sound to some in the context of a drug legalization discussion, provide realistic information on the values of abstinence and the joys of achieving highs without drugs. Social leaders would be saying to the people of the country what I have told virtually every meeting I have addressed of the National Organization to Reform Marijuana Laws: you really do not have to use this stuff to feel good, but if you do, I do not think you should be treated as criminals. These campaigns would not be like the current distortions put forth by the government and the Partnership for a Drug-Free America. Instead, they would accept the reality that the pursuit of highs is not evil but healthy, especially if done without drugs. Concrete information should be provided about the nondrug methods now in use that could be expanded. Even an increase in one

venerable method, disciplined meditation, could be beneficial to multitudes of people.

We also might bring back another old, seemingly scandalous, idea, the opium den, but we would reshape its function somewhat and give it a new name. If we think back and compare the gentle opium-smoking scenes of the past century with the rowdiness and violence of many modern alcohol bars and crack houses, the opium den would seem to be superior in the context of a harm-reduction strategy. We should also be guided by the wisdom of that opium-smoking prostitute who observed in 1884 that if opium houses were licensed like saloons, the society would benefit (Brecher 1972, 43).

The greatest danger here, in my opinion, is intoxicated people driving home from the drug bars at night, as in the case of alcohol bars. While none of the currently illegal drugs mentioned here should produce anything like the aggressive irresponsibility of the alcohol-impaired driver, all mind-altering drugs impair driving ability. Accordingly, all patrons of these new establishments would have to be impressed with the dangers to good driving posed by their drugs, with the fact that driving while intoxicated on any substance would continue to be a crime, and that at least one person in every car should be selected as a "designated driver" at the beginning of the evening, as should be done now with alcohol drinkers in bars. That person would not consume any mind-altering substance, except for perhaps some cappucino.

I worry more about the danger of an increase in drugged-driving deaths than I do about any single potential difficulty in the future under legalization. In large part, that is because the drunken driver has for decades been a greater threat to the safety of all of us than almost any other danger. Some of the best, and some of the worst, people in our society regularly drink and drive. Despite the magnitude of the danger, automobiles and alcohol remain quite legal. The same should be true of drugs. At the same time we must recognize that while the problem of impaired driving will not go away, we do not have to throw up our hands and lament that

that's the price of freedom. We must be constantly researching the matter and seeking new ways to reduce the harm from impaired driving, even though we cannot hope to stop the practice completely. For example, we should contemplate a coordinated national, state, and local campaign against impaired driving. This might involve, first, more punitive laws and regulations, particularly those that give greater power to the police to seize driving licenses of impaired drivers summarily under certain defined circumstances. Second, we should develop more effective educational and media programs to get the message across that driving while impaired by any substance constitutes the greatest threat of violent death and injury in modern society. Spot television commercials carrying such messages would be worthy substitutes for the misleading ads of the Partnership for a Drug-Free America. Thus we must constantly be striving for a rational balance in social relations. Greater freedom of choice for adults in regard to drugs should be balanced by more rational governmental intervention in related arenas—and also by greater personal attention by individual citizens to safety.

ARGUING AGAINST LEGALIZATION

James Inciardi

Tomorrow, like every other average day in the United States, about 11,449.3 babies will be born, 90 acres of pizza will be ordered, almost 600,000 M&M candies will be eaten, and some 95 holes-in-one will be claimed. At the same time, 171 million bottles of beer will be consumed, and almost 1.5 billion cigarettes will be smoked (Ruth 1992). In 1965, the annual death toll from smoking-related diseases was estimated at 188,000. By the close of the 1980s that figure had more than doubled, to 434,000, and it is expected to increase throughout the 1990s (Centers for Disease Control 1990, 1991b). And these figures do not include the almost 40,000 nonsmokers who die each year from ailments associated with the inhalation of passive smoke (*New York Times*, 1 February 1991, A14; *Time*, 11 February 1991, 58).

In addition, for millennia people have turned to alcohol to celebrate life's pleasures and to dull its pains. As a result, it is estimated that there are 10.5 million alcoholics in the United States, and that a total of 73 million adults have been touched by alcoholism (*Alcoholism and Drug Abuse Weekly*, 9 October 1991, 1). Each year there are some 45,000 alcohol-related traffic fatalities in the United States (Centers for Disease Control 1991a), and thousands of women who drink during pregnancy bear

children with irreversible alcohol-related defects (Steinmetz 1992). Alcohol use in the past year was reported by 54 percent of the nation's eighth graders, 72 percent of tenth graders, and 78 percent of twelfth graders, and almost a third of high school seniors in 1991 reported "binge drinking" (five or more drinks in a row) at least once during the two-week period prior to being surveyed (University of Michigan 1992). The cost of alcohol abuse in the United States for 1990 has been estimated at $136.31 billion (*Substance Abuse Report*, 15 June 1991, 3).

Keep the above data in mind, and consider that they relate to only two of the *legal* drugs. Now for some reason, numerous members of the pro-legalization lobby argue that if drugs were to be legalized, usage would likely not increase very much, if at all (see, for example, Chambliss 1988; Boaz 1990; Miller 1991). The reasons, they state, are that "drugs are everywhere," and that everyone who wants to use them already does. But the data beg to differ. For example, 56 percent of high school seniors in 1991 had never used an illicit drug in their lifetimes, and 73 percent had never used an illicit drug other than marijuana in their lifetimes; 50 percent of college students in 1991 had never used an illicit drug in their lifetimes, and 74 percent had never used an illicit drug other than marijuana in their lifetimes. True, these surveys did not include "dropout" populations in which usage rates are higher, but nevertheless, the absolute numbers in these age cohorts who have never even *tried* any illicit drugs are in the tens of millions. And most significantly for the argument that "drugs are everywhere," half of all high school students do not feel that drugs are easy to obtain.

Going further, most people in the general population do not use drugs. Granted, these data are limited to the "general population," which excludes such hard-to-reach populations as members of deviant and exotic subcultures, the homeless, and others living "on the streets," and particularly those in which drug use rates are highest. However, the data do document that the overwhelming majority of Americans do not use illicit drugs. This suggests two things: that the drug prohibitions may be working quite well; and that there is a large population who might, and I emphasize might, use drugs if they were legal and readily available.

The Problems with Illegal Drugs. Considerable evidence exists to suggest that the legalization of drugs could create behavioral and public health problems that would far outweigh the current consequences of drug prohibition. There are some excellent reasons why marijuana, cocaine, heroin, and other drugs are now controlled, and why they ought to remain so. What follows is a brief look at a few of these drugs. I have discussed this subject already on several occasions (see Inciardi and McBride 1989; Inciardi 1992, 244–47), but it warrants repeating in order that this essay stand by itself.

Marijuana. There is considerable misinformation about marijuana. To the millions of adolescents and young adults who were introduced to the drug during the social revolution of the 1960s and early 1970s, marijuana was a harmless herb of ecstasy. As the "new social drug" and a "natural organic product," it was deemed to be far less harmful than either alcohol or tobacco (see Grinspoon 1971; Smith 1970; Sloman 1979). More recent research suggests, however, that marijuana smoking is a practice that combines the hazardous features of both tobacco and alcohol with a number of pitfalls of its own. Moreover, there are many disturbing questions about marijuana's effect on the vital systems of the body, on the brain and mind, on immunity and resistance, and on sex and reproduction (Jones and Lovinger 1985).

One of the more serious difficulties with marijuana use relates to lung damage. The most recent findings in this behalf should put to rest the rather tiresome argument by marijuana devotees that smoking just a few "joints" daily is less harmful than regularly smoking several times as many cigarettes. Researchers at the University of California at Los Angeles reported early in 1988 that the respiratory burden in smoke particulates and absorption of carbon monoxide from smoking just one marijuana "joint" is some *four times greater* than from smoking a single tobacco cigarette (Macdonald 1988; Chaing and Hawks 1990). Specifically, it was found that one "toke" of marijuana delivers three times more tar to the mouth and lungs than one puff of a filter-tipped cigarette; that marijuana deposits four times more tar in the throat and lungs and increases carbon monoxide levels in the blood fourfold to fivefold.

There seem to be three distinct sets of facts about marijuana its apologists tend to downplay, if not totally ignore—those about its chemical structure, its "persistence-of-residue" effect, and its changing potency.

First, the *cannabis sativa* plant from which marijuana comes is a complex chemical factory. Marijuana contains 426 known chemicals which are transformed into 2,000 chemicals when burned during the smoking process. Seventy of these chemicals are *cannabinoids*, substances that are found nowhere else in nature. Since they are fat-soluble, they are immediately deposited in those body tissues that have a high fat content—the brain, lungs, liver, and reproductive organs.

Second, THC (delta-9-tetrahydrocannabinol), the active ingredient and most potent psychoactive chemical in marijuana, is soluble in fat but not in water, which has a significant implication. The human body has a water-based waste disposal system—through blood, urine, sweat, and feces. A chemical such as THC that does not dissolve in water becomes trapped, principally in the brain, lungs, liver, and reproductive organs. This is the "persistence-of-residue" effect. One puff of smoke from a marijuana cigarette delivers a significant amount of THC, half of which remains in the body for several weeks. As such, if a person is smoking marijuana more than once a month, the residue levels of THC are not only retained, but also building up—in the brain, lungs, liver, and reproductive organs.

Third, the potency of marijuana has risen dramatically over the years. During the 1960s the THC content of marijuana was only two-tenths of one percent. By the 1980s the potency of imported marijuana was up to 5 percent, representing a 25-fold increase. Moreover, California *sinsemilla*, a seedless, domestic variety of marijuana, has a THC potency of 14 percent. In fact, so potent is *sinsemilla* that it has become the "pot of choice" both inside and outside the United States. On the streets of Bogota, Colombia, *sinsemilla* has been traded for cocaine on an equal weight basis (*Street Pharmacologist*, May–June 1988, 5).

Finally, aside from the health consequences of marijuana use, recent research on the behavioral aspects of the drug suggests that it severely affects the social perceptions of heavy users. Findings from the Center for Psychological Studies in New York City, for example, report that adults who smoked marijuana daily believed the drug helped them to function better—improving their self-awareness and relationships with others (Hendin et al. 1987). In reality, however, marijuana had acted as a "buffer," enabling users to tolerate problems rather than face them and make changes that might increase the quality of their social functioning and satisfaction with life. The study found that the research subjects used marijuana to avoid dealing with their difficulties, and the avoidance inevitably made their problems worse, on the job, at home, and in family and sexual relationships.

What this research documented was what clinicians had been saying for years. Personal growth evolves from learning to cope with stress, anxiety, frustration, and the many other difficulties that life presents, both small and large. Marijuana use (and the use of other drugs as well, including alcohol), particularly among adolescents and young adults, interferes with this process, and the result is a drug-induced arrested development (see DuPont 1984, 80–83; Spencer and Boren 1990).

Alternatively, it has been argued that for humanitarian reasons, a reclassification of marijuana under the scheduling provisions of the Controlled Substances Act is in order. At present, marijuana is a Schedule I drug, which means that it has no recognized "accepted" medical use.[2] Cocaine, on the other hand, is a Schedule II drug, meaning that it can be legally obtained on a prescription basis under special circumstances. As such, with many AIDS patients saying that marijuana alleviates the nausea and vomiting caused by the syndrome and the drugs used to treat it (an argument also made by cancer chemotherapy patients), a reclassification of the drug into Schedule II would make it available for medical purposes (Van Pelt 1991). Moreover, this is one of the explicit positions of Arnold Trebach and the Drug Policy Foundation (1992). It is a position that I fully agree with; it is simply the humanitarian thing to do.

Cocaine. Lured by the Lorelei of orgasmic pleasure, millions of Americans use cocaine each year—a snort in each nostril and the user is up and away for 20 minutes or so. Alert, witty, and with it, the user has no hangover, no lung cancer, and no holes in the arms or burned-out cells in the brain. The cocaine high is an immediate, intensively vivid, and sensation-enhancing experience. Moreover, it has the reputation for being a spectacular aphrodisiac: it is believed to create sexual desire, to heighten

---

[2]Under federal regulations, Schedule I drugs are the most strictly controlled, have a high potential for abuse, no currently accepted use in the United States, and no acceptable safe level of use under medical supervision. Many narcotics, such as heroin and other opiates and opium derivatives, fall into this category. In addition, many hallucinogenic drugs that have no recognized medical value in this country, such as mescaline, peyote, and lysergic acid diethylamide (LSD), are listed in Schedule I.

it, to increase sexual endurance, and to cure frigidity and impotence.

Given all these positives, it is no wonder that cocaine became an "all-American drug" and a multibillion-dollar-a-year industry. The drug permeates all levels of society, from Park Avenue to the inner city: lawyers and executives use cocaine; baby boomers and yuppies use cocaine; college students and high school drop-outs use cocaine; police officers, prosecutors, and prisoners use cocaine; politicians use cocaine; housewives and pensioners use cocaine; Democrats, Republicans, Independents, and Socialists use cocaine; bartenders and stockbrokers and children and athletes use cocaine; even some priests and members of Congress use cocaine.

Yet, the pleasure and feelings of power that cocaine engenders in actuality make its use an unwise recreational pursuit. In very small and occasional doses it is no more harmful than equally moderate doses of alcohol, but there is a side to cocaine that can be very destructive. That euphoric lift, with its feelings of pleasure, confidence, and being on top of things, that comes from but a few brief snorts is short-lived and invariably followed by a letdown. More specifically, when the elation and grandiose feelings begin to wane, a corresponding deep depression is often felt, which is in such marked contrast to users' previous states that they are strongly motivated to repeat the dose and restore the euphoria. This leads to chronic, compulsive use. And when chronic users try to stop using cocaine, they are typically plunged into a severe depression from which only more cocaine can arouse them. Most clinicians estimate that approximately 10 percent of those who begin to use cocaine "recreationally" will go on to serious, heavy, chronic, compulsive use (Grabowski 1984; Kozel and Adams 1985; Erickson et al. 1987; Spitz and Rosecan 1987; Washton 1989; Washton and Gold 1987).

To this can be added what is known as the "cocaine psychosis" (see Weiss and Mirin 1987, 50–53; Satel et al. 1991). As dose and duration of cocaine use increase, the development of cocaine-related psychopathology is not uncommon. Cocaine psychosis is generally preceded by a transitional period characterized by increased suspiciousness, compulsive behavior, faultfinding, and eventually paranoia. When the psychotic state is reached, individuals may experience visual and/or auditory hallucinations, with persecutory voices commonly heard. Many believe that they are being followed by police or that family, friends, and others are plotting against them. Moreover, everyday events tend to be misinterpreted in a way that supports delusional beliefs. When coupled with the irritability and hyperactivity that the stimulant nature of cocaine tends to generate in almost all of its users, the cocaine-induced paranoia may lead to violent behavior as a means of "self-defense" against imagined persecutors.

Not to be forgotten are the physiological consequences of cocaine use. Since the drug is an extremely potent central-nervous-system stimulant, its physical effects include increased temperature, heart rate, and blood pressure. There are tens of thousands of cocaine-related hospital room emergency visits that occur each year.[3] In addition, there has been a gradual increase in the number of cocaine-related deaths in the United States, from only 53 in 1976 to 615 in 1985, to 2,483 in 1990 (National Institute on Drug Abuse 1986, 1991b). And while these numbers may seem infinitesimal when compared with the magnitude of deaths associated with alcohol- and tobacco-related diseases and accidents, it should be remembered that at present only a small segment of the American population uses cocaine. And too, in terms of numbers of overdose deaths, cocaine ranks higher than any other drug—legal or illegal (National Institute on Drug Abuse 1986, 1991b).

Finally, what has been said about cocaine also applies to crack, and perhaps more so. Crack's low price (as little as $2 per rock in some locales) has made it an attractive drug of

---

[3]In 1990, for example, there were more than 80,000 cocaine-related emergencies reported to the Drug Abuse Warning Network system (see National Institute on Drug Abuse 1991a). In 1991, this figure had increased to over 100,000 (*Substance Abuse Report*, 1 September 1992, 5–6).

abuse for those with limited funds. Its rapid absorption brings on a faster onset of dependence than is typical with other forms of cocaine, resulting in higher rates of addiction, binge use, and psychoses. The consequences include higher levels of cocaine-related violence and all the same manifestations of personal, familial, and occupational neglect that are associated with other forms of drug dependence. Issues related to crack are addressed in detail in a separate section of this essay.

Heroin. A derivative of morphine, heroin is a highly addictive narcotic, and is the drug historically associated with addiction and street crime. Although heroin overdose is not uncommon, unlike alcohol, cocaine, tobacco, and many prescription drugs, the direct physiological damage caused by heroin use tends to be minimal. And it is for this reason that the protagonists of drug legalization include heroin in their arguments. By making heroin readily available to users, they argue, many problems could be sharply reduced if not totally eliminated, including: the crime associated with supporting a heroin habit; the overdoses resulting from unknown levels of heroin purity and potency; the HIV and hepatitis infections brought about by needle-sharing; and the personal, social, and occupational dislocations resulting from the drug-induced criminal lifestyle.[4]

The belief that the legalization of heroin would eliminate crime, overdose, infections, and life dislocations for its users is for the most part delusional. Instead, it is likely that the heroin-use lifestyle would change little for most addicts regardless of the legal status of the drug, an argument supported by ample evidence in the biographies and autobiographies of narcotics addicts, the clinical assessments of heroin addiction, and the drug abuse treatment literature (for example, see Anonymous 1903; Burroughs 1953; Nyswander 1956; Street 1953; Hirsch 1968; Fiddle 1967; Smith and Gay 1971; Fisher 1972; Gould et al. 1974; Rettig, Torres, and Garrett 1977; Rosenbaum

1981; Peele 1985; Platt 1986). And to this can be added the many thousands of conversations I have had over the past 30 years with heroin users and members of their families.

The point is this. Heroin is a highly addicting drug. For the addict, it becomes life-consuming: it becomes mother, father, spouse, lover, counselor, and confessor. Because heroin is a short-acting drug, with its effects lasting at best four to six hours, it must be taken regularly and repeatedly. Because there is a more rapid onset when taken intravenously, most heroin users inject the drug. Because heroin has depressant effects, a portion of the user's day is spent in a semi-stupefied state. Collectively, these attributes result in a user more concerned with drug-taking and drug-seeking than health, family, work, relationships, responsibility, or anything else.

THE LEGACY OF CRACK COCAINE

The great drug wars in the United States have endured now for generations, although the drug legalization debates have less of a history—on again, off again since the 1930s, with a sudden burst of energy at the close of the 1980s. But as the wars linger on and the debates abide, a coda must be added to both of these politically charged topics. It concerns crack cocaine, a drug that has brought about a level of human suffering heretofore unknown in the American drug scene. The problem with crack is not that it is prohibited, but rather, the fact that it exists at all in the pharmacopoeia of intoxicants. The chemistry and psychopharmacology of crack, combined with the tangle of socioeconomic and psychocultural strains that exist in those communities where the drug is concentrated, warrant some consideration of whether further discussion of its legality or illegality serves any purpose. Focusing on crack as an example, my intent here is to argue that both the "drug wars" and "harm reduction effort" are better served by a shifting away from the drug legalization debate.

Crack Cocaine in the United States. Crack is not a particularly new drug to the United States,

---

[4]This point of view is most thoroughly articulated in Trebach (1982).

but goes back several decades, to a time when cocaine was still known as *charlie, corrine, bernice, schoolboy,* and the "rich man's drug." It was first reported in the literature during the early 1970s (Anonymous 1972), but even then it had been known for a number of years. At that time, however, knowledge of crack, known then as "base" or "rock" (not to be confused with "rock cocaine"—a cocaine hydrochloride product for intranasal snorting), seemed to be restricted to segments of cocaine's freebasing subculture. But since the drug contained many impurities, it was often referred to as "garbage freebase" by cocaine aficionados, and was quickly discarded. It was rediscovered at the beginning of the 1980s, and by the middle of the decade it had taken on a life of its own (see Inciardi 1992, 103–32).

For the inner cities across America, the introduction of crack couldn't have happened at a worse time. The economic base of the working poor had been shrinking for years, the result of a number of factors, including the loss of many skilled and unskilled jobs to cheaper labor markets, the movement of many businesses to the surburbs and the Sun Belt, and competition from foreign manufacturers. Standards of living, health, and overall quality of life were also in a downward direction, as consequences of suburbanization and the shrinking tax bases of central cities, combined with changing economic policies at the federal level that shifted the responsibility for many social supports to the local and private sectors. Without question, by the early to mid-1980s there was a growing and pervasive climate of hopelessness in ghetto America. And at the same time, as HIV and AIDS began to spread through inner-city populations of injectable drug users and their sex partners and as funding for drug abuse treatment declined, the production of coca and cocaine in South America reached an all-time high, resulting in high-purity cocaine at a low price on the streets of urban America. As I said, crack couldn't have come to the inner city at a worse time.

The next chapter in the story of crack is pretty well known, having been reported (and perhaps over-reported) in the media since early in 1986—the "highs," binges, and "crashes" that induce addicts to sell their belongings and their bodies in pursuit of more crack; the high addiction liability of the drug that instigates users to commit any manner and variety of crimes to support their habits. Also well known are the rivalries in crack distribution networks that have turned some inner-city communities into urban "dead zones," where homicide rates are so high that police have written them off as anarchic badlands; the involvement of inner-city youths in the crack business, including the "peewees" and "wannabees" (want-to-bes), those street-gang acolytes in grade school and junior high who patrol the streets with walkie-talkies in the vicinity of crack houses, serving in networks of lookouts, spotters, and steerers, and aspiring to be "rollers" (short for high-rollers) in the drug distribution business. Well known as well is the child abuse, child neglect, and child abandonment by crack-addicted mothers; and finally, the growing cohort of "crack babies" that appear troubled not only physically, but emotionally and behaviorally as well.

Drug Policy and the American Crack House. Drug policy is typically formulated and established by politicians and other government officials after input from the field, public hearings, various constituencies, and panels of advisers and experts. It is then deliberated and debated, pondered and argued by political and social observers of all types, and researchers and analysts from a variety of academic fields. Much of the deliberation and debate is typically based on what has appeared in the press, in the research literature, and from focused theoretical and empirical study. As such, policy formulation and subsequent discussions generally occur within the safe, secure, and existentially antiseptic confines of legislative chambers, government conference rooms, collegiate study halls, and the highest of academic roosts. It must be that way, for rational and measured thought has difficulty in the face of immediate chaos. But now and then, those who have the most to say about drug affairs ought to visit the mean and despairing streets.

It has been argued that you don't have to be a soldier to understand war, to live in the ghetto to understand poverty and hopelessness, to be a rape victim to understand sexual assault, or be a member of an oppressed minority to understand discrimination. But it sure can help. I know that the perspective and insight are different. Having seen the 1972 Warner Brothers epic *Deliverance* just doesn't convey the same experience as white-water rafting the wild and scenic Chattooga River through Georgia's Chattahoochee National Forest, where much of the movie was filmed. Or similarly, reading about a fatal automobile accident in the newspaper, no matter how vivid the description, is quite different from watching and listening to people burn to death, trapped in their overturned car. The cries of the dying seem to scream into your soul forever. As such, reading about crack houses, seeing pictures of crack houses, or even walking past a few on the street is entirely different from spending time in them. The ambiance is different. In the photo or the street scene, the aura of despair and hopelessness just isn't there, nor is the smell of fear, the constant threat of violence, and the degradation and suffering.

I've been doing street studies in Miami, Florida, for more years than I care to remember, and during that time I've had many an experience in the shooting galleries, base houses, and open-air drug and prostitution markets that populate the local drug scene. None of these prepared me, however, with what I was to encounter in the crack houses. As part of a federally funded street survey and ethnography of cocaine and crack use, my first trip to a crack house came in 1988.[5] I had gained entrée through a local drug dealer who had been a key informant of mine for almost a decade. He introduced me to the crack house "door man" as someone "straight but OK." After the door man checked us for weapons, my guide proceeded to show me around.

Upon entering a room in the rear of the crack house (what I later learned was called a "freak room"), I observed what appeared to be the forcible gang-rape of an unconscious child. Emaciated, seemingly comatose, and likely no older than 14 years of age, she was lying spread-eagled on a filthy mattress while four men in succession had vaginal intercourse with her. Despite what was happening, I was urged not to interfere.[6] After they had finished and left the room, another man came in, and they engaged in oral sex.

Upon leaving the crack house sometime later, the dealer/informant explained that she was a "house girl"—a person in the employ of the crack house owner. He gave her food, a place to sleep, some cigarettes and cheap wine, and all the crack she wanted in return for her providing sex—any type and amount of sex—to his crack house customers.

That was my first trip to a crack house. During subsequent trips to this and other crack houses, there were other scenes: a woman purchasing crack, with an infant tucked under her arm—so neglected that she had maggots crawling out of her diaper; a man "skin-popping" his toddler with a small dose of heroin, so the child would remain quietly sedated and not interrupt a crack-smoking session; people in various states of excitement and paranoia, crouching in the corners of smoking rooms inhaling from "the devil's dick" (the stem of the crack pipe); arguments, fist fights, stabbings, and shootings over crack, the price of crack, the quantity and quality of crack, and the use and sharing of crack; any manner and variety of sexual activity—by individuals and/or groups, with members of the opposite sex, the same sex, or both, or with animals, in private or public, in exchange for crack. I also saw "drug hounds" and "rock monsters" (some of the "regulars" in a crack house) crawling on their hands and knees, inspecting the floors for slivers of crack that may have dropped; beatings

[5]This research was supported by Health and Human Services grant # 1-R01-DA04862, "Crack Abuse Patterns and Crime Linkages," James A. Inciardi, Principal Investigator, from the National Institute on Drug Abuse.

[6]This incident, as well as a discussion of the methods, dangers, and ethics of crack house research, is examined in detail in Inciardi, Lockwood, and Pottieger (1993).

and gang rapes of small-time drug couriers—women, men, girls, and boys—as punishment for "messing up the money"; people in convulsions and seizures, brought on by crack use, cocaine use, the use of some other drug, or whatever; users of both sexes, so dependent on crack, so desperate for more crack, that they would do anything for another hit, eagerly risking the full array of sexually transmitted diseases, including AIDS; imprisonment and sexual slavery, one of the ultimate results of crack addiction (see Inciardi 1991; Inciardi, Lockwood, and Pottieger 1991, 1993). And then there was the time I was arrested in a Miami crack house.

It should be pointed out that not all of these activities occur all of the time, or even in all crack houses. But they do happen sufficiently often enough to make one wonder about it all.[7] Do these users who frequent crack houses represent some special breed of degenerate rarely seen elsewhere in the drug scene? Or is it something else? What is it about crack that engenders such behavior? To these three questions my answers are "no, not especially"; "yes, definitely"; and "a whole lot of things."

Crack has been called the "fast-food" variety of cocaine. It is cheap and easy to conceal, it vaporizes with practically no odor, and the gratification is swift: an intense, almost sexual euphoria that lasts less than five minutes. Smoking cocaine as opposed to snorting it results in more immediate and direct absorption of the drug, producing a quicker and more compelling "high," greatly increasing the dependence potential. Users typically smoke for as long as they have crack or the means to purchase it—money, personal belongings, sexual services, stolen goods, or other drugs. It is rare that smokers have but a single hit. More likely they spend $50 to $500 during a "mission"—a three- or four-day binge, smoking almost constantly, 3 to 50 rocks per day. During these cycles, crack users rarely eat or sleep. And once crack is tried, for many users it is not

long before it becomes a daily habit. Many crack users engage in sexual behaviors with extremely high frequency. However, to suggest that crack turns men into "sex-crazed fiends" and women into "sex-crazed whores," as sensationalized media stories imply, is anything but precise. The situation is far more complex than that.

A strong association between crack use and apparent "hypersexual behaviors" is evident in my observations and interviews in Miami, as well as other ethnographic analyses of the crack scene (for example, Bourgois and Dunlap 1991; Koester and Schwartz 1991; Ratner, in press). The crack-sex association has both pharmacological and sociocultural explanations (Inciardi, Lockwood, and Pottieger 1991). The former begins with psychopharmacology: one effect of all forms of cocaine, including crack, is the release of normal inhibitions on behavior, including sexual behavior. The disinhibiting effect of cocaine is markedly stronger than that of depressants such as alcohol, Valium, or heroin. While the latter drugs typically cause a release from worry and an accompanying increase of self-confidence, cocaine typically causes elation and an accompanying gross overestimation of one's own capabilities. Further, since crack effects have a rapid onset, so too does the related release of inhibitions. Medical authorities generally concede that because of the disinhibiting effects of cocaine, its use among new users does indeed enhance sexual enjoyment and improve sexual functioning, including more intense orgasms (Weiss and Mirin 1987; Grinspoon and Bakalar 1985). These same reports maintain, however, that among long-term addicts, cocaine decreases both sexual desire and performance.

Going further, the crack-sex association involves the need of female crack addicts to pay for their drug. Even this connection has a pharmacological component—crack's rapid onset, extremely short duration of effects, and high addiction liability combine to result in compulsive use and a willingness to obtain the drug through any means. Other parts of the economic crack-sex relationship, however, are strictly sociocultural. As in the legal job

---

[7]For descriptions of other crack houses in other cities, see Ratner (1993).

market, the access of women in the street sub-cultures to illegal income is typically more limited than that of men. Prostitution has long been the easiest, most lucrative, and most reliable means for women to finance drug use (Goldstein 1979).

The combined pharmacological and socio-cultural effects of crack use can put female users in severe jeopardy. Because crack makes its users ecstatic and yet is so short-acting, it has an extremely high addiction potential. Use rapidly becomes compulsive use. Crack acquisition thus becomes enormously more important than family, work, social responsibility, health, values, modesty, morality, or self-respect. This makes sex-for-crack exchanges psychologically tolerable as an economic necessity. Further, the disinhibiting effects of crack enable users to engage in sexual acts they might not otherwise even consider.

And what about the men, are they some special species of libertine, bent on degrading and exploiting women at every turn? Again, likely not. Most of the male crack users that I have interviewed, or observed in crack houses, are as forlorn and pathetic as the women. For some, it is indeed a "macho" thing, for the sake of dominating women, while others view the crack house as a vehicle for satisfying unfulfilled sexual fantasies. But for most, who have spent their lives in poverty or at its edge, attempting to cope with the series of tragedies and misfortunes that characterize existing and passing time in the inner city, trying to make lives for themselves in the cultures of terror and hopelessness that so often typify life in the street, the sex scene seems to provide a measure of influence and status. As one 44-year-old male put it in late 1990:

> I' been a loser all my life, except when I be in the *hut* [crack house] with a few dollars or some *cracks* [more than one rock]. Then I can tell the lady to get on her knees and put her face between my legs. It's the only time in my life I feel like I'm a little in control of things.

But the pathos of it all is that even then, the control is both limited and distorted. Only in the beginnings of a career in cocaine or crack use do men exhibit any sexual vitality, or experience sexual satisfaction. Chronic crack use engenders both impotence and the inability to climax. As such, in those crack houses where public sex is common, a customary sight is the seemingly never-ending oral stimulation of a flaccid penis.

In the final analysis, because of its chemistry, crack is easy to produce—mix a little bit of street cocaine, baking soda, and some additives for bulk with water, heat it in a microwave oven, and you have crack cocaine. It is also rather inexpensive to produce, and will likely remain that way for quite some time, regardless of its legal status. A benefit of its current criminalization is that since it *is* against the law, it doesn't have widespread availability, so proportionately few people use it.

So where does all of this take us? My point is this. Within the context of reversing the human suffering that crack has helped to exacerbate, what purpose is served by arguing for its legalization? Will legalizing crack make it less available, less attractive, less expensive, less addictive, or less troublesome? Nobody really knows for sure, but I doubt it.

References

Anonymous. 1903. *Twenty Years in Hell, or the Life, Experience, Trials, and Tribulations of a Morphine Fiend*, Kansas City, MO: Author's Edition.

Anonymous. 1972. *The Gourmet Cokebook: A Complete Guide to Cocaine*. White Mountain Press.

Benjamin, Daniel K., and Roger Leroy Miller. 1991. *Undoing Drugs: Beyond Legalization*. New York: Basic Books.

Boaz, David, ed. 1990. *The Crisis in Prohibition*. Washington: Cato Institute.

Bourgois, Phillipe, and Eloise Dunlap. 1991. "Sex-for-Crack in Harlem, New York." Paper presented at the Annual Meeting of the Society for Applied Anthropology, Charleston, South Carolina, 13–17 March.

Brecher, Edward M., and the Editors of Consumer Reports. 1972. *Licit and Illicit Drugs*. New York: Little, Brown.

Burroughs, William. 1953. *Junkie*. New York: Ace.

Centers for Disease Control. 1990. "Trends in Lung Cancer Incidence and Mortality," *Morbidity and Mortality Weekly Report* 39 (December 7): 875–83.

———. 1991a. "Annual and New Year's Day Alcohol-Related Traffic Fatalities: United States, 1982–1990," *Morbidity and Mortality Weekly Report* 40 (December 6): 821–25.

———. 1991b. "Cigarette Smoking Among Reproductive-Aged Women," *Morbidity and Mortality Weekly Report* 40 (October 25): 719–23.

Chaing, C. Nora, and Richard L. Hawks, eds. 1990. *Research Findings on Smoking of Abused Substances*, Rockville, MD: National Institute on Drug Abuse.

Chambliss, William J. 1988. "Testimony." In U.S. Congress. House. Select Committee on Narcotics Abuse and Control. *Hearings on Legalization of Illicit Drugs: Impact and Feasibility*. 100th Cong., 2d sess., 29 September.

Drug Policy Foundation. 1992. *National Drug Reform Strategy*. Washington: Drug Policy Foundation.

DuPont, Robert L. 1984. *Getting Tough on Gateway Drugs*. Washington: American Psychiatric Press.

Erickson, Patricia G., Edward M. Adlaf, Glenn F. Murray, and Reginald G. Smart. 1987. *The Steel Drug: Cocaine in Perspective*. Lexington, MA: Lexington Books.

Evans, Richard. 1990. "The Many Forms of Legalization: Beyond 'Whether' to 'How.'" *In The Great Issues in Drug Policy*, edited by Arnold S. Trebach and Kevin B. Zeese. Washington: Drug Policy Foundation.

Fiddle, Seymour. 1967. *Portraits from a Shooting Gallery*. New York: Harper & Row.

Fisher, Florrie. 1972. *The Lonely Trip Back*. New York: Bantam.

Goldstein, Paul J. 1979. *Prostitution and Drugs*. Lexington, MA: D.C. Heath.

Gould, Leroy, Andrew L. Walker, Lansing E. Crane, and Charles W. Litz. 1974. *Connections: Notes from the Heroin World*. New Haven, CT: Yale University Press.

Grabowski, John, ed. 1984. *Cocaine; Pharmacology, Effects, and Treatment of Abuse*. Rockville, MD: National Institute on Drug Abuse.

Grinspoon, Lester. 1971. *Marihuana Reconsidered*. Cambridge: Harvard University Press.

Grinspoon, Lester, and James B. Bakalar. 1985. *Cocaine: A Drug and Its Social Evolution*. New York: Basic Books.

Hendin, Herbert, Ann Pollinger Haas, Paul Singer, Melvin Ellner, and Richard Ulman. 1987. *Living High: Daily Marijuana Use Among Adults*. New York: Human Sciences Press.

Hirsch, Phil. 1968. *Hooked*. New York: Pyramid.

Inciardi, James A. 1979. "Heroin Use and Street Crime," *Crime and Delinquency* 25 (July): 335–46.

———. 1980. "Youth, Drugs, and Street Crime." In *Drugs and the Youth Culture*, edited by Frank R. Scarpitti and Susan K. Datesman. Beverly Hills, CA: Sage, 175–203.

———. 1986. *The War on Drugs: Heroin, Cocaine, Crime, and Public Policy*. Palo Alto, CA: Mayfield.

———. 1987. "Sociology and American Drug Policy," *American Sociologist* 18 (Summer): 179–88.

———. 1990. "Sociology and the Legalization of Drugs: Some Considerations for the Continuing Policy Debate." Paper presented at the 85th Annual Meeting of the American Sociological Association, 11–15 August, Washington, D.C.

———. 1991. "Kingrats, Chicken Heads, Slow Necks, Freaks, and Blood Suckers: A Glimpse at the Miami Sex for Crack Market." Paper presented at the Annual Meeting of the Society for Applied Anthropology, Charleston, South Carolina, 13–17 March.

———. 1992. *The War on Drugs II: The Continuing Epic of Heroin, Cocaine, Crack, Crime, AIDS, and Public Policy*. Mountain View, CA: Mayfield.

Inciardi, James A., Dorothy Lockwood, and Anne E. Pottieger. 1991. "Crack Dependent Women and Sexuality," *Addiction and Recovery* 11 (July–August): 25–28.

———. 1993. *Women and Crack-Cocaine*. New York: Macmillan.

Inciardi, James A., Steven S. Martin, Dorothy Lockwood, Robert M. Hooper, and Bruce M. Wald. 1990. "Obstacles to the Implementation of Drug Treatment Programs in Correctional Settings," National Institute on Drug Abuse Technical Review on Drug Abuse Treatment in Prisons and Jails, Rockville, Maryland, 24–25.

Inciardi, James A., and Duane C. McBride. 1989. "Legalization: A High Risk Alternative in the War on Drugs," *American Behavioral Scientist* 32 (January–February): 259–89.

———. 1991. *Treatment Alternatives to Street Crime (TASC): History, Experiences, and Issues*, Rockville, MD: National Institute on Drug Abuse.

Jones, Helen C., and Paul W. Lovinger. 1985. *The Marijuana Question*. New York: Dodd, Mead.

Koester, Stephen, and Judith Schwartz. 1991. "Crack Cocaine and Sex." *Paper presented at the Annual Meeting of the Society for Applied Anthropology.* Charleston, South Carolina, 13–17 March.

Kozel, Nicholas J., and Edgar H. Adams, eds. 1985. *Cocaine Use in America: Epidemiologic and Clinical Perspectives*. Rockville, MD: National Institute on Drug Abuse.

Kyvig, David E., ed. 1985. *Law, Alcohol, and Order: Perspectives on National Prohibition*. Westport, CT: Greenwood Press.

Macdonald, Donald Ian. 1988. "Marijuana Smoking Worse for Lungs," *Journal of the American Medical Association 259* (17 June): 3384.

Miller, Richard Lawrence. 1991. *The Case for Legalizing Drugs*. Westport, CT: Praeger.

National Institute on Drug Abuse. 1986. *Drug Abuse Warning Network Facility History File*. Rockville, MD: National Institute on Drug Abuse.

——— 1991a. *Annual Emergency Room Data From the Drug Abuse Warning Network*. Rockville, MD: National Institute on Drug Abuse.

———. 1991b. *Annual Medical Examiner Data From the Drug Abuse Warning Network*. Rockville, MD: National Institute on Drug Abuse.

Nyswander, Marie. 1956. *The Drug Addict as a Patient*. New York: Grune & Stratton.

Peele, Stanton. 1985. *The Meaning of Addiction*. Lexington, MA: Lexington Books.

Platt, Jerome J. 1986. *Heroin Addiction*. Malabar, FL: Robert E. Krieger.

Ratner, Mitchell. 1993. *Crack Pipe as Pimp: An Ethnographic Investigation of Sex-for-Crack Exchanges*. New York: Lexington Books.

Rettig, Richard P., Manual J. Torres, and Gerald R. Garrett. 1977. *Manny: A Criminal-Addict's Story*. Boston: Houghton Mifflin.

Rosenbaum, Marsha. 1981. *Women on Heroin*. New Brunswick, NJ: Rutgers University Press.

Ruth, Eric. 1992. "Leap Day: It's All in the Timing," Wilmington (Delaware) *News-Journal*, 29 February, 1A.

Satel, Sally L., Lawrence H. Price, Joseph M. Palumbo, Christopher J. McDougle, John H. Krystal, Frank Gawin, Dennis S. Charney, George R. Heninger, and Herbert D. Kleber. 1991. "Clinical Phenomenology and Neurobiology of Cocaine Abstinence: A Prospective Inpatient Study," *American Journal of Psychiatry* 148 (December): 1712–16.

Sloman, Larry. 1979. *Reefer Madness: The History of Marijuana in America*. Indianapolis: Bobbs-Merrill.

Smith, David E., ed. 1970. *The New Social Drug: Cultural, Medical, and Legal Perspectives on Marijuana*. Englewood Cliffs, NJ: Prentice-Hall.

Smith, David E., and George R. Gay, eds. 1971. *"It's So Good, Don't Even Try It Once."* Englewood Cliffs, NJ: Prentice-Hall.

Spencer, John W., and John J. Boren, eds. 1990. *Residual Effects of Abused Drugs on Behavior.* Rockville, MD: National Institute on Drug Abuse.

Spitz, Henry I., and Jeffrey S. Rosecan. 1987. *Cocaine Abuse: New Directions in Treatment and Research*. New York: Brunner/Mazel.

Street, Leroy. 1953. *I Was a Drug Addict*. New York: Random House.

Trebach, Arnold S. 1982. *The Heroin Solution*. New Haven, CT: Yale University Press.

———. 1987. *The Great Drug War*. New York: Macmillan.

———. 1989. "Legalization Versus the Law of the Jungle," Testimony in support of S. 1918, New York Senate (16 June).

Trebach, Arnold S., and Kevin B. Zeese, eds. 1989. *Drug Policy 1989–1990: A Reformer's Catalogue*. Washington: Drug Policy Foundation.

———, eds. 1990a. *Drug Prohibition and the Conscience of Nations*. Washington: Drug Policy Foundation.

———, eds. 1990b. *The Great Issues in Drug Policy*. Washington: Drug Policy Foundation.

———, eds. 1991. *New Frontiers in Drug Policy*. Washington: Drug Policy Foundation.

———, eds. 1992. *Strategies for Change*. Washington: Drug Policy Foundation.

Van Pelt, Dina. 1991. "AIDS Patients Seek a Legal High," *Insight* 14 (January): 50–51.

Washton, Arnold W. 1989. *Cocaine Addiction: Treatment, Recovery, and Relapse Prevention.* New York: W. W. Norton.

Washton, Arnold W., and Mark S. Gold, eds. 1987. *Cocaine: A Clinician's Handbook.* New York: Guilford Press.

Weiss, Roger D., and Steven M. Mirin. 1987. *Cocaine.* Washington: American Psychiatric Press.

In Re P.

LET THE 14-YEAR OLD GO, THE PROSTITUTION LAWS ARE UNCONSTITUTIONAL

MARGARET TAYLOR, JUDGE.

Respondent P. is a 14 year old female. The petition alleges that "Respondent did offer to perform a deviate sexual act for U.S. currency," an act which, if committed by an adult, would constitute the crime of prostitution. Paragraph Ten of the Bill of Particulars of the Corporation Counsel describes the incident as follows:

"On March 6, 1977, at about 8:30 P.M., respondent accosted complaining witness on the street and offered to engage in sexual acts with him for a fee of $10; he agreed and respondent took him to the Evans Hotel, 273 West 38 Street, New York City. Complaining witness paid $4 for the use of a room and went there with respondent."

It should be noted that the complaining witness was not charged with the violation of patronizing a prostitute. Nor was he charged with any other crime applicable to these facts.

> A person is guilty of prostitution when such person engages or agrees or offers to engage in sexual conduct with another person in return for a fee.

In re P 400 N.Y.S.2d 455 (1977). (This edited version retains original footnote numbers.)

A deviate sexual act is defined by the Penal Law as:

> "Deviate sexual intercourse" means sexual conduct between persons not married to each other consisting of contact between the penis and the anus, the mouth and penis, or the mouth and the vulva.

Deviate sexual intercourse, also a Class B misdemeanor, is a crime under the Penal Law:

> Consensual Sodomy: A person is guilty of consensual sodomy when he engages in deviate sexual intercourse with another person.

The threshold question in all juvenile delinquency proceedings is *not* whether a respondent committed a particular act but whether such an act would be a crime if committed by an adult. If not, then the court can go no further and must dismiss the petition. Accordingly, if acts committed by an adult would not constitute a crime because the criminal statute or statutes making such alleged acts a crime were unconstitutional, such acts could not be the basis for a charge of juvenile delinquency. A youth under the age of 16 may be found to be a juvenile delinquent only if an adult who engaged in the same conduct as the youth could be found to have committed a crime. If a statute is unconstitutional as applied to adults, a statute is unconstitutional as applied to juveniles.

Inasmuch as the petition alleges that the respondent offered to perform an act of consensual sodomy for a fee, the charges brought against respondent necessarily invoke the prostitution statute and the consensual sodomy law. Respondent is specifically charged with offering to perform a "deviate" sexual act for a fee. If she had been charged with offering to perform a "normal" sexual act (i.e. fornication) for a fee, it would have been necessary for the court to deal with the question of whether a crime can be committed by offering to perform a sexual act, which in and of itself is not illegal, for money.[4] Here, however, respondent is charged with offering to perform an act which in and of itself is prescribed by a criminal statute, the consensual sodomy law. It is necessary, therefore, for the court to examine those sections of the Penal Law and make a determination as to their constitutionality.

Respondent, by her attorney, has moved to dismiss the prostitution charge on constitutional and other grounds. For the reasons stated below, the court holds that sections 230.00, 130.38 and 130.00(2) of the Penal Law are unconstitutional under the New York State Constitution in that these statutes constitute a denial of equal protection and invade respondent's constitutionally protected right of privacy.

The equal protection clause is offended when the state discriminates between classes of citizens similarly situated on arbitrary and unreasonable grounds not related to the objective of the legislation.

The selective enforcement of a law against a particular class of individuals on the basis of sex is no less offensive to the equal protection clause than classification by sex on the face of the statute.

[4]See e.g. *In re Lane*, 58 Cal.2d 99, 22 Cal.Rptr. 857, 372 P.2d 897 (1962); *U. S. v. Moses*, 41 U.S.L.W. 2298 (D.C.Sup.Ct.1972) *rev'd* 339 A.2d 46 (D.C.App.1975).

Until 1964, a prostitute was defined as a "female person." The legislature amended the penal law to make the prostitution statute sex neutral in its wording and it enacted a statute proscribing the act of patronizing a prostitute. Although the prostitution laws were made facially sex neutral, their historical sex bias has endured.

A person may be found guilty of prostitution for simply "agreeing" to perform a sexual act, even if the patron is the solicitor. In contrast, patronizing a prostitute is merely a violation carrying a penalty of up to fifteen days imprisonment or up to $250 fine. The conduct engaged in by the prostitute and the patron is nearly identical and the wording of the respective statutes is quite similar.

The instant case presents clear evidence of intentional selective enforcement of the prostitution statutes against females. The overwhelming majority of arrests made under section 230.00 of the Penal Law are of female prostitutes. During the first six months of 1977, 3219 arrests were made in New York County under this statute. Of those arrested, 2,944 were females and only 275 were males. Of equal importance is the fact that although 3219 arrests were made for prostitution, only 62 persons were charged with patronizing a prostitute. Of the 2,944 female prostitutes arrested, only 60 of their male patrons were charged with a violation. This data supports the conclusion that those assigned the task of enforcing the law harbor the attitude that women who supply sex are immoral whereas the men who demand their services are considered blameless.

The methods of enforcement used by the police contribute to the selective enforcement of the prostitution laws against females. Arrests for prostitution are rarely made on the complaint of a private citizen. A police officer must be directly solicited to make an arrest. Male undercover police officers are assigned to pose as patrons to entrap streetwalkers. However, female plainclothes officers are not presently assigned to pose as prostitutes to entrap male patrons. Thus, the method of enforcement of the prostitution laws is sex biased, aimed only at punishing the female prostitute.[9]

. . . the prostitution statutes violate the equal protection clause. There is no, nor has the Corporation Counsel suggested any, reasonable justification for penalizing the conduct of female prostitutes more severely than the conduct of their male patrons.[10] The prostitution laws have undeniably been selectively enforced against females because of their sex. Discrimination by the state between different classes of citizens,

" 'must be reasonable, not arbitrary, and must rest upon some ground of difference having a fair and substantial relation to the object of the legislation, so that all persons similarly circumstanced shall be treated alike.' "

This court can find no real difference between the conduct of the prostitute and the patron. The patron pays and the prostitute receives compensation for her services. Yet, under the wording of the statute and frequently in practice, the patron may be the solicitor.[11]

As a court of this state observed over fifty years ago:

The men create the market; and the women who supply the demand pay the penalty. It is time that this unfair discrimination and injustice should cease. . . . The practical application of the law as heretofore enforced is an unjust discrimination against women in the matter of an offense, which in its very nature, if completed, requires the participation of men.

To the extent prostitution may cause a public nuisance by reason of offensive conduct on the streets or congested traffic, such nuisance is caused by prostitute and patron alike.

The respondent is charged with offering to perform a "deviate" sexual act for a fee. As indicated above, it is necessary, therefore, for the court to examine sections 130.38 and 130.00(2)

---

[9]In experimental programs in New York City and the District of Columbia, female undercover police officers were assigned to pose as prostitutes to entrap patrons. White, married, middle class and middle aged men were arrested. The public uproar of "respectable" citizens that ensued in response to these arrests caused the end of these experiments. See *N. Y. Times*, Nov. 16, 1977, at p. D17, col. 5. This commonplace selective enforcement tactic designed to punish the female streetwalker and leave unscathed her white, middle aged, middle class married male client (*Politics of Prostitution* supra at 52–3; Cooney & Quint. *Prostitution in New York City; Answers to Some Questions*, para. 3 (June, 1977)) is a very costly law enforcement practice. It violates the streetwalker's right to equal protection of the law. Moreover, community support for law enforcement is eroded when the streetwalker is repeatedly arrested while patrons, pimps, hotel owners and landlords go free. The court acknowledges the community concern over the street activity connected with prostitution. But inasmuch as it is the patron who is most sensitive to arrest and who is most likely to be deterred from engaging in allegedly disruptive public conduct, non-discriminatory enforcement of the prostitution laws against all participants—patrons, landlords, pimps, hotel owners and prostitutes alike—could resolve the constitutional infirmity *and* have a significant impact upon the street problems associated with prostitution.

[10]Unofficial sources report that the vast number of prostitutes arrested under Penal Law section 230.00 (and related statutes) are nonwhite streetwalkers. Their customers are predominately white males. Thus, it appears that Penal Law section 230.00 works an invidious racial discrimination.

[11]To borrow a succinctly worded observation from the Court of Appeals:

"[T]he conclusion seems inescapable that lurking behind the discrimination is the imputation that females who engage in misconduct, sexual or otherwise, ought more to be censured, and their conduct subject to greater control and regulation, than males. Somewhat similar moral presumptions have been squarely rejected as a basis or excuse for sexually discriminatory legislation. . . ."

Numerous commentators share the Court of Appeals' perspective that underlying the extremely harsh treatment meted out to females engaging in sexual "mis"-conduct or commercial sex are archaic notions that a woman's place is in the narrowly circumscribed, non-public world. When females wander out of this protective sphere into the public, they "get what they deserve". Or to state the same idea more pointedly, that females are chattel, the property of one male, and therefore, have no right to be promiscuous, to self-determine to whom and when they shall bestow their "sexual favors". See e.g., Wilkinson & White, *Constitutional Protection for Personal Life Styles.* 62 Cornell 563 (1976–7); Rosenbleet & Pariente, The Prostitution of the Criminal Law 11 *Am.Crim.L.Rev.* 373, 387 n. 84 (1973).

of the Penal Law and make a determination as to their constitutionality.

The Penal Law only makes unlawful acts of "deviate" sexual intercourse performed by unmarried persons, whether of the opposite or same sex. Thus, the consensual sodomy statute creates a distinction between the private consensual sexual conduct of married and unmarried persons.

As will appear more fully below, the private consensual sexual relations of married *and* unmarried persons involve a fundamental right of privacy protected by the New York State Constitution. The right of privacy does not attach to the marital relationship but to the individuals involved.

Since a fundamental interest involving life or liberty is involved in this challenge to the constitutionality of the consensual sodomy statute, this court will carefully examine the state interests claimed to be protected by the criminalization of consensual sodomy between unmarried adults. The court will not accept mere claims that "deviate" sexual intercourse is harmful and, therefore, is properly proscribed by a state statute. On the contrary, it must be demonstrated that consensual sodomy in fact harms the public health, safety or welfare.

It cannot be said that acts of deviate sexual intercourse are, in and of themselves, intrinsically harmful or unnatural, causing in the participants any deviation from fundamental human nature.[15] Since 1968, when the consensual sodomy law was amended, married persons in this state have been permitted to

engage in "deviate" sexual intercourse without criminal sanction. In these past nine years, no empirical evidence that consensual sodomy is intrinsically harmful has been produced. Such conduct may be freely engaged in by married persons without sanction and is a widely accepted form of sexual expression. In this state, affectional or sexual preference have not been found to be a controlling factor in matters of licensing, citizenship, or admission to the bar.

Since it cannot be demonstrated that there is anything intrinsically harmful in acts of consensual sodomy between unmarried adults, can Penal Law section 130.38 be legitimated as a mode of protecting the stability of marriage and the family? There is no empirical evidence that so-called "deviate" sex, an activity that has been engaged in for centuries, has been a factor of any significance affecting the stability of marriage and the family. On the contrary, in the 17 states where consensual sodomy has been decriminalized, and the 100 nations that permit consensual sodomy, cooperative social institutions like the family remain stable.

The court has searched for, but cannot find, a proper governmental objective served by the legislature in distinguishing between the marital status of persons engaging in so-called "deviate" sexual intercourse. Completely lacking is any evidence that the conduct proscribed is more harmful to unmarried participants or that such conduct between unmarried persons is more harmful to the public.

If the consensual sodomy law was designed to prevent sexual relations between unmarried people, then "normal" sexual relations between the unmarried would also be sanctioned by the Criminal Law. Fornication, however, is not a crime in this state. If the purpose of the law is to promote conventional sex it also fails in its objective since married persons are permitted to engage in unconventional or "deviate" sexual conduct. Thus, if morality vis a vis sexual norms or the promotion of marriage are the objectives of the legislation, there is no rational let alone substantial relationship between the law itself and these legislative ends. There is no logical or factual basis on which the marital status of the participants should be decisive

[15]In late 1973, the Board of Trustees of the American Psychiatric Association (A.P.A.) decided to remove homosexuality from the list of mental diseases. This action met with the approval of the A.P.A. membership in 1974. Studies indicate that most unmarried persons engage in the sexual conduct characterized as deviate sexual intercourse. Of unmarried heterosexual persons between the ages of 18 and 24 years old, 72% of those studied performed fellatio, 69% performed cunnilingus. One-sixth of all persons under 25 years of age who have ever had coitus have engaged in anal intercourse. Studies also reveal that 20 to 25% of all males over the age of 15 have engaged in oral or anal sex with another male and 10–20% of all females over 19 years of age have engaged in oral sex with another female.

as to whether a mode of sexual conduct is legal or criminal. Since the classification created by section 130.38 of the Penal Law and section 130.00(2) as incorporated therein has no rational basis, the criminalization of "deviate" sexual intercourse between persons who are not married to each other is an unconstitutional denial of equal protection of the laws.

As the framers of the Federal and New York State Constitutions realized, a tension exists between the rights and powers of the government as opposed to those rights reserved to the People. As the Supreme Court observed nearly a century ago:

> No right is held more sacred, or is more carefully guarded, by the common law, than the right of every individual to the possession and control of his own person, free from all restraint or interference from others, unless by clear and unquestionable authority of law.

It is the Bill of Rights that stands between the will of the majority and the individual. It declares that except in the direct pursuit of protecting the public health, safety or morals, the State may not interfere with the individual's right of self expression. As numerous commentators have noted, the right of privacy found in the Bill of Rights has, as its underpinnings, the concept that affording the maximum amount of opportunity for individual choice maximizes the ability of each person for self development.

Running counter to the majoritarian tide of laws is the Bill of Rights' protection of diversity and guarantee of opportunity for the disadvantaged, who are unable to gain redress through the political process, to gain expression of and protection for their views in the courts.

The Supreme Court only recently recognized in the Bill of Rights a right of privacy. But the parameters of this right are quickly being revealed. The right of privacy encompasses not just sexual conduct in the marital relationship but is broad in scope, including in its protection each individual's decision as to whether, when and in what manner he or she will engage in private intimate relations. The

mantle of constitutional protection surrounding personal intimacy is not, therefore, limited to married persons. It attaches to the individual not the relationship, and protects the individual's right to engage in non-procreative, recreational sex.

This court states at the outset the premise that private, intimate, consensual sexual conduct not harmful to others, even if it violates the personal moral code of many, does not violate public morality and is protected by the right of privacy. In determining whether the state has a legitimate interest in proscribing private consensual sexual conduct, "deviate" or "normal", the following questions must be dealt with:

1. What harm does such conduct pose to the public health, safety or morals?

2. Is there harm in fact? Can harm actually or empirically be shown?

3. Is the harm caused in fact by the proscribed conduct?

4. Is the legislation reasonably related to the state's legitimate objective or is the relationship between the protectible public interest and the proscribed conduct too attenuated?

This court will not accept at face value bald claims of harm to the public health, safety and morals, but will closely examine the reasonableness of the state objectives proffered by the Corporation Counsel.

In discussing above the equal protection challenge to the consensual sodomy statutes, this court discussed the harms to the public health, safety or welfare allegedly caused by "deviate" sexual intercourse. Assertions that "deviate" sexual intercourse is intrinsically harmful to the participants or that it has a deleterious effect on the moral fibre of the community by undermining the stability of marriage and the family were each shown to be unsubstantiated. Although other courts argue that the Bible prohibits "deviate" sexual conduct and therefore, such conduct is immoral, it is this court's view that absent empirical evidence demonstrating that private, consensual "deviate" sexual acts cause harm in fact to the public health, safety or welfare the state may not legitimately proscribe such conduct. Since there is no proof that public harm is caused by consensual sodomy, the government may not intrude in private, personal decisions regarding sexual preference.

Since it has been demonstrated that there is no legitimate basis for governmental interference in private, consensual sodomy, the balance of this opinion will deal with the remaining question of whether the state may legitimately proscribe commercial, recreational sex.

It is claimed that prostitution is indeed harmful in that it spreads disease, leads to ancillary criminal conduct, encourages criminal organization and generally may be characterized as anti-social behavior both offensive and injurious to the community.

It is urged that prostitution spreads venereal disease. Without question, venereal disease is a serious threat to public health and it has apparently now reached epidemic proportions. However, all empirical data supports the conclusion of Dr. Charles Winnick of the City University, President of the American Social Health Association, that "[T]he amount of venereal disease attributable to prostitution is remaining fairly constant at a little under 5%, which is a negligible proportion compared to the amount of venereal disease we now have." The state may have a legitimate interest in seeking to eradicate even this small incidence of disease, but the attenuated relationship between prostitution and venereal disease emphasizes that it would be unreasonable to prohibit all prostitution for the sake of eradicating 5% of the "VD" health hazard.

It is also claimed that prostitution leads to other crimes. Indeed, in this case respondent is also charged with acts which could constitute robbery and assault in the second degree if committed by an adult. Nonetheless, the Corporation Counsel has not come forward with any empirical evidence substantiating that prostitution is the cause-in-fact of ancillary crime. Indeed, it has been concluded by numerous social scientists that crimes ancillary to prostitution are a by-product of the environment to which society consigns prostitution.

The effects of the enforcement procedures on the prostitute clearly are negative. Jail is not a deterrent. It often encourages criminal conduct. Incarceration contributes little to rehabilitation while teaching the prostitute about genuine criminal activity. She learns that other more serious crimes may pay better; she begins to view herself as a criminal. Attaching the label "criminal" to prostitution and imposing heavy sentences blur the distinction between offering service and committing a theft.

Because prostitution and patronizing a prostitute are criminally sanctioned, prostitutes and their patrons alike fear reporting ancillary crimes for fear of prosecution. Moreover, 70% of the women in prison for felonies were first arrested for prostitution. Thus, there is a clear inference that it is the criminalization of prostitution and not prostitution itself that leads to ancillary crime.

This court knows of no study that has substantiated the allegation that sex for money in fact causes ancillary crime. Nor has the Corporation Counsel shed any light on this subject. Due process requires that a law be reasonably related and applied to some actual or manifest evil: it must have as its objective the eradication of harm in fact caused by the proscribed conduct. The constitution limits the extent to which the state can proscribe prostitution with the purpose of eradicating an entirely distinct, severable kind of conduct. The state must proceed against ancillary crimes directly by enforcing the specific sanctions against such conduct and may not rely on the blunderbuss approach of incarcerating all prostitutes.

Another type of harm attributed to prostitution is that it injures the community. Underlying this claim are the allegations that commercial sex undermines the stability of the family and is simply immoral.

The law may seek to legislate morality, but it must do so without offending the constitutional protections of the due process clause and the right of privacy.

The Penal Law should act to deprive an individual of liberty only when a real and demonstrable harm to the public can result from the proscribed conduct. The state cannot rely upon the bare assertion of immorality to justify a criminal prohibition. Attempts by the state to regulate lifestyle choices on the bare assertion that the regulation serves morality is impermissible. Conduct that does not interfere with the rights and interests of others may not be regulated by the state.

Preventing harm to what is believed by many to be the central institution for social cooperation, the family, may well be a legitimate objective of the state. Most male patrons of prostitutes are married. And it is the patron who creates the demand for the services of prostitutes. Thus, if the marital contract is breached by promiscuity or the family undermined by extra-marital sexual relations, the burden of responsibility lies with the patron, not the prostitute. Yet, the penal law punishes the prostitute most severely. If the state's objective is to promote the stability of the family and commercial sex has a direct impact upon the family, then the law should focus on the conduct of the patron. However, it has never been demonstrated that commercial sex has had any effect on the stability of marriage or the family. Indeed, although prostitution has been practiced for centuries, disruption of the family has never been causally related to prostitution. Several states and numerous foreign nations have decriminalized prostitution without any indication of a concomitant decline in the vitality of the marital or family institution. The decriminalization of fornication in this state has not led to any reported damage to the family. This court can find no reason why commercial fornication should have a less innocuous effect on these social institutions. Thus, there is no empirical connection between prostitution, whether involving ordinary or deviate sexual intercourse, and the stability of the family. Therefore, the state cannot reasonably assert protection of marriage and the family as legitimate objectives for its regulation of prostitution.

Sex for a fee is recreational, not procreational sex. Typically, it is the female participant who receives the fee. The arguments that prostitution harms the public health, safety or welfare do not withstand constitutional scrutiny. It may be that it is the fact that a woman is accepting a fee for recreational, sexual services that triggers the governmental intrusion upon this private consensual sexual conduct. If it is paternalism that prompts the legislature to protect women by proscribing prostitution,[26] that motive is ill served by the prostitution laws since women are not protected, but rather are penally punished. Society may find something offensive about having women perform sex for money. However offensive it may be, recreational commercial sex threatens no harm to the public health, safety or welfare and, therefore, may not be proscribed.

Finally, prostitution is said to offend public sensibilities. Individual members of the public may indeed be offended by the public conduct associated with prostitution: they may be solicited on the street by prostitutes, embarrassed by the advances of streetwalkers, or find their path on the sidewalks or thoroughfares blocked. Such conduct may, indeed, be a harm legitimately of interest to the state should it constitute public disorder. This court will not decide the question of who has a right to be on the public streets. However, the court will point out that this public conduct is not caused in fact by the act of engaging in sexual relations for a fee. This harm, if any, is caused by the solicitation aspect of prostitution. The *public* aspect of prostitution, solicitation, must be distinguished from its *private* aspect, the performance of consensual sexual relations for a fee in private. Street solicitation is a method of advertising the business of commercial sex. It is separable from the underlying activity. In

---

[26]Paternalism certainly could not be the motive in the instant case. Respondent is a 14 year old female. If the motive of this proceeding were to protect her, she would not be threatened with the loss of her liberty. Paternalism might dictate an Article Ten of the Family Court Act proceeding on her behalf. It clearly would dictate some charge against the patron, such as endangering the welfare of a minor, attempted statutory rape or criminal solicitation. None of these protective measures were taken in this case.

Nevada and Great Britain, for example, prostitution has been legalized, but street solicitation is proscribed by public order, breach of the peace—type statutes. Advertising is unoffensively and effectively accomplished through the use of discrete newspaper advertisements.

The prohibition of the offensive *public* conduct associated with the solicitation of prostitution may be a legitimate state objective. Since it has been demonstrated that only this public element of prostitution may make that conduct harmful, and that public conduct may be dealt with separately from the sexual conduct itself, it would be unreasonable for the state to completely proscribe private, sexual conduct in order to reach distinct public solicitation. Members of the public may have a protectable privacy interest: not to be repeatedly accosted on the streets by a prostitute any more than

a religious zealot, peddler, alcoholic or panhandler, and not to have a group of street musicians, noisy teenagers, solicitors for charities, or streetwalkers converging at his or her doorstep. These public interests can be protected, but by less intrusive means than those now employed by the state. Private, consensual sexual conduct between adults, whether or not performed for a fee, is protected by the right of privacy. If the state has a legitimate interest in curbing public disorder, it can and must accomplish this objective without depriving the individual of his or her right to engage in private, consensual, sexual relations. The constitutionally protected right of privacy makes it incumbent upon the state to implement its policy by more reasonable, less intrusive means.

For the reasons stated, the sexual conduct charge against respondent is dismissed.

Prostitution and Civil Rights

Catharine A. MacKinnon

The gap between the promise of civil rights and the real lives of prostitutes is an abyss which swallows up prostituted women. To speak of prostitution and civil rights in one breath moves the two into one world, at once exposing and narrowing the distance between them.

Women in prostitution are denied every imaginable civil right in every imaginable and unimaginable way,[2] such that it makes sense to understand prostitution as consisting in the denial of women's humanity, no matter how humanity is defined. It is denied both through

Catharine MacKinnon, "Prostitution and Civil Rights," vol. 1 Michigan Journal of Gender and Law (1993). Reprinted by permission from the *Michigan Journal of Gender and Law*, 13 (1993). Copyright © 1993 by Catharine A. MacKinnon. (Original footnote numbering retained in this edited version.)

the social definition and condition of prostitutes and through the meaning of some civil rights.

The legal right to be free from torture and cruel and inhuman or degrading treatment is recognized by most nations and is internationally guaranteed. In prostitution, women are tortured through repeated rape and in all the more conventionally recognized ways. Women are prostituted precisely in order to be degraded and subjected to cruel and brutal treatment without human limits; it is the opportunity to do this that is exchanged when women are bought and sold for sex. The fact that most legal prohibitions on torture apply only to official torture, specifically torture by state actors, illustrates the degree to which the legal design of civil rights has excluded women's experience of being denied them.

Security of the person is fundamental to society. The point of prostitution is to transgress women's personal security. Women in prostitution attempt to set limits on what can be done to them. But nothing backs them up. Pimps supposedly do, but it shows how insecure prostitutes' lives are that pimps can look like security. Nothing limits pimps, and, ultimately, anything can be done to their property for a price. As Andrea Dworkin has said, "whatever can be stolen can be sold."[3] In rape, the security of women's person is stolen; in prostitution, it is stolen and sold.

Liberty is a primary civil right. Kathleen Barry has analyzed female sexual slavery as prostitution one cannot get out of.[4] A recent study of street prostitutes in Toronto found that about ninety percent wanted to leave but could not.[5] If they are there because they cannot leave, they are sexual slaves. At the same time, liberty for men is often construed in sexual terms and includes liberal access to women, including prostituted ones. So while, for men, liberty entails that women be prostituted, for women, prostitution entails loss of all that liberty means.

The right to privacy is often included among civil rights. In the United States, one meaning privacy has effectively come to have is the right to dominate free of public scrutiny. The private is then defined as a place of freedom by effectively rendering consensual what women and children are forced to do out of the public eye. Prostitution is thus often referred to as occurring in private between consenting adults, as is marriage and family. The result is to extend the aura of privacy and protection from public intervention from sex to sexual abuse. In prostitution, women have no space they can call off-limits to prying eyes, prying hands, or prying other parts of the anatomy, not even inside their own skin.

Freedom from arbitrary arrest is also a civil right. Criminal prostitution laws make women into criminals for being victimized as women, so are arguably arbitrary in the first place. Then these laws are often enforced for bureaucratic, turf-protective, funding, political, or advancement reasons[6]—that is, arbitrarily, against women.

Property ownership is recognized as a civil right in many countries. Women in prostitution not only begin poor, they are systematically kept poor by pimps who take the lion's share of what they earn. They are the property of the men who buy and sell and rent them—placing the civil right, once again, in the hands of their tormenters.

Particularly in the United States, the right to freedom of speech is cherished. Prostitution as an institution silences women by brutalizing and terrorizing them so horribly that no words can form, by punishing them for telling the truth about their condition, by degrading whatever they do manage to say about virtually anything because of who they are seen as being. The pornography that is made of their violation—pimps' speech—is protected expression.[7]

One civil right is so deep it is seldom mentioned: to be recognized as a person before the law. To be a prostitute is to be a legal nonperson in the ways that matter. What for Blackstone and others was the legal nonpersonhood of wives is extended for prostitutes from one man to all men as a class. Anyone can do anything to you and nothing legal will be done about it. John Stoltenberg has shown how the social definition of personhood for men is importantly premised on the prostitution of women.[9] Prostitution as a social institution gives men personhood—in this case, manhood—through depriving women of theirs.

The civil right to life is basic. The Green River murders, the serial murders of women in Los Angeles, the eleven dead African-American women who had been in prostitution and were found under piles of rags in Detroit—these acts are "gender cleansing." Snuff films are part of it. When killing women becomes a sex act, women have no right to their lives. Women in prostitution, along with women cohabiting with men, are the most exposed.

Equality is also a civil right, both equal humanity in substance and formal equality before the law. In the United States, constitutional equality encompasses equal protection of the laws under the Fourteenth Amendment and freedom from slavery or involuntary servitude under the Thirteenth Amendment. Prostitution implicates both.

The Fourteenth Amendment provides for equal protection and benefit of the law without discrimination. What little equality litigation exists in the prostitution context misses the point of their unequal treatment in a number of illuminating ways. Some older prostitution statutes, challenged as sex discriminatory on their face, made prostitution illegal only when a woman engaged in it. For example, Louisiana provided that "[p]rostitution is the practice by a female of indiscriminate sexual intercourse with males for compensation."[10] Applying the sex discrimination test at the time, the court ruled that "[d]ifferences between the sexes does bear a rational relationship to the prohibition of prostitution by females."[11] In other words, defining prostitution as something only women do is simple realism. Women really do this: mostly only women do this: it seems to have something to do with being a woman to do this; therefore, it is not sex discrimination to have a law that punishes only women for doing this.

Here, the fact that most prostitutes are women is not a sex inequality, nor does equating prostitution with being a woman tell us anything about what being a woman means. That most prostitutes are women is the reason why legally defining the problem of prostitution as a problem of women is not a sex inequality. Thus does the soft focus of gender neutrality blur sex distinctions by law and rigidly sex-divided social realities at the same time. By now, most legislatures have gender neutralized their prostitution laws—without having done anything to gender-neutralize prostitution's realities.

The cases that adjudicate equal protection challenges to sex-discriminatory enforcement of prostitution laws extend this rationale. Police usually send men to impersonate tricks in order to arrest prostitutes. Not surprisingly, many more women than men are arrested in this way.[12] The cases hold that this is not intentional sex discrimination but a good faith effort by the state to get at "the sellers of sex,"[13] "the profiteer."[14] Sometimes the tricks

are even described by police as the women's "victim."[15] Courts seem to think the women make the money; in most instances, they are conduits from trick to pimp and the money is never theirs.[16] Sometimes the male police decoys wait to arrest until the sex act is about to happen—or, prostitutes complain, until after it happens.[17]

Another all-too-common practice is arresting accused prostitutes, women, while letting arrested customers, men, go with a citation or a warning. This, too, has been challenged as sex discrimination, and it sure sounds like it. Yet this, courts say, is not sex discrimination because male and female prostitutes are treated alike[19] or because customers violate a different, noncomparable, law from the one under which the women are charged.[20] There are some men in prostitution, most (but not all) prostituting as women. You can tell you have walked into the world of gender neutrality when the law treats men as badly as women when they do what mostly women do, and that makes treating women badly non-sex-based. Of course, compared with customers, prostitutes also more often fail to satisfy the gender-neutral conditions of release: good money, good name, good job, good family, good record, good lawyer, good three-piece suit. . . .

These cases represent the extent to which equal protection of the laws has been litigated for prostitutes. The disparity between the focus of this litigation and the civil rights violations inherent in prostitution is staggering. Behind the blatant sex discrimination these cases rationalize is the vision of equality they offer prostitutes—the right to be prostituted without being disproportionately punished for it. As unprincipled as the losses in these cases are, if they had been won, this is the equality they would have won.

Criminal laws against prostitution make women into criminals for being victimized as women, yet there are no cases challenging these laws as sex discrimination on this ground. Criminal prostitution laws collaborate elaborately in women's social inequality;[24] through them, the state enforces the exploitation of prostituted women directly. When legal victimization is piled on top of social victimization, women are dug deeper and deeper into civil inferiority, their subordination and isolation legally ratified and legitimated. Disparate enforcement combines with this discriminatory design to violate prostituted women's Fourteenth Amendment right to equal protection of the laws.

This is not to argue that prostitutes have a sex equality right to engage in prostitution. Rather, prostitution subordinates and exploits and disadvantages women as women in social life, a social inequality which prostitution laws then seal with a criminal sanction.

The argument to decriminalize trafficking women has no such support. Disadvantage on the basis of sex directly supports strict enforcement of laws against pimps, who exploit women's inequality for gain,[25] and against tricks, who benefit from women's oppressed status and subordinate individual women skin on skin.

Beyond eliminating discriminatory criminal laws and enforcing appropriate ones, it is time the law did something for women in prostitution. Getting the criminal law off their backs may keep the state from reinforcing their subordinate status but it does nothing to change that status. The Thirteenth Amendment, which applies whether or not the state is involved, may help.

The Thirteenth Amendment prohibits slavery and involuntary servitude. It, and its implementing statutes, was passed to invalidate the chattel slavery of African-Americans and kindred social institutions. The Thirteenth Amendment has been applied to invalidate a range of arrangements of forced labor and exploitive servitude.[27] The slavery of African-Americans is not the first or last example of enslavement, although it has rightly been one of the most notorious. To apply the Thirteenth Amendment to prostitution is not to equate prostitution with the chattel slavery of African-Americans but to draw on common features of institutions of forcible inequality in the context of the Thirteenth Amendment's implementation.

Compared with slavery of African-Americans, prostitution is older, more pervasive across

cultures, does not include as much non-sexual exploitation, and is based on sex, and sex and race combined. For Black women in the United States, the relation between prostitution and slavery is less one of analogy than of continuity with their sexual use under slavery.[28] Applying the Thirteenth Amendment to prostitution claims enslavement as a term and reality of wider application, which historically it has been. It also takes the view that the Thirteenth Amendment was intended to prohibit the forms slavery took for Black women just as much as those it took for Black men.

Thirteenth Amendment standards require a showing of legal or physical force, used or threatened, to secure service, which must be "distinctly personal service . . . in which one person possesses virtually unlimited authority over another."[30] Some cases predicated servitude on psychological coercion,[31] but the Supreme Court recently held that a climate of fear alone is not enough.[32] The vulnerabilities of the victims are still relevant to determining whether physical or legal coercion or threats compel the service, rendering it "slavelike." Recognized vulnerabilities have included mental retardation, being an illegal immigrant, not speaking the language, being a child, and being stranded in a foreign city without means of support.[34] Poverty has been pervasively understood as part of the setting of force.

The Thirteenth Amendment has often been found violated when a person is tricked into peonage or service through fraud or deceit and is then kept unable to leave, including through contrived and manipulated indebtedness.[36] Debt is not a requirement of servitude, but it is a common incident of it. One recent case found that victims—called victims in these cases—were forced into domestic service by enticing them to travel to the United States, where they were paid little for exorbitant work hours and had their passports and return tickets withheld, while they were required to work off, as servants, the cost of their transportation. Corroborating evidence has included extremely, poor working conditions.

Indentured servitude has long been legally prohibited in the United States, even prior to the passage of the Thirteenth Amendment.[39] In interpreting the Thirteenth Amendment in contemporary peonage contexts, courts have been far less concerned with whether the condition was voluntarily entered and far more with whether the subsequent service was involuntary.[40] That victims believe they have no viable alternative but to serve in the ways in which they are being forced has also supported a finding of coercion, and with it the conclusion that the condition is one of enslavement.[41] Involuntary servitude has embraced situations in which a person has made a difficult but rational decision to remain in bondage.[42]

If the legal standards for involuntary servitude developed outside the sexual context are applied to the facts of prostitution, the situations of most of the women in it are clearly prohibited. In prostitution, human beings are bought and sold as chattel for use in "distinctly personal service. Many women and girls are sold by one pimp to another as well as from pimp to trick and for pornography. Prostitution was not formerly called "white *slavery*" for nothing.[44]

Prostitution occurs within multiple power relations of domination, degradation, and subservience[45] of the pimp and trick over the prostitute: men over women, older over younger, citizen over alien, moneyed over impoverished, violent over victimized, connected over isolated, housed over homeless, tolerated and respected over despised. All of the forms of coercion and vulnerabilities recognized under the Thirteenth Amendment are common in prostitution, and then some. No social institution exceeds it in physical violence. It is common for prostitutes to be deprived of food and sleep and money, beaten, tortured, raped, and threatened with their lives, both as acts for which the pimp is paid by other men and to keep the women in line.[46] Women in prostitution are subject to near total domination. Much of this is physical, but pimps also develop to a high art forms of nonphysical force to subjugate the women's will. Their techniques of mind control often exploit skills women have developed to survive sexual abuse,

such as denial, dissociation, and multiplicity. They also manipulate women's desire for respect and self-respect.

Criminal laws against prostitution provide legal force behind its social involuntariness. Women in prostitution have no police protection because they are criminals, making pimps' protection racket both possible and necessary. In addition to being able to inflict physical abuse with impunity, pimps confiscate the women's earnings and isolate them even beyond the stigma they carry. The women then have nowhere but pimps to turn to bail them out after arrest, leaving them in debt for their fines which must be worked out in trade. Thus the law collaborates in enforcing women's involuntary servitude by turning the victim of peonage into a criminal. Such legal complicity is state action, raising a claim under the Fourteenth Amendment for sex discrimination by state law.

While it is dangerous to imply that some prostitution is forced, leaving the rest of it to seem free, as a matter of fact, most if not all prostitution is ringed with force in the most conventional sense, from incest to kidnapping to forced drugging to assault to criminal law. Sex-based poverty, both prior to and during prostitution, enforces it: while poverty alone has not been recognized as making out a case of coercion, it has been recognized as making exit impossible in many cases in which coercion has been found. If all of the instances in which these factors interacted to keep a woman in prostitution were addressed, there would be little of it left.

Beyond this, the Thirteenth Amendment may prohibit prostitution as an institution. In the words of The Three Prostitutes' Collectives from Nice, "*all* prostitution is forced prostitution . . . we would not lead the 'life' if we were in a position to leave it."[48] In this perspective, prostitution as such is coerced, hence could be prohibited as servitude. At the very least, there is authority for taking the victims' inequality into account when courts assess whether deprivation of freedom of choice is proven.[49]

On a few occasions in the past, the Thirteenth Amendment has been used to prosecute pimps for prostituting women.[50] In these federal criminal cases, the prostitution was forced in order to pay a debt the women supposedly owed the pimp. In one case, the defendant procured two women from a prison by paying their fines and then forced them to repay him by prostituting at his road house. In another, young Mexican women were induced to accept free transportation to jobs which did not exist and then were told they could not return home until they repaid the cost of the transportation through prostitution. These women were financially trapped, sometimes physically assaulted, always threatened, and in fear. Some complied with the prostitution; some were able to resist. In these cases, the prostitution as such was not considered involuntary servitude—the coercion into doing it was. But it is implicit in these cases that prostitution is not something a woman, absent force, would choose to do.

It is worth asking whether coercion of women into sex in a Thirteenth Amendment context would be measured by the legal standards by which courts have measured the coerciveness of nonsexual exploitation of groups that include men. The coercion of women into and within prostitution has been invisible because prostitution is considered sex and sex is considered what women are for. The standards for the meaning of women's "yes" in the sexual context range from approximating a dead body's enthusiasm, to fighting back and screaming "no," to pleading with an armed rapist to use a condom.[53] This being free choice, one wonders what coercion would look like. Sex in general, particularly sex for survival, is so pervasively merged with the meaning of being a woman that whenever sex occurs, under whatever conditions, the woman tends to be defined as freely acting.

Suits for prostitution as involuntary servitude confront the notion that women—some women who are "just like that" or women in general— are in prostitution freely. No condition of freedom is prepared for by sexual abuse in childhood, permits and condones repeated rapes and beatings, and subjects its participants to a risk of premature death of forty times the national average.[54] The fact that most women in prostitution were sexually abused as children,[55]

and most entered prostitution itself before they were adults,[56] undermines the patina of freedom and the glamour of liberation that is the marketing strategy apparently needed for most customers to enjoy using them. Such suits would also challenge freedom of choice as a meaningful concept for women under conditions of sex inequality. Women's precluded options in societies that discriminate on the basis of sex, including in employment, are fundamental to the prostitution context. If prostitution is a free choice, why are the women with the fewest choices the ones most often found doing it?[57]

When a battered woman sustains the abuse of one man for economic survival for twenty years, not even this legal system believes she consents to the abuse anymore. Asking why she did not leave has begun to be replaced by noticing what keeps her there.[58] Perhaps when women in prostitution sustain the abuse of thousands of men for economic survival for twenty years, this will, at some point, come to be understood as non-consensual as well. And many do not survive. They are merely kept alive until they can no longer be used. Then they are sold one last time to someone who kills them for sex, or they are OD'd in an alley or otherwise end up under those trash heaps in Detroit.

Fortunately for women, the Thirteenth Amendment has a civil application, meaning we can use it ourselves. Under §1985(3), prostituted women could allege that they have been subjected to a conspiracy to deprive them of civil rights as women. The conspiracy is the easy part—pimps never do this alone. In a supply-side conspiracy, they prostitute women through organized crime, gangs, associations, cults, families, hotel owners, and police. There is also a demand-side conspiracy, more difficult to argue but certainly there, between pimps and tricks.

Long unresolved is whether §1985(3) applies to conspiracies on the basis of sex. In a recent case, the Supreme Court held that the group "women who seek and receive abortions" was not an adequate class for purposes of §1985(3) because it was not based on sex.[59] The court did not say that sex-based conspiracies are not actionable under §1985(3): several members of the court said that they are. Prostituted women are an even more persuasive sex-based class. How hard can it be to prove that women are prostituted as women? Not only is prostitution overwhelmingly done to women by men, every aspect of the condition has defined gender female as such and as inferior for centuries. Evelina Giobbe explains how the status and treatment of prostitutes defines all women as a sex: "[T]he prostitute symbolizes the value of women in society. She is paradigmatic of women's social, sexual, and economic subordination in that her status is the basic unit by which all women's value is measured and to which all women can be reduced.[60] As Dorchen Leidholdt puts it: "What other job is so deeply gendered that one's breasts, vagina and rectum constitute the working equipment? Is so deeply gendered that the workers are exclusively women and children and young men used like women?[61] In addition, the fact that some men are also sold for sex helps make prostitution look less than biological, less like a sex difference. Treatment that is socially and legally damaging and stereotypical that overwhelmingly burdens one sex, but is not unique to one sex, is most readily seen as sex discrimination.

A civil action under §1985(3) would allow prostituted women to sue pimps for sexual slavery, refuting the lie that prostitution is just a job. Slavery is a lot of work, but that does not make it just a job, picking cotton being just picking cotton. The enforced inequality is the issue.

In addition to these legal tools, the law against pornography that Andrea Dworkin and I wrote gives civil rights to women in prostitution in a way that could begin to end that institution.[62] Pornography is an arm of prostitution. As Annie McCombs once put it to me, when you make pornography of a woman, you make a prostitute out of her. The pornography law we wrote is concretely grounded in the experience of prostituted women: women coerced into pornography are coerced into prostitution. It is also based on the experience of women in prostitution who

are assaulted because of pornography. Beyond this, under its trafficking provision, any woman, in or out of prostitution, who can prove women are harmed through the materials could sue pornographers for trafficking women. This provision recognizes the unity of women as a class rather than dividing prostituted women from all women. The precluded options that get women into prostitution, hence pornography, affect all women, as does the fact that pornography harms all women, if not all in the same way.

Subordination on the basis of sex is key to our pornography law. Pornography is defined as graphic sexually explicit materials that subordinate women (or anyone) on the basis of sex. Women in prostitution are the first women pornography subordinates. In its prohibition on coercion into pornography, in making their subordination actionable, this law sets the first floor beneath the condition of prostituted women, offers the first civil right that limits how much they can be violated. It does not do all that they need, but it is a lot more than the nothing that they have.

This law uses the artifact nature of pornography to hold the perpetrators accountable for what they do. Before this, the pictures have been used against women: to blackmail them into prostitution and keep them there, as a technologically sophisticated way of possessing and exchanging women as a class. Under this law, the pornography becomes proof of the woman's injury as well as an instance of it.

Because pornography affects all women and connects all forms of sexual subordination, so does this law. And this law reaches the pornography. The way subordination is done in pornography is the way it is done in prostitution is the way it is done in the rest of the world: rape, battering, sexual abuse of children, sexual harassment, and murder are sold in prostitution and are the acts out of which pornography is made. Addressing pornography in this way builds a base among women for going after prostitution as a violation of equality rights.

For years I have been saying that I do not know what to do, legally, about prostitution. I still do not. State constitutions and human rights remedies could be adapted to use the argument I offer here. The Florida statute Meg Baldwin wrote and got passed is brilliant and is beginning to be used by women.[63] Recent international initiatives build on superb long-term work and support these efforts.[64] I do know that we need to put the power to act directly in women's hands more than we have.[65]

NOTES

[This speech was given at a symposium "Prostitution: From Academia to Activism," University of Michigan Law School, Oct. 31, 1972. *Ed.*]

[2]This discussion builds upon prior presentations . . . in which the conditions of women in prostitution were documented. See generally Evelina Giobbe, *Juvenile Prostitution: Profile of Recruitment*, in Ann W. Burgess ed., *Child Trauma I: Issues and Research* 117 (1992); Evelina Giobbe, *Prostitution: Buying the Right to Rape* in Ann W. Burgess ed., *Rape and Sexual Assault III: A Research Handbook* 143 (1991); and citations throughout this article.

[3]See Andrea Dworkin, *Letters from a War Zone: Writings 1976–1986*, 229 (1989).

[4]See generally Kathleen Barry, *Female Sexual Slavery* (1979).

[5]Elizabeth Fry Society of Toronto, *Streetwork Outreach with Female Street Prostitutes* 13 (May 1987) (Approximately 90% of the women contacted indicated they wished to stop working on the streets at some point, but felt unable or unclear about how to even begin this process.).

[6]See generally *People v. Superior Court of Alameda County*, 562 P.2d 1315 (Cal. 1977).

[7]See generally *American Booksellers Ass'n v. Hudnut*, 771 F.2d 323 (7th Cir. 1985). aff'd, 475 U.S. 1001 (1986).

[9]See generally John Stoltenberg, Male Sexuality: Why Ownership Is Sexy, 1 *Mich. J. Gender & L.* 59 (1993).

[10]*State v. DeVall*, 302 So. 2d 909, 910 (La. 1974) (quoting La. Rev. Stat. Ann. §14:82 (West 1986).

[11]*DeVall*, 302 So. 2d at 913. See also City of Minneapolis v. Burchette, 240 N.W.2d 500, 505 (Minn. 1976) (arresting chiefly female violators of prostitution law is a rational way to meet the objective of controlling prostitution). This position has not changed significantly with elevated scrutiny. See, e.g., *State v. Sandoval*, 649 P. 2d 485. 487 (N.M. Ct. App. 1982) (ruling that there is no arbitrary enforcement of prostitution statute under state equal rights amendment): *Bolser v. Washington State Liquor Control Bd.*, 580 P.2d 629, 633 (Wash. 1978) (holding that male and female dancers are equally covered by restrictions on topless dancing, resulting in no violation of state equal rights amendment).

[12]I am told by women police officers that they loathe being decoys, although some of their work has resulted in spectacular arrests of pillars of the community. No woman should be forced to present herself as available for sexual use, whether as a prostitute or as a police officer ordered to pose as a prostitute as part of her employment.

[13]*United States v. Moses*, 339 A.2d 46, 55 (D.C. 1975). Another reason offered for not using women police decoys is that, due to past sex discrimination, there are few or no women to use. See *People v. Burton*, 432 N.Y.S.2d 312, 315 (City Ct. of Buffalo 1980).

[14]*People v. Superior Court of Alameda County*, 562 P.2d 1315, 1321 (Cal. 1977).

[15]*People v. Nelson*, 427 N.Y.S.2d 194, 195 (City Ct. of Syracuse 1980).

[16]Janice Toner, a former prostitute, argued that the money she made as a prostitute was not income to her because she was merely a conduit to her husband/pimp, who beat and threatened to kill her and their children. The Tax Court rejected the argument, although her husband was convicted of assault in a separate case. *Toner v. Commissioner*, 60 T.C.M. (CCH) 1016, 1019 (1990). The Court found that Toner did not show that her husband's abuse was causally connected to her earning of an income from prostitution and characterized her as an active, voluntary participant in some aspects of the prostitution business. Id. at 1021.

[17]*State v. Tookes*, 699 P.2d 983, 984 (Haw. 1985) (finding no denial of due process when civilian police agent had sex with woman for money before arresting her for prostitution).

[19]See Superior Court of Alameda County, 562 P.2d at 1323. See also *Morgan v. City of Detroit*, 389 F. Supp. 922, 928 (E.D. Mich. 1975).

[20]One court rejected this decisively in the 1920s:

> Men caught with women in an act of prostitution are equally guilty, and should be arrested and held for trial with the women. The practical application of the law as heretofore enforced is an unjust discrimination against women in the matter of an offense which, in its very nature, if completed, requires the participation of men.

People v. Edwards, 180 N. Y. S. 631, 635 (Ct. Gen. Sess. 1920). In 1980, the City Court of Syracuse, endorsing this reasoning, further rejected the dodge arguing that prostitute and patron are "not similarly situated" for equal protection purposes because they violate separate sections of the penal code. That court found that "the only significant difference in the proscribed behavior is that the prostitute sells sex and the patron buys it. Neither gender nor solicitation is a differentiating factor." *People v. Nelson*, 427 N. Y. S.2d 194, 197 (City Ct. of Syracuse 1980) (finding no evidence to discriminate, therefore no discrimination shown). Most courts that have considered sex-differential enforcement challenges on equal protection grounds have relied, for rejecting them, on the distinction in statutes under which prostitutes and patrons fall. See, e.g., Matter of Dora P., 418 N. Y. S. 2d 597, 604 (N. Y. App. Div. 1979) (prostitution and patronizing a prostitute are discrete crimes making differential treatment of women and men under them not discriminatory); Commonwealth v. King, 372 N. E. 2d 196 (Sup. Jud. Ct. Mass. 1977)

[24]As Margaret Baldwin has stressed to me, part of the complexity of this situation is that jail sometimes provides comparative safety for the women, and the criminal status of prostitution provides some barrier to recruitment and validation for the women's sense of violation. These concerns could be met without making women criminals.

[25]For a vivid description of the inequality between pimp and prostitute, see Dorchen Leidholdt. Prostitution: A Violation of Women's Human Rights, *1 Cardozo Women's I. J* 133 (1993).

[27]See *Bailey v. Alabama*, 219 U.S. 219, 241 (1911) ("[T]he words involuntary servitude have a 'larger meaning than slavery.'") (quoting The Slaughter-House Cases, 83 U. S. (16 Wall.) 36, 69 (1872)).

[28]See Vednita Nelson, Prostitution: Where Racism & Sexism Intersect, *1 Mich. I. Gender & L* 81, 84, 85 (1993).

[30]Hamilton, supra note 26, at 7.

[31]See. e.g., *United States v. Ancarola*, 1 F. 676, 683 (C.C.S.D.N.Y. 1880) (considering the case of an eleven-year-old Italian boy held in involuntary servitude by a padrone due to his youth and dependence which left him incapable of choosing alternatives).

[32]*United States v. Kozminski*, 487 U.S. 931, 949–950 (1988). For an analysis of combined psychological and economic coercion, see *United States v. Shackney*, 333 F.2d 475 (2d Cir. 1964).

[34]See id (mental retardation); *United States v. King*, 840 F.2d 1276 (6th Cir.), cert. denied, 488 U.S. 894 (1988) (children); *United States v. Mussry*, 726 F.2d 1448, 1450 (9th Cir.) cert. denied, 469 U.S. 855 (1984) (non-English speaking, passports withheld, paid little money for services); *Bernal v. United States*, 241 F. 339, 341 (5th Cir. 1917), cert. denied, 245 U.S. 672 (1918) (alienage, no means of support, "did not know her way about town"); Ancarold. 1 F. at 676 (child).

[36]See generally Mussry, 726 F.2d 1448.

[39]*Case of Mary Clark*, 1 Blackf. 122 (Ind. 1821).

[40]See, e.g., Mussry, 726 F.2d 1448. The later ruling by the Supreme Court in Kozminski, 487 U.S. 931, restricting Mussry doctrines does not cut back on this aspect of the courts' customary approach to this issue.

[41]*United States v. King*, 840 F.2d 1276, 1281 (6th Cir. 1988) cert. denied, 488 U.S. 894 (1988) (finding a conspiracy to deprive children living in a religious commune of rights under Thirteenth Amendment, in part because of a belief by the children that they "had no viable alternative but to perform service for the defendants."). When physical force is also present, *Kozminski* poses no barrier to prosecution. Id. at 1281.

[42]United States v. Bibbs, 564 F.2d 1165, 1168 (5th Cir. 1977), cert. denied, 435 U.S. 1007 (1978).

[44]This term was apparently used originally to parallel and distinguish prostitution of all women, including women of color, from slavery of Africans as such. *Traite des Noires*, trade in Blacks, referred to slavery of Blacks; in 1905. *Traite des Blanches*, trade in whites, was used at an international conference to refer to sexual sale and purchase of women and children. Marlene D. Beckman, The White Slave Traffic Act: The Historical Impact of a Criminal Law Policy on Women, 72 *Geo. L. J.* 1111 n.2 (1984).

[45]Here I draw on Akhil Amar's and Daniel Widawsky's proposed working definition of slavery. Akhil Amar & Daniel Widawsky, Child Abuse as Slavery: A Thirteenth Amendment Response to *DeShaney*, 105 *Harv. L. Rev.* 1359, 1365 (1992).

[46]See generally Leidholdt, *supra* note 25; Barry supra note 4, at 3–5: Activities for the Advancement of Women: Equality, Development and Peace, U.N. ESCOR. 1st Sess., Provisional Agenda Item 12, at 7–8, *U.N. Doc. E/1983/7* (1983).

[48]Activities for the Advancement of Women: Equality, Development and Peace, supra note 46, at 8 (quoting testimony by three "collectives" of women prostitutes given to the Congress of Nice on September 8, 1981).

[49]*The Peonage Cases*, 123 F. 671, 681 (M.D. Ala. 1903) (stating that the trier of fact "must consider the situation of the parties, the relative inferiority or inequality between the person contracting to perform the service and the person exercising the force or influence to compel its performance. . . .").

[50]See, e.g., *Pierce v. United States*, 146 F.2d 84 (5th Cir. 1944), cert. denied, 324 U.S. 873 (1945); Bernal v. United States, 241 F. 339 (5th Cir. 1917), cert. denied, 245 U.S. 672 (1918). See also United States v. Harris, 534 F.2d 207, 214 (10th Cir. 1975), cert. denied, 429 U.S. 941 (1976) (upholding conviction for involuntary servitude in prostitution context).

[53]A grand jury in Austin, Texas, failed to indict a man for rape where the victim asked him to wear a condom. Apparently, the woman's request somehow implied her consent. Ross E. Milloy, Furor Over a Decision Not to Indict in a Rape Case, N.Y. Times, Oct. 25, 1992, §1 at 30. A second grand jury did indict the man for rape and he was later convicted in a jury trial. Rapist Who Agreed to Use Condom Gets 40 Years. *N. Y. Times*, May 15, 1993, §1 at 6.

[54]For data on rape in prostitution, see Leidholdt supra note 25, at 138: Mimi H. Silbert & Ayala M. Pines, Occupational Hazards of Street Prostitutes, 8 *Crim. Just. Behav.* 395, 397 (1981) (70% of San Francisco street prostitutes reported rape by clients an average of 31 times); Council for Prostitution Alternatives, 1991 Annual Report 4 (48% of prostitutes were raped by pimps an average of 16 times a year, 79% by johns an average of 33 times a year). For data on beatings, see Silbert & Pines, supra at 397 (65% of prostitutes beaten by customers); Council for Prostitution Alternatives, supra, at 4 (63% were beaten by pimps an average of 58 times a year). For data on mortality, see *Pornography and Prostitution in Canada; Report of the Special Committee on Pornography and Prostitution*, Vol. II, 350 (1985) (finding that in Canada the mortality rate for prostituted women is 40 times the national average); Leidholdt, supra note 25, at 138 n. 15 (the Justice Department estimates that a third of the over 4,000 women killed by serial murderers in 1982 were prostitutes).

[55]See Mimi H. Silbert & Ayala M. Pines, Entrance into Prostitution, 13 *Youth & Society* 471, 479 (1982) (60% of prostitutes were sexually abused in childhood); Leidholdt, supra note 25, at 136 n.4 (quoting Mimi Silbert, Sexual Assault of Prostitutes: Phase One 40 (1980) (66% of subjects are sexually assaulted by father or father figure); The Council for Prostitution Alternatives, *1991 Annual Report* 3 (85% of clients have histories of sexual abuse in childhood, 70% most frequently by their fathers).

[56]See Cecilie Høigard & Liv Finstad, *Backstreets: Prostitution, Money, and Love* 76 (Katherine Hanson et al. trans., 1992) (average age of prostitutes interviewed in Norway began at 15 1/2 years). Compare Leidholdt, supra note 25, at 136 n.3 (citing Evelina Giobbe, founder of Minneapolis-based advocacy project, Women Hurt in Systems of Prostitution Engaged in Revolt [WHISPER]) (fourteen is the average age of women's entry into prostitution); Roberta Perkins, Working Girls: Prostitutes, *This Life and Social Control* 258 (1991) (finding in her Australian sample that almost half entered prostitution before age 20, and over 80% before age 25); Mimi H. Silbert & Ayala M. Pines, Occupational Hazards of Street Prostitutes, 8 *Crim. Just. Behav.* 395, 396 (1981) (68% were 16 years or younger when entered prostitution).

[57]For a superb discussion of the "choice" illusion, see Leidholdt, supra note 25, at 136–138.

[58]For an argument that domestic battery of women is involuntary servitude, see Joyce E. McConnell, Beyond Metaphor: Battered Woman, Involuntary Servitude, and the Thirteenth Amendment, 4 *Yale J.L. & Feminism* 207 (1992).

[59]*Bray v. Alexandria Women's Health Clinic,* 122 L. Ed. 2d 34, 46, 47 n.2 (1993).

[60]Evelina Giobbe, Confronting the Liberal Lies about Prostitution, in Dorchen Leidholdt & Janice G. Raymond eds., *The Sexual Liberty and the Attack on Feminism* 67, 77 (1990).

[61]Leidholdt, supra note 25, at 138–139.

[62]See Andrea Dworkin & Catharine A. Mackinnon, *Pornography & Civil Rights: A New Day for Women's Equality* apps. A, B, C (1988).

[63]Fla. Stat. ch. 796.09 (1992) (providing a cause of action for those coerced into prostitution to sue their pimps for compensatory and punitive damages). See Margaret A. Baldwin, Strategies of Connection: Prostitution and Feminist Politics, *1 Mich. J. Gender & L.* 65, 70 (1993) (reporting that several cases utilizing this statute are currently underway at the discovery stage prior to filing).

[64]See Gayle Kirshenbaum, A Potential Landmark for Female Human Rights, *Ms.*, Sept./Oct. 1991, at 13 (report on proposed U.N. Convention Against All Forms of Sexual Exploitation).

[65]The proposed Sexual Exploitation convention would require states' parties to adopt legislation to "hold liable" traffickers in pornography. International Convention to Eliminate All Forms of Sexual Exploitation, Sept. 1993, Art. 6(d).

International Committee for Prostitutes' Rights World Charter and World Whores' Congress Statements

International Committee for Prostitutes' Rights

WORLD CHARTER

Laws

Decriminalize all aspects of adult prostitution resulting from individual decision.

International Committee for Prostitutes' Rights World Charter and World Whores' Congress, Statement for Prostitutes' Rights; Draft Statements from the 2nd World Whores' Congress (1986).

Decriminalize prostitution and regulate third parties according to standard business codes. It must be noted that existing standard business codes allow abuse of prostitutes. Therefore special clauses must be included to prevent the abuse and stigmatization of prostitutes (self-employed and others).

Enforce criminal laws against fraud, coercion, violence, child sexual abuse, child labor, rape, racism everywhere and across national boundaries, whether or not in the context of prostitution.

Eradicate laws that can be interpreted to deny freedom of association, or freedom to travel, to prostitutes within and between countries. Prostitutes have rights to a private life.

Human Rights

Guarantee prostitutes all human rights and civil liberties, including the freedom of speech, travel, immigration, work, marriage, and motherhood and the right to unemployment insurance, health insurance and housing.

Grant asylum to anyone denied human rights on the basis of a "crime of status," be it prostitution or homosexuality.

Working Conditions

There should be no law which implies systematic zoning of prostitution. Prostitutes should have the freedom to choose their place of work and residence. It is essential that prostitutes can provide their services under the conditions that are absolutely determined by themselves and no one else.

There should be a committee to insure the protection of the rights of the prostitutes and to whom prostitutes can address their complaints. This committee must be comprised of prostitutes and other professionals like lawyers and supporters.

There should be no law discriminating against prostitutes associating and working collectively in order to acquire a high degree of personal security.

Health

All women and men should be educated to periodical health screening for sexually transmitted diseases. Since health checks have historically been used to control and stigmatize prostitutes, and since adult prostitutes are generally even more aware of sexual health than others, mandatory checks for prostitutes are unacceptable unless they are mandatory for all sexually active people.

Services

Employment, counseling, legal, and housing services for runaway children should be funded

in order to prevent child prostitution and to promote child well-being and opportunity.

Prostitutes must have the same social benefits as all other citizens according to the different regulations in different countries.

Shelters and services for working prostitutes and re-training programs for prostitutes wishing to leave the life should be funded.

Taxes

No special taxes should be levied on prostitutes or prostitute businesses.

Prostitutes should pay regular taxes on the same basis as other independent contractors and employees, and should receive the same benefits.

Public Opinion

Support educational programs to change social attitudes which stigmatize and discriminate against prostitutes and ex-prostitutes of any race, gender or nationality.

Develop educational programs which help the public to understand that the customer plays a crucial role in the prostitution phenomenon, this role being generally ignored. The customer, like the prostitute, should not, however, be criminalized or condemned on a moral basis.

We are in solidarity with all workers in the sex industry.

Organization

Organizations of prostitutes and ex-prostitutes should be supported to further implementation of the above charter.

DRAFT STATEMENTS FROM THE 2ND WORLD WHORES' CONGRESS (1986)

Prostitution and Feminism

The International Committee for Prostitutes' Rights (ICPR) realizes that up until now the women's movement in most countries has not, or has only marginally, included prostitutes as spokeswomen and theorists. Historically, women's movements (like socialist and communist movements) have opposed the institution of prostitution while claiming to support prostitute women. However, prostitutes reject support that requires them to leave prostitution; they object to being treated as symbols of oppression and demand recognition as workers. Due to feminist hesitation or refusal to accept prostitution as legitimate work and to accept prostitutes as working women, the majority of prostitutes have not identified as feminists; nonetheless, many prostitutes identify with feminist values such as independence, financial autonomy, sexual self-determination, personal strength, and female bonding.

During the last decade, some feminists have begun to re-evaluate the traditional anti-prostitution stance of their movement in light of the actual experiences, opinions, and needs of prostitute women. The ICPR can be considered a feminist organization in that it is committed to giving voice and respect to all women, including the most invisible, isolated, degraded, and/or idealized. The development of prostitution analyses and strategies within women's movements which link the condition of prostitutes to the condition of women in general and which do justice to the integrity of prostitute women is therefore an important goal of the committee.

1. Financial Autonomy

Financial autonomy is basic to female survival, self-determination, self-respect, and self-development. Unlike men, women are often scorned and/or pitied for making life choices primarily in the interest of earning money. True financial independence includes the means to earn money (or the position to have authority over money) and the freedom to spend it as one needs or desires. Such means are rarely available to women even with compromise and struggle. Financial dependency or despair is the condition of a majority of women, depending upon class, culture, race, education, and other differences and inequalities. Female compromises and struggles are traditionally considered reflections of immorality and misfortune rather than of responsibility, intelligence and courage. The financial initiative of prostitutes is stigmatized and/or criminalized as a warning to women in general against such sexually explicit strategies

for financial independence. Nonetheless, "being sexually attractive" and "catching a good man" are traditional female strategies for survival, strategies which may provide financial sustenance but rarely financial independence. All women, including prostitutes, are entitled to the same commercial rights as other citizens in any given society. *The ICPR affirms the right of women to financial initiative and financial gain, including the right to commercialize sexual service or sexual illusion (such as erotic media), and to save and spend their earnings according to their own needs and priorities.*

2. Occupational Choice

The lack of educational and employment opportunities for women throughout the world has been well documented. Occupational choice for women (especially for women of color and working-class women), and also for men oppressed by class and race prejudice, is usually a choice between different subordinate positions. Once employed, women are often stigmatized and harassed. Furthermore, they are commonly paid according to their gender rather than their worth. Female access to jobs traditionally reserved for men, and adequate pay and respect to women in jobs traditionally reserved for women are necessary conditions of true occupational choice. Those conditions entail an elimination of the sexual division of labor. Prostitution is a traditional female occupation. Some prostitutes report job satisfaction, others job repulsion; some consciously chose prostitution as the best alternative open to them; others rolled into prostitution through male force or deceit. Many prostitutes abhor the conditions and social stigma attached to their work, but not the work itself. *The ICPR affirms the right of women to the full range of education and employment alternatives and to due respect and compensation in every occupation, including prostitution.*

3. Alliance Between Women

Women have been divided into social categories on the basis of their sexual labor and/or sexual identity. Within the sex industry, the prostitute is the most explicitly oppressed by legal and social controls. Pornography models, strip-tease dancers, sexual masseuses, and prostitutes euphemistically called escorts or sexual surrogates often avoid association with prostitution labels and workers in an effort to elevate their status. Also among self-defined prostitutes, a hierarchy exists with street workers on the bottom and call girls on the top. Efforts to distance oneself from explicit sex work reinforce prejudice against prostitutes and reinforce sexual shame among women. Outside the sex industry, women are likewise divided by status, history, identity, and appearance. Non-prostitutes are frequently pressured to deliver sexual services in the form of sex, smiles, dress or affection; those services are rarely compensated with pay and may even diminish female status. In general, a whore-madonna division is imposed upon women wherein those who are sexually assertive are considered whores and those who are sexually passive are considered madonnas. *The ICPR calls for alliance between all women within and outside the sex industry and especially affirms the dignity of street prostitutes and of women stigmatized for their color, class, ethnic difference, history of abuse, marital or motherhood status, sexual preference, disability, or weight. The ICPR is in solidarity with homosexual male, transvestite and transsexual prostitutes.*

4. Sexual Self-Determination

The right to sexual self-determination includes women's right to set the terms of their own sexuality, including the choice of partner(s), behaviors, and outcomes (such as pregnancy, pleasure, or financial gain). Sexual self-determination includes the right to refuse sex and to initiate sex as well as the right to use birth control (including abortion), the right to have lesbian sex, the right to have sex across lines of color or class, the right to engage in sado-masochistic sex, and the right to offer sex for money. Those possibly self-determining acts have been stigmatized and punished by law or custom. Necessarily, no one is entitled to act out a sexual desire that includes another party unless that party agrees under conditions of total free will. The feminist task is to nurture self-determination both by increasing women's

sexual consciousness and courage and also by demanding conditions of safety and choice. *The ICPR affirms the right of all women to determine their own sexual behavior, including commercial exchange, without stigmatization or punishment.*

5. Healthy Childhood Development

Children are dependent upon adults for survival, love, and development. Pressure upon children, either with kindness or force, to work for money or to have sex for adult satisfaction, is a violation of rights to childhood development. Often the child who is abused at home runs away but can find no subsistence other than prostitution, which perpetuates the violation of childhood integrity. Some research suggests that a higher percentage of prostitutes were victims of childhood abuse than of non-prostitutes. Research also suggests that fifty percent of prostitutes were not abused and that twenty-five percent of non-prostitutes were abused. Child abuse in private and public spheres is a serious violation of human rights but it does not mean that the victims cannot survive and recover, especially given support and resources for development. A victim deserves no stigmatization either in childhood or adulthood. *The ICPR affirms the right of children to shelter, education, medical or psychological or legal services, safety, and sexual self-determination. Allocation of government funds to guarantee the above rights should be a priority in every country.*

6. Integrity of All Women

Violence against women and girls has been a major feminist preoccupation for the past decade. Specifically, rape, sexual harassment at work, battering, and denial of motherhood rights have been targeted as focal areas for concern, research, and activism. Within the context of prostitution, women are sometimes raped or sexually harassed by the police, by their clients, by their managers, and by strangers who know them to be whores. Prostitute women, like nonprostitute women, consider rape to be any sexual act forced upon them. The fact that prostitutes are available for sexual negotiation does not mean that they are available for sexual harassment or rape. *The ICPR demands that the prostitute be given the same protection. from rape and the same legal recourse and social support following rape that should be the right of any woman or man.*

Battering of prostitutes, like battering of non-prostitutes, reflects the subordination of women to men in personal relationships. Laws against such violence are often discriminately and/or arbitrarily enforced. Boyfriends and husbands of prostitutes, in addition to anyone else assumed to profit from prostitution earnings (such as family and roommates), are often fined or imprisoned in various countries on charges of "pimping" regardless of whether they commit a violent offense or not. Boyfriends and husbands of non-prostitute women are rarely punished for battering, even when the woman clearly presses charges against them. *The ICPR affirms the right of all women to relational choice and to recourse against violence within any personal or work setting.*

Women known to be prostitutes or sex workers, like women known to be lesbians, are regularly denied custody of their children in many countries. The assumption that prostitute women or lesbian women are less responsible, loving, or deserving than other women is a denial of human rights and human dignity. The laws and attitudes which punish sexually stigmatized women function to punish their children as well by stigmatizing them and by denying them their mothers. *The ICPR considers the denial of custodial rights to prostitutes and lesbians to be a violation of the social and psychological integrity of women.*

7. Pornography: "Writings of Harlots"

Sexually explicit material or pornography refers specifically in original Greek to the writing of harlots. Today, pornography has been taken over by a male-dominated production industry wherein the female models and actresses rarely determine the content of their products. Moreover, like prostitutes, pornography workers are stigmatized as whores, denied recourse after abuse, and are often blamed for abuse committed against them. They are also denied adequate financial compensation for distribution of products in which they appear. *The*

ICPR claims the right of sex workers (as opposed to managers) to determine the content, production procedure, and distribution procedure of the pornography industry. Such empowerment will require solidarity among sex workers, solidarity between women both within and outside the sex industry, and education of women in the production of sexually explicit material. In support of such a feminist self-determining movement, the ICPR calls for public education campaigns to change the demands of a market which eroticizes children and the abuse of women.

8. Migration of Women through Prostitution ("Trafficking")

Trafficking of women and children, an international issue among both feminists and non-feminists, usually refers to the transport of women and children from one country to another for purposes of prostitution under conditions of force or deceit. The ICPR has a clear stand against child prostitution under any circumstances. In the case of adult prostitution, it must be acknowledged that prostitution both within and across national borders can be an individual decision to which an adult woman has a right. Certainly, force or deceit are crimes which should be punished whether in the context of prostitution or not. Women who choose to migrate as prostitutes should not be punished or assumed to be victims of abuse. They should enjoy the same rights as other immigrants. For many women, female migration through prostitution is an escape from an economically and socially impossible situation in one country to hopes for a better situation in another. The fact that many women find themselves in another awful situation reflects the lack of opportunities for financial independence and employment satisfaction for women, especially for third world women, throughout the world. Given the increased internationalization of industry, including prostitution, the rights and specific needs of foreign women workers must be given special attention in all countries.

The ICPR objects to policies which give women the status of children and which assume migration through prostitution among women to be always the result of force or deceit. Migrant women, also those who work as prostitutes, deserve both worker rights and worker protections. Women who are transported under conditions of deceit or force should be granted choice of refuge status or return to their country of origin.

9. A Movement for All-Women's Rights

It is essential that feminist struggle include the rights of all women. Prostitutes (especially those also oppressed by racism and classism) are perhaps the most silenced and violated of all women; the inclusion of their rights and their own words in feminist platforms for change is necessary. *The ICPR urges existing feminist groups to invite whore-identified women into their leading ranks and to integrate a prostitution consciousness in their analyses and strategies.*

Prostitution and Health

Prostitute health and prostitute access to health care services are deeply affected by social stigma and legal discrimination. Those injustices function not only to deny healthy work conditions and effective services to prostitutes, but also to foster distorted beliefs about prostitutes among the general public. Historically, prostitutes have been blamed for sexually transmitted diseases and authorities have justified social and legal control of prostitutes as a public health measure. The assumptions that prostitutes are more responsible for disease transmission than other groups and that state control of prostitute behavior prevents such transmission are contrary to research findings. Presently, the assumption that prostitutes are carriers of AIDS and that forced AIDS testing will prevent the disease have been shown to be unfounded in the West. The situation in various third world countries is as yet unclear. Female prostitutes in the West are not a risk group for AIDS. The small minority of prostitutes who are needle-using drug addicts are at risk from shared needles, not from commercial sex.

The ICPR demands realistic portrayals of the health of diverse prostitutes and implementation of effective health education and treatment services. Those services must respect prostitute dignity and foster customer responsibility for disease prevention (i.e condom use) in sexual transactions. A list follows of injustices and rights which are crucial to prostitute health and public responsibility.

Human Rights Violations in Health Policy and Practice

I.   *Discrimination* against women in public health laws and practices is a basic violation of human rights. The ICPR demands:

A.   (1) Repeal of regulations which deny free choice of a doctor to prostitutes.

(2) Abolition of compulsory medical certificates.

(3) Repeal of laws to combat venereal disease which are invoked only against prostitutes.

(4) Prohibition of forced or incentive testing of prostitutes in prison for any purpose.

(5) Free, anonymous, and voluntary testing for venereal disease, including AIDS, at easily accessible health facilities available for all people, including prostitutes.

B.   Widespread education and regular screening for sexually transmitted diseases among all sexually active people. Note that venereal disease is a risk for different groups of sexually active people, that condoms are the best known preventive measure against VD, and that prostitutes are more likely to be aware of sexual health care than other persons.

C.   Health insurance and compensation benefits for all workers, including prostitutes. Note that the stigmas and regulations which prevent job mobility for prostitutes (such as the denial of required letters of good conduct to prostitutes) make it extremely difficult or impossible for prostitutes to change work when desired or when necessary for health reasons.

II. *Registration* of prostitutes with state and police authorities denies human rights to privacy and dignified employment. The ICPR demands:

A. Independent and confidential public health services for all people, including prostitutes. Collaboration between health providers and public authorities, such as police or researchers, should be illegal.

B. Abolition of mandatory registration of prostitutes and of unofficial pressure on prostitutes to register with the police.

III. *Criminalization* of prostitutes for purposes of public health is unrealistic and denies human rights to healthy work conditions. As outlaws, prostitutes are discouraged, if not forbidden, to determine and design a healthy setting and practice for their trade. The ICPR demands:

A. Decriminalization of all aspects of adult prostitution resulting from individual decision. Specifically, prostitutes must have the right to work indoors and the right to advertise; they must also have the right to solicit outdoors according to general zoning codes (i.e., active solicitation should be allowed in areas zoned for businesses). Denial of those rights forces prostitutes into medically unhygienic, physically unsafe, and psychologically stressful work situations.

B. Application of regular business codes to prostitution businesses, including codes for cleanliness, heating, and leave for sickness and vacation. Also, codes for mandatory condom use should be enacted. Regulations should be enforced by worker organizations and not by state authorities.

Medical and Counseling Services

I. *Education* of health workers about the realities of prostitution health issues is necessary to combat prejudice and misinformation within medical and counseling services. Prostitutes and ex-prostitutes should be employed to participate in such training.

II. *Integration* of prostitutes in the medical and counseling services is essential for effective policy-making and service delivery.

III. Vocational counselors must respect a woman's decision to *work as a prostitute or not.* Leaving prostitution must never be a prerequisite for counseling service.

IV. Health authorities should disseminate information about *safe sexual practices.* In particular, condom use should be recommended for all vaginal, oral, or anal sexual transactions.

Drugs and Alcohol

I. Those prostitutes who are addicts, a minority in most branches of prostitution, usually entered prostitution to support their habit. Inadequate drug policies are responsible for addicts practicing prostitution; *prostitution is not responsible for drug addiction.*

Social alternatives to prostitution are needed for addicted women. Both drug laws and drug treatment programs need to be re-evaluated. A clinical and social rather than a criminal model should be considered for controlling addictive substances. Treatment programs should be given adequate funding and research support.

II. There are no inherent connections between drug addiction and prostitution. Laws which criminalize both and practices which utilize addicted prostitutes as police informants are largely responsible for the connection between drugs and sex work on the streets. *Prostitution must be decriminalized and police must stop using prostitutes for illicit criminal investigations.*

III. Addicted prostitutes who use needles, like other needle-using addicts, must have *access to legal, inexpensive needles* in order to prevent the spread of disease (specifically, hepatitis and AIDS).

IV. It should be *illegal* for any employer, including managers of sex businesses, to *force employees to drink alcohol.*

Prostitution and Human Rights

The European Convention on Human Rights was drafted within the Council of Europe in 1950 and came into force in 1953. All twenty-one of the member States have ratified it. Those States include: Austria, Belgium, Cyprus, Denmark, France, Federal Republic of Germany, Greece, Iceland, Ireland, Italy, Liechtenstein, Luxembourg, Malta, the Netherlands, Norway, Portugal, Spain, Sweden, Switzerland, Turkey, and the United Kingdom. A published summary of the Convention is reprinted at the end of this statement.

The International Committee for Prostitutes' Rights (ICPR) demands that prostitutes, ex-prostitutes, and all women regardless of their work, color, class, sexuality, history of abuse, or marital status be granted the same human rights as every other citizen. At present, prostitutes are officially and/or unofficially denied rights both by States within the Council of Europe and by States outside of it. No State in the world is held accountable by any international body for those infractions. To the contrary, denial of human rights to prostitutes is publicly justified as a protection of women, public order, health, morality, and the reputation of dominant persons or nations. Those arguments deny prostitutes the status of ordinary persons and blame them for disorder and/or disease and for male exploitation of and violence against women. Criminalization or state regulation of prostitution does not protect anyone, least of all prostitutes. Prostitutes are systematically robbed of liberty, security, fair administration of justice, respect for private and family life, freedom of expression, and freedom of association. In addition, they suffer from inhuman and degrading treatment and punishment and from discrimination in employment and housing. Prostitutes are effectively excluded from the Human Rights Convention.

The World Charter of Prostitutes' Rights which was adopted by the ICPR in 1985 demands that prostitution be redefined as legitimate work and that prostitutes be redefined as legitimate citizens. Any other stance functions to deny human status to a class of women (and to men who sexually service other men).

The European Parliament recently took a step toward decriminalizing prostitution and prostitute workers by adopting a resolution on violence against women which includes the following clauses (see Hedy d'Ancona resolution, June session of Parliament, 1986):

"In view of the existence of prostitution the European Parliament calls on the national authorities in the Member States to take the necessary legal steps:

(a)   to decriminalize the exercise of this profession,

(b)   to guarantee prostitutes the rights enjoyed by other citizens,

(c)   to protect the independence, health and safety of those exercising this profession . . .

(d)   to reinforce measures which may be taken against those responsible for duress or violence to prostitutes . . .

(e)   to support prostitutes' self-help groups and to require police and judicial authorities to provide better protection for prostitutes who wish to lodge complaints . . ."

Concrete implementation of those steps requires specifications of the violations in each State. One goal of the Second World Whores' Congress is for prostitutes from countries represented within the Council of Europe and outside of it to specify those violations. The summarized list stated here will be elaborated at the congress.

Violations of the Human Rights of Prostitutes

1. The right to life. Murder of prostitutes is a common occurrence throughout the world. And, those murders are commonly considered less offensive than other murders, as evidenced by the fact that prostitute murderers are often not sought, found, or prosecuted.

2. The right to liberty and security of person. The physical safety of prostitutes is threatened by the criminal sphere in which they are forced to work.

The physical liberty of prostitutes is restricted by state and city regulations which prohibit their presence in certain districts or at certain times. For example, a woman standing on the street "looking as if she is a prostitute" can be fined for passive solicitation in France even if she is not negotiating a sexual transaction. Or, a prostitute in Toronto, Canada can be given a curfew (21:00) by the court if she hasn't paid three or four solicitation tickets; if she disobeys the order, she can be sentenced to six months in prison for disobeying a court order.

The right to liberty and security of persons is totally denied to women who are deceitfully or forcefully made to practice prostitution. In particular, the common transport of third world women to the West under false pretenses denies both liberty and security to women. The right *not* to work as a prostitute is as essential as the right to work if one so decides. Sexist and racist denial of both rights is widespread.

Prostitutes usually do not enjoy the same police protection of their liberty and security as other citizens. Due to the criminalization of their profession, they risk fines or arrests so they avoid calling upon police for protection. Police are frequently known to grant immunity from criminal action in exchange for information and/or sex, i.e. rape by the state as the cost for liberty.

Forced medical testing which denies choice of one's own doctor and medical facility denies liberty to prostitutes. Denial of worker's compensation prevents prostitutes from liberty and health security in case of illness.

Forced or pressured registration with the police stigmatizes prostitutes and frequently violates their privacy and liberty to change professions if they so choose. Prostitutes are denied job mobility by requirements for letters of good conduct which are granted only to those who can prove that they have not engaged in commercial sex for at least three years (for example, in Switzerland).

3. The right to fair administration of justice. Application of laws and regulations against prostitution is usually arbitrary, discriminatory, corrupt, and hypocritical. In Paris, for example, street prostitutes are given an average of three tickets per week for passive or active solicitation; at the same time, they are heavily taxed for their prostitution earnings.

Prostitutes who are raped or physically battered are unlikely to succeed in bringing charges against the rapist or batterer. The prostitute is considered fair game for abuse even by state and judiciary authorities.

Foreign women who were deceitfully or forcefully transported for purposes of prostitution rarely succeed in bringing charges against the violating party.

Male law enforcement officials, like other men, are frequently customers and/or violators of prostitute women. Police, for example, in the United States, Canada, and Great Britain, regularly entrap women by posing as customers and arresting them as soon as they mention a price for sex. Even if the prostitute is careful not to mention a price (many have learned to expect police deceit), she may be convicted because a police officer's word carries more credit than a whore's word in court.

Prostitution laws are discriminately enforced against women, especially third world and poor women, and against third world male associates of those women.

4. Respect for private and family life, home and correspondence. Laws which criminalize those who profit from the earnings of prostitutes are frequently used against the family of prostitutes, for example in the United States and France. Such "anti-pimping" laws violate a prostitute's right to a private life by putting all of her personal associates, be they lovers or children or parents or roommates, under (even more) risk of arrest than exploiters and physical violators.

Confiscation of personal letters or literary work of prostitutes, for example in the United States, is a clear denial of respect for home and correspondence, not to mention a denial of freedom of expression.

5. Freedom of expression and to hold opinions. The word of prostitutes is generally assumed to be invalid in public, for example as evidence in court. The opinions of prostitutes are rarely given a hearing, even in relation to their own lives.

In private, prostitutes are often used as police informants and as counselors to male customers. In public, be it on the street or in court, their testimony and opinion are silenced.

6. Freedom of peaceful assembly and association, including the right to join a trade union. Prostitutes are prevented from working together for purposes of safety, cooperation, and/or commercial advantage by specific statutes which criminalize "keeping a house" or other necessarily cooperative work forms.

Until prostitutes are recognized as legitimate workers, rather than as outlaws or vagrants or bad girls, they cannot officially form trade unions.

7. *The right to marry and found a family.* Both the right to marry and the right not to marry are frequently denied to women, in particular to the prostitute woman. Marriage is impossible if husbands thereby become outlaws, i.e. pimps. The denial of rights and legitimacy to unmarried women, on the other hand, can force women to marry against their will. A prostitute may also be denied the privilege of motherhood when the courts declare her unfit on the basis of her professsion.

8. *The right to peaceful enjoyment of possessions.* The possessions of prostitutes and their associates are confiscated on the ground that they were obtained with "illegal" money; they are also confiscated when a prostitute cannot pay the fines levied against her for the practice of her profession.

9. *The right to leave a country including one's own.* Prostitutes are denied the right to travel across national borders by signs or cuts on their passports (or identity cards) which indicate their profession. Also, police records registered on computers at certain borders will prevent prostitutes from leaving or entering the country.

10. *Prohibition of torture and inhuman or degrading treatment and punishment.* The above mentioned violations indicate inhuman treatment. Degradation of prostitutes is the norm both among official bodies, such as governmental and judiciary institutions, and among community bodies, such as neighborhood committees and social service agencies.

Forced prostitution should be recognized as a case of torture.

11. *Prohibition of slavery, servitude and forced labour.* Servitude exists both in cases of forced prostitution and in cases of voluntary prostitution under forced conditions. State regulated brothels such as found in Hamburg (Germany) and Nevada (United States) allow no choice in clientele, no right to refusal, no right to a fair share of the earnings, forced isolation, and forced overwork. Most brothels in the Netherlands force unhealthy practices such as no condoms (or less earnings for condom sex) and/or forced alcohol consumption.

Juvenile prostitution is a case of forced labour but the managers, be they managers of pornography or prostitution, are rarely prosecuted whereas the children are often stigmatized and punished.

12. *Prohibition of discrimination in the enjoyment of rights and freedoms guaranteed by the Convention.* Prostitutes are discriminated against in the enjoyment of every right and freedom. Prostitutes of color, foreign prostitutes, street prostitutes, drug addicted prostitutes, and juvenile prostitutes suffer extra and often extreme discrimination.

13. *Prohibition of the collective expulsion of aliens.* Expulsion of foreign women who entered the country under conditions of deceit or force and who often await persecution in their native country is a violation of human rights.

A Crime By Any Other Name . . .

Jeffrey Reiman

> If one individual inflicts a bodily injury upon another which leads to the death of the person attacked we call it manslaughter; on the other hand, if the attacker knows beforehand that the blow will be fatal we call it murder. Murder has also been committed if society places hundreds of workers in such a position that they inevitably come to premature and unnatural ends. Their death is as violent as if they had been stabbed or shot. . . . Murder has been committed if society knows perfectly well that thousands of workers cannot avoid being sacrificed so long as these conditions are allowed to continue. Murder of this sort is just as culpable as the murder committed by an individual.
>
> Frederick Engels, *The Condition of the Working Class in England*

WHAT'S IN A NAME?

If it takes you an hour to read this chapter, by the time you reach the last page, three of your fellow citizens will have been murdered. *During that same time, at least four Americans will die as a result of unhealthy or unsafe conditions in the workplace!* Although these work-related deaths could have been prevented, they are not called murders. Why not? Doesn't a crime by any other name still cause misery and suffering? What's in a name?

The fact is that the label "crime" is not used in America to name all or the worst of the actions that cause misery and suffering to Americans. It is primarily reserved for the dangerous actions of the poor.

In the February 21, 1993 edition of the *New York Times*, an article appears with the headline: "Company in Mine Deaths Set to Pay Big Fine." It describes an agreement by the owners of a Kentucky mine to pay a fine for safety misconduct that may have led to "the worst American mining accident in nearly a decade."

Jeffrey Reiman, "A Crime by Any Other Name . . .," *The Rich Get Richer and the Poor Get Prison*, 5th ed. (Reading, MA: Allyn & Bacon, 1998), pp. 51–53, 61–70. Reprinted by permission from Allyn & Bacon.

Ten workers died in a methane explosion, and the company pleaded guilty to "a pattern of safety misconduct" that included falsifying reports of methane levels and requiring miners to work under unsupported roofs. The company was fined $3.75 million. The acting foreman at the mine was the only individual charged by the federal government, and for his cooperation with the investigation, prosecutors were recommending that he receive the minimum sentence: probation to six months in prison. The company's president expressed regret for the tragedy that occurred. And the U.S. attorney said he hoped the case "sent a clear message that violations of Federal safety and health regulations that endanger the lives of our citizens will not be tolerated."[1]

Compare this with the story of Colin Ferguson, who prompted an editorial in the *New York Times* of December 10, 1993, with the headline: "Mass Murder on the 5:33."[2] A few days earlier, Colin had boarded a commuter train in Garden City, Long Island, and methodically shot passengers with a 9-millimeter pistol, killing 5 and wounding 18. Colin Ferguson was surely a murderer, maybe a mass murderer. My question is, Why wasn't the death of the miners also murder? Why weren't those responsible for subjecting ten miners to deadly conditions also "mass murderers"?

Why do ten dead miners amount to an "accident," a "tragedy," and five dead commuters a "mass murder"? "Murder" suggests a murderer, whereas "accident" and "tragedy" suggest the work of impersonal forces. But the charge against the company that owned the mine said that they "repeatedly exposed the mine's work crews to danger and that such conditions were frequently concealed from Federal inspectors responsible for enforcing the mine safety act." And the acting foreman admitted to falsifying records of methane levels only two months before the fatal blast. Someone was responsible for the conditions that led to the death of then miners. Is that person not a murderer, perhaps even a *mass murderer?*

These questions are at this point rhetorical. My aim is not to discuss this case but rather to point to the blinders we wear when we look at such an "accident." There was an investigation. One person, the acting foreman, was held responsible for falsifying records. He is to be sentenced to six months in prison (at most). The company was fined. But no one will be tried for *murder.* No one will be thought of as a murderer. *Why not?* Would the miners not be safer if such people were treated as murderer? Might they not still be alive? Will a president of the United States address the Yale Law School and recommend mandatory prison sentences for such people? Will he mean these people when he says,

> These relatively few, persistent criminals who cause so much misery and fear are really the core of the problem. The rest of the American people have a right to protection from their violence[?][3]

Didn't those miners have a right to protection from the violence that look their lives? *And if not, why not?*

Once we are ready to ask this question seriously, we are in a position to say that the reality of crime—that is, the acts we label crime, the acts we think of as crime, the actors and actions we treat as criminal—is *created:* It is

an image shaped by decisions as to *what* will be called crime and *who* will be treated as a criminal.

* * *

A CRIME BY ANY OTHER NAME . . .

Think of a crime, any crime. Picture the first "crime" that comes into your mind. What do you see? The odds are you are not imagining a mining company executive sitting at his desk, calculating the costs of proper safely precautions and deciding not to invest in them. Probably what you do see with your mind's eye is one person physically attacking another or robbing something from another via the threat of physical attack. Look more closely. What does the attacker look like? It's a safe bet he (and it is a *he*, of course) is not wearing a suit and tie. In fact, my hunch is that you—like me, like almost anyone else in America—picture a young, tough, lower-class male when the thought of crime first pops into your head. You (we) picture someone like the Typical Criminal described above. The crime itself is one in which the Typical Criminal sets out to attack or rob some specific person.

This last point is important. It indicates that we have a mental image not only of the Typical Criminal but also of the Typical Crime. If they Typical Criminal is a young, lower-class male, the Typical Crime is *one-on-one-harm*—where harm means either physical injury or loss of something valuable or both. If you have any doubts that this is the Typical Crime, look at any random sample of police or private eye shows on television. How often do you see the cops on "NYPD Blue" investigate consumer fraud or failure to remove occupational hazards? And when Jessica Fletcher (on "Murder, She Wrote") tracks down well-heeled criminals, it is almost always for garden-variety violent crimes like murder. A study of TV crime shows by The Media Institute in Washington, D.C., indicates that, while the fictional criminals portrayed on television are on the average both older and wealthier than the real criminals who figure in the FBI *Uniform Crime Reports.*

"TV crimes are almost 12 times as likely to be violent as crimes committed in the real world."[21] A review of several decades of research confirms that violent crimes are overrepresented on TV news and fictional crime shows, and that "young people, black people, and people of low socioeconomic status are underrepresented us offenders or victims in television programs"— exactly opposite from the real world in which nonviolent property crimes far outnumber violent crimes, and young, poor and black folks predominate as offenders and victims.[22] As a result, TV crime shows broadcast the double-edged message that the one-on-one crimes of the poor are the typical crimes of all and thus not uniquely caused by the pressures of poverty; *and* that the criminal justice system pursues rich and poor alike—thus, when the criminal justice system happens mainly to pounce on the poor in real life, it is not out of any class bias.[23]

In addition to the steady diet of fictionalized TV violence and crime, there has been an increase in the graphic display of crime on many TV news programs. Crimes reported on TV news are also far more frequently violent than real crimes are.[24] An article in *The Washingtonian* says that the word around two prominent local TV news programs is, "If it bleeds, it leads."[25] What's more, a new breed of nonfictional "tabloid" TV show has appeared in which viewers are shown films of actual violent crimes—blood, screams, and all—or reenactments of actual violent crimes, sometimes using the actual victims playing themselves! Among these are "COPS," "Real Stories of the Highway Patrol," "America's Most Wanted" and "Unsolved Mysteries." Here, too, the focus is on crimes of one-on-one violence, rather than, say, corporate pollution. The *Wall Street Journal*, reporting on the phenomenon of tabloid TV, informs us that "Television has gone tabloid. The seamy underside of life is being bared in a new rash of true-crime series and contrived-confrontation talk shows."[26] Is there any surprise that a survey by *McCall's* indicates that its readers have grown more afraid of crime in the mid-1980s—even though victimization

studies show a stable level of crime for most of this period?[27]

It is important to identify this model of the Typical Crime because it functions like a set of blinders. It keeps us from calling a mine disaster a mass murder even if ten men are killed, even if someone is responsible for the unsafe conditions in which they worked and died. One study of newspaper reporting of a food-processing plant fire, in which 25 workers were killed and criminal charges were ultimately brought, concludes that "the newspapers showed little consciousness that corporate violence might be seen as a crime."[28] I contend that this is due to our fixation on the model of the Typical Crime. This particular piece of mental furniture so blocks our view that it keeps us from using the criminal justice system to protect ourselves from the greatest threats to our persons and possessions.

What keeps a mine disaster from being a mass murder in our eyes is that it is not a one-on-one harm. What is important in one-on-one harm is not the numbers but the *desire of someone (or ones) to harm someone (or ones) else:* An attack by a gang on one or more persons or an attack by one individual on several fits the model of one-on-one harm; that is, for each person harmed there is at least one individual who wanted to harm that person. Once he selects his victim, the rapist, the mugger, the murderer all want this person they have selected to suffer. A mine executive, on the other hand, does not want his employees to be harmed. He would truly prefer that there be no accident, no injured or dead miners. What he does want is something legitimate. It is what he has been hired to get; maximum profits at minimum costs. If he cuts corners to save a buck, he is just doing his job. If ten men die because he cut corners on safety, we may think him crude or callous but not a murderer. He is, at most, responsible for an *indirect harm*, not a one-on-one harm. For this, he may even be criminally indictable for violating safety regulations—but not for murder. The ten men are dead as an unwanted consequence of his (perhaps overzealous or undercautious) pursuit of a legitimate goal. So, unlike the Typical Criminal, he has not committed the Typical Crime—or so we generally believe. As a result, ten men are dead who might be alive now if cutting corners of the kind that leads to loss of life, whether suffering is specifically aimed at or not, were treated as murder.

This is my point. Because we accept the belief—encouraged by our politicians' statements about crime and by the media's portrayal of crime—that the model for crime is one person specifically trying to harm another, we accept a legal system that leaves us unprotected against much greater dangers to our lives and well-being than those threatened by the Typical Criminal. Before developing this point further, let us anticipate and deal with some likely objections. Defenders of the present legal order are likely to respond to my argument at this point with irritation. Because this will surely turn to outrage in a few pages, let's talk to them now while the possibility of rational communication still exists.

The Defenders of the Present Legal Order (I'll call them "the Defenders" for short) are neither foolish nor evil people. They are not racists, nor are they oblivious to the need for reform in the criminal justice system to make it more evenhanded, and for reform in the larger society to make equal opportunity a reality for all Americans. In general, their view is that—given our limited resources, particularly the resource of human altruism—the political and legal institutions we have are the best that can be. What is necessary is to make them work better and to weed out those who are intent on making them work shoddily. Their response to my argument at this point is that the criminal justice system *should* occupy itself primarily with one-on-one harm. Harms of the sort exemplified in the "mine tragedy" are really *not* murders and are better dealt with through stricter government enforcement of safety regulations. The Defenders admit that this enforcement has been rather lax and recommend that it be improved. Basically, though, they think this division of labor is right because it fits our ordinary moral sensibilities.

The Defenders maintain that, according to our common moral notions, someone who tries to do another harm and does is really more evil than someone who jeopardizes others while pursuing legitimate goals but doesn't aim to harm anyone. The one who jeopardizes others in this way at least doesn't try to hurt them. He or she doesn't have the goal of hurting someone in the way that a mugger or a rapist does. Moreover, being directly and purposely harmed by another person, the Defenders believe, is terrifying in a way that being harmed indirectly and impersonally, say, by a safety hazard, is not—even if the resultant injury is the same in both cases. And we should be tolerant of the one responsible for lax safety measures because he or she is pursuing a legitimate goal, that is, his or her dangerous action occurs as part of a productive activity, something that ultimately adds to social wealth and thus benefits everyone—whereas doers of direct harm benefit no one but themselves. Thus, the latter are rightfully in the province of the criminal justice system with its drastic weapons, and the former appropriately dealt with by the milder forms of regulation.

Further, the Defenders insist, the crimes identified as such by the criminal justice system are imposed on their victims totally against their will, whereas the victims of occupational hazards chose to accept their risky jobs and thus have in some degree consented to subject themselves to the dangers. Where dangers are consented to, the appropriate response is not blame but requiring improved safety, and this is most efficiently done by regulation rather than with the guilt-seeking methods of criminal justice.

In sum, the Defenders make four objections: 1. That someone who purposely tries to harm another is really more evil than someone who harms another without aiming to, even if the degree of harm is the same. 2. That being harmed directly by another person is more terrifying than being harmed indirectly and impersonally, as by a safety hazard, even if the degree of harm is the same. 3. That someone who harms another in the course of an illegitimate and purely self-interested action is more evil than someone who harms another as a consequence of a legitimate and socially productive endeavor. 4. That the harms of typical crimes are imposed on their victims against their wills, while harms like those due to occupational hazards are consented to by workers when they agree to a job. This too is thought to make the harms of typical crimes evil in a way that occupational harms are not.

All four of these objections are said to reflect our common moral beliefs, which are a fair standard for a legal system to match. Together they are said to show that the typical criminal does something worse than the one responsible for an occupational hazard, and thus deserves the special treatment provided by the criminal justice system. Some or all of these objections may have already occurred to the reader. Thus, it is important to respond to the Defenders. For the sake of clarity I shall number the paragraphs in which I start to take up each objection in turn.

1. The Defenders' first objection confuses intention with specific aim or purpose, and it is intention that brings us properly within the reach of the criminal law. It is true that a mugger aims to harm his victim in the way that a corporate executive who maintains an unsafe workplace does not. But the corporate executive acts intentionally nonetheless, and that's what makes his actions appropriately subject to criminal law. What we intend is not just what we try to make happen but what we know is likely to happen as the normal causal product of our chosen actions. As criminal law theorist Hyman Gross points out: "What really matters here is whether conduct of a particular degree of dangerousness was done intentionally."[29] Whether we want or aim for that conduct to harm someone is a different matter, which is relevant to the actor's *degree* of culpability (not to whether he or she is culpable at all). Gross describes the degrees of culpability for intentional action by means of an example in which a sailor dies when his ship is fumigated while he is asleep in the hold. Fumigation is a dangerous activity: it involves spraying the ship with poison that is normally fatal to humans. If the fumigation was done in order to kill the sailor, we can say that his death is caused *purposely*. But suppose that the fumigation was done knowing that a sailor was in the hold but not in order to kill him. Then, according to Gross, we say that his death was brought about *knowingly*. If the fumigation was done without knowledge that someone was in the hold but without making sure that no one was, then the sailor's death is brought about *recklessly*. Finally, if the fumigation was done without knowledge that the sailor was there and some, but inadequate, precautions were taken to make sure no one was there, then the sailor's death is brought about *negligently*.

How does this apply to the executive who imposes dangerous conditions on his workers, conditions that, as in the mine explosion, do finally lead to death? The first thing to note is that the difference between purposely, knowingly, recklessly, or negligently causing death is a difference within the range of intentional (and thus to some extent culpable) action. What is done recklessly or negligently is still done intentionally. Second, culpability decreases as we go from purposely to knowingly to recklessly to negligently killing because, according to Gross, the outcome is increasingly due to chance and not to the actor; that is, the one who kills on purpose leaves less room to chance that the killing will occur than the one who kills knowingly (the one who kills on purpose will take precautions against the failure of his killing, while the one who kills knowingly won't), and likewise the one who kills recklessly leaves wholly to chance whether there is a victim at all. And the one who kills negligently reduces this chance, but insufficiently.

Now, we may say that the kernel of truth in the Defenders' objection is that the common street mugger harms on purpose, while the executive harms only knowingly or recklessly or negligently. This does not justify refusing to treat the executive killer as a criminal, however, because we have criminal laws against reckless or even negligent harming—thus the kid-glove treatment meted out to those responsible for occupational hazards and the like is no simple reflection of our ordinary moral sensibilities, as the Defenders claim. Moreover, don't be confused into thinking that, because all workplaces have some safety measures, all workplace deaths are at most due to negligence. To the extent that precautions are not taken against particular dangers (like leaking methane), deaths due to those dangers are—by Gross's standard—caused recklessly or even knowingly (because the executive knows that potential victims are in harm's way from the danger he fails to reduce). And Nancy Frank concludes from a review of state homicide statutes that "a large number of states recognize unintended deaths caused by extreme recklessness as murder.[30]

But there is more to be said. Remember that Gross attributes the difference in degrees of culpability to the greater role left to chance as we descend from purposely to recklessly to negligently harming. In this light it is important to note that the executive (say, the mine owner) imposes danger on a larger number of individuals than the typical criminal typically does. So while the typical criminal purposely harms a particular individual, the executive knowingly subjects a large number of workers to a risk of harm. But as the risk gets greater and the number of workers gets greater, it becomes increasingly likely that one or more workers will get harmed. This means that the gap between the executive and the typical criminal shrinks. By not harming workers purposely, the executive leaves more to chance; but by subjecting large numbers to risk, he leaves it less and less to chance that someone will be harmed, and thus he rolls back his advantage over the typical criminal. If you keep your workers in mines or factories with high levels of toxic gases or chemicals, you start to approach 100 percent likelihood that at least one of them will be harmed as a result. And that means that the culpability of the executive approaches that of the typical criminal.

A different way to make the Defenders' argument is to say that the executive has failed to protect his workers, while the typical criminal has positively acted to harm his victim. In general, we think it is worse to harm someone than to fail to prevent their being harmed (perhaps you should feed starving people on the other side of town or of the world, but few people will think you are a murderer if you don't and the starving die). But at least in some cases we are responsible for the harm that results from our failure to act (for example, parents are responsible for failing to provide for their children). Some philosophers go further and hold that we are responsible for all the foreseeable effects of what we do, including the foreseeable effects of failing to act certain ways.[31] While this view supports the position for which I am arguing here, I think it goes too far. It entails that we are murderers every time we are doing anything other than saving lives, which surely goes way beyond our ordinary moral beliefs. My view is that in most cases, we are responsible only for the foreseeable effects likely to be caused by our action—and not responsible for those caused by our inaction. We are, however, responsible for the effects of our inaction in at least one special type of case: where we have a special obligation to aid people. This covers the parent who causes his child's death by failing to feed him, the doctor who causes her patient's death by failing to care for her, and the coal mine owner who causes his employees' death by failing to take legally mandated safety precautions. It may also cover the society that fails to rectify harm-producing injustices in its midst. This is another way in which the moral difference between the safety-cutting executive and the typical criminal shrinks away.

Further on this first objection, I think the Defenders overestimate the importance of specifically trying to do evil in our moral estimate of people. The mugger who aims to hurt someone is no doubt an ugly character. But so too is the well-heeled executive who calmly and callously chooses to put others at risk. Compare the mine executive who cuts corners with the typical murderer. Most murders, we know, are committed in the heat of some passion like rage or jealousy. Two lovers or neighbors or relatives find themselves in a heated argument. One (often it is a matter of chance *which* one) picks up a weapon and strikes the other a fatal blow. Such a person is clearly a murderer and rightly subject to punishment by the criminal justice system. Is this person more evil than the executive who, knowing the risks, calmly chooses not to pay for safety equipment?

The one who kills in a heated argument kills from passion. What she does she probably would not do in a cooler moment. She is likely to feel "she was not herself." The one she killed was someone she knew, a specific person who at the time seemed to her to be the embodiment of all that frustrates her, someone whose very existence makes life unbearable. I do not mean to suggest that this is true of all killers, although there is reason to believe it is true of many. Nor do I mean to suggest that such a state of mind justifies murder. What it does do, however, is suggest that the killer's action, arising out of anger at a particular individual, does not show general disdain for the lives of her fellows. Here is where she is different from our mine executive. Our mine executive wanted to harm no one in particular, but he *knew his acts were likely to harm someone*—and once someone is harmed, the victim is someone in particular. Nor can our executive claim that "he was not himself." His act is done not out of passion but out of cool reckoning. Precisely here his evil shows. In his willingness to jeopardize the lives of unspecified others who pose him no real or imaginary threat in order to make a few dollars, he shows his general disdain for all his fellow human beings. Can it really be said that he is less evil than one who kills from passion? The Model Penal Code includes within the definition of murder any death caused by "extreme indifference to human life."[32] Is our executive not a murderer by this definition?

It's worth noting that in answering the Defenders here. I have portrayed harms from occupational hazards in their best light. They are not, however, all just matters of well-intentioned but excessive risk taking. Consider, for example, the Manville (formerly Johns Manville) asbestos case. It is predicted that 240,000 Americans working now or who previously worked with asbestos will die from asbestos-related cancer in the next 30 years. But documents made public during congressional hearings in 1979 show "that Manville and other companies within the asbestos industry covered up and failed to warn millions of Americans of the dangers associated with the fireproof, indestructible insulating fiber."[33] An article in the *American Journal of Public Health* attributes thousands of deaths to the cover-up.[34] Later in this chapter I document similar intentional cover-ups, such as the falsification of reports on coal dust levels in mines, which leads to crippling and often fatal black lung disease. Surely someone who knowingly subjects others to risks and tries to hide those risks from them is culpable in a high degree.

2. I think the Defenders are right in believing that direct personal assault is terrifying in a way that indirect impersonal harm is not. This difference is no stranger to the criminal justice system. Prosecutors, judges, and juries constantly have to consider how terrifying an attack is in determining what to charge and what to convict offenders for. This is why we allow gradations in charges of homicide or assault and allow particularly grave sentences for particularly grave attacks. In short, the difference the Defenders are pointing to here might justify treating a one-on-one murder as graver than murder due to lax safety measures, but it doesn't justify treating one as a grave crime and the other as a mere regulatory (or very minor criminal) matter. After all, although it is worse to be injured with terror than without, it is still the injury that constitutes the worst part of violent crime. Given the choice, seriously injured victims of crime would surely rather have been terrorized and not injured than injured and not terrorized. If that is so, then the worst part of violent crime is still shared by the indirect harms that the Defenders would relegate to regulation.

3. There is also something to the Defenders' claim that indirect harms, such as ones that result from lax safety measures, are part of legitimate productive activities, whereas one-on-one crimes are not. No doubt we must tolerate the risks that are necessary ingredients of productive activity (unless those risks are so great as to outweigh the gains of the productive activity). But this doesn't imply we shouldn't

identify the risks, or levels of danger, that are unnecessary and excessive, and use the law to protect innocent people from them. And if those risks are great enough, the fact that they may further a productive or otherwise legitimate activity is no reason against making them crimes—if that's what's necessary to protect workers. A person can commit a crime to further an otherwise legitimate endeavor and it is still a crime. If, say, I threaten to assault my workers if they don't work faster, this doesn't make my act any less criminal. And, in general, if I do something that by itself ought to be a crime, the fact that I do it as a means to a legitimate aim doesn't change the fact that it ought to be a crime. If acts that intentionally endanger others ought to be crimes, then the fact that the acts are means to legitimate aims doesn't change the fact that they ought to be crimes.

4. Cases like the Manville asbestos case show that the Defenders overestimate the reality of the "free consent" with which workers take on the risks of their jobs. You can consent to a risk only if you know about it, and often the risks are concealed. Moreover, the Defenders overestimate generally the degree to which workers freely consent to the conditions of their jobs. Although no one is forced at gunpoint to accept a particular job, virtually everyone is forced by the requirements of necessity to take some job. At best, workers can choose among the dangers present at various work sites, but they cannot choose to face no danger at all. Moreover, workers can choose jobs only where there are openings, which means they cannot simply pick their place of employment at will. For nonwhites and women, the choices are even more narrowed by discriminatory hiring, long-standing occupational segregation (funneling women into secretarial, nursing, or teaching jobs and blacks into janitorial and other menial occupations), not to mention subtle and not so subtle practices that keep nonwhites and women from advancing within their occupations. Consequently, for all intents and purposes, most workers *must* face the dangers of the jobs

that are available to them. What's more, remember that while here we have been focusing on harms due to occupational hazards, much of the indirect harm that I shall document in what follows is done not to workers but to consumers (of food with dangerous chemicals, and citizens (breathing dangerous concentrations of pollutants).

Finally, recall that the basis of all the Defenders' objections is that the idea that one-on-one harms are more evil than indirect harms is past of our common moral beliefs, and that this makes it appropriate to treat the former with the criminal justice system and the latter with milder regulatory measures. Here I think the Defenders err by overlooking the role of legal institutions in shaping our ordinary moral beliefs. Many who defend the criminal justice system do so precisely because of its function in educating the public about the difference between right and wrong. The great historian of English law, Sir James Fitzjames Stephens, held that a

> great part of the general detestation of crime which happily prevails amongst the decent part of the community in all civilized countries arises from the fact that the commission of offences is associated in all such communities with the solemn and deliberate infliction of punishment wherever crime is proved.[35]

One cannot simply appeal to ordinary moral beliefs to defend the criminal law because the criminal law has already had a hand in shaping ordinary moral beliefs. At least one observer has argued that making narcotics use a crime in the beginning of this century *caused* a change in the public's ordinary moral notions about drug addiction, which prior to that time had been viewed as a medical problem.[36] It is probably safe to say that in our own time, civil rights legislation has sharpened the public's moral condemnation of racial discrimination. Hence, we might speculate that if the criminal justice system began to prosecute—and if the media began to portray—those who inflict *indirect harm* as serious criminals, our ordinary moral notions would change on this point as well.

I think this disposes of the Defenders for the time being. We are left with the conclusion that there is no moral basis for treating *one-on-one harm* as criminal and *indirect harm* as merely a regulatory affair. What matters, then, is whether the purpose of the criminal justice system will be served by including in the category of serious crime, actions that are predictably likely to produce serious harm, yet that are done in pursuit of otherwise legitimate goals and without the aim of harming anyone.

What is the purpose of the criminal justice system? No esoteric answer is required. Norval Morris and Gordon Hawkins write that "the prime function of the criminal law is to protect our persons and our property."[37] *The Challenge of Crime in a Free Society*, the report of the President's Commission on Law Enforcement and Administration of Justice, tells us that "any criminal justice system is an apparatus society uses to enforce the standards of conduct necessary to protect individuals and the community."[38] Whatever else we think a criminal justice system should accomplish, I doubt if anyone would deny that its central purpose is to protect us against the most serious threats to our well-being. This purpose is seriously undermined by taking one-on-one harm as the model of crime. Excluding harm caused without the aim of harming someone in particular prevents the criminal justice system from protecting our persons and our property from dangers at least as great as those posed by one-on-one harm. This is so because, as I will show, there are a large number of actions that are not labeled *criminal* but that lead to loss of life, limb, and possessions on a scale comparable to those actions that are represented in the FBI Crime Index—and a crime by any other name still causes misery and suffering.

In the remainder of this chapter, I identify some acts that are *crimes by any other name*— acts that cause harm and suffering comparable to that caused by acts called crimes. My purpose is to confirm the first hypothesis: that the definitions of crime in the criminal law do not reflect the only or the most dangerous behaviors in our society. To do this, we will need some measure of the harm and suffering caused by crimes with which we can compare the harm and suffering caused by noncrimes. Our measure need not be too refined because my point can be made if I can show that there are some acts that we do not treat as crimes but that cause harm *roughly comparable* to that caused by acts that we do treat as crimes. For that, it is not necessary to compare the harm caused by noncriminal acts with the harm caused by *all* crimes. I need only show that the harm produced by some type of noncriminal act is comparable to the harm produced by *any* serious crime. Because the harms caused by noncriminal acts fall into the categories of death, bodily injury (including the disabling effects of disease), and property loss, I will compare the harms done by noncriminal acts with the injuries caused by the crimes of murder, aggravated assault, and theft.

According to the FBI's *Uniform Crime Reports*. in 1995, there were 21,597 murders and nonnegligent manslaughters, and 1,099,179 aggravated assaults. "Murder and nonnegligent manslaughter" includes all "willful (nonnegligent) killing of one human being by another." "Aggravated assault" is defined as an "attack by one person on another for the purpose of inflicting severe or aggravated bodily injury.[39] Thus, as a measure of the physical harm done by crime in 1995, we can say that reported crimes lead to roughly 21,000 deaths and 1,000,000 instances of serious bodily injury short of death a year. As a measure of monetary loss due to property crime, we can use $15.1 billion—the total estimated dollar losses due to property crime in 1995 according to the *UCR*.[40] Whatever the shortcomings of these reported crime statistics, they are the statistics upon which public policy has traditionally been based. Thus, I will consider any actions that lead to loss of life, physical harm, and property loss comparable to the figures in the *UCR* as actions that pose grave dangers to the community comparable to the threats posed by crimes. They are surely precisely the kind of harmful actions from which a criminal justice system whose purpose is to protect our persons and property ought to protect us. *They are crimes by other names.*

NOTES

[1]"Company in Mine Deaths Set to Pay Big Fine," *New York Times,* February 21, 1993, p. A19.

[2]"Mass Murder on the 5:33," *New York Times,* December 10, 1993, p. A34.

[3]Gerald R. Ford, "To Insure Domestic Tranquility: Mandatory Sentence for Convicted Felons," speech delivered at the Yale Law School Sesquicentennial Convocation, New Haven, Connecticut, April 25, 1975, in *Vital Speeches of the Day* 41, no. 15 (May 15, 1975), p. 451.

[21]*Washington Post,* January 11, 1983, p. C10.

[22]Voigt, Lydia, et al., *Criminology and Justice* (New York: McGraw-Hill, 1994), pp. 11–15; the quotation is at p. 15.

[23]This answers Graeme Newman, who observes that most criminals on TV are white, and wonders what the "ruling class" or conservatives have to gain by denying the criminality of Blacks." Graeme R. Newman, "Popular Culture and Criminal Justice: A Preliminary Analysis," *Journal of Criminal Justice* 18 (1990), pp. 261–74.

[24]Newman, "Popular Culture and Criminal Justice: A Preliminary Analysis," pp. 263–64.

[25]Barbara Matusow, "If It Bleeds, It Leads," *Washingtonian,* January 1988, p. 102.

[26]"Titillating Channels: TV Is Going Tabloid As Shows Seek Sleaze and Find Profits, Too," *Wall Street Journal,* May 18, 1988, p. 1.

[27]"Crime in America: The Shocking Truth," *McCall's,* March 1987, p. 144.

[28]John P. Wright, Francis T. Cullen, Michael B. Blankenship, "The Social Construction of Corporate Violence: Media Coverage of the Imperial Food Products Fire," *Crime & Delinquency* 41, no. 1 (January 1995), p. 32. I discuss this case in chapter 3.

[29]Hyman Gross, *A Theory of Criminal Justice* (New York: Oxford University Press, 1979), p. 78. See generally Chapter 3, "Culpability, Intention, Motive," which I have drawn upon in making the argument of this and the following two paragraphs.

[30]Nancy Frank, "Unintended Murder and Corporate Risk-Taking: Defining the Concept of Justifiability," *Journal of Criminal Justice* 16 (1988), p. 18.

[31]For example, see John Harris, "The Marxist Conception of Violence," *Philosophy & Public Affairs* 3, no. 2 (Winter 1974), pp. 192–220; Jonathan Glover, *Causing Death and Saving Lives* (Hammondsworth, England: Penguin, 1977), pp. 92–112; and James Rachels, *The End of Life* (Oxford: Oxford University Press, 1986), pp. 106–50.

[32]*Model Penal Code,* Final Draft (Philadelphia: American Law Institute, 1962).

[33]Russell Mokhiber, *Corporate Crime and Violence: Big Business Power and the Abuse of Public Trust* (San Francisco: Sierra Club, 1988), pp. 278, 285.

[34]David E. Lilienfeld, "The Silence: The Asbestos Industry and Early Occupational Cancer Research—A Case Study," *American Journal of Public Health* 81, no. 6 (June 1991), p. 791. This article shows how early the asbestos industry knew of the link between asbestos and cancer and how hard they tried to suppress this information. See also Paul Brodeur, *Outrageous Misconduct: The Asbestos Industry on Trial* (New York: Pantheon, 1985).

[35]Sir James Fitzjames Stephen, from his *History of the Criminal Law of England* 2 (1883), excerpted in *Crime, Law and Society,* eds., Abraham S. Goldstein and Joseph Goldstein (New York: Free Press, 1971), p. 21.

[36]Troy Duster, *The Legislation of Morality: Law, Drugs and Moral Judgment* (New York: Free Press, 1970), pp. 3–76.

[37]Norval Morris and Gordon Hawkins, *The Honest Politician's Guide to Crime Control* (Chicago: University of Chicago Press, 1970), p. 2.

[38]*Challenge,* p. 7.

[39]*UCR-1995,* pp. 13, 31.

The Brown and Williamson Documents

WHERE DO WE GO FROM HERE?

There is a massive body of evidence, derived from many scientific disciplines, that tobacco is addictive and kills smokers. Up to half of those who continue to smoke cigarettes will die prematurely from diseases caused by smoking, half of these deaths occurring in middle age.[1] Peto et al.[2] have calculated that of the 1.25 billion people now living in developed countries, 250 million will, if present tobacco consumption patterns are maintained, die from tobacco. With 3 million deaths worldwide each year currently due to tobacco use, the consequences of tobacco to the public health have been, and will continue to be, staggering, and the importance of bringing this hazard under control is correspondingly great.

It is against this background that *JAMA* publishes several highly unusual articles this week.

THE DOCUMENTS

On May 12, 1994, Stanton A. Glantz, PhD, a professor of medicine in the Division of Cardiology at the University of California, San Francisco (UCSF), and a scholar interested in the field of tobacco and the public health, received from an unknown source, "Mr Butts," approximately 4000 pages of memoranda, reports, and letters, covering a 30-year period, from the Brown and Williamson Tobacco Corporation (B&W) and its parent company, the British American Tobacco Company (now BAT Industries).[3] In the subsequent months,

Stanton Glantz, et al., "Looking Through a Keyhole at the Tobacco Industry: The Brown and Williamson Documents," *Journal of the American Medical Association* Volume 274 Number 3 (19 July 1995): 219–224, 256–258. Copyrighted 1995, American Medical Association.

Glantz received several thousand additional pages of documents from Congressman Henry Waxman's House Subcommittee on Health and the Environment and another few hundred pages of documents from the estate of the chief scientist of BAT. Glantz ultimately put all the documents into the library at UCSF.

This issue of *The Journal* is largely devoted to an analysis by Glantz and his colleagues of these three sets of documents.[4-8]

The documents show:

- that research conducted by tobacco companies into the deleterious health effects of tobacco was often more advanced and sophisticated than studies by the medical community.

- that executives at B&W knew early on that tobacco use was harmful and that nicotine was addictive and debated whether to make the research public.

- that the industry decided to conceal the truth from the public.

- that the industry hid their research from the courts by sending the data through their legal departments, their lawyers asserting that the results were immune to disclosure in litigation because they were the privileged product of the lawyer-client relationship.

- that despite their knowledge to the contrary, the industry's public position was (and continues to be) that the link between smoking and ill health was not proven, that they were dedicated to determining whether there was such a link and revealing this to the public, and that nicotine was not addictive.

We think that these documents and the analyses merit the careful attention of our readership because they provide massive, detailed, and damning evidence of the tactics of the tobacco industry. They show us how this industry has managed to spread confusion by suppressing, manipulating, and distorting the scientific record. They also make clear how the tobacco industry has been able to avoid paying a penny in damages and how it has managed to remain hugely profitable from the sale of a substance long known by scientists and physicians to be lethal. We hope that publication of the articles will encourage all our readers to become even more active in the campaign against tobacco.

The B&W documents Glantz first received are believed to be copies of documents themselves copied by a paralegal, Merrell Williams, who had once worked for one of B&W's outside counsel. Merrell Williams had, in 1993, turned the documents over to the attorney he had hired to make a claim for health damages against B&W. His ex-employers filed action against him in September 1993 to prohibit the use and dissemination of the B&W documents. In October 1993, B&W intervened as a plaintiff in the case, claiming that the documents were protected from disclosure to the public by the attorney-client privilege and the work product doctrine.[9]

The documents surfaced publicly on May 7, 1994, when Philip Hilts published the first of a series of articles in the *New York Times*,[10] and since then there have been reports in several national newspapers and on radio and television. In addition, Congressman Waxman made more documents public at hearings by the Subcommittee on Health and the Environment of the US House of Representatives in the summer of 1994. Since that time, in litigation in the District of Columbia, West Virginia, Massachusetts, Kentucky, and Mississippi, B&W has attempted to subpoena reporters and seal the documents. They have been unsuccessful. Judge Harold H. Greene of the US District Court for the District of Columbia quashed subpoenas directed at Congressmen Henry Waxman and Ron Wyden, concluding that B&W's course of conduct was "patently crafted to harass those who would reveal facts concerning B&W's knowledge of the health hazards of tobacco.[11]

In the case of the documents in the UCSF library, B&W has not only tried to remove the documents, but also sought to obtain the names of scholars who have used them, something the university has interpreted as a violation of the privacy rights of library patrons. In addition, the company hired private investigators to stake out the area in the UCSF library where the documents were kept, an action that had the effect of harassing and intimidating library personnel.[12] On May 25, 1995, Judge Stuart Pollak in the Superior Court of the State of California, without ruling on whether the documents were privileged, recognized that the documents were already in the public domain. The judge said that there was a strong public interest in permitting the information in the documents to remain available to the university and others. He noted that to grant B&W's application would have the effect of preventing the information from being used in the public dialogue bearing on public health, public law, and litigation. He denied B&W's application to take possession of all copies of the documents in the hands of the UCSF and its employees.[13] An appeal by B&W was unanimously rejected by the California Supreme Court on June 29, 1995. The documents, the authenticity of which is not in doubt, not least because of the actions B&W has taken to retrieve them, are therefore in the public domain because judges across the country say they should be.

WHO ARE THE AUTHORS?

The authors of the first five articles we publish in this issue of *JAMA* are people who have produced careful scholarship in the past, some of it published in *JAMA*.[14-16] They are academic researchers interested in national policy to reduce the toll from this devastating hazard to the nation's health.

THE ARTICLES

These five articles[4-8] provide a careful analysis of the documents. They detail the sharp disparities between the tobacco industry's private knowledge, developed by their own research during more than 30 years, and their public stance.

The articles show that the effect of tobacco company tactics, long suspected, has been to obfuscate the conclusions of scientists, to confuse the public, and to assist greatly the tobacco industry in its successful efforts to influence the political process in its favor. The surgeon general's report of 1964 would have been far more decisive in its conclusions and recommendations had the evidence available to the executives of B&W been available to the surgeon general's committee. We can only speculate how many lives would have been saved and how much suffering would have been averted.

JAMA hired Mr Tim Graham, a veteran editor with the Alameda Newspaper Group, which includes the *Oakland Tribune*. He, after reading the documents, has, according to usual journalistic practice, tried to contact executives of B&W and other interested parties to get their reactions. We publish Graham's article[17] together with the written questions he sent B&W and B&W's statement in response. We also publish an interview by Andrew Skolnick with Mr Victor Crawford, a lobbyist for the Tobacco Institute in Maryland, who is now dying of cancer of the oropharynx.[18]

WHY ARE WE PUBLISHING THE ARTICLES?

For many decades, the mission of the American Medical Association (AMA) has been to "promote the science and art of medicine and the betterment of public health." To remain silent about the B&W papers would be to deny our mission. Quite simply, we are publishing this research because it is the right thing to do.

Analysis of these papers suggests that we would have seen a very different picture of tobacco use today if the group knowing the most about the dangers of tobacco use, the industry, had been honest with its customers. The documents and the *JAMA* articles show us in a stark way that some of those who speak for the tobacco industry dissemble, distort, and deceive, despite the fact that the industry's own research is consistent with the scientific community's

conclusion that continued use of their product will endanger the lives and health of the public at home and abroad. The industry continues to use the same tactics: even now, it is suing the government over the release of the Environmental Protection Agency report that has classified environmental tobacco smoke as a group A carcinogen.[19] It is spending vast amounts of money to overturn antismoking laws.[20]

These papers show us how little the tobacco industry is to be trusted when they speak on health issues and that the "evidence" they put before regulatory and legislative bodies at the national, state, and local level is highly suspect.

WHERE DO WE GO FROM HERE?

The AMA maintains an unequivocal stance against tobacco.[21] The AMA reminds physicians, the public, and politicians that the damning evidence against tobacco makes opposition to its use a pressing, nonpartisan public health issue. If the industry uses political weapons, so shall we. The AMA will not relent in its opposition to tobacco use.

To accomplish this goal, the AMA recommends and will pursue the following steps:

1.   Further efforts should be made to educate physicians, the public, and policymakers about the consequences of tobacco use, the predatory nature of the tobacco industry, and ways individuals can break their addiction to tobacco.

2.   Medical schools and research institutions, as well as individual researchers, should refuse any funding from the tobacco industry and its subsidiaries to avoid giving them an appearance of credibility. The B&W documents affirm our belief that such tobacco industry entities as the Council for Tobacco Research, the Smokeless Tobacco Research Council, and the Center for Indoor Air Research are used by the tobacco industry to convince the public that there still is a controversy about whether tobacco has ill effects, to buy respectability, and to silence universities and researchers. We concur

with the recommendation of a subcommittee of the National Cancer Advisory Board that federal funding be withdrawn from cancer research organizations that accept tobacco industry support.[22]

3. Politicians should not accept money from the tobacco industry but should direct their efforts to protection of the nonsmoking majority. Those who do accept money should be identified publicly.

4. The federal Occupational Safety and Health Administration should move forward with its proposal to require smoke-free workplaces nationwide.

5. Local communities should continue to control smoking in public.

6. State legislatures should assume responsibility for ensuring smoke-free areas. Any preemptive tobacco laws should be repealed by public demand.

7. Purchase of tobacco should be strictly limited to adults, with severe penalties for those who transgress. Underage use of tobacco should carry consequences for the user. All tobacco advertising should be eliminated, and a vigorous counteradvertising campaign should be instituted.

8. The Justice Department should enforce the ban against indirect tobacco advertising such as televised sports events.

9. Tobacco itself should be considered a drug delivery vehicle and placed under the oversight of the Food and Drug Administration, with appropriate regulation as for other life threatening drugs.[23]

10. State and federal excise taxes on tobacco products should be dramatically increased, both to help defray costs of tobacco-induced diseases and to deter young people from becoming addicted.

11. The federal government should prevent the export of tobacco to other countries.

12. The continued contribution to knowledge of the control of tobacco by the National Cancer Institute should be strongly supported.

13. Physicians and the public should support legal action against the tobacco industry to recover billions of dollars in excess medical costs from tobacco-related diseases borne by Medicare, Medicaid, and the Department of Veterans Affairs.

14. All avenues of individual and collective redress should be pursued through the judicial system.

In summary, the evidence is unequivocal—the US public has been duped by the tobacco industry. No right-thinking individual can ignore the evidence. We should all be outraged, and we should force the removal of this scourge from our nation and by so doing set an example for the world. We recognize the serious consequences of this ambition, but the health of our nation is more important than the profits of any single industry.

On behalf of the physicians of this country and the people they serve, the AMA pledges its best efforts to the eradication of tobacco-related disease. We solicit the support of the public and our government in this endeavor. It is a worthy cause.

James S. Todd, MD	Palma E. Formica, MD
Drummond Rennie, MD	Michael S. Goldrich, MD
Robert E. McAfee, MD	William E. Jacott, MD
Lonnie R. Bristow, MD	Donald T. Lewers, MD
Joseph T. Painter, MD	John C. Nelson, MD, MPH
Thomas R. Reardon, MD	P. John Seward, MD
Daniel H. Johnson, Jr, MD	Randolph D. Smoak, Jr, MD
Richard F. Corlin, MD	Michael Suk, JD, MPH
Yank D. Coble, Jr, MD	Frank B. Walker, MD
Nancy W. Dickey, MD	Percy Wootton, MD
Timothy T. Flaherty, MD	George D. Lundberg, MD

NOTES

[1]Doll R, Peto R, Wheatly K, Gray R, Sutherland I. Mortality in relation to smoking: 40 years' observations on male British doctors. *BMJ*. 1994;309:901–911.

[2]Peto R, Lopez AD, Boreham J, Thun M, Heath C Jr. Mortality from tobacco in developed countries: indirect estimation from national statistics. *Lancet*. 1992;339:1268–1278.

[3]Glantz SA. Declaration to the Superior Court of the State of California for the County of San Francisco in *Brown and Williamson Tobacco Corporation v. Regents of the University of California*, May 15, 1995.

[4]Glantz SA, Barnes DE, Bero L, Hanauer P, Slade J. Looking through a keyhole at the tobacco industry: the

Brown and Williamson documents. *JAMA*. 1995;274: 219–224.

[5]Bero L, Barnes DE, Hanauer P, Slade J. Glantz SA. Lawyer control of the tobacco industry's external research program: the Brown and Williamson documents. *JAMA*. 1995;274:241–247.

[6]Barnes DE, Hanauer P, Slade J, Bero L, Glantz SA. Environmental tobacco smoke: the Brown and Williamson documents. *JAMA*. 1995;274:248–253.

[7]Hanauer P, Slade J, Barnes DE, Bero L, Glantz SA. Lawyer control of internal scientific research to protect against products liability lawsuits: the Brown and Williamson documents. *JAMA*. 1995;274:234–240.

[8]Slade J, Bero L, Hanauer P, Barnes DE, Glantz SA. Nicotine and addiction: the Brown and Williamson documents. *JAMA*. 1995;274:225–233.

[9]*Castano v. The American Tobacco Company, et al.* US District Court Eastern District of Louisiana.

[10]Hilts PJ. Tobacco company was silent on hazards. *New York Times*, May 7, 1994: A1.

[11]Greene HH, in *Maddox v. Williams*, June 6, 1994. DC District Court. 855 F Supp 406, pp 414–415.

[12]Balderson AJ. UCSF library has tobacco firm's documents under lock and key. *UCFS Newsbreak*, March 11–24, 1995;10c1.

[13]Pollack S. *Brown and Williamson v. Regents of the University of California*. Superior Court of the State of California for the County of San Francisco. May 25, 1996.

[14]Traynor M, Begay M, Glantz S. The tobacco industry strategy to prevent tobacco control. *JAMA* 1993; 270:479–488.

[15]Glantz S, Begay M. Tobacco industry campaign contributions are affecting tobacco control policymaking in California. *JAMA*. 1994;272:1176–1182.

[16]Glantz SA, Parmley WW. Passive smoking and heart disease: mechanisms and risk. *JAMA*. 1995;273:1047–1053.

[17]Graham T. The Brown and Williamson documents: the company's response. *JAMA*. 1995;274:254–255.

[18]Skolnick A. Cancer converts tobacco lobbyist: Victor L. Crawford goes on the record. *JAMA*. 1995;274:199.

[19]*Respiratory Health Effects of Passive Smoking; Lung Cancer and Other Disorders*. Washington, DC: US Environmental Protection Agency; December 1992. EPA/600-90-006F.

[20]Mallory M. Full-flavored, unfiltered statehouse shenanigans: Big Tobacco's big bucks can still turn antismoking laws around. *Business Week*. May 22, 1995:52.

[21]Lundberg GD. In the AMA, policy follows science: a case history of tobacco. *JAMA*. 1985;253:3001–3003.

[22]National Cancer Advisory Board, Subcommittee to Evaluate the National Cancer Program. *Cancer at a Crossroads: A Report to Congress for the Nation*. Washington, DC: National Cancer Institute; September 1994.

[23]Lundberg GD. Tobacco: for consenting adults in private only. *JAMA*. 1986;255:1051–1053.

Looking Through a Keyhole at the Tobacco Industry

THE BROWN AND WILLIAMSON DOCUMENTS

Stanton A. Glantz, PhD; Deborah E. Barnes; Lisa Bero, PhD; Peter Hanauer, LLB; John Slade, MD

Until now, the public's understanding of what the tobacco industry actually knew about the addictive nature of nicotine and the dangers

JAMA, July 19, 1995—Vol. 274, No. 3.

of smoking has been largely based on observation of the industry's behavior and suppositions by a few journalists and public health professionals. This situation changed dramatically in 1994, when several thousand pages of internal documents from the Brown and Williamson

Tobacco Corporation (B&W) and its parent company, BAT Industries (formerly British American Tobacco Company) of the United Kingdom, became available.[1-4] BAT is the second largest private cigarette manufacturer in the world. In 1992, the company sold 578 billion cigarettes,[5] 10.7% of the total world output and more than were consumed in the entire US market that year.[6] Its wholly owned US subsidiary, B&W, is the third largest cigarette maker in this country. It had an 11% share of the $48 billion US market in 1993.[7] B&W recently bought the domestic cigarette business of American Brands, adding another 6.7% to its US market share.

Some of these documents were delivered unsolicited to the authors from an anonymous source, some were obtained by Congress from B&W and subsequently made public, and some came from private papers of a deceased former BAT officer. While even these 1384 documents do not provide a complete picture, they provide the most detailed and candid look to date into one tobacco company's internal workings surrounding the smoking and health "controversy" during the last half of the 20th century.

The tobacco industry has used three primary arguments to deter further government regulation of its products and to defend itself in products liability lawsuits. First, it has consistently claimed that there is no conclusive proof that smoking causes diseases such as cancer and heart disease. Second, tobacco companies have claimed that nicotine is not addictive and that anyone who smokes makes a free choice to do so. Finally, tobacco companies have claimed that they are committed to determining the scientific truth about the health effects of tobacco, both by conducting internal research and by funding external research through jointly funded industry programs.

The documents provide a unique window—or, more precisely, a keyhole view—into how the tobacco industry has responded over the years to the evergrowing body of scientific evidence proving that its products kill. The documents show that, by the 1960s, B&W and BAT had proven in their own laboratories that cigarette tar causes cancer in animals. In addition,

by the early 1960s, BAT's scientists (and B&W's lawyers) were acting on the assumption that nicotine is addictive. BAT responded by secretly attempting to create a "safe" cigarette that would minimize dangerous ingredients and the associated damage to health, but would still deliver nicotine. Publicly, however, it maintained that cigarettes are neither dangerous nor addictive. The Table contrasts the tobacco industry's private knowledge, public statements, and views of the general scientific community on a variety of tobacco-related issues. To this day, despite overwhelming scientific evidence and official government reports to the contrary, the tobacco industry denies that tobacco products are addictive or that they cause any disease whatsoever.

B&W has pursued legal action to keep the documents out of the public eye. Nevertheless, when B&W had obtained subpoenas from the Superior Court for the District of Columbia to require Congressmen Henry Waxman (D, Calif) and Ron Wyden (D, Ore) of the House Subcommittee on Health and the Environment to produce documents from B&W allegedly held by these congressmen, US District Court Judge Harold H. Greene quashed the subpoenas. His opinion stated:

[The documents] may be evidence supporting a "whistle-blower's" claim that the tobacco company concealed from its customers and the American public the truth regarding the health hazards of tobacco products, and that he was merely bringing them to the attention of those who could deal with this menace. With the situation in that posture, to accept blindly the B&W "stolen goods" argument would be to set a precedent at odds with the law, with equity, and with the public interest.

If the B&W strategy were accepted, those seeking to bury their unlawful or potentially unlawful acts from consumers, from other members of the public, and from law enforcement of regulatory authorities could achieve that objective by a simple yet ingenious strategy: all that would need to be done would be to delay or confuse any charges of health hazard, fraud, corruption, overcharge, nuclear or chemical contamination, bribery, or other misdeeds, by focusing instead on inconvenient documentary evidence and labelling it as the product of theft, violation of proprietary information, interference with contracts, and the like. The result would be that even the most severe public health and safety dangers would be subordinated in litigation and in the public mind to the malefactor's tort or contract claims, real or fictitious.

The law does not support such a strategy or inversion of values. There is a constitutional right to inform the government of violations of federal laws—a right which under [United States Constitution] Article VI supersedes local tort or contract rights and protects the "informer" from retaliation [*Maddox v Williams* (1994, DC District Court) 855 Federal Supplement 406, p 414, 415].

In this spirit, the accompanying articles[8–11] summarize some of the B&W documents and the story that they tell.

Public vs Private Statements Made by the Tobacco Industry

Source	Statements
NICOTINE AND ADDICTION	
Summary	By the early 1960s, the British American Tobacco Company (BAT) and Brown and Williamson Tobacco Corporation (B&W) had developed a sophisticated understanding of nicotine pharmacology and knew that nicotine was pharmacologically addictive. Publicly, however, the tobacco industry has maintained and continues to maintain that nicotine is not addictive. The scientific community was much slower to appreciate nicotine addiction: the surgeon general did not conclude that nicotine was addictive until 1979.[12]
Surgeon general's reports	1964: "The tobacco habit should be characterized as an habituation rather than an addiction."[13,14]
	1979: ". . . It is no exaggeration to say that smoking is the prototypical substance-abuse dependency and that improved knowledge of this process holds great promise for prevention of risk."[12]
	1988: "After carefully examining the available evidence, this Report concludes that:
	• Cigarettes and other forms of tobacco are addicting.
	• Nicotine is the drug in tobacco that causes addiction.
	• The pharmacologic and behavioral processes that determine tobacco addiction are similar to those that determine addiction to drugs such as heroin and cocaine."[14(pp1,2)]
B&W/BAT research results	"There is increasing evidence that nicotine is the key factor in controlling, through the central nervous system, a number of beneficial effects of tobacco smoke, including its action in the presence of stress situations. In addition, the alkaloid [nicotine] appears to be intimately connected with the phenomena of tobacco habituation (tolerance) and/or addiction."—From *The Fate of Nicotine in the Body*, a report describing results of contract research conducted for BAT by Battelle Memorial Institute in Geneva, Switzerland, 1963 {1200.20}.
	"Chronic intake of nicotine tends to restore the normal physiological functioning of the endocrine system, so that ever-increasing dose levels of nicotine are necessary to maintain the desired action. . . . This unconscious desire explains the addiction of the individual to nicotine."—From *A Tentative Hypothesis on Nicotine Addiction*, an essay written by scientists at Battelle and distributed to senior executives at BAT and B&W, 1963 {1200.01, p 1}.
B&W/BAT private statements	"Moreover, nicotine is addictive. We are, then, in the business of selling nicotine, an addictive drug effective in the release of stress mechanisms."— Addison Yeaman, vice president and general counsel, B&W, 1963 {1802.05, p 4}.

Source	Statements
Tobacco industry public statements	"I do not believe that nicotine is addictive . . . nicotine is a very important constituent in the cigarette smoke for taste."—Thomas Sandefur, Chairman and CEO, B&W, testifying before the Health and Environment Subcommittee, Energy and Commerce Committee, House of Representatives, June 23, 1994.[15]

NICOTINE AND ADDICTION: LOW-TAR/LOW-NICOTINE CIGARETTES AND THE PHENOMENON OF SMOKER COMPENSATION

Source	Statements
Summary	Smokers compensate for the lack of nicotine in low-tar/low-nicotine cigarettes by puffing more frequently, by increasing the depth of duration of smoke inhalation, by smoking more cigarettes per day, and by smoking cigarettes to a shorter butt length. This means that smokers of low-tar/low-nicotine cigarettes are exposed to more "tar" and other harmful chemicals than would be indicated by an analysis of the cigarette smoke. This phenomenon, known as smoker compensation, was acknowledged internally in the tobacco industry by the early 1970s but was not appreciated in the scientific community until the 1980s.
Surgeon general's reports	1966: "The preponderance of scientific evidence strongly suggests that the lower the 'tar' and nicotine content of cigarette smoke, the less harmful would be the effect."[16]
	1979: "[The public] should be warned that, in shifting to a less hazardous cigarette, they may in fact increase their hazard if they begin smoking more cigarettes or inhaling more deeply."[12]
	1981: "Smokers may increase the number of cigarettes they smoke and inhale more deeply when they switch to lower yield cigarettes. Compensatory behavior may negate any advantage of the lower yield product or even increase the health risk."[16]
B&W/BAT research results	". . . whatever the characteristics of cigarettes as determined by smoking machines, the smoker adjusts his pattern to deliver his own nicotine requirements."—Minutes from BAT's Group Research & Development (R&D) conference held in Duck Key, Fla, 1974, taken by S. J. G. (S. J. Green of BAT R&D) {1125.01, p 2}.
	"Compensation study conducted by Imperial Tobacco Co., a BATCo affiliate, [shows that a smoker] adjusts his smoking habits when smoking cigarettes with low nicotine and TPM [total particulate matter] to duplicate his normal cigarette nicotine intake."—From document titled "Chronology of Brown & Williamson Smoking and Health Research," regarding research conducted in 1975. Chronology dated 1988 {1006.01, p 27}.
B&W/BAT internal statements	"In most cases, however, the smoker of a filter cigarette was getting as much or more nicotine and tar as he would have gotten from a regular cigarette." —Ernest Pepples, vice president and general counsel, B&W, 1976 {2205.01, p 2}.
Tobacco industry public statements	"All the fuss about smoking got me to thinking I'd either quit or smoke True. I smoke True."—Advertisement for Lorillard's True cigarettes in *Ms.* magazine, October 1975.
	"I like to smoke, and what I like is a cigarette that isn't timid on taste. But I'm not living in some ivory tower. I hear the things being said against high-tar smoking as well as the next guy. And so I started looking. For a low-tar smoke that had some honest-to-goodness taste. . . ."—Advertisement for Vantage cigarettes in *Time* magazine, November 9, 1977, pp 86–87.
	"The tobacco industry cannot find definitive evidence that tar above a certain level is harmful, and below it is not. At the same time, they are responding to what we might call the 'scare market.'"—William Kloepfer, Jr, Tobacco Institute spokesman, in a *New York Times* article, October 30, 1976.[17]

Source	Statements
	ROLE OF THE TOBACCO INDUSTRY RESEARCH COMMITTEE/COUNCIL FOR TOBACCO RESEARCH
Summary	The Tobacco Industry Research Committee (TIRC), later renamed the Council for Tobacco Research—U.S.A., Inc (CTR), was created by US tobacco companies in 1954. The tobacco industry has publicly claimed that TIRC/CTR is an independent organization that funds unbiased research into the health effects of smoking. Internally, however, tobacco industry representatives have stated that TIRC/CTR was created for public relations purposes and that it later fulfilled political and legal roles.
B&W/BAT private statements	"Originally, CTR was organized as a public relations effort. . . . The research of CTR also discharged a legal responsibility. . . . Finally the industry research effort has included special projects designed to find scientists and medical doctors who might serve as industry witnesses in lawsuits or in a legislative forum."—Ernest Pepples, vice president and general counsel, B&W, 1976 {2010.02, p 2}.
Tobacco industry public statements	"From the outset, the Tobacco Industry Research Committee has made clear that the object of its research program is to encourage scientific study for facts about tobacco use and health. Its position is that research will help provide the knowledge about lung cancer and heart disease for a full evaluation of all factors being studied in connection with these diseases."—Public relations document, circa 1963 {1903.03, p 1}.
	"The Council for Tobacco Research-U.S.A., Inc., is the sponsoring agency of a program of research into questions of tobacco use and health. . . . The Council awards research grants to independent scientists who are assured complete scientific freedom in conducting their studies. Grantees alone are responsible for reporting or publishing their findings in the accepted scientific manner—through medical and scientific journals and societies."[18]
	SMOKING AND DISEASE, 1960s
Summary	By the early 1960s, the scientific community had determined that smoking is causally related to lung cancer and probably related to heart disease. Results from tobacco industry laboratories supported these conclusions, but the tobacco industry publicly denied that the links had been proven.
Surgeon general's reports	1964: "Cigarette smoking is causally related to lung cancer in men; the magnitude of the effect of cigarette smoking far outweighs all other factors. The data for women, though less extensive, point in the same direction."
	"Cigarette smoking is the most important of the causes of chronic bronchitis in the United States, and increases the risk of dying from chronic bronchitis."
	"Male cigarette smokers have a higher death rate from coronary artery disease than non-smoking males, but it is not clear that the association has causal significance."
	"Cigarette smoking is a significant factor in the causation of cancer of the larynx [and] an association exists between cigarette smoking and cancer of the urinary bladder in man."[13]
B&W/BAT research results	"Scientists with whom I talked [at BATs laboratories in Great Britain] were unanimous in their opinion that smoke is weakly carcinogenic under certain conditions and that efforts should be made to reduce this activity." —Dr. R. B. Griffith, head of R&D, B&W, 1985 {1105.01, p 2}.
B&W/BAT private statements	"At the best, the probabilities are that some combination of constituents of smoke will be found conducive to the onset of cancer or to create an environment in which cancer is more likely to occur."—Addison Yeaman, vice president and general counsel, B&W, 1963 {1802.05, p 1}.

Source	Statements
Tobacco industry public statements	"The smoking of tobacco continues to be one of the subjects requiring study in the lung cancer problem, as do many other agents and influences in modern living. Science does not yet know enough about any suspected factors to judge whether they may operate alone, whether they may operate in conjunction with others, or whether they may affect or be affected by factors of whose existence science is not yet aware."—Public relations document, circa 1963 {1903.03, p 3}.

SMOKING AND DISEASE, 1970s

Source	Statements
Summary	Throughout the 1970s, B&W and BAT (and probably the other tobacco companies as well) privately engaged in a massive research campaign to identify and remove any toxic compounds identified in tobacco smoke. Privately, B&W and BAT scientists concluded there was no scientific controversy about smoking being dangerous. Their goal was to create a "safe" cigarette. However, their research showed that there were so many different toxic compounds in tobacco smoke that it would be very difficult to remove them all. Publicly, the industry continued to deny that smoking had been proven harmful to health.
Surgeon general's reports	1972: "Tobacco use is associated with increased risk of coronary heart disease; cerebrovascular disease (stroke); aortic aneurysm; peripheral vascular disease; chronic obstructive bronchopulmonary disease (COPD); cancers of the lung, lip, larynx, oral cavity, esophagus, urinary bladder, and pancreas; and gastrointestinal disorders such as peptic ulcer disease. In addition, maternal smoking during pregnancy retards fetal growth."[19] 1979: "The longer a smoker smokes, the higher the risk of dying prematurely. Death rates are higher for smokers who start smoking at young ages and for smokers who inhale. Life expectancy at any given age is significantly shortened by cigarette smoking. Cigar and pipe smoking also increase the risk of premature death. Although death rates are particularly high among cigarette smokers for such diseases as lung cancer, chronic obstructive lung disease, and cancer of the larynx, coronary heart disease is the chief contributor to the excess mortality among cigarette smokers."[12]
B&W/BAT research results	"Carbon monoxide [CO] will become increasingly regarded as a serious health hazard for smokers. The methods of control available are ventilation, diffusion and the choice of smoking materials. But the inverse relationship of polycyclic aromatics and carbon monoxide is still observed, e.g. lithium hydroxide reduced CO substantially but is coupled with an increase in tumorigenic activity."—Minutes from the Group Research & Development Conference held in Duck Key, Fla, 1974, taken by S. J. Green of BAT R&D {1125.01, p 3}.
B&W/BAT private statements	"There has been no change in the scientific basis for the case against smoking. Additional evidence of smoke-dose related incidence of some diseases associated with smoking has been published. But generally this has long ceased to be an area for scientific controversy."—Minutes from BAT's Group Research & Development Conference held in Sydney, Australia, 1978, taken by S. J. Green of BAT R&D {1174.01, p 1}.
Tobacco industry public statements	"Taking all the above into consideration, we believe there is sound evidence to conclude that the statement 'cigarettes cause cancer' is not a statement of fact *but merely an hypothesis.*" [emphasis in original—B&W public relations document, 1971 {2110.06, p 10}. "As for the lack of research on the "harmful" effects of smoking, the fact is there is good reason to doubt the culpability of cigarette smoking in coronary heart disease."—Ross R. Millhiser, president, Philip Morris Inc, in *New York Times* opinion editorial, January 12, 1978.[20] "There is still no basic answer to why people who smoke fall victim to some diseases in greater numbers than people who don't smoke."—Walker Merryman, Tobacco Institute spokesman, in *New York Times* article, September 22, 1979.[21]

Source	Statements
	SMOKING AND DISEASE, 1980s
Summary	B&W and BAT continued their efforts to develop a "safer" cigarette during the 1980s. The focus of their research was minimizing the "biological activity," or carcinogenic potential, of their products. Unfortunately, this proved more difficult than expected. In addition, as the scientific community noted, even if less carcinogenic cigarettes could be designed, these cigarettes would still cause some cancer, as well as heart disease and other noncancer diseases.
Surgeon general's reports	1981: "Smoking cigarettes with lower yields of 'tar' and nicotine reduces the risk of lung cancer and, to some extent, improves the smoker's chance for longer life, provided there is no compensatory increase in the amount smoked. However, the benefits are minimal in comparison with giving up cigarettes entirely.[16] 1989: "Smoking is responsible for more than one of every six deaths in the United States. Smoking remains the single most important preventable cause of death in our society."[22]
B&W/BAT research results	"Cigarette *brands* can be readily distinguished [in terms of mutagenicity as judged by an Ames test]. This is in contrast with the earlier mouse skin painting results. An unfortunate side-effect is that the sensitivity increases the probability of an Ames League Table appearing. A further unfortunate examination is that, to date, it is not uncommon for BAT brands to have a higher result [i.e., greater mitogenicity] than those from the opposition." —Minutes from BAT Biological Conference held in Southampton, England, 1984, author unknown {1181.06, p 1}.
B&W/BAT private statements	"Despite intense research over the past 25 years, the biological activity of smoke remains a major challenge. In particular, it is not known in quantitative terms whether the smoke from modern low and ultra-low delivery products has a lower specific biological activity than that from previous high delivery products. Nor is it clearly established . . . what are the main factors that influence biological [carcinogenic] activity."—Minutes from BAT Research Conference held in Montebello, Quebec, 1982, prepared by L. C. F. Blackman of BAT R&D {1179.01, p 4}.
Tobacco industry public statements	"Cigarette smoking has not been scientifically established to be a cause of chronic diseases, such as cancer, cardiovascular disease, or emphysema. Nor has it been shown to affect pregnancy outcome adversely."—Sheldon Sommers, MD, scientific director of the CTR in congressional testimony, March 1983.[23]
	MOUSE SKIN PAINTING EXPERIMENTS
Summary	Both the tobacco industry and the general scientific community have relied on mouse skin painting experiments to evaluate the carcinogenicity of elements in tobacco smoke. Publicly, however, the tobacco industry has criticized the validity of these tests.
Surgeon general's reports	1964: "[I]nduction of cancer by a compound in one species does not prove that the test compound would be carcinogenic in another species under similar circumstances. Therefore, tests for carcinogenicity in animals can provide only supporting evidence for the carcinogenicity of a given compound or material in man. Nevertheless, any agent that can produce cancer in an animal is suspected of being carcinogenic in man also."[13] "Almost every species that has been adequately tested has proved to be susceptible to the effect of certain polycyclic aromatic hydrocarbons identified in cigarette smoke and designated as carcinogenic on the basis of tests in rodents. Therefore, one can reasonably postulate that the same polycyclic hydrocarbons may also be carcinogenic in one or more tissues of man with which they come in contact."[13]

Source	Statements
B&W/BAT research results	"Studies in instant [fresh] condensate are showing a biological activity towards mouse-skin of the same order as that of stale condensate, suggesting that the biological activity is not time-dependent. The clear possibility of producing cigarettes with reduced mouse-skip biological activity therefore becomes of greater importance and a research solution to the whole problem is more likely."—Minutes from BAT Research Conference held in Hilton Head Island, SC, 1968, prepared by S. J. Green of BAT R&D {1112.01, p 1}.
	"The meeting agreed that it would be worthwhile to make a cigarette with lower biological activity on mouse skin painting, provided this did not adversely affect the position with respect to irritation and other factors. It was recognized that this implied certain assumptions about the relevance of mouse skin painting."—Minutes from BAT R&D Conference held in Montreal, Quebec, 1967, author unknown {1165.02, p 3}.
B&W/BAT private statements	"Historically, bioassay experiments were undertaken by the industry with the object of clarifying the role of smoke constituents in pulmonary carcinogenesis. The most widely used of these methods [was] mouse-skin painting. . . . (a) In the foreseeable future, say five years, mouse-skin painting would remain as the ultimate court of appeal on carcinogenic effects."—Minutes from BAT Research Conference held in Kronberg, Germany, 1969, prepared by S. J. Green of BAT R&D {1169.01, pp 2–4}.
Tobacco industry public statements	"Much of the experimental work involves mouse-painting or animal smoke inhalation experiments . . . *[T]hese condensates are artificially produced under laboratory conditions and, as such, have little, if any, relation to cigarette smoke as it reaches the smoker.* Further, the results obtained on the skin of mice should not be extrapolated to the lung tissue of the mouse, or to any other animal species. Certainly such skin results should not be extrapolated to the human lung."—B&W public relations document, 1971 [emphasis in original] {2110.06, pp 6–7}.

ENVIRONMENTAL TOBACCO SMOKE

Source	Statements
Summary	During the 1970s and 1980s, scientific evidence began to suggest that exposure to environmental tobacco smoke (ETS) could cause adverse health effects, such as lung cancer and cardiovascular disease, in nonsmokers. B&W and BAT responded by privately attempting to create a product that produced less hazardous sidestream smoke. Publicly, however, the industry has denied that passive smoking has been proven harmful to health.
Surgeon general's reports	1972: "1. An atmosphere contaminated with tobacco smoke can contribute to the discomfort of many individuals. 2. The level of carbon monoxide attained in experiments using rooms filled with tobacco smoke had been shown to be equal, and at times to exceed, the legal limits for maximum air pollution permitted for ambient air quality . . . 3. Other components of tobacco smoke, such as particulate matter and the oxides of nitrogen, have been shown in various concentrations to affect adversely animal pulmonary and cardiac structure and function. The extent of the contribution of these substances to illness in humans exposed to the concentrations present in an atmosphere contaminated with tobacco smoke is not presently known."[19]
	1982: Epidemiologic studies on ETS and lung cancer "raise the concern that involuntary smoking may pose a carcinogenic risk to the nonsmoker."[24]
	1986: "This review leads to three major conclusions: 1. Involuntary smoking is a cause of disease, including lung cancer, in healthy nonsmokers.

Source	Statements
Surgeon General's reports *(continued)*	2. The children of parents who smoke compared with the children of nonsmoking parents have an increased frequency of respiratory infections, increased respiratory symptoms, and slightly smaller rates of increase in lung function as the lung matures.
	3. The simple separation of smokers and nonsmokers within the same air space may reduce, but does not eliminate, the exposure of nonsmokers to environmental tobacco smoke."[25]
B&W/BAT research results	*"SIDESTREAM RESEARCH AND DEVELOPMENT.*
	Strategic objectives remain as follows:
	1. Develop cigarettes with reduced sidestream yields and/or reduced odour and irritation.
	2. Conduct research to anticipate and refute claims about the health effects of passive smoking."
	—Summary of BAT's Group Research and Development Centre Activities, 1984 {1181.12, p 1}.
B&W/BAT private statements	"We must get hard data both to help counter anti-smoking attacks, and to support the design of future products . . . We should keep within BAT:
	i) animal results on sidestream activity
	ii) thoughts on the biological activity [carcinogenicity] of sidestream [smoke]
	iii) research findings on the consumer annoyance aspects of environmental [tobacco] smoke—since these have potential commercial value."
	—Minutes from BAT Research Conference held in Montebello, Quebec, 1982, prepared by L. C. F. Blackman of BAT R&D {1179.01, p 7}.
Tobacco industry public statements	"[E]vidence relating ETS to health effects is scanty, contradictory and often fundamentally flawed. . . . [M]ore and better research needs to be done." [25(p1)]
	[E]xposure to environmental tobacco smoke has not been shown to cause lung cancer in nonsmokers. . . . [S]uch exposure has not been shown to impair the respiratory or cardiovascular health of nonsmoking adults or children, or to exacerbate preexisting disease in these groups, or to cause 'allergic' symptoms on a physiological basis."[26(p51)]

RESPECTING THE LIMITATIONS OF THE EVIDENCE

These documents provide our first look at the inner workings of the tobacco industry during the crucial period in which the scientific case that smoking is addictive and kills smokers solidified. However, it is important to remember that this view is a limited one.

The documents could be subject to a form of selection bias—they may have been picked by a whistle-blower with an eye toward smoking guns. Another limit of the evidence, which shows up particularly in the legal and public relations aspects, is that it is often difficult to tell from the discussion whether particular ideas were actually carried out. In some cases, the public record clearly shows that the contemplated actions were taken. In other cases, it is not obvious where the line between contemplated and actual action lies.

Many of the documents were prepared by lawyers. Lawyers by nature are asked to evaluate proposed courses of action in terms of their legal risks, but their advice is not always followed. Notwithstanding this fact, we were struck by the active role the lawyers had, not just as advisers, but also as managers, selecting which research would be done or not done, who would be funded, and what public relations and political actions would be pursued. Generally, the documents authored by attorneys do not outline possible courses of action or provide recommendations as to which course to follow, but rather strongly advocate that certain policies or actions be taken.

Finally, in preparing these articles we have not contacted any interested parties for comment (inside or outside the tobacco industry), but rather have concentrated on the story the documents themselves tell.

Despite these limitations, we are confident in the conclusions we draw from the documents. The documents showing lawyers steering scientists away from particular research avenues are inconsistent with the company's purported disbelief in the causation and addiction claims; if the company had been genuinely unconvinced by the causation and addiction hypotheses, then it should have had no concern that new research would provide ammunition for the enemy. Quite the contrary, the documents show that B&W and BAT recognized more than 30 years ago that nicotine is addictive and that tobacco smoke is "biologically active" (eg, carcinogenic).

. . . In an era in which public institutions are increasingly held in disdain, we would like to thank the University of California for providing an environment committed to academic freedom and the public interest. It would have been simpler—and cheaper—for the university to simply walk away from this project. After all, the history of the tobacco issue is one in which many institutions have followed the path of least resistance and failed to confront the issues raised in these documents. No administrator or other official ever told us to stop. Quite the contrary, we were encouraged and protected in our work. This behavior is what makes the University of California a great public institution.

References

[1]Hilts PJ. Tobacco company was silent on hazards. *New York Times*, May 7, 1994:A1.

[2]Hilts PJ. Way to make safer cigarette was found in 60's, but idea was shelved. *New York Times*. May 13, 1994:A10.

[3]Hilts PJ. Cigarette makers debated the risks they denied. *New York Times*. June 16, 1994:A1.

[4]Hilts PJ. Tobacco maker studied risk but did little about results. *New York Times*. June 17, 1994:A1.

[5]Maxwell JJ. *The Maxwell Consumer Report: Top World Cigarette Market Leaders*. Richmond, Va: Wheat, First Securities Inc; 1998.

[6]Maxwell JJ. *Historical Sales Trends in the Cigarette Industry*. Richmond, Va: Wheat, First Securities Inc; 1998.

[7]Weisz P. Smokes 'R' us: cigarette retailers are coming category among category killers. *Brandweek*. March 6, 1995:20–24.

[8]Slade J, Bero LA, Hanauer P, Barnes DE, Glantz SA. Nicotine and addiction: the Brown and Williamson documents. *JAMA*. 1995;274:225–233.

[9]Hanauer P, Slade J, Barnes DE, Bero LA, Glantz SA. Lawyer control of internal scientific research to protect against products liability lawsuits: the Brown and Williamson documents. *JAMA*. 1995;274:234–240.

[10]Bero LA, Barnes DE, Hanauer P, Slade J, Glantz SA. Lawyer control of the tobacco industry's external research program: the Brown and Williamson documents. *JAMA*. 1995;274:241–247.

[11]Barnes DE, Hanauer P, Slade J, Bero LA, Glantz SA. Environmental tobacco smoke: the Brown and Williamson documents. *JAMA*. 1995;274:248–253.

[12]US Dept of Health, Education and Welfare. *Smoking and Health: A Report of the Surgeon General*. Washington, DC: US Dept of Health, Education and Welfare, Public Health Services, Office of the Assistant Secretary for Health, Office on Smoking and Health; 1979. DHEW publication PHS 79-50066.

[13]US Dept of Health, Education and Welfare. *Smoking and Health: Report of the Advisory Committee to the Surgeon General of the Public Health Service*. Washington, DC: US Dept of Health, Education and Welfare; 1964. PHS publication 1103.

[14]US Dept of Health and Human Services. *The Health Consequences of Smoking: Nicotine Addiction: A Report of the Surgeon General*. Washington, DC: US Dept of Health and Human Services, Public Health Service, Centers for Disease Control, Center for Health Promotion and Education, Office on Smoking and Health; 1988. DHHS publication CDC 88-8406.

[15]Sandefur TJ. Testimony before the House Subcommittee on Energy and the Environment, June 23, 1994.

[16]US Dept of Health and Human Services. *The Health Consequences of Smoking: The Changing Cigarette: A Report of the Surgeon General*. Washington, DC: US Dept of Health and Human Services, Public Health Service, Office of the Assistant Secretary of Health, Office on Smoking and Health; 1981. DHHS publication PHS 81-50156.

[17]King W. Low-tar cigarettes creating a 'revolution.' *New York Times*. October 30, 1976:A8.

[18]Council for Tobacco Research. *Organization and Policy Statement*, New York, NY: Council for Tobacco Research; 1985.

[19]US Dept of Health, Education and Welfare. *The Health Consequences of Smoking: A Report of the Surgeon General*. Washington, DC: US Dept of Health, Education and Welfare, Public Health Service, Health Services and Mental Health Administration; 1972. DHEW publication HSM 72-7516.

[20]Millhiser RR. In defense of smoking. *New York Times*. January 1, 1978:A19.

[21]Associated Press. Study asserts nonsmokers live 2 years more by heeding alerts. *New York Times*. September 22, 1979:A6.

[22]US Dept of Health and Human Services. *Reducing the Health Consequences of Smoking: 25 Years of Progress*. Washington, DC: US Dept of Health and Human Services, Public Health Service, Centers for Disease Control, Center for Chronic Disease Prevention and Health Promotion, Office

on Smoking and Health; 1989. DHHS publication CDC 89-8411.

[23]Wolinsky H. When researchers accept funding from the tobacco industry, do ethics go up in smoke? *N Y State J Med.* 1985;85:451–455.

[24]US Dept of Health and Human Services. *The Health Consequences of Smoking: Cancer: A Report of the Surgeon General.* Washington, DC: US Dept of Health and Human Services, Public Health Service, Office on Smoking and Health; 1982. DHHS publication PHS 82-50179.

[25]US Dept of Health and Human Services. *The Health Consequences of Involuntary Smoking: A Report of the Surgeon General.* US Dept of Health and Human Services, Public Health Service, Centers for Disease Control; 1986. DHHS publication CDC 87-8898.

[26]Tobacco Institute. *Tobacco Smoke and the Nonsmoker: Scientific Integrity at the Crossroads.* Washington, DC: Tobacco Institute; 1986.

Cited Brown and Williamson Documents

As of this writing, these documents are being made available via the Internet at http://www.library.ucsf.edu/tobacco through the World Wide Web.

1006.01. Chronology of Brown & Williamson Smoking and Health Research, 1988.

1105.01. Griffith R. Report to Executive Committee, 1965.

1112.01. Green S. Research conference held at Hilton Head Island, SC. Minutes, September 24, 1968.

1125.01. Green S. Notes on the Group Research & Development Conference at Duck Key, Fla, January 12–18, 1974. Notes, January 12, 1974.

1165.02. BAT R&D conference, Montreal, Quebec, Proceedings, Wednesday, October 25, 1967. Minutes, 1967.

1169.01. Green S. Research conference held at Kronberg, Germany, June 2–8, 1969. Minutes, June 23, 1969.

1174.01. Green S. Notes on Group Research & Development Conference, Sydney, Australia, March 1978. Minutes, April 6, 1978.

1179.01. Blackman L. Research conference, Montebello, Quebec, August 30–September 3, 1982. Minutes, September 10, 1982.

1181.06. Biological conference, Southampton, England, April 9–11, 1984. BAT Research Conference 1984.

1181.12 Summary of GR&DC [Group Research & Development Centre] activities on: sidestream, psychology, 1984.

1200.01. Haselbach C, Libert O. *A Tentative Hypothesis on Nicotine Addiction.* London, England: British American Tobacco Co Ltd; 1963.

1200.20. Geinsbuhler H, Haselbach C. *The Fate of Nicotine in the Body.* Geneva, Switzerland: Battelle Memorial Institute (for BAT); 1983.

1802.05. Yeaman A. Implications of Battelle Hippo I & II and the Griffith filter, 1963.

1903.03. Tobacco Industry Research Committee organization and policy, 1967?

2010.02. Pepples E. Re: CTR budget. Letter to J. Edens, B&W Industries, C. McCarty, I. Hughes, and D. Bryant. April 4, 1978.

2110.06. Brown & Williamson. Project Truth: the smoking/health controversy: a view from the other side (prepared for the *Courier-Journal* and *Louisville Times*). Brown and Williamson Tobacco Company, 1971.

2205.01. Pepples E. Industry response to cigarette/health controversy, 1976.

Wisconsin v. Mitchell

A FEW OPINIONS ON SENTENCING ENHANCEMENT FOR HATE CRIMES

HEFFERNAN, CHIEF JUSTICE

This is a review of a published decision adjudging that Mitchell intentionally selected the battery victim because of the victim's race in

Wisconsin v. Mitchell 485 NW2d 807 (1992). (Original footnote numbers retained in this edited version.)

violation of the hate crimes penalty enhancer. Mitchell challenged the constitutionality and the court of appeals held that the statute was constitutional. The sole issue before the court is the constitutionality of the "hate crimes" statute. We hold that the statute violates the First Amendment and is thus unconstitutional.

The facts are not in dispute. On October 7, 1989, a group of young black men and boys was gathered. Todd Mitchell, nineteen at the time, was one of the older members of the group. Some of the group were at one point discussing a scene from the movie "Mississippi Burning" where a white man beat a young black boy who was praying.

Approximately ten members of the group moved outdoors, still talking about the movie. Mitchell asked the group: "Do you all feel hyped up to move on some white people?" A short time later, Gregory Reddick, a fourteen-year-old white male, approached the apartment complex. Reddick said nothing to the group, and merely walked by on the other side of the street. Mitchell then said: "You all want to fuck somebody up? There goes a white boy; go get him." Mitchell then counted to three and pointed the group in Reddick's direction.

The group ran towards Reddick, knocked him to the ground, beat him severely, and stole his "British Knights" tennis shoes. The police found Reddick unconscious a short while later. He remained in a coma for four days in the hospital, and the record indicates he suffered extensive injuries and possibly permanent brain damage.

Mitchell was convicted of aggravated battery. The jury separately found that Mitchell intentionally selected Reddick as the battery victim because of Reddick's race.

This case presents an issue which has spawned a growing debate in this country: the constitutionality of legislation that seeks to address hate crimes. Numerous articles have been published concerning the issue, some applauding hate crimes statutes and some vigorously in opposition.[5] Individuals and organizations traditionally allied behind the same agenda have separated on the issue of the legitimacy of hate crimes statutes.

The response to reports of bias related crime has been significant. Nearly every state in the country has enacted some form of hate crime legislation. The Wisconsin legislature's response was to enact sec. 939.645, Stats., which enhances the potential penalty for a criminal actor if the state proves that the actor intentionally selected the victim because of the victim's race, religion, color, disability, sexual orientation, national origin or ancestry.

The hate crimes statute violates the First Amendment directly by punishing what the legislature has deemed to be offensive thought and violates the First Amendment indirectly by chilling free speech.

The First Amendment of the United States Constitution states bluntly: "Congress shall make no law . . . abridging the freedom of speech." The First Amendment protects not only speech but thought as well. "[A]t the heart of the First Amendment is the notion that an individual should be free to believe as he will, and that in a free society one's beliefs should be shaped by his mind and his conscience rather than coerced by the State." Even more fundamentally, the constitution protects all speech and thought, regardless of how offensive it may be. "[I]f there is a bedrock principle underlying the First Amendment, it is that the government may not prohibit the expression of an idea simply because society finds the idea itself offensive or disagreeable." *Texas v. Johnson* (1989).[7] As Justice Holmes put it: "If there is any principle of the Constitution that more imperatively calls for attachment than any other it is the

[5]See, e.g., Susan Gellman, Sticks and Stones Can Put You in Jail, But Can Words Increase Your Sentence? *Constitutional and Policy Dilemmas of Ethnic Intimidation Laws*, 39 U.C.L.A.L. Rev. 333 (1991): and Tanya Kateri Hernandez, Bias Crimes: Unconscious Racism in the Prosecution of Racially Motivated Violence, 99 *Yale L.J.* 845 (1990). Similarly, numerous courts and commentators are currently struggling with the constitutional implications of college campus "hate speech" rules. See, e.g., *UWM Post,* *Inc. v. Board of Regents*, 774 F.Supp. 1163 (E.D.Wis. 1991); *Doe v. University of Michigan*, 721 F. Supp. 852 (E.D. Mich. 1989); Charles R. Lawrence. If He Hollers Let Him Go: Regulating Racist Speech on Campus 1990 *Duke L.J.* 431: Nadine Strossen. Regulating Racist Speech on Campus: A Modest Proposal?, 1990 *Duke L.J.* 484; and Katherine T. Bartlett and Jean O'Barr, The Chilly Climate on College Campuses; An Expansion of the "Hate Speech" Debate, 1990 *Duke L.J.* 574.

[7]See also *R.A.V. v. City of Saint Paul* (1992); *Hustler Magazine, Inc. v. Falwell* (1988).

principle of free thought—not free thought for those who agree with us but freedom for the thought we hate."[8]

Without doubt the hate crimes statute punishes bigoted thought. The state asserts that the statute punishes only the "conduct" of intentional selection of a victim. We disagree. Selection of a victim is an element of the underlying offense, part of the defendant's "intent" in committing the crime. In any assault upon an individual there is a selection of the victim. The statute punishes the "because of" aspect of the defendant's selection, the *reason* the defendant selected the victim, the *motive* behind the selection.

Construing the model hate crimes statute designed by the Anti-Defamation League of B'nai B'rith (ADL), upon which the Wisconsin hate crimes statute is apparently loosely based, one author provides the following insightful analysis:

> Under the ADL model, a charge of ethnic intimidation must always be predicated on certain offenses proscribed elsewhere in a state's criminal code. As those offenses are already punishable, all that remains is an additional penalty for the actor's *reasons* for his or her actions. The model statute does not address effects, state of mind, or a change in the character of the offense, but only the thoughts and ideas that propelled the actor to act. The government could not, of course, punish these thoughts and ideas independently. That they are held by one who commits a crime because of his or her beliefs does not remove this constitutional shield. Of course, the First Amendment protection guaranteed the actor's thoughts does not protect him or her from prosecution for the associated action. Neither, however, does the state's power to punish the action remove the constitutional barrier to punishing the thoughts.

Because all of the crimes under chs. 939 to 948, Stats., are already punishable, all that

remains is an additional punishment for the defendant's motive in selecting the victim. The punishment of the defendant's bigoted motive by the hate crimes statute directly implicates and encroaches upon First Amendment rights.

While the statute does not specifically phrase the "because of . . . race, religion, color, [etc.]" element in terms of bias or prejudice, it is clear from the history of anti-bias statutes, detailed above, that sec. 939.645, Stats., is expressly aimed at the bigoted bias of the actor. Merely because the statute refers in a literal sense to the intentional "conduct" of selecting, does not mean the court must turn a blind eye to the intent and practical effect of the law—punishment of offensive motive or thought.[11] The conduct of "selecting" is not akin to the

---

[11]There seems to be considerable confusion regarding the meaning and effect of "motive" in criminal law. As Black's Law Dictionary 810 (6th ed. 1990) states in its definition of "intent":

> Intent and motive should not be confused. Motive is what prompts a person to act, or fail to act. Intent refers only to the state of mind with which the act is done or omitted.

This confusion is manifested clearly in the dissenting opinion of Justice Bablitch, which correctly defines "intentionally" at p. 826 as "a purpose to do the thing or cause the result specified," correctly recognizes at pp. 821–822 n. 2 that the term "because of" implicates an actor's motive, and somehow concludes that the hate crimes statute involves ordinary criminal intent.

In this case the crime was aggravated battery, and the necessary intent under sec. 940.19(1m), Stats., is an "intent to cause great bodily harm." Quite clearly, Mitchell's intent to cause great bodily harm to Reddick is distinct from his motive or reason for doing so. Criminal law is not concerned with a person's reasons for committing crimes, but rather with the actor's intent or purpose in doing so.

As explained by Professor Gellman:

> "Motive," "intent," and "purpose" are related concepts in that they all refer to thought processes. They are legally distinct in crucial respects, however. Motive is nothing more than an actor's reason for acting, the "why" as opposed to the "what" of conduct. Unlike purpose or intent, motive cannot be a criminal offense or an element of an offense. . . . .

> The distinction becomes more clear upon consideration of the effect of altering the intent or purpose on the legal characterization of the same conduct, as compared to the effect (or lack thereof) of altering the motive.

(continued pg. 188)

---

[8]As was said in a statement attributed to Voltaire, surely one of the philosophical ancestors of our American constitution: "I disapprove of what you say but I will defend to the death your right to say it."

conduct of assaulting, burglarizing, murdering and other criminal conduct. It cannot be objectively established. Rather, an examination of the intentional "selection" of a victim necessarily requires a subjective examination of the actor's motive or reason for singling out the particular person against whom he or she commits a crime.[12]

In this case, Todd Mitchell selected Gregory Reddick because Reddick is white. Mitchell is black. The circumstantial evidence relied upon to prove that Mitchell selected Reddick "because" Reddick is white included Mitchell's speech—"Do you all feel hyped up to move on some white people?"—and his recent discussion with other black youths of a racially charged scene from the movie "Mississippi Burning." This evidence was used not merely to show the intentional selection of the victim, but was used to prove Mitchell's bigoted bias. The physical assault of Reddick is the same whether he was attacked because of his skin color or because he was wearing "British Knight" tennis shoes. Mitchell's bigoted motivation for selecting Reddick, his thought which impelled him to act, is the reason that his punishment was enhanced. In Mitchell's case, that motivation was apparently a hatred of whites.

The statute commendably is designed to punish—and thereby deter—racism and other objectionable biases, but deplorably unconstitutionally infringes upon free speech. The state would justify its transgression against the constitutional right of freedom of speech and thought because its motive is a good one, but the magnitude of the proposed incursion against the constitutional rights of all of us should no more be diminished for that good motive than should a crime be enhanced by a separate penalty because of a criminal's bad motive.[14]

The state admits that this case involves legislation that seeks to address bias related crime. The only definition of "bias" relevant to this case is "prejudice." A statute specifically designed to punish personal prejudice impermissibly infringes upon an individual's First Amendment rights, no matter how carefully or cleverly one words the statute. The hate crimes statute enhances the punishment of bigoted criminals because they are bigoted. The statute is directed solely at the subjective motivation of the actor—his or her prejudice. Punishment of one's thought, however repugnant the thought, is unconstitutional.[15]

In *R.A.V.*, the United States Supreme Court held that a Minnesota ordinance prohibiting bias-motivated disorderly conduct was facially invalid under the First Amendment. Accepting

---

Continuing with the example of burglary, changing the *purpose* of the break-in changes the very nature of the act: if *A* broke into *B*'s house for the purpose of getting *A*'s own property (not a criminal purpose), the act of breaking in is simply breaking and entering or trespass, not burglary, even if *A*'s motive was identical (the desire to pay his debts). By contrast, changing *A*'s *motives*, even to more sympathetic ones (say, the desire to buy a house for the homeless), while his *purpose* was that of committing the crime of theft in *B*'s house, does *not* change the nature of the act: it is still burglary.

Susan Gellman, 39 U.C.L.A. L.Rev. at 364–65 (emphasis in original). While the state speaks of the "intentional" aspect of the hate crimes statute, when the focus is on the "selects . . . because of" aspect of the law, it becomes clear that it is the actor's motive which is targeted and punished by the statute.

[12] In fact, on May 13, 1992, the legislature amended sec. 939.645, Stats., to apply specifically where the selection is "in whole or in part because of the actor's belief or perception regarding" the victim's status "whether or not the actor's belief or perception was correct."

Thus the legislature has removed any doubt that the aim of the statute is the actor's subjective motivation. The dissenting opinions ignore this legislative clarification in their refusal to recognize that the statute is focused upon and punishes the defendant's motive.

[14] As has long been recognized, the road to hell is paved with good intentions.

[15] Of course, freedom of speech is not absolute. For example, the government may regulate or punish "fighting words" that are "likely to provoke the average person to retaliation, and thereby cause a breach of the peace." *Chaplinsky v. New Hampshire* (1942). Also, the government may regulate expressive conduct where there is an important governmental interest and the regulation is narrowly tailored to address that interest. *United States v. O'Brien* (1968). The bigoted thought which is punished by the hate crimes statute fits neither category. While an individual's bigoted speech may occasionally provoke retaliation, a person's thought will not. Nor is it argued that a hate crime is protected expressive conduct. It is not. Rather, a person's bigoted thought, the very thing punished by the hate crimes statute, is entitled to the full protection of the First Amendment.

the Minnesota Supreme Court's determination that the ordinance reached only expressions that constituted "fighting words" within the meaning of *Chaplinsky*, the Court held that the government may not constitutionally regulate even otherwise unprotected speech on the basis of hostility towards the idea expressed by the speaker. In other words, while the government may regulate all fighting words, it may not regulate only those fighting words with which it disagrees. Such a prohibition is nothing more than a governmental attempt to silence speech on the basis of its content.

While the St. Paul ordinance invalidated in *R.A.V.* is clearly distinguishable from the hate crimes statute in that it regulates fighting words rather than merely the actor's biased motive, the Court's analysis lends support to our conclusion that the Wisconsin legislature cannot criminalize bigoted thought with which it disagrees. The Court stated:

[T]he only interest distinctively served by the content limitation is that of displaying the city council's special hostility towards the particular biases thus singled out. That is precisely what the First Amendment forbids. The politicians of St. Paul are entitled to express that hostility—but not through the means of imposing unique limitations upon speakers who (however benightedly) disagree.

The ideological content of the thought targeted by the hate crimes statute is identical to that targeted by the St. Paul ordinance—racial or other discriminatory animus. And, like the United States Supreme Court, we conclude that the legislature may not single out and punish that ideological content.

Thus, the hate crimes statute is facially invalid because it directly punishes a defendant's constitutionally protected thought.[17]

---

[17]The dissent of Justice Bablitch asserts that punishing motive is permissible, based upon *Dawson v. Delaware* (1992), wherein the United States Supreme Court indicated that evidence of a convicted murderer's bigoted motivation in committing the murder is a relevant inquiry in sentencing. The dissent is wrong. Of course it is permissible to consider evil motive or moral turpitude

The hate crimes statute is also unconstitutionally overbroad. A statute is overbroad when it intrudes upon a substantial amount of constitutionally protected activity. Aside from punishing thought, the hate crimes statute also threatens to directly punish an individual's speech and assuredly will have a chilling effect upon free speech. As we explained in *Bachowski:*

A [statute] is overbroad when its language, given its normal meaning, is so sweeping that its sanctions may be applied to constitutionally protected conduct which the state is not permitted to regulate. The essential vice of an overbroad law is that by sweeping protected activity within its reach it deters citizens from exercising their protected constitutional freedoms, the so-called "chilling effect."

The chilling effect need not be evident in the defendant's case; it is enough if hypothetical situations show that it will chill the rights of others.

The state admits as it must that speech may often be used as circumstantial evidence to prove the actor's intentional selection. This case is a perfect example. Mitchell's speech is the primary evidence of his intentional selection of Reddick. The use of the defendant's speech, both current and past, as circumstantial evidence to prove the intentional selection, makes it apparent that the statute sweeps protected speech within its ambit and will chill free speech.

The criminal conduct involved in any crime giving rise to the hate crimes penalty enhancer is already punishable. Yet there are numerous instances where this statute can be applied to convert a misdemeanor to a felony merely because of the spoken word. For example, if A strikes B in the face he commits a criminal battery. However, should A add a word such as "nigger, "honkey," "jew," "mick," "kraut," "spic," or "queer," the crime becomes a felony,

---

when sentencing for a particular crime, but it is quite a different matter to sentence for that underlying crime and then add to that criminal sentence a separate enhancer that is directed solely to punish the evil motive for the crime.

and A will be punished not for his conduct alone—a misdemeanor—but for using the spoken word. Obviously, the state would respond that the speech is merely an indication that A intentionally selected B. because of his particular race or ethnicity, but the fact remains that the necessity to use speech to prove this intentional selection threatens to chill free speech. Opprobrious though the speech may be, an individual must be allowed to utter it without fear of punishment by the state.

And of course the chilling effect goes further than merely deterring an individual from uttering a racial epithet during a battery. Because the circumstantial evidence required to prove the intentional selection is limited only by the relevancy rules of the evidence code, the hate crimes statute will chill every kind of speech. As Professor Gellman explains:

> In addition to any words that a person may speak during, just prior to, or in association with the commission of one of the underlying offenses, all of his or her remarks upon earlier occasions, any books ever read, speakers ever listened to, or associations ever held could be introduced as evidence that he or she held racist views and was acting upon them at the time of the offense. Anyone charged with one of the underlying offenses could be charged with [intentional selection] as well, and face the possibility of public scrutiny of a lifetime of everything from ethnic jokes to serious intellectual inquiry. Awareness of this possibility could lead to habitual self-censorship of expression of one's ideas, and reluctance to read or listen publicly to the ideas of others, whenever one fears that those ideas might run contrary to popular sentiment on the subject of ethnic relations.
>
> . . . .
>
> It is no answer that one need only refrain from committing one of the underlying offenses to avoid the thought punishment. Chill of expression and inquiry by definition occurs *before* any offense is committed, and even if no offense is *ever* committed. The chilling effect thus extends to the entire populace, not just to those who will eventually commit one of the underlying offenses.

Susan Gellman, 39 U.C.L.A. L.Rev. at 360–61 (emphasis in original) (citations omitted).

Thus, the hate crimes statute is unconstitutionally overbroad because it sweeps protected First Amendment speech within its reach and thereby chills free speech.

Finally, we consider the argument advanced by the *amici curiae* ADL, et. al., and embraced by the dissent that an analogy exists between the hate crimes statute and antidiscrimination laws, and that the numerous United States Supreme Court decisions upholding antidiscrimination laws lend support to the hate crimes statute. We disagree.

Discrimination and bigotry are not the same thing. Under antidiscrimination statutes, it is the discriminatory act which is prohibited. Under the hate crimes statute, the "selection" which is punished is not an act, it is a mental process. In this case, the act was the battery of Reddick; what was punished by the hate crimes statute was Mitchell's reason for selecting Reddick, his discriminatory motive.

As explained above, selection under the hate crimes statute is solely concerned with the subjective motivation of the actor. Prohibited acts of discrimination under Title VII of the Civil Rights Act of 1964, 42 U.S.C. § 2000e-2, and analogous state anti-discrimination statutes, such as refusal to hire, termination, etc., involve objective acts of discrimination. What is punished by the hate crimes penalty enhancer is a subjective mental process, not an objective act. The actor's penalty is enhanced not because the actor fired the victim, terminated the victim's employment, harassed the victim, abused the victim or otherwise objectively mistreated the victim because of the victim's protected status; the penalty is enhanced because the actor subjectively selected the victim because of the victim's protected status. Selection, quite simply, is a mental process, not an objective act.[21]

[21]The dissenting opinion of Justice Bablitch recites that it does not understand this "very complicated and elaborate distinction" between the hate crimes penalty enhancer and antidiscrimination statutes. That is interesting in light of the dissent's recognition that the statute applies to the defendant's "selection decision," an obviously subjective

Finally, there is a difference between the civil penalties imposed under Title VII and other antidiscrimination statutes and the criminal penalties imposed by the hate crimes law, and contrary to the dissent's protestations, it is a difference that matters. The difference is that while the First Amendment may countenance slight incursions into free speech where the overarching concern is protection from objective acts of bigotry in the employment marketplace and the adverse consequences of such acts on the civil rights of minorities, the First Amendment will not allow the outright criminalization of subjective bigoted thought. We have little doubt that an antidiscrimination statute which criminalized an employer's subjective discrimination, with nothing more, would be unconstitutional. This apparent schism in the First Amendment's protective shield is perhaps best understood in the context of overbreadth. A statute criminalizing the bigoted selection of a victim will chill free speech to a much greater extent than a statute imposing civil penalties for objective discriminatory acts.

In the wake of the Los Angeles riots sparked by the acquittal of four white police officers accused of illegally beating black motorist Rodney King, it is increasingly evident that racial antagonism and violence are as prevalent now as they ever have been. Indeed, added to the statistical compilation of bias related crimes could be the vicious beating of white truck driver Reginald Denny by black rioters, horrifyingly captured on film by a news helicopter. As disgraceful and deplorable as these and other hate crimes are, the personal prejudices

of the attackers are protected by the First Amendment. The constitution may not embrace or encourage bigoted and hateful thoughts, but it surely protects them.

Because we wholeheartedly agree with the motivation of the legislature in its desire to suppress hate crimes, it is with great regret that we hold the hate crimes statute unconstitutional—and only because we believe that the greater evil is the suppression of freedom of speech for all of us.

SHIRLEY S. ABRAHAMSON, JUSTICE (*DISSENTING*).

The Constitution teaches mistrust of any government regulation of speech or expression. Had I been in the legislature, I do not believe I would have supported this statute because I do not think this statute will accomplish its goal. I would direct the state's efforts to protect people from invidious discrimination and intimidation into other channels. As a judge, however, after much vacillation, I conclude that this law should be construed narrowly and should be held constitutional.

This case presents a very difficult question involving the convergence of three competing societal values—freedom of speech, equal rights, and protection against crime.

Freedom of speech is the most treasured right in a free, democratic society. Our constitution protects our right to think, speak and write as we wish. This freedom of expression encompasses all speech, pleasant or unpleasant, popular or unpopular. Even expressions of bigotry are protected. Our constitutional history makes clear that expression hostile to the values of our country should be addressed with more speech, not suppressed with police power.

Nevertheless, our law recognizes the harmful effects of invidious classification and discrimination. We acknowledge that when individuals are victimized because of their status, such as race or religion, the resulting harm is greater than the harm that would have been caused by the injurious conduct alone. In addition to the injury inflicted, the victim may suffer feelings of fear, shame, isolation and inability to enjoy

---

mental process. To state that a "decision" is analogous to the conduct proscribed by antidiscrimination statutes is untenable. We freely admit that antidiscrimination statutes are concerned with the actor's motive, but it is the objective conduct taken in respect to the victim which is redressed (not punished) by those statutes, not the actor's motive.

We repeat. The hate crimes statute does not punish the underlying criminal act, it punishes the defendant's motive for acting. Taking the dissent's explanation that the statute is concerned with the "decision" of the defendant, it is clear that the hate crimes statute creates nothing more than a thought crime. Apparently that dissent is comfortable with such an Orwellian notion; we are not.

the rights and opportunities that should be available to all persons. Furthermore, all members of the group to which the victim belongs may suffer when the individual is victimized. The state has determined that harms inflicted because of race, color, creed, religion or sexual orientation are more pressing public concerns than other harms. The state has legitimate, reasonable and neutral justifications for selective protection of certain people. "In light of our Nation's long and painful experience with discrimination, this determination is plainly reasonable. Indeed . . . it is compelling." The state has a compelling interest in combating invidiously discriminatory conduct, even when the conduct is linked to viewpoints otherwise protected by the First Amendment.

In addition, our government has a compelling interest in preserving the peace, in protecting each person from crime and from the fear of crime.

Section 939.645 addresses only those crimes committed "because of" the victim's "race, religion, color, disability, sexual orientation, national origin or ancestry." It does not punish all crimes committed by persons who have expressed bigoted beliefs. An individual may commit a criminal act. That same individual may possess or express bigoted beliefs. These two facts standing alone, however, do not subject that individual to punishment under sec. 939.645.

In my mind, it is the tight nexus between the selection of the victim and the underlying crime that saves this statute. The state must prove beyond a reasonable doubt both that the defendant committed the underlying crime and that the defendant intentionally selected the victim because of characteristics protected under the statute. To prove intentional selection of the victim, the state cannot use evidence that the defendant has bigoted beliefs or has made bigoted statements unrelated to the particular crime. Evidence of a person's traits or beliefs would not be permissible for the purpose of proving the person acted in conformity therewith on a particular occasion. The statute requires the state to show evidence of bigotry relating directly to the defendant's intentional

selection of this particular victim upon whom to commit the charged crime. The state must directly link the defendant's bigotry to the invidiously discriminatory selection of the victim and to the commission of the underlying crime.

Interpreted in this way, I believe the Wisconsin statute ties discriminatory selection of a victim to conduct already punishable by state law in a manner sufficient to prevent erosion of First Amendment protection of bigoted speech and ideas.

Read narrowly as the legislature intended, this statute is a prohibition on conduct, not on belief or expression. The statute does nothing more than assign consequences to invidiously discriminatory acts.

The state's interest in punishing biasrelated criminal conduct relates only to the protection of equal rights and the prevention of crime, not to the suppression of free expression. The enhanced punishment justly reflects the crime's enhanced negative consequences on society. Thus interpreted the statute prohibits intentional conduct, not belief or expression. The only chilling effect is on lawless conduct.

Bigots are free to think and express themselves as they wish, except that they may not engage in criminal conduct in furtherance of their beliefs. Section 939.645 does not punish abstract beliefs or speech. The defendant's beliefs or speech are only relevant as they relate directly to the commission of a crime.

The decision in *R.A.V. v. City of St. Paul* (1992) has not persuaded me to the contrary. In *R.A.V.*, the Supreme Court held unconstitutional a St. Paul ordinance prohibiting placing "on public or private property a symbol, object, appellation, characterization or graffiti, including, but not limited to, a burning cross or Nazi swastika, which one knows or has reason to know arouses anger, alarm or resentment in others on the basis of race, color, creed, religion or gender. . . ." The majority opinion in *R.A.V.* ruled the ordinance facially unconstitutional because, even assuming that the ordinance only regulated "fighting words," the ordinance was based on the content of the ideas expressed by a defendant. The four concurring justices found the ordinance unconstitutional on the ground that the statute was an over-broad prohibition of fighting words.

R.A.V. does not control this case. Section 939.645 is not similar to the St. Paul ordinance; its validity does not rely on the "fighting words" doctrine. The defendant in *R.A.V.* was also charged under a state statute much more similar to sec. 939.645 than the St. Paul ordinance, but the defendant did not challenge that charge.

For the reasons set forth, I dissent.

BABLITCH, JUSTICE (*DISSENTING*).

> Everywhere the crosses are burning,
> sharp-shooting goose-steppers around every
>   corner,
> there are snipers in the schools . . .
> (I know you don't believe this.
> You think this is nothing
> but faddish exaggeration. But they
> are not shooting at you.)
>   Lorna Dee Cervantes[1]

The law in question is not a "hate speech" law.

Nor is it really a "hate crimes" law as it has been somewhat inappropriately named.

It is a law against discrimination—discrimination in the selection of a crime victim.

Today the majority decides that the same Constitution which does not protect discrimination in the marketplace does protect discrimination that takes place during the commission of a crime. Numerous federal and state laws exist which prohibit discrimination in the selection of who is to be hired, or fired, or promoted. No one seriously (at least until today) questions their constitutionality. Yet the majority today gives constitutional protection to discrimination in the selection of who is to be the victim of a crime. Both sets of laws involve discrimination, both involve victims, both involve action "because of" the victim's status.

[1]Cervantes, Poem for the Young White Man Who Asked Me How I, An Intelligent Well Read Person Could Believe in the War Between Races, in M. Sanchez, *Contemporary Chicana Poetry* 90 (1986).

The majority says there is a difference in the two types of laws. They are wrong. There is no support in law or logic for their position. How can the Constitution not protect discrimination in the selection of a victim for discriminatory hiring, firing, or promotional practices, and at the same time protect discrimination in the selection of a victim for criminal activity? How can the Constitution protect discrimination in the performance of an illegal act and not protect discrimination in the performance of an otherwise legal act? How can the Constitution not protect discrimination in the marketplace when the action is taken "because of" the victim's status, and at the same time protect discrimination in a street or back alley when the criminal action is taken "because of" the victim's status?

These are laws against discrimination, pure and simple. Dictionaries do not disagree on the meaning of the term discrimination: to distinguish, to differentiate, to act on the basis of prejudice. Laws forbidding discrimination in the marketplace and laws forbidding discrimination in criminal activity have a common denominator: they are triggered when a person acts "because of" the victim's protected status. These exact words appear in most, if not all antidiscrimination laws. These exact words appear in the laws before us today.

Yet the majority says one is constitutional, one is not. I submit it is pure sophistry to distinguish the two. In its effort to protect speech, the majority's constitutional pen gets too close to the trees and fails to see the forest.

The majority rationalizes their conclusion by insisting that this statute punishes bigoted thought. Not so. The statute does not impede or punish the right of persons to have bigoted thoughts or to express themselves in a bigoted fashion or otherwise, regarding the race, religion, or other status of a person. It does attempt to limit the effects of bigotry. What the statute does punish is acting upon those thoughts. It punishes the act of discriminatory selection plus criminal conduct, not the thought or expression of bigotry. The Constitution allows a person to have bigoted thoughts and to express them, but it does not allow a person to act on them. The majority says otherwise. I disagree.

I conclude the statute in question is neither vague nor overbroad, nor does it offend equal protection. Accordingly, I dissent.

I.

Examples of shocking bias related crimes making headlines recently include:

> They pounced on two black women walking towards a shopping centre early in the morning. One escaped and ran for help, the other was beaten, stripped nearly naked, and sprayed with lighter fluid.

> In Kentucky this September, assailants beat a young gay man with a tire iron, locked him into a car trunk with a bunch of snapping turtles and then tried to set the car on fire.

> Amber Jefferson, a 15 year-old high school cheerleader almost lost her life because of the fact that she has one white and one black parent. Four attackers, allegedly all white, beat her with a baseball bat and split her face open with a shard of plate glass.

Wisconsin has also not been immune from reprehensible incidents of bias related crime:

> Anti-Semitic attacks erupt regularly, even at such supposedly progressive, enlightened institutions as the University of Wisconsin (Madison), where a Jewish student center has been pelted with rocks and bottles and where Jewish fraternities and sororities have been vandalized. Counselors at a Madison Jewish day camp discovered that the brake linings had been cut on a bus used to transport children—fortunately before the bus was used.

In 1987, the Wisconsin legislature acted to alleviate bias related crime. The Wisconsin legislature's response was to enact sec. 939.645, Stats., which enhances the penalty a perpetrator receives if the State of Wisconsin (State) proves that the perpetrator intentionally selected the victim because of the victim's race, religion, color, or other protected status.

I conclude that the First Amendment is not implicated in this case.

I reject the majority's and Mitchell's argument that sec. 939.645, Stats., punishes or has a chilling effect on free speech. The penalty enhancement statute is directed at the action or conduct of selecting a victim and committing a crime against that victim because of his or her protected status. The gravamen of the offense is selection, not the perpetrator's speech, thought, or even motive.[2] The statute does not impede or punish the right of persons to have thoughts or to express themselves regarding the race, religion, or other status of a person.

---

[2] One of the majority's chief contentions seems to be that the statute is unconstitutional because it punishes motive. Although I do not think that this statute punishes motive, even if it did, I have serious doubts about the majority's conclusion that punishing motive is impermissible under the First Amendment. The majority cites no authority to support its conclusion that punishing motive is impermissible under the First Amendment. In fact, the majority fails to explain why, under its analysis, it is impermissible for the penalty enhancer statute to punish a discriminatory motive, yet permissible for antidiscrimination statutes to punish a discriminatory motive. In fact one writer commenting on Title VII is at complete odds with the majority's analysis of motive under the criminal law. He writes:

> Title VII was passed because Congress perceived that actions resulting from bad thoughts were sufficiently pervasive to substantially limit economic opportunities of blacks. 'Bad thoughts' is, of course, shorthand for a wide range of interior activities which are the necessary predicate for disparate treatment liability. A more common terminology is 'prohibited considerations,' but 'bad thoughts' describes more graphically what disparate treatment entails.

> . . . .

> The notion of bad thoughts is not peculiar to disparate treatment discrimination under Title VII. It has played an important role in the Court's constitutional decisions over the last two decades in contexts ranging from equal protection to freedom of speech and religion. Nor is such concern new in the law.

> Modern criminal law has always manifested a concern for motivations under the rubric of mens rea. In the discrimination context, however, motivations are both more important and more elusive than in criminal law because the 'conduct' violating Title VII is neutral or positive except when it springs from bad thoughts. In the criminal context, much prohibited conduct is itself suspect. Charles A. Sullivan, Accounting For *Price Waterhouse:* Proving Disparate Treatment Under Title VII, Brooklyn L.Rev. 1107, 1139–1140 (1991).

The statute's concern is with criminal conduct plus purposeful selection. By enhancing the penalty, the penalty enhancer statute punishes more severely criminals who act with what the legislature has determined is a more depraved, antisocial intent: an intent not just to injure but to intentionally pick out and injure a person because of a person's protected status. The legislative concern expressed in this statute is not with the beliefs, motives, or speech of a perpetrator but with his or her action of purposeful selection plus criminal conduct.

Admittedly, the conduct prohibited by the penalty enhancer statute can be proven by an extensive combination of facts that might include words uttered by a defendant.[3] However, if words are used to prove the crime, the words uttered are not the subject of the statutory prohibition; rather, they are used only as circumstantial evidence to prove the intentional selection. Permitting the use of such evidence does not chill free speech. Just as words of defendants are frequently used to prove the element of intent in many crimes without violating the First Amendment, words may be used to prove the act of intentional selection. It is no more a chilling of free speech to allow words to prove the act of intentional selection in this "intentional selection" statute than it is to allow a defendant's words that he "hated John Smith and wished he were dead" to prove a defendant intentionally murdered John Smith.

[3]The majority essentially contends that the use of speech as circumstantial evidence impermissibly chills free speech. Once again the majority fails to explain why this is not also true in antidiscrimination cases. For example, under Title VII sexual harassment jurisprudence, an employee's or employer's sexist speech is not merely evidence of prohibited conduct; it is the prohibited conduct. See, e.g., *Volk v. Coler*, 845 F.2d, 1422, 1426–27 (7th Cir. 1988) (plaintiff alleged, among other things, that her supervisor called her and other female employees 'hon,' 'honey,' 'babe' and 'tiger.') *Andrews v. City of Philadelphia*, 895 F.2d 1469, 1485 (3d Cir. 1990) (pervasive use of derogatory and insulting terms relating the women generally and addressed to female employees personally may be sufficient to show a hostile work environment). See also *Robinson v. Jacksonville Shipyards, Inc.*, 760 F.Supp. 1486, 1535 (M.D.Fla.1991) ("pictures and verbal harassment are not protected speech because they act as discriminatory conduct in the form of a hostile work environment").

The use of speech under the penalty enhancer is not different than its use in prosecutions under antidiscrimination laws or fair housing discrimination laws. Antidiscrimination statutes often employ terms similar to those contained in the penalty enhancer. For instance, secs. 118.13, 111.321, 101.225, and 66.395, Stats., all prohibit certain conduct that occurs either "because of" or "on account of" or "on the basis of" a status of another person. Proof of violations of these statutes will often involve proof of words used by the violators. Under these statutes and the penalty enhancer, a particular action or conduct is being punished, and speech may be used to prove the conduct. Under the penalty enhancer statute, speech is simply probative of the element of intentional selection. The use of such evidence does not violate the First Amendment. The action of intentional selection is punished, and the words used by a defendant are merely evidence of an intentional selection.

Although the majority attempts to distinguish this statute and antidiscrimination statutes, its distinction is a distinction without a difference. The majority states that the penalty enhancer statute is unconstitutional because the statute does not punish only the conduct of intentional selection of a victim "[t]he statute punishes the 'because of' aspect of the defendant's selection, the *reason* the defendant selected the victim. . . ." The majority abandons this reasoning when applied to antidiscrimination laws. The majority posits that the distinction between the penalty enhancer statute and antidiscrimination laws is that antidiscrimination laws punish only the discrimination, i.e., the refusal to hire, not the discriminatory motive. The majority forgets a key requirement of antidiscrimination statutes. Antidiscrimination statutes do not prohibit a person from not hiring someone of a protected class, they prohibit a person from not hiring someone of a protected class *because* or *on the basis of* his or her protected class. It is not, as the majority suggests, the failure to hire that is being punished, it is the failure to hire because of status. How can the majority find the penalty enhancer statute unconstitutional because it punishes the "because of" aspect of a selection process, and at the same time conclude that antidiscrimination statutes, which do the same thing, are constitutional? The majority at the least ought to answer this question.

The majority also attempts to explain its very complicated and elaborate distinction between this statute and antidiscrimination laws based on some sort of difference between subjective motivations and objective acts. Although I do not quite understand the majority's use of the terms objective and subjective in the context of this case, I interpret the majority's argument to be that this statute is unconstitutional because it punishes the subjective motivations of the actor, while discrimination statutes involve objective acts of discrimination. This is merely the same distinction without a difference referred to above. Like antidiscrimination statutes, the penalty enhancer statute involves an "objective act"—the criminal conduct, e.g., the battery, etc. Likewise, despite the majority's contentions to the contrary, under the majority's analysis antidiscrimination statutes, because they require that the act be "because of" the protected status of the victim, implicate and punish the subjective motive of the actor. For example, in disparate treatment cases (cases in which the discrimination alleged is overt discrimination as opposed to disparate impact where the practices are fair in form, but discriminatory in operation) a person simply does not violate Title VII for refusing to hire a person of a protected status. The objective act alone does not invoke the provisions of the statute. Rather, the refusal must be "because of" the victim's protected status. Assuming that the majority is correct that this statute punishes motive, it fails to explain how the enhancer is any different from antidiscrimination laws.

If one assumes that the majority is correct that the penalty enhancer punishes motive there is only one distinction between it and antidiscrimination laws. The only distinction that exists between the penalty enhancer statute and antidiscrimination statutes is that the objective acts that are punished are different in that antidiscrimination laws punish legal conduct plus bad motive and the enhancer

punishes criminal conduct plus bad motive. While it is true that this is a distinction, the majority never explains why it is a distinction that matters. Why is it permissible to punish motive when it is accompanied by legal conduct and impermissible to punish motive when it is accompanied by illegal conduct. The majority does not give an answer to this question, it merely concludes that the distinction somehow makes a difference. Saying so, again and again, does not make it so.

Lastly, even assuming that the majority is correct in saying that this statute punishes motive, it has still failed to explain why punishing motive is impermissible. A recent case from the U.S. Supreme Court would seem to indicate that the majority is in error. In *Dawson v. Delaware* (1992), the United States Supreme Court held that "the Constitution does not erect a *per se* barrier to the admission of evidence concerning one's beliefs and associations at sentencing simply because those beliefs and associations are protected by the First Amendment." Although under the facts of *Dawson* the Court concluded that there was a First Amendment violation, its analysis lends considerable support to the conclusion that considering the perpetrator's motivations in determining the appropriate sentence is permissible. For example, in concluding that evidence that the defendant belonged to the Aryan Brotherhood was impermissibly submitted during the penalty phase of a capital case in violation of the First Amendment, the court stated:

> Even if the Delaware group to which Dawson allegedly belongs is racist, those beliefs, so far as we can determine, had no relevance to the sentencing proceeding in this case. For example, the Aryan Brotherhood evidence was not tied in any way to the murder of Dawson's victim. In *Barclay*, on the contrary, the evidence showed that the defendant's membership in the Black Liberation Army, and his consequent desire to start a "racial war," were related to the murder of a white hitchhiker. We concluded that it was most proper for the sentencing judge to 'tak[e] into account the *elements of racial hatred in this murder.*' In the present case, however, the murder victim was

white, as is Dawson: elements of racial hatred were therefore not involved in the killing.

The U.S. Supreme Court is clearly indicating that when racial hatred is relevant to the crime, i.e., the racial hatred is the perpetrator's reason for committing the crime, this information is completely relevant in sentencing. How then can the majority suggest that punishing motive is impermissible?

I repeat. Section 939.645, Stats., is not concerned with speech or thought. It is concerned with intentional selection. It becomes operative not just when a person's speech evinces the discriminatory selection, but rather anytime the choice of a victim from a protected class is shown to be selective rather than random, discriminating rather than indiscriminate, or designed rather than happenstance.

The penalty enhancer statute also does not seek to punish the motive of a perpetrator. Neither a perpetrator's bigoted beliefs, nor his or her motivation for intentionally selecting a victim because of a protected status are punished. Again, it is the act of selecting a victim because of his or her race, color, or etc., that is proscribed. If a perpetrator seeks out a Jewish person to physically assault, his intent is not just to injure, but to injure a Jewish person. He may be motivated by a hatred of Jewish people, a calling from God to sacrifice a Jewish person, or some other irrational motive. This law does not look to motive. This law does not look at why the perpetrator sought out a Jewish person. It looks only to whether the fact that the victim was Jewish was a substantial factor in the defendant's purposeful choice of the victim.

Similarly, under the facts of the present case, even if Mitchell could show that his motive was not a hatred of whites, his conduct would still be punishable under the statute. As the State points out, Mitchell's motive could have been to impress the group of boys that accompanied him. Nevertheless, the statute would still apply. Its focus is not on bigoted or hateful motivations. Rather, it punishes the action of intentionally selecting a victim on the basis of a protected status listed in the statute. As Mitchell himself emphasized at oral arguments, the term "hate crimes" statute is a misnomer. The crimes that fall under the statute may be motivated by many emotions; the intentional selection is what is prohibited. The statute looks at intent, and statutes are used in many ways to punish crimes differently based on the perceived seriousness of the intent of the perpetrator. For example, an intent to kill is punished greater than an intent showing utter disregard for human life. Likewise, a reckless intent is punished less than an intent showing utter disregard for human life.

Section 939.645, Stats., does not attempt to prohibit or punish bigotry, antisemitism, or the like. It does attempt to limit their effects. An individual's freedom to express his or her views in writing, speech, or otherwise is not regulated or chilled by this statute. What is prohibited is the act of intentionally selecting victims because of their protected status. Why a Black or a Jewish person or any other person of a protected class was chosen as the victim is not relevant. What is relevant is that the victim is intentionally chosen because of the victim's protected status.

I conclude that sec. 939.645, Stats., legitimately regulates criminal conduct, and raises no issue under the First Amendment. It does not punish speech, thought, or even motivation, nor does it sweep within its ambit actions which are constitutionally protected as to render it unconstitutionally overbroad.

II.

Regulation of harmful conduct is a legitimate exercise of a state's power. The function of the legislature in drafting criminal laws is always to make reasoned decisions concerning the social harm of particular conduct. The criminal laws are replete with similar legislative judgements involving enhanced penalties. For example, sec. 939.63, Stats., increases the penalty for a crime if the person possesses, uses, or threatens to use a dangerous weapon. Similarly, if a person commits a crime while his or her identity is concealed, the penalty for the underlying crime may be increased under sec. 939.641. See also, sec. 939.62 (increased penalty for habitual criminality): sec. 939.621 (increased penalty for certain domestic abuse offenses); sec. 939.64 (increased penalty for committing a felony while wearing a bullet-proof garment); sec. 948.02 (sexual contact or sexual intercourse with a person who has not attained the age of 13 years is guilty of Class B felony, while sexual contact or intercourse with a person who has not attained the age of 16 is a Class C felony); sec. 940.31 (kidnapping, a Class B felony under the statute is enhanced to a Class A felony when it is committed with the intent "to cause another to transfer property in order to obtain the release of the victim").

There is ample evidence to support the legislature's conclusion that intentional selection of a victim from a protected class causes a greater harm to its victims as well as to society than do crimes where the victim's status is not a factor. Many commentators have discussed the widespread psychological harms caused by crimes that appear to be bias related. See generally, Delgado, Words that Wound: A Tort Action for Racial Insults, Epithets, and Name-Calling, 17 *Harv. C.R.-C.L.L.Rev.* 133 (1982); Matsuda, Public Response to Racist Speech: Considering the Victim's Story, 87 *Mich.L.Rev.* 2320 (1989); Developments in the Law Sexual Orientation and the Law, 102 *Harvard L.Rev.* 1508, 1541 (1989). These theorists posit that bias related crimes cause injury and damage far beyond that created by similar criminal conduct which does not appear to be bias related because of their tendency to perpetuate prejudice and victimize classes of people. Crimes that appear to be based on intentional selection because of the victim's status create fear not only among those who share the victim's race, color, religion, etc; but they also threaten society in general. Reports of intentional selection, even if perhaps not motivated by bigotry, create the appearance of bigotry and hatred. These crimes breed fear, misunderstanding, misconceptions, and isolation between different classes of people. The Wisconsin legislature has attempted to hinder these crimes, not by regulating speech, thought, or even motivation, but rather by enhancing the criminal penalty for any crime, however motivated, where the perpetrator purposefully selects a victim because of a protected status. I conclude that the legislature's action was eminently reasonable and does not violate principles of equal protection.

Why Abortion Is Immoral

Don Marquis

The view that abortion is, with rare exceptions, seriously immoral has received little support in the recent philosophical literature. No doubt most philosophers affiliated with

Don Marquis, "Why Abortion Is Immoral," *Journal of Philosophy* 86, Number 4 (April 1989): 183–202. Reprinted by permission from the author and the *Journal of Philosophy.*

secular institutions of higher education believe that the anti-abortion position is either a symptom of irrational religious dogma or a conclusion generated by seriously confused philosophical argument. The purpose of this essay is to undermine this general belief. This essay sets out an argument that purports to show, as well as any argument in ethics can show, that abortion is, except possibly in rare cases, seriously immoral, that it is in the same moral category as killing an innocent adult human being.

The argument is based on a major assumption. Many of the most insightful and careful writers on the ethics of abortion—such as Joel Feinberg, Michael Tooley, Mary Anne Warren, H. Tristram Engelhardt, Jr., L. W. Sumner, John T. Noonan, Jr., and Philip Devine[1]—believe that whether or not abortion is morally permissible stands or falls on whether or not a fetus is the sort of being whose life it is seriously wrong to end. The argument of this essay will assume, but not argue, that they are correct.

Also, this essay will neglect issues of great importance to a complete ethics of abortion. Some anti-abortionists will allow that certain abortions, such as abortion before implantation or abortion when the life of a woman is threatened by a pregnancy or abortion after rape, may be morally permissible. This essay will not explore the casuistry of these hard cases. The purpose of this essay is to develop a general argument for the claim that the overwhelming majority of deliberate abortions are seriously immoral.

I.

A sketch of standard anti-abortion and pro-choice arguments exhibits how those arguments possess certain symmetries that explain why partisans of those positions are so convinced of the correctness of their own positions, why they are not successful in convincing their opponents, and why, to others, this issue seems to be unresolvable. An analysis of the nature of this standoff suggests a strategy for surmounting it.

Consider the way a typical anti-abortionist argues. She will argue or assert that life is present from the moment of conception or that fetuses look like babies or that fetuses possess a characteristic such as a genetic code that is both necessary and sufficient for being human. Anti-abortionists seem to believe that (1) the truth of all of these claims is quite obvious, and (2) establishing any of these claims is sufficient to show that abortion is morally akin to murder.

A standard pro-choice strategy exhibits similarities. The pro-choicer will argue or assert that fetuses are not persons or that fetuses are not rational agents or that fetuses are not social beings. Pro-choicers seem to believe that (1) the truth of any of these claims is quite obvious, and (2) establishing any of these claims is sufficient to show that an abortion is not a wrongful killing.

In fact, both the pro-choice and the anti-abortion claims do seem to be true, although the "it looks like a baby" claim is more difficult to establish the earlier the pregnancy. We seem to have a standoff. How can it be resolved?

As everyone who has taken a bit of logic knows, if any of these arguments concerning abortion is a good argument, it requires not only some claim characterizing fetuses, but also some general moral principle that ties a characteristic of fetuses to having or not having the right to life or to some other moral characteristic that will generate the obligation or the lack of obligation not to end the life of a fetus. Accordingly, the arguments of the anti-abortionist and the pro-choicer need a bit of filling in to be regarded as adequate.

Note what each partisan will say. The anti-abortionist will claim that her position is supported by such generally accepted moral principles as "It is always prima facie seriously wrong to take a human life" or "It is always prima facie seriously wrong to end the life of a baby." Since these are generally accepted moral principles, her position is certainly not obviously wrong. The pro-choicer will claim that

[1]Feinberg, "Abortion," in *Matters of Life and Death: New Introductory Essays in Moral Philosophy*, Tom Regan, ed. (New York: Random House, 1986), pp. 256–293; Tooley, "Abortion and Infanticide," *Philosophy and Public Affairs*, II, 1 (1972):37–65, Tooley, *Abortion and Infanticide* (New York: Oxford, 1984); Warren, "On the Moral and Legal Status of Abortion," *The Monist*, LVII, 1 (1973): 43–61; Engelhardt, "The Ontology of Abortion," *Ethics*, IXXXIV, 3 (1974):217–234; Sumner, *Abortion and Moral Theory* (Princeton: University Press, 1981); Noonan, "An Almost Absolute Value in History," in *The Morality of Abortion: Legal and Historical Perspectives*, Noonan, ed. (Cambridge: Harvard, 1970); and Devine, *The Ethics of Homicide* (Ithaca: Cornell, 1978).

her position is supported by such plausible moral principles as "Being a person is what gives an individual intrinsic moral worth" or "It is only seriously prima facie wrong to take the life of a member of the human community." Since these are generally accepted moral principles, the pro-choice position is certainly not obviously wrong. Unfortunately, we have again arrived at a standoff.

Now, how might one deal with this standoff? The standard approach is to try to show how the moral principles of one's opponent lose their plausibility under analysis. It is easy to see how this is possible. On the one hand, the anti-abortionist will defend a moral principle concerning the wrongness of killing which tends to be broad in scope in order that even fetuses at an early stage of pregnancy will fall under it. The problem with broad principles is that they often embrace too much. In this particular instance, the principle "It is always prima facie wrong to take a human life" seems to entail that it is wrong to end the existence of a living human cancer-cell culture, on the grounds that the culture is both living and human. Therefore, it seems that the anti-abortionist's favored principle is too broad.

On the other hand, the pro-choicer wants to find a moral principle concerning the wrongness of killing which tends to be narrow in scope in order that fetuses will *not* fall under it. The problem with narrow principles is that they often do not embrace enough. Hence, the needed principles such as "It is prima facie seriously wrong to kill only persons" or "It is prima facie wrong to kill only rational agents" do not explain why it is wrong to kill infants or young children or the severely retarded or even perhaps the severely mentally ill. Therefore, we seem again to have a standoff. The anti-abortionist charges, not unreasonably, that pro-choice principles concerning killing are too narrow to be acceptable; the pro-choicer charges, not unreasonably, that anti-abortionist principles concerning killing are too broad to be acceptable.

Attempts by both sides to patch up the difficulties in their positions run into further difficulties. The anti-abortionist will try to remove the problem in her position by reformulating her principle concerning killing in terms of human beings. Now we end up with: "It is always prima facie seriously wrong to end the life of a human being." This principle has the advantage of avoiding the problem of the human cancer-cell culture counterexample. But this advantage is purchased at a high price. For although it is clear that a fetus is both human and alive, it is not at all clear that a fetus is a human *being*. There is at least something to be said for the view that something becomes a human being only after a process of development, and that therefore first trimester fetuses and perhaps all fetuses are not yet human beings. Hence, the anti-abortionist, by this move, has merely exchanged one problem for another.[2]

The pro-choicer fares no better. She may attempt to find reasons why killing infants, young children, and the severely retarded is wrong which are independent of her major principle that is supposed to explain the wrongness of taking human life, but which will not also make abortion immoral. This is no easy task. Appeals to social utility will seem satisfactory only to those who resolve not to think of the enormous difficulties with a utilitarian account of the wrongness of killing and the significant social costs of preserving the lives of the unproductive.[3] A pro-choice strategy that extends the definition of 'person' to infants or even to young children seems just as arbitrary as an anti-abortion strategy that extends the definition of 'human being' to fetuses. Again, we find symmetries in the two positions and we arrive at a standoff.

There are even further problems that reflect symmetries in the two positions. In addition to

[2]For interesting discussions of this issue, see Warren Quinn, "Abortion: Identity and Loss," *Philosophy and Public Affairs*, XIII, 1 (1984):24–54; and Lawrence C. Becker, "Human Being: The Boundaries of the Concept," *Philosophy and Public Affairs*, IV, 4 (1975):334–359.

[3]For example, see my "Ethics and The Elderly: Some Problems," in Stuart Spicker, Kathleen Woodward, and David Van Tassel, eds., *Aging and the Elderly: Humanistic Perspectives in Gerontology* (Atlantic Highlands, NJ: Humanities, 1978), pp. 341–355.

counterexample problems, or the arbitrary application problems that can be exchanged for them, the standard anti-abortionist principle "It is prima facie seriously wrong to kill a human being," or one of its variants, can be objected to on the grounds of ambiguity. If 'human being' is taken to be a *biological* category, then the anti-abortionist is left with the problem of explaining why a merely biological category should make a moral difference. Why, it is asked, is it any more reasonable to base a moral conclusion on the number of chromosomes in one's cells than on the color of one's skin?[4] If 'human being', on the other hand, is taken to be a *moral* category, then the claim that a fetus is a human being cannot be taken to be a premise in the anti-abortion argument, for it is precisely what needs to be established. Hence, either the anti-abortionist's main category is a morally irrelevant, merely biological category, or it is of no use to the anti-abortionist in establishing (noncircularly, of course) that abortion is wrong.

Although this problem with the anti-abortionist position is often noticed, it is less often noticed that the pro-choice position suffers from an analogous problem. The principle "Only persons have the right to life" also suffers from an ambiguity. The term 'person' is typically defined in terms of psychological characteristics, although there will certainly be disagreement concerning which characteristics are most important. Supposing that this matter can be settled, the pro-choicer is left with the problem of explaining why *psychological* characteristics should make a *moral* difference. If the pro-choicer should attempt to deal with this problem by claiming that an explanation is not necessary, that in fact we do treat such a cluster of psychological properties as having moral significance, the sharp-witted anti-abortionist should have a ready response. We do treat being both living and human as having moral significance. If it is legitimate for the pro-choicer to demand that the anti-abortionist provide an explanation of the connection

between the biological character of being a human being and the wrongness of being killed (even though people accept this connection), then it is legitimate for the anti-abortionist to demand that the pro-choicer provide an explanation of the connection between psychological criteria for being a person and the wrongness of being killed (even though that connection is accepted).[5]

Feinberg has attempted to meet this objection (he calls psychological personhood "commonsense personhood"):

The characteristics that confer commonsense personhood are not arbitrary bases for rights and duties, such as race, sex or species membership; rather they are traits that make sense out of rights and duties and without which those moral attributes would have no point or function. It is because people are conscious; have a sense of their personal identities; have plans, goals, and projects; experience emotions; are liable to pains, anxieties, and frustrations; can reason and bargain, and so on—it is because of these attributes that people have values and interests, desires and expectations of their own, including a stake in their own futures, and a personal well-being of a sort we cannot ascribe to unconscious or nonrational beings. Because of their developed capacities they can assume duties and responsibilities and can have and make claims on one another. Only because of their sense of self, their life plans, their value hierarchies, and their stakes in their own futures can they be ascribed fundamental rights. There is nothing arbitrary about these linkages (op. cit., p. 270).

The plausible aspects of this attempt should not be taken to obscure its implausible features. There is a great deal to be said for the view that being a psychological person under some description is a necessary condition for having duties. One cannot have a duty unless one is capable of behaving morally, and a being's capability of behaving morally will require having

---

[4]See Warren, op. cit., and Tooley, "Abortion and Infanticide."

[5]This seems to be the fatal flaw in Warren's treatment of this issue.

a certain psychology. It is far from obvious, however, that having rights entails consciousness or rationality, as Feinberg suggests. We speak of the rights of the severely retarded or the severely mentally ill, yet some of these persons are not rational. We speak of the rights of the temporarily unconscious. The New Jersey Supreme Court based their decision in the Quinlan case on Karen Ann Quinlan's right to privacy, and she was known to be permanently unconscious at that time. Hence, Feinberg's claim that having rights entails being conscious is, on its face, obviously false.

Of course, it might not make sense to attribute rights to a being that would never in its natural history have certain psychological traits. This modest connection between psychological personhood and moral personhood will create a place for Karen Ann Quinlan and the temporarily unconscious. But then it makes a place for fetuses also. Hence, it does not serve Feinberg's pro-choice purposes. Accordingly, it seems that the pro-choicer will have as much difficulty bridging the gap between psychological personhood and personhood in the moral sense as the anti-abortionist has bridging the gap between being a biological human being and being a human being in the moral sense.

Furthermore, the pro-choicer cannot any more escape her problem by making person a purely moral category than the anti-abortionist could escape by the analogous move. For if person is a moral category, then the pro-choicer is left without the resources for establishing (noncircularly, of course) the claim that a fetus is not a person, which is an essential premise in her argument. Again, we have both a symmetry and a standoff between pro-choice and antiabortion views.

Passions in the abortion debate run high. There are both plausibilities and difficulties with the standard positions. Accordingly, it is hardly surprising that partisans of either side embrace with fervor the moral generalizations that support the conclusions they preanalytically favor, and reject with disdain the moral generalizations of their opponents as being subject to inescapable difficulties. It is easy to believe that the counterexamples to one's own moral principles are merely temporary difficulties that will dissolve in the wake of further philosophical research, and that the counterexamples to the principles of one's opponents are as straightforward as the contradiction between A and O propositions in traditional logic. This might suggest to an impartial observer (if there are any) that the abortion issue is unresolvable.

There is a way out of this apparent dialectical quandary. The moral generalizations of both sides are not quite correct. The generalizations hold for the most part, for the usual cases. This suggests that they are all *accidental* generalizations, that the moral claims made by those on both sides of the dispute do not touch on the *essence* of the matter.

This use of the distinction between essence and accident is not meant to invoke obscure metaphysical categories. Rather, it is intended to reflect the rather atheoretical nature of the abortion discussion. If the generalization a partisan in the abortion dispute adopts were derived from the reason why ending the life of a human being is wrong, then there could not be exceptions to that generalization unless some special case obtains in which there are even more powerful countervailing reasons. Such generalizations would not be merely accidental generalizations; they would point to, or be based upon, the essence of the wrongness of killing, what it is that makes killing wrong. All this suggests that a necessary condition of resolving the abortion controversy is a more theoretical account of the wrongness of killing. After all, if we merely believe, but do not understand, why killing adult human beings such as ourselves is wrong, how could we conceivably show that abortion is either immoral or permissible?

II.

In order to develop such an account, we can start from the following unproblematic assumption concerning our own case: it is wrong to kill *us*.

Why is it wrong? Some answers can be easily eliminated. It might be said that what makes killing us wrong is that a killing brutalizes the one who kills. But the brutalization consists of being inured to the performance of an act that is hideously immoral; hence, the brutalization does not explain the immorality. It might be said that what makes killing us wrong is the great loss others would experience due to our absence. Although such hubris is understandable, such an explanation does not account for the wrongness of killing hermits, or those whose lives are relatively independent and whose friends find it easy to make new friends.

A more obvious answer is better. What primarily makes killing wrong is neither its effect on the murderer nor its effect on the victim's friends and relatives, but its effect on the victim. The loss of one's life is one of the greatest losses one can suffer. The loss of one's life deprives one of all the experiences, activities, projects, and enjoyments that would otherwise have constituted one's future. Therefore, killing someone is wrong, primarily because the killing inflicts (one of) the greatest possible losses on the victim. To describe this as the loss of life can be misleading, however. The change in my biological state does not by itself make killing me wrong. The effect of the loss of my biological life is the loss to me of all those activities, projects, experiences, and enjoyments which would otherwise have constituted my future personal life. These activities, projects, experiences, and enjoyments are either valuable for their own sakes or are means to something else that is valuable for its own sake. Some parts of my future are not valued by me now, but will come to be valued by me as I grow older and as my values and capacities change. When I am killed, I am deprived both of what I now value which would have been part of my future personal life, but also what I would come to value. Therefore, when I die, I am deprived of all of the value of my future. Inflicting this loss on me is ultimately what makes killing me wrong. This being the case, it would seem that what makes killing *any* adult human being prima facie seriously wrong is the loss of his or her future.[6]

How should this rudimentary theory of the wrongness of killing be evaluated? It cannot be faulted for deriving an 'ought' from an 'is', for it does not. The analysis assumes that killing me (or you, reader) is prima facie seriously wrong. The point of the analysis is to establish which natural property ultimately explains the wrongness of the killing, given that it is wrong. A natural property will ultimately explain the wrongness of killing, only if (1) the explanation fits with our intuitions about the matter and (2) there is no other natural property that provides the basis for a better explanation of the wrongness of killing. This analysis rests on the intuition that what makes killing a particular human or animal wrong is what it does to that particular human or animal. What makes killing wrong is some natural effect or other of the killing. Some would deny this. For instance, a divine command theorist in ethics would deny it. Surely this denial is, however, one of those features of divine-command theory which renders it so implausible.

The claim that what makes killing wrong is the loss of the victim's future is directly supported by two considerations. In the first place, this theory explains why we regard killing as one of the worst of crimes. Killing is especially wrong, because it deprives the victim of more than perhaps any other crime. In the second place, people with AIDS or cancer who know they are dying believe, of course, that dying is a very bad thing for them. They believe that the loss of a future to them that they would otherwise have experienced is what makes their premature death a very bad thing for them. A better theory of the wrongness of killing would require a different natural property associated with killing which better fits with the attitudes of the dying. What could it be?

---

[6]I have been most influenced on this matter by Jonathan Glover, *Causing Death and Saving Lives* (New York: Penguin, 1977), ch. 3; and Robert Young, "What Is So Wrong with Killing People?" *Philosophy*, LIV, 210 (1979):515–528.

The view that what makes killing wrong is the loss to the victim of the value of the victim's future gains additional support when some of its implications are examined. In the first place, it is incompatible with the view that it is wrong to kill only beings who are biologically human. It is possible that there exists a different species from another planet whose members have a future like ours. Since having a future like that is what makes killing someone wrong, this theory entails that it would be wrong to kill members of such a species. Hence, this theory is opposed to the claim that only life that is biologically human has great moral worth, a claim which many antiabortionists have seemed to adopt. This opposition, which this theory has in common with personhood theories, seems to be a merit of the theory.

In the second place, the claim that the loss of one's future is the wrong-making feature of one's being killed entails the possibility that the futures of some actual nonhuman mammals on our own planet are sufficiently like ours that it is seriously wrong to kill them also. Whether some animals do have the same right to life as human beings depends on adding to the account of the wrongness of killing some additional account of just what it is about my future or the futures of other adult human beings which makes it wrong to kill us. No such additional account will be offered in this essay. Undoubtedly, the provision of such an account would be a very difficult matter. Undoubtedly, any such account would be quite controversial. Hence, it surely should not reflect badly on this sketch of an elementary theory of the wrongness of killing that it is indeterminate with respect to some very difficult issues regarding animal rights.

In the third place, the claim that the loss of one's future is the wrong-making feature of one's being killed does not entail, as sanctity of human life theories do, that active euthanasia is wrong. Persons who are severely and incurably ill, who face a future of pain and despair, and who wish to die will not have suffered a loss if they are killed. It is, strictly speaking, the value of a human's future which makes killing wrong in this theory. This being so, killing does not necessarily wrong some persons who are sick and dying. Of course, there may be other reasons for a prohibition of active euthanasia, but that is another matter. Sanctity-of-human-life theories seem to hold that active euthanasia is seriously wrong even in an individual case where there seems to be good reason for it independently of public policy considerations. This consequence is most implausible, and it is a plus for the claim that the loss of a future of value is what makes killing wrong that it does not share this consequence.

In the fourth place, the account of the wrongness of killing defended in this essay does straightforwardly entail that it is prima facie seriously wrong to kill children and infants, for we do presume that they have futures of value. Since we do believe that it is wrong to kill defenseless little babies, it is important that a theory of the wrongness of killing easily account for this. Personhood theories of the wrongness of killing, on the other hand, cannot straightforwardly account for the wrongness of killing infants and young children.[7] Hence, such theories must add special ad hoc accounts of the wrongness of killing the young. The plausibility of such ad hoc theories seems to be a function of how desperately one wants such theories to work. The claim that the primary wrong-making feature of a killing is the loss to the victim of the value of its future accounts for the wrongness of killing young children and infants directly; it makes the wrongness of such acts as obvious as we actually think it is. This is a further merit of this theory. Accordingly, it seems that this value of a future-like-ours theory of the wrongness of killing shares strengths of both sanctity-of-life and personhood accounts while avoiding weaknesses of both. In addition, it meshes with a central intuition concerning what makes killing wrong.

The claim that the primary wrong-making feature of a killing is the loss to the victim of the value of its future has obvious consequences for the ethics of abortion. The future of a standard fetus includes a set of experiences,

[7]Feinberg, Tooley, Warren, and Engelhardt have all dealt with this problem.

projects, activities, and such which are identical with the futures of adult human beings and are identical with the futures of young children. Since the reason that is sufficient to explain why it is wrong to kill human beings after the time of birth is a reason that also applies to fetuses, it follows that abortion is prima facie seriously morally wrong.

This argument does not rely on the invalid inference that, since it is wrong to kill persons, it is wrong to kill potential persons also. The category that is morally central to this analysis is the category of having a valuable future like ours; it is not the category of personhood. The argument to the conclusion that abortion is prima facie seriously morally wrong proceeded independently of the notion of person or potential person or any equivalent. Someone may wish to start with this analysis in terms of the value of a human future, conclude that abortion is, except perhaps in rare circumstances, seriously morally wrong, infer that fetuses have the right to life, and then call fetuses "persons" as a result of their having the right to life. Clearly, in this case, the category of person is being used to state the *conclusion* of the analysis rather than to generate the *argument* of the analysis.

The structure of this anti-abortion argument can be both illuminated and defended by comparing it to what appears to be the best argument for the wrongness of the wanton infliction of pain on animals. This latter argument is based on the assumption that it is prima facie wrong to inflict pain on me (or you, reader). What is the natural property associated with the infliction of pain which makes such infliction wrong? The obvious answer seems to be that the infliction of pain causes suffering and that suffering is a misfortune. The suffering caused by the infliction of pain is what makes the wanton infliction of pain on me wrong. The wanton infliction of pain on other adult humans causes suffering. The wanton infliction of pain on animals causes suffering. Since causing suffering is what makes the wanton infliction of pain wrong and since the wanton infliction of pain on animals causes suffering, it follows that the wanton infliction of pain on animals is wrong.

This argument for the wrongness of the wanton infliction of pain on animals shares a number of structural features with the argument for the serious prima facie wrongness of abortion. Both arguments start with an obvious assumption concerning what it is wrong to do to me (or you, reader). Both then look for the characteristic or the consequence of the wrong action which makes the action wrong. Both recognize that the wrong-making feature of these immoral actions is a property of actions sometimes directed at individuals other than postnatal human beings. If the structure of the argument for the wrongness of the wanton infliction of pain on animals is sound, then the structure of the argument for the prima facie serious wrongness of abortion is also sound, for the structure of the two arguments is the same. The structure common to both is the key to the explanation of how the wrongness of abortion can be demonstrated without recourse to the category of person. In neither argument is that category crucial.

This defense of an argument for the wrongness of abortion in terms of a structurally similar argument for the wrongness of the wanton infliction of pain on animals succeeds only if the account regarding animals is the correct account. Is it? In the first place, it seems plausible. In the second place, its major competition is Kant's account. Kant believed that we do not have direct duties to animals at all, because they are not persons. Hence, Kant had to explain and justify the wrongness of inflicting pain on animals on the grounds that "he who is hard in his dealings with animals becomes hard also in his dealing with men."[8] The problem with Kant's account is that there seems to be no reason for accepting this latter claim unless Kant's account is rejected. If the alternative to Kant's account is accepted, then it is easy to understand why someone who is indifferent to inflicting pain on animals is also indifferent to inflicting pain on humans, for one is indifferent to what makes inflicting pain wrong in both cases. But, if Kant's account is accepted, there

---

[8]"Duties to Animals and Spirits," in *Lectures on Ethics*, Louis Infeld, trans. (New York: Harper, 1963), p. 239.

is no intelligible reason why one who is hard in his dealings with animals (or crabgrass or stones) should also be hard in his dealings with men. After all, men are persons: animals are no more persons than crabgrass or stones. Persons are Kant's crucial moral category. Why, in short, should a Kantian accept the basic claim in Kant's argument?

Hence, Kant's argument for the wrongness of inflicting pain on animals rests on a claim that, in a world of Kantian moral agents, is demonstrably false. Therefore, the alternative analysis, being more plausible anyway, should be accepted. Since this alternative analysis has the same structure as the anti-abortion argument being defended here, we have further support for the argument for the immorality of abortion being defended in this essay.

Of course, this value of a future-like-ours argument, if sound, shows only that abortion is prima facie wrong, not that it is wrong in any and all circumstances. Since the loss of the future to a standard fetus, if killed, is, however, at least as great a loss as the loss of the future to a standard adult human being who is killed, abortion, like ordinary killing, could be justified only by the most compelling reasons. The loss of one's life is almost the greatest misfortune that can happen to one. Presumably abortion could be justified in some circumstances, only if the loss consequent on failing to abort would be at least as great. Accordingly, morally permissible abortions will be rare indeed unless, perhaps, they occur so early in pregnancy that a fetus is not yet definitely an individual. Hence, this argument should be taken as showing that abortion is presumptively very seriously wrong, where the presumption is very strong—as strong as the presumption that killing another adult human being is wrong.

III.

How complete an account of the wrongness of killing does the value of a future-like-ours account have to be in order that the wrongness of abortion is a consequence? This account does not have to be an account of the necessary conditions for the wrongness of killing. Some

persons in nursing homes may lack valuable human futures, yet it may be wrong to kill them for other reasons. Furthermore, this account does not obviously have to be the sole reason killing is wrong where the victim did have a valuable future. This analysis claims only that, for any killing where the victim did have a valuable future like ours, having that future by itself is sufficient to create the strong presumption that the killing is seriously wrong.

One way to overturn the value of a future-like-ours argument would be to find some account of the wrongness of killing which is at least as intelligible and which has different implications for the ethics of abortion. Two rival accounts possess at least some degree of plausibility. One account is based on the obvious fact that people value the experience of living and wish for that valuable experience to continue. Therefore, it might be said, what makes killing wrong is the discontinuation of that experience for the victim. Let us call this the *discontinuation account*.[9] Another rival account is based upon the obvious fact that people strongly desire to continue to live. This suggests that what makes killing us so wrong is that it interferes with the fulfillment of a strong and fundamental desire, the fulfillment of which is necessary for the fulfillment of any other desires we might have. Let us call this the *desire account*.[10]

Consider first the desire account as a rival account of the ethics of killing which would provide the basis for rejecting the anti-abortion position. Such an account will have to be stronger than the value of a future-like-ours account of the wrongness of abortion if it is to do the job expected of it. To entail the wrongness of abortion, the value of a future-like-ours account has only to provide a sufficient, but not a necessary, condition for the wrongness of killing. The desire account, on the other hand, must provide us also with a necessary condition

---

[9]I am indebted to Jack Bricke for raising this objection.

[10]Presumably a preference utilitarian would press such an objection. Tooley once suggested that his account has such a theoretical underpinning. See his "Abortion and Infanticide," pp. 44/5.

for the wrongness of killing in order to generate a pro-choice conclusion on abortion. The reason for this is that presumably the argument from the desire account moves from the claim that what makes killing wrong is interference with a very strong desire to the claim that abortion is not wrong because the fetus lacks a strong desire to live. Obviously, this inference fails if someone's having the desire to live is not a necessary condition of its being wrong to kill that individual.

One problem with the desire account is that we do regard it as seriously wrong to kill persons who have little desire to live or who have no desire to live or, indeed, have a desire not to live. We believe it is seriously wrong to kill the unconscious, the sleeping, those who are tired of life, and those who are suicidal. The value-of-a-human-future account renders standard morality intelligible in these cases; these cases appear to be incompatible with the desire account.

The desire account is subject to a deeper difficulty. We desire life, because we value the goods of this life. The goodness of life is not secondary to our desire for it. If this were not so, the pain of one's own premature death could be done away with merely by an appropriate alteration in the configuration of one's desires. This is absurd. Hence, it would seem that it is the loss of the goods of one's future, not the interference with the fulfillment of a strong desire to live, which accounts ultimately for the wrongness of killing.

It is worth noting that, if the desire account is modified so that it does not provide a necessary, but only a sufficient, condition for the wrongness of killing, the desire account is compatible with the value of a future-like-ours account. The combined accounts will yield an anti-abortion ethic. This suggests that one can retain what is intuitively plausible about the desire account without a challenge to the basic argument of this paper.

It is also worth noting that, if future desires have moral force in a modified desire account of the wrongness of killing, one can find support for an anti-abortion ethic even in the absence of a value of a future-like-ours account.

If one decides that a morally relevant property, the possession of which is sufficient to make it wrong to kill some individual, is the desire at some future time to live—one might decide to justify one's refusal to kill suicidal teenagers on these grounds, for example—then, since typical fetuses will have the desire in the future to live, it is wrong to kill typical fetuses. Accordingly, it does not seem that a desire account of the wrongness of killing can provide a justification of a pro-choice ethic of abortion which is nearly as adequate as the value of a human-future justification of an anti-abortion ethic.

The discontinuation account looks more promising as an account of the wrongness of killing. It seems just as intelligible as the value of a future-like-ours account, but it does not justify an anti-abortion position. Obviously, if it is the continuation of one's activities, experiences, and projects, the loss of which makes killing wrong, then it is not wrong to kill fetuses for that reason, for fetuses do not have experiences, activities, and projects to be continued or discontinued. Accordingly, the discontinuation account does not have the anti-abortion consequences that the value of a future-like-ours account has. Yet, it seems as intelligible as the value of a future-like-ours account, for when we think of what would be wrong with our being killed, it does seem as if it is the discontinuation of what makes our lives worthwhile which makes killing us wrong.

Is the discontinuation account just as good an account as the value of a future-like-ours account? The discontinuation account will not be adequate at all, if it does not refer to the *value* of the experience that may be discontinued. One does not want the discontinuation account to make it wrong to kill a patient who begs for death and who is in severe pain that cannot be relieved short of killing. (I leave open the question of whether it is wrong for other reasons.) Accordingly, the discontinuation account must be more than a bare discontinuation account. It must make some reference to the positive value of the patient's experiences. But, by the same token, the value of a future-like-ours account cannot be a bare future account either. Just having a future surely does not itself rule out killing the above patient. This account must make some reference to the value of the patient's future experiences and projects also. Hence, both accounts involve the value of experiences, projects, and activities. So far we still have symmetry between the accounts.

The symmetry fades, however, when we focus on the time period of the value of the experiences, etc., which has moral consequences. Although both accounts leave open the possibility that the patient in our example may be killed, this possibility is left open only in virtue of the utterly bleak future for the patient. It makes no difference whether the patient's immediate past contains intolerable pain, or consists in being in a coma (which we can imagine is a situation of indifference), or consists in a life of value. If the patient's future is a future of value, we want our account to make it wrong to kill the patient. If the patient's future is intolerable, whatever his or her immediate past, we want our account to allow killing the patient. Obviously, then, it is the value of that patient's future which is doing the work in rendering the morality of killing the patient intelligible.

This being the case, it seems clear that whether one has immediate past experiences or not does no work in the explanation of what makes killing wrong. The addition the discontinuation account makes to the value of a human future account is otiose. Its addition to the value-of-a-future account plays no role at all in rendering intelligible the wrongness of killing. Therefore, it can be discarded with the discontinuation account of which it is a part.

IV.

The analysis of the previous section suggests that alternative general accounts of the wrongness of killing are either inadequate or unsuccessful in getting around the anti-abortion consequences of the value of a future-like-ours argument. A different strategy for avoiding these anti-abortion consequences involves limiting the scope of the value of a future argument. More precisely, the strategy involves

arguing that fetuses lack a property that is essential for the value-of-a-future argument (or for any anti-abortion argument) to apply to them.

One move of this sort is based upon the claim that a necessary condition of one's future being valuable is that one values it. Value implies a valuer. Given this one might argue that, since fetuses cannot value their futures, their futures are not valuable to them. Hence, it does not seriously wrong them deliberately to end their lives.

This move fails, however, because of some ambiguities. Let us assume that something cannot be of value unless it is valued by someone. This does not entail that my life is of no value unless it is valued by me. I may think, in a period of despair, that my future is of no worth whatsoever, but I may be wrong because others rightly see value—even great value—in it. Furthermore, my future can be valuable to me even if I do not value it. This is the case when a young person attempts suicide, but is rescued and goes on to significant human achievements. Such young people's futures are ultimately valuable to them, even though such futures do not seem to be valuable to them at the moment of attempted suicide. A fetus's future can be valuable to it in the same way. Accordingly, this attempt to limit the anti-abortion argument fails.

Another similar attempt to reject the anti-abortion position is based on Tooley's claim that an entity cannot possess the right to life unless it has the capacity to desire its continued existence. It follows that, since fetuses lack the conceptual capacity to desire to continue to live, they lack the right to life. Accordingly, Tooley concludes that abortion cannot be seriously prima facie wrong (op. cit., pp. 46/7).

What could be the evidence for Tooley's basic claim? Tooley once argued that individuals have a prima facie right to what they desire and that the lack of the capacity to desire something undercuts the basis of one's right to it (op. cit., pp. 44/5). This argument plainly will not succeed in the context of the analysis of this essay, however, since the point here is to establish the fetus's right to life on other grounds. Tooley's argument assumes that the right to life cannot be established in general on some basis other than the desire for life. This position was considered and rejected in the preceding section of this paper.

One might attempt to defend Tooley's basic claim on the grounds that, because a fetus cannot apprehend continued life as a benefit, its continued life cannot be a benefit or cannot be something it has a right to or cannot be something that is in its interest. This might be defended in terms of the general proposition that, if an individual is literally incapable of caring about or taking an interest in some X, then one does not have a right to X or X is not a benefit or X is not something that is in one's interest.[11]

Each member of this family of claims seems to be open to objections. As John C. Stevens[12] has pointed out, one may have a right to be treated with a certain medical procedure (because of a health insurance policy one has purchased), even though one cannot conceive of the nature of the procedure. And, as Tooley himself has pointed out, persons who have been indoctrinated, or drugged, or rendered temporarily unconscious may be literally incapable of caring about or taking an interest in something that is in their interest or is something to which they have a right, or is something that benefits them. Hence, the Tooley claim that would restrict the scope of the value of a future-like-ours argument is undermined by counterexamples.[13]

Finally, Paul Bassen[14] has argued that, even though the prospects of an embryo might seem to be a basis for the wrongness of abortion, an embryo cannot be a victim and therefore cannot be wronged. An embryo cannot be a victim, he says, because it lacks sentience. His central argument for this seems to be that, even though plants and the permanently unconscious are alive, they clearly cannot be victims. What is the explanation of this? Bassen claims that the explanation is that their lives consist of mere metabolism and mere metabolism is not enough to ground victimizability. Mentation is required.

The problem with this attempt to establish the absence of victimizability is that both plants and the permanently unconscious clearly lack what Bassen calls "prospects" or what I have called "a future life like ours." Hence, it is surely open to one to argue that the real reason we believe plants and the permanently unconscious cannot be victims is that killing them cannot deprive them of a future life like ours; the real reason is not their absence of present mentation.

Bassen recognizes that his view is subject to this difficulty, and he recognizes that the case of children seems to support this difficulty, for "much of what we do for children is based on prospects." He argues, however, that, in the case of children and in other such cases, "potentiality comes into play only where victimizability has been secured on other grounds" (ibid., p. 333).

Bassen's defense of his view is patently question-begging, since what is adequate to secure victimizability is exactly what is at issue. His examples do not support his own view against the thesis of this essay. Of course, embryos can be victims: when their lives are deliberately terminated, they are deprived of their futures of value, their prospects. This makes them victims, for it directly wrongs them.

The seeming plausibility of Bassen's view stems from the fact that paradigmatic cases of imagining someone as a victim involve empathy, and empathy requires mentation of the victim. The victims of flood, famine, rape, or child abuse are all persons with whom we can empathize. That empathy seems to be part of seeing them as victims.[15]

---

[11]Donald VanDeVeer seems to think this is self-evident. See his "Whither Baby Doe?" in *Matters of Life and Death*, p. 233.

[12]"Must the Bearer of a Right Have the Concept of That to Which He Has a Right?" *Ethics*, XCV, 1 (1984):68–74.

[13]See Tooley again in "Abortion and Infanticide," pp. 47–49.

[14]"Present Sakes and Future Prospects: The Status of Early Abortion," *Philosophy and Public Affairs*, XI, 4 (1982): 322–326.

[15]Note carefully the reasons he gives on the bottom of p. 316.

In spite of the strength of these examples, the attractive intuition that a situation in which there is victimization requires the possibility of empathy is subject to counterexamples. Consider a case that Bassen himself offers: "Posthumous obliteration of an author's work constitutes a misfortune for him only if he had wished his work to endure" (op cit., p. 318). The conditions Bassen wishes to impose upon the possibility of being victimized here seem far too strong. Perhaps this author, due to his unrealistic standards of excellence and his low self-esteem, regarded his work as unworthy of survival, even though it possessed genuine literary merit. Destruction of such work would surely victimize its author. In such a case, empathy with the victim concerning the loss is clearly impossible.

Of course, Bassen does not make the possibility of empathy a necessary condition of victimizability; he requires only mentation. Hence, on Bassen's actual view, this author, as I have described him, can be a victim. The problem is that the basic intuition that renders Bassen's view plausible is missing in the author's case. In order to attempt to avoid counterexamples, Bassen has made his thesis too weak to be supported by the intuitions that suggested it.

Even so, the mentation requirement on victimizability is still subject to counterexamples. Suppose a severe accident renders me totally unconscious for a month, after which I recover. Surely killing me while I am unconscious victimizes me, even though I am incapable of mentation during that time. It follows that Bassen's thesis fails. Apparently, attempts to restrict the value of a future-like-ours argument so that fetuses do not fall within its scope do not succeed.

V.

In this essay, it has been argued that the correct ethic of the wrongness of killing can be extended to fetal life and used to show that there is a strong presumption that any abortion is morally impermissible. If the ethic of killing adopted here entails, however, that contraception is also seriously immoral, then there would appear to be a difficulty with the analysis of this essay.

But this analysis does not entail that contraception is wrong. Of course, contraception prevents the actualization of a possible future of value. Hence, it follows from the claim that futures of value should be maximized that contraception is prima facie immoral. This obligation to maximize does not exist, however; furthermore, nothing in the ethics of killing in this paper entails that it does. The ethics of killing in this essay would entail that contraception is wrong only if something were denied a human future of value by contraception. Nothing at all is denied such a future by contraception, however.

Candidates for a subject of harm by contraception fall into four categories: (1) some sperm or other, (2) some ovum or other, (3) a sperm and an ovum separately, and (4) a sperm and an ovum together. Assigning the harm to some sperm is utterly arbitrary, for no reason can be given for making a sperm the subject of harm rather than an ovum. Assigning the harm to some ovum is utterly arbitrary, for no reason can be given for making an ovum the subject of harm rather than a sperm. One might attempt to avoid these problems by insisting that contraception deprives both the sperm and the ovum separately of a valuable future like ours. On this alternative, too many futures are lost. Contraception was supposed to be wrong, because it deprived us of one future of value, not two. One might attempt to avoid this problem by holding that contraception deprives the combination of sperm and ovum of a valuable future like ours. But here the definite article misleads. At the time of contraception, there are hundreds of millions of sperm, one (released) ovum and millions of possible combinations of all of these. There is no actual combination at all. Is the subject of the loss to be a merely possible combination? Which one? This alternative does not yield an actual subject of harm either. Accordingly, the immorality of contraception is not entailed by the loss of a future-like-ours argument simply because there is no nonarbitrarily identifiable subject of the loss in the case of contraception.

VI.

The purpose of this essay has been to set out an argument for the serious presumptive wrongness of abortion subject to the assumption that the moral permissibility of abortion stands or falls on the moral status of the fetus. Since a fetus possesses a property, the possession of which in adult human beings is sufficient to make killing an adult human being wrong, abortion is wrong. This way of dealing with the problem of abortion seems superior to other approaches to the ethics of abortion, because it rests on an ethics of killing which is close to self-evident, because the crucial morally relevant property clearly applies to fetuses, and because the argument avoids the usual equivocations on 'human life', 'human being', or 'person'. The argument rests neither on religious claims nor on Papal dogma. It is not subject to the objection of "speciesism." Its soundness is compatible with the moral permissibility of euthanasia and contraception. It deals with our intuitions concerning young children.

Finally, this analysis can be viewed as resolving a standard problem—indeed, *the* standard problem—concerning the ethics of abortion. Clearly, it is wrong to kill adult human beings. Clearly, it is not wrong to end the life of some arbitrarily chosen single human cell. Fetuses seem to be like arbitrarily chosen human cells in some respects and like adult humans in other respects. The problem of the ethics of abortion is the problem of determining the fetal property that settles this moral controversy. The thesis of this essay is that the problem of the ethics of abortion, so understood, is solvable.

Abortion, Infanticide, and the Asymmetric Value of Human Life

Jeffrey Reiman

> Why . . . has it been imagined that to die is an evil—when it is clear that not to have been, before our birth, was no evil?
>
> —Voltaire

1. LOVE, RESPECT, AND THE ASYMMETRIC VALUE OF HUMAN LIFE

The pro-life position on abortion is that abortion is morally wrong because a fetus is an innocent human being, and killing it is, at least

Jeffrey Reiman, "Abortion, Infanticide, and the Asymmetric Value of Human Life," *Journal of Social Philosophy* 27, Number 3 (Winter 1996): 181–200. Reprinted by permission from the *Journal of Social Philosophy*.

morally speaking, murder.[1] This claim doesn't challenge our normal way of evaluating something morally as murder. On the contrary, it appeals to that normal evaluation and insists that, according to it, killing fetuses counts as murder. Our normal evaluation of a killing as murder hinges on our normal valuation of the lives of those whom we think it uncontroversially wrong to kill, namely, children and adults. Rational assessment of the pro-life position, then, requires determining whether there is something about fetuses that provides a plausible basis for applying to them the value we normally apply to the lives of children and adults.[2] In conducting this assessment, we are aided by a clue that has been largely overlooked in the abortion debate, namely, that the way we normally value human life is quite unusual, quite unlike the normal way in which we value other things. This has the consequence that only a very specific kind of feature of humans at any stage can provide a plausible basis for the normal valuation. I shall follow out this clue and show that there is something about children and adults that provides a plausible basis for the way we value their lives, but there is nothing about fetuses that will do the job. The result is a refutation of the pro-life position, and a defense of the pro-choice position on abortion.

The question whether killing fetuses is wrong for the same reasons we think it wrong to kill children or adults is more general than whether a fetus has a right to life. To avoid the mistake of thinking that having a right to life is the only moral basis for the wrongness of destroying a human life[3] we look for whatever might make it wrong to kill humans generally and see if this applies to fetuses. Of course, if it is not wrong to kill fetuses for the same reasons that it is wrong to kill humans generally, it might be wrong on other grounds.[4] I shall not pursue this, however, since it seems extremely unlikely that such grounds could be strong enough to justify requiring a woman to stay pregnant against her will (especially in these days of abundant reproduction). In any event, it is an implication of my argument here that there is nothing about fetuses which could provide a plausible basis for thinking that their lives should be protected in the way we protect the lives of children or adults.

There are some pro-choicers who think that the abortion dispute can be settled without addressing the moral status of the fetus. They think the fact (and I regard it as a fact) that a woman has a right to control her body is enough to justify her right to abortion. But, this is not enough because the right to control one's body ends if it comes up against a being with comparable moral status—"your right to

swing your fist ends where my nose begins," and all that.[5] So we shall still have to figure out if the fetus has a moral status comparable to that of the woman carrying it. On the other hand, there are even some arguments in favor of a woman's right to abortion that accept per argumentum that killing a fetus is as seriously wrong as killing a human adult. But such arguments can at best give a woman a right to expel an unwanted fetus from her body, and only to end its life if necessary for the expulsion.[6] As early as a living fetus can be safely and easily removed from a pregnant woman, her right to abortion might be transformed into a duty to provide extrauterine care for her expelled fetus. If (when!) medical technology pushes this point back toward the earliest moments of pregnancy, the right to abortion will disappear entirely. The surest way to secure a woman's right to abortion is to show that nothing about fetuses warrants including them under our normal way of valuing human life. And for this, we get some help from Voltaire.

Voltaire's question, quoted at the outset,[7] reminds us that we normally believe the moral wrongness of killing human beings to be something much worse than not creating them (if the latter is bad at all). This implies that the loss that results from ending a human life underway is much worse than the loss that would have been the result of not starting that life. In short, we normally think that murder is much worse than failure to procreate via contraception or voluntary abstinence. But, this means that the value of a human life is quite unusual: it is temporally *asymmetric*.

The standard kind of value is temporally *symmetric*. Normally, if something has x units of value, then destroying it (after it exists) and intentionally not producing it (before it exists) equally deprive the world of x units of value. Or, equivalently, that it has that value is equally a reason (before it exists) for a suitably situated moral agent to produce one and a reason (after it exists) for that agent to refrain from destroying it.

One way the value of something existing may seem not to be symmetric is that destroying the existent thing wastes the effort that already went into producing it, while not producing it does not. Likewise, trying to produce a new one courts a risk of failure, while an existing one is a sure thing. Thus, it would be more precise to say that the standard way in which something is thought to have value is symmetric except for considerations of wasted effort and uncertainty. However, these considerations are not large enough to account for the very large moral difference that people generally think exists between killing an existing human being and not bringing a new one into existence. Consequently, I shall say that a value is symmetric if the only difference between the value of producing it and the value of not destroying it stem from considerations of already invested effort and newly faced risk.[8] Thus, I will continue to say the value of normally valued things is symmetric, while the value we place on human life is asymmetric.

The upshot is that to determine whether killing a fetus is morally wrong for the same reasons that killing human beings generally is thought to be wrong, we need to figure out whether there is anything about the fetus that provides a plausible basis for thinking it is asymmetrically disvaluable—or, as I shall sometimes say, asymmetrically wrong—to end its life. Is there anything about the fetus that makes it seriously worse to kill it than not to have produced it, because of contraception or voluntary abstinence practiced by fertile couples? Though I don't argue for it here, I think that contraception and abstinence are not morally wrong at all. Nonetheless, my argument will work even if these are thought to be moderately wrong, since even people who think contraception is wrong think that abortion is much worse, and very few people who think that abortion is gravely evil think that abstinence is.

To help us think about the different ways in which things might have value, I want to distinguish roughly between the ways in which *love* and respect each value their objects. Love, though it may be triggered by the appeal of certain traits or properties of the beloved, comes to value the beloved as such—"unconditionally," we sometimes say—and thus values

the sheer existence of the beloved. Respect, though it is aimed at individuals, is, in my view, a way of honoring some property possessed by the respected one, where "honoring" involves at least not interfering with the normal functioning of that property. Thus, for Kant, we are to respect human beings because they possess the trait of rational agency, and we do so by honoring that property, which is to say, not interfering with or undermining the normal functioning of their rational agency.[9] Further, love is *given* freely by the lover, while respect is *deserved* by the respected because of the property she possesses. Love expresses the will of the lover, while respect responds to the worth of the respected.

Now, I think that there are only two possible ways in which something can have asymmetric value: either its existence itself (somehow) gives it a value that is not temporally symmetric, or its value is the value it has to itself or someone else. Some important writers—for example, Ronald Dworkin[10]—adopt the first alternative, and I think that the assumption that existence does add asymmetric value is tacitly held by many people who think that abortion is morally questionable. Consequently, I shall take it up in section 2, "The Priority of Morality over Metaphysics in the Abortion Question," and try to show that, to paraphrase Kant, existence is not a morally relevant property.[11] Since love cherishes the sheer existence of its object, while respect honors some property possessed by its object, I speculate that the widespread error of thinking that existence as such lends value is the result of confusing love with respect. And then "the priority of morality over metaphysics in the abortion question" implies "the priority of respect over love in the abortion question."

The second way in which something might have asymmetric value is more promising. if the value of something lies in its value to itself or to someone else, then its value only exists for itself or someone else. With our focus on the normal valuation of human life, we can eliminate the "someone else" from this formulation, since a human life is thought to have its value even if no one else cares about the individual whose life it is. If, then, the value of life is its value to the one whose life it is and who cares about its continuation, then its value only exists for the one who cares about it, and only once it is cared about and not before. And that gives us asymmetric value. Note that, here, respect has priority over love. It is not so much that we care about the one whose life it is, or care about what she cares about, as it is that we respect her because she possesses the property of caring about her life and we do so by honoring that property, which is to say, not interfering with or undermining her having what she cares about. I shall defend this account of the asymmetric value of human life in section 3. As confirmation, in section 4, I shall show how the account supports the widely held (but vaguely formulated) view that it is only once humans are *persons* that it is seriously wrong to kill them.

One implication of my argument that may trouble some readers is that the life of newborn infants is not yet asymmetrically valuable. However, this doesn't imply that it is okay to kill infants, but rather that, if infanticide is morally wrong, it is wrong on other grounds and in a different way than the killing of children and adults. I take this up in section 5, "The Priority of Love over Respect in the Infanticide Question."

2. THE PRIORITY OF MORALITY OVER METAPHYSICS IN THE ABORTION QUESTION

There are, broadly speaking, two ways to approach the question of abortion, which we can call the metaphysical way and the moral way. The metaphysical way is to start with a human being that it seems uncontroversially wrong to kill and work backwards to see if the fetus is, so to speak, a phase of this same individual entity. For example, up until the end of the first two weeks of pregnancy, a zygote or embryo may split into identical twins, who have the same genetic code and yet become two unique human beings. Noting this, Norman Ford maintains that starting at two weeks the fetus is the same individual entity which, in the normal

course of events, will become a full-fledged person and thus ought to have its life protected from then on.[12] One reason that this approach is bound to fail is that the assumption that being a human individual is enough to earn one moral protection of one's life smacks of *speciesism*— arbitrary or dogmatic preference for our own species.[13] Once we recognize that what makes the killing of human beings seriously wrong cannot be the sheer fact of their membership in the human species, the wrongness must be based on a property (it could be one or more features) that human beings normally have, but which could in principle turn up in other species.

Accordingly, we are looking for a property, not a kind. Of course, the property might be just that by which we identify beings as of a certain kind; but even then—even if the property is strictly coterminous with the kind (for example, rationality in the case of humans)— it will be the property that does the moral work, not the kind.[14] On the other hand, once it is clear that it is a property we seek, it cannot be taken for granted that the property is conterminous with the kind. We look for a property (ever) possessed by human beings which explains the wrongness of killing them, all the while leaving open the question whether the property is possessed by all human beings or at all stages. We answer the abortion question by determining whether that property is possessed by fetuses. This is the moral approach to the question, which I shall follow.

There is yet a deeper way in which morality has priority over metaphysics in answering the abortion question. Imagine that we found the special property that is the basis of our objection to killing humans, and suppose that this property is something (for example, a functioning cerebral cortex)[15] that emerges in the seventh month of pregnancy. Someone following the metaphysical approach outlined in the previous paragraphs might be tempted to say that the fetus from two weeks on is the same continuous self-identical individual as will have the special property at seven months, and thus it would be as wrong to kill it at two weeks as it is at seven months. If this were so, it would follow as well that the fetus is entitled to vote, since it is also the same continuous self-identical individual as will have that right at age eighteen. What's wrong in this argument is not the assumption that the being that traverses the span from conception to death is a self-identical individual. That is a more or less natural extension of the common belief that a human being from birth to death is a self-identical individual—the one named by its proper name.

The argument goes wrong by confusing metaphysical identity with moral identity, or assuming that the former entails the latter. Metaphysical identity from conception on means that the being is the same individual in all its temporal phases. Moral identity would mean that it has the same moral status in all its temporal phases, or at least, that earlier phases have a moral claim on the properties (and thus the moral status) possessed at later phases. If we are to grant the metaphysical identity of the human from conception on and avoid the inference that the fetus currently has the right to vote, we must grant that metaphysical identity is not equivalent to, and does not imply, moral identity. Here morality is prior to metaphysics in the sense that metaphysical identity will not supply us with the moral status needed to answer the abortion question: Rather than looking for the (metaphysical) beginning of the human individual that somewhere down the line has a life it is wrong to take, we must look for the (morally relevant) property that makes it wrong to take a human life, and see when the human individual starts to have that property.

The priority of morality over metaphysics has important implications for the significance of *existence* in the abortion debate. It may turn out that the fetus possesses from the moment of conception the property that makes killing it seriously wrong, and then its metaphysical and moral identity in this regard will coincide. However, given the possibility that this property is acquired later (either during pregnancy or later still), then the fetus may exist for some time without the property. Since the fetus's metaphysical identity with the human being

that will have the property does not entail their moral identity, it follows that the pre-property fetus has no moral claim to the property. Moreover, since what the property gives is precisely the moral wrongness of stopping the fetus from continuing on to later phases, there is nothing morally wrong with ending the fetus's life before the property is there. The fetus's existence prior to its possession of the property gives it no moral claim to continue existing. And, if the pre-property fetus has no moral claim to get the property, then there is no moral difference between a fetus that stops existing before it gets the property and a fetus that never starts to exist.

If this seems counterintuitive, I think it's because we tend to read a kind of personal identity backwards into fetuses, and personal identity carries connotations of moral identity beyond mere metaphysical identity. If we think of the pre-property fetus as a kind of quasi-person "who" loses the chance to have the special property, then we will think of the pre-property fetus as a person-like victim—which is a moral status that a not-yet-existing fetus lacks. Just because it is so natural to us to think this way, I believe that this ("retroactive empersonment") is the single greatest source of confusion in the abortion debate. If we resist it, then that the fetus has already been existing has no bearing on the moral status of its loss of future existence. Consequently, that loss is morally equivalent to the simple failure of that future stretch of fetal life to begin. And, then, it is no worse morally to end the life of a pre-property fetus than to refuse to produce a new one. Existence as such cannot provide asymmetrical value.

Mistakes about this are so common in the abortion dispute that I think that my argument will be strengthened by a plausible explanation of the appeal of the mistaken view. Recall the difference between the respect and (unconditional) love sketched earlier. Respect is something that we have toward some property that an individual has: reason, moral agency, what have you, and we respect that individual because of that property. Love, by contrast, is directed at individuals as such. Then, love naturally cherishes the sheer existence of its object. If this is so, then it is our natural love of our fellows (the sentiment that Hume called "humanity")[16] which leads us to cherish their sheer existence—before there is a moral warrant for this. And cherishing their sheer existence, we are naturally led to cherish their existence for as long as they can be said to exist as the same individual, metaphysically speaking. But that love is given freely by us, not deserved by the beloved. Thus, it does not imply anything about the beloved deserving to continue to exist. It tells us rather about our own sentiments. Consequently, the argument for the priority of morality over metaphysics is equally an argument for the priority of respect over love in the abortion question. This isn't to say that love counts for nothing in morality, only that it cannot justify the belief that its object possesses a moral standing of its own. Only possession of the appropriate property can do that.

3. VOLTAIRE'S QUESTION

Voltaire's question reminds us that we view the ending of a human life underway as much worse than the failure of a life to start. This gives us a surprisingly exclusive requirement because it rules out any attempt to explain the wrongness of killing human beings by invoking their "objectively" good properties—by which I mean properties whose appeal (roughly speaking) is that their existence makes the world a better place than it would be without them. Such objectively good properties are symmetrically valuable. That human beings possess such objectively good properties as rationality, or capacity for joy and attachment, cannot explain the serious wrongness of killing humans because contraception and abstinence also cause the nonexistence of these good properties. Then, these properties cannot be the basis of the asymmetric wrongness of killing human beings.

It might be thought that destroying an existing being that has objectively good properties is inherently worse than not creating a being with those properties. But this runs afoul

of the priority of morality over metaphysics because it counts existence itself as giving an existing being a moral claim to continue existing. Nor can the force of Voltaire's question be escaped by recourse to the so-called "acts-omissions" principle, which holds that acting to produce a bad outcome is always much worse than simply failing to prevent that same outcome. This principle is far from universally accepted, so we cannot assume that it holds in the controversial cases we are here considering. And, anyway, contraception and abstinence are acts, so they get no special dispensation from the principle.

The problem is to find a property whose nature involves existence in a way that makes the destruction of a being with that property significantly wrong while the noncreation of such a being is only mildly wrong if wrong at all. That this is just what objectively good properties lack suggests that it is a *subjective* property we need. I will argue that this suggestion is correct, but that not just any subjective property will do. For example, L.W. Sumner contends that sentience brings any creature into the realm of moral consideration, and therefore we should protect the lives of fetuses from the point at which they become sentient.[17] Now, aside from the fact that consistency would require that we extend the same protection to most animals, the most important fact for our purposes is that there is nothing about sentience as such that accounts for the asymmetric values of beings that possess it. It may be good that a six-month old sentient being continue on for another six months, but this is no better than ending it's life painlessly and replacing it with another that will have six months of sentience. There is nothing about being sentient that makes it worse to end a sentient being's life than to fail to create another sentient being.

The failure of sentience points us to the kind of subjective property that can do the job: The subjective awareness that one is already alive and counting on staying alive fits the requirement suggested by Voltaire's question. The loss to an aware individual of the life whose continuation she is counting on is a loss that can only exist once an aware individual exists. Moreover, it is a loss that remains a loss, a frustration of an individual's expectations, even if that individual is replaced by another equally aware one. And thus it is a loss that can explain why ending a human life is significantly worse than not creating one.

The point is precisely *not* to say that it is good that such awareness or such aware individuals exist. That would turn the property into one whose goodness is objective, and then we would lose the distinction needed to cope with Voltaire's question. It would then be just as good to create new aware individuals as to continue existing ones, and the harm of killing will be no worse than that of contraception or abstinence.

We need a way to say how it is valuable that individuals who care about their lives going on get to live on, without entailing that it is good that such aware individuals exist. We can do this by adverting to the moral attitude of respect: The asymmetric value of human life is a function of our respecting human beings because they possess the property of caring about the continuation of their lives; and we express that respect by honoring that property, which is to say by not interfering with or undermining people's ability to have or get what they care about. If it be thought that care about one's life is too thin a reed upon which to rest respect, remember that that care is the affective response to awareness of oneself as a being living out a life, so to speak, a minute or a day at a time—and that awareness is available only to rational beings. Consequently, respecting beings because they possess the property of caring about the continuation of their lives is respecting them for caring as only a rational being can care. Thus it can account for the asymmetric value we place on human life.

Note, that I am not arguing that ending the life of a human being who is aware of and caring about his life is wrong because it thwarts an occurrent desire to stay alive or a felt expectation that one will.[18] Rather, our inquiry has led us to a unique human vulnerability, and to a distinctive moral response to that vulnerability. Once a human being has begun to be aware of

her life, that life unfolds before a kind of inner audience that has an expectation of its continuation, an affective stake in living on. This expectation persists until the audience shuts down for good—even if, before that, the audience dozes off for a while. We defeat this expectation even if we kill a temporarily sleeping or comatose individual who has begun to be aware of her life. Because of this special awareness, humans are vulnerable to a special harm from the ending of a life already underway.[19] And we protect people from this harm because we respect them, not because we love them— though, of course, we may also do that.

My argument here should not be confused with the "logic-of-rights" approach used by Michael Tooley and S. I. Benn, to which it bears a certain surface resemblance.[20] Tooley has argued that a necessary logical condition for having a right is having some interest that the right protects, and—he contends—fetuses can't have an interest in staying alive. Consequently, fetuses are logically disqualified from possessing a right to life, and abortion is okay. As interesting as this strategy is, it relies too heavily on the logic of the concept of a right. Tooley's mistake is not just that his argument only works against a fetal right to life—but that he supposes us to be so much the prisoners of our existing moral concepts, that we need only determine what their logic allows to answer our moral questions. The simple fact is that if a moral concept logically excludes some case that there is good reason to include, we need only modify the concept or create a new one. Benn takes the logic of rights even further than Tooley. Benn thinks that the concept of a right is so exclusive that it only applies to agents. Then, since neither fetuses nor newborns are agents, they cannot have rights, and abortion and infanticide are okay. Benn's version seems to me extreme enough to qualify as a reductio ad absurdum of the "logic-of-rights" approach. Surely it cannot be that our concept of a right is so locked into its connection with agency that we cannot pry it loose and use it for other defensible purposes. Suppose we agreed that our concept of a right applied only to agents, and found that, say, people on respirators (or, in comas), though unable to act, ought to be protected against certain forms of molestation. What would happen if we simply modified the concept of a right so that it could cover such cases? Or, if we created a new concept with all the attributes of rights, except the restriction to agents? Would we slide into an abyss of incoherence? Would our lexicographers go on strike?

As I see it, the answer to the question of whether we should protect fetal life with a right to life or some other way hinges on whether there are good reasons for doing so, not on the logical preconditions of applying the concepts of rights or protection. My argument is that the interest that conscious human beings have in the continuation of the lives of which they are already aware is a good reason for protecting their lives morally in the asymmetric way that we do, and that no such good reason obtains in the case of fetuses. The loss suffered by the aborted fetus is precisely the same sort of loss caused by contraception or by abstinence, and thus provides no better reason for protecting fetuses than for prohibiting contraception or abstinence. Then, abortion can be no worse morally than these.

This train of argument may seem counterintuitive. It looks like abortion is different because it has a victim, while contraception and abstinence do not. But, recall the priority of morality over metaphysics: Since it is a property that makes it seriously wrong to kill something, the existing fetus before the property is not a victim in the morally relevant sense. The fetus's existence as such does not make the harm of depriving it of its future life morally different from the harm of the failure to produce a new fetus with its own future life, in the way that existing consciousness and expectation do for the harm of ending an aware human being's life.[21] *The loss to the fetus of its future life is no worse a loss than the loss to the world of any future life*

4. PERSONHOOD REVISITED

In an important article, Mary Anne Warren argues that it is personhood that warrants the right to life, and—appealing to common usage—she lists the traits of personhood as consciousness, reasoning, self-motivated activity, capacity to communicate, and the presence of self-concepts and self-awareness. Contending that the fetus lacks these elements, she concludes that the fetus doesn't have a right to life.[22] What we are not told is why any or all of these elements make it appropriate to hold the killing of a being with the elements seriously wrong. Warren's position then amounts to a report of our common practice of awarding rights to the beings we call persons.[23] And this renders her conclusion problematic because the pro-lifer can simply assert that the common practice is mistaken, or that there are grounds other than being a person for protecting fetuses. The only way out of these interminable disputes is to show that there is something about the nature of persons that explains the serious wrongness of killing them, and that there is no such thing about a fetus.

My argument to this point provides a way of showing what it is about persons that makes it asymmetrically wrong to kill them. Guided by Voltaire, I urged that the only plausible basis for asymmetrically valuing human life is that (and once) humans are aware of and counting on continuing the particular lives they already have. This is only possible for a being that is aware of his or her self as the same self enduring over time. And a hallowed philosophical tradition defines personhood by this very awareness. Locke defined a "person" as "a thinking intelligent being, that . . . can consider itself as itself . . . in different times and places."[24] And Kant wrote: "That which is conscious of the numerical identity of itself at different times is in so far a *person.*"[25]

Not only does this rescue the idea that it is persons who are morally entitled to protection against killing; it reinforces my claim that the asymmetric value of human life is based on our respect for our fellows as beings who care about their lives. Persons are commonly thought to be proper objects of respect.

5. THE PRIORITY OF LOVE OVER RESPECT IN THE INFANTICIDE QUESTION

The newborn infant does not yet have awareness that it is alive, much less that it is the self-same person enduring over time.[26] Its relationship to the future person that it is on the way to becoming is more like a fetus's than like an adult's or a child's relationship to the life of which she is already aware. If already being aware of one's life is the necessary condition of the objection to killing human beings, what follows about the moral status of infanticide? This question is important because some philosophers (and many nonphilosophers) take their intuition that infanticide is as wrong as killing adults or children so seriously as to rule out any account of the wrongness of killing that doesn't apply equally to infants.[27] What I shall say in response to this is not an attempt to settle the issue about the moral status of infanticide. I wish only to say enough to suggest how the wrongness of infanticide can be accounted for on terms that are compatible with what I have said about abortion and the wrongness of killing children and adults.

The attitude that we have when we think it wrong to kill a child or adult because they care about their lives going on is a form of respect. We respect the property of being aware of and caring about their lives (and all this brings in its wake), and we respect them for having this attribute. We show this respect by not undermining what they care about. We are not (necessarily) either caring about them independently of what they care about or directly caring about what they care about, either of which would characterize love rather than respect.[28]

Now, I think that the normal reaction to infants is a loving one (though of course it is not the only reaction, nor the only normal one). And, I think that this has probably been built into us as a result of evolution. Human babies are born at a very early stage of their development and must therefore be tended to by their parents (primarily their mothers, at least until recently) for a long time before they can get along on their own, and surely a long time before they can begin to pay their own way.[29] There are numerous evolutionary advantages from the long extrauterine development of humans. Most important, it allows adult human beings to have larger brains than could pass through a human female's birth canal. On the other hand, it is inconceivable that parents would have provided the necessary care for their helpless offspring over the hundreds of thousands of years of human evolution, if they had not developed a strong tendency to love infants. And this is love, rather than respect, precisely because it must happen automatically, before the infant can do anything to deserve or be worthy of it.

But there is more. The love that we naturally direct toward infants is arguably a necessary condition of the development of the infant into a being worthy of respect. This is so for at least two reasons, and probably more. First of all, by loving infants, we are moved to devote the energy and attention necessary to bring infants into the community of language users, which in turn brings infants to awareness of their lives, which is also a necessary condition of their caring about their lives and our respecting them for that.[30] (The *Oxford English Dictionary* gives the root of "infant" as *infans*, Latin for "unable to speak.") Second of all, by loving infants we convey to them a positive valuation of their sheer existence, which in turn underlies their valuation of their own particular lives once they are capable of it. Indeed, since it is precisely people's own valuation of their lives that is the condition of our respect for them, we can say that our loving infants is part of the process by which they become worthy objects of respect.

In short, we might say that we respect the lives of children and adults because they love their own lives, and loving infants prepares them for loving their own lives and thus for being worthy of respect. *Love is respect's pioneer.* It goes on ahead, clears the field and prepares the soil where respect will take root. Respect is what infants will get once they qualify for full membership in the human moral community, but love is what reaches out and brings them into that community and necessarily does so before they qualify.

This gives us enough to characterize the special status that infants have as natural objects of adults' love. As I suggested earlier, love cherishes the sheer existence of its object. Thus, love makes us want very much to protect infants and make sure that they survive. On the other hand, since that love is unconditional—given rather than deserved—it is not based on anything that makes the infants worthy of it. Thus, we find ourselves strongly inclined to believe that is wrong to kill infants, and unable to point to some property of infants (not shared by human fetuses, or even animals that we think may be acceptably killed) that justifies this belief.

If this is correct, then we can say that the strong belief in the wrongness of killing infants is the product of our natural love for them coupled with (or strengthened by) our respect for our fellows' love of them. And this love is worth supporting because it is respect's pioneer. That is, by loving infants we treat them as asymmetrically valuable before they really deserve it, but as part of the process by which they come really to deserve it. And then it will be wrong to kill infants because it will be wrong generally to block or frustrate this love, both because we and our fellows naturally feel it and because it is good that we feel it inasmuch as it is essential to infants' development into children and adults worthy of respect.

Note that this won't apply to fetuses. They may be objects of love, but not of such love as can play a role in their psycho-moral development. That requires a real, interactive social relation such as can only occur after birth. That is not to say that the fact that many people love fetuses counts for nothing. Much as respect for our fellows' love for infants justifies protecting infants' lives, respect for those who love fetuses, may, for example, justify treating aborted fetuses with special care. But since this is a matter of other people's love rather than fetuses' own worthiness for respect, it surely won't be enough to justify requiring women to stay pregnant against their wills.

This account does not say that killing infants is wrong for the same reasons as killing children or adults. Quite the contrary, killing children or adults is wrong because it violates the respect they are due as creatures aware of and caring about their lives. Killing infants is wrong because it violates the love we give them as a means to making them into creatures aware of and caring about their lives. The killing of children and adults is wrong because of properties they possess that make it wrong,

while the killing of infants is wrong because of an emotion which we naturally and rightly have toward infants. Then, it will be harder to justify exceptions to the rule against killing adults and children than to the rule against killing infants, because adults and children possess in their own right a property that makes it wrong to kill them. Infants, for the moment, do not. Killing them collides with our love for them, not their love for their lives. For this reason, there will be permissible exceptions to the rule against killing infants that will not apply to the rule against killing adults or children. In particular, I think (as do many philosophers, doctors, and parents) that ending the lives of severely handicapped newborns will be acceptable because it does not take from the newborns a life that they yet care about and because it is arguably compatible with, rather than violative of, our natural love for infants. But, of course, I have not proven this here.

NOTES

[1]A few words about terminology are in order: "Pro-life" and "pro-choice" are political labels, not technically accurate philosophical terms. I use them because of their familiarity, not because I think that only pro-lifers are pro-life or that only pro-choicers are pro-choice. Further, I use the term "murder" in its moral sense, meaning any killing that is bad for the same reasons it is bad to kill children and adults; and when I speak of it being bad or wrong to kill children or adults, I mean killing that takes place voluntarily and in the absence of such conditions as mental illness or duress that would normally block the imputation of wrongdoing. For the purpose of simplicity, I normally omit these necessary qualifications, and assume that the reader will fill them in where needed. Finally, I join in the widespread though technically incorrect practice of using the term "fetus" to refer to the being that develops in a pregnant woman from the moment of conception to the moment of birth. Speaking strictly, the single cell resulting from the fertilization of the egg is a zygote; shortly thereafter, when it becomes somewhat more complex, it is a blastocyst; when it implants in the uterine wall about six days after fertilization it is a called an embryo. It is only technically a fetus at about sixty days after conception. See Harold J. Morowitz and James S. Trefil, *The Facts of Life* (New York: Oxford University Press, 1992), p. 46.

[2]The claim is rightly understood and evaluated as a rational claim inasmuch as it is meant to persuade citizens of a modern secular state, since religious claims (such as that the fetus has an immortal soul from conception on) are

neither testable nor provable, and thus not (or, anyway, no longer) a plausible basis for securing widespread conviction or requiring compliance of nonbelievers.

[3]This mistake is all too prevalent in the literature on the abortion question, although, in a recent article, James Q. Wilson makes the mistake in reverse. He distinguishes the rights-based approach to abortion from the moral approach. Apparently, he's never heard of moral rights. I shall try to steer clear of both errors. See James Q. Wilson, "On Abortion," *Commentary* 27, no. 1 (Jan. 1994), pp. 21–29.

[4]Arguments which focus on the fact that the fetus is a *potential* human being or person make such a claim, but they are widely thought to fail because having the potential to realize a status does not entail having the rights that come with the actual status. (That newborn babies are potentially 18-year-olds doesn't give them the right to vote now.) Perhaps those pro-lifers who exhibit pictures of fetuses to show that they look like babies are making an argument of this sort, since being a baby is a property that adult humans don't have. But, being a baby is something that fetuses share with animals widely thought acceptable to kill. It's that fetuses look like baby humans that is thought to make them special, and their membership in the human species is something that fetuses share with adult humans. In any event, the positive emotional response that most people will have to pictures of babylike fetuses cannot decide their moral status, contrary to a claim recently made by James Q. Wilson. He proposes that we show people films of fetuses at different stages of gestation, and that we outlaw abortion at the point at which the fetus looks like a baby to most people, and, so to speak, engages their moral sentiments in its favor. If this really were a moral test, one wonders why Wilson doesn't also recommend that we show people films of women at different stages of legally enforced involuntary pregnancy, and that we permit abortion from the point at which the woman looks like a human being to most people and engages their moral sentiments in her favor. But, of course, it is not a moral test. Our emotional responses to what things look like is, at best, a hint about what they really are and really are entitled to. To determine that, we must use our reason. Mere feelings will not do. See Wilson, "On Abortion"; and my "The Impotency of the Potentiality Argument for Fetal Rights: Reply to Wilkins," *Journal of Social Philosophy* 24, no. 3 (Winter 1993), pp. 170–76.

[5]Put more technically: A pregnant woman has a right to control her body because she is a human being with the full complement of rights that humans are normally thought to have. If the fetus turns out to be a human being with the full complement of rights also, the woman's right will generally be thought to end at the point that it interferes with the fetus's control over its body. I am indebted to Karen Dolan for this clear statement of the principle.

[6]For example, Judith Thomson argues that, even if the fetus is already a person with a right to life (like a normal human adult), at least in most pregnancies and at least prior to viability, a woman has a right to abortion because a (fetus's) right to life doesn't entail a right to use another's resources (such as her uterus). Consequently, a woman has the right to expel the unwanted fetus, but only to kill it if that is the only way to expel it. Thomson's view might be thought to vindicate the idea, which I rejected above, that a woman's right to control her body suffices to establish her right to an abortion. However, Thomson's argument only works against the idea that the fetus has a right to life. It won't work if the fetus has some other special moral status which requires us to save it rather than merely not to kill it unjustly. (Suppose you found an abandoned baby on your doorstep and had no means of bringing it to other shelter. Would you have no duty to take it in, even if it had no right to use your resources?) It will still be necessary to determine the moral status of the fetus. See Judith Jarvis Thomson, "A Defense of Abortion," *Philosophy and Public Affairs* 1, no. 1 (1971), pp. 47– 66. Cf., Nancy Davis, "Abortion and Self-Defense," *Philosophy and Public Affairs* 13, no. 3 (1984), pp. 175–207. The question about the baby at the doorstep is raised by John Arthur, *The Unfinished Constitution: Philosophy and Constitutional Practice* (Belmont, CA: Wadsworth, 1989), pp. 198–200.

[7]The question is from Voltaire's article, "The Whys," *A Philosophical Dictionary*, vol. 10, in *The Works of Voltaire*, trans. W. F. Fleming (Paris: E. R. DuMont, 1901), vol. XIV, p. 214. I make no claim about what Voltaire actually meant by this question.

[8]Note that this formulation favors the pro-life camp. If the moral difference between killing and not procreating were due to the loss of investment that results from killing, then this will surely not be a large enough difference to make abortions as bad as killing children or adults, since abortions come when there is much less investment than goes into raising babies to become children and children to become adults. Similar things can be said about risk. The risk of not producing a fetus that reaches the stage at which most abortions occur is much less than the risk of not producing a being that survives until childhood or adulthood. In any event, until birth, both the investment and the risk are the pregnant woman's, and thus hers to waste or venture.

[9]When I observe the duty of respect," writes Kant, "I . . . keep myself within my own bounds in order not to deprive another of any of the value which he as a human being is entitled to put upon himself." Immanuel Kant, "The Metaphysical Principles of Virtue," Part 2 of *The Metaphysics of Morals*, in *Ethical Philosophy* (Indianapolis, IN: Hackett, 1983), p. 114; see also Kant's *Grounding for the Metaphysics of Morals* (Indianapolis, IN: Hackett, 1981), pp. 35–37. While I think my account of respect is in line with Kant's, I do not put it forth as a gloss on Kant's.

[10]In *Life's Dominion*, Ronald Dworkin maintains that we regard human life as sacred: "The hallmark of the sacred as distinct from the incrementally valuable is that the sacred is intrinsically *valuable because*—and therefore only once—*it exists*" (my emphasis). Dworkin gives two examples of things we value as sacred, works of great art and distinct animal species. What our valuation of these shares, and which Dworkin calls "the nerve of the sacred," is that we value the process that has brought them into existence. Individual human life is, for Dworkin, all the more eligible for sacredness than works of art or nature because it is,

so to speak, the product of both natural and human creative efforts. But our valuing of the natural processes and the human creative efforts that bring something into existence does not explain (much less justify) our asymmetric valuing of that thing. If it did, then we would value asymmetrically—find *sacred*—*every* product of human effort or natural process, which we obviously do not, and surely should not. See Ronald Dworkin, *Life's Dominion: An Argument About Abortion, Euthanasia, and Individual Freedom* (New York: Vintage Books, 1994), pp. 73–83.

[11]" '*Being*' is obviously not a real predicate; that is, it is not a concept of something which could be added to the concept of a thing." Immanuel Kant, *Critique of Pure Reason*, trans. Norman Kemp Smith (London: Macmillan, 1963), p. 504.

[12]Norman M. Ford, *When Did I Begin?* (Cambridge: Cambridge University Press, 1991). pp. xvi–xviii, inter alia. I suspect that Ford is a decent fellow trying to find a little space for a woman's autonomy within an otherwise strict rendition of the Roman Catholic condemnation of abortion. Nonetheless, it is difficult to understand why it would be okay to kill something while it still might become two things that it would be wrong to kill separately. Others who take some form of the metaphysical approach are: Richard Werner, "Abortion: The Moral Status of the Unborn," *Social Theory and Practice* 3, no. 2 (Fall 1974), pp. 201–222; Jean Beer Blumenfeld, "Abortion and the Human Brain," *Philosophical Studies* 32, no. 3 (Oct. 1977), pp. 251–68; Warren Quinn, "Abortion: Identity and Loss," *Philosophy and Public Affairs* 13, no. 1 (Winter 1984), pp. 24–54; Michael Lockwood, "Warnock Versus Powell (and Harradine): When Does Potentiality Count?," *Bioethics* 2, no. 3 (1988), pp. 187–213; John T. Noonan, "An Almost Absolute Value in History," Philip E. Devine, "The Scope of the Prohibition Against Killing," Norman C. Gillespie, "Abortion and Human Rights," and Joel Feinberg, "Potentiality, Development, and Rights," in Joel Feinberg, ed., *The Problem of Abortion*, 2nd ed. (Belmont, CA: Wadsworth, 1984), pp. 9–14, 21–42, 94–101, and 145–50.

[13]"That term, [speciesism], coined by the Oxford psychologist Richard Ryder in 1970, has now entered the *Oxford English Dictionary*, where it is defined as 'discrimination against or exploitation of certain animal species by human beings, based on an assumption of mankind's superiority'. As the term suggests, there is a parallel between our attitudes to nonhuman animals, and the attitudes of racists to those they regard as belonging to an inferior race." Peter Singer, *Rethinking Life and Death* (New York: St. Martin's Press, 1995), p. 173.

[14]I think this will hold even if, say, one thought of morality as an agreement among human beings to protect their shared interests. Such an agreement will have to identify the stage of development at which humans have an interest in being protected that is strong enough to override women's interest in being protected against forced pregnancy. This stage will have to coincide with the possession of some property that accounts for how humans become vulnerable to the sort of injury it would be reasonable for all to protect against.

[15]This is the defining property of our humanity according to Morowitz and Trefil, who then recommend that abortion be restricted from seven months on. Since this view cannot explain why it is worse to kill fetuses with functioning cerebral cortexes than to refuse to produce new ones who will have functioning cerebral cortexes, it is refuted by considerations raised in the present article. Morowitz and Trefi. *The Facts of Life*, pp. 17, 119, inter alia.

[16]David Hume, *An Enquiry Concerning the Principles of Morals* (Indianapolis, IN: Hackett Publishing, 1983), p. 75.

[17]Writes Sumner, "If the creatures we meet have interests and are capable of enjoyment and suffering, we must grant them some moral standing. We thereby constrain ourselves not to exploit them ruthlessly for our own advantage." On these grounds, he proposes that we treat the advent of fetal sentience (sometime in the second trimester of pregnancy) as bringing with it an entitlement to protection. L. W. Sumner, "A Third Way," in Feinberg, ed., *The Problem of Abortion*, pp. 71–93, esp. p. 84. Some scientists hold fetal sentience to be impossible before the beginning of the seventh month, that "before the wiring up of the cortex [around the twenty-fifth week], the fetus is simply incapable of feeling anything, including pain." See Morowitz and Trefil, *The Facts of life*, p. 158.

[18]The wrong involved in being killed is the loss of the life of which we have begun to be aware, it is not the pain of being aware of losing one's life. Causing this pain is a wrong to be sure, one that may make it worst to kill someone who is aware of what's happening than, say, to kill him in his sleep. But killing someone in his sleep is bad enough to count as murder, and that's what counts here.

[19]It isn't easy to capture the way in which staying alive becomes specially important to us once we are aware of it, though I think everyone can recognize it in his or her own experience. One writer who has given expression to part of what is at stake here is Richard Wollheim. Arguing that death is a misfortune even when life is bad, Wollheim writes, "it is not that death deprives us of some particular pleasure, or even of pleasure. What it deprives us of is something more fundamental than pleasure: it deprives us of that thing which we gain access to when, as persisting creatures, we enter into our present mental states. . . . It deprives us of phenomenology, and, having once tasted phenomenology, we develop a longing for it which we cannot give up: not even when the desire for cessation of pain, for extinction, grows stronger." Richard Wollheim, *The Thread of Life* (Cambridge: Harvard University Press. 1984), p. 269. I say that this captures part of what is at stake because I think that we long for more than phenomenology understood simply as perceptual experience. We would not, I think, care so much about continuing if we were and knew we were just experiencing fictional appearances, if our experience were, say, a continuing series of movies. It's because we seem to experience a real world in which people act and produce or fail to produce outcomes that matter, that we long for experience to go on. If philosophers' epistemological nightmare came true and we really were brains in vats, I think that our attachment to life would diminish.

[20]See Michael Tooley, *Abortion and Infanticide* (Oxford: Clarendon Press, 1983); and S. I. Benn, "Abortion, Infanticide, and Respect for Persons," in Feinberg, ed., *The Problem of Abortion*, pp. 135–44.

[21]This is what Don Marquis overlooks in holding that "loss of a future life" is what makes killing both human adults and human fetuses equally wrong: "Since the loss of the future to a standard fetus, if killed, is, however, at least as great a loss as the loss of the future to a standard adult human being who is killed, abortion . . . is presumptively very seriously wrong, where that presumption is very strong—as strong as the presumption that killing another adult human being is wrong." Don Marquis, "Why Abortion Is Immoral," *Journal of Philosophy* 86, 4 (April 1989), pp. 183–202, the quote is from p. 194. Responding to Marquis, Peter McInerney lists some of the many differences in the ways fetuses and adult humans are related to their futures. He concludes: "Although there is some biological continuity between them so that there is a sense in which the later person stages 'are the future' of the fetus, the fetus is so little connected to the later personal life that it can not be deprived of that personal life. At its time the fetus does not already 'possess' that future personal life in the way that a normal adult human already 'possesses' his future personal life." Peter K. McInerney, "Does a Fetus Already Have a Future-Like-Ours?," *Journal of Philosophy* 87, 5 (May 1990), pp. 266–67. While McInerney raises enough concerns about the difference between a fetus's relation to its future and an adult's to its to show that Marquis cannot simply assert that abortion does the same thing to a fetus that murder does to a normal adult, McInerney does not do enough to support his conclusion that a fetus cannot be deprived of its future personal life. Indeed, since he admits that there is at least biological continuity between the fetus and the future personal life it will have if not aborted, there remains at least some sense in which abortion does deprive the fetus of its future. The question whether the fetus's loss is enough to make killing it morally like killing an adult requires a moral comparison of the various losses, which McInerney doesn't undertake. Another case of failure to respect the priority of morality over metaphysics.

[22]Warren, "On the Moral and Legal Status of Abortion," in Feinberg ed., *The Problem of Abortion*, pp. 110–14.

[23]This fact enables Jane English to stymie Warren's attempt by claiming that, "as it functions in our actual practice of recognizing some creatures as persons, the concept of a person is too indefinite to be captured in a straitjacket of necessary and/or sufficient conditions." Jane English, "Abortion and the Concept of a Person," in Feinberg, ed., *The Problem of Abortion*, p. 152.

[24]John Locke, *An Essay Concerning Human Understanding* (London: Routledge & Sons, 1894), bk. II, chap. 27, sec. 9, p. 246.

[25]Kant, *Critique of Pure Reason*, p. 341.

[26]One expert on infant cognitive development writes: "it is a most un-Proustian life, not thought, only lived. Sensorimotor schemata . . . enable a child to walk a straight line but not to think about a line in its absence, to recognize his or her mother but not to think about her when she is gone. It is a world difficult for us to conceive, accustomed as we are to spend much of our time ruminating about the past and anticipating the future. Nevertheless, this is the state that Piaget posits for the child before one-and-a-half, that is, an ability to recognize objects and events but an inability to recall them in their absence. Because of this inability . . . the child cannot even remember what he or she did a few minutes ago. . . These observations have been made by others as well, but more recently there have been occasional suggestions that recall may occur considerably earlier than Piaget believed, perhaps in the second 6 months of life." Jean M. Mandler, "Representation and Recall in Infancy," in Morris Moscovitch, ed., *Infant Memory: Its Relation to Normal and Pathological Memory in Humans and Other Animals* (New York: Plenum Press, 1984), pp. 75–76.

[27]See, for example, Lockwood, "Warnock Versus Powell (and Harradine): When Does Potentiality Count?"; Werner, "Abortion: The Moral Status of Unborn"; Noonan, "An Almost Absolute Value in History"; Devine, "The Scope of the Prohibition Against Killing"; Feinberg, "Potentiality, Development, and Rights"—references in note 12, above. See also Loren E. Lomasky, "Being a Person—Does it Matter?," in Feinberg, ed., *The Problem of Abortion*, pp. 161–72.

[28]Of course, we will normally also be caring in these ways too. The point is that our doing so is not necessary to the way we value the lives of children or adults. For that, all that's necessary is that we respect their caring about their lives.

[29]"Human babies are the most helpless in the animal kingdom; they require many years of care before they can survive on their own." Mary Batten, *Sexual Strategies: How Females Choose Their Mates* (New York: G.P. Putnam's Sons, 1992), p. 142.

[30]"When infants become attached to their mothers many language-critical processes are encouraged: the desire to engage in playful vocalization, including vocal exploration, the emergence of turn taking and dialogue structure, and the desire to imitate vocal patterns. In turn, mothers who are attached to and feeling nurturant toward their infants provide them with a number of opportunities to learn. Among the other processes encouraged by attachment are the use of eye gaze and manual gestures to signal attentional focus and convey labels, and the use of voice to designate and convey." John L. Locke, *The Child's Path to Spoken Language* (Cambridge, MA: Harvard University Press, 1993), p. 107. Elsewhere Locke points out that infants who do not find this emotional responsiveness in their mothers seek it elsewhere (ibid., pp. 109–110).

Reiman on Abortion

Don Marquis

Jeffrey Reiman has argued that what makes killing us seriously wrong is that we care about the continuation of our lives. Because fetuses don't care about the continuation of their lives and because fetuses possess no other property that makes killing them wrong, abortion is morally permissible.[1]

There are counterexamples to Reiman's view. If what makes killing us wrong is that we care about our future lives, then because suicidal teenagers, some of the clinically depressed, and some of the brainwashed don't care about the continuation of their lives, killing them is morally permissible. Reiman might avoid these counterexamples by adopting the alternate view that, whether or not we *care* about our future lives, what makes killing us wrong is that we *expect* our lives to continue. However, because there are many things we expect to continue, such as starvation, cancer, and hate, which it plainly would not be wrong to eliminate, this alternative does not begin to explain the *wrongness* of killing. Reiman might avoid these further difficulties by assuming that the depressed, suicidal, and brainwashed will get psychiatric help and holding that what makes killing us wrong is that we either do now or *will* care about our lives if we survive. However, because fetuses will care about their lives if they get placental help, this alternative does not justify the moral permissibility of abortion. Thus, it seems that Reiman has no escape route from these counterexamples.

Counterexamples to a view are symptoms of a problem with the argument for it. Reiman's argument rests on this claim: "The standard kind of value is temporally *symmetric.*

Don Marquis, "Reiman on Abortion," *Journal of Social Philosophy* 29, Number 1 (Spring 1998): 143–145. Reprinted by permission from the *Journal of Social Philosophy.*

Normally, if something has *x* units of value, then destroying it (after it exists) and intentionally not producing it (before it exists) equally deprive the world of x units of value" (182–83). Because taking a life (from a child or an adult) is much worse than intentionally not producing a life, for example, practicing contraception, the value of a life is not symmetric. Therefore, an asymmetric value must be the basis for the wrongness of killing. Objectively good properties are symmetric. Thus, they cannot account for the wrongness of killing (188). This suggests that a subjective property, such as caring about one's life, is needed to account for that wrongness. But fetuses lack subjective properties.

That something is wrong with Reiman's argument can be seen by alternating the above Reimanian quote to insert mention of a subjective value. Then we get: "Destroying [a life that is cared about] (after it exists) and intentionally not producing it (before it exists) equally deprive the world of x units of value." This suggests that subjective values are just as symmetric as objective values so long as values are attributed primarily to *the world.* Reiman obtains asymmetry for the value of a life cared about by attributing that value to something other than "the world." Here is his move: "The loss *to an aware individual* of the life whose continuation she is counting on is a loss that can only exist once an aware individual exists"(189, my italics). This claim is true because *any* loss to an individual, aware or not, is a loss that can exist only if that individual exists. The loss to a plant of its well-being due to lack of water is a loss that can only exist if the plant exists. Thus, awareness drops out of the picture. Accordingly, Reiman's argument that only a subjective value could account for asymmetry the wrongness of killing is unsound.

Should we conclude that, because all values are symmetric and the wrongness of killing is asymmetric, no value at all can account for the wrongness of killing? That's hardly palatable. The source of this difficulty is Reiman's odd supposition that most value is attributed primarily to "the world" rather than primarily to some or all of the individuals in it. Even though certain utilitarians are fond of attributing value primarily to "the world", the rest of us do not. We attribute well being, for example, primarily to individuals. Reiman's odd supposition requires defense. Reiman gives none. The supposition that values are attributable primarily to "the world" leads to many difficulties in formulating an account of the wrongness of killing.[2] This, by itself, seems to be a good reason not to make it.

In addition, Reiman's theory of the wrongness of killing does not successfully account for the wrongness of infanticide. Reiman recognizes that because infants don't care about the continuation of their lives, his account requires a special justification of the wrongness of killing them.

Reiman claims that it is wrong to kill infants because we ought to love them. We ought to love them because love "bring(s) infants into the community of language-users, which in turn brings infants to awareness of their lives, which is also a necessary condition of their caring about their lives and our respecting them for that"(193). And "by loving infants we convey to them a positive valuation of their sheer existence, which in turn underlies their valuation of their own particular lives once they are capable of it"(193). Notice that both reasons appeal to the causal role the love of an infant plays in producing a property it will have when it becomes a child that is (according to Reiman) the basis of the wrongness of killing it.

It is certainly not obvious that such a causal role is the basis of an obligation. Reiman does not attempt to justify this assumption. In the absence of such a justification he has not *defended* the wrongness of infanticide. One might think that Reiman could easily have based a defense of such an obligation on the role the love of infants plays in contributing

to the well-being of the older children they will become. It is well he did not, for such a defense is successful only in the case of infants who actually survive to become older children. Therefore, it would have been of no help to Reiman in justifying the wrongness of having killed an infant who plainly won't survive to become an older child.

Reiman's account of the wrongness of infanticide faces another difficulty. Completing a pregnancy also plays a causal role in producing a property a human individual will later have that is the basis (according to Reiman) of the wrongness of killing that human individual when it becomes an older child. Accordingly, Reiman, to avert disaster for his defense of abortion, needs an account of why certain causal roles he regards as morally important are the basis for obligations and certain others are not. Reiman claims that the love of infants is different from completing a pregnancy because the love of infants "can play a role in their psycho-moral development. That requires a real, interactive social relation such as can only occur after birth"(194). But Reiman does not bother to explain (how could he?) why a causal process of *this* kind generates a duty, but the causal process of pregnancy does not. Therefore, his attempted defense of the wrongness of infanticide is ultimately arbitrary. Accordingly, it is not a defense at all.

There are counterexamples to the central claim in Reiman's defense of the moral permissibility of abortion. His argument for his view is unsound. He has failed to justify the wrongness of infanticide. Therefore, Reiman's defense of the moral permissibility of abortion is unsuccessful.

NOTES

[1] Jeffrey Reiman, "Abortion, Infanticide, and the Asymmetric Value of Human Life," *Journal of Social Philosophy*, Vol. 27, No. 3, Winter, 1996, 181–200. See especially 189 and 192. Page references in the text are to Reiman's essay.
[2] See Richard G. Henson, "Utilitarianism and the Wrongness of Killing," *Philosophical Review* Vol. 80 (1971), 320–37.

Abortion, Infanticide, and the Changing Grounds of the Wrongness of Killing: Reply to Don Marquis's "Reiman on Abortion"

Jeffrey Reiman

In "Reiman on Abortion,"[1] Don Marquis aims to refute the argument that I make for the moral permissibility of abortion in "Abortion, Infanticide, and the Asymmetric Value of Human Life."[2] There, I argue that a clue to the solution of the moral problem of abortion lies in the unusual way in which we value human life, namely, *asymmetrically.* We value human life in a way that implies that it is seriously wrong to end one that has already started, but not seriously wrong to refrain from producing a new one before it has started. This is unusual, since normally that we value something is about equally a reason for creating new ones and for not destroying existing ones. The normal way in which we value human life is to impute objective or inherent value to some distinctive trait or traits of human beings—rationality, creativity, capacity for loving attachment, and the like. But such valuing cannot account for the way that we think that killing humans is wrong or, equivalently, for how we think human life ought to be protected. Any of these valued traits is as much a reason for creating new humans as for not destroying existing ones, and thus would lead to the outcome that it would be about equally wrong to not procreate as to commit murder. We need, then, to find a reasonable

Jeffrey Reiman, "Abortion, Infanticide, and the Changing Grounds of the Wrongness of Killing: Reply to Don Marquis's 'Reiman on Abortion'," *Journal of Social Philosophy* 29, Number 2 (Fall 1998): 168–174. Reprinted by permission from the *Journal of Social Philosophy.*

way of valuing human life that does not yield this implication.

The asymmetry in asymmetric valuing of human life is that particular existing human lives are valued far above potential future lives, with the result that murder is far worse than not procreating. Now, since imputing objective or inherent value to human traits is not asymmetric valuing, I contend that the object of asymmetric valuing must be human beings' own subjective awareness of and caring about their own lives. Note, as a first step toward understanding this claim, that, unlike traits like rationality which in principle are equally valuable in existing and in future humans, human beings' conscious caring about their own lives is a caring about the particular lives that are theirs. This gives us, so to speak, a foot in the asymmetric door. Since conscious beings care about their particular lives, they care about themselves asymmetrically. Their caring about their own lives does not imply that it would be about equally good to preserve them as to produce a new one, or equally bad to murder them as not to procreate. For them, nothing is comparable to the loss of the particular lives they care about.

However, this is only part of the story. Since it is we who are valuing human beings when we think it seriously wrong to kill them, we must be valuing something about consciously caring beings that implies the asymmetric wrongness of killing them, that killing them is much worse than not procreating. And that means that we cannot simply value consciously cared-about lives as such, since that would imply that we think that one cared-about life is about as good as any other, even a future one, and thus that not producing a future one would cost the world about as much goodness as killing an existing one.

To arrive at the asymmetric valuing of human life, then, we must value something about consciously cared-about lives, but we must value this in a distinctive way. Instead of valuing the consciously cared-about life as such, I contend that we must value *that beings who consciously care about the continuation of their lives get what they care about.* This is an asymmetric way of valuing human life. We can value life in this way without thinking that it is good that there be or come into existence beings who care about their lives continuing, much as we can value that starving beings get fed without thinking that it is good that starving beings come into existence.

This is what Marquis misses when he tries to show that conscious caring about life is just as symmetric as imputing objective value to life by inserting "a life that is cared about" in my statement that "Normally, if something has x units of value, then destroying it (after it exists) and intentionally not producing it (before it exists) equally deprive the world of x units of value," to arrive at: "Destroying [a life that is cared about] (after it exists) and intentionally not producing it (before it exists) equally deprive the world of x units of value" (143)[3] Marquis would be correct here if the cared-about life was the object of our valuing. Then, our valuing would indeed be symmetric. But, the object of asymmetric valuing is *that beings that care about their lives get what they care about.* Such valuing does not imply that it would be about equally good to create new ones as to preserve existing ones, since what we are valuing is that existing caring be satisfied. And this does not imply that new caring ones should be brought into existence, because it implies nothing about whether it is better to care and be satisfied than never to have cared at all. Of course, I believe that it is almost always better to care and be satisfied than never to have cared at all. But that is a separate matter. As long as it is not implied by our valuing that caring

beings get what they care about, we have an asymmetric way of valuing human life.

Valuing that individuals who consciously care about the continuation of their lives get to continue satisfies the asymmetry condition because, once conscious caring has come on the scene, the ending of the life that is cared about causes a loss that cannot be made good by replacing that life with another living individual who is not yet conscious of or caring about his or her own continuation. This loss is not necessarily a felt loss. Once self-consciousness begins, our cares, desires, and reasons attach themselves to the ongoing "point of view" which constitutes our self, and which continues as our self even during periods of sleep or unconsciousness. It is the loss to this self, whether or not felt as a loss, that I have in mind here. Nothing more suspicious is involved in attributing a loss to a self, albeit unaware at the moment, than there is in holding that Einstein still knew modern physics while he slept, or in holding that, if Einstein's home had burned down while he was sleeping elsewhere, he would have undergone a loss at that very moment even if he didn't learn about the disaster until after he awoke. This does not, however, amount to saying that there can be a loss to a being who is never conscious of her cares and desires. Rather, once these come on the scene, they become abiding properties of the individual's self, against which a disappointment counts as a loss.

The loss of life to a being who has begun to care about living on cannot be made up for or made good by replacing the dead one with a new one who is not yet aware of or caring about his life. Consequently, valuing that beings vulnerable to this sort of loss be protected against suffering it implies the we believe that ending a life is far worse morally than not creating a new one, and thus it implies the asymmetric value of human life. But the only kind of being that can suffer this kind of loss is a conscious being. For us to value life in a way that implies the appropriateness of protecting it against this sort of loss, we must value *that* a consciously valuing being get what it values. In a wide sense of the term, we can think of this kind of valuing as a form of "respect" because respect is a kind of indirect valuing, a valuing of another's valuing. In the paradigmatic case, respect is a valuing of another's authority to set values for herself. Writes Kant, "[w]hen I observe the duty of respect, I . . . keep myself within my own bounds in order not to deprive another of any of the value which he as a human being is entitled to put upon himself."[4] I do not, by the way, try to prove that we should respect people's subjective valuation of their lives. Rather, I claim that *only* our respect for people's subjective valuation of their lives can account for the sort of protection to which we normally think human life is morally entitled.[5]

Since fetuses are not conscious that they are alive, they do not possess the property that is the object of asymmetric valuing, and thus there is no ground for according them the special protection to which we think human life (at some point) is entitled. Neither, of course, are infants conscious that they are alive. I claim in that case that the indirect valuing of respect is also at work—however, the respect is aimed not at the infants, but at the people who love them. People generally (not just parents or relatives) do (and I contend that it's good that they do) love infants—love that I link to the sentiment that Hume called "humanity" and which he understood as a general affection for our conspecifics. Respect for this love gives us a strong reason not to kill infants.[6]

Since asymmetric valuing of human life places special value on the particular living individual, it might seem that we could asymmetrically value a particular embryo. Insofar as each particular embryo is a distinct particular with its own genetic code, the line of thought runs, we could value the particular embryo itself and then regard its ending as a loss of a particular that cannot be made good by replacing it with a new one, since the new embryo will be a different one with a different genetic code. This implies, to be sure, that it is logically possible to value asymmetrically the particular embryo a pregnant woman is carrying. However, there is no reasonable ground for valuing that particular embryo asymmetrically. This is because,

until the embryo develops recognizable distinctive traits, its particularity is purely negative. We simply know that it has a distinct genetic code that is different from other ones. We do not know the positive content of this difference. And without that positive content, there is no reason to prefer this particular one over a new one, which will be particular in just the same way. Another way to see this is that in losing the particular embryo currently in a pregnant woman we lose no more than was lost when that woman did not conceive at another time. That, too, would have been a particular embryo with its own genetic code.

Marquis thinks that all that is necessary is that the embryo be a particular and thus that conscious caring is not necessary. He writes:

> Here is [Reiman's] move: "The loss to an aware individual of the life whose continuation she is counting on is a loss that can only exist once an aware individual exists." This claim is true because *any* loss to an individual, aware or not, is a loss that can exist only if that individual exists. The loss to a plant of its well being due to lack of water is a loss that can only exist if the plant exists. Thus, awareness drops out of the picture. Accordingly, Reiman's argument that only a subjective value could account for the asymmetry of the wrongness of killing is unsound. [144]

Marquis is correct that any loss to an individual is a loss that can exist only if that individual exists. The problem is to determine when an individual is vulnerable to a loss. That Marquis fails to see this problem is evident in the way in which he uncritically attributes *loss* to individual beings—even plants. Since his own argument for the immorality of abortion has the same problem, it will be useful to respond to this objection by referring to that argument, which is presented in Marquis's excellent article, "Why Abortion Is Immoral."[7] Marquis contends that murder is wrong because it causes its victim "to lose a future life like ours," and since abortion causes a fetus to lose a future life like ours it is, for all intents and purposes, murder—which fetuses should be protected against just as children and adults are. The problem with this claim is that it presupposes that a fetus is capable of *losing* something in a morally relevant way, and that amounts to assuming in advance that the fetus has moral standing—which is precisely what is denied by the pro-choicer.

Consider that we do not think that every premature stopping of a natural process is a loss. If a rose seed is planted but dies because not watered (intentionally or otherwise), we would not say that the seed has *lost* its rose-future. More accurate would be to say that its rose-future failed to occur. On the other hand, if an adult human being is murdered, we would surely say that she has *lost* the future life she would otherwise have had. Now, a pro-choicer thinks that the fetus is like the seed, and not like the murdered adult. Marquis has simply assumed the reverse. He has not provided an argument for why the fetus should count as a being that can *lose* its future, as opposed to counting merely as a being whose future phases may fail to occur. Marquis has begged the question by assuming in advance what he must prove instead. Thus, not only do I think that Marquis is wrong to reject the importance of conscious awareness and subjective valuation, I think his failure to see the need that such subjective valuation fulfills undermines his own argument about abortion.

In addition to his qualms about subjectively aware valuation, Marquis contends that there are counterexamples to my view: "If what makes killing us wrong is that we care about our future lives, then because suicidal teenagers, some of the clinically depressed, and some of the brainwashed don't care about the continuation of their lives, killing them is morally permissible" (143). This objection has gotten me to see a certain limitation of my argument as presented thus far. However, it is a limitation that can be repaired within the framework provided by the idea that our respect for people's subjective valuation of their lives accounts for the way in which we think human life should be protected.

Marquis's counterexamples appear to have considerable force until one realizes that their force rests on the assumption that there is one and only one continuing reason for the (asymmetric) wrongness of killing us. My argument does not assume this, since I distinguish the reasons against killing infants from the reasons against killing children and adults. Marquis's objection, however, has gotten me to see that yet additional distinctions are needed: the grounds of the wrongness of killing humans continue to change beyond the rudimentary caring that accounts for the wrongness of killing young children. Once this much is clear, the answer to Marquis's objection is that depressed or suicidal teens as well as brainwashed adults have autonomy rights that entitle them to protection of their lives *even if they have stopped caring positively about going on living*. What I have to show is that recognition of autonomy rights is also a form of respect for human beings' subjective valuation of their lives.

I follow the same clue that guided my original argument, namely, the protection of life that we think appropriate to human beings. The nature of this protection changes as children mature. We start protecting their lives as such (even, for example, against their own unwise choices) and we evolve in the direction of protecting their ability to make of their lives what they choose. In short, we move from protecting the child's security to protecting her autonomy. This evolution of protection is appropriate precisely because the child's attitude toward her life evolves as well. She starts off with little more than a blind attachment to the life that she is dimly aware of as hers. But, as she matures, she comes to view her life not just as the object of a desire to go on, but as the arena in which she will succeed or fail at living the life she wants to live. As self-awareness deepens to encompass recognition of oneself as having desires, recognition of the world as a place that does not dependably satisfy all one's desires, and recognition of one's mortality as an outer limit to living the life that is the object of one's desires, I contend that humans change from beings who simply desire that their lives go on to beings who (normally *also*, but sometimes *instead*) experience their lives as the theater of their own happening, the stage upon which is played out the drama of their one and only attempt to live the life they want to live. In response to this change, it is appropriate that our protection changes from protection of humans' lives to protection of their ability to make of their lives what they wish—*which necessarily includes protection of their lives, since unchosen death clearly frustrates people's ability to make of their live what they want.* Thus people's autonomy rights include their right to protection of their lives.

Note, however, that recognition of these autonomy rights is here accounted for as the appropriate moral response to the developed subjective awareness of older children and adults, and the increasingly complex way in which they value their lives. Thus, recognition of autonomy rights is a form of asymmetric valuing. That is, we can value *that* beings who experience themselves as wanting to live the lives they want to live get to do so, without having to value that there be or come into existence people who so experience themselves.

This is another a case of the indirect valuing that I have called respect. Indeed, valuing that people be able to make of their lives what they want is, as I've already suggested, the paradigmatic case of respect. But, notice that this respect does not depend on people's wanting to live. Rather, we respect them in a way that treats their lives as theirs to do with what they want, including (at least for liberals like me) their right to end their lives should they so choose. So, we protect depressed and suicidal teens because we view their lives as theirs to make of what they wish—and we try to treat their psychological problems precisely because such problems undermine their ability to live the lives they want. As for victims of brainwashing, their autonomy rights have already been violated by the brainwashing, and the resulting state surely cannot be used to justify depriving them of rights (that they can exercise or that others can exercise in their name) that they would have had without the brainwashing.

I will be brief about Marquis's objections to my discussion of infanticide. He writes, "Reiman claims that it is wrong to kill infants because we ought to love them. We ought to love them because love 'bring[s] infants into the community of language-users, which in turn brings infants to awareness of their lives, which is also the necessary condition of their caring about their lives and our respecting them for that'" (144). He takes this and other statements to mean that that our love plays such a causal role is the basis of an obligation to love infants and thus not to kill them. Then he asks why the same thing doesn't apply to the causal role that pregnancy plays toward bringing fetuses to the point where they will have properties worthy of respect and protection.

First, I do not say that it is wrong to kill infants because we ought to love them. I say it is wrong to kill infants because (we and) our fellows *do* love them and it is good that (we and) they do (for the causal reasons mentioned and others), *and we ought to respect our fellows' love.* By failing to see this crucial step in the argument, Marquis misses as well the way in which this argument establishes a weaker ground for prohibiting infanticide than for protecting the lives of children or adults. In the case of the latter, we protect them because we respect the caring that they experience. In the case of infants, we protect them because we respect the caring that others have for them—not because of something which they themselves possess or undergo. With this difference, it should be clear that this argument is not applicable to pregnancy (whatever it may cause) since respect for other people's love of what is inside a pregnant woman is not enough to justify forcing her to stay pregnant against her will with a fetus that itself does not care about its continuation.

NOTES

[1]Don Marquis, "Reiman on Abortion," *Journal of Social Philosophy* 29, no. 1 (Spring 1998): 143–45. Page references in the text are to this article.

[2]Jeffrey Reiman, "Abortion, Infanticide, and the Asymmetric Value of Human Life," *Journal of Social Philosophy* 27, no. 3 (Winter 1996): 181–200. This argument is developed in greater detail—along with critical analysis of the main abortion arguments on both sides and an historical survey of attitudes and laws about abortion—in Jeffrey Reiman, *Abortion and the Ways We Value Human Life* (New York: Rowman & Littlefield, forthcoming, 1999).

[3]Marquis faults me for speaking about values to the world. But this is just a way of speaking of what other philosophers call objective or inherent or intrinsic values, that is, things that have value independent of whether they are perceived to have it or of whether they serve some further purpose. This is quite common in moral philosophical discourse, and needs no special defense of the sort that Marquis chides me for not providing.

[4]Immanuel Kant, *The Metaphysical Principles of Virtue*, pt. 2 of *The Metaphysics of Morals*, in *Ethical Philosophy*, trans. James W. Ellington (Indianapolis, IN: Hackett, 1983; originally published 1797), 114.

[5]For those who think that sentiment is primary in morality, a similar point might be made in terms of sympathy rather than respect. Our sympathy for the consciously caring one leads us to want her to get what she cares about without implying that we want other consciously caring ones to come into existence. Since I hold a Kantian view in which the moral value of sentiments depends on their following the lead of correct moral judgments, I opt for respect since it is based on a rational judgment about the respectworthiness of its object.

[6]I think that a similar ground will provide a strong reason not to kill severely retarded individuals or victims of Alzheimer's disease, if they do not qualify for the additional grounds I shall spell out later in this paper.

[7]Don Marquis, "Why Abortion Is Immoral," *Journal of Philosophy 86*, no. 4 (April 1989): 183–202.

III
MORAL PROBLEMS
IN POLICING

Part three of *Criminal Justice Ethics* starts a review of important moral issues involved in the main functions of criminal justice: policing, judicial processing, and punishment. This section on policing opens with an article by John Kleinig, "Ethics and Codes of Ethics," from his book *The Ethics of Policing*. Kleinig traces the development of a police code of ethics in the larger context of the "general flowering" of professional codes. Ethical codes go beyond personal morality to help establish public trust and accountability, although Kleinig is well aware of their limitations. The Appendix of *Criminal Justice Ethics* contains more information about professional codes of ethics and information about finding the codes of ethics for professions the readers are most likely to enter.

The next several articles relate to the question of how far the police can go in using deception, seduction, and entrapment to catch criminals in the name of upholding the rule of law. In "The Ethics of Deceptive Interrogation," Jerome H. Skolnick and Richard A. Leo argue that tactics involving physical coercion are rare but that psychological persuasion and manipulation are "the most salient and defining features of contemporary police interrogation." They survey a range of police practices while drawing out three competing principles: ensuring reliable evidence, due process and fairness, and deterring police misconduct.

Readers who are interested in a case study should examine the case of *Brewer v. Williams* (1977), available in the Supreme Court opinion section of Findlaw <www.findlaw.com>. The police had agreed not to use a lengthy car ride to interrogate Williams about the disappearance of a 12-year-old girl, but an officer who knew that Williams was a former mental patient and deeply religious delivered the "Christian burial speech":

> I want to give you something to think about while we're traveling down the road. . . . they are predicting several inches of snow for tonight, and I feel that you yourself are the only person that knows where this little girl's body is, that you yourself have only been there once, and if you get a snow on top of it you yourself may be unable to find it . . . the parents of this little girl should be entitled to a Christian burial for the little girl who was snatched away from them on Christmas [E]ve and murdered.

Williams led them to the body, which was used as evidence to secure a conviction. The majority of the Court held the evidence inadmissible over a vigorous dissent.

Gary Marx elaborates on the questions of police tactics by posing the question, "When, if ever, is it appropriate to use friendship and the lure of sex as part of an investigation?" In his article, "Under-the-Covers Undercover Investigations," Marx sorts through issues relating to the use of the physical intimacy of sex and/or the psychological intimacy of friendship. He lays out a typology and discusses many perplexing, humorous, and troubling examples within each category to highlight what is at stake.

The next reading in this section on police tactics is Carl B. Klockars' "The Dirty Harry Problem." Many readers have seen the Clint Eastwood movie from which this article draws its name, although that is not required to appreciate the timeless moral question: "When and to what extent does the morally good end justify an ethically, politically, or legally dangerous means for its achievement?" Klockars affirms the reality of this question in police work and reviews the conditions that make it a true moral dilemma—one that will admit no final solution or resolution. He reviews some thoughtful, but defective, attempts at resolution. Ultimately, "the danger in Dirty Harry problems is never in their resolution, but in thinking that one has found a resolution with which one can truly live in peace."

United State v. Tobias deals with entrapment. Tobias called an organization that was a front for the Drug Enforcement Administration to place an order for material to make cocaine. He later canceled the order because he realized he did not have the background in chemistry, but he "just wanted to make some money." The DEA agent told him that making PCP was as easy as "baking a cake" and for $500 Tobias could have everything he needed. Tobias ordered the chemicals and the recipe, then called 13 times for technical advice before the DEA arrested him on drug charges. The majority opinion reasons that he had the prerequisite disposition to commit a crime and was not entrapped as a matter of law and that the government's involvement was not outrageous enough to violate due process; his 15-year prison term is affirmed. The dissent argues that if the government had stopped assisting Tobias he could not have produced the drug and that it is not acceptable that the government "vicariously manufactured PCP through Tobias in order to gather evidence to justify his prosecution."

The final readings on law enforcement involve the issue of police discretion and selective enforcement of the law. Laws are written in categorical language that calls for arrest and charging of persons doing legally prohibited acts, but police officers exercise a certain amount of discretion in deciding whether or not to arrest and/or charge individuals who in fact violate the law. For humanitarian reasons, a police officer may bring a juvenile home to his parents for discipline rather than to the station house where he will earn a lasting arrest record, or an officer may issue a warning for speeding rather than a summons. Sometimes, however, discretion is exercised to gain leverage over potential informants, sometimes in ways that appear to reflect racial bias against non-whites and/or class bias against the poor and unemployed. In the debate that follows, John Kleinig argues, in "Selective Enforcement and the Rule of Law," that police discretion is tacitly approved by the citizenry, that it allows the police to correct for unnecessarily harsh outcomes, and that it is not dangerous because it amounts to the police's using less than their full legal power rather than more. In "Against Police Discretion: Reply to John Kleinig," Jeffrey Reiman contends that discretionary enforcement amounts to the police's exercising powers that were not given them in law, that it renders the law vague and uncertain (is the speed limit the posted one, or is it the one that police are actually enforcing?), and that it gives the police unjust leverage over citizens from disadvantaged groups in our society.

For additional reading, *"Broken Windows" and Police Discretion*, by George L. Kelling, is published by the National Institute of Justice (NCJ 178259) and is available through the law enforcement documents section of the National Criminal Justice Reference Service <www.ncjrs.org>. The Criminal Justice Exploration Guide has links to a wide variety of other information on law enforcement <http://www.co.pinellas.fl.us/bcc/juscoord/explore.htm>.

All of the Internet resources and additional information are available through <http://www.paulsjusticepage.com>.

Ethics and Codes of Ethics[1]

John Kleinig

> Every code must be treated as a hypothesis to be tested and adapted while following it.
>
> John Kultgen[2]

Over the past hundred years—though particularly in the early decades of this century and from the 1960s on—associations of engineers, accountants, insurance agents, financial planners, realtors, public administrators, lobbyists, football coaches, journalists, social workers and psychologists, and organizations such as hospitals, chain stores, and credit unions have published "codes of ethics."[3] In these public statements, they have sought to articulate standards that should characterize their membership or operations and that would therefore mediate their provision of goods or services.[4]

John Kleinig, "Ethics and Codes of Ethics," *The Ethics of Policing*. (Cambridge: Cambridge University Press, 1996, Chapter 12.) © Cambridge University Press 1996. Reprinted with the permission of Cambridge University Press.

The precise reasons for this burgeoning interest in codes are probably various, though a confluence of social factors is likely to have had considerable influence. Advances in technology, increasing specialization, occupational autonomy and professionalization, rising corporatism, population growth, and rapid urbanization have considerably affected our social life. We are required increasingly to put our trust in people and organizations to whom we are significantly vulnerable and over whom we are able to exercise relatively little control. It is, as we have learned, a fragile trust, easily and far too often betrayed. The formation of occupational and professional associations, whose members are bound by a code of ethics, has been a partial response to this social breakdown. These associations offer to a consuming public some assurance that the services on which it depends will be delivered by its members in a manner that will not exploit or otherwise take advantage of its vulnerability.

In this chapter I propose to trace the rise of police codes of ethics, and, by setting them in the context of the more general flowering of such codes, will consider their purposes, problems, and value.

12.1 HISTORY*

Although something like a code of ethics was embedded in the 1829 *Instructions* given to Robert Peel's Metropolitan Police,[5] it was not until 1928 that a code of ethics was developed for U.S. police. Its background is interesting. On the recommendation of August Vollmer, the architect of the professionalization movement in American policing, his Californian protegé O. W. Wilson was appointed in 1928 as Chief of the Wichita (Kansas) Police Department. It was a troubled and much criticized department, and, full of Vollmer's spirit of professionalization, Wilson was provided with a context in which he could put into practice the ideas of his mentor. Among his early projects was what he called "Our 'Square Deal' Code," a public document designed in part to assure the citizens of Wichita that their much-criticized department was now there for them. Beyond that, Wilson rewrote the department's manual, establishing, in accordance with the conception of professionalization promoted by Vollmer, strict lines of authority, clear and efficient procedures, and rigid standards of conduct. The code did not replace the so-called ethical requirements that had traditionally been incorporated in departmental manuals. Rather, it gave public form to them.[6]

In 1937, the Federal Bureau of Investigation published its FBI Pledge for Law Enforcement Officers. Announced and printed in the December 1937 issue of the *FBI Law Enforcement Bulletin*, the director, J. Edgar Hoover, introduced the Pledge as being for "the voluntary consideration, acceptance, execution and adherence by all law enforcement officers." It was printed in poster format, and vigorously marketed to law enforcement agencies across the country. Police departments would get their sworn employees to sign, and then forward the signed pledges to the central office of the FBI, which then used the *Bulletin* to update the readership about its adoption across the country.

Then in 1955 the Police Officer's Research Association of California (PORAC), as part of a program to enhance the professional status of police, charged a subcommittee to prepare a code of ethics. Wilson, who had returned to Berkeley in 1947, was a member of PORAC and of its subcommittee. A final draft of the code was adopted by PORAC and the Californian Peace Officers Association in late 1955. Quite a bit of the phraseology comes from Wilson's 1928 code. The code gained wider attention, and in 1956 it was adopted by the National Conference of Police Associations. It was then considered for several months by an even more widely dispersed and prestigious body, the International Association of Chiefs of Police (IACP). Late in 1957, they too adopted the code, and published with it a short document called the Canons of Police Ethics, which sought to expand on some of the clauses and implications of the Code. Now known as the Law Enforcement Code of Ethics, the code was and still is adopted without change by many police departments, both in the United States and overseas.

Until the mid-1980s, the Code remained virtually unchallenged. But with the development of police accreditation in the early 1980s and the accreditation requirement that individual departments present a statement of their values, new ethical statements were formulated. There was, moreover, a growing discontent with the 1957 code. And so, in 1987 and 1989, the IACP adopted two new codes of ethics. The first was a Member Code of Ethics, tailored specifically to the situation of police executives. The second was designed to "replace" the 1957 code, which covered law enforcement officers generally. The attempt to replace the old code caused an unexpected uproar. Behind the uproar lay a sentimental grassroots attachment to the high-sounding phraseology of the 1957 code, though public

*Original section numbering system retained.

attacks on the new code were couched in various ways: It was seen as an executive action that had not been properly considered by the wider membership; it was too long for recital at police graduations; and its pragmatism was no longer inspirational. In 1991 the IACP developed a compromise solution that found general acceptance. It renamed the so-called replacement code the Police Code of Conduct; it restored the 1957 code to its place as the Law Enforcement Code of Ethics, but revised it in a few places to take account of some of the most serious deficiencies of the original.

The Law Enforcement Code of Ethics, with the 1991 changes to the italicized parts noted in brackets, reads as follows:

> As a Law Enforcement Officer, my fundamental duty is to serve *mankind* [the community]; to safeguard lives and property; to protect the innocent against deception, the weak against oppression or intimidation, and the peaceful against violence or disorder; and to respect the Constitutional rights of all *men* [ ] to liberty, equality and justice.
>
> I will keep my private life unsullied as an example to all; [, and will behave in a manner that does not bring discredit to me or my agency. I will] maintain courageous calm in the face of danger, scorn or ridicule; develop self-restraint; and be constantly mindful of the welfare of others. Honest in thought and deed, in both my personal and official life, I will be exemplary in obeying the laws *of the land* [ ] and the regulations of my department. Whatever I see or hear of a confidential nature or that is confided to me in my official capacity will be kept ever secret unless revelation is necessary in the performance of my duty.
>
> I will never act officiously or permit personal feelings, prejudices, [political beliefs, aspirations,] animosities or friendships to influence my decisions. With no compromise for crime and with relentless prosecution of criminals, I will enforce the law courteously and appropriately without fear or favor, malice or ill will, never employing unnecessary force or violence and never accepting gratuities.
>
> I recognize the badge of my office as a symbol of public faith, and I accept it as a public trust to be held so long as I am true to the ethics of *the law enforcement* [police] service. [I will never engage in acts of corruption or bribery, nor will I condone such acts by other police officers. I will cooperate with all legally recognized agencies and their representatives in the pursuit of justice.
>
> I know that I alone am responsible for my own standard of professional performance and will take every reasonable opportunity to enhance and improve my level of knowledge and competence.]
>
> I will constantly strive to achieve these objectives and ideals, dedicating myself before God to my chosen profession . . . law enforcement.

There is just one further dimension to be added to this brief historical overview. Besides the IACP, which is United States-dominated, there have been a number of other international initiatives to formulate police codes of ethics. A United Nations code was first suggested as early as 1961, but serious work did not begin until 1975. In 1979, after much debate, the United Nations adopted its Code of Conduct for Law Enforcement Officials. It has been used as the basis for code formation in a number of other countries. At about the same time, the Legal Affairs Committee of the Council of Europe developed a Declaration on the Police for its twenty-plus constituent members. The declaration, however, although adopted by the Parliamentary Assembly, was criticized in some of its parts, and in the member states it has never achieved the acceptance that was sought for it.

12.2 CODES AND THEIR KINDRED

Codes of ethics are variously described and come in a variety of formats. Like Wittgenstein's rope, they hang together as much by family resemblance as by any more formal features. What I think may come close to linking them is their function as commitments intended to mediate the formal relations between providers of goods and services and their public recipients.[7]

But as I have already noted, this emphasis on the public or mediatorial function of codes has been challenged by Michael Davis. For him, a professional code is first and foremost an internal document, a set of morally binding conventions intended by members of a profession to regulate and guide the pursuit of their professional activities. The important truth in this, I believe, is that drawing up the terms of a code of ethics is essentially and ultimately the task of the members of the profession or occupation (albeit in consultation with a wider public), for it is they who appreciate best what excellence in their specialty requires, what are the peculiar temptations that providers face, and what compromises are acceptable in their provision to a wider public. A particular code of ethics cannot be imposed on the members of a profession or occupation. But at the same time, I believe that the pressure for codes of ethics has almost always come from outside the profession or occupation, and that what is generally sought, in the development of such codes, is a document that is oriented to the wider public of consumers of the goods or services that the profession or occupation provides.

Even if I am right about the generally public character of codes of ethics, any survey of codes makes it abundantly clear that their forms and foci vary considerably. Not only do we have "codes" of "ethics," we have "canons" of "professional responsibility," "statements" of "values," "principles" of "conduct," "standards" of "practice" or "performance," and "oaths" of "office," along with "pledges," "vows," "maxims," "credos," "prayers," "tenets," and "declarations," in varying combinations. The rubrics are not strictly interchangeable, but neither are they precisely defined nor always clearly separable. At the same time, such commitments are sometimes found in association with but distinguished from statements of "goals," "mission," "philosophy," and "objectives," in which the scope of the service is articulated and generally set in the context of some wider social purpose.

It would be overly fastidious to attempt a neat differentiation of these different forms and foci, since some of them are treated interchangeably by their promulgators, and even where distinguished they may be accounted for in different ways. Nevertheless, some broad distinguishing features may be noted.

12.2.1 Codes

Pledges, credos, prayers, and oaths generally take the form of personal affirmations. Prayers are directed to God, and oaths more generally to some superior. Codes, canons, standards, maxims, declarations, and principles may be expressed personally, but they may just as easily be expressed impersonally. Codes and standards are often regulatory, whereas pledges and oaths tend to be aspirational. But there are, as I indicated, no hard-and-fast lines here.

Despite these differences, I think it is fair to understand most of these codes as public promises, vows or at least commitments by the provider of goods or services that certain standards will be observed in their provision. Indeed, I believe that this constitutes something of a raison d'être. Some codes, such as the 1957 Law Enforcement Code of Ethics, are explicitly formulated in a promissory fashion. They are really pledges. Others, such as the 1989 code intended as its successor, are expressed declaratively, the promise here being implicit, or perhaps explicit, as one enters into associational or adopting agency membership.

If codes are seen as promises or commitments, then it is easy to see how they bind. But there is an important objection to this account, based on the fact that professional codes are now used by courts as a basis for appraising practitioners who have never, explicitly or implicitly, affirmed them.[8] Thus, the American Medical Association (AMA) Code of Ethics may be invoked against a physician who has never joined the AMA, and its obligations may not be avoided by refusal to join. As Michael Davis puts it, the obligations of a professional "do not seem to rest on anything so contingent as a promise, oath or vow."[9] Professional obligations are, he thinks, only quasi-contractual, "resting not on an actual agreement (whether express or tacit) but on what it is fair to require of someone given what he has voluntarily done, such as accepted the benefits that go with claiming to be a [professional]."[10]

There is much to commend Davis's position, though not, as I shall suggest, as an alternative to what I have already suggested. Davis is correct to think that it should not be open to the beneficiary of a privileged social position to claim that his refusal to join a professional or occupational association should exempt him from the obligations articulated in the professional code. Codes, after all, are intended to *reflect* and *express* but not to *create* the public obligations of professional or occupational life. In an important sense, the professional code is a secondary rather than a primary expression of professional obligations. Nevertheless, this need not gainsay the fact that the code itself is primarily promissory in character, and that it is intended, by those who *affirm it*, to manifest a commitment to honor what the profession or occupation requires.

It is understandable that for purposes of public accountability codes should acquire the more general function of articulating not simply what members of a professional or occupational association have committed themselves to, but what a society may reasonably expect of those engaged in those professions or occupations. For the privilege of controlling what they do and, in some cases, of having a social monopoly on their activity, professionals and members of many other occupational groups must expect that with their privilege will also go a commensurate responsibility. Professional codes articulate that responsibility in a public manner.

But there is more to it than that. Those who explicitly promise—that is, those whose concern for professional advancement has brought them together—will articulate values and standards that will not only foster public trust, but will also provide assurance of excellent work. That is why professional codes seek to foster that trust through a commitment to excellence. And to the extent that that is so, it is not unreasonable for outside assessors to see such codes as manifesting a standard of performance for anyone who provides the service.

12.2.2 Ethics

If the reference to "codes" is complex, no less complex is their object, "ethics." Although the language of ethics, values, conduct, and practice is sometimes used interchangeably, it is just as often distinguished.

Statements of values tend to be broader than statements of ethics, and both may focus more pointedly on dispositional attitudes and character than do principles of conduct or practice. But to some extent at least we are dealing here with a difference of emphasis, since the interiority of values and ethical standards is intended to have external expression, and the enunciated principles of conduct or practice are generally associated with the possession of practical virtues. Nevertheless, statements of values and ethical standards are likely to be briefer and more general than codes of conduct or practice. The latter usually spell out in some detail what and how acts may or may not be done by service providers or associational members. And codes of practice or performance, as distinct from codes of conduct, may also embody some reference to technical standards (levels of competence) that the provider is expected to maintain.

Some writers have gone further to distinguish moral from ethical standards, by according universality to the former and group relatedness to the latter.[11] Honesty is seen as a *moral* requirement, truth in advertising as an *ethical* standard for business. And if we are talking about the *morality* of business people, we are not likely to be talking about exactly the same thing as their *ethics*. These are distinctions that can be made, and that might appropriately be made in certain contexts, albeit with only partial linguistic support. What I think is central to such a distinction is the concern in ethical codes to articulate moral values as they are relevant to the provision of particular goods or services.

Michael Davis, however, has argued that there is more to an ethical code than the situating of moral requirements within a specific professional or occupational context. The ethical requirements of codes, he believes, demand more of those for whom they are intended than is expected of others: "A code of ethics must set standards beyond ordinary morality if it is to be a code of ethics at all."[12] Unless a code of ethics demands more of those to whom it applies than can be ordinarily expected of others, it has no point. It goes without saying, he argues, that members of the professions are subject to the ordinary constraints of morality, that is, "those standards of conduct each of us wants every other to follow even if everyone else's following them means we must do the same."[13] And thus something more must be demanded of those to whom the codes apply. For this to be acceptable to those involved, Davis suggests, there must be some payoff or return. Codes must "buy" obedience.[14] Davis explains the purchase by characterizing codes as conventions between those whose wish to pursue a particular occupation is coupled with the recognition that the activity is most fruitfully pursued as a cooperative undertaking. Higher standards are the price one pays for the cooperation of others. If we accept that the professions necessarily provide a public service,[15] then the public's cooperation will also be needed, and the code will contain requirements that constrain practitioners in relation to their clientele.

If, for a moment, we accept this account, what should we say about police codes of ethics? For, as Davis notes, such codes do *not* seem to require of police anything more than might be expected of any decent human being. Police are to treat people with courtesy and respect, to be honest, and to exhibit integrity; they are not to use unnecessary force or act inequitably. Are not these reasonable expectations of anybody? Are police codes then an exception to the rule? Or, more radically, are their "codes" not genuine ethical codes after all?

In a section on "the problem of the missing higher standard," Davis accepts that police codes may be exceptional and, if so, that a large part of the reason for this may be due to the kind of work in which police are engaged. They see a side of life that encourages cynicism, and are subject to considerable temptations, and thus they "will do well to remain decent human beings."[16] What is demanded of the rest of us is, therefore, in some sense "more" for them. Even so, Davis is not entirely happy to accept that this is sufficient to save police codes, and so he suggests that the positive requirement found in some codes, requiring police to combat the misconduct and

corruption of fellow officers, might provide an appropriate "higher" standard.

I believe, however, that, by assuming that there would be no point to a professional code of ethics were such a code not to demand a higher standard of conduct of practitioners, Davis has created his own problem. It is true that what is demanded of professionals differs from what is demanded of others. But I do not think it follows or that Davis has shown that *more* is demanded of professionals than can be expected from others in similar circumstances, or that they are held to a higher standard. Or, to put the point slightly differently, I believe that if professionals are held to a higher standard, this *is* because of situational factors. As bearers of a public trust, it is important that they act and be seen to act in certain ways. Anyone else bearing the same trust could also be expected to act in those ways. What a code of ethics articulates is how someone confronting the kinds of choices, pressures, and temptations that a professional does, and bearing the trust with which a professional is vested, can be expected to behave.

Consider the one instance of a police code provision that Davis suggests does go beyond "what law, market, and ordinary morality exact": preventing and rigorously opposing violations of the code, reporting such violations to a superior or other appropriate authorities.[17] It is of course possible to question the propriety of such an expectation, seeing it as overzealous and maybe even insensitive to the loyalties that law enforcement work requires and fosters. But assuming that it is not an unreasonable expectation to have of police, might it not be argued that any person who is witness to the kinds of violations that are mentioned in the Code of Conduct (such as failures to respect human dignity or to be responsive to the suffering of those in one's care [custody], the infliction of torture or use of unnecessary force, or engagement in corruption) by someone in whom the public trust is vested—a witness who himself is a bearer of that trust—has a responsibility to prevent, oppose, or report such violations?

There is, however, a further distinction that Davis draws that has more importance for an understanding of ethical codes. He distinguishes between rules, principles, and ideals. It is a distinction between, roughly, those things that are to be regarded as mandatory or strictly obligatory, those that are to be seen as more general obligations or principles, and those forms of conduct that are to be seen simply as desirable or as ideals to be aspired to. Some codes restrict themselves to requirements of just one kind, others include all three indiscriminately, and yet others, such as some of the American Bar Association codes, have sometimes made an effort to distinguish them.[18]

Davis complains, properly so, that codes frequently confuse these different standards. What should be ideals are sometimes expressed as strict requirements, and what should be general principles are confused with rules.[19] Such confusions have practical significance. In the 1957 Law Enforcement Code of Ethics, for example, the pledge to "keep my private life unsullied as an example to all" is given the same status as obedience to the law and departmental regulations, hardly a reasonable expectation and liable to make the code an object of cynicism. It is, perhaps, reasonable for law enforcement officers to strive to keep their private lives "unsullied" and "an example to all," but this can hardly be demanded of them qua law enforcement officers. The 1989 Police Code of Conduct, though more discursive, manifests a similar failure to distinguish appropriate kinds of standards: "Force *should* be used only with the greatest restraint . . . ," an eminently reasonable principle, exists cheek by jowl with the statement: "The police officer's personal behavior *must* be beyond reproach" (emphases added).[20]

What drafters of codes need to ask themselves, Davis suggests, are the following questions: Does this provision state a minimum below which no officer may fall [except . . .]? Can an officer make good police decisions without giving some weight to this consideration? And if not, would it still be good for an officer qua officer to do as the provision suggests? Affirmative answers to the first question are likely to yield ethical rules; affirmative answers to the second are likely to yield ethical principles; and affirmative answers to the third are likely to yield ethical ideals.[21] Asking such questions, to anticipate what is to come, will not only inform a public of what it may and may not expect of police, and how to expect it, but also enables police to think through the ethical expectations associated with their role and to disentangle what is central and necessary from what must be taken into account and what is simply desirable.

12.3 CODES AND THEIR PUBLIC

I have suggested that it is a distinguishing feature of codes—as we currently understand them—that they do not function as purely internal documents, but manifest from within, or are intended to do so, the public accountability of organizations, agencies, and members of associations. Quite apart from various forms of external regulation and review to which the providers of goods and services are subject, codes are put forward as public evidence of a determination, on the part of the providers themselves, to serve in ways that are predictable and acceptable.

I referred earlier to Davis's distinction between morality and ethics, accepting that what is of significance in the distinction is the concern, in professional ethics, to articulate moral values in a manner that is relevant to the provision of particular goods or services. Professional ethics is not just general ethics writ small or in different garb, but ethical reflection that is articulated through the particular ideals and purposes that are constitutive of the profession. And it is precisely because of this that professionals are sometimes confronted with hard choices between the ethical demands of their professional excellence and other, or more general, ethical demands.[22]

Professional codes, too, are not to be seen as comprehensive codes of conduct. They view conduct primarily from the perspective of the professional services rendered. As Lon Fuller has expressed it, "a code of ethics must contain a sense of mission, some feeling for the peculiar role of the profession it seeks to regulate. A code that attempts to take the whole of right and wrong for its province breaks down inevitably into a mush of platitudes."[23] One unfortunate feature of some police codes of ethics is that they possess this platitudinous quality. What they commit their members to is not sufficiently articulated in terms of the services they provide. They uphold the virtues of public service, honesty, integrity, courtesy, nonpartisanship, and so on, without indicating in any significant way how these values might be expected to work themselves out in the concrete activities of police work.

12.4 THE PURPOSES OF POLICE CODES

When looking at the proliferation of occupational and professional codes, we need to keep distinct (though not completely separate) the issues of *explanation* and *justification*. Explanations of the formation of codes—whether in individual cases or as part of a general social phenomenon—look to the causal or historical factors in their production. Such factors might include the desire for social enhancement, the protection of turf, a defense against external controls, a heightened sense of moral and social accountability, or the desire to consolidate group identity and provide a group ethos. Explanatory factors may reflect well or badly or not at all on the organizations or associations in question. In other words, they may also function as justificatory reasons, though they need not do so.

Justificatory reasons, on the other hand, are directed to the question of normative desirability, to the legitimating grounds for promulgating or retaining a code. It is natural for organizations and associations to cast the reasons for formulating their codes in the language of justification, though in actual fact their motivations may be less commendable. Most likely, organizations will be moved to develop, retain, and revise their codes for a variety of reasons, some of which will be justificatory, but others of which will be of only explanatory significance—or, if also of justificatory significance, may serve only to call the organization's high purposes into question.

There is little doubt that one of the major impulses behind the development of police codes of ethics has been the desire for professional status. This was evident in O. W. Wilson's ambitions for his 1928 "Square Deal" Code, and has been behind subsequent initiatives of the IACP and other police organizations.

As noted earlier codes of ethics are often taken to be a hallmark of professional status. Occupations aspiring to or claiming professional status frequently seek to display this determination or achievement by promulgating a code. But although codes of ethics may be central to professionalization, they are not constitutive of it; and so, while many organizations and associations may seek to improve their social standing through the development of a code of ethics, this will not, of itself, achieve that end.

12.4.1 *External Functions*

Most codes of ethics are directed primarily to an indeterminate client public —its size largely a function of the number of people who wish or need to avail themselves of the goods or services provided. Sometimes, as in the case of police, the code will be of indirect as well as direct significance. Even if an individual does not actually require the direct services of a police officer, it may be important to know that certain standards are affirmed by those who provide police services. Otherwise one may be "caught in the crossfire" as police perform their otherwise legitimate tasks. But there may also be other groups to whom a code is partially directed. Codes of ethics sometimes seek to determine the forms of contact that their adherents may have with the media, with other professions, and even with government. More subtly, but no less really, a code may be intended to deflect or pre-empt judicial scrutiny.

What follows are some of the major external functions that codes are expected to have. Obviously, not all codes will have all of these functions. Indeed, most codes will not have all these functions, though most will have more than one. And the importance given to these various functions will differ from code to code. So will their justificatory value.

12.4.1.1 Assurance. Seekers and users of goods and services are to varying degrees dependent on others for the provision of those goods and services. For many goods and services the dependence can be very significant. And obtaining the goods or service may require considerable sacrifice and/or risk—of privacy, of resources, of effort, and/or of well-being. It is hardly surprising that people should want to be assured that the goods and services will meet certain expectations.

In the case of police, the need to provide assurance is demanded by the enormous social power that is vested in them. That need is reinforced by the media's relish for stories of police corruption and misconduct. Although there is probably more public trust in the police than police themselves recognize (for most of us there are, after all, few widely available alternatives), that trust must be secured in the face of ongoing (albeit uneven) media scrutiny. It is no doubt for this reason that a number of police codes (and regulations) restrict the liberty of first line officers in regard to their dealings with the media.[24]

In many cases the code of ethics has the appearance of a compact between the service-using public and the service provider. An exchange is involved. Service providers are accorded certain social privileges in virtue of the service they provide. Police, for example, have certain entitlements in respect of the use of coercive force, certain rights to command, and rights of entry. For the granting of such privileges the public can expect a certain return. Although codes of ethics generally originate from within the association and organizations to which they apply, and have not been formulated as the result of a public interchange, they may be couched as an appropriate exchange for the privilege that is given. One of the main privileges may be that of being the (almost) exclusive provider of a particular range of services.[25]

Codes provide assurance, not simply by notifying a public of what standards they may expect to find observed, but also, through their being enshrined in a public document, by giving service users a "handle" in the event that the service fails to live up to expectations. In some cases, the codes themselves indicate resources that are available for the handling of dashed expectations.

12.4.1.2 Improved Public Relations. To say that codes of ethics provide assurance is to view them from the perspective of service users. There is a flip side to this in the perspective of service providers. That is a public relations function. Associations and organizations frequently view the promulgation of a code of ethics as one of the ways in which they can improve their public image and increase their clientele. By assuring the public they enhance their standing and make their services more attractive. Several major police codes were drawn up in the wake of the scandals of the early 1970s, at a time when trust in the police was under severe challenge. Although law enforcement associations were motivated by a genuine concern to lift police performance and to reestablish trust, there is little doubt that the promulgation of these codes was also an exercise in public relations.

Although there has often been a mercenary dimension to the public relations function of codes, the ends have been as much social as financial. It has become a hallmark of professional status that one is governed by a code. The code speaks of self-governance, autonomy, and dedication. The acquisition of professional status is important to the self-image and social acceptance of those who have it. Thus one of the first projects of an occupation seeking to improve its place in the world—socially, as well as economically—is the formulation, adoption, and promulgation of a code of ethics.

12.4.1.3 Liability Limitation. To the extent that a police code of ethics sets out certain standards that are to operate in the provision of police services, it may be seen as constituting a constraint on excessive and unreasonable demands and in certain circumstances a hedge against liability for failures with which police may be charged. Where, as in the United States, the legal environment promotes contingency fee representation, and the judicial environment is often open to deep-pocket decision making, the police, as public employees with power to injure, are fair game for predators, both civilian and legal. In theory at least, and occasionally in practice, the code of ethics will constitute a public benchmark against which police conduct can be tested, and police can be secured against unwarranted—frivolous and vexatious—claims.[26]

There is a different way in which a code of ethics may limit liability. A hallmark of professionalism, at least in theory, is self-regulation. Those who provide professional services consider that they are best placed to appraise the delivery of those services. For the most part—except, perhaps, when blatantly criminal behavior is involved—professionals are strongly resistant to outside regulation. A code of ethics, particularly if it is associated with mechanisms for its monitoring and enforcement, is frequently appealed to as evidence that external review would be redundant and intrusive. Answerability within obviates the need for answerability without.

12.4.2 Internal Functions

Although the paradigm code format tends to mediate between providers and users, assuring each in relation to the other, it is becoming increasingly common for codes to be used as internal documents, setting out guidelines for individual providers and managers, and developing organizational or professional commitment and cohesion.

12.4.2.1 A Personal Standard. From the point of view of those who are members of an association or who are employees of an organization, the code of ethics might be expected to represent at least a minimum commitment—a standard of behavior that service users may demand, a commitment to which the provider must adhere. What, externally, users may *expect*, internally, providers *promise* to deliver. Of course the code may also gesture toward a maximum—it may comprise ideals as well as duties. What, externally, users may *anticipate* internally, providers *aspire* to.

In some cases these commitments may not seem to amount to very much. It is not uncommon for codes of ethics such as the 1957

Law Enforcement Code of Ethics to speak largely in generalities, pledging forms of conduct (self-restraint, courteousness, honesty) that might reasonably be expected of people in almost any situation. Nevertheless, we should not characterize them as merely platitudinous. For it is generally because the provision of a particular kind of service is associated with certain characteristic temptations that these ordinary forms of conduct are highlighted by a code.

In more detailed codes, declarations may involve distillations of practical wisdom that inexperienced practitioners are not likely to have, even if they are morally sensitive. As the working environment has become more complex and pluralistic, and traditions have become less evident, codes may constitute a beacon or anchor for service providers who do not yet or perhaps no longer have a sure sense of the normative constraints governing their work. There is an internal as well as external dimension to these normative constraints. In a complex and in some ways novel environment, providers of services may have no clear sense of "the thing to do." A code may help to crystallize issues and provide criteria for wise decision making. But as well as that, it may, in a pluralistic and normatively heterogeneous social milieu, provide something approaching a map of public expectations that will help the service provider to understand the social circumjacencies of decision making.

12.4.2.2 An Organizational Ethos. Codes, even if individually affirmed, are not constituted by individual declarations; they are associational and organizational constructs. And one function they try to serve is the unification of service providers through the creation or advancement of an associational or organizational ethos that is ostensibly promotive of the service to be provided. There are very few workplaces that can operate successfully simply by providing a location or vehicle for work. Associational ties and organizational cohesion generally require some sort of shared culture or ethos, and a code of ethics is frequently used to help foster that shared way of being. Where the providers of a service are at a geographical distance, and where there is a turnover of service providers, the code may be a major bonding agent, providing continuity from one generation to another. Professional and occupational loyalties are embedded in the ideology of code commitment.

The associational ethos usually involves a representation of the members to themselves that they are professionals. That may be interpreted in more than one way. One may see oneself as a privileged service provider; but equally one may understand it simply as a social status. For the social reality of being a professional is as much a matter of status as it is of expertise and service, even though the status purports to piggyback on expertise and service.

The duality here may create or at least embody a deep tension. On the one hand, the code serves the important sociopsychological purpose of binding and motivating service providers. On the other hand, it provides a moral framework and standard of conduct for what is done, one that is responsive to the concerns of a wider community. There is, therefore, an implicit tension between serving others as the binding raison d'être of the association or organization and a loyal commitment to fellow professionals or service providers. The stronger the organizational ethos, the more service to the public tends to be vulnerable to compromise, for personal loyalty to fellow professionals tends to take precedence over the commitment to a more impersonally construed public. In policing, this is a particularly acute problem; police officers will rarely turn in or testify against a fellow officer who violates the terms of his or her oath. This is so even if the code attempts to surmount the tension by explicitly demanding that police report violations by their fellows. Codes and other associational rituals may have a psychic and symbolic and social significance that is not strictly tied to their content. Many of those who bound themselves by and fought for the retention of the 1957 Law Enforcement Codes of Ethics not to "permit . . . friendships to influence [their] decisions" do not hesitate to exempt fellow officers from the normal consequences of traffic violations.

12.4.2.3 An Organizational Benchmark. Codes that are dedicated primarily to creating and promoting an organizational ethos tend to be aspirational. They enunciate ideals rather than establish obligatory standards. To the extent that a code's provisions are seen as aspirational, failure to live up to them may be viewed as a shortcoming, a reason for shame, perhaps, or even for others' social withdrawal. But where they are seen as benchmarks, as moral minima, they may serve a regulatory function. The more detailed and declarative a code is, the more likely it is that the standards it sets out will be regulatory (in intent, at least) rather than merely aspirational.

As an organizational benchmark, a code may function in any of at least four ways. (1) Generally the code is used to maintain membership quality control. By reference to its expectations, providers of a service may be admitted to or excluded from membership, and assessed, reprimanded, or ejected. Less formally, the code and its provisions may serve to deter unethical conduct. (2) The code may also be used to exercise control of a more political kind. Some years ago, Edwin T. Layton, Jr. observed that the AMA codes "have been used with great ruthlessness to punish dissidents who have taken the public's side on issues such as group medicine,"[27] and Philip Shuchman argued that the ABA Codes assert the power of "Big Law Firms" over "Little Lawyers."[28] In the policing context, the FBI Pledge was used to foster and assert the FBI's ideological dominance within American law enforcement. (3) There may, however, be a double edge to this, since ethics codes can also be used as vehicles for internal dissent, as means whereby members of an association or organization may hold their own hierarchy to account. (4) Less adversarially, codes may sometimes provide a basis for the adjudication of internal disputes.

12.4.2.4 A Teaching Device. It has not been uncommon for codes of ethics to function as the core of, or framework for, the ethical training of service providers. That at least has been one way in which medical and legal codes have been used in medical and law schools. Police academies have followed suit. A once widely used programmed text in police ethics, Allen P. Bristow's *You . . . and the Law Enforcement Code of Ethics*, is a particularly good expression of this approach.[29] Each of the clauses of the 1957 Law Enforcement Code of Ethics is articulated by means of problem cases in which trainee officers are called upon to think about what would constitute an ethically sensitive decision.

The use of professional codes in a teaching context has often left much to be desired. Whatever merit the codes themselves may have had, their use as a teaching device was often directed to keeping professionals out of trouble rather than to their ethical sensitization. The approach was legalistic rather than ethical.

In medical and legal ethics education, however, other less Sinaitic and self-serving approaches are now more common, and medical and law students are encouraged to develop ways of reflecting on what they are doing and on the hard cases that are likely to present themselves in the course of their work. They are taken behind and beyond what the traditional codes are able to provide. A similar change has been occurring in police training.[30]

12.5 CODES AND THEIR PROBLEMS

To say, as I have, that codes of ethics may have the various external and internal functions I have outlined is not to say that they always have or should have those functions, or that those functions are always compatible. Sometimes, indeed, individual codes give the appearance of being an uneasy compromise of several functions. But neither do I want to give the impression that these functions are always or easily separable. Thus, for example, unless there is some reasonable semblance of conformity with the provisions of a code, it is not likely that the code will constitute a very effective public relations document. Nevertheless, we should have no illusions that the foregoing catalogue provides an unproblematic justification for the promulgation of codes of ethics. Several difficulties need to be addressed.

Some of these problems tend to be associated with the code form itself, whereas others are more closely connected with contingent features of code formation and use. I will, somewhat artificially, distinguish the latter as contingent and the former as endemic problems.

12.5.1 Contingent Problems

There are several problems that bedevil many ethical codes, but which are potentially correctible.

12.5.1.1 Enforceability. Occupational and professional codes are "necessitated" by the exigencies and temptations of social life—the need to give assurance to a consuming clientele or public that the goods or services it is seeking will be provided in a spirit of service. Yet, just because of the circumstances that generate the "need" for a code, its provisions are most likely to be observed only if there is also some recourse to sanctions.

In some codes, the need for sanctions is recognized, and procedures for their imposition are set out. The IACP Member Code of Ethics (1987) includes elaborate provisions for enforcement. In some other codes, sanctioning procedures are contained in a separate document. But even where this is so, and more so where sanctions are not explicitly indicated, members of occupational associations are often extremely reluctant to support their enforcement. There is great unwillingness to report breaches or to testify against those who are the subject of a complaint. This is particularly true of ideologically cohesive groups such as the professions, but it is also characteristic of law enforcement-related organizations. The so-called blue wall of silence is notorious. The very code that evokes and reinforces group loyalty also encourages its ineffectiveness.

12.5.1.2 Cynicism. Whereas some codes are pretty matter-of-fact and realistic in their demands, others, especially those that are aspirational, may place global, unnecessary, or unreasonable demands on those who are called to affirm them. Police codes, particularly where police are made out to be communal role models, may sometimes make excessive demands and thereby encourage a cynical response. Police cannot be expected to enforce "all" the laws or, qua police, to keep their private lives "unsullied." They can be expected to maintain the public peace through the enforcement of laws, and to conduct their private lives in a manner that will not derogate from their public authority.

Cynicism, however, may have its source not only in the content of code provisions, but also in the manner of their introduction. Very often, codes of ethics are top-down productions, creations of boards or management, and not the result of cooperative dialogue and community consultation. Rightly or wrongly, they are seen as alien impositions, motivated not by a commitment to service, but by the desire for control, political exigencies, or just plain arrogance. This may have very little to do with the content of the code. The *Principles of Policing*, produced for the (London) Metropolitan Police in 1985, is one of the most remarkable and thoughtful attempts to offer police general and specific ethical guidance. Yet it caused barely a ripple, and by 1988 had been replaced by a brief, unelaborated statement of values. One reason for this was undoubtedly the manner in which it was disseminated—as though it were a Sinaitic deliverance whose acceptability needed no participation by those for whom it was intended. London police felt no "ownership," and in regard to what they did not own they experienced no loss.

Another source of cynicism can be found in the "do as I say not as I do" ethos that may accompany management directives. If a code of ethics is to be taken seriously—especially if it is a top-down creation—it needs to have not merely the endorsement but also the commitment of management. In police departments, where the chain of command is central, leadership by example will have as much to do with the effectiveness of a code as any provisions of the code itself.

12.5.1.3 The Danger of Minimalism. Although aspirational codes tend to bespeak a self-sacrificial ideal of dedication and service, codes that focus instead on the "mandatory" requirements of professional life may dissuade

sacrifice altogether. Practitioners may feel that so long as they stay within the mandated boundaries of the code they are doing all that may be expected of them. Though such requirements may deter conduct that is clearly detrimental to the users of goods and services, they may also discourage providers from giving more than is absolutely necessary. In occupations where the demands or competition are heavy and the threat of civil liability is constant, the pressure to stay with the minimum may be considerable.

12.5.2 Endemic Problems

Some of the problems that codes confront are much more deep-seated, and function as permanent dangers.

12.5.2.1 The Behavioral Bias. One of the more obvious features of many codes of ethics is their focus on outcomes—on ensuring that behavior meets certain standards. The emphasis tends to be on *doing* rather than *being*.

Codes are not always of this form. The more confessional statements are often interlarded with the language of virtue. Those who uphold the IACP Law Enforcement Code of Ethics, for example, pledge themselves to show "courageous calm in the face of danger," to be "honest in thought and deed," and so on. And the recent move toward "statements of values" also reflects a concern for the possession of certain attitudes and not simply the performance of certain behaviors.

Nevertheless, there is a natural gravitation toward behavioral standards. It is, after all, not easy to test dispositions, intentions, and motivations apart from their behavioral manifestations, and, furthermore, those behavioral manifestations do represent some sort of "bottom line" so far as the public function of the code is concerned.

Given the general regulatory purpose of codes, the emphasis on conduct is probably to be expected. After all, what a public seeks are certain assurances about the delivery of services, and not (usually) some general statement of character or whole-of-life guarantee. It is concern with the *dealings* between police and public that leads to the construction of such statements in the first place. Yet we should not confuse a certain kind of outcome optimization with acting ethically. *Moral* worth attaches to conduct not just by virtue of the good that it does or the evil that it prevents, but because it was done for certain kinds of reasons or was expressive of a certain kind of character. If a police officer pursues and apprehends a fleeing mugger, what motivates him is not relevant to our assessment of the good that was done. Indeed the same good could have been accomplished by a falling piece of timber. But motivation is relevant to any *moral* assessment of what he did. Concern that a violator was escaping is one possible motivating factor; so was his doing his duty; so was his delight in pursuit and dislike for perpetrators who belong to a particular minority group. Why we do what we do is of central moral importance, not just that we do it. Not that it should not be done at all if it is not done for the right reasons, but that our assessment of moral worth must take our reasons into account. There is more to morality than an optimization of outcomes.[31] Indeed, part of the point of a professional code must be to inspire *service*, to point members beyond economic and personal reward as the basis for their conduct.

12.5.2.2 The Encouragement of Inauthenticity. Morality, I have claimed, is not just a matter of conduct but of conduct that is informed by some reasons rather than others. Some contribute to moral praiseworthiness, others do not. But there is a further issue beyond that of the appropriateness of reasons to moral merit. It is also important that the reasons be *one's own*. Codes encourage an externalization of conduct not just by divorcing conduct from its appropriate springs, but by detaching it from a certain kind of subjectivity that makes it an authentic expression of the person whose conduct it is. The reasons for engaging in ethical conduct must express what is within, and not conform simply to what is demanded without. True, a code may prompt one to reflect in certain ways that one might not otherwise have anticipated. That is not being questioned and may, in fact, be an important value to be preserved in codes of ethics. But unless what is

ultimately done or not done is done or not done for reasons that are or have become one's own, rather than because "the conduct was prescribed or proscribed," it will lack authenticity and *moral* value, whatever other values it may possess. In some cases, no doubt, a person may be authentically committed to following the prescriptions and proscriptions of a code, and thus the conduct will possess an indirect authenticity. But there tends to be certain superficiality about this kind of authenticity, the kind of superficiality that made the Nuremberg defenses unworthy of human beings.

12.5.2.3 The Danger of Ossification. Associated with the foregoing deficiencies is a further one. Even if we grant—as I would—that ethical questions are generally amenable to definite and correct answers (there is a proper way to be, and a right thing to do), there is no decisive reason for assuming that those answers will be encapsulated in a given code of ethics. Actual codes do not usually exhaust the legitimate moral options and may even prescribe some illegitimate ones. Even if the provisions of a code reflect some widely shared understanding, that is no guarantee of their general correctness. We might, for example, consider how the Hippocratic Oath, for so long the physician's *Torah*, has now been "historicized" and called into question.[32] And although police officers who find their own understanding at variance with that of their code of ethics have a problem on their hands, we cannot just assume that all the provisions of a particular code are defensible. True, given the generality of most codified provisions, this is likely to be uncommon. But it will sometimes occur. And even when we are generally sympathetic to the provisions of a code, it is usually better to see them as presumptive than as absolute. For example, the commitment made in the IACP Law Enforcement Code of Ethics never to "permit personal feelings . . . or friendships to influence my decisions" and never to "accept gratuities" is probably reasonable enough if seen as a general statement of intent. But "never," as the code enjoins? We do not need to work too hard to think of situations in which conduct of the excluded kind would be, if not praiseworthy, then advisable, and even if not that, at least a matter for debate.[33] Few officers would ticket a fellow officer for a minor traffic violation. True, ticketing is discretionary, and there are surely limits to "professional courtesies,"[34] but when the renunciation is stated as baldly as it is in the Law Enforcement Code of Ethics it obscures the much finer nuancing that ethical reflection provides. And, of course, such absolutism lowers the code's status in the eyes of officers. There is an *ongoing* character to ethical reflection that is jeopardized by the institutionalized closure that often accompanies the adoption of a code.

12.5.2.4 The Failure to Prioritize. Even though codes sometimes provide fairly detailed guidance on specific issues, and may therefore assist the inexperienced, they are often of limited usefulness in those cases where assistance is most needed. "Hard cases" are not uncommon in police work. The very nature of the work often involves a careful assessment of individual and social interests that cannot be easily reconciled, and the wise exercise of discretion is required. Codes are rarely helpful to the making of such discretionary judgments. They enumerate goals and standards without indicating priorities or procedures for handling conflicts between code requirements. A police officer who must decide how to deal with a traffic violator needs to take into account not only the seriousness of the breach (itself a matter of judgment), but also the kinds of reasons that may have led to it, the sort of effects that a particular decision may have, the social and institutional environment in which the breach occurred, and so on. A police officer who has pledged to "keep the peace" and "enforce all the laws" is not likely to be greatly helped by such formulae. There is, after all, no simple choice between enforcing and not enforcing the law. There are several different ways in which the law may be enforced and not enforced, and though the officer's department may have, in addition to the code, some procedural regulations or rules of thumb, they are

unlikely to accommodate all the complexities with which the officer will be confronted.

In some respects, it is not surprising that codes fail to give this kind of detailed attention to priorities, exceptions, and situational factors. To do so would undermine some of the functions they are generally intended to have. The more a code is prepared to address specific issues, the more likely it is to arouse controversy both outside and within. And since codes are usually intended to inspire confidence without and unity within, there is a certain counterproductivity associated with detail. Both the ABA and AMA have found that to their cost.[35]

Despite the foregoing problems—contingent and endemic—they do not in themselves support the conclusion that codes ought not to be promulgated. The absence of a code is also problematic, and some of the problems of codes, if recognized, can be diminished, even if not always eliminated. To anticipate, I do not believe there is any fixed formula for occupational and professional codes, and, provided that we are aware of what we intend of them and of their limitations, they may serve valuable external and internal functions. What the problems referred to may do is point us in the direction of codes that, on the one hand, provide a more systematic and integrated statement of the standards that can be expected of service providers, along with a recognition of their own limitations.

12.6 THE VALUE OF CODES

In some respects ethical codes are like firearms. They have their value; they have their dangers. It is often difficult to maintain their value without risking their dangers; and it is difficult to eliminate their dangers without sacrificing their value.

Codes of ethics remind us that the provision of public services involves certain kinds of social cooperation, certain sharings of experience and insight, and that if these services are to be provided in an orderly manner their providers need to create an environment of trust. They remind us that trust requires a measure of trustworthiness. At the same time, however, as we examine "the life and times" of professional codes, they also remind us of the power of ideology—of the way in which an appearance can mask reality, and self-interest can exploit the conditions for social living.

Codes of ethics are also like barometers. They register fluctuations of pressure, of social pressure, and reflect a society's or service association's dominant concerns. The promulgation of a code constitutes one means whereby service providers may look at themselves to see what they are responsive to, and it thus represents an opportunity for them to assess and refocus their endeavors.

One of the most important functions that a code can fulfill is a processual one. The very task of drawing up a code should be an opportunity for an organization or association to look at itself—to ask itself what it is really about, what is reasonable to expect of its members, what standards should determine its internal as well as its external affairs. It should also be an opportunity for a wider community to ask itself what it may reasonably expect of the providers of particular goods and services. Too often, unfortunately, codes of ethics are seen statically, as outcomes or products, as fixed determinations, and not as active expressions of the self-awareness of a community within a community. They are, moreover, viewed as the deliverances of police management and not as documents of common ownership. Only if officers as a whole are able to participate in their formulation are they likely to consider such codes as *theirs*, as embodiments of a commitment *they* have made.

In a helpful overview of professional ethics and of professional codes, John Kultgen has remarked, in the epigraph to this chapter, that every code should be treated as a hypothesis to be tested and adapted while following it. This contains just about the right amount of paradox. At the point where he makes this remark, Kultgen challenges the mechanical application of codified rules. For even if the rules are adequate to a situation at hand, they do not obviate the need for a personal acceptance that enables following them to be an authentic expression of the decision maker. The judgment that the rule is adequate must be a judgment that the service provider makes. Authenticity, however, is not enough. Judgment too is required in applying the rule to the situation at hand. Courtesy may be a reasonable expectation to have of police. But there are many ways of being courteous, and some situations make some expressions of courtesy more appropriate than others. Firmness is not necessarily excluded. A police officer who recognizes that courtesy is grounded in a respect for the persons of those with whom he or she must deal will not confuse it with gentility but will see in it an expectation of considerateness in dealing with others.

The paradox implicit in Kultgen's advice is to be found in the conjunction of Rule following with the idea that rules are hypotheses to be tested. The conjunction is well chosen, however. There is no necessary opposition between fidelity to the standards that are implicit in the goals of a particular profession or occupation and a critical engagement with their articulation in specific provisions. A questioning faith need not be a doubting one. One may revise from within as from without.

In pledging themselves to their code of ethics, police officers signal their willingness to enter into an occupational culture that is defined by certain aims and standards. What is believed to justify this code—its creation and preservation—is the importance that a culture or ethos so defined has to the fulfillment of the ends of police service. In terms of their relations to each other and to their department and the public they serve, it is essential that there exists a framework of mutual understanding and trust. That at least seems to be something of the background to the pledge. But, as with other pledges, one does not sacrifice one's capacities and standing as a reflective being once the pledge has been made. And officers may well find, as they acclimatize themselves to their occupational environment, that their codes are not fully adequate to the situational and moral demands that are placed on them. To a degree, it is not inconsistent for them to press for some revision of their code. It is always appropriate for them to see the code itself as a resting point but not as the terminus in the ongoing deliberative enterprise that constitutes human life.

The very fact of variety in law enforcement (and other) codes should itself provide some reason for believing that, though codes may play a significant part in defining and preserving a police culture and in enabling police culture to flourish within a larger communal arrangement, they do not require a *sacrificium intellectus.* The police community is, as it must always be, a community of moral agents committed to the reflective and self-reflective task that is the task of every human being. That this reflection takes place within an environment shaped by the ends and tasks of policing need constitute no barrier to that deliberative enterprise, though it may well affect the way in which one goes about it. How one sets about repairing Theseus's ship will depend significantly on whether one is sailing in it on the high seas or one has it in dry dock.

NOTES

[1]The material in this chapter overlaps with the Introduction to John Kleinig, with Yurong Zhang (comps. and eds.), *Professional Law Enforcement Codes: A Documentary Collection* (Westport, CT: Greenwood, 1993). All the police codes referred to in this chapter are reproduced in that collection.

[2]John H. Kultgen, *Ethics and Professionalism* (Philadelphia: University of Pennsylvania Press, 1988), p. 216.

[3]See Michael Davis, "The Ethics Boom: What and Why" *The Centennial Review* 34 (1990), pp. 163–86.

[4]The earliest collection of which I am aware is Edgar L. Heermance's *Codes of Ethics: A Handbook* (Burlington, VT: Free Press Printing Co., 1924). Two significant recent collections are Rena A. Gorlin (ed.), *Codes of Professional Responsibility*, 3rd ed. (Edison, NJ: BNA Books, 1994); and Nigel G. E. Harris, *Professional Codes of Conduct in the United Kingdom: A Directory* (London: Mansell, 1989). None of them, however, contains any police code of ethics.

[5]*Maxims for the General Guidance of Members of the Police Force* (Sydney: Thomas Richards, NSW Government Printer, 1870).

[6]Wilson remained in Wichita for eleven years. For details, see William J. Bopp, *"O.W.": O.W. Wilson and the Search for a Police Profession* (New York: Kennikat Press, 1977), ch. 5.

[7]Wittgenstein's metaphor is explicated in *Philosophical Investigations,* trans. G. E. M. Anscombe (Oxford: Blackwell,

1958), sects. 66ff. For a criticism, which I accept, and which accounts for my reference to a unifying function, see Julius Kovesi, *Moral Notions* (London: Routledge & Kegan Paul, 1967), p. 22.

[8]As far as I know, police codes have not yet been used for this purpose. See, however, J. J. Fason, III, "Comment: The Georgia Code of Professional Responsibility: A Catalyst for Successful Malpractice Actions?" *Mercer Law Review,* 37 (1986), pp. 817–37; C. P. Edmonds, III and J. Shampton, "Codes of Ethics: A Basis for Evaluating Appraiser Liability," *Appraiser Journal* 58 (1990), pp. 168–79; C. A. Constantinides, "Note: Professional Ethics Codes in Court: Redefining the Social Contract Between the Public and the Professions," *Georgia Law Review* 25 (1991), pp. 1,327–73.

[9]Michael Davis, "Thinking Like an Engineer: The Place of a Code of Ethics in the Practice of a Profession," *Philosophy & Public Affairs* 20 (1991), p. 156.

[10]Ibid.

[11]See Michael Davis, "Do Cops Really Need a Code of Ethics?" *Criminal Justice Ethics* 10, 2 (Summer/Fall 1991), pp. 15–17.

[12]Davis, "Do Cops Really Need a Code of Ethics?" p. 20. Cf.: ". . . a code necessarily sets a standard higher than ordinary morality" (Davis, "Codes of Ethics, Professions, and Conflicts of Interest: A Case Study of an Emerging Profession, Clinical Engineering," *Professional Ethics* 1, 1 & 2 [Spring/Summer 1992], p. 186).

[13]Davis, "Do Cops Really Need a Code of Ethics?" p. 15.

[14]Ibid., p. 20.

[15]A point that Davis appears to concede in ibid., p. 23.

[16]Ibid., p. 24.

[17]This is taken from Article 8 of the United Nations' "Code of Conduct for Law Enforcement Officials."

[18]This is not the place to engage in an extended discussion of the appropriateness of each of these kinds of standards in an ethical code. Presumably, though, if a code is to have some practical bite, it will need to have some mandatory rules at its core. For an elaboration, see Davis, "Do Cops Really Need a Code of Ethics?"

[19]Ibid., pp. 18–19.

[20]I do not want to deny that a police officer's private life is of relevance to his or her public performance (see Chapter 10). However, the suggestion of these codified statements that a police officer must be a paragon of private virtue surely goes too far.

[21]Ibid., p. 20.

[22]See Davis, "Thinking Like an Engineer."

[23]Lon L. Fuller, "The Philosophy of Codes of Ethics," in Bernard Baumrin and Benjamin Freedman (eds.), *Moral Responsibility and the Professions* (New York: Haven Press, 1984), p. 83.

[24]Sometimes the restrictions are expressive of a fortress mentality. Yet there are quite legitimate concerns, such as the need to preserve the integrity and effectiveness of an investigation, and the correct representation of policy.

[25]Occasionally—though I do not have examples from policing—codes spell out rights and duties not only of service providers but also of service users.

[26]But of course a written document can be a two-edged sword. A document that may be used for protection in some situations may be used to convict in others. And so some organizations, including police departments, have at times shown an unwillingness to put standards (or more often procedures) in writing lest they be used against them at a later point. And, to the same end, when standards are reduced to written form, they are sometimes stated in a manner that will not allow breaches—even when they occur—to be easily established.

[27]"Engineering Ethics and the Public Interest," in Robert Baum and Albert Flores (eds.), *Ethical Problems in Engineering*, 2nd ed. (Troy, NY: Rensselaer Polytechnic Institute, 1980), vol. 2, p. 26.

[28]Philip Shuchman, "Ethics and Legal Ethics: The Propriety of the Canons as a Group Moral Code," *George Washington Law Review* 37 (1968), pp. 244–69. Cf. the cynical old-timer who is quoted as saying that "ethics are rules old men make to keep young men from getting any business" (in Jack McMinn, "Ethics Spun from Fairy Tales," in Baum and Flores [eds.], *Ethical Problems in Engineering*, vol. 1, p. 30).

[29]A. P. Bristow, *You . . . and the Law Enforcement Code of Ethics* (Santa Cruz, CA: Davis Publishing Co., 1975). See also George T. Payton, *Patrol Procedure and Enforcement Concepts*, 6th ed. (Los Angeles: Legal Book Co., 1982), ch. 1.

[30]It may, however, be occurring more slowly there, because police training is still academy-based rather than university-based. The openness to inquiry that should characterize university life is more difficult to create in the paramilitary environment of the police academy. This is a pity, since police on the street are still advised to "forget what you learned in academy."

[31]There is also more to morality than taking motivation into account *only* because it bears on the optimization of outcomes. Bernard Williams points to some of these difficulties in *Ethics and the Limits of Philosophy* (Cambridge, MA: Harvard University Press, 1985), ch. 6. There are further subtleties concerning motivation that make even apparently "moral" motivations inadequate. See Michael Stocker, "The Schizophrenia of Modern Ethical Theories," *Journal of Philosophy* 73, 14 (12 August, 1976), pp. 453–66.

[32]See, for example, Robert M. Veatch, *A Theory of Medical Ethics* (New York: Basic, 1981).

[33]See, for example, Richard Kania's discussion in "Should We Tell the Police to Say 'Yes' to Gratuities?" *Criminal Justice Ethics* 7, 2 (Summer/Fall 1988), pp. 37–49.

[34]See John Kleinig and Albert J. Gorman, "Professional Courtesies: To Ticket or Not to Ticket," *American Journal of Police* 11, 4 (1992), pp. 97–113.

[35]I would not, of course, want to deny that there have also been gains from such endeavors. One person's alienation is another's attraction.

The Ethics of Deceptive Interrogation

Jerome H. Skolnick and Richard A. Leo

I. INTRODUCTION

As David Rothman and Aryeh Neier have recently reported, "third degree" police practices—torture and severe beatings—remain commonplace in India, the world's largest

Jerome H. Skolnick and Richard A. Leo, "The Ethics of Deceptive Interrogation" (as appeared in *Criminal Justice Ethics* Volume 11, Number 1 [Winter/Spring 1992]: 3–12). Reprinted by permission of The Institute for Criminal Justice Ethics, 555 W. 57th St., New York, N.Y. 10019-1029.

democracy.[1] Police brutality during interrogation flourishes because it is widely accepted by the middle classes.[2] Although this may seem uncivilized to most Americans, it was not so long ago that American police routinely used physical violence to extract admissions from criminal suspects.[3] Since the 1960s, and especially since *Miranda*, police brutality during interrogation has virtually disappeared in America. Although one occasionally reads about or hears reports of physical violence during custodial questioning,[4] police observers and critics agree that the use of physical coercion during interrogation is now exceptional.

This transformation occurred partly in response to the influential Wickersham report,[5] which disclosed widespread police brutality in the United States during the 1920s; partly in response to a thoughtful and well-intentioned police professionalism, as exemplified by Fred Inbau and his associates; and partly in response to changes in the law which forbade police to "coerce" confessions but allowed them to elicit admissions by deceiving suspects who have waived their right to remain silent. Thus, over the last fifty to sixty years, the methods, strategies, and consciousness of American police interrogators have been transformed: psychological persuasion and manipulation have replaced physical coercion as the most salient and defining features of contemporary police interrogation. Contemporary police interrogation is routinely deceptive.[6] As it is taught and practiced today, interrogation is shot through with deception. Police are instructed to, are authorized to—and do—trick, lie, and cajole to elicit so-called "voluntary" confessions.

Police deception, however, is more subtle, complex, and morally puzzling than physical coercion. Although we share a common moral sense in the West that police torture of criminal suspects is so offensive as to be impermissible—a sentiment recently reaffirmed by the violent images of the Rodney King beating—the propriety of deception by police is not nearly so clear. The law reflects this ambiguity by being inconsistent, even confusing. Police are permitted to pose as drug dealers, but not to use deceptive tactics to gain entry without a search warrant; nor are they permitted to falsify an affidavit to obtain a search warrant.

The acceptability of deception seems to vary inversely with the level of the criminal process. Cops are permitted to, and do, lie routinely during investigation of crime, especially when, working as "undercovers," they pretend to have a different identity.[7] Sometimes they may, and sometimes may not, lie when conducting custodial interrogations. Investigative and interrogatory lying are each justified on utilitarian

crime control grounds. But police are never supposed to lie as witnesses in the courtroom, although they may lie for utilitarian reasons similar to those permitting deception at earlier stages.[8] In this article, we focus on the interrogatory stage of police investigation, considering (1) how and why the rather muddled legal theory authorizing deceptive interrogation developed; (2) what deceptive interrogation practices police, in fact, engage in; and—a far more difficult question—(3) whether police should ever employ trickery and deception during interrogation in a democratic society valuing fairness in its judicial processes.

II. THE JURISPRUDENCE OF POLICE INTERROGATION

The law of confessions is regulated by the Fifth, Sixth, and Fourteenth Amendments. Historically, the courts have been concerned almost exclusively with the use of *coercion* during interrogation. Although a coerced confession has been inadmissible in federal cases since the late nineteenth century, the Supreme Court did not proscribe physically coercive practices in state cases until 1936.[9] In *Brown v. Mississippi*, three black defendants were repeatedly whipped and pummelled until they confessed. This was the first in a series of state cases in which the Court held that confessions could not be "coerced," but had to be "voluntary" to be admitted into evidence.[10]

Whether a confession meets that elusive standard is to be judged by "the totality of the circumstances." Under that loose and subjective guideline, an admission is held up against "all the facts" to decide whether it was the product of a "free and rational will" or whether the suspect's will was "overborne" by police pressure. Over the years, however, certain police practices have been designated as presumptively coercive. These include physical force, threats of harm or punishment, lengthy or incommunicado interrogation, denial of food and/or sleep, and promises of leniency.[11] In 1940, the Supreme Court ruled—in a case in which a suspect was first threatened with mob violence, then continuously questioned by at least four officers for five consecutive days—that psychological pressure could also be coercive.[12]

One reason for excluding admissions obtained through coercion is their possible falsity. But, beginning with *Lisenba v. California*[13] in 1941, and followed by *Ashcraft v. Tennessee*[14] three years later, the Supreme Court introduced the criterion of *fairness* into the law. Whether in the context of searches or interrogations, evidence gathered by police methods that "shock the conscience" of the community or violate a fundamental standard of fairness are to be excluded, regardless of reliability.[15] This rationale is sometimes twinned with a third purpose: deterring offensive or unlawful police conduct.

In its watershed *Miranda* decision, the Supreme Court in 1966 prescribed specific limitations on custodial interrogation by police.[16] The five-to-four majority deplored a catalog of manipulative and potentially coercive psychological tactics employed by police to elicit confessions from unrepresented defendants. In essence, the court could not reconcile ideas such as "fairness" and "voluntariness" with the increasingly sophisticated and psychologically overbearing methods of interrogation. In response, it fashioned the now familiar prophylactic rules to safeguard a criminal defendant's fifth amendment right against testimonial compulsion. As part of its holding, *Miranda* requires that (1) police advise a suspect of her right to remain silent and her right to an attorney, and (2) the suspect "voluntarily, knowingly and intelligently" have waived these rights before custodial interrogation can legally commence. An interrogation is presumed to be coercive unless a waiver is obtained. Once obtained, however, the "due process-voluntariness" standard governs the admissibility of any confession evidence. In practice, once a waiver is obtained, most of the deceptive tactics deplored by the majority become available to the police.

In retrospect, *Miranda* seems to be an awkward compromise between those who argue that a waiver cannot be made "intelligently" without the advice of an attorney, who would usually advise her client to remain silent, and those who would have preferred to retain an unmodified voluntariness standard because police questioning is "a particularly trustworthy instrument for screening out the innocent and fastening on the guilty," and because the government's obligation is "not to counsel the accused but to question him."[17]

In sum, then, three sometimes competing principles underlie the law of confessions: first, the truth-finding rationale, which serves the goal of *reliability* (convicting an innocent person is worse than letting a guilty one go free); second, the substantive due process or *fairness* rationale, which promotes the goal of the system's integrity; and third, the related *deterrence* principle, which proscribes offensive or lawless police conduct.

The case law of criminal procedure has rarely, however, and often only indirectly, addressed the troubling issue of trickery and deceit during interrogation. We believe this is the key issue in discussing interrogation since, we have found, interrogation usually implies deceiving and cajoling the suspect.

Police deception that intrudes upon substantive constitutional rights is disallowed. For example, the Supreme Court has ruled that an officer cannot trick a suspect into waiving his *Miranda* rights. But apart from these constraints, the use of trickery and deception during interrogation is regulated solely by the due process clause of the Fourteenth Amendment, and is proscribed, on a case-by-case basis, only when it violates a fundamental conception of fairness or is the product of egregious police misconduct. The courts have offered police few substantive guidelines regarding the techniques of deception during interrogation. Nor have the courts successfully addressed the relation between fairness and the lying of police, or the impact of police lying on the broader purposes of the criminal justice system, such as convicting and punishing the guilty. As we shall see, the relations among lying, conceptions of fairness, and the goals of the criminal justice system raise intriguing problems.

III. A TYPOLOGY OF INTERROGATORY DECEPTION

Because police questioning remains shrouded in secrecy, we know little about what actually happens during interrogation. Police rarely record or transcribe interrogation sessions.[18] Moreover, only two observational studies of police interrogation have been reported, and both are more than two decades old.[19] Most articles infer from police training manuals what must transpire during custodial questioning. Our analysis is based on Richard Leo's dissertation research. It consists of a reading of the leading police training manuals from 1942 to the present; from attending local and national interrogation training seminars and courses; from listening to tape-recorded interrogations; from studying interrogation transcripts; and from ongoing interviews with police officials.

A. *"Interview" versus "Interrogate"*

The Court in *Miranda* ruled that warnings must be given to a suspect who is in custody, or whose freedom has otherwise been significantly deprived. However, police will question suspects in a "non-custodial" setting—which is defined more by the suspect's state of mind than by the location of the questioning—so as to circumvent the necessity of rendering warnings. This is the most fundamental, and perhaps the most overlooked, deceptive stratagem police employ. By telling the suspect that he is free to leave at any time, and by having him acknowledge that he is voluntarily answering their questions, police will transform what would otherwise be considered an interrogation into a non-custodial interview. Thus, somewhat paradoxically, courts have ruled that police questioning outside of the station may be custodial,[20] just as police questioning inside the station may be non-custodial.[21] The line between the two is the "objective" restriction on the suspect's freedom. Recasting the interrogation as an interview is the cleanest deceptive police tactic since it virtually removes police questioning from the realm of judicial control.

B. *Miranda Warnings*

When questioning qualifies as "custodial," however, police must recite the familiar warnings. The Court declared in *Miranda* that police cannot trick or deceive a suspect into waiving *Miranda* rights.[22] The California Supreme Court has additionally ruled that police cannot "soften up" a suspect prior to administering the warnings.[23] However, police routinely deliver the *Miranda* warnings in a flat, perfunctory tone of voice to communicate that the warnings are merely a bureaucratic ritual. Although it might be inevitable that police would deliver *Miranda* warnings unenthusiastically, investigators whom we have interviewed say that they *consciously* recite the warnings in a manner intended to heighten the likelihood of eliciting a waiver. It is thus not surprising that police are so generally successful in obtaining waivers.[24]

C. *Misrepresenting the Nature or Seriousness of the Offense*

Once the suspect waives, police may misrepresent the nature or seriousness of the offense. They may, for example, tell a suspect that the murder victim is still alive, hoping that this will compel the suspect to talk. Or police may exaggerate the seriousness of the offense—overstating, for example, the amount of money embezzled—so that the suspect feels compelled to confess to a smaller role in the offense. Or the police may suggest that they are only interested in obtaining admissions to one crime, when in fact they are really investigating another crime. For example, in a recent case, *Colorado v. Spring*, federal agents interrogated a suspect on firearms charges and parlayed his confession into an additional, seemingly unrelated and unimportant, admission of first-degree murder.[25] Despite their pretense to the contrary, the federal agents were actually investigating the murder, not the firearms charge. This tactic was upheld by the Supreme Court.

D. *Role Playing: Manipulative Appeals to Conscience*

Effective interrogation often requires that the questioner feign different personality traits or act out a variety of roles.[26] The interrogator routinely projects sympathy, understanding, and compassion in order to play the role of the suspect's friend. The interrogator may also try to play the role of a brother or father figure, or even to act as a therapeutic or religious counselor to encourage the confession. The best-known role interrogators may act out is, of course, the good cop/bad cop routine, often played out by a single officer. While acting out these roles, the investigator importunes—sometimes relentlessly—the suspect to confess for the good of her case, her family, society, or conscience. These tactics generate an illusion of intimacy between the suspect and the officer while downplaying the adversarial aspects of interrogation.

The courts have routinely upheld the legitimacy of such techniques—which are among the police's most effective in inducing admissions—except when such role-playing or manipulative appeals to conscience can be construed as "coercive," as when, for example, an officer implies that God will punish the suspect for not confessing.[27]

E. Misrepresenting the Moral Seriousness of the Offense

Misrepresentation of the moral seriousness of an offense is at the heart of interrogation methods propounded by Inbau, Reid, and Buckley's influential police training manual.[28] Interrogating officials offer suspects excuses or moral justifications for their misconduct by providing the suspect with an external attribution of blame that will allow him to save face while confessing. Police may, for example, attempt to convince an alleged rapist that he was only trying to show the victim love or that she was really "asking for it"; or they may persuade an alleged embezzler that blame for her actions is attributable to low pay or poor working conditions. In *People v. Adams*, for example, the officer elicited the initial admission by convincing the suspect that it was the gun, not the suspect, that had done the actual shooting.[29] Widely upheld by the courts, this tactic is advertised by police training manuals and firm as one of their most effective.

F. The Use of Promises

The systematic persuasion—the wheedling, cajoling, coaxing, and importuning—employed to induce conversation and elicit admissions often involves, if only implicitly or indirectly, the use of promises. Although promises of leniency have been presumed to be coercive since 1897, courts continue to permit vague and indefinite promises.[30] The admissibility of a promise thus seems to turn on its specificity. For example, in *Miller v. Fenton*, the suspect was repeatedly told that he had mental problems and thus needed psychological treatment rather than punishment. Although this approach implicitly suggested a promise of leniency, the court upheld the validity of the resulting confession.[31]

Courts have also permitted officers to tell a suspect that his conscience will be relieved only if he confesses, or that they will inform the court of the suspect's cooperation, or that "a showing of remorse" will be a mitigating factor, or that they will help the suspect out in every way they can if he confesses.[32] Such promises are deceptive insofar as they create expectations that will not be met. Since interrogating officials are single-mindedly interested in obtaining admissions and confessions, they rarely feel obliged to uphold any of their promises.

G. Misrepresentations of Identity

A police agent may try to conceal his identity, pretending to be someone else, while interrogating a suspect. In *Leyna v. Denno*, the suspect was provided with a physician for painful sinus attacks he begun to experience after several days of unsuccessful interrogation.[33] But the physician was really a police psychiatrist, who repeatedly assured the defendant that he had done no wrong and would be let off easily. The suspect subsequently confessed, but the Supreme Court ruled here that the confession was inadmissible. It would be equally impermissible for a police official or agent to pretend to be a suspect's lawyer or priest. However, in a very recent case, *Illinois v. Perkins*, a prison inmate, Perkins, admitted a murder to an undercover police officer who, posing as a returned escapee, had been placed in his cellblock.[34] The Rehnquist Court upheld the admissibility of the confession. Since Perkins was in jail for an offense unrelated to the murder to which he confessed, the Rehnquist Court said, Perkins was not, for *Miranda* purposes, "in custody." Nor, for the same reason, were his Sixth Amendment *Massiah* rights violated.[35] Thus, the profession or social group with which an undercover officer or agent identifies during the actual questioning may—as a result of professional disclosure rules or cultural norms—be more significant to the resulting legal judgment than the deceptive act itself.[36]

H. Fabricated Evidence

Police may confront the suspect with false evidence of his guilt. This may involve one or more of five gambits. One is to falsely inform the suspect that an accomplice has identified him. Another is to falsely state that existing physical evidence—such as fingerprints, bloodstains, or hair samples—confirm his guilt. Yet another is to assert that an eyewitness or the actual victim has identified and implicated him. Perhaps the most dramatic physical evidence ploy is to stage a line-up, in which a coached witness falsely identifies the suspect. Finally, one of the most common physical evidence ploys is to have the suspect take a lie-detector test and regardless of the results—which are scientifically unreliable and invalid in any event—inform the suspect that the polygraph confirms his guilt.[37] In the leading case on the use of police trickery, *Frazier v. Cupp*, the Supreme Court upheld the validity of falsely telling a suspect that his crime partner had confessed.[38]

IV. THE CONSEQUENCES OF DECEPTION

Although lying is, as a general matter, considered immoral, virtually no one is prepared to forbid it categorically. The traditional case put to the absolutist is that of the murderer chasing a fleeing innocent victim, whose whereabouts are known by a third party. Should the third party sacrifice the innocent victim to the murderer for the cause of truth? Few of us would say that she should. We thus assume a utilitarian standard regarding deception. So, too, with respect to police interrogation.

Interrogatory deception is an exceedingly difficult issue, about which we share little collective feeling. How are we to balance our respect for truth and fairness with our powerful concern for public safety and the imposition of just deserts? We are always guided by underlying intuitions about the kind of community we want to foster and in which we want to live. Which is worse in the long run—the excesses of criminals or the excesses of authorities?

Few of us would countenance torture by police in the interests of those same values. One reason is that violence may produce false confessions. As Justice Jackson observed in his dissent in *Ashcraft*: ". . . [N]o officer of the law will resort to cruelty if truth is what he is seeking."[39] But that is only partly correct. Cruelty can also yield incontrovertible physical evidence. We reject torture for another reason—we find it uncivilized, conscience-shocking, unfair, so most of us are repelled by it. That leads to a third reason for opposing torture. If effective law enforcement requires public trust and cooperation, as the recent movement toward community-oriented policing suggests, police who torture can scarcely be expected to engender such confidence.

What about police deception? Does it lead to false confessions? Is it unfair? Does it undermine public confidence in the police? A recent and fascinating capital case in the Florida Court of Appeal, *Florida v. Cayward*, the facts of which are undisputed, is relevant to the above questions.[40] The defendant, a nineteen-year-old male, was suspected of sexually assaulting and smothering his five-year-old niece. Although he was suspected of the crime, the police felt they had too little evidence to charge him. So they interviewed him, eventually advised him of his rights, and obtained a written waiver.

Cayward maintained his innocence for about two hours. Then the police showed him two false reports, which they had fabricated with the knowledge of the state's attorney.

Purportedly scientific, one report used Florida Department of Criminal Law Enforcement stationery; another used the stationery of Life Codes, Inc., a testing organization. The false reports established that his semen was found on the victim's underwear. Soon after, Cayward confessed.

Should this deception be considered as akin to lying to a murderer about the whereabouts of the victim? Or should police trickery, and especially the falsification of documents, be considered differently? We unsystematically put this hypothetical question to friends in Berkeley and asked about it in a discussion with scholars-in-residence at the Rockefeller Study Center in Bellagio, Italy. The answers, we discovered, revealed *no* common moral intuition. For some, the answer was clear—in either direction. "Of course the police should lie to catch the murdering rapist of a child," said one. "I don't want to live in a society where police are allowed to lie and to falsify evidence," said another. Most were ambivalent, and all were eager to know how the Florida court resolved the dilemma.

Citing *Frazier v. Cupp* and other cases, the court recognized "that police deception does not render a confession involuntary *per se.*" Yet the court, deeply troubled by the police deception, distinguished between "verbal assertions and manufactured evidence." A "bright line" was drawn between the two on the following assumption: "It may well be that a suspect is more impressed and thereby more easily induced to confess when presented with tangible, official-looking reports as opposed to merely being told that some tests have implicated him."[41]

Although we do not know the accuracy of the conjecture, it assumes that false police assertions such as "Your fingerprints were found on the cash register" are rarely believed by suspects unless backed up by a false fingerprint report. But in these deception cases, we do not usually encounter prudent suspects who are skeptical of the police. Such suspects rarely, if ever, waive their constitutional rights to silence or to an attorney. As in *Cayward*, and many deception cases, the suspect, young or old, white or black, has naively waived his right to remain silent and to an attorney.

Would such a suspect disbelieve, for example, the following scenario? After two hours of questioning, the telephone rings. The detective answers, nods, looks serious, turns to the suspect and says: "We have just been informed by an independent laboratory that traces of your semen were found, by DNA tests, on the panties of the victim. What do you say to that?"

A verbal lie can be more or less convincing, depending upon the authority of the speaker, the manner of speaking, its contextual verisimilitude, and the gullibility of the listener. False documentation adds to verisimilitude, but a well-staged, carefully presented verbal lie can also convince. The decision in *Cayward*, however well-written and considered, is nevertheless bedeviled by the classic problem of determining whether Cayward's confession was "voluntary."

No *contested* confession, however, is ever voluntary in the sense of purging one's soul of guilt, as one would to a religious figure. "The principal value of confession may lie elsewhere, in its implicit reaffirmation of the moral order," writes Gerald M. Caplan. "The offender by his confession acknowledges that he is to blame, not the community.[42] That observation focuses on the offender. Sometimes that is true, oftentimes it is not. Those who contest their confessions claim that they were unfairly pressured, and point to the tactics of the police. The claim is that the police violated the moral order by the use of unfair, shady, and thus wrongful tactics to elicit the confession. Had the police, for example, beaten a true confession out of Cayward, it would indeed seem perverse to regard his confession as a reaffirmation of the moral order.

If Cayward had been beaten, and had confessed, we would also be concerned that his confession was false. Assuming that all we know are the facts stated in the opinion, which say nothing of corroborating evidence or why Cayward was suspected, should we assume that his confession was necessarily true? However infrequent they may be, false confessions do occur. Moreover, they do not result *only* from physical abuse, threats of harm, or promises of leniency, as Fred Inbau and his associates have long maintained,[43] nor are they simply the result of police pressures that a fictionalized reasonable person would find "overbearing," as Joseph Grano's "mental freedom" test implies.[44] They may arise out of the manipulative tactics of influence and persuasion commonly taught in police seminars and practiced by police and used on Cayward.

Psychologists and others have recently begun to classify and analyze the logic and process of these false confessions,[45] which are among the leading causes of wrongful conviction.[46] Perhaps most interesting is the "coerced-internalized" false confession, which is elicited when the psychological pressures of interrogation cause an innocent person to temporarily internalize the message(s) of his or her interrogators and falsely believe himself to be guilty.[47] Although Cayward was probably factually guilty, he might have been innocent. Someone who is not altogether mature and mentally stable, as would almost certainly be true of a nineteen-year-old accused of smothering and raping his five-year-old niece, might also have a precarious and vague memory. When faced with fabricated, but supposedly incontrovertible, physical evidence of his guilt, he might falsely confess to a crime of which he has no recollection, as happened in the famous case of Peter Reilly,[48] and, more recently, in the Florida case of Tom Sawyer,[49] both of which were "coerced-internalized" false confessions.[50]

If Cayward was, in fact, guilty, as his confession suggests, the court was nevertheless willing to exclude it. Presumably, he will remain unpunished unless additional evidence can be produced. Characterizing the falsified evidence as an offense to "our traditional notions of due process of law," the Florida court was evidently alarmed by the *unfairness* of a system which allows police to "knowingly fabricate tangible documentation or physical evidence against an individual."[51] In addition to its "spontaneous distaste" for the conduct of the police, the court added a longer-range utilitarian consideration. Documents manufactured for such purposes, the court fears, may, because of their "potential of indefinite life and the facial appearance of authenticity,"[52] contaminate the entire criminal justice system. "A report falsified for interrogation purposes might well be retained and filed in police paperwork. Such reports have the potential of finding their way into the courtroom."[53] The court also worried that if false reports were allowed in evidence, police might be tempted to falsify all sorts of official documents "including warrants, orders and judgements," thereby undermining public respect for the authority and integrity of the judicial system.

Yet the slippery slope argument applies to lying as well as to falsification of documents. When police are permitted to lie in the interrogation context, why should they refrain from lying to judges when applying for warrants, from violating internal police organization rules against lying, or from lying in the courtroom? For example, an Oakland Tribune columnist, Alix Christie, recently received a letter from a science professor at the University of California at Berkeley who had served on an Alameda County (Oakland) murder jury. He was dismayed that a defendant, whom he believed to be guilty, had been acquitted because most of the jurors did not believe the police, even about how long it takes to drive from west to east Oakland. "The problem," writes Christie, "predates Rodney King. It's one familiar to prosecutors fishing for jurors who don't fit the profile of people who distrust cops." She locates the problem in "the ugly fact that there are two Americas." In the first America, the one she was raised in, the police are the "good guys." In the other, police are viewed skeptically.

Police misconduct—and lying is ordinarily considered a form of misconduct—undermines public confidence and social cooperation, especially in the second America. People living in these areas often have had negative experiences with police, ranging from an aloof and legalistic policing "style" to corruption, and even to the sort of overt brutality that was captured on the videotape of the Rodney King beating in Los Angeles. Community-oriented policing is being implemented in a number of American police departments to improve trust and citizen cooperation by changing the attitudes of both police and public.

Police deception may thus engender a paradoxical outcome. Although affirmed in the interest of crime control values by its advocates like Fred Inbau—who, along with his co-author John Reid, has exerted a major influence on generation of police interrogators—it may generate quite unanticipated consequences. Rarely do advocates of greater latitude for police to interrogate consider the effects of systematic lying on law enforcement's reputation for veracity. Police lying might not have mattered so much to police work in other times and places in American history. But today, when urban juries are increasingly composed of jurors disposed to be distrustful of police, deception by police during interrogation offers yet another reason for disbelieving law enforcement witnesses when they take the stand, thus reducing police effectiveness as controllers of crime.

Conservatives who lean toward crime control values do not countenance lying as a general matter. They approve of police deception as a necessity, measuring the cost of police deceit against the benefits of trickery for victims of crime and the safety of the general public. Police and prosecutors affirm deceitful interrogative practices not because they think these are admirable, but because they believe such tactics are necessary.[54]

The Florida police officers who fabricated evidence did so for the best of reasons. The victim was a five-year-old girl, and the crime was abhorrent and hard to prove. Nevertheless, the Florida court excluded the confession on due process grounds, arguing that police must be discouraged from fabricating false official documents. Many persons, but especially those who, like Fred Inbau, affirm the propriety of lying in the interrogatory context, tend to undervalue the significance of the long-term harms caused by such authorized deception: namely, that it tends to encourage further deceit, undermining the general norm against lying. And if it is true that the fabrication of documents "greatly lessens," as the Florida

court says, "the respect the public has for the criminal justice system and for those sworn to uphold and enforce the law,"[55] doesn't that concern also apply to interrogatory lying?

There is an additional reason for opposing deceitful interrogation practices. It does happen that innocent people are convicted of crimes. Not as often, probably, as guilty people are set free, but it does happen. Should false evidence be presented, a suspect may confess in the belief that he will receive a lesser sentence. In a study in 1986 of wrongful conviction in felony cases, Ronald Huff and his colleagues conservatively estimated that nearly 6,000 false convictions occur every year in the United States.[56] Hugo Bedau and Michael Radelet, who subsequently studied 350 known miscarriages of justice in recent American history, identified false confessions as one of the leading sources of erroneous conviction of innocent individuals.[57]

There are no easy answers to these dilemmas, no easy lines to suggest when the need to keep police moral and honest brushes up against the imperatives of controlling crime. Phillip E. Johnson, who has proposed a thoughtful statutory replacement for the Miranda doctrine,[58] would not allow police to "intentionally misrepresent the amount of evidence against the suspect, or the nature and seriousness of the charges,"[59] as well as other, clearly more coercive tactics. But he would allow reigned sympathy or compassion, an appeal to conscience or values, and a statement to the suspect such as "A voluntary admission of guilt and sincere repentance may be given favorable consideration at the time of sentence."[60] Johnson states no formal *principle* for these distinctions, but does draw an intuitively sensible contrast between, on the one hand, outright *misrepresentations*, which might generalize to other venues and situations; and, on the other, *appeals* to self-interest or conscience, which seem to draw upon commonly held and morally acceptable values. If, however, as we have argued, rules for police conduct, and the values imparted through these rules, produce indirect, as well as direct, consequences for police practices and the culture of policing, Johnson's distinctions are persuasive. This resolution, we suggest, is quite different from the direction recently taken by the Rehnquist Court.

We have earlier argued that when courts allow police to deceive suspects for the good end of capturing criminals—even as, for example, in "sting" operations—they may be tempted to be untruthful when offering testimony. However we think we ought to resolve the problem of the ethics of deceptive interrogation, we need always to consider the unanticipated consequences of permitting police to engage in what would commonly be considered immoral conduct—such as falsifying evidence. The Supreme Court has moved in recent years to soften the control of police conduct in interrogation. In *Moran v. Burbine*, for example, the Court let stand a murder conviction even though the police had denied a lawyer—who had been requested by a third party, but without the suspect's knowledge, prior to his questioning—to the suspect during interrogation. The dissenters decried the "incommunicado questioning" and denounced the majority for having embraced "deception of the shabbiest kind."[61]

More recently, the notoriety of the Rodney King beating overshadowed the significance of the Rehnquist Court's most significant self-incrimination decision, *Arizona v. Fulminante*.[62] Here, a confession was obtained when a prison inmate, an ex-cop who was also an FBI informer, offered to protect Fulminante from prison violence, but only if he confessed to the murder of his daughter. In a sharply contested five-to-four opinion, the Court reversed the well-established doctrine that a coerced confession could never constitute "harmless error." Whether the ruling will be as important in *encouraging* police coercion of confessions as the King videotape will be in discouraging future street brutality remains to be seen. But in concert with other recent U.S. Supreme Court decisions that have cut back on the rights of defendants, the *Fulminante* decision may also send a message that police coercion is sometimes acceptable, and that a confession elicited by police deception will almost always be considered "voluntary."

NOTES

For helpful advice, criticism, and counsel, we would like to thank the following individuals: Albert Altschuler, Jack Greenberg, James Hahn, Sanford Kadish, Norman LaPera, Paul Mishkin, Robert Post, Peter Sarna, Jonathan Sither, Amy Toro, Jeremy Waldron, and, especially, Phillip Johnson.

[1]Rothman & Neier, *India's Awful Prisons*, N.Y. Rev. Books May 16, 1991, at 53–56.

[2]Id. at 54.

[3]See E. Hopkins, *Our Lawless Police: A Study of Unlawful Enforcement* (1931), and E. Lavine, *The Third Degree: A Detailed and Appalling Expose of Police Brutality* (1930).

[4]"Confession at Gunpoint?" *20/20*, ABC News, March 29, 1991.

[5]National Commission on Law Observance and Enforcement, Lawlessness in Law Enforcement (1931).

[6]Richard Leo, From Coercion to Deception: An Empirical Analysis of the Changing Nature of Modern Police Interrogation in America (paper presented at the Annual Meeting of the American Society of Criminology, Nov. 19–23, 1991).

[7]See G. Marx, *Undercover: Police Surveillance in America* (1988).

[8]See Skolnick, Deception by Police, *Criminal Justice Ethics*, Summer/Fall 1982, at 40–54.

[9]*Brown v. Mississippi*, 297 U.S. 278 (1936).

[10]Caplan, Questioning Miranda, 38 *Vanderbilt Law Review* 1417 (1985).

[11]The Supreme Court's very recent ruling that coerced confessions may be "harmless error" will undermine this general rule. Arizona v. Fulminante, U.S. LEXIS 1854 (1991).

[12]*Chambers v. Florida*, 309 U.S. 227 (1940).

[13]314 U.S. 219 (1941).

[14]322 U.S. 143 (1944).

[15]See *Rochin v. California*, 342 U.S. 165 (1952), *Spano v. New York*, 360 U.S. 315 (1959), and *Rogers v. Richmond*, 365 U.S. 534 (1961).

[16]*Miranda v. Arizona*, 384 U.S. 436 (1961).

[17]Caplan, supra note 10, at 1422–23.

[18]The state of Alaska requires, as a matter of state constitutional due process, that all custodial interrogations be electronically recorded. See *Stephan v. State*, 711 P.2d 1156 (1985).

[19]Wald, et al., Interrogations in New Haven: The Impact of Miranda, 76 *Yale L. J.* 1519–1648 (1967), and N. Milner, *Court and Local Law Enforcement: The Impact of Miranda* (1971).

[20]*Orozco v. Texas*, 394 U.S. 324 (1969).

[21]See *Beckwith v. United States*, 425 U.S. 341 (1976), *Oregon v. Mathiason*, 429 U.S. 492 (1977), and *California v. Beheler*, 463 U.S. 1121 (1983).

[22]However, police may deceive an attorney who attempts to invoke a suspect's constitutional rights, as to whether the suspect will be interrogated, and the police do not have to inform the suspect that a third party has hired an attorney on his behalf. *People v. Moran*, 475 U.S. 412 (1986).

[23]*People v. Honeycutt*, 570 P.2d 1050 (1977).

[24]See O. Stephens, Jr., *The Supreme Court and Confessions of Guilt* 165–200 (1973) for a useful summary of studies assessing the impact of Miranda in New Haven, Los Angeles, Washington, D.C., Pittsburgh, Denver, and rural Wisconsin. These studies indicate that police obtain waivers from criminal suspects in most cases. Additionally, the Captain of the Criminal Investigation Division of the Oakland Police Department told one of the authors that detectives obtain waivers from criminal suspects in 85–90% of all cases involving interrogations.

[25]*Colorado v. Spring*, 107 S.Ct. 851 (1987).

[26]Consider the following passage from R. Royal and S. Schutt, *The Gentle Art of Interviewing and Interrogation* (1976): "To be truly proficient at interviewing or interrogation, one must possess the ability to portray a great variety of personality traits. The need to adjust character to harmonize with, or dominate, the many moods and traits of the subject is necessary. The interviewer/interrogator requires greater histrionic skill than the average actor. . . . The interviewer must be able to pretend anger, fear, joy, and numerous other emotions without affecting his judgment or revealing any personal emotion about the subject" (p. 65).

[27]*People v. Adams* 143 Cal.App.3d 970 (1983).

[28]F. Inbau, J. Reid, & J. Buckley, *Criminal Interrogation and Confessions* (1986).

[29]*People v. Adams*, supra note 27.

[30]*Bram v. United States*, 168 U.S. 532 (1897).

[31]*Miller v. Fenton*, 796 F.2d 598 (1986).

[32]Kaci & Rush, At What Price Will We Obtain Confessions? 71 *JUDICATURE*, 256–57 (1988).

[33]*Leyra v. Denno*, 347 U.S. 556 (1954).

[34]*Illinois v. Perkins*, 110 S.CT. 2394 (1990).

[35]In *Massiah v. United States*, 377 U.S. 201 (1964), the U.S. Supreme Court held that post-indictment questioning of a defendant outside the presence of his lawyer violates the Sixth Amendment.

[36]See Cohen, Miranda and Police Deception in Interrogation: A Comment on *Illinois v. Perkins, Criminal Law Bulletin* 534–46.(1990).

[37]See Skolnick, Scientific Theory and Scientific Evidence: Analysis of Lie Detection, 70 *Yale Law Journal* 694–728 (1961); and D. Lykken, *A Tremor in the Blood: Uses and Abuses of the Lie-Detector* (1981).

[38]*Frazier v. Cupp*, 394 U.S. 731 (1969).

[39]*Ashcraft v. Tennessee*, supra note 14, at 160.

[40]*Florida v. Cayward*, 552 So. 2d 971 (1989).

[41]Id. at 977.

[42]Caplan, Miranda Revisited, 93 *Yale L. J.* 1375 (1984).

[43]F. Inbau, Lie-Detection and Criminal Interrogation (1942).

[44]Grano, Voluntariness, Free Will, and the Law of Confessions, 65 *VA. L., REV.* 859–945 (1979).

[45]See Kassin & Wrightsman, Confession Evidence, in *The Psychology of Evidence and Trial Procedure* (S. Kassin & L. Wrightsman eds. 1986). G. Gudjonsson & N. Clark, *Suggestibility in Police Interrogation: A Social Psychological Model* (1986); Ofshe, Coerced Confessions: The Logic of Seemingly Irrational Action, 6 *Cultic Stud.* 6–15 (1969); Gudjonsson, The Psychology of False Confessions 57 *MedicoLegal J.* 93–110 (1989); R. Ofshe & R. Leo, The Social Psychology of Coerced-Internalized False Confessions (paper presented at the Annual Meetings of the American Sociological Association, August 23–27, 1991).

[46]Bedau & Radelet, Miscarriages of Justice in Potentially Capital Cases, 40 *Stan. L. Rev.* 21–79 (1987).

[47]Kassin & Wrightsman, supra note 45.

[48]*See* J. Bartel, *A Death in Canaan*, (1976); and D. Conery, *Guilty until Proven Innocent* (1977).

[49]*State of Florida v. Tom Franklin Sawyer*, 561 So. 2d 278 (1990). See also Weiss, Untrue Confessions, *Mother Jones*, Sept. 1989, at 22–24 and 55–57.

[50]Ofshe & Leo, supra note 45.

[51]*Florida v. Cayward*, supra note 40, at 978.

[52]Id.

[53]Id.

[54]Inbau Police Interrogation—A Practical Necessity, 52 *J. Crim. L., Criminology, & Pol. Sci.* 412 (1961).

[55]*Florida v. Cayward*, supra note 40, at 983

[56]Huff, Rattner & Sagarin, Guilty Until Proven Innocent: Wrongful Conviction and Public Policy, 32 *Crime & Delinq.* 518–44 (1986). See also Rattner, Convicted But Innocent: Wrongful Conviction and the Criminal Justice System, 12 *L. & Hum. Behav.* 283–93 (1988).

[57]Bedau & Radelet, supra note 46.

[58]P. Johnson, *Criminal Procedure* 540–50 (1988).

[59]Id. at 542.

[60]Id.

[61]*Moran v. Burbine*, 475 U.S. 412 (1986).

[62]*Arizona v. Fulminante*, supra note 11.

Under-the-Covers Undercover Investigations: Some Reflections on the State's Use of Sex and Deception in Law Enforcement

Gary T. Marx

I have no sympathy for those who are crybabies about the fact that police officers are selling to those who want to buy drugs. We use every legal means that we can. We want everybody to know that the next drug buy may be from a police officer.

—Mayor Marion Barry News Conference, 1988

Or it might be from a former girl friend working for police who has invited you to her hotel room. The arrest and trial of former Mayor Marion Barry after he had purchased drugs from an ex-girl friend raises a variety of ethical and policy issues involving police deception.[1] One of the most interesting involves friendship and undercover investigations. When, if ever, is it appropriate to use friendship and the lure of sex as part of an investigation?

State-sponsored deception, of course, raises all the ethical issues generally associated with deception.[2] It also raises some issues that are unique to the state as the symbolic repository of societal values (for example, the need to avoid setting bad examples). But when friendship and sex are present, as in the Barry case, the situation becomes more complex. Manipulation, temptation and deception (whether involving motives and/or identity) are joined in a potentially explosive[3] mix.

Gary T. Marx, "Under-the-Covers Undercover Investigations" (as appeared in *Criminal Justice Ethics*, Volume 11, Number 1, [Winter/Spring 1992]: 13–24). Reprinted by permission of The Institute for Criminal Justice Ethics, 555 W. 57th St., New York, N.Y. 10019-1029.

In this article I will focus on the limited topic of sex and undercover investigations. The deceptive use of sex may magnify the basic issue of the violation of trust found within the broader topic of "false friend deception." It might help our understanding of the larger topic if we focus on the narrower one. Here I ask: (1) What is at stake and what is different when undercover operations have a sexual component? (2) What are the main ways that sex is used in covert investigations? (3) How should we judge this behavior?

Some parallels exist between sexual and undercover activity. Both are private activities. Those not directly involved will not know much about what goes on. Secrecy and temptation may play important roles in each. Both romance and undercover activities can involve heightened efforts to create impressions, the keeping of secrets, and intense bonding. Prostitution, like undercover work, may involve role-playing and feigning emotions (and to judge from the classic scene in the film *When Harry Meets Sally*, faking it is not the exclusive preserve of professionals). Undercover activities, with their secret watching and audio and video recordings, have a voyeuristic quality. Terminology such as "deep penetration" and "access" have multiple referents. Targets of investigations frequently report being "screwed" by the agent after their arrest. Agents sometimes refer to the agency they work for as their "mistress." For some agents the excitement of undercover has a sexual parallel. As one highly experienced agent put it in an interview with a co-worker, "The best undercover is exalted in what he's doing; it's almost a sexual thrill."

In the case of the "mata-hari" phenomenon, undercover and sexual roles may be professionally interwined—although one recent account suggests that Mata-Hari may have been framed.[4] A possible link between homosexuality and spying, at least in the post-World War II British context, has often been noted. There seems to be a natural congruence between covert means and sex more generally.

I have identified a number of ethical justifications for, and objections to, undercover work.[5] Among the objections is that of lack of respect for the sanctity of intimate relations. Restrictions on the use of spousal testimony reflect this concern. Unlike the impersonal and instrumental relationships of the marketplace, intimate relationships are valued as (and assumed to be) ends in themselves. They flourish to the extent that individuals feel free to express themselves without suspiciousness or fear of others' ulterior motives.

In a larger sense, intimate relations can also have instrumental or functional consequences in positively linking the individual to others. Our sense of freedom, autonomy, and well-being depend partly on our ability to control information about the self and on our being able to voluntarily enter into relationships with others free from both coercion and deception.[6]

Undercover work exploits the cognitive and behavioral aspects of intimate relations by using them for purposes beyond the relationship itself. As Davis observes,[7] intimate relations inherently involve and develop trust based on the revelation and toleration of a wider range of attitudes, inclinations, and behavior than is the case with more casual relations. This trust leads to the exchange of "confidences," some of which will clash with the public image the individual would like to project.

Covert operations, with their duplicity and betrayal, trade on the trust that is essential to, and defines, these primary relations. Anything that debases that trust must be viewed as undesirable (if not necessarily always indefensible). It is in this regard that seduction is the moral equivalent of rape because they both deny the dignity and freedom of the individual.

By contrasting deceptive situations with respect to whether sexual intimacy (or the hint or promise of it) is present with those in which (from the point of view of the target of the investigation) psychological intimacy is, or is not, presumed to be present, we arrive at the four types of situation shown in Table 1.[8] The gravity of betrayal increases as we move from type 2 to type 4. The deception in type 4 "seduction" (psychological and sexual intimacy) is more unethical and troubling than in type 3 "platonic" (psychological but not sexual intimacy). These in turn are more troubling than

Table 1: Types of Intimacy in Undercover Enforcement

| | | *Sexual Intimacy?* | |
		No	Yes
Presumed Psychological Intimacy on Part of Target?	No	1	2 Decoys and prostitution
	Yes	3 Platonic friendships	4 Seduction

type 2 "prostitution" (sexual but not psychological intimacy), although there are ethical objections to this as well.

DECOYS AND PROSTITUTION

I will first consider the type 2 situation, where there is no psychological intimacy but there is implied or actual sexual intimacy. Other factors being equal, the use of undercover means is less troublesome here for three reasons: (i) the criminal violation itself involves sexual behavior, (ii) such acts are coercive or by definition commercial and instrumental, and (iii) the resulting arrests usually do not involve consummation.

The ethical objections (at least with respect to the sexual aspect) in using decoys as potential victims in response to a pattern of sexual assault and harassment are minimal. For example, after a series of rapes in a park, a female agent walks alone in the area with a backup team near by. After female patients complained of being assaulted by a dentist while they were under anesthesia, a policewoman poses as a patient and invites assault, with a backup team watching via a hidden video camera poised to intervene. Departments in a number of cities have recently used decoys in an effort to combat violence against homosexuals. Some departments (with the cooperation of the victim) arrange for rape and sexual harassment victims wearing a wire to return to their assailants and talk to them in order to gather evidence. Since those cases are likely to involve responses to crimes that have already been committed, coercion on the part of the offender, and a relatively passive response by the agent, they are acceptable. The fact that the bait is of a sexual rather than a monetary, or some other, nature is irrelevant. Directing undercover tactics against sexual predators in response to a pattern of victimization is appropriate.

What if those providing sexual services are the subjects of victimization unrelated to sex? Is it appropriate to use decoys where sex is only indirectly an issue? It is not uncommon for urban vice enterprises to be asked to pay organized crime for protection. In response to

the extortion of pornographers and brothel owners, police occasionally (as in Los Angeles and New York cases) act as pornographers and run brothels for a period of time. The goal is to gather evidence of extortion and racketeering. Again, the ethical objections we will note below do not apply.

Nor do these objections apply if those involved in the provision of sex are involved in other more serious crimes (rather than being victims themselves), and if agents facilitate, but are not directly involved, in providing sexual services. For example, in a Chicago investigation into links between organized crime and suburban prostitution, federal agents took over a credit card processing company (whose owner came to them complaining of an extortion threat). Over a four-year period they processed $30 million in customer payments for sexual services. These were shown on credit card records as expenditures for food, beverages, and office supplies, which could be taken as business tax deductions. The FBI-run firm paid the sex clubs from its own bank account and then collected from the customers' credit card company. It also had to pay out $100,000 to local police in bribes to stay in business. The main targets of the investigation were not the actual deliverers of sexual services but organized criminal groups linked to the illicit sex business and crimes of extortion, corruption of public officials, and tax fraud.[9]

With respect to prostitution and covert means, there is considerable disagreement about the appropriateness of criminalizing consenting behavior among adults. In enforcing such statutes the government engages in moral partisanship regarding the disputed relationship between sex and friendship/love. It hypocritically combats the separation it opposes through enforcement means that appear to further it.[10] Enforcing these laws may also waste scarce police resources, demean the enforcers, and have a variety of undesirable and unintended consequences.[11]

The use of covert means to enforce such laws (for example, an officer posing as a prostitute or the client of a prostitute, or as a buyer or seller of pornography) raises the problems that characterize any use of deception by the state. Propriety and the symbolic importance of a pristine governmental image may militate against certain extreme activities (such as the New York City case in which the government financed the making of a pornographic film and had a policewoman direct on-camera sex acts to ensure that they were sufficiently explicit to satisfy the legal definition of obscenity).[12]

Yet as long as these laws are on the books, *the substance of the violation (and its consensual and secret structure) practically requires a degree of participation by the state.* There is a distinction between situations in which sex is used in the direct enforcement of laws regarding sexual conduct (for example, prostitution or pornography) and situations in which sex is merely a tool to some other end. There is an obvious justification for using sex (to some degree at least) in the enforcement of laws requiring sexual conduct. In addition, targets may be protected by the entrapment defense. These factors are missing when sex is used as a resource against a person who faces unrelated, or no, charges.

Prostitution, of course, involves sexual intimacy but not emotional intimacy. In general prostitutes have no expectation of genuine emotional intimacy or commitment from their customers, nor do the customers expect it from them. Their role is strictly professional, and the operative principle is "Let the seller beware." Sex is separated from friendship. Indeed occupational folklore has it that when a prostitute starts enjoying sex with the customers, it's time to find a new line of work. With the publicity given to the use of policewomen posing as prostitutes, in an effort to arrest those who solicit them, the buyer must increasingly beware as well.

Prostitutes know their behavior is illegal and that police will use deception to arrest them. The prostitute chooses to convert sex into a marketable commodity. For law enforcement to use deception in the pretended, or real, purchase of sex is less morally questionable than to use deception in circumstances when it is not for sale, but instead, is voluntarily given out as part of what is presumed to be an intimate relationship.

To be sure, there are certainly questionable schemes to arrest prostitutes. Consider a newspaper advertisement in the *Los Angeles Free Press* which stated: "Sexy hostesses needed for gambling junket. Entails foreign travel. Expenses paid." Applicants were interviewed, and some were then invited to a party in a plush hotel suite. Those invited were told the party was being held so they could meet some of the gamblers who were going on the junket. The message to the girls was, "This is a run-through for the forthcoming trip; it's to your advantage to be liked by the men at the party." Fifty-four of the women went too far in their efforts to be liked and were arrested for solicitation. The ad had been placed by the Los Angeles Police Department, and the gamblers were all undercover police officers.

There are undoubtedly better ways to use police resources, but given laws against prostitution, this is not ethically very disturbing. It contrasts markedly with the ethical disaster that would exist if an undercover officer formed a relationship with a woman, convinced her to become a prostitute, and then had her arrested for prostitution. I have not encountered such a case, but undercover officers do sometimes play the role of pimp. In a Chicago case an agent had trouble leaving the role once the investigation came to an end. He was suspended for operating a prostitution ring.

An experienced undercover agent offers the following practical advice: "Never arrest anyone you sleep with." Most prostitution-related arrests do not involve consummation of a sexual act.[13] On that account at least, they are less objectionable than those in which the act is carried out. This is clearest when we consider the particularly egregious practice of an officer's consummating a sexual act and then arresting his partner. Apart from the personal temptation involved, completion of the act may offer clearer evidence of intent and permit higher charges to be brought.[14] In such (presumably statistically rare) cases, the association of the state's power with deception gives a double meaning to the notion of being screwed.

There is a theft of services and a terrible imbalance or lack of reciprocity that is not found with most other undercover encounters. Both parties participate in the criminal act, the male officer is paid by the state to have sex in the line of duty, and the participating female gets arrested.

Yet is the above situation any different from one in which a vice officer purchases drugs from a drug seller? The answer is "yes" because the former involves direct consumption (and to the benefit of the consumer, not the society on whose behalf he is authorized to act). However, if the agent consumes the drugs purchased the situations are more parallel. When the pursuit of private pleasures emerges as a new goal, the professional "disinterestedness" ideally associated with the role weakens or disappears.[15]

Still, there is an elusive difference which further indicates what is at stake when sex is deceptively "taken" under state sponsorship. In the first case (involving sex rather than drugs) the active participation of the other party is required. In that sense sexual acts are "personal," even in the absence of psychological intimacy. *Betrayal involving another's body adds an additional troubling element*, beyond that occurring with the mere exchange of tangible objects or the failure to keep a promise. Such betrayal is less distant and mediated and hence, whether engaged in coercion or deception, it is more violative.

Another ethical issue concerns equity in assignments regarding gender and sexual preference with respect to the role the agent plays and the likelihood of his or her becoming a suspect/target.

Playing an undercover sexual role and consummating a sexual act within it seems to be disproportionately a phenomenon of male heterosexuals. Greater undercover activity is directed at heterosexual than homosexual prostitution, and male agents are more likely to play the role of the "John" than female agents are that of the prostitute. Some critics also see a double standard (or at least a sexist outcome) in that when policewomen are asked to play such roles, it is that of female prostitute, while policemen rarely pose as male prostitutes.

Paid female heterosexual prostitution is of course much more common than its male equivalent. This represents culturally, and perhaps physiologically, shaped demand and supply factors. Men have traditionally expressed greater demand and also have been more willing to offer the supply without cash and other inducements. In this sense men in principle might be much more vulnerable to sexual exploitation for undercover purposes than are women. However, the double standards of our culture push in the opposite direction, and that helps to explain the empirical gender pattern.[16]

It is extremely rare for the male officers who pose as homosexuals to actually have sex with those they arrest. In my research for *Undercover* I did encounter one case in Atlanta. But this involved an untrained rookie officer who told his sergeant, "I thought you were supposed to go all the way." With increased efforts by departments to recruit homosexuals, actual homosexual activity may become more common.

While in recent decades there has been a marked increase (partly as a result of court challenges) in the number of policewomen posing as prostitutes who arrest the men who proposition them, I have not found equivalent accounts of actual sexual involvement. However, sexual involvement may occur indirectly when prostitutes serve as informers although such involvement is not usually for offenses related to the act of prostitution (for example, the Georgia case discussed later in this article).

SEDUCTION

The type 4 situation, labeled "seduction" in Table 1 (fake psychological intimacy and sexual intimacy), is the most troubling. I do not argue that such situations are always wrong as a law enforcement tool although I think they can rarely be justified. In reviewing type 4 situations I have identified five contexts (based on goals) in which seduction is most commonly found: (1) blackmail, (2) stigmatization and/or disruption, (3) general intelligence collection, (4) evidence collection for an offense that is suspected but not yet committed, and (5) evidence collection for a prior offense.

With respect to *blackmail* a distinction can be made between covert surveillance that permits documentation of sexually embarrassing facts, and the creation —morally even more troubling—of opportunities for such documentation. The secrecy surrounding both of these makes it difficult to know how widespread they are.

Every few years a case becomes public in which a vice detective is arrested for creating and documenting enticing situations that are subsequently used for blackmail purposes. But this use seems more common in international spying than domestically.[17]

The United States had its "honeypots" and the Soviet Union its "swallows," used for both blackmail and deceptive information collection, although the use of sex was probably not as widespread as those who write spy and detective novels would lead us to believe. Given the secrecy and the availability of the tactic to competing countries, it is sometimes difficult to decide just who was seduced and to determine who was the target and who was the agent. Sometimes the individuals involved are both.[18] Thus former FBI agent Richard Miller, who had an affair with a Russian emigre, was accused of spying for the Soviet Union. He claimed that he was trying to use the affair as a counter-intelligence strategy to infiltrate the K.G.B. The U.S. government saw a Soviet plot and claimed that the emigre, who pleaded guilty to spying, was working for the K.G.B.[19] (N.Y.T. May 8, 1985)

Domestically, the documentation of already existing embarrassing situations for purposes of blackmail is probably much more common than the effort to engineer them *ab initio*.[20] The former involves an invasion of privacy but not a violation of intimacy. J. Edgar Hoover was very adept at this. His voluminous files on important people contained information on sexual and other improprieties. Such information was rarely made public or used to prosecute. Instead the implied threat of exposure was used as a political resource.[21] Information from local police intelligence units in Chicago, Los Angeles, Detroit, Seattle, and many other cities has been used in this fashion.

A recent British military scandal offers an illustration of the expansionary strategy of coercively "turning" (upward if possible) ever more people involved in violations. A communications specialist serving in Cyprus was allegedly lured to a party, provided with drugs, and photographed having sex with two Arab males. He was then told that unless he delivered certain documents the photos would be made public. In a classic espionage technique, he was then pressured to recruit others in the military with whom he had been involved, under threat of exposing them. Seven servicemen were eventually charged with having passed important military secrets over a two-year period.[22]

With the declining importance of ideology as a motive for spying, sex, along with money and drugs, may take on increased importance. But this may be undercut by greater societal tolerance for homosexuality and other sexual practices once condemned by Victorian morality. This tolerance underlies new 1988 Department of Defense regulations requiring employees and contractors with security clearances to report if they have engaged in activities such as adultery, spouse swapping, and "group sex orgies." Under the new rules *acknowledged* homosexuals have received security clearances because they are not seen to be susceptible to blackmail.[23]

In the context of *stigmatization and/or disruption*, the goal is to create difficulties for a group without resort to legal sanctions. This is a classic tactic directed against politically suspect groups. For example, an informer who infiltrated the Dallas CISPES (Committee in Solidarity with the People of El Salvador), a group which regularly met in a church, reports that his FBI contact encouraged him to seduce one of the nuns in the group and film it. The Church Committee Investigation of the FBI's COINTEL program cites a Klan informant who testified that he was instructed "to sleep with as many wives as I could" in an attempt to break up marriages and gain information.[24]

In the context of *intelligence collection*, the official goal is preparedness and prevention. The infiltration of dissident political or criminal groups (or milieus) for monitoring purposes is a well-known tactic. In a Los Angeles example, an undercover agent who had infiltrated a local Maoist political organization became the boyfriend of one of the women he spied on. Under oath, the agent testified that, after consultation with his superiors, he regularly engaged in sexual intercourse with the woman. The relationship was used to help gather information about the woman and her associates and to establish the agent's credibility. He later testified that during the seventeen months he was undercover, he never heard anyone in the organization talk about committing crimes, nor did he see any weapons.[25]

In the fifth context an undercover operation is *directed against a particular group or individual there is reason to suspect of criminal activity.* For example an officer who successfully infiltrated an international drug ring was greatly aided by having an affair with one of the group's leaders.[26]

In a large Oklahoma corruption case the government's chief witness admitted she had had sexual relations with suspects in order to gather evidence. She stated: "At the time I was working for the government and I said and did anything to open up and get the information for the government."[27]

A further example can be seen in the FBI's effort to locate fugitives from the Weather Underground faction of Students for a Democratic Society.[28] A federal agent posing as a radical infiltrated a student milieu thought to be close to this faction. He developed a relationship with a political activist, and she became pregnant. After considerable indecision, and at the urging of the agent, she had an abortion. His efforts did not locate the fugitive. The agent's work then took him elsewhere, and he ended the relationship. The woman apparently never learned of his secret identity and true motives. The situation would have been more complicated had she decided to keep the child or died in childbirth or developed a sexually transmitted disease or become mentally unstable.[29]

In an equivalent example, Kim Paris, a young female investigator, established a specious relationship which led to a successful murder

prosecution. She contrived to meet a murder suspect and then dated him for two months. He proposed marriage to her. However, she told him she first wanted to know what it was that seemed to be troubling him. With Houston police listening through a transmitter in her purse, he confessed, was arrested and subsequently found guilty.[30]

How should we assess these five contexts? The first two can be quickly dismissed. Blackmail and disruption are both illegal and immoral, and there is little to discuss in a society in which conduct is governed by due process and political expression is protected. Of course controlling such conduct in organizations is another matter. But my concern here is with the ought rather than the actual.

The third context, the use of sex to gather general intelligence, should also be prohibited. Police resources are too scarce and the state-sponsored creation of specious intimate relations is too serious and potentially costly an undertaking to be used for fishing expeditions. This also violates the expectation that there should be specific grounds for suspicion before an investigation begins. In addition, in the post-Watergate age the infiltration of political groups may violate the law, or at least departmental guidelines.

In the other three cases, the mere fact that the goal is legal is not sufficient to conclude that it is sound as public policy. Legality is a necessary but certainly not a sufficient condition for the use of sex in an investigation. Here it is appropriate to recall Justice Potter Stewart's observation that just because there is a legal right to do something, it does not mean that it is the right thing to do.[31] After determining that the goal was legitimate we must next ask, How was sex used in the investigation?

Let us contrast two types of cases. First, there is the case of *"the beguiling serpent,"* in which sex is used as an inducement or incentive to encourage illegality on the part of the suspect. Sex is a resource offered in an exchange relationship.

In Florida a man was arrested after a female undercover agent offered him sexual favors if he would sell her marijuana.[32] He at least had possession of the marijuana, which suggests a presumption of guilt, leaving to one side the conditions under which the evidence was collected. More troubling is an Atlanta case involving a former nude dancer addicted to cocaine who worked with the Georgia Bureau of Investigation. Eighteen men were arrested as a result of her efforts. In a sworn statement she said many of those arrested had not previously used or purchased drugs until she enticed them. She approached male acquaintances with an offer of sex if they would purchase cocaine for her, and she steered them toward making purchases from an undercover agent.[33]

Such cases are troubling. But it is not immediately apparent why. The promise of casual sex certainly implied no serious emotional intimacy, so it can't be criticized on those grounds, and the purchase and use of cocaine is illegal.

A contrast of prostitution with drug use may help clarify why this example is troubling. The economic structure of the relationship is similar to that in prostitution. But there is a difference in that in the Georgia case the currency exchanged was an illegal substance, and the arrest that followed was unrelated to enforcing laws against prostitution.

The promise of sexual favors in return for procuring drugs (or participation in some other crime) is a different type of temptation from the promise of cash. We can imagine a continuum moving from more to less acceptable temptations. Temptations as public policy tools can be ranked by their ethical desirablity (or perhaps, more precisely, by their degree of undesirablity). One factor is of course how realistic or extreme the temptation is. Temptations should stay close to real-world settings. Also important is the degree of freedom of choice and absence of compulsion. In that regard using a physiological and/or psychological need such as sex seems less acceptable than the offer of cash. An extreme example is that of gaining the compliance of an addict experiencing withdrawal symptoms in an undercover scheme to buy or sell drugs. While the situations in which sex is employed generally do not go to this extreme, using it in this way seems

sleazy and exploitative because it draws upon an individual's vulnerability.

The above cases contrast with cases of the *facilitating serpent.* Sexual involvement is not directly tied to a crime. It is not bait held out in reward for participation in illegal activities. Instead, it is used to help the individual fit into a criminal environment or setting. The sexual behavior adds credibility and may be a means of gaining information. It can also be a self-protective device since not to become involved (whether with sex or drugs) would cast suspicion on the agent.[34] The offering of a woman can be a test and may create a dilemma for the agent. One agent notes: "Avoiding sexual compromise is no easy task when working undercover. It is, in fact, one of the job's greatest challenges."[35]

This second form certainly raises ethical issues, but they are ancillary to the criminal behavior. The violation of trust is a price paid to obtain, or at least not to block, obtaining some other end. This is not as abhorrent as using sex to tempt the target into illegality. It is also less morally unacceptable if the agent is a *passive respondent* rather than the *initiator.*

In contrast to the Georgia case, in neither the case of the faked romance to gain a confession nor the case of the search for the Weather Underground fugitives was sex used to *further* the commission of a crime. Nor were agents co-participants in a crime. Instead, a duplicitous relationship was established in order to *solve* a serious crime, and there was reason to choose the targets in question. These cases are also more acceptable than the infiltration of the Los Angeles Maoist group described above, which was undertaken for diffuse intelligence-gathering rather than in response to a particular crime that had a ready occurred. In contrasting the last three cases, does the successful confession in the murder case mean that use of the tactic was more acceptable than in the Weather Underground case, where the fugitives were not found? If the Los Angeles case had discovered a plot to blow up City Hall, the agent would likely have been a hero. But he apparently found nothing. It is tempting to make the end result the criterion for judgment. Yet such a criterion conflicts with the important principle that means have a moral component, apart from ends.

If, in pursuing the broader social good, harm is done to individuals (for example, in the cases of the duped pregnant women and the romantic partner in Los Angeles), should they be entitled to compensation as a result of being innocent third-party victims harmed by an undercover investigation?[36]

Given the potential of intimate relationships for gathering intelligence and evidence and our conventional assumptions about appropriate uses of sexuality, should agents be permitted, expected, or required to use sex if it will further an investigation? This involves the ethical issue of what can legitimately be asked of agents in situations where sexual deception may be justified. Given the unique character of such assignments they should certainly be voluntary. This is likely to be affected by gender, with men more likely to volunteer than women.

There is certainly resistance to this, but it is not universal. Thus in a novel drawing from her undercover experience, Kim Wozencraft recalls a conversation with her chief regarding evidence-gathering about a reputed crime leader, "I'll bet he'd give you anything you asked for." "Chief," I said, "you can get someone else to screw him, if that's what you're asking me to do. My job description says nothing about being a hooker."[37] This contrasts with the fictional account of a policewomen's eager infiltration of a radical group and the forming of a relationship with its leader.[38]

Let us return to the Barry case with which we began. An elected official who is believed flagrantly to have violated the standards he is charged with enforcing communicates cynicism and hypocrisy. The behavior of leaders is not only instrumental; it is also educational and symbolic. But when law enforcement resorts to trickery and exploits intimate relations to make a misdemeanor arrest, it in turn communicates the idea that the end justifies the means. This may hold in popular attitudes, but it is not the message of the law in its most exalted form. There is also communication when the suspect is from a minority group and the enforcers are not, and the case can be publicly perceived as a witch hunt. In the well-honored words of Justice Holmes, "For my part I think it a less evil that some criminals should escape than that the Government should play an ignoble part."[39]

To apply the criteria suggested here, the use of sex in the Barry case is ethically undesirable because it involves violation of psychological and sexual intimacy and was initiated by the state for an offense unrelated to statutes governing sex.

However, I do not suggest that there should be rigid rules against ever exploiting sex and friendship in an investigation.[40] There is need for flexibility and appreciation of the great variety in law enforcement situations. There are clear costs when the state introduces mistrust and suspiciousness into intimate relationships. But never to do this may also have costs. I don't think categorical prohibition is appropriate, but neither is unlimited permission. Instead, each case must be examined separately in light of questions touching the key issues.

Local departments should follow federal agencies in establishing guidelines and restrictions on the instrumental use of intimate sexual relations. In extreme cases an individual's constitutional rights may be violated. The courts may eventually offer clearer standards. Circuit courts have refused to dismiss charges when an informant had a sexual relationship with a defendant. However a different standard may apply when a sworn agent is involved.

The U.S. Court of Appeals for the Second Circuit recently set forth criteria for establishing when sexual relations between a government agent and a defendant constitute "outrageous conduct" that would require dismissal of an indictment. To rise to a level of a constitutional violation it must be shown that (1) the government "set out to use sex as a weapon in its investigatory arsenal," (2) a government agent initiated the sex or allowed it to continue to achieve a government goal, and (3) the sexual relationship occurred during or close to the period covered by the indictment and "was entwined with the events charged therein."[41]

In considering the ethics of sex as a part of an undercover investigation, I would take the same approach as I took to the general question of whether undercover tactics were ethical.[42] The answer depends on responses to a series of questions about the specific case. I argue that the greater the affirmative or "harm-avoiding" answers, the more justified undercover means are. The questions involve seriousness, alternatives, democractic decision making, spirit of the law, prosecution, clarity of definition, crime occurrence, grounds for suspicion, prevention, autonomy, degree of deception, bad lessons, privacy and expression, collateral harm, equitable target selection, realism, and relevance of the charges. Our assessment should also be conditioned by the goal of the investigation, the cost of taking no action, the degree of intrusion and the nature of the betrayal, the skill of the operatives, and the likelihood that the deception will be publicly judged in court. But in general there should be a strong presumption against trading in the currency of intimate relations, no matter how noble the goal.

NOTES

I am grateful to John Kleinig for his critical comments.

[1] For example is it wise to focus scarce resources on occasional users rather than dealers? If a case for indictment cannot be made before a grand jury or before a judge for permission to search, wiretap, or bug, is it appropriate to move to an undercover temptation for which there is no legal minimum threshold? Was the grand jury used in a manipulative way to obtain a felony indictment (Barry's allegedly lying to it about cocaine use is a felony, while his possession of cocaine was only a misdmeanor). Was the effort to get Barry on a drug charge undertaken after earlier efforts to obtain direct evidence of corruption against him failed? Is it sound social policy to use the criminal law not for prosecution but as a resource to be negotiated (e.g., the prosecutor's hint that he would exchange leniency in return for the Mayor's resignation)? Should special criteria be applied before a political figure becomes the target of an undercover investigation? What of the speculation that the highly visible prosecutor in the case has his own political aspirations? Is there a racial patterning in the selection of targets in recent sting operations or does the apparent pattern simply reflect greater black prominence in political life? Shouldn't the government try to block the flow of drugs rather than provide them? Should it have intervened after he purchased the drugs rather than letting him proceed to use them? What if he had suffered a heart attack or other serious health damage from the cocaine? Should the government be offering its citizens potentially toxic substances?

[2] The literature on the ethics of undercover investigations and the state is slim given the importance of the topic. See, e.g., Klockars, The Dirty Harry Problem, *Annals Am. Acad. Pol. & Soc. Sci.* (1980); C. Bok, *On the Ethics of Concealment and Revelation* (1982); Dworkin, The Serpent Did Beguile Me and I Did Eat: Entrapment and the Creation of Crime, *L. & Phil.* (1985); Schoeman, Privacy and Police Undercover Work, in *Police Ethics: Hard Choices in Law Enforcement* (W. Heffernan & T. Stroup eds. 1985); Skolnick, *Deception by Police*, and Stitt & James, Entrapment: An Ethical Analysis, in *Moral Issues in Polices Work* (F. Elliston & M. Feldberg, eds. 1985); G. Marx, *Undercover: Police Surveillance in America* (1988), and two special issues, 43 *J. Soc. Issues* ("Covert Facilitation of Crime") and *Crime, Law and Social Change*, ("Undercover Tactics") (forthcoming).

[3] The problem of undercover investigations in which the identity of the agent or informant is hidden adds an additional element to the more general category of exploitative sexual relationships. Ethical issues are of course present when the deception involves only motives, rather than also involving identity. Consider, for example, the anger and sense of betrayal shown by Michelle Pfeiffer in the film *Tequilla Sunrise* when she discovers that a detective (whose identity she knew) entered into a relationship with her in order to discover if she had "guilty knowledge that can help me do my job."

[4] W. Howe, *Mata-Hari: The True Story* (1986).

[5] G. Marx, supra note 2 (1988).

[6] Of course, the relations between the individual and others are dynamic. Individuality is partly a function of community attachments, and we value community to the extent that it sustains responsible individuality.

[7] M. Davis, *Intimate Relations* (1988).

[8] To keep things simple for the table, I have collapsed the distinction, important for some purposes, between the mere suggestion of sexual involvement and its actual occurrence.

These categories are, of course, not static. Individuals may move between them. This may change for targets as well as agents. As note 34, infra, suggests, the latter is potentially problematic (e.g., the conversion of a platonic to a sexual friendship or a sexually instrumental to a romantic relationship).

There is also movement in the opposite direction, in which what was initially a genuine relationship becomes one of betrayal. It is not uncommon for wives and lovers to turn to police with incriminating information about their partners, whether out of anger or of conscience. They may then be instructed to play along. When serious violations are present, is the betrayal of a friend who has a change of heart ethically better or worse than that of a stranger who seeks to become a friend in order to betray?

[9] *Chicago Tribune*, Aug. 29, 1984.

[10] Of course, in doing this it may also turn up Elmer Gantry-style personal hypocrisy on the part of those arrested. Thus the chief state prosecutor for the city of St. Louis, who had spent his 15 years in office crusading

against obscenity, pornography, and prostitution, was arrested on charges of soliciting sex from an undercover police officer. Among other things, he supported changes in the city's laws against prostitution to require mandatory jail sentences for second-time offenders (whether customers, prostitutes, or pimps). *N.Y. Times*, May 13, 1992.

[11]Morals squad work is often met with humorous jibes and derision. A college-educated Detroit policewoman states, "I studied hard to be a policewoman, but I don't think all the training was done so I could pose as a prostitute." A Boston officer hated the assignment and reported, "I just blanked out, went dead." She didn't like the station house jokes about "working the street," and male officers made her feel she was "doing in" innocent guys just out for a little fun." (G. Marx, supra note 2, at 168) [1988].) A vice officer whose job it was to arrest nude male dancers observed, "I hate to think that's my job in life, to go around telling guys to cover their buns and girls that they can't get their T-shirts wet." (M. Baker, *Cops: Their Lives in Their Own Words*) [1985].) One can imagine as well the great sense of satisfaction felt by the vigilant plainclothes detectives who arrested Pee Wee Herman for an act of indecent exposure in a Florida pornographic theater.

[12]*Boston Herald American*, June 25, 1982.

[13]Nor, conversely, do most on-duty sexual liaisons (whether undercover or not) result in arrests. When the officer's identity is known, the exchange of sexual favors and information may be traded for protection from arrest and from others in the criminal milieu. Brothels have a rich symbiotic history with police as places for intelligence, whether used on behalf of an investigation or (sometimes) of blackmail.

[14]Most such arrests stop short of consummation. The latter is thought to look bad to the court, juries, and the public, and to put the officer at risk of being an accomplice. The personality needs and structure of a person who engages in sex with another whom he then arrests is worthy of study.

Other ethical issues are present if the statutes are enforced in a discriminatory way. For example, in Los Angeles a top mayoral assistant was apparently targeted in a vice investigation because of his efforts at police reform. The scandal that subsequently resulted from his being arrested for lewd conduct under what appear to be contrived circumstances forced him to resign.

[15]Some agents consider the private pleasure they drive from their undercover work as a reward for a tough job. With respect to his drug use, one agent declared, "We're out here risking our lives to keep the fucksticks off the streets. But the job has a few fringe bennies." (K. Wozencraft, *Rush* 21) [1990].) One can also imagine agents who as "feigned accomplices" consummate sexual acts to gather evidence meeting in a tavern after work and saying "its a tough job but somebody's got to do it".

[16]But we must be aware of stereotypes about gender and sex. From the literature it appears that men find such work more enjoyable and less demeaning than women.

Yet it should not be assumed that seduction is invariably a pleasant task for a male agent in the face of lack of physical attraction, moral objections, and guilt. At the same time some women (like men) may enjoy the legally protected feigning, or acting out, of sexual fantasies that such roles can provide. It is an interesting question whether in our culture a male suspect seduced by a female agent or informer is perceived (and feels) violated to the same extent and in the same way as a female suspect seduced by a male agent.

[17]The standard for international behavior seems weaker than for domestic. While this may be justified in terms of expediency and reciprocity (we can get away with doing it to foreigners and the other side doesn't play fair, so why should we?), it is more difficult to justify in moral terms.

Of course such a strategy can backfire if it becomes public, leading to bad publicity for the agency. The criminal prosecution goal of law enforcement (with its judicial review and publicity) offers greater accountability than the intelligence and disruption goals of covert foreign intelligence. Accountability with respect to law enforcement may ironically conflict with the protection of privacy.

The tactic may also simply not work if the subject feels he has nothing to hide. Thus in one case a high government official was photographed in a contrived setting in bed with a prostitute. He rejected the threat of blackmail and was thrilled with the photos he was shown, even asking if he could obtain additional copies to show his friends. (Reported in V. Ostrovsky & C. Hoy, *By Way of Deception* [1990]).

[18]In an early 20th century situation in Chicago, concern over mashers led the chief to send "the best-looking flatfoot in the department" to walk the streets, and "bring in any female that attempted to flirt with him." He then sent out a "dashing policewoman" new to the force, to "pinch any man who made a pass at her." They ended up trying to arrest each other. (Z. Lait & J. Mortimer, *Chicago Confidential* [1950]). In a more contemporary example an agent reported striking up a conversation in a bar with an effeminate man wearing mascara. The men decide to go for a walk and after a series of suggestive comments, the agent announced, "You're under arrest." The other man said, "You can't arrest me. I was about to arrest you." He was another New York City policeman. (C. Whited, *Chiodo* [1974].)

[19]*N. Y. Times*, May 8, 1985.

[20]When the only ground for divorce was adultery, private detectives sometimes contrived to create evidence favorable to their clients, as well as simply documenting already existing embarrassing facts. In response to the suggestion that he did "all kinds of detective work," Philip Marlowe said, "Only the fairly honest kinds. . . . For one thing I don't do divorce business." (R. Chandler, *The Lady in the Lake* [Vintage Press ed. 1988].)

[21]See F. Donner, *The Age of Surveillance* (1980); R. G. Powers, *Secrecy and Power* (1987); A. Theoharis, *The Boss; J. Edgar Hoover and the Great American Inquisition* (1988).

[22]*Parade Magazine*, Aug. 18, 1985, at 14.

[23]*N. Y. Times*, May 14, 1988.

[24]U.S. Cong. (1976). While delegating an ethically questionable task to an informant insulates the government agent from direct involvement, the government's hands are sullied in either case, though perhaps not to the same extent.

Anonymous letters were also sent to spouses of activists accusing them of infidelities. For example, the wife of a black leader received a letter fictitiously reporting that her husband was committing adultery with women in his protest group.

[25]See G. Marx, supra note 2, at. 148 (1988).

[26]Such operations can take a great toll on family relations. Spouses are potential unseen victims. In the drug case described in the text, the agent's wife was proud of his heroic effort and the promotion it led to. But when the full details of the investigation became clear, she sought a divorce.

The Barry case offers a powerful illustration of the sweeping indiscriminate invasiveness of the video camera. While Effie Barry, the mayor's wife, sat in the courtroom, she (along with millions of television news watchers) saw her husband smoke crack, caress another woman on a hotel bed, ask her to engage in sex, and say, "I love you."

In those rare cases where sex is deemed appropriate for use in an investigation, there is a strong case for limiting such situations to ones in which both the agent and the suspect are single.

[27]*N. Y. Times*, Sept. 13, 1981.

[28]See G. Marx, supra note 2, at 148 (1988).

[29]C. Payne, *Deep Cover* (1979). In contrast, if she had undergone the far less offensive experience of merely having her phone tapped, authorities would have been legally required to notify her when the investigation ended.

[30]*Boston Globe*, Feb. 27, 1985.

[31]Consider a Kentucky case in which a fourteen-year-old boy serving as a decoy had sex with an older male who was arrested a few minutes later. The county attorney approved of the plan, the boy's mother signed a consent form and the judge found the tactic legally acceptable. An officer defended the tactic, saying, "he had not been exposed to anything he had not already done." (*N.Y. Times*, Sept. 17, 1984.)

[32]*Spencer v. State* (1972).

[33]She also reported having sex with the agent she worked with and his having looked the other way while she pocketed some of the drugs they seized. The chief drug investigator for the Georgia Bureau of Investigation reports that his agency does "not encourage or condone our agents sleeping with an informant." But neither does the agency have a written policy forbidding it. (Atlanta Constitution, March 31, 1991.) The operative principle here is "Lead us into temptation and deliver us to evil."

In the same "I don't want to hear about it" category is the response of a Florida IRS agent to a Congressional questioner about whether the agent had instructed informants to gather information about the sex and drinking habits of persons of interest. "I have never asked one of my informants to have sexual relations with a subject to gain information or for any other reason. . . . In the case of . . . Carmen [code name for an informant] she claimed to have had sexual relations in the performance of her information-gathering activities. *I did not condemn her for it. I did not encourage it and I did not discourage it.* (italics added) (Wise, 1976)

"[Carmen] . . . implied she was supposed to have sex with at least one of the targets but refused and quit instead." A Dade County Circuit Judge apparently targeted in the case said "My sex habits are not a taxable item. If anything, I think I'm depreciating and should get a tax writeoff. Cited in Block, forthcoming.

[34]Before entering the role, agents must anticipate how they will respond to the sexual advances (and emotional attachments) they may encounter. Among ways to avoid these are being accompanied by another agent of the opposite sex, claiming involvement with someone else, fatigue, illness or having a sexually transmitted disease. In many agencies (particularly at the federal level) sexual involvement with a target or informer could lead to dismissal on the pragmatic grounds of the danger of compromising the agent and/or tainting the evidence. But not in Los Angeles, where Chief Daryl Gates claims that to prohibit undercover officers from having sex in the line of duty might "seriously endanger" their lives.

There is also the danger of conversion or "going native," in which the agent in a deep undercover operation becomes ambivalent or has his judgment clouded. An illustration of this is in the film *Betrayed*, in which Debra Winger, playing an FBI agent who infiltrates a Klan-like group, falls in love with the suspect, with whom she has developed a relationship.

Equivalent judgment issues may also be present when agents "pretending" to be a couple actually become one. See the case in K. Wozencraft, supra note 15.

As Kurt Vonnegut observes in Mother Night, "We are what we pretend to be, so we must be careful about what we pretend to be."

[35]L. Wansley & C. Stowers, *FBI Undercover: The True Story of Special Agent "Mandrake,"* (1989). There is also the risk of discovery. An undercover agent sitting in a bar who was suddenly presented (by the target of his investigation) with an attractive and willing woman who began touching him, recalls thinking "Oh, God! How the hell am I gonna get out of this one? The woman's roaming fingers probed their way ever closer to my quivering genitals, where they might find more than anticipated. What eventually would be worse, I wondered, this woman telling Becker (the target) that Vinnie Muscio was wearing a hidden microphone in his crotch, or trying to explain to a long-suffering wife that one more momentous sacrifice had been required by the rigors of police work?" (V. Murano with W. Hoffer, *Cop Hunter* [1990].)

[36]Indemnification legislation to compensate third party victims of undercover operations has been suggested by the Senate Select Committee that investigated Abscam.

However the committee had in mind financial, not emotional, damage.

[37]K. Wozencraft, supra note 15, at 183.

[38]J. Mills, *Report to the Commissioner* (1973).

[39]*Olmstead v. United States*, 277 US 438, 470, 72 L. Ed 944, 952, 48 S Ct 564, 66 ALR 376 (1928) (dissenting).

[40]In contrast Schoeman, supra note 2, would exclude intimate personal relations (although not business or cordial social relations) from ever being the object of undercover

operations and would treat any information obtained from them as inadmissible.

[41]*US v. Cuervelo*, 90-1151. In the case in question, the defendant was sentenced to 30 years in prison for smuggling cocaine. She claimed "sexual entrapment" had violated her due process rights. According to the defendant, the DEA agent involved in the case wrote her love letters and gave her money, clothing, and jewelry as part of their ongoing sexual relationship.

[42]Marx, supra note 2, at 104–07.

The Dirty Harry Problem

Carl B. Klockars

THE ANNALS OF THE AMERICAN ACADEMY

When and to what extent does the morally good end warrant or justify an ethically, politically, or legally dangerous means for its achievement? This is a very old question for philosophers. Although it has received extensive consideration in policelike occupations and is at the dramatic core of police fiction and detective novels. I know of not a single contribution to the criminological or sociological literature on policing which raises it explicitly and examines its implications.[1] This is the case in spite of the fact that there is considerable evidence to suggest that it is not only an ineluctable part of police work, but a moral problem with which police themselves are quite familiar. There are, I believe, a number of good reasons why social scientists have avoided or neglected what I like to call the Dirty Harry problem in policing, not the least of which is that it is insoluble. However, a great deal can be

Carl Klockars, *The Annals*, 452, Nov 1980; 33–47. © 1980 by Sage Publications. Reprinted by permission of Sage Publications.

learned about police work by examining some failed solutions, three of which I consider in the

[1]In the contemporary philosophical literature, particularly when raised for the vocation of politics, the question is commonly referred to as the Dirty Hands problem after J. P. Sartre's treatment of it in *Dirty Hands*, (Les Maines Sales, 1948) and in *No Exit and Three Other Plays* (New York: Modern Library, 1950). Despite its modern name, the problem is very old and has been taken up by Machiavelli in *The Prince* (1513) and *The Discourses* (1519) (New York: Modern Library, 1950); by Max Weber, "Politics as a Vocation," (1919) in *Max Weber: Essays in Sociology*, eds. and trans. H. Gerth and C. W. Wills (New York: Oxford University Press, 1946); and by Albert Camus, "The Just Assassins," (1949) in *Caligula and Three Other Plays* (New York: Alfred A. Knopf, 1958). See Michael Walzer's brilliant critique of these contributions, "Political Action: The Problem of Dirty Hands" *Philosophy and Public Affairs*, 2(2) (winter 1972). Likewise the Dirty Hands/Dirty Harry problem is implicitly or explicitly raised in virtually every work of Raymond Chandler, Dashiel Hammett, James Cain, and other *Tough Guy Writers of The Thirties*, ed. David Madden (Carbondale, IL: Southern Illinois University Press, 1968), as they are in all of the recent work of Joseph Wambaugh, particularly *The Blue Knight*, *The New Centurions* and *The Choirboys*.

following pages. First, though, it is necessary to explain what a Dirty Harry problem is and what it is about it that makes it so problematic.

THE DIRTY HARRY PROBLEM

The Dirty Harry problem draws its name from the 1971 Warner Brothers film *Dirty Harry* and its chief protagonist, antihero Inspector Harry "Dirty Harry" Callahan. The film features a number of events which dramatize the Dirty Harry problem in different ways, but the one which does so most explicitly and most completely places Harry in the following situation. A 14-year-old girl has been kidnapped and is being held captive by a psychopathic killer. The killer, "Scorpio," who has already struck twice, demands $200,000 ransom to release the girl, who is buried with just enough oxygen to keep her alive for a few hours. Harry gets the job of delivering the ransom and, after enormous exertion, finally meets Scorpio. At their meeting Scorpio decides to renege on his bargain, let the girl die, and kill Harry. Harry manages to stab Scorpio in the leg before he does so, but not before Scorpio seriously wounds Harry's partner, an inexperienced, idealistic, slightly ethnic, former sociology major.

Scorpio escapes, but Harry manages to track him down through the clinic where he was treated for his wounded leg. After learning that Scorpio lives on the grounds of a nearby football stadium, Harry breaks into his apartment, finds guns and other evidence of his guilt, and finally confronts Scorpio on the 50-yard line, where Harry shoots him in the leg as he is trying to escape. Standing over Scorpio, Harry demands to know where the girl is buried. Scorpio refuses to disclose her location, demanding his rights to a lawyer. As the camera draws back from the scene Harry stands on Scorpio's bullet-mangled leg to torture a confession of the girl's location from him.

As it turns out, the girl is already dead and Scorpio must be set free. Neither the gun found in the illegal search, nor the confession Harry extorted, nor any of its fruits—including the girl's body—would be admissible in court.

The preceding scene, the heart of *Dirty Harry,* raises a number of issues of far-reaching significance for the sociology of the police, the first of which will now be discussed.

THE DIRTY HARRY PROBLEM I: THE END OF INNOCENCE

As we have phrased it previously, the Dirty Harry problem asks when and to what extent does the morally good end warrant or justify an ethically, politically, or legally dangerous means to its achievement? In itself, this question assumes the possibility of a genuine moral dilemma and posits its existence in a means-ends arrangement which may be expressed schematically as follows:

Means

		Morally Good (+)	Morally Dirty (−)
E N D S	Morally good (+)	A + +	B − + The Dirty Harry Problem
	Morally dirty (−)	C + −	D − −

It is important to specify clearly the terms of the Dirty Harry problem not only to show that it must involve the juxtaposition of good ends and dirty means, but also to show what must be proven to demonstrate that a Dirty Harry problem exists. If one could show, for example, that box B is always empirically empty or that in any given case the terms of the situation are better read in some other means-ends arrangement, Dirty Harry problems vanish. At this first level, however, I suspect that no one could exclude the core scene of *Dirty Harry* from the class of Dirty Harry problems. There is no question that saving the life of an innocent victim of kidnapping is a "good" thing nor that grinding the bulletmangled leg of Scorpio to extort a confession from him is "dirty."[2]

There is, in addition, a second level of criteria of an empirical and epistemological nature that must be met before a Dirty Harry problem actually comes into being. They involve the connection between the dirty act and the good end. Principally, what must be known and, importantly, known before the dirty act is committed, is that it will result in the achievement of the good end. In any absolute sense this is, of course, impossible to know, in that no acts are ever completely certain in their consequences. Thus the question is always a matter of probabilities. But it is helpful to break those probabilities into classes which attach to various subcategories of the overall question. In the given case, this level of problem would seem to require that three questions be satisfied, though not all with the same level of certainty.

In *Dirty Harry*, the first question is, Is Scorpio able to provide the information Dirty Harry seeks? It is an epistemological question about which, in *Dirty Harry*, we are absolutely certain. Harry met Scorpio at the time of the ransom exchange. Not only did he admit the kidnapping at that time, but when he

made the ransom demand, Scorpio sent one of the girl's teeth and a description of her clothing and underwear to leave no doubt about the existence of his victim.

Second, we must know there are means, dirty means and nothing other than dirty means, which are likely to achieve the good end. One can, of course, never be sure that one is aware of or has considered all possible alternatives, but in *Dirty Harry* there would appear to be no reason for Scorpio in his rational self-interest to confess to the girl's location without being coerced to do so.

The third question which must be satisfied at this empirical and epistemological level concedes that dirty means are the only method which will be effective, but asks whether or not, in the end, they will be in vain. We know in *Dirty Harry* that they were, and Harry himself, at the time of the ransom demand, admits he believes that the girl is already dead. Does not this possibility or likelihood that the girl is dead destroy the justification for Harry's dirty act? Although it surely would if Harry knew for certain that the girl was dead, I do not think it does insofar as even a small probability of her being saved exists. The reason is that the good to be achieved is so unquestionably good and so passionately felt that even a small possibility of its achievement demands that it be tried. For example, were we to ask, If it were your daughter would you want Harry to do what he did? it would be this passionate sense of unquestionable good that we are trying to dramatize. It is for this reason that in philosophical circles the Dirty Hands problem has been largely restricted to questions of national security, revolutionary terrorism, and international war. It is also why the Dirty Harry problem in detective fiction almost always involves murder.

Once we have satisfied ourselves that a Dirty Harry problem is conceptually possible and that, in fact, we can specify one set of concrete circumstances in which it exists, one might think that the most difficult question of all is, What ought to be done? I do not think it is. I suspect that there are very few people who would not want Harry to do something dirty in the situation specified. I know I would

---

[2]"Dirty" here means both "repugnant" in that it offends widely shared standards of human decency and dignity and "dangerous" in that it breaks commonly shared and supported norms, rules, or laws for conduct. To "dirty" acts there must be both a deontologically based face validity of immorality and a consequentialist threat to the prevailing rules for social order.

want him to do what he did, and what is more, I would want anyone who policed for me to be prepared to do so as well. Put differently, I want to have as policeofficers men and women of moral courage and sensitivity.

But to those who would want exactly that, the Dirty Harry problem poses its most irksome conclusion. Namely, that one cannot, at least in the specific case at hand, have a policeman who is both just and innocent. The troublesome issue in the Dirty Harry problem is not whether under some utilitarian calculus a right choice can be made, but that the choice must always be between at least two wrongs. And in choosing to do either wrong, the policeman inevitably taints or tarnishes himself.

It was this conclusion on the part of Dashiell Hammett, Raymond Chandler, Raoul Whitfield, Horace McCoy, James M. Cain, Lester Dent, and dozens of other tough-guy writers of hard-boiled detective stories that distinguished these writers from what has come to be called the "classical school" of detective fiction. What these men could not stomach about Sherlock Holmes (Conan Doyle), Inspector French (Freeman Wills Crofts), and Father Brown (Chesterton), to name a few of the best, was not that they were virtuous, but that their virtue was unsullied. Their objection was that the classical detective's occupation, how he worked, and the jobs he was called upon to do left him morally immaculate. Even the most brilliant defender of the classical detective story, W. H. Auden, was forced to confess that that conclusion gave the stories "magical function," but rendered them impossible as art.[3]

If popular conceptions of police work have relevance for its actual practice—as Egon Bittner and a host of others have argued that they do[4]—the Dirty Harry problem, found in one version or another in countless detective novels and reflected in paler imitations on countless

television screens, for example, "Parental Discretion is Advised," is not an unimportant contributor to police work's "tainted" quality. But we must remember also that the revolution of the tough-guy writers, so these writers said, was not predicated on some mere artificial, aesthetic objection. With few exceptions, their claim was that their works were art. That is, at all meaningful levels, the stories were true. It is this claim I should next like to examine in the real-life context of the Dirty Harry problem.

THE DIRTY HARRY PROBLEM II: DIRTY MEN AND DIRTY WORK

Dirty Harry problems arise quite often. For policemen, real, everyday policemen, Dirty Harry problems are part of their job and thus considerably more than rare or artificial dramatic exceptions. To make this point, I will translate some rather familiar police practices, street stops and searches and victim and witness interrogation, into Dirty Harry problems.

Good Ends and Dirty Means

The first question our analysis of street stops and searches and victim and witness interrogation must satisfy is. For policemen, do these activities present the cognitive opportunity for the juxtaposition of good ends and dirty means to their achievement? Although the "goodness" question will be considered in some detail later, suffice it to say here that police find the prevention of crime and the punishment of wrongful or criminal behavior a good thing to achieve. Likewise, they, perhaps more than any other group in society, are intimately aware of the varieties of dirty means available for the achievement of those good ends. In the case of street stops and searches, these dirty alternatives range from falsifying probable cause for a stop, to manufacturing a false arrest to legitimate an illegal search, to simply searching without the fraudulent covering devices of either. In the case of victim or witness interrogations, dirty means range all from dramaturgically "chilling" a *Miranda* warning by an edited or unemphatic reading to Harry's grinding a man's bulletshattered leg to extort a confession from him.

---

[3]W. H. Auden, "The Guilty Vicarage," in *The Dyer's Hand and Other Essays* (New York: Alfred A. Knopf, 1956) pp. 146–58.

[4]Egon Bittner, *The Functions of Police in Modern Society* (New York: Jason Aronson, 1975) and "Florence Nightingale in Pursuit of Willie Sutton," in *The Potential For Reform Of the Criminal Justice System*, vol. 3. ed. H. Jacob (Beverly Hills, CA: Sage Publications, 1974) pp. 11–44.

While all these practices may be "dirty" enough to satisfy certain people of especially refined sensitivities, does not a special case have to be made, not for the public's perception of the "dirtiness" of certain illegal, deceptive, or subrosa acts, but for the police's perception of their dirtiness? Are not the police hard-boiled, less sensitive to such things than are most of us? I think there is no question that they are, and our contention about the prevalence of Dirty Harry problems in policing suggests that they are likely to be. How does this "tough-minded" attitude toward dirty means affect our argument? At least at this stage it seems to strengthen it. That is, the failure of police to regard dirty means with the same hesitation that most citizens do seems to suggest that they juxtapose them to the achievement of good ends more quickly and more readily than most of us.

The Dirty Means Must Work

In phrasing the second standard for the Dirty Harry problem as "The dirty means must work," we gloss over a whole range of qualifying conditions, some of which we have already considered. The most critical, implied in *Dirty Harry*, is that the person on whom dirty means are to be used must be guilty. It should be pointed out, however, that this standard is far higher than any student of the Dirty Hands problem in politics has ever been willing to admit. In fact, the moral dilemma of Dirty Hands is often dramatized by the fact that dirty means must be visited on quite innocent victims. It is the blood of such innocents, for example, whom the Communist leader Hoerderer in Sartre's *Dirty Hands* refers to when he says, "I have dirty hands. Right up to the elbows. I've plunged them in filth and blood. But what do you hope? Do you think you can govern innocently?"[5]

But even if cases in which innocent victims suffer dirty means commonly qualify as Dirty Harry problems, and by extension innocent victims would be allowable in Dirty Harry problems, there are a number of factors in the nature and context of policing which suggest

that police themselves are inclined toward the higher "guilty victim" standard. Although there may be others, the following are probably the most salient.

1. The Operative Assumption of Guilt. In street stops and searches as well as interrogations, it is in the nature of the police task that guilt is assumed as a working premise. That is, in order for a policeman to do his job, he must, unless he clearly knows otherwise, assume that the person he sees is guilty and the behavior he is witnessing is evidence of some concealed or hidden offense. If a driver looks at him "too long" or not at all or if a witness or suspect talks too little or too much, it is only his operative assumption of guilt that makes those actions meaningful. Moreover, the policeman is often not in a position to suspend his working assumption until he has taken action, sometimes dirty action, to disconfirm it.

2. The Worst of all Possible Guilt. The matter of the operative assumption of guilt is complicated further because the policeman is obliged to make a still higher-order assumption of guilt, namely, that the person is not only guilty, but dangerously so. In the case of street stops and searches, for instance, although the probability of coming upon a dangerous felon is extremely low, policemen quite reasonably take the possibility of doing so as a working assumption on the understandable premise that once is enough. Likewise the premise that the one who has the most to hide will try hardest to hide it is a reasonable assumption for interrogation.

3. The Great Guilty Place Assumption. The frequency with which policemen confront the worst of people, places, and occasions creates an epistemological problem of serious psychological proportions. As a consequence of his job, the policeman is constantly exposed to highly selective samples of his environment. That he comes to read a clump of bushes as a place to hide, a roadside rest as a homosexual "tearoom," a sweet old lady as a robbery looking for a place to happen, or a poor young black as someone willing to oblige her is not a

---

[5]Sartre, *Dirty Hands*, p. 224.

question of a perverse, pessimistic, or racist personality, but of a person whose job requires that he strive to see race, age, sex, and even nature in an ecology of guilt, which can include him if he fails to see it so.[6]

4. The Not Guilty (This Time) Assumption. With considerable sociological research and conventional wisdom to support him, the policeman knows that most people in the great guilty place in which he works have committed numerous crimes for which they have never been caught. Thus when a stop proves unwarranted, a search comes up "dry," or an interrogation fails, despite the dirty means, the policeman is not at all obliged to conclude that the person victimized by them is innocent, only that, and even this need not always be conceded, he is innocent this time.

Dirty Means as Ends in Themselves

How do these features of police work, all of which seem to incline police to accept a standard of a guilty victim for their dirty means, bear upon the Dirty Harry problem from which they derive? The most dangerous reading suggests that if police are inclined, and often quite rightly inclined, to believe they are dealing with factually, if not legally, guilty subjects, they become likely to see their dirty acts, not as means to the achievement of good ends, but as ends in themselves—as punishment of guilty people whom the police believe deserve to be punished.

If this line of argument is true, it has the effect, in terms of police perceptions, of moving Dirty Harry problems completely outside of the fourfold table of means—ends combinations created in order to define it. Importantly as well, in terms of our perceptions. Dirty Harry problems of this type can no longer be read as cases of dirty means employed to the

achievement of good ends. For unless we are willing to admit that in a democratic society a police arrogates to itself the task of punishing those who they think are guilty, we are forced to conclude that Dirty Harry problems represent cases of employing dirty means to dirty ends, in which case, nobody, not the police and certainly not us, is left with any kind of moral dilemma.

The possibility is quite real and quite fearsome, but it is mediated by certain features of police work, some of which inhere in the nature of the work itself and others, imposed from outside, which have a quite explicit impact on it. The most important of the "naturalistic" features of policing which belie the preceding argument is that the assumption of guilt and all the configurations in the policeman's world which serve to support it often turn out wrong. It is precisely because the operative assumption of guilt can be forced on everything and everyone that the policeman who must use it constantly comes to find it leads him astray as often as it confirms his suspicions.

Similarly, a great many of the things policemen do, some of which we have already conceded appear to police as less dirty than they appear to us—faked probable cause for a street stop, manipulated *Miranda* warnings, and so forth—are simply impossible to read as punishments. This is so particularly if we grant a hard-boiled character to our cops.

Of course, neither of these naturalistic restrictions on the obliteration of the means-ends schema is or should be terribly comforting. To the extent that the first is helpful at all assumes a certain skill and capacity of mind that we may not wish to award to all policemen. The willingness to engage in the constant refutation of one's working worldview presumes a certain intellectual integrity which can certainly go awry. Likewise, the second merely admits that on occasion policemen do some things which reveal they appreciate that the state's capacity to punish is sometimes greater than theirs.

To both these "natural" restrictions on the obliteration of the means-ends character of Dirty Harry problems, we can add the exclusionary rule. Although the exclusionary rule is

---

[6]One of Wambaugh's characters in *The Choirboys* makes this final point most dramatically when he fails to notice that a young boy's buttocks are flatter than they should be and reads the child's large stomach as a sign of adequate nutrition. When the child dies through his mother's neglect and abuse, the officer rightly includes himself in his ecology of guilt.

the manifest target of *Dirty Harry*, it, more than anything else, makes Dirty Harry problems a reality in everyday policing. It is the great virtue of exclusionary rules—applying in various forms to stops, searches, seizures, and interrogations—that they hit directly upon the intolerable, though often, I think, moral desire of police to punish. These rules make the very simple point to police that the more they wish to see a felon punished, the more they are advised to be scrupulous in their treatment of him. Put differently, the best thing Harry could have done for Scorpio was to step on his leg, extort his confession, and break into his apartment.

If certain natural features of policing and particularly exclusionary rules combine to maintain the possibility of Dirty Harry problems in a context in which a real danger appears to be their disappearance, it does not follow that police cannot or do not collapse the dirty means–good ends division on some occasions and become punishers. I only hold that on many other occasions, collapse does not occur and Dirty Harry problems, as defined, are still widely possible. What must be remembered next, on the way to making their possibility real, is that policemen know, or think they know, before they employ a dirty means that a dirty means and only a dirty means will work.

Only a Dirty Means Will Work

The moral standard that a policeman know in advance of resorting to a dirty means that a dirty means and only a dirty means will work, rests heavily on two technical dimensions: (1) the professional competence of the policeman and (2) the range of legitimate working options available to him. Both are intimately connected, though the distinction to be preserved between them is that the first is a matter of the policeman's individual competence and the second of the competence of the institutions for which (his department) and with which (the law) the policeman works.

In any concrete case, the relations between these moral and technical dimensions of the Dirty Harry problem are extremely complicated. But a priori it follows that the more competent a policeman is at the use of legal means, the less he will be obliged to resort to dirty alternatives. Likewise, the department that trains its policemen well and supplies them with the resources—knowledge and material—to do their work will find that the policemen who work for them will not resort to dirty means "unnecessarily," meaning only those occasions when an acceptable means will work as well as a dirty one.

While these two premises flow a priori from raising the Dirty Harry problem, questions involving the moral and technical roles of laws governing police means invite a very dangerous type of a priori reasoning:

> Combating distrust [of the police] requires getting across the rather complicated message that granting the police specific forms of new authority may be the most effective means for reducing abuse of authority which is now theirs; that it is the absence of properly proscribed forms of authority that often impels the police to engage in questionable or outright illegal conduct. Before state legislatures enacted statutes giving limited authority to the police to stop and question persons suspected of criminal involvement, police nevertheless stopped and questioned people. It is inconceivable how any police agency could be expected to operate without doing so. But since the basis for their actions was unclear, the police—if they thought a challenge likely—would use the guise of arresting the individual on a minor charge (often without clear evidence) to provide a semblance of legality. Enactment of stopping and questioning statutes eliminated the need for this sham.[7]

Herman Goldstein's preceding argument and observations are undoubtedly true, but the danger in them is that they can be extended to apply to any dirty means, not only illegal arrests to legitimate necessary street stops, but dirty means to accomplish subsequent searches and seizures all the way to beating confessions out of suspects when no other means will work.

[7]Herman Goldstein, *Policing a Free Society* (Cambridge, MA: Ballinger Publishing, 1977), p. 72.

But, of course, Goldstein does not intend his argument to be extended in these ways.

Nevertheless, his a priori argument, dangerous though it may be, points to the fact that Dirty Harry problems can arise wherever restrictions are placed on police methods and are particularly likely to do so when police themselves perceive that those restrictions are undesirable, unreasonable, or unfair. His argument succeeds in doing what police who face Dirty Harry problems constantly do: rendering the law problematic. But while Goldstein, one of the most distinguished legal scholars in America, can follow his finding with books, articles, and lectures which urge change, it is left to the policeman to take upon himself the moral responsibility of subverting it with dirty and hidden means.

Compelling and Unquestionable Ends

If Dirty Harry problems can be shown to exist in their technical dimensions—as genuine means–ends problems where only dirty means will work—the question of the magnitude and urgency of the ends that the dirty means may be employed to achieve must still be confronted. Specifically, it must be shown that the ends of dirty means are so desirable that the failure to achieve them would cast the person who is in a position to do so in moral disrepute.

The two most widely acknowledged ends of policing are peace keeping and law enforcement. It would follow, of course, that if both these ends were held to be unworthy, Dirty Harry problems would disappear. There are arguments challenging both ends. For instance, certain radical critiques of policing attempt to reduce the peace-keeping and law-enforcing functions of the police in the United States to nothing more than acts of capitalist oppression. From such a position flows not only the denial of the legitimacy of any talk of Dirty Harry problems, but also the denial of the legitimacy of the entire police function.[8]

Regardless of the merits of such critiques, it will suffice for the purpose of this analysis to maintain that there is a large "clientele," to use Albert Reiss's term, for both types of police function.[9] And it should come as no surprise to anyone that the police themselves accept the legitimacy of their own peace-keeping and law-enforcing ends. Some comment is needed, though, on how large that clientele for those functions is and how compelling and unquestionable the ends of peace keeping and law enforcement are for them.

There is no more popular, compelling, urgent, nor more broadly appealing idea than peace. In international relations, it is potent enough to legitimate the stockpiling of enough nuclear weapons to exterminate every living thing on earth a dozen times over. In domestic affairs, it gives legitimacy to the idea of the state, and the aspirations to it have succeeded in granting to the state an absolute monopoly on the right to legitimate the use of force and a near monopoly on its actual, legitimate use: the police. That peace has managed to legitimate these highly dangerous means to its achievement in virtually every advanced nation in the world is adequate testimony to the fact that it qualifies, if any end does, as a good end so unquestionable and so compelling that it can legitimate risking the most dangerous and dirtiest of means.

The fact is, though, that most American policemen prefer to define their work as law enforcement rather than peace keeping, even though they may, in fact, do more of the latter. It is a distinction that should not be allowed to slip away in assuming, for instance, that the policeman's purpose in enforcing the law is to keep the peace. Likewise, though it is a possibility, it will not do to assume that police simply enforce the law as an end in itself, without meaning and without purpose or end. The widely discretionary behavior of working policemen and the enormous underenforcement of the law which characterizes most police agencies simply belie that possibility.

---

[8]See, for example, John F. Galliber, "Explanations of Police Behavior: A Critical Review and Analysis," *The Sociological Quarterly*, 12:308–18 (summer 1971); Richard Quinney, *Class, State, and Crime* (New York: David McKay, 1977).

[9]Albert J. Reiss, Jr., *The Police and the Public* (New Haven, CT: Yale University Press, 1971), p. 122.

An interpretation of law enforcement which is compatible with empirical studies of police behavior —as peace keeping is—and police talk in America—which peace keeping generally is not—is an understanding of the ends of law enforcement as punishment. There are, of course, many theories of punishment, but the police seem inclined toward the simplest: the belief that certain people who have committed certain acts deserve to be punished for them. What can one say of the compelling and unquestionable character of this retributive ambition as an end of policing and policemen?

Both historically and sociologically there is ample evidence that punishment is almost as unquestionable and compelling an end as peace. Historically, we have a long and painful history of punishment, a history longer in fact than the history of the end of peace. Sociologically, the application of what may well be the only culturally universal norm, the norm of reciprocity, implies the direct and natural relations between wrongful acts and their punishments.[10] Possibly the best evidence for the strength and urgency of the desire to punish in modern society is the extraordinary complex of rules and procedures democratic states have assembled which prevents legitimate punishment from being administered wrongfully or frivolously.

If we can conclude that peace and punishment are ends unquestionable and compelling enough to satisfy the demands of Dirty Harry problems, we are led to one final question on which we may draw from some sociological theories of the police for assistance. If the Dirty Harry problem is at the core of the police role, or at least near to it, how is it that police can or do come to reconcile their use of—or their failure to use—dirty means to achieve unquestionably good and compelling ends?

---

[10]These two assertions are drawn from Graeme Newman's *The Punishment Response* (Philadelphia: J. B. Lippincott Co., 1978).

PUBLIC POLICY AND POLICE MORALITY: THREE DEFECTIVE RESOLUTIONS OF THE DIRTY HARRY PROBLEM

The contemporary literature on policing appears to contain three quite different types of solution or resolution. But because the Dirty Harry problem is a genuine moral dilemma, that is, a situation which will admit no real solution or resolution, each is necessarily defective. Also, understandably, each solution or resolution presents itself as an answer to a somewhat different problem. In matters of public policy, such concealments are often necessary and probably wise, although they have a way of coming around to haunt their architects sooner or later. In discovering that each is flawed and in disclosing the concealments which allow the appearance of resolution, we do not urge that it be held against sociologists that they are not philosophers nor do we argue that they should succeed where philosophers before them have failed. Rather, we only wish to make clear what is risked by each concealment and to face candidly the inevitably unfortunate ramifications which must proceed from it.

Snappy Bureaucrats

In the works of August Vollmer, Bruce Smith, O. W. Wilson, and those progressive police administrators who still follow their lead, a vision of the perfect police agency and the perfect policeman has gained considerable ground. Labeled "the professional model" in police circles —though entirely different from any classical sense of profession or professional—it envisions a highly trained, technologically sophisticated police department operating free from political interference with a corps of well-educated police responding obediently to the policies, orders, and directives of a central administrative command. It is a vision of police officers, to use Bittner's phrasing, as "snappy bureaucrats,"[11] cogs in a

---

[11]Bittner, p. 53.

quasi-military machine who do what they are told out of a mix of fear, loyalty, routine, and detailed specification of duties.

The professional model, unlike other solutions to be considered, is based on the assumption that the policeman's motives for working can be made to locate within his department. He will, if told, work vice or traffic, juvenile or homicide, patrol passively or aggressively, and produce one, two, four, or six arrests, pedestrian stops, or reports per hour, day, or week as his department sees fit. In this way the assumption and vision of the professional model in policing is little different from that of any bureaucracy which seeks by specifying tasks and setting expectations for levels of production—work quotas—to coordinate a regular, predictable, and efficient service for its clientele.

The problem with this vision of *sine ira et studio* service by obedient operatives is that when the product to be delivered is some form of human service—education, welfare, health, and police bureaucracies are similar in this way—the vision seems always to fall short of expectations. On the one hand the would-be bureaucratic operatives—teachers, social workers, nurses, and policemen—resent being treated as mere bureaucrats and resist the translation of their work into quotas, directives, rules, regulations, or other abstract specifications. On the other hand, to the extent that the vision of an efficient and obedient human service bureaucracy is realized, the clientele of such institutions typically come away with the impression that no one in the institution truly cares about their problems. And, of course, in that the aim of bureaucratization is to locate employees' motives for work within the bureaucracy, they are absolutely correct in their feelings.

To the extent that the professional model succeeds in making the ends of policing locate within the agency as opposed to moral demands of the tasks which policemen are asked by their clients to do, it appears to solve the Dirty Harry problem. When it succeeds, it does so by replacing the morally compelling ends of punishment and peace with the less human, though by no means uncompelling, ends of bureaucratic performance. However, this resolution certainly does not imply that dirty means will disappear, only that the motives for their use will be career advancement and promotion. Likewise, on those occasions when a morally sensitive policeman would be compelled by the demands of the situational exigencies before him to use a dirty means, the bureaucratic operative envisioned by the professional model will merely do his job. Ambitious bureaucrats and obedient timeservers fail at being the type of morally sensitive souls we want to be policemen. The professional model's bureaucratic resolution of the Dirty Harry problem fails in policing for the same reason it fails in every other human service agency; it is quite simply an impossibility to create a bureaucrat who cares for anything but his bureaucracy.

The idealized image of the professional model, which has been responded to with an ideal critique, is probably unrealizable. Reality intervenes as the ideal type is approached. The bureaucracy seems to take on weight as it approaches the pole, is slowed, and may even collapse in approaching.

Bittner's Peace

A second effort in the literature of contemporary policing also attempts to address the Dirty Harry problem by substituting an alternative to the presently prevailing police ends of punishment. Where the professional model sought to substitute bureaucratic rewards and sanctions for the moral end of punishment, the elegant polemics by Egon Bittner in *The Functions of Police in Modern Society* and "Florence Nightingale in Pursuit of Willie Sutton: A Theory of the Police" seek to substitute the end of peace. In beautifully chosen words, examples, and phrasing, Bittner leads his readers to conclude that peace is historically, empirically, intellectually, and morally the most compelling, unquestionable, and humane end of policing. Bittner is, I fear, absolutely right.

It is the end of peace which legitimates the extension of police responsibilities into a wide variety of civil matters—neighborhood disputes, loud parties, corner lounging, lovers' quarrels, political rallys, disobedient children, bicycle registration, pet control, and a hundred other types of tasks which a modern "service" style police department regularly is called upon to perform. With these responsibilities, which most "good" police agencies now accept willingly and officially, also comes the need for an extension of police powers. Arrest is, after all, too crude a tool to be used in all the various situations in which our peace-keeping policemen are routinely asked to be of help. "Why should," asks Herman Goldstein, in a manner in which Bittner would approve, "a police officer arrest and charge a disorderly tavern patron if ordering him to leave the tavern will suffice? Must he arrest and charge one of the parties in a lovers' quarrel if assistance in forcing a separation is all that is desired?"[12] There is no question that both those situations could be handled more peacefully if police were granted new powers which would allow them to handle those situations in the way Goldstein rhetorically asks if they should. That such extensions of police powers will be asked for by our most enlightened police departments in the interests of keeping the peace is absolutely certain. If the success of the decriminalization of police arrests for public intoxication, vagrancy, mental illness, and the virtually unrestricted two-hour right of detention made possible by the Uniform Law of Arrest are any indication of the likelihood of extensions being received favorably, the end of peace and its superiority over punishment in legitimating the extension of police powers seem exceedingly likely to prevail further.

The problem with peace is that it is not the only end of policing so compelling, unquestionable, and in the end, humane. Amid the good work toward the end of peace that we increasingly want our police to do, it is certain that individuals or groups will arise who the police, in all their peace-keeping benevolence,

will conclude, on moral if not political or institutional grounds, have "got it coming." And all the once dirty means which were bleached in the brilliant light of peace will return to their true colors.

Skolnick's Craftsman

The third and final attempt to resolve the Dirty Harry problem is offered by Jerome Skolnick, who in *Justice Without Trial* comes extremely close to stating the Dirty Harry problem openly when he writes:

> . . . He (the policeman) sees himself as a craftsman, at his best, a master of his trade . . . [he] draws a moral distinction between criminal law and criminal procedure. The distinction is drawn somewhat as follows: The substantive law of crimes is intended to control the behavior of people who wilfully injure persons or property, or who engage in behaviors having such a consequence, such as the use of narcotics. Criminal procedure, by contrast, is intended to control authorities, not criminals. As such, it does not fall into the same *moral* class of constraint as substantive criminal law. If a policeman were himself to use narcotics, or to steal, or to assault, *outside the line of duty*, much the same standards would be applied to him by other policemen as to the ordinary citizen. When, however, the issue concerns the policeman's freedom to carry out his *duties*, another moral realm is entered.[13]

What is more, Skolnick's craftsman finds support from his peers, department, his community, and the law for the moral rightness of his calling. He cares about his work and finds it just.

What troubles Skolnick about his craftsman is his craft. The craftsman refuses to see, as Skolnick thinks he ought to, that the dirty means he sometimes uses to achieve his good ends stand in the same moral class of wrongs as those he is employed to fight. Skolnick's craftsman reaches this conclusion by understanding that his unquestionably good and compelling

---

[12]Ibid., p. 72.

[13]Jerome Skolnick, *Justice Without Trial*, 2nd ed. (New York: John Wiley & Sons, 1975), p. 182.

ends, on certain occasions, justify his employment of dirty means to their achievement. Skolnick's craftsman, as Skolnick understands him, resolves the Dirty Harry problem by denying the dirtiness of his means.

Skolnick's craftsman's resolution is, speaking precisely, Machiavellian. It should come as no surprise to find the representative of one of the classic attempts to resolve the problem of Dirty Hands to be a front runner in response to Dirty Harry. What is worrisome about such a resolution? What does it conceal that makes our genuine dilemma disappear? The problem is not that the craftsman will sometimes choose to use dirty means. If he is morally sensitive to its demands, every policeman's work will sometimes require as much. What is worrisome about Skolnick's craftsman is that he does not regard his means as dirty and, as Skolnick tells us, does not suffer from their use. The craftsman, if Skolnick's portrait of him is correct, will resort to dirty means too readily and too easily. He lacks the restraint that can come only from struggling to justify them and from taking seriously the hazards involved.

In 1966, when *Justice Without Trial* first appeared, Skolnick regarded the prospects of creating a more morally sensitive craftsman exceedingly dim. He could not imagine that the craftsman's community, employer, peers, or the courts could come to reward him more for his legal compliance than for the achievement of the ends of his craft. However, in phrasing the prospects in terms of a Dirty Harry problem, one can not only agree with Skolnick that denying the goodness of unquestionably good ends is a practical and political impossibility, but can also uncover another alternative, one which Skolnick does not pursue.

The alternative the Dirty Harry problem leads us to is ensuring that the craftsman regards his dirty means as dirty by applying the same retributive principles of punishment to his wrongful acts that he is quite willing to apply to others! It is, in fact, only when his wrongful acts are punished that he will come to see them as wrongful and will appreciate the genuine moral—rather than technical or occupational—choice he makes in resorting to them. The prospects for punishment of such acts are by no means dim, and considerable strides in this area have been made. It requires far fewer resources to punish than to reward. Secondly, the likelihood that juries in civil suits will find dirty means dirtier than police do is confirmed by police claims that outsiders cannot appreciate the same moral and technical distinctions that they do. Finally, severe financial losses to police agencies as well as to their officers eventually communicate to both that vigorously policing themselves is cheaper and more pleasing than having to pay so heavily if they do not. If under such conditions our craftsman police officer is still willing to risk the employment of dirty means to achieve what he understands to be unquestionably good ends, he will not only know that he has behaved justly, but that in doing so he must run the risk of becoming genuinely guilty as well.

A FINAL NOTE

In urging the punishment of policemen who resort to dirty means to achieve some unquestionably good and morally compelling end, we recognize that we create a Dirty Harry problem for ourselves and for those we urge to effect such punishments. It is a fitting end, one which teaches once again that the danger in Dirty Harry problems is never in their resolution, but in thinking that one has found a resolution with which one can truly live in peace.

CASE STUDY
United States v. Tobias

IT IS NOT ENTRAPMENT FOR AN UNDERCOVER OFFICER TO TELL THE DEFENDANT THAT MAKING PCP IS AS "EASY AS BAKING A CAKE"

HATCHETT, CIRCUIT JUDGE:

We again examine the extent to which the government may become involved in a criminal enterprise without being found guilty of entrapment or having its conduct declared so outrageous as to violate a criminal defendant's due process rights under the fifth amendment. Finding the government's conduct in this case to be within lawful bounds, we affirm.

FACTS

In order to pursue undercover investigations of clandestine laboratory operators, the Drug Enforcement Administration (DEA), established a chemical supply company in a midwestern state which shall be known herein as the supply company. The supply company operated in the same way as any legitimate chemical supply company. It had a business location and received orders via telephone and mail for various chemicals which could be used in the manufacture of controlled substances.

In the April 1980 edition of *High Times Magazine*, the DEA supply company placed an advertisement offering over-the-counter sales of chemicals and laboratory equipment. On March 18, 1980, supply company received a letter from Thomas C. Tobias, the defendant, requesting "more information" and giving his name and address. A catalog was sent to Tobias in Mobile, Alabama. On March 26, 1980, Tobias telephoned the supply company and placed an order for various chemicals. On April

Case Study: *US v Tobias* 662 F.2d 381 (1981).

15, 16, 17, and 24, 1980, Tobias telephoned the supply company to check on his order and to order additional chemicals.

On April 25, 1980, Tobias again called the supply company about his order. According to Tobias's testimony, he telephoned to cancel his order because he had discovered from reading drug literature that he could not manufacture cocaine without "more knowledge . . . and a lot of equipment." Before Tobias could cancel his order, however, Special Agent Schabilion asked him what he was trying to do. Tobias admitted that he wanted to make cocaine but had encountered difficulties. Pretending to empathize with Tobias, Schabilion stated that he too found cocaine to be extremely difficult and expensive to manufacture. To this, Tobias said he was not necessarily interested in manufacturing cocaine, but "just wanted to make some money." Agent Schabilion advised Tobias that "almost anything would be cheaper and easier to manufacture than cocaine," including amphetamines. Schabilion then suggested that Tobias make Phencyclidene (PCP). Schabilion explained that making PCP was as easy as "baking a cake" and that for $500 he would send Tobias everything he needed to get set up. Stating that he might have a market for PCP in Mobile, Tobias agreed. He cancelled his order for the original chemicals and told Special Agent Schabilion to send him everything he needed to manufacture PCP.

The supply company shipped the formula and some of the chemicals needed to manufacture PCP to the DEA office in Mobile for delivery to Tobias. It is undisputed that the chemicals provided by the DEA were not difficult to obtain and could have been purchased at other chemical supply houses. After receiving the chemicals and formula from the DEA, Tobias telephoned the supply company thirteen times to discuss problems encountered in the manufacturing process and to obtain advice for overcoming them. On May 9, 1980, when DEA agents executed a search warrant on Tobias's residence in Mobile they found PCP in a liquid state.

Tobias was convicted in a non-jury trial and received sentences totaling fifteen years in prison.

I.

Tobias complains that the record is devoid of any evidence indicating that he entertained the thought of making drugs prior to reading the government's advertisement for chemicals. He also argues that even after he sought to abandon his scheme to manufacture cocaine, the DEA agents suggested that he make a "cheaper and easier" drug and provided him with the necessary precursors, equipment, and know-how. Thus, he argues that he was entrapped as a matter of law.

"[W]hen entrapment is at issue, the focal point of the inquiry is on the predisposition of the defendant." Thus, a defendant who wishes to assert an entrapment defense must initially come forward with evidence "that the Government's conduct created a substantial risk that the offense would be committed by a person other than one ready to commit it." Once the defendant has carried this burden, the government must, if it is to prevail, prove beyond a reasonable doubt that the defendant was predisposed to commit the crime charged.

"A prosecution cannot be defeated merely because a government agent has provided the accused with the opportunity or facilities for the commission of the crime. It is only when the government's deception actually implants the criminal design in the mind of the defendant that the defense of entrapment comes into play."

On this record, we cannot say that Tobias was entrapped. Even assuming Tobias produced sufficient evidence to raise the issue of entrapment, we are satisfied that the government carried its burden of proving, beyond a reasonable doubt, that Tobias was predisposed to commit the charged offenses. The government's proof showed that Tobias responded to a simple advertisement offering the over-the-counter sale of chemicals which could be purchased without any difficulty in chemical houses in Mobile, Alabama. This advertisement served only to provide one so disposed the opportunity to obtain the necessary precursors and equipment to manufacture controlled substances. Tobias seized this opportunity by writing the supply company for "more information" and telephoning the supply company on many occasions to place and check on his order. The DEA did nothing else to solicit Tobias's business. A prosecution may not be defeated because the government provides the accused with the opportunity to commit the crimes charged.

Tobias also contends that agent Schabilion's suggestion that PCP would be "cheaper and easier" to manufacture implanted the criminal design in his mind at a time when he sought to cancel his order for chemicals necessary to manufacture cocaine.

The record simply does not bear out Tobias's contention. The record shows that although Tobias sought to cancel his original order, he indicated to agent Schabilion that he was not interested in manufacturing any particular drug but was only interested in making money. At that point, agent Schabilion suggested that amphetamines, including PCP, would be "cheaper and easier" to manufacture. Tobias then indicated that there might be a market for PCP in Mobile and asked Schabilion to send him the formula, equipment, and precursors necessary to manufacture PCP. This evidence shows that Tobias was predisposed to manufacture a controlled substance, although no one drug in particular.

If law enforcement agents are precluded from discussing the particulars of how a criminal enterprise is to be conducted, the undercover work that is essential to the investigation and prosecution of drug offenses becomes impossible. Suggestions regarding the particulars of manufacturing one drug or another did not vitiate the predisposition which is best shown by Tobias's continuance of the conversation.

II.

Tobias next argues that if the government had not provided him with the formula, necessary precursors, and continuing advice during the manufacturing process, he would have been unable to manufacture PCP. Thus, he argues that the government's involvement in this scheme was so outrageous that due process principles bar his convictions. This presents a tougher question.

In *Russell*, the Supreme Court held that the defense of entrapment was foreclosed to one who was predisposed to commit a crime, regardless of the type and degree of government activity involved. The Court, however, expressed the possibility that due process principles might prohibit an excessive degree of government involvement, stating: "[W]e may some day be presented with a situation in which the conduct of law enforcement agents is so outrageous that due process principles would absolutely bar the government from invoking judicial processes to obtain a conviction. . . ." While the Court pointed out that in certain situations the conduct of the government may bar prosecution, it emphasized that the defendant must show that the challenged government conduct violates "'that fundamental fairness, shocking to the universal sense of justice,' mandated by the due process clause of the fifth amendment."

In certain circumstances, the government's conduct may be so outrageous as to violate due process however, "[p]olice overinvolvement in crime would have to reach a demonstrable level of outrageousness before it could bar convictions."

In the recent case of *United States v. Gray*, this court was presented with the question whether the government's conduct was so outrageous as to require reversal of convictions for violation of due process. In *Gray*, two government agents suggested a smuggling scheme to defendants and provided them with repair services, an airstrip, and a crew. The court, although acknowledging that the government agents suggested the scheme and aided in arranging the air transportation, held that "the providing of essential services is not misconduct."

In *United States v. Leja*, the defendant approached a government informant and suggested that the two produce PCP in a laboratory. They entered into an agreement which provided that the government informant would obtain the necessary chemicals and the other two defendants would supply glassware, money, and technical expertise. Not only did the government informant provide the chemicals necessary to produce PCP, but another government informant provided technical instructions concerning the manufacturing process when one of the defendants encountered difficulties. The Sixth Circuit, relying on the fact that the government agent neither solicited the defendants nor provided them with chemicals and information which they could not have obtained elsewhere, held that the due process clause did not require reversal of their convictions.

In *United States v. Twigg*, however, the Third Circuit found the government's conduct so outrageous as to violate due process because the government agent suggested the establishment of a drug laboratory, provided the place, equipment, supplies and know-how, and then ran the entire operation with only meager assistance from the defendants.

From these cases emerges the basic proposition that government infiltration of criminal activity is a "recognized and permissible means of investigation." "This proposition remains true even though the . . . government agent . . . supplies something of value to the criminal." This is necessary so that the agent "will . . . be taken into the confidence of the illegal entrepreneurs." On the other end of the spectrum, however, the government may not instigate the criminal activity, provide the place, equipment, supplies and know-how, and run the entire operation with only meager assistance from the defendants without violating fundamental fairness.

Although the DEA provided the formula and some of the chemicals for the manufacture of PCP, the chemicals were not difficult to obtain and, in fact, some were ordered from a chemical supply house in Mobile. DEA provided no financial aid for Tobias's operation. In sum, "[t]he law enforcement conduct here stops far short of violating that 'fundamental fairness, shocking to the universal sense of justice,' mandated by the due process clause of the fifth amendment."

The cases demonstrate that outrageous involvement turns upon the totality of the circumstances with no single factor controlling. Although a totality of the circumstances standard must be applied, it is beneficial to review the parts that make up the whole. The DEA, in this case, did not initiate contact with Tobias. May the government be held to have involved itself in outrageous conduct by placing the ad in *High Times*? Similarly, may the government be condemned for shipping the necessary chemicals, even at cut-rate prices? Or, was it outrageous for DEA to deliver the chemicals to Tobias's home? We think not. The crucial factor in this total fact picture is the step-by-step advice given by the DEA agents. This advice was given to Tobias or his wife on more than thirteen occasions. On each occasion, however, Tobias or his wife contacted the DEA. This would be a more difficult case if the DEA had pursued Tobias by repeated phone calls and encouragement. But here, the drug transaction would have stopped at any time that Tobias made no further calls. Instead of being a *predisposed inactive participant* in this scheme to manufacture and distribute PCP (a cheap mind bending drug) primarily sold to youngsters, Tobias was a *predisposed active participant* motivated solely by a desire to make money. It is this predisposition plus active and insistent participation that sets this case apart from cases finding a due process violation. We are mindful of the Supreme Court's admonition that due process can only be invoked in the rarest and most outrageous circumstances. Yet, this case does set the outer limits to which the government may go in the quest to ferret out and prosecute crimes in this circuit.

FRANK M. JOHNSON, JR., CIRCUIT JUDGE, DISSENTING:

Because I conclude that the Drug Enforcement Agency's (DEA) "overinvolvement" in the commission of the crime for which defendant was convicted precludes prosecution, I am unable to agree with the majority's opinion and therefore respectfully dissent.

Tobias is a 21- or 22-year-old married man employed as a house painter. With the exception of a minor exchange of fisticuffs, he has no prior record of any kind and had never been convicted of a drug related offense. In early 1980 Tobias responded to an advertisement in *High Times*, an over-the-counter drug culture periodical, and sought information concerning the purchase of chemicals necessary to make cocaine. Defendant requested a catalogue from the chemical supply company and eventually ordered what he thought were chemicals needed to manufacture cocaine. Unbeknownst to Tobias, the chemical supply company, located in a mid-western state, was owned and operated by the DEA. On April 25, 1980, Tobias called the company to cancel his order and spoke to DEA Agent Schabilion. He advised Schabilion that he intended to use the chemicals to manufacture cocaine but had concluded that he lacked the requisite knowledge and equipment necessary to make the drug. Indeed, the record reflects that Tobias was ineptly suited to make cocaine. His education extended only as far as high school, whereas manufacturing cocaine requires a "sophisticated chemical background." Further, it appears that Tobias never had even a basic understanding of what was needed to manufacture the drug, both in terms of the necessary chemicals and in terms of the necessary knowledge of chemistry.[1] During

---

[1] Tobias originally ordered four chemicals from the supply company and later added two more. According to counsel for the Government. DEA officials did not ship the chemicals because they were unable to tell from the order what Tobias was trying to manufacture. Apparently Tobias' list of chemicals was either incomplete or inaccurate, indicating that he did not know the proper ingredients. Further, it was Agent Schabilion during the April 25 phone call who had to explain to Tobias about the chemicals, precursors, expense and technical knowledge necessary to make cocaine.

the course of the conversation, Schabilion emphasized the difficulty and expense involved in manufacturing cocaine and suggested a number of "cheaper" and "easier" alternatives. "I advised him [Tobias] that almost anything would be cheaper and easier to manufacture than cocaine, and suggested that any of the amphetamines, speed or PCP would be easier." Until that statement, nothing in the record reveals any intent or disposition on the part of Tobias to attempt the manufacture of any drug other than cocaine. Tobias admitted to Schabilion that there might be a market for PCP in the Mobile area but expressed reservations about making the drug, stating that he had no background in chemistry. At that point in the conversation Agent Schabilion explained that manufacturing PCP was as easy as "baking a cake." The agent, according to defendant, also told him that selling the drug would be profitable. Without any discussion as to particular chemicals or quantities, Schabilion promised to supply Tobias with everything necessary to make PCP, including the formula, at a total cost of $500. Tobias then agreed to purchase the chemicals and delivery was made in Mobile, Alabama, by a DEA agent acting as an employee of a fictitious delivery company. The defendant received two separate deliveries on the same day and paid $101 for the chemicals, the total amount requested by the DEA. The DEA supplied Tobias with all of the necessary ingredients of PCP except diethyl ether, which Tobias obtained at a local chemical supply store.

Utilizing the chemicals provided by the DEA and the formula provided by the DEA, Tobias attempted to manufacture a drug suggested by the DEA. However, the agency's encouragement, pervasive influence, and active participation did not end there. Still uncertain about how to actually make the drug, from April 29 through May 9 Tobias telephoned the supply company 13 times and his wife called on three other occasions to obtain information and additional advice concerning the procedure at each stage of the manufacturing process. It is undisputed that Tobias did not know how to make PCP and that during those phone calls the DEA agents instructed him as

to each step in the process. Agents for the Government, therefore, guided the defendant in every stage of the process, from inception to termination. Tobias was ultimately arrested and, despite his status as a first-time drug offender, his youthful age and his family situation, was cumulatively sentenced to fifteen years' incarceration and ten years' special parole.

Government involvement and assistance in the criminal activities of others are sometimes necessary to enforce the laws. The degree of Government involvement is not, however, boundless. The Supreme Court observed that, when involvement by federal agents in the commission of a crime is so outrageous as to shock the conscience, either due process or the Court's supervisory powers will preclude prosecution. These decisions make clear that as a general rule infiltration and "limited involvement" by Government agents in a drug related enterprise do not run afoul of the due process clause and in fact constitute a legitimate method of apprehending offenders. The Supreme Court also admonished that due process is not meant to provide federal courts with a "chancellor's foot" veto over investigatory techniques that lack judicial approbation. The two cases read in tandem demonstrate that only extreme and outrageous Government involvement in the commission of a crime will justify reversing for that reason a conviction under the due process clause.

Although providing a rudimentary framework for analysis, neither *Russell* nor *Hampton* delineated with clarity the point at which Government involvement becomes shocking and outrageous. However, some lower court decisions have found the requisite level of outrageous involvement and provide useful guidance. In *Greene v. United States*, a case cited by the Supreme Court in *Hampton*, the defendants contacted a Government agent concerning the possibility of manufacturing and selling bootleg whiskey. The agent represented himself to be a member of the "syndicate" and agreed to both provide financial assistance and buy all of the whiskey produced. Extensive communications transpired between the parties, with the agent providing the defendants with substantial assistance. He helped search for an appropriate site for the still, agreed to provide equipment and an operator for the still, and made available two thousand pounds of sugar at wholesale prices. The agent also tried to prompt the defendants by intimating that he was receiving pressure for the whiskey from his syndicate boss. On appeal, the court noted that the defendants evinced a predisposition to commit the crime and could not, therefore, invoke the "usual entrapment defense." However, because of the extensive and aggressive overinvolvement by the agent in the crime, the conviction was reversed. "[W]hen the Government permits itself to become enmeshed in criminal activity, from beginning to end, to the extent which appears here, the same underlying objections which render entrapment repugnant to American criminal justice are operative."

Similarly in *United States v. Twigg* DEA agents initiated contact with the defendants and suggested that they construct a laboratory for manufacturing amphetamines. The DEA agents supplied the defendants with the necessary chemicals at a discount price, supplied a portion of glassware to be used, and provided a barn as the situs for the laboratory. The agents facilitated defendants' ability to purchase chemicals from other supply companies and made available the necessary funds to make the purchases. A DEA agent also supervised the entire manufacturing process, with the defendants providing only minor production assistance. The Third Circuit rejected the defense of entrapment, finding evidence of predisposition. However, the court reversed the conviction and held that "the nature and extent of police involvement in this crime was so overreaching as to bar prosecution of the defendants as a matter of law."

The cases demonstrate that outrageous involvement turns upon the totality of the circumstances with no single factor controlling. Under such a standard, it is my judgment that the DEA's overinvolvement in this case requires reversal of the conviction. The DEA agents placed the advertisement for the chemicals in *High Times* magazine. The majority justifies this conduct by observing that it was for

the purpose of pursuing "undercover investigations of clandestine laboratory operators . . .". While that may have been the purpose of the operation of the chemical supply house, in this case the advertisement constituted the initial contact with a young man that had up until then indicated no predisposition to manufacture drugs. When it became apparent that Tobias was completely stymied in his predisposition to manufacture cocaine, the agents advanced the idea of manufacturing an "easier" and "cheaper" drug. Tobias was provided with almost all of the necessary chemicals at apparently cut-rate prices, was provided with the formula for manufacturing the PCP and was persuaded to make PCP in part by the statement that the process was no more difficult than "baking a cake." The DEA agents personally delivered the chemicals to his home and gave technical advice concerning the amount and sequence of combining each separate ingredient at every step of the manufacturing process. Admittedly, the agents did not other than the advertisement initiate contact with Tobias, but that fact is not dispositive.[2]

This case does not merely involve law enforcement officers supplying Tobias with an "item of value" necessary to make the prohibited drug. Such a practice is universally recognized as an acceptable investigative technique. Here, Tobias amounted to little more than a conduit. Had the Government agents at any point ceased providing Tobias with assistance and encouragement, the record indicates that he would have been incapable of manufacturing the illicit drug. Thus Government agents

[2]The majority indicates that the DEA's failure to provide Tobias with "financial aid" distinguishes the case from prior decisions dealing with Government overinvolvement. The record indicates, however, that the Government did provide Tobias with "financial assistance." Tobias was originally informed that the chemicals would cost $500. Nonetheless, when the DEA agent delivered the chemicals, he charged Tobias only $101. Moreover, the DEA agent made a second delivery on the same day and did not charge Tobias *anything* for the additional chemicals. Thus, although the record is not totally clear, the Government appears to have provided "financial assistance" to Tobias in the form of reduced prices for the chemicals used to manufacture the PCP.

vicariously manufactured PCP through Tobias in order to gather evidence to justify his prosecution. The instant case therefore involves that rare degree of Government involvement in the commission of a crime that *Hampton and Russell* intended to prevent. I do not, of course, propose that federal courts be accorded a "chancellor's foot" veto over law enforcement techniques that are disapproved.

I do suggest, however, that the majority goes too far by holding, in effect, that no matter how egregious and shocking the degree of Government involvement in the commission of a crime, neither the due process clause nor the court's supervisory powers will ever be invoked to preclude prosecution.

Courts are rightfully loathe to overturn convictions on the basis of Governmental over-involvement in the commission of a crime,

recognizing that law enforcement officials need wide latitude in devising appropriate methods and tactics for apprehending violators. However, judicial tolerance of Governmental involvement in criminal activity should not constitute a *carte blanche;* there is still a point beyond which law enforcement officials cannot go. As Justice Brandeis observed, "[t]o declare that in the administration of criminal law the end justifies the means—to declare that the Government may commit crimes in order to secure the conviction of a private criminal—would bring terrible retribution." The direct, continual involvement by Government agents in the creation, maintenance and commission of a crime, to the extent reflected in this case, goes beyond the perimeter of permissible conduct and should not be countenanced by this Court.

Selective Enforcement and the Rule of Law

John Kleinig

"Is it justifiable in a free society to allow police officers freedom to determine whether or not to arrest someone when they legally and physically can make the arrest?" This is the question to which Jeffrey Reiman has recently answered an unambiguous "no."[1] It is not the first time that the question has been answered this way,[2] though Reiman's robust defense must once again give pause to those who, like myself,

believe that some discretion in this regard ought to be allowable.

One of the merits of Reiman's discussion lies in his attempt to embed his defense within the larger framework of political philosophy. Using as his base Plato's account of the rule of law in *The Statesman*, Reiman makes three observations. First, the purpose of laws is not simply to ensure justice to citizens, but also to protect us from the vagaries of rulers; second, the rule of law generally works out well, though not perfectly: what it loses in just results in particular cases it gains in the protection that it provides against tyranny; and third, this trade-off is necessitated by the fact that

John Kleinig, "Selective Enforcement and the Rule of Law," *Journal of Social Philosophy* 29, Number 1 (Spring 1998): 117–31. Reprinted by permission of the *Journal of Social Philosophy*.

"ideal rulers" are not only few and far between, but cannot be readily identified.[3]

What Plato holds to be true is reinforced by contemporary political theorizing. Here the very idea of an "ideal" or "natural" ruler is called into question. The probability of tyranny is thus increased, and the practical importance of the rule of law is heightened. In a world that lacks natural rulers, each person must be accorded an equality of status and be recognized as having a natural authority over only his or her own actions. Political authority, if it is to be justified at all, can be justified only if it can be seen as a reasonable bargain on the part of those who are subject to it. It constitutes a reasonable bargain only if it is constrained by rules that exclude its arbitrary exercise. And this, Reiman insists, amounts to an acceptance of the rule of law.[4]

Political authority as we now understand it is not primarily goal-oriented, but contractual. It does not authorize those in power to achieve some desirable end by whatever means they consider appropriate, but is a limited *authorization* to secure certain specified ends (as enshrined in law) by means that are limited. That being so, Reiman argues, any discretionary authority that police exercise can be justified in only two ways: either as an explicit grant by citizens or as the conclusion of an argument showing that it would be reasonable to make such a grant. He takes it that there is no basis for believing the former: police are "simply and explicitly authorized to enforce the law that the people's representatives enact, and no more."[5]

Is there any good reason to think that people *should* give police some discretion about whether or not to enforce the law? Reiman offers four reasons for thinking that no good grounds exist for giving them that discretion: (1) it would render the laws "vague and uncertain"; (2) it would effectively give police the power to amend laws that the people's representatives had passed; (3) it would almost certainly be used discriminatorily; and (4) it would be used coercively as a form of leverage. In what follows I shall attempt to meet the challenge posed by Reiman's arguments, and shall argue that it is reasonable to allow to police a limited discretionary authority in regard to their enforcement of law.

LAW ENFORCEMENT AND ORDER MAINTENANCE

First of all, however, I need to address what I believe to be a very problematic qualification that Reiman makes near the beginning of his discussion. There he notes that police are "commonly charged with the dual task of enforcing law and maintaining order," and that in fulfillment of the latter goal "they disperse unruly crowds, quiet noisy neighbors, break up fights before they begin, clear the streets of prostitutes, and so on."[6] In situations such as these, he believes it appropriate that police exercise discretion—perhaps by choosing not to arrest where the law would allow them to.

This is no small concession. If we are to believe James Q. Wilson, "[t]he patrolman's role is defined more by his responsibility for *maintaining order* than by his responsibility for enforcing the law."[7] Wilson characterizes order maintenance as intervention in situations that disturb or threaten to disturb the public peace, an account that sits well with Reiman's examples.[8] So, despite Reiman's unambiguous "no" to his initial question, a great deal of police work may in fact constitute an exception to it. This surely represents not only an "important" (his term) but a dramatic qualification of his opposition to selective enforcement. For there is nothing in his later arguments that provides a basis for such exceptions. It is, moreover, these added dimensions of the police task (whether characterized as order maintenance, peacekeeping, or social service functions) that have provided one of the traditional rationales for selective enforcement.

But that is not all. Wilson makes it clear that the order maintenance function no longer figures in cases in which "there is no dispute."[9] When an infraction of the law is observed, such as a traffic violation, it is no longer possible to appeal to order-maintenance as a reason for not enforcing the law (in the sense of making an arrest or issuing a ticket). Yet I believe that selective enforcement *may* be justifiable in these cases as well—where there is no victim or there are believed to be extenuating circumstances. And perhaps Reiman would also want to make exceptions in such cases. But if that is so he cannot make them under the rubric of the police order-maintenance function.

THE RULE OF LAW

As Reiman rightly observes, the idea of "a government of laws, not men" is of ancient pedigree.[10] Not only Plato but also Aristotle was convinced that "the rule of law is preferable to that of any individual."[11] And in liberal democratic regimes, the rule of law has been appealed to as the main bulwark against tyranny. Any theoretical doubts that people have had about its appropriateness have usually been allayed by the spectacle of what happens in societies that have rejected it.

Nevertheless, appeals to the rule of law are neither as transparent nor as compelling as Reiman seems to believe. First of all, there is considerable debate about what is encompassed by the rule of law, and for this reason it can be questioned whether a rule of law excludes the recognition of limited discretionary authority; and second, there is a tension between the rule of law and democratic expectations.

The rule of law is a political ideal. Essentially, it sets forth conditions for government that are intended to preserve the governed from the tyranny of arbitrary power. For some writers this is understood *formalistically*, as requiring no more than the existence of and subscription to fixed and preannounced formal rules, rules that are articulated with sufficient clarity to enable exercises of governmental authority to be predicted with some certainty.[12] But for other writers, the rule of law is interpreted more *substantively* to require that rules promulgated by governmental authority be broadly concordant with a particular conception of human entitlements. Thus "rule of law values" (as catalogued by Michael Moore)— the separation of powers, equality and formal justice, liberty and notice, substantive fairness, procedural fairness, and efficient administration—are intended to secure citizens not only

against arbitrariness but also against oppressive rules.[13]

Reiman does not explicitly join this debate, though he is clearly concerned about both oppression and arbitrariness. He accepts that respect for human freedom and human equality need to be preserved in—indeed, constitute the *raison d'être* for—civil society. It could be that freedom and equality can be protected not only by adherence to the rule of law but also by commitment to a conception of human rights or personal sovereignty, the latter pressed as political demands additional to that of the rule of law. But I think that he implicitly accepts the richer, more substantive view of the rule of law, for he quotes with approval Locke's contention that "*where-ever law ends, tyranny begins,*" and that the person who "exceeds the power given him by the law . . . may be opposed, as any other man, who by force invades the right of another."[14] This strongly suggests that Reiman sees the rule of law as securing us not merely against arbitrariness but also against (other?) violations of our rights.[15]

Because of this, Reiman believes that in a free society adherence to the rule of law will preclude the grant of discretionary authority to police. It is only if such authority has been explicitly granted, or if it is reasonable to expect it to be granted, that we may reconcile police discretion with the rule of law. He takes it that the former has not occurred, and believes the latter to be lacking in merit.

Consider now the second issue: the coherence of the rule of law with democratic or contractual processes. Reiman seems to take it for granted that there is an easy fit between the rule of law and its modern expression in liberal democratic society. Yet a little reflection indicates that this is not the case. The rule of law, at least according to Reiman's conception, seems to require that laws be applied exceptionlessly. Democratic and contractarian theories, on the other hand, emphasize the value of the majority will, and that will need not be limited to or even be compatible with the substantive requirements of law. After all, the rulers envisaged in Plato's *The Statesmen* or Aristotle's *Politics*, though enjoined to rule through law rather than the deliverances of individual judgment, were not conceived of as democratically elected incumbents.

The seriousness of this potential tension between the rule of law and democratic values is not unrelated to the way in which we construe both the rule of law and democracy. If democracy and the rule of law are both thought of formalistically—as no more than a crude majoritarianism, on the part of one, and a law of rules, on the part of the other—then the tension could be quite significant. But if democratic rule is anchored instead in the values of equality and freedom, and the rule of law is likewise anchored in a theory of human rights, the rule of law may be seen as expressing one of the conditions under which (liberal) democratic aspirations may be realized.

Have people actually withheld discretionary authority from the police? Reiman might have referred to the full enforcement statutes that have been passed in many states.[16] If the people have not spoken, then their representatives certainly have, and they have charged police with responsibility to arrest anyone who violates a law.[17] What more appropriate evidence could we want in a democratically ordered society? Strong as this consideration is, however, I am not entirely convinced that we should take it as our only—or even as decisive—evidence of what the people have chosen.

First of all, a great number of violations are dealt with informally by police, and for the most part their choice not to arrest or summons or cite does not meet with public disapproval. We all know that many of those who are stopped for traffic offenses—such as speeding or having defective tail lights—are let off with a warning rather than a summons, and yet, unless the case is an egregious one, we do not complain. Maybe our failure to protest can be put down to naked self-interest—the recognition of our own propensity to speed or our failure to make regular checks of our car's condition, and the desire that we should be treated leniently if caught. But I think there is rather more to it than that. For we also recognize that people exceed the speed limit or fail to ensure that their car is not in violation of laws relating

to its condition for many different reasons, and in some of these cases we would feel that an injustice had been done were a ticket to be issued or the driver arrested. For the most part, we would be more upset were someone who was speeding for a "legitimate" reason to be ticketed than we would be were someone not to be ticketed for a comparable offense for which there were no "legitimating" reasons.

Reiman alludes to the possibility of a public acceptance of discretion, but says that it does not amount to a public grant of authority. In the circumstances which he has in mind—the nonarrest of drug dealers and prostitutes on condition that they become informants[18]—I am at least sympathetic. But this is probably a special case; at least it is a more controversial one. What we might ask is whether the circumstances in which the discretion is exercised are such that the discretion could (though not necessarily will) be sustained in a public forum. In the case of the circumstances under which the services of drug dealers and prostitutes are obtained, I can imagine that there would be a significant division of opinion. But in the cases to which I earlier alluded, in which traffic laws are violated, I think that the argument for publicly defending an exercise of discretion not to arrest or ticket is much stronger.

Second, there is some reason to view full enforcement statutes only as broad statements of purpose and not as rigid requirements. This is not to say that they would be modified if challenged. They are, however, products of a political process, a process that is sometimes best served if statements are made in categorical and unqualified terms. Lending credence to this view is the finding that despite provisions for doing so, full enforcement statutes are rarely enforced and, further, this fact per se brings with it no public outcry. It is only when the discretion is exercised in what seem to be *inappropriately* lenient ways that complaints are heard.[19] Although we are all aware that the police exercise discretion, when it is not felt to be oppressive it is rarely opposed. Furthermore, it is not uncommon for the police to publicize in broad terms the fact that they selectively enforce the law.[20] What generally sticks in people's craw is not less than full enforcement per se, but the discriminatory way in which that is sometimes practiced and the disregard for victims that it sometimes displays.

Third, although legislation sometimes mirrors a social consensus (or at least social majority), it does not always do so. It may be progressive or lag behind social change. There are many reasons for the hiatuses that occur between legislation and social values—some understandable, some reprehensible—and sometimes police are left with the task of making informal adjustments so that social peace may be preserved. Statutes outlawing sodomy, adultery, and fornication may remain on the books for political reasons, yet police would alienate significant sections of their community and generate considerable social turmoil were they to enforce them.

For these reasons, I do not think it unreasonable to argue that the purpose of full enforcement statutes is not so much to require that every law be enforced on every occasion on which it can be, but to place an onus on police to enforce.[21] The difference is important. Those who violate the law know that police have a defeasible obligation to enforce it. Enforcement is not optional; but neither is it mandatory. It is a defeasible obligation on the part of police to investigate law breaking and to take some action with regard to all violations that are called to their attention.

As I noted earlier, there is a sense in which full enforcement statutes are politically necessary. To pass laws and not require that they be enforced or to indicate explicitly that whether or not they will be enforced will be left to the discretion of the police, would be to undermine their force as law. *Even if* it is left to the discretion of police whether or not to enforce the law by means of arrest or summons, the law needs to be magisterially asserted. Otherwise those who break the law will not see their fate as a consequence of their violating the law but only as a matter of negotiation between themselves and the police. Allowing police discretion to enforce the law selectively is not intended to sanction the latter.

Let us now look in more detail at Reiman's four objections.

VAGUENESS AND UNCERTAINTY

Reiman's first claim is that any acceptance of discretion will render the law "vague and uncertain." Why should we think this to be the case? If the law says that the speed limit is 55 mph, and police do not generally ticket people unless they are traveling 10 mph over the speed limit, the law is not thereby rendered vague and uncertain. Nor does it suggest that the speed limit is really 65 mph and not 55 mph. A person who is traveling at 70 mph will be charged with traveling 15 mph over the speed limit, not 5 mph. And a person who happens to get picked up for traveling at 60 mph cannot complain that he wasn't traveling over 65 mph, and therefore should not have been picked up. Of course, he might wonder why he, of all the people who travel over 55 and under 65 mph, was picked up. But if at 60 mph this person was creating a risk, then there does not seem to be any problem about the police picking him up and not others.

This having been said, it might still be reasonable for us to agree that the police generally wait until people are about 10 mph over the limit before they move in. The reasons here are practical. Our speedometers may be slightly off. The instrumentation used by the police may not be completely accurate. The road may be straight and clear, and visibility good, and no risk may be involved. We may have simply allowed the car to drift above the speed limit, easy to do when one has been driving for a while. It involves a better use of police resources to target those who are more than 10 mph over. And, finally, there may be all sorts of personal reasons why we were traveling above the limit—to get someone to hospital, because we are late picking up the children, we need to get to a bathroom, and so on.[22] Unless there is some special reason to give the law strict liability status, its rigid application in some of these cases would be obnoxious, and would do little to advance the purpose of the law. Laws are not contextless requirements but embedded in social purposes, and although they provide clear guidelines, they are not, or at least should not be, impervious to the social purposes that have informed them. "Overreach" of the law, as Klockars calls it, the working of injustice because laws are expressed too specifically or generally, is correctable by means of discretionary judgments. The correction doesn't make the law vague or uncertain, but allows factors relevant to the law's purpose (both in general and in particular cases) to be incorporated into its enforcement.

Another way of putting this is to say that humans are rational beings, capable of understanding not only the terms of laws (their letter), but also the purposes (or spirit) that led to their promulgation. A person who is "given a break" when traveling at 63 mph, because he was responding to an anxious call from his wife, is not going to go on his way less certain about the law, because he understands not only the letter of the law but also the spirit that infuses it.

CONFUSION OF POWERS

Would selective enforcement in effect give police the power to amend the law, and thus subvert the purposes that have made the doctrine of a separation of powers so valuable to sustaining liberal democratic structures? Reiman certainly thinks so, and he is not alone in this. The virtue that informs the doctrine of separation of powers is the dispersal of power and thus a diminished likelihood of its being used tyrannically: "liberty will be best protected if police, judges, and law makers each do what they are mandated to do."[23] Whereas it is the task of the legislature to make and amend the law, it is the task of the police to enforce it.[24]

It is worth noting that the matter of separation has been discussed at great length in regard to judicial decision making. There has been a longstanding controversy between defenders of a mechanical jurisprudence, strict constructionists, who believe that the task of judges is to "discover" the law and then to apply it, and those "activists" who believe that judges have a more creative role to play. That

debate has been closely linked to another debate, namely, whether "law" should be understood positivistically as rules promulgated by a duly constituted authority, devoid of normative presumptions, or whether law must be thought of normatively, as embodying not merely formal requirements but as also expressive of or at least subject to certain normative "principles," the latter to be understood as either political or legal. Some members of the positivist group would want to limit judicial discretion to those cases not covered by law, and which can be settled *only* by appealing to extralegal (moral or political) principles.[25] Members of the second group, on the other hand, see judicial discretion as both generated and guided by the normative principles that inform law.[26] In other words, the law, though anchored to the words of a text (or texts), is not a contextless set of assertions, but needs to be understood and applied with an eye to the broader social canvas in which it is embedded. This is not to endorse "Humpty Dumpty,"[27] but it is to oppose a contextless literalism.

I believe that the debate over police discretion has significant parallels to that concerning judicial discretion, and that the reasons which favor the latter also favor the former. But two factors are sometimes thought to indicate crucial differences. One concerns publicity. The other concerns competence. With regard to the first, whereas the discretionary decisions of judges are "public," and therefore open to scrutiny, those of individual police officers are often "private" and therefore veiled from public scrutiny. This clearly poses a problem, for if police are to be given the power to make discretionary judgments, they need to be accountable for exercises of that power, and that will be very difficult to achieve if their decisions are made out of public view.[28]

But what I think we should conclude from this—and what is to some extent manifest in practice—is that police discretion needs to be much more carefully circumscribed than judicial discretion. We should note what this means and what it doesn't. Since police discretion is private in the sense that much of what police do is unsupervised, this will remain the case whether or not they have the formal power to act in a discretionary manner. So removing, circumscribing, or not granting them the power to make discretionary judgments about whether or not to arrest will have no effect on the visibility of their conduct. The question we must ask then is: Is it better that police not have that formal discretionary power (even though they may privately act as though they do), or that they be granted a formal discretionary power, although one that is circumscribed (even though we may not be able to keep a close eye on how they use it)?

How we answer this question goes to the very heart of our aspirations for policing. If we see the largely paramilitary structure of contemporary policing as necessary or desirable, then, whether or not it is possible to provide better supervision, the denial of discretionary authority will better reflect the discipline of police work. But if we wish to encourage greater professionalism in policing, then the answer will most likely be the grant of discretionary authority, along with efforts to educate police in its wise use.[29]

In addition, we should note that although it may be practically difficult to give the decisions of individual police officers the same kind of scrutiny as the decisions of judges, there is nothing to stop the general practice of police decision making from being publicly reviewed, and nothing to stop certain general kinds of discretionary decisions from being discussed in a public forum. Indeed, there often is such discussion when the assumed discretion is exercised in a way that is thought to be harmful to the legitimate interests of those involved—whether they be citizens who believe that they have been discriminatorily targeted, suspects who feel they have been harshly treated, or victims who consider that their legitimate expectations have not been met. I have no problem with greater publicity in this regard, and indeed would think it highly desirable.

As noted, police discretion generally is more tightly circumscribed than judicial discretion, both because of significant court cases that have limited the way in which police may go about their work and because of internal constraints that have been placed on police procedures. What Kenneth Culp Davis popularized as "administrative rule making" colors much of what they may do.

What I have said in relation to publicity also bears on the question of competence. Judges certainly are more experienced "practitioners" of the law than police. Yet the strategies adopted to make police discretion more public or less arbitrary—the openness of discretionary policies to public discussion, and the promulgation of discretionary guidelines—also serve to deal with the lesser sophistication of police.

But Reiman, I suspect, would oppose the grant of discretion *even were* there to be such discussion, *even were* it to be generally agreed that some such discretion would be utilitarianly desirable, and *even were* discretionary guidelines to be publicly promulgated. His reason for this would probably be that powers that should be separate would here be conjoined, that the checks and balances so important to preserving a free society would here be compromised. But this assumes a separation of powers that has never existed; nor could it have. Judges are appointed by politicians; police chiefs are appointed by mayors; funding for the judicial and executive branches of government is usually determined by the legislative branch; and so on. The question is not so much: What separation can we achieve? but: What of importance is secured by whatever arrangement that exists? What we want and need is not a complete separation of powers but sufficient separation—sufficient, that is, for independence and strength—so that we can ensure that the values of a free society are nurtured and preserved. I do not see any virtue in the separation of powers *in abstracto*, but only insofar as it is able to safeguard citizens against tyranny. If it is possible to do well (even better) with less than complete separation, then there should be no decisive objection to that being so.

Of course it would be different if police acted as though they had the discretionary authority to add to our current stock of laws. That indeed would make the exercise of discretion tyrannical. But what we have in mind in talking of selective enforcement is a lessening of the grip of law, an easing of the burdens it imposes, and this, provided that, as a result, victims do not go unrequited, should not be seen as an instance of tyranny. Indeed, I am arguing almost the opposite, viz., that a form of tyranny (or certainly harshness) may reside in always applying the law as written in the circumstances as given.

Reiman is correct to identify the issue of police discretion as an area of concern. But the appropriate response, I believe, is not to condemn that discretion as a transgression of proper boundaries, but to bring it into the public domain for monitoring and discussion, as necessary.

What I think should be more worrying from Reiman's perspective is some form of departmentally sanctioned discretion—where, for example, a police chief promulgates as departmental policy a qualification of the law as written. Suppose, for example, the law forbids the possession of marijuana, but the police chief informs members of the department that no action should be taken against those who have less than 1 oz. of marijuana in their possession. Here, it might be argued, the chief exercises a form of discretion that effectively "amends" the law as written. Is *this* justifiable?

Although it may not be legally provided for, I do not see why it should not be morally justifiable, though there are clearly problems if a decision of this kind is cloaked in secrecy. Although a public *announcement* might well send the wrong message, it is not too difficult to see how a police department could justify this way of husbanding its resources.

Davis gives the example of a police department that, in the face of a law prohibiting gambling, promulgates to its members the following rule:

> In the absence of special circumstances, we do not ordinarily arrest for social gambling in the absence of (a) a complaint, (b) a profit from the gambling other than gambling winnings, or (c) extraordinarily high stakes. When we receive a complaint, we ordinarily investigate, but for first offenders we may break up social gambling without making arrests.[30]

What is going on here? I think it is reasonable to suggest that the legislature did not have as its focus the weekly game of cards played by a group of friends, where only a few dollars change hands over the course of an evening—although there is nothing in the statute to exclude such activities from its purview.[31] With good reason we might also suggest that were the legislature to have attempted to qualify its prohibition so that activities such as these were excluded from its purview, it would have gotten into legislative quicksand. It could not have used the above wording, since it invites inquiries into the meaning of "special circumstances," "extraordinarily," and "ordinarily," and even then is expressed permissively. As Reiman recognizes, human behavior and the circumstances in which it occurs are extraordinarily diverse, and good legislative practice usually involves the drawing of relatively bright lines.[32] My contention is that a police organization that has one ear open to the legislature and one to the community will be able to develop reasonable guidelines for the exercise of discretion.[33]

The foregoing case also touches upon another point that often guides police discretion: the presence or absence of a complaint. Of course, the presence or absence of a complainant is not a decisive feature in deciding whether to go ahead with an arrest, for sometimes victims refuse to lay a complaint for reasons that have nothing to do with the seriousness of a situation.[34] Yet, in the absence of a complaint that would assist in any case for prosecution, arrest may achieve very little. So, although police may have a legally sufficient reason for making an arrest, they may choose not to arrest if the charges are minor and the case will otherwise have a very uncertain future. Scarce resources are expended that might have been more productively used elsewhere.

DISCRIMINATION

It is the possibility of using discretion in a discriminatory way that troubles me most. It troubles me, not just because of the *possibility* of discretion being exercised discriminatorily, but because *appeals to discretionary power have often been used* to cloak discrimination. Yet we may wonder whether removal of whatever assumed discretionary competence that police have with regard to arrest will resolve this problem, or even go any way toward alleviating it.

As I indicated earlier, the unsupervised nature of much police work will not change just as a result of some change in policy with respect to arrest/nonarrest. If police deviate from discretionary guidelines by claiming that they are only exercising a discretion they have, they will just as readily claim that they have or do not have legally clear grounds for arrest when they act discriminatorily under a full enforcement policy. The poor and ethnically different will still tend to attract disproportionate attention, and not just because they may be in violation of the law more frequently. For the source of discrimination is not to be found in the power to use discretion but in the disposition to act with prejudice, and there is probably no greater difficulty involved in showing that guidelines for exercising discretion were ignored than in showing whether legally sufficient grounds for arrest were present.

Once again, to the extent that it is possible, the best counter to poorly or discriminatorily exercised discretion is not to outlaw it but to reeducate its users and to require that, where decisions or patterns develop that appear discriminatory, they be justified. Given the absence of supervision, this will not guarantee anything, but it may function to deter the development of entrenched practices of discrimination. Ultimately, the issue is not one of having or not having full enforcement laws. It is a matter, rather, of police who want to make fair decisions.

IMPROPER LEVERAGE

Reiman is concerned that discretionary authority will be used in a tyrannical fashion. In particular, he is concerned that the additional power that discretion to arrest gives to police beyond their power to arrest enables them to coerce people into doing things that they would otherwise be unwilling to do. In other words, it allows for the tyrannical exercise of power. He instances the cooption of someone as an informant in exchange for nonarrest.[35]

Why does this constitute a tyrannical use of power? Reiman writes that

> if we are not ready to endorse a law requiring all citizens to give the police whatever information they want, then such use of discretion as leverage to get information amounts to allowing police to exercise a power over some citizens that we would not allow them to exercise over all.[36]

One thing to note about this criticism is that it is leveled at a particular use of discretion, and not at selective enforcement as such. The police officer who allows a speeding motorist to go unsummonsed after a stern reprimand about the dangers of speeding is not exploiting that power to gain something to which he would not otherwise have had access. We could, therefore, forbid police from using their power as leverage without denying them the power to enforce the law selectively.

So why does Reiman use this argument? It seems to me that the importance of the argument is that it gives *some* plausibility to the idea that the power not to arrest might contribute to tyranny. It is necessary to give plausibility to that claim because, at first blush, the power not to arrest those who have done that which would justify arrest appears to be the very antithesis of a *tyrannical* use of power. I am sure that the motorist who gets off with just a warning or reprimand feels relieved rather than oppressed.[37] Tyranny would be involved were the officer to take the view that even though the speed limit was 55 mph, he would ticket people who were traveling only at 50 mph. Or because the color of their car was displeasing to him. Those would be tyrannical police acts. So the additional leverage that a police officer may gain as a result of his discretionary authority is necessary to give some credence to the idea that it is a tyrannical power.

But as far as I know, defenders of police discretion have not argued that police should be able to impose *greater* burdens on others than the law allows. The argument for selective enforcement is always an argument that police should be permitted, in appropriate circumstances, to impose less than a full enforcement policy would dictate.

Maybe a greater burden could be imposed in cases in which informants are coopted. But I do not think it necessary that this should occur. Note that there is a considerable difference between there being a law requiring that we give police whatever information they want, and the choice offered to offenders to avoid arrest by becoming informants. In the first case, the threat of arrest attends the refusal to provide information per se. In the second case, the threat of arrest attends the violation of some other law, but may be removed if a person is willing to provide information. To the person in the latter situation, becoming an informant may represent an acceptable bargain and, if there are no significant victims involved, the arrangement may represent good social value. If the person does not wish to become an informant, then the arrest that follows will be sufficiently justified by the initial offense, and does not need additional support from the refusal to provide information.

Most of us are aware that police frequently gain informants by means such as these. Yet for the most part their use evokes from us no angered or resentful response. Reiman takes our reaction to manifest no more than the lack of respect we have for drug dealers and prostitutes, and our acquiescence in their being treated "in a tyrannical fashion."[38] But I think we need to distinguish two different kinds of case. One is the situation in which the police officer says something like: "If you are prepared to give me a certain piece of information, I won't take you in." The other is where the officer uses arrest as a *continuing threat* in order to have the person become an ongoing informant. In such cases, where the offender might be looking at a few years in prison, and becoming an informant has significant risks and no clear endpoint, the arrangement may well be seriously exploitative of a vulnerable person.

What Reiman establishes, I think, is that the discretion not to arrest can be easily misused, and needs to be monitored. Officers who make

use of informants should be required to submit for approval the uses they make of them and the conditions under which they retain their services.[39]

CONCLUSION

It is important that a free society be governed by rules, not men. But the adherence to rules need not be mechanical, for the rules, apart from curbing governmental arbitrariness, also serve important social purposes beyond themselves. If those wider purposes are not being served, then either the rules should be amended or, if that poses problems, there should be granted to those who administer them the power to make discretionary judgments concerning their application and enforcement. Provided that those who make such judgments can be held accountable for them, it should be possible to secure a greater just freedom than would be the case were no such discretion permitted.

NOTES

[1] Jeffrey Reiman, "Is Police Discretion Justified in a Free Society?" in John Kleinig (ed), *Handled With Discretion: Ethical Issues in Police Decision Making*, Lanham, MD: Rowman & Littlefield, 1996, p. 71. I shall assume that what Reiman has in mind includes not only arrest but also other formal procedures (citation, summons) that might be provided for as responses to particular breaches, and that what he proposes to exclude are departmental policies of nonenforcement, or individual decisions not to enforce (by ignoring or merely reprimanding).

[2] A powerful statement can be found in Ronald J Allen's critique of Kenneth Culp Davis's *Police Discretion*: "The Police and Substantive Rulemaking: Reconciling Principle and Expediency," *University of Pennsylvania Law Review*, 125 (1976), pp. 62–118, and his rejoinder to Davis's reply: "The Police and Substantive Rulemaking: A Brief Rejoinder," *University of Pennsylvania Law Review*, 125 (1977), pp. 1172–81. Davis's critique, however, is primarily legal, and only secondarily philosophical. Cf also Joseph Goldstein, "Police Discretion Not to Invoke the Criminal Process: Low Visibility Decisions in the Administration of Justice," *Yale Law Journal*, 69 (1960), 543–94.

[3] Reiman, "Is Police Discretion Justified in a Free Society?" p 74.

[4] Ibid, pp. 76–77.

[5] Ibid, p. 78.

[6] Ibid, p. 71.

[7]James Q Wilson, *Varieties of Police Behavior: The Management of Law and Order in Eight Communities*, Cambridge, MA: Harvard University Press, 1968, p. 16.

[8]Ibid Wilson also allows that "some or all of these examples of disorderly behavior involve infractions of the law" (ibid., p. 17).

[9]Ibid, p. 17.

[10]Though the phrase was coined by John Adams (*Constitution of Massachusetts: Declaration of Rights*, Art 30 [1780]).

[11]Aristotle, *Politics*, Bk 3, Ch. 16.

[12]See, for example, Friedrich von Hayek, *The Road to Serfdom*, Chicago: University of Chicago press, 1944, p 54.

[13]Michael S Moore, "A Natural Law Theory of Interpretation," *Southern California Law Review*, 58 (1985), pp. 313–18.

[14]Locke, *Second Treatise of Civil Government*, quoted by Reiman on p 77.

[15]Henry Jordan's famous remark regarding Vince Lombardi—"he treated us all the same, like dogs"—captures the problem of formalism.

[16]See Allen, "The Police and Substantive Rulemaking: Reconciling Principle and Expediency," pp 71–72.

[17]We should not lose sight of the distinctively North American character of this argument. For the British police, a limited selective enforcement is well entrenched in the legal tradition. It is explicitly acknowledged in the judgment of Lord Devlin in *Shaaban bin Hussein v. Chong Fook Kam* (1969) 3 AER 1626, and in the *obiter* of Lord Denning in *R. v. Metropolitan Police Commissioner ex parte Blackburn* 1968 2 WLR 893, at 902, and again in *R. v. Metropolitan Police Commissioner ex parte Blackburn* 1973 QB 241, at 254. Cf. also *Arrowsmith v. Jenkins* 1963 QB. It is also explicitly provided for by the Police and Criminal Evidence Act in cases where a "reasonable suspicion" exists that a person has committed an offense.

[18]Reiman, "Is Police Discretion Justified in a Free Society?" p 79.

[19]There has, for example, been some public concern expressed about the police issuing only warnings in domestic dispute and sexual abuse cases, presumably out of a desire not to disrupt families. See, for example, James J. Fyfe, "Structuring Police Discretion," in Kleinig (ed.), *Handled with Discretion*, pp. 183–205; anon., "Police forces allow rapists to go free with a caution," *The Times* (London), Feb. 18, 1996, pp. 1, 4.

[20]For example, the IACP "Police Code of Conduct" includes among the fundamental duties of a police officer: "serving the community; safeguarding lives and property; protecting the innocent; keeping the peace; and ensuring the rights of all to liberty, equality and justice." Then, under the heading "Discretion," it notes *inter alia* that "it is important to remember that a timely word of advice rather than arrest . . . can be a more effective means of achieving a desired end."

[21]It might also be argued that if "the people" were really serious about full enforcement they would also provide the resources for full enforcement. But since they do not provide the resources for full enforcement, they could not be serious about it. However, I do not think that this argument will work. Law enforcement has to be weighed against other social priorities, and the people's representatives might reasonably allocate a lesser amount of resources than will be sufficient for full enforcement *while yet believing that, within the limitations of those resources, full enforcement should be practiced.*

[22]Carl Klockars offers a whole brace of such reasons in *The Idea of Police*, Beverly Hills, CA: Sage, 1985, p 97.

[23]Reiman, "Is Police Discretion Justified in a Free Society?" p 80.

[24]Some legal regimes are quite explicit about this. However, I take it that the basis for the doctrine is to be found in political or moral theory and not in the existence of legislation that affirms it.

[25]HL.A. Hart represents a notable example. See *The Concept of Law*, Oxford: Clarendon, 1961.

[26]Ronald Dworkin sees the principles as essentially political. See his *Taking Rights Seriously*, London: Methuen, 1967; Steven J. Burton believes that the background principles are essentially legal. See his *Judging in Good Faith*, Cambridge: Cambridge University Press, 1992.

[27] " ' . . There's glory for you!'
'I don't know what you mean by "glory," ' Alice said.
Humpty Dumpty smiled contemptuously. 'Of course you don't—till I tell you. I meant "there's a nice knock-down argument for you!" '
'But "glory" doesn't mean "a nice knock-down argument," ' Alice objected.
'When *I* use a word,' Humpty Dumpty said, in rather a scornful tone, 'it means just what I choose it to mean—neither more nor less.'
'The question is,' said Alice, 'whether you *can* make words mean so many different things'
'The question is,' said Humpty Dumpty, 'which is to be master—that's all.' "
Lewis Carroll, *Through the Looking-Glass, Ch. 6.*

[28]The problem is said to be exacerbated by the fact that whereas judges are highly educated and experienced practitioners, those who will exercise most discretion in policing will be those with least training and experience.

[29]It is at least arguable that efforts being made to loosen the paramilitary structure of policing, the development of more "educative" training systems, and attempts to attract recruits with higher educational levels, signal a publicly accepted commitment to policing that acknowledges the need for wise discretion.

[30]Kenneth Culp Davis, *Police Discretion*, St Paul, MN: West, 1975, pp 141–42. Reiman would probably see nonarrest in such cases as a legitimate expression of the police order-maintenance function. However, I do not see any significant difference between this case and one in which a police department chooses not to enforce an anti-drug law in cases where small quantities of marijuana are involved, or a can of beer is being consumed in public.

[31]Allen considers it out of place to appeal to an alleged "purpose" of a statute as a basis for limiting its scope. The

legislature may have had a number of purposes in mind, and a limiting "interpretation" that takes one purpose into account may "amend" the statute with respect to other "conceivable" purposes ("The Police and Substantive Rulemaking: Reconciling Principle and Expediency," p. 80). But it is not enough that the purposes be merely "conceivable." We need some reason to think that the other purposes would have been legitimately satisfied by a rule of the kind in question.

[32]We need to remember that the drafting of legislation is through and through *political*, and that legislators expect that those charged with enforcement of the law will use good judgment in acting on it.

[33]In his response to Davis, Allen complains that such cases are plausible (to the extent that they are) only because, as it happens, the police department makes a common-sensical decision. There is nothing, however, to prevent a chief from deciding not to prosecute rapists when the victim has been dressed "provocatively" ("The Police and Substantive Rulemaking: A Brief Rejoinder," p. 1176). But of course there is everything to prevent

that assumption of discretionary power—there are victims who will be unrequited and as public that is almost certain to protest. Poor discretionary guidelines may be instituted, but if they are open to scrutiny they are likely to be modified or removed.

[34]Domestic disputes are a good example.

[35]Reiman, "Is Police Discretion Justified in a Free Society?" p 79.

[36]Ibid.

[37]One of Allen's complaints against police "rulemaking" is that the discretionary rules are not likely to come up for public or judicial scrutiny. And the reason for that is that "no individual will be affected adversely by such rules" ("The Police and Substantive Rulemaking: Reconciling Principle and Expediency," p. 85). The charge that they are tyrannical needs to be made out.

[38]Ibid. In many such cases I would think it would more likely be exploitative than tyrannical.

[39]Many police departments do in fact have informant policies in place.

Against Police Discretion: Reply to John Kleinig

Jeffrey Reiman

In "Selective Enforcement and the Rule of Law," John Kleinig has presented a powerful rejoinder to my argument that police discretion has no rightful place in a liberal democratic state.[1] He replies to the four reasons which I give for the undesirability of police discretion. Those reasons are: (1) that police discretion renders the laws vague and uncertain. Rather than stating forthrightly what will and what will not be permitted, laws subject to discretionary enforcement effectively contain the additional wild-card proviso "if a police officer judges it

Jeffrey Reiman, "Against Police Discretion: Reply to John Kleinig," *Journal of Social Philosophy* 29, Number 1 (Spring 1998): 132–42. Reprinted by permission of the *Journal of Social Philosophy*.

appropriate . . . "; (2) that by adding this proviso, police discretion effectively amends the laws as passed by the people's representatives, and thus usurps the exercise of legislative authority; (3) that police discretionary power is almost certain to be used frequently in ways that discriminate (in effect, if not in intent) against the poor, powerless, and unpopular in our society[2]—undermining the legitimacy of the law where it is most in need of legitimacy; (4) that granting police discretion to decide whether or not to enforce the law gives police officers the ability to use that discretion as leverage over other citizens, say, by threatening arrest if a citizen won't reveal some desired information.

In what follows, I shall start with some general observations about the issues. Then, I shall respond to Kleinig's specific replies to my four reasons for finding police discretion undesirable, and show why I think these replies are unsatisfactory. I shall close with some final comments on the issue, including a further argument against police discretion, namely, that it is incompatible with treating us as citizen-sovereigns of a liberal democratic polity and that it is an affront to our dignity as responsible agents.

1. GENERAL OBSERVATIONS

A large part of my objection to police discretion is that it usurps the legislative authority of the people and their elected representatives. Consequently, if there are laws that the people truly want enforced with discretion, I have no objection if the people through their representatives include express provision for discretion in the law when they enact it. Quite the contrary, that is exactly what I think they should do. It follows that, even where I might agree with Kleinig that discretionary enforcement serves some valuable social aim, my view will be that it is still wrong that that discretion is simply taken by the police as their right. If discretionary enforcement is what the citizens want, then let them say so in the law. They and their elected representatives are the only ones with both the right and the duty to do so. What's more, doing so in the visible arena of the legislature will force open discussion of the proposal. Hence it is irresponsible of the legislature to refrain from providing for discretion in the law when they want it and instead to leave it to police to build it in in the far less visible realm in which they work.

In the essay to which Kleinig is replying, I defined "police discretion" as "the freedom of police officers to decide whether or not to arrest an individual when the conditions that would legally justify that arrest are present and when the officer can make the arrest without sacrificing other equally or more pressing legal duties." Consequently, if the police must prioritize their enforcement activities because of limited resources (so long as this prioritization reflects the choice to enforce other equally or

more important laws), I do not count this as discretion for purposes of this discussion. I think in general that the legislature should keep the number of laws down to a number that the police can effectively enforce. If they don't, then the police will have no choice but to prioritize and my objection will be to the irresponsibility of the lawmakers in forcing this on the police rather than making the hard choices for which they were elected. Thus, when, as he does at numerous points, Kleinig justifies police discretion as needed to husband limited resources, my difference with him will not be over what the police do so much as over what the legislature has failed to do.

Because he is a fair-minded fellow, Kleinig has offered me additional ammunition for my argument by pointing out that many states have passed full enforcement statutes charging "police with responsibility to arrest anyone who violates a law." I was content to think that simply passing laws that state categorically that people doing such and such will be arrested, and so forth, was enough to show that the people and their representatives have not given the police discretionary authority. That they have in many cases gone further and expressly mandated full enforcement only strengthens my claim here—for which I thank Kleinig. He, however, takes the fact that there is no public outcry when the police handle violations without arrest as indicating that even explicit full enforcement statutes do not express what the people have chosen. This seems a stretch to me. If the people's representative pass *both* categorical criminal laws calling for arrest *and* laws that insist that those criminal laws be fully enforced, then it seems that the people have done enough to show their will. That there is little or no public outcry over much selective enforcement nonetheless is better explained as apathy (or perhaps frustration at having twice tried and failed to get the police to enforce the laws), than as indication of yet a different public will than that already twice expressed in the laws. Indeed, that the police and Kleinig think that it is okay to second guess the public in the face of two layers of laws is evidence, in my view, of the way in which police discretion undermines the people's role in a liberal democratic polity.

Kleinig occasionally speaks of the denial of discretionary authority as implying that the police are to apply the law mechanically. And, in the same spirit, he suggests that we will want to grant the police discretionary authority if we would like to "encourage greater professionalism in policing." I think that the use of the term "mechanical" in this context is misleading. As Kleinig himself suggests in his essay, determination of whether legally sufficient grounds for arrest exist is as complex a matter as judging whether or not to arrest when one has the discretionary authority to do so. Police work will always require intelligence and judgment, and denial of discretionary authority is not going to change that. The use of the term "professionalism" is, in my view, even more problematic. Since the opposite of professionalism appears to be amateurism, it's hard to deny that one wants to encourage professionalism in policing. However, traditionally, professionals (doctors, lawyers, and the like) have successfully asserted the right to exercise authority at their discretion and to be accountable only to fellow members of their profession for that exercise. This model has no place in policing. The authority that doctors and lawyers possess is that of *knowledge* (they are authorities *on* health or the law). Such authority is rightly judged by others who are equally authorities in those areas. Police have this sort of authority, they are authorities *on* law and perhaps *on* order as well. However, the authority that police have that Kleinig would have them exercise with discretion is, by contrast, that of *power* (police have authority *over* other citizens, the right to arrest them and use force in the process). Allowing authority of this sort to be exercised with discretion is a dangerous thing even if Kleinig is correct that we should allow it.[3] In any event, we should not be fooled by the positive sound of the term professionalism into thinking it appropriate to treat the authority that police exercise as including discretion in the way that the authority of doctors and lawyers does.

2. SPECIFIC REASONS, REPLIES, AND RESPONSES

I turn now to Kleinig's responses to the four reasons I offered for the undesirability of police discretion. For ease of identification, I shall number the first paragraph in which each of the four reasons is discussed.

(1) In response to my claim that discretion renders the laws vague and uncertain, Kleinig writes:

> If the law says that the speed limit is 55 mph, and police do not generally ticket people unless they are traveling 10 mph over the speed limit, the law is not thereby rendered vague and uncertain. Nor does it suggest that the speed limit is really 65 mph and not 55 mph. A person who is traveling at 70 mph will be charged with traveling 15 mph over the speed limit, not 5 mph. And a person who happens to get picked up for traveling 60 mph cannot complain that he wasn't traveling over 65 mph, and therefore should not have been picked up.

Now, before responding to Kleinig's claim that this poor fellow cannot complain, consider a different question: What is the *real* speed limit in this example? It seems to be sometimes 65 mph and sometimes 55 mph. Does a driver in this situation get clear guidance about how fast to drive from the legal system, that is, the *whole* legal system from lawmaker to law enforcer? Clearly not. If he drives at 55 mph, he will find everyone passing him in full view of the police. If he drives at 60 mph, he probably won't get a ticket except when some police officer thinks he should. That he cannot complain if this happens makes things worse rather than better. The situation that Kleinig describes is one in which a person is asked to think that he may in fact drive 60 mph *while he has no grounds to complain if he gets penalized for doing so.* This is precisely what police discretion does. It sends a mixed and confusing signal that takes it largely out of the citizen's hands whether he gets penalized or not.

That the citizen can avoid being ticketed by driving 55 mph is no better answer here than that he could avoid being ticketed by not driving at all. Why should he drive at 55 mph, allowing all cars to pass him, when he sees others driving above 55 mph in full view of the police? The law is not just words on a lawbook page or numbers on a speed limit sign. It is a whole system which includes these words and numbers in a real human practice that the citizen confronts as a whole. The speed limit signs tell him one thing and the police practice tells him another. Consequently, his ability to control his fate is weakened by the contradictory and confusing message that he receives from the legal system as a whole.

Can this driver rightly complain? Perhaps not in our discretion-ridden legal system. But, morally speaking, I think he can complain because the legal system failed to do what it was supposed to do. It failed to give him clear guidance about how to avoid getting penalized—just the flaw for which laws are sometimes found unconstitutional because of vagueness. Did this driver have reason to think he was courting a ticket by driving 60 in a 55 mph zone? The answer seems to me to be: yes and no. *Yes*, because he knew that the posted speed limit was 55 mph. *No*, because he didn't know that going five miles over that limit was in fact treated as breaking the law. *Yes and no:* how much more uncertain can the law be than that?

(2) Regarding my claim that police discretion effectively amends the laws that the people's representatives have passed, Kleinig describes a situation in which, though the law prohibits all gambling for money, a police department promulgates a rule among its officers that excludes arresting people for social gambling for moderate stakes. Of this, Kleinig writes:

> What is going on here? I think it is reasonable to suggest that the legislature did not have as its focus the weekly game of cards played by a group of friends, where only a few dollars change hands over the course of an evening—although there is nothing in the statute to exclude such activities from its purview. With good reason we might also suggest that were the legislature to have attempted to qualify its prohibition

so that activities such as these were excluded from its purview, it would have got into legislative quicksand.

I don't deny that the police in this example are modifying the legislature's work in a good way, and maybe even in a way that the legislature would have wanted its work modified. But, good or bad, the police are modifying the law. The people's representatives passed a law against gambling, and the police have transformed it into a law against certain kinds of gambling and not against others. The police have taken over a job that is not theirs to take. That a blanket law against gambling is a bad law, I am the first to admit. But it is the people's law, and they will never make better laws if they can leave it to the police to clean up their poor lawmaking. For this reason, we should not so quickly accept that the legislature couldn't have made a law closer to their real intention without getting into "legislative quicksand." Quite the reverse. Trying to spell out just what it is about gambling that makes it the appropriate target of a criminal law would have been a good exercise for the legislature and for the people whose representatives they are. Because police discretion will patch up their incomplete lawmaking, the people and their representatives are deprived of a valuable exercise in democratic governance and allowed to shirk the responsibility to make good and adequately specific laws. If, instead of covering up for their poor lawmaking, the police enforced the law as the lawmakers wrote it and, say, started arresting well-to-do surburbanites at their weekly gin rummy games, the lawmakers would soon be back at the drawing board trying to make a law that clearly targeted the kind of gambling the people want penalized. The short-term costs to those suburbanites would, in my view, be far outweighed by the benefits of making the lawmakers make the law express the people's real will. And, knowing that the police will not clean up their sloppy work will make the lawmakers more careful in future lawmaking as well.

If the legislature finds that it cannot specify what kind of gambling is illegal, then that is grounds for wondering whether it should be illegal after all—wondering that doesn't occur because the police have patched the law. Moreover, if the legislature cannot specify what kind of gambling is illegal but make a law against it wholesale expecting the police to do the specifying, then they fail to make a law that can guide the citizens in their behavior and thus they fail at what they were elected to do. All of this is covered up—and kept insulated from change—by police discretion. Some gambling will lead to arrest and other gambling will not, and the distinction between them will be made by the police, not by the people's representatives.

(3) In response to my claim that discretion will be used discriminatorily against the poor, powerless, and unpopular in our society, Kleinig proposes that discretion be limited by guidelines promulgated by police departments. As to whether this will be effective in preventing discrimination, Kleinig contends that it will be no less effective than a full enforcement policy:

> If police deviate from discretionary guidelines by claiming that they are only exercising a discretion they have, they will just as readily claim that they have or do not have legally clear grounds for arrest when they act discriminatorily under a full enforcement policy. . . . For the source of discrimination is not to be found in the power to use discretion but in the disposition to act with prejudice, and there is probably no greater difficulty involved in showing that guidelines for exercising discretion were ignored than in showing whether legally sufficient grounds for arrest were present.

Kleinig's response seems to me to be unsatisfactory on several grounds. First of all, as his account shows, guidelines for discretion place an additional layer of desiderata on top of the determination of whether legally sufficient grounds for arrest are present. Even if it is true that "there is probably no greater difficulty involved in showing that guidelines for exercising discretion were ignored than in showing whether legally sufficient grounds for arrest were present," there is surely greater difficulty

in showing that *both* sets of rules were misapplied than in showing that the law alone has been misapplied. At very least, Kleinig's proposal gives the police two levels at which they can deny that they were acting discriminatorily, instead of one. Second, if there were a full enforcement policy, then citizens would come to expect it and they would be able to protest where it was violated, particularly if it were violated in a discriminatory fashion. Under a policy that allows discretion, the citizens have additional grounds for uncertainty about what the police are actually doing, and thus it will be more difficult for them to complain about what appears to be discrimination. And finally, if guidelines for discretion can be formulated that are satisfactory, then they will express the implicit will of the lawmakers and the people who elected them. But, then, the lawmakers should have bitten the bullet and formulated those guidelines themselves as part of the laws they were making, rather than make incomplete laws and let the unelected police fill in the blanks.

(4) I argued that discretion gives police officers a kind of leverage over citizens that can be used tyrannically. What I have in mind here are cases—seen commonly in film and television portrayals of police work—in which the police hold the threat of arrest over some small-time crook as a way of compelling that individual to become an informant. This is clearly a power that police have only when they can refrain from arresting someone who is legitimately subject to arrest. And it is a power which we would not grant to police over all citizens, since if we wanted that we would pass a law requiring all citizens to give police whatever information the police want. Consequently, police discretion here gives police a special power over some citizens which the lawmakers have not given the police over those citizens and which the lawmakers would not give the police over all citizens.

Against this, Kleinig's reply has three parts. First, he takes it that we could simply forbid the police to use their discretion this way, while leaving the rest of their discretionary authority intact. He does not, however, explain how this would work, and it seems that his earlier observation on the difficulty of controlling police decisions of this sort would work against it. As I said earlier, it seems that outright prohibition of discretion would give citizens the best and clearest weapons against such leverage. For example, imagine a small-time crook who had been "leveraged" into becoming an informant by the threat of arrest not carried out. Suppose that this fellow decides he no longer wants to be an police informant, and the police officer involved decides to arrest him. If there were no discretion allowed, the would-be noninformant could point to earlier cases when the police officer could have but didn't arrest him. This would give him a weapon against continued exploitation. However, as long as discretion is allowed, the police officer will always be able to explain the earlier nonarrests as appropriate discretion. Even if, as Kleinig has suggested, the police officer would always be able to claim that legally sufficient grounds for arrest didn't exist in the earlier case, the fact remains that allowing discretion gives the police two levels of protection of their actions, whereas forbidding discretion leaves them only with one.

Second, Kleinig maintains that the occasional trade of nonarrest for information (as opposed to the continuing threat of arrest to make someone an ongoing informant, which Kleinig admits "may well be seriously exploitative of a vulnerable person") is an acceptable practice. To the individual who has violated a law for which he could be rightly arrested and who is offered nonarrest in return for information, writes Kleinig,

> becoming an informant may represent an acceptable bargain and, if there are no significant victims involved, the arrangement may represent good social value. If the person does not wish to become an informant, then the arrest that follows will be sufficiently justified by the initial offense . . .

But, if the initial offense justified arrest, how was it justified not to arrest him? Did the law say that people who commit this offense will be arrested unless they can provide some "good social value"? Either the legislature which passed the relevant law wanted people to be arrested who violated it, or the legislature wanted the police to be able to use this law sometimes not to arrest but to get information. If the former, then, in not arresting, the police officer violates the wishes of the legislature and the people they represent. If the latter, then the legislature has misled the citizenry by passing a law saying one thing while wishing and expecting something different. Either way, the citizens are swindled out of real democratic control of the agents of their government.

Third, Kleinig makes here a point he makes generally, namely, that discretion is not tyrannical because it amounts to allowing the police, not "to impose *greater* burdens on others than the law allows," but, rather "to impose less than a full enforcement policy would dictate." Naturally, allowing the latter is not as bad as allowing the former, but that doesn't mean that allowing the latter is good. It still modifies undemocratically the laws as made by the people's representatives; it still renders unclear what really is going to be treated as illegal; and it still leaves room for continued leverage against small-time crooks to make them into ongoing informants—which both Kleinig and I regard as exploitation of the vulnerable, but which he thinks and I doubt can be eliminated surgically while leaving police discretion intact.

3. CONCLUDING COMMENTS

I conclude, now, with a more general observation about the significance of police discretion and its incompatibility with law as an instrument of self-governance by the citizens of a liberal democratic state. In his discussion of the discretionary administration of speed laws, Kleinig refers to the driver let off without a summons as one who has been "given a break." And later, Kleinig adds: "I am sure that the motorist who gets off with just a warning or reprimand feels relieved rather than oppressed." Now, I think that there is something inappropriate in our thinking of the police as "giving us a break"—however natural it is for us to want to get one. What it suggests is that the power to arrest is the police officer's own power and we, his subjects, are relieved that he has shown the mercy not to impose the full force of his power. What's wrong here is that, in a liberal state, the police officer's power belongs to the citizens. It is *our* power, not the police officer's own. Thus, Locke said of the extent of the political authority in a legitimate state, that it is "the joint power of every member of society."[4] And John Rawls has written that, in liberal democratic polities, "political power, which is always coercive power, is the power of the public, that is, of free and equal citizens as a collective body."[5]

We are not to be thankful to the police officer for giving us a break, as if his mercy were a gift to us from him. Rather, his "mercy" is his disobedience of our will as expressed in our laws; he has twisted into his own shape (for however good a reason) a power which we gave him in a shape that we designed. Such mercy (however natural it is to desire it) is an insult to us as citizens of a democracy. If we want speeding laws to be administered mercifully, then it is our business to build mercy into our laws. If we want speeding laws to be administered with discretion, then it is our business to build discretionary authority into our laws. If we make laws, we should expect them to be carried out as we make them. Anything less fails to take us seriously as the sovereign citizen-rulers of a democratic polity.

But discretion is not only an insult to us as citizen-sovereigns of a liberal democratic state, it is an insult to us as responsible agents. The distinguished philosopher of law, Lon Fuller, catalogued eight features of what he called the "internal morality of law." Among these are that the law be clear enough to guide citizens in choosing how to conduct themselves, and that there be congruence between official action and declared rule.[6] I think that I have shown that discretion undermines both of these features. Interestingly, Fuller thought of these features of law as a morality because he thought of law as a purposive enterprise, one that implicitly treats the people subject to it as responsible agents. He wrote:

To embark upon the enterprise of subjecting human conduct to the governance of rules involves of necessity a commitment to the view that man is, or can become, a responsible agent, capable of understanding and following rules, and answerable for his defaults.

Every departure from the principles of the law's inner morality is an affront to man's dignity as a responsible agent.[7]

To the extent that police discretion makes the law unclear and opens a gap between the stated rule and the official actions done in its name, it does not address the citizens as individuals capable of governing themselves in light of public rules. Rather it subjects citizens to an ill-defined and unpredictable police authority in the face of which citizen self-governance is reduced to guessing what the laws will actually mean in the hands of this or that police officer.

In closing, I want to acknowledge the very important fact that instituting a policy of full enforcement will require significant changes in our legal system if this policy is not to bring worse evils than the discretion it is meant to replace. For instance, police often refrain from arresting individuals because they may have to spend a night in jail until they can see a judge and because, even if they are acquitted, they will end up with a damaging arrest record. Consequently, for full enforcement to work, we will have to staff our courts with enough judges so that arrestees can see them in short order, and we will have to eliminate the practice of holding acquitted persons' arrest records against them. Since jailing arrestees because there's no judge around and holding arrest records against acquitted people amount to punishing people who are either presumed or legally innocent, these changes seem long overdue.

The most important change that full enforcement requires, however, is that we reduce dramatically the number and complexity of our criminal laws. And this too seems long overdue. In this regard, it is interesting to note that two of the greatest liberals in the English-speaking tradition, John Locke and John Stuart Mill, had different conceptions of the relation between law and liberty. Locke's view was that law limits the arbitrary acts of others and thus that, to maintain liberty, we should insist that officials act according to the laws and exercise no authority beyond them.[8] Mill's view was that law limits liberty and thus that, to enlarge liberty, we should shrink the reach of the law.[9] Both views are correct: The simple fact is that a free society should have few and clear criminal laws that the police should be expected to enforce wherever they apply.

In short, full enforcement is part of a "package deal." If, as I expect, we can't have the whole package—if we are not about to limit criminal law to a small number of clear statutes or to provide resources for speedy, nonpunitive treatment of arrestees, and so on—then Kleinig is right: We should keep police discretion and try to curb its abuses. But, then, we should admit that we have failed to stand up to the full measure of our roles as citizen-sovereigns of a liberal democratic polity. Instead of controlling the exercise of our public power by means of rules we have democratically enacted, we have handed this job over to the police and can only hope that they perform it fairly to the disadvantaged, and mercifully to us all.

NOTES

[1]Jeffrey Reiman, "Is Police Discretion Justified in a Free Society?" in John Kleinig, ed., *Handled With Discretion: Ethical Issues in Police Decision Making* (Lanham, Md.: Rowman & Littlefield, 1996), pp. 71–83; the article is reprinted with minor stylistic changes in Jeffrey Reiman, *Critical Moral Liberalism: Theory and Practice* (Lanham, Md.: Rowman & Littlefield, 1997), pp. 221–34. In the article just mentioned, I qualify my opposition to police discretion to allow police to refrain from arresting those they legally might arrest when the police are executing their order-maintenance function, that is, dispersing unruly crowds, quieting noisy neighbors, breaking up fights before they begin, clearing the streets of drunks or prostitutes, and so on. In the context of such order maintenance, the police power to arrest is not so much a power to limit citizens' freedom as it is a threat available to police to back up their attempts to get troublesome individuals to desist from offending behavior or to clear the area. In his essay, Kleinig contends that I give no basis for this exception. On the contrary, however, I point out that in these cases the threat

of arrest is not being used to limit people's freedom substantially but to give the police authority to maintain order, and I indicate that whenever arrest is used to set in motion a series of events aimed at seriously limiting citizens' freedom, or when the threat of arrest itself seriously limits citizens' freedom, I contend that police ought not to have discretion. Needless to say, it will not always be possible to keep this line clear in practice, but then I urge—for all the reasons in the previous article and the present reply—that the benefit of the doubt go against discretionary enforcement.

[2]See, for example, Dennis D. Powell, "A Study of Police Discretion in Six Southern Cities," *Journal of Police Science and Administration* 17, no. 1 (1990): 1–7; as well as the studies reported in my *The Rich Get Richer and the Poor Get Prison: Ideology, Class, and Criminal Justice*, 5th ed. (Needham, Mass.: Allyn & Bacon, 1998), pp. 106–110. For a general overview of the problem and recent attempts to solve it, see Samuel Walker, *Taming the System: The Control of Discretion in Criminal Justice, 1950–1990* (New York: Oxford University Press, 1993), especially chapter 2, "Police Discretion."

[3]In correspondence, Kleinig points out that this authority is consented to by the citizenry. And, of course, it is. I am not questioning the legitimacy of police authority as such. I am questioning whether this authority includes the right to enforce the law discretionarily. To that, I contend, the citizens have not and ought not to consent. Evidence that they *have not* is given, inter alia, by Kleinig himself in talking about the "full enforcement" statutes that many states have enacted. That they *ought not* to consent to it follows if my argument against police discretion is sound.

[4]John Locke, *Second Treatise of Government* (Indianapolis, Ind.: Hackett, 1980; originally published 1690), p. 70 (emphasis in original).

[5]John Rawls, *Political Liberalism* (New York: Columbia University Press, 1993), p. 216.

[6]Lon Fuller, *The Morality of Law*, rev. ed. (New Haven, Conn.: Yale University Press, 1969), pp. 39, 63–65, 81–91, et passim.

[7]Ibid., p. 162.

[8]Wrote Locke, "for *law*, in its true notion, is not so much the limitation as *the direction of a free and intelligent agent* to his proper interest, and . . . freedom is not, as we are told, *a liberty for every man to do what he lists:* (for who could be free, when every other man's humor might domineer over him?) but a *liberty* to dispose, and order as he lists, his person, actions, possessions, and his whole property, within the allowance of those laws under which he is, and therein not to be subject to the arbitrary will of another, but freely follow his own." Locke, *Second Treatise*, p. 32 (emphasis in original).

[9]This is implicit in Mill's attempt to limit legal prohibitions in defense of liberty. See John Stuart Mill, *On Liberty* (Indianapolis, Ind.: Hackett, 1978; originally published 1859).

IV
MORAL ISSUES IN JUDICIAL PROCESSING AND JURISPRUDENCE

Responsibility for processing cases in a manner consistent with justice falls on lawyers. Yet people are profoundly cynical about lawyers and the concept of lawyers' ethics. This sentiment is expressed in jokes like: "Why are all the toxic dumps in New Jersey and all the lawyers in California? New Jersey got the first pick." "Why didn't the sharks eat the lawyer who fell overboard? Professional courtesy." The *Sourcebook of Criminal Justice Statistics, 1998* indicates that public belief in the honesty and ethical standards of lawyers has declined in the last 20 years, and that people see the ethical standards of lawyers as being about the same as those of labor union leaders, Congress members, advertising practitioners, and insurance salespeople. Lawyers come out slightly ahead of car salespeople (Tables 2.21 and 2.22, p 108: <http://www.albany.edu/sourcebook/>).

Paul Haskell is well aware of the public perception about lawyers and seeks to tell the untold story in "The Behavior of Lawyers" from his book, *Why Lawyers Behave As They Do*. Haskell presents 23 example scenarios—from those illustrating the exploiting of mistakes and lying in negotiations to those showing lawyers helping to achieve immoral objectives—to discuss how lawyers should behave and the rules of professional responsibility that govern each case. The American Bar Association's Center for Professional Responsibility has a links page to which interested readers may refer to find the model rules of lawyers' conduct for many different states <http://www.abanet.org/cpr/links.html>.

Haskell notes that "aspect's of a lawyer's exclusive dedication to the interests of the client are considered by some moral philosophers to be morally unjustifiable." This concern is exactly the topic of Ted Schneyer's "Moral Philosophy's Standard Misconception of Legal Ethics." Schneyer reviews many articles written by moral philosophers to develop a standard conception or critique of legal ethics that centers on principles of neutrality (performing services for anyone) and partisanship (only considering the client's interests). He shows the complexity and variety of moral principles and professional rules that might apply to a situation, and he challenges moral philosophers to mine the "hard-won understandings" of the legal profession that "so frequently involves moral risks."

Readers interested in this article should explore the materials that James R. Elkins has collected on the Internet for a law school class entitled Practical Moral Philosophy for Lawyers <http://www.wvu.edu/~lawfac/jelkins/syllabus.html>. Additional information about many current issues in legal ethics is available through Findlaw <http://www.findlaw.com/01topics/14ethics/index.html>.

The remaining articles shift the focus from lawyers to policies and practices involved in processing defendants through the courts. O. J. Simpson attorney Johnnie J. Cochran and Yale Law professor Akhil Reed Amar debate the timeless question, "Do Criminal Defendants Have Too Many Rights?" Actually, they debate several additional questions as well: the lawyer's exercise of power in using challenges to shape the composition of the jury, the value of excluding illegally gathered evidence, and whether criminal defendants should be made to speak. Cochran argues his ideas are formed "in the trenches" rather than in an "ivory tower with a pipe"; Amar states that he can "call it as I see it" because "I don't make money off the system one way or another."

In "Criminal Justice and the Negotiated Plea," Kenneth Kipnis examines the coercion present in plea bargaining, through which the vast majority of criminal cases are settled (in real life, if not on television dramas). Kipnis states that "[I]n the gunman situation I must choose between very certain loss of my money and the difficult-to-assess probability that my assailant is willing and able to kill me if I resist. As a defendant I am forced to choose between a very certain smaller punishment and a substantially greater punishment with a difficult-to-assess probability." Under such circumstances, is the plea "voluntary"? Readers who are struggling with a response to this reasoning can read Alan Wertheimer, "The Prosecutor and the Gunman," *Ethics* 89, no. 3 (April 1979): 269–79.

The Sixth Amendment to the Constitution provides that an accused person shall be tried by a jury of his peers. The need for a finding of guilt by citizens of the community is part of the shield to protect defendants from the power of the state. Indeed, juries can engage in "nullification"—refusing to follow the law and return a not guilty verdict even when the facts point to guilt. Judge Jack B. Weinstein discusses the uses and abuses of this discretion by juries in "Considering Jury 'Nullification': When May and Should a Jury Reject the Law To Do Justice." Our trust in juries to be the conscience of a community is put to the test by the question of whether juries should be informed of their right to nullify. Weinstein does not believe in such instructions and likens giving them to "telling children not to put beans in their noses." The opposing argument is made by the Fully Informed Jury Association <http://nowscape.com/fija/fija_us.htm>.

All of the Internet resources mentioned in this introduction and other materials are available through <http://www.paulsjusticepage.com>.

The Behavior of Lawyers

Paul Haskell

In recent years I have been teaching a course to law students titled "Professional Responsibility," which deals with the rules governing the conduct of lawyers.[1] This subject is also described as legal ethics; the terms are used interchangeably. The term "legal ethics" is misleading, however, because the primary definition of ethics is morality. The secondary definition is the rules of conduct governing a profession. It is the secondary definition that applies here. The professional rules sometimes impose duties that are moral in nature, but many have only attenuated moral significance, if any at all. Indeed, aspects of the lawyer's exclusive dedication to the interests of the client are considered by some moral philosophers to be morally unjustifiable.

In teaching the course I have been struck by the realization that it contains a story that has not been told to the public, at least not adequately. The lawyer in his professional role is perceived by the public as devious and manipulative, perhaps hypocritical or dishonest, and sometimes unconcerned with the harm done to others or to society in general. Lawyers' conduct certainly is not always so, but it is so often enough to justify the perception.

The rules governing lawyers' conduct permit or require such behavior in myriad circumstances. The untold story is the rationale for such conduct. On its face the conduct is immoral or destructive, but it is maintained that there are societal purposes being served, the value of which justifies the behavior. Most in the profession who think about the matter believe this, but not all. The rationale is controversial, as we shall see. If the rationale fails,

the behavior is indefensible. The object of this book is to explain the rationale for lawyers' behavior and to assess its validity.

The first step is to describe specifically what the rules governing lawyers require or permit them to do. The examples that follow illustrate how lawyers may or must behave under the professional rules that govern them. The first group of examples describe a variety of tactics, techniques, and practices of lawyers. The next several examples illustrate the consequences of the lawyer's duty to maintain the confidentiality of information acquired in the representation of the client, and the concluding examples deal with the representation of clients who are pursuing objectives that are legal but morally questionable.

1. DISCREDITING THE TRUTHFUL WITNESS

At one o'clock in the morning Mugger knocked a pedestrian to the ground and took his money at a lighted intersection. Witness observed the crime from across the street. Within thirty seconds a patrol car came upon the scene, and Witness described Mugger to the officers. The officers promptly arrested Mugger several blocks away. Mugger protested his innocence when arrested. He was prosecuted for the crime of robbery. Mugger did not testify at the trial; a criminal defendant has the constitutional right not to testify. The prosecutor has the burden at the trial of convincing the jury that the defendant is guilty beyond a reasonable doubt.

Mugger told his lawyer that he committed the act. Witness testified for the prosecution that Mugger was the culprit. In an effort to discredit Witness's testimony, the lawyer on cross-examination brought out that she had several convictions for shoplifting, that she had been drinking for several hours that evening, and that she had had a violent argument with Mugger at a bar earlier in the evening.

The lawyer's conduct is proper; he is permitted to attempt to discredit the testimony of a witness he knows is telling the truth.[2] A lawyer is permitted to advance the objectives of his client by all means within the law and the professional rules. Efforts to discredit the testimony of an opposing witness which is known to be false or the truthfulness of which is in doubt, are, of course, permissible. If a lawyer is not permitted to discredit the testimony of a truthful witness, the client is penalized for telling his lawyer the truth because it is from that information that the lawyer learns that the testimony is truthful.

A lawyer is not permitted to present evidence he knows to be false,[3] but that has not been done here. A lawyer is also not permitted to cross-examine an opposing witness in a manner that has no substantial purpose other than to humiliate or harass,[4] but that has not been done here because the information about Witness that has been disclosed reflects adversely upon her character and the credibility of her testimony. This reasoning may seem sophistic, but it is used to justify a lawyer's efforts to impeach the credibility of an opposing witness under these circumstances. Unquestionably the purpose and effect of such conduct are to blur the truth and mislead the jury.

Here is a similar example. A lawyer represented Killer, who admitted to his lawyer that he committed the homicide for which he was being prosecuted. The prosecution obtained drops of blood from the scene of the crime and submitted them to a laboratory for DNA identification. The laboratory identified the blood as being, in all likelihood, that of Killer. The lawyer cross-examined the laboratory technicians for the purpose of revealing flaws in their procedures, even though she knew the lab's work had produced an accurate result.

The lawyer's conduct is professionally permissible. She is not presenting false evidence; she is merely trying to discredit valid evidence. Again, the consequence may be to blur the truth and mislead the jury.

2. EXPLOITING THE ADVERSARY'S MISTAKE

A lawyer represented Mugger, who was charged with robbery. Mugger told her that he knocked Victim to the ground, stunning him, and stole his watch and wallet. Victim testified that he was robbed at ten o'clock. In fact, the incident occurred at nine o'clock, but Victim's condition and the loss of his watch caused him to lose track of time the night of the crime. Mugger did not testify at his trial, which was his constitutional right. Two of his acquaintances testified truthfully that Mugger was at a bar with them at ten o'clock.

The lawyer is permitted to present that testimony because it is truthful; a lawyer is only forbidden to present evidence that he knows to be false. The fact that the testimony has the effect of obfuscating the truth and misleading the jury makes no difference. A lawyer is entitled to take advantage of the error in the prosecution's case by the use of truthful evidence.[5]

3. BETTER NOT TO PROBE

A lawyer represented Wife in divorce and child custody litigation. The lawyer lived in the same neighborhood as the family and knew the husband slightly. Wife told the lawyer of shocking neglect and psychological abuse of the children, aged 3 and 4, by the husband and stated her intention to testify to this effect. Wife also identified two friends who were prepared to testify that they had observed such abuse and neglect. The lawyer spoke to the friends; they confirmed Wife's statement. The lawyer was skeptical of the truthfulness of these allegations, but he did not probe further to confirm their accuracy; he went ahead and presented the testimony.

The professional rules provide that "A lawyer shall not knowingly . . . offer evidence that the lawyer knows to be false."[6] The definitional section of the rules states that "'Knowingly' . . . denotes actual knowledge of the fact in question."[7] The lawyer did not have actual knowledge that the allegations were false. The lawyer might have discovered that they were false or exaggerated if he had inquired of others, but the rules did not require the lawyer to do this. In this circumstance many lawyers would probe further, but it is common practice not to do so.[8]

4. STATING THE LAW BEFORE ASKING FOR THE FACTS

Mother, a widow, died and left a will that disposed of her entire estate to her Daughter. Son, Mother's only other child, was very unhappy. If the will was invalid, under the law Daughter and Son would share the estate equally. Son retained a lawyer for the purpose of contesting the validity of the will. The lawyer told Son that the usual grounds for contesting a will are lack of mental capacity to make a will and undue influence exercised upon the person making the will.

In his business Son had been involved in litigation and knew that if he said something to his lawyer that was damaging to his case, any subsequent modification would be problematic because of the rule that a lawyer is prohibited from presenting evidence that he knows to be false. Before Son provided the lawyer with any facts, Son asked her for a legal definition of mental capacity and undue influence. (The definitions contain a number of elements and are somewhat technical.) The lawyer complied with Son's request, thereby providing Son with information that would enable him to tailor his "recollection" of the facts to suit his best interests, if he were so inclined. That is to say, Son might opt to "recall" events that satisfied the definition of incapacity or undue influence.

Lawyers are permitted to assist witnesses in presenting their testimony in an orderly and convincing manner. Counseling a witness to lie is, of course, impermissible,[9] as is allowing a witness to testify in a manner that the lawyer knows is perjurious. The problematic area is where counseling with respect to the significance or consequences of certain testimony may have the effect of suggesting that the client commit perjury.

The lawyer's conduct here is permissible. Son is entitled to a statement of the law before he tells what he knows. The lawyer is not required to withhold information on the law until

after Son has told him the facts. Son may misuse what the lawyer tells him, but that does not make the lawyer's conduct improper. Many lawyers, however, would decline to set out the law before receiving the facts from the client.

Suppose the lawyer initiated the discussion by telling Son that if Mother, who was elderly, was lucid and alert the day she executed the will, incapacity would be difficult to establish, and that if Mother was a strong-willed person, undue influence would be difficult to establish. A statement by the lawyer of the legal consequence flowing from a hypothesized fact, without having been asked about it, may be considered a suggestion that the client create a "fact" to support his case. Such behavior probably violates professional rules.[10]

5. DILATORY TACTICS

Drug Company produced a popular drug that was used for five years for respiratory ailments. A federal agency had been investigating the effects of the drug on blood pressure; there were strong indications that in the near future distribution of the drug would be prohibited. A number of studies had concluded that the drug had a dangerously adverse effect upon blood pressure in some circumstances, but there were several responsible scientists who were skeptical of the validity of the studies because of the methodologies employed. Drug Company had a large inventory of the drug and would suffer a significant loss if the ban were to be imposed soon.

The lawyer advised the president of Drug Company that he could delay the ban for several months by petitioning for a hearing to present the testimony of the skeptical scientists. The lawyer also told the president that continued sales in this circumstance might increase the potential of liability for harm to consumers of the product. Neither the president nor the lawyer believed that the testimony would prevent the ban from being imposed. The president told the lawyer to petition for a hearing. The lawyer complied with the direction. This action was taken solely to obtain the delay in the application of the ban.

The lawyer's advice and conduct are professionally proper. The rules provide that "A lawyer shall not bring . . . a proceeding . . . unless there is a basis for doing so that is not frivolous."[11] A proceeding is not frivolous "even though the lawyer believes that the client's position ultimately will not prevail."[12] The expert testimony to be offered in the hearing may be the position of only a few scientists, but it is not frivolous.

The rules also prohibit lawyers from engaging in dilatory tactics, but a proceeding that has a substantial purpose other than to delay is permissible despite the fact that it has a dilatory effect.[13] The presentation of the testimony of responsible scientists constitutes a substantial purpose.

The rules provide that "A lawyer . . . may take whatever lawful and ethical measures are required to vindicate a client's cause or endeavor. A lawyer should act with commitment and dedication to the interests of the client and with zeal in advocacy upon the client's behalf."[14] In this context, the term "ethical" means within the rules governing the profession. Conduct that is within the law and within the professional rules is permissible regardless of its consequences. A lawyer may use all legal and professionally permissible means to further the interests of her client.

Although the lawyer's actions are within the rules, many lawyers would decline to comply with the president's decision. It is professionally obligatory to inform the client of the legal options available, but many lawyers would recommend against petitioning for the hearing because of the potential for harm to consumers that may be caused by the delay and because the dilatory purpose impedes the proper functioning of the legal process. If the president nevertheless insisted upon proceeding with the hearing, the lawyer is permitted to decline and terminate the representation of the client.[15]

6. DESCRIBING THE CONSEQUENCES OF CRIMINAL CONDUCT

A lawyer represented a manufacturing corporation, whose liquid discharge contained chemicals. The president of the corporation called him in to discuss recent federal regulations dealing with chemical effluents. The lawyer described the operation of the regulations, the willful violation of which could result in criminal prosecution. The president commented that compliance would be very expensive and asked the lawyer what the realities of governmental enforcement were. He responded that in his experience government inspectors who detected a violation usually provided the violator with a period of time within which to come into compliance if the violation did not exceed by more than thirty percent the limits allowed by law. In addition, due to understaffing, the government did not attempt to impose sanctions on violators whose discharge did not exceed the legal maximum by more than fifteen percent.

The lawyer's conduct is professionally permissible. The lawyer is forbidden to "counsel a client to engage, or assist a client, in conduct that the lawyer knows is criminal or fraudulent, but a lawyer may discuss the legal consequences of any proposed course of conduct."[16] The lawyer is permitted to respond to the president's question concerning the realities of enforcement because that is a discussion of the legal consequences of a proposed course of conduct. The lawyer would not be permitted to suggest that the client need not comply with the law, for this would constitute counseling the client to commit a crime.[17] The line between discussing the consequences of criminal or fraudulent conduct and counseling or assisting such conduct is not always clear.

It should also be noted that sometimes the penalty for failure to comply with a governmental regulation is characterized as a civil penalty in the form of a fine rather than as a criminal penalty. The difference between them has to do primarily with the procedural requirements for enforcement. In addition, a crime has greater stigmatizing effect than a civil penalty, both socially and legally. If the only sanction for violation of an environmental regulation is a civil penalty, in most states the lawyer is free to counsel and assist the client with respect to violation.

7. COUNSELING TO BREACH A CONTRACT

Manufacturer and Supplier had a contract that stated that Supplier would furnish raw materials to Manufacturer at a price of two million dollars over five years. They had been operating under the contract for two years. Manufacturer recently discovered another material that was almost as good as the contract material and cost half as much. Manufacturer's president asked his lawyer if there was anything that could be done about its contractual commitment to Supplier. The lawyer asked the president if Supplier had consistently fulfilled its contractual obligations. The president replied that occasionally the deliveries had been late and occasionally the quality had not been up to standard, but most of the time Supplier had been in compliance.

The lawyer advised the president that the instances of Supplier's noncompliance in all likelihood did not entitle Manufacturer legally to terminate the contract. On the other hand, she stated that if Manufacturer terminated, the instances of noncompliance and the expense of litigation could be used as bargaining tools to bring about a settlement with Supplier that, considering the price of alternative materials, would be advantageous to Manufacturer. She also told the president that if Supplier chose not to settle and carried through to litigation, the net financial result, considering legal fees, would be unfavorable. The lawyer told the president that, based on her experience, the odds were great that a satisfactory settlement would be reached. The president decided to inform Supplier that further deliveries would not be accepted. The lawyer agreed to represent Manufacturer in the negotiations.

The lawyer's conduct is permissible under the professional rules. The rules provide that "A lawyer shall not counsel a client to engage, or assist a client, in conduct that the lawyer knows is criminal or fraudulent."[18] The lawyer is counseling her client to breach its contract with Supplier. A breach of contract is not a crime. A crime is an act for which an individual may be prosecuted by the state and, if found

guilty, fined or jailed. Breach of contract is only a violation of civil (as distinguished from criminal) law. The party to the contract who commits the breach may be sued by the other party for damages to compensate for the loss occasioned by the breach.

Fraud is a willful misrepresentation that induces reliance. There is no fraud here; there is simply a statement that Manufacturer will no longer perform its side of the contract, which is accurate. Lawyers can counsel or assist clients in breaches of contract as long as neither the client nor the lawyer lies to the other party.

Many lawyers would not participate in the breach of contract. The lawyer has an obligation to tell her client what his options are and what the consequences of those actions may be, but she may recommend that the client perform his legal obligation. If the client chooses to breach, the lawyer can terminate the relationship if she chooses.

8. LYING IN NEGOTIATIONS

(A) A lawyer represented Construction Company, whose employees negligently caused an explosion that damaged an adjacent building. Construction Company clearly was liable; the only issue concerned the amount of damages. Suit was brought against Construction Company. The owner gave the lawyer authority to settle for $600,000. In a negotiating conference with the attorney for the party whose building was damaged, the lawyer made a settlement offer of $400,000. The other party's attorney asked the lawyer if he was authorized to negotiate a settlement for more than that figure. The lawyer responded that he was not.

The lawyer's misrepresentation appears to be professionally permissible. The rules provide that in representing a client a lawyer shall not "knowingly make a false statement of material fact or law to a third person.[19] However, an explanatory comment to the rule states, "Under generally accepted conventions in negotiation, certain types of statements ordinarily are not taken as statements of material fact. Estimates of price or value placed on the subject of a transaction and a party's intentions as to an acceptable settlement of a claim are in this category."[20]

The attorney for the injured party stated that the cost of repairing the building would be about $300,000 and the loss of business would amount to about $200,000. In fact, the attorney was told by his client that the repairs were likely to cost about $200,000, and that the interruption of business would probably cost about $100,000. This statement is probably permissible puffing under the professional rules as an estimate of "price or value placed on the subject of a transaction." The rules seem to accept the ethics of the marketplace in negotiations.

(B) A lawyer represented Owner, whose business was ruined by the wrongful conduct of a bank, causing him substantial economic loss. Owner also suffered some emotional distress, but it was not severe. He got his business back on track and brought suit against the bank. Liability was clear; the only issue was the amount of damages. In negotiations for settlement of the litigation, Owner's lawyer stated that her client suffered severe emotional distress.

This was an exaggeration, but should it be considered a professional violation? In a study conducted several years ago, this question was put to a group of fifteen lawyers (nine law professors, four trial lawyers, and two federal judges). Eight said it was impermissible to make the statement; five said it was permissible; two were equivocal.[21]

9. CUSTODY BLACKMAIL

A lawyer represented Husband in a divorce proceeding. Wife wanted the custody of the children, as well as alimony and child support. Husband had no interest in the custody of the children, and wanted to minimize the alimony and child support. His lawyer advised Husband that a custody demand could be a bargaining device in negotiations to reduce alimony and child support because of Wife's fear of losing exclusive custody of the children. The lawyer told Husband that if Wife called their bluff by not yielding on alimony and child support and insisting on custody, they would withdraw the custody demand. Husband agreed to the strategy, and it turned out as planned—Wife settled for lower alimony and child support in exchange for exclusive custody.

This has been referred to as "custody blackmail." It is often done, and it may be professionally permissible.[22] It is a misrepresentation of Husband's state of mind, but it has become a negotiating convention that may legitimize the tactic under the professional rules.

10. USING A FALSE IDENTITY

A lawyer represented Driver, who was being sued for negligently driving his car, which ran into the plaintiff's car and caused her bodily injury. The plaintiff owned her own business, which required some travel. An aspect of the plaintiff's damage claim was that the injury prevented her from conducting some of her business functions. The lawyer was suspicious of the truthfulness of that aspect of the damage claim and hired a private investigator to check it out.

The lawyer was aware that the private investigator used false identities in the course of making investigations; in many cases it was the only way to obtain the information being sought. In fact, the private investigator used a false identity in this case, which enabled him to obtain information establishing that the business aspect of the plaintiff's damage claim was false, as the lawyer had suspected.

The professional rules prohibit the lawyer from engaging in dishonest or fraudulent conduct.[23] The lawyer's knowledge of the investigator's subterfuge certainly involves him in dishonest conduct. Nevertheless it has been maintained that the broad language of the rules was not meant to cover the use of subterfuge for the purpose of establishing an adversary's falsification.[24] In any event, it is a common practice. Indeed, criminal prosecutors are aware that the police often use undercover agents who misrepresent their identities to detect crime. Acquiescing in the use of a false identity by another to discover the truth may be professionally permissible.

It should be noted that this form of deception serves a different end from the forms of deception described in the other examples. Here the deception is for the purpose of achieving what the client is entitled to under the law; deception more often serves the end of obtaining an advantage to which the client is not entitled under the law.

11. INSERTING AN ILLEGAL CLAUSE

Landlord owned a number of apartment houses. His lawyer prepared a lease form that every tenant must sign. The lease contains a provision to the effect that Landlord has no obligation to make any repairs during the period of the lease or any renewal of the lease. This provision is in conflict with a state statute that requires landlords to make specific repairs and in general to maintain the apartments in a habitable condition—obligations that cannot be modified by the terms of a lease. Landlord and his lawyer are aware of the statute. The tenants never consult a lawyer before signing the lease. Most tenants are unaware of their statutory rights. The purpose of the inclusion of the clause is to discourage tenants from asking for or insisting upon repairs to be made by Landlord.

The professional rules forbid lawyers from assisting their clients in criminal or fraudulent activity and from engaging in dishonest, deceitful, or fraudulent conduct. The inclusion of the provision in the lease is not a crime. This practice is certainly a form of deception, however, as its purpose is to mislead the tenant into believing that the lease denies him any legal claim for repairs. Of course, tenants could discover the invalidity of the provision by consulting a lawyer.

Lawyers often overreach by including in contracts unenforceable provisions favorable to their clients in order to induce or discourage certain conduct when their bargaining position permits it. It is not clear that this relatively mild form of deception is covered by the prohibition against fraudulent, dishonest, and deceitful conduct. Its frequent use and the absence of any specific prohibition in the rules suggest that it is professionally permissible.[25]

12. TAKING ADVANTAGE OF ANOTHER LAWYER'S IGNORANCE

Mechanic replaced the worn brakes on Customer's car. Customer picked up the car and drove off at a speed of 50 miles per hour in a 30-mile-per-hour zone. As he approached a red light at that speed, the brakes malfunctioned and the car swerved, smashing into a tree. Customer was injured and the car was totaled. It was clear that both Customer and Mechanic had been negligent.

The traditional rule had been that a negligent party (defendant) was absolved from liability if the party suing (plaintiff) was also guilty of negligence that contributed to the injury. This was true even if the negligence of the defendant contributed more substantially to the accident than the negligence of the plaintiff. However, in recent years, most states have changed the traditional rule to provide that in circumstances like these the defendant is liable to the plaintiff in accordance with his proportionate share of the responsibility for the accident. That is, if the plaintiff's damages are $100,000, the plaintiff's negligence contributed 20 percent, and the defendant's negligence contributed 80 percent, the defendant is liable for $80,000.

In this case, the state changed the traditional rule six months ago. In the negotiations for settlement of Customer's claim against Mechanic, it became clear to Mechanic's lawyer that Customer's attorney was inexperienced in personal injury work and was unaware of the change in the law. Mechanic's negligence probably contributed 80 percent to the accident, but apparently Customer's attorney believed that any proof of his client's negligence would bar his claim. Mechanic's lawyer did not inform his counterpart of the change in the law. The parties entered into a settlement in an amount that was far less than what Customer would have received had his attorney been aware of the change in the law.[26]

Mechanic's lawyer's silence is professionally permissible. He has no duty to educate the opposing attorney. It should be noted, however, that the professional obligation to a judge is different. The rules provide, "A lawyer shall not knowingly . . . fail to disclose to the tribunal legal authority known to the lawyer to be directly adverse to the position of the client and not disclosed by opposing counsel."[27]

13. DEALING WITH THE UNREPRESENTED PERSON

A lawyer represented Computer Programming, a company in the business of selling programming services to commercial enterprises. The lawyer prepared a form contract that was very favorable to Computer Programming, dealing with matters of copyright, warranties, and a variety of risks. In most cases the purchaser of the services retains an attorney who negotiates changes in the terms of the contract to make it more balanced. The lawyer intended the form contract to be a starting point for negotiation between lawyers. Occasionally a small businessperson did not retain an attorney and accepted the form contract without any change. The lawyer assumed that such a businessperson did not appreciate the one-sided nature of the contract and the risks to which he was exposed. The lawyer never advised such a businessperson that he should consult an attorney.

The lawyer's conduct is professionally permissible. The rules provide that a lawyer who is dealing on behalf of a client with a person not represented by counsel must not state or imply that the lawyer is looking out for the interests of that person. The rules also state that in this circumstance the lawyer "should not give advice to an unrepresented person other than the advice to obtain counsel."[28] It is permissible to advise the person to obtain counsel but it is not required. Some lawyers would advise a person to consult a lawyer in this circumstance.

14. ARGUING PRO AND CON

A lawyer represented a manufacturer of an appliance in a suit in a state court brought by an injured consumer against the company. In the course of the trial, the lawyer argued for a certain interpretation of an applicable statute. The trial judge accepted that interpretation. On that basis the lawyer obtained a judgment for her client in the trial, and the consumer did not appeal the judgment to a higher court.

Six months later the same lawyer represented another injured consumer in a suit against a different manufacturer of a similar appliance. The case was heard in the same state court but before a different trial judge. This time the lawyer argued for an interpretation of the same statute opposite to the interpretation she had advocated in the prior suit.

The lawyer's reversal of position is permissible. There is no hypocrisy here. Lawyers are not to be identified with the positions they take, nor are they expected to believe in the arguments they make. Lawyers are actors playing roles in the theater of law. A lawyer is obligated to take whatever position the needs of her client require, regardless of inconsistency with positions taken in past litigation. As a matter of business prudence, however, many lawyers would not accept the second representation because of concern for the appearance of disloyalty to the interests of the first client, but this is an entirely different consideration from professional permissibility.

There is a limitation that is applicable here: A lawyer may not take conflicting positions on a legal issue in courts in the same state at the same time. The reasoning here is that the immediacy of the simultaneous conflicting arguments may reduce the chance of success for one client or the other. This would constitute a form of impermissible disloyalty to the client.[29]

15. CONFIDENTIALITY: LIFE-THREATENING INJURY

Driver negligently drove through a red light and struck Pedestrian. Pedestrian suffered a fractured arm and ribs. Driver was clearly at fault legally; the only issue related to the amount of damages. A physician retained by Driver's lawyer examined Pedestrian and discovered that in addition to the fractures, Pedestrian suffered an aortic aneurysm that was life-threatening. In light of Pedestrian's medical history and records, there was no doubt the aneurysm was caused by the accident.

The negotiations between Pedestrian's attorney and Driver's lawyer involving the amount of the settlement indicated that Pedestrian, his attorney, and his physician were unaware of the aortic aneurysm. The amount demanded by Pedestrian's attorney did not reflect the life-threatening nature of the injury. The physician hired by Driver's lawyer did not disclose the aneurysm to Pedestrian or his attorney because he considered that the contractual context of his examination preempted any medical ethical obligation that would otherwise apply, committing him to disclose what he knew only to Driver's lawyer. The lawyer for Driver did not disclose the aneurysm because of his duty of loyalty to his client's interests[30] and his duty of confidentiality. Driver's lawyer is obligated to maintain the confidentiality of information acquired in the professional relationship.[31]

Driver's lawyer also represented Driver's insurance company. He asked the senior officer of the insurance company responsible for matters of this nature whether she wanted the aneurysm to be disclosed to Pedestrian. The officer told the lawyer to enter into the settlement at the amount asked by Pedestrian's attorney as soon as possible, and then to disclose the aneurysm to Pedestrian. The lawyer acted in accordance with those instructions.

As a matter of contract law, a party to a settlement agreement is usually not required to disclose information bearing on the settlement that is unknown to the other side, although he may, of course, if he wishes to.[32] The lawyer is bound not to disclose this confidential information under the professional rules unless the client authorizes such disclosure.

The silence of Driver's lawyer endangered Pedestrian's life and resulted in a settlement that inadequately compensated Pedestrian. As we can see, a very high moral price may be paid for the duty of confidentiality. Unquestionably many lawyers would disclose the information immediately upon learning of it; the risk to life would outweigh the professional obligation of confidentiality in the moral scales.

In some states, as a matter of contract law, a party to a settlement agreement may be obligated to disclose information of this nature bearing upon the settlement; if the disclosure is not made, the settlement agreement may be invalidated for failure to disclose. A lawyer must advise the client of this consequence. If the client chooses to remain silent, the lawyer must remain silent pursuant to his duty of confidentiality. It is provided in the professional rules that fraud does not include "failure to apprise another of relevant information."[33] For professional purposes the lawyer's silence in the aneurysm situation does not constitute fraud by him, nor does it constitute assistance of the client in fraudulent conduct.[34]

16. CONFIDENTIALITY: PAST FRAUD

Computer, Inc., bought computers and leased them out. Computer financed its purchases with bank loans. A lawyer represented Computer in its dealings with banks for several years. During this time, through the creation of false documents, Computer borrowed from banks for "purchases" of computers that never occurred. The lawyer had no knowledge of the fraud. She and the banks had relied upon certifications by Computer's accounting firm, which had also been deceived.

One day a senior officer of the accounting firm advised the lawyer that Computer had defrauded the banks and that in due course this would be disclosed. When she confronted the president of Computer with this charge, he admitted that wrongs had been committed but assured her that the banks would be paid and that the practice had stopped. Shortly thereafter she terminated her representation of Computer. Computer proceeded to retain another law firm to represent it in future borrowings. The lawyer never told the successor law firm or the banks her reason for terminating her representation. More fraudulent loans were made. The successor law firm had no knowledge of the fraud. Several months later all the fraudulent activity came to light.

The lawyer's failure to advise the successor law firm or the banks of what she knew was proper under the professional rules. She learned of the fraud in connection with her representation of Computer, and she was forbidden to disclose such information without the consent of the client.[35] Confidentiality of information acquired in the professional relationship is a cardinal principle of the profession.

The lawyer's silence in this situation allowed the fraud upon the banks to continue. It also involved the successor law firm in a situation that was potentially damaging; even innocent association with fraudulent activity may affect one's reputation. There was also the possibility that the successor law firm would be charged, however improperly, with complicity in the fraud. Nevertheless, the professional rules place enormous value upon confidentiality of client information. The price for this principle can obviously be very high.

There is an exception to the duty of confidentiality that provides that the lawyer may (not must) reveal the intention of the client to commit a crime and provide the information necessary to prevent it.[36] Acquiring loans by fraud is a crime. The lawyer, in her discretion, would have been permitted to warn others if she believed that the fraudulent practices would continue, but she would not be required to do so.

It should be emphasized that the lawyer's unwitting participation in her client's fraudulent conduct did not violate the professional rules because she did not know that the conduct was fraudulent at the time.[37]

17. CONFIDENTIALITY: CHILD ABUSE

Mother was divorced and had custody of her two children, aged four and six. Her lawyer was assisting her in connection with various financial matters, including securing social service benefits available to her and child support payments from the defaulting father. In the course of the representation the lawyer learned that Mother was unstable and sometimes beat the children. There was a state law that required an

individual who learned of child abuse to report the information to a public authority. The law made no reference to the lawyer's duty of confidentiality.

There is a legal issue as to whether such a statute supersedes the lawyer's duty of confidentiality. In a substantial majority of states the professional rules governing lawyers provide that in the absence of a judicial decision to the contrary, it should be presumed that such a law does not supersede the duty of confidentiality.[38]

18. CONFIDENTIALITY: UNPROSECUTED HOMICIDE

A lawyer represented Client, who had been indicted for a homicide. In the course of discussing Client's personal history, the lawyer learned from Client that five years ago he had committed a murder for which another person was convicted and was serving a life sentence. Client was never prosecuted for that crime. The lawyer did not reveal what he had learned to the public authorities. Despite the miscarriage of justice for the imprisoned individual, the lawyer's conduct in this matter was professionally required by her duty of confidentiality to Client.[39]

19. IMMORAL OBJECTIVE: STATUTE OF LIMITATIONS

Investor entered into a contract with Contractor for the construction of an office building. Shortly before construction was to begin, Contractor decided to undertake another project and notified Investor that he wasn't going to perform the contract. Investor made other arrangements for the construction but incurred substantial additional expenses and lost considerable income on account of Contractor's breach of contract. Investor threatened that if Contractor did not compensate him for such losses he would sue. From time to time they discussed a settlement but never agreed on a figure. Negotiations broke down, time passed, and finally Investor contacted an attorney to bring suit.

In all states, there are statutes—known as statutes of limitations—that place a time limit for bringing a law suit. In this state, suit for breach of contract must be brought within two years of the breach. It is up to the person being sued to plead the statute or not, as he sees fit. Investor contacted the attorney two years and five days following the breach. The attorney promptly brought suit, hoping to convince the trial judge that the statutory period should be extended in this instance.

Contractor retained a lawyer who informed Contractor of the two-year statute. Contractor admitted to his lawyer that he had no legal justification for failure to perform the contract. The lawyer asked Contractor if he wanted to litigate the question of damages, settle out of court, or plead the two-year statute of limitations. Pleading the statute is optional for the Contractor. Contractor instructed the lawyer to plead the two-year statute. She complied with the instruction. The trial judge ruled in favor of Contractor.

The best reason for statutes of limitations is to protect the person being sued who is not, or may not, be liable, but has difficulty establishing his defense because of the passage of time; his witnesses may have forgotten, moved, or died, or other evidence may be unavailable or difficult to obtain years after the event. The statutes are unconditional, however, and are available to parties who have no defense and are clearly liable. The unconditional nature of the statutes eliminates the trouble and expense of examining the justification in each case. Its use is often harsh and unfair, as in this case, but that use is allowed under the law. Some lawyers would decline to plead the statute and would opt to withdraw from representation in this circumstance.

20. IMMORAL OBJECTIVE: TELEVISION TRASH

A lawyer was asked by Television Producer to represent him in contract negotiations with a cable television network, directors, actors, writers, and others, in connection with the production of a television series that would emphasize violence, sadism, and promiscuous sex. The lawyer believed that such television fare contributed to anti-social behavior, degraded women, and was culturally decadent. Nevertheless she agreed to represent Television Producer.

The lawyer believed that whatever the nature of the subject of her representation, it was legal, the client was entitled to what the law permitted, and legal representation was necessary to the realization of what the law permitted. Certainly many lawyers would not accept Producer as a client.

21. IMMORAL OBJECTIVE: GAMBLING ENTERPRISES

Recently a state legalized gambling casinos in certain locations. A lawyer represented Casinos, Inc., in all aspects of its legal gambling operations. The lawyer believed that commercial gambling was exploitative of human weakness, destructive of the character of those who participate, and that the economic benefits to the community did not justify the harm done. Nevertheless he squared representation with his conscience on the grounds that the law permits what Casinos, Inc., was doing, and that if he did not represent Casinos, Inc., some other lawyer would. Representing a cigarette manufacturer would present a similar dilemma, substituting harm to health for harm to character.

22. IMMORAL OBJECTIVE: NAZI SPEECH

A Nazi organization applied for a permit to conduct a march through the downtown area of a suburb that had a substantial Jewish population. Many of those citizens had family members who died in the Nazi holocaust. The marchers planned to carry placards advocating genocide. The city denied the permit. The Nazi organization then retained a lawyer to file suit to require the city to grant the permit.[40]

Although the lawyer was appalled by Nazi ideology, she believed correctly that the freedom-of-speech provision of the First Amendment entitled the Nazi group to a permit. She also believed that everyone, including the Nazi organization, was entitled to what the law allowed. In addition, she believed that if the Nazi group were denied the right to express themselves, there would be a danger that others wishing to voice unpopular but worthy ideas might meet with such denials as well. In the specific instance, although the lawyer's action would further the Nazi ideology, she took the case in service of a broader social objective.

Lawyers are permitted to select their clients, but the professional rules encourage the representation of unpopular clients. Nonetheless, many lawyers would decline to represent the Nazi organization because they would not want to assist in the dissemination of a viewpoint they find to be abhorrent.

23. IMMORAL OBJECTIVE: SEEKING ACQUITTAL OF A RAPE-MURDERER

Laypersons often ask how a lawyer with any decency can seek to obtain an acquittal for a client who admits to him that he has committed a heinous crime, such as a rape-murderer. As we have stated, the lawyer is not permitted to present evidence that he knows to be false, but he can present evidence whose genuineness he doubts so long as he doesn't *know* it to be false. The lawyer can attempt to cast doubt upon the credibility of a prosecution witness who he knows to be telling the truth, or he may attempt to discredit physical evidence that he knows to be valid, so long as he does not engage in falsification. Are such tactics justifiable? Most lawyers think they are. Most lawyers also believe that representation of the guilty is justifiable.

Conviction for committing a serious crime is devastating. For that reason, in a criminal case, the prosecution is required to prove beyond a reasonable doubt that the defendant has committed the crime, the jury must be unanimous in concluding that the defendant is guilty, and the defendant cannot be forced to testify. Our social philosophy accepts that it is better to have a guilty person go free under this standard than to have an innocent person be convicted under

a lesser standard. (By contrast, in a civil—that is, noncriminal—suit, the jury need only find that the plaintiff has proved his case by a preponderance of the evidence, i.e., that it is more likely than not that the plaintiff's account is true.)

The defendant is entitled to whatever the law allows. The law requires that the state prove guilt beyond a reasonable doubt. The lawyer for the defendant sees to it that the defendant gets what the law allows, and the law allows him to go free if the state is unable to prove guilt in accordance with the standard. The system is designed to protect the innocent defendant, but the guilty defendant often gets the benefit of it also. Once again, better that the guilty go free than an innocent be convicted.

Many lawyers do not find criminal defense work attractive for a variety of reasons; the defense of the guilty is definitely one of them. Such lawyers believe that it is fine for some other lawyer to defend the guilty, because they accept the social principle underlying such representation, but they do not want to be a part of it.

SUMMARY OF PRINCIPLES

The behavior described in the preceding examples is founded upon three interrelated principles: (1) The lawyer's relationship to the client is that of an agent and fiduciary exclusively and zealously dedicated to the advancement of the client's interests; (2) the lawyer is unconcerned with the morality or social consequences of the client's objective; and (3) the lawyer may use all means within the professional rules to achieve the client's objective, regardless of their impact upon others or their relationship to justice.

Almost two centuries ago, in his defense of Queen Caroline, Lord Brougham portrayed the lawyer as an advocate who

. . . in the discharge of his duty knows but one person in all the world, and that person is his client. To save that client by all means and expedients, and at all hazards and costs to other persons, and, amongst them, to himself, is his first and only duty; and in performing this duty he must not regard the alarm, the torments, the destruction which he may bring upon others.[41]

The professional rules express this position more moderately:

A lawyer should pursue a matter on behalf of a client despite opposition, obstruction or personal inconvenience to the lawyer, and may take whatever lawful and ethical measures are required to vindicate a client's cause or endeavor. A lawyer should act with commitment and dedication to the interests of the client and with zeal in advocacy upon the client's behalf.[42]

The examples discussed are illustrative of the lawyer's exclusive and zealous dedication to the client's interests. The lawyer may assert a claim or position for which there is some factual or legal basis however remote the possibility that the claim or position will be sustained by a court or other arbiter and without regard to the cost that may be inflicted upon others by such an assertion or any dilatory effects the assertion may have.

The lawyer may counsel and assist the client in the violation of law as long as the client is not engaged in conduct that constitutes a crime or that constitutes fraud (misrepresentation or other form of deception). Consequently, the lawyer may counsel or assist the client in committing a breach of contract, engaging in negligent behavior, or violating regulations or statutes that carry only civil penalties because such conduct is neither criminal nor fraudulent.

Although the lawyer is forbidden to counsel or assist the client in conduct that is criminal or fraudulent, the lawyer may inform the client of the potential consequences of conduct contemplated by the client that is criminal or fraudulent, including whether there is significant likelihood of detection and what the severity of possible criminal sanctions (fines or incarceration) might be. Clearly the statement of the potential consequences of criminal or fraudulent activity may in certain circumstances induce such activity.

The lawyer may not present evidence that he *knows* is false, but he may present evidence that he suspects, but does not know, is false. The lawyer may prepare his client or a witness for his client by telling him what the law is on the matter in question before asking him about what happened. This allows the lawyer to convey to the client or witness the consequences of his recollection of events. The lawyer may advise the client or witness to respond to questions from opposing counsel as narrowly as possible and to avoid volunteering information; an excess of truth may be damaging. The lawyer may attempt to impeach the credibility of opposing witnesses that he knows are telling the truth. The lawyer may make an argument to a judge or jury based on evidence that the lawyer does not believe is true, but does not *know* to be false.

Although the lawyer is generally forbidden to lie, in negotiations she is permitted to misrepresent the value of the subject matter of a transaction and to misrepresent the authorization she has received from her client with respect to settlement as well as her client's intentions with respect to settlement.

The lawyer may decline to alert an unrepresented person to the need for legal assistance to avoid risks to which that person may unwittingly be subjecting himself. In dealing with an attorney for an opposing party, the lawyer may decline to alert his counterpart to recent changes in the law of which his counterpart is obviously uninformed, even though that knowledge is essential to the proper representation of his counterpart's client. The lawyer is generally free to exploit the ignorance or mistakes of opposing counsel.

Subject to several exceptions, the lawyer must not disclose information obtained in the representation of her client, without regard to the physical or financial harm that may result to an opposing party or to third parties because that information has been withheld. One exception is that the lawyer may (but need not) disclose the client's intention to commit a crime in the future. Another exception is that the lawyer may disclose information necessary to collect her fee or to enable the lawyer to defend herself against charges stemming from the representation of her client. Another is that the lawyer must disclose that her client intends to testify perjuriously and that evidence she has previously presented believing it at that time not to be false, is, in fact, false.

The lawyer may seek to achieve the lawful objective of his client regardless of the immoral or socially harmful nature of that objective.

It is emphasized that most of the conduct described above is permitted but not required. Many lawyers would not assert marginal claims or participate in a breach of contract. Many lawyers probe their clients to determine the facts, rather than accepting the client's self-serving statements at face value. Many lawyers would advise an unrepresented adversary to hire a lawyer. Many lawyers would not attempt to impeach the credibility of an opposing witness the lawyer knows is telling the truth. Many lawyers would not lie in negotiations. Many lawyers would not represent a client whose objective is socially harmful. Nonetheless, the various practices that have been described are widespread in the profession.

There is language of moderation in the professional rules. There are several references to the appropriateness of advice that goes beyond strictly legal advice. For example: "In rendering advice, a lawyer may refer not only to law but to other considerations such as moral, economic, social and political factors that may be relevant to the client's situation."[43]

There is also recognition that the lawyer is not required to go the limit in her exclusive and zealous dedication to the client's interests: "A lawyer should act with commitment and dedication to the interests of the client and with zeal in advocacy upon the client's behalf. However, a lawyer is not bound to press for every advantage that might be realized for a client."[44]

The professional rules make it clear that the client has the final decision concerning the objectives of the representation, such as the terms of the contract that is being negotiated, whether to bring a law suit, or whether to settle a pending suit and what the terms of that settlement should be. The lawyer has the final

decision with respect to the means used in pursuit of the objective, but she is obligated to consult with the client.[45] With respect to means, the rules also provide that the lawyer "should defer to the client regarding such questions as the expense to be incurred and concern for third persons who might be adversely affected."[46]

We should also emphasize that there are firm constraints upon the conduct of lawyers. The lawyer is forbidden to lie (except in negotiations); to assist the client in criminal or fraudulent conduct; to present evidence known to be false; to destroy evidence in litigation; to commit crimes involving moral turpitude; to assert frivolous claims; or to use tactics that have no justification in fact or law solely for the purpose of harassment or delay. There are many opportunities legitimately available to the lawyer to mislead or harm others, but there are ultimate limits to the deception and harm that the lawyer is permitted to effect.

The Anglo-American system of freedom under law is the finest form of governance in human history. It imposes order as well as limitations upon state power that assure intellectual, aesthetic, spiritual, and economic freedom. It provides for the orderly transition of power based on majoritarian principles. It includes a system of fundamentally just substantive and procedural principles for the resolution of disputes between individuals and between individuals and the state. In sum, it creates a balance between authority and liberty that honors both community and individual dignity. It has been durable, resilient, and adaptive. It is indeed a system of wise restraints that make men free.

Every orientation program for incoming law students speaks of the contribution of the profession to the development of our remarkable system of governance and of the profession's service on behalf of civil rights, the less fortunate, and the environment. It is all true.

There is, of course, a less glamorous but no less worthy side. Many lawyers serve society in ways that go unheralded, rarely, if ever, compromising personal ethics in the process. They assist in the transfer of property, prepare wills and assist in the planning and administration of estates, and prepare and negotiate contracts in an atmosphere of compromise and accommodation. They assist in the creation of business enterprises and counsel in dealings between parties in a spirit of fairness and candor. If disputes arise they try to settle them in an equitable manner; if settlement efforts fail, they conduct litigation in a manner that minimizes offense and assists in a just resolution.

The practice of law at its best is a caring and productive profession. In the courtroom it can determine truth and achieve justice. In personal matters it can provide security and harmony. In commercial affairs it can facilitate the production of wealth. It can protect the individual and the environment from the misuse of power by the state and private interests.

Then there is what may be viewed as the dark side of the practice of law, in which the lawyer serves the unworthy objective of his client, or employs deception and obfuscation, or harms others in the course of serving the client's objective, whether good, bad, or indifferent. Is such conduct worthy of a profession? Can such conduct be justified in moral or social terms? We now deal with the responses to these questions.

NOTES

[1]In 1908 the American Bar Association (ABA) promulgated the Canons of Professional Ethics. The ABA is a private organization that has no legal authority over the profession. The Canons constituted a recommendation to the states and many adopted them, usually by action of the highest court of the state, sometimes by the legislature. In 1969 the ABA promulgated the Model Code of Professional Responsibility, replacing the 1908 Canons. Almost all states adopted the Model Code, which was much more detailed than the Canons. In 1983 the ABA promulgated the Model Rules of Professional Conduct, replacing the 1969 Model Code; a number of substantive changes were made, but for the most part the differences were in style and form. The 1983 Model Rules have been adopted in about three-fourths of the states. Throughout this book the 1983 Model Rules are used as the basis for discussion. The Model Rules referred to in the text are contained in the Appendix.

[2]This practice by criminal defense counsel is defended by a prominent commentator on legal ethics, Monroe Freedman, in his book *Understanding Lawyers' Ethics* 161–171 (Matthew Bender, 1990). Another authority, Charles W.

Wolfram, in *Modern Legal Ethics* 651 (West, 1986), suggests that this practice may be justified in criminal defense, but should not be professionally permissible in civil trials. There is no doubt, however, that it is professionally permissible in the civil trial as well. The use of this tactic by criminal defense counsel is supported in the American Bar Association Standards Relating to the Administration of Criminal Justice, The Defense Function § 4–7.6(b). Those same Standards dealing with The Prosecution Function § 3–5.7(b) provide that it is impermissible for the prosecutor to use this tactic. The prosecutor's role "is to seek justice, not merely to convict" § 3-1.2(c). The American Bar Association Standards Relating to the Administration of Criminal Justice are not part of the formal rules of professional behavior such as the 1983 Model Rules, but are intended to provide unofficial guidance to practitioners and courts in the area of criminal justice.

[3]Model Rule 3.3(a)(4).

[4]Model Rule 4.4.

[5]Ethics committees of state bars issue opinions on actual ethical problems presented to them by lawyers. This problem reflects the facts and conclusions of Michigan Ethics Opinion CI-1164 (1987).

[6]Model Rule 3.3(a)(4).

[7]Model Rules, Terminology.

[8]Federal courts and most state courts have a procedural rule in civil cases that the lawyer filing a pleading or a motion must undertake a reasonable inquiry concerning the facts stated in the pleading or motion. (Rule 11 of Federal Rules of Civil Procedure.) Accepting the client's story without further inquiry may not suffice unless it is impracticable to verify through other sources. It is emphasized that this duty is limited to documents filed in a court proceeding. Corroboration by the client's two friends would satisfy this rule. The court may sanction the lawyer monetarily for violation of the rule. The Model Rules of Professional Conduct do not contain any provision requiring investigation of the client's story.

[9]Model Rule 3.4(b).

[10]Model Rule 1.2(d) and 3.4(b). The practices described in this problem are disapprovingly discussed in Marvin Frankel, Partisan Justice 16 (Hill & Wang, 1980), and Charles W. Wolfram, *Modern Legal Ethics* 648 (West, 1986). Monroe Freedman takes a more sympathetic view of telling the client the law before asking for the facts in his book Understanding Lawyers' Ethics 155–160 (Matthew Bender, 1990).

[11]Model Rule 3.1.

[12]Model Rule 3.1, Comment.

[13]Model Rule 3.2, Comment.

[14]Model Rule 1.3, Comment.

[15]Rule 11 of the Federal Rules of Civil Procedure applicable to civil suits in federal courts provides that a pleading or a motion must have some basis in fact and law, and must not have been filed for an improper purpose such as delay. Most state courts have adopted the same rule. The court may impose monetary sanctions against the lawyer for

violation. Literally this rule states that a pleading or motion that has a basis in fact and law but which is filed for dilatory purposes would be sanctionable. Except in unusual circumstances, however, this rule has generally been interpreted to mean that a pleading or motion which is not frivolous (i.e., has some substantive basis) is not a violation although delay may be the motivation.

This problem is patterned after one presented in Alan H. Goldman, The Moral Foundations of Professional Ethics 102 (Rowman & Allenheld, 1980).

[16]Model Rule 1.2(d).

[17]Model Rule 1.2(d).

[18]Model Rule 1.2(d).

[19]Model Rule 4.1(a).

[20]Model Rule 4.1, Comment.

[21]Larry Lempert, *In Settlement Talks, Does Telling the Truth Have Its Limits?* 2 Inside Litigation 1 (Prentice-Hall Law and Business, 1988).

[22]For a discussion of this technique and its prevalence, see Richard Neely, The Primary Caretaker Parent Rule: Child Custody and the Dynamic of Greed, 3 *Yale Law and Policy Review* 168, 177–79 (1984). See also Jane B. Singer and William L. Reynolds, A Dissent on Joint Custody 47 *Maryland Law Review* 497, 515–516 (1988); Lenore J. Weitzman, *The Divorce Revolution* 310 (Free Press, 1985); Eleanor E. Maccoby and Robert H. Mnookin, *Dividing the Child* 154–59 (Harvard, 1992).

The American Academy of Matrimonial Lawyers has published a set of standards for matrimonial lawyers entitled Bounds of Advocacy (1991). These standards are stated to be "ethical standards . . . that go beyond those required by the American Bar Association and state ethics codes." In essence, they are recommendations to the bar in that area of practice. One of the standards (§ 2.25) states that "An attorney should not contest child custody or visitation for either financial advantage or vindictiveness."

[23]Model Rules 8.4, 4.1(a).

[24]This is the position taken by Robert E. Keeton, formerly professor of law at Harvard, and currently Federal District Judge, in his book Trial Tactics and Methods 326 (Little, Brown, 2d ed. 1973).

[25]The only formal ethics opinion that has been found on this point states that the inclusion of a clause in a legal document that is clearly contrary to law is unethical as a deception to the other party and as a form of disloyalty to the law. Association of the Bar of the City of New York and the New York County Lawyers Association, Committee on Professional Ethics, Opinions on Professional Ethics 435–36 (1956) (Opinion No. 722, December 6, 1948). The 1908 Canons of Professional Ethics were in effect at the time.

[26]This problem is patterned after one presented in Alan H. Goldman, The Moral Foundations of Professional Ethics 103 (Rowman & Allenheld, 1980).

[27]Model Rule 3.3(a)(3).

[28]Model Rule 4.3, Comment.

[29]See Model Rule 1.7, Comment.

[30]Model Rule 1.3, Comment.

[31]Model Rule 1.6.

[32]Restatement 2d of Contracts § 161 (1981); Restatement 2d of Torts § 551 (1977); Charles W. Wolfram, Modern Legal Ethics 722 (West, 1986); E. Allan Farnsworth, *Contracts* § 4.11 (Little, Brown, 1990); William L. Prosser and W. Page Keeton, *Law of Torts* § 106 (West, 5th ed., 1984).

[33]Model Rules, Terminology.

[34]This problem is patterned after the case of *Spaulding v. Zimmerman*, 263 Minn. 346, 116 N.W.2d 704 (Minnesota Supreme Court 1962).

[35]Model Rule 1.6(a).

[36]Model Rule 1.6(b)(1) permits the lawyer to reveal information to prevent the client "from committing a criminal act that the lawyer believes is likely to result in imminent death or substantial bodily harm." Intention to commit a financial or commercial crime cannot be revealed. However, a majority of states permit the lawyer to reveal the client's intention to commit any crime.

[37]Model Rule 1.2(d). This problem is derived from the story of O.P.M. Leasing Services, Inc., whose frauds are described in Geoffrey C. Hazard, Susan P. Koniak, and Roger C. Cramton, *The Law and Ethics of Lawyering* 300 (Foundation Press, 1994).

[38]Model Rule 1.6, Comment. See Robert P. Mosteller, Child Abuse Reporting Laws and Attorney-Client Confidences: The Reality and the Specter of Lawyer as Informant, 42 *Duke Law Journal* 203 (1992).

[39]A lawyer was faced with this problem following the notorious conviction in Georgia of Leo Frank, a Jewish factory owner, for the murder of his 14-year old employee, Mary Phagan. Frank was sentenced to death. Later Arthur Powell, an Atlanta attorney, was told by a client that he had committed the murder, not Frank. Powell told the Governor of Georgia that he knew Frank was innocent but did not disclose his source. The Governor commuted Frank's sentence to life in prison. Shortly thereafter a lynch mob hanged Frank. Arthur G. Powell, Privilege of Counsel and Confidential Communication, 6 *Georgia Bar Journal* 334 (1944); Leonard Dinnerstein, *The Leo Frank Case* 125 (Columbia, 1987); Robert S. Frey and Nancy Thompson-Frey, *The Silent and the Damned: The Murder of Mary Phagan and the Lynching of Leo Frank* 85–99 (Madison, 1988).

[40]This problem is based on the case of *Collin v. Smith*, 578 F.2d 1197 (7th Circuit Court of Appeals 1978), certiorari denied, 439 U.S. 916 (1978), in which it was held that such speech was protected under the First Amendment.

[41]2 Trial of Queen Caroline 5 (Shackell and Arrowsmith, 1821).

[42]Model Rule 1.3, Comment.

[43]Model Rule 2.1.

[44]Model Rule 1.3, Comment.

[45]Model Rule 1.2(a).

[46]Model Rule 1.2, Comment.

Moral Philosophy's Standard Misconception of Legal Ethics

Ted Schneyer

Since Watergate, and maybe because of it, moral philosophers have taken a serious interest in lawyers' ethics. Most have been very critical of the legal profession's thinking on the subject. The critics include Richard Wasserstrom[1] and recently, Michael Bayles,[2] Alan Goldman,[3] David Luban[4] and Gerald Postema.[5] In addition, William Simon, though a lawyer rather than a philosopher by trade, published a major article in 1978[6] that faulted the legal profession for doing no "fundamental questioning" of its ethical premises and criticized in the moral philosophers' idiom much of what lawyers had ever written about legal ethics.

Practicing lawyers have traditionally maintained a very limited interest in legal ethics, perhaps wondering from time to time whether

Ted Schneyer, "Moral Philosophy's Standard Misconception of Legal Ethics," *Wisconsin Law Review* (1984), excerpts from: 1529–1573. Reprinted by permission of the author. (In this edited version footnotes have not been renumbered.)

[1]Wasserstrom, Lawyers as Professionals: Some Moral Issues, 5 *Human Rights 1* (1975).

[2]Bayles, Professionals, Clients, and Others, in *Profits and Professions: Essays in Business and Professional Ethics* 65–73 (1983). Bayles has also written a textbook on professional ethics which emphasizes law and medicine but provides an overview of ethical issues in the professions generally. *See* M. Bayles, *Professional Ethics* (1981).

[3]Goldman's work on legal ethics is found largely in one chapter in his book on ethics in various professions. See A. Goldman, *The Moral Foundations of Professional Ethics* ch. 3 (1980). For a thoughtful review of this essay, see Kaufman, Book Review, 94 *Harv. L. Rev.* 1504 (1981).

[4]Luban, The Adversary System Excuse, in *The Good Lawyer: Lawyers' Roles and Lawyers' Ethics* 83–122 (D. Luban ed. 1983).

[5]Postema, Moral Responsibility in Professional Ethics 55 *N.Y.U.L. Rev.* 63 (1980).

[6]Simon, The Ideology of Advocacy: Procedural Justice and Professional Ethics, 1978 *Wis. L. Rev.* 29.

a certain course of action would be forbidden, permitted or required under the prevailing rules, but rarely considering whether their everyday conduct could be justified in any broader ethical sense. The moral philosophers' attention may prod lawyers and law students to take a deeper interest in legal ethics, just as it has encouraged doctors in recent years to take a deeper interest in medical ethics.

But for all its potential significance the philosophers' work on lawyers' ethics has been disappointing in two respects. For one thing, Wasserstrom, Bayles, Goldman, Luban, Postema and Simon approach their subject in a temper that blinds them to the possibility of learning anything of use to non-lawyers. They find nothing of general value in the way lawyers address their ethical problems, and no solutions to specific problems which would be valuable as analogies in other ethical domains. This is not only curious, since in other respects philosophers have been eager to generalize from their study of law and legal institutions, but regrettable as well. Because law practice so frequently involves moral risks, lawyers' reflections on ethics just might contain, like law itself, a vein of hard-won understanding that philosophers could mine for the benefit of non-lawyers. But mining cannot be expected from those who come to new territory as missionaries rather than prospectors. And missionaries bent on converting the bar are what the philosophers have mostly been. Only the late Charles Frankel has emphasized the need for philosophers looking at legal ethics to be prepared to criticize the moral principles of lawyers *and* of non-lawyers when the two clash.[14]

[14]Frankel, Review, 43 *U. Chi. L. Rev.* 874, 883–84 (1976) (Frankel reviews the ABA Code of Professional Responsibility).

And no philosopher has staked out the position (paralleling Alasdair MacIntyre's views on medical ethics)[15] that legal ethics, with its emphasis on concrete roles and relationships, presently has more to teach moral philosophy as a general field than moral philosophy can teach legal ethics.

A second and more serious flaw reduces the value of the philosophers' work for lawyers in particular. It is the tendency to rely on some dubious empirical claims about law practice and about legal ethics as a body of lawyers' thought. My aim in this Article is to identify those claims, explain why they are unwarranted, and show how they distort the philosophers' analysis.

I. THE PHILOSOPHERS' INDICTMENT

Starting from their shared conception of the central problem in the field, Wasserstrom, Bayles, Goldman, Luban, Postema and Simon present more or less the same indictment. First, they claim that lawyers routinely do things for clients that harm third parties and would therefore be immoral, even in the lawyers' eyes, if done for themselves or for non-clients. Such actions constitute "role-differentiated behavior" in the sense that the actors, if asked to justify themselves, would claim that their role as a lawyer required them to "put to one side [moral] considerations . . . that would otherwise be relevant if not decisive." A lawyer's role-differentiated behavior could involve helping a client pursue a morally objectionable aim, or using a hurtful or unfair tactic to give a client an advantage. Specific examples might include invoking the statute of frauds to help a client avoid paying a debt he really owes, attacking an honest person's veracity in order to discredit him as a witness, taking advantage of an opponent's misunderstanding of the applicable law in settlement negotiations, or suggesting

that a corporate client lay off some of its workers until the Justice Department comes to see the merits of the company's merger proposal. Off duty, lawyers would presumably not think it appropriate to avoid repaying a debt, impugn a truthful person's honesty, take advantage of another's mistake, or exploit workers. On duty, the philosophers say, lawyers routinely do such things for their clients.

Next, the philosophers claim that lawyers do this to conform to their profession's ethical principles and not just to make money, earn a promotion, win a contest, pick a fight, or be doggedly loyal to someone in trouble. Lawyers, in other words, are not only tempted by self-interest and other prosaic motives to engage in morally questionable behavior for their clients. They are motivated to do so by professional principles which, far from being the solution to lawyer misbehavior, turn out to be a large part of the problem. As Goldman puts it: "The central problem . . . is not that [lawyers] often fail to live up to their unique official codes and professional principles; nor that they lack the will to enforce them. It is rather that they often assume without question that they ought to live up to them."

What are the principles of legal ethics and where are they found? The philosophers consider legal ethics a highly specialized body of lawyers' and judges' thought found in codes drafted by the organized bar (notably the ABA Code of Professional Responsibility and, before 1970, the ABA Canons of Professional Ethics),[21] as well as in bar association ethics

---

[15]See MacIntyre, What Has Ethics to Learn from Medical Ethics? 2 *Phil. Exchange* 37 (1978) (criticizing the attitude that moral philosophers are "a kind of intellectual peace corps, the medical profession a morally underdeveloped country").

[21]The ABA adopted its first ethics code for lawyers, the Canons of Professional Ethics [hereinafter cited as Canons], in 1908. American Bar Association (ABA), 39 Annual Report 559–70 (1914: The Canons were amended on a number of occasions and then supplanted by the Code, which the ABA promulgated in 1969 see ABA, 94 *Annual Report* 728 (1969), and which was quickly adopted by court rule in nearly all states, with only minor amendments. ABA, 97 *Annual Report* 268, 272 (1972). The Code was most recently published as the ABA Model Code of Professional Responsibility. The Model Code has now been supplanted by the Model Rules, which the ABA adopted in 1983. See supra note 10. The philosophers' essays on which this Article focuses were written before the Model Rules were adopted.

opinions, case law, and scholarly texts. The philosophers claim that legal ethics, so understood, has at least in this century been built around one "Standard Conception" or "Official View" of the lawyer's role. This Standard Conception boils down to two principles: Neutrality and Partisanship. Neutrality requires a lawyer to practice without regard to her personal views concerning either a client's character or the moral status of his objectives. Partisanship commits a lawyer to the aggressive and single-minded pursuit of her client's objectives, "[w]ithin, but all the way *up to*, the limits of the law." Together these principles mean that on the job the lawyer's moral universe may be—indeed, must be—defined solely by the law and by client interests.

We can now better examine the concept of role-differentiated behavior as it is used in several of the philosophers' critiques. The concept is obviously meant to appeal to our desire for moral consistency. But its power is limited by the fact that we have no single dimension for gauging the consistency of a lawyer's actions. For instance, when we think of lawyers as if they were public officials, like judges, consistency seems to mean acting on the same principles other lawyers would employ; equal protection by lawyers becomes nearly as attractive as equal protection of the law. When we think of them as providing services in the marketplace, however, consistency means that their behavior be reconcilable with that of other service providers.

Adopting the latter standpoint for a moment, notice that lawyers adhering to the Neutrality Principle would not behave differently than the providers of most services. Doctors generally feel they should accept and treat patients without regard to the ends to which those patients will put their improved health. And cab drivers, even if they consider prostitution an evil, will not hesitate to deliver a garishly dressed fare to Forty-Second and Broadway at midnight. In this sense one might say that lawyering by the Neutrality Principle is not role-differentiated behavior. And, if one felt that lawyers should not adhere to the Neutrality Principle, one would have to distinguish

legal services from other services, perhaps by showing that the former are relatively likely to jeopardize important third-party interests.[26] (After all, helping a client win a lawsuit always makes a loser of the opposing party.) One would then be arguing that lawyers' actions *should* be role-differentiated, i.e., not based on the Neutrality Principle that appears to govern other service providers.

Obviously, this cannot be the sense in which our philosophers usually speak of role-differentiated behavior, for they regard Neutrality-based lawyering as strongly role-differentiated, and as undesirable. In their usage a lawyer's professional actions are role-differentiated if contrary to principles that would govern that same lawyer's non-professional actions. This usage suggests that the philosophers place moral consistency across each individual's actions above consistency among lawyers or between occupations. This priority may be defensible, but the philosophers never adequately defend it.

In any event, though the concept of role-differentiated behavior does little to strengthen their indictment, the philosophers still conclude that the principles of legal ethics encourage lawyers to do things that cost society too much. The costs of course include harm to third parties—the foiled creditor, the humiliated witness, the laid-off workers—whose interests the Standard Conception ignores. But they may also include more subtle harm, first to the integrity of lawyers who cannot reconcile their on-duty and off-duty behavior, and then even to clients, who, though ostensibly the beneficiaries of the Standard Conception, may find themselves dealing with, and being represented in public by,

---

[26]Michael Bayles briefly develops such an argument: Should professionals assist clients in achieving legally permissible ends that are contrary to ordinary morality? Can any legally permissible means be used to assist clients, regardless of their conformity to the dictates of ordinary morality? Since the conduct of lawyers in assisting their clients almost always affects others, whereas the conduct of other professionals is less likely to do so, these issues are more pressing for lawyers. . . .

someone who is not playing with a full moral deck.[39]

Such, in brief, is the philosophers' indictment. Before I develop my objections to it, I should say that I agree with the indictment in a key respect: a lawyers' ethic that treats Neutrality and Partisanship as absolutes is inappropriate. Rather than restate all of the criticisms of such an ethic here, I shall simply identify the three most conventional justifications for exalting Neutrality and Partisanship above other values and mention a few of the problems raised by each justification.

First, one might argue that Neutrality and Partisanship ought to be overriding principles because of their value in safeguarding client autonomy from the state, particularly when the client is a criminal defendant. As the philosophers generally acknowledge, criminal defendants should have the power to put the state, with its vast resources, to its proof, even at the risk of acquitting some who are guilty. Having criminal defense lawyers act on the principles of Neutrality and Partisanship will certainly help assure that defendants have this power. On the other hand, cases pitting a party's freedom or property against the resources of the state are not representative of all litigation, let alone all lawyering situations. And even criminal cases do not involve these interests alone. The complaining witness humiliated during relentless cross-examination in a rape case is not exactly Leviathan. Her interests are distinct from those of the state and deserve to be recognized. A defense lawyer acting solely on

the principles of Neutrality and Partisanship would ignore them.

Second, one might defend Neutrality and Partisanship as overriding principles on the ground that they enable citizens to fully exercise all their legal rights. After all, even recognizing one's rights often requires legal advice, and exercising rights may require zealous representation as well. But although each citizen has a constitutional claim to effective assistance of counsel in criminal cases, he has no moral or political claim to legal assistance in every exercise of a legal right, let alone to the zealous assistance of a lawyer who has qualms about what the citizen proposes. Why not? Because not every exercise of a legal right has a moral justification. Even the most ardent believer in the correspondence between law and morality should recognize that law tolerates certain behavior only because legal rights are embodied in rules, which by their nature must be somewhat over- and under-inclusive, or because a ban could not be satisfactorily enforced. While judges must stick to the law in these situations, it does not follow that lawyers should be encouraged to help parties pursue their legal rights. For example, Wisconsin's law against aiding a felon by destroying incriminating evidence exempts the aided felons themselves and their close relatives, in an apparent concession to their desperation. Although a desperate felon could certainly benefit from a lawyer's help in deciding how and when to destroy evidence, no one believes the statute should exempt lawyers too, so they can help client-felons "fully" exercise this legal right.

Of course, this may be a special case; the statute presumably excluded legal assistance when it gave felons a right to destroy evidence, and Partisanship only encourages a lawyer to help his client up to the limits of the law. What about the more common case, in which lawyers could lawfully help? Without a professional ethic based on Neutrality and Partisanship moralistic lawyers could conceivably nullify legal rights by refusing to accept certain clients or to take certain perfectly legal steps for others. But the chance seems remote; in our pluralistic society very few attempts to exercise a

---

[39] . . . today's moral philosophers stand in marked contrast to those of an earlier day who regarded the creation of ethics codes by professional associations as desirable. See supra note 12. Of course, philosophers are not the only ones who have soured on this enterprise. The same political evaluation is more or less explicit in a number of studies of legal ethics codes by legal scholars. See, e.g., Abel, Why Does the ABA Promulgate Ethical Codes? 59 *Tex. L. Rev.* 639 (1981); Morgan, The Evolving Concept of Professional Responsibility, 90 *Harv. L. Rev.* 702 (1977); Rhode, Why the ABA Bothers: A Functional Perspective on Professional Codes, 59 *Tex. L. Rev.* 689 (1981); Wolfram, Barriers to Effective Public Participation in Regulation of the Legal Profession, 62 *Minn. L. Rev.* 619 (1978).

legal right would be morally repugnant to every available lawyer. And when every lawyer is repelled, an ethic that broadly encourages representation may not be desirable. In view of the importance of free speech rights, Neutrality and Partisanship might concededly serve society well in the unlikely case in which they were the only reasons any lawyer would help the Ku Klux Klan obtain a parade permit.[43] More often, however, no such fundamental rights are implicated, and the calculus of social advantage seems different. For example, when a statute designed to protect against fraudulent contract claims also shields some defendants who are not being defrauded, society may be better off with a professional ethic that does not encourage lawyers to invoke the statute on behalf of those defendants.

The final argument for Neutrality and Partisanship as overriding principles is that they are required by our commitment to an adversary system of justice. A tribunal's decision is likely to be an informed one, factually and legally sound, only when each litigant has the opportunity to present his case in the best possible light and to bring out weaknesses in his opponent's case. This, it is said, requires a lawyer's full commitment to the client's objectives and to the use of every lawful tactic for attaining them, whatever the lawyer's personal opinion about the propriety of those objectives and tactics may be.

One possible problem with this argument is that advocacy motivated by a commitment to Neutrality and Partisanship might contribute less to a judge's decision than advocacy motivated by belief in the justice of its own claims. But the main problem is again overgenerality. Though Neutrality and Partisanship might promote wise and informed decisions when both parties are represented by equally well-equipped lawyers whose performance is closely monitored by an impartial judge, such ideal lawsuits are only the tip of our legal iceberg. Consider the rest. Cases are hardly uncommon in which, for example, a large real estate operation wants to sue a tenant who cannot obtain counsel or whose lawyer can only devote minimal time and effort to the matter. In such a case, if Neutrality and Partisanship spurred the landlord's lawyer to act as an aggressive and single-minded advocate, not only might the proceeding strike the tenant (and us) as unfair, but on the adversary system's own assumptions the decision might be *less* informed than if the landlord's lawyer had considered the tenant's claims sympathetically. Moreover, it is not litigating, but counseling, negotiating and drafting that make up the largest chunk of the legal iceberg. Here lawyers are very often free of the constraints that check their behavior in court: an impartial decision-maker and a watchful opposing counsel. Consequently, in these activities, what Luban calls the "adversary system excuse" cannot begin to justify an ethic based solely on Neutrality and Partisanship.[47]

Thus, as evaluations of one possible conception of the lawyer's role, the philosophers' critiques are appealing. But the essays in question are not just evaluative. They make important empirical claims or assumptions about law practice and about legal ethics as a body of lawyers' thought. I quarrel with five of those claims or assumptions: 1) that lawyers characteristically are willing to do things for clients that show no regard for the welfare of others; 2) that the need or desire to conform to authoritative principles of legal ethics is a prime determinant of lawyer behavior; 3) that the principles of legal ethics are elaborated in a set

---

[43] I call this an "unlikely case" because the Klan, like the Nazi Party, has found lawyers who take parade permit cases out of a commitment to the first amendment rather than a commitment to the Neutrality Principle—the notion that one should always disregard the morality of a client's aims. The point was brought home recently when a black lawyer recommended by the American Civil Liberties Union represented the Klan after the initial denial of the Klan's application for a permit to hold a parade in a small Alabama town. "I grew up in Mobile and of course I have some emotions about the Klan," the lawyer said, "but I had to set them aside for the sake of preserving the First Amendment." Reaves, It's Part of the Job: Black Lawyer Defends KKK, *A.B.A.J.*, Mar. 1984, at 43.

[47] For development of this point, see Schwartz The Professionalism and Accountability of Lawyers 66 *Calif. L. Rev.* 669 (1978).

of rules and doctrines that predetermine lawyers' responsibilities, leaving little or no room for individual discretion; 4) that legal ethics is a highly autonomous and specialized field, uninfluenced by external ethical, political or theological ideas; and 5) that the ethical thought of the legal profession strives uniformly to ground the lawyer's role on Neutrality and Partisanship.

I want to argue, to the contrary, that lawyers to a surprising degree do not engage in exclusively client-regarding behavior, and that when they do, their actions can seldom be chalked up to legal ethics understood as an autonomous field. In addition to presenting evidence about the way lawyers behave, I shall try to make three points. First, some lawyers' texts on legal ethics appear to be heavily influenced by ideas taken from other fields. Second, whatever the provenance of its texts, legal ethics is a much less coherent, and so a less controlling, body of rules and principles than the philosophers acknowledge; their Standard Conception is really only one, and never a completely dominant, strand of thought in a vague and sometimes contradictory field.[50] Third, the common financial, psychological and organizational pressures of law practice explain the exclusively client-regarding behavior of lawyers better than the rules of legal ethics. For, ineffective as those rules may be, some are clearly designed to discourage such behavior rather than encourage or legitimize it.

My argument is based on the traditional legal ethics literature and the sociological literature on the legal profession. My conclusion is that moral philosophers will not develop a sufficiently nuanced picture of lawyers' ethics until they take a closer look at both.

II.   HOW LAWYERS BEHAVE

I begin with the philosophers' claim that lawyers are characteristically willing to help clients achieve morally objectionable aims and to use any hurtful or unfair (but legal) tactic to gain their client an advantage. The degree to which lawyering would have to fit this pattern before the claim would be confirmed is unclear. But the claim is strong; Wasserstrom asserts, for example, that "for most lawyers, most of the time," single-mindedly pursuing the interests of one's client is an "attractive and satisfying way to live." The claim is broad too; it covers more than just the way lawyers behave in lawsuits. Thus, Luban insists that lawyers "commonly act as though *all* their functions [as adviser, negotiator and draftsman, as well as advocate] were governed" by the principles of Neutrality and Partisanship. Assertions to the contrary—that lawyers in any role deviate substantially from those principles—Luban dismisses as "bad sociology." In fact, however, some perfectly respectable sociology supports just such assertions.

Take criminal defense work. Sociologist Abraham Blumberg found, in what remains one of the most important empirical studies of the field, that defense lawyers sometimes behave more like professional wrestlers than zealous combatants.[54] Generally, criminal defense lawyers represent their clients on a one-shot basis and are paid by a third party. For these structural reasons, Blumberg found, defense lawyers are understandably tempted to sacrifice individual clients, or even their clients as a class, in order to maintain good personal relations with the prosecutors, police, and court and jail personnel with whom they must deal on a long-term basis. Moreover, they sometimes succumb to the temptation, foregoing meritorious defenses to avoid antagonizing busy prosecutors and judges, and even acting as "double agents" for the criminal justice bureaucracy by advising clients to cop pleas when it might not be in their interest and by "cooling out" clients who fail at first to see the wisdom of the advice.

Blumberg's article is a valuable reminder that many criminal defendants do not receive the no-stone-unturned defense received by, say, John DeLorean. It also helps us see certain

---

[50]My view of the field, particularly the ABA Canons and Code, is in this respect similar to that of Andrew Kaufman See Kaufman, A Professional Agenda, *6 Hofstra L. Rev.* 619, 621–23 (1978).

[54]Blumberg The Practice of Law as Confidence Game: Organizational Cooptation of a Profession, *1 L. & Soc'y Rev.* 15 (1967).

provisions in the Code of Professional Responsibility differently than the philosophers do. Some of their favorite whipping boys are the Code provisions requiring a lawyer to represent his client "zealously." These include DR 7-101(A)(1), a disciplinary rule which says that a lawyer "shall not intentionally fail to seek the lawful objectives of his client through reasonably available means permitted by law." Though this rule goes on to make it clear that a lawyer need not use "offensive tactics" on a client's behalf, the philosophers believe that such provisions are intended to stifle whatever moral qualms lawyers may have about seeking certain objectives or using certain tactics for their clients; they regard these provisions as embodiments of the principles of Neutrality and Partisanship. After reading Blumberg, however, one sees that the provisions may serve largely as a corrective against indifferent advocacy by lawyers whose institutional position inclines them to be unduly deferential to certain third parties and whose personal interests—rather than scruples—are stacked against clients. A society that considers effective representation of counsel a fundamental value in criminal cases should welcome such a corrective.

Similarly, legal ethics has long been concerned with assuring the availability of counsel to represent those accused of illegal political activity or heinous crimes. The Code contains several provisions on this point, including Ethical Consideration 2-27, which states that "a lawyer should not decline representation because a client or a cause is unpopular or community reaction is adverse." Although these provisions do not impose on any individual lawyer an ethical, let alone a legal, duty to represent an "unpopular" client (except in extraordinary circumstances),[61] the philosophers are again apt to see them as embodiments of the Neutrality Principle. Yet the pertinent survey data and case studies suggest that the main obstacle to finding a lawyer to represent an unpopular client is not personal repugnance toward such a person or his deeds, but fear that becoming associated with the client in the minds of other lawyers and the public will damage one's practice or reputation.[63] So once more the Code can be read chiefly as exhorting lawyers to transcend their interests, not their personal morality.

The vivid and influential ties Blumberg observed between criminal defense lawyers and third parties can sometimes be found in civil litigation as well. Sociologist Donald Landon recently interviewed 200 trial lawyers who practice in small communities and often know an opposing party or counsel personally.[64]

Landon's advocates were sometimes reluctant to accept cases, not because of moral qualms, but because it would make them unpopular in their community and be bad for business; one lawyer, for instance, called his decision to handle a malpractice suit against the local doctor a ruinous mistake he would never repeat. Landon's advocates were also reluctant to pursue their clients' initial aims without considering the appropriateness of those aims. Indeed, they often approached their cases as mediators. One such lawyer described himself as presently working on a church-split case that "has all the makings of a community-wide confrontation" and said that he and the opposing attorney were "trying very hard to cool things down." Finally, Landon's advocates were unwilling to use sharp tactics to gain an advantage over a lawyer they knew and regularly dealt with. As one said: "You don't file a five-day motion on Charley Jones when he's on a two-week vacation, or try to take advantage of him. If he's forgot to file an answer, you don't ask the judge for default. You call him. . . . [F]airness is more important than winning."

---

[61]EC 2-26 makes it clear that a lawyer has no obligation to represent any particular client, though he should never "lightly decline" employment. Only when a lawyer is appointed by a court to represent a person otherwise unable to obtain counsel does the Code take a different position. In that situation the lawyer should not seek to be excused from handling the matter except for "compelling reasons," not including the "repugnance of the subject matter of the proceeding." ABA Code EC 2-29.

[63]See, Ball, Freedom of the Bar *32 Cal. St. B.J.* 109 (1957); Pollitt, Timid Lawyers and Neglected Clients, *Harpers*, Aug. 1964, at 81; Douglas. The Black Silence of Fear *N.Y. Times*, Jan. 13, 1952, § 6 (Magazine), at 7, 37–38.

[64]D. Landon, Clients, Colleagues and Community: The Shaping of Zealous Advocacy in Country Law Practice (n.d.) (unpublished manuscript). vacation).

[T]he findings say something about legal ethics as well as small-town life, namely, that the Code does not dictate the sort of behavior Landon originally expected from litigators and is too vague and self-contradictory to seal lawyers hermetically inside a role, impervious to broader cultural and moral influences.

Notice, for example, that the behavior reported by Landon's interviewees is at least arguably consistent with the Code even though it may have been aimed at accommodating client to third-party interests. In the church litigation, the lawyer was apparently pressing his client to take a conciliatory tone for the good of the community. This was hardly unethical, at least on its face; while the Code indicates that the decision to forego legally available objectives is "ultimately" for the client, it encourages the lawyer, in advising his client, to "point out those factors which may lead to a decision that is morally just" and to "emphasize the . . . harsh consequences that might result from assertion of legally permissible positions." As for the lawyer who refused to use sharp tactics to gain an advantage over an opponent, the Code does prohibit a lawyer from failing to seek "the lawful objectives of his client through reasonably available means" (presumably including motions for default judgment and the like); but the same rule permits a lawyer to accede to "reasonable requests of opposing counsel," to shun "offensive tactics," and to treat "with courtesy and consideration all persons involved in the legal process," (presumably including the opposing counsel who files a pleading a bit late or is briefly away on vacation). The Code also encourages lawyers to "follow local customs of courtesy or practice."

Putting criminal and civil litigation aside, consider the way lawyers behave as negotiators, advisers and draftsmen. Regarding negotiations, several years ago my colleague Stewart Macaulay surveyed 100 Wisconsin lawyers practicing in a wide range of settings who had experience representing buyers or sellers in the settlement of minor consumer complaints. His conclusions about the way lawyers behave in the negotiation process were these:

Rather than playing hired gun for one side, lawyers often mediate between their client and those not represented by lawyers. They seek to educate, persuade and coerce *both* sides to adopt the best available compromise rather than to engage in legal warfare. Moreover, in playing all of their roles, . . . lawyers are influenced by their own values and self-interest.[73]

Macaulay found these patterns, incidentally, among business lawyers, who were apt to have an ongoing relationship with their clients, and among consumers' lawyers, who were not.

With regard to the behavior of lawyers as advisers and draftsmen, we may look to sociological studies of corporate practice in large-city law firms, since corporate lawyers spend most of their time counseling clients on matters of corporate governance or on the legal aspects of business transactions, and preparing documents for those transactions or for submission to government agencies. On the whole these studies do not support the view that the principles of Neutrality and Partisanship account for the behavior of corporate lawyers. Among the older studies is Erwin Smigel's examination of practice at twenty Wall Street firms. Smigel found good reason to agree with Talcott Parsons that lawyers often operate as a "kind of buffer between the illegitimate desires of clients and the social interest," inducing clients to abandon or moderate their morally questionable as well as their illegal aims. Similarly, in tracing the rise of the modern corporate lawyer, historian Willard Hurst found that Elihu Root had not been too far off when he said that "about half the practice of a decent lawyer consists in telling would-be clients that they are damned fools and should stop."[78]

---

[73]Macaulay, Lawyers and Consumer Protection Laws, *14 L. & Soc'y Rev.* 115 (1979).

[78]J.W. Hurst, *The Growth of American Law: The Law Makers 345* (1950). Of course, Root, like the profession generally, may not have been of one mind on the subject of lawyer-client relations. He is also reported to have said: "The client never wants to be told he can't do what he wants to do; he wants to be told how to do it, and it is the lawyer's business to tell him how." R. Swaine, *The Cravath Firm and its Predecessors* 667 (1946).

More recently, lawyer and sociologist Robert Nelson interviewed 222 corporate lawyers practicing in large Chicago firms. He asked if they had ever refused work because it was contrary to their personal values. Only thirty-six lawyers or sixteen percent of the sample had done so, and only twelve had done so more than once.[79] This might suggest that most respondents were willing to do morally questionable things for their clients. In fact, however, nearly all those who had never refused a task said this was because their tasks had never contravened their personal values. Most tasks were so technical that no value question seemed to be involved. When this was not the case, when moral or political issues were implicated, clients' wishes and lawyers' sensibilities jibed. Whether this means that the clients of corporate lawyers in Chicago are above reproach, or that the lawyers are beneath contempt, is beside the point. The point is that Nelson's lawyers, in deciding what matters to handle, exhibit no pattern of laying aside their personal values in favor of Neutrality. True, fourteen of the 186 lawyers who had never turned down an assignment did cite as a reason their view that personal values should have no bearing on such decisions. These individuals conform to the philosophers' image of the bar. But a greater number of lawyers (eighteen) had rejected a task precisely because it would have required them to do something which, though legal, might foster racial discrimination, pollution, or some other practice that was contrary to their personal values.

III.   WHY LAWYERS BEHAVE AS THEY DO

Together, these empirical studies show that lawyers in their various roles do not as a matter of course do things for clients that are contrary to the lawyers' personal values or harmful to the legitimate interests of third parties. But the studies do not prove that lawyers never do such things. Nor could they prove it; such behavior undoubtedly occurs frequently. So my aim now shifts to accounting for the exclusively client-regarding behavior one does find in law practice. How well, I want to ask, do the prevailing rules and the motivational force of legal ethics explain that behavior?

A. *Lawyers' Tactics*

I begin by discussing lawyers' tactics, reserving the problem of accounting for the willingness of lawyers to pursue objectionable ends for their clients. Consider some of the objectionable litigation tactics lawyers have been said to use: encouraging personal injury plaintiffs to lie about the extent of their injuries and assuring them that this is "how the game is played," failing to disclose directly adverse legal authority to the court, recording conversations without the participants' knowledge in order to gain evidence, and relentlessly cross-examining rape victims about their prior sexual conduct even when this will obviously be degrading to the witnesses and should be irrelevant in determining whether rapes have occurred. These tactics are not only morally suspect; they are likely to violate the Code, which, therefore, cannot be read simply as a set of elaborations on the Partisanship principle.

Having personal injury clients lie under oath about the extent of their injuries is suborning perjury and violates the DRs that prohibit illegal conduct as well as those that bar a lawyer from creating false evidence and using perjured testimony.[88] Of course, since these rules may only prohibit conduct already proscribed by law, they are consistent with the Partisanship principle. But suppose a lawyer

---

[79]R. Nelson, Practice and Privilege: The Social Organization of Large Law Firms 314–19 (June 1983) (unpub. Ph.D. dissertation). See also Heinz, The Power of Lawyers, 17 *Ga. L. Rev.* 891, 902–03 (1983) (summarizing Nelson's data).

[88]*See* ABA Code DRs 7-102(A)(4), 7-102(A)(6). These rules clearly oblige lawyers to make some threshold judgments about the truth-value of potential evidence. This belies an assumption implicit in at least some of the philosophers' essays, namely, that in our adversary system only judges and juries are concerned with "truth" while lawyers do not vouch at all for the truth-value of their pleadings or the evidence they introduce.

encourages her client to lie, or exaggerates the extent of the client's injuries herself, in settlement negotiations. These actions presumably are not crimes. Yet they appear to violate the DRs that prohibit a lawyer from: 1) knowingly making a false statement of fact; 2) engaging in conduct involving dishonesty, fraud, deceit, or misrepresentation; or 3) assisting a client in carrying out a fraud.

The Code also covers our other examples. Deliberate failure to disclose adverse legal authority to a tribunal violates DR 7-106(B)(1).[93] An ABA ethics opinion has construed the Code rule against "conduct involving dishonesty, fraud, deceit or misrepresentation" to prohibit a lawyer from recording a telephone conversation without the knowledge of the participants, even if the recording is lawful. This implies that a lawyer may not use or recommend at least some of the devious evidence-gathering tactics a party may lawfully employ in his own behalf. As for cross-examining a rape victim about her prior sexual conduct, irrelevant questions intended to degrade a trial witness violate DR 7-106(C)(2). A Code footnote suggests that this rule was meant to encourage the respect for adverse witnesses and parties which Canon 18 of the Canons of Ethics had earlier and more explicitly promoted. Canon 18 may not have had much bite, but even a philosopher would be hard pressed to reconcile its bark with the Partisanship principle. Canon 18 provided:

> A lawyer should always treat adverse witnesses and suitors with fairness and due consideration, and he should never minister to the malevolences or prejudices of a client in the trial or conduct of a cause. The client cannot be made the keeper of the lawyer's conscience in professional matters. He has no right to demand that his counsel shall abuse the opposite party or indulge in offensive personalities. Improper speech is not

excusable on the ground that it is what the client would say if speaking in his own behalf.

Since these litigation tactics are likely to violate the prevailing rules of legal ethics, the motivation to use them is likely to lie outside the *field* of legal ethics. A number of legal scholars sensibly attribute their use to other forces, such as the urges to satisfy clients, to make money, and to win what is too often mistaken for a contest. Many ethics rules seem designed to counteract rather than instill or legitimize those urges. In some measure, the prevailing rules of legal ethics not only protect the integrity of the judicial process but help lawyers withstand the pressure to do things in practice, such as advise people to lie, that conscience tells them would be wrong to do outside of practice. Moral philosophers who fail to acknowledge this are not likely to be taken seriously by the bar.

EC 7-4 states that in litigation an advocate is not justified in asserting a frivolous position, though he "may urge any permissible construction of the law" favorable to his client. The Code allows a lawyer to withdraw from representing a client who "insists, in a matter not pending before a tribunal, that the lawyer engage in conduct contrary to the lawyer's judgment or advice;" so the lawyer whose client demands that he use some sleazy but lawful tactic in, say, negotiating a contract "may continue" in the representation but need not do so.

[W]henever the Code can be read either to require lawyers to use a sharp tactic or merely to allow it, the philosophers are apt to grasp at the first interpretation without considering the second. Goldman, for instance, takes DR 7-106(C)(2)'s ban on degrading witnesses by asking irrelevant questions to imply that a lawyer not only may but "perhaps must" degrade witnesses whenever it would be "helpful to his client's cause." This is plausible in view of DR 7-101(A)(1)'s general requirement that a lawyer not "fail to seek the lawful objectives of his client through reasonably available means permitted by law and the Disciplinary Rules," but hardly inescapable, since DR 7-101(A)(1)

---

[93] DR 7-106(B) provides: "In presenting a matter to a tribunal, a lawyer shall disclose: (1) Legal authority in the controlling jurisdiction known to him to be directly adverse to the position of his client and which is not disclosed by opposing counsel." Id.

immediately adds that a lawyer may forego "offensive tactics" and "treat with courtesy and consideration all persons involved in the legal process."

Of course, these points of Code interpretation are relatively minor. The Code does at least tolerate many litigation tactics that can not only harm witnesses or adverse parties, but make judicial decisionmaking less reliable to boot. Examples include discrediting a truthful witness on cross-examination; counseling a client not to retain certain records because they could be damaging in future litigation; cultivating an expert witness by feeding her only favorable information until she is locked in to supporting the client's position; and using pretrial motions, refusals to stipulate, and discovery requests to exploit a client's greater staying power.

[I]f lawyers do have too much ethical leeway to use sharp tactics, the philosophers may be unfair in blaming this on a "peculiar ethical orientation" whereby the typical lawyer "explicit[ly] refus[es] to be bound by personal and social norms which he considers binding on others."[115] Why unfair? Because lawyers' justifications for using sharp tactics may often have nothing to do with "the needs of the adversary system" or any other rationale that would appeal to lawyers alone. The lawyer's ethical outlook, in other words, may not rest upon as specialized or autonomous a body of thought as the philosophers suppose. This point requires elaboration.

In a much discussed article, law professor Charles Fried argued that the lawyer-client relationship, involving as it does a personal service, is much like a friendship, so that what lawyers should do for their clients is analogous to what friends should do for one another, especially in times of trouble.[116] For Fried this analogy justified many, though not all, of the disturbing tactics lawyers use. Fried's argument is certainly open to attack, mainly for failing

to acknowledge either the limits on what one should do for a friend or the implausibility of viewing every client (even, say, a profiteering landlord in an eviction case) as a friend, let alone a friend in trouble. Still, the argument offers a useful insight into a lawyer's conscience; it shows that lawyers will sometimes try to justify themselves by appealing to a value—here, loyalty to a friend—that is not unique to them. (Non-lawyers have friends too.) This undercuts the criticism that legal ethics exempts lawyers from having to consider "ordinary" moral principles. Indeed, it suggests that the opposite criticism may be more appropriate: that legal ethics has so far failed to insulate lawyers from some of the sentiments that ordinarily motivate people, such as the impulse to be loyal to intimates at others' expense.[119] Perhaps the legal profession's ethical orientation is not peculiar enough!

Fried's insight into the lawyer's conscience parallels that of another legal scholar, Thomas Shaffer. Shaffer treats criminal defense lawyers, not in terms of their duties to defendants as advocate and to the state as officer of the court, but rather in terms of a Christian responsibility to minister to their clients as individuals forsaken by the community at large.[120] Ministry means providing companionship and encouraging the client to be good, but also refusing to write off one's client as a lost soul and, therefore, running the risk of inadvertently furthering his schemes. This has implications, according to Shaffer, for how one represents the guilty. As an expression of faith in her client the lawyer

---

[115]Simon, supra note 6, at 30.

[116]Fried, supra note 31.

[119]This criticism is implicit in Sissela Bok's study of the morality of lying, which attributes the willingness of lawyers to use perjured testimony on a client's behalf in part to a "tribal ethic of avoiding harm to oneself and one's own," S. Bok *Lying* 159 (1980). See also Newton, Professionalization: The Intractable Plurality of Values in *Profits and Professions: Essays in Business and Professional Ethics,* supra note 2, at 23, 32 (one-to-one relationship evokes in lawyers a "natural sympathy" for their clients as against third parties). Cf. R. Niebuhr, Moral Man and Immoral Society 28 (1932) (ethical regard for others often turns crucially on personal contacts and direct relations).

[120]T. Shaffer, On Being a Christian and a Lawyer 35–104 (1981).

should allow him to testify even if he has expressed an intention to commit perjury. Moreover, when a client does commit perjury the lawyer should not feel obliged to reveal the lie to the court; doing so would break faith with the client and be inconsistent with the responsibility to continue to minister to the client after the lie occurs.

Many people would object to a lawyer's use of perjured testimony and her failure to rectify a client's fraud on a court. These acts may also violate the prevailing rules of legal ethics. Nevertheless, to the extent that Shaffer's views represent the thinking of some criminal lawyers, we are again confronted with professionals acting on principles whose origins and appeal lie outside their profession. Christian theology is not the stuff of a specialized and autonomous lawyers' ethic.

B. Clients' Ends

I have so far spoken mostly about lawyers' tactics, not clients' objectives. I have tried to show that the prevailing rules of legal ethics generally do not require, and sometimes do not permit, lawyers to use morally objectionable tactics, even when those tactics are otherwise lawful. I have also tried to show that when lawyers use disturbing tactics their motives are likely either to have nothing to do with values or to involve values that are not unique to the bar. Many of the same points apply to the pursuit of immoral ends. To avoid repetition, however, I shall make only three direct responses to the philosophers' charge that lawyers pursue such ends for clients out of a commitment to a Neutrality Principle that is supposedly central to legal ethics.

First, one cannot substantiate the charge, as the philosophers seem to think, just by pointing to situations in which lawyers have served some arguably unworthy goal by helping a client. The problem with such proof is not failure to identify a moral arbiter, because the philosophers are obviously concerned about lawyers helping clients pursue ends the lawyers themselves consider wrong. Rather, the problem is that more than one of a lawyer's values are implicated in many lawyering situations,

leaving it far from clear when the lawyer's conduct is wrong in his terms. True, there is no trick to coding Wasserstrom's hypothetical lawyer who disapproves of smoking and thinks it should be banned, yet gladly helps a new cigarette manufacturer to incorporate; he definitely goes into the moral compromisers' box. But he may also be a stick figure. What about the more complicated, truer-to-life lawyer who agrees to represent the new manufacturer despite her disapproval of smoking but who also believes that as long as adults are permitted to smoke they should be able to buy cigarettes at competitive prices? I would hesitate to say that she was compromising herself, since her actions further at least one of her social goods—competition in business.

To take the point further, consider the lawyers who help the Klan get parade permits. Realistically, they might be of two types: racists whose actions are plainly consistent with their own twisted values; and ACLU lawyers who report that they are acting in order to preserve free speech, not in a broader belief that everybody is entitled to a lawyer, and certainly not to promote the racism they abhor. The Klan's purposes are wrong from the ACLU lawyer's standpoint, but his own objective is not. The lawyer's self-reported motive could be a pretext or a rationalization, I suppose, but I see no reason to presume that it is either.

We might speculate briefly about why the philosophers seem so oblivious to the moral complexities of lawyering. Wasserstrom puts the case of lawyer L, who is asked to prepare a will; the would-be testator is L's longtime client; she wants to disinherit her son for being a draft resister; L would not consider this an acceptable reason to disinherit his own child. For Wasserstrom the case poses only one issue: whether L should turn down the client and remain true to his *moral* principles or should instead disregard his principles and help the client to effectuate her *legal* rights. On this analysis one must concede that by preparing the will L would, in his own terms, be helping the client to do something wrong. But the analysis may be inadequate. The legal right to disinherit is not merely a legal right; it is grounded, as Alan Goldman to his credit points out, on a widely recognized *moral* right to dispose of one's legitimately gained property as one sees fit. If L agrees to prepare the will in the recognition that his client has this moral right, then it seems inappropriate to tax L with betraying his principles, even though he would consider it wrong to disinherit his own son for being a draft resister. Wasserstrom may have overlooked this complication because *he* sees the legal right to disinherit—and perhaps many legal rights—as having no moral underpinning. Behind his view of legal ethics may lurk some unarticulated and debatable assumptions about law itself.

My first response to the philosophers' charge could be wrong, of course. Maybe many lawyers at one time or another unequivocally disserve their personal values by pursuing client objectives. My second response is this: even if these lawyers are generally motivated by some conception of their professional responsibilities and not simply by the desire to earn a living (a very dubious assumption), that conception may have nothing to do with Neutrality. It may rest instead on a more morally defensible view of the lawyer-client relationship. To develop this response let me refer again to the last hypothetical.

Suppose L would consider it wrong to disinherit his son for resisting the draft and also believes that his client has no moral right to disinherit her son on that ground, but senses that the client believes she has this right. I presume that Wasserstrom would still not want L to prepare the will, and if L simply proceeded to do so, I might be as critical as Wasserstrom. On the other hand, if L refused without fully discussing the client's position and his own, this would, in my view, be an act of arrogance, a failure to respect the client's status as a moral agent. And if L refused after a full discussion, even though he was convinced that disinheriting the son was proper by the client's moral lights, I would be inclined to see the refusal as an act of intolerance, at least in this instance, since the client's moral lights are as unexceptional as a 60-watt bulb. Moreover, I suspect that many lawyers and non-lawyers would see the matter this way.

As Thomas Shaffer might put the point: the lawyer-client relationship has moral value as a relationship; each party should therefore accept the risk that some actions taken in the name of the relationship will conflict with the moral principles he would apply if acting independently; the opportunity to discuss moral differences and sway one another is a justification for accepting that risk and, ideally, a key point of the relationship; and refusing to carry out a client's wishes where there is a genuine moral disagreement settles things by an exercise of power, not principle. To be sure, this exercise of power may be warranted if a disagreement remains fundamental after the matter has been fully aired. But there will be cases where the lawyer comes to feel that the client's position, though different from his own, is at least morally defensible. Here, in the interest of preserving a valuable relationship, carrying out the client's wishes may give less cause for regret than refusing to do so. Those of us who take this view reject the principle of lawyer Neutrality but still believe the rules of legal ethics are wise not to treat as categorically wrong a lawyer's representation of a client, of whose ends he disapproves.

According to the philosophers, however, the prevailing rules of legal ethics do not just recognize the value of this sort of representation in some cases; they extol its value in all, by proclaiming, for example, that "[h]istory is replete with instances of distinguished and sacrificial services by lawyers who have represented unpopular clients and causes." If the philosophers' reading were correct, one would have to concede that the rules do rest fundamentally on the Neutrality Principle. However, my final criticism of the link the philosophers draw between legal ethics and the pursuit of immoral client aims is that no such concession is in order; the prevailing rules are much more equivocal than the philosophers acknowledge.

The issue of whether to help a client achieve a morally troubling objective can confront a lawyer in three forms: whether to accept a client's case or matter at all; whether, in taking a case, to press the client to accept limits on the objectives to be achieved (even though other lawyers with different values might not do so); and whether to withdraw when the client insists on pursuing an objective the lawyer considers improper.

[T]he Code says that "a lawyer is under no obligation to [represent] every person who may wish to become his client," except in the rare instance in which one is appointed to represent a client who cannot otherwise obtain counsel.[143] True, lawyers are admonished not to turn down a client "lightly," but refusing a case for reasons of conscience hardly seems like whimsy. My Code also says that, except when a matter is pending before a tribunal, a lawyer may withdraw whenever a client "insists . . . that the lawyer engage in conduct that is contrary to the [lawyer's] judgment and advice," and this undoubtedly includes moral judgment and advice. Since most legal tasks do not involve litigation this is a rule of broad application. Finally, although the Code is not explicit on the point, it has been construed to permit a lawyer, at the time he accepts a client, to limit on moral grounds the objectives he will pursue for her.[147]

In short, on any fair inspection the Code leaves considerable room for a lawyer's values to be taken into account, if he is not by circumstance or disposition too "squeamish" to try to hammer out a moral *modus vivendi* with his clients. Concededly, the Code does little to highlight the lawyer's status as a full moral partner and may obscure that status by making some shallow bows in the direction of Neutrality. However, even this will misdescribe the prevailing rules of legal ethics as soon as the Model Rules supplant the Code around the country. The Model Rules openly invite the lawyer to bring his personal values into play. They not only permit him to refuse clients on moral grounds, but give him explicit authority to "limit the objectives of the representation if the client consents after consultation" and to use such limitations to "exclude objectives . . . the lawyer regards as repugnant or imprudent." (This presumably means, for example, that a lawyer who feels strongly that divorcing fathers should never get sole custody of their children may condition his acceptance of a male divorce client on the client's willingness not to seek sole custody.) And in another generous concession to the lawyer's sensibilities, the Model Rules allow withdrawal from any matter in which "a client insists upon pursuing an objective that the lawyer considers repugnant or imprudent," and they allow this (unless a court orders the lawyer to continue) even if the client's interests will be adversely affected.

IV.   CONCLUSION

This Article has attacked the claim that lawyers generally adhere to a Standard Conception of legal ethics which motivates them to act for their clients up to the limits of the law and without regard for the interests of anyone but their clients. The reader who finds my attack convincing may wonder how the philosophers ever came to believe that lawyers share such an ethic. Since some legal scholars hold the same belief, the answer can hardly be that the philosophers have designed the Standard Conception out of whole cloth. Instead, I suspect that philosophers and legal scholars alike have fallen prey to the notion that legal ethics must, as an intellectual field, be dominated by a single overarching theory or set of principles—a paradigm. Unable to define a plausible rival paradigm they have too quickly accepted the evidence that supports the Standard Conception's dominance in legal ethics and too easily

---

[143]ABA Code EC 2–29. See also Wolfram, *A Lawyer's Duty to Represent Clients Repugnant and Otherwise*, in *The Good Lawyer: Lawyers' Roles and Lawyers' Ethics*, supra note 4, at 214, 216–18.

[147] Model Rules Rule 1.2(c) permits this kind of limitation, and the drafters cite the Code's DR 7-101(B)(1) ("lawyer may, where permissible, exercise his professional judgement to waive or fail to assert a right or position of his client") as a comparable provision. Model Rules Rule 1.2(c) comment and code comparison. *Cf.* ABA Comm. on Professional Ethics and Grievances, Formal Op. 90 (1932) (criminal defense attorney may withdraw when client confides that he is guilty, but only if lawyer originally reserved the right to withdraw under these circumstances). This opinion predates the Code, but the Code does not disavow it. Goldman cites the opinion for the bald proposition that a defense lawyer may never withdraw upon learning of a client's guilt and must continue to raise all available defenses. See A. Goldman, supra note 3, at 100.

dismissed the adverse evidence. They have consequently made findings of fact about lawyers' behavior and legal ethics that are no sounder than the findings of any judge who too quickly forms a theory of his case and never really hears the contrary arguments.

One sees this not only in the philosophers' treatment of the Code, as I have already shown, but also in their highly selective references to legal ethics commentators. They love to quote Lord Brougham's intemperate remarks to the effect that an advocate's sole duty is to his client,[155] as if that long-dead English barrister were a central figure in the American bar's living ethical tradition. They often refer to Charles Curtis, a practitioner who argued in the 1950's that disputes are more or less sporting contests in which lawyers should sometimes lie for their clients and should almost never disclose damaging information, since the outcome is of interest only to the parties themselves.[156] And some appear to attribute to the whole profession legal scholar Monroe Freedman's highly controversial view that using perjured testimony for a client is justified whenever a lawyer has learned the testimony will be false through a confidential communication.[157]

The field, however, must be evaluated as a whole. For every Lord Brougham there has been a Louis Brandeis, who believed that lawyers should sometimes think of themselves as "counsel for the situation" rather than try to serve the interests of only one party.[158] For every Charles Curtis there is a Marvin Frankel, an ex-judge who contends that the conduct and results of lawsuits are a matter of public concern and that litigators should be expected to disclose adverse evidence as well as adverse legal authority in the interests of truth.[159] And for every Monroe Freedman there is a John Noonan, who argues that a lawyer's duty of confidentiality must be balanced against the goal of promoting informed judicial decisions and cannot justify the use of perjured testimony.[160]

If Brougham, Curtis and Freedman—the high priests of Neutrality and Partisanship—have found a place in the ABA's ethics codes, so have Brandeis, Frankel and Noonan. If we take the ABA codes as our best evidence of the legal profession's ethical values—a reasonable step since the codes have been the product of broad professional effort[164]—then we must conclude that the philosophers' Standard Conception is really a *mis*conception; for it obscures the vague and often contradictory nature of the field it is meant to illuminate. Whatever may be the case in other fields, legal ethics has no paradigm, only some fragmentary conceptions of the lawyer's role vying inconclusively for dominance[166]—the lawyer as "hired gun," to be sure, but the lawyer also as "officer of the

---

[155.]Lord Brougham said: An advocate, in the discharge of his duty, knows but one person in all the world, and that person is his client. To save that client by all means and expedients, and at all hazards and costs to other persons, and amongst them, to himself, is his first and only duty. . . .

[156.]See Curtis, The Ethics of Advocacy, 4 *Stan. L. Rev.* 3, 8, 17 (1951).

[157]See M. Freedman, supra note 132, at 27–42; Freedman, Professional Responsibility of the Criminal Defense Lawyer: The Three Hardest Questions, 64 *Mich. L. Rev.* 1469, 1475–78 (1966).

[158]See Frank, The Legal Ethics of Louis D. Brandeis, 17 Stan. L. Rev. 683, 698 (1965). A lawyer might serve appropriately as "counsel for the situation," for example, in helping parties put together a business deal or in mediating among a group of creditors who are trying to keep their debtor's business afloat.

[159]See Frankel, The Search for Truth: An Umpireal View, 123 *U. Pa. L. Rev.* 1031, 1055–59 (1975).

[160]Noonan, supra note 111, at 1487. See also Ordover, The Lawyer as Liar, 2 *Am. J. Trial Advoc.* 305 (1979).

[164]Philosopher Lisa Newton, however, makes the intriguing argument that professional ethics codes are really addressed to the public rather than the members of a profession, tend to express values the profession believes the public will accept, and are not reliable evidence of the profession's own ethical views. Newton, supra note 119, at 34.

[166]Cf. Greenbaum supra note 98, at 627 (finding two contradictory lawyering models running through the legal ethics literature—a "client-oriented" and a "public interest" model); D'Amato & Eberle, Three Models of Legal Ethics 27 *St. Louis U.L.J.* 761, 761–63 (1983) (noting that most scholarly analysis of legal ethics is built on either an "autonomy" model or an opposing "socialist" model of professional responsibility, and calling for the recognition of a "deontological" third model that may explain certain anomolies in the field).

court," "counsel for the situation," "friend," "minister," and so forth. As a result the organized bar, for all its attention to ethics rules, has been able to do very little "predetermining" of the individual lawyer's responsibilities, at least when it comes to reconciling his duties to clients and to third parties.

This is not to suggest that the legal profession is already in the best of all ethical worlds or that moral philosophers have nothing to contribute to legal ethics. On the contrary, the philosophers' contribution has been significant and should become more so once they abandon their mistaken empirical assumptions. As I noted at the outset, most of their criticisms of a "hired-gun" ethic—an ethic built on Neutrality and Partisanship—are well-founded. The criticisms have also been worth making, since *some* lawyers are surely animated by that ethic, even if it is not nearly as pervasive or constraining as the philosophers suppose. For the same reason, the philosophers could profitably explore and criticize other broad conceptions of the lawyer's role—the lawyer as state functionary or "officer of the court," for example.

Philosophers can also help lawyers to look at some of the narrower issues in legal ethics from a fresh perspective. One such issue pits the inviolability of client confidences against the protection of third parties by blowing the whistle on a client who plans to commit a crime. The pertinent provision in the ABA's new Model Rules, Rule 1.6(b)(1), goes to the extreme of forbidding the disclosure of any information related to the representation of a client, except as needed to prevent the client from committing a crime likely to involve "imminent death or substantial bodily harm," in which case the lawyer may, but need not, tell somebody what she knows. (Thus, a divorce lawyer cannot warn anyone that her client plans to "snatch" his children, and a corporate lawyer may do no more than withdraw in an effort to prevent his client from defrauding hundreds of investors, even when the lawyer has inadvertently aided the client's

scheme.)[168] In contrast, the Code,[169] the preliminary versions of the Model Rules,[170] and the Model Rules as adopted so far by the state supreme courts all give the client's interest in confidentiality much less protection.

As the bar's flip-flops suggest, lawyers have not achieved a stable consensus on the issue. They debate the matter endlessly, but the debate has become stale. Defenders of Rule 1.6(b)(1) say it will encourage clients to be candid, thereby giving lawyers a chance to discourage them from committing crimes, and thus protect the public (a rationale, notice, that emphasizes third-party, not client, interests). Opponents claim the rule will have no such effect, and that if it did, then the last crimes lawyers should be allowed to warn people about may be precisely the serious, violent ones the rule lets them disclose. Defenders say that by promoting candid lawyer-client communications Rule 1.6(b)(1) at least helps to ensure that clients receive effective legal assistance. Opponents reply that a client's criminal plans are rarely the sort of information a lawyer

---

[168]But a lawyer may in withdrawing make public the fact of his withdrawal and "disaffirm any opinion [or] document" he prepared for the client. Model Rules Rule 1.6 comment. See also Rotunda, The Notice of Withdrawal and the New Model Rules of Professional Conduct: Blowing the Whistle and Waving the Red Flag, 63 *Or. L. Rev.* 455 (1984).

[169]The Code permits a lawyer to reveal "the intention of his client to commit a[ny] crime and the information necessary to prevent the crime." ABA Code DR 4-101(C)(3).

[170]The first published version of the Model Rules *required* disclosure of confidential information to the extent "necessary to prevent the client from committing an act that would result in death or serious bodily harm" and permitted disclosure when "necessary to prevent . . . a deliberately wrongful act by the client." ABA Comm. on Evaluation of Professional Standards, Model Rules of Professional Conduct Rule 1.7 (Discussion Draft 1980). A later version permitted disclosures when necessary "to prevent the client from committing a criminal or fraudulent act that the lawyer believes is likely to result in death or substantial bodily harm, or substantial injury to the financial interest or property of another." ABA Comm. on Evaluation of Professional Standards, Model Rules of Professional Conduct Rule 1.6(b)(2) (Proposed Final Draft 1981).

needs in order to give effective assistance and that in any event we should not be so solicitous of clients as to make effective assistance of counsel entail a vow of silence about their illicit plans.

Issues are thus joined but not resolved. Nor are things likely to be resolved without an infusion of fresh approaches from outside the legal profession: efforts, for example,to compare the values at stake in defining norms of secrecy for lawyers and for others,[174] as well as inquiries into the source of the client's interest in lawyer secrecy (Is it grounded on some inherent feature of legal services, or simply on traditional lawyer assurances of confidentiality?). These are

topics moral philosophers seem eminently qualified to address.

Of course, it would also help to have some empirical data on the effects of various confidentiality rules on lawyer-client communication. And this brings me to my final point. I have argued that when lawyers unduly favor their clients at the expense of third parties (or vice-versa) they often do so because of financial, psychological or organizational pressures and not because of professional ethics. Simply tinkering with ethics rules, or even with lawyers' moral sensibilities, may not effectively counter these pressures. The legal profession therefore needs the sustained attention not only of moral philosophers but of social scientists and journalists as well. We need studies of the constraints and incentives that operate on lawyers in various settings and of measures that might be taken to alter those constraints and incentives.

---

[174]For a comprehensive survey of secrecy norms and their rationales in professional, business, military and other settings, see S. Bok, *Secrets: On the Ethics of Concealment and Revelation* (1983).

Do Criminal Defendants Have Too Many Rights?

Professor Akhil Reed Amar vs. Johnnie J. Cochran, Jr.
Moderated By: Nina Totenberg

Stephanie Pickels: I am pleased to introduce tonight Professor Akhil Reed Amar, the Southmayd Professor of Law at Yale Law School. Professor Amar is a leading scholar and prolific

Akhil Amar and Johnnie Cochran, "Do Criminal Defendants Have too Many Rights?" *American Criminal Law Review* Volume 33, (1996): 1193–1218. Reprinted with permission of the publisher, Georgetown University and *American Criminal Law Review.* © 1996. (This version has been edited.)

writer in the fields of constitutional law, criminal procedure, American legal history, and federal jurisdiction. He is the author of more than forty articles in leading law reviews, including over a dozen lead articles on topics covering everything from voting rights and affirmative action to the Vice Presidency and Presidential succession.

Professor Amar is what we would affectionately call a hot-shot. After graduating *summa cum laude* from Yale College in 1980, Professor Amar received his law degree from Yale Law School in 1984. Following a clerkship with then Judge

Steven Breyer, Professor Amar went on to become the second youngest scholar in history to receive an endowed Chair at Yale. In addition to delivering endowed lectures at fifteen universities in the last five years, Professor Amar was awarded the 1993 Paul M. Bator Award of the Federalist Society and was named one of the *National Law Journal's* forty rising stars in the law in 1995. Given such impressive credentials, it would be easy to cast Professor Amar as locked away in an intellectual ivory tower.

However, it is important to note that Professor Amar's influence extends beyond the academic world and into real life. At the request of Senator Hatch, he recently testified before the Senate Judiciary Committee on the Crime Bill and the exclusionary rule. The popular media has sought his opinions and comments on a variety of issues, including recent Supreme Court rulings, challenges by the gun lobby and the Tennessee Militia to interpretations of the Second Amendment, and even the O. J. Simpson case. He has appeared on PBS, NPR, C-SPAN, and MTV, and has contributed to many magazines and newspapers, including *The Washington Post*, *The New Republic*, *Washington Monthly*, and the *Policy Review.*

The New Yorker has recognized him as a leader of the "truth school" in criminal procedure—a position which, among other things, asserts that constitutional protection of the guilty should come only as an incidental by-product of protection of the innocent. To put it another way, although the guilty will often have the same rights as the innocent, they should never have more, and never because they are guilty. Professor Amar is the author of the forthcoming book from Yale University Press entitled *The Constitution and Criminal Procedure—First Principles*, and we are honored to have him with us tonight. Clem.

Clem Turner: You may think that the next man to speak at this podium needs no introduction. Referred to succinctly as "The Man" by commentators on the O.J. Simpson trial, Johnnie Cochran's name is practically a household word. You've read about him in many publications, such as *Ebony*, *The New Yorker*, *Time*, and *Newsweek.* You have seen him on *20/20*, *The Evening News with Dan Rather*, *Nightline*, and *Good Morning*

America, to name a few. His list honors includes being cited in the Fifth Edition of the *Best Lawyers of America*. He was voted Attorney of the Year by the Los Angeles Trial Lawyers' Association, and Civil Rights Lawyer of the Year by the Los Angeles Chapter of the NAACP. His client list reads like Who's Who in Los Angeles and includes Michael Jackson, Eddie Murphy Productions, and Jim Brown.

However, there is a lesser-known side of Johnnie Cochran—a firm believer that injustice anywhere is a threat to justice everywhere. Mr. Cochran has always fought for fameless people who don't sing, dance, or score touchdowns. In one of his landmark cases, Mr. Cochran won a large jury award for a little girl who was the victim of grievous sexual misconduct by a police officer. In another case, police insisted that a student athlete arrested for a traffic violation had committed suicide in his cell. Mr. Cochran forced another inquest, which revealed that the boy's death was at the hands of another—probably a police chokehold. Cases like these, as well as his own experience as a victim of an illegal traffic search in 1979, have shown Mr. Cochran that it is always necessary to question the official version of events, and have caused him to champion the rights of defendants who have no one else to speak for them.

His current clients include the families of the 300 Oklahoma City bombing victims and 2,000 to 3,000 Black residents of Bogalusa, Louisiana, whose land and health has been affected by a toxic spill. Furthermore, his commitment to those less fortunate extends beyond his legal practice. Acts, such as establishing a low-income housing complex in South Central Los Angeles and creating a scholarship for African-Americans at UCLA, his alma mater, earned him the prestigious Golden Bell Award for community service in 1994. Johnnie Cochran is motivated by the premise that one man can make a difference in this world, and you need only look at his life to see that this is true. Mike.

Michael Carroll: It's my pleasure to introduce our moderator for tonight, Nina Totenberg. Ms. Totenberg is the award-winning journalist for National Public Radio. She is the Legal Affairs Correspondent and also a correspondent for

ABC's program, *Nightline.* As one of the most respected journalists in Washington, Ms. Totenberg is well known for her coverage of the Supreme Court and the Supreme Court nomination process. It was Ms. Totenberg who first reported on Anita Hill's allegations of sexual harassment during the confirmation hearings of Clarence Thomas. It was Ms. Totenberg who first reported on Judge Douglas Ginsberg's marijuana use during his youth.

Nina Totenberg is both a reporter and a media personality in her own right. One of her colleagues at NPR described her as "a character with a lot of character," and the editors of *Esquire* twice named her as one of the "Women We Love." Ms. Totenberg brings with her tonight the perspective developed from covering the Supreme Court for more than twenty years. During that time, she has reported on the Court as it has struggled with many of the issues that will be debated here tonight, and we are very pleased that Ms. Totenberg could be here with us tonight. At this point I'd like to ask her to take over and tell us about tonight's topic. Please welcome Nina Totenberg.

Nina Totenberg: Thank you, folks. I also bring you the perspective of somebody who never went to law school and doesn't have a college degree. So with that caveat, we are blessed this evening by having two great debaters and a subject that increasingly has become the focus of debate from the living room to the law schools all over the country. The debate, of course, is not entirely new. Judges, lawyers, and politicians have for the last half century been debating whether criminals or accused criminals have too many rights. Justice Benjamin Cardozo, before he was a Justice, as all law students know, is the author of the famous phrase "the criminal is to go free because the constable blundered"—a principle that Chief Justice Warren Burger and others would later call "handcuffing the police."

Of late, critics of the criminal justice system have come to focus not just on the exclusionary rule, but also on the way juries are selected, and even on the hallowed Fifth Amendment and how far it should go. This evening we are going to divide our debate into these three controversies, starting with jury selection.

They have given me three minutes for my overview, but you don't want to hear me anyway. So, I will tell you I will not give you a big broad overview like that. I will tell you that last night I had occasion to be talking to Judge Abner Mikva, the former Chief Judge of the U.S. Court of Appeals here in Washington, who resigned to become White House Counsel, and I told him that I was moderating this debate and that the debaters were Akhil Amar and Johnnie Cochran. Judge Mikva remarked with a grin, "Sounds pretty boring to me. What do they have to disagree about?"

"Everything," I said, "starting with Amar's opposition to the exclusionary rule."

And Mikva looked at me and said, "Is that the Akhil Amar that I know, the young guy at Yale, the one who used to be a law clerk?"

"Yeah," I said, and I noted that Amar recently testified before the Senate Judiciary Committee in support of Senator Hatch's bill doing away with the exclusionary rule.

"Hmmm," said Judge Mikva, "times really have changed."

So, with that, let me introduce Akhil Amar for a two-minute overview of the subject for tonight, "Do accused criminals have too many rights?" The debaters don't have a lot of rights, because I've got the stopwatch. Two minutes, Professor Amar.

Akhil Amar: Thank you, Nina. So, the short answer is yes, sometimes they do. The longer, more precise answer is: and often they don't. Most precisely still, they have the wrong kind of rights. We have rights right now that often benefit the guilty without helping the innocent and that indeed sometimes make the innocent worse off. Judge Mikva notwithstanding, I still count myself a liberal and I think liberals should really care about protecting innocent people from erroneous conviction, but the current rules that we have often make their plight worse in order to help guilty people escape conviction.

So, let's just take the Fourth, Fifth, and Sixth Amendments in sort of constitutional order. Fourth Amendment. The exclusionary rule basically says (and Judge Cardozo was actually an opponent of it, interestingly, that phrase was meant to deride the rule a bit) if the cops find extremely reliable evidence, the exclusionary rule says sometimes we toss that out even though it can help us get at the truth. That's a great rule if you happen to be guilty because the more evidence the cops find, the more they exclude, the more you benefit. It doesn't help you at all, of course, if they don't find any reliable evidence against you, if you are innocent—if they know you are innocent, if they just want to hassle you because of your race or your sex or your politics.

The exclusionary rule is upside down. It protects the guilty and it doesn't protect the innocent at all, and worse, it actually often leads judges to constrict the scope of the Fourth Amendment right. If we have to exclude, we'll deny the Fourth Amendment was violated—see Judge Baer—and what that means is innocent people are worse off because we have a narrow Fourth Amendment. Okay, Fourth.

Fifth Amendment self-incrimination. Right now, when Ollie North is forced to testify, if he confesses that he embezzled $50,000 and the gold bars are in his garage with his fingerprints on them, we can't introduce it at trial; if he was obliged to tell the truth before a hearing outside of the jury's earshot, we can't introduce the confession. That might make some sense—maybe he was innocent but he had a slip of the tongue, as one of us might have tonight. But we also exclude the reliable, physical evidence—the gold bars with fingerprints on them—and that's a mistake that doesn't help innocent people at all and in fact makes them worse off because of the current Fifth Amendment rules in place. Under these rules, if you are innocent and you know who did it, right now you're not able to force that guilty person to take the stand because of that person's overly broad Fifth Amendment immunity. I'll explain how that works a little bit later.

Finally, for the Sixth Amendment, how we pick juries. Right now, we let the parties pick, and we let the parties often sort of stack the jury using race and all sorts of other things, even though they try to deny that that's what they are doing, but they are trying to manipulate jury composition. This may help some guilty defendants go free, with a designer jury, but it also means the defendants are doing this with jury consultants, but so are the prosecutors. Having

the prosecutors manipulate the system with peremptory challenges ends up hurting innocent defendants too. So, in all these cases, it's upside down. We have too many rights for guilty defendants and not enough for innocent defendants. How did I do on time?

Nina Totenberg: Before the O.J. Simpson trial I, quite frankly, only knew about Johnnie Cochran sort of vaguely by reputation. But I remember early, before the trial really had begun, I was chatting with a lawyer friend who handles only first degree murder cases, and we were speculating about who would take the lead role in the trial. And I remember very clearly her saying that it would be Cochran, if O.J. wants to win, she said. I raised an eyebrow. "Just wait and see," she said. I waited, I saw, and so did the rest of the country. So, to rebut Akhil Amar, Mr. Cochran.

Johnnie Cochran: Thank you and good evening to everyone. I've been a criminal defense attorney for almost thirty-three years. During this time I've fought and spent time in the trenches trying to give a life to the principles of justice outlined in the Constitution. It is one thing to sit in an ivory tower and, pipe in mouth, textbook in hand, to think about some of the drastic changes that have come about in our system of justice. It is quite another to truly appreciate and understand that judges are human, police officers sometimes lie, innocent people are sometimes charged with crimes.

That many of these people are often poor, black, brown adds yet another dimension to the complexity of ensuring that justice is truly for all in this great country. When the question is posed—"Do criminal defendants have too many rights?"—what really is being asked is, "Do guilty people have too many rights?" Implicit in the original question is the latent belief that this generic criminal defendant is really a guilty heathen hiding behind our Constitution. It was written really to protect innocent people, not guilty ones. But the Constitution bestows its protections upon all American citizens, and the only way that you and I can be assured of a fair trial is if every citizen in this land is assured of his or her right to a fair trial.

Our system of justice demands that all persons charged with a crime be presumed innocent.

Since that is so, and surely no one here would argue against that, do innocent people charged with crimes have too many rights? This is the real question, because while you may guarantee that you will not commit a crime, you cannot guarantee that you will not someday be charged with a crime. If you were charged with a crime in this country, or if your mother or your father or your sister or your brother were charged with a crime, wouldn't you want every protection afforded you by the Constitution, or would you feel then that you have too many rights?

The short answer is that criminal defendants do not have too many rights. This is a system that has worked well. As we talk about this tonight, I hope that will become abundantly clear to you. During the Simpson trial we talked a lot about a rush to judgment. H. L. Menken once said that for every problem, there is an obvious solution that is quick, easy, and wrong. Just as in the Simpson case, I caution again tonight against this rush to judgment in seeking solutions after the verdict to perceive problems by solutions that many times will only compound those problems. Thank you.

Nina Totenberg: Alright, now, we have picked three basic topics, and I'm allowed to interrupt anytime I feel like it. We are going to divide it into thirteen-minute segments. The first one is about the jury. Should lawyers, through peremptory challenges, essentially pick jurors? Why don't you start, Professor Amar?

Akhil Amar: Thanks. I believe in the Constitution. I've studied it for the last ten years. I admit it's been in an ivory tower. On the other hand, I don't make any money off the system one way or the other, and so I try to call it as I see it.

And I might be wrong, but the ideas should just stand or fall, I think, on their own merit, rather than on where the ideas come from, whether they come from the ivory tower or someone else. I always thought that these ideas came from the Constitution itself. They come from England. So, I want to persuade you that there's nothing wrong with our Constitution, it doesn't need amending at all. I do think that some of our interpretations have been erroneous.

Now, the Supreme Court is clear that there is no Constitutional right to peremptory challenges.

The lawyers don't have to have a right to design or pick the jury. And some of our greatest civil libertarians have been really concerned about peremptory challenges because they allow lawyers to use race and sex and religion and other factors to try to manipulate jury composition. The great Thurgood Marshall opposed peremptory challenges precisely because he thought it enabled lawyers and jury consultants and all the rest to rig the system.

Here's the fundamental constitutional idea—and England does this today—and it's the idea, I think, at the heart of the Bill of Rights. The jury should represent the people, not the parties. Juries should represent public justice. So, the way they do it in England is they pick their petit juries very similar to the way they pick their grand jurors. You know, the defendant doesn't get to hand-pick the grand jury, he doesn't get to hand-pick the judge who tries the case, or the legislature that passes the law, or the appellate court that rules finally. And neither does the prosecutor. Basically, those institutions are picked by the people. So, in England, basically, voters names are put into a drum, they pull out twelve. If you are a friend of one of the parties, if you're the brother-in-law, you're excluded in the same way that you would have to recuse yourself as a judge, but otherwise you sit in judgment, and the jury looks like America, not like the plaintiff, not like the defendant.

Johnnie Cochran: Well, I think—and I'm glad the Professor mentioned England, because I recently was in England, and many of the lawyers there are chaffing at the bit at the unfairness of this system of randomly picking individuals—to suggest that juries should be selected randomly is to ignore the complexities of a multiracial society. We live in America, a melting pot. I don't think that Professor Amar would quarrel with the fact that if there were twelve members of the KKK and a black defendant—you want those first twelve people? That's why we have voir dire. That's why we probe their minds.

Now certainly there have been abuses throughout, but the peremptory challenges allow you to exclude those people where the judge denies a challenge for cause. I believe, quite frankly, that the challenges for cause should be expanded. Again, leaving the ivory tower and going into the practicalities, you have people from all walks of life, and they bring biases into that courtroom, civil or criminal. And so when they bring their biases in there, what you want, Professor Amar, is a fair trial.

For a litigant who's been waiting two or three years for his day in court, or whose life hangs in the balance, who could quarrel about that? One of the fairest things that Judge Ito did in the Simpson case was allow the lawyers an opportunity in this important case to query these jurors where there's so much publicity in the case. Everybody has an opinion. You need to ferret out that. Just take the first twelve? Let me tell you, that's part and parcel of a thought that you have this guilty heathen defendant. It doesn't make any difference . . .

Nina Totenberg: Professor Amar, do you envision questioning of jurors, after they are randomly selected, to see if there are biases?

Akhil Amar: Well, of course you have to have challenges for cause, just like you have . . .

Nina Totenberg: But I asked you, do you envision questioning jurors? Lawyers questioning jurors?

Akhil Amar: Well, that's a different question. For example, lawyers don't always have to do the questioning, judges can do the questioning. And so, you have to make sure that they don't know the brother and they're not friends with the brother-in-law . . .

Nina Totenberg: Or that they're a member of the KKK?

Akhil Amar: Well, I wouldn't want members of the NAACP excluded from some white racist defendant's trial. I basically think, ordinarily, we don't exclude grand jurors or judges because they happen to have a race. Everyone does. Or a sex, or a political affiliation. We trust the jury basically, and the Simpson case, of course, is unusual in the amount of publicity. Here's a grand jury. It sits and it issues multiple indictments over a whole range of cases . . .

Nina Totenberg: But nobody goes to jail because of what happens in a grand jury.

Akhil Amar: Well, when a grand jury indicts you, you are subject to great anxiety. It's a huge event in your life. You're . . .

Nina Totenberg: But you're not going to lose your liberty yet.

Johnnie Cochran: That'll be later.

Nina Totenberg: Mr. Cochran, would you trust a judge to do the questioning for you?

Johnnie Cochran: Absolutely not. Again, in practicality, the problem is the judge is basically out of practice. Let me tell you what the real world is like. The judge is sitting there and he's worried about his next case. This is your litigant's one day in court. You know the facts. The judge will ask a generic question, he's sitting in an elevated or she's sitting in an elevated position, jurors will say what the judge wants to hear, he moves on. He doesn't follow up. He doesn't find out anything that way. The lawyer has an interest in his case and you've got to be about that.

Let me just tell you a question that I ask always in these cases to determine the mindset of a juror: Would you be comfortable being tried by a person in your present frame of mind? And that's what you're looking at. We're not trying to carve out any boutique jury. You're trying to get some people who say they can be fair. And even with that, they don't always tell you the truth. But certainly the judge, his interest is, "Let's move this case along, I've got this heavy calendar, I've got things to do"—and you move along.

So you look at this from a practical standpoint. This is a system that has worked, and worked very, very well. If there are abuses, what the judge will do is to sit down with the lawyers and say, "Look, I want you to submit those questions, I want to see no running afield, don't ask the same questions over and over again, don't do such and such . . ."

That's alright. But to take away the right and say that you're going to accept questioning by the judge is to bury your head in the sand. The last thing I'd like to say if I could, is that I don't think you can very well equate the KKK with the NAACP.

Nina Totenberg: Would you be so anxious to be asking a lot of questions of jurors, and would you be so excited by the notion of random selection of jurors if there was a universal ban on jury consultants and you couldn't use them at all?

Johnnie Cochran: No, I'd still want to do that. The Simpson case is the first time in thirty-three years that I used a jury consultant. Normally you use your own visceral reaction or gut reaction, how you feel about this person when they look you in the eye, and that's really the question. You want to find out, "Can my client receive a fair trial?" That's all you're really asking. And how bad is that? But people bring biases, and this is a realization. You see, what I believe, and rooted in what the Professor has told us, is that we start off believing these defendants are guilty, so why do we need a trial? Pretty soon we could put it in the computer and have it spew out . . .

Akhil Amar: Hang on.

Johnnie Cochran: It's truth that we're talking about, and I don't want to do that, you know.

Akhil Amar: I don't remotely believe that. That's such a straw-man argument. Now here's the point. Okay, first of all, if this is so bad, then Thurgood Marshall was crazy and England is crazy and the Supreme Court has been crazy when it says there's no Constitutional right to this at all. Now, I understand that the lawyers want to manipulate the system. They like to pick, because that gives them a lot more power. I'm not sure, though, that the American people are well served by that kind of manipulation.

The point is if it's peremptory, peremptory means never having to say you're sorry, never having to explain it. So if *you* can exclude someone peremptorily, the problem is so can the prosecutor, and the prosecutor can exclude someone because she's a member of the NAACP. With peremptories, both sides use them to manipulate and create unrepresentative juries that don't look like the people. We want our juries to be representative of the society.

Johnnie Cochran: No, I don't think you could peremptorily excuse someone because they belong to the NAACP. I don't think you go with that. In fact, if you excuse a juror . . .

Akhil Amar: You don't have to explain!

Johnnie Cochran: Oh yes, you do.

Nina Totenberg: You do. Yeah, you do.

Johnnie Cochran: In California, you do have to explain. This is the reality.

Akhil Amar: You have to explain that you're not doing it because of someone's race, but if you say it's because of their attitude, it's because they looked at me the right way, they didn't look at me in the eye, they looked the other way.

Johnnie Cochran: Let me give you an example, Professor, again. Let me return to the reality of the courtroom. When the prosecutors in the Simpson case excused—ten of the eleven first challenges were black people. I started at the second challenging them. And that's why they finally stopped because, you're right, they have to make up reasons. The prosecutors can't say they excused someone because they're black because they can't do that under *Batson* and in California under *Wheeler*.

But you stop them every time—they become offended—but you stop and so they say, "Well, I didn't like the way she looked at me." And you are absolutely right. Where there are abuses, the judge can stop it.

I had a case where there were two blacks on a panel, and the prosecutors excused both blacks, and the judge stopped it under a *Wheeler* motion in California. He brought a new panel from downtown to Torrence. And that's what you have to have . . .

Akhil Amar: And lots of judges don't. With peremptory challenges, it's just a loaded gun. Again, lots of prosecutors in lots of other courtrooms with different judges get away with that all the time.

Johnnie Cochran: But the idea is that you've got to have a fair shot at this. You've got to understand and look at it from a standpoint that racism is endemic in the system. If we lived in a perfect society where people didn't bring these biases, then so be it. We could just have this underway. But people bring their biases in. Just as this is . . .

Akhil Amar: Then let's have them cancel out in a conversation around the jury room where we have black and white and brown and yellow and red and male and female and all religions and all classes together. That's America.

Johnnie Cochran: That would be nice, Professor, except the jury panel doesn't look like that. The jury panels are chosen from voters, and you take an area, even in Los Angeles, you have a jury panel that looks like it's 70% or 80% white; very, very few Hispanics, very few blacks. It doesn't work that way. And with a few peremptory challenges, unless you can really force their hand, you're not going to get that jury you're talking about.

Akhil Amar: Well, if the panel is mainly white, here's the real problem. If each side has an equal number of peremptory challenges, and the prosecutor is looking to exclude the minorities, and there are fewer of them in the pool, this is a pro-prosecution device in a lot of situations, and that's why Thurgood Marshall opposed peremptory challenges.

Nina Totenberg: There's nothing in the law that says jurors have to be from the voting rolls, and in some places, many places, they're not.

Johnnie Cochran: In California they are, and they don't have to be, but generally that's a good way of certainly picking them in California. I think that Professor Amar and I might agree with what we'd like to see in the end result. I just . . . My practice tells me you're never going to get that. Let me just talk about this area.

A trial really isn't so much the search for truth. The great Clarence Darrow, hero of many, once said that a courtroom is not a place where truth and innocence inevitably triumph. It is only an arena where contending lawyers fight not for justice, but to win. Now he said that long before Professor Amar and I came on the scene. This was years and years ago that he said that. These lawyers are there trying to win. Now, it's nice to have this truth, but in the courtroom you're not going to have the same level of truth that you have in a scientific lab. We're going to have to talk about that somewhere along the way. We may not disagree about the end result, it's how we get there. The judge is not going to help you get there. You know your case best, you know which jurors are going to best help you do that. That's what gives confidence to the system. If you bring . . .

Akhil Amar: Even if it's not true.

Johnnie Cochran: I think that's what gives confidence. If you bring citizens in who are set up to lose—who never think they can get justice—believe me, your way is going to make the system a lot worse. And we have seen that in Los Angeles.

Nina Totenberg: Mr. Cochran, most of the jury studies that have been done do not bear out trial lawyers' contentions that their tummy instincts are right. Their tummy instincts are frequently wrong.

Johnnie Cochran: Sometimes they are, but you know, after thirty-three years you get a pretty good feeling about people. I'll still put my tummy instincts up against these consultants and others, because, you know, in the final analysis, you look back over your career and certainly sometimes you've been wrong, but by in large, what you feel about a person will generally carry the day.

Akhil Amar: But let's talk about these prosecutors' tummy instincts that blacks think a certain way and Jews think a certain way and women think a certain way. The problem isn't just one person's tummy instincts, it's that there are two sides here, both trying to manipulate the system, and the people get cut out of the process. And I understand why lawyers do this—it's lucrative, it gives them a lot more control over the whole proceeding. But I'm not sure that it's conducive to truth or democracy or a sense of public confidence that public justice is done in public courtrooms.

Johnnie Cochran: May I ask you this: In any court in this country, you can take the same facts and go into one courtroom and get one result. You can go right next door with the same facts and get a directly opposite outcome, and that's the way the system has always worked. You know, being an advocate means you're doing the best you can for your client. That's all we're talking about. This isn't like some lottery, we just go in there and say, "Let's just take the first twelve that are randomly picked." These people bring their biases, some don't want to be there. You know, that's unspeakable or unthinkable that you would go along and do that and rely upon the judge who wants to finish this case and get to the next case.

Akhil Amar: England has thought it and done it.

Johnnie Cochran: England is changing. I want you to know, Professor, they are now asking for diversity in jurors because they said it is unfair for the people who formerly served as colonists, the people who were the colonizing ones, to have all the power and sit on juries. I just came back from there, and I've seen it. And the whole world is going to change. The view you're talking about would be a nice view in another time and place, but this is a new world now, and people now want some fundamental fairness. If they don't get that, it causes a lot of unrest. And that's not what we want in our law. We want a system where there's not unrest and chaos. We want law and order, not anarchy.

Nina Totenberg: Well, my unrest is to move on to the next subject. And the subject is the exclusionary rule. As far as I know, I don't think evidence was ever excluded, certainly in this country, until about 1886. But the notion, the concept of the exclusionary rule, at least in the federal system, goes back to 1914 in the *Weeks* case. That's a very long time ago. Almost a century ago.

No judge has ever liked the rule particularly. Not even Chief Justice Earl Warren or Justice William J. Brennan, but they finally came to the conclusion that it was the only effective tool to sort of knock upside the head the police and get their attention so that they wouldn't engage in police misconduct, that there was no reward for police misconduct, and that the only way to get there was to throw out the evidence. Now, Professor Amar thinks that's an unfortunate conclusion for the courts to have reached, and I would like you, Professor Amar, to tell us why you think that damage suits, in place of the exclusionary rule, are a real-life option.

Akhil Amar: Two things that I agree with: no court in America for the first hundred years ever excluded evidence. The Framers—none of them believed in exclusion. England has never had exclusion in two hundred years; Canada didn't until 1985, and they have a much more modest version. The Supreme Court has recently, I think, made it clear that exclusion is not constitutionally required. If you have a real substitute that protects the Fourth Amendment, and England has

been based on that and so was the Fourth Amendment, then exclusion isn't required.

Now exclusion can never be your sole mechanism, because too many times the cops are going to do things that don't lead to evidence, but they're abusive. They punch people in the nose. They do chokeholds in Los Angeles—and I'm sure Johnnie Cochran will agree with me—and there's nothing to exclude. You've got to have damage remedies; when they whup Rodney King upside the head, there's nothing to exclude in that case. So, for better or worse, you're going to have to have a damage system with punitive damages for outrageous conduct and the like to protect all the innocent people in the world.

The cops actually, even with the exclusionary rule, benefit tremendously. They've always, for two hundred years, been able to introduce the evidence in a civil case against the target or in a criminal case against someone other than the party searched. They get to keep the drugs (which is a lot of money); they can sell them for medicinal uses, they can return . . . This is big bucks, people! They can return stolen goods to their rightful owners, even without exclusion. So, we have all of that right now. Exclusion could never be the only or the sole mechanism.

Now, what has happened in the last century, as courts built up exclusion, is they whittled away damage schemes, punitive damages, administrative sanctions, and the like, that would have protected all these innocent folks. And, we need to bring those back and, in fact, the Hatch Bill does do that, and I applaud it for that. I'm a liberal Democrat, but this is great for civil libertarians to give us something that we haven't had before, which is the ability to be free of governmental immunity. There are all sorts of technical immunities of government and of individuals that are preventing recovery for people who have been abused.

Johnnie Cochran: I think that our courts for some time have recognized that the exclusionary rule is an important tool to prevent rampant police overreaching and police misconduct. Without the threat of some serious sanctions for the violation of basic Fourth Amendment rights, no citizen would be safe from unbridled police actions;

we would move toward a police state. However distasteful the thought—and let's not dance around it tonight—there's some law enforcement officers who would be willing to corrupt the process to convict defendants whom they feel are guilty anyway, including by manufacturing evidence. The exclusionary rule provides protection against that potential abuse.

So, the one thing that the Professor forgets is that there are times police officers plant evidence. So, when that happens, an illegal search and seizure, it's not going to help. This man's in prison for thirty years under the federal sentencing guidelines; that doesn't help. So again, you've got to look at the realities of what happens out there in the streets when the ends justify the means. You've got to look at that—and all of us then are less safe. And so it's easy to say, well, it's just, you know, only innocent people should be worried about this. Well, I think it protects equally the guilty and the innocent.

We don't start again on the premise that most people are guilty. The Constitution was set up in a way that protected all of us, and so I feel real strongly that in our justice system, the exclusionary rule plays a very, very important role. The Fourth Amendment has been very, very effective and good. Sure, it's been chipped away, and clearly it will continue to be chipped away. But we need this. We don't want a police state under the guise that we live, and we have these heathen defendants out there who should've all been taken away, and we need to take whatever is illegally seized. Some of the things seized have been planted by the police. That does in fact happen.

In the real world we have to be mindful of that and stop tiptoeing around. And the other thing—and I agree with the Professor about this—is that there is too much looking away that corrupts the process. Judges will sit there and see police officers lie to establish probable cause, and you know what? They look the other way. The best example of this is the embarrassing situation of Judge Baer recently in New York City. That is an embarrassment for all of us; and none of us want to see that, neither Professor Amar nor myself, but this happens. You have this lying and this corrupting.

In the Simpson case, some people said that only two people in America thought that the

police went there to save lives and look for O.J. Simpson and notify him regarding his ex-wife's death—and that was Judge Kathleen Kennedy Powell and Judge Lance Ito. They were the only two—the rest of us knew that was an illegal search and seizure.

Nina Totenberg: Mr. Cochran, you concede that judges look the other way.

Johnnie Cochran: Yes.

Nina Totenberg: Anybody who's spent any time in criminal courts knows that there are terms of art even for the way police deal with evidence. Things like "dropsy"; you say they dropped the drugs if that's what you need to do; you say they picked up the drugs if that's what you need to do. If you're really not protected by the exclusionary rule because the police have come up with all kinds of artifices to get around it when they need to, and judges have come up with all kinds of artifices to get around it when they need to, doesn't that mean that the rule has failed?

Johnnie Cochran: No, I don't think so. I think we need better judges. Judges who have some integrity, who'll stand up. And you're absolutely right. When the Supreme Court came down and said that if you could stop a defendant where you saw him making a furtive move or the so-called "dropsy" cases, the numbers in New York City went from like 14% before to 50%. In California, when the Supreme Court said that if you smelled ether from a PCP lab, with every case, the police officer driving down the street would smell ether from the middle of the street—that's what happens. Yet the judges look the other way.

It's all because of this mentality in this country. You are presumed to be innocent, and we've got to get ahold of that. What we ought to be debating tonight is what's happened to this country—in the interest of putting everybody in jail, we've gone far too far. It seems to me we ought to be talking about that and a better caliber of judge who's going to be honest and upright in what they're doing, rather than passing a litmus test to see who can be the toughest on anybody charged with a crime.

Nina Totenberg: Professor Amar, how would your idea really concretely work? And let me just follow that up by saying, most times—if I walk out of here tonight and I'm strip searched by a policeman on the street, and I sue him, the likelihood is he doesn't have a lot of money for me to get, and that's not really a huge deterrent. When, was the *Bivens* case?

Akhil Amar: 1973.

Nina Totenberg: I wrote a story as a young journalist saying—I hate to admit I was around then, but I was—this would open the door, provide a new remedy. Warren Burger proclaimed it as a new era in the criminal law. It ain't happened.

Akhil Amar: Great. Two thoughts: First, here's why the exclusionary rule is affirmatively bad, and second, here's why damages are so much better—and it's not really my scheme; it's the Framers'. Let's get that clear; just because I have spent a little bit of time studying what they did and it's England so, it's not just some ivory tower theory. Okay.

Law professors can be very arrogant, and I want to claim very little credit for any originality here. This is not my idea. Here's why it's affirmatively bad. One—Johnnie Cochran just told you—because we see the problem of throwing out reliable evidence. It tempts judges to lie, to say that the Fourth Amendment wasn't violated, and that is a bad thing. It's a corrupting thing, and it hurts innocent defendants and these subsequent *Bivens* suits because it generates a very bad precedent.

It encourages the police to lie, because ordinarily honest cops—some are not ordinarily honest, but the ones that are—often will tell a small lie to get the larger truth, because it really wasn't planted evidence and they want to get that in. And so there becomes a police culture of lying, of winking in order to get actual honest evidence in, and that creates a very bad culture. Evidence is planted but that almost never has anything to do with whether you had a warrant. You can plant evidence with a warrant or without, so it has nothing to do with whether the search or seizure was constitutionally reasonable. It's a red herring. Planting evidence is different from the exclusionary rule.

The exclusionary rule says even if there's no planted evidence, no remote possibility of planted evidence, it's utterly reliable—we exclude it, and

that's a mistake. The exclusionary rule creates this culture of corruption and dishonesty in courts and by the police, and society then becomes very disheartened. Now, precisely because right now they say, "Well, you can sue the officer but the officer has no money," and you might not even know which officer did it to you—the exclusionary rule helps you not at all in your situation because they didn't find anything. Maybe they just wanted to hassle you because they were offended by your last NPR piece. That officer works for someone—that's the government. Follow the money. You sue the government directly, and—if you think there's not enough deterrence—just start adding zeros to the punitive damages until the lawyers start to take interest, you know. If you build it, they will come.

And that's what the Framers recognized in the O.J. Simpson case of its era—*Wilkes v. Wood*. It's the most famous case in the Anglo-American world: Wilkes-Barre, Pennsylvania; Wilkes County, North Carolina; Wilkes County, Georgia. The judge is Camden, as in Camden Yards where the Orioles play; Camden, New Jersey; Camden, South Carolina.

This was a case where it was an outrageous government search and seizure, almost a strip search, in someone's home. He sued, got massive punitive damages from the government itself. He socked it to 'em. And that was the principle that gave us, and the case, that gave us the Fourth Amendment.

Nina Totenberg: Let me just ask one question. When you were testifying before Senator Hatch, were you also testifying against caps on punitive damages at that time?

Akhil Amar: Indeed, yes—and they got rid of them to their credit. Again, I'm of the other party, and they got rid of them when I said, "If you mean to take seriously the Fourth Amendment, you have to provide some real effective deterrents." And they said, "By gosh, you're right."

Johnnie Cochran: Let me . . . Certainly, this is one area where I find the Professor and I are closer than the other areas. But let me just combine two things. Certainly, you should have the right to bring these damage suits. For fifteen years I've done an awful lot of that in Southern California. And let me tell you . . .

These are the toughest lawsuits you can ever bring as young lawyers. You need to bring them. But it's fighting City Hall.

It's very, very tough. And believe you me, if you have a random selection of jurors, you'll never win. First of all, let's start with that—I want to combine two things. But more important than that, the other problem is I think the Professor underestimates how the police really stand together. Let me just read something very quickly in that regard.

Let me just refer to this fellow, Detective Fuhrman, who is someone you've heard about. You know, we talk about these internal investigations and suing and everything. Here's what he had to say—I want to give you just two quick quotes, which I think the Professor will find instructive. He was describing the arrest of a black man in Westwood, California, where UCLA is, and he said, "So, you're allowed to just pick somebody up that you think doesn't belong in an area and arrest him?" That's what Kenny asked him.

The answer: "I don't know. I don't know what the Supreme Court or the Superior Court says. And I don't really give a so-and-so. If I was pushing this thing, why I did it, I'd say suspicion of burglary. I'd be able to correlate exactly what I said into a reasonable, probable cause for an arrest." That's the mentality of these police officers. But even more than that, on the issue of "let's just sue 'em," here's what happens.

Here's what he says to his partner one day in the car: "Don't tell me because you've got a wife and a kid—you're either my partner all the way or you get the blank out of this car. We die for each other. We live for each other. And that's how it is in this car. You lie for me, up to six months' suspension."

So, believe you me, it's not like you just run off into court and have this judge ask these questions, get a random selection of jurors, have the police officer still lie, and you collect anything. It's not practical. It doesn't work under those circumstances. We know there aren't easy answers, but you've got to look at the practicality of how it is. And I applaud the fact there are no limits on the damages, but that's not going to work and

really solve the problem either, I think. And that's what I'm concerned about.

Akhil Amar: There are other mechanisms in addition to civil jury options. Remember, we're talking about civil suits brought by aggrieved citizens who may not have been even charged with any wrongdoing. They may have been utterly innocent, and even the cops knew they were innocent . . .

You know, and the cops want to hassle them. So, these are civil suits. In civil suits we can easily structure the thing to give citizen plaintiffs, when they're suing the government, a choice. Do you want a jury, or would you prefer this to be a judge trial? No problem whatsoever on the Seventh Amendment. And you give the citizen the choice. Her option.

There are administrative schemes, sanctioning schemes, and the like. For example, if you're hurt in the workplace, we have OSHA and worker's compensation and the like. There are many civil models for enforcing the Fourth Amendment in addition to juries. But, here's the fundamental other disagreement. I basically have more confidence in a random selection of my fellow citizens and their ability, with proper instructions from the judge, who will sometimes say this is unreasonable as a matter of law, this is not unreasonable as a matter of law.

Within the confines of that judicial grid of what is and isn't reasonable, I have more confidence in my fellow citizens trying to decide what police conduct they consider reasonable, what police conduct they consider unreasonable, what they consider outrageous.

Nina Totenberg: I just want to ask one question on this idea of internal discipline. Why would we have any reason to think that that would work when, for example, take the case of Mark Fuhrman. I've never been able to figure out why the Los Angeles Police Department fought him when he was trying to get early retirement essentially, disability on the basis that he was an unredeemed bigot, then put him on the Homicide Squad in one of the creme-de-la-creme positions with enormous power over people's lives. Why would we think that police departments who behave that way for, not necessarily even evil reasons, often bureaucratic reasons, because they're going to get sued by the officer, or they'll be up before the State Employment Board, or whatever; what makes you think that your value will trump other values?

Akhil Amar: The problem is bureaucracy, which creates a certain kind of density and solidarity and a culture of "us" against "them." And one way you break it is by trying to bring sunshine in, oversight. So you could have—and this is a jury-like idea, but not technically the jury—citizen oversight panels. You have either community leaders, respected community leaders, that's like a blue-ribbon jury; or random cross-sections of citizens or grand juries who monitor and are involved in that oversight process when citizens come and bring complaints against police officers. They're not handled just by the police department bureaucracy, but by the citizenry monitoring its government officials.

Johnnie Cochran: Ms. Totenberg, what I was going to say—and a good example is again, Detective Fuhrman, who was charged with some sixty-six counts, resulting in the beatings that he talks about on the tape, of the Hispanics in East Los Angeles. He took great pride in the fact that he was the last one they talked to, which meant that he was the real heavy. And he said that he was acquitted, absolved of every last one of the them. Because he knew he would. The officers said, "We knew how to lie for each other. We stood up for each other together." That's why these tapes are so chilling.

That's why all of America needed to hear these tapes because there are Mark Fuhrmans in every department in America—not the majority of officers, make no mistake about it, it's not about being anti-police. But they are there, and they do exist, and it doesn't help us to engage in this national epidemic of denial. What the Professor again talks about would be nice in a perfect world, but it's not going to work. It's not a remedy that's going to work until we overcome and come to grips with the issue of race in America that nobody ever wants to talk about. Racism is endemic.

Nina Totenberg: That's the last word on this subject. Moving on to the next, which is confessions and self-incrimination. Should defendants be forced to speak? And when? And to what degree? So, we'll start with you again, Professor Amar, since you want to curtail this to some degree.

Akhil Amar: Yeah, I want to construe the Fifth Amendment correctly is another way of saying that. Start by reading the words of the Amendment. But the basic idea here is that in any criminal case, no person shall be compelled to be a witness against himself, okay? I've moved the words around, but that's the key concept. Now, here's one thing, for example, that we can compel people to do. We can compel people to give their blood, their hair, voice exemplars, and the like—and the Supreme Court said that's not forcing them to be witnesses against themselves; that's reliable, physical evidence, and it can come in. Now, under that theory—that's the famous *Schmerber* case—my suggestion is that so long as someone outside the courtroom—in a grand jury proceeding, in a civilized deposition, the same way we have civil discovery on the civil side, with their lawyer present, with Brendan Sullivan whispering in your ear (he's not a potted plant)—you're asked questions and you have to answer them.

Those answers aren't introduced in a criminal case because then you would in effect be a witness against yourself by affidavit. But if your answers lead to other physical evidence—you know, where is that bloody knife, where is that smoking gun, where are those gold bars with your fingerprints on them? Just like, where is your blood? And give it to us—those bits of reliable, physical evidence can come in the courtroom because that's not witnessing, that's fruit.

Now, why do we exclude words and allow fruit? Again, it's all about truth-seeking and reliability. Under pressure, you're just an ordinary person, and you're confronted with a very clever lawyer who's trying to make a monkey out of you and make you look guilty when you're not. You might not be particularly educated; you might slip up and actually say something that looks quite incriminating and hang yourself. And we're really worried about protecting innocent people from that, so we don't force people to take the stand because even though they're innocent, they might look bad; they might look guilty; they might slip up. So we exclude their testimony.

They have a right to not have those words come in. But reliable, physical evidence is altogether different: blood, hair samples, bloody knives, smoking guns, gold bars.

Nina Totenberg: So, wait a minute, before you answer, I need you to spin this out one step further. Blood and hair we all know about. I mean, you don't have any right to not give that to the police. But what are you saying more than that?

Akhil Amar: Okay. Outside your criminal case, there's a deposition, and you're there, and you're Ollie North, and you're given in Congress even a certain immunity. Here's the immunity that you get: your words will never be introduced against you in the criminal case. You will never have been made a witness against yourself in the criminal case. But fruit leads that are generated by that testimony—the identity of other witnesses, all of that comes in. That's the English rule. It always has been. That's the Canadian rule.

Here's why this is affirmatively good for innocent defendants. Right now, here's what happens. I'm on trial for my life, and I know who did it. I have an explicit Sixth Amendment right to compel the production of witnesses in my favor, but right now, when I try to put that person on the stand, that person invokes the Fifth Amendment. We saw a variant of this in a case that Mr. Cochran is aware of, and the problem right now is that person's Fifth Amendment rights are trumping my Sixth Amendment right to compel the production of witnesses.

The reason that person's Fifth Amendment right trumps is because I can't immunize that person and say, "Okay, I confer immunity on you, and so then tell them you did it so I can go free." And the reason I can't is right now, once immunity is given, it basically means we can never prosecute that person at all. That's why Oliver North is free today, rather than the convicted criminal that he would be if the other evidence were allowed to come in. So, innocent defendants right now are worse off because we've overbroadly construed Fifth Amendment immunity in a way that helps the guilty and hurts the innocent.

Johnnie Cochran: Well, I disagree.

Nina Totenberg: Surprise!

Johnnie Cochran: Surprise! Surprise! And even though one might think that certainly Oliver North's political views are worlds apart from mine, I respect his right to not have a statement made before Congress used against him because he was advised that it would not be used against him, and I understand that. And I think that's part of our system that he was told that—it would be unfair, and the appellate court so ruled. The problem is, I think the press has it all wrong. Let's go back to practicalities again. In a criminal case, the burden is upon the prosecution. The defendant doesn't have to do anything to *help* his conviction.

Akhil Amar: Except give his blood.

Johnnie Cochran: He doesn't have to do it; there's been chipping away—certainly blood and hair and that sort of thing—from the old *Rochin* case in California, but Professor Amar wants to go further than that. You see, implicit in what we've been hearing tonight is the fact that somebody can make a judgment of who's innocent and who's guilty. I started off by saying that's what this is about. We have now come so far to the right that we now believe that everybody is basically a guilty, heathen defendant hiding behind the Constitution, so, let's just wipe them out and let's only try to protect the innocent. But the truth, it doesn't work that way.

Truth in the courtroom doesn't work that way. Who's to say what the truth is? I dare say, in any given case, unless you or I were there, especially in the circumstantial evidence case, nobody knows for sure. And that's the issue. When the jury goes back and votes, they're not voting on whether they feel most likely this person is guilty, or it's probable that they were guilty. It's whether or not they're guilty beyond a reasonable doubt and to a moral certainty. That's what we're talking about. You know, somebody else said it really, really well when they said what is really a trial—a trial is simply a struggle for an acceptable level of human certainty.

In criminal cases, we call that beyond a reasonable doubt and to a moral certainty. So let's not turn this Fifth Amendment on its head in the interest of trying to get at only the innocent people—who's going to make that determination?

Now to the Professor's credit, he's been talking about this and expostulating these ideas long before Simpson. But for the majority of people—and the reason why I am so disturbed by it—it's only after Simpson that they decided to have all these ideas because they didn't like the result. They didn't have these same issues and weren't worrying about it with William Kennedy Smith or Claus von Bulow or John DeLorean. But in regard to the Professor, he has long thought this.

His arguments are well thought out. The only problem that I find is that I don't think they're necessarily going to work, and I think that in many instances it changes the whole burden, making it easier for the prosecution. That's what I see as the agenda; it makes it easier for the prosecution. And, you know, let me just say this, that's what makes it so beautiful in this country. The thing about the Simpson case—unless we took a vote here it's not important what you thought about that verdict—what's important is that if the jurors thought they were doing their job, and even if it's unpopular, isn't that what makes our system great in America?

That's what we're talking about—you don't talk about one case. And please, the other thing, if I can leave one thought with you, don't use Simpson for changes to the system—Simpson is an aberration in many particulars. When did you ever see any defendant who could fight on an equal field with the prosecution? What we ought to be thinking about, and let me not get too far afield, is how do we give more resources to other poor defendants out there? That's what we ought to be thinking about.

Nina Totenberg: Let me ask you a hypothetical, a so-called hypothetical. You have a rape defendant, and there are seventeen other young women who are willing to testify that he has date-raped them. I really almost don't know a court in this country where that would be permissible evidence under current rules. The notion being that the other evidence would be so inflammatory to the jury that the jury would be unable to rule on this case and this case alone, where the evidence is being introduced about this case. Under your theory, as I understand it, all seventeen of those women would come in and testify that way. Right?

Akhil Amar: Hmm, I don't think that actually my theory had much to say about that. But let me tell you how it would play out here. First of all, I do not challenge the presumption of innocence or the *Winship* idea that the prosecutor has to prove things beyond a reasonable doubt. Precisely because that is such a heavy burden and rightly so, the question is whether we're going to allow reliable evidence in the courtroom that can help establish that. That's why we force the defendant to give his own blood, even if he doesn't want to, because that can actually help us decide who did it. And in a rape case, not a date-rape case, but another case where the question might not be consent, but identity. The . . .

Nina Totenberg: There's no consent in a date-rape.

Akhil Amar: Right, that's . . . the issue is consent rather than identity in date-rape, but the end of the so-called stranger-rape situation, the question is who did it. And that's where, again, reliable physical evidence can be absolutely critical, like sperm. We force people to give over their bodily fluids, even though it may convict them, because it's reliable evidence—DNA, for example. It can also help clear the innocent. There are people who were on death row who now are free because the blood, because the DNA has proved it was someone else.

I don't want to say anything at all about whether the person you've heard about in the media actually committed the so-called Unabomber crimes, but I can tell you that in any trial about the Unabomber, what ultimately will be perhaps among the most decisive pieces of evidence will be saliva. Because there's saliva on the back of a stamp, and they will be able, if they ever do catch the person who did it, they will be able to prove that person's guilt literally from that person's own mouth. From saliva. But not in order to compel that person's words, because words are less reliable than saliva. So, the whole point is words can be unreliable in a way that physical evidence is much more trustworthy and can acquit the innocent.

Nina Totenberg: I'd like to remind the witness that he's not answered my question. I don't care whether you want it to be stranger-rape and there's seventeen women who say, "That guy is the guy who raped me" or you want it to be date-rape. It doesn't really matter. Eyewitness testimony is not DNA, and, as far as I know, usually, I don't know a court in the country where, unless the defendant is charged with that crime . . .

Akhil Amar: Uh huh. But that has nothing to do with coerced confessions or compelled self-incrimination. It is an interesting issue, and I'll talk about it, but it really isn't . . .

Nina Totenberg: Well, . . .

Akhil Amar: Now here's what's interesting about my . . .

Nina Totenberg: You've written about it in connection with it, you're just trying to avoid it.

Akhil Amar: In . . . And I thought you were a moderator.

Nina Totenberg: A moderator is supposed to hold both your feet to the fire. I hope I can do that.

Akhil Amar: Okay. And they're both being held. Now, the point is in a lot of cases what will make us very confident about guilt or innocence, and also clearing other suspects, is reliable physical evidence—blood, hair, fingerprints, and the like. Date-rape is unusual in one respect because the question isn't, "Who were the relevant parties?" The question there is, "Who do you believe?"—he said/she said. And that's something as to which reliable physical evidence doesn't tell us much.

It's possible it could tell us something if we were able through some examination of the relevant parties to try to deduce whether force had occurred or not. Typically, that's going to be an examination of the woman complainant victim, rather than the defendant. So again, self-incrimination doesn't come in. But if it all turns on who you believe—he said/she said—then it is quite possible to ask the following, and it's a symmetric question: "Has she ever cried rape before?" and "Has he ever been accused of date-rape before?" That might help us, actually, on a jury, try to figure out who we believe. When the physical evidence doesn't adjudicate, it's he said/she said. And there is actually interesting legislation—I think Senator Kyle has introduced it—on this question of prior bad acts.

Johnnie Cochran: Let me just respond briefly to prior bad acts. No, that should not come in, I don't believe. I think that, again, very often the courts will engage in a balancing process, and where you have these prior bad acts, certainly under that circumstance, you can't have seventeen other little trials. And the probative value of that is far outweighed by the prejudicial factor of that evidence. So I think it stays out. Much in the same way we argued that, in the Simpson case, that acts of previous alleged domestic discord, as we call it, shouldn't come in. Now, of course the Judge let it all come in. The prosecutors themselves decided not to do that, but Judge Ito said they could use many of these acts, and we thought that was an outrageous ruling, we thought, at the time. So, the short answer is no, I don't think that should come in.

But, I want to enlarge upon the topic of confessions. If, again, you think with me for a minute, this idea of letting the defendant, or making the defendant speak or use his statement, will lead to coerced confession—that's been a real problem in this country. Where the defendant is then, you're going to see it, the courts say that comes along, believe me, every defendant is going to confess in every case. Whether it takes a rubber hose or whatever, you're going to see more and more and more of that. And I can see these, I can just conjure up in my mind, the things that are going to happen again out in the street.

So again, I don't think you can shift the burden and I think it really is a shifting of burden. What my learned adversary talks about from a standpoint of chipping away, the courts always do that. They will carve out these little exceptions, and we've come to live with the fact that hair and blood are things that are going to . . .

Nina Totenberg: But Mr. Cochran, the Supreme Court was one vote, one vote away, from not permitting blood and hair, and as we now know, DNA, and all kinds of really probative evidence that, once you get it, is really only subject to debate over how it's tested, etc. But it is not like an eyewitness. It is not completely deceptive evidence. We were one vote away from that not being acceptable, and just as Professor Amar's theories conceivably, as you spin them out, could go to putting all kinds of innocent people in prison, I suppose your theories could go to putting an enormous number of guilty people back on the street to victimize other people.

Johnnie Cochran: Now, let me just say this, and the Framers have said this for years: better to let ten guilty people go than one innocent person be convicted. And that's another reason why we can argue another time about the death penalty. Some people may think that's just the cost of business. But when you're in criminal law, when you're in the court, when you have somebody's life in your hands, these principles become very real. For it's no longer a theory at that point—when some innocent person is put to death, all of us are less safe. And the Framers were concerned about that, and that's really what we're talking about here. So, sure there probably are some guilty people who go free.

Nina Totenberg: But not every case is a capital case.

Johnnie Cochran: Not every case is a capital case, but that obviously is the ultimate, and if it applies for the smaller case, it certainly applies for the larger case. And that's really the problem, because really, if you think about everything we've talked about here tonight, what we're talking about is making it easier for the police. Doesn't it have to do with the tenor of the times? Isn't this really a political discussion? We talk about these bills before Congress. We talk about testifying. How many of these Congresspeople try cases every day? Or are actually out there dealing with jurors?

They need to talk with people who've actually been out there doing it and understand what this means to everyday Americans and their belief in their society. They need to understand that, it seems to me, before we talk about these changes. You know, you talked about the Unabomber—one of the things I'm concerned about the Unabomber is the fact that, again, in this country, you know, I don't know all the facts, and he's still alleged to be guilty or he's allegedly innocent at this point—but how's he going to get a fair trial when every night, Nina, your colleagues come up with all this . . .

Nina Totenberg: And me. And me.

Johnnie Cochran: Let's get her now, okay? So, every night your colleagues, however, come on television and give us some more evidence. I'm pretty particularly sensitive of that because, having lived through that, where you're tried in the media—the media does a great job and at the end, when the media was wrong, and the jurors didn't listen to that evidence that the media was speculating about, and you get an acquittal—then you have trouble in the country having people understand what took place. So, I think we need to look at that also, another subject perhaps.

Nina Totenberg: Well, we're out of time and I'm supposed to wrap this up. And so I will wrap it up this way, since I'm neither brilliant practitioner nor brilliant scholar. My area of knowledge is really journalism and the press, and what I can tell you is, even understanding that this will be shown in classrooms around the country, that the British system sucks vis-à-vis the press. Once somebody is arrested in Great Britain, you can't write anything about the crime, what police are doing, what prosecutors are doing.

That is allegedly meant to protect the innocent defendant, but it also protects the vicious prosecutor. Similarly, when there is a trial, you may only report exactly the words that go on in the trial. You may not even report what the prosecutor looked like, or the body language of somebody. You may not use what small amount of creative language we in journalism might have. The result is that in Great Britain there have been, in large numbers of cases, really many more than in this country proportionately, railroad jobs that succeed for many years, often decades, and are not exposed by the press because there are mechanisms to keep it a secret.

Criminal Justice
and the Negotiated Plea

Kenneth Kipnis

In recent years it has become apparent to many that, in practice, the criminal justice system in the United States does not operate as we thought it did. The conviction secured through jury trial, so familiar in countless novels, films, and television programs, is beginning to be seen as the aberration it has become. What has replaced the jury's verdict is the negotiated plea. In these "plea bargains" the defendant agrees to plead guilty in exchange for discretionary consideration on the part of the state. Generally, this consideration amounts to some kind of assurance of a minimal sentence. The well-publicized convictions of Spiro Agnew and Clifford Irving were secured through such plea bargains. In 1974 in New York City, 80 percent of all felony cases were settled as misdemeanors through plea bargains.[1] Only 2 percent of all felony arrests resulted in a trial.[2] It is at present a commonplace that plea bargaining could not be eliminated without substantial alterations in our criminal justice system.

Plea bargaining involves negotiations between the defendant (through an attorney in the standard case) and the prosecutor as to the conditions under which the defendant will enter a guilty plea.[3] Both sides have bargaining power in these negotiations. The prosecutor is ordinarily burdened with cases and does not have the wherewithal to bring more than a fraction of them to trial. Often there is not sufficient evidence to ensure a jury's conviction. Most important, the prosecutor is typically under administrative and political pressure to dispose of cases and to secure convictions as efficiently as possible. If the defendant exercises the constitutional right to a jury trial, the prosecutor must decide whether to drop the charges entirely or to expend scarce resources to bring the case to trial. Since neither prospect is attractive, prosecutors typically exercise their broad discretion to induce defendants to waive trial and to plead guilty.

From the defendant's point of view, such prosecutorial discretion has two aspects: it darkens the prospect of going to trial as it brightens the prospect of pleading guilty. Before negotiating, a prosecutor may improve his bargaining position by "overcharging" defendants[4] or by developing a reputation for severity in the sentences he recommends to judges. Such steps greatly increase the punishment that the defendant must expect if convicted at trial. On the other hand, the state may offer to reduce or to drop some charges, or to recommend leniency to the judge if the defendant agrees to plead guilty. These steps minimize the punishment that will result from a guilty plea. Though the exercise of prosecutorial discretion to secure pleas of guilty may differ somewhat in certain

Kenneth Kipnis, "Criminal Justice and the Negotiated Plea," *Ethics* Volume 86 (January 1976): 93–106.

[1]Marcia Chambers, "80% of City Felony Cases Settled by Plea Bargaining," *New York Times* (February 11, 1975), p. 1.

[2]Tom Goldstein, "Backlog of Felonies Rose Sharply Here Despite Court Drive," *New York Times* (February 12, 1975), p. 1.

[3]Often the judge will play an important role in these discussions, being called upon, for example, to indicate a willingness to go along with a bargain involving a reduction in sentence. A crowded calendar will make the bench an interested party.

[4]In California, for example, armed robbers are technically guilty of kidnapping if they point a gun at their victim and tell him to back up. Thus, beyond the charge of armed robbery, they may face a charge of kidnapping which will be dropped upon entry of a guilty plea (see Albert W. Alschuler, "The Prosecutor's Role in Plea Bargaining," *University of Chicago Law Review* 36 [Fall 1968]: 88).

jurisdictions and in particular cases, the broad outlines are as described.

Of course a defendant can always reject any offer of concessions and challenge the state to prove its case. A skilled defense attorney can do much to force the prosecutor to expend resources in bringing a case to trial.[5] But the trial route is rarely taken by defendants. Apart from prosecutorial pressure, other factors may contribute to a defendant's willingness to plead guilty: feelings of guilt which may or may not be connected with the charged crime; the discomforts of the pretrial lockup as against the comparatively better facilities of a penitentiary; the costs of going to trial as against the often cheaper option of consenting to a plea; a willingness or unwillingness to lie; and the delays which are almost always present in awaiting trial, delays which the defendant may sit out in jail in a kind of preconviction imprisonment which may not be credited to a postconviction sentence. It is not surprising that the right to a trial by jury is rarely exercised.

If one examines the statistics published annually by the Administrative Office of the U.S. Courts,[6] one can appreciate both the size of the concessions gained by agreeing to plead guilty and (what is the same thing) the size of the additional burdens imposed upon those convicted without so agreeing. According to the 1970 report, among all convicted defendants, those pleading guilty at arraignment received average sentences of probation and/or under one year of imprisonment. Those going to a jury trial received average sentences of three to four years in prison.[7] If one looks just at those convicted of Marijuana Tax Act violations with no prior record, one finds that those pleading guilty at arraignment received average sentences of probation and/or six months or less of imprisonment while those going to trial received average sentences more than eight times as severe: four to five years in prison.[8] Among all Marijuana Tax Act convictions, defendants pleading guilty at the outset had a 76 percent chance of being let off without imprisonment, while those who had gone to trial had only an 11 percent chance.[9] These last two sets of figures do not reflect advantages gained by charge reduction, nor do they reflect advantages gained by electing a bench trial as opposed to a jury trial. What these figures do suggest is that the sentences given to convicted defendants who have exercised their constitutional right to trial are many times as severe as the sentences given to those who do not. In *United States v. Wiley*[10] Chief Judge Campbell laid to rest any tendency to conjecture that these discrepancies in sentences might have explanations not involving plea bargains.

> . . . I believe, and it is generally accepted by trial judges throughout the United States, that it is entirely proper and logical to grant some defendants some degree of leniency in exchange for a plea of guilty. If then, a trial judge grants leniency in exchange for a plea of guilty, it follows, as the reverse side of the same coin, that he must necessarily forego leniency, generally speaking, where the defendant stands trial and is found guilty.
>
> . . . I might make general reference to a "standing policy" not to consider probation where a defendant stands trial even though I do not in fact strictly adhere to such a policy.

No deliberative body ever decided that we would have a system in which the disposition of criminal cases is typically the result of negotiations between the prosecutor and the defendant's attorney on the conditions under which the defendant would waive trial and plead guilty to a mutually acceptable charge. No legislature ever voted to adopt a procedure in which defendants who are convicted after trial typically receive sentences far greater than those received by defendants charged with similar offenses but

[5]Arthur Rosett, "The Negotiated Guilty Plea," *Annals of the American Academy of Political and Social Science* 374 (November 1967): 72.

[6]Administrative Office of the United States Courts, *Federal Offenders in the United States District Courts* (Washington, D.C., 1970).

[7]Ibid., pp. 57, 59.

[8]Ibid., pp. 57, 65.

[9]Ibid., p. 60:

[10]184 F. Supp. 679 (N.D. Ill. 1960).

pleading guilty. The practice of plea bargaining has evolved in the unregulated interstices of our criminal justice system. Its development has not gone unnoticed. There is now a substantial literature on the legality and propriety of plea bargaining.[11] But though philosophers do not often treat issues arising in the area of criminal procedure, there are problems here that cry for our attention. In the preceding pages I have been concerned to sketch the institution of plea bargaining. In what follows I will raise some serious questions about it that should concern us. I will first discuss generally the intrinsic fairness of plea bargains and then, in the final section, I will examine critically the place of such bargains in the criminal justice system.

I

As one goes through the literature on plea bargaining one gets the impression that market forces are at work in this unlikely context. The terms "bargain" and "negotiation" suggest this. One can see the law of supply and demand operating in that, other things being equal, if there are too many defendants who want to go to trial, prosecutors will have to concede more in order to get the guilty pleas that they need to clear their case load. And if the number of prosecutors and courts goes up, prosecutors will be able to concede less. Against this background it is not surprising to find one commentator noting:[12] "In some places a 'going

rate' is established under which a given charge will automatically be broken down to a given lesser offense with the recommendation of a given lesser sentence." Prosecutors, like retailers before them, have begun to appreciate the efficiency of the fixed-price approach.

The plea bargain in the economy of criminal justice has many of the important features of the contract in commercial transactions. In both institutions offers are made and accepted, entitlements are given up and obtained, and the notion of an exchange, ideally a fair one, is present to both parties. Indeed one detects something of the color of consumer protection law in a few of the decisions on plea bargaining. In *Bailey v. MacDougal*[13] the court held that "a guilty plea cannot be accepted unless the defendant understands its consequences." And in *Santo Bello v. New York*[14] the court secured a defendant's entitlement to a prosecutorial concession when a second prosecutor replaced the one who had made the promise. Rule 11 of the Federal Rules of Criminal Procedure (effective August 1, 1975) requires that "if a plea agreement has been reached by the parties which contemplates entry of a plea of guilty or nolo contendere in the expectation that a specific sentence will be imposed or that other charges before the court will be dismissed, the court shall require the disclosure of the agreement in open court at the time the plea is offered." These procedures all have analogues in contract law. Though plea bargains may not be seen as contracts by the parties, agreements like them are the stuff of contract case law. While I will not argue that plea bargains are contracts (or even that they should be treated as such), I do think it proper to look to contract law for help in evaluating the justice of such agreements.

The law of contracts serves to give legal effect to certain bargain-promises. In particular, it specifies conditions that must be satisfied by bargain-promises before the law will recognize and enforce them as contracts. As an example,

---

[11]Some of the the most significant treatments of plea bargaining are Alschuler; Arnold Enker, "Perspectives on Plea Bargaining," in *Task Force Report: The Courts,* by the President's Commission on Law Enforcement and Administration of Justice (Washington, D.C., 1967), p. 108; "The Unconstitutionality of Plea Bargaining," *Harvard Law Review,* 83 (April 1970): 1387; Donald J. Newman, *Conviction: The Determination of Guilt or Innocence without Trial* (Boston, 1966); Abraham S. Blumberg, *Criminal Justice* (Chicago, 1967); National Advisory Commission on Criminal Justice Standards and Goals, *Task Force Report: The Courts* (Washington, D.C., 1973); American Bar Association Project on Minimum Standards for Criminal Justice, *Standards Relating to Pleas of Guilty, Approved Draft* (New York, 1968).

[12]Rosett, p. 71.

[13]392 F.2d 155 (1968).

[14]404 U.S. 257 (1971).

we could look at that part of the law of contracts which treats duress. Where one party wrongfully compels another to consent to the terms of an agreement the resulting bargain has no legal effect. Dan B. Dobbs, a commentator on the law in this area, describes the elements of duress as follows: "The defendant's act must be wrongful in some attenuated sense; it must operate coercively upon the will of the plaintiff, judged subjectively, and the plaintiff must have no adequate remedy to avoid the coercion except to give in. . . . The earlier requirement that the coercion must have been the kind that would coerce a reasonable man, or even a brave one, is now generally dispensed with, and it is enough if it in fact coerced a spineless plaintiff."[15] Coercion is not the same as fraud, nor is it confined to cases in which a defendant is physically compelled to assent. In Dobb's words: "The victim of duress knows the facts but is forced by hard choices to act against his will." The paradigm case of duress is the agreement made at gunpoint. Facing a mortal threat, one readily agrees to hand over the cash. But despite such consent, the rules of duress work to void the effects of such agreements. There is no legal obligation to hand over the cash and, having given it over, entitlement to the money is not lost. The gunman has no legal right to retain possession even if he adheres to his end of the bargain and scraps his murderous plans.

Judges have long been required to see to it that guilty pleas are entered voluntarily. And one would expect that, if duress is present in the plea-bargaining situation, then, just as the handing over of cash to the gunman is void of legal effect (as far as entitlement to the money is concerned), so no legal consequences should flow from the plea of guilty which is the product of duress. However, Rule 11 of the Federal Rules of Criminal Procedure requires the court to insure that a plea of guilty (or nolo contendere) is voluntary by "addressing the defendant personally in open court, determining that the

plea is voluntary and not the result of force or promises *apart from a plea agreement*" (emphasis added). In two important cases (*North Carolina v. Alford* and *Brady v. United States*)[16] defendants agreed to plead guilty in order to avoid probable death sentences. Both accepted very long prison sentences. In both cases the Supreme Court decided that guilty pleas so entered were voluntary (though Brennan, Douglas, and Marshall dissented). In his dissent in *Alford*, Brennan writes: ". . . the facts set out in the majority opinion demonstrate that Alford was 'so gripped by fear of the death penalty' that his decision to plead guilty was not voluntary but was the 'product of duress as much so as choice reflecting physical constraint.'" In footnote 2 of the *Alford* opinion, the Court sets out the defendant's testimony given at the time of the entry of his plea of guilty before the trial court. That testimony deserves examination: "I pleaded guilty on second degree murder because they said there is too much evidence, but I ain't shot no man, but I take the fault for the other man. We never had an argument in our life and I just pleaded guilty because they said if I didn't they would gas me for it, and that is all." The rule to be followed in such cases is set out in *Brady*: "A plea of guilty entered by one fully aware of the direct consequences, including the actual value of any commitments made to him by the court, prosecutor or his own counsel, must stand unless induced by threats (or promises to discontinue improper harassment), misrepresentation (including unfilled or unfillable promises), or perhaps by promises that are by their very nature improper as having no proper relationship to the prosecutor's business (e.g. bribes)." Case law and the Federal Rules both hold that the standard exercise of prosecutorial discretion in order to secure a plea of guilty cannot be used to prove that such a plea is involuntary. Even where the defendant enters a guilty plea in order to avert his death at the hands of the state, as in *Alford*, the Court has not seen involuntariness. Nevertheless, it may be true

---

[15]Dan B. Dobbs, *Handbook on the Law of Remedies* (Saint Paul, 1973), p. 658.

[16]400 U.S. 25 (1970) and 397 U.S. 742 (1970), respectively.

that some guilty pleas are involuntary in virtue of prosecutorial inducement considered proper by the Supreme Court.

Regarding the elements of duress, let us compare the gunman situation with an example of plea bargaining in order to examine the voluntariness of the latter. Albert W. Alschuler, author of one of the most thorough studies of plea bargaining, describes an actual case:

> San Francisco defense attorney Benjamin M. Davis recently represented a man charged with kidnapping and forcible rape. The defendant was innocent, Davis says, and after investigating the case Davis was confident of an acquittal. The prosecutor, who seems to have shared the defense attorney's opinion on this point, offered to permit a guilty plea to simple battery. Conviction on this charge would not have led to a greater sentence than thirty days' imprisonment, and there was every likelihood that the defendant would be granted probation. When Davis informed his client of this offer, he emphasized that conviction at trial seemed highly improbable. The defendant's reply was simple: "I can't take the chance."[17]

Both the gunman and the prosecutor require persons to make hard choices between a very certain smaller imposition and an uncertain greater imposition. In the gunman situation I must choose between the very certain loss of my money and the difficult-to-assess probability that my assailant is willing and able to kill me if I resist. As a defendant I am forced to choose between a very certain smaller punishment and a substantially greater punishment with a difficult-to-assess probability. As the size of the certain smaller imposition comes down and as the magnitude and probability of the larger imposition increases, it becomes more and more reasonable to choose the former. This is what seems to be occurring in Alschuler's example: "Davis reports that he is uncomfortable when he permits innocent defendants to plead guilty; but in this case it would have been playing God to stand in the defendant's way. The attorney's assessment of

the outcome at trial can always be wrong, and it is hard to tell a defendant that 'professional ethics' require a course that may ruin his life." Davis's client must decide whether to accept a very certain, very minor punishment or to chance a ruined life. Of course the gunman's victim can try to overpower his assailant and the defendant can attempt to clear himself at trial. But the same considerations that will drive reasonable people to give in to the gunman compel one to accept the prosecutor's offer. Applying the second and third elements of duress, one can see that, like the gunman's acts, the acts of the prosecutor can "operate coercively upon the will of the plaintiff, judged subjectively," and both the gunman's victim and the defendant may "have no adequate remedy to avoid the coercion except to give in." In both cases reasonable persons might well conclude (after considering the gunman's lethal weapon or the gas chamber) "I can't take the chance." A spineless person would not need to deliberate.

That prosecutors could exercise such duress apparently seemed plain to the authors of the *Restatement of Contracts*.[18] Their summarization of the law of contracts, adopted in 1932 by the American Law Institute, contained the following: "A threat of criminal prosecution . . . ordinarily is a threat of imprisonment and also . . . a threat of bringing disgrace upon the accused. Threats of this sort may be of such compelling force that acts done under their influence are coerced, and the better foundation there is for the prosecution, the greater is the coercion." While it is always true that even in the most desperate circumstances persons are free to reject the terms offered and risk the consequences, as Morris Raphael Cohen put it: "such choice is surely the very opposite of what men value as freedom."[19]

Indeed if one had to choose between being in the position of Davis's client and facing a fair-minded gunman, I think that it would be reasonable to prefer the latter. While the law

---

[17]Alschuler, p. 61.

[18]American Law Institute, *Restatement of Contracts* (Saint Paul, 1933), p. 652.

[19]Morris Raphael Cohen, "The Basis of Contract," in *Law and the Social Order* (New York, 1933), p. 86.

permits one to recover money upon adverting to the forced choice of the gunman, it does not permit one to retract a guilty plea upon adverting to the forced choice of the prosecutor. This is the impact of *Brady* and Rule 11.

Note that the duress is not eliminated by providing defendants with counsel. While a good attorney may get better concessions and may help in the evaluation of options, in the end the defendant will still have to decide whether to settle for the smaller penalty or to risk a much heavier sentence. One does not eliminate the injustice in the gunman situation by providing victims with better advice.

Nor does it help matters to insure that promises of prosecutorial concessions are kept. The gunman who violates his part of the bargain—murdering his victims after they give over their money—has compounded his wrongdoing. Reputations for righteousness are not established by honoring such bargains.

Nor is it legitimate to distinguish the prosecutor from the gunman by saying that, while the gunman is threatening harm unless you hand over the cash, the prosecutor is merely promising benefits if you enter a guilty plea. For, in the proper context, threats and promises may be intertranslatable. Brandishing his pistol, the holdup man may promise to leave me unharmed if I hand over the cash. Similarly, the prosecutor may threaten to "throw the book" at me if I do not plead guilty to a lesser charge. In the proper context, one may be compelled to act by either form of words.

One might argue that not all "hard choices" are examples of duress. A doctor could offer to sell vital treatment for a large sum. After the patient has been cured it will hardly do for her to claim that she has been the victim of duress. The doctor may have forced the patient to choose between a certain financial loss and the risk of death. But surely doctors are not like gunman.

Two important points need to be made in response to this objection. First, the doctor is not, one assumes, responsible for the diseased condition of the patient. The patient would be facing death even if she had never met the doctor. But this is not true in the case of the gunman, where both impositions are his work.

And in this respect the prosecutor offering a plea bargain in a criminal case is like the gunman rather than like the doctor. For the state forces a choice between adverse consequences that it imposes. And, of course, one cannot say that in the defendant's wrongdoing he has brought his dreadful dilemma upon himself. To do so would be to ignore the good reasons there are for the presumption of innocence in dispositive criminal proceedings.

Second, our laws do not prohibit doctors from applying their healing skills to maximize their own wealth. They are free to contract to perform services in return for a fee. But our laws do severely restrict the state in its prosecution of criminal defendants. Those who framed our constitution were well aware of the great potential for abuse that the criminal law affords. Much of the Constitution (especially the Bill of Rights) checks the activity of the state in this area. In particular, the Fifth Amendment provides that no person "shall be compelled in any criminal case to be a witness against himself." If I am right in judging that defendants like Alford and Davis's client do not act freely in pleading guilty to the facts of their cases, that the forced choice of the prosecutor may be as coercive as the forced choice of the gunman, that a defendant may be compelled to speak against himself (or herself) by a prosecutor's discretion inducing him to plead guilty, then, given the apparent constitutional prohibition of such compulsion, the prosecutor acts wrongfully in compelling such pleas. And in this manner it may be that the last element of duress, wrongfulness, can be established. But it is not my purpose here to establish the unconstitutionality of plea bargaining, for it is not necessary to reach to unconstitutionality to grasp the wrongfulness of that institution. One need only reflect upon what justice amounts to in our system of criminal law. This is the task I will take up in the final section of this paper.

II

Not too long ago plea bargaining was an officially prohibited practice. Court procedures were followed to ensure that no concessions had been given to defendants in exchange for guilty pleas. But gradually it became widely known that these procedures had become charades of perjury, shysterism, and bad faith involving judges, prosecutors, defense attorneys and defendants. This was scandalous. But rather than cleaning up the practice in order to square it with the rules, the rules were changed in order to bring them in line with the practice. There was a time when it apparently seemed plain that the old rules were the right rules. One finds in the *Restatement of Contracts:*[20] "... even if the accused is guilty and the process valid, so that as against the State the imprisonment is lawful, it is a wrongful means of inducing the accused to enter into a transaction. To overcome the will of another for the prosecutor's advantage is *an abuse of the criminal law which was made for another purpose*" (emphasis added). The authors of the *Restatement* do not tell us what they were thinking when they spoke of the purpose of the criminal law. Nonetheless it is instructive to conjecture and to inquire along the lines suggested by the *Restatement*.

Without going deeply into detail, I believe that it can be asserted without controversy that the liberal-democratic approach to criminal justice—and in particular the American criminal justice system—is an institutionalization of two principles. The first principle refers to the intrinsic point of systems of criminal justice.

A. Those (and only those) individuals who are clearly guilty of certain serious specified wrongdoings deserve an officially administered punishment which is proportional to their wrongdoing.

In the United States it is possible to see this principle underlying the activities of legislators specifying and grading wrongdoings which are serious enough to warrant criminalization and, further, determining the range of punishment appropriate to each offense; the activities of policemen and prosecutors bringing to trial those who are suspected of having committed such wrongdoings; the activities of jurors determining if defendants are guilty beyond a reasonable doubt; the activities of defense attorneys insuring that relevant facts in the defendant's favor are brought out at trial; the activities of judges seeing to it that proceedings are fair and that those who are convicted receive the punishment they deserve; and the activities of probation officers, parole officers, and prison personnel executing the sentences of the courts. All of these people play a part in bringing the guilty to justice.

But in liberal-democratic societies not everything is done to accomplish this end. A second principle makes reference to the limits placed upon the power of the state to identify and punish the guilty.

B. Certain basic liberties shall not be violated in bringing the guilty to justice.

This second principle can be seen to underlie the constellation of constitutional checks on the activities of virtually every person playing a role in the administration of the criminal justice system.

Each of these principles is related to a distinctive type of injustice that can occur in the context of criminal law. An injustice can occur in the outcome of the criminal justice procedure. That is, an innocent defendant may be convicted and punished, or a guilty defendant may be acquitted or, if convicted, he or she may receive more or less punishment than is deserved. Because these injustices occur in the meting out of punishment to defendants who are being processed by the system, we can refer to them as internal injustices. They are violations of the first principle. On the other hand, there is a type of injustice which occurs when basic liberties are violated in the operation of the criminal justice system. It may be true that Star Chamber proceedings, torture, hostages, bills of attainder, dragnet arrests, unchecked searches, *ex post facto* laws, unlimited invasions of privacy, and an arsenal of other measures could be employed to bring more of the guilty to justice. But these steps lead to a dystopia where our most terrifying nightmares can come true. However we limit the activity of

---

[20]American Law Institute, p. 652.

the criminal justice system in the interest of basic liberty, that limit can be overstepped. We can call such infringements upon basic liberties external injustices. They are violations of the second principle. If, for example, what I have suggested in the previous section is correct, then plea bargaining can bring about an external injustice with respect to a basic liberty secured by the Fifth Amendment. The remainder of this section will be concerned with internal injustice or violations of the first principle.

It is necessary to draw a further distinction between aberrational and systemic injustice. It may very well be that in the best criminal justice system that we are capable of devising human limitations will result in some aberrational injustice. Judges, jurors, lawyers, and legislators with the best of intentions may make errors in judgment that result in mistakes in the administration of punishment. But despite the knowledge that an unknown percentage of all dispositions of criminal cases are, to some extent, miscarriages of justice, it may still be reasonable to believe that a certain system of criminal justice is well calculated to avoid such results within the limits referred to by the second principle.[21] We can refer to these incorrect outcomes of a sound system of criminal justice as instances of aberrational injustice. In contrast, instances of systemic injustice are those that result from structural flaws in the criminal justice system itself. Here incorrect outcomes in the operations of the system are not the result of human error. Rather, the system itself is not well calculated to avoid injustice. What would be instances of aberrational injustice in a sound system are not aberrations in an unsound system: they are a standard result.

This distinction has an analogy in the area of quality control. Two vials of antibiotic may be equally contaminated. But depending upon the process used to produce each, the contamination may be aberrational or systemic. The first sample may come from a factory where every conceivable step is taken to insure that such contamination will not take place. The second vial may come from a company which uses a cheap manufacturing process offering no protection against contamination. There is an element of tragedy if death results when all possible precautions have been taken: there just are limits to human capability at our present level of understanding. But where vital precautions are dropped in the name of expediency, the contamination that results is much more serious if only because we knew it would take place and we knew what could be done to prevent it. While we have every reason to believe that the first sample is pure, we have no reason to believe that the second sample is uncontaminated. Indeed, one cannot call the latter contamination accidental as one can in the first case. It would be more correct to call it an accident if contamination did not take place in the total absence of precaution.

Likewise, systemic injustic in the context of criminal law is a much more serious matter than aberrational injustice. It should not be forgotten that the criminal sanction is the most severe imposition that the state can visit upon one of its citizens. While it is possible to tolerate occasional error in a sound system, systematic carelessness in the administration of punishment is negligence of the highest order.

With this framework in mind, let us look at a particular instance of plea bargaining recently described by a legal aid defense attorney.[22] Ted Alston has been charged with armed robbery. Let us assume that persons who have committed armed robbery (in the way Alston is accused of having committed it) deserve five to seven years of prison. Alston's attorney sets out the options for him: "I told Alston it was possible, perhaps even probable, that if he went to trial he would be convicted and get a prison term of perhaps five to seven years. On the other hand, if he agreed to plead guilty to a low-grade felony, he would get a probationary sentence and not go to prison. The choice

[21]My discussion here owes much to John Rawls's treatment of "imperfect procedural justice" in his *A Theory of Justice* (Cambridge, 1971), pp. 85–86.

[22]Robert Hermann, "The Case of the Jamaican Accent," *New York Times Magazine* (December 1, 1974), p. 93 (© The *New York Times* Company).

was his." Let us assume that Alston accepts the terms of the bargain and pleads guilty to a lesser offense. If Alston did commit the armed robbery, there is a violation of the first principle in that he receives far less punishment than he deserves. On the other hand, if Alston did not commit the armed robbery, there is still a violation of the first principle in that he is both convicted of and punished for a crime that he did not commit, a crime that no one seriously believes to be his distinctive wrongdoing. It is of course possible that while Alston did not commit the armed robbery, he did commit the lesser offense. But though justice would be done here, it would be an accident. Such a serendipitous result is a certain sign that what we have here is systemic injustice.

If we assume that legislatures approximate the correct range of punishment for each offense, that judges fairly sentence those who are convicted by juries, and that prosecutors reasonably charge defendants, then, barring accidents, justice will *never* be the outcome of the plea-bargaining procedure: the defendant who "cops a plea" will never receive the punishment which is deserved. Of course legislatures can set punishments too high, judges can oversentence those who are convicted by juries, and prosecutors can overcharge defendants. In these cases the guilty can receive the punishment they deserve through plea bargaining. But in these cases we compensate for one injustice by introducing others that unfairly jeopardize the innocent and those that demand trials.

In contrast to plea bargaining, the disposition of criminal cases by jury trial seems well calculated to avoid internal injustices even if these may sometimes occur. Where participants take their responsibilities seriously we have good reason to believe that the outcome is just, even when this may not be so. In contrast, with plea bargaining we have no reason to believe that the outcome is just even when it is.

I think that the appeal that plea bargaining has is rooted in our attitude toward bargains in general. Where both parties are satisfied with the terms of an agreement, it is improper to interfere. Generally speaking, prosecutors and defendants are pleased with the advantages they gain by negotiating a plea. And courts, which gain as well, are reluctant to vacate negotiated pleas where only "proper" inducements have been applied and where promises have been understood and kept. Such judicial neutrality may be commendable where entitlements are being exchanged. But the criminal justice system is not such a context. Rather it is one in which persons are justly given, not what they have bargained for, but what they deserve, irrespective of their bargaining position.

To appreciate this, let us consider another context in which desert plays a familiar role; the assignment of grades in an academic setting. Imagine a "grade bargain" negotiated between a grade-conscious student and a harried instructor. A term paper has been submitted and, after glancing at the first page, the instructor says that if he were to read the paper carefully, applying his usually rigid standards, he would probably decide to give the paper a grade of D. But if the student were to waive his right to a careful reading and conscientious critique, the instructor would agree to a grade of B. The grade-point average being more important to him than either education or justice in grading, the student happily accepts the B, and the instructor enjoys a reduced workload.

One strains to imagine legislators and administrators commending the practice of grade bargaining because it permits more students to be processed by fewer instructors. Teachers can be freed from the burden of having to read and to criticize every paper. One struggles to envision academicians arguing for grade bargaining in the way that jurists have defended plea bargaining, suggesting that a quick assignment of a grade is a more effective influence on the behavior of students, urging that grade bargaining is necessary to the efficient functioning of the schools. There can be no doubt that students who have negotiated a grade are more likely to accept and to understand the verdict of the instructor. Moreover, in recognition of a student's help to the school (by waiving both the reading and the critique), it is proper for the instructor to be lenient. Finally, a quickly assigned grade enables the guidance personnel and the registrar to respond rapidly and appropriately to the student's situation.

What makes all of this laughable is what makes plea bargaining outrageous. For grades, like punishments, should be deserved. Justice in retribution, like justice in grading, does not require that the end result be acceptable to the parties. To reason that because the parties are satisfied the bargain should stand is to be seriously confused. For bargains are out of place in contexts where persons are to receive what they deserve. And the American courtroom, like the American classroom, should be such a context.

In this section, until now I have been attempting to show that plea bargaining is not well calculated to insure that those guilty of wrongdoing will receive the punishment they deserve. But a further point needs to be made. While the conviction of the innocent would be a problem in any system we might devise, it appears to be a greater problem under plea bargaining. With the jury system the guilt of the defendant must be established in an adversary proceeding and it must be established beyond a reasonable doubt to each of twelve jurors. This is very staunch protection against an aberrational conviction. But under plea bargaining the foundation for conviction need only include a factual basis for the plea (in the opinion of the judge) and the guilty plea itself. Considering the coercive nature of the circumstances surrounding the plea, it would be a mistake to attach much reliability to it. Indeed, as we have seen in *Alford*, guilty pleas are acceptable even when accompanied by a denial of guilt. And in a study of 724 defendants who had pleaded guilty, only 13.1 percent admitted guilt to an interviewer, while 51.6 percent asserted their innocence.[23] This leaves only the factual basis for the plea to serve as the foundation for conviction. Now it is one thing to show to a judge that there are facts which support a plea of guilty and quite another to prove to twelve jurors in an adversary proceeding guilt beyond a reasonable doubt. Plea bargaining substantially erodes the standards for guilt and it is reasonable to assume that the sloppier we are in establishing guilt, the more likely it is that innocent persons will be convicted. So apart from having no reason whatever to believe that the guilty are receiving the punishment they deserve, we have far less reason to believe that the convicted are guilty in the first place than we would after a trial.

In its coercion of criminal defendants, in its abandonment of desert as the measure of punishment, and in its relaxation of the standards for conviction, plea bargaining falls short of the justice we expect of our legal system. I have no doubt that substantial changes will have to be made if the institution of plea bargaining is to be obliterated or even removed from its central position in the criminal justice system. No doubt we need more courts and more prosecutors. Perhaps ways can be found to streamline the jury trial procedure without sacrificing its virtues.[24] Certainly it would help to decriminalize the host of victimless crimes—drunkenness and other drug offenses, illicit sex, gambling, and so on—in order to free resources for dealing with more serious wrongdoings. And perhaps crime itself can be reduced if we begin to attack seriously those social and economic injustices that have for too long sent their victims to our prisons in disproportionate numbers. In any case, if we are to expect our citizenry to respect the law, we must take care to insure that our legal institutions are worthy of that respect. I have tried to show that plea bargaining is not worthy, that we must seek a better way. Bargain justice does not become us.

[23]Blumberg, p. 91.

[24]John Langbein has suggested that we look to the German legal system to see how this might be done. See his "Controlling Prosecutorial Discretion in Germany," *University of Chicago Law Review* 41 (Spring 1974): 439.

Considering Jury "Nullification": When May and Should a Jury Reject the Law to Do Justice?

The Honorable Jack B. Weinstein*

I. INTRODUCTION

There seems to be a good deal of distress expressed today about perceived "jury nullification."[1] Nullification occurs when a jury—based on its own sense of justice or fairness—refuses to follow the law and convict in a particular case even though the facts seem to allow no other conclusion but guilt.[2] Such concerns

Jack Weinstein, "Considering Jury 'Nullification': When May and Should a Jury Reject the Law To Do Justice?" *American Criminal Law Review* Volume 30 Number 2 (1993): 239–254. Reprinted with permission of the publisher, Georgetown University and *American Criminal Law Review.* © 1993.

*United States District Judge, Eastern District of New York. This essay expands on a speech originally delivered at the 1992 District of Columbia Circuit Conference in Williamsburg, Virginia. I acknowledge with thanks the able assistance of my law clerk, Jessica C. Vapnek.

[1]See, e.g., Terence Moran, Maybe the Jury was White, *Conn. L. Trib.*, June 15, 1992, at 15 (discussing concern that Rodney King verdict reflected views of community, rather than adjudication of facts).

[2]Although there may be examples of nullification by conviction, as by a refusal to follow instructions on justification or the requirement of *mens rea*, the possibility seems to be remote in practice except as an expression of extreme prejudice based on race or the appalling nature of the issue. See Jon M. Van Dyke, The Jury as a Political Institution, 16 *Cath. Law.* 224, 238–39 (1970) (nullification by conviction is unlikely because courts can reverse conviction unsupported by facts and reason). *But see* Irwin A. Horowitz & Thomas E. Willging, Changing Views of Jury Power, 15 *L. & Hum. Behav.* 165, 172–73 (1991) (studies suggest juries receiving nullification instructions treat unsympathetic defendants more harshly than other juries). Such prejudicial conviction are, I believe, much rarer today than in times past, partly as a result of post-World War II improvements in our justice system and partly due to a society more tolerant of diversity. Nullification by conviction of a defendant who should under the law have been acquitted cannot be tolerated.

about jury nullification in my district—the most densely populated district in the country after Washington, D.C.—are unwarranted.

The legitimacy of the jury process demands respect for its outcomes, whatever they may be. Attempting to distinguish between a "right" outcome—a verdict following the letter of the law—and a "wrong" one—a "nullification" verdict—can be dangerous, and this endeavor depends largely upon personal bias. Nullification is but one legitimate result in an appropriate constitutional process safeguarded by judges and the judicial system. When juries refuse to convict on the basis of what they think are unjust laws, they are performing their duty as jurors. Once judges and courthouse personnel have set the stage and parameters for fair decision-making, the result is not nullification but vindication of the process.

Current concern with jury nullification reflects disturbing trends in society. Racial disharmony and antagonism are perceived by some to threaten many institutions, including the jury.[3] This tendency has not been manifested in the Eastern District of New York. Our jurors—who are of many diverse ethnic groups and origins—are excellent. Our prosecutors tend to screen out those cases that are

[3]See, e.g., L.A. Lawless, *The Nation*, May 18, 1992, at 651 ("Racial fears and prejudices are planted so firmly in [the Rodney King jury's] unconscious (not one of them was black) that nothing prejudicial need be said to produce the desired effect."); Daniel Klaidman, Racial Politics in the Jury Room, *Legal Times*, Apr. 23, 1990, at 1 ("[a] D.C. Superior Court jury's acquittal . . . offers a rare and palpable glimpse of how emotionally charged views on race have seeped into the ultimate sanctum of the criminal justice system—the jury room.").

not significant from a law enforcement point of view and that might invite nullification.

Even if the problem should manifest itself here or elsewhere, it is neither necessary nor desirable to attempt to prevent nullification through strict controls. The jury room is not the place to counteract society's larger problems. Trial by jury retains its legitimacy precisely because of its long history of impermeability to the vicissitudes of politics and fashion.

There is the troubling question of whether juries should be informed that they have the power to nullify.[4] Fervent supporters of nullification seek a forthright instruction from the judge that the jury may disregard the charge and nullify the law.[5] Others oppose even the barest of hints from the judge that the jury may take that route and still arrive at a fair outcome.[6] It is my view that, although juries should not be instructed that they have the power to nullify, judges can and should exercise their discretion to allow nullification by flexibly applying the concepts of relevancy and prejudice and by admitting evidence bearing

on moral values. Professor R. Kent Greenawalt's discussion of morality and law, referred to below, provides a useful model for the exercise of that discretion.[7]

II. DISCUSSION

Our jury system deserves admiration. My respect for it is based not on the fact that my juries and I generally reach the same result but on the meticulous and responsible process by which jurors follow the evidence, deliberate fully, and ask the right questions during deliberations. Some of the juries with which I have worked have devoted months to the most difficult scientific and criminal issues, effectively deciding the facts and assiduously following instructions on the law. Most trial judges are in this respect biased—they believe in the historical American jury system of which they are a part.

A. Disobeying Unjust Laws

Nullification is British in origin,[8] yet quintessentially American. The power of the jury to nullify was approved in 1670 in *Bushell's Case*[9] when Chief Justice Vaughan released from jail British jurors who had had the audacity to ignore a trial judge and acquit William Penn of unlawful assembly.[10] Along with its sibling, civil disobedience, jury nullification was an integral feature of the birth of our nation.[11] The Boston Tea Party and the acquittal of dissident John Peter Zenger on charges of libel both might

---

[4]This essay focuses on nullification in criminal cases, although it can occur in civil cases as well. See generally Roger W. Kirst, The Jury's Historic Domain in Complex Cases, 58 *Wash. L. Rev.* 1, 12 (1982) ("[jury] nullification argument has some value as a reminder of the American jury's political role, but it will not long be a defensible position in the complexity debate"); Noel Fidel, Preeminently a Political Institution: The Right of Arizona Juries to Nullify the Law of Contributory Negligence, 23 *Ariz. St. L.J.* 1, 6–7 (1991) (arguing that jury nullification is "constitutionally embroidered into Arizona's law of torts").

[5]One group, the Fully Informed Jury Association (FIJA), has lobbied several state legislatures for statutes requiring judges to inform juries of their powers of nullification. Katherine Bishop, Diverse Group Wants Juries to Follow Natural Law, *N.Y. Times*, Sept. 27, 1991, at B16; see also William M. Kunstler, Jury Nullification in Conscience Cases, 10 *Va. J. Int'l. L.* 71, 83 (1969) (juries should be told they have power to nullify); Alan W. Scheflin & Jon M. Van Dyke, Merciful Juries: The Resilience of Jury Nullification, 48 *Wash. & Lee L. Rev.* 165, 183 (1991) (same); Robert J. Stolt, Note, Jury Nullification: The Forgotten Right, 7 *New Engl. L. Rev.* 105, 120–22 (1971) (same).

[6]See e.g., Gary J. Simson, Jury Nullification in the American System: A Skeptical View, 54 *Tex. L. Rev.* 488, 525 (1976) (juries should not be instructed on their power to nullify); Eleanor Tavris, The Law of an Unwritten Law: A Common Sense View of Jury Nullification, 11 *W. St. L. Rev.* 97, 114–15 (1983) (same).

[7]See infra notes 60–64 and accompanying text (discussing Professor Greenawalt's model).

[8]Thomas Andrew Green, *Verdict According to Conscience, Perspectives on the English Criminal Trial Jury, 1200–1800* xviii (1985) ("[n]ullification begins in the medieval period with jury mitigation in routine felonies").

[9]124 Eng. Rep. 1006 (P.C. 1670).

[10]Id.

[11]For an in-depth historical view of jury nullification, see Mark DeWolfe Howe, Juries as Judges of Criminal Law, 52 *Harv. L. Rev.* 582, 583–96 (1939); Alan Scheflin & Jon Van Dyke, Jury Nullification: The Contours of a Controversy, 43 *Law & Contemp. Probs.* 51, 56–63 (Autumn 1980).

be called founding acts of civil disobedience and nullification.[12]

The American nullification tradition was ratified by the Supreme Court in *Sparf and Hansen v. United States*.[13] The Court recognized that judges had no recourse if jurors acquitted in the face of overwhelming inculpatory evidence and law.[14]

In the nineteenth century the practice of nullifying to avoid capital punishment for minor offenses became so widespread in England that Parliament eventually had to act to follow the jury's views in reducing the number of capital crimes.[15] In the United States during that same period, the federal government feared that Northern juries would nullify the fugitive slave laws, while Southern juries were prone to nullify laws designed to prevent mistreatment of slaves.[16] In many states, the failure of numerous juries to find defendants guilty in the face of overwhelming evidence helped influence Congress and state legislatures to reject mandatory death penalty schemes.[17]

During the Vietnam-era disturbances, there was a good deal written on the right of citizens in a democracy to ignore "unjust" laws.[18] Martin Luther King, Jr. acted in the highest ideals of the nullification and civil disobedience tradition. Recall his eloquent letter from the Birmingham jail:

> An individual who breaks a law that conscience tells him is unjust, and willingly accepts the penalty . . . to arouse the conscience of the community over its injustice, is in reality expressing the very highest respect for the law. . . . It was "illegal" to aid and comfort a Jew in Hitler's Germany: But I am sure that if I had lived in Germany during that time I would have . . . comforted . . . the Jewish people.[19]

Recently, "pro choice" and "pro life" forces have mounted barricades in violation of injunction and statute.[20] When Americans feel deeply, they speak out and they act out. It is doubtful that juries would return convictions in these abortion clinic interdiction

---

[12]See Scheflin & Van Dyke, supra note 11, at 57 (acquittal of Zenger is "most famous colonial example of jury nullification"); Steven M. Bauer & Peter J. Eckerstrom, The State Made Me Do It: The Applicability of the Necessity Defense to Civil Disobedience, 39 *Stan. L. Rev.* 1173, 1175–76 (1987) (Boston Tea Party began American tradition of civil disobedience).

[13]156 U.S. 51 (1895).

[14]Id. at 80.

[15]See generally Jerome Hall, *Theft, Law & Society* 127–32 (2d ed. 1952). "By the middle of the eighteenth century the practice of returning fictitious verdicts was so widespread that it was generally recognized as a typical feature of English administration of criminal justice." *Id.* at 127.

[16]See Paul D. Carrington, The Seventh Amendment: Some Bicentennial Reflections, 1990 *U. Cal. Legal F.* 33, 45–46 (discussing federal concerns of jury nullification in the nineteenth century).

[17]See *Woodson v. North Carolina*, 428 U.S. 280, 288–304 (1976) (discussing history); *McGautha v. California*, 402 U.S. 183, 199 (1971) ("legislature . . . forthrightly grant[ed] juries the discretion which they had been exercising in fact") (citation omitted); see also *Furman v. Georgia*, 408 U.S. 238, 333–42 (1972) (Marshall, J., concurring) (tracing history of the death penalty in United States). The Supreme Court recently considered mandatory sentencing schemes in *Walton v. Arizona*, 497 U.S. 639 (1990). In

Walton, an Arizona statute provided for a separate sentencing hearing in first degree murder cases, at which the prosecution had the burden of proving the existence of aggravating circumstances and the defendant had the burden of proving the existence of mitigating circumstances. A majority of the Court held that this sentencing scheme did not violate the Sixth Amendment. Id. at 649. Further, a plurality held that the sentencing scheme did not violate the Eighth and Fourteenth Amendments. Id.

[18]See, e.g., Stanford Jay Rosen, Civil Disobedience and other Such Techniques: Law Making through Law Breaking, 37 *Geo. Wash. L. Rev.* 435, 444 (1969) (discussing the importance of civil disobedience as a way of preventing violent dissent); Lawrence R. Velvel, Freedom of Speech and the Draft Card Burning Cases, 16 *Kan. L. Rev.* 149, 152 (1968) ("strong case" for protecting peaceful opposition to the Vietnam War and the draft); Stolt, supra note 5, at 119–20 (jury nullification needed to protect important right of civil disobedience).

[19]Martin Luther King, Jr., Letter from a Birmingham Jail, in *Christian Century*, June 12, 1963, at 80, reprinted *in* Robert T. Hall, *Morality and Disobedience* 767–73 (1971).

[20]See, e.g., John W. Whitebread, Civil Disobedience and Operation Rescue: A Historical & Theoretical Analysis, 48 *Wash & Lee L. Rev.* 77, 107–22 (1991) (criticizing the tactics of Operation Rescue); Eric Harrison, Kansas Protesters Defy Court, Block Abortion Clinic. *L.A. Times*, Aug. 10, 1991, at A1 (discussing the Operation Rescue demonstration in Wichita, Kansas).

cases.[21] Other modern moral dilemmas face citizens and jurors: How should we treat those who keep drugs for personal use? Should we punish battered women who strike back, harming or killing their batterers? Must tax protesters be prosecuted?

The heritage of refusing to obey laws regarded as unjust in their operations is honored today within all branches of the federal government, often for the "good of the Republic." Presidents and their minions, enthralled with a particular policy goal, sometimes violate laws, mislead Congress and the public, and try to cover it up.[22] Legislators sometimes consider themselves above their own rules and abuse their privileges. Members of the Supreme Court of the United States twist or ignore precedent in pursuit of higher views of justice. From time to time, the Courts of Appeals so distort the facts of cases that the trial judges cannot recognize the cases they tried. Finally, district court judges have been known to nullify when, for example, they seek to escape the rigors of guideline sentencing or when the outcome of a trial totally offends their sense of justice.[23]

The difficulty with any tendency to ignore laws is that whether a particular law is unjust may depend entirely on the view of the beholder. One person might feel compelled to disobey a judge's injunction and approach women at abortion clinics. Another might refuse to pay taxes. Our system of law is grounded on the general assumption that people will obey laws voluntarily. Chaos results if each person feels it appropriate without limit to pick and choose which laws to recognize.

This is one reason the jury system embodies group decision-making. It is unlikely that twelve persons chosen at random from the community will at the same time be struck with a collective will to ignore a just law or with the same burning political zeal. As Judge Bazelon wrote, dissenting in a case arising from the Vietnam War:

> I do not see any reason to assume that jurors will make rampantly abusive use of their power. Trust in the jury is, after all, one of the cornerstones of our entire criminal jurisprudence, and if that trust is without foundation we must reexamine a great deal more than just the nullification doctrine.[24]

Jurors help keep us sensitive to wrong, immoral, and unjust laws. Nullification arising from idealism is good for the American soul. It prevents the perversion of morality by an Eichmann who so conforms to the law as to compromise the individual's responsibility for developing and living in a way consonant with truth, justice, and love for fellow man.[25]

When our jurors retire to the jury room they understand their job is to find the just result and reach a consensus. Professor Uviller

[21]However, efforts to advocate jury nullification in these cases have sparked controversy. For example, in January 1990, the publisher of the *San Diego Reader* placed an ad in his newspaper urging jury nullification of pro-life protesters who violate statutes or injunctions as part of their demonstrations against abortion. The National Organization of Women immediately responded by requesting that major advertisers pull their ads from the paper. A board member of the local chapter of NOW stated, "We think [the publisher] is doing something self-serving as well as threatening to our legal system." Michael Granberry, NOW Urges Advertisers to Drop Reader, *L.A. Times*, Feb. 3, 1990, at B1.

[22]The verdicts in the trial of Lieutenant Colonel Oliver North might be considered by some to be nullification verdicts: he was convicted of three felonies concerning cover-ups of earlier activities, but acquitted on the nine counts concerning his activities in Nicaragua. The jury arguably disregarded the dangers of encouraging the executive to ignore congressional limitations. See also Louis B. Schwartz, "Innocence"—A Dialogue with Professor Sundby, 41 *Hastings L.J.* 153, 155–56 (1989) (discussing the presumption of innocence in criminal procedures).

[23]Recently, when a district court judge refused to let a guilty verdict stand and ordered a new trial because he "could not abide the police [officers' perjured] testimony,"

the government accused him of acting as the "Thirteenth Juror." The circuit court reversed the order, finding that perjury alone was not enough to upset the conviction. See, e.g., Joel Cohen, Does the Justice System Bear False Witness, *N.Y. L.J.*, Sept. 8, 1992, at 2 (discussing *United States v. Sanchez*, 969 F.2d 1409 (2d Cir. 1992)).

[24]*United States v. Dougherty*, 473 F.2d 1113, 1142 (D.C. Cir. 1972) (Bazelon, J., dissenting).

[25]See Hannah Arendt. *Eichmann in Jerusalem: A Report on the Banality of Evil* 3 (1964) (reporting on the trial of Adolf Eichmann in Jerusalem for his crimes during World War II).

writes that "[m]ost former jurors report that the process of deliberation was unique in their experience. Never had they been in a situation where so many different sorts of people tried so hard for so long to reconcile such various views of reality—and with such remarkable success."[26] The exercise of the nullification power does not cast doubt on the jury process; rather, it reaffirms the liberty of a free society upon which it is based. "Jury nullification, rather than destroying the law, is necessary to protect it."[27]

When jurors return with a "nullification" verdict, then, they have not in reality "nullified" anything: they have done their job. "[N]ullification is inherent in the jury's role as the conscience of the democratic community and a cushion between the citizens and overly harsh or arbitrary government criminal prosecution."[28] Juries are charged not with the task of blindly and mechanically applying the law, but of doing justice in light of the law, the evidence presented at trial, and their own knowledge of society and the world. To decide that some outcomes are just and some are not is not possible without drawing upon personal views.[29]

Given the procedural safeguards and requirements of group decision-making, we can remain confident that, first, instances of nullification will continue to be rare, and second, if twelve individuals decide to "nullify," they will have a good reason for so doing.

B. The Perceived Problem

Jury nullification can take several forms. In Professor R. Kent Greenawalt's comprehensive discussion of the conflicts between law and morality, he points out that nullification, what he calls "amelioration" of the criminal process, takes place through non-prosecution, judge or jury nullification, and pardon.[30] Pardon or amnesty, one of the executive's forms of nullification, seldom is used for that purpose in this

---

[26]H. Richard Uviller, Acquitting the Guilty: Two Case Studies on Jury Misgivings and the Misunderstood Standard of Proof, 2 *Crim. L.F.* 1, 21 (1990) (citation omitted); see also Nancy S. Marder, Note. Gender Dynamics and Jury Deliberation, 96 *Yale L.J.* 593, 594–98 (1987) (discussing the role of gender in jury deliberations and the danger that female members participate less actively than male counterparts).

[27]Scheflin & Van Dyke, supra note 11, at 89.

[28]Milton Heumann & Lance Cassak, Not-So-Blissful Ignorance: Informing Jurors About Punishment in Mandatory Sentencing Cases, 20 *Am. Crim. L. Rev.* 343, 386 (1983) (citation omitted).

[29]See Uviller, supra note 26, at 1–6 (discussing concepts of true and false verdicts); *cf.* Akhil Reed Amar, The Bill of Rights as a Constitution, 100 *Yale L.J.* 1131, 1191–95 (1991) (distinguishing between refusing to follow laws thought unjust and laws thought unconstitutional); Michael Polanyi, *The Study of Man* (1959). Polanyi writes:

> Mental passions are a desire for truth, or more generally, for things of intrinsic excellence. . . . The theory of personal knowledge says that . . . a valid choice can be made by submitting to one's own sense of responsibility. Herein lies the self-compulsion by which, in

the ideal case of a purely mental achievement, the utmost straining of every clue pointing towards the true solution finally imposes a particular choice upon the chooser. In view of the unspecifiabilty of the particulars on which such a decision will be based, it is heavily affected by the participation of the person pouring himself into these particulars and may in fact represent a major feat of his originality. Yet since this act is called forth by the agent's utmost submission to his intimations of reality, it does not abridge the universal intent of its own outcome. Such are the assumptions of human responsibility and such the spiritual foundations on which a free society is conceivable.

Id. at 62–63. See also Ernest L. Weinrib, Law as a Kantian Idea of Reason, 87 *Colum. L. Rev.* 472, 494–95 (1987):

> The duty of juridical honor is incumbent on the free will as a law of its own being, and it is expressed in the imperative "Do not make yourself into a mere means for others, but be at the same time an end for them." Kant conceived of juridical honor as a kind of defensive imperialism, whereby the actor, to realize his nature as a bundle of self-determining energy, presses out into the world and thus resists the pressures that other actors exert upon him.

[30]R. Kent Greenawalt. *Conflicts of Law and Morality* 349–73 (1987); see also Kenneth C. Davis, *Discretionary Justice* 189–214 (1969) (discussing immense discretion held by prosecutors to refuse to prosecute); Green, supra note 8, at 28–64 (discussing the early history of jury nullification in England, in which juries exercised discretion by refusing to convict when they felt the death sentence too severe); Mortimer Kadish & Sanford Kadish. *Discretion To Disobey* 51 (1973) (explaining the moral legitimacy of juries departing from the law when the law is contrary to justice); George C. Christie. Lawful Departures from Legal Rules: "Jury Nullification" and Legitimated Disobedience, 62 *Cal. L. Rev.* 1289, 1289–1310 (1974) (criticizing the reasoning of *Discretion to Disobey*).

country.[31] A striking recent example was President Ford's action exonerating President Nixon.[32]

Judicial nullification through sentencing, directed verdicts, or findings on evidence is rare. It probably has some impact in prosecutions such as those during World War II for statutory rape, when the community was sympathetic toward young people involved in a romance, or in the prosecution of draft avoiders or card burners during the Vietnam War.[33] In civil cases, such as landlord-tenant disputes or evictions for mortgage defaults, judges stretch the law to some extent out of sympathy for the litigants and a sense of justice. And, as Professor Jerome Hall notes, English judges often cooperated with juries in circumventing the death penalty in simple larceny cases.[34] The reluctance of judges in the North to enforce fugitive slave laws is also well known.[35]

By far the greatest nullification takes place as a result of decisions not to prosecute or to reduce charges.[36] Our prosecutors have enormous discretion because of the great number of crimes found in our over-expansive criminal laws. For example, prosecution for possession of marijuana for private use or for growing or dealing in small amounts is rare. The police also exercise discretion—at times invidiously—by failing to arrest, for example, in cases of suspected domestic violence.[37]

Compared to prosecutorial nullification, grand jury refusal to indict and petit jury refusal to find guilt are of minor significance.[38] Jurors have generally become more sophisticated about people and the law. Our jurors are not obtuse. In the 1960s, FBI agents were regarded as infallible. During the Vietnam period, some of the younger jurors disbelieved them merely because they were agents. This generational gap was temporary. Now New York police and DEA agents tend to be more professional and believable. Their testimony generally is treated with critical but fair-minded neutrality.

Some jurors want to follow the law but think that the police and society are so biased that they find it difficult to consider law enforcement officers credible.[39] Our society is increasingly

[31]See Daniel T. Kobil, The Quality of Mercy Strained; Wresting the Pardoning Power from the Ring, 69 *Tex. L. Rev.* 569, 602 (1991) (use of the pardon is declining and, even when used, is normally used post-sentence to rehabilitate person's criminal record).

[32]See Pardon of Richard M. Nixon and Related Matters: Hearings Before the Subcomm. on Criminal Justice of the House Comm. on the Judiciary, 93d Cong., 2d Sess. 151 (1974) (statement of President Gerald Ford); see also Editorial, A Bush Pardon Now: Unforgivable. *N.Y. Times*, Nov. 12, 1992, at A24 (urging then-President Bush not to pardon any defendants charged in the Iran-contra investigation because it would prompt suspicion of his involvement).

[33]See Irwin A. Horowitz, Jury Nullification: The Impact of Judicial Instructions, Arguments, and Challenges on Jury Decision Making 12 *L. & Hum. Behav.* 439, 441 (1988) ("The evidence reveals that juries convicted at a higher rate in draft evasion cases when a war was popular than when the war (Vietnam and Korea) lost public support.").

[34]See Hall, supra note 15, at 80–92.

[35]See William W. Fisher III, Ideology, Religion, and Constitutional Protection of Private Property, 39 *Emory L.J.* 65, 121–31 (1990) (discussing actions taken in Northern courts to avoid enforcing Fugitive Slave laws).

[36]See Alan Scheflin, Jury Nullification: The Right to Say No, 45 *S. Cal. L. Rev.* 168, 181 (1972) (arguing that jury nullification as an exercise of juror discretion "may be a useful check on prosecutorial indiscretion"). Compare the German system of lack of discretion described in Davis, supra note 30, at 191: Professor Davis suggested review of prosecutors by administrative appeals, supervision by an outsider and increased judicial authority.

[37]See Thomas Bell, Support Grows for Domestic Violence Curbs. *Wash Post*, June 21, 1990, at J1 (group lobbies for mandatory arrest of batterers); Tom Coakley, Man Allegedly Detailed Fatal Stabbing of Wife, *Boston Globe*, July 18, 1992, at 19 (police failed to arrest suspect for whom warrant issued, and eight days later the suspect killed his wife).

[38]Compare James Bennet, Juries Reflect Fears of Crime, *N.Y. Times*, Aug. 25, 1992, at B3 (describing a few instances of grand jury and petit jury decisions treating defendants who kill to defend themselves or their families with compassion because of "growing tendency of juries and prosecutors to recognize the terrible strain that fear of urban crime can place on people who would otherwise obey the law") with DAVIS, supra note 30, at 189–214 (describing widespread and relatively unchecked prosecutorial discretion).

[39]See Editorial, The Crown Heights Acquittal, *N.Y. Times*, Oct. 31, 1992, at A20 (describing a Brooklyn jury's acquittal of a black youth accused of murdering a Hasidic scholar as a "powerful warning about the dangers of allowing many citizens to lose faith in the police"); Shawn G. Kennedy, Accused and Police Given Equal Weight, Poll Finds, *N.Y. Times*, Feb. 15, 1993, at A8 (survey of jurors by *National Law Journal* revealed that 51% were as likely to believe defendants as to believe police officers and 70% stated that police officers' testimony would not carry more weight); see also *United States v. Sanusi*, No. CR 92-410, 1992 U.S. Dist. LEXIS 17741, at 33 (E.D.N.Y. Nov. 23, 1992) (invitation to CBS by Secret Service to accompany them on a search of defendant's home may provide the jury with the basis for a not guilty verdict).

divided along racial, ethnic, economic, and social lines. We are facing difficulties unimagined ten or twenty years ago. There is an undercurrent of fear that the community has broken down.

Juries, which are drawn from a cross-section of the community, are not impervious to the problems outside the courtroom. Juries cannot be "the conscience of the community"[40] if there is no community. Will white jurors convict white police of brutality? Will African-American jurors convict African-American defendants for violent acts, particularly in conflicts with police? These are the fears behind the renewed interest in jury nullification.

Many consider the Rodney King verdict ample proof that such premonitions have been realized. Others argue that such a verdict does not reflect the breakdown of the jury system or rampant nullification, but rather is "a case of an inept prosecution and a non-representative jury."[41] Not having seen and heard the evidence, I have no view on the outcome of that trial.

If more than negligible racial bias is infecting the courts, the disease has not yet reached the federal courts in the Eastern District of New York. The resentments of the poorest segments of our population have not yet created widespread observable distortions, but that may be because the poorest tend not to vote, are not on jury rolls, and therefore do not serve. But there are suspicions and racial tensions that are impossible to deny.

The problems we have inherited have certainly been exacerbated by a decade of greed and excessive attention to the acquisition of personal wealth at the expense of our civic duties. Increasingly we have turned into a nation of classes with limited power to escape inherited poverty and with circumscribed dreams of upward mobility. Something is amiss in our society when so many have lost faith in the visions of those, like Thurgood Marshall or Martin Luther King, Jr., who once led the valiant struggle to create genuine equality and integration.

In a sense, the possibility of nullification based upon race is not surprising. We are all citizens of a country conceived upon the most fundamental and terrible social division, that of the free person and the slave. Professor Judith Shklar eloquently wrote that "[citizenship in] America has in principle always been democratic, but only in principle. From the first the most radical claims for freedom and political equality were played out in counterpoint to chattel slavery, the most extreme form of servitude, the consequences of which still haunt us."[42] Legally, we are doing better with minorities, with women, with the disabled, and with family and sexual orientations once deemed unacceptable because out of the mainstream. The schisms in our country, though great, have not incapacitated our judicial institutions as have similar societal divisions in some areas of the world.

Given structural gaps and a lack of consensus, we could expect nullification to be much more prevalent in this country. This suggests that, first, more than some predict, our people are disciplined and accepting of the need for law to be applied without regard to race or creed; and second, centripetal social forces in society are much more powerful than the centrifugal. Bitter ethnic divisions and the absence of liberty would render juries unworkable in many countries; they still work in the United States.

The critical factor in avoiding nullification along racial and other structural schisms is to heal ourselves of the cancerous inequality of real opportunity that pervades much of our society. Our goal should be "to discover the cement to bond the heterogeneous strains into one nation, one polity, one civilization."[43]

Against this background, courts can take only small ameliorative steps. Even were the problems of race to affect the court system more visibly, nullification should not be prevented

---

[40]*United States v. Spock*, 416 F.2d 165, 182 (1st Cir. 1969).

[41]Scheflin & Van Dyke supra note 11, at 94 n.173 (using as an example the acquittal of former Supervisor Dan White in the murder of San Francisco Mayor and Supervisor).

[42]Judith Suklar. *American Citizenship: The Quest for Inclusion* 1 (1991).

[43]Leslie Gordon Fagen, Preface to *Simon Rifkind, At 90, On the 90s* iii (1992) (quoting Judge Rifkind).

through strict jury controls. If society is sick, then the jury system may be infected, but society's problems cannot be solved by controlling what takes place in the jury room. The concept of trial by jury has remained consistent over this country's long history because it is almost impervious to petty concerns and even to the tides of popular belief.

C. *Allowing Nullification Without Fostering It*

Proceedings in the courtroom should encourage a sense that the participants are sharing in a search for justice. Seemingly trivial things such as the manner in which we greet the jurors, care for them during their time in the courthouse, and instruct them can be helpful. When respected as colleagues in a mutual search for truth, jurors tend to listen to judges and follow their advice. When pushed to accept a judge's view or when treated with disdain, they rebel.

When judges take further initiatives to prevent nullification beyond such simple house-keeping measures, they run a serious risk of interfering with the jury system and with defendants' constitutional rights.[44] For example, courts sometimes excuse potential jurors who appear prone to nullify, particularly in death penalty cases.[45] Federal Rule of Evidence 606(b) prohibits questioning jurors on the hows and whys of their decisions.[46] Jurors have

a recognized privacy right.[47] Access to the jury room—opening the black box—would not likely decrease the level of jury nullification. Jurors could always internalize and rationalize their actions.

Limiting defense evidence on the grounds that it is irrelevant to a particular legal theory and may therefore prompt nullification is a dubious route. Defendants indicted for quasi-political acts, for example, are often not permitted to explain their reasons for acting since those reasons usually are not relevant to the legal case.[48] In my view these defendants are entitled to tell their story to the jury. The courtroom is their public forum. They should be permitted to explain their intent and state of mind as relevant to *mens rea* in the broadest sense.

The question whether juries should be informed that they have the power to nullify raises the most heated debate among judges and lawyers. Fervent supporters of nullification seek an outright instruction from the judge that the jury may disregard the charge and nullify the law.[49] Others oppose even hints

---

[44]Cf. Chaya Weinberg-Brodt, Note, Jury Nullification and Jury-Control Procedures, 65 *N.Y.U. L. Rev.* 825, 841–46 (1990) (proposing a defendant-centered rather than jury-centered view of nullification).

[45]Cf. Scott W. Howe, Resolving the Conflict in the Capital Sentencing Cases: A Desert-Oriented Theory of Regulation, 26 *Ga. L. Rev.* 323, 418 (1992) ("[r]egulating capital sentencing under the Eighth Amendment requires a standard to determine when a death sentence in an individual case is just").

[46]Federal Rule of Evidence 606(b) states:

Upon an inquiry into the validity of a verdict or indictment, a juror may not testify as to any matter or statement occurring during the course of the jury's deliberations or to the effect of anything upon that or any other juror's mind or emotions as influencing the juror to assent to or dissent from the verdict or indictment or concerning the juror's mental processes in connection therewith, except that a juror may testify on the question of whether extraneous prejudicial

information was improperly brought to the jury's attention or whether any outside influence was improperly brought to bear on any juror. Nor may a juror's affidavit or evidence of any statement by the juror concerning a matter about which the juror would be precluded from testifying be received for these purposes.

Fed. R. Evid. 606(b).

[47]See Marc O. Litt, "Citizen Soldiers" or Anonymous Justice: Reconciling the Sixth Amendment Right of the Accused, the First Amendment Right of the Media and the Privacy Right of Jurors, 25 *Colum. J.L. & Soc. Probs.* 371, 389–98 (1992) (discussing the contours of a juror's right to privacy).

[48]See Weinberg-Brodt, supra note 44, at 857–65 (discussing examples, such as *United States v. Montgomery*, 772 F.2d 733 (11th Cir. 1985), in which trespassers at a nuclear facility were forbidden from explaining implications of nuclear power and nuclear weapons because the sole purpose of the evidence was to cause nullification).

[49]See generally Kunstler, supra note 5, at 83 (juries should be told they have power to nullify); *Scheflin & Van Dyke*, supra note 11, at 111 (same) see also Heumann & Cassak, supra note 28, at 386–89 (considering possible constitutional right to inform jury of mandatory sentencing scheme or of its power to nullify).

from the judge that the jury may stray from the black letter of the law.[50] Still others take an intermediate position.[51]

I would not instruct juries on the power to nullify or not to nullify. Such an instruction is like telling children not to put beans in their noses. Most of them would not have thought of it had it not been suggested. As Judge Leventhal wrote:

> To tell [a juror] expressly of a nullification prerogative . . . is to inform him, in effect, that it is he who fashions the rule that condemns. That is an overwhelming responsibility, an extreme burden for the jurors' psyche.
>
> . . . .
>
> An explicit instruction to a jury conveys an implied approval that runs the risk of degrading the legal structure requisite for true freedom, for an ordered liberty that protects against anarchy as well as tyranny.[52]

In relatively infrequent extreme cases, the jurors will be distressed and exercise the power themselves. Nullification should occur only after the jury has struggled with it, as occurred in the television documentary about jury deliberations, "Inside the Jury Room."[53] The jurors dissolved in tears when they returned to the jury room after delivering a nullification verdict.[54] The jury itself will

"identify the case as establishing a call of high conscience. . . ."[55]

The judge may, and sometimes should, exercise some leniency in defining relevance in order to permit an argument for nullification. By construing relevance liberally, judges can admit evidence which might allow a jury to consider nullification sensibly. Jurors will then have the information and freedom necessary to ignore the judge's instructions to follow the law if the jurors think the law as applicable to the case before them is unjust.[56]

Often jurors will already have enough background so that they do not need any new information. Nullification of slavery in the North or defiance of Vietnam-era draft laws illustrate this. But the jury may be affected by the fact that a particular draft avoider may have had special reasons for his behavior which he would like to put before the jurors.

Addressing the jury or judge is the best chance a defendant may have to obtain publicity for his or her views. Arguably, the opportunity verges on a First Amendment right. A less stringent relevancy definition than the rigid and logical one in Rules 401, 402, and 403 of the Federal Rules of Evidence is justified in such cases.[57]

There is a danger, however. A defendant may so open the door to prejudicial material

[50]See, e.g., John E. Coons, Consistency, 75 *Cal. L. Rev.* 59, 79 (1987) ("[when] jurors ignore their instructions and smuggle in their private preferences, thereby defeating the intent of legislative and judicial rules . . . [t]hey simply violate their oath to uphold the law"); Simson, supra note 6, at 490 (arguing that nullification is neither historically nor functionally appropriate); Uviller, supra note 26, at 43 ("juries . . . need not reach the blissful state of perfect certainty in order to render a true verdict according to the evidence").

[51]See, e.g., *United States v. Dougherty*, 473 F.2d at 1135–37 (jurors perceive the power to nullify through informal channels and overall culture but they should not be informed outright since they might not reserve it for rare cases).

[52]Id. at 1136–37.

[53]*Frontline*, 410 (WGBH Boston, Apr. 8, 1986).

[54]See *Judicial Conference—Second Circuit*, 141 F.R.D. 573, 660–61 (Sept. 7, 1991) (discussing the videotape).

[55]*United States v. Dougherty*, 473 F.2d at 1136.

[56]Accord Kadish & Kadish, supra note 30, at 66; Paul H. Robinson, Legality and Discretion in the Distribution of Criminal Sanctions, 25 *Harv. J. on Legis.* 393, 403–04 (1988) (nullification occurs when there is a strong moral component of the decision and the jury perceives that applying rules would conflict with its normative sense of justice).

[57]Rule 401 defines relevant evidence as "evidence having any tendency to make the existence of any fact that is of consequence to the determination of the action more probable or less probable than it would be without the evidence." *Fed R. Evid.* 401. Relevant evidence is generally admissible. *Fed. R. Evid.* 402. Rule 403 limits this general rule by providing that "Although relevant, evidence may be excluded if its probative value is substantially outweighed by the danger of unfair prejudice, confusion of the issues, or misleading the jury, or by considerations of undue delay, waste of time, or needless presentation of cumulative evidence." *Fed. R. Evid.* 403.

by the prosecution or so turn a simple issue-of-fact trial into a political debate as to warrant the court's employing a strict view of relevancy even where a reasonable nullification argument exists. Judges will have to use their discretion sensibly under the Rules.

The example in "Inside the Jury Room" illustrates, I believe, a justifiable approach to a liberal view of relevancy.[58] Under the law, the only relevant facts were whether the defendant had been convicted of a felony and whether he possessed a gun. Both facts had to be conceded by the defense. The court, however, allowed proof that the defendant had voluntarily turned the gun over to the sheriff, that his intelligence and schooling were limited, and that he wanted to be a detective and was under the impression that a person studying for this profession needed a gun. The jury refused to convict, presumably based on all of this information which was not relevant under the statute.[59] I believe the judge was sensible in admitting the evidence.

Some might argue that loosening the rules of evidence is inconsistent with providing the federal judges' standard instruction that the jury must accept the law as stated by the judge even if the jury disagrees with it and that the jury should (not must) find the defendant guilty if all elements of the case have been proved beyond a reasonable doubt.[60] Professor R. Kent Greenawalt presents a narrow and justifiable view of what the law should logically be and suggests that "[d]efendant's counsel can neither argue that the jury should disregard those instructions nor present evidence in favor of the proposition that the defendant should be acquitted despite violating the law."[61]

But pure logical analysis without regard for ameliorative techniques such as jury nullification is unsatisfactory. It fails to appreciate fully the purpose of procedure and technique in modifying the effects of substantive law.

Professor Greenawalt does concede, "a jury's obligation to apply the law could be outweighed by its duty to do what is morally just in an individual case."[62] If this is so, and I believe it is, then should the jury not have the data necessary to decide whether morality requires nullification? And, if the jury should have this data, how is it to be presented except through a loosening of relevancy rules in those cases where an issue of morality in conflict with law exists? The judge should recognize, at the request of counsel, the question of when such an issue of morality should be considered as having arisen.

As already suggested, jurors bring a good deal of information with them —about slavery, the Vietnam War, police abuses in the community, the prevalent use of alcohol (during Prohibition) and of marijuana in recent years. This common knowledge is probably the most typical basis for nullification. To this store of information is added defense counsel's insinuation of non-relevant considerations into the case. Finally, the judge may make a deliberate decision to loosen relevancy controls to allow nullification.

Professor Greenawalt describes, but would not tell the jury, what the limits of nullification should be:

> A juror should not acquit unless he is firmly convinced that a gross injustice would be done by conviction. . . . He must think that the actor was performing an act that was clearly justified or was exercising an undeniable moral right. Ordinarily, he would have to think either that the law

---

[58]See supra notes 53–54 and accompanying text (discussing the videotape).

[59]See *Frontline* supra note 53.

[60]See, e.g. 1 Hon. Leonard B. Sand et al. *Modern Federal Jury Instructions: Criminal* 2–5 (1988) ("You should not, any of you, be concerned about the wisdom of any rule that I state. Regardless of any opinion that you may have as to what the law may be - or ought to be - it would violate your sworn duty to base a verdict upon any other view of the law than that which I give you.").

[61]Greenawalt, supra note 30, at 361; see also id. at 367 ("no evidence or argument in the possibility of nullification should be permitted").

[62]Id. at 364.

on which the prosecution is based is itself highly unjust or that the particular circumstances of the case are so far outside what the legislature had in mind that the law's application in this case would be unconscionable.[63]

This statement is a good guide for the judge as to when relevancy should be liberally construed to admit evidence which might permit nullification by the jury.

In the main, the nullification threat, like so many of our democracy's inconsistencies and compromises, is one that we can live with because it is used sensibly by responsible jurors, judges, and lawyers to help make the system work. As in the apparent conflict between justice and mercy, the dilemma is bridged if we concede that there are times when the law should recognize that it is reasonable to temper one with the other.[64] So, too, nullification built into the system and conceded to be reasonable and appropriate at times becomes a proper exercise of power within the law, not a nullification of the law.

[63]Id. at 365. For the full text of Greenawalt's statement, with further refinements, see id.

[64]Cf. H.L.A. Hart. *Punishment and Responsibility* 24 (1968) (Even though "like cases" should be "treated alike," "[j]ustice requires that those who have special difficulties to face in keeping the law which they have broken should be punished less."). See also Norman Lamm. *"Peace and Truth": Strategies for Their Reconciliation—A Meditation in Reverences, Righteousness and Rahamanut, Essays in Memory of Rabbi Dr. Leo Jung* 193–99 (Jacob J. Schacter ed., 1992).

III.   CONCLUSION

My view is simply summarized: jury nullification is not a substantial problem. Where it is a problem, it is probably because, first, the society is so sick that urgent remedial steps outside the courthouse are needed; second, trial judges have failed to provide the courthouse conditions under which jurors will decide within the confines of the law; or third, law enforcement is poor—that is to say, police and law enforcement agents are acting lawlessly or with racial bias, or prosecutors are not screening out poor cases or are not trying cases well.

Almost all jurors are doing just what we tell them to do—following the law not to find the defendant guilty unless each element of the crime has been proved beyond a reasonable doubt. Judges should permit jurors to hear the evidence that will allow them to reach a just result.

Some may not see this as a tidy view of the law. There is, however, a deep and profound sense of many Americans that they have the duty to revolt in large and small ways.[65] This is our ultimate protection against tyranny and injustice. Nullification is one of the peaceful barricades of freedom.

[65]Cf. *John Locke, Second Treatise of Government* 107–24 (C.B. McPherson ed., 1980) (discussing distribution of government as the ultimate nullification).

V
PENOLOGY

Penology is the study of punishment and is broader in scope than just prisons or "corrections." Criminal offenders do deserve to suffer, but how and how much? Currently, the United States relies heavily on prisons and has one of the highest incarceration rates in the world, although the uses and abuses of incarceration raise moral problems in many nations [see Vivien Stern, *A Sin Against the Future: Imprisonment in the World* (Boston: Northeastern University press, 1998)]. The search for alternatives occurs within a context of becoming increasingly harsh and "tough on crime," so this section examines chain gangs, corporal punishment, and the death penalty.

Graeme Newman reviews some of the history of punishment and "civilization" in the selections from his book, *Just and Painful: A Case for the Corporal Punishment of Criminals*. Newman is in favor of implementing corporal punishment in the form of public electric shocks for many minor crimes. His argument does not rest on "tough-on-crime" attitudes, but rather on a review of utilitarian and retributive philosophies, as well as on a concern that prison is a violent punishment that the United States. uses to excess. Newman advocates taking responsibility for the punishment by establishing the number of shocks, the voltage, and their duration and by attempting to match these to the harm of the crime. For him, this system is more just than sentencing someone to, say, three to five years in a violent warehouse of a prison that is frequently a "school for crime." More information can be found at the World Corporal Punishment Research Website <http://www.corpun.com/expl.htm>. Interested readers may wish to read about Michael Matthews' different perspective on the permissibility of corporal punishment in "Caning and the Constitution: Why the Backlash against Crime Won't Result in the Back-lashing of Criminals" 14 *New York Law School Journal of Human Rights* 571, Spring 1998.

The next article is Tessa Gorman's "Back on the Chain Gang: Why the Eighth Amendment and the History of Slavery Proscribe the Resurgence of Chain Gangs." Gorman examines some of the history of race and racism in criminal justice that furnish a backdrop for chain gangs and other current concerns about the disproportionate numbers of minorities in prison. Her article reviews current revivals of the chain gang against the Eighth Amendment, which needs to be interpreted in light of "evolving standards of decency." She concludes that "punishment must reflect the progression of society, not regress to the days of institutionalized racial oppression." The Supreme Court cases mentioned in this article can be found at Findlaw, <www.findlaw.com>.

The next readings are about the death penalty. Americans remain ambivalent about the death penalty as a punishment for murder; they believe strongly that some murderers deserve the death penalty, and yet they are reluctant to impose it. In public opinion polls, a majority insist that they support the death penalty and do not want it abolished. Nonetheless, in the courts, prosecutors ask for far fewer death sentences than they legally might, and juries return death sentences in only a fraction of the cases in which they have been asked for. Moreover, when states allow juries the possibility of sending murderers to prison for their whole lives *without chance of parole*, the rates at which juries return death sentences plummet dramatically.

In the debate that follows, philosophers Stephen Nathanson and Jeffrey Reiman argue for the abolition of the death penalty from unusual angles. In "Is the Death Penalty What Murderers Deserve?" Nathanson contends that even if some murderers do deserve to die, the decision as to which ones do is extremely complex and difficult to make, with the result that juries in some jurisdictions will return death sentences for murderers who in other jurisdictions would have been spared. For Nathanson, this means that death sentences are subject to serious error and are handed out arbitrarily. From this he concludes that "[t]o recognize the likelihood of error and arbitrariness here is to recognize the possibility that people will be executed who do not deserve to die, and this must be something that people who have the highest respect for human life must oppose."

In "Against the Death Penalty," Jeffrey Reiman defends the *lex talionis* ("an eye for an eye,") as a valid standard of desert—criminals deserve punishment that harms them roughly the same amount they tried to impose on their victims. However, he points out that this principle also implies that torturers deserve to be tortured and rapists to be raped, both of which penalties are normally judged to be too brutal to be imposed by a civilized society. Thus, Reiman concludes that while criminals deserve harm equivalent to what they attempt to cause, it is not unjust to punish them less harshly (down to some limit), and the state's example in refraining from executing even those murderers who deserve death "contributes to reducing our tolerance for cruelty and thereby fosters the advance of human civilization as we understand it." Reiman also contends that the evidence fails to show that capital punishment is necessary to deter murder, and that the continued existence of race and class bias in the handing out of death sentences constitutes an independent reason for refraining from capital punishment.

In the third part of this debate, Ernest van den Haag rejects Nathanson's idea that, since it is hard to determine desert, society should not try. He contends that the fact that different juries will issue different sentences is an unavoidable consequence of having different lawyers and different individuals on the juries in different cases. Van den Haag holds that we take numerous precautions to try to avoid injustice in our courts, but that we must accept that they are staffed by fallible human beings and, as in every human endeavor, face some risk of error. Against both Nathanson and Reiman, van den Haag contends that the fact that some who deserve capital punishment get it and others equally deserving of it do not is not unjust to the ones who were sentenced to death—they still got what they deserved even if others who deserved the same did not. Also against Reiman, van den Haag rejects the idea that it is just to give criminals less than the punishment they deserve, and he has a different reading of the deterrence research. He claims it is reasonable to suppose that capital punishment will deter some murderers not deterred by imprisonment, so it is both just and prudent to continue the practice.

For many readers, religious principles and ethics furnish the basis for an opinion about capital punishment. Although some scriptural passages can be interpreted to support the death penalty, the high-ranking policy bodies within Christian denominations and Judaism have statements opposing executions. The National Council of the Churches statement, "Abolition of the Death Penalty," is one such example. For interested readers, Sister Helen Prejean's book, *Dead Man Walking* (New York: Vintage Books, 1993), is a thoughtful application of Catholic social thought to the death penalty and many of the issues that surround it, including racism and poverty. Her opinion about capital punishment is also notable because she has worked extensively with families of murder victims as well as with men on death row.

The existence of a death penalty creates moral dilemmas for individuals who must work with condemned men and must make life-and-death decisions—or even bring about a premeditated death. Prejean, for example, ponders the conflicts between being a good Christian and an executioner. The last two articles in this chapter explore the issues of professional ethics facing doctors who participate in executions and psychiatrists who have condemned men as clients. In "Physician Participation in Capital Punishment," the Council on Ethical and Judicial Affairs of the American Medical Association states that a physician's opinion on capital punishment is a personal matter, but that as members of a profession dedicated to preserving life they should not participate. Marianne Kastrup's article, "Psychiatry and the Death Penalty" reviews a range of ethical concerns including evaluation for competence, predictions of future dangerousness, and the treatment of the incompetent who will be executed when restored to competence.

Further information about capital punishment is available from many sources. We especially recommend the Death Penalty Information Center, which has an interesting section on international attitudes about capital punishment and the use of it by the United States <http://www.essential.org/dpic/>. American Society of Criminology's Division on Critical Criminology has a helpful collection of death penalty resources <http.//sun.soci.niu.edu/~critcrim/>. This organization also has information on peacemaking criminology and restorative justice, both of which are efforts to search for less punitive responses to crime and crime prevention.

The Internet sources mentioned in the introduction and other related materials are available through <http://www.paulsjusticepage.com>.

Just and Painful

Graeme Newman

In *Harm in American Penology*, Todd Clear calls the popular and political belief in the statistical relationship between punishment and crime rates, "the ideology of harm." It is not an ideology, but a popular myth that is the exterior form of a deeper need to punish in Western culture (in fact probably all complex societies and cultures).[7] Clear asks, "Why is harm needed to teach moral lessons?" The question answers itself, although his use of the word "harm" instead of "punishment" muddies the waters a little. The history of Western culture leaves no doubt that the nexus between crime and punishment which produces a moral spirit in a society is cemented by suffering. In fact the one cannot exist without the other. There is a large body of history and literature that I surely do not even need to cite to affirm this fact. The moral fiber of our culture depends on the constant affirmation of this nexus, like it or not. The exact mechanics of this process are still a matter for debate, but that punishment is deeply embedded in moral feeling is without question.[8] It is one thing to hope for a culture that does not depend on this deep human need for its moral fiber and spirit. But after a few thousand years, in which the suffering of punishment has served to identify and affirm morality (both in the secular and sacred realms), the prospects for a dream society without punishment are not good.

In this book I face up to the reality of the public demand for punishment. I advocate a humane way in which this demand can be harnessed, made even more just, and its penchant for excess kept under control. That's right. I argue that corporal punishment is *the* most humane punishment we have. This is not a semantic trick. It is easily demonstrated in this book. All it requires is for the reader to put aside past prejudices about what punishment is and should be.

In a nutshell, the case for the corporal punishment of criminals is as follows.

The Problem: In America today it is quite possible to receive probation for shooting someone because he would not turn down his radio, yet it is also possible to receive a life sentence for stealing $229.11. There has to be something terribly wrong with a system that allows such grossly disproportionate sentences.

The Root of the Problem: Liberal penologists have tried to reduce the prison population for some fifty years. They tried to do this by introducing alternatives to prison which were not alternatives at all because they lacked the credibility of punishments. That is, they were not painful enough. Examples of such punishments are probation and work release. Further, they destroyed the credibility of prisons by trying to minimize the pains of imprisonment, introducing prison farms and minimum security prisons for Watergate type offenders. This resulted in the paradoxical situation in which opinion polls show that people do not believe that prisons are tough enough, even though penologists know that even the mildest of them are horrible places.

The public's demand for more punishment and the conservative reformers' swing to "just deserts" in the late seventies resulted in more people being put in prison, yet at the same time, researchers found that prisons do not rehabilitate, nor do they deter (above a minimum level).

The Crisis: There is a crisis both moral and fiscal. Prisons are overcrowded, violent, vicious places—yet the conservatives call for more of the same. Judges, because they are required to

Graeme Newman, *Just and Painful; A Case for the Corporal Punishment of Criminals*, 2nd ed. (Albany: Harrow & Heston, 1983), excerpts, pp. 6–13, 56–67. Reprinted by permission of the Criminal Justice Press. (Original footnote numbering retained.)

uphold the law, keep sending more persons to prison—yet taxpayers are not prepared to throw more money after bad. The liberals wring their hands, pleading for prisoners to be released early or given probation. They cling to the hope that one day, treatment will be found to work. What they do not understand is that, even if treatment did work, the public would not accept it in most cases because it is not demonstratively painful.

Both the conservative and liberal approaches are doomed to repeat the failures of the past because they will not face up to reality. This reality is that prisons are the most expensive and least morally defensible form of severe punishment. In their present form they are an aberration of the twentieth century which historians of the future will look back on and view as barbaric.

The Solution: We must find a punishment alternative that is truly credible—that is, which the public can believe is properly painful, which can be proportioned to the offense, which is humane, and which is less expensive. This punishment must be directed to the majority of offenders who fall in between the terrible, terrible few who must be locked up and the minor offenders who may continue with probation.

Corporal punishment which applies a non-lasting intense pain, such as electric shock can do the job. It can be over in seconds, not years as is the case with the long, drawn out punishment of prison. It can be adjusted so that pain is felt without any lasting consequences to speak of—at least in comparison to the severe long term effects of prison.

It punishes the offender, and only the offender for the offense. Prison in contrast punishes innocent people, such as the offender's family, by depriving it of his or her support.

It ensures that the pain to be applied to the offender is applied directly in proportion to the offense, and there is no other hidden punishment. When a person is sentenced to prison, especially a young drug offender, the chances are very high that he will be raped and assaulted. Using the strictly controlled punishment of electric shock, this cannot happen.

It is clearly more equitable in comparison to prison. Pain is, of course, subjectively felt. However, research clearly demonstrates that the variation in the way physical pain is felt is much less than the variation in reaction to prison. Indeed, when one considers that corporal punishment can be over in a matter of minutes rather than years, the variation in reaction to these experiences is clearly going to be much greater for prison than for corporal punishment. Thus, corporal punishment can be applied in the same amounts, for the same crimes, no matter the age, sex or social class of the offender.

It is sometimes argued that corporal punishment would have to be limited to youthful and physically strong offenders. But there is no evidence that older people can stand pain less, and in fact the threshold of pain could be established easily enough so that all people could stand it, but still feel it as very painful. Once again, we must compare this to what we have. No one asks whether older people can stand prison less than others—although it is often argued that the young should not be imprisoned which has led to the excessive use of probation for such offenders. And no one seriously asks whether offenders are medically fit to receive prison.

Corporal punishment may deter crime. Although I do not defend corporal punishment on the grounds of deterrence (for complex philosophical reasons explained in this book), I have no serious objection (though many misgivings) if there turns out to be a secondary deterrent effect. Studies in the laboratory suggest quite clearly that corporal punishment is a very effective suppresser of unwanted behavior. One may argue about the interpretations of these research data, but certainly the weight of the evidence is not enough to advocate the abolition of corporal punishment. It is unfortunate that corporal punishment in criminal justice was abolished prematurely before studies could be conducted to test it.

There are circumstances under which I strongly object to the use of corporal punishment as a deterrent, and that would be its use within prison or prison-like settings, such as a mental asylum or jails administered by police departments. The reason for this is that all punishment has a tendency to escalate (for many reasons), and history makes clear that the worst examples of this have occurred under conditions of secrecy. Public scrutiny is the best means of control, and as well it ensures that we all take direct responsibility for the punishment. In the use of corporal punishment, we could not electrocute someone to death for a minor crime and shirk responsibility for it. This is not the case with prisons where the sentence amounts to a quasi-death penalty when some offenders either commit suicide as a result of their prison experience, or are murdered by other inmates. We pretend that this violent part of prison is not really part of the punishment because it is not stated as part of the sentence. We need *real* truth in sentencing which acknowledges that the prison sentences currently handed down by judges bear little relationship to the actual punishment suffered by the offender.

Similarly, I do not favor the use of corporal punishment in families because they are not subject to public scrutiny. As well, children do not enjoy "due process" within the family (nor should they). This is a good reason to protect them from corporal punishment.

REPLIES TO COMMON CRITICISMS

Corporal punishment would be a violation of the Eighth Amendment of the Constitution against cruel and unusual punishment. **Reply:** Corporal punishment of the carefully controlled type described in this book has never been found to be cruel and unusual by the U.S. Supreme Court. The case that comes closest is that of *Bishop* in which a leather strap was used. But this concerned the use of corporal punishment in a prison, and it is argued by some interpreters of that case that corporal punishment was found unconstitutional because of the way it was used in the system (several rules were broken) not because it was corporal punishment *per se.* I am adamantly opposed to the use of corporal punishment in prison settings for the reasons stated above.

If the Court can find that a life sentence in prison for possessing 672 grams of cocaine is not a disproportionate sentence (as it did in a recent case, *Harmelin v. Michigan*, 1991), and that it is not cruel and unusual to use corporal punishment on innocent (as against criminal) school children (*Ingraham v. Wright*) there would seem to be plenty of room to maneuver. Given that the Court is reticent to interfere in the States' rights to enact their own crimes and punishments, there is every chance, provided that a law was carefully written, that it would pass the test of constitutionality. Some states have had corporal punishment statutes up to as late as 1972.

Corporal punishment will unleash a kind of fury of the masses and get out of control. **Reply:** Criminal punishment is already out of control in the form of prison. At least 1,000,000 lives, and in addition those of their families, right now are being unnecessarily ruined by the excessive use of prison as a punishment. It is not the vengefulness of people that has caused prison to get out of control. Rather it is its separation from the people, its loss of credibility, and the failure to take direct responsibility for the punishment that has caused its use in barbaric proportions. Corporal punishment as described in this book offers the chance to get punishment under control, and reduce the excesses of prison.

Corporal punishment will be added on to prison and the prison population will not decrease. **Reply:** Legislatures must be mindful of the fiscal costs of such punishments. Corporal punishment must never be used in conjunction with a prison term, since this would defeat the whole purpose of non-lasting corporal punishment, and subject it to the same criticisms now made against prison. The combination of these two punishments is therefore morally and fiscally indefensible. It is possible that corporal punishment could take the place of some probation. This is desirable, since probation has lost its credibility as a punishment. However, because corporal punishment is a credibly painful punishment, it is more likely to offer a genuine alternative to prison, so that the chances of it being an add-on to prison are much less. There is a real chance that it will reduce prison rates.

Corporal punishment will encourage violence by setting a bad example. **Reply:** This is probably the most common criticism. In spite of claims to the contrary, an unbiased review of the research shows that whether or not children learn aggression from watching others use it is still unclear, and in cases where it has been shown to affect children, these are not long term effects. Just in case though, we should not let children watch the corporal punishment of criminals unless this experience is accompanied by a clear explanation of the crime and why the individual is being punished. This criticism, and much of the research used to back it up, fails to examine carefully the context in which corporal punishment is used, which, when properly administered, is in the context of discipline. It is not wanton violence. If a delinquent (along with radical criminologists who make the same argument) says, "I beat up this little old lady, but so what? The cops use violence too," then one must point out that violence is clearly not deserved by the old lady, but it may well be deserved by the delinquent. He is fortunate that we are sufficiently civilized not to visit on him harm that is anywhere near the amount of harm he has caused his victim— even when we use electric shock.

Corporal punishment amounts to a return to torture. **Reply:** Torture is a process which requires total control of the individual's body and mind over an extended period of time, with the goal of extracting confession, proving guilt and punishing all at the same time. Non-lasting corporal punishment has no interest in such matters. The control of a person's mind, which was indeed the horror of Orwell's *1984* is exactly what prisons try to accomplish. Therefore it is prison that is more like torture, not corporal punishment. Another feature of torture is excessive use of pain. This book makes clear that it is against the excessive use of any punishment, and advocates the highly controlled application of pain as punishment. This is not torture by any stretch of the imagination.

Plea bargaining over the number of volts to be administered would amount to a sick joke. **Reply:**

Every day lawyers callously bargain away years of an offender's life. Bargaining over the number of volts of electricity which may involve only a couple of hours of the person's life, is a far more humane and sensitive approach to the offender's plight.

Corporal punishment has severe negative side-effects. **Reply:** There is no research to support this assertion. In fact, in regard to use of electric shock as punishment, while some mild negative side effects have been observed (such as aversion to the implement that delivers the shock) the positive effects far outweigh the negative effects. . . . Once again, compared to the punishment of prison, the negative side effects of corporal punishment are negligible, especially if delivered in accordance to the guidelines suggested in this book.

Corporal punishment humiliates the offender. **Reply:** There is no evidence that it does any more than any other severe punishment, especially prison, whose requirement of subordination of the inmate for reasons of prison control humiliates the offender 24 hours a day, 7 days a week. Opportunities to humiliate an offender in prison begin from the very first moment of admission, when inmates are routinely made to remove their clothes and are subject to cursory physical examinations, without privacy. In fact the currently popular shock incarceration (a kind of prison boot camp) is essentially founded on the infliction of humiliation on the offender with such activities as "cleaning latrines with a toothbrush," "carrying heavy logs around with them everywhere they go," or "wearing baby bottles around their necks" (*New York Times*, March 4, 1988, p. 15). If this isn't humiliation, I don't know what is. It is a far cry from the corporal punishment advocated in this book.

Corporal punishment is a return to barbarism. **Reply:** What is barbaric? The cultural arrogance of this position I have already noted. But the hypocrisy of it I have not. Injury to the body of the accused already occurs in uncontrolled proportions within prisons, through rape, beatings, and protection rackets in prison. Corporal punishment as described in this book makes sure that we are publicly accountable for the punishment we administer and any injury that occurs to the inmate. This is not what happens with prisons, which are secret, allowing many hidden punishments for which society avoids responsibility because these injuries were "unintended" (though predictable).

Newman is out of step with modern sensibilities. **Reply:** David Garland made this observation in his excellent book *Punishment and Society*. It is not really a criticism, since it does not challenge my argument, only its timing, I am inclined to agree with it, although I remain puzzled by the theory that it implies. Garland uses the word "sensibilities" as though it is synonymous with "manners" or "taste." For example, he reviews the work of Norbet Elias on the history of manners and tries to apply it to the history of punishment. This fascinating work attempts to explain why we abide by everyday habits of behavior such as using a knife and fork, not defecating in public or urinating at the dinner table (which Elias shows were quite common not too long ago). Would the use of corporal punishment be like farting in public? On closer analysis, we see that this criticism is actually the same as the "barbarism" criticism. As one Chinese student of mine observed: it is amusing to see that a Western scholar (Elias) should think that the use of a fork is the sign of a civilized society. Yet I admit that the outraged reactions I received in response to my book made me think that I had indeed committed an act of gross indecency.

It's a fantasy. **Reply:** A reviewer called the first edition of this book a "fantasy." It is fantastic, no doubt about that. But it is much less of a fantasy than the unrealistic programs advanced by the wishful thinking of liberal penologists who try to deny the basic force that drives Western culture: punishment. By denying that force, liberal penologists who will not punish, simply create a greater demand for it. The liberals blame the excesses of prison on all kinds of woes, such as the tyranny of the State, inequality, racism, class conflict, capitalism. The list goes on. But the responsibility for the excesses of prison today lies squarely with the liberal reformers who have fiddled with the punishment processes in society. The liberal reformers of the 18th and 19th centuries created prisons as we know them today. Ashamed of punishing, they have swept punishment behind the secret walls of prison. There it has grown and festered like a huge ulcer. Guilty about punishing, they have invented programs to negate the punitive might of prison. Deeply concerned with control, they have invented community programs of non-punishment to add on to prison. All of the forms of criminal punishment in use today have been invented by liberal reformers. The only exception to that historical fact is the death penalty. And if they had their way, they would get rid of that too.

NOTES

[7]Newman, Graeme. *The Punishment Response: 2nd Edition.* (NY: Harrow and Heston, 1985)

[8]Garland, D. *Punishment and Modern Society.* (Chicago: University of Chicago Press, 1990). See especially his chapter on Durkheim.

ELECTRIC SHOCK: THE FAIREST PUNISHMENT OF ALL

THE ACUTE PUNISHMENT of electric shock is easily demonstrated to be superior in every respect to our current punishment practices. Compare a typical occurrence in today's courtroom with what we would have in the future if only we could get it straight that it is pain, pure and simple, that is the essence of punishment.

The judge peers out over his glasses at the pathetic woman who sits across the courtroom. In a violent outburst she has just called him a heartless tyrant or something to that effect. The public defender and a courtroom guard restrain her.

"Mrs. Washington," says the judge. "This is your third shoplifting offense. You leave me no choice. . ."

He hesitates, expecting another outburst. Mrs. Washington's three year old daughter sits next to her, eyes wide and watery. The judge tries to avoid her gaze.

"Mrs. Washington, it is the judgment of this court that you be sentenced to a minimum of six months in the penitentiary and a maximum of one year. Your daughter will be turned over to the care of the Department of Youth, since the pre-sentence report indicates that you have no husband or relatives who could care adequately for her. . ."

The mother is led, crying, out of the courtroom. The child pulls at her mother's skirt, crying "Mama! Mama!" But the hands of the court are upon her, and an innocent child is about to be punished for the crime of having a guilty mother.

Every day, all across America many, many families and relatives of offenders suffer in this way. This means that literally thousands of people are punished for other people's crimes.

Now, an example of what punishment of the future could be like.

Twenty-year old John Jefferson stands beside his lawyer, the public defender.

"John Jefferson," says the judge, "the court has found you guilty of burglary in the first degree. Because this is your first offense, but the damage you did was considerable, I sentence you to. . ." The judge pushes a few buttons at his computer console. The average sentence for similar cases to Jefferson's flashes on the display, ". . . five shock units."

"You will be taken immediately to the punishment hall to receive five shock units. Next case."

The victim of this crime is sitting at the back of the court. He approaches the court clerk, who directs him to the punishment hall where he will be able to watch the administration of the punishment.

Jefferson's wife and child are ushered to the waiting room where they will await Jefferson's return after he has been punished.

Meanwhile, in the punishment hall, Jefferson is seated in a specially designed chair. As part of the arrest procedure he has already received a medical examination to establish that he was fit to receive punishment.

In addition to the victim, a few members of the press are seated on the other side of the glass screen. The punishment technician, having settled the offender in the chair, returns to an adjoining room where he can observe the offender through a one way screen. A medic is also present.

The technician sets the machine at the appropriate pain level, turns the dial to "5," and presses the button.

Jefferson receives five painful jolts of electricity to his buttocks. He screams loudly, and by the time the punishment is over, he is almost crying with pain.

The technician returns and releases the offender. "Stand and walk a little," he says.

Jefferson walks around, rubbing his buttocks. A shade drops over the spectators' screen.

"Do you still feel the pain?" asks the medic.

"Goddam, I sure do! But it's getting better. Can I go now?"

"Just sign here, and you've paid your dues."

Jefferson sighs happily and asks, "Which way to the waiting room?"

"Straight down the passage and second left."

Jefferson enters the waiting room where his wife rushes into his arms, crying, "I'm so glad it's over! Thank goodness you weren't sent to prison."

We see in this example that only the guilty person is punished. The punishment administered is clean, simple, and most importantly, convincingly painful. It is over in a brief time, and the offender is able to return to his family and his job. Punishment is confined only to the guilty. The side effects of punishment are minimized.

There is little doubt that such punishment procedures are more than feasible. Yet as we saw in Chapter 1, a major objection to it has been that, because it is subjective, it would be felt so differently by each individual that it would be an inequitable punishment. Although it is true that people do respond differently to pain, it is also true that in the area of physical pain these differences can be more easily overcome than with other kinds of pain.

Let us look at the evidence.

MEASURING DIFFERENCES IN RESPONSE TO PAIN

In general, it has been found that individuals vary according to the threshold at which they report pain (that is, the point of severity in the painful stimulus at which they report that it "hurts" or request that it be stopped). The kinds of painful stimuli applied to subjects in these experiments have been:

1. Application of pressure to tissue or bone, such as the use of a blood pressure arm band with a hard object sewn into it.

2. Application of electric shock which can be carefully calibrated.

3. Application of heat to various parts of the body, which can be calibrated in terms of skin temperature at the site of application.

4. Field studies where persons in hospitals who are in pain, either through chronic illness, or perhaps as a result of an operation (post operative pain) may be studied to see how they perceive and report upon their pain, such as how often they request pain killing drugs.

We should make an important distinction here between pain threshold and tolerance of pain.

Pain threshold refers to the point on the scale of severity of the pain stimulus (for example, heat) at which the person reports that he "feels" it as pain (in this case, prickly heat). This may, of course, vary somewhat among individuals, but it should be realized that it is usually only a painful stimulus at a very low level of intensity. As we increase the intensity of the painful stimulus the person will soon decide where along that scale to say "stop."

There is an additional advantage in the administration of physical pain in that one does not need to rely exclusively on verbal reports to ascertain when it "hurts." Rather, there are physiological reactions such as sweating and pupil dilation, which are good indicators that the painful stimulus is indeed having a painful effect. In this way we are able to eliminate at least one aspect of the complicated process of the person's perception of pain (that is, we do not have to depend on him to tell us when it hurts).

Tolerance of pain is not necessarily related to a person's pain threshold. While a person may call out "stop" relatively early in the application of a gradually increasing amount of pain, he may nevertheless be able to stand certain levels of pain for quite some time. The tolerance of pain refers to the time element in pain. Again, people may vary in the extent to which they can stand pain over time, and it has generally been found that the variations in tolerance of pain are greater than the variations in pain threshold.[1]

MAKING PAIN THE SAME FOR EVERYONE

Since pain in these experiments is almost always at a very low level of intensity, people will cry out or ask for it to be stopped long before it reaches a point where they can no longer stand it. Thus, we would expect variations among individuals as to the point at which they called "stop." However, if one were to administer a painful stimulus which was, say, twenty times that of the lowest pain threshold, the extent to which this pain was felt differently among individuals would be "levelled." That is, it would be felt the same (very painful) by everyone. And if we used a physiological indicator we could be even more certain.

For example, suppose we have established from our experiments that the range at which people display a high sweat reaction is from a low of 5 volts to a high of 20 volts, with most people at about the middle, that is, 12 volts. We could safely administer 30 volts for a one second duration, and be sure that everyone felt the shock, and that it was very painful. This would have the effect of levelling the punishment in that we could be absolutely sure that the punishment really hurt every person to whom it was applied, and hurt them equally.

The important point about this method of applying an amount of pain is that not only is it of brief duration, but it is certainly painful. Furthermore, the scientific studies have found that the variations in perceptions of pain are much greater for chronic pain (that is, drawn out pain, or pain tolerance) than for acute pain.[2] We are on much safer ground using momentary application of a painful stimulus that we know will really hurt every person who receives it, than to apply some other form of pain which by its nature requires that it be administered over long periods of time. The longer the time period, the more the concept of pain tolerance will override the notion of pain threshold. And the longer the time period, the harder it is to control the amount of pain administered, and the way it is perceived.

With the application of acute pain, intensity depends much more on the amount of electric shock, the amount of heat, or amount of pressure. Only as a secondary device need time be used to vary the amount of pain. Thus, we may apply our 30 volts of shock for as brief a time as a fraction of a second. And, for some offenses, this may be sufficient.[3]

DOES PAIN DIFFER ACCORDING TO SOCIAL AND ETHNIC BACKGROUND?

There have been a number of studies by various anthropologists and psychologists which claim to have found differential responses to pain and suffering according to religious and ethnic background. One well known study conducted in the 1950's found that "old Americans" (that is, your everyday WASP) were more likely to put up with pain for a longer period and of more intensity without complaining than were Irish or Italian Catholics and Jews.[4] There were a number of control problems with this study, so that definitive conclusions cannot be drawn from it.

Others have found that Eskimos will tolerate more pain than whites, and that whites will tolerate more pain than blacks. However, all these studies have been severely criticized on the basis of their very small samples and their reliance on cultural stereotypes to select their groups.[5] Although a few studies have found some support for the claim of differences in response to pain according to religious background, other reviews of this research have generally concluded that while different cultural or social groups may be said to respond to and interpret pain differently, there is every chance that they actually feel pain in about the same way. In fact, all these studies are irrelevant because they measure tolerance of pain, rather than pain threshold. They simply suggest the obvious: that particular ethnic or religious groups complain differently about pain. They do not show that these groups *feel* the intensity of pain differentially. In fact, the most recent evaluation of all research conducted into the cultural differences in response to pain concluded:

> There is no evidence suggesting that the neurophysiologic detection of pain (i.e., pain threshold) varies across cultural boundaries.[6]

It is reasonable for us to conclude that pain is not differentially distributed in society according to social class or race, as is money. Certainly, if there were any differences, these would be *comparatively* much less than are those of economics. Pain is a great leveller.

In sum, people's physiological reaction to painful stimuli is pretty much the same. The way they deal with the pain varies according to the way they have been brought up. In other words, all people feel pain as pain. The ways they react to this pain may vary.

DIFFERENCES IN REACTION TO CHRONIC PAIN

Are there differential responses to the effects of prison (that is, chronic pain and pain tolerance) according to social and ethnic background? There are drastic variations. Not only do people (including inmates) perceive time differently (and it is time that is the main element of pain in prison), but inmates also experience prison life in widely differing ways. Some, indeed, see no difference between life on the inside and life on the outside:

> It's not a matter of a guy saying, 'I want to go to jail or I am afraid of jail.' Jail is on the street just like it is on the inside. The same as, like, when you are in jail, they tell you, 'Look, if you do something wrong you are going to be put in the hole.' You are in jail, in the hole or out of the hole. You are in jail in the street or behind bars. It is the same thing.[7]

Differences in tolerance of prison are also demonstrated by the fact that hispanics have the highest suicide rate in prison, and the highest rate of self-inflicted injury. They are followed by whites, then by blacks. One should add that it will probably never be known whether inmates of differing backgrounds experience the pain of prison differently because it is impossible to measure the pain threshold of prison. This is because prison is such an abstruse and complex pain provider: it applies many different kinds of pain, such as restriction of liberty, time, diet and space, denial of sexual gratification, corporal mutilation (from other inmates), enforced obedience etc., all of which are mixed in together.

THE FAIRNESS OF ACUTE PAIN

One can immediately see the inherently attractive features of acute pain such as electric shock, as opposed to prison. It ensures that all persons receive the same amount of punishment. All people, rich or poor, black or white, will suffer the same amount of pain. This surely fulfills the requirements of equity and fairness. People will truly receive the same amount of punishment for the same crimes. No longer will it be possible to claim that the punishment favors the rich or poor, since we know that we have, by the scientific selection of an intensely painful stimulus, ensured that each individual will experience the same amount

of pain. And for those purists who would insist that no matter at what level of intensity of shock, each one will feel it differently, one may reply that even if this is so, it is demonstrably clear that in comparison with the punishment of prison, the application of physically acute pain to the body is far more equitable, and far less susceptible to variations in effects. It achieves its object, then stops.[8]

WOULD MINORITIES SUFFER MORE THAN THEY DO NOW?

The number of people in prison has increased over the last twenty years at an astronomical rate, from approximately 177,113 in 1971 to 1.5 million in 1994. The number of minorities in state prisons has always been disproportionately high: 47.8% in 1979, during a period when there was supposedly more sensitivity to the plight of minorities in the United States.[9] The U.S. Bureau of Justice Statistics reports that in 1993 minorities made up 61.7% of the prison population (44.1% blacks and 17.6% hispanics). When we consider that blacks comprise only about 12% of the total United States population, we see that the proportion of blacks in prison is tremendous. And in some regions of the United States the proportions are even higher. The chances are that every black in the country has at least one relative in prison and probably more.

The trouble is that these figures do not have much impact because the ordinary person is not likely to be confronted by the silent process that keeps people—of all colors—in prison. Criminals can be funnelled into this archipelago and forgotten about by the majority of people who are happy that someone will keep them locked up, and preferably silent. Only from time to time do prison riots break this silence, but after a brief spilling of blood, the silence returns, and we hear nothing more.[10]

Clearly, if corporal punishment can become a viable alternative to prison, then blacks stand to gain more than any other group. A reviewer of the first edition of this book castigated me for making this statement. But I stand by it. The biggest challenge to minorities has always been to convince the American public that they are being treated badly. For the entire period I have been involved in criminal justice (longer than I would care to admit) blacks have complained of discrimination and abuse at the hands of the police. Not until the highly public Rodney King beating did this issue become a public (and political) cause. But it is impossible to publicize the tremendous suffering caused by imprisonment because it is by design administered *in secret*. If blacks were punished in public with corporal punishment to the differential extent that they are currently punished with prison, there would be a public outcry. It would be *too much*. It would force us to be accountable for our excesses in punishment. Right now, we are not accountable for the excesses of prison, because it is a secret and silent punishment. The differential rate of black imprisonment is a *silent statistic*.

WHAT ABOUT WOMEN AND CHILDREN?

It is a popular belief that women are able to withstand more pain than men, although there is no research data to support this claim.

It is also argued on occasion that the young could withstand severe acute pain more easily than the old, but once again there is no research data to support this claim.

But there is evidence to show that women and children suffer more than do adult men from the punishment of prison. Studies have shown that women suffer the separation from their families much more than do men,[11] and it is a well established fact that the young who are sent to prison are those who are preyed on by rapists, and if they are not raped, they are turned into hardened criminals by older inmates.[12]

Therefore, it would seem to be much more preferable to administer acute pain in the same quantities for women and children as for men. In this way we have truly fair punishments, and all, regardless of race, age, or sex, receive the same penalty. Isn't this politically correct? In addition, the law could be considerably simplified, since in many cases, separate laws have

had to be made for children so that they could be given more lenient (and recently more severe) punishments.

It may seem callous and brutal to suggest administering the same corporal punishment to children as compared to adults. But a moment's reflection reveals that this is a deep and abiding hypocrisy. If we are to believe Straus's surveys, it seems that over 90% of American parents at some time in their lives spanked their own children.[13] Some half of American school districts still allow corporal punishment of school children. So, this is not at all an "unusual" punishment for children. In the celebrated Michael Fay case of the American teenager in Singapore caned for vandalism, some 49% of Americans surveyed actually approved of the caning.[14] What *is* unusual about the punishment schedule outlined in this chapter is that I am advocating it for *adults*.

It might reasonably be argued that, given the facts of the widespread corporal punishment of children in America, I am therefore treating adults like children when I advocate corporal punishment for all offenders. This is a fair criticism. The solution, though, is to stop hitting kids, so that we can't any longer claim that corporal punishment is a children's punishment. In fact, I strongly oppose the use of corporal punishment on children within the family, because they have no recourse. It is punishment administered in secret (the sanctity of the home) and thus full of the same dangers of excess as found in the use of corporal punishment in prisons. There is no ready accountability, no "due process" one might say, within the traditional family household.[15] Corporal punishment is a very severe punishment. It should only be used against those who have broken the law. There is no justification for its use otherwise.

IN SUM . . .

It is clear that, where appropriate to the crimes, the use of an acute corporal punishment instead of the vague use of prison as punishment is preferable, since the application of acute pain can be scientifically controlled both in terms of duration and intensity. The way it is physically felt does not vary, although reactions to it may: but even these reactions vary far less than reactions to prison.

Prisons conditions vary so much, that there is no reliable way to control their quality or intensity. Convicts are well aware of the ways in which prisons differ from each other, as is well documented in any prison diaries and books about prison. And these variations occur within prisons that are supposed to be of one type, such as "maximum security."[16]

This chapter suggests another defect in the use of prison as punishment. It is difficult to vary the intensity and duration of prison in a clear cut way. The most common way to vary intensity of prison is to vary the length of prison term. But this mixes up duration with intensity. Another way to vary the intensity of prison is to introduce various types or degrees of "security"—such as maximum security down to minimum security prisons. However, such variations in intensity are not specific enough for our purposes, for we wish to control the administration of pain as carefully and fully as possible.

Varying the intensity of prisons also affects the credibility of prisons as a punishment since minimum security prisons are easily portrayed as "resorts for white collar criminals." "Perks" such as gym equipment, TV, or even libraries, convey the (mistaken) idea that prison is not that bad a place. Varying the intensity of prison in this way undermines its credibility as a punishment, and paradoxically feeds the public's demand for more and more punishment, which under the present system can only be prison.

We have seen that we can minutely control both the intensity and duration of electric shock. If we are to control the intensity of prison, we must look closely at the types of pain that occur in prison—diet, hard labor, isolation cells—and consider systematically grading these so that the intensity of prison may be adjusted to the punishment deserved by the crime.[17]

Up to this point, we have considered what punishments are appropriate for what crimes, but we have not considered whether certain kinds of criminals deserve particular kinds of punishments. Rather, we have stayed on what could be called a "superficial" level in our attempt to match the crimes with the punishments. Here we are confronted with the most difficult of all questions in criminal punishment: which criminals (as opposed to crimes) deserve punishments of the chronic proportions of prison; which ones deserve the lesser ones of acute pain; and are there any that deserve both?

Matching *criminals* to punishments is a much more difficult problem than matching *crimes* to punishments, and gets us into hot water when it comes to using retribution as the justification for administering painful punishment. For it is one thing to reflect the elements of crimes in punishments, but it is another to reflect the elements of criminals in the punishments. The latter would virtually mean concocting punishments which were unique to each criminal.

Such an "individualization of punishment" is not new, and was advocated around the turn of the century.[18] It has been found by and large to be unrealistic, and that those who advocate it in fact do not really practice it. Researchers have found that judges tend to apply similar punishments for similar crimes and similar criminals.

The solution to this problem lies in repackaging the notion of retribution by using the knowledge we now have about the range of pains and punishments.

NOTES

[1]Sternback, *Pain: A Psychophysiological Analysis.* See also, Zatzick, D.F. and Joel M. Dinsdale, "Cultural Variations in Response to Pain Stimuli." *Psychosomatic Medicine,* 52:544–557, 1990.

[2]Kosterlitz, *Pain and Society.*

[3]It would be necessary to avoid another phenomenon that appears to occur naturally in the body when pain is experienced over a long period of time, which is that the body's defensive apparatus manufactures substances that interfere with the brain's processing of painful stimuli. It may be that people will adapt to the level of painful stimulus over time, and thus may not "feel" it as much as in the immediate and momentary onset of pain. Indeed, some torture victims have referred to this very phenomenon and even said in retrospect that the torture was not all that bad. This

is why the best torturers make cunning use of time, and will vary torture sessions over some weeks or months.

Some experimentation may also be necessary as to the appropriate parts of the body to attach the electrodes, and the amount of voltage and current to apply without causing tissue damage. Considerable research has been conducted on dogs in relation to the use of electricity in the death penalty, but little data is available on its use as a means of administering pain. See T. Bernstein, "Theories of the Causes of Death by Electricity," *Medical Instrumentation* 9 (November–December, 1975): 6; and by the same author, "A Grand Success," *IEEE Spectrum*, (February, 1973). The most research in the use of electric shock has been in the field of seriously disruptive behavior among retarded individuals. None of this research has been shown to have serious negative side effects. Most of it has shown that electric shock is an effective punishment in controlling undesirable behavior. See: Matson, J.L. and Marie E. Taras, "A 20 Year Review of Punishment and Alternative Methods to Treat Problem Behaviors in Developmentally Delayed Persons." (*Research in Developmental Disabilities.* Vol. 10, pp. 88–104, 1989); Kenneth L. Lichstein and Laura Schreibman, "Employing Electric Shock with Autistic Children: A Review of the Side Effects." (*Journal of Autism and Childhood Schizophrenia.* Vol. 6. No. 2., 1976); Sandra L. Harris and Robin ErsnerHershfield, "Behavioral Suppression of Seriously Disruptive Behavior in Psychotic and Retarded Patients: A Review of Punishment and its Alternatives." (*Psychological Bulletin.* Vol. 85, No. 6, 1352–1375, 1978).

[4]M. Zborowski, *People in Pain* (San Francisco: Jossey Bass, 1969).

[5]B. B. Wolff and S. Langley, "Cultural Factors and Response to Pain: A Review," *American Anthropologist* 70 (1968): 495–501.

[6]Zatzick and Dimsdale, "Cultural Variations in Response to Painful Stimuli." See also: J. J. Bonica and D. Albe-Fessard eds., *Proceedings of the First World Congress on Pain* (St. Florence: World Health Organization, 1975).

[7]Quoted in J. Braithwaite, *Prisons and Work* (Brisbane: University of Queensland Press, 1980).

[8]See in this regard A. Petrie, *Individuality in Pain and Suffering* (Berkeley, California: University of California Press, 1961) who has identified "augmenters" and "reducers" in the perception of pain and suffering. This differentiation, though not yet shown to be related to any class or ethnic background, may nevertheless tell us that the way in which prison is perceived is unquestionably different according to each individual. The augmenters are those whose perceptual processes must increase the intensity with which they feel a stimulus. The reducers are those whose perceptual processes do the opposite, and so reduce the amount of intensity of the stimulus.

Petrie observes that the augmenters are those who are most likely to suffer from being isolated in prison, since they must constantly augment or add to their stimulation. They are the ones who suffer severely from boredom, and for whom lack of stimulation of any kind is a severe form of punishment. On the other hand the reducers find even the minimal amount of stimulation enough, and so are less likely to suffer from the isolation of prison—provided, of course, they are able to live out their time in a prison that fosters individual isolation. In today's overcrowded conditions, this is doubtful.

[9]See S.Christianson, "Our Black Prisons," *Crime and Delinquency* (July, 1981):364–375.

[10]Prison riots are as old as prisons themselves. See T. Kabealo and S. Dinitz, "Prison Riots and Revolts in the U. S. 1951–1971," *Quaderni di Criminotogia Clinica* 15 (1973): 305–328; D. Asiz, *Historical Review of Prison Disturbances* 1970–1980 (Unpublished report to the New York State Department of Corrections, 1981).

[11]See, for example, T. Foster, "Make Believe Families: A Response of Women and Girls to the Deprivations of Imprisonment," *International Journal of Criminology and Penology* 3 (1975): 7178.

[12]J. Irwin, *Prisons in Turmoil* (Boston: Little Brown and Co., 1980).

[13]Straus, M. *Beating the Devil out of Them.*

[14]This case and the relevant polls were widely reported in both national and local media. Polls conducted by the media reported roughly similar findings: 49% of Americans approved of the sentence, although only 36% said they would approve of such a punishment being introduced into American Criminal Justice. (*L.A. Times*, Thursday, April 21, 1994). Polls conducted by other national media reported similar findings.

[15]In fact, this is why corporal punishment is often identified in research on child abuse as the beginning of a slippery slope of violence against children by their parents. This is well documented by Straus, *Beating the Devil out of Them*

[16]Irwin, *Prisons in Turmoil.*

[17]Recent innovative research on the effectiveness of prison is an exciting start in this direction. See: United States Bureau of Justice Statistics, *Performance Measures for the Criminal Justice System.* (NCJ-143505, 1993. Washington, D.C.). Also: Charles H. Logan, *Criminal Justice Performance Measures for Prisons.* (NCJ-139458, 1993. Washington, D.C.). While these papers focus on the performance of prisons in terms of fulfilling their basic mission of providing a secure environment for inmates, they do begin to show how the varying conditions of prison may be systematically identified and measured.

[18]R.Salleilles, *The Individualization of Punishment* (Boston: Little Brown and Co., 1911).

Back on the Chain Gang: Why the Eighth Amendment and the History of Slavery Proscribe the Resurgence of Chain Gangs

Tessa M. Gorman

"Tsarist Russia had its Siberia; the Balkans has its underground inquisition; Venezuela its torture chamber; France its Devil's Island—and America its Chain Gang."[1]

On display in the Mobile Public Library in Alabama is an interesting relic from the days of slavery. Discovered in the thicket near the East Head of Pigeon Creek, Greenville, Butler County, Alabama, this savage contraption from the past is a "Bell Rack."[2] This apparatus, a reminder of racial terrorism, consists of an iron collar that was closed by a bolt, attached to an upright bar or post. A belt went around the slave's waist and through an iron loop. When in use, a bell hung from a hook at the top, above the slave's head. This hook kept the slave confined to the highways and open places, for it would catch in the limbs of the trees and cause the bell to ring if the slave tried to run away through the woods. The slave could move around, but had no chance to make a getaway.

Tessa Gorman, "Back on the Chain Gang: Why the Eighth Amendment and the History of Slavery Proscribe the Resurgence of Chain Gangs." © 1997 by *California Law Review, Inc.* This article first appeared in its full, unedited version in Volume 85 Number 2 (March 1997): 441–478 of the *California Law Review*. Reprinted by permission of the *California Law Review* and the author. (Original footnote numbering retained in this edited version.)

[1] Walter Wilson, *Forced Labor in the United States* 68 (1933) (quoting the editor of the *Southern Worker*).

[2] See *The American Slave: A Composite Autobiography* (George P. Rawick ed., Supp. 1 1977).

The Bell Rack represents America's darkest chapter—one that should have closed over 100 years ago.

However, the legacy of the Bell Rack continues. Outside the walls of Alabama's Limestone Correctional Facility stands a tall U-shaped metal bar, called "the hitching post," to which an inmate is chained when he refuses to work on the chain gang.[8] The inmate can move around, but has no chance to make a getaway. The man remains on the hitching post, with hands cuffed above his head, from 8:30 a.m. until 6:30 p.m.[10] This is Alabama, 1996.

Four hundred convicts, who will form that day's chain gangs, are being led in groups of forty from their mass barracks to the yard. Nearly seventy percent of the men are African American.[12] They wear white uniforms with the words "CHAIN GANG" stamped across their backs in large, black letters.[13] From the yard, they move toward the road that encircles

[8] See Peter Morrison, The New Chain Gang, *Nat'l L. J.*, Aug. 21, 1995, at A1.

[10] See id.; William Booth, Show Time: It's the Sound of the Men Working on the Chain Gang. Oooh. Aaaah, *Wash. Post*, Dec. 17, 1995, at F1, F4.

[12] See Anne Hull, Chained to a New Kind of Justice, *St. Petersburg Times*, June 25, 1995, at 1A.

[13] See William Booth, The Return of the Chain Gangs: Work Crews of Alabama Prisoners Form a Link to the South's Past, *Wash. Post*, May 4, 1995, at A1.

the prison, where guards await, shotguns balanced on their hips. The prisoners approach the guards and then kneel before them. The bright metal chains come out of their wooden boxes, clinking and rattling, and then the men are bound, ankle to ankle, shackled for their day's work.

The rattling of chains stirs old memories. An image of slavery is inescapable. This Comment argues that chain gangs invoke an historical association with slavery and therefore should be deemed cruel and unusual punishment under the Eighth Amendment, which requires that a method of state punishment be consistent with societal notions of dignity, to wit: it "must draw its meaning from the evolving standards of decency that mark the progress of a maturing society."[16] The chain gang springs from an historical context that attaches a cruel meaning to this form of punishment. Chain gangs are inextricably bound to a legacy of racial injustice in this country and therefore should be proscribed by the Eighth Amendment.

I   TRACING THE HISTORY OF SLAVERY AND THE HISTORY OF THE CHAIN GANG

The chain gang has largely been an instrument with which to terrorize, torture, and exploit Africans and African-Americans. Its beginnings can be traced to the roots of slavery in this country, as it was adopted in the colonies as a way to control and transport slaves. Former slave holders embraced the chain gang at the end of the Civil War as a means of placing the recently "freed" blacks back into bondage.[18]

Slavery was a large business. Investors around the world put up considerable sums of money for the opportunity to trade in human flesh.[19] Backers wagered that a ship could get to Africa, trade for or capture slaves, transport them across the Atlantic, and sell them at a high price in the Western Hemisphere. Ships left from various European nations with their trade goods—firearms, gunpowder, rum, beads, trinkets, tools—and visited trading posts on the west coast of Africa. Once there, they traded the rum and other goods for slaves. The slaves "were chained, leg to leg, arm to arm," to prevent escape, rebellion, and suicide.

Such treatment pales when compared with the treatment of slaves aboard the slave ship. The trips across the "middle passage," the six- to ten-week journey to the Western Hemisphere, chronicle some of history's most egregious human atrocities. The deplorable images of the slave ships are inseparably intertwined with chains:

> On many of these ships, the sense of misery and suffocation was so terrible in the 'tween-decks—where the height was only 18 inches, so that the unfortunate slaves could not turn round, were wedged immovably, . . . and *chained to the deck by the neck and legs*—that the slaves not infrequently would go mad before dying or suffocating.[25]

A doctor aboard a slave ship in the mid-eighteenth century described his harrowing impressions:

> The wretched Negroes are immediately fastened together, two and two, by handcuffs on their wrists and by irons rivetted on their legs. . . . They are frequently stowed so close as to admit of no other position than lying on their sides. Nor will the height between decks allow them to stand.[26]

Perhaps a slave's own words best capture the mental and physical horrors. Gustavus Vassa was eleven when he was captured into slavery:

> I was soon put down under the decks and there I received such asalutation in my nostrils as I had never experienced in my life; so that with the loathsomeness of the stench and crying together, I became so sick and low that I was not able to eat, nor had I the least desire to taste anything. I now wished for the last friend, death, to relieve

---

[16]*Trop v. Dulles*, 356 U.S. 86, 101 (1958).

[18]See Wilson, supra note 1, at 68.

[19]See Robert Liston, *Slavery in America* 32 (1970).

[25]Id. at 35–36 (emphasis added).

[26]Id. at 36 (emphasis added).

me. . . . The closeness of the place, and the heat of the climate, added to the number in the ship, which was so crowded that each had scarcely room to turn himself, almost suffocated us. This produced copious perspiration, so that the air soon became unfit for respiration, from a variety of loathsome smells, and brought on a sickness among the slaves, of which many died, thus falling victims to the improvident avarice, as I may call it, of their purchasers.

This wretched situation was again aggravated by the galling of the chains, now become insupportable; and the filth of the necessary tubs, into which the children often fell, and were almost suffocated. The shrieks of the women, and the groans of the dying, rendered the whole scene of horror almost inconceivable.[27]

Many slaves fought the hideous captivity by attempting suicide and fratricide. They begged chainmates to choke or suffocate them; "[t]hey tore at their chains until they were maimed for life."[29]

After arriving in the New World, the slaves were delivered to various locations in the Western Hemisphere. Those delivered to the British colonies were sold on auction blocks where they were displayed in chains. The atrocious images of the auction blocks are intimately intertwined with the images of chains. Since these images are inseparable, an inquiry into the events of a slave auction illuminates what images are retrieved when viewing a chain gang.

The auction blocks, "niggah tradahs' yahds,"[31] were used to systematically humiliate and dehumanize the slaves. The slaves were stripped half or sometimes entirely naked.[32] The auctioneer would describe each slave offered for sale as akin to an animal: "strong, healthy, choice stock, a willing worker."[34] The auctioneer might laud the women slaves as good breeders, referring to their ability to bear more slaves. Since no buyer would spend money without guarantee of the quality, the auction also included an inspection. Recalls one ex-slave: "They 'zamine you just like they do a horse; they look at your teeth, and pull your eyelids back and look at your eyes, and feel you just like you was a horse."[37] Conducted "amid jests and catcalls from the spectators," the inspection was inevitably the highlight of the auction.[38]

Slave auctions are wedded to images of chains, as slaves were transported to and from such auctions chained together. As one account chronicles:

[T]he women were tied together with a rope about their necks, like a halter, while the men wore iron collars, fastened to a chain about one hundred feet long, and were also handcuffed. The men in double file went ahead and the women followed in the same order. The drivers rode wherever they could best watch and direct the coffle. At the end of the day all, without being relieved of their collars, handcuffs, chains or ropes, lay down on the bare floor, the men on one side of the room and the women on the other.[39]

Elsewhere, "the men were linked by chains fastened to iron collars around their necks. In addition, they were handcuffed in pairs, with about a foot of chain between. In this [chained] fashion, the slaves trudged the hot, dusty roads of the South."[40]

After the purchase at the auction, the slaves usually traveled to their new "homes" bearing chains. J. K. Spaulding, Secretary of the Navy under President Van Buren, recounted his encounter with a group of chained slaves:

The sun was shining out very hot, and in turning an angle of the road we encountered. . . . three men, bareheaded, half naked, and chained together with an ox-chain. Last of all came a

---

[27]Id. at 37–38 (emphasis added).

[29]Id.

[31]Frederic Bancroft, *Slave Trading in the Old South* 282 (1959).

[32]See Liston, supra note 19, at 84.

[34]Id.

[37]Id.

[38]Id.

[39]Bancroft, supra note 31, at 282 (footnote omitted).

[40]Liston, supra note 19, at 85.

white man on horseback, carrying pistols in his belt.[42]

The systematic dehumanization of the American slaves involved far more than breaking them physically with toil and terrorizing them with the whip and auction block. In innumerable, perhaps unknowable, ways, the slave was humiliated and degraded. He was denied virtually every human dignity. If a slave was starved, mutilated by a whip, sold away from his or her spouse, parents, or children, he had no recourse to appeal to for help. Slaves could not own property, enter into contracts, vote, or testify under oath in a court. Slave marriages had no legal standing, and slaves had no legal claim upon their children. In essence, the slave in America was a thing, and "[a]bout the only significant difference between the planter's treatment of his slaves and his cattle was the fact that he did not slaughter his slaves for food."[47] Significantly, chains were a tangible symbol of this dehumanization and were prevalent throughout the ante-bellum South.

For many African-Americans living in the United States at the end of the Civil War, the transition from bondage to freedom was more theoretical than real, and life for African-Americans "was punctuated with reminders that 'freedom' was essentially a change in form rather than in substance."[48] Although slavery ended in 1865, the various mechanisms for race control, including statutes and court decisions, as well as the underlying rationales for the law of slavery, continued to influence Southern law: "[t]he slave codes of the ante-bellum period were the basis of the black codes of 1865–66 and later were resurrected as the segregation statutes of the period after 1877. The legal heritage of slavery did not end with its demise. . . ."[49] Most pertinent to this Comment is that in the antebellum South, chain gangs were pervasive and were used as a method to control freed blacks.

Even though slavery was officially over after the Civil War, mechanisms to control blacks remained. Blacks were either forced into labor contracts or compelled to enter the convict labor system.[50] It became impossible to escape the spiral of imprisonment. If the laborer refused to work on the farm, he was forced to work as a "convict." The labor contract system "so strictly and legally bound the farm workers to the plantation owners that it seemed like another form of slavery."[53] The black laborers "were at the mercy of [the] owners and local law-enforcement officers"[54] and were being held "in a worse state then [sic] when they were slaves."[55] In 1888, Booker T. Washington observed that "colored people on these plantations are held in a kind of slavery that is in one sense as bad as the slavery of ante bellum days."[56]

This system of forced labor also continued during and after Reconstruction through convict labor. There were few choices for "convicts." The state either leased the convicts to private interests, forced them into criminal surety contracts under which a period of servitude for a private employer was exchanged for the payment of a criminal fine, often based on petty or exaggerated charges, or placed them on state or county chain gangs.[60] A prison official, writing in 1904, noted the conditions of convicts and related that "The Negro

---

[42]Id.

[47]Id. at 81–82.

[48]Milfred C. Fierce, *Slavery Revisited* 3 (1994).

[49]Paul Finkelman Exploring Southern Legal History 64 *N.C. L. Rev.* 77, 90 (1985) (footnote omitted).

[50]See Pete Daniel, *The Shadow of Slavery: Peonage in the South, 1901–1969*, at 25 (1972).

[53]Rhoda Lois Blumberg, *Civil Rights: The 1960s Freedom Struggle* 19 (rev. ed. 1991).

[54]Daniel, supra note 50, at 5.

[55]Id. (quoting W. O. Butler, a Pensacola, Florida, lawyer).

[56]Benno C. Schmidt, Jr., Principle and Prejudice: The Supreme Court and Race in the Progressive Era, (pt. 2: The Peonage Cases), 82 *Colum. L. Rev.* 646, 653 (1982).

[60]See id. at 651. A laborer who signed a contract and then abandoned his job could be arrested for a criminal offense. As punishment, he could either work out his contract or go to the chain gang. See Daniel, supra note 50, at 25. In such cases, the fines were often less than one dollar, but as William W. Armbrecht, U.S. Attorney in Mobile, Alabama, pointed out in the early twentieth century, "the prosecution is not instigated with any idea of up-holding the majesty of the law, but with the idea of putting these negroes to work." Id. at 27.

Convict Is A Slave,"[61] and the state, a collective slavemaster.

During this time, a large number of blacks became convicts for the first time.[62] This type of bondage was supported by an unequal justice system "in which a black person could never successfully challenge a white person's word."[63] In addition, former slaves' petty theft, vagrancy, unemployment and contract violations earned them fines they could not pay, resulting in a convict labor system comprised of up to ninety percent African-Americans,[64] thereby making involuntary membership in such a system a realistic possibility for African-Americans.[65] Convict labor was so widespread and essential to the Southern economy that local sheriffs commonly arrested able-bodied African-Americans and falsely charged them with crimes, forcing them into labor as "convicts."[66] One contemporary commentator reported that "[o]ne reason for the large number of arrests . . . lies in the fact that the state and the counties make a profit out of their prison system," and therefore, the "natural tendency is to convict as many men as possible."[67]

Even for African-Americans never caught in the toils of Southern justice, the threat of being forced into the convict labor system kept them in involuntary servitude under their labor contracts. "Contract breaches, switching jobs, failure to pay debts and simple idleness were surrounded with the threat of false accusations and criminal sanctions—a potent weapon in the hands of white employers who sought to bend blacks to their bidding."[68] As one black activist noted, "[t]he horror of ball and chain is ever before [blacks], and their future is bright with no hope."[69]

After the war, the system of convict leasing began to grow and prosper, and by the mid-1870s, almost every Southern state had developed some type of convict leasing.[70] The general description of the fate that befell the mostly black convicts leased to private interests is worth noting:

> Colored men are convicted in magistrates' courts of trivial offenses, such as alleged violation of contract or something of the kind, and are given purposely heavy sentences with alternate fines. Plantation owners and others in search of labour, who have already given their orders to the officers of the law, are promptly notified that some available labourers are theirs to command and immediately appear to pay the fine and release the convict from [jail] only to make him a slave. If the negro dares to leave the premises of his employer, the same magistrate who convicted him originally is ready to pounce down upon him and send him back to [jail]. Invariably poor and ignorant, he is unable to employ counsel or to assert his rights (it is treason to presume he has any) and he finds all the machinery of the law, so far as he can understand, against him. There is no doubt . . . that there are scores, hundreds perhaps, of couloured men in the South today who are vainly trying to repay fines and sentences imposed upon them five, six or ten years ago.[71]

Many former slaves, jailed for petty offenses or kidnapped, were seized by the convict leasing so soon after the adoption of the Thirteenth Amendment that they never knew

[61] Fierce, supra note 48, at 251.

[62] See Schmidt, supra note 56, at 651.

[63] Blumberg, supra note 53, at 19.

[64] See Fierce, supra note 48, at 88, 147. "At the present time, especially in the county chain gangs, the Negroes still furnish a quota greatly out of proportion to the part which they form of the population." Jesse F. Steiner & Roy M. Brown, *The North Carolina Chain Gang* 14–15 (1927) (relying on data from 1875–1878).

[65] See Jennifer Roback, Southern Labor Law in the Jim Crow Era: Exploitative or Competitive?, 51 *U. Chi. L. Rev.* 1161, 1163–69 (1984).

[66] See Fierce, supra note 48, at 85–87.

[67] Schmidt, supra note 56, at 651 (quoting R. Baker, *Following the Color Line* 50 (1964)).

[68] Id. at 653.

[69] Fierce, supra note 48, at 233 (quoting Mary Church Terrell, Peonage in the United States: The Convict Lease System and the Chain Gangs, in *The Nineteenth Century* 62, 308 (1907)).

[70] See id. at 9.

[71] Id. at 232 (quoting Mary Church Terrell, Peonage in the United States: The Convict Lease System and the Chain Gangs, in *The Nineteenth Century* 62, 308 (1907)).

freedom.[72] For these slaves, "convict leasing was not a revisit to slavery because they had never left it: freedom's interlude completely passed them by."[73] Assistant Attorney General Charles W. Russell, the Justice Department's special investigator, concluded that the convict leasing system was "largely a system of involuntary servitude—that is to say, persons are held to labor as convicts under those laws who have committed no crime."[74]

Those "convicts" who served their time on the chain gangs also suffered severe hardships and disrespect. Such conditions are in an account of the Bibb County chain gang in Georgia:

> The sufferers wear the typical striped clothing of the penitentiary convict. Iron manacles are riveted upon their legs. These can be removed only by the use of the cold chisel. The irons on each leg are connected by chains. . . . Their progress to and from their work is public, and from dawn to dark, with brief intermission, they toil on the public roads and before the public eye. About them, as they sleep, journey, and labor, watch the convict guards, armed with rifle and shotgun. This is to at once make escape impossible, and to make sure the swift thudding of the picks and the rapid flight of the shovels shall never cease. If the guards would hesitate to promptly kill one sentenced for petty violations of city law should he attempt to escape, the evidence does not disclose the fact. And the fact more baleful and more ignominious than all— with each gang stands the whipping boss, with the badge of his authority.[75]

Life on the chain gang reached such an abominable level that in 1919, Alabama Governor Thomas E. Kilby declared his state's chain gangs and convict-lease system "a relic of barbarism . . . a form of human slavery."[76]

In 1933, chain gangs became more common as Southern states outlawed convict leasing and replaced it with chain gangs.[77] New legislation required that convicts be confined to labor on "public works."[78] One evil thereby replaced another, and convict leasing systems were legally replaced with chain gangs.

The chain gangs of the 1930s were marked by the same humiliation and dehumanization as those of the ante-bellum era. The convicts were usually harnessed together with chains at all times, even while eating or sleeping.[79] The chains were riveted around their legs and could only be removed with a chisel at the time of the prisoners' release from the gang.[80] John L. Spivak, in his book *Georgia Nigger*, paints a vivid picture of life on a South Carolina prisoner chain gang:

> In Buzzard's Roost [a Georgia chain gang] there were vermin and stench, cursings and beatings and stocks but out of Slatternville seventeen Negroes went into the wilderness of the South Carolina hills in a floating cage, a cage drawn by four mules, a swaying, creaking, rumbling prison of thick wood with no bars or windows for air on nights that choked you, and bunks of steel with rungs for master chains to lock you in at night. Bedbugs slept with you in that cage and lice nestled in the hair of your body and you scratched until your skin bled and the sores on your body filled with pus. Meat for the floating kitchen wrapped in burlap bags, stinking meat swarming with maggots and flies, and corn pone soaked by fall rains, slashing rains that beat upon the wooden cage through the barred door upon the straw mattresses until they were soggy.[81]

A 1927 look at the chain gang chronicled the shame involved, noting that chain gangs were "frequently criticized on the ground that the use of chains . . . in public places is unduly

---

[72]See id. at 51.

[73]Id.

[74]Schmidt, supra note 56, at 651 (quoting C. Russell, *Report on Peonage* 17 (1908)).

[75]Id. at 652 (quoting *Jamison v. Wimbish* 130 F. 351, 355–56 (W.D. Ga. 1904)).

[76]Id. at 651 (alteration in original).

[77]See Fierce, supra note 48, at 12–13.

[78]See id. at 13.

[79]See Wilson, supra note 1, at 70.

[80]See id.

[81]Id.

humiliating to the prisoners as well as degrading to those who are forced to witness such a spectacle when passing along the highways."[82]

Chain gangs continued building public works for the Southern states until widespread abuses led to reform and, finally, extinction.[83] They were seen more as public humiliation than punishment.[84] However, in 1995, the chain gang returned to Alabama.

II   CHAIN GANGS TODAY

A. May 1995–May 1996

On any particular Alabama summer day, it is nearly 100 degrees outside when inmates, most of them black, get off the bus beside Interstate 65.[85] These men will form the day's chain gang. Guards with mirrored sunglasses overlook the long stretches of hot road, while nearby tracking dogs howl in their cages.[86] The inmates drop to their knees so their ankles can be linked with the chains.[87] Three guards, armed with 12-gauge shotguns, carefully watch the inmates.

This notorious method of punishment returned to Alabama on May 3, 1995.[89] Alabama became the first state in the nation to reinstitute chain gangs. The chains went on for political reasons, returning after newly elected Alabama Governor Fob James, Jr. suggested them on a radio talk show in the final weeks of his 1994 campaign.[91] He kept his election promise. Polling showed that an overwhelming majority of Alabamans approved of the idea.[92]

Approximately 700 inmates make up the Alabama chain gang.[93] The inmates are usually sent to work on the chain gang as punishment for violating parole or for breaking prison rules. However, state judges also have the discretion to impose time on a chain gang as part of the original sentence. Recidivists work on the chain gang for between six months and one year, while disciplinary offenders stay on the chain gang for up to forty-five days. Either way, members of the chain gangs are "forced to labor for ten hours a day."[97]

When the chain gangs at Limestone Correctional Facility first began, members cut weeds and picked up trash along highways; today, however, most of the chain gang members spend their days doing the stereotypical chore at the rock pile, pounding big rocks into little pebbles with sledgehammers.[98] Since it would be cheaper to buy crushed rocks, the only goal of the rock-crushing program must be to increase the level of punishment and humiliation for prisoners. After the prisoners kneel and are shackled, they walk a few hundred feet from the prison walls into a new enclosure, "sort of a cattle pen of barbed wire."[100] Although the men are enclosed securely, the guards also have orders to shoot escaping prisoners. During their tenure, the chain gang members are at substantial risk of receiving snake and insect bites.[102]

---

[82]Steiner & Brown, supra note 64, at 8.

[83]See Francis Butler Simkins, A History of the South 512 (3d ed. 1963).

[84]See John Pillow, Chain Reaction . . . Even Shackled for Work, Inmates Like Outdoors, *Courier-Journal*, Aug. 23, 1995, at B1.

[85]See Rhonda Cook, Back to Hard Labor, *Atlanta J. & Const.*, Aug. 20, 1995, at D4.

[86]See Hull, supra note 12.

[87]See Cook, supra note 85.

[89]See John David Morley, Back on the Chain Gang, *Times Mag.* (London), Aug. 5, 1995, at 22, 24.

[91]Plaintiffs' Second Amended Complaint at 4, *Austin v. James* (M.D. Ala. 1996) (No. 95-T-637-N) [hereinafter Plaintiffs' Complaint].

[92]See Eric Harrison, The Chain Gang Is Resurrected in Alabama, *L.A. Times*, May 3, 1995, at A5 (reporting that 70% of the state's residents support the chain gangs); Morley, supra note 89 (reporting that 75% of those polled said they were in favor of putting people in chains);.

[93]Plaintiffs' Complaint, supra note 91, at 4.

[97]Id. at 5.

[98]See Booth, supra note 10.

[100]Id.

[102]See Plaintiffs' Opposition to Defendants' Motion for Summary Judgment at 12–13, Austin v. James (M.D. Ala. 1996) (No. 95-T-637-N) [hereinafter Plaintiffs' Opposition].

When the first chain gangs were reintroduced, the brainchild behind the gangs' resurrection, then Commissioner of Corrections Ronald Jones,[105] presided over the event. Hundreds of reporters and photographers from around the world came to Alabama to witness this spectacle. Alabama convicts have long performed cleanup work on the roads.[106] So why all the attention?

The chains create an intentional spectacle—a deliberate and obvious association with a different era. Alabama is not a place stuck in time. Just down the road in nearby Huntsville, passers by who just gawked at the chain gang will be able to see a NASA installation and dozens of aerospace and defense companies.[107] However, with tobacco chewing officers, tough talking Southern lawmen, "this redneck scene . . . is straight outta Hollywood," commented one inmate.[108]

Alabama chain gangs are part of an environment created to appease society's hostility to prisoners, dissatisfaction with criminal justice, and intolerance of further crime. The following paragraphs and pages are not meant to draw overbroad generalizations about the people of Alabama, but rather to highlight the peculiar context of the chain gangs. They chronicle the Alabama that the Alabama Department of Corrections has deliberately presented to the American public. The message being sent is clear: Alabama is tough on crime because Alabama is tough on criminals.

Each person at the Alabama Department of Corrections plays his part to perfection, from the shotgun toting guards to the colorful Prison Commissioner. Commissioner Jones looks the part of the lawman—smoking menthols and wearing a bad tie that does not cover his stomach.[110] Jones spoonfeeds the press the stereotypical role of a lawman they have come to see, hollering that "[w]e're going to make prison as miserable as we can and that's not a threat, that's a promise."[111] His image has been broadcast everywhere. The world has seen the heavy chain and sixty-five-pound ball that grace the walls of his office in the state capital of Montgomery.[112] It has heard him glibly state that "[i]t became real humane on my part to put these inmates out there in leg irons because they have virtually no chance of escaping. Therefore they're not going to get shot"[113] Jones continues, "I don't want them shot. It's not that I'm a softy. It's expensive. You shoot someone and you send him to the hospital and it costs $100,000 to patch him up."[114]

Jones rails against in-prison education, drug counseling and therapy, calling them "freebies," and arguing that they have transformed inmates into a "class of parasites on the welfare wagon."[115] Jones loves the press, welcoming the attention. "The more press the better."[116]

Although Commissioner Jones justified the chain gangs as more cost effective, commenting "[m]y reality is budget cuts and a taxpayer

---

[105]Jones resigned from his post on April 26, 1996. *See* Deborah L. Rhode. Is There Sexual Parity For Prisoners? *Nat'l L.J.* July 8, 1996, at A19. Jones' fate as Alabama's Prison Commissioner was sealed when he proposed in the spring of 1996 that women prisoners be put on chain gangs, joining their male counterparts. See id. In response to a lawsuit challenging Alabama's resurrection of chain gangs as unlawful sex discrimination, Jones agreed, concluding that "[t]here's no real defense for not [including] females." Id. (second alteration in original). In response, Governor James demanded Jones' resignation and reassured worried citizens that "[t]here will be no women on any chain gang in the state of Alabama today, tomorrow, or any time under my watch." Id. The governor then named Joe Hopper as acting Prison Commissioner. See Les Payne, Old Times Here Are Not Forgotten, *Newsday*, May 5, 1996, at A42. Hopper quickly pledged to continue placing male inmates on chain gangs. See id.

[106]See Michael Dorman, On the Chain Gang *Newsday*, June 18, 1995, at A7.

[107]See Booth, supra note 13, at A14.

[108]Hull, supra note 12.

[110]See Booth, supra note 10.

[111]Katherine M. Skiba, Bustin' Rock: Alabama Resurrects Chain Gangs Under Scrutiny of Guards, Critics, *Milwaukee J. Sentinel*, Nov. 12, 1995, at 1.

[112]See Booth, supra note 10.

[113]John Leland, Back on the Chain Gang *Newsweek*, May 15, 1995, at 58; see Cohen, supra note 101, at 26.

[114]Booth, supra note 13, at A14.

[115]Skiba, supra note III, at 1.

[116]Booth, supra note 10, at F1.

revolt,"[122] it remains uncertain whether the chain gangs are saving Alabama any money.[123] Jones also claimed that the chain gang is successful because it deters crime.[124] However, it is widely disputed whether the chain gang program will decrease recidivism, discourage parole violations, or reduce disciplinary violations.[125]

There is something going on in Alabama, something to do with the public's feelings regarding the nature of punishment. The resurrection of chain gangs comes at a time when the nation is weary of the rehabilitation programs of the 1970s and eager for retribution.[126] The public yearns to see prisoners work, desires *real* punishment instead of cable television and weights. "There is something about the notion of hard labor, punishment for punishment's sake, that appeals to an electorate scared of crime, fed up with what it sees as coddling."[127] And the politicians are responding. They are quite willing to show the public what it desires to see.

B. Current Status of Chain Gangs

On June 19, 1996, without being ordered to do so by the Court, the State of Alabama, in a settlement with the Southern Poverty Law Center, agreed to end the practice of chaining inmates together in the state prison system.[128]

The State did not concede that there was an Eighth Amendment violation, and in fact the settlement explicitly stated that "no evidence has been adduced of any violation of the Eighth Amendment with regard to the practice of chaining inmates together."[129]

The absence of group chaining does not eliminate the "cruel and unusual" historical association of chain gangs with slavery and convict leasing. Viewers still observe a disproportionate number of African-American men wearing chains and performing labor. The image evokes the same connotation of slavery. A chain gang still exists—different form, same substance. For instance, although Arizona's chain gangs are comprised of inmates shackled at the ankle, but not to each other, they are nonetheless called "chain gangs."[131] Also, the projected image is the same despite the actual method of chaining, as evidenced by Senator Sandra Kennedy's comment while viewing an Arizona chain gang: "This reminds me of the old days of slavery."[132]

Even before the court agreement was reached in June, the prison commission had ceased chaining inmates together, in large part due to safety concerns.[133] Alabama did not stop the practice because of its inherent inhumanity, nor because of political pressure. To the contrary, Alabama prison officials try to appease a general public that overwhelmingly supports chaining inmates. Indeed, Alfred Sawyer, Governor James' spokesperson, insists that individual chains are not much of a departure from Governor James' original promise to put prisoners in leg irons.[135] Alabama did not "agree"

---

[122]Booth, supra note 13, at A14.

[123]See Plaintiffs' Opposition, supra note 102, at 5.

[124]See Cook, supra note 85.

[125]See Plaintiffs' Opposition, supra note 102, at 5.

[126]See Morrison, supra note 8.

[127]Booth, supra note 10.

[128]See Stipulation at 1, Austin v. James (M.D. Ala. 1996) (No. 95-T-637-N) [hereinafter Stipulation]. This resettlement was the result of a suit filed in 1996 by the Southern Poverty Law Center (SPLC) against Fob James and Ron Jones, seeking injunctive relief to end chain gangs and hitching posts. The SPLC argued that "[t]hese practices deprive prisoners of their associational rights and innate human dignity and are barbaric, cruel and unusual." Plaintiffs' Opposition, supra note 102, at 1. The SPLC's arguments focused on 1) the inmates' increased exposure to substantial risk of physical injury and death due to traffic accidents, inmate violence, injuries at the rock pile, and snake and insect bites; 2) the unsanitary and uncivilized conditions of the toilet facilities; and 3) the grave psychological pain suffered by chain gang members. See Plaintiff's Opposition, supra note 102, at 7–13.

[129]Stipulation, supra note 128, at 1, *Austin* (No. 95-T-637-N).

[131]See Norm Parish, Chain Gangs a Link to Slavery? *Ariz. Republic*, May 29, 1995, at A1.

[132]Id. Senator Kennedy is an African-American Democrat representing southern Phoenix, Arizona See id.

[133]As of May 21, 1996, Alabama ceased chaining inmates together after a guard fatally shot an inmate who attacked a fellow chain gang member. Alabama Alters Chain Gang Rules *Phoenix Gazette*, June 21, 1996, A4.

[135]See *Alabama Court Case Settled over Chain Gang Dispute* (National Public Radio broadcast, June 21, 1996) [hereinafter *Alabama Court Case*].

to end chaining inmates together for fear of losing the litigation.[136] Alabama ended the practice because of administrative concerns.

As Governor Fob James commented in a public statement, "[w]e determined individual chains allow for more efficient management of inmates, especially with regard to safety."[137] According to one official, the "change was due to safety concerns as well as to the relatively inefficient use of time spent chaining and unchaining inmates for transportation and work purposes."[138] In essence, the chaining together of inmates was not as logistically facile as the state had hoped. There were problems, major problems: chain gang inmate Abraham McCord was shot and killed by a correctional officer after he attacked a fellow chain gang inmate with an ax; many inmates were injured with tools because they were unable to escape the fighting.[139] Moreover, two inmates escaped from the gangs.[140]

Chain gangs still exist and continue to prosper in Alabama. The Alabama Department of Corrections still has high-risk prisoners working on the roads, and they still are bound in chains.[141] Each prisoner on the chain gang has his legs shackled together, but is not chained to other inmates. In August 1996, Alice Ann Byrne, Assistant General Counsel of the Alabama Department of Corrections, wrote a letter to *Newsweek* correcting the magazine on its article about the discontinuation of Alabama's chain gangs in which she said, "Your article stated that Alabama has discontinued the use of chain gangs. Not only is this incorrect, but just the opposite is true. As individual chains have

proved to be more efficient, Alabama is increasing the number of inmates on its chain gang by at least 10 percent."[143]

The use of chain gangs endorses a mode of punishment that is both a cruel barb and an unusual indignity to the class of persons most likely to suffer the penalty. Chain gangs are a loaded symbol. They evoke the horror of countless racial indignities, from slave ships to forced labor. Since chain gangs have been used as instruments in such barbaric systems, they now cannot be used as part of a "legitimate" system, seeking to administer justice. Such a punishment, one which fits into a repertoire of repression, cannot satisfy the mandate of decency demanded by the Eighth Amendment.

III   TRACING THE HISTORY OF THE EIGHTH AMENDMENT AND ITS JURISPRUDENCE

The cruel and unusual punishments clause included in England's Declaration of Rights was subsequently adopted in various colonial declarations of rights.[167] The federal government inserted it into the Northwest Ordinance of 1787, and in 1791 it became the Eighth Amendment to the United States Constitution.[171] The Eighth Amendment provides that "[e]xcessive bail shall not be required, nor excessive fines imposed, nor cruel and unusual punishments inflicted."[172] The American amendment was adopted almost word-for-word from the English version. In fact, the only change James Madison made in writing the American version was to replace the English "ought not" with the imperative "shall not."[173]

Although the similar wording of the two documents indicates that the English Declaration of

---

[136]The state has never conceded that the practice is cruel and unusual. See id.

[137]Alabama Drops its Chain Gangs, Opts for Individual Chains. *Agence France-Presse*, June 21, 1996, available in Westlaw, AGFRP database.

[138]Letters: Chain Gangs *U.S. News & World Ref.*, Aug. 19, 1996, at 6 [hereinafter Letters] (letter written by Alice Ann Byrne, Asst. Gen. Counsel, Alabama Department of Corrections).

[139]See Plaintiff's Opposition, supra note 102, at 10–11.

[140]See The Nation: Unchained *USA Today* Jan. 18, 1996. at 3A.

[141]*See Alabama Court Case*, supra note 135.

[143]Letters, supra note 138.

[167]See *Ingraham v. Wright*, 430 U.S. 651, 664 (1977); Granucci, supra note 144, at 852–53.

[171]See Note, The Cruel and Unusual Punishment Clause and the Substantive Criminal Law, 79 *Harv. L. Rev.* 635, 636–37 (1966).

[172]*U.S. Const.* amend. VIII.

[173]See Larry Charles Berkson, *The Concept of Cruel and Unusual Punishment* (1975).

Rights influenced the Framers, debate surrounds what the Founding Fathers intended in adopting the clause. There is very little record of the Framers' discussion of the Clause and scholarship on the Framers' intent is inconclusive.[174] Thus, an examination of the history of prohibitions against cruel methods and excessiveness of punishments offered little guidance to the Supreme Court's Eighth Amendment analysis.[179] The lack of historical evidence made it difficult for the Supreme Court to determine what the clause was intended to prohibit, which in turn made it difficult for the Court to announce exacting, consistent standards to govern its application.[180]

Following the adoption of the Cruel and Unusual Punishments Clause in 1791, both state and federal jurists seemed to accept the view that the Clause prohibited the more cruel methods of punishment such as pillorying, disemboweling, decapitation, and drawing and quartering.[181] However, since the United States never resorted to the barbarous punishments used in Stuart England, by the nineteenth century, some considered the Eighth Amendment to be obsolete.[182] Accordingly, the Clause was rarely invoked in court.[183]

The Supreme Court first applied the Eighth Amendment by comparing the challenged methods of execution to concededly cruel methods of punishment, such as torture. The Court defined the scope of the Cruel and Unusual Punishments Clause for the first time in *Wilkerson v. Utah*.[186] *Wilkerson* involved a defendant convicted of murder in the first degree and condemned to death by shooting. Although acknowledging that defining the scope of the Eighth Amendment with "exactness" was difficult, the Court found that punishment should not entail "terror, pain, or disgrace." The Court was resolute that the Eighth Amendment condemned torture, stating that "it is safe to affirm that punishments of torture . . . and all others in the same line of unnecessary cruelty, are forbidden."

The Court concluded that shooting was an acceptable method of punishment and did not constitute unnecessary cruelty. To guide its inquiry, the Court indulged in a two-page historical analysis, chronicling the historical acceptability of certain practices and examining traditional means of death. The Court found shooting to be a legitimate method because it was a common military practice. It denounced unacceptable practices—such as public burning, disembowelment, drawing and quartering—and attempted to differentiate these from acceptable practices by focusing on torture and unnecessary cruelty. Ultimately, it found that the custom of shooting did not offend contemporary standards of decency, and therefore execution by shooting was not cruel.

More than a decade later, in *In re Kemmler*, a condemned convict asserted that death by electrocution was cruel and unusual and that New York's arbitrary adoption of such punishment violated his right to due process.[197] In the *Kemmler* opinion, relying upon the rationale of *Wilkerson*, the Court acknowledged that the mere fact that a punishment was "unusual" or novel was not sufficient reason for its condemnation under the Eighth Amendment. Rather, to violate due process, the punishment must be considered *excessively* cruel.

After discussing manifestly cruel punishments such as "burning at the stake, crucifixion, [and] breaking on the wheel," the Court found that "common knowledge" is sufficient to render certain punishments unusually cruel. Although the Court introduced a standard stating that "[p]unishments are cruel when they involve torture or a lingering death," the opinion as a whole suggests that an unpleasant visceral response to punishments may provide a starting point for Eighth Amendment analysis.

---

[174]See *Weems v. United States*, 217 U.S. 349, 368–69 (1910); John B. Wefing, Cruel and Unusual Punishment, 20 *Seton Hall L. Rev.* 478, 482 (1990).

[179]See Wefing, supra note 174, at 481–82.

[180]See Schwartz & Wishingrad, supra note 177, at 789.

[181]See Granucci, supra note 144, at 842.

[182]See Note, supra note 171, at 637.

[183]See Granucci, supra note 144, at 842.

[186]99 U.S. 130(1878).

[197]See In re *Kemmler*, 136 U.S. 436, 439, 441–42 (1890).

In 1910, a revolutionary expansion of the Eighth Amendment occurred. In *Weems v. United States*,[203] the Court for the first time rejected the notion that the Eighth Amendment is limited to punishments that are inhumane, barbarous, or torturous. Instead, *Weems* addressed the excessiveness of a punishment, noting that the Eighth Amendment was not designed merely to prohibit the cruel methods of punishment employed by the Stuarts in England.

In *Weems*, a court convicted a civil servant for falsifying an entry in a public document. Weems was sentenced to an extremely harsh, but common, form of punishment called *cadena temporal*. The punishment directed that Weems "carry a chain at the ankle, hanging from the wrists . . . [and that he] be employed at hard and painful labor" for fifteen years. The statute also restricted his personal rights, resulting in his loss of marital and parental rights, inability to pass property inter vivos, and subjection to life-long surveillance.

The Court found that punishment could no longer be justified on the basis of tradition alone. It recognized that the Eighth Amendment is "progressive, and is not fastened to the obsolete, but may acquire meaning as public opinion becomes enlightened by a humane justice." The *Weems* Court acknowledged that "[t]ime works changes, brings into existence new conditions and purposes." These sentiments set the tone for future Eighth Amendment inquiries by suggesting that the Amendment should be interpreted in a flexible manner to comport with the developments of time: "[for] a principle to be vital[, it] must be capable of wider application than the mischief which gave it birth." In effect, whether a punishment is constitutional depends on dynamic societal standards of justice.

Forty years later, the dissenters in a death penalty case, *Louisiana ex. rel. Francis v. Resweber*, addressed whether the psychological effects of a punishment can prompt a violation of the Eighth Amendment.[213] Convicted murderer Willie Francis was sentenced to die by electrocution. Francis' life was spared, however, when the electric chair malfunctioned in the course of his execution. Although the switch was repeatedly thrown, the electric chair continued to fizzle. Francis groaned, jumped, and finally demanded that the current be turned off and he be allowed to breathe.

Francis presented the issue of whether it was constitutional to allow a second attempt at electrocution. Francis claimed that a second attempt would force him to repeat the severe psychological strain of preparing for electrocution, thereby subjecting him to a "lingering or cruel and unusual punishment." A majority of the Court rejected Francis' argument, holding that the Constitution prohibits cruelty only in the method of punishment. The State therefore was held to be morally blameless for any cruelty that resulted from the "unforeseeable accident." The majority holding sent Francis back to the electric chair, where he died in a second electrocution. Four Justices dissented in *Francis*, dismissing the majority's reliance on official intent, focusing instead on pain and mental anguish.[220]

In the next significant Supreme Court case, the *Weems* principle of the changing nature of Eighth Amendment prohibitions reached full articulation. In *Trop v. Dulles*,[225] the Court held that a non-death penalty, non-physical punishment could violate the Eighth Amendment. Trop was a wartime deserter, and as a consequence of a provision of the Nationality Act of 1940, he lost his citizenship. Trop protested that the Eighth Amendment prevented divestment of citizenship, and the Court confronted the issue of whether denationalization was cruel and unusual within the meaning of the Eighth Amendment. Relying on the sentiments of *Weems*, a plurality of the Court announced a flexible governing principle: "[t]he

---

[203]217 U.S. 349 (1910).

[213]See Louisiana *ex rel. Francis v. Resweber*, 329 U.S. 459, 477 (1947) (Burton, J., dissenting).

[220]See id. at 477. Finding intent immaterial in its determination of whether a second attempt at execution is cruel and unusual, the dissenters argued that "[t]he intent of the executioner cannot lessen the torture or excuse the result." Id.

[225]356 U.S. 86 (1958).

Amendment must draw its meaning from the evolving standards of decency that mark the progress of a maturing society."

In analyzing the constitutionality of Trop's punishment, the Court found that, although denationalization does not involve any "physical mistreatment [or] primitive torture," it still offends modern sensibilities, and therefore violates the Eighth Amendment. The Court considered the psychological effects of forced denationalization on an individual, including "fear and distress," in holding this form of punishment unconstitutional. The Court contemplated civilized standards of decency and asserted that "[t]he basic concept underlying the Eighth Amendment is nothing less than the dignity of man."

In 1962, in *Robinson v. California*,[233] the Court followed its interpretation of the Eighth Amendment, and held, as in *Trop*, that a non-death penalty punishment violated the Eighth Amendment. *Robinson* involved a California law which declared drug addiction to be illegal. When the defendant was sentenced to jail after being convicted of drug addiction, even though he did not have any drugs in his possession, the Court held that the sentence violated the Eighth Amendment.

The judicial interpretation involved in these landmark Eighth Amendment cases reveals three significant themes. First, the Court made it clear in *Trop* and *Weems* that the Eighth Amendment is not chained to history. Rather, the Eighth Amendment is a fluid concept, guided by contemporary standards of decency. Second, *Wilkerson* and *In re Kemmler* highlight the Court's consideration of the historical context of certain forms of punishment. These cases hint that an intuitive reaction, based on historical association, to a particular punishment can be a factor in determining whether that punishment is cruel and unusual. Finally, *Wilkerson* and *In re Kemmler* introduce the concept that cruel and unusual punishments may encompass more than just purely physical punishments. *Trop* and *Francis* confirm the Court's

recognition that the psychological impact of punishment is a factor in determining whether it is unconstitutional. Although the *Trop* Court found the psychological evidence persuasive, while the *Francis* Court did not, mental anguish was central in both. In sum, the cases suggest that the historical importance and psychological impact of chain gangs are central to a constitutional analysis of whether the punishment satisfies evolving standards of decency.

With the exception of *Francis* and *Robinson*, all of the foundational cases discussed above considered the constitutionality of a particular criminal sanction. However, the Eighth Amendment also reaches beyond inmates' sentences. A prisoner's condition of confinement can also give rise to an Eighth Amendment violation.[238]

The prisoners' rights movement of the 1960s transformed the status of a prisoner from that of a "slave of the state," having scarcely any rights at all,[239] into that of a "legal person." This transformation fostered new challenges under the Cruel and Unusual Punishments Clause. After being convicted and incarcerated, many prisoners found the conditions of their confinement, as well as their treatment by prison officials, inhumane.[240] They turned to the Eighth Amendment for relief and the Court eventually responded by acknowledging that conditions of confinement could give rise to a violation.[241] Therefore, because serving on a chain gang is a condition of an inmate's confinement, chain gangs are subject to the scrutiny of the Eighth Amendment.

---

[238]See *Rhodes v. Chapman*, 452 U.S. 337 (1981) (finding that certain conditions of confinement may be proscribed by the Eighth Amendment); *Hutto v. Finney*, 437 U.S. 678 (1978) (discussing prison conditions that affect the prison population generally); *Estelle v. Gamble*, 429 U.S. 97 (1976) (finding that the Cruel and Unusual Punishments Clause could be applied to some deprivations that were not specifically part of the sentence).

[239]*Ruffin v. Commonwealth*, 62 Va. (21 Gratt.) 790, 796 (1871).

[240]See *Rhodes*, 452 U.S. 337; *Hutto*, 437 U.S. 678; *Estelle*, 429 U.S. 97.

[241]See *Rhodes*, 452 U.S. 337.

---

[233]370 U.S. 660 (1962).

IV THE EIGHTH AMENDMENT PROSCRIBES THE USE OF CHAIN GANGS AS PUNISHMENT

As an examination of the case law demonstrates, precise formulae do not exist for determining when a punishment offends the Eighth Amendment. However, the ultimate inquiry in any Eighth Amendment case seems to be whether the punishment is consistent with "evolving standards of decency."[242] This enunciation has become a guidepost for virtually all Eighth Amendment analyses subsequent to *Trop*.[243]

The "evolving standards of decency" doctrine recognizes that times change and that the Constitution must allow for the moral evolution of our nation. A punishment must reflect the progression of society, not regress to the days of institutionalized racial oppression. Chain gangs were eliminated in the 1960s because this country could no longer tolerate their inhumanity. Society expressed its notion of decent punishment, and the chain gang failed to meet this standard.

A. Historical Association Should Matter

It can be argued that the Eighth Amendment "was intended to safeguard individuals from the abuse of legislative power."[244] Thus, "legislative judgments alone cannot be determinative of Eighth Amendment standards."[245] Despite how state legislatures have treated certain punishments, the Court should always inquire further when evaluating whether a punishment is consistent with evolving standards of decency.

In determining whether a punishment comports with the constitutional standard, a court should consider a number of objective factors, including "whether the punishment . . . is *historically* associated with repression or

tyranny."[246] A court should "[employ] the tools of philosophy, religion, logic, and *history*, in an effort to obtain a full understanding of the nature of a civilized society."[247] Both the *Wilkerson* and *Kemmler* opinions factored history into their decisions, focusing on atrocities of the past and perhaps signaling the intuitive notion that historical connotation should matter in Eighth Amendment analysis. *Kemmler* and *Wilkerson* are formative cases, for they establish a foundation for defining the parameters of "cruel and unusual." Both decisions mention history in their analyses, and both voice standards based on intangible, inchoate, perhaps visceral factors. Since the severe and agonizing punishments paraded and rejected in *Wilkerson* and *Kemmler*—disembowelment, beheading, and burning at the stake—can be considered "historical throwbacks to times of tyranny and repression,"[248] perhaps part of the Court's intuitive rejection of such punishments was their unique and horrific historical connotation.

What is disturbing about these punishments, besides their obvious physical atrociousness, is their use as instruments of oppression. For instance, Judge Reinhardt of the Ninth Circuit recently engaged in a historical analysis of hanging, discussing its horrifying historical associations:

> Hanging is associated with lynching, with frontier justice, and with our ugly, nasty, and best-forgotten history of bodies swinging from the trees or exhibited in public places. To many Americans, judicial hangings call forth the brutal images of Southern justice. . . . Yet to all of us, hangings are a remnant of an earlier, harder time, a time when in meting out punishment we were far less concerned with human dignity and decency.[249]

Judge Reinhardt calls attention to the historical significance of hanging and notes its

---

[242]*Trop v. Dulles*, 356 U.S. 86, 101 (1938) (plurality opinion).

[243]Federal courts have cited the "evolving standards of decency" language used in *Trop* over 500 times. Search of Westlaw, Allfeds database.

[244]*Gregg v. Georgia*, 428 U.S. 153, 174 n.19 (1976) (opinion of Stewart, Powell, and Stevens, JJ.).

[245]Id.

[246]*Campbell v. Wood*, 18 F.3d 662, 697 (9th Cir. 1994) (Reinhardt, J., concurring and dissenting) (emphasis added).

[247]Id. (emphasis added).

[248]McLaughlin, supra note 199, at 185.

[249]*Campbell*, 18 F.3d at 701 (Reinhardt, J., concurring and dissenting).

connection to crude Southern justice.[250] In condemning its use, he emphasizes that such a connotation should not be invoked in current forms of punishment.[251]

This analysis and reasoning, in which history is a factor that aids in evaluating "evolving standards of decency," implies that knowledge of past racial discrimination must be an integral part of a present analysis of chain gangs. The chain gang is not only a mechanism of punishment, but a symbol of slavery. Today's images of chains conjure up images of the past. For instance, Flossie Hodges, an elderly white woman who has lived in Limestone County, Alabama her whole life, watched a gang intently, commenting that "I love seeing `em in chains. They ought to make them pick cotton all day."[252] Indeed, today's chain gangs should be denounced because of a shameful past when chains were used to humiliate and dehumanize blacks. Slaves were chained in the abominable hulls of slave ships, chained on their way to and from the shameful auction blocks, chained as working slaves, and chained to maintain bondage in a time of supposed "freedom."[253]

Considering that minority criminals in general and black criminals in particular are disproportionately subjected to the chain gang, chain gangs have particular meaning to the typical inmate punished by such a method and to the society that witnesses such cruelty.[254] At present, nearly seventy percent of the members on Alabama's chain gangs are black.[255] The black inmates say they feel like slaves and the white inmates say they feel they are being treated like blacks.[256] Says one black chain gang member, "These white boys are just like sprinklings on a cake." The composition of Alabama's prison population suggests that men in chains observed by thousands of passing citizens along Alabama's highways will be mostly African-American.

Blacks as a group continue to grapple with the American experience of slavery, and chain gangs mock the history of racial injustice in this country. The potency of the image of men in chains undeniably draws power from the history of chain gangs, yet that history is one of racism and barbarism. They are a throwback to a time of oppression, repression, and hate. They remind us of the worst chapter in our national history. Racism and hate continue to exist in this country. Chain gangs, reminders of a time when racism was legal, feed this hate.

Chain gangs are particularly repugnant in Alabama, a state infamous for its history of civil rights atrocities. In the 1950s and 1960s, out of all the southern states, Alabama remained the stronghold of resistance to the civil rights movement in the United States.[263] It was in Alabama that two prosperous brothers were found guilty of holding blacks in slavery. The date was May 14, 1954.[264] It was the Alabama State Legislature that called the Court decision of *Brown v. Board of Education* "null, void and of no effect."[265] It was in Montgomery, Alabama, that Mrs. Rosa Parks refused to give up her seat in the bus. The march that has lived in American memories as "Bloody Sunday" took place from Selma to Montgomery.[266] Eugene "Bull" Connor, Birmingham, Alabama's police

---

[250]See id.

[251]See id. Reinhardt, in his effort to emphasize the connection between hanging and lynching, quotes a Billie Holiday song, "Strange Fruit":

> Black bodies swingin'
> In the Southern breeze
> Strange fruit hanging
> From the poplar trees.

Id.

[252]Leland, supra note 113, at 58.

[253]See supra Parts I.A-B.

[254]See Hull, supra note 12.

[255] See id.

[256] See Booth, supra note 10.

[263]See Fierce, supra note 48, at 211.

[264]See Len Cooper, *Wash. Post*, June 16, 1996, at Fl.

[265]The Damned: Slavery Did Not End with the Civil War. One Man's Odyssey Into a Nation's Secret Shame, Blumberg, supra note 53, at 58.

[266]Heading into Montgomery, the marchers were greeted by armed troopers with gas masks. See id at 131. One young girl later recalled, "I saw those horsemen coming toward me and they had those awful masks on; they rode right through the cloud of teargas [that they had thrown]. Some of them had clubs, others had ropes, or whips, which they swung about them like they were driving cattle." Id.

commissioner, became the nation's most nefarious symbol of police authority. Under his command, Freedom Riders were dumped beside a highway in Tennessee and beaten unconscious, and protesters were deterred through the use of electric cattle prods, high-pressure hoses, billy clubs, and police dogs.[267] Also, it was Alabama Governor George Wallace who made history as he stood in the doorway at the University of Alabama, blocking black students from registering, and proclaiming, "Segregation now! Segregation tomorrow! Segregation forever!"[268] Alabama was the location of the Ku Klux Klan bombing of the all-black Sixteenth Street Baptist Church in Birmingham which killed four girls who were attending Bible school.[269]

The history of civil rights abuses in Alabama is long and particularly disgraceful. Thirty years ago, Alabama's governor blocked the school house door.[270] Now, Alabama is the leader in resurrecting the chain gang. In Alabama today, images of the past are prevalent. A guard racks a round into his shotgun to hurry inmates along.[271] Restrained dogs howl from the sidelines, their clinking chains adding to the music of those of the inmates.[272] "They're treating us like . . . slaves," said William Cook, a 28 year old member of the rockbreaking detail in Alabama.[273] As one reporter lamented, "[w]atching the chain gang at work, it's impossible to wipe away the images of the Old South."[274]

The chains serve as a reminder more than a restraint. "I think it's a reminder of the way it used to be, putting the African-American male in chains," states Alabama State Representative John Hilliard.[275] Representative Alvin Holmes insists that "[t]he only reason they're doing it is because an overwhelming majority of the prisoners are Black."[276] Growing up outside of Montgomery, Holmes recalls never seeing a white man on the chain gang: "The only people you ever saw were Black. The whole purpose of having the chain gang is racist to the core. . . . [Certain white people] want things back the way they used to be."[277]

Bruce Jackson, professor of English and sociology at the State University of New York at Buffalo and author of ten books on crime and prison conditions, agrees, commenting that "[t]he whole image of the chain gang is part of the image of slavery. That is one of the reasons it is so offensive. There is a link."[278]

An association to hideous practices of the past can give power and meaning to a current form of punishment. Historical association is especially important when "history" presents a clear and conscious pattern of abuses based on race. This historical background should be a factor in Eighth Amendment analyses of cruel and unusual punishment.

B. The Psychological Trauma of Chain Gangs Degrades the "Dignity of Man"

In evaluating punishments under the Eighth Amendment, the Court has taken due care in upholding dignity in the punishment. Whether the punishment upholds the dignity of those affected seems to be a requisite factor in evaluating whether the punishment comports with society's standards of decency. Judge Reinhardt advocates considering whether a punishment "may fairly be characterized as dehumanizing or degrading."[279]

It is not only the individual's dignity that is at stake, but the nation's and society's as well. Reinhardt emphasizes this social dignity in his

---

[267]See Anna Kosof, *The Civil Rights Movement and It's Legacy* 46, 51–52 (1989).

[268] Id. at 52.

[269]See id. at 57–58.

[270]See id. at 52.

[271]See Hull, supra note 12.

[272]See id.

[273]Bechetta A. Jackson. Is The Alabama Prison System's Return to the Chain Gang Unfair to Blacks? *Jet*. Sept. 18, 1995 at 17 (alteration in original).

[274]Hull, supra note 12.

[275]Jackson, supra note 273, at 12.

[276]Id. at 13.

[277]Id. at 14.

[278]Parish, supra note 131.

[279]See *Campbell v. Wood*, 18 F.3d 662, 697 (9th Cir. 1994) (Reinhardt, J., concurring and dissenting).

analysis, commenting that "[w]e reject barbaric forms of punishment as cruel and unusual not merely because of the pain they inflict but also because we pride ourselves on being a civilized society."[280] In his *Furman v. Georgia* concurrence, Justice Brennan agreed that, "[w]hen we consider why [barbaric punishments] have been condemned, . . . we realize that the pain involved is not the only reason. The true significance of these punishments is that they treat members of the human race as nonhumans. . . ."[281]

The institution of slavery treated humans like nonhumans.[282] Since chain gangs draw on the historical connection to slavery, the punishment similarly absorbs the connotations surrounding slavery. Members of chain gangs support this notion, expressing that they feel like slaves.[283] Therefore, the punishment must be cruel, for as Justice Brennan articulated, the Constitution condemns punishments that treat people as nonhumans, robbing people of their dignity.

Both the *Wilkerson* and *Kemmler* decisions establish that punishment cannot be tantamount so "terror, pain, or *disgrace*,"[284] establishing that, at its core, the Cruel and Unusual Punishments Clause seeks to preserve the "dignity of man."[285] The Court has found a lack of this dignity in certain punishments that are unduly humiliating. For instance, in *Trop*, the Court took offense at the psychological effects of a punishment on an individual. Indeed, the Court explicitly linked the cruelty of a punitive measure with its emotional effects and political connotations. Even in *Francis*, although the Court ultimately did not find that a punishment was cruel and unusual, Justices were nonetheless willing to consider psychological impact in their determination of whether

the punishment violates common standards of decency.[288]

Notably, the *Trop* and *Francis* courts did not limit their inquiries to whether the punishments involved unnecessary infliction of pain. Indeed, even the most painless punishments may still evidence utter disregard for "the dignity of man."[289] For example, although no pain is involved,

> the Eighth Amendment prohibits the public exhibiting of carcasses on yardarms, . . . the stringing up of bodies in public squares. . . . the dragging by caissons of corpses through the public streets after a state-sponsored execution. . . . drawing and quartering not only before but after the death sentence has been fully carried out.[290]

Since pain is not the objective of these punishments, perhaps they were chosen for their symbolic value. What is cruel about these punishments is their manifest indignity. Such practices could be considered atrocities because of their symbolic use as instruments of repression:

> There is no torture involved in the act of beheading, but no American court would uphold its constitutionality. There is no lingering death in a mock execution, but the ritual is roundly condemned. On the other hand . . . malfunctions of the electric chair have caused incidents of slow, singeing deaths. Yet no court has questioned the propriety of electrocution.[291]

---

[280]Id. at 701.

[281]*Furman v. Georgia*, 408 U.S. 238, 273 (1972) (Brennan, J., concurring).

[282]See supra notes 47 and accompanying text.

[283]See supra text accompanying notes 256, 282.

[284]*Wilkerson v. Utah*, 99 U.S. 130, 135 (1878) (emphasis added).

[285]*Trop v. Dulles*, 356 U.S. 86, 100 (1958).

[288]See Louisiana *ex rel. Francis v. Resweber*, 329 U.S. 459, 464 (1947).

[289]As Justice Reinhardt notes, the guillotine is a relatively painless method, but no court would hold that beheading is consistent with our current standards of decency. See *Campbell v. Wood*, 18 F.3d 662, 706 (9th Cir. 1994) (Reinhardt, J., concurring and dissenting). Additionally, any punishments involving postmortem mutilation would be proscribed by the Eighth Amendment, although they would not cause any infliction of pain. See Id.

[290]Id. at 702 (citing *Wilkerson v. Utah*, 99 U.S. 150, 135–36 (1879)).

[291]McLaughlin, supra note 199, at 186 (footnotes and internal quotations omitted). On May 4, 1990, during a bungled execution, a defective sponge in Florida's electric chair caused Jesse Tafero to be slowly burned alive as twelve-inch blue and orange flames burst from the sides of his

As Flossie Hodges' quotation suggests, the citizen sees the chain gang and makes an historical association to slavery and oppression. Because of this historical connotation, the chain gang punishment, though relatively painless, unduly removes an inmate's dignity, thus falling short of the constitutional standard. If a black man bound by chains prompts memories of slavery or black oppression, his dignity is violated. Therefore, in light of remarks like Hodges', it is difficult to reconcile chain gangs with the Eighth Amendment's mandate that a punishment uphold the "dignity of man."

Like being expatriated, being a black member of an Alabama chain gain implicates the inmate's status in society. With an undeniable reference to the days of slavery and forced labor, chain gangs are both humiliating and degrading. The inmate receives more than punishment; he receives a disproportionate stigma from society, reducing him again to the role of a slave. The political and social connotations of a chain gang harken to days of explicit racial injustice in this country—days when blacks were forced to work, forced to leave family and loved ones, and callously bred to bear more slaves.

The humiliation of the cruel punishment extends also to those who witness such indignity, and to society as a whole. Like public hangings in the nineteenth century, people drive miles to view the spectacle of the chain gang.[293] On many days, tour buses carrying curious citizens drive through the entrance of the Limestone Facility to catch a glimpse of the chain gangs. On one occasion, an officer directed a chain of five to line up and face the bus. The men stood there for ten minutes as the tourists observed them. On that particular chain, most of the prisoners were black, and most of the tourists were white.

CONCLUSION

Their undeniable historical association with oppression, compounded by the accompanying humiliation, renders chain gangs repugnant to civilized notions of common decency and a violation of prisoners' dignity and humanity. Therefore, chain gangs offend the Eighth Amendment's tenet of "evolving standards of decency."

Resurrection of the chain gangs offends a progression of decency rooted in American history. A devolution to the chain gang contradicts the constitutional mandate that we must progress away from punishments that society has already found to offend the "dignity of man." There is an unambiguous historical connection between chain gangs and slavery. Advocates of the modern chain gang in Southern states trade on this historical connection. Says one native Alabaman, "One of my lingering hometown memories [of Tuscaloosa, Alabama] is of a chain gang decked out in white herded about by armed guards on horseback. Laying aside the lynching bee, no other image was as vivid a reminder of the days of the slave South terror and its ensuing oppressiveness."[295]

Slavery's image is inescapable. Resurrecting a punishment so intimately connected with American slavery offends the mandate of decency. We cannot ignore the fact that chains are loaded with symbolism. The sad story of a past of chaining African-Americans and a currently disproportionate number of incarcerated African-Americans have filtered into the collective consciousness. The image of chains and African-Americans is the image of slavery. We must evolve from this history. "[A] penalty that was permissible at one time in our Nation's history is not necessarily permissible today."[296]

Using chains as punishment in a culture where chains are intimately connected with the subjugation of a race implicitly embraces slavery. The enslavement of people is unacceptable by any standard of decency.

---

head. See id. at 186 n.49 (citing Jacob Weisberg. This Is Your Death: Capital Punishment. What Really Happens. *New Republic*, July 1, 1991, at 23). A 1989 malfunction of Alabama's electric chair also caused "an agonizing death" for the inmate. Id. (citing Note, The Madness of the Method: the Use of Electrocution and the Death Penalty, 70 *Tax. L. Rev.* 1039, 1050–54 (1992)).

[293]Christi Parsons, Tourists, Other States Curious About Alabama Chain Gangs, *Chi. Trib.*, May 10, 1996, at 10.

[295]Payne, supra note 105, at A42.

[296]*Furman v. Georgia*, 408 U.S. 238, 329 (1972) (Marshall, J., concurring).

To the litany of such historically disfavored punishments as drawing and quartering, disemboweling, and beheading, society has added another—chain gangs. Just as beheading represented state-sanctioned oppression, so do chain gangs represent this nation's physically, emotionally, and mentally oppressive system of black slavery and forced labor. Chain gangs' close association with racial inequality, deliberate humiliation, and intentional dehumanization puts it in a category with other historically repressive punishments, and thus should render the punishment cruel and unusual by Eighth Amendment standards. As a direct descendent from slavery and as a symbol of human degradation, chain gangs fail to pass the constitutional mandate that punishments must meet a current standard of decency. This country must break its shackles of racial inequality and leave the chains where they were left thirty years ago: abandoned as relics of a shameful past.

Is the Death Penalty What Murderers Deserve?

Stephen Nathanson

THE ARGUMENT FROM DESERT

In this paper, I am going to focus on one issue in the debate about the death penalty. The issue is whether we ought to have the death penalty because people who commit murder deserve to die.

In focusing on this one issue, I will be ignoring many other important aspects of the death penalty debate.[1] Still, because this issue is so central to many people's thinking, it deserves careful attention, and making progress in understanding it can help us to decide whether the death penalty is a morally justified form of punishment.

Many people think it is obvious that at least certain people who are guilty of murder deserve to die. In addition, they think it is obvious

"Is the Death Penalty What Murderers Deserve?" from *Living Well: Introductory Readings in Ethics* by Stephen Luper © 1999 by Harcourt, Inc., reprinted by permission of the publisher.

that if some people deserve to die for their crimes, then we ought to institute the death penalty as the legal punishment for them.

Indeed, the truth of these claims seems so obvious to some people that they often don't feel a need to state their argument. Instead, they think they can prove their case simply by reciting the names of particularly evil and horrifying people—whether they be political leaders like Hitler, Stalin, and Pol Pot or especially vile murderers like Jeffrey Dahmer, Theodore Bundy, or Timothy McVeigh. Simply to recall these names and the crimes perpetrated by these people is supposed to be enough to show that the death penalty is a morally justified form of punishment.

I assume that when people recall these names, they are implicitly appealing to the argument from desert, the view that the death penalty is legitimate and desirable because some murderers deserve to die. In the pages that follow, I will try to show that this argument and the conclusion it supports are mistaken.

TWO BAD REPLIES

Opponents of the death penalty sometimes respond to this argument by charging that it simply expresses a desire for vengeance and that vengeful desires are base and unworthy—especially for those who claim to be civilized and to respect the value of human life.

This is not an effective reply. First, while it charges advocates of the death penalty with an undesirable motive, it does not show that they actually have such a motive. After all, people who favor the death penalty, even if they are mistaken about what justice requires, may still be motivated by a desire for justice. They may cherish human life and think that killing is the only punishment that responds appropriately to the evil of unjustifiably taking a life. Even if they are mistaken about this, there is no justification for assuming that undesirable motives underlie their support for the death penalty.

A second bad reply might try to show that even people who commit the vilest acts are essentially good and hence that they deserve no evil. It is hard to see how this argument could be persuasively developed. If the only way to show that murderers do not deserve to die is by arguing that they are really good people, then the argument would be doomed to failure. Just as it is implausible to argue that no actions are wrong, so is it implausible to argue that all people are fundamentally good.

WHY THE ARGUMENT FROM DESERT IS FLAWED

One of the main problems with the argument that the death penalty is required because (at least some) murderers deserve to die is that it oversimplifies and takes as obvious what is actually a very complex matter. It says: Some murderers deserve to die, and we, acting through our legal system, should kill them. End of discussion.

The argument assumes (a) that we know with certainty what people deserve and (b) that what people deserve is the only consideration that matters in the debate about capital punishment. Each of these assumptions is false. It is often difficult to know what people deserve, and there are other matters that need to be considered when deciding on the appropriate legal punishment for murder and other crimes.

The argument ignores other relevant matters because it thinks of the death penalty only as an act of ending a convicted criminal's life. But the death penalty is also an institution. It is a set of legal rules and practices that authorize certain people to take legal steps that can lead to the killing of a convicted criminal. Once we start to think about the death penalty as an institution and not as an individual act, we are less likely to overlook the fact that other things may matter in addition to whether a particular person deserves death.

There are often reasons why we don't institutionalize a particular practice, even if we would like certain people to be treated in a particular way. For example, some people oppose the institution of "physician-assisted suicide" even though they think that some individuals would be better off if someone helped them to die. Yet, fears about the impact of this practice on the doctor/patient relationship and about possible abuses of this practice lead some people to oppose it, even though they might want it to be permitted in particular cases.[2]

What this example shows is that we cannot move automatically from judgments that an act would be good in a particular case to judgments that we ought to establish a practice to carry out that act. Advocates of the death penalty who appeal to the argument from desert are generally thinking about the execution of a particular person, but they neglect the difficult institutional issues that arise in writing the death penalty into our laws and legal practices.

DETERMINING WHAT PEOPLE DESERVE

We have the illusion that it is easy to tell what people deserve because in some cases, what people deserve depends entirely on two things: (1) their actions or traits and (2) some set of accepted criteria. If, for example, a student answers all the questions on a test correctly and if getting a perfect score is the criterion for an "A" grade, then the student deserves an A. Or, if a prize is offered to the tallest person at a party, the one who is tallest deserves the prize. In each case, the combination of an action or a trait and a criterion yields a simple determination of what people deserve. People who think it obvious that murderers deserve to die may have this model in mind, and this may explain their confidence in their judgment.

There are several sources of complications, however. In some cases, deciding whether the person has performed the required action may not be so easy. So, for example, a student who writes an excellent essay may deserve an "A" grade, but the criteria for an excellent essay are more complicated that the criteria for a perfect score on a multiple choice test. Coherence, clarity, originality, understanding, etc. (which are some of the features of an excellent essay) are matters of degree, and competent evaluators may differ on the degree to which a particular essay exhibits these qualities. Even if everyone agrees that some essays are in the good-to-excellent range and that others are poor, competent evaluators may still disagree about whether a particular essay merits an A, an A−, or a B+. Likewise, determining who is the most beautiful person in a group is trickier than determining who is the tallest one, even if there is general agreement about who the top contenders are.

These cases may seem irrelevant to judging murderers, but in fact they are quite analogous. Judging whether the action of a particular murderer deserves death, life in prison, or some other punishment is more like evaluating an essay than it is like grading a multiple choice test, more like deciding who is most beautiful than it is like deciding who is tallest.

Things would be simpler, of course, if we believed that everyone who illegally kills another human being deserves to die. If, for example, we really believed in the maxim "an eye for an eye," that would give us a criterion that would permit killing everyone who kills another human being. But that is not what we think, and it is not the rule on which our legal system is based. (If we really accepted the "eye for an eye" principle, we would have

to accept the idea that executioners ought to be executed.)

Some killings are not illegal at all—for example, those done in self-defense. Even among those that are crimes, we distinguish between manslaughter and murder, and murders are classified as first or second degree, while cases of manslaughter may be divided into various categories: voluntary, involuntary, reckless, etc.

Because we differentiate among types of killings, prosecutors have to decide not just whether there is evidence that Tom killed Dick; they also have to decide what degree of homicide to charge Tom with. Their charge is extremely important because only people who are charged with first degree murder are eligible for the death penalty.[3] Likewise, juries must decide not only that there is evidence beyond a reasonable doubt that Tom killed Dick; they must also decide if the circumstances were such that Tom is guilty of first degree murder, second degree murder, or some other grade of homicide. Finally, even if Tom is convicted of first degree murder, the jury and/or the judge must decide whether Tom satisfies the legal criteria for being sentenced to death or whether he ought to be sentenced to prison.

In one sense, of course, all homicides are equally serious, since all involve the death of a human being. But we do not actually judge all of them to be equally bad. If a person was severely provoked or acted in a rage, we may not think his deed is as terrible as it would be if he had coldly planned the murder in advance. Even cases of prior planning differ among themselves. Think of the woman who, after years of cruelty and abuse, makes a plan to kill her husband and then carries it out.

So, deciding whether someone deserves to die is quite different from deciding that all the answers on a multiple choice test are correct or that one person is the tallest in a room. For this reason, prosecutors, juries, and judges often end up treating people who have committed apparently similar crimes in very different ways. Some are sentenced to die while others are given prison terms. Others of us might judge these same cases in different ways entirely, just as different evaluators might disagree about the degree of excellence in a particular piece of writing or the beauty of a particular contestant.[4]

Notice that there are at least two different sources of disparities. People may judge the particular cases differently, but they may also understand the criteria differently. Where criteria are unclear, so many different understandings may be possible that the criteria don't provide genuine guidance. People may feel that they are following them, but each follows his or her own understanding of them. The legal scholar Charles Black, Jr., has argued that the legal criteria for determining who should be executed are so unclear that they are not genuine rules or guidelines at all.[5]

WHY DISPARITIES ARE TROUBLING

The fact that people who have committed similar crimes often receive different punishments is troubling for a number of reasons. Even if a person who is executed does deserve to die, it is troubling if other people who are equally deserving are treated more leniently. This is because whether a person's punishment is just or not depends not simply on what he or she deserves but also on how the punishment compares with the punishments of others. So, what a person deserves is not the only factor that determines whether that person's punishment is just. A punishment can be deserved and still be unjust.[6]

If one student in a class receives a failing grade for cheating while another is simply warned not to do it again, then even if the first student deserved to fail, the infliction of this punishment is unjust. Or, to take an example from recent news reports, if low-ranking members of the military are typically imprisoned or receive dishonorable discharges for committing adultery while high-ranking officers are generally reprimanded, the punishment of those with lower rank seems unfair, even if (given military rules), they deserve a severe punishment.

What is common to both these cases is that arbitrary reasons—reasons that have nothing to do with the criteria of desert—play an important role in determining whether people will be treated as they deserve. In the case of military personnel who are guilty of adultery, the arbitrary reasons may by systematic, creating a system of advantaged and disadvantaged parties.

Similar charges, supported by considerable research, have been made about the death penalty. The severity of the punishment imposed on people convicted of homicide depends not just on the awfulness of their crimes but also on factors like their race, the race of their victims, and whether they have the money to acquire skillful legal representation. Yet none of these factors is relevant to what they deserve.[7]

In 1972, the Supreme Court thought these problems were so serious that, by a vote of 5–4 in *Furman v. Georgia*, it ruled the death penalty unconstitutional. Four years later, in *Gregg v. Georgia*, it ruled that some new state laws that authorize the death penalty were consistent with the Constitution. These new laws, the Court argued, provided clear guidelines for jurors to use and thus insured that the sentencing of murderers would no longer be arbitrary or capricious.

In reinstating the death penalty, the justices in the majority seemed to be making two false assumptions. First, they assumed that changing the laws could succeed in weeding out the influence of arbitrary factors from the judicial process. Second, they also mistakenly assumed that judgments of desert could be made with an extraordinary degree of precision.

To see why these are false, imagine that two people are guilty of first degree murder and that juries are asked to determine whether they deserve to die or whether they deserve life imprisonment. Both have committed terrible crimes so if one is justifiably sentenced to prison and the other is justifiably sentenced to death, there must be some fairly precise scale that can be used to distinguish them. It is as if there were a point system and everyone who commits first degree murder has at least 95 out of a potential 100 points. Only those who score 98 or more, however, deserve to die. Juries then are judging where between 95 and 100 a particular murderer falls. Such judgments are totally different from the judgments about desert that we make in ordinary life. In ordinary circumstances, our judgments about what people deserve are quite crude and rough. We have no experience with the kind of precise calculations of desert that are required in these kinds of sentencing decisions.

Even if we are confident that we can classify some murders as worse than others, we should not feel confident that we can make precise discriminations between different people who have committed dreadful crimes. As the judgments required become more and more complex (not just judging that Tom killed Dick but rather that Tom's killing Dick should be rated as a 97 rather than a 98), our degree of confidence should diminish. Human fallibility becomes a more significant feature. Prejudices and irrelevant factors can play a role because the criteria are so murky. The punishment people receive begins to look more like the result of the "luck of the draw" rather than the result of a reasoned assessment of desert. It is this randomness that led Supreme Court Justice Stewart to write in *Furman v. Georgia* that receiving a death sentence was like "being struck by lightning."[8] It happened to some people who committed murders but not to others, even though there was no discernible difference between their crimes. This degree of fallibility and randomness may be acceptable in the evaluating of essays or beauty contests, but it is not acceptable on a matter of life and death.

Why is it not acceptable? Because death penalty advocates claim that they only want to execute those who deserve to die. They also claim that they have the highest respect for life and that this respect is what motivates their support of the most severe punishment for taking a life. This is a contradictory view, however, once one recognizes the fallibility of these judgments and the impossibility of meaningful, precise standards of desert. To recognize the likelihood of error and arbitrariness here is to recognize the possibility that people will be executed who do not deserve to die, and this must be something that people who have the highest respect for life must oppose. Only if we could make judgments about what people deserve in a precise, reliable way can support of the death penalty be compatible with a proper respect for human life.

Consider one other factor. Juries and judges don't actually get to examine the murder itself in order to determine the degree of guilt and blameworthiness. What they get to consider is the account of the murder that is presented and described by the prosecutor, the defense lawyer, and the witnesses who are called to testify. Yet the ability of lawyers to present a case effectively varies considerably, and impoverished defendants are often represented by inexperienced lawyers who are assigned to the case and who may lack both the resources and the skills to represent the defendant effectively.

The judgment about what a particular murderer deserves, then, is not directly based on the nature of the crime and the killer themselves. Rather, it is based on these factors as they are filtered through the abilities of the lawyer who represents the defendant, adding one more element of complexity to the context in which these judgments are made.

The simple model of judging desert, then, does not really fit what goes on in death penalty cases, even if we look primarily at the actions that people perform. For reasons that I will now explain, the situation is even more murky than I have so far suggested.

IT'S NOT JUST ACTIONS THAT MATTER

Judgments of desert are even more complicated than I have so far discussed. We can see this in the following kind of case.

Suppose that Jill has written a paper that everyone thinks is excellent, while Jack wrote a paper that everyone agrees is weak. Looking at the papers alone, the teacher gives Jill an A and Jack a C. Jill, however, wrote her paper in a very short time and put very little effort into it, while Jack put in long hours doing research, wrote a first draft, consulted with his teacher, edited and revised his paper, and did everything in his power to write an excellent paper. While it is perhaps proper that Jill gets a higher grade, it is not so obvious that she is morally more deserving of a high grade than Jack. He worked hard (a morally relevant factor), while she took advantage of natural gifts or superior earlier schooling (both of which are matters of luck).

Or consider the beauty contest participants. Even if we had a precise scale of beauty so that everyone agreed on who was most beautiful, would it follow that the winner really deserves the prize? Isn't the winner's beauty just a matter of luck and not really deserved at all?

Similar issues arise in criminal cases. Even if a person has committed a brutal murder, we may still have reason to wonder whether he or she actually deserves the punishment for that crime.

In one area, the law recognizes this. When murders are committed by people who are judged to be criminally insane, the judgment is made that they are not responsible for their actions. People who are criminally insane cannot be held responsible for their actions and hence cannot deserve to be punished. We may confine them to protect others from them, but this is a misfortune, since it involves imposing severe limits on the liberty of people who do not deserve such deprivations.

What makes people criminally insane? Two criteria that have traditionally been important are (a) the inability to tell right from wrong or to appreciate the wrongness of the action they commit and (b) the inability to control one's impulses.[9]

In fact, only a small number of people are judged to be so lacking in their moral capacities that they are thought to be beyond being judged to deserve punishment. But the case of the criminally insane makes it clear that we cannot tell what someone deserves simply on the basis of what they do. We also have to know that they have the capacities to act as moral agents. In particular, they have to be able to know that their action is wrong, and they have to be able to exercise control over their impulses.

So, when we judge that a particular murderer deserves to die, we are judging not just the awfulness of the kind of murder that this person committed; we are also making a judgment about the capacity of this person to act as a moral agent.

Critics of the death penalty often suggest that judges and juries are not very good at making these complex judgments, and they believe that persons who are undeserving of death are sometimes executed. In making this argument, they are not denying the dreadfulness of the crime the person committed. Rather, they are claiming that we cannot tell what people morally deserve just by looking at features of their actions. Even where the action is genuinely horrific, there may be facts about the person that diminish responsibility and blameworthiness. These facts may not be taken seriously enough within the legal process.

That is the conclusion reached in a study of the death penalty in the United States published by Amnesty International, the international human rights organization. This study claimed that many of these who have been executed have in fact been mentally ill or had features that diminished their personal blameworthiness for their deeds. Here are the report's descriptions of some of the people who have been executed in the United States:

Arthur Goode: Mentally unstable; documented history of mental illness since age of three.

David Funchess: Vietnam veteran; . . . Left army with heroin addiction. Several years after conviction was found to be suffering from post-traumatic stress syndrome, a psychological disorder not properly understood at [the] time of his trial.

John Young: His psychiatric trauma from witnessing [his] mother's murder at age three and subsequent neglected childhood [were] not mentioned at his trial; . . . Young [was] alleged to have been under the influence of drugs at [the] time of crime.

Jerome Bowden: Diagnosed as mentally retarded, with IQ of 65.

David Martin: History of drug/alcohol addiction. Reportedly suffered mental/physical abuse as a child . . .

James Terry Roach—Minor at [the] time of crime. Trial record acknowledged Roach acting under [the] domination of [an] older man, and that he was mentally retarded. Later evidence that he was suffering from hereditary degenerative disease that could have affected mental state.[10]

What shall we say about these people? Admittedly, our picture of them is limited, but if we reflect on the features of these people, we may come to doubt that people with these features could truly deserve to die, even if there is no doubt that they committed terrible crimes.

And once we realize that we cannot fully tell what someone deserves just by knowing what dreadful acts they committed, then we can see that no recitation of the names of terrible murderers is sufficient to prove anything. A person can fail to be fully blameworthy, even if he has intentionally and maliciously committed the most vile crimes.

This does not mean that people should not be punished or held responsible. The defense of social order and personal security seems to require the institution of punishment, and punishment can be at least partly defended on this basis. But we ought not to feel confident that we can judge the precise degree of punishment that people morally deserve, and even if we could do this, we ought not to feel confident that our criminal justice system actually does so.

To affirm that the people listed above deserved to die, we would have to judge that factors like a history of mental illness, mental retardation, post-traumatic stress syndrome, childhood trauma, and abuse are irrelevant to determinations of what people deserve. Yet our legal system appears to sanction just such judgments, raising strong doubts that it takes seriously the questions of determining what people deserve in all its complexity. It is hard to imagine, for example, that if there is an infinitely wise God who judges such people for their crimes, such a God would dismiss mental illness, retardation, and trauma as irrelevant to what people deserve. Once we recognize their relevance, however, it becomes clear that the snap judgments we sometimes make about what people deserve do not do justice to the complexity of the factors that are relevant to judging what people morally deserve.

A SERIOUS OBJECTION

Faced with arguments of the sort I have raised, some people simply stand pat. They reaffirm their confidence in their own and other people's judgments about what murderers deserve, and they dismiss as irrelevant the flaws in our legal system and the influence of arbitrary factors on the imposition of the death penalty. I have tried throughout this paper to argue against this mindset and have nothing further to add.

There is another response, however, which is important for me to acknowledge and reply to briefly. Some people hear these arguments, recognize the inadequacy of our judgments about what people deserve, and acknowledge the role that race, poverty, and other irrelevant factors play in the death penalty system.

But, they say, these same factors play a role throughout our system of judicial punishment. If showing the complexity of desert judgments and the influence of arbitrary factors is a good argument against the death penalty, then isn't it a good argument against the whole system of punishment? Doesn't my argument reduce itself to absurdity when we see that it implies the illegitimacy of all punishment?

Nonetheless, we cannot and should not abolish the system of punishment. At least at present, it plays a necessary role in sustaining and enforcing the rules of civilized life. Without it, we would be likely to see more widespread violations of people's rights and a serious loss of security for most people. So, punishment is a necessary institution and one which we should retain.[11]

In responding to this objection, let me first agree that the factors I have discussed do operate at all levels and that they do indeed raise serious worries about our system of justice. Putting people in prison for long periods is a grievous punishment, and no one should be happy about the influence of race, social status, and wealth on the distribution of punishment.

It does not follow, however, that we should retain the death penalty. There are two reasons for this, which I will simply state without defending fully. First, punishing by death is a significantly more severe punishment than imprisonment and so needs to be treated differently from other punishments by people who claim to have civilized and humane values. One reason, though not the only one, for this is that the death penalty cannot be corrected in any way. Any errors, any executions of innocent people cannot be undone or compensated for, while imprisonment permits reversals and at least partial corrections.

Second, while the argument above assumes that we need punishment to protect people's lives and safety, the same cannot be said for the death penalty. There is no solid evidence that the death penalty provides greater safety or security than long term imprisonment or life imprisonment without parole.[12]

Because of the extraordinary severity of the death penalty, then, and because it provides no extra measure of safety for our citizens, the arguments raised in this paper count against it with special force. They should, in addition, spur us on to seek greater justice throughout our legal system, but only in the case of the death penalty do they constitute such a powerful case for abolition.

THE BASIC QUESTION

I have been discussing the question of what people morally deserve because advocates of the death penalty say that moral justice will only be done if the law takes the lives of (at least some) murderers. Advocates of the death penalty say that they care about doing what is morally right and that they want the law to be patterned on the demands of morality. Thinking that it is obvious that murderers morally deserve to die, they want death to be the legal punishment for murder.

I have tried to show that the belief on which this argument rests—the belief that murderers deserve to die—is far from obviously true. Even if it is true of some murderers, the judgment that it is true of them is complicated, and there is much room for error in arriving at that judgment.

In addition, the legal system as it actually operates is a kind of filtering device that deeply influences the kinds of facts that emerge about particular people, and the set of social attitudes prevalent in society deeply influences the way in which different kinds of murderers and their victims are regarded.

People who favor the death penalty often overlook the fact that they are approving a system that may execute some murderers who they themselves would not judge to be deserving of death. Once the system is in place, death penalty supporters don't get to pick and choose who will live and who will die. Other people, with perhaps different criteria, get to make those decisions.[13]

It is very difficult to know about a particular murderer that he or she deserves to die, and it is impossible to design a system that makes such judgments in a reliable way. Recognizing the fallibility of our judgments in individual cases and of the system as a whole, we would do best to express our commitment to respecting human life and human dignity by forsaking the practice of killing those who kill. Every legitimate social need for the defense of human life can be accomplished with other punishments that are sufficiently severe and that allow for the correction of error and injustice.[14]

NOTES

[1]In *An Eye for an Eye?—The Immorality of Punishing by Death* (Lanham, Md.: Rowman and Littlefield, 1987) I try to consider all of the major arguments both for and against the death penalty. For a valuable source of much relevant information, see the various editions of Hugo Bedau, ed., *The Death Penalty in America* (New York: Oxford University Press, various years).

[2]I don't mean to take any stand here on physician-assisted suicide. The example is only intended to bring out the distinction between an individual act and a general practice.

[3]For an interesting description that brings out some of these classification problems see Steven Phillips, *No Heroes, No Villains* (New York: Random House, 1977).

[4]For a discussion of these problems that includes many examples of similar cases handled differently, see Ursula Bentele, "The Death Penalty in Georgia: Still Arbitrary," *Washington University Law Quarterly* 62 (1985): 573–646.

[5]This argument is put forward by Black in *Capital Punishment: The Inevitability of Caprice and Mistake*, 2d ed. (New York: W. W. Norton, 1981), pp. 26–29.

[6]On this point, see my article, "Does It Matter If the Death Penalty Is Arbitrarily Administered?" *Philosophy and Public Affairs* 14 (1985): 149–64. For a contrary view, see

Ernest van den Haag, "The Collapse of the Case against Capital Punishment," *National Review* March 31, 1978.

[7]For studies of the influence of race on sentencing, see William Bowers and Glen Pierce, "Racial Discrimination and Criminal Homicide under Post-Furman Capital Statutes," *Crime and Delinquency* 26 (1980): 563–635; and Samuel Gross and Robert Mauro, *Death and Discrimination* (Boston: Northeastern University Press, 1989).

[8]Reprinted in Hugo Bedau, ed., *The Death Penalty in America*, 3rd ed. (New York: Oxford University Press, 1982), p. 263.

[9]For a philosophical analysis of criminal insanity, see Herbert Fingarette, *The Meaning of Criminal Insanity* (Berkeley: University of California Press, 1972).

[10]From Amnesty International, *United States of America: The Death Penalty* (London: Amnesty International Publications, 1987), pp. 196—203.

[11]My argument here echoes familiar points whose classic expression can be found in Thomas Hobbes's *Leviathan*, especially Chapters 13–17. For a contrary view by a defender of anarchism, see Peter Kropotkin, "Law and Authority," in Roger Baldwin, ed., *Kropotkin's Revolutionary Pamphlets* (New York: Dover Books, 1970).

[12]For a brief survey of the evidence on the deterrent power of the death penalty, see Chapter 2 of my book, *An Eye for an Eye?* For fuller overviews of this debate, see the third and fourth editions of Bedau, ed., *Death Penalty in America*.

[13]For other points about the systematic nature of the death penalty; see my "How (Not) to Think about the Death Penalty," *The International Journal of Applied Philosophy* 11 (Winter/Spring 1997): 7–10.

[14]I'd like to express my appreciation to Bill Bowers and Ben Steiner for insightful comments on an earlier draft and for sharing their research on the process of jury deliberations, to Ursula Bentele for keeping me accurate on legal matters and to Steven Luper for the invitation to write the paper and for helpful feedback on an earlier draft.

Against the Death Penalty

Jeffrey Reiman

My position about the death penalty as punishment for murder can be summed up in the following four propositions:

1. Though the death penalty is a just punishment for some murder, it is not unjust to punish murderers less harshly (down to a certain limit);
2. Though the death penalty would be justified if needed to deter future murders, we have no good reason to believe that it is needed to deter future murders; and
3. In refraining from imposing the death penalty, the state, by its vivid and impressive example, contributes to reducing our tolerance for cruelty

"Against the Death Penalty" from *Living Well: Introductory Readings in Ethics* by Stephen Luper © 1999 by Harcourt, Inc., reprinted by permission of the publisher.

and thereby fosters the advance of human civilization as we understand it.

Taken together, these three propositions imply that we do no injustice to actual or potential murder victims, and we do some considerable good, in refraining from executing murderers. This conclusion will be reinforced by another argument, this one for the proposition:

4. Though the death penalty is *in principle* a just penalty for murder, it is unjust *in practice* in America because it is applied in arbitrary and discriminatory ways, and this is likely to continue into the foreseeable future.

This fourth proposition conjoined with the prior three imply the overall conclusion that it is good in principle to avoid the death penalty and bad in practice to impose it. In what follows, I shall state briefly the arguments for each of these propositions.[1] For ease of identification, I shall number the first paragraph in which the argument for each proposition begins.

1. Before showing that the death penalty is just punishment for some murders, it is useful to dispose of a number of popular but weak arguments against the death penalty. One such popular argument contends that, if murder is wrong, then death penalty is wrong as well. But this argument proves too much! It would work against all punishments since all are wrong if done by a regular citizen under normal circumstances. (If I imprison you in a little jail in my basement, I am guilty of kidnapping; if I am caught and convicted, the state will lock me up in jail and will not have committed the same wrong that I did.) The point here is that what is wrong about murder is not merely that it is killing per se, but the killing of a legally innocent person by a nonauthorized individual—and this doesn't apply to executions that are the outcome of conviction and sentencing at a fair trial.

Another argument that some people think is decisive against capital punishment points to the irrevocability of the punishment. The idea here is that innocents are sometimes wrongly convicted and if they receive the death penalty there is no way to correct the wrong done to them. While there is some force to this claim, its force is at best a relative matter. To be sure, if someone is executed and later found to have been innocent, there is no way to give him back the life that has been taken. Whereas, if someone is sentenced to life in prison and is found to have been innocent, she can be set free and perhaps given money to make up for the years spent in prison—however, those years cannot be given back. On the other hand, the innocent person who has been executed can at least be compensated in the form of money to his family and he can have his name cleared. So, it's not that the death penalty is irrevocable and other punishments are revocable; rather, all punishments are irrevocable though the death penalty is, so to speak, relatively more

irrevocable than the rest. In any event, this only makes a difference in cases of mistaken conviction of the innocent, and the evidence is that such mistakes—particularly in capital cases—are quite rare. And, further, since we accept the death of innocents elsewhere, on the highways, as a cost of progress, as a necessary accompaniment of military operations, and so on, it is not plausible to think that the execution of a small number of innocent persons is so terrible as to outweigh all other considerations, especially when every effort is made to make sure that it does not occur.

Finally, it is sometimes argued that if we use the death penalty as a means to deter future murderers, we kill someone to protect others (from different people than the one we have executed), and thus we violate the Kantian prohibition against using individuals as means to the welfare of others. But the Kantian prohibition is not against using others as means, it is against using others as *mere* means (that is, in total disregard of their own desires and goals). Though you use the bus driver as a means to your getting home, you don't use her as a mere means because the job pays her a living and thus promotes her desires and goals as it does yours. Now, if what deters criminals is the existence of an effective system of deterrence, then criminals punished as part of that system are not used as a mere means since their desires and goals are also served, inasmuch as they have also benefited from deterrence of other criminals. Even criminals don't want to be crime victims. Further, if there is a right to threaten punishment in self-defense, then a society has the right to threaten punishment to defend its members, and there is no more violation of the Kantian maxim in imposing such punishment than there is in carrying out any threat to defend oneself against unjust attack.[2]

One way to see that the death penalty is a just punishment for at least some murders (the cold-blooded, premeditated ones) is to reflect on the *lex talionis*, an eye for an eye, a tooth for a tooth, and all that. Some regard this as a primitive rule, but it has I think an undeniable element of justice. And many who think that the death penalty is just punishment for murder are responding to this element. To see what the element is consider how similar the *lex talionis* is to the Golden Rule. The Golden Rule tells us to do unto others what we would have others do unto us, and the *lex talionis* counsels that we do to others what they have done to us. Both of these reflect a belief in the equality of all human beings. Treating others as you *would* have them treat you means treating others as equal to you, because it implies that you count their suffering to be as great a calamity as your own suffering, that you count your right to impose suffering on them as no greater than their right to impose suffering on you, and so on. The Golden Rule would not make sense if it were applied to two people, one of whom was thought to be inherently more valuable than the other. Imposing a harm on the more valuable one would be worse than imposing the same harm on the less valuable one—and neither could judge her actions by what she would have the other do to her. Since *lex talionis* says that you are rightly paid back for the harm you have caused another with a similar harm, it implies that the value of what you have done to another is the same as the value of having it done to you—which, again, would not be the case if one of you were thought inherently more valuable than the other. Consequently, treating people according to the *lex talionis* (like treating them according to the Golden Rule) affirms the equality of all concerned—and this supports the idea that punishing according to *lex talionis* is just.

Furthermore, on the Kantian assumption that a rational individual implicitly endorses the universal form of the intention that guides his action, a rational individual who kills another implicitly endorses the idea that he may be killed, and thus, he authorizes his own execution thereby absolving his executioner of injustice. What's more, much as above we saw that acting on *lex talionis* affirms the equality of criminal and victim, this Kantian-inspired argument suggests that acting on *lex talionis* affirms the rationality of criminal and victim. The criminal's rationality is affirmed because he is treated as if he had willed the universal form of his intention. The victim's rationality is affirmed because the criminal only authorizes his own killing if he has intended to kill another rational being like himself—then, he implicitly endorses the universal version of that intention, thereby authorizing his own killing. A person who intentionally kills an animal does not implicitly endorse his own being killed; only someone who kills someone like himself authorizes his own killing. In this way, the Kantian argument also invokes the equality of criminal and victim.

On the basis of arguments like this, I maintain that the idea that people deserve having done to them roughly what they have done (or attempted to do) to others affirms both the equality and rationality of human beings and for that reason is just. Kant has said: "No one has ever heard of anyone condemned to death on account of murder who complained that he was getting too much [punishment] and therefore was being treated unjustly; everyone would laugh in his face if he were to make such a statement."[3] If Kant is right, then even murderers recognize the inherent justice of the death penalty.

However, while the justice of the *lex talionis* implies the justice of executing some murderers, it does not imply that punishing less harshly is automatically unjust. We can see this by noting that the justice of the *lex talionis* implies also the justice of torturing torturers and raping rapists. I am certain and I assume my reader is as well that we need not impose these latter punishments to do justice (even if there were no other way of equaling the harm done or attempted by the criminal). Otherwise the price of doing justice would be matching the cruelty of the worst criminals, and that would effectively price justice out of the moral market. It follows that justice can be served with lesser punishments. Now, I think that there are two ways that punishing less harshly than the *lex talionis* could be unjust; it could be unjust to the actual victim of murder or to the future victims of potential murderers. It would be unjust to the actual victim if the punishment we mete out instead of execution were so slight that it trivialized the harm that the murderer did. This would make a sham out of implicit affirmation of equality that underlies the justice of the *lex talionis*. However, life imprisonment, or even a lengthy prison sentence—say, 20 years or more without parole—is a very grave punishment and not one that trivializes the harm done by the murderer. Punishment would be unjust to future victims if it were so mild that it failed to be a reasonable deterrent to potential murderers. Thus, refraining from executing murderers could be wrong if executions were needed to deter future murderers. In the following section, I shall say why there is no reason to think that this is so.

2. I grant that, if the death penalty were needed to deter future murderers, that would be a strong reason in favor of using the death penalty, since otherwise we would be sacrificing the future victims of potential murderers whom we could have deterred. And I think that this is a real injustice to those future victims, since the we in question is the state. Because the state claims a monopoly of the use of force, it owes its citizens protection, and thus does them injustice when it fails to provide the level of protection it reasonably could provide. However, there is no reason to believe that we need the death penalty to deter future murderers. The evidence we have strongly supports the idea that we get the same level of deterrence from life imprisonment, and even from substantial prison terms, such as 20 years without parole.

Before 1975, the most important work on the comparative deterrent impact of the capital punishment versus life in prison was that of Thorsten Sellin. He compared the homicide rates in states with the death penalty to the rates in similar states without the death penalty, and found no greater incidence of homicide in states without the death penalty than in similar states with it. In 1975, Isaac Ehrlich, a University of Chicago econometrician, reported the results of a statistical study which he claimed proved that, in the period from 1933 to 1969, each execution deterred as many as eight murders. This finding was, however, widely challenged. Ehrlich found a deterrent impact of executions in the period from 1933

to 1969, which includes the period of 1963 to 1969, a time when hardly any executions were carried out and crime rates rose for reasons that are arguably independent of the existence or nonexistence of capital punishment. When the 1963–1969 period is excluded, no significant deterrent effect shows. This is a very serious problem since the period from 1933 through to the end of the 1930s was one in which executions were carried out at the highest rate in American history—before or after. That no deterrent effect turns up when the study is limited to 1933 to 1962 almost seems evidence *against* the deterrent effect of the death penalty!

Consequently, in 1978, *after Ehrlich's study*, the editors of a National Academy of Sciences study of the impact of punishment wrote: "In summary, the flaws in the earlier analyses (i.e., Sellin's and others) and the sensitivity of the more recent analyses to minor variation in model specification and the serious temporal instability of the results lead the panel to conclude that the available studies provide no useful evidence on the deterrent effect of capital punishment."[4] Note that, while the deterrence research commented upon here generally compares the deterrent impact of capital punishment with that of life imprisonment, the failure to prove that capital punishment deters murder more than does incarceration goes beyond life in prison. A substantial proportion of people serving life sentences are released on parole before the end of their sentences. Since this is public knowledge, we should conclude from these studies that we have no evidence that capital punishment deters murder more effectively than prison sentences that are less than life, though still substantial, such as 20 years.

Another version of the argument for the greater deterrence impact of capital punishment compared to lesser punishments is called *the argument from common sense*. It holds that, whatever the social science studies do or don't show, it is only common sense that people will be more deterred by what they fear more, and since people fear death more than life in prison, they will be deterred more by execution than by a life sentence. This argument for the death penalty, however, assumes without argument or evidence that deterrence increases continuously and endlessly with the fearfulness of threatened punishment rather than leveling out at some threshold beyond which increases in fearfulness produce no additional increment of deterrence. That being tortured for a year is worse than being tortured for 6 months doesn't imply that a year's torture will deter you from actions that a half-year's torture would not deter—since a half-year's torture may be bad enough to deter you from all the actions that you can be deterred from doing. Likewise, though the death penalty may be worse than life in prison, that doesn't imply that the death penalty will deter acts that a life sentence won't because a life sentence may be bad enough to do all the deterring that can be done—and that is precisely what the social science studies seem to show. And, as I suggested above, what applies here to life sentences applies as well to substantial prison sentences.

I take it then that there is no reason to believe that we save more innocent lives with the death penalty than with less harsh penalties such as life in prison or some lengthy sentence, such as 20 years without parole. But then we do no injustice to the future victims of potential murderers by refraining from the death penalty. And, in conjunction with the argument of the previous section, it follows that we do no injustice to actual or potential murder victims if we refrain from executing murderers and sentence them instead to life in prison or to some substantial sentence, say, 20 or more years in prison without parole. But it remains to be seen what good will be served by doing the latter instead of executing.

3. Here I want to suggest that, in refraining from imposing the death penalty, the state, by its vivid and impressive example, contributes to reducing our tolerance for cruelty and thereby fosters the advance of human civilization as we understand it. To see this, note first that it has been acknowledged that the state, and particularly the criminal justice system, plays an educational role in society as a model of morally accepted conduct and an indicator

of the line between morally permissible and impermissible actions. Now, consider the general repugnance that is attached to the use of torture—even as a punishment for criminals who have tortured their victims. It seems to me that, by refraining from torturing even those who deserve it, our state plays a role in promoting that repugnance. That we will not torture even those who have earned it by their crimes conveys a message about the awfulness of torture, namely, that it is something that civilized people will not do even to give evil people their just deserts. Thus it seems to me that in this case the state advances the cause of human civilization by contributing to a reduction in people's tolerance for cruelty. I think that the modern state is uniquely positioned to do this sort of thing because of its size (representing millions, even hundreds of millions of citizens) and its visibility (starting with the printing press that accompanied the birth of modern nations, increasing with radio, television, and the other media of instantaneous communication). And because the state can do this, it should. Consequently, I contend that if the state were to put execution in the same category as torture, it would contribute yet further to reducing our tolerance for cruelty and to advancing the cause of human civilization. And because it can do this, it should.

To make this argument plausible, however, I must show that execution is horrible enough to warrant its inclusion alongside torture. I think that execution is horrible in a way similar to (though not identical with) the way in which torture is horrible. Torture is horrible because of two of its features, which also characterize execution: intense pain and the spectacle of one person being completely subject to the power of another.[5] This latter is separate from the issue of pain, since it is something that offends people about unpainful things, such as slavery (even voluntarily entered) and prostitution (even voluntarily chosen as an occupation). Execution shares this separate feature. It enacts the total subjugation of one person to his fellows, whether the individual to be executed is strapped into an electric chair or bound like a laboratory animal on a hospital gurney awaiting lethal injection.

Moreover, execution, even by physically painless means, is characterized by a special and intense psychological pain that distinguishes it from the loss of life that awaits us all. This is because execution involves the most psychologically painful features of death. We normally regard death from human causes as worse than death from natural causes, since a humanly caused shortening of life lacks the consolation of unavoidability. And we normally regard death whose coming is foreseen by its victim as worse than sudden death because a foreseen death adds to the loss of life the terrible consciousness of that impending loss. An execution combines the worst of both. Its coming is foreseen, in that its date is normally already set, and it lacks the consolation of unavoidability, in that it depends on the will of one's fellow human beings not on natural forces beyond human control. Indeed, it was on just such grounds that Albert Camus regarded the death penalty as itself a kind of torture: "As a general rule, a man is undone by waiting for capital punishment well before he dies. Two deaths are inflicted on him, the first being worse than the second, whereas he killed but once. Compared to such torture, the penalty of retaliation [the *lex talionis*] seems like a civilized law."[6]

4. However just in principle the death penalty may be, it is applied unjustly in practice in America and is likely to be so for the foreseeable future. The evidence for this conclusion comes from various sources. Numerous studies show that killers of whites are more likely to get the death penalty than killers of blacks, and that black killers of whites are far more likely to be sentenced to death than white killers of blacks. Moreover, just about everyone recognizes that poor people are more likely to be sentenced to death and to have those sentences carried out than well-off people. And these injustices persist even after all death penalty statutes were declared unconstitutional in 1972[7] and only those death penalty statutes with provisions for reducing arbitrariness in

sentencing were admitted as constitutional in 1976.[8] In short, injustice in the application of the death penalty persists even after legal reform, and this strongly suggests that it is so deep that it will not be corrected in the foreseeable future.

It might be objected that discrimination is also found in the handing out of prison sentences and thus that this argument would prove that we should abolish prison as well as the death penalty. But I accept that we need some system of punishment to deter crime and mete out justice to criminals, and for that reason even a discriminatory punishment system is better than none. Then, the objection based on discrimination works only against those elements of the punishment system that are not needed either to deter crime or to do justice, and I have shown above that this is true of the death penalty. Needless to say we should also strive to eliminate discrimination in the parts of the criminal justice that we cannot do without.

Other, more subtle, kinds of discrimination also affect the way the death penalty is actually carried out. There are many ways in which the actions of well-off people lead to death which are not counted as murder. For example, many more people die as a result of preventable occupational diseases (due to toxic chemicals, coal and textile dust, and the like, in the workplace) or preventable environmental pollution than die as a result of what is treated legally as homicide.[9] So, in addition to all the legal advantages that money can buy a wealthy person accused of murder, the law also helps the wealthy by not defining as murder many of the ways in which the wealthy are responsible for the deaths of fellow human beings. Add to this that many of the killings that we do treat as murders, the ones done by the poor in our society, are the predictable outcomes of remediable social injustice—the discrimination and exploitation that, for example, have helped to keep African Americans at the bottom of the economic ladder for centuries. Those who benefit from injustice and who could remedy it bear some of the responsibility for the crimes that are predictable outcomes of injustice—and that implies that plenty of well-off people share responsibility with many of our poor murderers. But since these more fortunate folks are not likely to be held responsible for murder, it is unfair to hold only the poor victims of injustice responsible—and wholly responsible to boot!

Finally, we already saw that the French existentialist, Albert Camus, asserted famously that life on death row is a kind of torture. Recently, Robert Johnson has studied the psychological effects on condemned men on death row and confirmed Camus's claim. In his book *Condemned to Die*, Johnson recounts the painful psychological deterioration suffered by a substantial majority of the death row prisoners he studied.[10] Since the death row inmate faces execution, he is viewed as having nothing to lose and thus is treated as the most dangerous of criminals. As a result, his confinement and isolation are nearly total. Since he has no future for which to be rehabilitated, he receives the least and the worst of the prison's facilities. Since his guards know they are essentially warehousing him until his death, they treat him as something less than human—and so he is brutalized, taunted, powerless, and constantly reminded of it. The effect of this on the death row inmate, as Johnson reports it, is quite literally the breaking down of the structure of the ego—a process not unlike that caused by brainwashing. Since we do not reserve the term "torture" only for processes resulting in physical pain, but recognize processes that result in extreme psychological suffering as torture as well (consider sleep deprivation or the so-called Chinese water torture), Johnson's and Camus's application of this term to the conditions of death row confinement seems reasonable.

It might be objected that some of the responsibility for the torturous life of death row inmates is the inmates' own fault, since in pressing their legal appeals, they delay their executions and thus prolong their time on death row. Capital murder convictions and sentences, however, are reversed on appeal with great frequency, nearly ten times the rate of reversals in noncapital cases. This strongly supports the idea that such appeals are necessary to test the legality of murder convictions and death penalty sentences. To hold the inmate somehow responsible for the delays that result from his appeals, and thus for the (increased) torment he suffers as a consequence, is effectively to confront him with the choice of accepting execution before its legality is fully tested or suffering torture until it is. Since no just society should expect (or even want) a person to accept a sentence until its legal validity has been established, it is unjust to torture him until it has and perverse to assert that he has brought the torture on himself by his insistence that the legality of his sentence be fully tested before it is carried out.

The worst features of death row might be ameliorated, but it is unlikely that its torturous nature will be eliminated, or even that it is possible to eliminate it. This is, in part, because it is linked to an understandable psychological strategy used by the guards in order to protect themselves against natural, painful, and ambivalent feelings of sympathy for a person awaiting a humanly inflicted death. Johnson writes: "I think it can also be argued . . . that humane death rows will not be achieved in practice because the purpose of death row confinement is to facilitate executions by dehumanizing both the prisoners and (to a lesser degree) their executioners and thus make it easier for both to conform to the etiquette of ritual killing."[11]

If conditions on death row are and are likely to continue to be a real form of psychological torture, if Camus and Johnson are correct, then it must be admitted that the death penalty is in practice not merely a penalty of death—it is a penalty or torture until death. Then the sentence of death is more than the *lex talionis* allows as a just penalty for murder—and thus it is unjust in practice.

I think that I have proven that it would be good in principle to refrain from imposing the death penalty and bad in practice to continue using it. And, I have proven this while accepting the two strongest claims made by defenders of capital punishment, namely, that death is just punishment for at least some murderers, and that, if the death penalty were a superior deterrent to murder than imprisonment, that would justify using the death penalty.

NOTES

[1] The full argument for these propositions, along with supporting data, references, and replies to objections, is in Louis Pojman and Jeffrey Reiman, *The Death Penalty: For and Against* (Lanham, Md: Rowman & Littlefield, 1998), pp. 67–132, 151–163. My essay in that book is based upon and substantially revises my "Justice, Civilization, and the Death Penalty: Answer van den Haag,* *Philosophy and Public Affairs* 14, no. 2 (Spring 1985): 115–148; and my "The Justice of the Death Penalty in an Unjust World," in *Challenging Capital Punishment: Legal and Social Science Approaches*, ed. by K. Haas & J. Inciardi (Beverly Hills, Calif.: Sage, 1988), pp. 29–48.

[2] Elsewhere I have argued at length that punishment needed to deter reasonable people is *deserved* by criminals. See Pojman and Reiman, *Death Penalty*, pp. 79–85.

[3] Immanuel Kant, "The Metaphysical Elements of Justice," Part 1 of *The Metaphysics of Morals*, trans. by J. Ladd (Indianapolis: Bobbs-Merrill, 1965; originally published 1797), p. 104, see also p. 133.

[4] Alfred Blumstein, Jacqueline Cohen, and Daniel Nagin, eds., *Deterrence and Incapacitation: Estimating the Effects of Criminal Sanctions on Crime Rates* (Washington, D.C.: National Academy of Sciences, 1978), p. 9.

[5] Hugo Bedau has developed this latter consideration at length with respect to the death penalty. See Hugo A. Bedau, "Thinking about the Death Penalty as a Cruel and Unusual Punishment." *U.C. Davis Law Review* 18 (Summer 1985): 917. This article is reprinted in Hugo A. Bedau, *Death Is Different: Studies in the Morality Law and Politics of Capital Punishment* (Boston: Northeastern University Press, 1987); and Hugo A. Bedau, ed., *The Death Penalty in America: Current Controversies* (New York: Oxford University Press, 1997).

[6] Albert Camus, "Reflections on the Guillotine," in Albert Camus, *Resistance, Rebellion, and Death* (New York: Knopf, 1961), p. 205.

[7] *Furman v. Georgia*, 406 U.S. 238 (1972).

[8] *Gregg v. Georgia*, 428 U.S. 153 (1976).

[9] Jeffrey Reiman, *The Rich Get Richer and the Poor Get Prison: Ideology, Class, and Criminal Justice*, 5th ed. (Boston: Allyn and Bacon, 1998), pp. 71–78, 81–87.

[10] Robert Johnson, *Condemned to Die: Life under Sentence of Death* (New York: Elsevier, 1981), p. 129.

[11] Robert Johnson, personal correspondence.

A Response to Reiman and Nathanson

Ernest van den Haag

I had the pleasure on prior occasions to respond to essays on the death penalty by Messrs. Reiman and Nathanson. Here they have greatly enriched their arguments. (I hope to have done the same.) Neither, however, has changed his basic view. Which goes to show that my attempt to rehabilitate them was futile—as I have long believed most such attempts are. If two mild mannered professors of philosophy cannot be reformed, what chance do we have with hardened criminals? Since it may not be obvious from my response

"A Response to Reiman and Nathanson" from *Living Well: Introductory Readings in Ethics* by Stephen Luper © 1999 by Harcourt Inc., reprinted by permission of the publisher.

let me make it explicit now that I have respect and affection for Jeffrey Reiman. However wrong his views be they are always interesting and original in their wrongness.

RESPONSE TO REIMAN: SHOULD HUMANENESS REPLACE JUSTICE?

Reiman believes that the death penalty is just, because deserved for murder (via the *lex talionis*). But, he thinks it would not be unjust to punish murderers less harshly, and, for various reasons, of which anon, it would be more humane to do so. Being humane, Reiman opposes the death penalty.

Reiman has an odd notion of "deserved" which allows him to think it justice to give less than what is deserved as a punishment, or, I presume, as a reward. But it is not justice to give anyone less, or more, than is deserved. If you won a race you deserve the trophy promised and should get no less, even if you are morally repugnant. Nor should you get the trophy merely because you have moral merits irrelevant to the race. If you have done something wrong you get the deserved (and prescribed) punishment. *Suum cuique tribue.* To everyone what he deserves. It is not just to give less than what is deserved. Charity is desirable as other forms of love are, but is not justice, precisely because it need not be deserved. So with generosity, or "humanness." The murderer knew what his punishment would be and volunteered to risk suffering it. (If he didn't volunteer he didn't commit a crime.)

I do not mean to suggest that he calculates his risk. Thank God he doesn't, because the risk of suffering the death penalty is exceedingly small. What deters most people is a generalized dread both of the crime and of the punishment. That dread ultimately goes back to the death penalty. Probability calculations are no more involved than they are when people buy a lottery ticket. The size of the punishment, or of the reward, seems to matter more than the probability of receiving it, in determining deterrence or attractiveness. A case for clemency can be made in some cases. But clemency (Reiman's humaneness?) cannot take the place of justice and should not be confused with it.

Because the death penalty is applied arbitrarily and discriminatorily, Reiman says it is unjust in practice. *Non sequitur.* The arbitrary or discriminatory application of the penalty does not make those who receive it less guilty, or less deserving of the penalty, than they would be if everyone (or no one) else in their position also would receive it. How does any murderer become less deserving of execution because other murderers are not executed, whether because of luck (they were not caught or the evidence was insufficient) or because of discrimination? Unequal punishment is not unjust, if those who deserve it get the punishment they deserve. Unequal justice is justice

still and the only justice available to us. The inequality of distribution is undesirable and unconstitutional if deliberate but not remedied by abolishing just punishments.

By not imposing the death penalty, Reiman contends, we would reduce social intolerance for cruelty. One could as well say: By not imposing the death penalty we display more tolerance for the cruelty of murderers than we should and thereby we encourage it.[1] (Incidentally, Reiman confuses reversing and revoking penalties. Except for fines, penalties cannot be reversed. The death penalty is not exceptional in this. It is exceptional only because it cannot be revoked as other penalties can.)

If the death penalty is morally deserved for murder, it should be imposed even if it does not deter future murderers (as long as it does not encourage them). However, I disagree with Reiman on the empirical question of deterrence. I don't think it has been shown, or can be shown, that the death penalty does not, or cannot, deter more than imprisonment. What has been shown is that its greater deterrent effect has not been proven beyond controversy. But not proving deterrence is not the same as disproving it, as Reiman comes perilously close to contending. He also argues that the threat of imprisonment anyway will deter all those that can be deterred. Maybe. But it seems quite possible that some prospective murderers not deterred by the threat of life imprisonment will be deterred by the threat of execution. Even if not probable surely this is possible. And the possibility is enough to make it prudent as well as just to execute those who deserve the death penalty.

Reiman also believes that execution is painful and undignified because it totally subjects one person to the power of another. Both these arguments seem weak. If, as it is currently done in most states, the criminal receives first an injection that anesthetizes him and then two lethal injections, he cannot feel pain any more than an anesthetized patient does during a surgical operation. Actually his death is likely to be less painful than the death of most persons; and he is not more, or less, in the power of his executioner than a patient is in the power of his surgeon.

Finally on the matter of poverty. It is true, as Reiman contends, that the poor commit proportionately more violent crimes than the rich. There are many reasons for this, the main one being that the rich can obtain most of what they want by buying it whereas the poor, by definition, cannot. They are more tempted therefore to obtain what they want by violence. Reiman assumes that somehow this is the fault of the rich, which is not much better than assuming that the suffering of the ill is the fault of the healthy. There are rich and poor in any system. Even if everyone, diligent or lazy, were to get the same income, some will impoverish themselves by spending it immediately, and others will enrich themselves by saving. Motives for crime will remain abundant.

In any case temptation is an explanation, not a justification. The purpose of the criminal law is to dissuade people who are tempted from committing crimes. There is no point in threatening the untempted. Unlike compulsion, temptation can be resisted and is not exculpatory.

RESPONSE TO NATHANSON: SHOULD EQUALITY REPLACE JUSTICE?

Professor Nathanson promises to focus on whether "people who commit murder deserve to die." He does not keep his promise. On the contrary, his paper is so unfocussed I found it hard to follow. He describes desert as difficult to determine and complex, but never tells whether, if desert were simple and easy to determine, it could justify the death penalty. He never suggests what he means by "deserve" beyond simply "should get:" He also insists that the death penalty is not an individual act but an institution. It is both, but so what? What follows? I know of no philosopher who neglects (as Nathanson implies) the obvious, that we cannot move from a particular act to a general practice.

Professor Nathanson's favorite analogy is between sentencing and grading a true and false test on the one hand or an essay test on the other. He never tires of reiterating that sentencing is more like grading an essay test. I don't know of anyone who would contest his point. Analogies are not proofs but, at best, helpful illustrations. But many of Nathanson's analogies are misleading or themselves based on error. This is true of his arguments as well. He writes "If we really accepted the eye for an eye principle we would have to accept the idea that executioners ought to be executed." Not so. A few lines before Nathanson indicates that he is aware that the *lex talionis* was applicable only to murder (illegal killing) but not to execution (legal killing). Otherwise it would justify the infinite vendettas it was meant to avoid.

Elsewhere Nathanson asserts that whether a person's punishment is just or not does not depend simply on what is deserved, but also on how "the punishment compares with the punishment of others." Not so. If others got a different punishment for the same crime it merely follows that the punishments were unequal, both may be unjust, or one of them may be just and the other not. The just punishment is the one deserved, whether or not it is also received by others.

Nathanson also asserts "a punishment can be deserved and still be unjust: I can't see that at all. If the punishment is deserved it is just by definition. "To give everyone what is deserved is to do justice" (Domitianus Ulpianus). Nathanson illustrates his point "if one student receives a failing grade for cheating while another is simply warned, then even if the first student deserved to fail, the infliction of this punishment is unjust." Why? The fact that someone else who deserved the same punishment did not get it does not make the deserved punishment unjust. Nathanson also objects to the fact (and it is a fact) that two murderers having committed the same crime may get different sentences. This inequality is regrettable but unavoidable and true for all punishments. The two murderers appear before different courts evaluating different evidence have different prosecutors and defense lawyers and different juries. Our system of justice rests on the belief that we can punish people as nearly as they deserve as can be done. Nathanson's demand, that punishment be exactly what is deserved and that we somehow must find ways of determining desert precisely, seems bizarre. It is impossible to do that whether we are dealing with a burglary or a murder.[2] Only God can have the kind of judgment Nathanson would like all of us to have. That is no reason for giving up the justice system, including the death penalty. We exclude hearsay evidence, insist that jurors have no detectable bias and require them to be unanimous in finding a defendant guilty only if none has a reasonable doubt of his guilt. I do not see how we can do more to avoid error, except by giving up punishment.

Nathanson also points out that courts do not directly witness crimes but must rely on testimony and circumstances reported by witnesses and analyzed by attorneys. Quite so. For the greater part of our life we have to rely on indirect experiences. When he teaches, Professor Nathanson expects his students to rely on indirect experiences and reports.

Returning to his favorite analogy Professor Nathanson laments that two students get the grades they get when one of them writes a brilliant paper with little effort and the other writes a not so brilliant paper, although he spends much more effort and time on it. Somehow, Nathanson feels the first student should not get an A and the second a C because, after all, the second student made more efforts. But the task of the teacher (after kindergarten) is not to grade students according to the efforts they made but rather to grade the results of their efforts. We cannot grade efforts nor should we. As Nathanson notes, the winner of a beauty contest may be morally inferior to the loser. And beauty or talent are largely matters of luck. But beauty is what the contest judges are to grade. In a sense this applies to crime as well. The judges (or professors) do not have the task of correcting the injustices of life but a more restricted one of determining who wins or loses according to the preestablished rules. Is the defendant guilty as charged? The court determines this and the sentence as well, on the basis not of the defendant's beauty or efforts or wealth or talent but on the basis of the gravity of his crime and his culpability in committing it. This is what is meant by equality before the law.

Professor Nathanson is certainly right in affirming that it is difficult to determine more merit, but fortunately we are called upon mostly to determine what people deserve for specific acts. Did he run faster than the others? He deserves to win—even though other runners may be more deserving in other respects, and made greater efforts.

The vagueness of Professor Nathanson's criteria of desert becomes apparent when we consider the instances of misjudgment he cites. (These misjudgments were listed by Amnesty International, an organization opposed to the death penalty. Nathanson seems to rely entirely on the arguments of the defense; he does not mention what prosecutors, or courts, contended. He also accepts unquestioningly all facts alleged by the defense.) Consider some of Nathanson's instances.

Arthur Goode, "mentally unstable, documented history of mental illness at the age of three." Wherein does that show that Goode should not suffer the death penalty? Obviously the courts held that he was mentally competent when he committed the act for which he was tried. The court may have been wrong, but wherein does mental instability at the age of three show this?

David Funchess, "Vietnam veteran, left army with heroin addiction, suffering post traumatic stress syndrome, a psychological disorder not properly understood at the time of trial." It is still not properly understood and may not exist. If it does, how does it exculpate?

John Young, "His psychiatric trauma from witnessing his mother's murder at the age of three and subsequent neglected childhood were not mentioned at the trial. Alleged to have been under the influence of drugs at the time of the crime." The court found that these things, mentioned or not mentioned in the trial, were no reasons for not imposing the death penalty. Nathanson never shows wherein the court is wrong.

Jerome Borden, "Diagnosed as mentally retarded with an IQ of 65." An IQ of 65 is not sufficient to indicate that the person did not understand what he was doing or did not know or could not know that it was wrong.

David Martin, "History of drug/alcohol addiction. Reportedly (!) suffered from mental, physical abuse as a child." Abuse is regrettable but why should it exempt from the death penalty? Many people unfortunately are abused as children but do not become criminals and many criminals have never been abused. Thus abuse is neither a necessary nor a sufficient reason for not punishing crimes.

Reading the essay to which I am responding has persuaded me that Professor Nathanson is opposed to the death penalty. The arguments he offers have not persuaded me that he should be.

NOTES

[1] Theologians and philosophers such as Thomas Aquinas, Immanuel Kant, G. F. W. Hegel, John St. Mill, and Thomas Jefferson have felt that we have a duty to execute murderers for the sake of their human dignity which is affirmed by recognizing their responsibility.

[2] Criminals in Pakistan get different punishments than they do in the United States, and punishments in Manhattan differ from the sentences judges mete out in Alabama. Some states have the death penalty, others don't.

Abolition of the Death Penalty

Adopted by the General Board September 13, 1968

A Policy Statement of the National Council of the Churches in the U.S.A.

In support of current movements to abolish the death penalty, the National Council of Churches hereby declares its opposition to capital punishment. In so doing, it finds itself in substantial agreement with a number of member denominations which have already expressed opposition to the death penalty.

Reasons for taking this position include the following:

1. The belief in the worth of human life and the dignity of human personality as gifts of God;
2. A preference for rehabilation rather than retribution in the treatment of offenders;
3. Reluctance to assume the responsibility of arbitrarily terminating the life of a fellow-being

National Council of the Churches, "Abolition of Death Penalty" (Policy Statement).

solely because there has been a transgression of law;

4. Serious question that the death penalty serves as a deterrent to crime, evidenced by the fact that the homicide rate has not increased disproportionally in those states where capital punishment has been abolished;
5. The conviction that institutionalized disregard for the sanctity of human life contributes to the brutalization of society;
6. The possibility of errors in judgment and the irreversibility of the penalty which make impossible any restitution to one who has been wrongfully executed;
7. Evidence that economically poor defendants, particularly members of racial minorities, are more likely to be executed then others because they cannot afford exhaustive legal defenses;

8. The belief that not only the severity of the penalty but also its increasing infrequency and the ordinarily long delay between sentence and execution subject the condemned person to cruel, unnecessary and unusual punishment;

9. The belief that the protection of society is served as well by measures of restraint and rehabilitation, and that society may actually benefit from the contribution of the rehabilitated offender;

10. Our Christian commitment to seek the redemption and reconciliation of the wrongdoer, which are frustrated by his execution.

Seventy-five nations of the world and thirteen states of the United States have abolished the death penalty with no evident detriment to social order. It is our judgment that the remaining jurisdictions should move in the same humane direction.

In view of the foregoing, the National Council of Churches urges abolition of the death penalty under federal and state law in the United States, and urges member denominations and state and local councils of churches actively to promote the necessary legislation to secure this end, particularly in the thirty-seven states which have not yet eliminated capital punishment.

Physician Participation in Capital Punishment

Council on Ethical and Judicial Affairs, American Medical Association

BACKGROUND

The question of physician participation in capital punishment has a long history.[1] Physicians have helped develop execution methods that were more humane than conventional methods. The most famous example is that of Dr Joseph Guillotin, who developed a mechanism for execution that he believed to be far more humane and civilized than other contemporary methods.[2] However, other physicians have disagreed with any physician participation in the death penalty.[1] The Oath of Hippocrates has historically been interpreted as prohibiting

Council on Ethical and Judicial Affairs, "Physician Participation in Capital Punishment," *JAMA* Volume 270 Number 3 (July 21, 1993): 365–368. Copyrighted 1993, American Medical Association.

physician participation in executions. The Oath states in part:

> I will use treatment to help the sick according to my ability and judgment, but never with a view to injury and wrong-doing. Neither will I administer a poison to anyone when asked to do so nor will I suggest such a course.[1]

During the 1970s, states began to consider use of lethal injection when executing condemned prisoners. By 1980, four states had selected lethal injection as the method by which executions would take place,[1] and in 1982 Texas became the first state to execute a person using this method (*Washington Post.* December 11, 1990:Z15).

Although physicians had been concerned with the possibility that states might require their presence or assistance with legal executions by other means, execution by lethal injection presents special problems for the medical profession (*Am Med News*. September 21, 1990:3).[1,3,4] Death by lethal injection requires that mechanisms that are ordinarily used to preserve life in a medical setting be used to cause death and that a person with at least some medical knowledge perform the procedure.[1]

In 1980, the American Medical Association's (AMA's) Council on Ethical and Judicial Affairs (then Judicial Council) issued a report that prohibited the participation of physicians in capital punishment. The Council considered all aspects of the problem and decided that physicians as professionals committed to "first of all do no harm," *primum non nocere*, could not ethically participate in executions. The Council's report was used as the basis for Current Opinion 2.06, which states the following.

CAPITAL PUNISHMENT

An individual's opinion on capital punishment is the personal moral decision of the individual. A physician, as a member of a profession dedicated to preserving life when there is hope of doing so, should not be a participant in a legally authorized execution. A physician may make a determination or certification of death as currently provided by law in any situation.[5(p3)]

At about the same time or subsequent to the Council's original report, several other medical associations, including the World Medical Associations,[6] the American College of Physicians,[7] the American Public Health Association,[8] the medical societies of the Nordic countries (Norway, Finland, Denmark, Iceland, and Sweden),[9] the American Psychiatric Association,[10] and the Committee on Bioethical Issues of the Medical Society of the State of New York,[11] adopted policies that prohibit physician participation in executions. In addition, the guidelines of the National Commission on Correctional Health Care prohibit participation of prison health care staff in execution.[12]

Today, the death penalty can be administered for some federal crimes[13] as well as for certain nonfederal crimes in 36 states. Thirteen states and the US government specify lethal injection as the execution method, 12 require electrocution, and one uses the gas chamber. In addition, 10 states allow the condemned person to choose between lethal injection and electrocution, the gas chamber, hanging, or a firing squad (written communication, National Coalition to Abolish the Death Penalty, Washington, DC, April 1993; *Los Angeles Times*. August 29, 1992:A17).

Since the Council's report in 1980, many commentators have asked organized medicine to provide a clarification as to what constitutes "participation" by the physician.[14-16] This report specifies what is meant by participation. In updating its explanation of physician participation in execution, the Council does not abandon the principle that each individual physician has the right to his or her own personal view on the issue of capital punishment. This report addresses only the question of the extent to which a physician may ethically participate in, assist, or associate with the process of execution. This report does not take a position on the ethical propriety or morality of capital punishment.

RATIONALE AND OPPOSING VIEWS

Rationale

A physician's role is to use his or her medical knowledge and skills to alleviate pain and prolong life.[17] The medical tools and technology used by physicians are meant to facilitate the realization of this role.[1] Physician's participation in executions contradicts the dictates of the medical profession by causing harm rather than alleviating pain and suffering.

Participation by physicians in execution by lethal injection is especially troublesome.[1,2,4] The process of execution by lethal injection employs the same devices and methods used by physicians to preserve life.[1] Using medical devices and methods for execution distorts the life-saving purposes of medical technology and medical tools. Physician participation in a process that has medical overtones, but ultimately causes involuntary death, further distorts the purpose and role of medicine and its professionals in the preservation of life. The use of physicians and medical technology in execution presents a conceptual contradiction for society and the public. The image of physician as executioner under circumstances mimicking medical care risks the general trust of the public.[1]

It is not simply the participation in a death-causing process that makes physician participation in capital punishment unethical. In other contexts, physicians may ethically act in ways that contribute to the death of a patient. The Council has previously stated that a physician may, with the informed consent of the patient, withhold or withdraw treatment even if the treatment is life-sustaining.[17] Discontinuation of life-sustaining treatment can be distinguished from participation in capital punishment in at least two ways. First, although death may ensue from the physician's actions, the individual patient is voluntarily choosing to risk death upon the withdrawal or withholding of care. With capital punishment, the physician is causing death against the will of the individual. Second, when life-sustaining treatment is discontinued, the patient's death is caused primarily by the underlying disease; with capital punishment, the lethal injection causes the prisoner's death. When physicians withdraw or withhold life-sustaining treatment at the request of the patient, they do not violate the fundamental ethical principle *primum non nocere*. Physician participation in capital punishment, however, does violate that principle. Deliberately causing a death or participating in the process that intentionally causes death is a harm to the person executed.

Opposing Views

Opposing views hold that, when physicians decline to participate in executions, they are breaching their obligations as physicians and citizens.[1,2,11,18,22] According to one argument, physicians have a moral duty to ensure[2] that the execution is carried out in the most humane and painless way possible, particularly if the condemned requests physician participation.[3,23] Physician participation would not

signal approval of the taking of a life, but compassion for the person to be executed. Further, the physician's duty as a citizen requires participation because the executions take place with the authorization of the government.[11]

These arguments are not sufficiently compelling to justify physician participation in capital punishment. The procedures used for executions do not require the skills of a physician. Even when the method of execution is lethal injection, the specific procedures can be performed by nonphysicians with no more pain or discomfort for the prisoner. While physician participation may potentially add some degree of humaneness to the execution of an individual, it does not outweigh the greater harm of causing death to the individual. A request by the prisoner for physician participation would not overcome objections to physician participation. Although the physician's involvement would occur with the will of the prisoner, the prisoner's death would still be caused against the will of the prisoner. In addition, the physician's obligation to refrain from causing death is a duty to the profession and to society in general that cannot be waived by individuals. Finally, the AMA's Principles of Medical Ethics do recognize that physicians have civic duties.[22] However, medical ethics do not require the physician to carry out civic duties that contradict fundamental medical ethical principles, such as the duty to avoid doing harm. Further, government approval or authorization of an act does not constitute a requirement on the part of any citizen to take action. For instance, voting in an election is authorized by the government but is not mandatory.

DEFINITION OF PARTICIPATION

Proposed Definitions of Physician Participation

Although several other medical societies and associations have stated that physicians should not participate in executions, only a few have defined participation with a significant degree of specificity.[13,14] Resolution 5 (December 1991), which requested that the Council develop a definition of participation, asked that the following be included as actions constituting participation: selecting fatal injection sites; starting intravenous lines as a port for a lethal injection device, prescribing or administering preexecution tranquilizers and other psychotropic agents and medications, injection drugs, or their doses or types; inspecting, testing, or maintaining lethal injection devices; consulting with or supervising lethal injection personnel; monitoring vital signs on site or remotely (including monitoring electrocardiograms); attending, observing or witnessing executions as a physician; providing psychiatric information to certify competence to be executed; providing psychiatric treatment to establish competence to be executed; and soliciting or harvesting organs for donation by condemned persons.[14]

Also, the Council of the Medical Society of the State of New York approved a statement on May 10, 1990, that defined participation as including, among other things, (1) the determination of mental and physical fitness for execution; (2) the rendering of technical advice regarding execution; (3) the prescription, preparation, administration, or supervision of doses of drugs in jurisdictions where lethal injection is used as a method of execution; and (4) the performance of medical examinations during the execution to determine whether or not the prisoner is dead.[11] The Council of the Medical Society of the State of New York specifically excludes the following from its definition of participation: (1) to serve as a witness in a criminal trial prior to the rendering of a verdict to determine guilt or innocence of an accused person; (2) to relieve acute suffering of a convicted prisoner while he is awaiting execution; (3) to certify death, *provided that* [emphasis in original] the prisoner has been declared dead by someone else; and (4) to perform an autopsy following the execution.[11]

Clarifications to the AMA Prohibition on Participation

There is a consensus among most medical societies that physician participation in executions is unethical.[5-12,14] There is also consensus that the following actions constitute physician participation in executions: directly injecting a lethal agent into a person, starting an intravenous line that conducts a lethal agent, or rendering technical advice for the individuals performing the execution. However, in several other contexts, the distinction between forbidden participation and permissible conduct requires special explanation or clarification.

Determination vs Certification of Death. Determining death includes monitoring the condition of the condemned during the execution and determining the point at which the individual has actually died.[11] Certifying death includes confirming that the individual is dead after another person has pronounced or determined that the individual is dead.[11] Certifying death takes place after the execution procedure is complete, is a neutral medical act, does not implicate the moral beliefs of the physician concerning capital punishment, and cannot be construed to constitute physician participation in the death penalty.

Determining death has the potential to require physician involvement in the actual execution process.[1,15] There have been several cases where a condemned person did not die immediately upon being injected, gassed, electrocuted, or hanged.[23] A physician charged with determining death where initial attempts at execution failed would have to signal that death was not achieved and indicate that the execution attempt must be repeated. In some cases, the physician might have to specifically indicate which drug, what amount of electricity, or what amount or type of gas must be added or repeated to complete the execution.[15]

Determining death might require the physician to use his or her medical knowledge or skills in a participatory fashion in the execution (*Washington Post*. December 11, 1990:Z12). The physician would potentially be put in the position of directing the specific action that would cause death to the condemned person.[15] For these reasons, determining death constitutes physician participation in execution and is unethical. Certifying death after another person has determined or pronounced death, however, would not involve the physician in the execution process and is permitted.

Supervising or Overseeing the Preparation or Administration of the Execution Process. Supervising execution proceedings implicates concerns similar to those raised by determining the death of the condemned. If improper application of the chosen execution method occurred, the physician would be placed in the position of using his or her medical skills to assist the execution. The physician might be required to take specific corrective action that would contribute directly to the taking of life.[15] Supervising the preparation or administration of the execution process is therefore unethical.

Physician Participation in the Legal Processes Leading to Condemnation and Execution. There are several ways in which physicians may be asked to participate in the legal processes that lead to the conviction, sentencing, and execution of an individual. A physician may be asked to evaluate and testify about a defendant's criminal responsibility or competence to stand trial. If the defendant is convicted, testimony may be requested about potentially aggravating or mitigating factors that are considered during the sentencing phase of the proceedings. Physicians may also be asked to evaluate competence to be executed or to provide treatment in order to restore competence so that the execution may take place.[16,18,24–26]

Testifying as to competence to stand trial or competence to be executed presents particular ethical dilemmas for psychiatrists, as psychiatrists are ordinarily the only medial professionals called on to make such competency determinations. The American Psychiatric Association stated in 1980 that "[t]he physician's serving the state as executioner, either directly or indirectly, is a perversion of medical ethics and of his or her role as a healer and comforter."[27]

A physician who testifies to the competence of an individual to stand trial in a capital proceeding may ultimately contribute in some way to the individual's execution.[18] Had the physician not provided testimony supportive of a finding of competence, then the individual might not have stood trial, been convicted, and been sentenced. However, the physician's

responsibility for the execution is attenuated. Defendants who are found competent to stand trial may be acquitted or, if found guilty, may be sentenced to a penalty less severe than death. In addition, the physician does not make the formal determinations that lead to the defendant's execution. The judge determines whether the defendant is competent to stand trial. Similarly, other parties, including the judge, the trial jury, and the sentencing jury, decide whether the defendant is guilty and whether the death penalty should be imposed. The psychiatrist is not using medical skills to cause the death of the accused, and the psychiatrist's actions do not directly result in a death.

Similar considerations apply when a physician provides testimony during the trial in a capital case or during the sentencing phase of a capital case. Although the physician's actions may ultimately influence the decision to execute an individual, the actual determination to execute is made by the jury, which has the option of accepting or rejecting the psychiatrist's testimony. In addition, the psychiatrist's testimony may help exculpate the defendant.

In all cases where a physician is called upon to testify before and during the trial and sentencing of the accused, the physician is ethically obligated to give an objective medical evaluation of the accused or of the medical evidence in the case. Physicians may not allow personal beliefs regarding the morality of capital punishment to influence their medical evaluation.

Different concerns are raised when the psychiatrist asked to testify to the competence of a condemned prisoner to be executed. A longstanding legal tradition, in both statutory and common law, prohibits the execution of the incompetent.[24] In *Ford v Wainwright*, the Supreme Court held that executing an incompetent individual is also unconstitutional.[25] When a psychiatrist testifies to an individual's competence to be executed, the psychiatrist is put in a position where his or her actions could set the process of execution in motion.[26] If a psychiatrist's testimony results in a finding of competence, the effect may be to remove the last barrier to execution.[15] Accordingly, the death of the condemned may depend directly upon the psychiatrist's use of medical skills. On the other hand, if a psychiatrist's testimony results in a finding of incompetence, the psychiatrist's involvement has the effect of halting the process of execution. In addition, the formal competency determination is typically made by a judge or jury rather than by psychiatrists.[28] Consequently, it may not be appropriate to characterize a physician's testimony regarding a prisoner's competence to be executed as participation in capital punishment.

Given the complexity of the ethical issues and the importance of the role of psychiatrists, the Council will defer guidelines on physician involvement in evaluations of a prisoner's competence to be executed until the Council has consulted further with the ethics committee of the American Psychiatric Association. The Council also will defer guidelines on the question whether physicians may treat an incompetent prisoner to restore the prisoner's competence to be executed.

Actions Associated With Executions That Do Not Constitute Physician Participation in Executions. A physician's obligation to do no harm does not require him or her to abandon a condemned individual or to refrain from providing comfort or medical care to a person on death row. A physician may provide medical care to a condemned person if the individual gives informed consent, the medical care is used to heal, comfort, or preserve the life of the condemned individual, and the medical care would not enable or facilitate the execution of the condemned person. One often-cited example is that a physician may perform an appendectomy on a condemned person who has acute appendicitis. Ethically, this is permissible because performing the appendectomy prolongs the life of the condemned individual, if even only for a short period.[13]

The wait for execution on death row may be long, and a variety of illnesses or maladies may manifest themselves. Under the foregoing analysis, a physician may counsel or treat an individual for anxiety or depression with the patient's informed consent.[29] Any acute or chronic medical conditions that arise could be tended to, and the physician may use medical or personal skills to comfort the condemned person. For instance, the condemned individual might request medication that would relieve acute anxiety that had occurred as a result of anticipating the impending execution.

Although the physician may not participate in an execution, he or she may witness the execution in a nonprofessional capacity. The physician may also witness the execution at the specific voluntary request of the condemned person as long as the physician takes no action that would cause the death of the condemned individual, assists in no way in the process that is used to execute the condemned individual, and does not otherwise violate the definition of physician participation in execution in this report.

A General Definition of Physician Participation

From the foregoing discussion, a general definition of physician participation can be constructed that would include the specific actions previously described while providing guidelines for determining whether other actions not mentioned or as yet unanticipated might also constitute physician participation in executions. A general definition of physician participation in executions would be as follows:

An action by a physician that would fulfill one or more of the following conditions: (1) an action that would directly cause the death of the condemned (eg, administering a lethal injection); (2) an action that would assist, supervise, or contribute to the ability of another individual to directly cause the death of the condemned (eg, prescribing the drugs necessary for a lethal injection); and (3) an action that could automatically cause an execution to be carried out on a condemned prisoner (eg, determining whether death has occurred during an execution).

This definition would exclude actions such as testifying as to competence to stand trial, certifying death (after another party had declared death), and providing medical care to the condemned for medical problems before the execution.

GUIDELINES

For the reasons described in this report, the Council on Ethical and Judicial Affairs issues the following guidelines:

1. An individual's opinion on capital punishment is the personal moral decision of the individual. A physician, as a member of a profession dedicated to preserving life when there is hope of doing so, should not be a participant in an execution. Physician participation in execution is defined generally as actions that would fall into one or more of the following categories: (1) an action that would directly cause the death of the condemned; (2) an action that would assist, supervise, or contribute to the ability of another individual to directly cause the death of the condemned; and (3) an action that could automatically cause an execution to be carried out on a condemned prisoner.

2. Physician participation in an execution includes, but is not limited to, the following actions: prescribing or administering tranquilizers and other psychotropic agents and medications that are part of the execution procedure; monitoring vital signs on site or remotely (including monitoring electrocardiograms); attending or observing an execution as a physician; and rendering of technical advice regarding execution.

3. In the case where the method of execution is lethal injection, the following actions by the physician would also constitute physician participation in execution: selecting injection sites; starting intravenous lines as a port for a lethal injection device; prescribing, preparing, administering, or supervising injection drugs or their doses or types; inspecting, testing, or maintaining lethal injection devices; consulting with or supervising lethal injection personnel.

4. The following actions do not constitute physician participation in execution: (1) testifying as to competence to stand trial, testifying as to relevant medical evidence during trial, or testifying as to medical aspects of aggravating or mitigating circumstances during the penalty phase of a capital case; (2) certifying death, provided that the condemned has been declared dead by another person; (3) witnessing an execution in a totally nonprofessional capacity; (4) witnessing an execution at the specific voluntary request of the condemned person, provided that the physician observes the execution in a nonphysician capacity and takes no action that would constitute physician participation in an execution; and (5) relieving the acute suffering of a condemned person while awaiting execution, including providing tranquilizers at the specific voluntary request of the condemned person to help relieve pain or anxiety in anticipation of the execution.

References

[1]Curran WJ, Casscells W. The ethics of medical participation in capital punishment. *N. Engl. J. Med.* 1980; 302:226–230.

[2]Weiner DB. The real Dr Guillotin. *JAMA.* 1972; 220: 85–89.

[3]Bolsen B. Strange bedfellows: death penalty and medicine. *JAMA.* 1982;248:518–519.

[4]Casscells W, Curran WJ. Doctors, the death penalty, and lethal injections. *N. Engl. J. Med.* 1982;307:1532–1533.

[5]Council on Ethical and Judicial Affairs, American Medical Association. *Code of Medical Ethics: Current Opinions.* Chicago, Ill: American Medical Association; 1992.

[6]World Medical Association. *Handbook of Declarations,* Ferney-Voltaire, France: World Medical Association Inc; 1993:20.6/81.

[7]American College of Physicians Ethics Manual; third edition. *Ann. Intern. Med.* 1992;117:947–960.

[8]American Public Health Association, Policy statement No. 8521: participation of health professionals in capital punishment. In: *American Public Health Association Public Policy Statements: 1948–Present Cumulative,* Washington, DC: American Public Health Association; 1993.

[9]Hovedbestyrelsen: Nordisk resolution om laegers medvirken ved henrettelser. Ugesker Laesaer. 1986; 148:1929. Cited by: Thornburn KM. Physicians and the death penalty. *West J Med.* 1987;146:638–640.

[10]American Psychiatric Association. *The principles of Medical Ethics. With Annotations Especially Applicable to Psychiatry.* Washington, DC: American Psychiatric Association; 1992.

[11]Committee on Bioethical Issues of the Medical Society of the State of New York. Physician involvement in capital punishment. *N Y State J Med.* 1991;91:15–18.

[12]National Commission on Correctional Health Care. *Standards for Health Services in Prisons.* Chicago, Ill: National Commission on Correctional Health Care; 1992:10.

[13]28 CFR §§26.1–26.5.

[14]American Medical Association. *Proceedings of the House of Delegates: 15th Interim Meeting,* Chicago, Ill: American Medical Association; 1991:355–356.

[15]Thorburn KM. Physicians and the death penalty. *West J Med.* 1987;146:638–640.

[16]Clare AN. Doctors and the death penalty: an international issue. *BMJ.* 1987;294:1180–1181.

[17]Council on Ethical and Judicial Affairs. American Medical Association. Decisions near the end of life. *JAMA.* 1992;267:2229–2233.

[18]The death penalty: dillemmas for physicians and society—a panel discussion. *Pharos.* 1987;50(3):23–27.

[19]Danckers UF. State executions and the physician. *Chicago Med.* 1991;94:12.

[20]Wishart DL. Physicians and the death penalty. *West J Med.* 1987;147:207.

[21]Minkin W. Involvement of physicians in capital punishment. *N Y State J Med.* 1991;91:271–272.

[22]Entman H. First do no harm. *JAMA.* 1989;261:134.

[23]Weisberg J. This is your death; capital punishment: what really happens. *New Republic.* 1991;205(1):23–27.

[24]Salguero RG. Medical ethics and competency to be executed. *Yale Law J.* 1986;96:166–187.

[25]*Ford v Wainwright.* 106 SCt 2595 (1986).

[26]Sargent DA. Treating the condemned to death. *Hastings Cent Rep.* 1986;16(6):5–6.

[27]American Psychiatric Association. Position statement on medical participation in capital punishment. *Am J Psychiatry.* 1980;137:1487.

[28]Enzinna PF, Gill JL. Capital punishment and the incompetent: procedures for determining competency to be executed after *Ford v. Wainwright. Florida Law Rev.* 1989;41:115–152.

[29]National Medical Association Section on Psychiatry and Behavioral Sciences. *Position Statement on the Role of the Psychiatrist in Evaluating and Treating Death Row Inmates.* Washington, DC: National Medical Association.

Psychiatry and the Death Penalty

Marianne Kastrup

The issue of capital punishment has produced considerable controversy in society with regard to both its effectiveness as a deterrent and the ethics of its use (1). Society's fear of crime and the mass-media emphasis on violent crime encourage the public to view violent crimes as more of a problem than they actually are. Over the years a number of arguments have been put forward in the public debate *pro et contra* the death penalty including that: the death penalty is a deterrent because a person tempted to commit a capital offence will desist to avoid the possibility of execution; the death penalty provides justice by meeting society's need to revenge itself for its loss; serious offenders

Marianne Kastrup, "Psychiatry and the Death Penalty," *Journal of Medical Ethics* Volume 14 (1988): 179–183. Reprinted by permission of the BMJ Publishing Group.

deserve to die because they have committed acts which have put them outside the rights of the human race (1).

The arguments used against the death penalty often focus upon the view that it contravenes the right to life as stated in human rights declarations. Also, it is argued, the death penalty is immoral and violates the modern teaching of most major religions; the death penalty is cruel, inhuman and degrading; it is unfair as it almost always will fall on minorities; the death penalty is irrevocable; it is obstructive of attempts to apply modern criminology, and it condones violence as a means of coping with society's problems.

Furthermore, the death penalty has no preventive effect and it risks providing a false sense of protection and is wasteful, not only of human life, but also because of the cost of the endless legal machinery it requires (1).

RESISTANCE TO ABOLITION

It may be difficult for many people to come to a rational decision on the death penalty as the primary resistance to the abolition of the death penalty is not rational but is connected to strong emotional feelings, conscious or unconscious. One such feeling may be that of the need for a 'scapegoat': that the person whose misdeed is discovered and who is punished by death serves to expiate the guilt engendered by the crimes of all.

Alternately, society may use the death penalty to focus upon the condemned as the embodiment of human sinfulness (the 'sacrificed lamb') and, at the same time, magically to insinuate the survivors into the grace of God by the sacrifice.

Finally, reference can be made to the need felt by individuals to develop defences against their own secret destructive impulses. The average person senses his basic instinctual relationship to the violent criminal and may become anxious that if the death penalty is eliminated he/she will be forced to rely more on his/her own internal control and less upon fear of punishment (2).

THE PARTICIPATION OF HEALTH PROFESSIONALS

There is nothing new about the medical profession's participation in executions. Doctors and other professionals have been present at, and have had roles in, official executions for centuries. As an example, the guillotine was invented by a physician who opposed the death penalty and thought the guillotine a more humane method of killing. Further, a commission of American doctors opposed execution by hanging in 1887 because it frequently prolonged suffering, and recommended more humane forms of killing, favouring electrocution (3).

The death penalty is still an issue for medical professionals. Physicians and other medical personnel are reported to take part in the execution process by examining prisoners prior to execution, by staying in the death chamber, and by monitoring the prisoners' condition either during electrocution or lethal injections and advising whether or not to continue the execution. Often they have been charged with functions such as examining the prisoner (4) or placing a mark on the chest of the prisoner before shooting (5). In several countries, execution cannot take place without the participation of doctors even when the traditional methods are used. A minimum requirement is that the doctor certifies death.

There have, however, been several examples of very active participation of doctors. In one case in the USA, a physician and a medical assistant helped to strap the prisoner to the electric chair, and the struggle was reported to last for seven minutes. In another case a physician monitored the prisoner's heartbeat, indicating that the execution should continue for a few more minutes (6).

To summarise, doctors may be called on to participate in executions by, among other things, determining fitness for execution, giving technical advice, prescribing, preparing, and administering or supervising the injection of poison and making medical examinations during the execution in order to advise continuation of the execution if the prisoner is not yet dead (1).

DILEMMAS

These problems, amongst others, imply that a physician may easily find himself in an ethical dilemma. One problem is the so-called 'fit-for-execution' certificate. Treating prisoners on death row may result in grotesque situations where an execution cannot take place because the prisoner has fallen ill and the doctor's task is to restore him or her to a condition which allows execution. In this way the physician may easily find himself in a key position where his evaluation is the decisive factor determining whether the prisoner is executed or not and he may be required to use professional skills for the sole purpose of restoring the prisoner to a condition which makes him fit for execution.

Finally it needs emphasis that the presence of a physician can be used to lend credibility to the act of execution and deflect the responsibility from those who have ordered the execution.

THE PARTICIPATION OF PSYCHIATRISTS

One basic principle of forensic psychiatry is that it is morally unjust to evaluate and judge mentally ill persons by the same legal rules as people who are mentally fit, punishing them for acts which are a consequence of their disorder.

The function of the psychiatrist is that of providing the court with a medical answer to whether any significant psychiatric disease or mental deficiency is present. The verdict 'guilty but insane', that is not responsible, is a legal task and has yielded protection against the imposition of a death sentence (7).

From a legal point of view (8) two areas of concern are raised by psychiatric participation.

The first concerns the examination of the defendant without making reasonable efforts to assure that he has full understanding of the significance of this examination, *that is the examiner's opinion as to his dangerousness.* Traditionally, this problem has been approached by asking whether the subject has any right to refuse co-operation. From an ethical point of view it is offensive to encourage a criminal defendant, especially one who is unaware of the true nature of the situation, to participate in an interview the end result of which may be to cause him to be put to death. It may thus be concluded that no prosecution psychiatric testimony should be admitted on the death penalty issue if that testimony is based upon an interview with the defendant unless it is shown that prior to the interview the defendant recognised his privilege against self-incrimination.

The second area of concern is the inadequate cross-examination of psychiatric testimony presented in capital trials. Lawyers provided for defendants by the court may fail to cross-examine witnesses or present contrary testimony by other psychiatrists.

Furthermore one should be concerned with the quality of the psychiatric examinations and testimonies. Of major concern here is whether psychiatrists are particularly qualified to give opinions on future dangerousness.

FUTURE DANGEROUSNESS

In some states with death penalty statutes (for example Texas) one factor which leads to the imposition of the death penalty on the convicted prisoner is the probability that he or she will commit similar acts of violence in the future. To determine likely future dangerousness, evidence from psychiatrists may be intoduced and this testimony has been an influential and, in some cases the key, factor in convincing the jury to vote for the death penalty (6).

The role and capacity of psychiatrists in assessing future dangerous acts has been examined in detail in a number of cases. An important example was the case of *Barefoot versus Estelle.* At his trial two psychiatrists testified that someone of Barefoot's character would probably commit further acts of violence and that therefore he represented a continuing threat to society. This evidence led to Barefoot being sentenced to death. He subsequently appealed, claiming that the use of psychiatric testimony was unconstitutional because a psychiatrist had no special competence to make evaluations of future dangerousness. The American Psychiatric Association (APA) also rejected the use of psychiatric testimony based on hypothetical questions, asserting that research indicates that even under the best of conditions psychiatric predictions of long-term future dangerousness are wrong in at least two out of every three cases. They concluded that in the Barefoot case, a psychiatrist was allowed to masquerade personal preferences as 'medical' views (9). On the other hand, it should be recognised that there is little evidence that those other than psychiatrists are good at predicting dangerousness either.

Furthermore, recent research indicates that the most reliable predictor of future violent behaviour are factors that have nothing to do with mental illness such as age, sex and past dangerous behaviour and that the forecast of future dangerousness is primarily not an expert psychiatric one (8). The US Supreme Court has made the observations that 'neither the prisoner nor the American Psychiatric Association suggests that psychiatrists are always wrong with respect to future dangerousness, *only most of the time*' (9).

Psychiatrists have given a number of rationales for their participation in this process including that more conservative and prosecution-prone colleagues would then take over. This is, however, like saying good people should do bad things because otherwise only bad people will do bad things.

ASSESSMENT OF COMPETENCE

It is accepted practice in many states that insane prisoners should not be executed. Psychiatrists take an active part in evaluating a defendant's competence to stand trial and in assessing the convicted person's capacity for psychiatric rehabilitation. Generally no ethical problem is seen with such activities.

Another more difficult issue is the psychiatric assessment of the mental condition of the prisoner to be executed. This procedure to determine competence varies in the USA from a full court hearing to an evaluation according to the assessment of the prison warden. A dilemma exists for psychiatrists as to what extent they should participate in determining competence (8). Some psychiatrists may argue that an assessment of competence to be executed does not differ from other tasks psychiatrists are called upon to perform. Another position recognises profound differences between this evaluation and other evaluations since the assessment has life-and-death implications for the subject. Psychiatrists who support this approach emphasise that the standards used for determining competence should be clarified and that the prisoner should be allowed to call his own expert. Finally, some psychiatrists reject the idea of participating in evaluations of competence of prisoners condemned to be executed. They stress that the only purpose of such an evaluation is to facilitate the administration of punishment, which is a role that psychiatrists should avoid.

In the US, the Supreme Court ruled in 1985 that states must provide free psychiatric assistance in preparing an insanity claim and, in 1986, that it is unconstitutional to execute a prisoner who becomes insane while awaiting execution (6).

Here a possibility may arise that psychiatrists become doctors at risk. It has been suggested that the court in which the prisoner is presenting evidence concerning his sanity need not be presided over by a judge. This would mean that psychiatrists perform an evaluation and also present evidence, thus acting as the ultimate decision-makers as to whether the prisoner is to be executed. Regardless of whether the right is constitutionally based or not, determination of competence to be executed presents a difficult problem for mental health professionals.

TREATMENT OF THE INCOMPETENT

It is, as mentioned, in many states required that prisoners be competent before the execution. Psychiatrists may therefore find themselves in a dilemma when a prisoner is found incompetent—either at the time of the trial or as a consequence thereof. Should the psychiatrist accept the task and treat the prisoner, well aware that a successful treatment may result in the person's execution (8)? No easy answer can be given. Some clinicians believe that their responsibility as psychiatrists is to treat mental illness whenever possible, without regard to the prisoner's status as a condemned prisoner. Others reject the idea that they should be asked to restore a prisoner to a mental state which would allow an execution to proceed. For them the relief of suffering in the short-term must be weighed against the long-term interest of the prisoner. Psychiatrists who favour this position might argue that it is more humane to let a person suffer from a psychosis than to treat the psychosis, thereby threatening the life of the prisoner. Finally some favour an intermediate position; they are willing to treat those prisoners who themselves want to be treated (8).

Different ways exist out of the dilemma. One possibility might be automatically to commute a death sentence to life imprisonment in cases where a prisoner is shown to be incompetent. Another possibility might be to abolish the requirement that prisoners must be competent when executed (though, in the US, this would contravene the US Supreme Court's ruling on the constitutionality of executing insane prisoners).

PSYCHIATRIC PROBLEMS OF DEATH ROW

Two kinds of psychiatric problems are to be found on death row: 1) problems that are present in prisoners on death row, and 2) problems that are caused by the conditions on death row.

1. An important issue is psychiatric disorders suffered by condemned prisoners. In a recent survey (10) the neuropsychiatric characteristics of 15 men and women who were sentenced to death in the US between 1976 and 1984 were presented. The study represents the first systematic clinical investigation of individuals waiting to be executed and the subjects were selected not because of any evident psychopathology but because of the imminence of their executions.

All were psychiatrically evaluated and detailed neurological histories were obtained. All 15 had histories of head injuries. Five subjects had major neurological impairments such as paralysis or cortical atrophy and a further seven had histories of black-outs and psychomotor epileptic symptoms. All but one of the eleven subjects psychologically tested were of normal intelligence.

As regards the psychiatric symptoms, nine of the 15 subjects suffered psychiatric symptoms during childhood of a nature so severe that they had needed consultation. Six subjects were found to be chronically psychotic, and their psychotic history antedated their imprisonment. Three more subjects were episodically psychotic, and two subjects suffered from symptoms consistent with **DSM-III** criteria for bipolar mood disorder (manic-depressive).

It may of course be questioned whether these prisoners indeed were representative of death row prisoners. The authors imply that a majority of death row prisoners have longstanding neurological or psychiatric disorders, many of them associated with traumata in early life and that they would have had much to gain

by convincing the examiners they were impaired. The question is: Why were these serious disorders not identified during the trials? One answer suggested by the authors is that nobody suspected them and thus nobody looked for them. The fact that the disorders were not previously identified conflicts with the view that murderers are sociopaths who will feign any illness to escape their punishment. The possibility remains that these prisoners constitute a severely impaired population of prisoners who are less able to get competent attorneys to defend their cases, though undoubtedly socio-economic factors play an important role here.

2 The anticipation of death at a specific time is an extremely stressful factor that has been studied in a survey of inmate response to death row confinement (11). A number of psychological symptoms can be observed in death row inmates: both clinical evaluations and psychological testings demonstrate a 'hardening' of psychological defences over time. Some condemned prisoners went on manifesting marked symptomatic responses in relation to stress, but more described a lowering of perceived stress. The findings suggest that it is possible to adapt to some extent to the death row experience, but the adjustment may result in a socially undesirable position.

HOW TO CHANGE THE SITUATION

Is it morally justifiable that psychiatrists participate in trials in which their testimony may be decisive for the life or death of another human being? Is it morally justifiable that psychiatrists should decide who is fit for execution, or that psychiatrists treat the psychotic person with the consequence that he/she gets so well that he/she is found fit for execution? Can we as psychiatrists accept this situation? And if not, how do we change it? It is my hope that psychiatrists and other medical professionals worldwide will condemn medical participation in capital punishment unconditionally.

At the World Medical Association's assembly in Lisbon in 1981, a resolution was passed including the passage 'it is unethical for physicians to participate in capital punishment although this does not preclude physicians certifying death'. The United Nations' principles of Medical Ethics specifically preclude the participation of physicians in any cruel, inhuman or degrading treatment or punishment.

The medical associations of 17 countries have indicated their support of the World Medical Association resolution opposing involvement of doctors in the death penalty. In June 1986 a resolution was passed by representatives of all Nordic medical associations, declaring it indefensible for any physician to participate in any act connected to and necessary for the administration of capital punishment. The American Psychiatric Association has resolved that the physician serving the state as executioner is a perversion of medical ethics and the association strongly opposes any participation by psychiatrists in capital punishment. In the annotated *Principles of Medical Ethics* (12) it is mentioned that a psychiatrist who regularly practises outside his/her area of professional competence should be considered unethical.

Determination of professional competence should be made by peer review boards or other appropriate bodies. Such and other similar principles for ethical conduct could be a safeguard against psychiatrists overlooking disorders or giving inappropriate evidence in court.

If a complaint of unethical conduct is sustained the psychiatry member should receive a sanction. These sanctions could take many forms, from admonishment to expulsion from a professional organisation, and the intensified debate thus sparked off might lead to an increased awareness of the ethical dilemmas.

'Doctors at risk', which comprises those who work for authorities and who risk committing human rights violations, may be under considerable stress if refusing to co-operate, and the establishment of a professional network to provide support is essential.

This could be helpful for psychiatrists who in court are ordered to reveal confidences of patients and who reserve the right to raise the question of need for disclosure; or in cases where psychiatrists feel that their testimony is being used by the legal profession outside the context for which it was meant.

This is encouraging but more needs to be done. Professional associations have much to contribute to the defence of human rights and to the objective of removing doctors from the execution chambers and associated legal processes.

References

1. Amnesty International, Canadian Section Medical Network. *Health care and human rights.* Toronto: 1987, 5, 1.

2. West L J. Psychiatric reflections on the death penalty. *American journal of orthopsychiatry,* 1975; 45: 689–700.

3. Curran W J, Casscells W. The ethics of medical participation in capital punishment by intravenous drug injection. *New England journal of medicine* 1980; 302: 226–230.

4. Hussain A H, Tozman S. Psychiatry on death row. *Journal of clinical psychiatry* 1978; 39: 183–188.

5. Dix G E. Psychiatric testimony in death penalty litigation. *Bulletin of the American Academy of Psychiatry Law* 1977; 5: 287–293.

6. Amnesty International. *The death penalty in the United States of America: an issue for health professionals.* London: Amnesty International, 1987.

7. Reich W. Psychiatric diagnosis as an ethical problem. In: Bloch S, Chodoff P, eds. *Psychiatric ethics* Oxford: Oxford University Press, 1981.

8. Appelbaum P S. Competence to be executed: another conundrum for mental health professionals. *Hospital and community psychiatry* 1986; 37: 682–384.

9. Brief for Amicus Curiae, American Psychiatric Association. Supreme Court of the United States, Oct term 1982. *Barefoot v Estelle.*

10. Lewis D O, Pincus J H, Fledman M et al. Psychiatric, neurological and psychoeducational characteristics of 15 death row inmates in the US, *American journal of psychiatry.* 1986; 143: 838–845.

11. Gallemore J L, Panton I H. Inmate responses to lengthy death row confinement. *American journal of psychiatry* 1972; 129: 167–172.

12. American Psychiatric Association. *The principles of medical ethics.* 1986.

VI
EMERGING ISSUES

Much can be learned from studying moral problems that have existed long enough to be the subject of considerable thought and reflection. Yet society is changing rapidly, driven by evolving technological capabilities. It is a substantial challenge to identify new moral issues and make sense of how old moral understandings may or may not apply to new situations. The readings in this chapter were chosen because they describe novel and challenging situations that require moral judgments; they describe significant moral issues that are neglected in the traditional scope of criminal justice ethics and start the difficult process of applying accumulated wisdom to new generations of problems. Although this is the final chapter in *Criminal Justice Ethics*, we hope it is a starting point for the study of problems we must face to establish ethical communities in real life and to ensure that social justice remains an important principle as technology changes our lives in unprecedented ways.

The first reading is by Harvard Law Professor Lawrence Tribe and entitled "The Constitution in Cyberspace: Law and Liberty Beyond the Electronic Frontier." Tribe is well known for his scholarship on the Constitution and its interpretation. This article is the text of a keynote address he gave at a conference on Computers, Freedom and Privacy. He describes some recent problems and outlines a useful series of principles of the Constitution that can help with its application to computer networks. Ultimately, Tribe argues for an additional Constitutional Amendment that would read:

> This Constitution's protections for the freedoms of speech, press, petition, and assembly, and its protections against unreasonable searches and seizures and the deprivation of life, liberty, or property without due process of law, shall be construed as fully applicable without regard to the technological method or medium through which information content is generated, stored, altered, transmitted, or controlled.

The text of this speech came from the archives of the Electronic Frontier Foundation <www.eff.org>, which has a wide range of resources and breaking news on related topics. Both Findlaw <www.findlaw.com> and *The Jurist: The Law Professors' Network* <http://jurist.law.pitt.edu/> have growing sections on the topic of "cyberlaw."

One of the main concerns related to technology is how increasingly sophisticated databases and methods of record keeping pose a threat to individual privacy. Jeffrey Reiman uses the example of the Intelligent Vehicle Highway Systems—where people are passive passengers in cars moved more efficiently by computer direction—to explore this issue in "Driving to the Panopticon: A Philosophical Exploration of the Risks to Privacy Posed by the Highway Technology of the Future." The Panopticon was a plan for a prison that involved the extensive use of surveillance as a mechanism of control. Reiman is concerned with the forms of social control that accompany the surveillance of where people drive all the time. Interested readers can search the Internet for recent updates on the progress of IVHS and explore a range of related issues at the Center for Democracy and Technology <http://www.cdt.org/>.

If technology poses danger to adults, then it has even more potential to harm vulnerable children. Computers create new ways for sex offenders to victimize children, but the Internet may also have the potential to help by notifying communities about offenders. Ernie Allen is the C.E.O of the National Center for Missing and Exploited Children, and he debates Nadine Strossen, President of the American Civil Liberties Union in "Megan's Law and the Protection of the Child in the On-Line Age." They start by debating the merits of Megan's law, which requires community notification of sex offenders. The second debate topic is the recent Supreme Court decision in *Kansas v. Hendricks*, which allowed the involuntary civil commitment of sex offenders when their prison terms expired. The final topic for their debate is the Communications Decency Act, which Congress passed to protect children from indecency on the Internet and which the Supreme Court struck down in *Reno v. ACLU.*

The National Center for Missing and Exploited Children can be found at <http://www.missingkids.com/> and the American Civil Liberties Union at <www.aclu.org>. The debate mentions the National Center on Institutions and Alternatives, which has many resources available on the Internet <http://www.ncianet.org/ncia/index.html>. The Supreme Court cases mentioned in the debate are available through Findlaw <www.findlaw.com>. The Criminal Justice Exploration Guide section on sex offender information includes sites at which people can type in their zip codes and see a list of sex offenders in their area; other sites include information about child protection, sex offender treatment, and initiatives for thwarting sex offenders who use cyberspace to find victims <http://www.co.pinellas.fl.us/bcc/juscoord/explore.htm>.

The next article is Julian Dibbell's "A Rape in Cyberspace: Or, How an Evil Clown, a Haitian Trickster Spirit, Two Wizards, and a Cast of Dozens Turned a Database into a Society." The first of many intriguing questions is the appropriateness of the term *rape* for an event that takes place in the computer chat room—a "virtual" encounter in which suffering was caused though no one's real-life body was harmed. The second main issue is that of finding an appropriate response from the virtual community to the offense, and Dibbell chronicles the odd collection of cyber-characters as they create a criminal justice system for their community. This work is part of a growing genre called the cyber-biography and is the first chapter of Dibbell's book, *My Tiny Life: Crime and Passion in a Virtual World* (New York: Henry Holt, 1998).

The last two essays are about the media's power to shape perceptions about crime and justice. Debra Seagal took a job at a "reality-based" police show and tells how the show was put together in "Tales From the Cutting-Room Floor." The show has film crews in several cities and "story analysts" like Seagal sift through thousands of hours of tape, which provide a detailed empirical study of police behavior. Readers should identify what they see as the ethical issues and violations on the part of the police. Seagal is insightful about the values that go into deciding what goes into the program and what gets left out, including instances of too much reality for the "reality-based" program. Her short article speaks volumes about media ethics and the ideological distortions in the "reality" it creates. *Picturing Justice: The On-Line Journal of Law and Popular Culture* is devoted to exploring related issues and can be found at <http://www.usfca.edu/pj/>.

People on all sides of the capital punishment debate have advocated televising an execution; Paul Leighton examines this idea in "Fear and Loathing in an Age of Show Business: Reflections on Televised Executions." Television is present in 98 percent of households—more homes than have indoor plumbing—so a televised execution has the potential to save lives through deterrence and undermine support for capital punishment by exposing viewers to the reality of executions. Leighton tries to identify both the assumptions behind such claims and the data relevant to assessing the likely effects. He also explores the possibility that a televised execution may cause additional deaths because of brutalization dynamics or imitation effects.

The Internet resources mentioned above and other related materials are available through <http://www.paulsjusticepage.com>.

The Constitution in Cyberspace: Law and Liberty Beyond the Electronic Frontier

Laurence H. Tribe

My topic is how to "map" the text and structure of our Constitution onto the texture and topology of "cyberspace." That's the term coined by cyberpunk novelist William Gibson, which many now use to describe the "place"—

Laurence Tribe, "The Constitution in Cyberspace," Prepared remarks for his keynote address at the First Conference on Computers, Freedom & Privacy (1991). Available from the archives of the Electronic Frontier Foundation, *http://www.eff.org*. Reprinted by permission of Laurence Tribe.

a place without physical walls or even physical dimensions—where ordinary telephone conversations "happen," where voice-mail and e-mail messages are stored and sent back and forth, and where computer-generated graphics are transmitted and transformed, all in the form of interactions, some real-time and some delayed, among countless users, and between users and the computer itself.

Some use the "cyberspace" concept to designate fantasy worlds or "virtual realities" of the sort Gibson described in his novel *Neuromancer*, in which people can essentially turn their minds into computer peripherals capable of perceiving and exploring the data matrix. The whole idea of "virtual reality," of course, strikes a slightly odd note. As one of Lily Tomlin's most memorable characters once asked, "What's reality, anyway, but a collective hunch?" Work in this field tends to be done largely by people who share the famous observation that reality is overrated!

However that may be, "cyberspace" connotes to some users the sorts of technologies that people in Silicon Valley work on when they try to develop "virtual racquetball" for the disabled, computer-aided design systems that allow architects to walk through "virtual buildings" and remodel them *before* they are built, "virtual conferencing" for business meetings, or maybe someday even "virtual day care centers" for latchkey children. The user snaps on a pair of goggles hooked up to a high-powered computer terminal, puts on a special set of gloves (and perhaps other gear) wired into the same computer system, and, looking a little bit like Darth Vader, pretty much steps into a computer-driven, drug-free, 3-dimensional, interactive, infinitely expandable hallucination complete with sight, sound and touch—allowing the user literally to move through, and experience, information.

I'm using the term "cyberspace" much more broadly, as many have lately. I'm using it to encompass the full array of computer-mediated audio and/or video interactions that are already widely dispersed in modern societies—from things as ubiquitous as the ordinary telephone, to things that are still coming on-line like computer bulletin boards and networks like Prodigy, or like the WELL ("Whole Earth 'Lectronic Link"), based here in San Francisco. My topic, broadly put, is the implications of that rapidly expanding array for our constitutional order. It is a constitutional order that tends to carve up the social, legal, and political universe along lines of "physical place" or "temporal proximity." The critical thing to note is that these very lines, in cyberspace, either get bent out of shape or fade out altogether.

The question, then, becomes: when the lines along which our Constitution is drawn warp or vanish, what happens to the Constitution itself?

SETTING THE STAGE

To set the stage with a perhaps unfamiliar example, consider a decision handed down nine months ago, *Maryland v. Craig*, where the U.S. Supreme Court upheld the power of a state to put an alleged child abuser on trial with the defendant's accuser testifying not in the defendant's presence but by one-way, closed-circuit television. The Sixth Amendment, which of course antedated television by a century and a half, says: "In all criminal prosecutions, the accused shall enjoy the right . . . to be confronted with the witnesses against him." Justice O'Connor wrote for a bare majority of five Justices that the state's procedures nonetheless struck a fair balance between costs to the accused and benefits to the victim and to society as a whole.

Justice Scalia, joined by the three "liberals" then on the Court (Justices Brennan, Marshall and Stevens), dissented from that cost-benefit approach to interpreting the Sixth Amendment. He wrote: "The Court has convincingly proved that the Maryland procedure serves a valid interest, and gives the defendant virtually everything the Confrontation Clause guarantees (everything, that is, except confrontation). I am persuaded, therefore, that the Maryland procedure is virtually constitutional. Since it is not, however, actually constitutional I [dissent]."

Could it be that the high-tech, closed-circuit TV context, almost as familiar to the Court's youngest Justice as to his even younger law clerks, might've had some bearing on Justice Scalia's sly invocation of "virtual" constitutional reality? Even if Justice Scalia wasn't making a pun on "virtual reality," and I suspect he wasn't, his dissenting opinion about the Confrontation Clause requires us to "confront" the recurring puzzle of how constitutional provisions written two centuries ago should be construed and applied in ever-changing circumstances.

Should contemporary society's technology-driven cost-benefit fixation be allowed to water down the old-fashioned value of direct confrontation that the Constitution seemingly enshrined as basic? I would hope not. In that respect, I find myself in complete agreement with Justice Scalia.

But new technological possibilities for seeing your accuser clearly without having your accuser see you at all—possibilities for sparing the accuser any discomfort in ways that the accuser couldn't be spared before one-way mirrors or closed-circuit TVs were developed—should lead us at least to ask ourselves whether two-way confrontation, in which your accuser is supposed to be made uncomfortable, and thus less likely to lie, really is the core value of the Confrontation Clause. If so, "virtual" confrontation should be held constitutionally insufficient. If not—if the core value served by the Confrontation Clause is just the ability to watch your accuser say that you did it—then "virtual" confrontation should suffice. New technologies should lead us to look more closely at just what values the Constitution seeks to preserve. New technologies should not lead us to react reflexively either way—either by assuming that technologies the Framers didn't know about make their concerns and values obsolete, or by assuming that those new technologies couldn't possibly provide new ways out of old dilemmas and therefore should be ignored altogether.

The one-way mirror yields a fitting metaphor for the task we confront. As the Supreme Court said in a different context several years ago, "The mirror image presented [here] requires us to step through an analytical looking glass to resolve it" (*NCAA v. Tarkanian*). The world in which the Sixth Amendment's Confrontation Clause was written and ratified was a world in which "being confronted with" your accuser necessarily meant a simultaneous physical confrontation so that your accuser had to perceive you being accused by him. Closed-circuit television and one-way mirrors changed all that by decoupling those two dimensions of confrontation, marking a shift in the conditions of information-transfer that is in many ways typical of cyberspace.

What does that sort of shift mean for constitutional analysis? A common way to react is to treat the pattern as it existed prior to the new technology (the pattern in which doing "A" necessarily included doing "B") as essentially arbitrary or accidental. Taking this approach, once the technological change makes it possible to do "A" without "B"—to see your accuser without having him or her see you, or to read someone's mail without her knowing it, to switch examples—one concludes that the "old" Constitution's inclusion of "B" is irrelevant; one concludes that it is enough for the government to guarantee "A" alone. Sometimes that will be the case; but it's vital to understand that, sometimes, it won't be.

A characteristic feature of modernity is the subordination of purpose to accident—an acute appreciation of just how contingent and coincidental the connections we are taught to make often are. We understand, as moderns, that many of the ways we carve up and organize the world reflect what our social history and cultural heritage, and perhaps our neurological wiring, bring to the world, and not some irreducible "way things are." A wonderful example comes from a 1966 essay by Jorge Louis Borges, "Other Inquisitions." There, the essayist describes the following taxonomy of the animal kingdom, which he purports to trace to an ancient Chinese encyclopedia entitled "The Celestial Emporium of Benevolent Knowledge". On those remote pages it is written that animals are divided into: (a) those belonging to the Emperor (b) those that are embalmed (c) those that are trained (d) suckling pigs (e) mermaids (f) fabulous ones (g) stray dogs (h) those that are included in this classification (i) those that tremble as if they were mad (j) innumerable ones (k) those drawn with a very fine camel's hair brush (l) others (m) those that have just broken a water pitcher (n) those that, from a great distance, resemble flies.

Contemporary writers from Michel Foucault, in "The Archaeology of Knowledge", through George Lakoff, in "Women, Fire, and Dangerous Things," use Borges' Chinese encyclopedia to illustrate a range of different propositions, but the core proposition is the supposed arbitrariness—the political character, in a sense—of all culturally imposed categories.

At one level, that proposition expresses a profound truth and may encourage humility by combating cultural imperialism. At another level, though, the proposition tells a dangerous lie: it suggests that we have descended into the nihilism that so obsessed Nietzsche and other thinkers—a world where everything is relative, all lines are up for grabs, all principles and connections are just matters of purely subjective preference or, worse still, arbitrary convention. Whether we believe that killing animals for food is wrong, for example, becomes a question indistinguishable from whether we happen to enjoy eating beans, rice and tofu.

This is a particularly pernicious notion in a era when we pass more and more of our lives in cyberspace, a place where, almost by definition, our most familiar landmarks are rearranged or disappear altogether—because there is a pervasive tendency, even (and perhaps especially) among the most enlightened, to forget that the human values and ideals to which we commit ourselves may indeed be universal and need not depend on how our particular cultures, or our latest technologies, carve up the universe we inhabit. It was my very wise colleague from Yale, the late Art Left, who once observed that, even in a world without an agreed-upon God, we can still agree—even if we can't "prove" mathematically—that "napalming babies is wrong."

The Constitution's core values, I'm convinced, need not be transmogrified, or metamorphosed into oblivion, in the dim recesses of cyberspace. But to say that they need not be lost there is hardly to predict that they will not be. On the contrary, without further thought and awareness of the kind this conference might provide, the danger is clear and present that they will be.

The "event horizon" against which this transformation might occur is already plainly visible:

Electronic trespassers like Kevin Mitnik don't stop with cracking pay phones, but break into NORAD—the North American Defense Command computer in Colorado Springs—not in a "War Games" movie, but in real life.

Less challenging to national security but more ubiquitously threatening, computer crackers download everyman's credit history from institutions like TRW; start charging phone calls (and more) to everyman's number; set loose "worm" programs that shut down thousands of linked computers; and spread "computer viruses" through everyman's work or home PC.

It is not only the government that feels threatened by "computer crime"; both the owners and the users of private information services, computer bulletin boards, gateways, and networks feel equally vulnerable to this new breed of invisible trespasser. The response from the many who sense danger has been swift, and often brutal, as a few examples illustrate.

Last March, U.S. Secret Service agents staged a surprise raid on Steve Jackson Games, a small games manufacturer in Austin, Texas, and seized all paper and electronic drafts of its newest fantasy role-playing game, "GURPS [reg.t.m.] Cyberpunk," calling the game a "handbook for computer crime." By last Spring, up to one quarter of the U.S. Treasury Department's investigators had become involved in a project of eavesdropping on computer bulletin boards, apparently tracking notorious hackers like "Acid Phreak" and "Phiber Optik" through what one journalist dubbed "the dark canyons of cyberspace."

Last May, in the now famous (or infamous) "Operation Sun Devil," more than 150 secret service agents teamed up with state and local law enforcement agencies, and with security personnel from AT&T, American Express, U.S. Sprint, and a number of the regional Bell telephone companies, armed themselves with over two dozen search warrants and more than a few guns, and seized 42 computers and 23,000 floppy discs in 14 cities from New York to Texas. Their target: a loose-knit group of people in their teens and twenties, dubbed the "Legion of Doom."

I am not describing an Indiana Jones movie. I'm talking about America in the 1990s.

THE PROBLEM

The Constitution's architecture can too easily come to seem quaintly irrelevant, or at least impossible to take very seriously, in the world as reconstituted by the microchip. I propose today to canvass five axioms of our constitutional law—five basic assumptions that I believe shape the way American constitutional scholars and judges view legal issues—and to examine how they can adapt to the cyberspace age. My conclusion (and I will try not to give away too much of the punch line here) is that the Framers of our Constitution were very wise indeed. They bequeathed us a framework for all seasons, a truly astonishing document whose principles are suitable for all times and all technological landscapes.

Axiom 1: There is a Vital Difference Between Government and Private Action

The first axiom I will discuss is the proposition that the Constitution, with the sole exception of the Thirteenth Amendment prohibiting slavery, regulates action by the government rather than the conduct of private individuals and groups. In an article I wrote in the *Harvard Law Review* in 1989 on "The Curvature of Constitutional Space," I discussed the Constitution's metaphor-morphosis from a Newtonian to an Einsteinian and Heisenbergian paradigm. It was common, early in our history, to see the Constitution as "Newtonian in design with its carefully counterpoised forces and counterforces, its [geographical and institutional] checks and balances."

Indeed, in many ways contemporary constitutional law is still trapped within and stunted by that paradigm. But today at least some post-modern constitutionalists tend to think and talk in the language of relativity, quantum mechanics, and chaos theory. This may quite naturally suggest to some observers that the Constitution's basic strategy of decentralizing and diffusing power by constraining and fragmenting governmental authority in particular has been rendered obsolete.

The institutional separation of powers among the three federal branches of government, the geographical division of authority between the federal government and the fifty state governments, the recognition of national boundaries, and, above all, the sharp distinction between the public and private spheres, become easy to deride as relics of a simpler, pre-computer age. Thus Eli Noam, in the First Ithiel de Sola Pool Memorial Lecture, delivered last October at MIT, notes that computer networks and network associations acquire quasi-governmental powers as they necessarily take on such tasks as mediating their members' conflicting interests, establishing cost shares, creating their own rules of admission and access and expulsion, even establishing their own de facto taxing mechanisms. In Professor Noam's words, "networks become political entities," global nets that respect no state or local boundaries. Restrictions on the use of information in one country (to protect privacy, for example) tend to lead to export of that information to other countries, where it can be analyzed and then used on a selective basis in the country attempting to restrict it. "Data havens" reminiscent of the role played by the Swiss in banking may emerge, with few restrictions on the storage and manipulation of information.

A tempting conclusion is that, to protect the free speech and other rights of users in such private networks, judges must treat these networks not as associations that have rights of their own against the government but as virtual "governments" in themselves—as entities against which individual rights must be defended in the Constitution's name. Such a conclusion would be misleadingly simplistic. There are circumstances, of course, when nongovernmental bodies like privately owned "company towns" or even huge shopping malls should be subjected to legislative and administrative controls by democratically accountable entities, or even to judicial controls as though they were arms of the state—but that may be as true (or as false) of multinational corporations or foundations, or transnational religious organizations, or even small-town communities, as it is of computer-mediated networks. It's a fallacy to suppose that, just because a computer bulletin board or network or gateway is something like a shopping mall, government has as much constitutional duty—or even authority—to guarantee open public access to such a network as it has to guarantee open public access to a privately owned shopping center like the one involved in the U.S. Supreme Court's famous "PruneYard Shopping Center" decision of 1980.

The rules of law, both statutory and judge-made, through which each state allocates private powers and responsibilities themselves represent characteristic forms of government action. That's why a state's rules for imposing liability on private publishers, or for deciding which private contracts to enforce and which ones to invalidate, are all subject to scrutiny for their consistency with the federal Constitution. But as a general proposition it is only what governments do, either through such rules or through the actions of public officials, that the United States Constitution constrains. And nothing about any new technology suddenly erases the Constitution's enduring value of restraining government above all else, and of protecting all private groups, large and small, from government.

It's true that certain technologies may become socially indispensable—so that equal or at least minimal access to basic computer power, for example, might be as significant a constitutional goal as equal or at least minimal access to the franchise, or to dispute resolution through the judicial system, or to elementary and secondary education. But all this means (or should mean) is that the Constitution's constraints on government must at times take the form of imposing affirmative duties to assure access rather than merely enforcing negative prohibitions against designated sorts of invasion or intrusion.

Today, for example, the government is under an affirmative obligation to open up criminal trials to the press and the public, at least where there has not been a particularized finding that such openness would disrupt the proceedings. The government is also under an affirmative obligation to provide free legal assistance for indigent criminal defendants, to assure speedy trials, to underwrite the cost of counting ballots at election time, and to desegregate previously segregated school systems. But these occasional affirmative obligations don't, or shouldn't, mean that the Constitution's axiomatic division between the realm of public power and the realm of private life should be jettisoned.

Nor would the "indispensability" of information technologies provide a license for government to impose strict content, access, pricing, and other types of regulation. Books are indispensable to most of us, for example—but it doesn't follow that government should therefore be able to regulate the content of what goes onto the shelves of bookstores. The right of a private bookstore owner to decide which books to stock and which to discard, which books to display openly and which to store in limited access areas, should remain inviolate. And note, incidentally, that this needn't make the bookstore owner a "publisher" who is liable for the words printed in the books on her shelves. It's a common fallacy to imagine that the moment a computer gateway or bulletin board begins to exercise powers of selection to control who may be on line, it must automatically assume the responsibilities of a newscaster, a broadcaster, or an author. For computer gateways and bulletin boards are really the "bookstores" of cyberspace; most of them organize and present information in a computer format, rather than generating more information content of their own.

Axiom 2: The Constitutional Boundaries of Private Property and Personality Depend on Variables Deeper Than Social Utility and Technological Feasibility

The second constitutional axiom, one closely related to the private-public distinction of the first axiom, is that a person's mind, body, and property belong to that person and not to the public as a whole. Some believe that cyberspace challenges that axiom because its entire premise lies in the existence of computers tied to electronic transmission networks that process digital information. Because such information can be easily replicated in series of "1"s and "0"s, anything that anyone has come up with in virtual reality can be infinitely reproduced. I can log on to a computer library, copy a "virtual book" to my computer disk, and send a copy to your computer without creating a gap on anyone's bookshelf. The same is true of valuable computer programs, costing hundreds of dollars, creating serious piracy problems. This feature leads some, like Richard Stallman of the Free Software Foundation, to argue that in cyberspace everything should be free—that information can't be owned. Others, of course, argue that copyright and patent protections of various kinds are needed in order for there to be incentives to create "cyberspace property" in the first place.

Needless to say, there are lively debates about what the optimal incentive package should be as a matter of legislative and social policy. But the only constitutional issue, at bottom, isn't the utilitarian or instrumental selection of an optimal policy. Social judgments about what ought to be subject to individual appropriation, in the sense used by John Locke and Robert Nozick, and what ought to remain in the open public domain, are first and foremost *political* decisions.

To be sure, there are some constitutional constraints on these political decisions. The Constitution does not permit anything and everything to be made into a *private commodity*. Votes, for example, theoretically cannot be bought and sold. Whether the Constitution itself should be read (or amended) so as to permit all basic medical care, shelter, nutrition, legal assistance and, indeed, computerized information services, to be treated as mere commodities, available only to the highest bidder, are all terribly hard questions—as the Eastern Europeans are now discovering as they attempt to draft their own constitutions. But these are not questions that should ever be confused with issues of what is technologically possible, about what is realistically enforceable, or about what is socially desirable.

Similarly, the Constitution does not permit anything and everything to be socialized and made into a public good available to whoever needs or "deserves" it most. I would hope, for example, that the government could not use its powers of eminent domain to "take" live body parts like eyes or kidneys or brain tissue for those who need transplants and would be expected to lead particularly productive lives. In any event, I feel certain that whatever constitutional right each of us has to inhabit his or her own body and to hold onto his or her own thoughts and creations should not depend solely on cost-benefit calculations, or on the availability of technological methods for painlessly effecting transfers or for creating good artificial substitutes.

Axiom 3: Government May Not Control Information Content

A third constitutional axiom, like the first two, reflects a deep respect for the integrity of each individual and a healthy skepticism toward government. The axiom is that, although information and ideas have real effects in the social world, its not up to government to pick and choose for us in terms of the content of that information or the value of those ideas.

This notion is sometimes mistakenly reduced to the naïve child's ditty that "sticks and stones may break my bones, but words can never hurt me." Anybody who's ever been called something awful by children in a schoolyard knows better than to believe any such thing. The real basis for First Amendment values isn't the false premise that information and ideas have no real impact, but the belief that information and ideas are too important to entrust to any government censor or overseer.

If we keep that in mind, and only if we keep that in mind, will we be able to see through the tempting argument that, in the Information Age, free speech is a luxury we can no longer afford. That argument becomes especially tempting in the context of cyberspace, where sequences of "0"s and "1"s may become virtual life forms. Computer "viruses" roam the information nets, attaching themselves to various programs and screwing up computer facilities. Creation of a computer virus involves writing a program; the program then replicates itself and mutates. The electronic code involved is very much like DNA. If information content is "speech," and if the First Amendment is to apply in cyberspace, then mustn't these viruses be "speech"—and mustn't their writing and dissemination be constitutionally protected? To avoid that nightmarish outcome, mustn't we say that the First Amendment is inapplicable to cyberspace?

The answer is no. Speech is protected, but deliberately yelling "Boo!" at a cardiac patient may still be prosecuted as murder. Free speech is a constitutional right, but handing a bank teller a hold-up note that says, "Your money or your life," may still be punished as robbery. Stealing someone's diary may be punished as theft—even if you intend to publish it in book form. And the Supreme Court, over the past fifteen years, has gradually brought advertising within the ambit of protected expression without preventing the government from protecting consumers from deceptive advertising. The lesson, in short, is that constitutional principles are subtle enough to bend to such concerns. They needn't be broken or tossed out.

Axiom 4: The Constitution is Founded on Normative Conceptions of Humanity That Advances in Science and Technology Cannot "Disprove"

A fourth constitutional axiom is that the human spirit is something beyond a physical information processor. That axiom, which regards human thought processes as not fully reducible to the operations of a computer program, however complex, must not be confused with the silly view that, because computer operations involve nothing more than the manipulation of "on" and "off" states of myriad microchips, it somehow follows that government control or outright seizure of computers and computer programs threatens no First Amendment rights because human thought processes are not directly involved. To say that would be like saying that government confiscation of a newspaper's printing press and tomorrow morning's copy has nothing to do with speech but involves only a taking of metal, paper, and ink. Particularly if the seizure or the regulation is triggered by

the content of the information being processed or transmitted, the First Amendment is of course fully involved. Yet this recognition that information processing by computer entails something far beyond the mere sequencing of mechanical or chemical steps still leaves a potential gap between what computers can do internally and in communication with one another—and what goes on within and between human minds. It is that gap to which this fourth axiom is addressed; the very existence of any such gap is, as I'm sure you know, a matter of considerable controversy.

What if people like the mathematician and physicist Roger Penrose, author of "The Emperor's New Mind," are wrong about human minds? In that provocative recent book, Penrose disagrees with those Artificial Intelligence, or AI, gurus who insist that it's only a matter of time until human thought and feeling can be perfectly simulated or even replicated by a series of purely physical operations—that it's all just neurons firing and neurotransmitters flowing, all subject to perfect modeling in suitable computer systems. Would an adherent of that AI orthodoxy, someone whom Penrose fails to persuade, have to reject as irrelevant for cyberspace those constitutional protections that rest on the anti-AI premise that minds are not reducible to really fancy computers?

Consider, for example, the Fifth Amendment, which provides that "no person shall be . . . compelled in any criminal case to be a witness against himself." The Supreme Court has long held that suspects may be required, despite this protection, to provide evidence that is not "testimonial" in nature—blood samples, for instance, or even exemplars of one's handwriting or voice. Last year, in a case called *Pennsylvania v. Muniz*, the Supreme Court held that answers to even simple questions like "When was your sixth birthday?" are testimonial because such a question, however straightforward, nevertheless calls for the product of mental activity and therefore uses the suspect's mind against him. But what if science could eventually describe thinking as a process no more complex than, say, riding a bike or digesting a meal? Might the progress of neurobiology and computer science eventually overthrow the premises of the Muniz decision?

I would hope not. For the Constitution's premises, properly understood, are normative rather than descriptive. The philosopher David Hume was right in teaching that no "ought" can ever be logically derived from an "is." If we should ever abandon the Constitution's protection for the distinctively and universally human, it won't be because robotics or genetic engineering or computer science have led us to deeper truths, but rather because they have seduced us into more profound confusions. Science and technology open options, create possibilities, suggest incompatibilities, generate threats. They do not alter what is "right" or what is "wrong." The fact that those notions are elusive and subject to endless debate need not make them totally contingent on contemporary technology.

Axiom 5: Constitutional Principles Should Not Vary With Accidents of Technology

In a sense, that's the fifth and final constitutional axiom I would urge upon this gathering: that the Constitution's norms, at their deepest level, must be invariant under merely technological transformations. Our constitutional law evolves through judicial interpretation, case by case, in a process of reasoning by analogy from precedent. At its best, that process is ideally suited to seeing beneath the surface and extracting deeper principles from prior decisions. At its worst, though, the same process can get bogged down in superficial aspects of preexisting examples, fixating upon unessential features while overlooking underlying principles and values.

When the Supreme Court in 1928 first confronted wiretapping and held in *Olmstead v. United States* that such wiretapping involved no "search" or "seizure" within the meaning of the Fourth Amendment's prohibition of "unreasonable searches and seizures," the majority of the Court reasoned that the Fourth Amendment "itself shows that the search is to be of material things—the person, the house, his papers or his effects," and said that "there was no searching" when a suspect's phone was

tapped because the Constitution's language "cannot be extended and expanded to include telephone wires reaching to the whole world from the defendant's house or office." After all, said the Court, the intervening wires "are not part of his house or office any more than are the highways along which they are stretched." Even to a law student in the 1960s, as you might imagine, that "reasoning" seemed amazingly artificial. Yet the Olmstead doctrine still survived.

It would be illuminating at this point to compare the Supreme Court's initial reaction to new technology in Olmstead with its initial reaction to new technology in *Maryland v. Craig*, the 1990 closed-circuit television case with which we began this discussion. In Craig, a majority of the Justices assumed that, when the 18th-century Framers of the Confrontation Clause included a guarantee of two-way physical confrontation, they did so solely because it had not yet become technologically feasible for the accused to look his accuser in the eye without having the accuser simultaneously watch the accused. Given that this technological obstacle has been removed, the majority assumed, one-way confrontation is now sufficient. It is enough that the accused not be subject to criminal conviction on the basis of statements made outside his presence.

In *Olmstead*, a majority of the Justices assumed that, when the 18th-century authors of the Fourth Amendment used language that sounded "physical" in guaranteeing against invasions of a person's dwelling or possessions, they did so not solely because physical invasions were at that time the only serious threats to personal privacy, but for the separate and distinct reason that intangible invasions simply would not threaten any relevant dimension of Fourth Amendment privacy.

In a sense, *Olmstead* mindlessly read a new technology out of the Constitution, while *Craig* absent-mindedly read a new technology into the Constitution. But both had the structural effect of withholding the protections of the Bill of Rights from threats made possible by new information technologies. *Olmstead* did so by implausibly reading the Constitution's text as though it represented a deliberate decision not to extend protection to threats that 18th-century thinkers simply had not foreseen. *Craig* did so by somewhat more plausibly—but still unthinkingly—treating the Constitution's seemingly explicit coupling of two analytically distinct protections as reflecting a failure of technological foresight and imagination, rather than a deliberate value choice.

The *Craig* majority's approach appears to have been driven in part by an understandable sense of how a new information technology could directly protect a particularly sympathetic group, abused children, from a traumatic trial experience. The *Olmstead* majority's approach probably reflected both an exaggerated estimate of how difficult it would be to obtain wiretapping warrants even where fully justified, and an insufficient sense of how a new information technology could directly threaten all of us. Although both *Craig* and *Olmstead* reveal an inadequate consciousness about how new technologies interact with old values, *Craig* at least seems defensible even if misguided, while *Olmstead* seems just plain wrong.

Around 23 years ago, as a then-recent law school graduate serving as law clerk to Supreme Court Justice Potter Stewart, I found myself working on a case involving the government's electronic surveillance of a suspected criminal—in the form of a tiny device attached to the outside of a public telephone booth. Because the invasion of the suspect's privacy was accomplished without physical trespass into a "constitutionally protected area," the Federal Government argued, relying on *Olmstead*, that there had been no "search" or "seizure," and therefore that the Fourth Amendment "right of the people to be secure in their persons, houses, papers, and effects, against unreasonable searches and seizures," simply did not apply.

At first, there were only four votes to overrule *Olmstead* and to hold the Fourth Amendment applicable to wiretapping and electronic eavesdropping. I'm proud to say that, as a 26-year-old kid, I had at least a little bit to do with changing that number from four to seven—and with the argument, formally adopted by a seven-Justice majority in December 1967, that

the Fourth Amendment "protects people, not places." In that decision, *Katz v. United States,* the Supreme Court finally repudiated *Olmstead* and the many decisions that had relied upon it and reasoned that, given the role of electronic telecommunications in modern life, the First Amendment purposes of protecting free speech as well as the Fourth Amendment purposes of protecting privacy require treating as a "search" any invasion of a person's confidential telephone communications, with or without physical trespass.

Sadly, nine years later, in *Smith v. Maryland,* the Supreme Court retreated from the *Katz* principle by holding that no search occurs and therefore no warrant is needed when police, with the assistance of the telephone company, make use of a "pen register," a mechanical device placed on someone's phone line that records all numbers dialed from the phone and the times of dialing. The Supreme Court, over the dissents of Justices Stewart, Brennan, and Marshall, found no legitimate expectation of privacy in the numbers dialed, reasoning that the digits one dials are routinely recorded by the phone company for billing purposes. As Justice Stewart, the author of Katz, aptly pointed out, "that observation no more than describes the basic nature of telephone calls. . . . It is simply not enough to say, after *Katz,* that there is no legitimate expectation of privacy in the numbers dialed because the caller assumes the risk that the telephone company will expose them to the police." Today, the logic of Smith is being used to say that people have no expectation of privacy when they use their cordless telephones since they know or should know that radio waves can be easily monitored!

It is easy to be pessimistic about the way in which the Supreme Court has reacted to technological change. In many respects, *Smith* is unfortunately more typical than *Katz* of the way the Court has behaved. For example, when movies were invented, and for several decades thereafter, the Court held that movie exhibitions were not entitled to First Amendment protection. When community access cable TV was born, the Court hindered municipal attempts to provide it at low cost by holding that rules requiring landlords to install small cable boxes on their apartment buildings amounted to a compensable taking of property. And in *Red Lion v. FCC*, decided twenty-two years ago but still not repudiated today, the Court ratified government control of TV and radio broadcast content with the dubious logic that the scarcity of the electromagnetic spectrum justified not merely government policies to auction off, randomly allocate, or otherwise ration the spectrum according to neutral rules, but also much more intrusive and content-based government regulation in the form of the so-called "fairness doctrine."

Although the Supreme Court and the lower federal courts have taken a somewhat more enlightened approach in dealing with cable television, these decisions for the most part reveal a curious judicial blindness, as if the Constitution had to be reinvented with the birth of each new technology. Judges interpreting a late 18th century Bill of Rights tend to forget that, unless its terms are read in an evolving and dynamic way, its values will lose even the static protection they once enjoyed. Ironically, fidelity to original values requires flexibility of textual interpretation. It was Judge Robert Bork, not famous for his flexibility, who once urged this enlightened view upon then Judge (now Justice) Scalia, when the two of them sat as colleagues on the U.S. Court of Appeals for the D.C. Circuit.

Judicial error in this field tends to take the form of saying that, by using modern technology ranging from the telephone to the television to computers, we "assume the risk." But that typically begs the question. Justice Harlan, in a dissent penned two decades ago, wrote: "Since it is the task of the law to form and project, as well as mirror and reflect, we should not . . . merely recite . . . risks without examining the desirability of saddling them upon society" (*United States v. White*). And, I would add, we should not merely recite risks without examining how imposing those risks comports with the Constitution's fundamental values of freedom, privacy, and equality.

Failing to examine just that issue is the basic error I believe federal courts and Congress have made: in regulating radio and TV broadcasting without adequate sensitivity to First Amendment values; in supposing that the selection and editing of video programs by cable operators might be less than a form of expression; in excluding telephone companies from cable and other information markets; in assuming that the processing of "0"s and "1"s by computers as they exchange data with one another is something less than "speech"; and in generally treating information processed electronically as though it were somehow less entitled to protection for that reason.

The lesson to be learned is that these choices and these mistakes are not dictated by the Constitution. They are decisions for us to make in interpreting that majestic charter, and in implementing the principles that the Constitution establishes.

CONCLUSION

If my own life as a lawyer and legal scholar could leave just one legacy, I'd like it to be the recognition that the Constitution as a whole "protects people, not places." If that is to come about, the Constitution as a whole must be read through a technologically transparent lens. That is, we must embrace, as a rule of construction or interpretation, a principle one might call the "cyberspace corollary." It would make a suitable Twenty-seventh Amendment to the Constitution, one befitting the 200th anniversary of the Bill of Rights. Whether adopted all at once as a constitutional amendment, or accepted gradually as a principle of interpretation that I believe should obtain even without any formal change in the Constitution's language, the corollary I would propose would do for technology in 1991 what I believe the Constitution's Ninth Amendment, adopted in 1791, was meant to do for text.

The Ninth Amendment says: "The enumeration in the Constitution, of certain rights, shall not be construed to deny or disparage others retained by the people." That amendment provides added support for the long-debated, but now largely accepted, "right of privacy" that the Supreme Court recognized in such decisions as the famous birth control case of 1965, *Griswold v. Connecticut*. The Ninth

Amendment's simple message is: The text used by the Constitution's authors and ratifiers does not exhaust the values our Constitution recognizes. Perhaps a Twenty-seventh Amendment could convey a parallel and equally simple message: The Technologies familiar to the Constitution's authors and ratifiers similarly do not exhaust the *threats* against which the Constitution's core values must be protected.

The most recent amendment, the twenty-sixth, adopted in 1971, extended the vote to 18-year-olds. It would be fitting, in a world where youth has been enfranchised, for a twenty-seventh amendment to spell a kind of "childhood's end" for constitutional law. The Twenty-seventh Amendment, to be proposed for at least serious debate in 1991, would read simply: "This Constitution's protections for the freedoms of speech, press, petition, and assembly, and its protections against unreasonable searches and seizures and the deprivation of life, liberty, or property without due process of law, shall be construed as fully applicable without regard to the technological method or medium through which information content is generated, stored, altered, transmitted, or controlled."

Driving to the Panopticon: A Philosophical Exploration of the Risks to Privacy Posed by the Highway Technology of the Future

Jeffrey H. Reiman

. . . the major effect of the Panopticon [is] to induce in the inmate a state of conscious and permanent visibility that assures the automatic functioning of power.

Michel Foucault

If we can never be sure whether or not we are being watched and listened to, all our actions will be altered and our very character will change.

Hubert Humphrey

Experience should teach us to be most on our guard to protect liberty when the government's purposes are beneficent.

Louis Brandeis

Jeffrey Reiman, "Driving to the Panopticon: A Philosophical Exploration of the Risks to Privacy Posed by the Highway Technology of the Future," *Santa Clara Computer and High Technology Law Journal* Number 11 (1995): 27–44. Reprinted by permission of the author.

According to the IVHS AMERICA Legal Issues Committee, "IVHS [Intelligent Vehicle-Highway Systems] information systems [will] contain information on where travelers go, the routes they use, and when they travel. This information could be used to disadvantage individuals, and should be secure."[1] This is from a list of what the Privacy Task Group of the Legal Issues Committee calls, interestingly, "'Strawman' Privacy Principles." I hope that my title, "Driving to the Panopticon," indicates to you that I don't regard the threat to privacy posed by Intelligent Vehicle-Highway Systems as a strawman at all. Nor do I think that vague reference to use of information to individuals' disadvantage does any more than begin to hint at the nature of that threat.

The Panopticon was Jeremy Bentham's plan for a prison in which large numbers of convicts could be kept under surveillance by very few guards. The idea was to build the prison cells in a circle around the guard post. All the prisoners would be silhouetted against light coming into the cells from windows on the outside of the circle. Their movements would be visible to a single guard in the center. The French philosopher Michel Foucault used Bentham's Panopticon as an ominous metaphor for the mechanisms of large-scale social control that characterize the modern world.[2] He contended that it became, perhaps subconsciously, the model for institutions in nineteenth-century Europe and America. "Is it surprising," asked Foucault, "that prisons resemble factories, schools, barracks, hospitals, which all resemble prisons?"[3]

As Bentham realized and Foucault emphasized, the system works even if there is no one in the guard house. The very fact of general visibility—being see*able* more than being seen—will be enough to produce effective social control.[4] Indeed, awareness of being visible

makes people the agents of their own subjection. Writes Foucault,

He who is subjected to a field of visibility, and who knows it, assumes responsibility for the constraints of power; he makes them play spontaneously upon himself; he inscribes in himself the power relation in which he simultaneously plays both roles; he becomes the principle of his own subjection.[5]

Foucault went on to stretch the panopticon metaphor beyond architecture to characterize the practices of conventional medicine, psychology and sex education, all of which he thought subject us to increasing social control because they create a world in which the details of our lives become symptoms exposed to a clinical gaze—even if no one is actually looking.[6] I want to stretch the panopticon metaphor yet further, to emphasize not just the way it makes people visible, but the way that it makes them visible *from a single point.*

An intriguing and illuminating feature of the suspicion about the threat to privacy posed by IVHS is that the information that would be accumulated by it is public. Wherever we drive, we drive in the public world, and thus normally subject to unobjectionable public observation. Courts have held that normal observation by police officers in or from public places does not intrude on a person's private affairs. And this has been specifically applied to "the following of an automobile on public streets and highways,"[7] even when the following was done by tracking a beeper planted on an object in the driver's possession. In *U.S. v. Knotts*, the Supreme Court held that "While in [their] vehicles on public roads . . . , [t]he defendants had no privacy interest in what could be visually observed in these public places."[8]

<hr/>

[1] IVHS AMERICA Legal Issues Committee, 'Strawman' Privacy Principles—Comment Form, at 2.

[2] Michel Foucault, *Discipline and Punish: The Birth of the Prison* 195–228 (Alan Sheridan trans., New York: Vintage Books 1979) [Hereinafter Discipline] See p. 200 for a description of the architecture envisioned by Bentham.

[3] Id. at 228.

[4] "[I]t is at once too much and too little that the prisoner should be constantly observed by an inspector: too little, for what matters is that he knows himself to be observed; too much, because he has no need in fact of being so," Discipline, at 201.

[5] Id. at 202–03.

[6] "The panoptic schema . . . was destined to spread throughout the social body: its vocation was to become a generalized functions", Id. at 207; see also 211–16.

[7] *U.S. v. Knotts*, 460 U.S. 276, 281 (1983).

[8] Id.

If there is a threat to privacy from IVHS, it comes from the fact that—as readers of detective fiction well know—by accumulating a lot of disparate pieces of public information, you can construct a fairly detailed picture of a person's private life. You can find out who her friends are, what she does for fun or profit, and from such facts others can be inferred, whether she is punctual, whether she is faithful, and so on. Richard Wasserstrom observes, in an article first published in 1978, that the information already collected in data banks at that time, if gathered together, could produce a "picture of how I had been living and what I had been doing . . . that is fantastically more detailed, accurate, and complete than the one I could supply from my own memory."[9]

There is, then, something to learn about privacy from the sort of threat that IVHS represents: namely, that privacy results not only from locked doors and closed curtains, but also from the way our publicly observable activities are dispersed over space and time. If we direct our privacy-protection efforts at reinforcing our doors and curtains, we may miss the way in which modern means of information collection threaten our privacy by gathering up the pieces of our public lives and making them visible from a single point. This is why the panopticon is a more fitting metaphor for the new threat to privacy than, for example, that old staple, the fishbowl.

But a threat to privacy is only worrisome insofar as privacy is valuable or protects other things that are valuable. No doubt privacy is valuable to people who have mischief to hide, but that is not enough to make it generally worth protecting. However, it is enough to remind us that whatever value privacy has, it also has costs. The more privacy we have, the more difficult it is to get the information that society needs to stop or punish wrongdoers. Moreover, the curtain of privacy that is traditionally brought down around the family has often provided cover for the subjugation and abuse of women and children. Privacy is not a free

lunch. To believe, as I do, that privacy is essential to a free society is to believe that it is worth its costs. But then freedom, itself, is not a free lunch. A free society is a dangerous and often chaotic one. Let us then look at the value of privacy.

By *privacy*, I understand the condition in which other people are deprived of access to either some information about you or some experience of you. For the sake of economy, I will shorten this and say that *privacy is the condition in which others are deprived of access to you*. I include experience alongside information under access, since I think that privacy is about more than information. Your ability to take a shower unwatched is part of your privacy even though watchers may gain no information about you that they didn't already get in their high school biology course. Or, if you think that they might after all gain some information about your particular physiognomy, I would say that it is a matter of privacy that you are able to keep your body unobserved even by people who have already seen it and thus who already have that particular information. This said, I shall primarily speak of the value of privacy regarding information, since it is information about us that will be collected by IVHS.

Note that I have defined privacy in terms of the condition of others' lack of access to you. Some philosophers, for example Charles Fried, have claimed that it is your *control* over who has access to you that is essential to privacy. According to Fried, it would be ironic to say that a person alone on an island had privacy.[10] I don't find this ironic at all. But more importantly, including control as part of privacy leads to anomalies. For example, Fried writes that "in our culture the excretory functions are shielded by more or less absolute privacy, so much so that situations in which this privacy is violated are experienced as extremely distressing."[11] But, in our culture one does not have control over who gets to observe one's performance of the excretory functions, since it is generally prohibited to execute them in

---

[9]Richard Wasserstrom, Privacy: Some Arguments and Assumptions, in *Philosophical Dimensions of Privacy*, 325–26 (Ferdinand Schoeman, ed., 1984) [hereinafter *PDOP*].

[10]Charles Fried, Privacy, in *PDOP*, supra note 9, at 209–10.
[11]Id. at 214.

public.[12] Since prying on someone in the privy is surely a violation of privacy, privacy must be a condition independent of the issue of control.[13]

It's easy to get confused here since there are some private matters in which control is of great importance. For example, we don't simply want to restrict access to our naked bodies, we want to be able to decide who gets to see or touch them. The privy should remind us, however, that cases like these do not exhaust our interest in privacy. To include control in the definition of privacy would restrict our understanding of the value of privacy to only that part of privacy in which control is important—which is precisely the result in Fried's case. He ends up taking privacy to be a value because it gives us a kind of scarce resource (access to ourselves) to distribute. And he claims that our ability to distribute this resource is the key to our ability to have intimate relations.[14] I think that Fried is wrong about intimate relations, since I think that intimate relations are a function of how much people care about each other, not how much they know about each other. One may have an intensely intimate relationship with someone without—or at least before—sharing a lot of private information with them; and one can share private information with one's shrink or priest or even with a stranger on an airplane without thereby having an intimate relationship with them.

If we include control in the definition of privacy we will find the value of the sort of privacy we want in the bedroom, but not of the sort we want in the bathroom. In our bedrooms, we want to have power over who has access to us; in our bathrooms, we just want others deprived of that access. But notice here that the sort of privacy we want in the bedroom presupposes the sort we want in the bathroom. We cannot have discretion over who has access to us in the bedroom unless others lack access at their discretion. In the bathroom, that is all we want. In the bedroom, we want additionally the power to decide at our discretion who does have access. What is common to both sorts of privacy interests, then, is that others not have access to you at their discretion. If we are to find the value of privacy generally, then it will have to be the value of this restriction on others. Sometimes its value will lie precisely in the fact that the restriction leaves room for our own control. But other times it will lie just in that others lack the access. And this is important for our purposes, since the information that IVHS systems will gather is not the sort which it will be terribly important for us to be able to give out at our discretion. It will be information that we simply do not want others to have.

From the definition of privacy just given follows a specific conception of the *right* to privacy. The right to privacy is not my right to control access to me—it is my right that others be deprived of that access.[15] In some cases,

---

[12]If it is said that such prohibition doesn't take away your ability to display such functions, it only ups the cost of doing so, then it will follow that no one has any privacy in his home since crooks can break in even though it is prohibited. On the other hand, it might be objected that I can after all invite someone to watch me perform my excretory functions, and in this sense even the privacy that I have here includes my control over who gets access to me. But to think that this shows that such privacy necessarily includes control, one would have to maintain that if I couldn't invite a witness in to watch (say, because of draconian laws or unfailing taboos against doing so), that would mean that those functions were no longer shielded by privacy—and that sounds quite implausible.

[13]Ruth Gavison gives additional reasons for excluding control from the definition of privacy. Ruth Gavison, Privacy and the Limits of Law, in *PDOP*, supra note 9, at 349–50.

[14]"But intimacy is the sharing of information about one's actions, beliefs, or emotions which one does not share with all, and which one has the right not to share with anyone. By conferring this right, privacy creates the moral capital which we spend in friendship and love" Fried, supra note 10, at 211. I criticize this view in Privacy, Intimacy and Personhood, 6 Philosophy & Public Affairs 26–44(Fall 1976) reprinted in *PDOP*, at 300–16.

[15]It might be objected that, if I have a right that others be deprived of access to me, then I can waive that right, and thus effectively I would have the right to grant individuals access to me. This would bring control back in, not back into the definition of privacy, but into the definition of the right to privacy. But, there are rights that people have but cannot waive in the sense here needed. For example, my right to life is not generally taken as one that I can waive and thereby have a right to stop living; and my right to not be enslaved is not generally taken as one that I can waive and thereby have a right to sell myself into slavery.

though not all, having this right will protect my ability to control access to me.

Having privacy is not the same thing as having a right to privacy. I can have either without the other. I can have privacy without the right to privacy, say, when I successfully conceal my criminal activities. And, I can have a right to privacy and not have privacy, say, when others successfully violate the right.

For there to be a right to privacy, there must be some valid norm that specifies that some personal information about, or experience of, individuals should be kept out of other people's reach. Such norms may be legal. I've already quoted some of the legal norms governing the right to privacy in the United States.[16] If, however, we think that people ought to have others deprived of access to some of their personal affairs whether or not a law says so, then we think that there is (something like) a moral right to privacy. And we will want our laws to protect this moral right by backing it up with an effective legal right. Since I think that IVHS threatens our privacy in ways that go beyond current legal rights, I am concerned to defend a moral right to privacy.

To say that someone has a moral right to privacy doesn't say much unless we know what the scope of that right is, what things or activities a person has a right to keep out of other people's view. For anyone who doesn't live in a cave or in a desert, a completely private life is impossible. Normally, we will think that some things are rightly within the scope of a person's privacy (say, their religious beliefs), and other things (say, the color of their eyes) are not. Often, as cases like *Roe v. Wade*[17] and *Bowers v. Hardwick*[18] show, precisely what should or should not come under the scope of the right to privacy is controversial. As these cases testify, some will argue that citizens of a free society should have as extensive a right to privacy as is compatible with reasonably safe social coexistence, while others will argue that only certain specific areas of people's lives (for example,

bodily processes, intimate relationships, activities relating to the formation of political opinions and plans) should be protected. And, as the tension between current law and fears about IVHS shows, there is disagreement over whether the accumulation of bits of public information should come under the scope of privacy.

To resolve such disagreements, we must get clear on the value of privacy. If we know why having privacy, or, equivalently, having an effective right to privacy, is an especially important and good thing for human beings, we will be able to determine what must come under the scope of privacy for that value to be realized.

To do this, I propose that we imagine together the world in which the full IVHS project is completed, and then see what losses we might suffer as a result of the information about us that would then be gathered. Here it is of great importance that a fully developed IVHS will not exist in an informational vacuum. IVHS's information will exist alongside that provided by other developments already in existence and likely to grow, such as computerization of census and IRS information, computer records of people's credit-card purchases, their bank transactions, their credit histories generally, their telephone calls, their medical conditions, their education and employment histories, and of course the records of their brushes with the law, even of arrests that end in acquittal. Add to this the so-called "information highway" on which we will all soon be riding, with its automatic recording of all interactions, not to mention the FBI's desire to keep it eternally wiretappable.[19] It has been observed, by the way, that as people conduct the business of their daily live's more and more via digital communications, mere knowledge of who people call—knowledge now readily available to police agencies—"would give law enforcers extensive access to people's habits and daily activities."[20]

[16]See notes 7 and 8 above, and accompanying text.

[17]*Roe v. Wade*, 410 U.S. 113 (1973).

[18]*Bowers v. Hardwick*, 478 U.S. 186 (1986).

[19]Interestingly, the "information highway" is the inverted image of IVHS: here the intelligence comes first and then the roadways.

[20]John Schwartz, Industry Fights Wiretap Proposal: Group Says Clinton Plan Would Scare Consumers Off 'Data Highway', *Wash. Post*, Mar. 12, 1994, at C1, C7.

It is this whole complex of information-gathering that I think threatens us. It is this whole complex that, in its potential to make our lives as a whole visible from a single point, brings to mind the panopticon. Accordingly, it is as helping to bring about this whole complex that I shall consider the threat posed by IVHS.

It might seem unfair to IVHS to consider it in light of all this other accumulated information—but I think, on the contrary, that it is the only way to see the threat accurately. The reason is this: We have privacy when we can keep personal things out of the public view. Information-gathering in any particular realm may not seem to pose a very grave threat precisely because it is generally possible to preserve one's privacy by escaping into other realms. Consequently, as we look at each kind of information-gathering in isolation from the others, each may seem relatively benign.[21] However, as each is put into practice, its effect is to close off yet another escape route from public access, so that when the whole complex is in place, its overall effect on privacy will be greater than the sum of the effects of the parts. What we need to know is IVHS's role in bringing about this overall effect, and it plays that role by contributing to the establishment of the whole complex of information-gathering modalities.

I call this whole complex of which IVHS will be a part the *informational panopticon*. It is the risks posed to privacy by the informational panopticon as a whole that I shall explore.

Ride with me, then, into the informational panopticon and consider what we stand to lose if our lives become generally visible. I think that we can characterize the potential risks under four headings: *First*, the risk of extrinsic loss of freedom; *second*, the risk of intrinsic loss of freedom; *third*, symbolic risks; and, *fourth*, the risk of psychopolitical metamorphosis. All these strange titles will become clear in due course. I have given the last category a particularly unwieldy and ugly title precisely because it is the one that I regard as least familiar, most speculative and most ominous. The reference to Kafka is intentional. This said, I should add that these headings are not put forth as airtight metaphysical divisions. They are meant simply to get unruly ideas under control. Like many philosophical categories, they will crumble if pressed too hard. If, however, we see them for what they are, they will give us an orderly picture of the risks that IVHS and the rest of the informational panopticon pose to privacy. But, more, this picture will be just a negative image of the value of privacy.

I.   THE RISK OF EXTRINSIC LOSS OF FREEDOM

By extrinsic loss of freedom, I mean all those ways in which lack of privacy makes people vulnerable to having their behavior controlled by others. Most obviously, this refers to the fact that people who want to do unpopular or unconventional actions may be subject to social pressure in the form of denial of certain benefits, jobs or promotions or membership in formal or informal groups, or even blackmail, if their actions are known to others. And even if they have reason to believe that their actions *may* be known to others and that those others *may* penalize them, this is likely to have a chilling effect on them that will constrain the range of their freedom to act.[22] Remember, it is by inducing the consciousness of visibility that the panopticon, in Foucault's words, "assures the automatic functioning of power."

Ruth Gavison writes, "Privacy . . . prevents interference, pressures to conform, ridicule, punishment, unfavorable decisions, and other forms of hostile reaction. To the extent that privacy does this, it functions to promote liberty of

---

[21]Fried observes in a note that "so long as the mails are still private, wire tapping may not be so severe an imposition, particularly if people do not in any case consider telephone conversations as necessarily private", Fried, supra note 10, at 221 n. 18.

[22]"The usual arguments against wiretapping, bugging, a National Data Center, and private investigators rest heavily on the contingent possibility that a tyrannical government or unscrupulous individuals might misuse them for blackmail or victimization. The more one knows about a person, the greater one's power to damage him", Stanley I. Benn, Privacy, Freedom, and Respect for Persons, in *PDOP*, supra note 9, at 226.

action, removing the unpleasant consequences of certain actions and thus increasing the liberty to perform them."[23] This is not just a matter of the freedom to do immoral or illegal acts. It applies equally to unpopular political actions which have nothing immoral or illegal about them.

Moreover, in a free society, there are actions thought immoral by many or even a majority of citizens that a significant minority thinks are morally acceptable. The preservation of freedom requires that, wherever possible, the moral status of these actions be left to individuals to decide for themselves, and thus that not everything that a majority of citizens thinks is immoral be made illegal. (Think here of pornography, gambling, drunkenness, homosexual or pre- or extramarital heterosexual sex.) If it would be wrong to force people legally to conform to the majority's views on such issues, it will be equally wrong to use harsh social pressure to accomplish the same effect. For this reason, Mill argued in *On Liberty* against both legal enforcement of morality and its informal social enforcement by stigmatization or ostracism.[24]

Mill was not, by the way, against people trying to persuade one another about what is moral. Actually, he thought we should do more of that than we normally do. He distinguished, however, between appeals to reason and appeals to force or its equivalent, harsh informal social penalties. Trying to persuade the minority by making arguments and producing evidence can be done in public forums without pointing fingers, and thus without putting any particular person at risk. Most importantly, it leaves the members of the minority free to make up their own minds.[25] Threatening the minority with stigmatization or ostracism works like force because it changes people's actions by attaching painful consequences to them, without changing their minds at all.

Privacy protects people from the operation of this force, and thus preserves their freedom.

Some may wonder whether the idea that people need privacy to act freely is based on too dim a view of human character. Those who raise this doubt think that people with strong characters will be able to resist social pressure, and thus only those with weak characters need dark private corners in order to act freely. In different ways, this objection can be raised against all the risks to privacy that I shall describe, and so I want to give a general answer to it. The answer has three parts:

First, laws and social practices generally have to be designed for the real people that they will govern, not for some ideal people that we would like to see or be. Just as Madison observed that if people were angels we wouldn't need government at all,[26] so we might add that if people were heroes we wouldn't need privacy at all. Since people are neither angels nor (except in a few instances) heroes, we need both government and privacy.

Second, just because people are not angels, some will be tempted to penalize those who act unconventionally. Even if people should ideally be able to withstand social pressure in the form of stigmatization or ostracism, it remains unjust that they should suffer these painful fates simply for acting in unpopular or unconventional ways. In any actual society we will need privacy to prevent this injustice.

Third, suppose we wanted to make our citizens into the sorts of strong-willed people who could resist social pressures. We would still have to give them experience in formulating their own judgments and in acting upon those judgments. And this experience will have to be given to them before they have the strong characters we hope them to attain. They will have to be sheltered from the pressures toward social conformity while they are still vulnerable, in order to become the sorts of people who are not vulnerable. They will need privacy in order to become the sorts of people who don't

---

[23]Gavison, supra note 13, at 363–64.

[24]John Stuart Mill, *On Liberty* 9 (Hackett Publishing Company, 1978; originally published in 1859), inter alia.

[25]It also forces the majority to test its own beliefs in the open court of public discussion.

[26]Federalist No. 51(James Madison).

need it.[27] Much as Mill felt that liberty was a school for character,[28] so too is privacy. And, since this school must provide continuing education for adults as well as for children, we will need privacy as an abiding feature of the society. In short, the vast majority of actual people need privacy for free action, and those who do not will need privacy to become that way. With or without heroes, we will need privacy.

II. THE RISK OF INTRINSIC LOSS OF FREEDOM

By intrinsic loss of freedom, I point to ways in which denial of privacy limits people's freedom directly, independently of the ways in which it makes them susceptible to social pressure or penalties. Put differently, I want here to suggest that privacy is not just a means of protecting freedom, it is itself constitutive of freedom in a number of important ways.

To start, recall the discussion about the place of control in the definition of privacy.[29] I concluded there that control is not part of privacy, but in some cases it is part of what privacy makes possible. For me to be able to decide who touches my body, or who knows the details of my personal history, those things must be generally not accessible to others at their discretion. That means that if those things are not shielded by privacy, I am automatically denied certain important choices. This is what I mean by an intrinsic loss of freedom. I am not here denied the choices by fear of certain consequences; I am denied them directly because privacy is the condition of their being choices for me in the first place.

Another intrinsic loss of freedom is the following. A number of writers have emphasized the ways in which some actions have a different nature when they are observed than they do when they are not.[30] This is clearest in cases that are distant from IVHS: Criticizing an individual in front of others is a different act than uttering the same critical words to him in private. And, of course, making love before an audience is something quite different from the same act done in private. In the case of our informational panopticon the alteration is more subtle. Every act, say, driving to destination X at time T, is now a more complex event: It now becomes driving to X at T and *creating a record of driving to X at T*. These differ from one another as leaving a message on someone's answering machine differs from rehearsing the same words in one's imagination. If my every driving act (not to mention all the other acts visible in the informational panopticon) is also the depositing of a record, not only are my acts changed, but my freedom is limited: I am no longer free to do the act of simply driving to X at T *without leaving a record*.

With this, I lose as well the freedom of acting spontaneously. In a society which collected data on all of an individual's transactions, Richard Wasserstrom writes,

> one would be both buying a tank of gas and leaving a part of a systematic record of where one was on that particular date. One would not just be applying for life insurance; one would also be recording in a permanent way one's health on that date and a variety of other facts about oneself. No matter how innocent one's intentions and actions at any given moment . . . persons would think more carefully before they did things that would become part of the record. Life would to this degree become less spontaneous and more measured.[31]

---

[27]"[P]rivacy also contributes to learning, creativity and autonomy by insulating the individual against ridicule and censure at early stages of groping and experimentation," Gavison, supra note 13, at 364.

[28]"He who lets the world, or his own portion of it, choose his plan of life for him has no need of any other faculty than the ape-like one of imitation. He who chooses his plan for himself employs all his faculties", Mill, *On Liberty* 56.

[29]See notes 10 through 15 above, and accompanying text.

[30]"The observer makes the act impossible . . . in the sense that the actor now sees it in a different light", Benn, supra note 22, at 226. "Aware of the observer, I am engaged in part in viewing or imagining what is going on from his or her perspective. I thus cannot lose myself as completely in the activity", Wasserstrom, supra note 9, at 324. See also, the sensitive discussion in Robert S. Gerstein, Intimacy and Privacy, in *PDOP*, supra note 9, at 265–71.

[31]Wasserstrom, supra note 9, at 328.

When you know you are being observed, you naturally identify with the outside observer's viewpoint, and add that alongside your own viewpoint on your action. This double vision makes your act different, whether the act is making love or taking a drive. The targets of the panopticon know and feel the eye of the guard on them, making their actions different than if they were done in private. Their repertoire of possible actions diminishes as they lose those choices whose intrinsic nature depends on privacy.

III.   SYMBOLIC RISKS

Elsewhere I have argued that privacy is a social ritual by which we show one another that we regard each person as the owner of herself, her body, her thoughts.[32] It is for this reason that privacy is generally absent from organizations like monasteries, armies, communist cells and madhouses, where individuals are thought to belong to some larger whole or greater purpose. This is also why invasions of privacy are wrong even when they don't pose any risk to reputation or freedom, even when the invader will not use what he observes in any harmful way, even when the individual is unaware that her privacy is being invaded. Aside from any harms that invasions of privacy threaten, such invasions are, in addition, *insults*. They slight an individual's ownership of himself, and thus insult him by denying his special dignity. The peeping tom treats his prey with unmerited, and thus unjust, contempt.

Privacy conveys to the individual his self-ownership precisely by the knowledge that the individual gains of his ability and his authority to withdraw himself from the scrutiny of others. Those who lose this ability and authority are thereby told that they don't belong to themselves; they are specimens belonging to those who would investigate them.[33] They are

someone else's data. It is no accident that the panopticon was a design for a prison, an institution which in effect suspends a person's ownership of himself because he committed a crime. And since our informational panopticon effectively suspends self-ownership though no crime has been committed, it conveys an unmerited, and thus unjust, insult.

I said earlier that I wanted to emphasize the way in which the panopticon makes our lives visible from a single point. Here it is worth noting that that point is outside of us, where the guardian stands. The panopticon symbolizes a kind of draining of our individual sovereignty away and outside of us into a single center. We become its data to observe at its will—our outsides belong to its inside rather than to our own.

I have called this a symbolic risk because it affects us as a kind of message, a message inscribed in an institutional structure. We are not deprived of our self-ownership in the way that slaves are deprived permanently or the way that prisoners are deprived temporarily. Rather, the arrangement of the institution broadcasts a image of us, to us, as beings lacking the authority to withdraw ourselves from view. It conveys the loss of self-ownership to us by announcing that our every move is fitting data for observation by others. As a symbolic message, it insults rather than injures.

But, of course, what is symbolic is almost never merely symbolic. By such symbols do we come to acquire our self-conceptions. They shape the way we identify ourselves to ourselves and to one another, and thus they shape our identities themselves. Growing up in the informational panopticon, people will be less likely to acquire selves that think of themselves as owning themselves. They will say *mine* with less authority, and *yours* with less respect. And I think that selves that think of themselves as owning themselves are precisely what we understand as "moral selves." They are selves that naturally accept ownership of their actions and

---

[32]Jeffrey Reiman, Privacy, Intimacy, and Personhood, *Phil. & Pub. Aff.* 26–44 (1976), reprinted in *PDOP*, supra note 9, at 300–16.

[33]"A man whose home may be entered at the will of another, whose conversation may be overheard at the will of another, whose marital and familial intimacies may be

---

overseen at the will of another, is less of a man, has less human dignity, on that account." Edward J. Bloustein, Privacy As an Aspect of Human Dignity: An Answer to Dean Prosser, in *PDOP*, supra note 9, at 165.

thus responsibility for them. They naturally insist on ownership of their destinies and thus on the right to choose their own way. Here the loss of privacy threatens an incalculable loss. What will it be worth if a man should gain the world but lose his soul?

IV. THE RISK OF PSYCHO-POLITICAL METAMORPHOSIS

The risk just discussed is not that we shall lose something we now enjoy, but that we will become something different than we currently are, something less noble, less interesting, less worthy of respect. This is the fear expressed in the quote from Hubert Humphrey.[34] What I shall say now continues in this vein.

The film *Demolition Man* portrays a future society characterized by wide-spread information gathering, including a full IVHS system. However, to me, the most interesting feature of the film is that the denizens of the society depicted there speak, and thus seem to think, in a way that can only be described as childish. They have an oversimplified way of labeling things and experiences, and appear to have a repertoire of responses that is limited in number and nuance. Their emotional lives are, you might say, reduced to the primary colors, without shade or tone, disharmony or ambiguity. I want to suggest that this is a product of the informational panopticon in which they live. Total visibility infantilizes people. It impoverishes their inner life and makes them more vulnerable to oppression from without.

There is already a widely recognized correlation between privacy and adulthood. But it is normally understood in the reverse direction: The less mature a person is the less privacy he gets, and he gets more privacy as he moves toward adulthood. I want to suggest that this is a two-way street. The deprivation of privacy stunts maturity, keeps people suspended in a childish state.

How does this happen? Consider the words of Edward Bloustein, President of Rutgers University:

The man who is compelled to live every minute of his life among others and whose every need, thought, desire, fancy or gratification is subject to public scrutiny, has been deprived of his individuality and human dignity. Such an individual merges with the mass. His opinions, being public, tend always to be conventionally accepted ones; his feelings, being openly exhibited, tend to lose their quality of unique personal warmth and to become the feelings of every man. Such a being, although sentient, is fungible; he is not an individual.[35]

But this is only the beginning. Consider the process and where it leads: To the extent that a person experiences himself as subject to public observation, he naturally experiences himself as subject to public review. As a consequence, he will tend to act in ways that are publicly acceptable. People who are shaped to act in ways that are publicly acceptable will tend to act in safe ways, to hold and express and manifest the most widely-accepted views, indeed, the lowest-common denominator of conventionality.[36] (Think here of the pressure that TV sponsors exercise against anything unconventional, in their fear of offending any segment of the purchasing population.) But, thought and feeling follow behavior. (Pascal said: "Kneel down, move your lips in prayer, and you will believe.")[37] Trained by society to act conventionally at all times, people will come so to think and so to feel. Their inner lives will be impoverished to the extent that their outer lives are subject to observation. Infiltrated by social convention, their emotions and reactions will become simpler, safer, more predictable, less nuanced, more interchangeable. This much is noted by Bloustein, but I think the process goes further.

As the inner life that is subject to social convention grows, the still deeper inner life that is separate from social convention contracts and,

---

[34]Hubert H. Humphrey, Forward to Edward V. Long, *The Intruders*, at viii (New York, 1967).

[35]Bloustein, supra note 33, at 188.

[36]"In the absence of privacy we would dare less, because all our failures would be on record," Gavison, supra note 13, at 364.

[37]This is attributed to Pascal, without citation. Louis Althusser, *Lenin and Philosophy* (B. Brewster trans., 1971).

given little opportunity to develop, remains primitive. Likewise, as more and more of your inner life is made sense of from without, the need to make your own sense out of your inner life shrinks. You lose both the practice of making your own sense out of your deepest and most puzzling longings, and the potential for self-discovery and creativity that lurk within a rich inner life. Your inner emotional life is impoverished, and your capacity for evaluating and shaping it is stunted.

Thus will be lost—and this is the most ominous possibility of all—the inner personal core that is the source of criticism of convention, of creativity, rebellion and renewal. To say that people who suffer this loss will be easy to oppress doesn't say enough. They won't have to be oppressed, since there won't be anything in them that is tempted to drift from the beaten path or able to see beyond it. They will be the "one-dimensional men" that Herbert Marcuse feared.[38] The art of such people will be insipid decoration, and their politics fascist.

Here, I think, we reach something deep and rarely noted about the liberal vision—something that shows the profound link between liberalism and privacy, and between those two and democracy. The liberal vision is guided by the ideal of the autonomous individual, the one who acts on principles which she has accepted after critical review rather than simply absorbing them unquestioned from outside.[39] Moreover, the liberal stresses the importance of people making sense of their own lives, and of having authority over the sense of those lives. All this requires a kind of space in which to reflect on and entertain beliefs, and to experiment with them—*a private space*.

Deeper still, however, the liberal vision has an implicit trust in the transformational and ameliorative possibilities of private inner life. Without this, neither democracy nor individual freedom have worth. Unless people can

form their own views, democratic voting becomes mere ratification of conventionality, and individual freedom mere voluntary conformity.[40] And, unless, in forming their own views, people can find within themselves the resources for better views, neither democracy nor individualism can be expected to improve human life.

This concludes my catalogue of the risks posed by loss of privacy. As I suggested earlier, the risks give us a negative image of the value to us of maintaining privacy. I can sum up that value as: the protection of freedom, moral personality, and a rich and critical inner life. If IVHS endangers these values, then we will have to bring the heretofore public information about travel on public streets under the scope of privacy.

But that is just the beginning of what is necessary. Here we should remember Bentham's and Foucault's recognition that the panopticon works even if no one is in the guard house. The risks that are posed by the informational panopticon come not from being seen, but from the knowledge that one is visible. And this means that protecting ourselves from the risks I have described will be harder than we might imagine.

Consider that privacy can be protected in two ways, which I shall call, respectively, the formal conditions of privacy and the material conditions. By the *formal* conditions of privacy, I mean generally the rules that either specifically give one a right to privacy or that have a similar effect (such as conventions of modesty or reserve, of appropriate levels of curiosity or prying). Such rules might be legal or customary or moral, or some combination of these. By the *material* conditions of privacy, I mean physical realities that hinder others in gathering information about or experiences of you,

---

[38]Herbert Marcuse, *One-Dimensional Man* (Beacon Press. 1964).

[39]See Benn, supra note 22, at 241 for a statement of this ideal and a discussion of its relation to privacy.

[40]"Part of the justification for majority rule and the right to vote is the assumption that individuals should participate in political decisions by forming judgments and expressing preferences. Thus, to the extent that privacy is important for autonomy, it is important for democracy as well," Gavison, supra note 13, at 369–70.

things like locks, fences, doors, curtains, isolation and distance.

It should be clear that one might have formal conditions without the material, and that the formal conditions might be effective without the material being in place. For example, people packed like sardines in a rush-hour subway train have a way of respecting each other's privacy even though they have, materially, extensive access to one another's bodies. On the other hand, one can have the material conditions of privacy without the formal, and the material conditions might be effective without the formal being in place. For example, after my students are duly shocked by Hobbes' defense of absolute political authority,[41] I remind them that, when Hobbes wrote, it took about a week to travel from the west coast of England to the east coast, and about two weeks from north coast to south.[42] An absolute sovereign in Hobbes' time, without any formal constraints, surely had less actual ability to invade his subjects' lives than, say, a contemporary U.S. president, even with all our constitutional safeguards.

That constitutional safeguards can be and have been ignored by the powerful bears a lesson for us: Material conditions of privacy more reliably prevent invasions of privacy than formal conditions can. Material conditions have a kind of toughness that the formal conditions never can match. Thus, formal conditions of privacy can never fully guarantee protection of privacy when the material conditions for invading privacy are at hand. The material conditions for invading privacy are a kind of power, and power is always tempting, often corrupting, and, to paraphrase Lord Acton, the more power there is the more corrupting it is likely to be.

This is important because the accumulation of detailed information about people's goings and comings is a material condition for invading privacy. What's more, the continued and increasing amassing of this and all the other sorts of information that make up the informational panopticon seems to me to be inevitable. This is for the simple reason that, as with IVHS, all of the elements of the informational panopticon serve good purposes and can and will be put in place with the best of intentions. Here we should remember Louis Brandeis's warning, quoted at the outset, and watch out for threats of liberty dressed in beneficent intentions. The existence of all this collected information and of the technical ability to bring these different records together will add up to an enormous capacity to amass detailed portraits of people's lives—in short, material conditions for invasion of privacy on unheard-of scale. One has to be very optimistic indeed about the power of rules, to think that formal guarantees of privacy will protect us. And, to the extent that we are not so optimistic, we will experience ourselves as visible even if we are not being observed, which will bring in its train all the risks earlier described.

To the extent that the material conditions for our virtually total visibility come ineluctably into place in the years ahead, we will need not only to prevent the misuse of information *but to prevent the fear that it is being misused.* That is the lesson of the Panopticon. We will have to protect people not only from being seen but from feeling visible. Thus, we will need more than ever before to teach and explain the importance of privacy, so that respect for it becomes second nature, and violation of it repugnant. And, of course, we will need more than ever to make sure that our fellows are complying with the formal rules that protect privacy. If we are going to protect privacy in the informational panopticon, we're really going to have to keep an eye on one another!

[41]Thomas Hobbes, *Leviathan* (Prometheus Books, 1988) (1651).

[42]J. Crofts, *Packhorse, Waggon and Post: Land Carriage and Communications Under the Tudors and Stuarts* 84–88, 122–24, 141–142 (Routledge and Kegan Paul, 1967); and Sidney and Beatrice Webb, *The Story of the King's Highway* 62–84, (Vol. V of English Local Government)(Archon Books, 1963)(1913). I am indebted to my colleague Terence Murphy of the American University Department of History for these references.

Megan's Law and the Protection of the Child in the On-Line Age

Professor Nadine Strossen v. Professor Ernie Allen
Moderated by Mr. Walter Pincus

Robert Kwak: Thank you. My name is Robert Kwak and I'm the Executive Editor of the *American Criminal Law Review*. On behalf of the Journal let me also welcome our distinguished speakers, students, faculty, and members of the administration to our annual debate, this year entitled "Megan's Law and the Protection of the Child in the On-Line Age."

Ernie Allen is the co-founder, president, and CEO of the National Center for Missing & Exploited Children. Based in Arlington, the National Center is a private, non-profit organization which has aided in the recovery of close to thirty-nine thousand missing and abducted children. In addition, his organization helps to train local law enforcement to combat child abduction and exploitation, operate the child pornography tip line in cooperation with the United States Postal Service, and has recently established the Cyber Tip Line, allowing individuals to report incidents of child pornography and sexual exploitation through current on-line services.

Prior to his current post, Mr. Allen worked in public service in his native Kentucky as Director of Public Health and Safety for the city of Louisville, and Director of the Louisville Jefferson County Crime Commission. Mr. Allen, a graduate of the University of Louisville and the University of Louisville School of Law is a member of the Kentucky Bar. In addition to teaching

Nadine Strossen and Ernie Allen (debate), "Megan's Law and the Protection of the Child in the On-Line Age," *American Criminal Law Review* Volume 35 Number 4, (1998): 1319–1341. Reprinted with permission of the publisher, Georgetown University and *American Criminal Law Review*. © 1998. (Some introductory remarks and procedure instructions have been deleted.)

at his alma mater, he has held faculty positions at the University of Kentucky, Indiana University, and has served as visiting faculty at Northeastern and the University of Wisconsin. We are honored to have him here today.

Debating against Mr. Allen is Ms. Nadine Strossen, President of the American Civil Liberties Union. Founded in 1920, the ACLU is considered the nation's foremost advocate of individual rights. It has been involved in some of the most famous and infamous litigation in our nation's history, including the *Scopes* anti-evolution case, the forced relocation of Japanese-Americans during World War II, and most recently in overturning the Communications Decency Act. Ms. Strossen was elected to her current position with the ACLU in 1991 after serving as general counsel to the organization since 1986.

In addition to her duties at the ACLU, she is a professor of law at New York Law School, where she teaches constitutional law and international human rights. She is the author of numerous articles and books, including *Defending Pornography: Free Speech, Sex, and the Fight for Women's Rights*. A native of Minneapolis, Professor Strossen graduated with high honors from Harvard Law School, where she was an editor of the *Law Review*.

Finally, our moderator today is Walter Pincus, senior correspondent for the *Washington Post*. In his four decades in journalism he has worked for a variety of major newspapers, television networks, and has served as the Executive Editor for the *New Republic*. Mr. Pincus has covered some of the most important stories of the last half of the twentieth century for the *Washington Post*, including the Watergate hearings, the hostage crisis in Iran, the Iran-Contra Affair, and the Aldridge Ames espionage case. In 1981 he received an

Emmy for writing on a CBS News documentary series on defense of the United States.

In addition to his responsibility as a journalist, Mr. Pincus serves as a consultant to the Washington Post Corporation, where he's helping to steer the newspaper into the non-print ventures of television and the World Wide Web. A graduate of Yale University, Mr. Pincus is currently a student here at Georgetown in the Law Center's evening division. It is a pleasure to have all three participants join us today and, without further ado, I turn the lectern over to Mr. Walter Pincus.

Walter Pincus: In late July of 1994 a seven-year old New York girl named Megan Kanka was abducted, raped, and murdered by a twice-convicted sex offender who, unknown to her parents, lived just across the street with two other men who had been convicted of sex offenses. Public outrage about Megan's murder was immediate, intense, and inevitably political. Within two weeks New Jersey's governor and the State General Assembly were considering bills for registration and community notification. By October, the Governor had signed the registration and community notification laws, which had quickly passed both the State Senate and General Assembly.

The horror of the event had been carried into every home in the country, by television, by radio, and by print. The resultant fear within every household with young children created a political wildfire. Similar laws were rapidly passed in other states, so that by the time the first court challenge to Megan's Law reached New Jersey's courts in 1996, forty-nine states, according to a recent *Washington Post* article, had adopted similar sex offender registration laws, and thirty-seven had maintained some form of community notification program.

Congress had its own version, which President Clinton signed in May of 1996. Last year, the Third Circuit Court of Appeals rejected arguments that Megan's Law violated constitutional guarantees against double jeopardy and ex post facto punishment. Registration and notification were approved. One court decision said the danger of recidivism requires a system of registration which will permit law enforcement

officials to identify previous offenders and alert the public, when necessary, for public safety. It rejected the notion that the law was punitive against convicted sex offenders. The dissenting judge, however, said it was punitive, notwithstanding the Legislature's subjective intent to the contrary. Early this year the Supreme Court refused to hear an appeal on the New Jersey decisions. So Megan's Law as passed, and modified by court decisions, is enforced.

We hope today through discussion and debate, to allow you to understand the pros and cons of the laws, as well as the conflicts inherent in the implementation of them. These are untested laws. They exist in widely different forms throughout the country, but they were put together out of honest fears.

Not for the first time in our history will laws reduce the rights of some—in this case, the over one hundred seventy-five thousand classified as sexual offenders—in the name of protecting others. We'll focus on various forms of notification adopted in jurisdictions around the country, including not only distribution of handbills, law enforcement announcements, publication of notices, but the newer techniques of CD-ROM, the Internet, and 900 telephone numbers.

Megan's Law statutes have been justified as a necessary means of protecting the public from a group of individuals who may be likely to repeat their crimes. These laws have also been attacked as a way to continue punishing offenders after they've served their sentences. What do you say is the purpose of Megan's Law? Do these laws protect the public or punish offenders?

Ernie Allen: Mr. Pincus, these laws protect the public. That is their purpose. They are not punitive; they are regulatory. We are dealing with a category of offenders who represent the highest risk to the community, and particularly, to the most vulnerable sections of the community.

Let me try to provide a little perspective. Megan's Law is one element of comprehensive state sex offender policy. That policy includes aggressive enforcement, prosecution, meaningful sentencing, treatment as a matter of opportunity, not right, and then follow-up in the community for these released offenders. Follow-up includes registration for all convicted offenders and notification for the most serious of those offenders.

Now, a question I suppose one could ask is "why sex offenders?" Well, our view is that sex offenders are different. We would not support, and do not support such approaches and such legislation for auto thieves or bad check artists, but sex offenders are different. Sex offenders create enormous fear among the public. The nature of their act conveys a kind of psychological menace or harm. Sex offenders prey upon the most vulnerable segments of our population.

The majority of the victims of America's sex offenders are kids, and research has shown that a significant subset of the sex offender population represents the highest risk of reoffense. They are coming back into our communities. Therefore, is it not appropriate that government, as an exercise of its legitimate public purpose of maintaining public health and safety, should provide that extra measure of protection to communities, to people at risk?

Now, the concept is simple, and the numbers have evolved since that *Washington Post* article. Today, fifty states have sex offender registry laws requiring every convicted sex offender to register their presence in the community with local law enforcement. Today, forty-five states have enacted some version of community notification, or Megan's Law. It is our view that these laws are not punitive. Criminal history is already public record. However, historically, the public's not been able to get to it and doesn't know to ask for it. This is a legitimate exercise of state power. There is no question that there is some invasion of that convicted sex offender's privacy, but it's important for people to understand that only the most serious offenders are subjected to the broadest kind of public and community notification.

The standard in the model statutes that are being enacted across the country is that offenders are assessed based upon their level of risk. With every offender required to register with law enforcement, only the most serious offender is subject to community notification. We believe there is a rational basis for such distinctions and that these laws are regulatory and not punitive. Any stigma that flows from this notification is a product not of the registration and notification, but of the criminal offenses for which these offenders have been convicted. Megan's Law's purpose is to protect, not to punish.

Nadine Strossen: Well, certainly the purpose of all *criminal* laws is also to protect, and I think it's very interesting that Mr. Allen has stressed the fact that these laws we're discussing apply to convicted offenders. That is precisely the basis for singling them out. I think it's an exercise in legal fiction to label as "non-punitive" a law that clearly has a punitive effect—imposing a mark of Cain or a scarlet letter upon one selected group of offenders who have served out their time, let me emphasize that.

Such a law is inconsistent with a whole range of constitutional guarantees, including the prohibition against ex post facto or retroactive punishments and double jeopardy. The reason why advocates of these laws strain so mightily to put the label "regulatory" upon them is precisely to escape the constitutional guarantees that go with our criminal justice process.

Now, I want to stress, these are people who have committed very serious crimes. The appropriate way to deal with those crimes is to prosecute them, to punish them to the full extent of the law. If we feel that they need additional punishment, or if we feel that they need additional treatment or rehabilitation, that has to be done within the context of the criminal justice system.

I have to emphasize, I don't think we have to make a trade-off here between the constitutionally-guaranteed rights of all citizens, including those who are convicted of crimes, on the one hand, and protecting our communities and our children, on the other hand. One of the reasons why the ACLU objects to these laws is we think they are as ineffective as they are unconstitutional. They give the community a false sense of security; they divert resources away from constructive measures, measures such as those that are pursued by Mr. Allen's organization to actually prevent and educate in a more meaningful sense.

Walter Pincus: If I can pick it up from there, if you say the idea of community notification doesn't work, that there is a perception that there's a high risk with these people in the community, what's your formula for protecting people with children?

Nadine Strossen: You say there's a perception of a high risk of reoffense, and I'm glad you used the word "perception," because public perception and political statements about the likelihood of reoffense have been grossly exaggerated. The National Center for Institutions and Alternatives has recently released a study that reviews the meta-analyses that have been done of recidivism rates. The recidivism rates of sex offenders are actually quite low, and lower than those of any offenders other than murder. I say that because we are going down a slippery slope here. If the rationale that is asserted for imposing additional punishments on sex offenders, including registration and prolonged incarceration, if those rationales are based on a notion of likelihood or possibility of committing crimes again, then I think we are talking about a radical change in our entire criminal justice system.

Now, what do I propose we do that would provide meaningful and constitutionally acceptable protection for our communities, which they certainly deserve? One approach is, as I already indicated, to use the criminal justice system. There is no reason why legislatures cannot extend the amount of incarceration, cannot enact habitual offender statutes so that repeat offenders would be subject to longer incarceration.

Most importantly, the professionals who work with sex offenders have argued that there are many treatment modalities that offer great promise. Unfortunately, only a tiny percentage of people who are convicted of sex offenses now are receiving any kind of treatment or rehabilitation while they are incarcerated. You know, to release them to the community and to say, "Well, we're going to warn you about this person who is still dangerous, but we're not going to do anything to treat that person, either within prison or outside of prison," that's like just telling the community that we've got a poisoned water supply. We're notifying you about it, but we're not doing anything to deal with the underlying harm.

So, that's what I would say in terms of the perpetrators—let's treat them, let's incarcerate them, but let's not pretend that we are releasing them and then in fact continue life-long punishment in one fashion or another.

From the perspective of children and others in our society, how do we meaningfully protect them? Unfortunately, it's not by notifying them of the tiny percentage of sex offenders who have actually been convicted and released. Every study shows, sadly, tragically, that about eighty percent of all sex offenses, including against children, are committed not by strangers, not by people who have been convicted and released, but rather by people who have never been arrested or prosecuted, and who are even within their own families. Unfortunately, it is a sad reality that if we want our children to be safe, we have to educate them about the dangers of sex abuse, we have to warn them against contact, unwanted contact, with every adult, including those—indeed, particularly those—that they know and trust.

And here is something where I know from having read information from Mr. Allen's fine organization: they agree. They have argued that it gives a false sense of security to focus on stranger danger rather than comprehensive programs of educating all children and all parents, through the homes and through the schools, about exercising caution when dealing with any adult, regardless of whether you have been specifically warned about that particular person.

Ernie Allen: Let me briefly rebut. I agree with a lot of that. Certainly I agree with the premise that the stranger danger aspect is a myth, and you are right, Professor Strossen. However, it's important to note that even though seventy to ninety percent of those who prey upon children are not strangers in the eye and the mind of the child, neither are they necessarily family members. HHS research established that only one-third to one-half of sexual abuse cases against girls are perpetrated by family members and only ten to twenty percent of those against boys. Jesse Timmendequas was not a pure stranger to Megan Kanka. He was her neighbor. This whole premise of the risk to kids from people they know is one of the key reasons why Megan's Law is so important. It's one of the key reasons why we need to know the people who are coming into day-care centers and working in schools and living on the block.

Second, and I don't mean to get into a statistical quarrel, but let me respond briefly on the issue of recidivism and on the issue of extent of the problem. Justice Department data indicate that six out of every ten convicted child molesters has a prior conviction, prior history. One out of every four has a history of violent sexual offenses. Forty-eight percent of convicted sex offenders in America's prisons will be arrested for a felony or serious misdemeanor within three years of their release. Of the quarter of a million sex offenders currently under the care and control of correctional agencies in the United States, sixty percent of them today are in the community, and virtually all of them are coming back to the community. The reality is Megan's Law is not a panacea. But don't we owe that little extra measure of protection and information to families potentially faced with an offender who could represent a threat to them and their child and their community? Again, Megan's Law focuses only on the most serious risks, not on everybody.

Walter Pincus: States define "sex offender" in various ways. For example, under some state statutes "sex offender" is defined as any individual who commits sexual assault or endangers the welfare of the child. Other statutes include within their definition individuals convicted of consensual sodomy. Who should define what offenders are covered by Megan's Law? What should the definition be?

Ernie Allen: Mr. Pincus, the answer to who should define it is the legislative body of each individual state, under our Tenth Amendment premise of leaving those decisions to them. Now, we share the concerns and the implications of your question. I think it's important to understand that Megan's Law is new law. Most states have enacted these statutes within the past two years, and one of the great problems, as you indicated in your introductory remarks, is the lack of uniformity.

We, as an organization, are working very hard to try to bring about greater uniformity and greater consistency from state to state. There are federal guidelines. Congress provides guidelines for states in terms of what the covered offenses should be. And clearly we think those offenses should be proscribed sexual offenses

against children, including kidnapping and false imprisonment, criminal sexual conduct, solicitation of a minor for a sexual performance, for prostitution and rape and those offenses that speak to sexually-violent predators.

However, even with those kinds of statutory inconsistencies and the current problems we face, I think it's important to focus on the processes that are developing and that a lot of us are arguing need to be in place. For example, there are some model states, Minnesota is one, Washington State is one, that have established levels of risk. That process begins with an end-of-sentence review panel in which a multi-disciplinary group of professionals, including corrections and mental health professionals, take a look at the totality of the issues affecting this particular offender.

They look at his prior history. They look at the nature of the offenses, the age of his victims, any violence associated with it. They look at the prospects and the risks associated with reoffense. They look at offender characteristics, whether he has participated in treatment, how he's performed in prison. They look at whether he has community supports and resources, whether he has neighborhood or family or other kinds of employment prospects when he gets out. They look at what he says, and an astounding, an alarming number of these offenders say, "Yeah, if you let me go, I may do it again; I'm not sure I can control my behavior." They look at personal traits and characteristics like age and whether he has debilitating illnesses that affect that release decision.

Based upon that process, and this is one that we think ought to be in place across America, they make a judgment, they assign a rating that determines this offender's level of risk. The low-risk offenders are subject only to the registration requirement. They register their presence with law enforcement in that community. The moderate-risk offenders are subject to notification only in a very targeted way: to schools, to community organizations, but not in a public sense. And only the highest risk, or level three offenders, are subject to the broadest kind of notification.

We think that is a model that works. All sex offenders are not alike. It's a way to minimize the potential intrusion on a sex offender's privacy.

And my response to your question, Mr. Pincus, in the circumstance that you cite in which consenting adult statutes would be included on this list under this process is that, it is virtually inconceivable that community notification would be made in such a case.

We'd like to see greater uniformity. We don't see the need for those kinds of statutes to be in play. But even with them, these processes are very unlikely to intrude on the individual privacy of those offenders, other than requiring them to register with law enforcement.

Walter Pincus: If I can add one point to that, New Jersey has registration every three months for fifteen years. Is that a rational approach?

Ernie Allen: I think one of the risks is we don't want to create such a massive bureaucracy that the bureaucracy impedes on common sense. I think every three months is probably too frequent.

Now, let me say we think, frankly, that the California registration law has some merit, which is a lifetime registration law. Most of the new laws are ten-year requirements for registration with the potential to challenge or revisit. The reason we think that's so important is that recidivism and treatment research indicates that for a certain category of offender, for the traditional pedophile offender, this is a life-long problem. They may not re-offend periodically, but treatment research shows that even when an offender is caught and prosecuted at a youthful age and treated, there is still a propensity for that behavior to appear far later in life.

Nadine Strossen: Well, that shows the ongoing importance of treatment, and it seems to me by branding somebody as a pariah, you are very likely—as all mental health organizations have pointed out in testifying against this law—you are very likely to drive that person away from treatment, away from the kind of family support structure, away from the kind of job support structure that is most likely to increase that person's chances of reintegrating productively into society.

I think it's quite ironic that Mr. Allen cites the three states that he mentioned as models of how this process of supposedly selecting the most dangerous offenders is working. The three states he mentioned are California, Minnesota, and Washington. The actual experiences in those states, I think, afford us no ground for celebration in terms of human rights—and that means both the human rights of the convicted offender who has served his time and the human right to safety for the rest of us.

Take California, for example. In California, for the first two years that its revamped version of Megan's Law was in effect (I say "revamped" because California has had sex offender registration since the 1940s), it was enforced upon everybody who had ever been convicted of any sex offense, including consensual sodomy between adults, including statutory rape, at a time that the laws on those subjects were still in effect, even though those acts are not crimes now. People who were convicted back in the 1940s and 50s, including in sting operations against gay men, have had to register and have been subject to community notification. Many of them have had their lives destroyed, their marriages destroyed, and finally came to the ACLU. Fortunately, we were able to persuade the California legislature to amend the law.

But that's not an aberration. The Third Circuit case that's been alluded to from New Jersey involved a man named Alexander Artway. His conviction was for having consensual sodomy with an adult woman. At the time that had happened, many years ago, that was a crime in New Jersey. So, you know, it reminds me a little bit of Justice Potter Stewart's famous epigram about pornography: "I may not be able to define it, but I know it when I see it." Well, these states are each seeing a different "it" in terms of sexual offenses that they consider so heinous and so dangerous that they are subjecting people who were convicted of those crimes—including many, many years ago—to lifelong registration and notification procedures.

In terms of being able to predict who is the most dangerous, the professional literature indicates that even the best trained experts are wrong most of the time, more than fifty percent of the time. Worse yet, in New Jersey, for example, it is the prosecutor who is deemed to be an expert. And let me submit to you, no matter who is making that determination, there is such an enormous incentive to find anybody being evaluated—who, after all, by definition, has been convicted of a heinous sex crime—there is such an enormous pressure not to release that person without some kind of notification. I'm not surprised by what's happened in my state of New York, and I think it's typical, it's going to happen everywhere: that the vast, vast, vast majority of all sex offenders are labeled as the highest category of risk.

Walter Pincus: Accepting the fact that you don't believe in notification in these cases, the fact is we have a law. Define what you would like to see done, given the fact that there is registration, and notification becomes a second part of it. What's the least restrictive way to enforce the kinds of laws that clearly the public wants on the books?

Nadine Strossen: Well, the least restrictive would obviously be registration only with police, and in fact, the ACLU has not opposed those kinds of registration requirements, so long as there are certain basic procedural protections, such as making sure that you've got the right person and making sure that you are not talking about offenses such as consensual sodomy. In fact, the purpose of the registration statutes that have existed for a while, including the one in California, was to aid *law enforcement officers* in monitoring and, in the worst-case scenario, if there actually is a crime, to look for a likely offender.

The difference with the community notification is that it removes or displaces responsibility from law enforcement into citizens' hands. This is a plain call for vigilante "justice." That's an oxymoron, of course. And in every state in which we've had community notification, there have been tragic instances of vigilantism—in some cases, misdirected against somebody who turned out not even to have been a convicted sex offender.

If forced to choose the least intrusive kind of notification, I would say it's one aspect of what California now has, which is a 900 number that you can access to seek information about a particular person only under two conditions. One is that you specifically identify that person. In other words, this is not a dragnet request for information. You give that person's name, address, and other identifying characteristics. Second, and even more importantly, you identify a particular reason

why you have a focused safety concern. For example, "I'm thinking about hiring this person as a babysitter to take care of my children in our home." I think that kind of notification is the least intrusive and also the most effective.

I keep submitting, as a constant theme of my remarks, that we don't have to make a tradeoff between protecting rights of people convicted of crime and who have served their time, on the one hand, and on the other hand protecting the community, because I believe other kinds of notification (that go beyond the "least intrusive" California approach I just described) are ineffective.

On the one hand you could have vary targeted notification, right? You could notify people who live in the immediate surroundings of the released sex offender. That means people who live beyond the immediate surroundings could potentially be easy targets, under the rationale for this law, right? Because they're not going to be on particular notice about this person. At the other end of the spectrum, the more widely dispersed you make the notice, the less impact it has in another sense, because how are the recipients going to be able to sort through all of the information? Depending on how wide the notice is, you are going to be driving the convicted sex offenders out of particular communities into other communities where there either will not be any notice at all or it will be part of such a huge list of names that the notice is going to be meaningless. Which brings me full circle to a point I started with, which is that the only meaningful protection is to be on your guard against everybody who engages in inappropriate conduct.

Ernie Allen: A couple of brief responses. First of all, on the California issue, we do not recommend California as the model, and in fact, our view is that the model for community notification is a state that allows some basic active notification. California, right now, only has a passive notification system, which allows people to query a 900 number or a CD-ROM disc or a database of registered offenders. The California law is fifty years old and is lifetime registration in terms of Mr. Pincus's point about a ten or fifteen-year life span of such a requirement.

We don't agree on the point, however, about the other models. One of the points you made about targeting the notification, frankly, we support that. The Minnesota law, for example, talks about the issue of "likely to encounter." We think it does make sense, on the basis of this levels of risk process, to target where you're going to provide the information, to target those people most likely to come into contact with this particular offender, meaning the neighborhood in which he lives, the area in which he works. We would like to preserve the ability to do broader notification with the most serious offenders. But I think there is a continuum here. There are a range of responses, including community-based treatment availability for youthful offenders or offenders who are non-violent first offenders, registration for all convicted offenders, and then targeted notification for those offenders who present the highest risk.

Walter Pincus: Ms. Strossen, in her response, brought up this question of the effect that notification has in a negative way. In Washington State, for example, a child rapist's house is burned down before he is to be released from prison, and there are other examples. A Texas man who was released from prison after serving eleven years for a girl's murder is driven out of six towns, denied entry to more than two hundred halfway houses. How do you answer that particular criticism, that the statutes provoke vigilante action . . . harassment?

Ernie Allen: I respond in two ways. Obviously, vigilante violence and harassment are outrageous, should not be tolerated, and it's the obligation of law enforcement, the obligation of the state to deal with them, to prosecute those who violate the laws. Burning down somebody's house is just as unlawful if the occupant is a convicted sex offender as if he were anybody else. However, opponents of these laws have waved the bloody shirt from the beginning. They prophesied chaos and violence and all kinds of disruption. Well, the first Megan's Law, four years before Megan Kanka was murdered, was the Washington State law passed in 1990. There is at least, as a result of the research from the Washington State Institute of Public Policy, six years' worth of tracking data. Let me illustrate that data just to show a couple of points. During that six-year period,

there were nearly ten thousand sex offenders who were registered sex offenders in the state of Washington. Of that group, roughly nine hundred forty were subject to community notification, level two and level three, about two-thirds of their notifications were just to schools and community groups, three hundred twenty-seven of them were more broad-based community notification. Of that number there were thirty-three reported incidents of harassment. Now, that's terrible, there shouldn't be any. But thirty-three is barely three percent of the total number of offenders who were subject to community notification during those six years in the State of Washington.

Of everybody subject to community notification—ten thousand registered sex offenders—only nine hundred forty were deemed, through the process in the State of Washington, to be appropriate for notification to the community, only three hundred twenty-seven viewed as the highest-risk offenders. So, this is not a law where everybody is being exposed and everybody is being subjected. Vigilantism should not be tolerated. We don't support it, nobody supports it, and we need to make sure it doesn't happen.

One other quick point, Mr. Pincus. One of the reasons for the success of the Washington State program and the other programs in terms of minimizing the incidents of vigilantism is that those programs have community meetings, they go to the community to have discussions before the offender is ever released. They answer the questions, they tell people in the affected community who is coming into the community, what their history is. The message is, people can deal with it, they can assimilate the information, they can use it to say to their children, "Avoid where this guy lives." If the Kankas had known that, Megan would probably not have gone into her neighbor's house and been victimized. So, vigilantism has not been the level of problem that is prophesied, but we still shouldn't tolerate it.

Nadine Strossen: Well, it's interesting that Mr. Allen talks about the success of the Washington program and cites the Washington State Institute of Public Policy review. I'm familiar with that study too, which also shows that there is no positive impact in reducing sex crimes or recidivism as a result of this law. So, it may be successful in slightly reducing the incidents of vigilantism, but it's not successful in terms of its avowed purpose, which is to provide greater protection to the community.

I think there's a double standard here too when we say, as Mr. Allen and others have said, that to save the life of even one child it is worth whatever the downsides are of this law. Certainly, I put infinite value on the life of any human being. But that also includes human beings who are accused of crime and convicted of crime—or falsely believed to have been convicted of crime, because some of the victims of vigilantism have been completely innocent. They have been victims of mistaken identity.

You know, there's also harassment in addition to the most flagrant examples of houses being burned and people being physically assaulted. There's a lower level of harassment here that is extremely pernicious, in terms of community safety as well as concerns about the released sex offender, who is being ostracized, being isolated, being denied jobs, being denied a place to live. This is going to drive these people underground. According to the psychological experts, it's going to minimize rather than maximize the chance that they will seek treatment, the chance that they will be safely reintegrated into our communities.

One other thing I'd like to point out in this vein: the State of California, which has the longest experience with sex registration, is completely unable to keep track of about eighty percent of all people who are supposedly registered, as a result of the notification requirement. Notification is going to decrease the likelihood that somebody is going to register and face the ostracism or vigilantism or worse, and therefore, the public safety rationale of the law is undermined.

Walter Pincus: I want to move on to a slightly different part of the same subject. In *Hendricks v. Kansas*, the Supreme Court upheld that State's law which allowed sex offenders to be committed to psychiatric institutions at the end of their prison terms. If a convicted criminal is released from prison, has a mental disorder rendering him dangerous to himself or others, he can be civilly confined to a mental institution by his family or

the state. What is wrong with doing this in the context of sex offenders?

Nadine Strossen: *Kansas v. Hendricks* was a terrible decision and I'm glad I have an opportunity to comment on it, because I think it hasn't received nearly the public attention and concern that it should. What is being talked about is not our ordinary processes of civil commitment, which the Supreme Court previously has upheld. The constitutional requirements are: Number one, somebody has to be mentally ill, that is, have a dysfunction that is subject to treatment. Number two, he must be a danger to himself or others. Then the rationale for involuntary commitment is both to protect that person from himself and to protect the community by providing treatment, which maximizes the likelihood that this person is going to be rehabilitated.

That is not at all the rationale of the Kansas law or of the others that the Supreme Court has now validated. In fact, the Kansas law's legislative history, along with other such statutes, precisely says, because this person cannot be institutionalized pursuant to our normal civil commitment procedures, we have to come up with a new approach. Also, this person cannot be subject to criminal punishment, because by definition he has already completely served out his sentence. Therefore, we are going to come up with a brand new term, not at all recognized by mental health professionals—namely, a "mental disorder" or "abnormality."

As experts testified—again, I want to cite the mental health organizations that uniformly opposed this kind of law—it's a circular definition. You basically say, the evidence of abnormality is that he's committed a crime in the past and therefore we are going to put him away, essentially for life, indefinitely. The reason I say "essentially for life" is that he is put away until or unless the fact-finder, the judge, determines that this person is no longer a threat to the community. To make matters worse, in the *Hendricks* case, the individual was put away in a state prison facility where he was not offered any treatment at all.

Now the reason I say this case is so profoundly dangerous to our notion of liberty, our notion of justice, our notion of the purposes of the mental health system on the one hand and the prison system on the other hand, is that this is nothing short of shades of the Soviet gulag: using psychiatric hospitals as places to put away people who are deemed to be undesirable or dangerous for various reasons.

Again, I want to emphasize that if somebody is truly mentally ill and can be treated and is a danger, that person should be subject to the civil commitment procedures that already exist in Kansas and in other states. But let's not put a veneer, a rationale, a euphemism of some kind of mental health purpose onto a procedure that is in fact nothing but prolonged incarceration for the purpose of punishment and specific deterrence, removing a social undesirable from our midst, merely on the prediction of future dangerousness—a very dangerous legal fiction.

Ernie Allen: Prior history many times is a very good predictor of future behavior. The reality is Leroy Hendricks has a lifetime of offending children. Leroy Hendricks has been in and out of prison his whole life and this issue is bigger than Leroy Hendricks. But let's just focus on him.

There's no question. Leroy Hendricks was a pedophile. Leroy Hendricks said, "If you let me go, I'm probably going to do it again; when I get under stress, this is what I do." The reality is, the purpose of civil commitment is exactly as Professor Strossen articulated, it is to deal with someone who has an uncontrollable behavioral problem, as a result of mental illness or mental abnormality, who represents a danger to himself and others, who has a prior history of sexually violent pathology, sexual violent criminality, and you address the issue of does that person represent a threat to the community?

The fact that he has completed his sentence, in our view and in the Court's view, does not make it punitive. It doesn't meet the test. The traditional test of punishment is not met. It is not retribution because his prior criminal history is only used for evidentiary purposes. It's not deterrence, because if he's truly mentally ill or has a mental abnormality, the threat of commitment isn't going to deter future behavior. The issue here is, is this the sort of thing that can be done to protect the community in a very narrow slice of cases? Now, Professor Strossen talked about the controversy within the mental health community. I

think it's important to note that the American Psychiatric Association views pedophilia as a condition—a mental condition—and that it is a prescribed condition in the DSM-4, the Diagnostic Manual.

Walter Pincus: Let me go on to just fill out one part of this. If we accept the Kansas view that the way they're recommitting people is to provide treatment to sex offenders, shouldn't that treatment have taken place during their prison sentence, at the same time?

Ernie Allen: We support treatment in the prison setting, we support treatment post-release, we support it in the community for low-risk non-violent offenders. My answer to your question is "yes." However, I think within the context that the court looked at this there are two primary purposes. The primary purpose of this civil commitment statute is to protect the community.

The second purpose is treatment. Now, one of the tough issues here is, what if you cannot successfully treat this sort of offender? Well, my argument would be, and I think there are lots of examples in the law and in public policy on this point, that the absence of a cure or the absence of a successful intervention or treatment doesn't necessarily obviate the desirability to commit the particular person. If there's some kind of dread virus and you need to quarantine someone to avoid it, they're infecting everybody else, would you say, "We don't have a cure for this; we don't have a silver bullet for this; we'll just have to let you go?" I think the point is very basic here.

Now, in the *Hendricks* decision, Justice Kennedy's concurrence, the key point that he made, was that this cannot be and should not be used to correct the results of inadequate sentencing, to modify the product of the criminal justice process. In our view, civil commitment should be used rarely and only for the most dangerous offenders. Again, if you look at this continuum of offenders, these offenders should be more dangerous than the high-risk offenders for community notification under Megan's Law.

One final point here is that this is not retribution, and Professor Strossen makes the point about being housed or committed within the prison facility. The model for these, and now

484 Emerging Issues

nine states have them, and even Mr. Hendricks was not under the control of the state corrections agency, these offenders should be housed in the same sort of settings as other civilly committed individuals under the control of mental health systems or social services systems, and every effort should be made to treat within the limits of available treatment. These laws provide for annual reviews in order to assess their progress through treatment. The mere absence of a cure or successful treatment we don't think obviates the need or the appropriateness to have a civil commitment availability for these kinds of high-risk offenders.

Nadine Strossen: I'm not arguing, nor are the mental health professionals, including the American Psychiatric Association, which also opposed this (Mr. Allen cited it, so I want to underscore that), none of us is arguing that the absence of a cure is the problem here. To the contrary, we are arguing that it's the absence of a mental illness that is a problem. Kansas acknowledged in its law's legislative history that there is no mental illness here, so we're going to come up with this other new-fangled term: "disorder." Yes, it is true that pedophilia, along with alcoholism, along with too much caffeine, a whole lot of things that a lot of people do, are classified as disorders, but that is certainly not the same as a mental illness.

I think there are a lot of dangers to community safety, as well as individual rights, if we blur the distinguishing rationales that to this point had existed between the civil commitment system for mentally ill people and the criminal justice system for people who have been adjudicated guilty of having committed a criminal act in the past. The danger is that we are now moving toward a system of massive preventive detention. That is, because of an admittedly inexact, speculative prediction that a particular person is likely to commit a crime in the future, that somehow is deemed enough to detain this person forever.

It is also a diversion of resources from treating people who are actually mentally ill, and that is one of the reasons why mental health professionals oppose this.

Walter Pincus: I want to move on now to a new sort of area, that is "communications decency

acts" that have been introduced in the Congress. The protection of children is not limited to just Megan's Law statutes. What's the most effective way to protect children from on-line dangers?

Nadine Strossen: Well, there are two kinds of on-line dangers. First, through on-line communications a child can actually be targeted for some kind of contact, including criminal contact, in the three-dimensional, real world. Here I really want to congratulate the National Center for Missing & Exploited Children, which has worked very effectively with the FBI, in using existing law enforcement authority and existing investigative approaches to find those people who are in fact using the Internet, as they have used other communications media in the past, to try to develop exploitative relations with, or to endanger, actual children. So we need to continue to devote law enforcement resources to actual prosecution of those who victimize actual children.

What parents have to do in this new medium is the "same old same old,"—to give their children the same kinds of warnings that they had given in previous contexts: "Don't talk to strangers; don't give out your home address; never agree to meet a stranger." It's very, very important that parents be educated and that children be educated about the dangers of actual contacts that can begin in an on-line environment.

The second kind of danger that is said to threaten children from on-line activities is the supposed harm that results from exposure to expression, to ideas, to depictions, and to words. Most concerns seem to be about sexually-oriented expression. Violence is also a concern. These are the same kinds of expression that many parents have not wanted their children to view in more traditional media.

And here again, our response is, use in the present the same tried-and-true tactics that have been used in the past. As a parent you want to maintain, certainly when you're dealing with a young child—I think the older the young person becomes, the more independent he or she is and as the Supreme Court has recognized, begins to have free-speech rights and autonomy of his or her own—but certainly when their children are at a young age, parents have a constitutional right, as well as a responsibility, to shield the education and upbringing of their children, and they should monitor what their children do on-line.

Parents are certainly also free to choose to install any of the freely available software programs that screen out certain materials. Here, the ACLU's concern is that much of that software is extremely overbroad and misleading when it tells parents that all that's going to be filtered out is, for example, hard-core pornography; yet surveys continue to show that many of these software programs, in fact, filter out much valuable information that many concerned parents would want their children to have access to. Many of them screen out any reference whatsoever to any sexually-oriented material, even if it's artistic, even if it's got very serious value.

Last, let me say I think rather than negatively blocking or blacklisting certain materials that are deemed to be dangerous, we should instead use the same kind of affirmative approach that has worked in other media, empowering parents and children themselves to make affirmative selections of materials that they consider to be particularly valuable or useful. The American Library Association has always given recommendations and guidelines of books that are particularly educationally valuable for children of various ages. They're now performing an analogous function on-line.

Ernie Allen: I agree.

Walter Pincus: Some of the recent legislation that's been introduced in Congress take two different ways of approaching the problem. One is limiting access by sexual offenders to the Internet, while another seeks to protect children from material, just sexually-explicit material that's on-line. To what extent should the responsibility be left primarily to the parents, but most importantly, what should be the role of the state?

Ernie Allen: Well, as Professor Strossen indicated, we certainly think the role of the parent is very key and very important. Our organization, now for four years, has been promulgating and disseminating information to help parents catch

up to this technological age and emphasizing the role of parenting, talking to your kids, finding out what your kids are involved in. We also share and support the notion of development of technology access tools and controls. Probably the one point I do want to elaborate on that she raised is the whole issue of overbroad control in terms of access to content. I think much of that is going to be a function of evolving technology, technology software tools, access controls that don't just block out words but can now deny access to children by Web address, by URL. That evolution of technology, I think, will help us address this problem.

We do think that there's a significant role for the state, and that role is primarily in the area of enforcement. Professor Strossen mentioned this. I think one of the important things that came from the *Reno* decision is the reaffirmation by the Court that child pornography and obscenity, wherever they are, including cyberspace, is unlawful—in the adult bookstore, in the mails, in the shopping mall, or on the Internet.

What that means is that the state has to do a better job of catching up. You know, law enforcement in many ways is still in the horse-and-buggy days. It does not have the technology access and the tools to really deal with the misuse of the Internet. One of the things that we've certainly seen since the *Ferber* decision in the 1980's on child pornography—which said that child pornography is not protected speech, it's child abuse—is that that decision forced child pornography out of the adult bookstores. The United States Postal Service has cracked down on the use of the mails, and what we've seen is a sense of the Internet, or cyberspace, as a sanctuary for pedophiles who feel that they can operate with anonymity, that they can disseminate and distribute unlawful images, non-protected speech.

Law enforcement is catching up. Since the "Innocent Images" task force at the FBI and the Customs Service initiative, there are now more than four hundred convictions in the past two years. In the concurrence and the dissent to the *Reno v. ACLU* case, I thought some very important points were made: Technology will evolve. There's a fundamental challenge here and the challenge is that in the physical world you can zone areas where kids can't go and reach content. In the world of cyberspace you can't do that without also denying adults access to what is adult-allowable or appropriate information. As technology evolves through the development of gateways and other technology tools, one of the roles of the state that we see in the future and in partnership with the private industry is the development of zoning-type applications on the Internet. Clearly we need to deal more effectively with that content which is unlawful, but even with content that is protected speech. That's a challenge.

Nadine Strossen: Well, I'm glad that Mr. Allen referred to one of my favorite Supreme Court decisions, *Reno v. ACLU!* It gives me an opportunity to say that the ACLU did not challenge in that case the aspects of the Communications Decency Act that simply carried forward into the on-line environment prohibitions on expression that are already illegal in other kinds of communications media—namely, obscenity, child pornography, or threatening or harassing expression. But, to the extent it went beyond that, criminalizing "indecent" and "patently offensive" expression, we think it was a tragic diversion of resources, scarce law enforcement resources, from prosecution of actual on-line stalkers and those who actually abuse and exploit children.

I saw testimony that Mr. Allen gave, along with Louis Freeh, the Director of the FBI, in the Senate last month (March, 1998) and they were talking about how they don't yet have enough resources to get enough computers to do enough training of state and local law enforcement authorities all over the country to protect actual children from actual crimes. That's because Congress, as well as state and local governments, are busily drafting and passing unconstitutional laws that go beyond obscenity and child pornography and criminalize "indecent" or "patently offensive" expression, notwithstanding our victory in the Supreme Court, as well as in a number of lower federal courts around the country.

So, for those of us who really care about protecting actual children, there is another reason

to oppose censorial measures that continue to be aimed at the Internet at every level of government. That is, the waste of time and the waste of resources. That money should be going instead to the National Center for Missing & Exploited Children and to actual law enforcement.

Walter Pincus: Can you define what you would see as a constitutional law that deals with the problem of pornography in cyberspace?

Nadine Strossen: Well, I have to say I question what the "problem" of pornography in cyberspace is. Pornography is just sexually-oriented expression. Pornography by definition is constitutionally protected expression. Not all sexually-oriented expression falls within the category of "obscenity," which the Supreme Court has carved out and said this relatively narrow category is not going to receive constitutional protection. Among other things, obscenity has to lack serious literary, artistic, political or scientific value. So, when you go beyond that and talk about pornography, by definition, you are talking about constitutionally protected expression. And even concerning unprotected obscenity, recall Justice Potter Stewart's famous "definition": "I cannot define it, but I know it when I see it."

Our clients in *Reno v. ACLU*, which the government admitted would all be subject to criminal prosecution under the Communications Decency Act, included such hard-core pornographers as Planned Parenthood of America, Human Rights Watch, and my favorite, the National High School Journalism Educators Association. Why? Because they gave information about sex, because they used some graphic images or vulgar language.

There are many parents who think it is important for their kids to have access to that information. But, there seems to be such a presumption that if it has to do with sex, if you can slap that "p" word, which is an epithet, on it—"pornography"—then it must be harmful to minors. Well, the government didn't put in any evidence that any of that material that they sought to criminalize could be harmful to any minors. Conversely, we put in evidence that much of that material would be affirmatively beneficial—indeed, even life-saving, to minors. When you consider the tragic spread of HIV and other STD's among teenagers, the record-breaking numbers of unwanted teen pregnancies, and of lesbian and gay teenagers who commit suicide, then you have to recognize that the kinds of information and opportunity to exchange with others that some of our clients provided on-line, far from endangering teens' welfare, would be positive to their welfare.

The bottom line for us, as in every other situation, is individual freedom of choice on the part of consenting adults. And with respect to families, it is a family matter to decide, consistent with their own values and educational priorities and views about sexuality, and their other views about morality and religion and so forth. They should decide what their children should have access to. It is none of the government's business.

Ernie Allen: Just briefly—and I certainly will not attempt to defend the classification of the category of indecent speech as proposed by the Communications Decency Act, the Court said it was overbroad. I think the case was well made by the ACLU and others. However, a hundred million people are on the Internet today. The numbers of people of the Internet have doubled every 100 days. The capacity, the volume, the numbers of users have grown exponentially, unparalleled in American history. The challenge is most American families don't have a clue what their kids are doing on the computer. There's a false sense of security, there's a sense that my kid's in his own room, he's doing something good for his future, he's not out there where he's at risk. Kids are making those decisions, parents aren't making those decisions. And while I completely support the point that we need to emphasize parental responsibility, get parents involved in their kid's lives, it is not enough to say "families need to make those decisions and let's let kids fend for themselves." There are risks. We need to strengthen the protections for kids on-line, and the CDA might not have been the best way to do it, but we need a real dialogue to address these problems because kids are being harmed.

Walter Pincus: It's time for our summary and Professor Strossen, you go first.

Nadine Strossen: I'd like to end where I began. It posits a false choice to suggest that we have to choose between, on the one hand, safety for our children and safety for our communities, and, on the other hand, civil liberties.

Conversely, I would argue that the kinds of laws that we oppose—Megan's Law, the Kansas so-called "civil commitment" statute, the Communications Decency Act—these laws not only violate civil liberties of adults, not to mention civil liberties of minors, but also are ineffective in actually advancing safety for children and adults in our communities. They are ineffective because they are merely symbolic. They are pandering to public fears. They are creating scapegoats. They are allowing politicians to say, "I care about children; I'm doing something for children." In fact, they are at best ineffective and at worst counter-productive.

I've explained to you why Megan's Law is ineffective, giving us a false sense of security. It is counter-productive because it diverts resources from more constructive measures. I don't think that the diversion of resources issue here is at all a trivial one. As a result of procedural due process protections that the courts have (correctly) insisted upon, and that indeed I heard Mr. Allen advocate, tremendous amounts of resources are going into an inevitably unsuccessful and futile attempt to predict which particular person in the future is going to pose a high risk of danger.

In New Jersey, for example, every single prosecutor's office has to deputize one prosecutor full-time to do nothing but handle classification hearings under Megan's Law. Likewise, one judge in every jurisdiction has to do that. Meanwhile, the statistics about the number of arrests that are made—let alone successful prosecutions and convictions—of those who commit actual crimes, are frighteningly low. We can't afford this dangerous diversion of resources.

And, I also want to emphasize that what we're talking about here are not only the rights and welfare of adults, but also the rights and welfare of children. If we turn to the on-line aspect of our debate, I think it's important to note that the Supreme Court many years ago said constitutional rights do not magically spring into being when somebody happens to attain the state-defined age of majority. Young people have been pioneers in using the Internet. I think we talk too often about the potential dangers lurking out there in cyberspace and we don't talk often enough about the wonderfully positive, liberating, enlightening, and empowering aspects of the Internet for young people. So, let's not deny them of the educational and other benefits through censorship.

I like to say that the ACLU is a pro-family organization. We simply don't believe that Big Brother is an appropriate member of "the traditional American family." So we would like to rest protection of families and children where it belongs—in their own hands, through education and through prevention; not through scapegoating, not through stigmatizing, not through depriving anybody of rights. Public safety and civil liberties can go hand-in-hand under our Constitution. Thank you.

Ernie Allen: Thank you, Mr. Pincus. You may be shocked to hear this, but for one two-hour period on PBS, Professor Strossen and I were man and wife, and I think PBS thought that would be amusing and create some interesting conflict. But during that session, Arthur Miller, the moderator, came to me after we'd engaged in some particularly heated exchange, and said "are you still proud of her?" I made some kind of smart-aleck retort, but basically, I said, "Yes." I think it's important to note that I am glad that she does what she does and I'm glad that there's an ACLU. We at the Center and other child advocates are fiercely pro-Constitution. We believe in privacy rights. We believe in due process. We are not in favor of trashing the Constitution for any reason. I think the differences between Professor Strossen and me are very basic. They're about limits and they're about balance.

Our view is that these freedoms are not absolute. Our view is that in the case of convicted offenders who've established a pattern of behavior and who represent a threat to the public—that it is not unreasonable to limit their privacy rights a little bit, to carve away in the more compelling public interest.

Let me talk about that balance. I'm glad the ACLU defends the rights of convicted child

molesters and others, that they defend and advocate for the rights of the most difficult to advocate and the most difficult to defend. But there's balance in play here. Let me try to show you briefly what's at stake, balanced against the privacy rights of a convicted child molester. Sixty-one percent of the rape victims in America are less than eighteen, twenty-nine percent less than eleven. A majority of the victims of sex offenses in America are kids. Two-thirds of the sex offenders in American prisons today committed their offenses against children. We talked about the California sex offender registry. There are seventy thousand registered sex offenders in California today. I asked the Attorney General of California how many of them were convicted of offenses against kids. The answer is sixty-one percent of them. And another eighteen percent committed their offenses against kids and adults. Kids today in this country are hidden victims, and while we hope that these sex offenders are reintegrated into the community, that they stay crime-free, the reality is that the worst thing we can do is to provide them anonymity.

The worst thing that we can do is take someone out of prison and say, "Go forth and sin no more," because even the ones that are well-intentioned, and again, all sex offenders are not alike, I'm not trying to over-generalize, but even the ones that are well-intentioned come back to the communities where they have access to kids and women and they begin to fantasize, and these offenses reoccur. My point is, we're not saying, "Lock them away forever." All of them don't need to be. We are saying, in the interest of balance and reason, is it not rational and reasonable to say that, at least in the most serious cases, we can provide the information of their presence in the community to the people most likely to be affected by it?

I think that's what our debate's about. Our debate is about where you draw the lines. And we believe that there is a compelling public interest for the state to do more, to protect the most vulnerable section of our population, other than just saying to high-risk offenders who've served their time, that we hope they don't do it again, and if they do, we're going to do the best we can to catch them. Thanks.

A Rape in Cyberspace: Or, How an Evil Clown, A Haitian Trickster Spirit, Two Wizards, and a Cast of Dozens Turned a Database into a Society

Julian Dibbell

They say he raped them that night. They say he did it with a cunning little doll, fashioned in their image and imbued with the power to make them do whatever he desired. They say that by manipulating the doll he forced them to have sex with him, and with each other, and to do horrible, brutal things to their own bodies. And though I wasn't there that night, I think I can assure you that what they say is true, because it all happened right in the living room—right there amid the well-stocked bookcases and the sofas and the fireplace—of a house I've come to think of as my second home.

Call me Dr. Bombay. Some months ago—let's say about halfway between the first time you heard the words *information superhighway* and the first time you wished you never had—I found myself tripping with compulsive regularity down the well-traveled information lane that leads to LambdaMOO, a very large and very busy rustic chateau built entirely of words. Nightly, I typed the commands that called those words onto my computer screen, dropping me with what seemed a warm electric thud inside the mansion's darkened coat closet, where I checked my quotidian identity, stepped into the persona and appearance of a minor character from a long-gone television sitcom, and stepped out into the glaring chatter of the crowded living room. Sometimes, when the mood struck me, I emerged as a dolphin instead.

Julian Dibbell, "A Rape in Cyberspace," (as it appears in Mark Dery, ed., *Flame Wars*). Reprinted by permission of the author.

I won't say why I chose to masquerade as Samantha Stevens's outlandish cousin, or as the dolphin, or what exactly led to my mild but so-far incurable addiction to the semifictional digital otherworlds known around the Internet as multi-user dimensions, or MUDS. This isn't my story, after all. It's the story of a man named Mr. Bungle, and of the ghostly sexual violence he committed in the halls of LambdaMOO, and most importantly of the ways his violence and his victims challenged the thousand and more residents of that surreal, magic-infested mansion to become, finally, the community so many of them already believed they were.

That I was myself one of those residents has little direct bearing on the story's events. I mention it only as a warning that my own perspective is perhaps too steeped in the surreality and magic of the place to serve as an entirely appropriate guide. For the Bungle Affair raises questions that—here on the brink of a future in which human life may find itself as tightly enveloped in digital environments as it is today in the architectural kind—demand a clear-eyed, sober, and unmystified consideration. It asks us to shut our ears momentarily to the techno-utopian ecstasies of West Coast cyberhippies and look without illusion upon the present possibilities for building, in the online spaces of this world, societies more decent and free than those mapped onto dirt and concrete and capital. It asks us to behold the new bodies awaiting us in virtual space undazzled by their phantom powers, and to get to the crucial work of sorting out the socially meaningful differences between those bodies and our physical ones. And most forthrightly it asks us to wrap our late modern ontologies, epistemologies, sexual ethics, and common sense around the curious notion of rape by voodoo doll—and to try not to warp them beyond recognition in the process.

In short, the Bungle Affair dares me to explain it to you without resort to dime-store mysticisms, and I fear I may have shape-shifted by the digital moonlight one too many times to be quite up to the task. But I will do what I can, and I can do no better, I suppose, than to lead with the facts. For if nothing else about Mr. Bungle's case is unambiguous, the facts at least are crystal clear.

The facts begin (as they often do) with a time and a place. The time was a Monday night in March, and the place, as I've said, was the living room—which, due to the inviting warmth of its decor, is so invariably packed with chitchatters as to be roughly synonymous among LambdaMOOers with a party. So strong, indeed, is the sense of convivial common ground invested in the living room that a cruel mind could hardly imagine a better place in which to stage a violation of LambdaMOO's communal spirit. And there was cruelty enough lurking in the appearance Mr. Bungle presented to the virtual world—he was at the time a fat, oleaginous, Bisquick-faced clown dressed in cum-stained harlequin garb and girdled with a mistletoe-and-hemlock belt whose buckle bore the quaint inscription "KISS ME UNDER THIS, BITCH!" But whether cruelty motivated his choice of crime scene is not among the established facts of the case. It is a fact only that he did choose the living room.

The remaining facts tell us a bit more about the inner world of Mr. Bungle, though only perhaps that it couldn't have been a very comfortable place. They tell us that he commenced his assault entirely unprovoked, at or about 10 p.m. Pacific Standard Time. That he began by using his voodoo doll to force one of the room's occupants to sexually service him in a variety of more or less conventional ways. That this victim was legba, a Haitian trickster spirit of indeterminate gender, brown-skinned and

wearing an expensive pearl gray suit, top hat, and dark glasses. That legba heaped vicious imprecations on him all the while and that he was soon ejected bodily from the room. That he hid himself away then in his private chambers somewhere on the mansion grounds and continued the attacks without interruption, since the voodoo doll worked just as well at a distance as in proximity. That he turned his attentions now to Starsinger, a rather pointedly nondescript female character, tall, stout, and brown-haired, forcing her into unwanted liaisons with other individuals present in the room, among them legba, Bakunin (the well-known radical), and Juniper (the squirrel). That his actions grew progressively violent. That he made legba eat his/her own pubic hair. That he caused Starsinger to violate herself with a piece of kitchen cutlery. That his distant laughter echoed evilly in the living room with every successive outrage. That he could not be stopped until at last someone summoned Zippy, a wise and trusted old-timer who brought with him a gun of near wizardly powers, a gun that didn't kill but enveloped its targets in a cage impermeable even to a voodoo doll's powers. That Zippy fired this gun at Mr. Bungle, thwarting the doll at last and silencing the evil, distant laughter.

These particulars, as I said, are unambiguous. But they are far from simple, for the simple reason that every set of facts in virtual reality (or VR, as the locals abbreviate it) is shadowed by a second, complicating set: the "real-life" facts. And while a certain tension invariably buzzes in the gap between the hard, prosaic RL facts and their more fluid, dreamy VR counterparts, the dissonance in the Bungle case is striking. No hideous clowns or trickster spirits appear in the RL version of the incident, no voodoo dolls or wizard guns, indeed no rape at all as any RL court of law has yet defined it. The actors in the drama were university students for the most part, and they sat rather undramatically before computer screens the entire time, their only actions a spidery flitting of fingers across standard QWERTY keyboards. No bodies touched. Whatever physical interaction occurred consisted of a mingling of electronic signals sent from sites spread out between New York City and Sydney, Australia. Those signals met in LambdaMOO, certainly, just as the hideous clown and the living room party did, but what was LambdaMOO after all? Not an enchanted mansion or anything of the sort—just a middlingly complex database, maintained for experimental purposes inside a Xerox Corporation research computer in Palo Alto and open to public access via the Internet.

To be more precise about it, LambdaMOO was a MUD. Or to be yet more precise, it was a subspecies of MUD known as a MOO, which is short for "MUD, Object-Oriented." All of which means that it was a kind of database especially designed to give users the vivid impression of moving through a physical space that in reality exists only as descriptive data filed away on a hard drive. When users dial into LambdaMOO, for instance, the program immediately presents them with a brief textual description of one of the rooms of the database's fictional mansion (the coat closet, say). If the user wants to leave this room, she can enter a command to move in a particular direction and the database will replace the original description with a new one corresponding to the room located in the direction she chose. When the new description scrolls across the user's screen it lists not only the fixed features of the room but all its contents at that moment—including things (tools, toys, weapons) and other users (each represented as a "character" over which he or she has sole control).

As far as the database program is concerned, all of these entities—rooms, things, characters—are just different subprograms that the program allows to interact according to rules very roughly mimicking the laws of the physical world. Characters may not leave a room in a given direction, for instance, unless the room subprogram contains an "exit" at that compass point. And if a character "says" or "does" something (as directed by its user-owner), then only the users whose characters are also located in that room will see the output describing the statement or action. Aside from such basic constraints, however, LambdaMOOers are allowed a broad freedom to create—they can describe

their characters any way they like, they can make rooms of their own and decorate them to taste, and they can build new objects almost at will. The combination of all this busy user activity with the hard physics of the database can certainly induce a lucid illusion of presence—but when all is said and done the only thing you *really* see when you visit LambdaMOO is a kind of slow-crawling script, lines of dialogue and stage direction creeping steadily up your computer screen.

Which is all just to say that, to the extent that Mr. Bungle's assault happened in real life at all, it happened as a sort of Punch-and-Judy show, in which the puppets and the scenery were made of nothing more substantial than digital code and snippets of creative writing. The puppeteer behind Bungle, as it happened, was a young man logging in to the MOO from a New York University computer. He could have been Al Gore for all any of the others knew, however, and he could have written Bungle's script that night any way he chose. He could have sent a command to print the message "Mr. Bungle, smiling a saintly smile, floats angelic near the ceiling of the living room, showering joy and candy kisses down upon the heads of all below"—and everyone then receiving output from the database's subprogram #17 (a/k/a the "living room") would have seen that sentence on their screens.

Instead, he entered sadistic fantasies into the "voodoo doll," a subprogram that served the not exactly kosher purpose of attributing actions to other characters that their users did not actually write. And thus a woman in Haverford, Pennsylvania, whose account on the MOO attached her to a character she called Starsinger, was given the unasked-for opportunity to read the words "As if against her will, Starsinger jabs a steak knife up her ass, causing immense joy. You hear Mr. Bungle laughing evilly in the distance." And thus the woman in Seattle who had written herself the character called legba, with a view perhaps to tasting in imagination a deity's freedom from the burdens of the gendered flesh, got to read similarly constructed sentences in which legba, messenger of the gods, lord of crossroads and communications, suffered a brand of degradation all-too customarily reserved for the embodied female.

"Mostly voodoo dolls are amusing," wrote legba on the evening after Bungle's rampage, posting a public statement to the widely read in MOO mailing list called *social-issues*, a forum for debate on matters of import to the entire populace. "And mostly I tend to think that restrictive measures around here cause more trouble than they prevent. But I also think that Mr. Bungle was being a vicious, vile fuckhead, and I . . . want his sorry ass scattered from #17 to the Cinder Pile. I'm not calling for policies, trials, or better jails. I'm not sure what I'm calling for. Virtual castration, if I could manage it. Mostly, [this type of thing] doesn't happen here. Mostly, perhaps I thought it wouldn't happen to me. Mostly, I trust people to conduct themselves with some veneer of civility. Mostly, I want his ass."

Months later, the woman in Seattle would confide to me that as she wrote those words posttraumatic tears were streaming down her face—a real-life fact that should suffice to prove that the words' emotional content was no mere playacting. The precise tenor of that content, however, its mingling of murderous rage and eyeball-rolling annoyance, was a curious amalgam that neither the RL nor the VR facts alone can quite account for. Where virtual reality and its conventions would have us believe that legba and Starsinger were brutally raped in their own living room, here was the victim legba scolding Mr. Bungle for a breach of "civility." Where real life, on the other hand, insists the incident was only an episode in a free-form version of Dungeons and Dragons, confined to the realm of the symbolic and at no point threatening any player's life, limb, or material wellbeing, here now was the player legba issuing aggrieved and heartfelt calls for Mr. Bungle's dismemberment. Ludicrously excessive by RL's lights, woefully understated by VR's, the tone of legba's response made sense only in the buzzing, dissonant gap between them.

Which is to say it made the only kind of sense that *can* be made of MUDly phenomena.

For while the *facts* attached to any event born of a MUD's strange, ethereal universe may march in straight, tandem lines separated neatly into the virtual and the real, its meaning lies always in that gap. You learn this axiom early in your life as a player, and it's of no small relevance to the Bungle case that you often learn it between the sheets, so to speak. Netsex, tinysex, virtual sex—however you name it, in real-life reality it's nothing more than a 900-line encounter stripped of even the vestigial physicality of the voice. And yet, as many a player can tell you, it's possibly the headiest experience the very heady world of MUDS has to offer. Amid flurries of even the most cursorily described caresses, sighs, and penetrations, the glands do engage, and often as throbbingly as they would in a real-life assignation—sometimes even more so, given the combined power of anonymity and textual suggestiveness to unshackle deepseated fantasies. And if the virtual setting and the interplayer vibe are right, who knows? The heart may engage as well, stirring up passions as strong as many that bind lovers who observe the formality of trysting in the flesh.

To participate, therefore, in this disembodied enactment of life's most body-centered activity is to risk the realization that when it comes to sex, perhaps the body in question is not the physical one at all, but its psychic double, the bodylike self-representation we carry around in our heads. I know, I know, you've read Foucault and your mind is not quite blown by the notion that sex is never so much an exchange of fluids as it is an exchange of signs. But trust your friend Dr. Bombay, it's one thing to grasp the notion intellectually and quite another to feel it coursing through your veins amid the virtual steam of hot netnookie. And it's a whole other mind-blowing trip altogether to encounter it thus as a college frosh, new to the net and still in the grip of hormonal hurricanes and high-school sexual mythologies. The shock can easily reverberate throughout an entire young worldview. Small wonder, then, that a newbie's first taste of MUD sex is often also the first time she or he surrenders wholly to the slippery terms of MUDish ontology, recognizing in a full-bodied way that what happens inside a MUDmade world is neither exactly real nor exactly make-believe, but profoundly, compellingly, and emotionally meaningful.

And small wonder indeed that the sexual nature of Mr. Bungle's crime provoked such powerful feelings, and not just in legba (who, be it noted, was in real life a theory-savvy doctoral candidate and a longtime MOOer, but just as baffled and overwhelmed by the force of her own reaction, she later would attest, as any panting undergrad might have been). Even players who had never experienced MUD rape (the vast majority of male-presenting characters, but not as large a majority of the female-presenting as might be hoped) immediately appreciated its gravity and were moved to condemnation of the perp. legba's missive to *social-issues* followed a strongly worded one from Zippy ("Well, well," it began, "no matter what else happens on Lambda, I can always be sure that some jerk is going to reinforce my low opinion of humanity") and was itself followed by others from Moriah, Raccoon, Crawfish, and evangeline. Starsinger also let her feelings ("pissed") be known. And even Jander, the Clueless Samaritan who had responded to Bungle's cries for help and uncaged him shortly after the incident, expressed his regret once apprised of Bungle's deeds, which he allowed to be "despicable."

A sense was brewing that something needed to be done—done soon and in something like an organized fashion—about Mr. Bungle, in particular, and about MUD rape, in general. Regarding the general problem, evangeline, who identified herself as a survivor of both virtual rape ("many times over") and real-life sexual assault, floated a cautious proposal for a MOO-wide powwow on the subject of virtual sex offenses and what mechanisms if any might be put in place to deal with their future occurrence. As for the specific problem, the answer no doubt seemed obvious to many. But it wasn't until the evening of the second day after the incident that legba, finally and rather solemnly, gave it voice: "I am requesting that Mr. Bungle be toaded for raping Starsinger and I. I have never done this before, and have thought about it for days. He hurt us both."

That was all. Three simple sentences posted to *social*. Reading them, an outsider might never guess that they were an application for a death warrant. Even an outsider familiar with other MUDs might not guess it, since in many of them "toading" still refers to a command that, true to the gameworlds' sword-and-sorcery origins, simply turns a player into a toad, wiping the player's description and attributes and replacing them with those of the slimy amphibian. Bad luck for sure, but not quite as bad as what happens when the same command is invoked in the MOOish strains of MUD: not only are the description and attributes of the toaded player erased, but the account itself goes too. The annihilation of the character, thus, is total.

And nothing less than total annihilation, it seemed, would do to settle LambdaMOO's accounts with Mr. Bungle. Within minutes of the posting of legba's appeal, SamIAm, the Australian Deleuzean, who had witnessed much of the attack from the back room of his suburban Sydney home, seconded the motion with a brief message crisply entitled "Toad the fukr." SamIAm's posting was seconded almost as quickly by that of Bakunin, covictim of Mr. Bungle and well-known radical, who in real life happened also to be married to the real-life legba. And over the course of the next 24 hours as many as 50 players made it known, on *social* and in a variety of other forms and forums, that they would be pleased to see Mr. Bungle erased from the face of the MOO. And with dissent so far confined to a dozen or so antitoading hard-liners, the numbers suggested that the citizenry was indeed moving toward a resolve to have Bungle's virtual head.

There was one small but stubborn obstacle in the way of this resolve, however, and that was a curious state of social affairs known in some quarters of the MOO as the New Direction. It was all very fine, you see, for the LambdaMOO rabble to get it in their heads to liquidate one of their peers, but when the time came to actually do the deed it would require the services of a nobler class of character. It would require a wizard. Masterprogrammers of the MOO, spelunkers of the database's deepest code-structures and custodians of its day-to-day administrative trivia, wizards are also the only players empowered to issue the toad command, a feature maintained on nearly all MUDS as a quick-and-dirty means of social control. But the wizards of LambdaMOO, after years of adjudicating all manner of interplayer disputes with little to show for it but their own weariness and the smoldering resentment of the general populace, had decided they'd had enough of the social sphere. And so, four months before the Bungle incident, the archwizard Haakon (known in RL as Pavel Curtis, Xerox researcher and LambdaMOO's principal architect) formalized this decision in a document called "LambdaMOO Takes a New Direction," which he placed in the living room for all to see. In it, Haakon announced that the wizards from that day forth were pure technicians. From then on, they would make no decisions affecting the social life of the MOO, but only implement whatever decisions the community as a whole directed them to. From then on, it was decreed, LambdaMOO would just have to grow up and solve its problems on its own.

Faced with the task of inventing its own self-governance from scratch, the LambdaMOO population had so far done what any other loose, amorphous agglomeration of individuals would have done: they'd let it slide. But now the task took on new urgency. Since getting the wizards to toad Mr. Bungle (or to toad the likes of him in the future) required a convincing case that the cry for his head came from the community at large, then the community itself would have to be defined; and if the community was to be convincingly defined, then some form of social organization, no matter how rudimentary, would have to be settled on. And thus, as if against its will, the question of what to do about Mr. Bungle began to shape itself into a sort of referendum on the political future of the MOO. Arguments broke out on *social and elsewhere that had only superficially to do with Bungle (since everyone agreed he was a cad) and everything to do with where the

participants stood on LambdaMOO's crazy-quilty political map. Parliamentarian legalist types argued that unfortunately Bungle could not legitimately be toaded at all, since there were no explicit MOO rules against rape, or against just about anything else—and the sooner such rules were established, they added, and maybe even a full-blown judiciary system complete with elected officials and prisons to enforce those rules, the better. Others, with a royalist streak in them, seemed to feel that Bungle's as-yet unpunished outrage only proved this New Direction silliness had gone on long enough, and that it was high time the wizardocracy returned to the position of swift and decisive leadership their player class was born to.

And then there were what I'll call the technolibertarians. For them, MUD rapists were of course assholes, but the presence of assholes on the system was a technical inevitability, like noise on a phone line, and best dealt with not through repressive social disciplinary mechanisms but through the timely deployment of defensive software tools. Some asshole blasting violent, graphic language at you? Don't whine to the authorities about it—hit the @gag command and the asshole's statements will be blocked from your screen (and only yours). It's simple, it's effective, and it censors no one.

But the Bungle case was rather hard on such arguments. For one thing, the extremely public nature of the living room meant that gagging would spare the victims only from witnessing their own violation, but not from having others witness it. You might want to argue that what those victims didn't directly experience couldn't hurt them, but consider how that wisdom would sound to a woman who'd been, say, fondled by strangers while passed out drunk and you have a rough idea how it might go over with a crowd of hard-core MOOers. Consider, for another thing, that many of the biologically female participants in the Bungle debate had been around long enough to grow lethally weary of the gag-and-get-over-it school of virtual-rape counseling, with its fine line between empowering victims and holding them responsible for their own suffering, and its shrugging indifference to the window of pain between the moment the rape-text starts flowing and the moment a gag shuts it off. From the outset it was clear that the technolibertarians were going to have to tiptoe through this issue with care, and for the most part they did.

Yet no position was trickier to maintain than that of the MOO's resident anarchists. Like the technolibbers, the anarchists didn't care much for punishments or policies or power elites. Like them, they hoped the MOO could be a place where people interacted fulfillingly without the need for such things. But their high hopes were complicated, in general, by a somewhat less thoroughgoing faith in technology ("Even if you can't tear down the master's house with the master's tools"—read a slogan written into one anarchist player's self-description—"it is a damned good place to start"). And at present they were additionally complicated by the fact that the most vocal anarchists in the discussion were none other than legba, Bakunin, and SamIAm, who wanted to see Mr. Bungle toaded as badly as anyone did.

Needless to say, a pro-death-penalty platform is not an especially comfortable one for an anarchist to sit on, so these particular anarchists were now at great pains to sever the conceptual ties between toading and capital punishment. Toading, they insisted (almost convincingly), was much more closely analogous to banishment; it was a kind of turning of the communal back on the offending party, a collective action which, if carried out properly, was entirely consistent with anarchist models of community. And carrying it out properly meant first and foremost building a consensus around it—a messy process for which there were no easy technocratic substitutes. It was going to take plenty of good old-fashioned, jawbone-intensive grassroots organizing.

So that when the time came, at 7 p.m. PST on the evening of the third day after the occurrence in the living room, to gather in evangeline's room for her proposed real-time open conclave, Bakunin and legba were among the first to arrive. But this was hardly to be an anarchist-dominated affair, for the room was

crowding rapidly with representatives of all the MOO's political stripes, and even a few wizards. Hagbard showed up, and Autumn and Quastro, Puff, JoeFeedback, L-dopa and Bloaf, HerkieCosmo, Silver Rocket, Karl Porcupine, Matchstick—the names piled up and the discussion gathered momentum under their weight. Arguments multiplied and mingled, players talked past and through each other, the textual clutter of utterances and gestures filled up the screen like thick cigar smoke. Peaking in number at around 30, this was one of the largest crowds that ever gathered in a single LambdaMOO chamber, and while evangeline had given her place a description that made it "infinite in expanse and fluid in form," it now seemed anything but roomy. You could almost feel the claustrophobic air of the place, dank and overheated by virtual bodies, pressing against your skin.

I know you could because I too was there, making my lone and insignificant appearance in this story. Completely ignorant of any of the goings-on that had led to the meeting, I wandered in purely to see what the crowd was about, and though I observed the proceedings for a good while, I confess I found it hard to grasp what was going on. I was still the rankest of newbies then, my MOO legs still too unsteady to make the leaps of faith, logic, and empathy required to meet the spectacle on its own terms. I was fascinated by the concept of virtual rape, but I couldn't quite take it seriously.

In this, though, I was in a small and mostly silent minority, for the discussion that raged around me was of an almost unrelieved earnestness, bent, it seemed, on examining every last aspect and implication of Mr. Bungle's crime. There were the central questions, of course: thumbs up or down on Bungle's virtual existence? And if down, how then to insure that his toading was not just some isolated lynching but a first step toward shaping LambdaMOO into a legitimate community? Surrounding these, however, a tangle of weighty side issues proliferated. What, some wondered, was the real-life legal status of the offense? Could Bungle's university administrators punish him for sexual harassment? Could he be prosecuted under California state laws against obscene phone calls? Little enthusiasm was shown for pursuing either of these lines of action, which testifies both to the uniqueness of the crime and to the nimbleness with which the discussants were negotiating its idiosyncrasies. Many were the casual references to Bungle's deed as simply "rape," but these in no way implied that the players had lost sight of all distinctions between the virtual and physical versions, or that they believed Bungle should be dealt with in the same way a real-life criminal would. He had committed a MOO crime, and his punishment, if any, would be meted out via the MOO.

On the other hand, little patience was shown toward any attempts to downplay the seriousness of what Mr. Bungle had done. When the affable HerkieCosmo proposed, more in the way of a hypothesis than an assertion, that "perhaps it's better to release . . . violent tendencies in a virtual environment rather than in real life," he was tut-tutted so swiftly and relentlessly that he withdrew the hypothesis altogether, apologizing humbly as he did so. Not that the assembly was averse to putting matters into a more philosophical perspective. "Where does the body end and the mind begin?" young Quastro asked, amid recurring attempts to fine-tune the differences between real and virtual violence. "Is not the mind a part of the body?" "In MOO, the body IS the mind," offered HerkieCosmo gamely, and not at all implausibly, demonstrating the ease with which very knotty metaphysical conundrums come undone in VR. The not-so-aptly named Obvious seemed to agree, arriving after deep consideration of the nature of Bungle's crime at the hardly novel yet now somehow newly resonant conjecture "All reality might consist of ideas, who knows."

On these and other matters the anarchists, the libertarians, the legalists, the wizardists— and the wizards—all had their thoughtful say. But as the evening wore on and the talk grew more heated and more heady, it seemed increasingly clear that the vigorous intelligence being brought to bear on this swarm of issues wasn't going to result in anything remotely like resolution. The perspectives were just too varied, the meme-scape just too slippery. Again and again, arguments that looked at first to be heading in a decisive direction ended up chasing their own tails; and slowly, depressingly, a dusty haze of irrelevance gathered over the proceedings.

It was almost a relief, therefore, when midway through the evening Mr. Bungle himself, the living, breathing cause of all this talk, teleported into the room. Not that it was much of a surprise. Oddly enough, in the three days since his release from Zippy's cage, Bungle had returned more than once to wander the public spaces of Lambda MOO, walking willingly into one of the fiercest storms of ill will and invective ever to rain down on a player. He'd been taking it all with a curious and mostly silent passivity, and when challenged face to virtual face by both legba and the genderless elder statescharacter PatGently to defend himself on *social, he'd demurred, mumbling something about Christ and expiation. He was equally quiet now, and his reception was still uniformly cool, legba fixed an arctic stare on him—"no hate, no anger, no interest at all. Just . . . watching." Others were more actively unfriendly. "Asshole," spat Karl Porcupine, "creep." But the harshest of the MOO's hostility toward him had already been vented, and the attention he drew now was motivated more, it seemed, by the opportunity to probe the rapist's mind, to find out what made it tick and if possible how to get it to tick differently. In short, they wanted to know why he'd done it. So they asked him.

And Mr. Bungle thought about it. And as eddies of discussion and debate continued to swirl around him, he thought about it some more. And then he said this:

> "I engaged in a bit of a psychological device that is called thought-polarization, the fact that this is not RL simply added to heighten the affect of the device. It was purely a sequence of events with no consequence on my RL existence."

They might have known. Stilted though its diction was, the gist of the answer was simple, and something many in the room had probably already surmised: Mr. Bungle was a psycho.

Not, perhaps, in real life—but then in real life it's possible for reasonable people to assume, as Bungle clearly did, that what transpires between word-costumed characters within the boundaries of a makebelieve world is, if not mere play, then at most some kind of emotional laboratory experiment. Inside the MOO, however, such thinking marked a person as one of two basically subcompetent types. The first was the newbie, in which case the confusion was understandable, since there were few MOOers who had not, upon their first visits as anonymous "guest" characters, mistaken the place for a vast playpen in which they might act out their wildest fantasies without fear of censure. Only with time and the acquisition of a fixed character do players tend to make the critical passage from anonymity to pseudonymity, developing the concern for their character's reputation that marks the attainment of virtual adulthood. But while Mr. Bungle hadn't been around as long as most MOOers, he'd been around long enough to leave his newbie status behind, and his delusional statement therefore placed him among the second type: the sociopath.

And as there is but small percentage in arguing with a head case, the room's attention gradually abandoned Mr. Bungle and returned to the discussions that had previously occupied it. But if the debate had been edging toward ineffectuality before, Bungle's anticlimactic appearance had evidently robbed it of any forward motion whatsoever. What's more, from his lonely corner of the room Mr. Bungle kept issuing periodic expressions of a prickly sort of remorse, interlaced with sarcasm and belligerence, and though it was hard to tell if he wasn't still just conducting his experiments, some people thought his regret genuine enough that maybe he didn't deserve to be toaded after all. Logically, of course, discussion of the principal issues at hand didn't require unanimous belief that Bungle was an irredeemable bastard, but now that cracks were showing in that unanimity, the last of the meeting's fervor seemed to be draining out through them.

People started drifting away. Mr. Bungle left first, then others followed—one by one, in twos and threes, hugging friends and waving goodnight. By 9:45 only a handful remained, and the great debate had wound down into casual conversation, the melancholy remains of another fruitless good idea. The arguments had been well-honed, certainly, and perhaps might prove useful in some as-yet-unclear long run. But at this point what seemed clear was that evangeline's meeting had died, at last, and without any practical results to mark its passing.

It was also at this point, most likely, that JoeFeedback reached his decision. JoeFeedback was a wizard, a taciturn sort of fellow who'd sat brooding on the sidelines all evening. He hadn't said a lot, but what he had said indicated that he took the crime committed against legba and Starsinger very seriously, and that he felt no particular compassion toward the character who had committed it. But on the other hand he had made it equally plain that he took the elimination of a fellow player just as seriously, and moreover that he had no desire to return to the days of wizardly fiat. It must have been difficult, therefore, to reconcile the conflicting impulses churning within him at that moment. In fact, it was probably impossible, for as much as he would have liked to make himself an instrument of LambdaMOO's collective will, he surely realized that under the present order of things he must in the final analysis either act alone or not act at all.

So JoeFeedback acted alone.

He told the lingering few players in the room that he had to go, and then he went. It was a minute or two before ten. He did it quietly and he did it privately, but all anyone had to do to know he'd done it was to type the @who command, which was normally what you typed if you wanted to know a player's present location and the time he last logged in. But if you had run a @who on Mr. Bungle not too long after JoeFeedback left evangeline's room, the database would have told you something different.

"Mr. Bungle," it would have said, "is not the name of any player."

The date, as it happened, was April Fool's Day, and it would still be April Fool's Day for another two hours. But this was no joke: Mr. Bungle was truly dead and truly gone.

They say that LambdaMOO has never been the same since Mr. Bungle's toading. They say as well that nothing's really changed. And though it skirts the fuzziest of dream-logics to say that both these statements are true, the MOO is just the sort of fuzzy, dreamlike place in which such contradictions thrive.

Certainly whatever civil society now informs LambdaMOO owes its existence to the Bungle Affair. The archwizard Haakon made sure of that. Away on business for the duration of the episode, Haakon returned to find its wreckage strewn across the tiny universe he'd set in motion. The death of a player, the trauma of several others, and the angst-ridden conscience of his colleague JoeFeedback presented themselves to his concerned and astonished attention, and he resolved to see if he couldn't learn some lesson from it all. For the better part of a day he brooded over the record of events and arguments left in *social*, then he sat pondering the chaotically evolving shape of his creation, and at the day's end he descended once again into the social arena of the MOO with another history-altering proclamation.

It was probably his last, for what he now decreed was the final, missing piece of the New Direction. In a few days, Haakon announced, he would build into the database a system of petitions and ballots whereby anyone could put to popular vote any social scheme requiring wizardly powers for its implementation, with the results of the vote to be binding on the wizards. At last and for good, the awkward gap between the will of the players and the efficacy of the technicians would be closed. And though some anarchists grumbled about the irony of Haakon's dictatorially imposing universal suffrage on an unconsulted populace, in general the citizens of LambdaMOO seemed to find it hard to fault a system more purely democratic than any that could ever exist in real life. Eight months and a dozen ballot measures later, widespread participation in the new regime has produced a small arsenal of mechanisms for dealing with the types of violence that called

the system into being. MOO residents now have access to a @boot command, for instance, with which to summarily eject berserker "guest" characters. And players can bring suit against one another through an ad hoc arbitration system in which mutually agreed-upon judges have at their disposition the full range of wizardly punishments—up to and including the capital.

Yet the continued dependence on death as the ultimate keeper of the peace suggests that this new MOO order may not be built on the most solid of foundations. For if life on LambdaMOO began to acquire more coherence in the wake of the toading, death retained all the fuzziness of pre-Bungle days. This truth was rather dramatically borne out, not too many days after Bungle departed, by the arrival of a strange new character named Dr. Jest. There was a forceful eccentricity to the newcomer's manner, but the oddest thing about his style was its striking yet unnameable familiarity. And when he developed the annoying habit of stuffing fellow players into a jar containing a tiny simulacrum of a certain deceased rapist, the source of this familiarity became obvious:

Mr. Bungle had risen from the grave.

In itself, Bungle's reincarnation as Dr. Jest was a remarkable turn of events, but perhaps even more remarkable was the utter lack of amazement with which the LambdaMOO public took note of it. To be sure, many residents were appalled by the brazenness of Bungle's return. In fact, one of the first petitions circulated under the new voting system was a request for Dr. Jest's toading that almost immediately gathered 52 signatures (but has failed so far to reach ballot status). Yet few were unaware of the ease with which the toad proscription could be circumvented—all the toadee had to do (all the urBungle at NYU presumably had done) was to go to the minor hassle of acquiring a new Internet account, and LambdaMOO's character registration program would then simply treat the known felon as an entirely new and innocent person. Nor was this ease generally understood to represent a failure of toading's social disciplinary function. On the contrary, it only underlined the truism (repeated many times throughout the debate over Mr. Bungle's fate) that his punishment, ultimately, had been no more or less symbolic than his crime.

What *was* surprising, however, was that Mr. Bungle/Dr. Jest seemed to have taken the symbolism to heart. Dark themes still obsessed him—the objects he created gave off wafts of Nazi imagery and medical torture—but he no longer radiated the aggressively antisocial vibes he had before. He was a lot less unpleasant to look at (the outrageously seedy clown description had been replaced by that of a mildly creepy but actually rather natty young man, with "blue eyes . . . suggestive of conspiracy, untamed eroticism and perhaps a sense of understanding of the future"), and aside from the occasional jar-stuffing incident, he was also a lot less dangerous to be around. It was obvious he'd undergone some sort of personal transformation in the days since I'd first glimpsed him back in evangeline's crowded room—nothing radical maybe, but powerful nonetheless, and resonant enough with my own experience, I felt, that it might be more than professionally interesting to talk with him, and perhaps compare notes.

For I too was undergoing a transformation in the aftermath of that night in evangeline's, and I'm still not entirely sure what to make of it. As I pursued my runaway fascination with the discussion I had heard there, as I pored over the *social debate and got to know legba and some of the other victims and witnesses, I could feel my newbie consciousness falling away from me. Where before I'd found it hard to take virtual rape seriously, I now was finding it difficult to remember how I could ever not have taken it seriously. I was proud to have arrived at this perspective—it felt like an exotic sort of achievement, and it definitely made my ongoing experience of the MOO a richer one.

But it was also having some unsettling effects on the way I looked at the rest of the world. Sometimes, for instance, it was hard for me to understand why RL society classifies RL rape alongside crimes against person or property. Since rape can occur without any physical pain or damage, I found myself reasoning,

then it must be classed as a crime against the mind—more intimately and deeply hurtful, to be sure, than cross-burnings, wolf whistles, and virtual rape, but undeniably located on the same conceptual continuum. I did not, however, conclude as a result that rapists were protected in any fashion by the First Amendment. Quite the opposite, in fact: the more seriously I took the notion of virtual rape, the less seriously I was able to take the notion of freedom of speech, with its tidy division of the world into the symbolic and the real.

Let me assure you, though, that I am not presenting these thoughts as arguments. I offer them, rather, as a picture of the sort of mindset that deep immersion in a virtual world has inspired in me. I offer them also, therefore, as a kind of prophecy. For whatever else these thoughts tell me, I have come to believe that they announce the final stages of our decadeslong passage into the Information Age, a paradigm shift that the classic liberal firewall between word and deed (itself a product of an earlier paradigm shift commonly known as the Enlightenment) is not likely to survive intact. After all, anyone the least bit familiar with the workings of the new era's definitive technology, the computer, knows that it operates on a principle impracticably difficult to distinguish from the pre-Enlightenment principle of the magic word: the commands you type into a computer are a kind of speech that doesn't so much communicate as *make things happen*, directly and ineluctably, the same way pulling a trigger does. They are incantations, in other words, and anyone at all attuned to the technosocial megatrends of the moment—from the growing dependence of economies on the global flow of intensely fetishized words and numbers to the burgeoning ability of bioengineers to speak the spells written in the four-letter text of DNA—knows that the logic of the incantation is rapidly permeating the fabric of our lives.

And it's precisely this logic that provides the real magic in a place like LambdaMOO—not the fictive trappings of voodoo and shapeshifting and wizardry, but the conflation of speech and act that's inevitable in any computer-mediated world, be it Lambda or the increasingly wired world at large. This is dangerous magic, to be sure, a potential threat—if misconstrued or misapplied—to our always precarious freedoms of expression, and as someone who lives by his words I do not take the threat lightly. And yet, on the other hand, I can no longer convince myself that our wishful insulation of language from the realm of action has ever been anything but a valuable kludge, a philosophically damaged stopgap against oppression that would just have to do till something truer and more elegant came along.

Am I wrong to think this truer, more elegant thing can be found on LambdaMOO? Perhaps, but I continue to seek it there, sensing its presence just beneath the surface of every interaction. I have even thought, as I said, that discussing with Dr. Jest our shared experience of the workings of the MOO might help me in my search. But when that notion first occurred to me, I still felt somewhat intimidated by his lingering criminal aura, and I hemmed and hawed a good long time before finally resolving to drop him MOO-mail requesting an interview. By then it was too late. For reasons known only to himself, Dr. Jest had stopped logging in. Maybe he'd grown bored with the MOO. Maybe the loneliness of ostracism had gotten to him. Maybe a psycho whim had carried him far away or maybe he'd quietly acquired a third character and started life over with a cleaner slate.

Wherever he'd gone, though, he left behind the room he'd created for himself—a treehouse "tastefully decorated" with rare-book shelves, an operating table, and a life-size William S. Burroughs doll—and he left it unlocked. So I took to checking in there occasionally, and I still do from time to time. I head out of my own cozy nook (inside a TV set inside the little red hotel inside the Monopoly board inside the dining room of LambdaMOO), and I teleport on over to the treehouse, where the room description always tells me Dr. Jest is present but asleep, in the conventional depiction for disconnected characters. The not-quite-emptiness of the abandoned room invariably instills in me an uncomfortable mix of melancholy and the creeps, and I stick around only on the off

chance that Dr. Jest will wake up, say hello, and share his understanding of the future with me.

He won't, of course, but this is no great loss. Increasingly, the complex magic of the MOO interests me more as a way to live the present than to understand the future. And it's never very long before I leave Dr. Jest's lonely treehouse and head back to the mansion, to see some friends.

I won't pretend I knew what I was doing when I wrote "A Rape in Cyberspace." I thought, to be honest and if you can believe it, that I was setting down little more than an engaging true-life fable, played out in a realm of experience so circumscribed and so unique that no one (except perhaps the residents of LambdaMOO itself) could possibly take it as anything but a curiosity, a traveler's tale brought back from strange climes and only barely pertinent to the world as we know it. The philosophical excursions woven into the piece reached for a certain universal relevance, to be sure, but they were almost an afterthought, added at the last moment in hopes of teasing from the story a broader significance I wasn't entirely sure it had.

I needn't have bothered, though. For in the deluge of online responses to which I was soon exposed, very few readers remarked directly on my transparent attempts at intellectual provocation. It was the story itself that provoked them, or elements of the story anyway. And it was the story seen not as a piece of exotica but as a dispatch from a place maybe a little too close to home: the busy intersection of sex, violence, and representation around which late twentieth-century American culture hovers like a soul obsessed.

That the story tapped such a deep vein of anxieties is a development I look on now with some sense of gratification, yet I can't say I was exactly enjoying myself as those anxieties began flooding in my general direction. Opinions ran strong, and those that reflected not-so-very-well on me—or on the acts and attitudes of the tiny, textual world I had tried to represent as accurately as possible—seemed to run strongest. "Media culture keeps blurring the line between real offense and imaginary offense, but this is ridiculous," wrote one participant in a lengthy discussion on the haut-cachet New York bulletin-board system ECHO. "That article had no journalistic value whatsoever" added another ECHO-dweller, fuming at what many in that virtual community saw as crass exploitation of the unsettling and admittedly problematic notion of "virtual rape": "It was just using the RAPE catchphrase to SELL PAPERS . . . and it brutally trivializes people who have suffered through the real thing."

This hurt. The trivialization charge was an argument I recognized as part of the rhetorical arsenal of pro-sex feminists in their righteous battle against legal scholar Catharine MacKinnon's creepy redefinitions of porn as rape (and more broadly, of word as deed), and I didn't feel at all good about being placed conceptually in her camp. Compared to this insult, one Echoid's crudely worded announcement that he had used a copy of my article to tidy himself after a bowel movement seemed a friendly chuck under the chin. So I was relieved when West Coast feminist pornographer (and disaffected former MacKinnonite) Lisa Palac posted on ECHO in the article's favor, downplaying any fuss over its use of the word *rape* as essentially semantic, and finding in it an effective illustration of "how online worlds and identities reflect . . . RL socialization":

> I can't tell you how often I am interviewed by reporters who are under the assumption that taking on an online identity is "risk-free." And that for some reason, going online will be free from the social/cultural shapes as we know them. . . . [The subject of] this article may be extreme, but it disproves the "all is safe in cyberspace" notion.

Palac's note signaled, or so I thought, that the debate was mellowing and would soon enough be off my screen and out of my life. In fact, though, what it mainly signaled was that the debate had reached the other side of the country and would soon become fodder for the topic-hungry habitués of the WELL, a Bay Area bulletin-board system even more vigorously literate than ECHO. Once there, the discussion grew a notch more thoughtful, though no less contentious. Even more than the ECHO conference, the WELL's discussion seemed haunted by the ghosts of nearly every nineties polemic to have grappled with the issue of dangerous expression, from Anita Hill to the campus curriculum battles to the *succès de scandale* of "Beavis and Butt-head." The twists and turns of the arguments grew so convoluted that at one point, if I followed correctly, my account of Mr. Bungle's fate was determined to imply that Shakespeare, Sophocles, and Ibsen should also have been lynched on grounds of subjecting countless audience members to the emotional violence of catharsis.

More effectively critical, though, were the comments of R. U. Sirius, cofounder and guiding light of the magazine *Mondo 2000*. "The conflation of language and mediated activity with real activity seems to be more or less complete," wrote Sirius, in a formulation not at all surprising to anyone familiar with *Mondo 2000*'s reputation as a nest of giddy, pop-Baudrillardian armchair prophets stoned out of their minds on the ascendancy of digital simulation. What might have surprised those unable or unwilling to look past that caricature, however, was the entirely characteristic moral rigor Sirius then brought to bear on LambdaMOO's own giddy romp through the conflations of the hyperreal:

> These people all volunteered to act in a theater of the imagination and then got scared. Do we want Disney World? As the simulacrum becomes a bigger part of our lives, do we demand that people clip their imaginations at the place where it feels comfortable? . . . I think that freedom would be well served by simple toughening up.

And this hurt too. It was bad enough feeling like a rhetorical football, after all, without feeling part of me wanting to agree with some of those landing the hardest kicks.

Days of online discussion started piling up into weeks, and I began to wonder: How long could this go on? And how long would it be before the turbulence of the debate spilled over into less neatly compartmentalized venues for social interaction, like my more casual online encounters on the MOO, or the offline interactions I still respectfully referred to as real life? The WELL conference slowed down eventually, but controversy over the tale of Mr. Bungle spread into other online conferencing forums: Internet mailing lists. Usenet newsgroups, Compuserve. To this day, in fact, four months after its original publication, the story (stripped down to ASCII and turned loose to wander the nets) continues to find new pockets of interest and to gather online discussion around itself. Yet in the end, what I had dreaded most—the general irruption of the controversy into other areas of my life—has failed to materialize. LambdaMOOers, for the most part, seem to have accepted my interpretation of their world as true to their own experiences and left it at that. Most real-lifers unacquainted with any form of cyberspace, on the other hand, have found in the story a fascinating glimpse of a realm too distant from their own to pass judgment on—a parallel universe perhaps, or maybe a hint of their own future.

Which leaves only the denizens of the bulletin-board cybercosm to argue over the meaning of the life and crimes of Mr. Bungle. And, frankly, the fact that they have done so with such vociferous gusto remains something of a puzzle to me. Certainly, arguing is what people mainly do in such settings, and certainly, as I suggested earlier, the bleedthrough from larger cultural concerns about texts and violence has fed much of the fracas. Yet the more I ponder the furious online response to my story, the more I suspect the real object of that fury is neither LambdaMOO nor America's latest culture wars, but the ambiguous nature of online discourse itself.

Perched on a tightwire between the reasoned deliberation of text and the emotional immediacy of conversation, online communication sets itself up for a fall that is constantly realized. Fooled by the cool surface of electronic text, people lob messages cast in aggressively forensic impersonality into the midst of this combustibly personal medium, and the result, routinely, is just the sort of flame war I found myself embroiled in: a heatedly antagonistic exchange fueled by the most livid of emotions yet pretending in its rhetorical strategies to the most rational of dialogue. And in some sense, I think, the two sides of the Bungle war have taken up the two sides of this basic tension: the rational recognition (on the part of those who found the story ridiculous) that ultimately anything that happens online is "only words on a screen" countered by the emotional understanding (on the part of those who found the story compelling) that words can have powerful and deeply felt effects. It's too much to hope, I suppose, that this tension will ever really be resolved. Still, it's comforting to think that the noisy dialogue sparked by my article has not been only sound and fury. On its surface, of course, the discussion has provided more than its share of insight into a story I myself didn't fully understand when I wrote it. But deeper down, in the very structure of the debate, I have sometimes imagined I can hear the sound of cyberspace groping toward an end to flame wars.

Tales from the Cutting-Room Floor

THE REALITY OF "REALITY-BASED" TELEVISION

Debra Seagal

MAY 6, 1992

Yesterday I applied for a job as a "story analyst" at *American Detective*, a prime-time "reality-based" cop show on ABC that I've never seen. The interview took place in Malibu at the program's production office, in a plain building next door to a bodybuilding gym. I walked past rows of bronzed people working out on Nautilus equipment and into a dingy array of padded dark rooms crowded with people peering into television screens. Busy people ran up and down the halls. I was greeted by the "story department" manager, who explained that every day the show has camera crews in four different cities trailing detectives as they break into every type of home and location to search, confiscate, interrogate, and arrest. (The crews have the right to do this, he told me, because they have been "deputized" by the local police department. What exactly this means I was not told.) They shoot huge amounts of videotape and it arrives every day, rushed to Malibu by Federal Express. Assistants tag and time-code each video before turning it over to the story department.

After talking about the job, the story-department manager sat me in front of a monitor and gave me two hours to "analyze" a video. I watched the camera pan through a dilapidated trailer while a detective searched for incriminating evidence. He found money in a small yellow suitcase, discovered a knife under a sofa, and plucked a tiny, twisted marijuana

butt from a swan-shaped ashtray. I typed each act into a computer. It took me forty-five minutes to make what seemed a meaningless record. When I got home this afternoon there was a message on my phone machine from the story-department manager congratulating me on a job well done and welcoming me to *American Detective*. I am pleased.

MAY 18, 1992

Although we're officially called story analysts, in-house we're referred to as "the loggers." Each of us has a computer/VCR/print monitor/TV screen/headphone console looming in front of us like a colossal dashboard. Settling into my chair is like squeezing into a small cockpit. The camera crews seem to go everywhere: Detroit, New York, Miami, Las Vegas, Pittsburgh, Phoenix, Portland, Santa Cruz, Indianapolis, San Jose. They join up with local police teams and apparently get access to everything the cops do. They even wear blue jackets with POLICE in yellow letters on the back. The loggers scrutinize each hour-long tape second by second, and make a running log of every visual and auditory element that can be used to "create" a story. On an average day the other three loggers and I look at twenty to forty tapes, and in any given week we analyze from 6,000 to 12,000 minutes—or up to 720,000 seconds of film.

The footage comes from handheld "main" and "secondary" cameras as well as tiny, wire-like "lock-down" cameras taped to anything that might provide a view of the scene: car doors, window visors, and even on one occasion—in order to record drug deals inside an undercover vehicle—a gear-shift handle. Once a videotape is viewed, the logger creates a high-light reel—a fifteen-minute distillation of the overall "bust" or "case." The tapes and scripts are then handed over to the supervising producer, who in turn works with technical editors to create an episode of the show, each of which begins with this message on the screen: "What you are about to see is real. There are no re-creations. Everything was filmed while it actually happened."

There are, I've learned, quite a few of these reality and "fact-based" shows now, with names like *Cops*, *Top Cops*, and *FBI: The Untold Stories*. Why the national obsession with this sort of voyeuristic entertainment? Perhaps we want to believe the cops are still in control. The preponderance of these shows is also related to the bottom line: they are extremely inexpensive to produce. After all, why create an elaborate car-chase sequence costing tens of thousands of dollars a minute when a crew with a couple of video cameras can ride around with the cops and get the "real" thing? Why engage a group of talented writers and producers to make intelligent and exciting TV when it's more profitable to dip into the endless pool of human grief?

I've just participated in my first "story meeting" with the supervising producer. He occupies a dark little room filled with prerecorded sounds of police banter, queer voice-over loops, segments of the *American Detective* theme song, and sound bites of angry drug-busting screams ("Stop! Police! Put your hands up, you motherfucker!"). A perpetual cold wind blows from a faulty air duct above his desk. He is tall, lanky, in his fifties; his ambition once was to be a serious actor. His job is to determine what images will be resurrected as prime-time, Monday-night entertainment. He doesn't look miserable but I suspect he is.

There are six of us in the story meeting, the producer, four loggers, and the story-department manager. Each logger plays high-light reels and pitches stories, most of which are rejected by the producer for being "not hot enough," "not sexy." Occasionally, I learned today, a highlight reel is made of a case that is still in progress, such as a stakeout. Our cameramen then call us on-site from their cellular phones during our story meeting and update us on what has been filmed that day, sometimes that very hour. The footage arrives the next morning and then is built into the evolving story. This process continues in a flurry of calls and Federal Express deliveries while the real drama unfolds elsewhere—Pittsburgh or San Jose or wherever. We are to hope for a naturally dramatic climax. But if it doesn't happen, I understand, we'll "work one out."

MAY 26, 1992

I'm learning the job. Among other tasks, we're responsible for compiling stock-footage books—volumes of miscellaneous images containing every conceivable example of guns, drugs, money, scenics, street signs, appliances, and interior house shots. This compendium is used to embellish stories when certain images or sounds have not been picked up by a main or secondary camera: a close-up of a suspect's tightly cuffed wrists missed in a rush, a scream muffled by background traffic noise. Or, most frequently, the shouts of the cops on a raid ("POLICE! Open the door! Now!") in an otherwise unexciting ramrod affair. Evidently the "reality" of a given episode is subject to enhancement.

Today the story-department manager gave me several videotapes from secondary and lock-down cameras at an undercover mission in Indianapolis. I've never been to Indianapolis, and I figured that, if nothing else, I'd get to see the city.

I was wrong. What I saw and heard was a procession of close-up crotch shots, nose-picking, and farting in surveillance vans where a few detectives waited, perspiring under the weight of nylon-mesh raid gear and semi-automatic rifles. Searching for the scraps of usable footage was like combing a beach for a lost contact lens. The actual bust—a sad affair that featured an accountant getting arrested for buying pot in an empty shoe-store parking lot—was perhaps 1 percent of everything I looked at. In the logic of the story department, we are to deplore these small-time drug busts not because we are concerned that the big drugs are still on the street but because a small bust means an uninteresting show. A dud.

Just before going home today, I noticed a little list that someone tacked up on our bulletin boards to remind us what we are looking for:

DEATH
STAB
SHOOT
STRANGULATION
CLUB
SUICIDE

JUNE 3, 1992

Today was the first day I got to log Lieutenant Bunnell, which is considered a great honor in the office. Lieutenant Bunnell is the show's mascot, the venerated spokesperson. Only two years ago he was an ordinary narcotics detective in Oregon. Today he has a six-figure income, an agent, fans all over the country, and the best voice coach in Hollywood. He's so famous now that he's even stalked by his fans, such as the strange woman who walked into our office a few days ago wearing hole-pocked spandex tights, worn-down spike-heeled backless pumps, and a see-through purse. She'd been on his trail from Florida to California and wanted his home phone number. She was quietly escorted out the door to her dilapidated pickup truck.

At the beginning of each episode, Lieutenant Bunnell sets the scene for the viewer (much like Jack Webb on *Dragnet*), painting a picture of the crime at hand and describing the challenges the detectives face. He also participates in many of these raids, since he is, after all, still a police lieutenant. The standard fare: Act I, Bunnell's suspenseful introduction; Act II, Bunnell leads his team on a raid; Act III, Bunnell captures the bad suspect and throws him in the squad car, etc. The format of each drama must fit into an eleven-minute segment. So it is that although *American Detective* and its competitors seem a long way from *Dragnet*, *The Mod Squad*, *The Rookies*, et al.—all the famous old cop shows—they follow the same formula, the same dramatic arc, because this

is what the viewers and advertisers have come to expect.

JUNE 10, 1992

The producers are pleased with my work and have assigned me my own beat to log—Santa Cruz in northern California. Having spent several summers there as a teenager, I remember its forests, its eucalyptus and apple orchards. But today, two decades later, I strap on earphones, flip on the equipment, and meet three detectives on the Santa Cruz County Narcotic Enforcement Team. Dressed in full SWAT-team regalia, they are Brooks, an overweight commander; Gravitt, his shark-faced colleague; and Cooper, a detective underling. The first image is an intersection in Santa Cruz's commercial district. While an undercover pal negotiates with a drug dealer across the street, the three detectives survey an unsuspecting woman from behind their van's tinted windows. It begins like this:

[*Interior of van. Mid-range shot of Commander Brooks, Special Agent Gravitt, and Detective Cooper*]

Cooper: Check out those volumptuous [*sic*] breasts and that volumptuous [*sic*] ass.

Brooks: Think she takes it in the butt?

Cooper: Yep. It sticks out just enough so you can pull the cheeks apart and really plummet it. [*Long pause*] I believe that she's not beyond fellatio either.

[*Zoom to close-up of Cooper*]

Cooper: You don't have true domination over a woman until you spit on 'em and they don't say nothing.

[*Zoom to close-up of Gravitt*]

Gravitt: I know a hooker who will let you spit on her for twenty bucks . . . [*Direct appeal to camera*] Can one of you guys edit this thing and make a big lump in my pants for me?

[*Zoom to close-up of Gravitt's crotch, walkie-talkie between his legs*]

JUNE 15, 1992

I'm developing a perverse fascination with the magic exercised in our TV production sweatshop. Once our supervising producer has picked the cases that might work for the show, the "stories" are turned over to an editor. Within a few weeks the finished videos emerge from the editing room with "problems" fixed, chronologies reshuffled, and, when necessary, images and sound bites clipped and replaced by old filler footage from unrelated cases.

By the time our 9 million viewers flip on their tubes, we've reduced fifty or sixty hours of mundane and compromising video into short, action-packed segments of tantalizing, crackfilled, dope-dealing, junkie-busting cop culture. How easily we downplay the pathos of the suspect; how cleverly we breeze past the complexities that cast doubt on the very system that has produced the criminal activity in the first place. How effortlessly we smooth out the indiscretions of the lumpen detectives and casually make them appear as pistol-flailing heroes rushing across the screen. Watching a finished episode of *American Detective*, one easily forgets that the detectives are, for the most part, men whose lives are overburdened with formalities and paperwork. They ambush one downtrodden suspect after another in search of marijuana, and then, after a long Sisyphean day, retire into red-vinyl bars where they guzzle down beers among a clientele that, to no small degree, resembles the very people they have just ambushed.

JUNE 23, 1992

The executive producer is a tiny man with excessively coiffed, shoulder-length blond hair. He is given to wearing stone-washed jeans, a buttoned-to-the-collar shirt, and enormous cowboy boots; he also frequently wears a police badge on his belt loop. As I log away, I see his face on the screen flashing in the background like a subliminal advertisement for a new line of L.A.P.D. fashion coordinates. He sits in on interrogations, preens the detectives' hair, prompts them to "say something pithy for the camera." He gets phone calls in surveillance vans and in detective briefing rooms. With a cellular phone flat against his ear, he even has conversations with his L.A. entourage—Lorimar executives, ABC executives, other producers—while he runs in his police jacket behind the cops through ghettos and barrios.

I am beginning to wonder how he has gained access to hundreds of cop cars from California to New Jersey. Clearly the cops don't fear they will be compromised; I see the bonding that takes place between them and the executive producer, who, after a successful raid, presents them with *American Detective* plaques that feature their own faces. Their camaraderie is picked up continuously by the cameras. One of my colleagues has a photograph of our executive producer and Lieutenant Bunnell with their arms around a topless go-go dancer somewhere in Las Vegas; underneath it is a handwritten caption that reads, "The Unbearable Lightness of Being a Cop."

JUNE 25, 1992

Today I logged in several hours of one detective sitting behind a steering wheel doing absolutely nothing. How a man could remain practically immobile for so long is beyond my comprehension. He sat and stared out the window, forgetting that the tiny lock-down camera under his window visor was rolling. After an hour, it seemed as though I had become the surveillance camera, receiving his every twitch and breath through the intravenous-like circuitry that connects me to my machine and my machine to his image. There was, finally, a moment when he shifted and looked directly at the camera. For a second our eyes met, and, flustered, I averted my gaze.

JUNE 26, 1992

Today would have been inconsequential had not the supervising producer emerged from his air-conditioned nightmare and leaned over my desk. "We'll have a crew covering Detroit over the weekend," he said. "Maybe we'll get a good homicide for you to work on." I was speechless.

I've never seen a homicide, and I have no interest in seeing one. But I'm working in a place where a grisly homicide is actually welcomed. I am supposed to look forward to this. After work, I prayed for benevolence, goodwill, and peace in Detroit.

JUNE 29, 1992

My prayers must have worked—no Detroit homicide case came in today. That doesn't mean, however, that I'm any less complicit in what is clearly a sordid enterprise. This afternoon I analyzed a tape that features detectives busting a motley assortment of small-time pot dealers and getting them to "flip" on their connections. The freshly cuffed "crook" then becomes a C.I. (confidential informant). Rigged with hidden wires and cameras, the C.I. works for the detectives by setting up his friends in drug busts that lead up the ladder. In exchange for this, the C.I. is promised a more lenient sentence when his day comes up in court. Some of the C.I.'s have been busted so many times before that they are essentially professional informants. Ironically, some have actually learned how the game is played by watching reality-based cop shows. This is the case with a nervous teenage first-time pot seller who gets set up and busted in a bar for selling half an ounce of pot. When the undercover cop flashes his badge and whips out his cuffs, a look of thrilled recognition brightens the suspect's face. "Hey, I know you!" he gasps. "You're what's-his-name on *American Detective*, aren't you? I watch your show every week! I know exactly what you want me to do!"

The cops are flattered by the recognition, even if it comes from a teenage crook caught selling pot. They seem to become pals with the C.I.'s. Sometimes, however, they have to muscle the guy. The tape I saw today involves a soft-spoken, thirtysomething white male named Michael who gets busted for selling pot out of his ramshackle abode in the Santa Cruz mountains. He's been set up by a friend who himself was originally resistant to cooperating with the detectives. Michael has never been arrested and doesn't understand the mechanics

of becoming a C.I. He has only one request: to see a lawyer. By law, after such a request the detectives are required to stop any form of interrogation immediately and make a lawyer available. In this case, however, Commander Brooks knows that if he can get Michael to flip, they'll be able to keep busting up the ladder and, of course, we'll be able to crank out a good show.

So what happens? Hunched in front of my equipment in the office in Malibu, this is what I see, in minute after minute of raw footage:

[*Michael is pulled out of bed after midnight. Two of our cameras are rolling and a group of cops surround him. He is entirely confused when Brooks explains how to work with them and become a confidential informant.*]

Michael: Can I have a lawyer? . . . I don't know what's going on. I'd really rather talk to a lawyer. This is not my expertise at all, as it is yours. I feel way outnumbered. I don't know what's going on. . . .

Brooks: Here's where we're at. You've got a lot of marijuana. Marijuana's still a felony in the state of California, despite whatever you may think about it.

Michael: I understand.

Brooks: The amount of marijuana you have here is gonna send you to state prison. . . . That's our job, to try to put you in state prison, quite frankly, unless you do something to help yourself. Unless you do something to assist us. . . .

Michael: I'm innocent until proven guilty, correct?

Brooks: I'm telling you the way it is in the real world. . . . What we're asking you to do is cooperate . . . to act as our agent and help us buy larger amounts of marijuana. Tell us where you get your marijuana. . . .

Michael: I don't understand. You know, you guys could have me do something and I could get in even more trouble.

Brooks: Obviously, if you're acting as our agent, you can't get in trouble. . . .

Michael: I'm taking your word for that? . . .

Brooks: Here's what I'm telling you. If you don't want to cooperate, you're going to prison.

Michael: Sir, I do want to cooperate—

Brooks: Now, I'm saying if you don't cooperate right today, now, here, this minute, you're going to prison. We're gonna asset-seize your property. We're gonna asset-seize your vehicles. We're gonna asset-seize your money. We're gonna send your girlfriend to prison and we're gonna send your kid to the Child Protective Services. That's what I'm saying.

Michael: If I get a lawyer, all that stuff happens to me?

Brooks: If you get a lawyer, we're not in a position to wanna cooperate with you tomorrow. We're in a position to cooperate with you right now. Today. Right now. Today. . . .

Michael: I'm under too much stress to make a decision like that, I want to talk to a lawyer. I really do. That's the bottom line.

[*Commander Brooks continues to push Michael but doesn't get far.*]

Michael: I'm just getting more confused. I've got ten guys standing around me. . . .

Brooks: We're not holding a gun to you.

Michael: Every one of you guys has a gun.

Brooks: How old is your child?

Michael: She'll be three on Tuesday.

Brooks: Well, children need a father at home. You can't be much of a father when you're in jail.

Michael: Sir!

Brooks: That's not a scare tactic, that's a reality.

Michael: That is a scare tactic.

Brooks: No, it isn't. That's reality. . . . And the reality is, I'm sending you to prison unless you do something to help yourself out. . . .

Michael: Well, ain't I also innocent until proven guilty in a court of law? . . . You know what, guys? I really just want to talk to a lawyer. That's really all I want to do.

Brooks: How much money did you put down on this property? . . . Do you own that truck over there?

Michael: Buddy, does all this need to be done to get arrested? . . .

Brooks: Yeah. I'm curious—do you own that truck there?

Michael: You guys know all that.

Brooks: I hope so, 'cause I'd look good in that truck.

Michael: Is this Mexico?

Brooks: No. I'll just take it. Asset-seizure. And you know what? The county would look good taking the equity out of this house.

Michael: Lots of luck.

[*Commander Brooks continues to work on Michael for several minutes.*]

Michael: I feel like you're poking at me.

Brooks: I *am* poking at you.

Michael: So now I really want to talk to a lawyer now.

Brooks: That's fine. We're done.

[*Brooks huffs off, mission unaccomplished. He walks over to his pals and shakes his head.*]

Brooks: That's the first white guy I ever felt like beating the fucking shit out of.

If Michael's case becomes an episode of the show, Michael will be made a part of a criminal element that stalks backyards and threatens children. Commander Brooks will become a gentle, persuasive cop who's keeping our streets safe at night.

JULY 1, 1992

Today I got a video to analyze that involves a car chase. It includes the three Santa Cruz cops and a few other officers following two Hispanic suspects at top speed through a brussels-sprout field in the Central Valley. Our cameramen, wearing police jackets, are in one of their undercover vans during the pursuit. (One of them has his camera in one hand and a pistol held high in the other. The police don't seem to care about his blurred role.) When the suspects stop their car and emerge with their arms held high, the detectives bound out of their vans screaming in a shrill chorus ("Get on the ground, cocksucker!" "I'll blow your motherfucking head off."). I watch. Within seconds, the suspects are pinned to the ground and held immobile while cops kick them in the stomach and the face. Cooper is particularly angry because his van has bounced into a ditch during the pursuit. He looks down at one of the suspects. "You bashed my car," he complains. "I just got it painted, you motherfucker." With that he kicks the suspect in the head. Our main cameraman focuses on the detectives ambling around their fallen prey like hunters after a wild-game safari; a lot of vainglorious, congratulatory back-slapping ensues. Our secondary cameraman holds a long, extreme close-up of a suspect while his mouth bleeds into the dirt. "I feel like I'm dying," he wheezes, and turns his head away from the camera. I watch.

This afternoon, in the office, the video drew a crowd. One producer shook his head at the violence. "Too bad," he said. "Too bad we can't use that footage." This was clearly a case of too much reality for reality-based TV. I couldn't help but wonder what the producers would do if these two suspects were beaten so badly that they later died. Would they have jeopardized their own livelihoods by turning over the video to the "authorities"?

SEPTEMBER 21, 1992

I'm losing interest in the footage of detectives; now it is the "little people" who interest me, the people whose stories never make it past a highlight reel. I am strangely devoted to them. There is "the steak-knife lady" who waves her rusty weapon in front of a housing project in Detroit. I replay her over and over again. There is something about her: her hysteria, her insistence on her right to privacy, and her flagrant indignation at the cameras ("Get those cameras outta my face, you assholes!"); the way she flails her broken knife in self-defense at a drunk neighbor while her gigantic curlers unravel; the way she consoles her children, who watch with gaping mouths. This woman is *pissed*. She is *real*. Little does she know I'm going to be watching her in Malibu, California, while I sip my morning cappuccino,

manipulating her image for my highlight reel. I feel like I'm in the old Sixties movie *Jason and the Argonauts*, in which Zeus and Hera survey the little humans below them through a heavenly pool of water that looks, oddly enough, like a TV screen.

And there is a skinny, mentally disturbed redhead who took in a boyfriend because she was lonely and friendless. Unknown to her, he is selling heroin out of her apartment. But in the eyes of the law she is considered an accomplice. When the cops interrogate her, all she can say about her boyfriend is, "I love him. I took him in because I love him. He's a little bit retarded or something. I took him in." Later she breaks down sobbing. She is terrified that her father will throw her into a mental institution. "I need love. Can't you understand that?" she cries to the policeman who is trying to explain to her why they are arresting her boyfriend. "I need love. That's all I need, sir."

There are, too, the hapless Hispanic families living in poverty, stashing marijuana behind tapestries of the Virgin Mary and selling it to some of the same white middle-class couch potatoes who watch reality-based cop shows. There are the emotionally disturbed, unemployed Vietnam veterans selling liquid morphine because their SSI checks aren't enough to cover the rent. And there are AIDS patients who get busted, their dwellings ransacked, for smoking small quantities of pot to alleviate the side effects of their medication.

In our office the stories of people like these collect dust on shelves stacked with *Hollywood Reporters*, cast aside because they are too dark, too much like real life. I feel overwhelmed by my ability to freeze-frame their images in time-coded close-ups. I can peer into their private lives with the precision of a lab technician, replaying painful and sordid moments. I am troubled that something of their humanity is stored indefinitely in our supervising producer's refrigerated video asylum. Some of their faces have even entered my dreamworld. This afternoon when I suggested that such unfortunates might be the real stars of our show, my boss snapped, "You empathize with the wrong people."

SEPTEMBER 28, 1992

This morning I realized that watching hour after hour of vice has begun to affect me. After a raid, when the detectives begin to search for drugs, money, and weapons while our cameras keep rolling, I find myself watching with the intensity of a child foraging through a grassy backyard for an exquisitely luminous Easter egg. The camera moves through rooms of the unknown suspect as the detectives poke through bedrooms with overturned mattresses and rumpled, stained sheets, through underwear drawers and soiled hampers; into the dewy, tiled grottoes of bathrooms, past soap-streaked shower doors and odd hairs stuck to bathtub walls, clattering through rows of bottles, creams, tubes, and toothbrushes, their bristles splayed with wear. The exploration continues in kitchens, past half-eaten meals, where forks were dropped in surprise moments earlier, past grime-laden refrigerators and grease-pitted ovens, past cats hunched frozen in shock, and onward, sometimes past the body of a dog that has recently been shot by the police, now stiffening in the first moments of rigor mortis.

In the midst of this disarray the police sometimes find what they are so frantically looking for: abundant stacks of $100 bills stuffed in boots, behind secret panels and trap doors; heroin vials sealed in jars of cornmeal stashed in the dank corners of ant-infested cupboards; white powders in plastic Baggies concealed behind moldy bookshelves; discarded hypodermic needles in empty, economy-size laundry-detergent boxes; and thin, spindly marijuana plants blooming in tomato gardens and poppy fields. And, finally, on a lucky day, the guns: the magnums, automatics, shotguns, machine guns, and, in one case, assault rifles leaned against walls, their barrels pointed upward.

I feel as though my brain is lined with a stratum of images of human debris. Sitting at home in my small bungalow, I have begun to wonder what lurks behind the goodwill of my neighbors' gestures, what they are doing behind their porches and patios.

SEPTEMBER 30, 1992

Today was stock-footage day. I spent ten hours finding, cutting, and filing still-shots of semi-automatic rifles and hypodermic needles. I am starting to notice signs that I am dispirited and restless. I spend long moments mulling over camera shots of unknown faces. Today I took my lunch break on the Malibu pier, where I sat transfixed by the glassy swells, the kelp beds, and minnows under the jetty. I know I can't go on much longer, but I need to pay the rent.

OCTOBER 1, 1992

I've just worked through a series of videos of the Las Vegas vice squad as they go on a prostitute rampage with our cameramen and producers. Pulling down all-nighters in cheesy motel rooms, the detectives go undercover as our camera crew, our producers, and some of the detectives sit in an adjacent room, watching the live action through a hidden camera. It is, essentially, a voyeur's paradise, and definitely X-rated. The undercover cops' trick is to get the call girls into a position where they are clearly about to accept money for sexual acts. The scam goes something like this: "Hi, I'm John. Me and my buddies here are passing through town. Thought you gals might be able to show us a good time . . ."

"What did you have in mind?" they ask. The detectives respond with the usual requests for blow jobs. Maybe the undercover cops ask the girls to do a little dancing before getting down to real business. They sit back and enjoy the show. Sometimes they even strip, get into the motel's vibrating, king-size bed, and wait for just the right incriminating moment before the closet door bursts open and the unsuspecting woman is overwhelmed by a swarm of detectives and cameramen.

"He's my boyfriend!" many insist as they hysterically scramble for their clothes.

"What's his name?" the cops respond while they snap on the cuffs.

"Bill. Bob. Uh, John . . ."

It doesn't matter. The police get their suspect. The camera crew gets its footage. The cameras keep on rolling. And what I see, what the viewer will never see, is the women—disheveled, shocked, their clothes still scattered on musty hotel carpets—telling their stories to the amused officers and producers. Some of them sob uncontrollably. Three kids at home. An ex who hasn't paid child support in five years. Welfare. Food stamps. Some are so entrenched in the world of poverty and pimps that they are completely numb, fearing only the retribution they'll suffer if their pimps get busted as a result of their cooperation with the cops. Others work a nine-to-five job during the day that barely pays the rent and then become prostitutes at night to put food on the table. Though their faces are fatigued, they still manage a certain dignity. They look, in fact, very much like the girl next door.

I can't help but see how each piece or the drama fits neatly into the other: one woman's misery is another man's pleasure; one man's pleasure is another man's crime; one man's crime is another man's beat; one man's beat is another man's TV show. And all of these pieces of the drama become one big paycheck for the executive producer.

OCTOBER 5, 1992

Today the executive producer—in the flesh, not on tape—walked into the office and smiled at me. I smiled back. But I was thinking: one false move and I'll blow your head off.

OCTOBER 9, 1992

It would seem that there could not be any further strangeness to everything that I've seen, but, in fact, there is: almost all of the suspects we film, including the prostitutes, sign releases permitting us to put them on TV. Why would they actually want to be on TV even when they've been, literally, caught with their pants down? Could it be because of TV's ability to seemingly give a nobody a certain fleeting, cheap celebrity? Or is it that only by participating in the non-reality of TV can

these people feel *more* real, more alive? I asked around to understand how the release process happens.

Usually a production coordinator—an aspiring TV producer fresh out of college—is assigned the task of pushing the legal release into the faces of overwhelmed and tightly cuffed suspects who are often at such peak stress levels that some can't recognize their own faces on their driver's licenses. "We'll show your side of the story," the production coordinator might say. Sometimes it is the police themselves who ask people to sign, suggesting that the cameras are part of a training film and that signing the form is the least of their present concerns. And to anyone in such a situation this seems plausible, since the entire camera crew is outfitted with police jackets, including the executive producer, who, with his "belt badge," could easily be mistaken for a cop in civilian attire. And, clearly, many of those arrested feel that signing anything will help them in court. In the rare event that a suspect is reluctant to sign the release, especially when his or her case might make for a good show, the *American Detective* officials offer money; but more frequently, it seems, the suspect signing the release form simply doesn't adequately read or speak English. Whatever the underlying motive, almost all of the arrested "criminals" willingly sign their releases, and thus are poised—consciously or not—to participate in their own degradation before the American viewing public.

OCTOBER 16, 1992

Today I saw something that convinced me I may be lost in this netherworld of videotape; I did, finally, get a homicide. The victim lived in Oregon and planned to save up to attend Reed College. She was a stripper who dabbled in prostitution to make ends meet. On the tape the cops find her on her bed clutching a stuffed animal, her skull bludgeoned open with a baseball bat. A stream of blood stains the wall in a red arc, marking her descent just three hours earlier.

The guy who killed her was a neighbor—blond, blue-eyed, wore a baseball cap, the kind of guy you'd imagine as the head of a Little League team, or a swim coach. He has that particularly American blend of affability, eagerness, and naiveté. When the cops ask him why he bludgeoned her repeatedly after clubbing her unconscious with the first stroke, he replies, "I don't know. I don't really know."

She was Asian, but you would never have known it from what was left of her. What one sees on the tape is that bloody red stain on the wall. We never know why he killed her. We never really know who she was. But it doesn't really matter. She is "just another prostitute." And she will be very good for the show's ratings.

OCTOBER 19, 1992

This morning I explained my feelings to my boss. I said I "didn't feel good" about the work and had decided to quit. He understood, he said, for he'd once had certain ideals but had eventually resigned himself to the job.

Before departing, I asked a colleague if he was affected by the grief and vice on our monitors. "They're only characters to me," he replied. I noted this quietly to myself, and, with barely a good-bye to my other co-conspirators, I slipped out of the *American Detective* offices into the noon blaze of the California sun, hoping to recover what it is I've lost.

Editors' Note: American Detective was canceled last summer by ABC, despite good ratings.

Fear and Loathing in an Age of Show Business: Reflections on Televised Executions

Paul Leighton

One must kill publicly or confess that one does not feel authorized to kill—Camus (1960: 187)

Hey, man, you shouldn't be killing people for no four hundred dollars—condemned man speculating on his final words to the executioner (in Prejean 1993: 182)

Paul Leighton, "Fear and Loathing in an Age of Show Business," © 2000 Paul Leighton. Reprinted by permission of the author. Permission is freely given to distribute paper copies at or below cost. All other rights, including electronic, are reserved. Small portions or this paper appeared in "Televising Executions, Primetime 'Live'?" *The Justice Professional* Volume 12 Number 2 (1999).

The idea of televising executions seems like a bad joke—a satiric comment on media values, audience taste, or the latest in tougher-than-thou political campaigning. Any media cynic can quickly apply the logic of television to executions and create instant dark humor about summer reruns and slow motion reverse angles. What is an appropriate commercial to broadcast with capital punishment, or would a World Wrestling Federation pay-per-view program be the model?

Grim humor aside, there are good reasons to start examining televised executions: They could easily become reality, and human lives are at stake. Televised executions may not be inevitable, but their prohibition rests on dated case law. A suit from the press, or even an Internet entertainment group, might prevail in a court, especially one with a maverick tough-on-crime judge. Strange bedfellows like victim's rights and open-government advocates could form a coalition to broadcast at least one execution, or someone could take advantage of miniaturized surveillance equipment to make a bootlegged movie for television or the Internet.

Politicians suggest that televising executions would be an effective part of a tough-on-crime agenda that would increase deterrence and save lives. The possibility also exists that televised executions would brutalize some viewers and precipitate copycat murders. The chance to be executed before a national, or even international, audience might tempt some people to commit spectacular crimes. Even though a televised execution would be the first in the United States, the potential effects (good and bad) are international, since the broadcast would go out to the global village. Internet sites would ensure wide dissemination of the execution and preserve it for countless others in the future. Also at issue is public opinion and how televised executions would affect support for capital punishment. Would the televised image make the taking of a life "real" in a way that undermines support for the death penalty, or would it make people complacent with an administrative death that is quite mild when compared to the myriad violence seen so regularly on television? Can the United States maintain credibility when railing against human rights abuses after broadcasting to the world our use of a sanction that other industrialized democracies renounce?

This paper cannot hope to resolve many of the issues surrounding televised executions, nor does it intend to. The purpose is to incite discussion. My belief is that footage of an execution will appear on television or the Internet in the future. If this event really holds the promise of saving lives, then we should enact laws to make a televised execution happen as part of our legislative program to build a better world. If the event is going to touch off further violence, then there needs to be a debate about how to weigh that against a possible First Amendment right to free press or a belief that open government ideals require just such questionable practices to be carried out before the public. If a televised execution is going to touch off further violence, I think we should try to figure out what kind and how to minimize the harm done by the broadcast. (The possibility of this state-sponsored "snuff film" being seen by billions and having no effect is both too disturbing and remote to be considered further.)

In the next section, I sketch a brief history of public and private executions then examine current arguments supporting televised executions. Subsequently, I consider the claims that a televised execution would help deter people from committing homicide and the counterclaim that it might brutalize people or somehow encourage further violence. The final section analyzes the potential effect of televised executions on public opinion and our "evolving standards of decency."

PATHWAYS TO TELEVISED EXECUTIONS

In the past, executions were public events attended by tens of thousands of people who had such a good time that one of our terms for celebration—gala—comes from the word gallows (Johnson 1998). States started to restrict public access in the 1830s through "private execution" statutes aimed at reducing unsightly public spectacles and thus undermining growing sentiment to abolish the death penalty (Bessler 1993). Courts accepted paternalistic justifications due to an argument about the detrimental effects on the public from witnessing executions. One court, in upholding a fine for publishing details of a hanging that took almost 15 minutes to complete, stated that the execution needed to be surrounded "with as much secrecy as possible, in order to avoid exciting an unwholesome effect on the public mind. For that reason it must take place before dawn, while the masses are at rest, and within an enclosure, so as to debar the morbidly curious" (quoted in Bessler 1993: 365), But even denied direct access to the execution, people in the 1940s gathered in places like Mississippi, "late at night on the courthouse square with chairs, crackers and children, waiting for the current to be turned on and the street lights to dim" (in Oshinsky 1996: 207).

People still meet at the prison gates to celebrate an execution (Parker 1989a and b), but aside from a handful of witnesses the closest most people will come to an execution is watching a fictional television show. Although media representatives are official witnesses to an execution, the state statutes or prison media policies prohibit cameras. In 1977, Garrett had wanted to televise Texas' first execution since 1964 and claimed that if a reporter with a notebook is allowed, then a broadcast journalist with a camera should also be admitted. The federal Court of Appeals denied the request and held that there were no First Amendment issues because Garrett was still free to make his report by other means, including "by simulation" (in Bessler 1993: 375, quoting *Garrett v. Estelle*).

This precedent is binding only in the Fifth Circuit and could easily be overruled on the basis of other cases in which courts have held that transcripts of proceedings are no substitute for television coverage. Indeed, in the two decades since this decision, CSPAN coverage of Congress supplements the *Congressional Record* and Court-TV broadcasts judicial proceedings. Further, "with television stations in the United States already broadcasting assassinations and executions in other countries . . . it is ironic and contrary to the First Amendment principles that executions performed by our own government are deemed inappropriate for television audiences in the United States" (Bessler 1993: 403).

Claims that executions should be televised because of the First Amendment or principles of open government share a basis in the importance of an informed public to democratic self-governance. They differ, however, in that one claims the *right of television to show* the execution; the other claims a *right of the general public to view* the workings of government (and television is the medium through which the information is carried). Courts have stated that visual impressions add dimensions that print does not and that "the importance of conveying the fullest information possible increases as the importance of the particular news event or news setting increases" (in Bessler 1993: 402 n. 273). Because the death penalty is a dramatic display of state power—whether it is the first in many years or one of several dozen a state will do this year—citizens should have the fullest information possible from a televised proceeding. Indeed, Bessler notes that Eighth Amendment jurisprudence requires the prohibition on cruel and unusual punishment to be evaluated against the "evolving standards of decency that mark the progress of a maturing society" (1993: 423, quoting *Trop v. Dulles*, 356 US 86 at 101, 1958). He argues that only with public executions can people have "full access" to information regarding capital punishment, and only on this basis can a court determine whether the sanction violates contemporary standards of decency.

Arguments opposing public executions suggest that the spectacle will be harmful and that people can be informed about executions without a broadcast. Many concerns about the harmful nature of public executions are based on earlier times' paternalistic distaste of crowd behavior. The suggestion that "harm" might befall a contemporary audience watching a lethal injection is difficult to support given what one media critic describes as "the tube's day and night splatterings of brutality, grossness, commercialism, exploitation and inanity" (Goodman 1991: C18). The same could be said of the notion that an execution would be "shocking" or "offensive," but these concerns are weak and problematic reasons for not televising executions. The lower court in *Garrett* noted: "If government officials can prevent the public from witnessing films of governmental proceedings solely because the government subjectively decides that it is not fit for public viewing, then news cameras might be barred from other public facilities where public officials are involved in illegal, immoral, or other improper activities that may be 'offensive,' 'shocking,' 'distasteful' or otherwise disturbing to viewers of television news" (in Bessler 1993: 375).

The larger context to this discussion is the extent to which television is critical to being "informed" in the sense important to a democratic country. Executions are one of many possible areas which raise questions about television's ability to educate citizens about public policy. Already, there exists what Johnson (1998) calls a "cottage industry" of people viewing executions and *writing* about them. People can view simulated executions in many movies and television crime dramas. But the argument is that the visual depiction of an actual execution provides additional knowledge and that it is more likely to be seen than a newspaper or book. One media critic even asserts that "for most of the nation, all those beer-and-pretzel people, the picture is the thing and television is the source" (Goodman 1991: C18).

Debate about televising executions thus involves many more values than simple support for or dissent of capital punishment. Combined with other arguments about the potential of broadcast executions to deter and/or create abhorrence for executions, people on different sides of the capital punishment debate can find themselves united on the issue of televising it. For example, in Sister Helen Prejean's *Dead Man Walking*, one of the condemned decided he would like his electrocution televised because it "would change some minds" when people "see what they are really doing" (1993: 207). The father of one of his victims believes "what we should do is fry the bastards on prime-time" to "see if that doesn't give second thoughts to anybody thinking of murder" (1993: 235).

Their positions represent others who favor televising executions. For example, now-retired talk show host Phil Donahue expressed his desire to televise a 1994 execution on the assumption that the exposure would reduce support for capital punishment (Goodman 1994: C15).

Senator Mark Hatfield proposed public executions for federal death penalty cases because he believed people would turn against capital punishment once they saw the execution (Bessler 1993: 368 n. 60). Other legislators, though, suggest televising executions as part of tough-on-crime public policy (Bowers and Pierce 1980: 453; Gugliotta 1994: A13; Varney 1995: B3). More recently, Mike Wallace of *60 Minutes* suggested coverage of McVeigh's execution for his part in the Oklahoma City bombing that killed 168 people: "If it's a public policy to take an individual's life, why in the world shouldn't the American public be allowed to see it?" The executive producer—who would later agree to air footage of Dr. Jack Kevorkian assisting in a suicide—said it would happen "over my dead body. . . . don't see any point except shocking people" (in Turner 1997: 83).

Many of the assumptions underlying the various positions are open to question and explored in subsequent sections, but an important conclusion to be reached is that people with opposing views on capital punishment could become strange bedfellows in the politics of televising an execution. They could even have drastically different reasons, but still work together to support legislation, litigation, or a mission to capture an image and distribute it.

SCARED STRAIGHT

Deterrence is the notion that the pain of punishment prevents other crimes; it can be part of a utilitarian justification for punishment because of the larger good it does by saving lives. Deterrence is premised on a rational-choice model in which people weigh the pleasures or gains of a crime against the certainty, severity, and swiftness of a possible punishment. Empirical studies have failed to find support for a deterrent effect from capital punishment as opposed to life imprisonment, but the question here is how publicity affects deterrence. Importantly, though, few people revoke their support for the death penalty if asked to assume that it has no deterrent effect (Ellsworth and Gross 1994: 27). Retribution thus drives support for the death penalty, and discussions about promoting public good and crime reduction may mask troublesome questions about our society's voyeuristic interest in punishment.

Empirical evidence, derived from a variety of methods in several countries, suggests that there is no greater deterrent effect from capital punishment than from imprisonment (Blumstein, Cohen, and Nagin 1978; Bailey and Peterson 1994; Camus 1960: 192; Kappler, Blumberg, and Potter 1996: 308–16). The few findings of a greater deterrent effect are not robust, but rather fragile artifacts of methodology, assumptions, and data construction (Bowers and Pierce 1975, 1980; Kappler, Blumberg, and Potter 1996: 315; McGahey 1980). The argument about televising the death penalty, though, assumes that deterrence is low because executions occur out of public view and that capital punishment *would* deter if only more people knew of its use. Indeed, Camus suggested that if deterrence were a serious argument in favor of capital punishment, then people should be shown more photographs of it or the scaffold should be moved to the town square. "The entire population should be invited," he said "and the ceremony should be put on television for those who couldn't attend" (1960: 181).

Camus' sarcastic comment is argued in earnest by contemporary politicians because part of deterrence is related to communications theory. Punishment needs to be certain, swift, and severe—and these attributes need to be made salient to a potential law breaker. Television is ideal to "get out the word" because it is present in 98 to 99 percent of households—more homes than have indoor plumbing or refrigerators (Surette 1992: 33). People watch frequently and for a long duration; they regard TV as the most credible "complete," "intelligent," and "unbiased" source of news (Bailey 1990: 628; see Postman 1985 for an eloquent dissent). However, anecdotal evidence from people with intense exposure to capital punishment does not suggest a deterrent effect. European pickpockets frequently plied their trade at the hanging of other pickpockets (Camus 1960: 189); both inmates and law enforcement officers who have been around

executions have gone on to commit capital murders (Espy 1980; Senate Committee on the Judiciary 1968). More controlled and systematic research on publicized executions and deterrence bears out the anecdotal findings. Bailey, for example, examines the deterrent effect of newspaper and television coverage of executions, controlling for whether the news included graphic details. The correlations for publicity and deterrence (and its opposite, brutalization) are not statistically significant, and they do not become significant in any model with lag effects ranging from one to twelve months (Bailey 1990).

The deterrent effect is weak because the "rational choice" model does not always apply to homicidal situations. Rationality can be short term rather than take into account punishments many years down the road after a seemingly unlikely capture and conviction. Decisions also involve irrational elements and situational seductions (Katz 1988; Barak 1998). People kill in the heat of passion; they get drunk and/or drugged. Some may be violent due to brain damage, including damage from childhood abuse (Lewis 1986). Others live in the midst of such violence that they—like those in a war zone—plan and think about their own funerals (Brown 1993: A1). Children who say, "*if* I grow up, Mr. Kemp, I want to be a bus driver" obviously experience other threats to their lives with such salience that they will not be deterred by a state-ordered execution, whether televised or not (Weisskopf 1996: A1; emphasis supplied). The argument about deterrence further assumes that execution footage would stand out in a medium in which violence is more rampant than it is in the real world. The methods of execution, especially lethal injection, seem tame by comparison to thousands of other televised deaths played to viewers and gruesome mutilation many have performed in video games.

The United States has already experimented with a "scared straight" program in the form of a television documentary based on the Juvenile Awareness Project (created by the Lifers' Group at Rahway Prison, New Jersey). Rap sessions between convicts and the high school students were meant to explain the consequences of crime and "demonstrated the unpleasantness and brutality of prison life by verbal abuse and physical intimidation directed towards the juveniles" (Cavender 1981: 433). This program that "scared the hell" out of juveniles received extensive favorable media coverage and widespread calls for replications of its design (ibid: 437). One set of inmates replicating the "Scared Straight" program even wanted a drama coach for maximum effect (Cavender 1981: 438 n. 4). Serious evaluation of the program, however, found no deterrent effect from the harassment and threats of violence that included rape. Some research indicated that participants did slightly worse in terms of frequency and severity of subsequent offenses compared to a control group (ibid: 434–35).

A replication involving broadcasting an execution raises serious issues about deterrence and the media. At what point does "communicating the consequences" for a crime become an exercise in terrorizing people into submission? What are the ethical issues involved for the media in dramatizing an execution for heightened deterrence (or ratings)? To what extent should the media—the National Entertainment State in the form of a "user-friendly" Big Brother[4] (in Barak 1998: 270–71)—add to "law and order" when the social order is heavily marked by racial and class inequality?

BRUTALIZATION BACKFIRE EFFECTS

If more publicity creates greater deterrence, then logic would suggest maximum effect from grisly executions that are frequently replayed. The rather obvious flaw is that at some point people may well become desensitized to violence or even brutalized, so televised executions might result in increased homicides. Although most research finds neither a deterrent nor a brutalization effect following executions, a brutalization effect shows up more frequently in research, indicating that executions have an effect on the homicide rate. The question, as with deterrence, is what potential publicity has to magnify the effect. Brutalization

research has not specified a single dynamic at work to explain why there are greater numbers of homicides following an execution. This section explores several possible paths through which a deterrent effect could be undermined or negated, such as murder-suicide, copycat or imitation, and celebrity criminals.

One of the strongest brutalization findings is from research by Bowers and Pierce, who conclude that the brutalization effect for non-televised executions is "two homicides one month later and one homicide two months later," which they believe to be a minimal estimate (1980: 481). Their analysis applied only to New York State, yet publicity about executions may carry a brutalization effect beyond its geographical boundaries and for longer than two months. Televising executions would certainly have this effect by making the image available across the nation—perhaps the world— *and* for unlimited future replay. Bowers and Pierce suggest that the results of their study are "ominous," and that the "cost in innocent lives would be outstanding" if death rows were emptied through execution (1980: 483). Even those who do not give full credence to these findings may wish for additional study before televising executions. A brutalization effect for publicized executions seems at least likely enough that media planning to televise the spectacle have some moral duty to ensure that their actions—however well-intentioned and within First Amendment rights—will not result in increased slaughter.

While deterrence rests on the notion that executions convey the message "crime doesn't pay," may also tell the audience that "a man's life ceases to be sacred when it is thought useful to kill him" (quoted in Camus 1960: 229). Executions can strengthen social solidarity by "drawing people together in a common posture of anger and indignation" (in Reiman 1998: 40). A person who identifies with the state may then associate "the person who has wronged him with the victim of an execution" and see "that death is what his despised offender deserves" (Bowers and Pierce 1980: 456). The issue is not simply about devaluing life, but also about modeling and imitation, which are most likely when the violence is "presented as 1) rewarded, 2) exciting, 3) real, and 4) justified; when the perpetrator of violence is 5) not criticized for his behavior and is presented as 6) intending to injure his victim" (Phillips 1983: 561). Indeed, Phillips' work on boxing—another example of acceptable and rewarded violence—is especially disconcerting in finding a greater increase in homicides following a heavily publicized boxing prizefight than after a less publicized one and finding that homicide victims bear at least some resemblance to the loser of the prizefight (Phillips 1983). This research certainly adds another strong reason for caution in approaching a televised execution.

Another chilling possibility is that the publicity about an offender's misdeeds that accompanies a televised execution could unleash great harm to the family and associates of the condemned—people who neither have done harm nor share guilt. Although the issue is not frequently discussed, hostility targeted at the condemned spills over onto others, those who serve as proxies for rage that may continue even after the murderer has been executed. Mikal Gilmore writes about the aftermath of his brother Gary's execution in Utah—the first in the nation after the Supreme Court lifted the death penalty moratorium in 1976:

> I took comment after comment from people who betrayed their own intelligence and grace with the remarks and jokes they made, and each time, something inside me flinched. I felt that nobody would ever forget or forgive me for being the dead fucking killer's brother. I learned a bit of what it is like to live on in the aftermath of punishment: as a living relative, you have to take on some of the burden and legacy of the punishment. People can no longer insult or hurt Gary Gilmore, but because you are his brother—even if you're not much like him—they can aim at you (1994: 357–58).

Mikal notes that he received letters from people who told him he had no right to hold a job with *Rolling Stone* where he had the attention of young people; others wrote that he should be shot alongside his brother (1994: 356). Hours after the bars closed, people would pull up outside of the trailer where Gary's mom lived: "she would hear voices, whispers, laughs, profanities, threats. Some people would yell horrible things, some people threw bottles or cans at the trailer" (1994: 359).

Sister Helen Prejean notes that her mother "gets angry phone calls about her daughter's misplaced kindness'" in being spiritual advisor to condemned men (1993: 68). The mother of one condemned man found a dismembered cat on her front porch one morning (1993: 107), and one of the attorneys had garbage dumped all over his yard (1993: 161). The examples make clear that misplaced public retaliation already occurs. Televising an execution has serious potential to expand such behavior by widely publicizing the offender's misdeeds.

Further, backfire effects can happen when people identify with the condemned and see him as a hero. Kooistra's fascinating work *Criminals as Heroes* notes that hero status occurs when an audience finds "some symbolic meaning in his criminality" (1989: 152), for example, when substantial segments of the public feel " 'outside the law' because the law is no longer seen as an instrument of justice but as a tool of oppression wielded by favored interests" (1989: 11). At such times, or among groups with this perception, there is a "market" for symbolic representations of justice and "a steady need for the production of celebrities" (Kooistra 1989: 162; Barak 1998: Chapter 11). These dynamics suggest that the execution of an African-American activist like Mumia Abu-Jamal could elevate his status among some to a martyr and hero, thus precipitating racial strife reminiscent of what followed the verdict in the Rodney King beating case (see Abu-Jamal 1995).

Another mechanism through which televised executions could contribute to violence is known as the "murder/suicide" phenomenon. This clinically recognized syndrome is characterized by suicidal individuals who kill thinking that "the State will execute him and thereby accomplish what he himself cannot bring about by his own hand" (Strafer 1983: 863 n. 12). In this sense the death penalty "breeds murder" and becomes "a promise, a contract, a covenant between society and certain (by no means rare) warped mentalities who are moved to kill as part of a self-destructive urge" (in Strafer 1983: 864 n. 13; Bowers and Pierce 1980: 458; Parker 1989a). For example, Ted Bundy *went* to Florida and Gary Gilmore *went* to Utah; they intentionally chose states that had capital punishment. Jeffrey Dahmer told the judge at his 1992 sentencing, "I wanted death for myself" (quoted in Barak 1998). This dynamic may not have much of an effect at present because of capital punishment's infrequent and freakish application, but a televised execution would advertise this "contract" broadly and potentially stimulate the more self-destructive amongst us (Farberow 1980).

The potential infamy and attention stemming from a televised execution may have an impact on those whose violence comes out of a sense of powerlessness and need for attention. For severely neglected people, negative attention in the form of mass hatred is better than continued neglect. If part of the "contract" is not just a desired death but also nationwide media exposure, might there not be people motivated to kill by the promise of publicity and made-for-TV movies? Indeed, Sellers suggests that power and attention contribute to capital murder where the murderer's sense of wrongdoing can be assuaged only at the hands of

> someone greater than himself. His private despair and desirable suicide turn a mean face upon him, he wishes to resolve his puniness and make of his death something grand; all his life's prospects have drained into the ignoble, and nothing less than mass hatred and execution can vindicate his will (1990: 36).

Research on serial killers seems to confirm this dynamic, including Hickey's observation that "society gave Ted [Bundy] what he so eagerly sought throughout his life: infamy, notoriety, and the attention of millions of people" (1997: 162). Bundy, "like some other serial killers," found his fortune in "recognition and celebrity status" (ibid); he was "reveling in the notoriety" (1997: 164).[2]

Seltzer asks many intriguing questions about "death as theater for the living" (Seltzer 1998: 22) and argues that the U.S. already has a "pathological public sphere" characterized by a "wound culture." "The public fascination with torn and open bodies and torn and opened persons, a collective gathering around shock, trauma, and the wound" (ibid: 2). Such a culture is a breeding ground, he argues, for serial killers like Dennis Nilsen, who dismembered bodies while listening to Aaron Copeland's *Fanfare for the Common Man*. Nilsen described "his final public service as a mass spectacle of pathology and abjection. He was a black hole of violation and pollution about which the contemporary national body gathers, spectates, and discharges itself: in his words, he was 'a national receptacle into which all the nation will urinate'" (Seltzer 1998: 19). The question, then, is whether televised executions would create more characters like Nilsen. Does the U.S. want to indulge him—and ourselves—in gathering, spectating, and discharging on a television event being broadcast to the world?

TELEVISION AND THE "EVOLVING STANDARD OF DECENCY"

Another possibility is that televised executions will be such an unsettling spectacle that they will add support for the movement to abolish the death penalty. As Johnson (1998) notes, executions are not the hallmarks of civilization, so exposure has the potential to spread the idea that capital punishment is a regrettable lapse of civility. Publicity could fuel the abolitionist movement by increasing the salience of premeditated killing being done in the name of the people, especially when the condemned is young, severely mentally retarded, or female. If the reality of killing in our name is not enough, then perhaps the actual methods, when seen on television, will seem inconsistent with our self-image as a civilized nation and world leader on human rights.

In the scope of history, current executions are very secret events. The act of hiding execution "suppresses the horror," which needs to be undone by showing—perhaps forcing—people to look at the executioner's hands *each time*, as Camus said. This principle is extended to all of those who have responsibility for bringing the executioner into being (1960: 187; see also Prejean 1993: 197), and death penalty opponents have used this logic to suggest that judges and juries be required to witness the executions they impose as sentences (Hentoff 1995: A19). Support for the death penalty drops if people are required to be an "active participant" such as juror or executioner (Howells et al. 1995: 413; Zakhari and Ransom 1999), so the increased awareness of executions could especially undermine support with people who want to "preserve the symbolism of capital punishment without having to witness a bloodbath" (Costanzo and White 1994: 7). Publicity "simply makes the reality inescapable, and our role undeniable. If we want it, we should be able to look at it. If we can't bear to look at it, maybe it's time to rethink our desires" (in Howells et al. 1995: 414). Goodman, though, notes that people may have a difficult time with consistency in determining which atrocities to televise in the name of democracy (1991: c18)—an issue he raises with respect to the Gulf War but which is more problematic when applied to abortion.

This argument about television highlighting the reality of the death penalty is independent of the actual method used for the execution. The method is important, but executions are ultimately ugly because people representing them cooperate in the premeditated killing of a helpless person (Amnesty International 1989; Prejean 1993: 216). Those who participate in the process display discomfort and at times acute stress in spite of their efforts to see it as "just doing their job" and trying to do it professionally (Johnson 1998; Prejean 1993). Although their feelings might not come across in a televised execution, people watching have to confront the reason for their distress—taking the life of a helpless person.

Further, the methods used for execution may create revulsion, and although lethal injection is tame, television would expose mistakes or irregularities that might offend the audience's sense of justice. When Camus suggested that "the man who enjoys his coffee while reading that justice has been done would spit it out at the least detail" [1960: 187; also quoted in *Glass v. Louisiana* 471 US 1080, 1086 (1985)], he meant the guillotine in France. Now, execution mostly involves a pinprick (preceded by an alcohol swab to prevent infection) rather than "the sound of a head falling," although crude depictions of dismembered bodies have increasingly become part of public entertainment on television and computer games advertised as "decapitating, spine-crushing fun!" (*Interaction Magazine*, Holiday 1996, p. 46; see generally Bok 1998). The television program *The Day After* did have a modest impact on social consciousness about the effects of nuclear holocaust, but reactions included at least one person disappointed that "there weren't a lot of people with their faces melting away" (in Oskamp 1989: 296). Electrocutions would be more intense, but they cause few outward signs of pain more extreme than the "gasp or yawn" exhibited by the condemned in a lethal injection (Prejean 1993: 217). Indeed, electrocutions and lethal injections *appear* to be less painful than they are, which might produce complacency with contemporary methods (Johnson 1998: Chapter 2; *Glass v. Louisiana* 471 US 1080; Trombley 1992).

Complacency can also be generated because the effect of decades on death row is difficult to capture on television, yet it is a crucial part of the pain caused by capital punishment. Indeed, the stress of life on death row is the reason the European Court of Human Rights refused to extradite a person to the U.S. for execution on the grounds that it was "in human and degrading punishment" and violated article 3 of the European Convention on Human Rights (in Johnson 1998: 222; Grant 1998: 25). Research on the effects of showing executions is inconclusive. Howells et al. (1995) showed subjects seven minutes of footage from the commercial videotape that depicts execution by gas chamber and by electrocution. Twice as many viewers became less supportive of capital punishment than more supportive (57 percent and

27 percent), though the authors note that the condemned were nameless and anonymous people. A televised execution could acquaint viewers with the details of the crime and/or the human qualities of the defendant, and this context might contribute heavily to the net effect. The execution will always be more subdued than the crimes it is punishing, which could diffuse potential abolitionist sentiments. Further, a televised re-enactment of the crime prior to the showing of the execution is likely to undermine both the potential deterrent or abhorrent effects because there is less reaction to real violence when it follows the viewing of fictional aggression (Howells et al. 1995: 423).

Abolitionist sentiment may get a boost from mistakes or flaws in the execution process that offend public sensibilities and generate "suddenly realized grievances" (Haines 1992). Modern execution protocols are heavily bureaucratic affairs designed to drain much of the emotion out of the event; they create a certain etiquette of dying that ensures cooperation from the condemned and helps the execution team "face the morning of each new execution day" (in Haines 1992: 126; Johnson 1998). Ruptures in the execution routine that make the procedure more difficult and traumatic both for the participants and spectators include ones: 1) that are technically botched, 2) where the condemned do not play the expected calm and non-combative role, 3) where solemnity of the death chamber is compromised, and 4) involving legal irregularities that come to light (Haines 1992; Weyrich 1990). Haines does note that flaws, especially if only sporadic, may be interpreted as a need for technological improvement or as part of what a subhuman offender "had coming" (1992: 127).

Abhorrence also may be generated by spectators' glee or exuberance at another's death. For example, the last public execution was in 1936, when the hanging of a 19-year-old black youth named Rainey Bethea attracted an estimated 15,000 to 20,000 people. Espy notes that the disorderliness of the crowd (and general scathing manner of the press) was one of the reasons for halting public hangings for rape (1980: 540). More recent executions have attracted people to the prison gates, where they register sometimes intense support for the sanction, but the involvement of television adds to the possibilities for generating indignities both through its own sensationalism and by allowing new forms of collective celebration. Imagine people celebrating executions at "happy hour" in bars with large-screen televisions or local football-style tailgate parties.

Television also shows our use of capital punishment to all of our neighbors in the global village, where the trend has been to renounce the use of the death penalty even in cases of mass murder, like genocide. The Parliamentary Assembly of the Council of Europe expressed the view that "the death penalty has no legitimate place in the penal system of modern civilized societies . . . its application may well be compared with torture" (in Grant 1998: 20). Grant exposes the problem in her aptly titled article "A Dialogue of the Deaf?" (1998): the United States already demands exceptions to various international human rights conventions to be able to continue with the executions of juveniles and the mentally retarded—even as it demands other countries make drastic changes in their legal systems. The claim the U.S. has to leadership in the area of human rights is in jeopardy here because countries that have abolished the death penalty see the U.S. as violating a basic human right. And, "the point of human rights language is that it maintains there are no culturally appropriate excuses for cruelty, inhuman and degrading punishment. . . . The political culture of Texas is no less exempt from human rights scrutiny than that of Tehran or Baghdad" (in Grant 1998: 29; see also Prejean 1993: 197).[3]

Lastly, attitudes may change from exposure to information about the death penalty in the commentary and discussions that surround the actual broadcast. However, little evidence exists to support the notion that exposure to information has a significant impact on people's attitudes (Bohm et al. 1993). Social scientists have examined what has become known as the Marshall hypothesis, so named after a remark by Justice Thurgood Marshall in *Gregg v. Georgia*, suggesting that the "opinion of an informed citizenry" would oppose the death penalty (in Haney and Logan 1994: 81; Bohm et al. 1991). Justice Marshall had in mind certain facts about the arbitrary and unjust administration of the death penalty (Fitzpatric 1995: 1072), and no matter what facts researchers use to measure 'informed opinion', "most people care a great deal about the death penalty but know little about it, and have no particular desire to know" (Ellsworth and Gross 1994:40). In fact, "a large proportion of the American public already believes the death penalty is unfair, but supports it nonetheless" (ibid: 36). Justice Marshall thus seems mistaken; further, when people have been exposed to an environment rich in conflicting information—such as would characterize a televised execution—they have most often assimilated the "evidence that favored the position they already held, and rejected the contrary evidence" (Ellsworth and Gross 1994: 34). A televised execution is thus not likely to be a significant source of opinion change because attitudes are "fundamentally noninstrumental symbolic attitudes, based on emotions and ideological self-image" (ibid: 31), including our "basic political and social attitudes regarding liberalism, authoritarianism" (Howells et al. 1995: 413).

Also, television is a commercial enterprise that makes a profit through the audience size. Television is "an institution that exists primarily to translate the phenomenon of simultaneous mass viewing into a commodity that can be sold to advertisers" (in Cummings 1992), so televised executions would be driven by concerns about marketable images and audience share.[4] At a time when 80 percent of the population supports the death penalty, no network would create a program that would possibly alienate such a substantial segment of its viewers. Rather, networks would be likely to give viewers what they want—or what the television executives *think* viewers want.

CONCLUSION

Johnson tells the story about a sailor who is shipwrecked alone on an uncharted island. His apprehension about the inhabitants, though, is relieved when he sees a gallows: "At last, I've reached civilization!" (1996, 1998). Only people who were well-settled would build an apparatus for punishment, but the assumption of "civilization" is simultaneously undermined by the suggestion of deliberate and ceremonious killing. Does the theater of punishment attract large numbers of "civilized" people, and how do they react to the spectacle of suffering?

The story can be updated because televising executions requires the sophisticated technology of an "advanced" society, but the content of the broadcast serves to call into question how civilized the society is. One can imagine, for example, the sailor in contemporary times returning from a tour of duty and checking on e-mail from friends washed up on other corners of the globe. The sailor navigates the Internet to check out the latest promotional spin-offs from the *COPS* television show, then follows a link to information about an imminent execution. After reading a description of the crime and some statements from the victim's family, the cybernaut feeds the data into the high definition television set and programs the VCR to record the event. The sailor logs onto an Internet chat room to converse with the virtual community while watching the televised execution.

"Ah, civilization!"—?

NOTES

[1]McKenna discusses "electronic drugs" in a chapter entitled "Heroin, Cocaine and Television" (1992). He argues it is a high-technology drug that creates an "alternative reality by acting directly on the user's sensorium, without chemicals being introduced into the nervous system" (1992: 218). He continues: "No epidemic or addictive craze or religious hysteria has ever moved faster or made as many converts in so short a time . . . no drug in history has so quickly or completely isolated the entire culture of its users from contact with reality. And no drug in history has so completely succeeded in remaking in its own image the values of the culture that it has infected. Television is by nature the dominator drug par excellence" (ibid: 218–220).

[2]The execution of serial killer Ted Bundy, for example, attracted many people with T-shirts reading "The Bundy BBQ," "Toast Ted," and "Burn Bundy Burn," one person passed out electric chair lapel pins while another held a sign saying "Roses Are Red, Violets Are Blue. Good

Morning, Ted. We're Going to Kill You," state officials approved a vanity license plate reading "FRY TED" (Parker 1989a; 1989b). Perhaps Bundy and others are like the protagonist in Camus' novel *The Stranger*. "For all to be accomplished, for me to feel less lonely, all that remained to hope was that on the day of my execution there should be a huge crowd of spectators and that they greet me with howls of execration" (in Montague and Matson 1983: 36).

[3]I already received a cartoon of Secretary of State Albright in China being introduced: "The emissary from the country with the world's largest prison population wishes to criticize our justice system, sir." (Signe Wilkinson/*Philadelphia Daily News*). But then the world has already heard an Alabama Department of Corrections official say of the state's chain gang that "[i]t became real humane on my part to put these inmates out there in leg irons because they have virtually no chance of escaping. Therefore, they're not going to get shot . . . It's not that I'm a softie. It's expensive" (in Gorman 1997: 455). More on the international view of U.S. and capital punishment can be found in the Death Penalty Information Center's International section http://www.essential.org/dpic.

[4]Certainly violence, suffering, and death are subjects that historically capture our attention, so some of this inquiry needs to focus on television as a medium for mass communication. In his brilliant work, Postman argues that entertainment is the super-ideology of television (1985). Not all programming will be entertaining, but what television does best is show dramatic pictures—such as sex and/or violence—that are visually stimulating to keep the viewer tuned in for the commercial. Television is not completely bereft of information; Postman suggests, however, that the ever-changing, almost hyper-active pace of images creates decontextualized and fragmented information. It is like a game of peek-a-boo with subjects appearing then vanishing, and its foundation in show business means that good television seeks "applause, not reflection" (Postman 1985: 77, 91). Television amuses but cannot challenge the viewer the way a book can challenge a reader who makes a commitment to sit down by herself in a state of intellectual readiness to "be confronted with the cold abstractions of printed sentences" (ibid: 50). Less charitably, Charren and Sandler (1983: 38) state: "What speaks in the great tragedies speaks through the word, speaks to the imagination, speaks for the understanding of human life—its misery—its wonder. But in television, the word is void and the violence is there as violence—like raw sewage in a river."

REFERENCES

Abu-Jamal, Mumia. 1995. *Live from Death Row*. Reading: Addison-Wesley.

Amnesty International. 1989. *When the State Kills . . . The Death Penalty: A Human Rights Issue*. New York: Amnesty International Publications.

Bailey, William. 1990. "Murder, Capital Punishment, and Television: Execution Publicity and Homicide Rates," *American Sociological Review* v. 55, 628–33.

Bailey, William, and Ruth Peterson. 1994. "Murder, Capital Punishment and Deterrence: A Review of the Evidence and an Examination of Police Killings," *Journal of Social Issues* v. 50 #2, 53–74.

Barak, Gregg. 1998. *Integrating Criminologies*. Boston: Allyn & Bacon.

Barkan, S., and S. Cohen. 1994. "Racial Prejudice and Support for the Death Penalty by Whites," *Journal of Research in Crime and Delinquency* v. 31 #2, 202–209.

Bessler, J. D. 1993. Televised Executions and the Constitution: Recognizing a First Amendment Right of Access to State Executions," *Federal Communications Law Journal* v. 45 #3, 355.

Blumstein, Alfred, Jacqueline Cohen, and Daniel Nagin. 1978. *Deterrence and Incapacitation: Estimating the Effects of Criminal Sanctions on Crime Rates*. Washington, DC: National Academy of Sciences.

Bohm, Robert, Louise Clark, and Adrian Aveni. 1991. "Knowledge and Death Penalty Opinion: A Test of the Marshall Hypothesis," *Journal of Research in Crime and Delinquency* v. 28, 360–87.

———, Ronald Vogel, and Albert Maisto. 1993. "Knowledge and Death Penalty Opinion: A Panel Study," *Journal of Criminal Justice* v. 21, 29–45.

Bok, Sissela. 1998. *Mayhem: Violence as Public Entertainment*. Reading, MA: Perseus Books.

Bowers, William and Glenn Pierce. 1975. "The Illusion of Deterrence in Isaac Ehrlich's Research on Capital Punishment," *Yale Law Journal* v. 85, 187–208.

———. 1980. "Deterrence or Brutalization: What Is the Effect of Executions?" *Crime and Delinquency* v. 26, 453–84.

Brown, DeNeen. 1993. "Getting Ready to Die: Children in Violent D.C. Neighborhoods Plan Their Own Funerals," *The Washington Post* 1 November, A1.

Brownlee, Shanon, Dan McGraw, and Jason Vest. 1997. "The Place for Vengeance," *US News & World Report* 16 June, 25–32.

Cameron, Deborah. 1992. "'That's Entertainment'?: Jack the Ripper and the Selling of Sexual Violence," in Jill Radford and Diana Russell (eds.),

Femicide: The Politics of Woman Killing. New York: Twayne Publishers.

Camus, Albert (Justin O'Brien, trans.). 1960. *Resistance, Rebellion, and Death.* New York: Alfred A. Knopf.

Cavender, Grey. 1981. " 'Scared Straight': Ideology and the Media," *Journal of Criminal Justice* v. 9 #6, 431–39.

Charren, Peggy, and Martin Sandler. 1983. *Changing Channels: Living (Sensibly) with Television.* Reading: Addison-Wesley.

Cohn, Steven, Steven Barkan, and William Halteman. 1991. "Punitive Attitudes Toward Criminals: Racial Consensus or Racial Conflict?" *Social Problems* v. 38 #2, 287–96.

Costanzo, Mark, and Lawrence White. 1994. "An Overview of the Death Penalty and Capital Trials: History, Current Status, Legal Procedures and Cost," *Journal of Social Issues,* v. 50 #2, 1–18.

Cummings, Bruce. 1992. *War and Television.* London: Verso.

Deveny, Kathleen. 1992. "Despite AIDS and Safe-Sex Exhortations, Sales of Condoms in U.S. Are Lackluster," *The Wall Street Journal* 24 November, B1.

Ellsworth, Phoebe, and Samuel Gross. 1994. "Hardening of the Attitudes: Americans' Views on the Death Penalty," *Journal of Social Issues* v. 50 #2, 19–52.

Espy, M. Watt. 1980. "Capital Punishment and Deterrence: What the Statistics Cannot Show," *Crime and Delinquency* v. 26, 537–44.

Farberow, Nelson (ed.) 1980. *The Many Faces of Suicide: Indirect Self-Destructive Behavior.* New York: McGraw-Hill.

Fitzpatric, Tracy. 1995. "Justice Thurgood Marshall and Capital Punishment: Social Justice and the Rule of Law," *American Criminal Justice Law Review* v. 132, 1065.

Gilmore, Mikal. 1994. *Shot in the Heart.* New York: Anchor/Doubleday.

Goodman, Walter. 1991. "Executions on TV: Defining the Issues," *The New York Times* 30 May, C18.

———. 1994. "Viewing an Execution from the Sofa," *The New York Times* 13 June, C15.

Gorman, Tessa. 1997. "Back on the Chain Gang: Why the Eighth Amendment and the History of Slavery Proscribe the Resurgence of Chain Gangs," *California Law Review* v. 85, 441.

Grant, Judith. 1992. "Prime Time Crime: Television Portrayals of Law Enforcement," 15 *Journal of American Culture* 57.

Grant, Stephanie. 1998. "A Dialogue of the Deaf? New International Attitudes and the Death Penalty in America," *Criminal Justice Ethics* v. 17 #2, 19.

Gugliotta, Guy. 1994. "Puffing Some Bite Into Crime (Bill)," *The Washington Post* 2 August, A13.

Haines, Herb. 1992. "Flawed Executions, the Anti-Death Penalty Movement, and the Politics of Capital Punishment," *Social Problems* v. 39 #2, 125–38.

Haney, Craig, and Deana Logan. 1994. "Broken Promise: The Supreme Court's Response to Social Science Research on Capital Punishment," *Journal of Social Issues,* v. 50 #2, 75–101.

Hentoff, Nat 1995. "This Dismal Spectacle," *The Washington Post* 30 December, A19.

Hickey, Eric. 1997. *Serial Murderers and Their Victims,* 2nd ed. Belmont: Wadsworth.

Howells, Gary, Kelly Flanagan, and Vivian Hagan. 1995. "Does Viewing a Televised Execution Affect Attitudes Toward Capital Punishment?" *Criminal Justice and Behavior* v. 22 #4, 411–24.

Johnson, Robert. 1996. *Hard Time: Understanding and Reforming the Prison,* 2nd ed. Pacific Grove: Brooks/Cole.

———. 1998. *Death Work: A Study of the Modern Execution Process,* 2nd ed. Pacific Grove: Brooks/Cole.

Kappler, Victor, Mark Blumberg, and Gary Potter. 1996. *The Mythology of Crime and Criminal Justice,* 2nd ed. Prospect Heights: Waveland.

Katz, Jack. 1988. *Seductions of Crime.* New York: Basic Books.

Kooistra, Paul. 1989. *Criminals as Heroes: Structure, Power and Identity.* Bowling Green: Bowling Green State University Popular Press.

Lewis, D. O. 1986. "Psychiatric, Neurological, and Psychoeducational Characteristics of Fifteen Death Row Inmates in the United States," *American Journal of Psychiatry* v. 143 #7, 838–45.

Matthews, Jay. 1991. "TV Barred from Filming Executions," *The Washington Post* 8 June, A10.

McGahey, Richard. 1980. "Dr. Ehrlich's Magic Bullet: Economic Theory, Econometrics, and the Death Penalty," *Crime and Delinquency* v. 26, 485–502.

McKenna, Terence. 1992. *Food of the Gods: The Search for the Original Tree of Knowledge: A Radical History of Plants, Drugs and Human Evolution.* New York: Bantam Books.

Minow, Martha. 1998. *Between Vengeance, and Forgiveness: Facing History After Genocide and Mass Violence.* Boston: Beacon Press.

Montagu, Ashley, and Floyd Matson. 1983. *The Dehumanization of Man.* New York: McGraw-Hill.

Morrow, Lance. 1992. Television Dances with the Reaper," *Time* 4 May, 84.

Oshinsky, David. 1996. *"Worse Than Slavery": Parchman Farm and the Ordeal of Jim Crow Justice.* New York: Simon and Schuster.

Oskamp, Stuart. 1989. "Nuclear War on Television: The Impact of 'The Day After,'" in *Public Communication and Behavior,* volume 2. Orlando: Academic Press.

Parker, Laura. 1989a. "Bundy's Bizarre Quest for Punishment," *The Washington Post* 23 January A3.

———. 1989b. "2,000 Cheer Execution of Killer Bundy," *The Washington Post* 25 January 1989 A1.

Phillips, David. 1983. "The Impact of Mass Media Violence on Homicides," *American Sociological Review* v. 48, 560.

Postman, Neil. 1985. *Amusing Ourselves to Death: Public Discourse in the Age of Show Business,* New York: Penguin Books.

Prejean, Sister Helen. 1993. *Dead Man Walking.* New York: Vintage/Random House.

———. 1995. [No title given to transcript of speech posted on Internet]. Radical Catholic Page, <http://www.bway.net/~halsall/radcath/prejean1.html> Accessed 19 Feb 1999.

Radalet, Michael. 1989. "Executions of Whites for Crimes Against Blacks: Exceptions to the Rule?" *Sociological Quarterly* v. 30 #4, 529–44.

Reiman, Jeffrey. 1998. *The Rich Get Richer and the Poor Get Prison* 5th ed. Boston: Allyn and Bacon.

Seagal, Debra. 1993. "Tales from the Cutting-Room Floor. The Reality of "Reality-Based" Television," *Harper's* November, 50.

Sellers, Terence. 1990. *The Correct Sadist: The Memoirs of Angel Stern.* New York: Grove.

Seltzer, Mark. 1998. *Serial Killers: Death and Life in America's Wound Culture.* New York: Routledge.

Senate Committee on the Judiciary. 1968. *To Abolish the Death Penalty: Hearings Before the Subcommittee on Criminal Laws and Procedures* (S. 1760), 90th Congress, 2nd session; 20 and 21 March and 2 July.

Surette, Ray. 1992. *Media Crime and Criminal Justice: Images and Realities.* Pacific Grove: Brooks/Cole.

Strafer, G. Richard. 1983. "Volunteering for Execution: Competency, Voluntariness and the Propriety of Third Party Intervention," *Journal of Criminal Law and Criminology* v. 74 #3, 860–912.

Thomas, Jo. "McVeigh Talks, but Fleetingly and Obscurely," *New York Times* 15 August, A1.

Trombley, Steve. 1992. *The Execution Protocol: Inside America's Capital Punishment Industry.* New York: Anchor Books.

Turner, Richard. 1997. "Death Penalty Taboos," *Newsweek* 30 June, 83.

Varney, James. 1995. "Officials Urge TV Executions After Killer Dies," *Times-Picayune* (Louisiana) May 17, B3.

Weisskopf, Michael. 1996. "Kemp's Racial Awakening: Candidate's Experience in Pro Football Led Him Away from Republican Mainstream," *The Washington Post* 9 October, A1.

Weyrich, Dawn. 1990. "Debating a Fate Worse Than Death," *Insight* 2 July, 21–23

Zakhari, Beatrix, and Rainey Ransom. 1999. "Jurors in Capital Cases: What Can One Maryland Jury Teach Us?" *Criminal Justice* (American Bar Association Section on Criminal Justice) v. 14 #2, 18–24.

APPENDIX: PROFESSIONAL CODES OF ETHICS

Paul Leighton and Donna Killingbeck

The editors of *Criminal Justice Ethics* conceive of the topic as related to both social justice and professional ethics. Criminal justice is about enforcing law and order, but social justice demands asking questions like, Whose law and what order? Further, criminal justice is limited in its ability to achieve justice if the laws being enforced are unfair or inappropriate restrictions on freedom. Even when laws are appropriate, the quest for justice can be undermined by policies involved with law enforcement, judicial processing, or punishment. Lastly, social justice requires that individuals acting within criminal justice conduct themselves as ethical professionals.

Professional ethics is about obligations related to a job or professional role, such as a police officer or social worker. People engaged in these jobs have important decision-making power over the lives of others, and professional codes of ethics discuss how this power should be used. At their best, codes acknowledge this power and make a public commitment that the power will not be misused, especially for personal gain. Ideally, codes provide guidance about the guiding values of the profession, specific ethical principles, and specific standards.

Codes vary widely in how thoroughly and intelligently they accomplish these tasks, so we have taken helpful language from several well-developed codes to help explain the structure of a professional code of ethics. This Appendix then reproduces specific sections of codes that will be of general relevance to readers of this book, for example, competence, cultural diversity, sexual relationships, sexual harassment, and reporting information. At the end of this Appendix are Internet addresses for a variety of professional organizations that have codes of ethics and a code of ethics library. We invite students to research a code of ethics for a profession they are thinking of entering, or better still several complete codes of ethics. The code for the national Association of Social Workers is especially notable for its advocacy of individual self-determination and social justice.

Studying ethical codes does not guarantee ethical behavior on the part of professionals. As the National Association of Social Work (NASW) code states, "a code of ethics cannot resolve all ethical issues or disputes or capture the richness and complexity involved in striving to make responsible choices within a moral community. Rather, a code of ethics sets forth values, ethical principles, and ethical standards to which professionals aspire and by which their actions can be judged." The American Psychological Association (APA) code adds: "The development of a dynamic set of ethical standards for a psychologist's work-related conduct requires a personal commitment to a lifelong effort to act ethically; to encourage ethical behavior by students, supervisees, employees, and colleagues, as appropriate; and to consult with others, as needed, concerning ethical problems."

THE STRUCTURE OF ETHICAL CODES

The better and more detailed codes of ethics start with a preamble, which explains the role of the profession for society and acknowledges the power and responsibilities that it has. For example, the code of ethics for Child Welfare Professionals (CWP) states:

> Society delegates to the child welfare field and to those who become members of the field the authority to intervene in the lives of families with the goals of ensuring the safety of abused and neglected children, assisting parents in meeting minimum parenting standards, and planning alternative permanent care when parents are incapable of or unwilling to meet those standards. When individuals accept the role of child welfare professional and the delegated authority inherent in that role, they publicly acknowledge having the professional responsibilities which accompany that authority. Society and agency clients, therefore, have legitimate expectations about the nature of professional intervention as it occurs in one-on-one professional/client interactions, in the management and administration of those providing intervention, and in policy decision-making. Because of their special knowledge and authority, all professionals are in a position of power in inherently unequal relationships with their clients. The power of child welfare professionals is particularly daunting because of their delegated state authority and the mandated nature of their professional/client relationships.

The introductions of many codes state general objectives of the profession. The NASW code announces social workers "enhance human well-being and help meet the basic human needs of all people, with particular attention to the needs and empowerment of people who are vulnerable, oppressed, and living in poverty." In addition, social workers "promote the general welfare of society, from local to global levels," and "advocate for living conditions conducive to the fulfillment of basic human needs and should promote social, economic, political, and cultural values and institutions that are compatible with the realization of social justice."

The code then moves from general statements to a set of "core values" service, social justice, dignity, and worth of the person, importance of human relationships, integrity, competence. In turn, the core values are the foundation for more specific ethical principles. The core value of service produces the ethical principle: "Social workers' primary goal is to help people in need and to address social problems." The core value of social justice produces the ethical principle that social workers challenge social injustice. The core value of competence produces the ethical principle: "Social workers practice within their areas of competence and develop and enhance their professional expertise."

The ethical principles of any code are meant to articulate a common set of values for the profession and provide some goals to which members should aspire. In addition, the ethical principles provide the foundation for a more specific set of *ethical standards* that are the basis for charging someone with an ethical violation before the professional association's ethics committee. The specific language also provides concrete detail for guidance in situations. Most codes, for example, have an ethical principle against non-exploitation, and the APA sets specific ethical standards that therapists cannot enter into sexual relationships with former therapy patients for two years following the termination of treatment—and then only under a specific set of circumstances (see APA standard reproduced below).

Ethical standards are not exhaustive and cannot be made to cover all situations. The American Society of Criminology (ASC) proposed code adds a helpful note that: "Ethical standards are not simply determined by whether an action is legally actionable; behavior that is technically legal may still be unethical." The APA code also tries to be helpful about the relationship between ethical standards and legal standards:

> Whether or not a psychologist has violated the Ethics Code does not by itself determine whether he or she is legally liable in a court action, whether a contract is enforceable, or whether other legal consequences occur. These results are based on legal rather than ethical rules. However, compliance with or violation of the Ethics Code may be admissible as evidence in some legal proceedings, depending on the circumstances.

Even the specific ethical standards cannot cover the wide variety of real-life situations that create ethical dilemmas. Most of the codes note that context is crucial to making a decision, and the NASW code is most helpful about how to resolve conflicts:

> In addition to this *Code*, there are many other sources of information about ethical thinking that may be useful. Social workers should consider ethical theory and principles generally, social work theory and research, laws, regulations, agency policies, and other relevant codes of ethics, recognizing that among codes of ethics social workers should consider the *NASW Code of Ethics* as their primary source. Social workers also should be aware of the impact on ethical decision making of their clients' and their own personal values and cultural and religious beliefs and practices. They should be aware of any conflicts between personal and professional values and deal with them responsibly. For additional guidance social workers should consult the relevant literature on professional ethics and ethical decision making and seek appropriate consultation when faced with ethical dilemmas. This may involve consultation with an agency-based or social work organization's ethics committee, a regulatory body, knowledgeable colleagues, supervisors, or legal counsel.

Professionals who know the ethical course of conduct may face many impediments to implementing it. Readers interested in the question of how to do the right thing and still keep a job can consult Nan DeMars, *You Want Me to Do What? When, Where & How to Draw the Line at Work* (New York: Simon & Schuster, 1997).

ETHICAL STANDARDS

The full text of the codes is available at the Internet addresses provided below. Please note that the codes for the American Society of Criminology (ASC) and the Academy of Criminal Justice Sciences (ACJS) are *proposed;* the language has not been ratified by the membership of those organizations at the time this Appendix is being written.

Informed Consent

CWP: Child welfare professionals should inform clients as soon as feasible and in language that is understandable about the nature of the professional relationship, the nature of the professional intervention, the professional's delegated authority and the limits of that authority, which decisions the client can make and which decisions the child welfare professional will make.

ASC: Criminologists should take culturally appropriate steps to secure informed consent and to avoid invasions of privacy. In addition, special actions will be necessary where the individuals studied are illiterate, are mentally ill, are minors, have low social status, are not comfortable or familiar with the language being used in the research, are under judicial or penal supervision, or are unfamiliar with social research and its constraints and purposes.

Competence

APA: Psychologists who engage in assessment, therapy, teaching, research, organizational consulting, or other professional activities maintain a reasonable level of awareness of current scientific and professional information in their fields of activity, and undertake ongoing efforts to maintain competence in the skills they use.

Cultural Competence and Social Diversity

NASW: a) Social workers should understand culture and its function in human behavior and society, recognizing the strengths that exist in all cultures. b) Social workers should have a knowledge base of their clients' cultures and be able to demonstrate competence in the provision of services that are sensitive to clients' cultures and to differences among people and cultural groups. c) Social workers should obtain education about and seek to understand the nature of social diversity and oppression with respect to race, ethnicity, national origin, color, sex, sexual orientation, age, marital status, political belief, religion, and mental or physical disability.

Colleague's Impairment or Incompetence

NASW: Social workers who have direct knowledge of a social work colleague's impairment [or incompetence] that is due to personal problems, psychosocial distress, substance abuse, or mental health difficulties and that interferes with practice effectiveness should consult with that colleague when feasible and assist the colleague in taking remedial action.

Privacy and Confidentiality

NASW: Social workers should take precautions to ensure and maintain the confidentiality of information transmitted to other parties through the use of computers, electronic mail, facsimile machines, telephones and telephone answering machines, and other electronic or computer technology. Disclosure of identifying information should be avoided whenever possible.

ASA: Sociologists use extreme care in delivering or transferring any confidential data, information, or communication over public computer networks. Sociologists are attentive to the problems of maintaining confidentiality and control over sensitive material and data when use of technological innovations, such as public computer networks, may open their professional and scientific communication to unauthorized persons.

Conflict of Interest

APA: A psychologist refrains from entering into or promising another personal, scientific, professional, financial, or other relationship with such persons if it appears likely that such a relationship reasonably might impair the psychologist's objectivity or otherwise interfere with the psychologist's effectively performing his or her functions as a psychologist, or might harm or exploit the other party.

Non-exploitation and Discrimination, General

NASW: Social workers should not take unfair advantage of any professional relationship or exploit others to further their personal, religious, political, or business interests.

ACJS: Members of the Academy should not coerce or obtain through manipulation personal or sexual favors or economic or professional advantages from any person, including students, respondents, clients, patients, research assistants, clerical staff or colleagues. In addition, members of the Academy should recognize that romantic or intimate relationships with individuals vulnerable to manipulation, such as current students in their programs or employees under their supervision, may create the appearance of, or opportunities for, favoritism and/or exploitation, and thus such relationships should be avoided.

Sexual Relationships

ASC: Criminologists do not have sexual relationships with anyone over whom they exercise evaluative or supervisory power because of the potential for exploitation and harm. Exercising professional authority over someone with whom there has been a relationship should be avoided whenever possible because of the likelihood of impaired judgment and the difficulty in maintaining professional boundaries.

NASW: Social workers should not engage in sexual activities or sexual contact with clients' relatives or other individuals with whom clients maintain a close personal relationship when there is a risk of exploitation or potential harm to the client. Sexual activity or sexual contact with clients' relatives or other individuals with whom clients maintain a personal relationship has the potential to be harmful to the client and may make it difficult for the social worker and client to maintain appropriate professional boundaries. Social workers—not their clients, their clients' relatives, or other individuals with whom the client maintains a personal relationship—assume the full burden for setting clear, appropriate, and culturally sensitive boundaries.

APA: a) Psychologists do not engage in sexual intimacies with a former therapy patient or client for at least two years after cessation or termination of professional services. b) Because sexual intimacies with a former therapy patient or client are so frequently harmful to the patient or client, and because such intimacies undermine public confidence in the psychology profession and thereby deter the public's use of needed services, psychologists do not engage in sexual intimacies with former therapy patients and clients even after a two-year interval except in the most unusual circumstances. The psychologist who engages in such activity after the two years following cessation or termination of treatment bears the burden of demonstrating that there has been no exploitation, in light of all relevant factors, including 1) the amount of time that has passed since therapy terminated, 2) the nature and duration of the therapy, 3) the circumstances of termination, 4) the patient's or client's personal history, 5) the patient's or client's current mental status, 6) the likelihood of adverse impact on the patient or client and others, and 7) any statements or actions made by the therapist during the course of therapy suggesting or inviting the possibility of a post-termination sexual or romantic relationship with the patient or client.

Sexual Harassment

ASC: Sexual harassment includes advances, solicitation, or requests for sexual favors from those over whom an individual exercises professional authority or with whom one attends classes or works. Harassment may consist of a single intense act or multiple persistent acts that are unwelcome, offensive, and/or that create a hostile work, school, or professional environment. Harassment can include written or electronic communications and nonverbal conduct such as touching, staring, or physically following an individual. It can also include verbal behavior that reflects excessive attention to physical appearance, especially after notice has been given that such attention is unwelcome.

ASA: Sociologists do not engage in harassment of any person, including students, supervisees, employees, or research participants. Harassment consists of a single intense and severe act or of multiple persistent or pervasive acts which are demeaning, abusive, offensive, or create a hostile professional or workplace environment. Sexual harassment may include sexual solicitation, physical advance, or verbal or non-verbal conduct that is sexual in nature. Racial harassment may include unnecessary, exaggerated, or unwarranted attention or attack, whether verbal or non-verbal, because of a person's race or ethnicity.

APA: a) Psychologists do not engage in sexual harassment. Sexual harassment is sexual solicitation, physical advances, or verbal or nonverbal conduct that is sexual in nature, that occurs in connection with the psychologist's activities or roles as a psychologist, and that either: 1) is unwelcome, is offensive, or creates a hostile workplace environment, and the psychologist knows or is told this; or 2) is sufficiently severe or intense to be abusive to a reasonable person in the context. Sexual harassment can consist of a single intense or severe act or of multiple persistent or pervasive acts. b) Psychologists accord sexual-harassment complainants and respondents dignity and respect. Psychologists do not participate in denying a person academic admittance or advancement, employment, tenure, or promotion, based solely upon their having made, or their being the subject of, sexual harassment charges. This does not preclude taking action based upon the outcome of such proceedings or consideration of other appropriate information.

Research Subjects

ACJS: Human subjects have the right to full disclosure of the purposes of the research as early as it is appropriate to the research process, and they have the right to an opportunity to have their questions answered about the purpose and usage of the research. Members should not deceive research participants about significant aspects of the research that would affect their willingness to participate such as physical risks, discomfort, or unpleasant emotional experiences.

APA: Psychologists trained in research methods and experienced in the care of laboratory animals supervise all procedures involving animals and are responsible for ensuring appropriate consideration of their comfort, health, and humane treatment. Psychologists make reasonable efforts to minimize the discomfort, infection, illness, and pain of animal subjects. A procedure subjecting animals to pain, stress, or privation is used only when an alternative procedure is unavailable and the goal is justified by its prospective scientific, educational, or applied value. When it is appropriate that the animal's life be terminated, it is done rapidly, with an effort to minimize pain.

Authorship, Acknowledgment and Plagiarism

ASC: When a criminologist is involved in a joint project with others—including students, research assistants, and employees, there should be mutually accepted explicit agreements at the outset with respect to division of work, compensation, access to data, rights of authorship, and other rights and responsibilities. Such agreements may need to be modified as the project evolves and such modifications must be agreed upon jointly. Authorship of a completed article or product should reflect the relative contribution of authors in terms of data gathering, analysis, text, and original work and not the relative professional status of the authors. Students should normally be the principal authors of any work that substantially derives from their thesis or dissertation.

APA: Principal authorship and other publication credits accurately reflect the relative scientific or professional contributions of the individuals involved, regardless of their relative status. Mere possession of an institutional position, such as Department Chair, does not justify authorship credit. Minor contributions to the research or to the writing for publications are appropriately acknowledged, such as in footnotes or in an introductory statement.

ASA: In publications, presentations, teaching, practice, and service, sociologists explicitly identify, credit, and reference the author when they take data or material verbatim from another person's written work, whether it is published, unpublished, or electronically available. In their publications, presentations, teaching, practice, and service, sociologists provide acknowledgment of and reference to the use of others' work, even if the work is not quoted verbatim or paraphrased, and they do not present others' work as their own whether it is published, unpublished, or electronically available.

Teaching

ASC: When acting as teachers, criminologists should provide students an honest statement of the scope and perspective of their courses, clear expectations for student performance, and fair, timely and easily accessible evaluations of their work.

APA: Psychologists responsible for education and training programs seek to ensure that there is a current and accurate description of the program content, training goals and objectives, and requirements that must be met for satisfactory completion of the program. This information must be made readily available to all interested parties.

ASA: Sociologists do not permit personal animosities or intellectual differences with colleagues to foreclose students' or supervisees' access to these colleagues or to interfere with student or supervisee learning, academic progress, or professional development.

Reporting Research and Information

ASA: Sociologists do not fabricate data or falsify results in their publications or presentations. In presenting their work, sociologists report their findings fully and do not omit relevant data. They report results whether they support or contradict the expected outcomes. Sociologists take particular care to state all relevant qualifications on the findings and interpretation of their research. Sociologists also disclose underlying assumptions, theories, methods, measures, and research designs that might bear upon findings and interpretations of their work.

APA: Psychologists do not make public statements that are false, deceptive, misleading, or fraudulent, either because of what they state, convey, or suggest or because of what they omit, concerning their research, practice, or other work activities or those of persons or organizations with which they are affiliated. As examples (and not in limitation) of this standard, psychologists do not make false or deceptive statements concerning 1) their training, experience, or competence; 2) their academic degrees; 3) their credentials; 4) their institutional or association affiliations; 5) their services; 6) the scientific or clinical basis for, or results or degree of success of, their services; 7) their fees; or 8) their publications or research findings. . . . Psychologists do not compensate employees of press, radio, television, or other communication media in return for publicity in a news item.

Social and Political Action

NASW: Social workers should engage in social and political action that seeks to ensure that all people have equal access to the resources, employment, services, and opportunities they require to meet their basic human needs and to develop fully. Social workers should be aware of the impact of the political arena on practice and should advocate for changes in policy and legislation to improve social conditions in order to meet basic human needs and promote social justice. Social workers should act to expand choice and opportunity for all people, with special regard for vulnerable, disadvantaged, oppressed, and exploited people and groups. Social workers should promote conditions that encourage respect for cultural and social diversity within the United States and globally. Social workers should promote policies and practices that demonstrate respect for difference, support the expansion of cultural knowledge and resources, advocate for programs and institutions that demonstrate cultural competence, and promote policies that safeguard the rights of and confirm equity and social justice for all people. Social workers should act to prevent and eliminate domination of, exploitation of, and discrimination against any person, group, or class on the basis of race, ethnicity, national origin, color, sex, sexual orientation, age, marital status, political belief, religion, or mental or physical disability.

FOR MORE INFORMATION

American Psychological Association http://www.apa.org/
American Sociological Association http://www.asanet.org/
American Society of Criminology http://www.asc41.com/
International Association of Police Chiefs http://www.theiacp.org/
National Association of Social Workers http://www.naswdc.org
Code of Ethics Library http://csep.iit.edu/codes/index.html
Code of Ethics Toolbox http://www.chowan.edu/acadp/ethics/ethics_toolbox.htm